CAMBRIDGE LIBRARY COLLECTION

Books of enduring scholarly value

Technology

The focus of this series is engineering, broadly construed. It covers technological innovation from a range of periods and cultures, but centres on the technological achievements of the industrial era in the West, particularly in the nineteenth century, as understood by their contemporaries. Infrastructure is one major focus, covering the building of railways and canals, bridges and tunnels, land drainage, the laying of submarine cables, and the construction of docks and lighthouses. Other key topics include developments in industrial and manufacturing fields such as mining technology, the production of iron and steel, the use of steam power, and chemical processes such as photography and textile dyes.

The Mining Industry

The mining industry was a fundamental part of the economy of South Africa in the late nineteenth century, and control of the region's gold mines was a significant factor in the tension between Dutch and English settlers that led to the Second Boer War in 1899. In 1889 the Witwatersrand Chamber of Mines had been formed to promote the industry's development. Economic problems in the region led the Volksraad of the South African Republic to set up a Commission of Enquiry in 1897 to investigate high tariffs, labour and transport costs which were adversely affecting the mining industry. The 1897 report reissued here was not that of the commission itself, but contains much of the evidence and statistical material presented to it, in the hope that the mining industry would adopt its recommendations. As such, this detailed resource remains relevant to economic historians of South Africa and the British Empire.

T0300493

Cambridge University Press has long been a pioneer in the reissuing of out-of-print titles from its own backlist, producing digital reprints of books that are still sought after by scholars and students but could not be reprinted economically using traditional technology. The Cambridge Library Collection extends this activity to a wider range of books which are still of importance to researchers and professionals, either for the source material they contain, or as landmarks in the history of their academic discipline.

Drawing from the world-renowned collections in the Cambridge University Library and other partner libraries, and guided by the advice of experts in each subject area, Cambridge University Press is using state-of-the-art scanning machines in its own Printing House to capture the content of each book selected for inclusion. The files are processed to give a consistently clear, crisp image, and the books finished to the high quality standard for which the Press is recognised around the world. The latest print-on-demand technology ensures that the books will remain available indefinitely, and that orders for single or multiple copies can quickly be supplied.

The Cambridge Library Collection brings back to life books of enduring scholarly value (including out-of-copyright works originally issued by other publishers) across a wide range of disciplines in the humanities and social sciences and in science and technology.

The Mining Industry

Evidence and Report of the
Industrial Commission of Enquiry

COMPILED BY
THE WITWATERSRAND CHAMBER OF MINES

CAMBRIDGE
UNIVERSITY PRESS

University Printing House, Cambridge, CB2 8BS, United Kingdom

Published in the United States of America by Cambridge University Press, New York

Cambridge University Press is part of the University of Cambridge.
It furthers the University's mission by disseminating knowledge in the pursuit of
education, learning and research at the highest international levels of excellence.

www.cambridge.org
Information on this title: www.cambridge.org/9781108062343

This edition first published 1897
This digitally printed version 2013

ISBN 978-1-108-06234-3 Paperback

Evidence and Report

of the

Industrial Commission of Enquiry,

With an Appendix.

THE MINING INDUSTRY.

EVIDENCE AND REPORT

OF THE

INDUSTRIAL COMMISSION OF ENQUIRY,

WITH AN APPENDIX

CONTAINING

The Letter of the Chamber of Mines to the Commission,
The Principal Laws of the Republic Affecting the Mining Industry,
And other Documents of Interest Appertaining to the
Evidence Given at the Enquiry.

Compiled and Published by

THE WITWATERSRAND CHAMBER OF MINES, JOHANNESBURG, S.A.R.

Johannesburg:
TIMES PRINTING AND PUBLISHING WORKS.
—
1897.

JOHANNESBURG :

PRINTED AT THE JOHANNESBURG TIMES PRINTING AND PUBLISHING WORKS.

PREFACE.

SINCE its formation in 1889 the Chamber has been mainly engaged in endeavouring to secure the mines relief from the heavy burdens imposed on them. The cost of living, and hence the rate of wages of the white employees, has been rendered unduly high by the duties on the necessaries of life and on all articles of ordinary requirement, while heavy railway tariffs and the dynamite monopoly, and the difficulty of obtaining an adequate supply of native labour at reasonable pay, have militated against the profitable working and development of the industry as a whole. As is shown in the letter of the Chamber to the Industrial Commission all these matters have again and again been brought to the notice of the Government and the Legislature, but on the most important questions redress has not been obtained.

At the annual meeting of the Rand Mines, Ltd., in March last, especial stress was laid by the Chairman on the manner in which the development of the industry was being retarded by the excessive rates for transport of coal and other articles of prime necessity for mining, by the extortionate price charged for explosives, by the high cost of white labour, due to the duties on foodstuffs, and of native labour, consequent on the inefficient administration of the Pass and Liquor Laws and the scant assistance afforded by the Government in connection with procuring a sufficient supply at moderate wages. Subsequently at meetings of other companies similar complaints were made, and it was pointed out that unless relief were obtained many mines which were barely paying expenses would be forced to shut down, while others, which under favourable conditions could and would be profitably worked, would continue inactive.

Meanwhile the disastrous effects of rinderpest on the farmers and of bad trade on the urban population were becoming evident in a constantly widening area of acute distress.

Among the Executive Council minutes presented to the Volksraad is one which records, that, on the 24th March the Executive Council considered a complaint regarding the excessive tariffs charged in the South African Republic and other States of South Africa, and deeming it desirable to institute an enquiry into the state of affairs generally of the mining industry of the Witwatersrand, resolved to appoint a commission for that purpose. Accordingly on the 14th April the following notice appeared in the *Government Gazette* :—

"It is hereby made known for general information that the Executive "Council has seen fit to institute an enquiry with reference to the present "alleged state of affairs in connection with the mining industry of the Wit-"watersrand diggings in general, and to furnish the Executive Council with a "report regarding all matters that may have stood in the way, or have "hindered, and still may hinder the development of the mining industry, and "further, so soon as possible, to make such recommendations as may tend to "the improvement and amendment of such matters."

"The Commission, charged with this enquiry, consists of the following "gentlemen :—S. W. BURGER, member of Executive Council; J. S. SMIT, "Commissioner of Railways ; C. J. JOUBERT, Minister of Mines ; G. SCHMITZ-"DUMONT, Acting State Mining Engineer : and J. F. DE BEER, First Special "Judicial Commissioner, Johannesburg, as ordinary members, with Mr. THOMAS "HUGO, as financial expert ; Messrs. E. BROCHON, J. PIERCE, and A. BRAKHAN "shall either jointly as a Commission, or severally, support the permanent "members of the Commission with their advice, whenever requested. In order "to make the work of the Commission as wide as possible they are authorised "to take evidence on all those matters that can forward the aim of the "Commission."

"The Government desires to bring under the notice of all persons con-"cerned that the willing tendering of evidence and information by each and "every one, no matter from whom required, will greatly assist the above "described aim.

(Signed)   C. VAN BOESCHOTEN,

Acting State Secretary.

Government Office, Pretoria,
    14th April, 1897."

Messrs. H. Bosch and E. Levy were appointed Secretaries, and with the consent of the Government, Messrs. James Hay (President of the Chamber of Mines) and George Albu (Chairman of the Association of Mines) were later added to the Commission as advisory members.

From the minute of the Executive Council of the 30th March it is clear that the duties of the financial expert and of the advisory members were intended to be of a very limited character. Mr. Hugo was not to be an ordinary member of the Commission, but was to sit merely as financial expert and as such to have the right of voting on financial matters ; the advisory members were appointed as members to assist the Commission, whenever desired so to do, with information, explanation and advice.

But when the Commission started work it became evident that the advisory members by their knowledge of the questions under consideration were able to render indispensable service in eliciting evidence and examining and cross-examining witnesses, and they assumed and were accorded in all respects the same rights as those exercised by the ordinary members, eventually taking part in the drafting of the report and attaching their signatures to it.

The Commission opened their sittings, for the taking of evidence, on the 20th April and closed them on the 4th June : the actual time devoted to the hearing of witnesses having been twenty days. Their report was signed and presented to Government on the 27th July, and was laid before the Volksraad by the Government on the 9th August, with a request that that body would appoint a committee to act in conjunction with the Government in considering the various points contained therein, and make such recommendations as they might deem reasonable and desirable : and to refer to the Second Volksraad all such subjects as would properly come under the cognizance of that House.

After a protracted debate the proposal of the Government was adopted on the 10th August and the following committee, with instructions to submit its recommendations during the current session, was appointed, viz : Messrs. F. H. G. Wolmarans, A. D. W. Wolmarans, B. J. Vorster, C. J. Tosen, and L. Botha.

The mining industry responded willingly to the request of the

Government to give evidence before the Commission, and a mass of valuable statistical data in connection with the working of the mines, and the way in which the low grade properties were kept idle by the various burdens and administrative shortcomings which artificially raise working costs, was submitted.

With the object of preserving this important evidence and rendering it available for the mining companies for purposes of reference, the Chamber determined upon publishing it in book form. It was also deemed advisable to embody in the volume the different laws of the State bearing directly on the mining industry and the agreements entered into by the Government in connection with the railway concession and the dynamite monopoly, which formed the subject of frequent reference by many of the witnesses; while population and other statistics have been added as being of interest in relation to the questions dealt with by the Commission.

For the convenience of the reader the evidence of those witnesses, whose examination did not proceed continuously, has been brought together; marginal notes have been furnished throughout, and the index has been arranged to facilitate reference to the various subjects covered by the enquiry.

It had been hoped that the report of the Volksraad Commission would have been published in time to have been included in this volume, but that expectation has not been realised. The report has still to be presented, and it remains to be seen to what extent the Legislature will then approve and give effect to the recommendations of the Commission. These recommendations, though not proceeding so far as the Chamber would have desired, are generally regarded by the industry as liberal and statesmanlike; and it is clear that if adopted they will do much towards permitting that expansion of mining operations which would result from the working of the poorer mines of the Witwatersrand.

By their condemnation of monopolies and concessions, by their recommendations for the lightening of the duties on foodstuffs and of the railway rates on coal and other articles, in their plea for the better and more effective administration and enforcement of the Pass Law, the

Liquor Law, and the Gold Thefts clauses of the Gold Law, the Commissioners appointed by the Government to enquire into the state of affairs of the gold mining industry of the Witwatersrand have testified in the fullest possible way to the reality of the grievances which are bearing so heavily on the mines and to the justice of the demands for redress, which unfailingly, year by year, the Chamber has laid before the Government and the Legislature of the Republic.

Chamber of Mines,
    20th September, 1897.

LIST OF WITNESSES.

ERRATUM.

On page 425, in the first marginal note, "Simmer and Jack Shafts" should read "Simmer and Jack East Shafts."

TABLE OF CONTENTS.

PART I.

EVIDENCE GIVEN BEFORE THE INDUSTRIAL COMMISSION OF ENQUIRY AND THE REPORT OF THE COMMISSIONERS.

PART II.

APPENDIX.

PART I.

EVIDENCE GIVEN BEFORE THE INDUSTRIAL COMMISSION OF ENQUIRY AND THE REPORT OF THE COMMISSIONERS.

PART II.

APPENDIX.

THE INDUSTRIAL COMMISSION

OF ENQUIRY.

The Members of the Commission, Messrs. SCHALK W. BURGER, Member Executive Members of the Commission.
ouncil (Chairman); J. S. SMIT, Government Railway Commissioner; CHRISTIAAN
)UBERT, Minister of Mines; SCHMITZ-DUMONT, Acting State Mining Engineer;
F. DE BEER, First Special Judicial Commissioner, Johannesburg; THOS. HUGO,
eneral Manager National Bank (financial advisor); E. BROCHON, A. PIERCE,
anager Natal Bank, Johannesburg; A. BRAKHAN, (advisory members,) opened
e enquiry at Johannesburg on the 20th April, 1897. On the 27th of the month
r. JAS. HAY, President of the Chamber of Mines, and Mr. G. ALBU, Chairman of
e Association of Mines, were added to the Commission as advisory members.

The CHAIRMAN explained that, in accordance with the powers entrusted to it by the Appointment of Commission.
xecutive Council, Minute B 4,365 of 1897, this Commission took upon it to institute
thorough and searching inquiry into the alleged grievances of the mining industry
set forth by those interested; and the latter, as many of them as should give in
eir names to the Secretary, would be called upon to inform the Commission
rsonally of their grievances and difficulties. As necessarily consequent upon
d connected with the mining industry, the following subjects would be taken into Scope of Enquiry.
nsideration, namely, the labour question, traffic rates, taxation, dynamite, trade,
riculture, and other matters associated with the said industry. To those who were
terested opportunity would be given personally and by way of evidence to en-
hten the Commission on these points, in order to place it in a position to lay before
e Government a true report of affairs, and, where possible, to recommend the desired
erations and improvements. The purpose and tendency of the Commission had
ready appeared from the notice in the *Staatscourant* and from the resolution already
opted by the Commission. But since the scope of the Commission embraced a great
al, and was of the highest importance for the land in general, and for the gold-fields
particular, and as he understood its results were anticipated with interest, he took
e liberty, and deemed it not out of place, at the commencement of its proceed-
gs, to offer a few further remarks on behalf of himself and fellow-members. He
d noticed that the press had already indulged in all manner of reflections and
edictions regarding the labours of the Commission.

Objects of Commission.

I hope, continued the Chairman, I shall not render myself guilty of anticipatin the result of our labours; but I desire to limit myself to the following points, wit the object of making our position clear to you, so that we may be able to recke the more upon your valued assistance and co-operation :

(a) The *raison d'être* of the Commission.

(b) Ascertaining the causes of the alleged grievances.

(c) The bringing to light of the actual state of the mining industry of th Witwatersrand Goldfields in general, and the reason for the same.

(d) After inquiry into and investigations of affairs, to propose amendmen to the Government.

For the rest, the Commission was prepared to deal with the requirements of th mining industry in a sympathetic manner, but it must first appear to the Commissio what the actual cause was of the alleged condition of affairs, and if this cause was be ascribed to the high rate of wages, bad administration, burdensome taxatio excessive rates of transport, foreign influence and policy, or to one or other the said causes.

The Chairman enumerated the *personnel* of the Commission, and explained tha Mr. Thomas Hugo was financial expert, and Messrs. Brochon, Pierce, and Brakha were advisory members of the Commission.

Wishes of Government.

The Government was keenly alive to the importance of the mining industry, an for that reason was determined to probe the alleged grievances to the bottom. Wh he said "alleged" was because neither the Commission nor the Government wer certain that any such grievances existed. What the Government and Commissione wanted was a clear statement of fact, and if there was any blame or culpability to placed on the side of the Government, such as excessive taxation, etc., and oth burdens, the Commission would promptly advise the Government on those point

The Industry's Duty.

with the view of having matters remedied. On the other hand, they wanted cle and unreserved and honest statements from the other side as to what was the origi or cause of the present depression. The evidence would have to be given fully an boldly and without reserve, for the Commission wanted to know whether th depression or reaction was due to over-speculation or other causes.

Over Speculation.

It was by the mining industry and those interested that the grievances woul have to be enumerated. The present condition of things was not wholly unexpecte by him (the Chairman). Those who had seen the wild and hysterical state of affai during the boom had expected a reaction. He was of opinion that in some instanc more capital had been put into the ground than certain tracts of ground reall justified. Capital had been invited from European centres; the thousands who ha since flocked into Johannesburg thought that gold was to be picked up in the street The present state of affairs was not unknown or unprecedented in other countrie indeed, in South Africa the same thing had occurred in the Diamond Fields. Fir there was a period of excessive speculation and then the reaction, until conditio were restored to their normal state.

Reasons for Depression.

Mr. J. F. DE BEER read the second portion of the Chairman's speech, which stat that the Commission was keenly desirous of obtaining a true statement of affairs, an to know whether the present depression was ascribable to excessive taxatio dynamite, railway rates, labour question, or other burdens, foreign interference, et They expected from the mining industry evidence that would be accompanied b accredited statistics. It seemed to him that half the trouble was due to the matter white labour, which absorbed 50 per cent. of the total working cost. He als referred to the machinery contracts which were invariably placed in England America. If this machinery were made here it would create work for many wh ere at present deprived of their employment on the mines. He hoped for the earty co-operation of the mining industry in these matters, and trusted that the perations of the Commission would be conducted with harmony, and that some plan, might be evolved by which the industry would be restored to its brilliant, normal tate.

The first witness called was Mr. JAMES HAY, who was sworn by Mr. J. F. de Beer nd said: I am the Chairman of the Chamber of Mines in Johannesburg.

Mr. *de Beer.*

You have seen that various memorials have been presented from the Chamber f Mines to the Government regarding the grievances alleged to exist in connection with the mining industry?—Yes.

Will you give us evidence upon the points raised in those memorials?—At the resent moment we have only as yet heard, that is since Friday afternoon, about the ittings of the Commission. It is a very wide Commission. The question is, what vidence do you wish me to give?

We want to know everything about these grievances, everything in your power o give. And we look to you to furnish such information as representing the Chamber f Mines and, of course, the mining industry.—The Chairman has made a statement s to the objects of the Commission and what it ought to embrace, and I think he said t would be for the benefit of the people that they might know all the points. do not understand Dutch sufficiently well to follow all that has been said, but if he points are put before me that I am required to answer, I will come prepared o do so. It is a very wide subject and, generally, I do know all about the ndustry, but there may be many points about which the Commission require infor- mation, technical and otherwise, which, if I only knew what was required, could asily be provided.

Chairman.

The first notice was published on the 14th inst.

Mr. *de Beer.*

We want the fullest particulars, as a copy will be submitted to the Volksraad. We would like you to speak about what is contained in the memorials.—This *producing paper)* begins with the liquor law. We approve of that law, and only sk that it be more efficiently administered. That is what the memorial embraces. here is another matter, that of dynamite. The report of the Commission appointed y the Volksraad shows that the concessionaires have not complied with their onditions, and that they have secured very large profits from their concession. he principal point in the memorial is that the Government should afford relief by a eduction being made in the price of dynamite.

Liquor Law.

Dynamite.

Chairman.

That is one of the points upon which we can begin, and about which the Com- mission wishes to hear evidence. The required reduction of the cost is said to be one f the existing grievances, its expense being one of the alleged causes of the epression, and it now rests with you and the representatives of the industry to show hat to be a fact.—I will be able to produce evidence and statistics with that object.

Witness.] I think, perhaps, it would simplify matters very much if I put my iews forth as to what the industry requires, and then it would be for you to say hat meets with your approval, and what can be pursued further as you wish. We ad better follow some plan or we shall get into hopeless confusion before we have one.

Mr. James Hay's Evidence.

Chairman.

We do not want to ask you anything you do not know; but you must understand that this is a Commission of Investigation. There are certain alleged grievances, which must be reported upon to the Government. There are several complaints as you know yourself; but the *onus* lies on the mining industry to show where the grievances lie in order to enable the Government to deal with those grievances.

Classification of Mines.

Witness.] If you will allow me to make my statement first it will simplify matters very much. The mining industry here consists of practically two classes of mines; those that pay and those that don't pay. What I understand this Commission is to enquire into is whether it is possible to work those mines in such a way

Mining Costs. as to return a profit. Now, in working those mines the cost is divided into two classes, wages and material used in those mines. Wages are also divided into two

White Wages. classes, whites' wages, and blacks'. The cost of white wages depends upon the law of supply and demand, and the cost of the living of the white people. If the Commission desire to go into the question of the wages of the white people, we can prepare tables as required. The cost of living of the white people depends upon the price of the food they consume, and that is made up in this country largely by the charges of railway carriage and Customs dues, in addition to the original cost of the goods

Native Wages. at the place where they came from. The next question is that of native wages and it is a very important one, not only for the mines, but for the farmers, and everybody who requires labour. I think we are all agreed that the natives are too highly paid in this country. But the difficulty is, how can the wages be reduced, and I am not sufficiently acquainted with the natives of the Transvaal, and to the North, and in the Portuguese territory, to speak definitely on the matter but it is quite possible for the Commission to have those here who are better able to say whether these wages can be reduced or not. Then another question is the cost of goods, which are supplied to the mines. That divides itself into several minor

Dynamite. questions. The first probably that we could deal with would be that of dynamite because that is an article which is a subject of monopoly in the country, and the price at which it is sold is beyond our control. The Volksraad appointed a commission to inquire into this question, and they made a report which is embodied in the translation I now hand in. It gives the quantity which is used, the price at which it is supplied to the Government, and the profit made by the concessionaires over and above the profit made by the manufacturer of the goods in Europe. If the Commission wish it we can supply further evidence. Then the next item of large use at

Coal. the mines is coal, and the price at which it is delivered is affected by the railway charges. The whole question of the railway matter will be gone into by the Commission, I presume, because that question increases the cost of the goods, food, and stores which are required at the mines, and I think we are quite right in saying that

Railway Profits. the railways, not only of the Transvaal, but of Natal, Cape Colony and the Free State have made very handsome profits out of the carriage of the goods for the industry, and that they could reduce their tariffs without great injury to themselves Broadly, that is the position of the mining industry. There are other questions

Gold and Liquor Laws. involved. The Volksraad have already passed a new Liquor Law, which has acted favourably to the mining industry; they have also passed a Gold Law, and these two laws if efficiently and properly carried into effect would be of great advantage. The natives would not be able to get drink and would give full work, and if we had a good detective department we would be able to retain the gold which we now believe is being stolen from us. That practically sums up the position from the mining industry point of view, and on these heads we can supply the Commission with

y information that is required to facilitate their investigations. I should like to
ow if the Commission wish to approach the subject in that way, or if they have
ne arrangement of their own.

Mr. *Joubert.*

We seem to be starting in the middle of the matter. What I would like to Flotation of
ow first is if the child was born a healthy child ; whether the primary intention Mines.
many of the mines was fair and honest. Were they floated according to value ?—
at would be impossible for me to say.

Mr. *Smit.*

Are you interested in mining other than as Chairman of the Chamber of Mines ?—
m a director of four companies—the Robinson, the Ferreira, the Jumpers and Paarl
ntral, and also of a coal company.
Are they paying mines ?—The first two are absolutely paying; the Jumpers has
id at intervals, and the Paarl Central has never paid.
Is there only one Chamber of Mines ?—There are two. Formerly they were one,
t there was a split.
Why ?—For various reasons. One object, however, both have in view. After the
turbances which occurred in the beginning of last year feeling ran rather strong
ween different parties interested in the mines, with the result that some members
ided to have a new Chamber of Mines for themselves.
Were they political differences ?—No.
What are their different names ?—One is called the Witwatersrand Chamber of
nes, the other the Association of Mines of the South African Republic. I am chair-
n of the Chamber of Mines. Mr. Albu is chairman of the Association of Mines.
You say in a petition that the liquor law operated at first very satisfactorily, Working of Li-
t not afterwards.—At first the people were afraid to sell liquor to the natives quor Law.
ause they felt they would be apprehended and punished, but now they find
police supervision is not as good as it ought to be, and they are selling liquor to
tives now at a higher price and making a profit.
The police supervision has not ceased, but the people used to be more afraid of
law ?—Yes.
If there were a better staff of police and detectives it would be carried out
perly ?—I believe so.
Before the dynamite monopoly existed, what was the price of dynamite ?— Dynamite.
annot say ; from memory I think it about £5.
At present ?—About £5 7s. 6d. Of course the conditions of the country are altered
ce that time, the nearest point of the railway then being Kimberley.
At what price at the present moment could dynamite be landed here ?—At less
n 40s.
What guarantee have you that the manufacturers would not form a ring to keep
the price if the present monopoly was removed ?—There are sufficient manufacturers
w in the world, and the competition is so great that we could make contracts for
supply at reasonable prices. There are no patents in existence. Anybody can
ke dynamite.

Mr. *Joubert.*

What is the price of dynamite at the factory ?—At the factory, 85s.
What is the imported price ?—40s. or less.

Mr. *Schmitz Dumont.*

Railway Rates.   You have also said the freight charges are too high; what reductions do you w
made in order to make the poorer class of mines pay ?—The rates on coal ought to
reduced to the lowest price the railway can afford to carry it for.

And as to machinery and other things ?—I am not a railway expert, and canr
particularize what ought to be reduced specially.

What is your opinion as to the reductions on food and machinery carriage,
order to make the poorer mines pay ?—I think the railways could make a reduction
30 per cent.

What is the price of a ton of coals delivered at the mines ?—About a pound.

How much could be saved out of that ?—From Brakpan the cost of carriage
5s. 1d. per ton; then there are siding charges of 2½d. per ton, and additional charg
on taking it from the sidings to the mines.

What is the objection to coal being delivered in sacks instead of in bulk ?—T
Railway Company declines to give sidings where the trucks can be off-loaded.   T
train comes along with the coal, and they give you about ten minutes to take all t
coal off, and unless it is in bags it cannot be taken off in time, and the line would
blocked.

Would it be better in bulk ?—Yes.   The saving in case of bags would be 1s. 6
per ton; the filling and stowing another 6d. per ton and another advantage wou
be that the coal, when it is taken out of the mine, could be taken up in big block
instead of being broken up small, and causing the waste of coal, which, of course, h
to be paid for by the industry.

Could you suggest a remedy against that, and also to bring about a reduction
kaffir wages ?—I think you could get someone who could more satisfactorily answ
these questions.

Kaffir Wages.   What do the kafirs get ?—About 2s. a day and their food.

What do you think a fair wage ?—I think they ought to work for 1s. 3d. or 1s. 6
per day and their food.

Is there much trouble to get kafirs to work ?—At times.   Just now they a
plentiful.

Mr. *Smit.*

Railway Divi-   Do you mean that the railways in this State or outside are paid too much ?
dends.   Speaking from memory, on the Cape line they make a profit of nine per cent. on the
capital, the result of carrying goods for the Transvaal; they make about a million
year profit; and in Natal, last year, their profit was about three-quarters of a millio
the bulk of which is made out of carriage of goods for the Transvaal.

In arriving at the thirty per cent., have you taken into consideration the relatio
between the capital and the earning power ?—The question I answered was on goo
used by the mines; the railway carries everything.

Do you mean they would make nine per cent. if they deducted thirty per ce
What would remain for the railways after thirty per cent. was deducted ?—It wou
be impossible for me to say.   At any rate less than nine.

Ferreira and   What dividend does the Robinson mine pay ?—13½ per cent.   The Ferreira pa
Robinson Cap-   275 per cent.   The capital of this company is £90,000, that of the Robinson
itals.   £2,750,000.

Is it fair to take off from the 9 per cent. railways and nothing off these mine
—If all the companies were like the Robinson and Ferreira there would be nothi
to say.   I do not come here to ask for a reduction solely on their account.

Would it not be fair to make the good-paying companies pay for those that do not pay ?—The question from the capital point of view has not been arrived at that way. The Ferreira, for instance, has a small capital ; when they wanted money to open out, and working machinery, they were able to sell shares at a very high price to provide the necessary capital. The cost to open up the Ferreira was £450,000 ; that is, the cash required to provide machinery and to open out ; and if you calculate the profit on that, you will find that reduced the profits very much.

The Jumpers—did that pay better than at present ?—No.

Did neither Jumpers nor Paarl Central pay from the beginning ?—The Jumpers *Jumpers Dividends.* paid a dividend the first month, but not another for about four years, and then it paid a dividend ; another in about two years more, and there has been no dividend since January last year.

Can you explain why the Jumpers paid a dividend in the first month, and then no other for four years ?—They had a very rich leader on the surface of the ground, and when they took that out, it was several ounces to the ton ; the capital being small, they paid a dividend, as it cost next to nothing to get out the gold. Now that rich leader disappeared, and the reef is very much poorer. I may explain it thus : A reef may be profitable, it may be rich, and the cost of getting out a ton of ore is not so great as the gold obtained ; if that reef becomes poorer the cost would be the same per ton, and you would have less or no profit ; then comes the question that the reefs are not all continuous. [*The witness here exemplified his meaning by plan.*] It is the dead work which increases so largely the cost, it being one of the things no one knows until they get down. Some of the reefs are so broken up that the cost is more than the value of the gold in them when extracted.

Since when has the cost of dynamite been reduced ?—Just about the time the *Reduced Cost Dynamite.* concession was given the last time. About 1893. That was brought about by the fact that, when we proved that the dynamite was not being made in the country, the Government issued permits, and we were able to go and get the dynamite elsewhere. Nobels came in and sold at a lower price.

Mr. *Brakhan.*

Can you tell us the railway freights on bulky articles in Europe and elsewhere ?—Mr. Albu will be able to give you that information.

Chairman.

I would very much like to get some statistics.—If the Commission would state what they require, I will have it got ready.

We would like statistics on everything in connection with the importation *Statistics* by railway. As far as the matter has gone now, it does not bring us to the point *quired.* yet. We must have figures before us to show that dynamite can be sold cheaper, also the railway charges, not the profit the railway makes. We want to know if a certain reduction be made, what effect that will have on the working of the mines.

Mr. *de Beer.*

We want reliable statistics, and I want to ask you whether you know what percentage of expenditure the labour forms. Please divide it into white and black labour.—Mr. Eckstein, at the Rand Mines meeting, recently, made the following *Percentage of* statement :—He says these costs are mainly made up by half-a-dozen principal items ; *Mining Costs.* white labour, 28 per cent., or 8s. 3d. per ton ; black labour, 23 per cent., or 6s. 9½d. per ton ; explosives, 2s. 11½d. per ton ; coal, 2s. 4½d. per ton. I hand you the report as read at the meeting.

Would these remarks apply to all mines, or only those working under ex ceptionally favourable conditions ?—Mr. Eckstein made his report from twenty seve outcrop companies.

If we take the mines in general, would it be right to take 14s. for whites, an 11s. 6d. for blacks per ton ?—No, that would be too high.

Do you consider the statement you just handed in to be a fair statement ? Ca we take it as reliable statistics ?—Yes, I think so. I have not checked it.

According to your statement, the cost of some mines, labour alone, is over 50 pe cent., so that more than half the cost is for labour ?—Yes.

Is labour then the only question to be solved ?—Yes, the question is how can it k solved.

That is why we want your co-operation in the matter. Amongst the expenses c labour, do you include all salaries ?—Yes.

All directors' fees, etc. ?—I cannot say. I should think so.

Native Labour Difficulties. You say the native labour is far too high. You will admit that other industrie cannot possibly compete with it at the present price of native labour. Has th Chamber of Mines ever inaugurated any scheme to get cheaper labour ?—Yes, man schemes. We have had a separate inquiry in the matter to see if natives could not b brought from anywhere cheaper, but so far the matter has not been a success.

Is not one reason, that the native is not willing to work, and cannot be compelle to work ?—Yes, especially in the Transvaal.

Forced Native Labour. Have you ever submitted a scheme for compulsory labour by natives ?—N I think not.

Do you think it would be desirable to get forced labour ?—Yes.

Against fair pay ?—Of course.

So that the salaries would be equitable, comparing favourably with what the could earn elsewhere ?—Yes.

Of course any statement you make here is in the capacity of representative of th Chamber of Mines and director of four companies ?—Well, it must be taken as m opinion. There may be many members of the Chamber of Mines who do not agre with my opinion.

About the liquor question, you say it is a good law for the industry; do you mea generally or as far as the mines are concerned. ?—Both.

Number of Li- quor Licenses. There are about 400 licences in Johannesburg proper. According to the new la there ought to be only 60 or 70. Do you think it would be to the interest of Johannes burg and the inhabitants that the remainder should be abolished ?—I think the 60 o 70 embrace wholesale as well as retail licences, and in that case there would be too few because there must be enough not to give the wholesale houses a monopoly, and th hotels should have a larger proportion in Johannesburg than in smaller towns.

Do you consider wholesale liquor licences as commercial licences ?—Yes.

Mr. *Joubert.*

You have a book here showing the position of 27 companies ?—Yes.

There are 200 mines, and only reference is made to 27.—Yes. I have onl referred to the Robinson and Ferreira, that is why I brought the book.

Nothing about all the other mines not referred to in the report ?—No, but : anything more is wanted it can easily be supplied.

Action of Gov- ernment to relieve Native Labour Diffi- culties. In response to the complaint about high wages, have the Government taken n steps to give relief ?—The Government have expressed their willingness to do so.

The Commissioner of Natives was here to inquire into the matter some tim ago ?—Yes, I was out of town at the time.

It was done after consulting the Chamber of Mines ?—Yes.

The kaffirs are prepared to accept a reduction of wages as proposed ?—Yes. Reduction of Native Wages.
e pay was reduced and the kaffirs agreed to it; but we want a further reduction.

You must admit that the Government have assisted as far as possible in
e matter ?—Yes, in that matter.

Mr. *Hugo.*

Regarding this question of cost in wages and materials, has not the falling in
e grade of the ore something to do with it ?—That depends upon the way the ore is
ken out in many cases. There is no uniformity. In some mines you have what is
lled a south reef, which is sometimes rich, and then you might have a reef to the
rth of that, which would be poorer. There may be more south reef crushed one
ne than north, and of course that would affect the question.

You have handed in a report, and we must go by it ?—I came here unprepared,
d put my hand on that document as one that could be relied on at once. We can
epare whatever is required. That report merely gives some of the ideas.

Mr. GEO. ALBU, Chairman Association of Mines, was put into the witness chair. Mr. Albu's Evidence.
He stated he was a Director of several companies, and held a very large
interest in the mining industry.

Mr. *de Beer.*

The object of the Commission was fully explained by the Chairman yesterday.
re you prepared to give your evidence *seriatim* ?—Yes.

Just as you like, as Mr. Hay did yesterday ?—Yes ; I should like to make a state-
ent first.

Chairman.

I would like any declaration of that kind to be made in writing and handed in.
would contain more information than a verbal statement.

Mr. Albu then made the following statement.] Mr. Chairman and Gentlemen,— Commission approved in Europe.
fore submitting to your questions, I think it would be right to say a few words
out the work which is before us. I can assure you, I and my people in Europe have
iled with great satisfaction the appointment of this Commission to go into the
lady, as it were, of the mining industry. The position which you are called upon
perform is that of the operating surgeon, together with the members of the mining
dustry, who will act in a like capacity. The mining industry is at present ailing,
d that the Government is cognisant of the fact is proved by the appointment of this
quiry. I can assure you it is my earnest desire, unbiassed by any party feeling, to
re you such information as will give you a free and open bird's eye view of the
sition of the mining industry at the present moment. It is my desire to see the
ength of the State and the strength of the mining industry renovated, as it were.
an only compare these two, the State and the mining industry, as twins—twins not
the ordinary sense, but which, by some freak of nature, have grown together at one
int. The welfare of one must of necessity affect the welfare of the other. The
ning industry, I may say in answer to Mr. Joubert, is a child healthily born, but is
ginning to ail for want of proper nourishment—then the welfare of the State must
fer as well. Now, going boldly into the question generally—it is no earthly use Mining Industry to be dealt with as a whole
king out one or two mines of exceptional wealth—these are not the pillars of the
ate. The State is supported by the whole of the mining industry—the mining
dustry from east to west, for a distance of about 40 miles. It was simply a fallacy
pick out just one, two, or half-a-dozen mines which are rich. In illustration of this,

if the conditions are not changed, and changed soon, the pillars of the State must fa
and the whole burden will be put down upon the shoulders of these few rich min
and which you will agree with me are not strong enough to carry the burden of t
State, and they must in consequence fall too. It is, therefore, advisable in deali

Advantages of rich Mines to whole Mining Industry.

with the question, as I said before, not to pick out a few mines. You must not forg
that it has been the most fortunate day for the Transvaal that such mines as t
Robinson, Ferreira, and Wemmer were the first mines to be discovered. If one of t
poorer mines had been the first to be discovered, you could never have induced t
capitalists at Home in Europe to invest any money here; therefore it was a fortuna
thing that the gold was found in these rich mines first. So far then, these rich min
had served their purpose in having drawn the attention of the European capitalis

Importance of Mining Industry to the Republic.

to the Transvaal, and in enabling us to try the poor mines and open them up. Y
must understand further that an industry like the one in the Transvaal has nev
existed before in the world. I do not say that in order that you should have
exalted idea of the industry, but I would simply point out to you the importance
this industry to the Republic. Now, you must further understand that we have be
novices in working this industry. We could only gain our experience, if I may say
by the capital which we have put into the mines. We have found out where we ha
made mistakes and where we have been successful. To earn experience costs a lot

Support of European capitalists.

money, and it is still costing us a lot of money. We have not attained perfection
the working of our mines yet. I know that the European capitalist is perfect
willing to support us financially to earn this experience, provided that the Gover
ment will treat this industry in a fair and equitable manner. You have no idea t
impression which the appointment of this Commission has made at Home. I si
cerely regret that we have not come together—the mining industry and the Gover
ment—years ago. If we had, many sad hours might have been saved to both partie
Now, as I said before in the beginning of my explanation, two surgeons are necessar
to operate upon this healthily-born child. The Government is one physician and t
leaders of the mining industry the other. I know the seat of the disease, and yo
have to operate upon this child immediately. I would point out to my colleague, t
other surgeon, the Government, the two questions which affect the ultimate success
the mining industry are the Railway question and the Dynamite question. Now,
assure you I do not point out these things in order to blow into the same horn
everybody, but that is the seat of the disease which can be treated by the Governmer

Railway tariff.

To start with the railway tariffs. In European countries the Government who ow
the railway does everything in its power to bring the goods which are necessary for
certain industry at as cheap a rate as possible. I will give you a small instance whi
came under my notice only the other day. English firms used to send coal in gre
quantities to the northern part of Germany. The nearest coal mine in Germany w
about 340 miles away. In order to compete with the English coal, the Governmer
immediately reduced the freight on coal to a quarter of a penny per ton per mile—
fact, the railway is regarded in Europe as the means of bringing all that is necessar
to foster a factory or industry, and to bring the necessary machinery and necessar
material to the site of that industry at as low a cost as possible. What have you g
here, gentlemen? Our coal transport costs us from the coal mines to the gold min
about 6s. per ton, or an average of about 2½d., and including the charges made f
trucks, 3d. per ton per mile. I say the railway should, if it is absolutely necessary
foster the mining industry here, bring that coal to the mine at cost price even, f
they will be amply compensated by the flourishing state of the industry, and the
profits will be derived from other sources. I will give you a few instances. Fir
that of galvanised corrugated iron from England. The shipment from there cos

pproximately, free on board, £900. The approximate freight—the ship freight—to Delagoa Bay is £150. Now we come to the railway carriage from Delagoa Bay to ohannesburg, which is £580. From Durban and East London it is £660, and from 'ort Elizabeth to Johannesburg £700; so that the shipping charges from England re increased by 100 per cent. Then, as to pitch pine. 825 tons of this material cost in America £1,100; freight to Delagoa Bay £1,300. It is expensive n account of these 825 tons almost filling the ship. From Delagoa Bay to ohannesburg the charge is £3,093, so that the railway fare from Delagoa Bay to ohannesburg is three times the amount of the original cost of the stuff in America. 'rom Durban to Johannesburg it costs £3,650, and that means that the wood, which ost in America £1,100, costs, if you ship it by Durban, about £6,000. A cask of ement, which weighs 400lbs., costs 5s. 6d., freight to Durban 4s. 4d., Durban to Johannesburg £1 7s., and duty 12s. 3d. The duty alone on that commodity, which we equire for building here, is 250 per cent. on the original cost. Pipes, that is iron ipes, cost in Europe £10 per ton. The freight is £2 10s., and from Port Elizabeth to ohannesburg £8. One more item is that of deals, which generally come from Sweden. cargo of 3in. x 9in. deals costs free on board £1,000. The freight to Delagoa Bay, urban, and Port Elizabeth is £500; and railway carriage to Johannesburg is £1,600. 'rom Delagoa Bay and Durban is £1,900, and from Port Elizabeth to Johannesburg 2,000. I am giving you details concerning these materials simply because they equire those heavy materials to build over batteries and timber over shafts. If we ould do these things with cheese, I might give you the price of cheese, but it is heavy material which is necessary. In those tremendous charges of the Netherlands Rail- *Rates of Cape and Natal Railways.* vay you give the Colony and Natal a very good handle to turn the same organ. It ad been repeatedly said that the whole of South Africa considered the Transvaal an range, and everybody sucks it, and they will suck until the juice has been sucked out f it and there will be nothing left. You cannot blame the other States for saying: Vhy should we reduce our railway rates if you don't do it ? In fact, the colonies go urther. Not only are they not satisfied with charging us heavy railway rates, they harge us transit dues as well. This is not done anywhere, so far as my knowledge oes, in the world. They excuse themselves by saying that they are building large ocks, etc., but they forget that they are charging very handsome dock dues, and the ery fact of them charging us transit dues is a piratical act committed on the State. ut you cannot blame them. It is for the Government to see that these railway rates re reduced, and then we have a just case for the colonies to do likewise. Is it not ufficient and conclusive proof to you, gentlemen, that the Cape Government Railway ade last year 9 per cent. profit—divisible profit—and all from this northern line, for happen to know myself that the other lines did not pay. Is it an argument to say *Distinction between Mining and Railway Companies.* nat because the Robinson and the Ferreira companies are paying large dividends why hould we expect the railway companies to reduce their profits ? You must always onsider, gentlemen, it is not the railways which make the gold mines, it is the gold ines which make the railways. If we had no gold mines here we would have no ailways, and, all over the world, if the Government derives from its railways $3\frac{1}{2}$ or 4 er cent. then they are perfectly satisfied. The Government's duty is to foster the ndustry which is the staple industry of the country, and if that industry flourishes, nen the welfare of the State is assured. Now, gentlemen, another important item. don't want to go into details as to what profits the concessionaire is making; I only *Cost of Dynamite* ish to point out, gentlemen, that an article which costs to manufacture at Home 3s. 6d. per case should be paid for by us 85s. And it is not an article which is used a small quantities. The Transvaal is about the largest consumer in the world of this rticle, and must not we look idiotically foolish—that we, as the largest consumer, pay (for an article that costs 18s. 6d.) 85s., and when the Government only makes 5s. per case over that. I don't think you can find its equal anywhere in the world, and think the Government will see the fallacy of upholding a concession which is not carrying out in the first instance its object, and which has so far shown an utter apathy to trying to meet the mining industry here. Years ago, when the railway was built, you fixed a certain rate of tariff for the work which had to be done then by

Consumption of Dynamite. the railways. The same with the dynamite. You fixed the rate years ago when the consumption was about 40,000 cases. It had run to the respectable quantity of 108,000 cases last year. I can assure you if the industry is supported by the Government as it ought to be, then the consumption of dynamite will soon increase within a short time to 300,000 cases. This fact alone should have dictated to the dynamite monopolists quite a different policy to the one which they have carried on so far. The same argument applies to the railway people. To illustrate the case to you. If I go to my municipality and ask them to allow me to build a tramline, the price they will allow me to charge for each person will be high if the traffic is but a limited one. If the Government does its best, and we do our best, the work can be accomplished. Opinions on this matter, of course, differ, say 10s. per ton, some 6s. per ton, and others 5s. per ton. In this way we will be enabled to work the mines, which, at the present moment, work without any profit, profitably. We do not complain of the fact, gentle-

Effects of economic relief. men, that there are a good many mines in the Transvaal that won't pay if they got dynamite and native labour for nothing. But these mines we can well leave out entirely in our calculations. They were concerned mostly with the mines between the eastern and western portions of the Witwatersrand, and if these can work at a reduction of 5s. only per ton, then you will see that prosperity will return to Johan-

Probable effect of depression. nesburg. I don't know whether you are aware that we are at present in a condition of great depression, and there is no improvement in the state of affairs, as the European capitalists are tired of putting in more money in a place which has to pay enormous prices for its principal commodity, dynamite, and where such extraordinary tariffs exist as those shown by our railway tariff. As a friend of the Government I can only point out to you, gentlemen, that if this depression lasts you will soon feel the effects in your own Budget. It is, therefore, necessary for our benefit as well as for the sake of the welfare of the State, that we should work hand in hand together to foster this industry, and to bring it to its height. There are a few minor questions

Liquor Law and its administration. gentlemen. For instance, take the Liquor Law, which was a very good one, but the administration of the law was very lax. What does it matter to a man when he has paid his £50 fine. You have the best proof of this in a case in the Meyer & Charlton in Jeppestown. There is a canteen there that has been trapped no less than three times last year, and has received its licence, only in a different name this time.

Chairman.

Its name?—The name was Judellsen, and the place used to be called the Park Bar. The drink, gentlemen, is the curse of the place, and unless the law is strengthened so that there is more severe punishment than a fine of £50, the traffic will continue rampant as it is at the present moment, and will only increase. Another question which affects us, and cuts very, very deep into the mining industry, is gold thefts. What we want, therefore, is an honest Detective Department, without which you will never be able to detect the criminals. The other questions we have to deal with are native labour, white labour, and the general management of our affairs, and

Over-capitalisation. I can assure you that the leaders of the industry are working to see whether we can improve matters. It is no use, gentlemen, saying, "Are there not mines which have been over-capitalised?" There may be mines over-capitalised, and I not ashamed to

that there are mines which are over-capitalised, and there are also mines in
existence which have no gold, although the property was reported to be very rich at
the time of the flotation. We would have been a very extraordinary community if
there had not been some of us who had taken advantage of the people who were
ready to put in money from Home. This sort of thing you find when there is a boom.
You have had this in America and Europe. It is always in such times, flourishing
ones, that flotations are made, the basis of which is not very sound, but that has
nothing to do with our mining industry whether there are mines over-capitalised.
The question is " can you work a mine with a profit? " Never mind what its capital

By way of instance, I may mention to you that I myself floated a company a few
years ago, the property of which consisted of 250 claims, for a sum of £10,000 cash
working capital, and the total capital of the company was only £10,000. Although
they had £10,000 cash and 250 claims, I lost all the same, for the rich reef I thought
I had, had given out, therefore whether it had been a million or £10,000 capital I
would have lost everything. Mr. Chairman and gentlemen, I thank you for the
patient hearing you have given me, and I can assure you from the bottom of my
heart it is only my desire to see this State flourish, together with the mining
industry.

I would like to have reliable statistics of the freight of coal, etc., in the Transvaal
and Colony.—I will work out whatever statistics are required, and hand the same in
to the Secretary.

Mr. *Joubert.*

I would like to hear the resolution passed by us in our meeting at Pretoria, as
in what order we are going to work, so that I cannot again be said to be out of
order like yesterday.

Mode of proce-
dure of Com-
mission.

Mr. *de Beer.*

You gave us a very full explanation, Mr. Albu, as to what you expect from the
one side, the Government; but I would like to know what is going to be done from
the other side, the industry.

Mr. *Joubert.*

Before we go any further I want to hear that resolution of ours, else, I won't ask
another question. I do not want to be insulted again.

Chairman.

Any member can ask any question, but I think I, as Chairman, can correct
anybody if out of order.

Mr. *Joubert.*

I appeal to the internal regulations of the Commission.

In order to give Mr. Joubert an insight into the regulations as desired, the
Chairman adjourned the sitting for a quarter of an hour, and the public, as well as
the press, were asked to leave the room.

Mr. *de Beer.*

On resuming the sitting, Mr. de Beer repeated his question to Mr. Albu, and
asked his opinion about the reduction of native wages.

Witness.] The reduction of native labour is necessary for two reasons, the one is
reduce our whole expenditure, and the second has a very far-reaching effect upon
the conditions which may prevail with regard to native labour in the future. The

native at the present moment receives a wage which is far in excess of the exigenc of his existence. The native earns between 50s. and 60s. per month, and then he pa nothing for food or lodging, in fact he can save almost the whole amount he receiv At the present rate of wages the native will be enabled to save a lot of money in couple of years. If the native can save £20 a year, it is almost sufficient for him go home and live on the fat of his land. In five or six years' time the nati population will have saved enough money to make it unnecessary for them to wo any more. The consequences of this will be most disastrous for the industry and t State. This question applies to any class of labour, and in any country, whether it in Africa, Europe, or America. I think if the native gets sufficient pay to save £ɛ year, that sum is quite enough for his requirements, and will prevent natives fro becoming rich in a short space of time.

You say the native does not require luxuries, and if he has worked for a year has saved enough to go back to his kraal and remain idle ?—Yes.

Can you suggest any remedy for this ?—The only remedy I can suggest is th we pay the natives a wage which, whilst enabling him to save money, will hinder hi becoming exceptionally rich.

Why were not the wages reduced before ?—For years and years we we labouring under a scarcity of native labour, which to a great extent is now abate At the present moment we have sufficient labour. Secondly, we have come to t conclusion that it is absolutely impossible to pay these high wages. We have eith to reduce our expenses, or we have to shut down the greater number of our mines.

Reduction of cost of Native Labour. Is it in the control of the mining industry to regulate the wages of kafirs ?— a great extent it is, provided that the Government assists us in bringing labour this market. The difficulties which the mining industry has to contend with in th **Supply of Native Labour.** respect are numerous. Native Commissioners up North want to receive a certa amount of compensation for every native which they send down. I do not kno **Remuneration demanded by Native Commissioners.** whether the Government is cognisant of this, but it is always a question of 10s. or ɛ per head which the mining industry has to pay to someone to collect natives an forward them here.

What amount is generally charged ?—It varies. It depends upon the deman If there is a great need of natives, the amount is a large one. Another difficulty **Railway charges for transport of Natives.** occasioned by the Railway Department exacting a large amount per head to bring t native to his destination. They ought to carry everything that is necessary for t mining industry at as low a rate as possible.

That is a question of opinion.—The native, as a rule, who wants to come dov to work, has no money, and the mining industry has to advance his fare ; and, wh the native comes here, we have so little control over him that he can easily desert. has occurred to companies who have brought down 500 natives at a cost of £1,25 that 300 have deserted after a week. The suggestion which one could make to t Railway Department is that they should bring down natives at a nominal rate, an charge him the full rate when he returns to his country ; and that the Governme should see that its servants in the native districts are sufficiently honest.

Is there no competition in the wages paid to the natives amongst t companies, or have they agreed on a certain scale ?—They agreed about eig months ago to reduce the native pay, but we find that even that amount is far in exce of the value of the work which they render to their respective companies. As I sa before, we cannot make both ends meet, and, sooner than pay thousands of pounds wages, and be unable to make a return to our shareholders, we will close down t mines.

Is there competition amongst the mines with regard to the wages ?—I don't think at the present moment.

You said nothing about white labour; is it a fact there are thousands of white miners out of employment at the present moment ?—I think there are a good many workmen out of employment.

Are you of the opinion that the wages paid to miners at the present moment are abnormal ?—In some instances they are abnormal.

Is there any chance of getting these abnormal wages reduced now that there are so many out of work? Certainly there is; I think the white labourers are prepared to accept the lesser of two evils. If we close down the mines a lot of white labourers will be thrown out of employment. *Reduction of white wages.*

What is the wage of the ordinary white man? —From £18 to £22 per month.

If I can show from statistics that white labour costs £40 per head per month, would I be right?—That includes managers' and secretaries' salaries, and so forth.

We must get the average cost of white labour in that way?—There are men who are paid £40 and £35 per month who do not deserve more than £25 and £30. I do not propose to attack the miner who receives £18; he does not receive very much in excess of what he ought. *Wages of Miners.*

What is the average wage of white miners in Europe?—I think about £4 per month.

How can you account for the difference in wage of £14?—It is much more expensive living in this country. A man pays for his board alone £5 and £6 per month, and, if he be a married man, his rent is a very heavy item.

Does not the company in most instances supply quarters?—Yes, in some instances; but where there is an excess of married men they could not supply accommodation. Another thing why a man wishes to earn more than in his own country; he comes 7,000 miles from home, and he has got to pay for that, and he thinks of paying a visit to his home.

What is the reason of some miners receiving £18 and others receiving abnormal wages?—Well, there are workmen and workmen, you must remember as well as managers and managers. One man may be cheap at £200, and another may be cheap at £1,500. It always depends on the mental work, as well as the physical work. We can reduce white wages if the railway tariffs are reduced, as the necessities of life would be made cheaper in this place.

Is £1,500 the maximum wage paid to mine managers and consulting engineers ?—There are bigger salaries paid. *Salaries of Mine Officials.*

Can you give us the maximum figure?—Well, I should say the highest salary paid to managers is about £3,000. Only a few receive that amount, and they are good men, or, at least, they are supposed to be.

And the engineers?—Well, those men who receive £3,000 are supposed to be engineers.

Do you know of any higher salaries paid than £3,000?—Higher salaries were paid, but I don't know whether they are still paid. There may be such as to the men in high positions, such as the consulting engineers of financial corporations.

Are these wages included as wages paid to white labour ?—No, they don't rank in any statistics.

Do they appear in the cost of white labour in the mining companies' expenses ?—Oh! yes.

What do these financial corporations want with a consulting engineer ?—They require a consulting engineer to examine the mines, and, unfortunately in some cases, on their reports most of the financial corporations put their money into the mines.

Do these financial corporations charge for the services of their engineers?—No, the engineer is for their own purposes.

Is not the ground sufficiently developed yet for local men to report on?—There are local men certainly, but these financial corporations are mostly floated in Europe and the directors choose men of whose ability they have knowledge, and they send them to South Africa. I may say I have engaged a consulting engineer in this place.

Purchase of machinery. Who has charge of the purchase of machinery on the mine?—The Board, under the advice of the consulting engineer. In companies honestly managed, tenders are asked for for the machinery which is necessary.

And in other companies again it is simply done on the recommendation of the directors?—The directors will never undertake to order machinery unless they have the advice of their engineer. The boards in most cases consist of laymen.

Charges of Foreign Railways. You have been talking about the railways in other countries being only in existence to foster the industries. Do you include England and Holland in these countries?—Yes.

Can you quote any railway in England or Holland that does it?—I have never lived a sufficient time in England, and have never lived in Holland, but I know an instance in Germany. Yes, I do know an instance in England that only came to my knowledge yesterday. There is a railway in the south of Wales of the length of 25 miles. This railway has been built for the purpose of bringing coal from a certain coal district to supply the docks. This railway, although of a length of 25 miles, has, with its various tracks and link lines, a total mileage of 120 miles. The capital of this railway is eight and-a-half millions. They charge only 1s. 3d. per ton for 25 miles, and, if the wagon is not supplied by the coal mine, 6d. per ton for the 25 miles. The total cost is therefore ·84d. per ton per mile, and it would be less if it were reasonable to expect that those who pay the money into this railway concern should receive less than a dividend of, for 1894, 3¼, and for 1895, 3⅛ per cent. I have pointed out in my address to you that the German Government, in order that their coal mines should compete with foreign mines, have reduced the coal tariff to a quarter of a penny per ton per mile.

Cape Colony and Natal Railway tariffs. Speaking about the height of the tariff here and in Cape Colony and Natal, supposing the tariffs here were lowered, what about the tariffs of Cape Colony and Natal?—I always took it that Natal co-operates, or is influenced to a great extent by the tariff which is charged by the Netherlands Railway, and if the Netherlands railway were to reduce its tariff, Natal would follow suit, and Cape Colony would be forced, in order to retain some trade, to also reduce the rates. The Netherlands Railway has got a good lever in the Delagoa Bay line.

Delagoa Bay route. Do you think the mining industry would support the Delagoa Bay line supposing the neighbouring Colonies would not support a reduced tariff?—Yes, provided Delagoa Bay would give it facilities for landing goods, and forwarding goods the same as those given by Natal and the Cape Colony. But the arrangements at the present moment in Delagoa Bay are frightfully bad. The administration is very unreliable there, and we are therefore compelled to get our materials through other ports, and we prefer paying a little more than having the uncertainty which prevails through the administration of Delagoa Bay.

If there were good administration in Delagoa Bay you would prefer that route with a reduced tariff?—Being the shortest route, certainly.

Number of Mines on Witwatersrand. Can you give the Commissioners the exact number of mines in existence?—No, that I cannot.

How many companies are there, can you say?—That I really don't know by heart. There are, I should say, about 170 on the Witwatersrand.

Can you give us the number of mines which pay dividends and mines which Dividend and non-dividend paying Mines.
not pay dividends?—Approximately I can. I think there are about 25 companies
t pay dividends, and the rest consist of mines that just cover their working
enses; mines that are working at a loss; and mines which are in the course of
elopment.

Are all those mines *bona fide* mining concerns?—On the Witwatersrand, yes.

And also on other reefs, such as the Black Reef?—Yes. Of these 150 companies Bogus Companies.
ich are not paying dividends there are about 25 floated in London during the
m, and the reefs of which exist in the imagination of the floaters, or the promoters.

Do you know how many Main Reef companies there are—outcrop and deep- Main Reef Mines
els?—There are about 120 companies in all, I think, on the Main Reef.

Your opinion is that all the companies on the Main Reef are *bona fide*?—Yes.

There are a number of companies which are not payable?—Yes.

Generally known as wild cats?—Yes.

You just now observed that the capital of the company in no way affected the
t of working the company?—Is it not a fact that too much money has gone into
pockets of the vendors and promoters?—That may have been the case years ago.

What does reconstruction imply?—Reconstruction means that if a company after Reasons for reconstructions.
ving opened up work for some time has found out its machinery is obsolete, they
ve to raise fresh capital in order to get machinery of later pattern.

Is that the only reason?—No, there are other reasons. Five or six years ago, as
ted in my address to you, being novices at gold mining, in floating the company
y provided it with too small working capital, and not being able to judge the
uirements of such a company in the shape of machinery, the consequence was they
nted more capital to complete the installations.

Was it never a reason for reconstruction that there was too little working
ital?—Yes, but there are other reasons. Granted that the working capital was
ficient to develop the mine to a certain depth and to put up machinery and installation,
company may find on going down to that depth that the reef breaks off and forms to
north or south, and so all calculations as to the number of tons required to be moved
the developing work prove a failure. That is, in consequence of these breaks and
ms in the reefs, they require more working in order to go down to greater depth
l to take up the reef.

Are there no other reasons?—Of these reasons one or the other, although other
sons may have been faulty management. Also to acquire additional ground.
sometimes occurred that in days gone by, when the laws in this place were not
good for the mining community, the ground and titles were at fault through no
lt of the promoters, and the ground was jumped and had to be bought back.

The cost of labour will be greatly increased when the deep levels are at work?— Cost of Deep Levels.
you mean the opening of the deep levels?

The cost of native labour and general expenses?—The general expenditure, yes,
some extent, certainly.

Could you give a percentage?—No, but I may say that it will be counter-
anced by the using of the latest machinery. Engineers are at work to improve
on the methods adopted of extracting gold with regard to the expenditure, as well
to the actual extraction, and they will counterbalance to a great extent the greater
t of deep level mining.

Will you explain to the Commission whether deep levels stand on their own Deep Levels.
und, or whether they are only subsidiary to the outcrop companies.—They are not
nected, and work quite independently.

They are floated in different companies?—Yes.

Did I understand you aright when you said that there were two levels to
struck ?—No, I only said there was one.

You said that there were capitalists in Europe, and these found that in eve
community there were people who were desirous of "squeezing the lemon"?—Y
I made that comparison about squeezing the lemon, and compared this industry to t
lemon, and the high rates and charges over the whole of South Africa—transit duti
dynamite profits—to the squeezing. So long as the industry, which I compared
the lemon, has anything in it, it will be squeezed till it is perfectly dry and useless.

Working of Liquor Law. In the beginning the Liquor Law worked satisfactorily as regards the mines
In some districts yes, where the supervision was good. In the Krugersdorp distr
it never worked well.

Liquor licenses. Do you think that in a community like this 60 licences is enough for the wh
of Johannesburg ?—The town is a very thirsty place.

Leaving alone that question, take a normal view of the matter. Don't you thi
that 60 would be too few ?—I cannot give you an opinion on that.

What is your opinion about wholesale licences ; are they commercial licences
liquor licences ?—They are commercial licences.

It is not the case that the Park Bar at the Meyer and Charlton has
licence. The licence has been provisionally transferred by the Chairman. I wi
to state that for your information.—How I came to the conclusion was, that whe
went down yesterday to the mine I saw the bar opened in another name.

Mr. *Joubert.*

Is it not a fact that the confidence of capitalists in Europe has be
shaken ?—Yes.

Effects of redress of grievances. If the Government give a reduction in the railway tariffs; if the Governme
tries to do its utmost to get labour wages reduced, and make an arrangement abo
dynamite, will that confidence be restored, in your opinion ?—Decidedly.

Will the capitalist again invest his money ?—Yes.

Without getting a clear statement as to whether their capital here is invested
payable mines ?—Yes.

Will do it blindly ?—The capitalists in Europe have representatives here ;
myself, represent a financial group in Europe, and they have asked me whether it w
not the time now to invest money ?

And the confidence in Europe will be restored without proper proof being p
duced that companies are floated on an honest basis ?—Well, the flotations which ha
not been done on an honest basis are finished with. They cannot get that mon
back.

Still it has shaken the confidence of capitalists ?—Well, it may have contribut
to the reasons.

Why has nothing been said about that ?—I am always speaking about it.

But there never has been any complaint to the Government ?—Certainly y
cannot expect a woman who sells fish to tell her customers it is stinking fi

But the unexpected happens occasionally ?—Yes, somebody finds it o

Don't you think it would be desirable for the Commission to point out to t
investing public what has been done with the money in the past which has be
lost ?—They know themselves how it has been lost.

They don't know generally ?—By Jove ! I think they do.

Mr. *Smit.*

Of which Companies are you a director or manager ?—I am managing director

...e Meyer and Charlton, Roodepoort United Main Reef, George Goch Amalgamated, ...d Aurora West, besides director of the Coal Trust, Steyn Estate, Midas East Estate. ...don't think any more.

What dividends have these Companies paid, more or less?—Only three of these companies have paid dividends, namely, the Meyer and Charlton, Roodepoort United ...ain Reef, and the Coal Trust.

Of what amount during the last year?—The Meyer and Charlton paid 20 per ...nt. during 1896, Roodepoort United 35 per cent., I believe, and the Coal Trust 5 per ...nt. in 1896.

Do you know anything about gold mining in other countries?—No.

Do you know anything about taxation levied by the Civil Government on gold ...ines in other countries?—No.

So you cannot say whether the taxation comes heavy or light?—No.

Are any taxes imposed by the Government direct which form the subject of ...bjection or grievances here?—With the exception of a few where special taxation ...kes place, I don't think we can complain very much.

I do not allude to import duty, but to personal taxes and taxes levied by the ...tate.—I don't think we have anything to complain of.

In respect to claim licences or prospecting licences. Are these considered ...xcessive?—No, I don't think so.

Don't you think prospecting licences might be reduced?—Well (after considera-...ion), the present charge for prospecting licences is 5s., isn't it? No, I don't think ...ney need be reduced.

You think that charge is reasonable?—I think it is sufficient, but I don't think ... is too much, especially in bad times such as we have at present.

You stated this morning that the charge for railage of coal is too heavy, and that ...the Railway Company were to carry coal at a cost just enough to cover expenditure ...ey would reap benefit from other sources. What sources do you refer to?—First of ...l, the very fact of not only the coal tariff but others being reduced would make ...ining in itself cheaper. This would prevent, in the first instance, mines which are ...ill at work having to close down, and mines which are not working at the present ...oment on account of the heavy burdens, will be able to start work. These mines, ...hich will re-start working, will require new machinery, and this would swell the ...venue, of course, of the railway. In fact, if we get these reforms which we are ...sking, it would impart a new impetus to the mining industry. Fresh capital ...ould be brought into the country again, and it is a well-known fact that workmen ...nd men of science follow in the train of capital.

That would affect more the outside railways than the railways within the ...tate, because they have a bigger mileage outside than inside the State?—So long as ...is railway makes a good profit, you cannot be jealous of the profit which the other ...ilways make from legitimate traffic.

You see it would help to reduce the freight from here to Vereeniging to a ...inimum, whereas the greater portion is paid from Vereeniging to East London.—...es, but they would also reduce. You see, although the line of the Netherlands ...ailway is but a short distance, I may point out that the dividend paid for ...895 came to 36½ per cent. on the capital of the Netherlands Railways. That was ... 1895, and if I take the figures of receipts as a guide for the profits which the ...etherlands will make for 1896, the dividend of the Netherlands Railway will ...mount to 100 per cent.; of course, including the share of the profit which the ...overnment gets.

The report of the Netherlands Company, which I have got before me, for 1895 shows a dividend of 8·4.—Yes, I have got down approximately 9 per cent.

In the 8·4 is included the amount paid to the Government.—No. After you paid the amount to the Government, 8·4 is left to the shareholders. You paid to the Government in 1895 £322,327 13s. 4d. This item alone comes t 27½ per cent. on the capital of the Netherlands Railway. The capital of th Netherlands is £1,166,666 13s. 4d. The shareholders received a dividend the of 9 per cent., or 8·4. The clear profit for 1896 on the Netherlands Railway will b at least a million. Now, I will point out to you the Netherlands Company has in vested a share capital (apart from debenture issue, of course) of £1,166,666—a littl over a million. They have earned a million net profit last year. That is what i will come to. The mining industry has invested anything between 75 and 12 millions. This varies according to the value of the shares. And they have paid ou last year a little over a million and a half. So this illustration will go a long way to prove to you that we not only pay too much to the railway companies, but that th request of the industry that the Netherlands Company should reduce its rates is bu reasonable and justified. I still maintain that it is the duty of a railway company t bring the materials which are necessary for opening up and working an industry a as low a price as possible. And in some countries they even go so far as to bring thi material at a loss to the seat of the industry. In the long run they make a profit.

Are these Companies belonging to the State or private Companies?—On th State railways on the Continent there is an enormous traffic, but it does no return the Government more than 3 to 3½ per cent. On the private railway in England I think the shareholders are highly pleased if they make 4½ pe cent. Now, go to the railways in America. Still, there is not a single one that ha paid a dividend yet.

Those Companies which carry necessities for the mines at a loss, are the companies belonging to the State or private Companies?—On the Continent the belong to the State.

So the State is there to help the industry?—Certainly.

Are there any private Companies which carry goods at a loss in order to foste the industry?—Well, I suppose there must be, because in England, where the railway belong to private Companies, if the earning power is only 3 to 4 per cent., I thinl they must to some extent carry goods at a loss.

A private Company which owns a railway is on an equal footing with a privat Company which runs a mine?—Yes.

And why should then a railway company carry goods of an oppositio company at a loss?—In the first instance we do not ask the Netherland Company to reduce its rates. We ask the Government to do that, one way or the other, for the simple reason that if nothing is done in that respect th Netherlands Company will be a much heavier loser, and the State with it.

What would be the object of a company in England carrying goods for othe industries—for private companies—at a loss?—If the industry prospers under certai conditions, these conditions must be considered by the railway, and they get a profi out of other traffic created in consequence of the industry.

In short, they lose in one way and gain in another?—Quite so. I don't say th Netherlands Company need carry anything at a loss, the margin is so enormously great.

Can you quote any industry which is supported by the railway at Home b carrying goods at loss in order to foster the industry?—The railway in Silesia carrie coal at a loss.

Mr. G. Albu's Evidence.

21

Where do they carry it to ?—They carry it right through the country. It is the
arest coal mine to the northern part of Germany, and the railway carries the coal
: a quarter of a penny per ton per mile. If the Government had not done that,
ese coal mines would have been compelled to close down, and the population would
ry likely leave the country.

What benefit does the railway derive in other directions ?—Well, the population *Advantages of low freights to Railways.*
increased in that part of the country, not alone by the various marriages which
te place there, and they require food stuffs. You know that sort of thing is like
chain, one link fitting into another.

Do you mean to say people get married because there is a cheap coal tariff ?—
at is it.

Can you explain why it is that dynamite formerly, before the concession existed, *Dynamite Concessions. Former prices of Dynamite.*
.s not cheaper than it was ?—First of all we had no railway communication
th the Transvaal, and it was sent by ox-wagon; secondly, the consumption was very
all, and we were not sufficiently large consumers to dictate to the powerful trust
mpany. To-day we are large consumers; we have railway communication, and
facility for bringing the dynamite to the mines. I think therefore we ought
get dynamite at a price which would allow the dynamite factory a reasonable
ofit. If this monopoly were not in existence we could get other people to supply
at a price very much less than Nobels are supplying it to-day.

There was a time when the dynamite factory could not supply the wants of the *Permits to import Dynamite*
ning industry, and the Government gave permits to importers. What was the price
dynamite then, was it high or low ?—I don't think it was much less than what it is
day. These permits, strange to say, found their way into the pockets of merchants,
that if a company required 50 cases per month and could not import the stuff
mselves they had to go to the merchants, who formed a little ring themselves.

If the permits got into the merchants' hands the representatives of the mining
lustry had only themselves to blame.—I believe others were in the same position as
vas. I was quite new here and did not know the circumstances. My time was
ficiently taken up in looking after the mines I became connected with, so I had not
ne to look after the dynamite question. The De Beers Company, for instance, pay *Price of Dynamite at De Beers.*
s. 6d. or 60s. for dynamite, and 12s. 6d. of that goes to the Cape Government, and
pay 80s. in the Transvaal. The De Beers Company consume about 80,000 cases in
e year. I am buying dynamite myself for a company I am connected with in the
mberley district for 55s.

Now ?—Yes. If De Beers required a larger consumption they could get it very
ich cheaper.

Now, formerly, I understand, that the sellers tried to get as much as possible out *Advantages of competition in trade.*
the sale of dynamite, and now the Government contract has been made at a certain
ure, they are all prepared to undersell.—Of course, competition is good for trade,
d if we close competition there is no business. Suppose, for instance, I came 20
ars ago to the Transvaal Government and got a concession from them to work
e gold in the Transvaal, and said I would give them £100,000, I think the
vernment would have done it. I would then have started to work the gold mines,
t do you think the place would have been so far ahead now. The Government
uld have had £100,000, and that is all. The Government's income is now about
,000,000 a year, simply through competition from the Transvaal Government having
rown open the fields to all, and invited everyone to come and prospect by merely
ying their licences. I see Pretoria flourishing, and a place like Johannesburg which
s sprung up within ten years, railways and bridges being built, and I can assure

you, sir, that if you only help the industry, this will be one of the most flourish
States in the world.

You said this morning that if the dynamite were cheaper there would be mo
carriage of it and a greater consumption ?—Yes.

As far as you know, are there any mines that cannot be worked because of t
price of dynamite ?—There are mines which I know which will have to be shut dov
if the Government will not grant these reforms, and we do not do something in t
matter of labour.

What can the Government do to prevent these mines shutting down ?—T
cheapening of dynamite, the reduction of the railway tariff so that we can get co
cheaper to the mine, and machinery and timber. These are the two importa
questions.

Do you think that will be sufficient assistance to work the mines which wou
otherwise be forced to lie idle ?—Yes, if we do our portions as well. We have
reduce native labour, and see that the managers exercise that tact and knowledge
the work in order to bring about the reduction of cost in the working. Only th
will we be able to work in such a way as to return a profit on the money invested
the mines.

Do you intend to cheapen kaffir labour ? How do you propose to effect that ?.
By simply telling the boys that their wages are reduced. The maximum at present
2s. 3d. a shift, and we can reduce that to 1s. 6d., that is for skilled labour. F
ordinary labour 1s. or less for the shift.

Suppose the kaffirs retire back to their kraals ? Now, in case that happened, a
that you were without black labour, would you be in favour of asking the Gover

ment to enforce labour ?—Certainly. A kaffir cannot live on nothing.

You would make it compulsory ?—Yes, I would make it compulsory, and witho
using force a tax could be levied. If a white man loiters about without doing an
thing he is run in. Why should a nigger be allowed to do nothing. If there is
famine in a district the Government has to pay for it, and that falls back again on t
industry. Therefore, I think a kaffir should be compelled to work in order to ea
his living.

Do you think that you would get the majority of the people on the Rand wi
you in trying to make the kaffirs work at a certain pay ?—I think so.

Would it not be called slavery ?—Not so long as the men earned a certain amou
of money.

If a man can live without work, how can you force him to work ?—Tax hi
then. If I have £5 per month to spend, I don't want to do any work; but if t
Government passes a law that all gentlemen at large whom you may know
South Africa, who often call themselves that, must pay £3 per month tax, the
only remains £2, and I am forced to work.

Then you would not allow the kaffir to hold land in the country, but he mu
work for the white man to enrich him ?—He must do his part of the work of helpir
his neighbours. How would the Government like us to sit down and say that w
have enough money; where would the State drift to? There is always competitio
in labour, and when a man once tastes the fruits of his labour he will work.

You said that the capital does not affect the working of the mines ?—That is
As I pointed out this morning, in my own case, I had a mine with £10,000 workir
capital, and that represented the whole of the capital of the company.

Suppose the mine had paid something, it would be far easier to return
£10,000 than £100,000 ?—Then the value of the shares would always be in proportic
to the profits. It does not matter whether I get £5 for £1 shares, the proportion

he same, and it makes no difference if the mine has been over-capitalised. Don't you Native locations. hink that with regard to native labour, if natives were allowed locations around ohannesburg it would be a good way of getting Kafirs here?

The kraal kafirs won't do this. Only Colonial boys will do it perhaps. If the ines came together to reduce wages to a certain figure, will it not harm the mines a great extent?—It will do harm to a certain extent, but we will have to get over his in some way or other. If, for instance, we want natives from Delagoa Bay, we Cost of procuring native labour. ave to pay 27s. 6d. to get a boy there. Who receives this money, I don't know, ut somebody gets it. Then we have to pay 20s. 6d. for railway expenses, and nother 10s. a head for collecting the boys and feeding them. Thus bringing a boy rom Komati Poort to here costs about 62s. 6d.

Can you give any instance where a Native Commissioner has charged for kafirs Exactions by Native Commissioners for supply of natives. ent to the mines?—No, but I am more or less certain that this is done. We pay he agents, and the agents again pay the officials.

Has it ever been attempted to import poor whites from Europe to labour ere, and to pay the expenses?—No, we have at present too many labourers here on ccount of the many mines that have stopped work.

As you said this morning, you have to pay high wages here because the living is Comparison of white wages and Railway rates. expensive, but can you then expect the railways which carry coal here to do it at he same rates as in other countries?—No, it must be done at a higher rate here, but ood wages have to be paid at Home as well, for if not, we will have more clever anagers here.

I know of cases where our Government pays engineers £100 per month, whereas hey only received £300 per year in Europe.—This is the case with the majority of .s.

Mr. *Brakhan.*

You told us this morning the loss to the mining industry by gold thefts is very Gold thefts. onsiderable. Can you inform us what amount per annum would they come to?— Well I think we can reckon, on what has been divulged lately, 10 per cent.

What amount would that be?—About 20,000 ozs. per month. Amount of gold thefts.

That would be about three-quarters of a million per year?—Yes.

You consider that an absolute loss which otherwise would be paid in dividends to he shareholders?—Yes.

Can you suggest any ways and means by which gold thefts can be prevented Prevention of gold thefts. ltogether or minimised?—The only way I think would be by an efficient detective epartment. I don't think any law will ever prevent or minimise the crime. I think a law were introduced which would deal very severely with the miscreants, and an onest detective department established in which we can have trust and repose onfidence, then I think we can minimise the gold thefts.

Do I understand that you suggest a separate detective department should be stablished simply to deal with gold thefts?—Yes, I would suggest that a separate etective department should be established, which would comprise advisory members ppointed by the mining industry.

With regard to native labour, do you consider that in the cold weather there Supply of native labour. ould be a sufficiently continuous supply unless locations were formed on the Rand? —My experience is that it was never owing to winter that we had less natives than the summer. There are always other reasons why the natives went home— loughing, sowing, or getting married.

Do you consider that if there are locations on the Rand you would have an Native locations ncreased supply of skilled labour?—Yes, I think they would stay here.

I have very often heard that the labour which comes to the Rand is to a great extent very inefficient and very incapable, and the natives have to be taught.—I think if the natives had their locations here, and had their wives and families, they would make this place their home.

I suppose in considering this question of locations you are in favour of compensation being given to the burghers of the State who give ground for the purpose of the locations ?—No; I think it a question for the Government to decide.

Salaries of Mine Engineers and Officials. You also alluded this morning to the excessive salaries paid to experts on the Rand; do you consider—I am speaking only of those who are really capable—that their salaries are very excessive in comparison with the salaries paid in Europe ?—That is a very difficult question to answer; brain power is a very expensive commodity, and a rare commodity too. A clever engineer may be satisfied with £2,000 a year, while another is not satisfied with £4,000.

Well then, I should think that these men who are well paid here could also command very good salaries in Europe and other parts of the world ?—Yes.

And they could live under more favourable conditions than they are doing here —Quite so.

You have mentioned that the industry is not heavily burdened by direct taxation, such as claim licences ?—That is my opinion.

Taxation of Mynpachts. We know, under the Gold Law, there is a provision where mynpachts may be taxed to the extent of $2\frac{1}{2}$ per cent. on the gold produced; now, do you consider if the Government compelled the owners of mynpachts to pay this $2\frac{1}{2}$ per cent., the owners of mines are at a disadvantage compared with those companies that merely hold claims ? —Well, I know some mynpachts that would not pay 6d. to the Government if the 2 per cent. were levied.

I mean in the majority of cases ?—You put a very awkward question, which I prefer not to answer.

Diggers' and claim licenses. Then, with regard to diggers' licences and claim licences, lately diggers' licences have been asked for prospecting claims which are not worked. What is your opinion with regard to that ?—My opinion is that the Government should not impose diggers' licences on prospectors' claims.

Profits on Dynamite. With regard to dynamite, you have told us that the cost to Nobel and other manufacturers is about 18s. ?—Yes, about £1; and the blasting gelatine for which we pay £5 7s. 6d., costs about 25s. or 30s. per case. If the Government want exact figures on this matter, they can simply apply to the agent of the Transvaal at home to collect them.

In other words, Nobel is satisfied with a profit of 5s. per case in Europe ?—I don't think he is satisfied at all. Nobel takes what he can get.

According to your figures he gets a profit of 48s. per case on the dynamite ?—I don't know what profit Nobel gets, but if these figures are correct he must make an enormous profit; and, by reason of having this monopoly in South Africa, he simply controls the whole market at home, because he gets such a tremendous profit here.

Do you consider a market like the Transvaal, which consumes about 180,000 cases of dynamite annually, would be sufficient to break a monopoly ?—I think so. The position in the Transvaal is strong enough to break the monopoly of Nobel, and the industry is strong enough to break any monopoly in the world.

Permits to import Dynamite Then you also mentioned about permits issued some time ago when the factory in this country was not in a position to deliver sufficient dynamite. How do you explain that greater advantage did not accrue to the mining industry. Was it from excess of

ty or any other charge ?—I really do not know the circumstances. I was new
re. I do not know what duty was charged, but somebody made money out of it.

Mr. *Brochon.*

You told us that about 25 mines are paying dividends, and you also told us *Mines which could pay Dividends.*
at if certain reforms took place some more mines which do not pay could work
a profit. Can you give us any exact figures about them ? Can you tell us
w many mines would be able to pay dividends under other circumstances ?—I think
least 50 mines. That does not include mines which are at present developing. They
ll also pay dividends when they are ready.

You think about 50 mines more will be able to pay dividends on the introduction
new reforms ?—Almost immediately.

We have about 150 mines here, so that would give 75 mines paying dividends ?—
ere are about 25 mines north of the reef which are failures.

So there would be very few which would not be able to pay ?—I maintain that
arly all the mines on the Main Reef, if we get these reforms which we are now
aying for, should, if the Directors see that they are worked honestly, make profits.

Can you suggest any measures to the Government to deal with the native labour *Remedies for administration of Pass Law.*
oblem ?—I would suggest that the administration of the Pass Law should be applied
t by the Government alone, but also by the members of the mining industry, who
ould form a body. I think it is quite impossible for the Government to know what
necessary ; what is required for us, and I would also suggest, as the mining industry *Representation of Mines and of Commerce.*
s no representation in the Volksraad, that the Government should have represen-
tives of the industry to consult with them on questions which appertain to the
ining Industry ; that they should also choose members from the Mercantile Associa-
n for a similar purpose—to consider questions which affect commercial interests.
is sort of thing is done in Europe, besides the fact that you have got in the Houses
Parliament in Europe men who represent the various industries. I think if the
vernment were to act upon these suggestions, a much better understanding would
evail between the so-called *uitlander* classes and the Government.

You mean cousulting members ?—Yes.

Mr. *Hugo.*

Kafir labour is a very heavy item in the expenditure ?—Yes.

Are you able to give us the percentage of the expenditure on that item alone ?— *Cost of native labour.*
comes roughly to about 25 per cent.

Including food ?—Yes. Of course, with some mines, I must explain, it entirely
pends upon the nature of the reef; if the reef worked is a wide one it requires less
our to break it ; if the reef is a narrow one you require more labour to feed the
ll with a certain amount of ore. In some mines it may be 25 per cent., and in some
may be more.

That being so is it possible to replace kaffir labour by white miners ?—That is
t possible. I don't think a white man can do considerably more work than a skilled
ffir.

For underground work it has been suggested that white labour should be em-
yed ?—They would find it a failure, and too expensive.

Yesterday you suggested that, in order to obtain kaffirs, locations should be *Compound system.*
ablished, but that does not seem quite feasible ; what do you think of the com-
und system that prevails in Kimberley ?—I would not recommend the compound
tem.

Why ?—Because I think it would hurt the commercial industry.

In Kimberley a contract is entered into to keep the kaffirs for six months in t
compound ?—Yes. I think it would have a bad effect upon the commercial industr
which, after all, is a great factor in the progress of the country.

For that reason you would not recommend the introduction of the compou
system ?—Yes. The main reason why, in Kimberley, the compound system was intr
duced was in order to evade the theft of diamonds. I can speak with experience
the subject because I have lived for twelve years in Kimberley, and was engag
in mining there.

Coming to dynamite, there was a report in the newspapers this morning that
a certain occasion the Chamber of Mines were on the point of entering into a contra
to supply dynamite at 45s. Just about the time the monopoly was entered into ?
I have some slight knowledge of what occurred at the time. When this contract w
submitted to my Companies I opposed it.

Was the price then proposed 45s. ?—I think it was 45s. plus duty. I don't spe
with any absolute knowledge on the subject.

At any rate you are convinced at the present moment that dynamite can
supplied at 40s ?—Yes. Dynamite for which we are paying 80s. costs about 18s. 6
in Europe. I have here the annual report of the Alaska Mexican Gold Minir
Company in America, and under the items of disbursements, dynamite costs 28s. 1
per case of 50 lbs. That is the price under an old contract; they are now payir
25s. per case, and that is in the centre of North America.

What do you think would be a fair cost for dynamite delivered here, rough
speaking ?—It is difficult for me to say; naturally, these people want a profit and
fair profit.

Mr. Hay, in his evidence, stated that dynamite could be delivered here at le
than 40s. ?—I believe he is correct.

There is no fear of a ring being formed ?—No. The mining industry is qui
rich enough to erect its own factory somewhere in Europe; the various Compani
would be willing to contribute the necessary amount for this purpose.

You also referred in your evidence to the gold thefts. Would you recommen
the Commission to submit a special law dealing with this, the same as the I.D.B. A
in Kimberley ?—Certainly.

You estimate the loss to the companies at a very enormous sum—10 per cent.
think ?—A large number must be thriving on the ill-gotten gains of I.G.B. The pro
of that we have in the quantity of the people who are doing absolutely nothing, an
they live in a very good manner. I have been in South Africa 21 years, and I prett
well know them all.

You referred to the establishment of a detective department. Can you make an
recommendation as to how it is to be constituted ?—I would suggest that the Gover
ment should request the members of the mining industry to co-operate and make som
proposal to the Government as to the best method of choosing a detective departmen

What do you think a reduction in the coal tariff would effect a saving of ? Hav
you any idea of the total cost of transport ?—I would rather give you the expen
from Brakpan to the George Goch; the Netherlands Railway charges for runnir
trucks into the siding at the Transvaal Coal Trust $2\frac{1}{2}$d. per ton.

You put it down at 3d. all told ?—Yes.

Can you give, more or less, the aggregate sum paid for the transport of coal
the mining industry per month or per annum ?—From £350,000 to £360,000 p
annum.

In your opinion, how much can be saved in that ?—I think about 2s. 3d. can
saved.

You estimate about £200,000 can be saved by transport alone to the mining ~~dustry~~?—Yes. This saving could be effected if the Netherlands Railway put in ~~lings~~ for the various companies and delivered the coal in bulk. That alone would ~~ve~~ about 2s. 6d. per ton, because the bag item is a very heavy one.

Reduction possible in Coal freight.

Mr. Joubert.

To a question of Mr. Smit's yesterday you replied that a railway company and a ~~ld~~ mining company are on one footing. Was that what you said?—I don't know what connection. I said the industry, perhaps, and the railway were on the same ~~oting~~. If the gold mines do not pay any more, and they have to close down, then ~~e~~ railway companies will not pay.

Comparison of Gold and Railway Companies.

What I mean is, that you replied to Mr. Smit that if a gold company was an ~~dustrial~~ company so was a railway company.—A railway in this country is so far an ~~dustrial~~ concern.

You don't say there is any competition between the two?—No. There should be ~~mpetition~~ between the railway lines, but there ought to be none between a gold ~~mpany~~ and a railway.

You make no difference between monopoly and competition?—I make a great ~~fference~~.

Then the two classes of companies cannot be treated as standing on the same ~~atform~~?—Of course not; but a monopoly in a railway department means that there only one railway allowed. I dare not build a line to compete with the present line. ~~herefore~~ the railway company can have it all their own way.

And, therefore, according to my opinion, you cannot deal with a gold mining ~~mpany~~ as standing on the same platform as a railway company?—No, of course not.

Then you cannot have understood Mr. Smit's question, because he plainly asked— a railway company is a company and a gold mining company also a company, both ~~ive~~ to do their utmost to earn profits?—Yes, therefore I answered that the railways ~~any~~ other country are run to promote the interests of the staple industry of the ~~nd~~.

But you can never put a railway company on the same platform as a gold mining ~~mpany~~?—As long as you establish the fact that a railway in this country, being a ~~mpany~~ must try to earn as much as possible, then they are on the same footing.

But still they have got a monopoly, there is no competition!—All the worse ~~r~~ it.

Netherlands Railway a monopoly.

That is why I do not want to admit they are on the same footing.—If Mr. Joubert ~~dmits~~ it is unjust that it should be a private company and make as much profit out ~~the~~ concern as possible, then he is right.

I won't admit it is unjust, but I want to say you cannot put the two on the same ~~vel~~, to be considered from the same standpoint.—I can gauge the feeling of Mr. Jou~~ert~~, when he does wish to say it is unjust. The object of the Commission is not only ~~look~~ after the interests of the country, but also to look after the credit of the coun~~y~~ outside, and as a commercial man I cannot admit that a railway company is on the ~~me~~ level as a gold mining company, because in the gold mining there is competition ~~d~~ in a railway there is not. The credit of the country can and will only suffer when ~~e~~ staple industry of the country is proved to be unpayable, and this can only be ~~tered~~, and they could only enhance the value of their properties when they were able ~~work~~ at a profit. As long as such abnormal conditions prevail—all these enormously ~~igh~~ rates and cost of dynamite and other mining items—our properties will not be ~~ole~~ to pay a return to the shareholders, the consequences of which must be that the ~~redit~~ of the State suffers.

But what possibility do you see for the Government to bring about a reductio after your declaration that the railway company stands on the same level as a gol

Railway a private company. mining company ?—I don't say that. When you acknowledge the railway compan must exist as a private company, then I say, of course the railway people have a righ to charge as much as possible. But it is unjust that the Government should support monopoly of that kind, and if the Government acknowledges that, and say we canno allow this company to exist any longer as a private company, and we must, therefor

Expropriation of Railway. expropriate or buy the railway—so long as you acknowledge that, I say the Goverr ment will say, "All right. Now, after expropriating the railway we reduce th charges to such and such an extent." But as long as the Government says this is private company, then I don't blame the directors of the private company for chargin as much as possible.

But it is always a privileged company.—Which is ?

The Netherlands.—Yes ; that is their good fortune.

Because there is no competition ?—And because it is a private company.

That is what makes it so difficult to understand your declaration that the tw stand on the same level.—As long as the Government will recognise this company a a private company, then I say they are quite right in charging as much as possible The only way I can see out of that is that the Government expropriates the railway

You acknowledge that a gold company is a private company, and a railway also private company, and that every company will do its best to make as much profit a possible. Now, the question is, have both got the same chance of doing it ?—Well, yo know it is rather difficult to answer this question, for the simple reason that such

No Competition in Gold Mining. thing as competition does not exist in gold mining. The more gold that is put out th better it is. But if you substitute diamond for gold mining, competition in the diamon industry is disastrous. The more diamonds that are found the less value are they. I

Railway competition prohibited. we were allowed to build one or two more railway lines in this country to compet with the Netherlands line, then, although they might be private concerns, we woul have better conditions prevailing.

You say, then, in gold mining there is no competition ?—Yes.

But still there ought to be ?—Well, the more gold mines the better for th country.

The more competition there is the better ?—Well, I don't know. If I had th choice of being the owner of one gold mine or 10, I think I would be the owner o the 10.

What is the reason there is no competition in gold mining ? It is only putting ir

No monopoly in Gold Mining. money in order to take out gold. Why cannot there be competition ?—It lies in th very fact that such a thing cannot exist. When an article which increases in valu the more it is discovered or found, you cannot call it competition. If you increas the article which you are manufacturing and thereby reduce its value, that mean competition.

My idea was that everyone was at liberty to do with his money as he likes ?— The word competition denotes that one man competes with the manufacture of a article to do better and cheaper. But gold has a standard value. This has beer proved, as you will see, in the price of silver, which has fallen for the reason that mor silver has been produced than necessary, but gold has a standard value.

Suppose a company is floated which developes a property well and has a goo output. Nothing prevents another company starting work with a good capital ?—Nc I wish I could find a few mines more.

Then that is competition ?—No, it does not reduce the value of the article produce.

It means that one has not got the monopoly to dig for gold ?—Such a monopoly s not exist.

Gold has got its value to day, but a sovereign is nearly worth £100 as compared h last year ?—Yes, but I don't admit it. You must say that money is dearer to-day n a year ago.

So gold does not get the same value ?—Times would be like last year if we had the cessions to work the mines better.

Exactly so. The competition makes it go up and down and get cheaper and rer, according to competition.—So many things cause money to be dear or cheap. itical questions and commercial questions affect the money market. The question ongs rather to national or political economy.

You said yesterday that if a law could be made for enforced labour it would be a *Forced labour.* at assistance. Is that your opinion ?—Yes.

Is there a law in England to get forced labour ?—No ; nowhere in the world as far I know.

Then why would you like it here ?—I have not asked for it. But I told you at the consequence would be if we reduced the price of labour and the natives used to work here. Then I suggested to impose a head tax, and I think Mr. Smit *Taxation of na-* ked me if it would be a good thing to have forced labour. I, as an employer of *tives.* our, say it would be a good thing to have forced labour, but another question is ether you could get it. You could exercise a certain amount of force amongst the ives if you impose a certain tax upon each native who does not work, or if he has t shown he has worked a certain length of time.

Mr. Smit pointed out to you that you cannot tax a kaffir higher than a white n.—No, you only tax him to make him work.

How can you make a law for two ? The law of the Republic will be the same everyone. Do you think the people would consent to such a law ?—I do not know. m not a legislator. The law is not the same for the kaffir as for the white man.

How can you say so ?—The native, for instance, has to wear a badge, and he must be out after nine o'clock. If you say the same law exists for the native as for the ite man a kafir ought to appeal against this.

From the beginning of the country the principle was laid down that the white n was a burgher and the kafir was not. The same law does not apply to the ite man.—The law then should be for the native, that if he does not work for a tain number of years, or if he is too rich to work, he must pay.

You know of no other country where there is such a law ?—There are no kaffirs in y country I have been in, but the rich man who does not work has to pay a higher than the poor man who has to work. In fact, the man who earns a certain amount money pays no tax at all, and the proportion of taxes goes up in proportion to a n's wealth. If a native does not work he ought to be taxed.

If he has no money and does not work ?—I do not know how such a man can live.

But although there are in London no kaffirs, there are poor whites ?—Oh, yes.

Are these compelled to work ?—You do not need to tell a man to work there, he ll work if he can only get it.

Is it the same here ?—No. A kaffir can get work if he will come.

But still they live ?—Who ?

The poor at Home—Oh ! yes, they live.

Do you know that two-thirds of the natives in the mines are not subjects of this *Nationality of* te ?—Yes. *mine boys.*

How can we go and tax natives who are not our subjects ?—No, of course not. e native who comes here would not get taxed ; he works.

So. Consequently the kaffir coming in from outside would have the privilege ov
the one here ?—I do not know what the other countries would do. In the Colony the
is a law which compels natives to work. It is the Glen Grey Act.

Chairman.

I want to be clear with regard to the grievances, and what you expect t
Government to assist the mining industry in. To start with the railway.
understand that if we lower the tariff as far as material for the mines is concern
and machinery, that this would be of great assistance to the industry ?—Yes.

Reduction of Railway rates.

Then this question does not include a general lowering of tariff for gene
merchandise ?—Yes, we ask for a lowering of the tariff all round.

Then we come again to the question discussed casually between you and M
Joubert, that, through the reduction of certain articles, I do not believe that any grea
impression would be made on the revenue of the railway. I can well understand th
on the promoting of the interests of the industry, the prosperity of the commerce a
the whole Republic depends. Consequently, when we go into these questions, we mu
remember that, although the Railway Company is a private company, still the Gover
ment have a great interest in it, and exercise supervision over it. It is well know
that the Government is a big shareholder in the company. Still, when the tariffs a
lowered, no matter whether it belongs to a company or to the Government, they cou

Railway profits. not be so far lowered as to preclude the Railway Company paying expenses.—B
the margin between the profits and the cost of working the railway is so enormo
that the railway tariff might be reduced considerably—very considerably—and y
the Railway Company would make a large profit. I can give the Chairman a f
figures for 1896.

The Chairman said he preferred to have the figures with the other statistics whi
had been asked for, and said : You have pointed out the transport of oth
countries. I don't take that as an argument in favour of a reduction here, because
must keep in view the expenses of living here, and the expenses of articles to be land
here, which are so much cheaper in other countries. The same rule applies to the ra
way, so far as it concerns the importation of railway material, and the salaries a
wages of its employees.—May I say one thing about that ? In spite of all the Chairm
has said, and in spite of the enormous cost of bringing material here, living here, &c., t
Railway Company made a profit last year of £1,298,000. From this you can gauge t
heavy burden borne by this industry. The Railway Company, moreover, made th
profit after allowing 6 per cent. interest on the share capital, and on the debentu
stock. This will give you an idea, Mr. Chairman, that this industry is not only ove
charged; it is not only unfairly treated; it is simply strangled. I don't exaggerate, a
I assure you that such a state of things does not exist in any other part of the wor
of a company with a capital of £1,166,666 making a profit of £1,298,000 after maki
allowance for interest and debenture stock. I am glad you have pointed out how ve
expensive it is to run a railway, as you will now gain an idea of how expensive it is
run a gold mine.

Necessity for re-dress of griev-ances.

Of course, we must probe this question to its very depth.—I can only answ
the Chairman this. I speak feelingly, and I know that the end of my examinati
is nearing ; but the State will have such ample proof that, unless they me
us in such a way that we can work the industry at reasonable prices,
will never be required again, inasmuch as most of the mines—and I don't sa
this by way of holding out a threat—as I speak as a man who has got a large inter
at stake in this country, and it may hurt me to admit the fact I am about to reveal
you—that our interests will not be worth the paper they are written on, unless t

overnment agree to give us the reforms which are really and fairly required by the mining industry. Figures will prove anything to you, but you can twist figures as you like, the facts will be very bitter, and they will prove much more than figures.

I understand that the question of dynamite is a serious one in the development the industry ?—It is, sir.

These are really the two big questions ?—Just so ; but I would like to give you Railway rates on foodstuffs. he lot of figures. A merchant here has brought me a bill of lading for 180 bags of our. From Bloemfontein to the Bridge, a distance of 210 miles, the railway charge £4 15s. 6d., but from Vereeniging to Johannesburg it cost £6, or 50 per cent. dearer, nd only quarter the distance. These are the items which make our foodstuffs very dear. herefore, I say the tariffs must be reduced all round. The Government need not fear at the receipts of the Netherlands Railway Company will be reduced if they reduce heir tariff, and I would guarantee that the receipts will be more than doubled, and at the Netherlands Company will still make a big profit; indeed, I should not be rprised to see the profit almost as high as last year. The Netherlands Company as not yet felt the effects of the calamity which has befallen the Rand. There are ill millions of pounds to be spent on machinery, which is coming out in a few onths' time. When this is finished, then the country will awaken to the fact that e are going to have disastrous times here, and the only way you can prevent that is, y the Government and the mining industry acting as surgeons, and consulting as to e best means and methods to operate on the sick patient, which is the mining dustry.

But, in order to cure the disease, we must know where it lies. As to the Cost of native labour. bour question, I understand that is one of the biggest before us ?—The native bour question is a very big one, and the mining industry will deal with it. ll we request is, that the Government will help us to get the natives in a Duty of Government. ir and reasonable manner. That we should not be compelled to pay every ative Commissioner 10s. or £1 for his goodwill; that the railway should not arge too much ; and that the administration of the Pass Law—which in itself is a ood law, with slight alterations—should be properly administered. Its administra- on should always be a matter for discussion between the leaders of the mining dustry and the Government officials. As I have stated before, it would be very lvantageous, and would have a salutary effect upon the mining industry and the untry at large, if the Government were to consult on questions which affect the ining industry with the members of the mining industry, and on questions which fect the commercial community with members of the commercial community, and I me back to your question that we shall be able to deal with the native labour ques- on if you give us only the slight help we ask you for.

All kaffirs who come here come over the border ?—They come from Komati d from the Cape Colony. The main question is, we will reduce native wages, d the support which we ask from the Government is a minor question then ; e working of the Pass Law must be thoroughly gone into ; the Liquor Law is one f the side issues of that question.

The proper enforcement of the Pass Law will not help you very much, as before ou enforce it you must have the niggers here ?—We have got the niggers here.

And there is no difficulty in getting kaffirs ?—No.

And then the great difficulty is taken away from our side about the labour uestion ?—Yes, that question affects us ; for this disease we are to be the surgeon.

I think you said it would be desirable that you should be better represented in Representation of Mining In- dustry. e Volksraad or Executive Council ?—I have said, unfortunately we have no voice in e Volksraad or in the legislation of the country, and I therefore have recommended that the Government should elect consulting members for the mining industry an the commercial representatives.

The burghers in Johannesburg have the same representation as the rest of th country.—Johannesburg has a very small number of members, and then the membe are burghers whom you don't expect to understand the requirements of the minin industry.

Mr. Jeppe understood the requirements of the industry.—Mr. Jeppe was by pr fession an advocate, and not a mining man. If such an advisory Board existed, think it would be almost unnecessary to have a Commission appointed. The advisor members and the representatives of the Government would long ago have come to th conclusion at which I hope we will come to now.

There was nothing prevented the industry before now from trying to bring abou the appointment of a Commission, or the conclusion which we are arriving at now ?— can only say I wish it had been done years ago.

That is not a reply to my question.—I can only say I would it had been don years ago.

I put my question in order to show that the Executive and the Governmen were, always prepared to receive any deputation from the goldfields in th interests of the goldfields. The Minister of Mines is not only prepared, as he is i duty bound, whenever he is called here by the Chamber of Mines or the Chamber o Commerce or the public in general, to put before the Government any communication made to him, and the grievances reported to him. It is a pity that we have neve before come as far as we have to-day. These are matters belonging to the past, an we will try to improve them. There is one question I wish to put to you : You hav acknowledged the Government must meet the industry and the industry must mee part of the difficulties themselves ?—Yes.

Duty of Mining
Leaders re-
garding reduc-
tion of working
costs. And you even went so far as to say that if the Government were to giv you everything you ask for, and the leaders of the mining industry would no exert themselves from their side, then all the efforts would be in vain.—The would not help to a great extent, but I think it would reflect very badly o us if the Government were to give us what we require, and we do nothin in order to bring about a reduction in general expenses, and I assure yo there would be such an uproar in Europe among shareholders that the task o managers-directors and directors of mines would be most unpalatable. Besides, yo must not forget one fact, that the men who are living here, the leaders of the minin industry, have every penny they possess invested in spite of the big boom which too place in 1895. You see all these men like Robinson, Barnato, and others have com out here to look after their interests. Do you think they would do that if they ha no shares or no interest in this place. I venture to state their interests are as large a ever they have been, and they will do their utmost to make the money they hav invested here remunerative—quite apart from the duty they owe to the shareholder in Europe.

Attitude of Gov-
ernment. I put my question in order to explain to you that now is the opportunit on your side to put whatever you require from the Government before th Commission, and then it will be necessary for the Government to know exactl what mistakes were made on your side. Therefore, it will be necessary for us late on to enter into details of the management of mines, and any mistakes made in th management.—Yes. We, at the present moment, are engaged in bringing about thes reforms that we can bring about.

You knew all the difficulties on your side for some time past, why didn't yo move first, and then come to the Government ? Now you want the Governmen

make the first move, and then the mines will follow suit.—It is not a question
the Government moving first and the mines following suit. We could not,
instance, reduce the wages if we have to pay these high tariffs. We anticipated
ong time ago that the Government would see the necessity of granting the
orms asked for by the industry. The Government will very soon find out, and
convinced of the necessity, by their own budget.

The Government has seen the necessity, and we all understand that the interests
l progress of the industry are the interests and progress of the country.

Mr. *Smit*.

What did you mean just now when you said that you cannot decrease wages Railway rates on
ile you are still paying high railway rates ?—I have just quoted an instance, that foodstuffs.
flour, which comes from Bloemfontein to the bridge. For instance, during the
ught we imported mealies from America. They cost us, landed in Durban,
, and delivered on the mine 22s. 6d. How can the mining industry, which requires
000 sacks per month, pay if they have to pay on a commodity of that kind more
n 100 per cent. for railway transit for 350 miles, after these mealies have come
usands of miles from America.

Yesterday and to-day you pointed out frequently that the Railway Company has Railway profits.
apital of £1,666,000, and to that you compare the high revenue. You know that
railway cost seven millions, so that we have not got to pay interest on one million,
t on seven millions.—I can answer to this, that if the Transvaal Government's
dit is good enough, provided that the industry is in a flourishing state—which
in, I think depends upon the Government of the State—the Transvaal Govern-
nt's credit is good enough to issue debentures for the whole of this railway, say
nine million pounds sterling at 3½ per cent. per annum, which would mean an
penditure of £300,000 a year. That is what it would cost you. What is the good
the credit of the State when the State does not employ that credit ?

I differ from you. In order to keep the credit of the State good you must make use
it as little as you can. Here, too much use has been made of credit, and that is the
son that you are now going back.—If the Transvaal had made use of its credit in
h a way as a State can make use of its credit, for the purpose of building railways,
n I think the credit of the Rand would have been better. You have two bank
nagers present, Messrs. Hugo and Pierce, who, I think, will bear me out in that.

You speak of profit. Do you mean nett profit or gross profit ?—The actual Gross and nett
eipts of the Netherlands for 1896 came to £2,970,000; working expenses came to Railway pro-
237,000, and that left over £1,700,000 for distribution, for the payment of debentures, fits.
l for dividends to be paid to the shareholders. Now, supposing you had to pay 6
cent.—I believe the State could get money for 3 per cent.—but say you had to pay
er cent. You give the debenture holders 6 per cent.; that would require £435,000.
e working expenses for 1896, £1,237,000, total interest of 6 per cent., and working
penses come to £1,672,000. The actual receipts were £2,970,000, therefore there
nains an excess of £1,298,000.

I want to go back to the report of 1895. In taking the nett profit you have left Railway divi-
of account the enormous expenses for permanent works, improving stations, &c.— dends for 1895.
at is capital expenditure. For 1895 you paid dividends to the shareholders of
ost 9 per cent., besides which the Government receives its share of the 85 per cent.
22,000. That makes altogether a total on the capital of the Netherlands—without the
entures of course, for these you had to pay first—that makes a total of 36½ per
t. dividend for 1895. First you pay the debentures, then you pay the shareholders
er cent., then the Government get their share of the 85 per cent., and then there

is a division again to the shareholders out of the 15 per cent. after the payment of 85 per cent. It has always been a commercial maxim that if you reduce the amounts, if the burdens which the industry has to bear are lessened and brought down to a level, it will enable us to live on, and your profits will not diminish.

Mr. *de Beer.*

Do you know whether the Glen Grey Act works well ?—I think so.

Nominal capitals

Now, can you give me a definition of the nominal capital of companies ?—The nominal capital is that capital represented by the property and working capital including the reserve shares.

Flotations.

Suppose, now, a company of £150,000 nominal capital. Is all that money in circulation, or would it be used in the development of the mine ?—If a company is floated with a nominal capital of £150,000 there will be a certain amount of the capital which would go to pay the vendors for the ground.

Can you tell us how much ?—That entirely differs. All the rest would be devoted for the development of the mine and for the erection of machinery. The remainder is the cash or working capital.

Would I be wrong in such a case if I supposed that £75,000 would go to the vendors out of £150,000 as an average ?—That would entirely depend on the value of the ground, and in order to answer this question correctly I must refer you to flotations which have taken place four, five, and eight years ago. In those days it was

Amount of working capital.

thought that a working capital of £50,000 was a large amount, but since we have gained the knowledge that the amount to equip a mine with 50 heavy stamps, with machinery of the latest type, and to develop this mine, costs alone about £120,000. Since we have gained that knowledge we do not float any more companies, the work-

Cost of Mine equipment.

ing capital of which would only be £50,000. It would be quite impossible to equip the mines in a manner which from the outset would guarantee a certain amount of success, without most of these mines issuing their reserve shares or increasing the

Reserve shares.

capital. These reserve shares were not issued at par, but at very large premium varying from £2 to £20 per share. Now, to give an illustration, the capital of

Meyer & Charlton flotation.

Meyer and Charlton is now £85,000. In order to equip the mine we raised the capital two years ago, which was £75,000, by 10,000 shares, bringing up the capital to £85,000. For these 10,000 shares certain firms have paid the company at the rate of £7 per share. That is almost as much as the whole capital was at the time. If I had been compelled to create the £70,000 cash at par, I should have increased the capital of the Meyer and Charlton from £75,000 to £150,000.

This is an isolated case ?—No it is not an isolated case, but occurs almost in

George Goch reserve shares.

every company. In the George Goch Company, firms have taken up only a little over 30,000 shares for £90,000 cash, and so I can give examples in any quantity.

Ferreira reserve shares.

The Ferreira Company for instance, four or five years ago sold their reserve shares in

Modderfontein reserve shares.

order to equip the mine properly, at £15 a share. The Modderfontein Company sold their reserve shares at £6 per share.

On which do you pay dividends, speaking of the first company ?—On £85,000.

How would the company with £150,000 capital pay ?—On all shares issued. Only the reserve shares do not receive dividends.

Now, with the Company with £150,000 capital, on how much would you have to pay dividends ?—As I said, on all shares issued.

You say that seven or eight years ago £50,000 would have been considered sufficient working capital ?—Yes.

Payments of Dividends.

Taking the company with the capital of £150,000, how would the profits be paid out ?—The dividends would be paid from the profits on the whole of the capital.

I have nothing against the system, I only wanted to show that the mines were very wealthy, and the dividends paid did not represent the riches of the mine, or the money invested in them.—The shares given to the owners of the ground are also in circulation. We cannot possibly expect them to put the ground in without. ^{Vendors' shares.}

Does the working capital, plus the ground, make £150,000 ?—The promoters, of course, get something.

How are they paid ?—Some are floated high and others low.

You keep £50,000 as a cash working capital. Now there is £100,000 left. Is the mine represented by £100,000 ?—The promoters, and the vendors, and the middlemen get paid out of the amount. In some instances they have received 80,000 shares. The promoter who pays down £50,000 cash may sometimes receive 20,000 shares, for you must remember that mining is at best only a speculation, and after he puts in £50,000 he does not know whether he will get it back. The shares may be worth pounds or shillings, and the man who gets the 80,000 shares takes the risk. There is no business which carries such great risks as mining, and that is a recognised fact, and it is for this reason that people all over the world who invest money in mining expect to get a bigger return than those who invest money in railways. ^{Flotations.}

Now, coming to the labour question. You do not quote lump sums in this ?—The labour takes more than 50 per cent. of the money in mining companies on the Rand. We will say between 51 and 52 per cent. ^{Percentage of labour costs.}

What is the percentage of railway carriage in working costs ? We have got 52 per cent as labour costs; now, which is the percentage for carriage ?—To give an exact or approximate estimate is impossible. For ever copper penny you spend in mining carries a certain proportion of freight. ^{Percentage of freight on working costs.}

You complain that freight charges are high. There are certain things charged direct to carriage and freight ?—No, nothing is charged direct. If we order machinery from Home it is entered in the books costing so much delivered at the mine, including the price paid the engineering firm, shipping charges, and railway freight.

Don't you enter the expenditure in the books under different headings ?—Yes, items are debited so much under cyanide, or hauling charges, or shipping charges. But we often get machinery and timber through the agent here, and as to how much of the charges went to carriage and shipping he could not say exactly, but would only repeat the statement he gave the other day, that the shipping of a load of timber that cost £1,100 cost £6,000 landed here. ^{Rates of freight.}

It is an isolated case.—In the case of mealies bought in America, they cost six times as much delivered at the mines.

That does not explain. I want the percentage or exact total.—The cost is 100 per cent. more than I can buy at Home. If I pay £25,000 for machinery in England, it costs £50,000 here.

You can tell us that labour represents 50 per cent., and now in the case of carriage you give us an isolated case.—It is difficult to say ; but all I can tell you, sir, is that the railway charges are so tremendous on the original cost, that, not only are installations excessively dear, but living is also, in consequence, dearer than it would be if we had cheaper rates.

The system in which you keep your books is not known to me. So far as I know the receipts and expenditure are booked under different headings, especially such an important item, freight, which ought to have a heading to itself.—I have explained we don't buy machinery at all. The commercial people who supply us make us a charge delivered at the mine. I think you will to some extent get this information from the people in the commercial business.

The direct complaint is against the railway company, and, in order to test that we must know which proportion of expenditure constitutes freight.—It is quite impossible to state, and if it is not a sufficient illustration that the mining industry which has invested between 75 and 100 millions has made a visible profit of one-and-a-half millions, whilst the railway company, which has actually invested £1,166,000 has made a profit for 1896 of over a million—then if this is not a sufficient illustration of circumstances, and if these figures don't appeal to you, the figures you seek to obtain, and which are almost impossible to obtain, will never illustrate to you the necessity of reducing railway charges.

Profits of Netherlands Railway. You quoted one million. Mr. Smit later on said it was seven millions.—Yes, but the six millions are debentures of the Government, which is after all the guardian of its people, and must look after the interests of its people. It has been appointed by the people, and should study the interests of the industry of the land. If they can get money at 4 per cent. then I think it is a suicidal policy which the Government pursues if they take from the people 36 per cent. dividends. If you will allow me, that is with regard to the income of the Netherlands Railway, I will give you the figures of the profits made by the Cape Government Railway.

Profits of Cape Colony and Natal Railways. Have you brought these forward before?—No. As you are all aware, the progress which the Cape Colony and Natal have made of late years is only due to the industry of the Transvaal. The figures will show what this industry is taxed with. I will first give you the figures of the Cape Government Railway. They expended on their railway lines 20½ millions. The interest on the capital expenditure was 4 per cent., which is a very handsome amount. That will make £820,000. The actual working expenses, as published in their accounts for 1896, amount to £1,922,000, so if you take the interest on the capital and the working expenses, these two items come to £2,742,000. Now, will you believe me when I tell you that the gross receipts for 1896 for the Cape Government Railway—including the Free State, of course—amounted to £4,079,000. After paying interest of 4 per cent. and after paying working expenses, they have still a surplus of £1,337,000, and those railways did not pay before the Transvaal existed. I do not want to weary you too much with figures. A similar statement applies to the Natal Government Railway. Their surplus, after paying 4 per cent. on their capital, and after paying all their working expenses, amounted to almost half a million pounds. You also know the Natal Railway did not pay until it was brought up to Charlestown. These two surpluses amount to £1,800,000, and that simply comes out of the Transvaal.

Freights. What proportion of expenses is the freight on coal?—The percentage of expenses at one mine with which I am connected, for coal, is 15 per cent., and the carriage of it is 50 per cent.

You don't follow me. We have got the percentage of labour at 50 per cent. Now, we want to make up the 100 per cent. What is the cost of freight on coal alone?—It is between 7½ and 10 per cent. That includes, of course, the carriage to the sidings of the various works.

Can you give us statistics. We want to get the division of percentage to make up the 100 per cent.?—I can give it to you roughly now.

Mr. de Beer said he could hand them in later on.

Mr. *Brakhan.*

Profits on Dynamite. I should like to revert to two questions put to you yesterday. The first is, that about two or two and a half years ago the Government issued permits to the mining industry to import dynamite. Then, I think, the cost of dynamite was between 40s. and 45s. per case, delivered in Johannesburg, exclusive of duty. Can you explain

me why the difference occurs, because the mines had not the advantage of these
import tariffs ?—I could not give information yesterday on the point, but I have since
been ascertained from various permit holders the reason why we had to pay so much
for dynamite at that time when permits were granted by the Government. The
Government exacted from 37s. 6d. to 40s. per case duty, which we had to pay, and
which was added to the cost price of the imported stuff. It is a very curious fact,
however, that the Government only gets now 5s. per case. Two and a half years ago,
the period you are alluding to, the Government received about 40s. per case duty.

Then I wish also to ask you with regard to the Gold Law. The mining industry Taxation of Myn-pachts.
pays licences on claims, whilst on mynpachts the Gold Law provides that the Government is entitled to charge 2½ per cent. on gold produced by companies which have
mynpachts. My question was, but I may not have made it very clear, whether, in
your opinion, if this 2½ per cent. were charged on the gold produced by mynpacht
companies—I do not speak of the poor ones—would it be a great disadvantage
against those companies which merely work their claim properties ?—As comparatively but few—only one or two—mynpachts are rich, I can only come to the conclusion that if Government were to exact 2½ per cent. on the mynpacht, then the
result would be very disastrous to the mynpacht companies. If they were all rich
mynpachts—and when I talk of rich mynpachts the Robinson is a rich mynpacht—
they were all similarly or even approximately as rich as that, it might not hurt
them so much, but as I have stated before, most mynpachts are too poor, and a charge
that kind would be a serious loss to the company.

Reverting to the evidence of this morning, I should like to ask you whether it Percentage of mining costs.
not a fact that the proportion of wages to the proportion paid for stores and
material in the working expenses of mining in other parts of the world is also very
considerable, that is to say that the proportion paid for wages is larger than that
which is paid for stores ?—You mean in this country ?

No; in other parts, because here it is 51 per cent.—You want to know if the proportion of stores used here—

I want to know your opinion generally—whether in other parts of the world the
percentage of wages to material—what you call here stores, is also not greater ? Is
the 51 per cent. in this country normal ?—I have not had very much experience
mining at Home, because when I came to this country I came almost from school,
but from what I have been able to gather from the reports, I find in Europe, and
America as well, the heaviest proportion is always the wages paid to workmen.

Therefore you do not consider 51 per cent., which falls here for wages—white
and native, excessive ?—No. I do not think so. If the mines are managed with the
most care we may be able to reduce this item a little, but I don't think we can
reduce it very much—comparatively much, I mean. On the other hand, if our
requests are granted as regards railway rates, dynamite, etc., then the amount for
wages will be a smaller one.

One question with regard to flotations years ago when this mining industry was Flotation.
its infancy. You say that the working capital was moderate, and that the
promoters in these companies got certain shares for putting in the ground, and also for
putting in the money. Now I want to know from you whether they were well
informed about the value of these reefs. Do you consider the shares which these
promoters took in loan for their working capital which they put in, and also for the
ground, whether they were too high considering that at that time one did not know
what those £50,000 would bring ?—I have explained to Mr. de Beer that I consider
capitalists are the people who put in capital in those days, and ran the risk of losing
their money they put in. And to show you how uncertain we were of the quality of

our mines, I may simply point out to you that in 1887 or 1888 a very eminent mini
engineer, Mr. Gardner Williams, came up to the Rand to report for Messrs. Wernhe
Beit, and Co., and that his reports were unfavourable, and to the effect that he d
not think the conglomerate bed would be continuous and that it was only a surfa
wash. I may say here that this opinion advanced by Mr. Gardner Williams
the time does not in the least reflect upon his ability as a mining engineer, becau
the conglomerate bed as found here had never been met with anywhere in the worl
and that his conclusions were at the time perfectly justified. Does it not strike yo
as being very plucky for men to put in £50,000 or £5,000 at the time, and as t
profit is always in proportion to the risk which a commercial man takes, that t
money which these men in the early days made they were justly entitled to mak
If you have a mine you can get your working capital subscribed at par, or eve
people are willing to pay premiums, or, as I have pointed out to Mr. de Beer, t
reserve shares were subscribed for at premiums varying from 200 per cent. to 2,00
per cent.

Now must I understand that those premiums paid lately have been paid by t
public, by groups of financiers, or by the promoters of the mines ?—The issues have be
guaranteed and generally subscribed for by financiers.

Then those who formerly had no shares have lately paid for shares considerab
over par ?—Just so.

Chairman.

I must now thank you, Mr. Albu, for the manner in which you gave evidenc
and I can assure you that you have assisted us materially in our work. So far we ha
finished with you, although I think we shall recall you later on.

Mr. Edward Way's evidence.

MR. EDWARD J. WAY, manager of the George Goch Mine, was called. Mr. W
stated that he was manager of the George Goch for three years past, a
prior to that he had been manager of the Eastleigh Mines at Klerksdorp.

Chairman.

On the lines indicated by you, the Commission, after your statement, will put oth
questions.

Cost of native labour.

Witness.] With regard to the question of mining costs there are four or five chi
headings to engage one's attention upon which reductions can be made. The mo
important is kaffir wages. Taking the figures of my mine as a criterion, the avera
wage paid to each boy amounts to about 2s. 1d. per shift and his food. Previous
November, 1896, it amounted to from 2s. 7d. to 2s. 8d. per shift. The natives of n

Reduction of native wages.

own mine draw monthly from £3,500 to £3,900. Most of the managers have notifi
their Boards that in their opinion these wages should be reduced one-third, and t
matter is now under serious consideration. On the George Goch Mine this would me
a reduction of £1,300 per month. The wages then would even be higher than we
paid by me ten years ago in Pilgrim's Rest.

Mr. *Hugo.*

How much higher ?—The average wage paid in 1889 was about 27s. per calend
month, with food. The wage now, if this reduction takes place, will be about 40s. p
calendar month. That is the maximum. The next question is dynamite. The Geor

Dynamite costs.

Goch Company pays at present about from £1,000 to £1,200 per month for dynami
If it were possible to reduce this dynamite from about £5 per case to 50s. per case, it wou
save us from five to six hundred pounds per month, which is about 1s. per ton on t

e treated per month. The next question is the question of coal. At present we pay *Coal freights.*
is. 3d. per ton for nut coal—that is small coal—and 18s. 9d. for the large coal, all
;livered in bags. It would be possible to get this coal, if not delivered in bags, at from
is. to 16s. per ton. I think it is possible to deliver coal to the centre of the Witwaters-
nd at from 12s. to 13s. per ton, provided the railway freight be reduced. This would
ean a saving to the George Goch Mine of 5s. 6d. per ton on about 2,000 tons of coal
-about £1,000 per month. My present coal bill is about £1,900 per month. Coal,
ynamite, and native labour wages, which I have just given you, if reduced in the way
 have suggested, would mean a saving of approximately £36,000 a year to my
mpany. This would be entirely profit, and is equal to over 10 per cent. upon the
pital of the company, which at the present moment is not paying any dividends at
l. With regard to the question of further reduction of white wages, I think the high
st of living must be seriously taken into consideration before any steps are taken in
at direction. If we can reduce the cost of living, and make a reduction in the other *White wages.*
ems which I have mentioned, I think we shall have reasonable grounds for attacking
hite wages. At the present time, upon the George Goch Mine, wages alone are 55 per
nt. of the total expenditure.

Mr. *de Beer.*

Everything included ?—Yes.

Mr. *Smit.*

White and black labour ?—Yes. Native labour, with food, comes to about *Percentage of mining cos*
7 per cent., and the white labour to about 28 per cent. The actual stores consumed,
ich as drill steel, machinery, mealie meal, and other items which make up the trade
counts of the mine, could be possibly very greatly reduced. The trade accounts,
clusive of dynamite, amount to about from £2,800 to £3,300 per month. Ten or 20
r cent. reduction on this amount would mean a further saving of from £300 to £600
r month, so that if you add these figures together—the £3,000 I have mentioned and
e other reductions—it would come to £3,600 per month. That is equal to about from
. 8d. to 7s. 3d. per ton, and would reduce our expenses to about 15s. per ton, including
erything. The two items of dynamite and coal on the George Goch Mine come to
36,000 a year; the whole item of wages would amount to from £80,000 to £90,000 a
ar; the proposed reduction of native wages would mean a saving of about £16,000 a
ar on the George Goch.

Mr. *Joubert.*

Supposing it to be possible that the Government were to give low railway
tes, make a reduction in the price of dynamite and the price of kafir labour, would
e mines then be prepared, when any further complaint was made, to co-operate
ith the Government, and show the outside world that such complaint was ground-
ss ?—I should say that the matters which are being brought up before this Commission
r redress will be complete, and I should not anticipate that anything further will be
ought up. It depends entirely on the scope of the enquiry.
   The question is: Would the mines be prepared, if the Government does its best to *Co-operation of mining leaders*
eet these grievances, and then, if any further complaint was made, to co-operate with
e Government to convince the public at large that such complaints were groundless ?—
hat is a question I hardly can answer.
   I simply want to know your opinion on the subject ?—It strikes me that question
ould be answered more readily by the heads of the mining groups. My opinion is
at if the Government and the mining industry co-operate together and act together,
don't see how there can be any further cause of complaint.

I want to be assured in case I make recommendations to the Government, and the recommendations are adopted, that the Government can then depend on the support the mines.—I should say they will be supported by the mines if their recommendation are adopted.

One of the objects of the Commission is to put matters on such a basis that t mines can co-operate with the Government to bring them all to a good state, and I, a member of the Committee, would like to know from the managers if the Governmei redress these grievances, whether the mines would co-operate with the Government ?— I should say most certainly.

Mr. *de Beer.*

White and native wages.

You say the wages are £80,000 per annum ?—Yes.

As far as I understand it is divided pretty equally among black and white ?—Ye including the food of the natives.

How many white employees have you got ?—180 ; but I must say, in continuatio: that at least 70 or 80 of that number are employed upon what we call capital expend ture—what we call construction. In an ordinary way we have 105.

How many kafirs have you got ?—At the present moment in my compound I hav 1,335.

What is the aggregate per head for white labour ?—Do you include managers ?- Are they included in the 105 ?—Yes.

Average of white wages and salaries.

What is the aggregate wage of the 105 ?—From £25 to £27 per month.

I make it over £30.—That may be owing to the fact that in the amount I name I included town salaries, directors' fees, and the head office in Berlin and the Londo office expenses. The actual number of white employees stated by me is 105, and Mr. de Beer is dividing the amount I gave by that number, I must include seven eight more, because they are not under my control. I am merely speaking of tho: under my control. There is the secretary in town, for instance, and his staff. M figures are approximate : I have no notes.

Average native wages.

What would the average kaffir wages per head be per year ?—The average woul be something under £35 per year ; we don't pay them all the same.

Then you think that the amount of wage paid to your 1,335 kaffirs per year ca be reduced by about one-third ?—Yes.

Reduction of white wages.

You see no chance of reducing the wages of white labour—those who get a average of £30 per month ?—The possible average of my mine probably differs fro other mines ; I am merely taking the figures of the George Goch Mine. It may I that other mines pay higher or lower as the case may be.

It is rumoured that there are thousands of white miners out of employmen This being so, is there no chance to reduce wages ?—That is not my experience. have the greatest difficulty in getting good miners. I will give the Commission a example. I advertised in the *Star* for two pump men, and I had only one applicatio: and the applicant was absolutely incompetent. I can understand that there are great many men out of employment, but they are not competent, and so long as w have not got an over-abundance of competent white miners, we cannot hope to redu their wages unless we can reduce the cost of living.

Rates of white wages.
Contract work.

Do you consider that £340 a year is an abnormal salary for a white man ?—. depends entirely upon the work he does. If he is employed on contract work ai relies upon his own efforts, I personally have no objection to a man earning £35 to £4 per month. If I employ a cheaper man to do this work he would probably bur twice as much dynamite, so that the difference between the men is thus balance My experience is that if you can get together a good body of men and pay them we

money which they save in other departments a great deal more than covers the
:eased wage they may be earning.

Do I understand that these 105 are skilled labourers ?—It depends on what line
demarcation you draw between skilled and unskilled labour. The only unskilled
1 we have are the actual miners.

And their salary ?—£4 10s. per week.

And you consider that with the high cost of living it is difficult to reduce that ?— *Wages of married miners.*
comes particularly heavy on married men. A single man can possibly save, if he
es everything possible, perhaps £100 a year. But the married man has several
advantages. As a rule he does not get a house free upon the company's property.
has house rent to pay, and there is the keep of his wife and possibly a family,
l he cannot live under a margin of £18 or £20 per month. A very large percentage
the men who live as single men on the Rand, particularly among the Cornish
1ers, have wives and families in Cornwall, so that the apparent saving, so far as
know it, possibly goes to keep a wife and family in Cornwall. Most of the miners
the George Goch are Cornishmen.

Do you order your machinery direct from the manufacturers ?—Does Mr. de *Purchase of machinery.*
3r mean me personally.

Your company ?—Yes, from agents in Johannesburg.

What do the agents charge on that do you know ?—As a rule the work is given
to contract, and the lowest tender is accepted. If the nature of the work
icludes it being given out to contract it is supplied on what is called prime cost,
t is to say, the principals of the agents in Johannesburg send the exact cost of.
king the work, together with their profit, to which is added freight and railage,
l, as a rule, the agent here gets 5 per cent. on that.

Do the railway charges always appear as separate items ?—In our accounts
tainly. I understood you to refer to prime cost when you spoke about railage. If
buy stores from merchants in town we know nothing about railage.

I am speaking of machinery ?—Yes, in regard to machinery.

Mr. *Smit.*

One of the biggest items of your expenditure is labour, which means 55 per *Percentage of labour costs.*
t. ?—Yes.

Amongst which is 27 per cent. for kafir labour, and 28 for white ?—Yes.

Are any steps being taken by the George Goch, in conjunction with other *Reduction of white and native wages.*
ipanies, to get the wages reduced ?—Yes.

What steps are being taken ?—As I pointed out to the Commission, the managers
'e recommended ther directors to go into the question of further reducing kaffir
ges by 33 per cent. The question of the reduction of white wages is also under
sideration.

Can you tell what the mine managers will get ?—They will get anything from *Salaries of Mine Managers.*
000 to £4,000 a year.

There is no case where they get more than £4,000 ?—I cannot tell that.

On the different savings suggested by you, what would be the total amount in
ing effected by the George Goch after all the reductions were made ?—Over
),000 a year.

Wages come to 55 per cent. How do you make up the rest ?—Dynamite, about *Percentage of mining costs.*
per cent. ; coal, about 11 per cent.—that is coal and carriage.

How much of the 11 per cent. belongs to carriage ?—About one-half, roughly.

And how is the remainder of the total made up ?—It would be taken up in
ieral stores, such as candles, fuse, pipe fittings, cyanide. Cyanide amounts to about

2 to 3½ per cent. Mine timber would amount to 3 or 4 per cent. The price of mi
timber largely depends upon the source from which it is obtained. At the prese
moment our supplies are mostly coming from Natal, as the farmers of the Transv
have not been bringing in large quantities lately. I believe a pole which costs ab
1s. in Natal costs 8s. or 9s. by the time we get it.

Percentage of freight on working costs. At any rate, the charge for railway carriage debited to general expenditu
account would only be on coal, 5½ per cent. ?—It is very difficult in buying fr
merchants in Johannesburg to know what has been paid for railage, freight, Custom
and transit dues. As a rule, the mine manager makes a contract with a mercha
and, as far as he possibly can, he accepts the lowest possible figure. He does n
concern himself at all as to the actual way in which the cost is made up.

Chairman.

Have you had occasion lately to dismiss white labour ?—No.
I mean fixed miners on the mine ?—No.

Mr. Schmitz-Dumont.

You have said that of the price of coal one-half ought to be debited to railage ?
I said approximately.
You say 11 per cent. is the proportion of your expenditure used by coal ?—Yes.
The salaries of white people are so high because the cost of living is so high, a
the Commission would like to know what the amount is which the mines pay
railage to the railway company indirectly through their consumption on differe
articles ?—I cannot say. In my opinion I would say that is a question for t
merchants.
It is impossible to fix the amount which goes to the railway in proportion to t
salaries of white men ?—From my point of view it is impossible.
Scarcity of competent miners. You say it is difficult to get competent miners for the mines ?—Yes.
What class of people are they, now, who walk about Johannesburg and witho
work ?—I think they are more of the more artisan class.
It is a certain fact that really competent men are scarce ?—In my opini
competent miners are scarce. The State Mining Engineer should know almost as w
as I do.

Mr. Brakhan.

Percentage of freight on working costs. Am I to understand from you that the books at the mine, or the books of t
company show to no material extent the railage, that is to say, the cost which rea
goes to the railway company on all the various articles used ?—In hardly o
particular case.
Then I am to understand from you that the cost actually paid to the railway d
not so much come from the mine, but from the merchants who supply the vario
machinery, wood, and various other plant and stores ?—Yes.
Therefore if the mines were to compile out of the books the amount of freight p
direct to the railway company this would give no idea whatever of the situation ?
None whatever.
In other words, the amount of material, whatever it might be, imported direct
the company is a very small one ?—Very small. Coal, for instance, is delivered a
contract price; it is delivered at the different works at a fixed price, and we are
informed how much it cost per mile to carry it.
Reduction of native wages. You have informed us that the mine managers have advised the Boa
to reduce the kaffir wages by one-third. Has that advice come from all t

managers along the reef ?—In the first place the Council of the Mine Managers' Association unanimously decided that it was an opportune time that the reduction should take place. It was then brought before the Chamber of Mines, Association of Mines, and the Rand Native Supply Association, and a meeting was held and a committee formed. At the same time the mine managers had a general meeting, at which it was unanimously decided that the time was opportune that the reduction should take place, and that the reduction should be 33 per cent.

It has not come to your knowledge that any mine managers who were not present at that general meeting, hold a different opinion ?—I have heard that is so.

Can you inform us whether the good supply of black labour on the Witwatersrand is general ?—I think it depends to a large extent upon the locality and upon the compound management. I think, at the present time, the central part of the Rand has more natives than it requires. I have heard that the outside districts are short, but I cannot understand how this can be when the Native Supply Association informs us they have natives on hand whom no one wants. *Supply of native labour.*

Is it not a fact that kafirs are at times unwilling to go to certain parts of the Rand—in fact, I may say insist on coming to the centre part ?—I should think it is largely a question of management.

What is your opinion as to the quality of the native labour which is general here —I speak more especially with regard to drill boys ?—In my experience, they are very inferior to what they were six or seven years ago. *Quality of native labour.*

In other words, boys who used to work formerly here do not come back in such large proportion, or the demands of the industry are so much greater ?—I think many of the boys have become demoralised by the high wages which they receive. I have boys working in my compound who did twice the work for 25s. a calendar month, eight years ago, which they do now for £3.

In other words, the boys know they are to some extent masters of the situation ? —They may think so, but I cannot admit they know it for a fact.

Are not lower wages paid to natives in other districts—Pilgrim's Rest—than on the Rand ?—The latest information is that in Pilgrim's Rest wages are about equal to what they are here, if not higher. *Wages at Pilgrims' Rest.*

With regard to Barberton ?—I cannot say.

Is the number of skilled drill boys very limited ?—I don't think it is a question of skill so much as unwillingness to work. There is a sort of understanding that in the hard rock their work for the day should be one hole approximately 3 feet deep, and that is so rooted in their minds that if a shift boss or mine foreman or manager tries to get any more he loses his boys, because they will go at once to mines where such labour is scarce. *Drill boys.*

Can you suggest any plan by which a permanent supply could be relied upon for the Rand, skilled principally ?—The only way is to give natives facilities for family life. We do it to a certain extent on the George Goch, and we get into considerable trouble for doing it. We have a location upon our lower claims, and I have boys who have their wives and families, who have been working at the mine for the last eight years. If locations could be established somewhere in the neighbourhood of the mines —within walking distance—so that the natives could bring down their wives and families, I think you would have a far greater supply than you require. *Native locations.*

I notice in your evidence you put native pay per month at £3. I think the other mines' average is a higher one. You also say you have a good supply of boys. Do you attribute these two points to the fact that you have a small location?—I attribute it to that, and to the fact that we give considerable attention to our compound management. *Compound management.*

MR. SYDNEY J. JENNINGS, General Manager of the Crown Reef Gold Minin Company, stated he had been General Manager of the Company since the 1 September, 1896. Before then he was manager of the Crown Deep and Lan laagte Deep.

Chairman.

You know the line of enquiry the Committee is pursuing, and I would be please if you would give your own statement on the different points, and afterwards th Members of the Commission will put questions.

Pass Law.

Witness]. It seems to me the three chief points which affect the mines which a not on the verge of paying dividends are these. The first is native wages. We have her a most excellent law, in my opinion—namely the Pass Law—which, if properly carrie out, and efficiently administered, will enable us to get complete control over our kaff labourers. The Pass Law, as it is carried out at present, does not give any satisfactio From the Crown Reef, where I am manager, no fewer than 1,030 kaffirs deserted sin the 1st June, 1896, and it is impossible for us to trace these kaffirs. If we take native to the Pass Office, and ask whether he has ever been registered before, it impossible for the officials to give us any information. If every kaffir could be traced if it could be told whether they have been registered before, or been in the service a company, then we would have control over them. We can get kaffirs here from othe places on a contract for twelve months, but they work for only two weeks and the leave, and it is impossible for us to find them. We have another law, which is a ve

Liquor Law.

good one, viz., the Liquor Law. When this law was first enforced, in January an February, we received great benefit from it, in that the kaffirs were never drunk, suffering from the effects of drink, and consequently worked their full week, and di better work than at the present time. The Liquor Law is not enforced now, or th keepers of eating-houses, or dealers in drink think it will not be enforced; consequent the kaffirs now get, freely and openly, drink of the most vile compounds, and th

Native wages.

makes them so that they cannot work as well as before. I have a list here whic shows that the total sum paid in wages to kaffirs at the Crown Reef during 189 amounts to £63,902, 6s. 1d., and this is about 24 per cent. of the total costs of the wor Then the cost of supplying the kaffirs with food was £12,503 for the same year, and th is nearly 1s. 3d. per ton, or 4½ per cent. of the total cost. Therefore, the native labour an native food amounted to 2s. 10d. per shift. If the Pass Law were properly and efficient administered, and the Liquor Law likewise, we could reduce this to 1s. 6d. per shif Again, if we had complete control over the native labour, we could teach the kaffirs do all lower forms of work that are now done by white men. By these reductio other mines would be brought into operation, and more white men of greater ski would come into the country. The lower classes of labour, mostly unskille would be done by kaffirs. This would be a permanent benefit to the country in man directions. You would have more mines at work; you would cause more goods to carried over the railroad, and the man who had invested his money in the mines woul

Coal.

receive greater dividends. The second point is the cost of coal. The Crown Reef pa last year £25,909, 14s., which amounts to 2s. 7¼d. per ton. I am informed that we pa an average of 19s. per ton for coal I am informed, but I don't know it of my ow knowledge, that of that amount 9s. is carriage, or not quite one half. Therefore, if th carriage is reduced to a figure at which a great many think it possible to carry coal, should be reduced by 6s. per ton, or, on our expenses, about one-third of our coal bill,

Dynamite.

10d. per ton working costs. The third point is dynamite. The Crown Reef spent o dynamite last year £24,225, which amounts to 2s. 5d. per ton, or 9 per cent of the tot cost. Having had considerable experience in dynamite, I should say that dynami be delivered here, exclusive of duty, at 36s. per case. The Crown Reef uses sting gelatine, for which it pays £5 9s. 3d. per case, delivered on the mine. If we nt the dynamite should pay even a large duty, we should at least get it for half amount we get it at now, which would mean a saving of about 1s. 2d. per ton at Crown Reef. The other items of expenditure on the Crown Reef are made up of Mining costs. nide, and what might be called general stores, such as candles, steel, oils, pipes, and e fittings, fuses, and detonators. These all pay railway carriage, which, in my nion, is very high, but of which I have no accurate statistics to give the Committee. th regard to white labour, the salaries on the Crown Reef include directors' fees, nager, consulting engineer, secretary, and every other white man working on the Salaries of ne, came to £77,222, or 29 per cent. of the total cost. This amounts to Whites. 4 1s. 10d. per month per man. In my opinion, unless a great reduction is de in the cost of living, it is impossible to reduce that amount. It seems to me that policy should be to open up and make it possible for a great many more mines to y, so that we should be able to use more white labour of the very highest skill, to White wages. om it would be cheap to pay a high wage. I would like to hand in this statement, that the Commission will have accurate statistics so far as the Crown Reef is ncerned.

Chairman.

What is the dividend paid by the Crown Reef?—We paid 140 per cent. on our Dividends of pital, and in that connection I would like to make a statement. The capital of the Crown Reef. own Reef is only £120,000. The total expenses of equipping and developing the Capital of Crown Reef. ne in such a way that it is possible to pay dividends, was £480,000 odd. Therefore, e 140 per cent. dividend on £120,000 capital is only about 35 per cent. on the money ent in equipping it.

As regards kaffir labour, there is no difficulty in getting a sufficient supply?— Supply of native labour. ere is no difficulty if we can keep those we get.

Your remedy for that is that the Liquor Law be properly carried out, and also the ss Law?—Yes.

As regards white labour, have you any difficulty in getting skilled white labour? Scarcity of skilled white labour. It is very difficult to get skilled white labour.

Have you had any occasion to dismiss white labourers lately?—Yes.

Can you tell us how many and why?—About four or five, who have got sick or ne home, or wanted to go home to England.

Have you got any great trouble about stealing amalgam?—Not to my know- ge.

Is there any general complaint about I.G.B.?—Yes, the complaint is very great. Gold thefts. has been shown in the case of the City and Suburban that an organised gang of eves has been at work, which, in that case, stole a large quantity of amalgam, and is fair to assume that that is not the only company.

Is it not possible to improve the labour conditions by importing better machinery? Improved mach- That has been done to the very highest extent by the Crown Reef Company. inery.

Mr. Smit.

Has your company ever participated in any effort to import white labour?—No, t to my knowledge.

Mr. Joubert.

Is there any complaint about the quality of the dynamite made in this country? Quality of dyna- Not that I have heard of. Not in my mine. mite.

You work with dynamite ?—We do not use dynamite at all. We use blast[ing] gelatine.

Is it also manufactured here ?—That I do not know.

Do you know where you get it from ?—We buy it from the Explosives Compan[y].

You have worked with different kinds of dynamite before in other countries. [Is] there any appreciable difference between these and that you work with now ?—The[re] is a large difference in the effect of blasting gelatine and dynamite.

You have worked with gelatine in different countries, you say. Is there a[ny] difference in the quality of the stuff you used there and the stuff you use here ?—No.

Mr. *Schmitz-Dumont.*

Wages of married and unmarried miners.
Do you think that an unmarried miner gets a wage which enables him to l[ive] very well ?—He gets a wage that if he is really single, that is living here without [a] wife, enables him to live well.

And how about the married miner ?—It is very difficult for him to make b[oth] ends meet.

You have a lot of experience of the compound system in Kimberley ?—Yes.

Compound system.
Would you think it would be advisable to apply the same here ?—Taking [all] considerations, the commercial community and the good of the land into considerati[on] I should say no. We could get sufficient control over the kaffirs if the Pass Law w[ere] efficiently administered, without the compound system.

Native locations.
And how about establishing kaffir locations along the Rand ?—I say it would b[e a] most excellent idea if the sale of liquor in the locations was absolutely prohibited, a[nd] no licences were allowed for the sale of anything for a long distance round, so th[at] there would be no possibility or pretext whatever of introducing drink.

I think you have experience of mining in America ?—Yes.

Cost of dynamite in America.
Can you tell us the cost of dynamite there ?—In the Alaska Treadwell and Alas[ka] Mexican mines, which are very large concerns, the dynamite costs 15·3 cents per [lb.] (about 7½d. per lb.) That would amount to about 26s. per case.

Is that a quality which equals No. 1 sold here at 85s. ?—That equals No. 1 so[ld] here at 85s.

You mean to say it has the same power ?—It has the same power.

Mr. *Brochon.*

Wages of unmarried miners.
You think a single man can live very well here with the salary he gets ; can y[ou] tell us what he has to pay for his board and lodging ?—It all depends on where [he] lodges. The average board on the mine is £5 10s. per month, I should say, but mo[st] of the mines furnish skilled men with quarters free, although some charge 10s. p[er] month.

Is that all the expense ?—He would have to clothe himself and he would have [to] have some amusement I suppose.

His salary we will take as your average, for the miner it will be about £20. Y[ou] told us he paid £5 10s. for his board and 10s. for lodging, that makes £6. That leav[es] him £14 out of which he has to pay for clothes. How much do you think that mig[ht] be ?—I would think about £5 per month. I am merely estimating how much, but [of] course a miner could tell you with more accuracy than I could.

How much do you think he saves a month ?—I should say about eight or ni[ne] pounds.

Wages of married miners.
When a man is married the mines do not give him free lodging ?—No, not as [a] rule.

So he has naturally large expenses ?—Yes.

How much do you think he has to pay?—About £3 or £4 per month for three rooms and a kitchen.

And food for himself and his family, how much would that be?—Well, it would depend upon how many children he has, and how good a manager his wife is. I should say about £11 or £12 per month.

So a married man has very little to save?—He has nothing, I should say. That is if he has only £20.

Mr. Jennings was thanked by the Chairman.

Margin for saving.

Mr. JAMES PERCY FITZPATRICK, the next witness called, said that he was an employé of Messrs. Eckstein & Co.

Mr. Fitzpatrick's evidence.

Chairman.

By this time you know what are the objects of the Commission, and that it has been the rule for witnesses first to give their statement of the case and then to answer any questions.—Yes. I have not written a statement but I shall deal with the whole subject.

How long have you been in Johannesburg?—I have been in Johannesburg continuously for the last five years.

And before that?—I was away for a little time. I was several years in Barberton, and prior to that at Pilgrim's Rest and Lydenburg. I have been in the country since 1884. In order to make the position clear, I would like to follow on the lines taken by other witnesses, going first into the working costs of the company.

If you have perused the other evidence which has been given, you will understand that it will not be necessary to repeat it. If you can confirm what Mr. Albu or what Mr. Hay has stated you may just simply say so.—It was my intention to take the different items, and, where possible, to say simply that I endorse the statements made, and where I think the statements are not sufficiently full to give other details. I take the proportion of mining costs to be as follows:—White labour, 28 per cent. of the total; black labour, 23 per cent.; explosives, 10 per cent.; and coal, 8 per cent.; these are the principal items. The 31 per cent. remaining is made up of materials, office expenses, chemicals, and many other little outlays, which, I think, the professional witnesses will deal with in detail. The white labour, making up 28 per cent., I don't think it would be possible to reduce much at present, and I think that the reason is that the cost of living for the white miner is very high. I know that the wages are in favour of the single man—that is, that the single man can save money, whereas the married man with a wife and two children cannot. In order to deal with the question, I have got an estimate from two men whom I believe to be thoroughly honest. I take it this way. The average day of a white miner is 16s. or 20s. a shift.

Percentages of costs of mines.

Reduction of white wages not now feasible owing to cost of living.

Average daily wage of white miner.

Mr. Hugo.

How many working hours?—Eight hours. According to one estimate I find that, all details being given, the cost of living for a white married miner amount to £18 17s. 6d. per month. That makes no allowance for life insurance, education of children, smoking, drink, amusements, native servant, newspapers, books, or cost of coming to this country. That is for a man with a wife and two children coming from England. Food and clothes, you will see, come to nearly double, and house-rent to five times what they pay in Europe. In face of these conditions, most married men leave their wives and families in England and on the Continent; and, although they may appear to be saving money, this is not the case, as they have to continuously remit money to their wives. Another estimate brings out the cost at £20. I think

Average number of working hours per day of white miner

Average cost of living for white married miner

Comparative cost of living in England and on Rand.

Families of married miners often in Europe.

that practical miners would be able to throw more light upon the subject, and they will be here to give you information. With that I will leave the white labour question.

Native labour.

As regards the black labour, an arrangement was come to last week, whereby

30 per cent. reduction of native wages.

it was agreed to reduce the black labour by 30 per cent. We have a considerable

Present supply of native labour.

number of kaffirs here just at present, and I think the reduction can be accomplished. I consider that the cause of the number of kaffirs being here just now is largely due to the bad times, and to the closing down of certain mines. I hope that we shall be able to maintain the supply, but unless we get that help in the proper carrying out of the Pass Law, the Liquor Law, and get those general facilities the Government is able to give, I am afraid we shall have again a shortness, and that we shall suffer.

Pass Law.

About the Pass Law, others have already spoken. I can only say that it is a very

Pass Law is good but the administration bad. Desertion.

good law badly carried out. Of course, it is a difficult law, but what we wish to point out is, that the points that we had in view, such as desertion, are exactly the points on which the law has failed. For instance, the Robinson Company, since the law has been brought into operation, had over 1,600 boys desert from their service, and not a single one had been re-captured. I will leave the Pass Law now, as I do not think there is very much more to say, and other witnesses will speak on the point, so that I will not take up your time unnecessarily.

The Liquor Law.

The next thing is the Liquor Law, because it is in connection with the kaffir labour question. I have here numerous complaints sent in by the various Companies regarding drunkenness amongst the kaffirs, which I will hand in if you like.

The *Chairman.*

Illicit sale of liquor at Jumpers Mine

Yes, please, let us have them.—The Jumpers advise that the sale of liquor to natives was going on in the most barefaced manner out there, and gangs of boys were

Inefficiency of detectives.

being continually met in a helpless state of intoxication, and so far the detectives had

Illicit sale of liquor at New Heriot and Robinson mines.

done nothing. The New Heriot advised in the same way, and the Robinson Gold Mining Company wrote exactly similar. They say that the kaffirs have little difficulty in obtaining liquor from the canteens and illicit hawkers, and unless steps are taken to put down this trade, they will lose all the advantages they thought they

Illicit sale of liquor at New Rietfontein Mine.

would gain by the law. I have been favoured by the Consolidated Investment Company with a statement from the Rietfontein Company of what goes on there. They say that native labour is plentiful, but the sale of liquor is in full swing. They have reported the fact to the Landdrost, but no relief had been afforded. Mr. De

Illicit sale of liquor at Worcester Mine.

Roos, of the Worcester Company, writes that nothing has been done to check the illicit sale of liquor, which is more rampant than ever. Boys can be seen in squads drunk, and carrying liquor openly through the streets. On the 8th of March, 300 of our boys were drunk and incapable, and the liquor was mostly supplied by the bars.

Illicit sale of liquor at Robinson Mine

The Good Luck Bar, situated next to the Robinson G. M. Co., is notorious, and this can be said directly of nearly all the bars in the vicinity, and indirectly of the kaffir eating-houses. I think the Sanitary Board should take the matter in hand, and

Illicit sale of liquor and kaffir eating houses.

licence the eating-houses so as to get them under control. While they are allowed to carry on this nefarious business, it will be hopeless for us to come out satisfactorily in our kaffir labour.

Letter of Mr. de Roos to Commandant van Dam regarding illicit sale of liquor.

Mr. De Roos also says that he has written to Commandant Van Dam on the subject. The letter to Commandant Van Dam names certain bars here. The Wiltshire Bar, just below the Ferreira, the Princess Bar, near our mine, do a roaring trade. "There are kaffir eating-houses in the neighbourhood, and most of them sell liquor; one in particular near the Oliver Mill, on the Booysen's road, is doing an extensive illicit business. And so are the bars at Ophirton. I shall be pleased to give any assistance in trapping the offenders, but I think it will be better to employ your own ps. However, just as you please. I confidently hope you will give this matter ur serious and early attention, as our work is greatly hindered by the drunkenness the natives."

The Minerva Company also writes to say that although the boys do not get unk on this property, they appear to have discovered that it is obtainable in hannesburg, and at the end of the week they clear out in considerable numbers to at place, notwithstanding the Pass Law, and that it is in a different district. "On onday morning I was forty of my hammer boys short from this cause." *(Illicit sale of liquor in Johannesburg.)*

There is a letter from the Wolhuter Company complaining of the same:—"Illicit uor traffic has been prevalent on our property, and interferes with native labour." *(Illicit sale of liquor at Wolhuter Mine.)*

There is one also from the City and Suburban, but it is followed up by the statement that the police have taken up the case complained of, and have closed the ahamstown Bar. I think I have said enough regarding the Liquor Law. *(Illicit sale of liquor at City and Suburban Mine. Closure of Grahamstown bar by the police.)*

I come now to the question of gold thefts—I.G.B. I don't think I need take up e time of the Commission very long. I think the case just finished exemplifies *(Gold thefts.)* irly well the difficulties we have to deal with. I don't feel justified in making any timate as to the quantity of gold stolen, because I haven't the least indication to go on, and I don't think it possible to make an estimate. It may be one per cent. and may be 10 per cent. But it is a perfect certainty that there is I.G.B. going on. It *(Amount of gold stolen impossible to estimate.)* notorious that there are a number of persons nominally engaged in the watchmaking d jewellery business, but who are doing a much better business than their capital d apparent energy warrant. They sit still all day, and yet prosper exceedingly. he President of the Chamber of Mines, I may say, has received letters on the subject peatedly, but, of course, such letters do not give absolute evidence. We do the best e can, but there are very serious difficulties in the way of detection. In the City *(Difficulty of detecting gold thefts.)* d Suburban case, just tried in the Circuit Court, we were told beforehand that there as practically no fear of a conviction, because the operators had arranged matters. don't mean that they had arranged with the higher officials; but that they said they ere in with the police. I cannot tell you if that was true or not; I only give you *(Alleged collusion of police with City and Suburban gold thefts.)* hat they said; but in view of the developments of the case, I think they were stified in their boast. It seems hard when private individuals do all the work, end their money, and even risk their lives, as I think the Battery Manager of the *(Discouragement of private persons who assist the police in detecting gold thefts.)* ity and Suburban has risked his life, in order to supplement the work of the partment, to find that all their labour has been thrown away. It is very, very scouraging. Now, in these three matters, the Pass Law, the Liquor Law, and the ld thefts, the suggestion has been made that the Government should constitute a *(Local Board representing the mining interests advisable for administration of matters regarding the Pass and Liquor laws, and gold thefts.)* cal board—some board or permanent Commission in which you could enlist the telligence, the interests, and the energies of the people who desire to protect themlves. There is absolutely no idea of assuming any part of the duty or to trench upon e privileges of Government in this suggestion; but we do think that where our terests are so much concerned, and where it is our business to understand every tail, we could do good work in carrying out the laws which the Government has ven us. And I would like to say that the Pass Law and the Liquor Law are very *(Pass and Liquor laws are good laws but the administration is bad.)* od laws, only they want good administration. I don't think that there is any other testion in this but that of good administration. I put it to you this way. If you ant a house built, you employ a mason; and when you want an industry properly anaged which calls for the highest training and intelligence, I think the abilities of e people ought to be made use of, and I think it would help the Government quite much as it would help us. I must make one other allusion here to the Pass Law; d that is that the Pass Law is very complicated. By it a department was created *(Complexity of Pass Law.)* hich really requires at its head a man with a great capacity for organisation and

D

management, a man with plenty of tact and judgment. When we made th suggestion of this Pass Law, we did hope that we should have a really competent ma at the head of its administration, but the appointment was filled up and these hop were not realised. Well, gentlemen, if you should be able to recommend to Govern ment the establishment of such a board as has been suggested I do hope that you wi also be able to recommend the appointment of men who will secure good admini tration. The best of laws is no good to us if it is not carried out properly.

Inefficiency of the head of the Pass Law administration.

Able men required for local board.

Dynamite.

Dynamite concession — Report of Raad. Commission on dynamite.

Government required to cancel dynamite concession.

Next I come to the dynamite question. The position of the dynamite questic appears to us to be exceedingly simple. A certain concession was granted. A Raa Commission reported to the Government that its terms were not being carried ou The Government have the right to cancel that concession, and we ask them exercise their right. We put it to the Government that it is not only their right cancel it, but that it is even good policy and also their clear duty to do so. Goin into the figures in connection with dynamite and the railway, I would like to poir out to you one of our difficulties. *The onus is thrown on us of showing what the two monopolies are doing.* With infinite difficulty we get hold of many of th details. There may be trifling inaccuracies, but we know that we have got at th principle of it. We know that the representatives of the monopolies will have a opportunity of criticising the evidence we give, and it is quite right that they shoul But they will speak with an intimate knowledge, and we can only quote wha we have discovered by our energies *in the face of every obstacle and difficult deliberately placed in our way.* Why I think this is *a wrong position is becau Government has the right to call upon the two monopolies to expose the whole of the business to the full light of public criticism.* Government can compel the dynamit agents to show how much dynamite they are making (if indeed they are making an at all), what the materials cost them, and what the dynamite, blasting gelatine, c whatever it is, actually costs them free on board at Hamburg; and whether, whe they say it costs them 40s., it is not a fact that Nobel makes it at 18s. 6d. i Hamburg and charges Nobel in Johannesburg 40s. for it, and calls that the cost pric Now it is *in the power of the Government* to make them produce that evidence. must remind you that when Nobel was fighting Mr. Lippert and trying to get market for his goods, he offered to sell—bound himself in fact to sell—down to 40s. case, and reserved to himself the right to sell under 40s.; and I don't think he woul have reserved that right, if he could not have done it with advantage. That pric was for dynamite in bond in Johannesburg without the duty. And I will tell yo why he could do it. At the beginning of this year, dynamite was selling free o board at Hamburg at £43 per ton, which is equal to 21s. 6d. a case. Ocean freight i 4s., landing charges 6d. a case at Port Elizabeth, agency 6d., Colonial duty 2s. 1d railage 4s., which brought it up to 32s. 7d. a case, and in that price Nobel had mad his European profit. I must also in this connection refer to the alleged intervie with Dr. Leyds in the Paris *Temps*.

Difficulty of proving specific misdeeds of dynamite and railway monopolists.

Right of Government to demand a full account of their business from dynamite and railway monopolists.

Nobel's offer to sell dynamite free in bond at Johannesburg at 40s. per case

Price of dynamite at the commencement of this year, free on board at Hamburg.

Charges on dynamite from Hamburg to Johannesburg.

Alleged interview with Dr. Leyds in the Paris *Temps* regarding dynamite.

Chairman.

We want simply local information.

Witness.] I will leave out Dr. Leyds then, and put it this way. A statemen has been made then in a foreign newspaper that the Chamber of Mines was read four years ago to enter into a contract with Nobel for 16 years for the deliver of dynamite at 90s. per case. That is perfectly true, and the explanation is this: tha whereas Mr. Lippert was selling us dynamite at 90s., and the Government was onl getting 5s., Mr. Nobel was going to sell us dynamite at 52s., and the Government wer going to get 38s., and if the contract had been made, the Government would hav

Alleged proposed contract between Chamber of Mines and Nobel's for dynamite at 90s. per case.

ade about £1,200,000 in duty during the past four years instead of, say, £150,000. If these figures are too vague I will undertake that the Chamber of Mines will give you the exact calculations, within a few pounds. I think it is a very great pity that statements like that should be made without quoting the facts which put the truthful complexion on them.

Mr. *de Beer.*

You have introduced a statement which the Commission know nothing of. They have no evidence of it, and the Commission would not be influenced by a newspaper statement, but only by evidence.—I do not mean to insinuate that the Commission would be influenced by this information, but we should have the right to refute a misstatement. Now, in looking at the dynamite, and also at other things, I do not think it is right to calculate, as an argument to the Government, how much the cancellation of the monopoly would benefit us. I go back to the point that the Government have certain rights and duties. I do not suggest to the Government to ignore anybody else's rights, no matter how obtained, but these people have also certain responsibilities. They have failed to carry out these responsibilities, and the Government have the right to cancel that monopoly. We only ask them to exercise that right. I think we might ask that of them, even if it did not benefit us at all, but just fairly to hold people to their contract. There is a great deal of ancient history in the dynamite question which would be interesting to the Commission, but I think we can safely deal with it simply as a fact. It is not necessary now to go into the question of how the dynamite monopoly was created. I would rather deal with the practical question.

Failure of concessionaires to carry out dynamite contract.

Right of Government to cancel dynamite contract.

Request to Government to exercise right of cancellation.

Chairman.

What the Commission want to know is the cost of dynamite here at present, what price can it be landed at here, and how far this price for which dynamite can be sold would influence the cheaper working of the mines?—Certainly. I have given you one set of figures which I think is the most effective, because they are the figures of the same people when they were playing a different game, and to the best of my belief they represent the price at which dynamite monopolists get their dynamite here. Of course I do not believe that if they attempted to *manufacture* dynamite they could make it for 32s. 7d. In the first place, I believe their raw materials will make up about three times as much weight and bulk as the manufactured article, and in that connection they would suffer from railway charges the same as we do. We have an offer from an American firm of manufacturers guaranteeing the same efficiency in the dynamite as that which we call No. 1. I keep No. 1 as a standard. If we talk about blasting gelatine, all the figures will have to be proportionately raised. It will prevent confusion to stick to No. 1. We can deliver No. 1 from San Francisco, of the same quality as obtained here, at 37s. 6d.; and if we had called for tenders a fortnight earlier than we did, we could have obtained it at one penny per lb. cheaper, because lately they decided to increase the price by that much. Had we obtained it one penny cheaper, it would have reduced the price to 33s. 4d. per case, whereas, as I have said, we now quote 37s. 6d. From an average of the working costs of some of the principal mines, taking the same analysis that I gave you at the beginning, the cost of explosives to us comes to 2s. 11½d. per ton. If we had free trade, we would save on explosives alone, 1s. 9d. per ton on the working costs, that is assuming that the working cost is 29s. 6d. per ton. If the old duty, which we agreed to pay some three or four years ago, were put into force on top of the price I have quoted, the Government would make about £500,000 sterling per annum instead of about £60,000. I think the duty we undertook to pay was 8½d. per lb., together

What is present price of dynamite.

How would reduction of cost of dynamite lessen working costs of mines.

Price of dynamite manufactured in Transvaal,

Price of No 1 dynamite imported.

Average percentage of cost of explosives on working costs. Percentage of working costs to be possibly saved in reducing cost of explosives.

Comparison of revenue accruing to Govern-

with 7½ per cent. *ad valorem*. This duty would come to about 38s. or 40s. per cas
I might draw your attention to a statement in the Rand Mines Annual Report, whic
illustrates how this comes home to the companies. The dynamite monopoly last yea
cost the subsidiary companies of the Rand Mines £54,000 for plunder alone. (
course, it will be considerably more as the companies get fully to work. There wa
only one company actually milling during the time I speak of. Just think over the
illustration.

ment through duty on explosives formerly agreed to, and actual duty.
Cost of dynamite monopoly to Rand Mines group in 1896.

Mr de Beer.

Do you speak of only one group, namely, the Rand Mines group ?—I am onl
speaking of the companies I know well. I am perfectly ready to give the Commissio
all names and references. The £54,000 refers to the subsidiary companies of the Ran
Mines. Now, for the next item, I will take you, gentlemen, to coal. Coal costs at th
pit's mouth—that is the price at which the companies sell it—about 9s. to 9s. 6d. pe
ton. I have taken coal separately, that is apart from the rest of the railwa
expenses, because it is a big item in mining expenses, to which we can trace the exac
proportion of working costs. We suggest to the Commission that coal should b
carried at the lowest possible rate, and that every facility should be given to th
mining companies for cheap delivery. When we complain that an average of 100 pe
cent. is put on coal between the time it leaves the pit mouth and reaches the bunker
of the mining companies, we do not mean to say that the N.Z.A.S.M. takes all tha
money. They impose very heavy tariff and heavy terminal charges, but there are
great many items of costs which do not profit the N.Z.A.S.M. at all. We want mor
facilities, and the Netherlands Company will have to give up a portion of its revenu
for a time, and to foster and encourage the mining companies, and presently b
increased carriage, because of cheaper rates, they will find their revenue brought u
to the present standard. We consider that we should have coal delivered at an averag
cost of from 12s. to 13s. per ton instead of from 19s. to 20s., which is, so far as we ca
ascertain, the present average cost of coal per ton delivered on the mines. If we ha
our carriage reduced to the rate I have suggested, I believe it would be a saving o
about 10d. per ton in our working cost. Now, those two items together, dynamite an
coal, if reduced, would make a total saving in the working expenses of about 2s. 7d
per ton. The question has been discussed as to whether in the event of the dynamit
and coal being reduced, companies could work at a profit—that is an increased profi
for those companies now working, and the difference between profit and loss to thos
companies who are not working or are about to shut down. In my opinion, thi
saving of 2s. 7d., which, with the fractions will be 2s. 8d., in the working expenses wil
not make much difference, for we have to go further into matters and not deal wit
the mere questions of dynamite and coal, and for that reason I will give the Commissio
more figures on other points. But, before proceeding to go into other matters, I wi
give you an idea of what difference that 2s. 8d. would mean to certain companie
There is a long list of them, which I hand you.

Coal.
Price of coal at pit's mouth.
Charges on coal before delivery
Share of Netherlands Railway in coal charges
More facilities required for delivery of coal
Loss of Netherlands Railway only temporary by reduction of coal charges.
Delivery prices of coal per ton, possible and actual.
Probable saving in percentage of working costs by reduction in price of coal.
Total saving in percentage of working costs by reduction in coal and dynamite.
Value of reductions on coal and dynamite in percentages to certain paying and non-paying companies.

Company.		Tons crushed in 1896.		Issued Capital 000 omitted.		Additional Dividend possible in the case of a reduction in the working costs per ton of		No. of months crushing*
				£		2s. 8d.		
Crown Reef	...	198,236	...	120	...	21·98	...	12
Durban Roodepoort	...	109,735	...	125	...	12·00	...	12
Ferreira	...	120,772	...	90	...	17·32	...	12
Ginsberg	...	21,529	...	152½	...	1·74	...	12
Henry Nourse	...	92,143	...	125	...	9·32	...	12

Company.	Tons crushed in 1896.	Issued Capital 000 omitted. £	Additional Dividend possible in the case of a reduction in the working costs per ton of 2s. 8d.	No. of months crushing*
Johannesburg Pioneer	33,194	21	21·32	12
New Heriot	92,799	112	10·66	12
Nigel	27,449	200	2·66	12
Princess	42,339	165	3·33	12
Robinson	177,500	2,750	·88	12
Simmer & Jack	156,930	4,700	·45	12
Wemmer	74,945	80	12·48	12
Worcester	43,293	937	6·16	12
Champ d'Or	55,808	128½	5·79	12
City & Suburban	202,850	1,360	2·66	12
Geldenhuis Estate	178,439	200	12·00	12
Geldenhuis Main Reef	35,018	150	3·09	12
George Goch	103,515	325	4·16	12
Glencairn	87,275	225	6·90	9
Jubilee	59,880	50	12·40	12
Jumpers	108,720	100	14·66	12
Block B	92,773	632	1·94	12
Langlaagte Estate	236,229	470	6·69	12
Langlaagte Royal	83,689	180	10·59	7
May	130,050	275	6·67	12
Meyer & Charlton	101,397	85	12·40	12
Minerva	27,643	200	2.77	7
New Chimes	42,451	100	5.33	12
New Primrose	268,428	280	13·33	12
New Rietfontein	42,347	270	2·08	12
Salisbury	58,257	100	7·36	12
Stanhope	19,300	35	8·82	10
United Main Reef	87,226	150	7·36	12
Van Ryn	53,916	170	4·24	12
Wolhuter	139,273	835	2·21	12
Kleinfontein	7,132	185	3·04	2
Porges Randfontein	21,763	437½	1·60	5
Bonanza	19,652	200	2·92	5
Geldenhuis Deep	144,059	280	6·85	12
Langlaagte Star	29,533	240	2·67	7
New Comet	44,844	225	4·00	8
New Crœsus	69,289	500	2·21	10
New Midas	19,083	150	2·88	7
Modderfontein	60,000	900	1·69	7
Roodepoort (Kimberley)	23,551	125	3·73	8
Roodepoort Deep	39,445	180	3·50	10
Treasury	55,228	540	1·81	9

     Total   ...   3,938,928.

Two or three other companies crushed small quantities in 1896, bringing the total ore crushed to 4,000,000 tons.

*All dividends are reckoned on twelve months' milling.

Many of the companies on the list pay no dividends at all at present. When I say in one breath what increase of dividends the saving would mean for the company, and in the next that it is not enough, the explanation is this:—Where in this list a great

dividend is shewn it means that the company has a small capital, and the shares are
high premiums, so that the dividend on the capital is nominally big. The result to
shareholders is not nearly so large as you would imagine at first sight, judging by
figures. The unalterable bedrock fact is that the two items I mentioned would me
a saving to the companies of 2s. 8d. per ton on their working expens

Railway rates. The next item bearing on the cost is the railway charges. I would like to take
Netherlands Railway, first dealing with the rates, then referring to classification a

Railway rates on Coal. the want of facilities, and then the profits. I have to refer again, first of all, to

Comparison of charge of Netherlands Railway on coal transport to Geldenhuis Deep Mine per ton per mile and English Railway coal freight. tariff on coal: I take the Geldenhuis Deep. The transport on coal, including the charg
is 3½d. It is a little over the 3½d., the figures being 3·58d. per ton per mile, on the
of which there is a charge of 1 per cent. for keeping acccounts. The rate in England ov
an equal distance on the Barry Railway is a little over ½d. a ton per mile, so that if t
English charges had prevailed instead of the Netherlands' charges, it would have mad
difference of 5s 8½d. per ton of coal, or nearly 1s. per ton on the ore milled by the Compa
The Commission will remember that that is a little bit higher than the average of all t
companies. That would have paid 2½ per cent. dividend on the capital of the Compa
The exact figures are, from the Cassel Collieries to the Geldenhuis Deep, 7s. 5½d. T
same distance carried under the same conditions in South Wales is charged at 1s.
The N.Z.A.S.M. charge per mile is 3½d. per ton, and the other is about ¾d. The act
cost of carrying the coal cannot be more than ¼d. per ton per mile, and it is a fact t

Railway rates on coal carried for departmental purposes in Orange Free State and Cape Colony. under the agreement between the Free State and the Cape Colony they carry the c
for departmental purposes at *one-seventh of a penny* per ton per mile, which the Ca
Colony and the Free State consider to be just about cost price. I don't want to ta

Netherlands Railway rate for rough goods from Vereeniging to Johannesburg. up the time of the Commission with a great number of instances in connection w
the rates; but I will quote one—about the worst—the rough goods rate from Veree
ging to Johannesburg, which, I believe, for the distance and conditions, is absolutely

Rates of Cape Railway for rough goods. world's record. It is 7·7d. per ton per mile. That includes, I think, the cost of ladi
The Cape rate for the same class is 1⅓ per ton per mile. The Free State rate is t

Orange Free State, Natal, and Portuguese rates, and Netherlands Railway rates from Natal and Delagoa Bay for rough goods. same as that of the Cape Colony. The Natal rate is very nearly 2d. The Portugue
rate is 2½d. The Z.A.S.M. rate from Natal is 3½d., and the Z.A.S.M. rate from Delag
Bay is 2½d. So that the highest rate charged anywhere else, even by the Z.A.S.M.,
not half the rate from Vereeniging to Johannesburg. I wish to lay a great deal
stress on that fact, because that little distance should bring down the rat

Comparison of through and terminal rates from Vereeniging to Johannesburg. tremendously. What is so curious about that tariff, is that, if you load up a thing
Vereeniging, and bring it on to Johannesburg, when they have double terminals, t
rates are from 3d. up to 6d., but when they have no trouble and a through rate, t
carriage is 7¾d. It really comes down to this, that the Netherlands Company do abo
from six to seven per cent. of the work, and they take from 24 to 25 per cent. of t
money. If they would charge the same rates as the Cape Colony, the through ra
from the Cape ports would be reduced by 18 per cent. straight away. To quote o
or two samples of how the heavy rates work out, I may say they tell most on timb

Railway rates from Delagoa Bay on timber and machinery Expenses of mine equipment. The article that the tariff tells next heavily on is machinery, so that it presses a
tells more on the equipment of a company than on the actual working cost. I w
give you a few examples of importations from the Baltic and America. I will give y
the prime cost and the railage from Delagoa Bay, showing the comparison between t
cost and the railage, which you will see supports my contentions as to the excessi
rates. We will take pitch pine. The prime cost of a consignment was £1,722. T

Railway rates from Delagoa Bay of consignments of galvanised iron, sheet lead and candles. railage amounted to £7,234. Oregon pine, prime cost £2,988; railage from Delag
Bay £14,500. Baltic deals cost £2,679; railage £4,170. Galvanized iron cost £25
railage £210. I will give you some instances where the difference is smaller. She
lead £61 10s.; railage £40. Cotton waste, prime cost £92; railage £32 15s. Candl

very largely used on the mines) £1,337 ; railage £313. There are others, but I will and in the statement to the Commission if they like. Those figures are American. There is another statement showing the cost of Australian material.. On a first cost of £1,855, the railage from Durban was £4,100. The expense is considerably added to by wrong classification. For instance, steel plates and angle iron, taking one particular ot, were charged exactly the same rate as a steam regulator, which is a very delicate nstrument, and which only weighs 400-lbs. The steel plates are only worth 10s. 7d. er 100-lbs. and the other is worth £7 15s. per 100-lbs., yet they are charged at the ame rate. Another thing is that there is no allowance made for large lots. The same ate, for instance, is charged for 300-lbs. of rails as for 30 tons, but there is no doubt it s more economical for the Company to handle them in one lot than in 20 lots. Now here are other charges which we consider unnecessary charges and particularly heavy. Many of these charges come in and they do not show in the rate. They add to our osts, and we never see it in the rate. For instance, at the Geldenhuis Deep, 4s. a ruck is charged for bringing the trucks and taking them away. In other countries it s done for less than 1s. But here there is an additional charge of 3s. 4d. to 6s. 8d. per ruck for shunting, and that is not charged anywhere else at home. There is another hing. The Jumpers Company buys coal, and they are charged the full rate into Johannesburg, which is 1s. 3d. per ton more than they ought to pay for the distance. The only reason for it is that there is no official station at the Jumpers. I do not know what an official station is, but although they deliver at this un-official station direct, hey charge for a journey to Johannesburg and back, which is never made. The Jumpers station is therefore official on the down journey, but un-official on the up. Then a very curious thing is that the Z.A.S.M. charges the coal companies one per cent. for keeping their accounts. It is generally considered the duty of every man to keep his own accounts. Another irritating and vexatious tax—one which adds up very much n the costs—is this. The Railway Company allows two hours for the off-loading of rucks at a siding, after which they impose a fine of 1d. per axle per hour. I can only quote what is done in England, as I have no American or Continental statistics here. n England they allow 48 hours for off-loading coal without any extra charge, and even then they do not strictly enforce it. Here the Company never takes the trucks away after the two hours nor even the same day ; but if the consignees fail to off-load within two hours, they get fined just the same. It pays, you will see, to keep a man o watch for these things. Now, there doesn't seem to us to be any justification at all or that.

Mr. *De Beer.*

Supposing they left a wagon the whole day, would they demand the fine ?— cant say that ; but it's a fact that the fine is levied. Of course, I would not know if it when they failed to charge it. If they leave the trucks through their own fault, you understand the Z.A.S.M. do not charge us ; but they fine us for the time over two hours that we neglect to off-load. If we failed by four hours to off-load, they charge he fine even if they leave the trucks for another 48 hours. Here are a couple of other instances. The Herman Conglomerate Company sent a truck-load of material o the Jumpers Deep on March 17. That load is still coming. A substitute lot was ordered, and took five days to arrive at the Jumpers Deep. The same Company has an arrangement with the Cassel Coal Company to get eight trucks a week. The Cassel Company carries out the agreement, but the Railway Company very seldom brings eight trucks a week. The trucks accumulate at Elandsfontein, and the Railway Company brings on a train of twenty-four trucks at a time. The consequence s, that the work on the mine is all put out in order to off-load, and the demurrage or charge for delay has got to be paid by the Jumpers Deep, because they cannot off load twenty-four trucks in the time they undertake to off-load eight. There are also some very unaccommodating regulations. I will give you an instance about excess

Regulations of Netherlands Railway as to excess goods.

goods. People sending large consignments often send a little more than actually appears in the invoice. Sometimes an important part of machinery happens to be left out. The Railway Company weighs all that, and charges for what it actually carries; but they do not deliver the excess article. I don't say that they keep them for their own benefit, but they will not give you them, that is all. Now, the question

Sidings.

of sidings is most important to the Companies, and the delay in obtaining permission to build them, causes the mines a great deal of trouble. The plans do not in any way give trouble to the Companies' engineers here, but still one believes that the plans must be sent to Holland. I do not say that that is so, but the time that lapses between the day on which they are sent to Pretoria, and the day on which they are returned, leaves nothing to prevent them being sent to Holland. I will give you an instance of the vexation Companies have to undergo on the question of sidings. It is

Siding of Violet Consolidated Company.

in connection with the Violet Consolidated Company, a Company with which I am not in any way connected, but the information is correct, given to me by one of the directors. This Company's mine is situated two miles from Krugersdorp, and eight miles from Randfontein. They wished to put down a siding, about 1,000 yards long at a cost of £900. The plans were approved of by the engineers of the company, but were refused by the management at Pretoria. When asked for a reason, the answer the company got was, that they could put up a platform along the main line, and the train would be allowed to stop there twenty minutes in order to off-load. Now, the company has to put up a battery of 100 stamps, and if one mortar box could be un-loaded in twenty minutes it would be smart work. So it was simply impossible. Then the Railway Company said they could put down a siding, *but they would have to connect with Krugersdorp Station,* two miles distant, instead of connecting where the line passed the mine, and at a cost, according to their quotations, of £11,600. You must understand that they wanted to put down a line duplicating their line to Krugersdorp, *besides* making the siding proposed their main line. Another difficulty the mines have to contend with is the fact that we cannot get bottom discharge trucks. If we did not have to put the coal in bags we should save breaking; we should have the coal in bulk, and it would save handling at both ends, because we could get the trucks to discharge automatically. The Geldenhuis Deep and the

Automatic discharge trucks disallowed by Netherlands Railway.

Jumpers Deep went to a cost of, respectively, £4,000 and £2,600 to carry out this arrangement, but they could not get it to work, as the Company refused to provide or permit bottom discharge trucks. I will now give you an instance of how the cost of

Cost free on board and Netherlands Railway charges on a consignment of timber American railway rates on timber sets.

timber worked out on a mine. In the working shafts the timber has to be in what are called sets, which cost on the ship £2 4s. each, and on the mine £13 11s. If the Railway Company charged 1d., which is twice the American rates, the sets would have only cost £9 6s., or being a saving per set of £4 5s., or a saving on the sets put in the two shafts on the Ferreira Deep Mine of £2,000, and that only in the timber of the main shafts. I obtained from a merchant in Johannesburg a statement of the cost

Prime cost and railway rates on a consignment of furniture.

of furniture, which is also a factor in the men's wages. Nine cases of furniture cost £68 19s., and landed here, £128. The railage was £17 2s. 2d.; nine cases of bedsteads cost £59 13s., and landed here, £138—the railage being £34. Now comes the question

Profits of the Netherlands Railway.

of the Netherlands Company's profits. They have a capital of £1,666,660.

The Chairman.

We are all acquainted with the figures, and it will not benefit us to hear them

ain. It will save time if you pass over that question. It will be a matter for us
decide.

Witness.] I cannot get at the possible saving in working cost of the mines unless
o. I will be as brief as possible. I will put it this way. Last year, over and above
e working capital, and the interest on guaranteed loans, the Netherlands Company
de a profit of £1,330,000, and that on a capital of £1,166,660. This, of course, in-
des the Government share, which is shown in the Revenue returns at about
50,000, but as far as I can see, should have been over £700,000; and I say that, by
eping up the rates, they are able to, and I think it fair to say that they do force
tal and the Cape Colony to do the same. Last year the colonies made £1,800,000
re than they ought to have done, allowing 4 per cent. on their capitals—that is,
er £3,000,000 was made, and nearly all of it out of us, for although all the profits
not go to the N.Z.A.S.M., all the loss comes out of our pockets all the same. In
nsequence of the discussion about the railways and the protests made by the
dustry here, there have been some statements made in the Cape and Natal. In this
tter we are entirely dependent upon the goodwill of the Government, because we as
community have no means of compelling neighbouring systems of railways to reduce
tes. It has been stated by the Commissioner of Railways at the Cape that if they
st the whole of the through trade they would still make six per cent. Well, I have
t got the figures to check that, but they never made five per cent. before they had
is through trade, and since they felt the benefit of it they lowered the rates within
e Colony, and they built lines which they did not think they were justified in build-
g when they had to pay for it themselves. So I judge their position is not "all their
ncy paints." They seem at the same time to be willing to reduce rates in a straight-
rward and friendly manner, if allowed to do so for our benefit. I do not think
yone can get away from the fact that nine per cent. is a monstrous profit to make,
sides which they have a transit duty which this community has to pay. In con-
ction with the Natal Railway, there was a statement made by the Commissioner of
blic Works, that Natal was not so badly off as people made out, because half their
nnage was due to the internal trade of Natal. I do not care anything about the
nnage, and it doesn't matter, for it depends upon how much you pay per ton. A ton
rried from Durban to Maritzburg earns very little comparatively with a ton carried
om Durban to Charlestown. This is the point. Before they had their through con-
ction, their revenue was £366,000. In the year 1896, when they got the through
affic, their revenue was £996,000, an increase of £630,000. Of this, general
erchandise contributed £284,000, timber £136,000, and imported mealies £99,000.
at is £500,000 out of £600,000. I think they can talk as much as they like about
nnage, but if they look at the sovereigns—we pay. All the railway systems together
ke about £3,000,000 more than they ought to do. I cannot say that the Transvaal
ade pays for every bit of that, because we would have to see their books, but it pays
r three-quarters of it. Every now and then they have meetings of the Commissioners,
d the only thing they do is to congratulate each other, except when they propose, as
ey did the other day in Durban, to increase the rates. Well, considering that this
mmunity is paying so much of it, we would ask the Government to allow us to make
me suggestions at such meetings if nothing else can be done, because it is simply
ushing the business of the place, and Government will feel the result of it in the long
n as surely as we are feeling it now. I have mentioned those other railways, but
ough they do take a great deal too much, I do not think they are free agents. It
s been stated on behalf of the Cape Railways that it is only allowed certain rates on
e condition that it shall maintain its transit duty. The Cape now say publicly that
ey are willing to reduce, but they are prevented by the Netherlands and Natal.

Marginal notes:

Government share of profits of Netherlands Railway.

Natal and Cape Colony forced to keep up railway rates by Netherlands Railway.

Profits of Natal and Cape Railways for 1896.

Mining industry dependent on goodwill of Government regarding railway rates of neighbouring States.

Position of Cape railways.

Apparent willingness of Cape railways to reduce rates.

Excessive profit of Cape railways.

Transit duty.

Position of Natal Railway.

Total excessive profits of railway systems.

Excessive contribution of Transvaal trade to railway profits.

Representation of mining industry at meetings of Commissioners of railway systems demanded of Government.

Coercion of Cape and Natal Railways by Netherlands Railway so as to maintain high rates.

The Natal Government shuffles and smiles. And if you look at the rate I quoted fro Vereeniging it does look like it. Natal is afraid to reduce without consent. Now, can understand perfectly well that the Z.A.S.M., as a commercial concern, wants

Three courses open to Government in dealing with Netherlands Railway. make as much profit as it can—that is perfectly natural; but there is a means checking it, and we ask the Government to take the necessary steps. There are thr courses open. In the first case Government may leave the Company alone to do as likes, and I don't think that would be in the interest of the State or the communit or any other interest except that of the Z.A.S.M. Or it can expropriate the railwa

Expropriation by Government possible. or else it can tell the Company that the rates must be reduced, and if not that tl Company must be expropriated. Government is not without means of making tl

Government can compel reduction of rates of Netherlands Railway. Railway Company reduce its rates, and the Company is suffering no injustice, becau it has made a certain agreement giving the Government the right to do so. I think tl Commission knows enough about the terms of expropriation, and I need not enter in them at present. If the concession had been taken over in 1895, it would have co

Cost of expropriation in 1895. the Government £1,785,000 to expropriate the 1,166,660 shares. Of course, the loa would also have had to be paid; but they are all practically safe.

Chairman.

It is not for us to go into these matters now. These are not grievances of tl mines—they are things that we must afterwards find out for ourselves.

Extent of reduction of (mining) working costs dependent on Government action regarding Netherlands Railway. *Witness.*] It would depend on what course is adopted with regard to the railways a to what extent we could reduce our working costs; and unless we have some basis to g upon we can make no estimate. Railway charges amount to a very big proportion c the equipment of a company, and they, as far as I can make out, make up about 5 to 1

Percentage of Railway charges on working costs of mines. per cent. of the working costs of the mines. That is a very big margin, I know; bu it is an extremely difficult item to estimate, and I have given the outside figure That is on material. I do not touch on how white or black labour expenses could b reduced in this connection, though that, of course, is a very serious question. But shall leave the railway question now, since the Commission wishes it. The nex

General taxation question which affects our costs of working is that of the general taxation. I don want to take up your time by going into each item. I can get at what I want in a fe

Comparative growth of revenue and population, 1885-1897. figures. The revenue of the State in 1885 was £177,876, and in 1897—twelve year later—£4,886,000. Well, the population has only increased in that time from 50,00 to 250,000, according to the State returns, but where the people paid £3 15s. per hea then, they now pay £17 13s., on the basis of all the whites contributing equally. It rather difficult for me to explain this matter without getting on to subjects which w

Incidence of taxation. would rather avoid; but if you look into the incidence of taxation, you will find tha the taxation per head of the industrial population comes out £23, after allowing £5 pe head for the 70,000 forming the rural population. Well, I would submit to you tha it is quite impossible for a community to keep on contributing like this. That amoun is not paid out of our earnings, because we don't earn enough to pay it. When w have paid our working expenses, there is not difference enough to pay the taxatior

Taxation of mining community exceeds margin of profits. Therefore the money must be paid out of the capital. The money—that is our point— is being stopped from going into the ground, and we would particularly ask the Com

Economic reform required. mission to suggest a plan by which the expenditure of the State might be brough down to the limit that we can bear. To take an illustration—if you were farmin with a man on certain terms, you would not take half of his seed oats and se them, and then reap his half-grown crop for green forage. Yet that is just wha is being done with us. If the money went into the ground and the valu was got out of it, the State could share out of the profits as much as it gets now. would not come the first year, nor perhaps the second; but it would come, and that

that we ask the Commission to consider carefully. The harvest would be enough for all. A million and a half a year should serve to carry on the work of the State—it now takes four and a half millions. Then there are such things as heavy purchases and permanent works, and, though we could pay the interest on them, we don't think it right that we should pay for the capital out of revenue. It is not very difficult to say exactly where the money comes from; where you have only one real industry in the State and such an enormous revenue, you can fairly assume, in the absence of all evidence to the contrary, that the latter is paid by the former. All the money that we have had to pay, £3,000,000 to the railway, and the £3,000,000 which the State has unnecessarily had out of us, has come from European capital, and ought to have gone into the ground. It has not all come out of our earnings, because we have never earned it. We lay so much stress on the questions of dynamite and coal, because they are such clear cases that it is impossible to pass them over, and because we have to look into every detail that can bring down our costs. If we neglected them we should be doing, what we are sometimes accused of doing, not attending to our own business. But the real pinch is in the great items of the railways and the general taxation, and we ask that the Commission would consider those matters—we are told that they are not matters to be argued about in public—but consider them, and talk them over carefully. It is impossible for the industry to keep on contributing like this—nothing but ruin stands ahead if it has to do so. Two points I want to mention to show that it would be possible to reduce our burdens largely. Take the Free State. They have more than a quarter of the Transvaal population, and therefore our expenditure, if on the same lines, should be less than four times as much. Their expenditure, including £100,000 of special expenditure, was last year £430,000. If you exclude the special expenditure, ours should be a lot less than 1½ millions. Including everything, it should be under two millions. Then the net Government revenue, striking out the profits of the Netherlands Company and State profits on dynamite, was £3,600,000; the dynamite, over and above what we ought to have paid, was £500,000; railways, £2,500,000; imports, £12,000,000. We have paid the railway system £3,000,000; transit dues, £300,000; coal, £500,000. We pay for the produce of the country, £1,000,000; the interest to European shareholders in dividends, £1,500,000; white wages, £1,500,000; native wages, £2,000,000; and it brings the total up to over £28,000,000, and the State only produces £8,000,000. It is true a great deal of that is capital expenditure, but the enormous difference which remains must make you see that it cannot go on. That is all I have to say on the immediate causes of the present state of affairs.

Marginal notes: Excessive State expenditure. State capital expenditure charged to revenue. Absorption of European money by railways and by taxation. Railway and taxation the chief grievances of mining industry. Comparison of Orange Free State and Transvaal populations and expenditure. Payments of mining industry.

Chairman.

Did I rightly understand you this morning, on the dynamite question, when you said that the factory was, at the present moment, connected with Nobel's ?—Yes, that is certainly what we understand, and it has been publicly stated that Nobel's bought out Mr. Lippert, and it is known that the agents of Nobel's are associated with the factory here.

Will you repeat the figures you gave us to-day as to the actual price of dynamite made, delivered, and the expenses on it ?—I do not think I quoted the price at which it was made. I said the price of No. 1 placed on board at Hamburg was 21s. 6d. I believe that Mr. Albu said it could be made at 18s. 6d., and I daresay he is perfectly right.

Can you prove to us by reliable statistics at what price the dynamite was sold at Hamburg ?—I can prove that it was sold this year, or within the last six months, at Hamburg at 21s. 6d., that is £43 per ton.

Marginal notes: Connection of dynamite factory with Nobel's. European price of dynamite.

Percentage of
working costs.
This morning you made the statement that the percentage of the wages of the whites was 28 per cent. ?—Yes.

And that of the kaffirs 23 per cent. ?—Yes.

That 10 per cent. went for explosives ?—Yes.

Coal, 8 per cent. ?—True.

Now that makes it 69 per cent., and you said that 31 per cent. went in stores and material, &c. ?—I did.

Later on you said that railway rates came to from 5 to 10 per cent. ?—Yes.

Did you include that in the 31 per cent. ?—Yes.

Percentage of railway rates on working costs. But not the 8 per cent. for coal ?—No. Coal works out at 8 per cent. carriage paid. We arrive at the carriage on stores this way. We take an item, oil, £1,300. go to the merchant in town and we get his figures, and can thereby easily estimate the railage. I do the same with regard to all stores, and then I obtain from all the companies their figures and strike an average. The reason why I gave the margin from 5 to 10 per cent. is that some companies are putting up cyanide vats, sheds, and adding to their machinery, and the proportion of railway rates in these would be heavy. One company might give 5 per cent. and another fifteen per cent., and to get at the working costs as they are year by year, to obtain a fair result—you must take the average.

Reduction of white wages. Now with regard to the 28 per cent. for white wages, do you consider that that could be reasonably reduced ?—I think it is possible to have it reduced, but that could only be done by getting in a great many men who can live here cheaper than the men we have got at present, and who will work at a much lower wage. It would mean men without families or starvation wages. But no matter how much they were paid they would still want the necessaries of life. You see in white wages everything comes in, such as railway carriage and general taxation.

Percentage of white wages on working costs. Does the 28 per cent. include the wages paid to every white man, from the director to the lowest man employed on the mine ?—Yes. That is the average amongst the principal companies on the Rand, and I think it is the fairest average because their conditions of working are the conditions which all the other companies are trying to attain. If you take the average of all the mines on the Rand you may get one or two per cent. either way. Sometimes a mine varies because of the different character of the reefs, but that is a fair average.

Scarcity of native labour. As regards coloured labour, I understand you to say there is no want of black labour at the present moment ?—Not at present.

How many white labourers have you discharged at any of the mines you are connected with ?—I really cannot tell you now, but I can find out. It is not a matter that comes before the directors.

Under whose department does it come ?—Under the manager's.

Taxation. You are the first witness who makes any mention of any further burdens pressing on the mines, and I would like to have more information on that point because I have a different opinion about the case. You want it to appear that the burdens are only borne by the mining industry, and that nearly all is paid out of the capital which is introduced into the country. We have made a calculation—our income is so much and the revenue so much. Then you put down the taxation at about £23 per head. You stated £17 13s. first and then £23.—Yes, I did, but the explanation is this: the £17 13s. is the contribution per head calculated on the total of white inhabitants of the State. But that is not a sound calculation, because the country population do not contribute anything like as much as the industrial population. In order then to get at the truth as nearly as possible—I take the Government *Staats Almanak* figures—the official records of population and the rural

pulation, I allow taxation of £5 per head—a figure which errs greatly on the liberal
.e, but I take it because it is the figure of the contribution per head of the total
aite population in the Orange Free State towns and country, industrial and rural ;
rely that is most liberal. And on this basis the new population here pay £23 per
ad per annum.

I want to be clear on this point. Has there been any increase of taxation
tween 1885 and 1897 ?—I do not suggest that, Mr. Chairman. That is why I say
at the taxation comes out of capital, because the people do not and cannot pay it
ect. What I suggest is this, if I may put it this way—the duty of the Govern- *State revenue and expenditure.*
ent is to adjust the revenue to real necessities of the State. If you can conduct the
ate on two millions, the rest of the taxation, or the revenue, ought to be remitted,
cause it pays the State to do so. It does not matter whether sugar or tobacco or
gars is raised or lowered in a calculation of this sort. What I suggest is that there
very much more raised in the State than is absolutely necessary for the Govern-
ent. I can suggest to you, for instance, permanent works, and other points will
cur to yourselves. This we do not consider to be necessary out of revenue.

The increase of revenue does not arise from any direct taxation being put on the *Sources of State revenue.*
pulation, but it arises from the increased population of the country itself, from the
tension of all branches of industry, and the largest increase in the revenue is on
port duty. Why is this, but because the consumption and the use of imported
ods is increasing. It is not the mines which pay that, but the country generally,
d every individual inhabitant of the country. I will agree with you that the
xation ought to be regulated according to the expenditure of the State itself. But
the present moment the expenditure and revenue still go like ebb and flood in this
untry. It is not regulated properly yet. It cannot be shown there is any direct
x pressing upon any individual.—I would suggest that a fat year for the State is a
ry lean year for the industry.

I cannot see that, because the fat year for the State has to come from the cow—
hich is the industry.

Mr. *Joubert.*

I understood from your evidence that the Government, through the dynamite *Dynamite monopoly.*
ntract, has suffered a loss of £4,000,000 during the last four years.—I think I said
at if we had paid the duty of about 38s. a case, which we offered to pay in that
oposed contract with Nobel four years ago, the Government would have obtained
out £1,000,000 out of that duty—£1,200,000 I said, according to the shorthand
iter's report.

You say the Pass Law is a good law ?—Yes. *Pass Law.*

But that the man who is at present in charge is not able to carry out the *Administration of Pass Law.*
ministration properly ?—Yes.

Can you adduce any facts to show that he is not competent ?—The condition of
s department indicates it.

Every man puts his own construction on the law ?—Well, the first intention of the
w was to prevent desertions and to get back those who desert, and I have given you
e instance of the Robinson Company of 1,600 deserters, and not one captured.

That surely is not the fault of the Distributor of Passes ?—No ! I did not say
at. The Distributor is only one of the minor officials, who has got certain work
do.

However good the law might be, still the kaffir could "scoot" with his pass ?—
ere are safeguards against that. He has to show a discharge and district pass
fore he can travel. At present it is only an extra tax-collecting agency. We'll take

the Customs Law.   Here you have officials that give receipts for the Customs, ye
have an inspector on the border, and also have a high official who organises the who
thing.   If you only had an inspector and no collector, and no prosecutions, the la
would be a failure.

I would like to know in the interest of the high official where you put the blan
on him ?—As we have not the working of the department we cannot exactly say, b
it is the first duty of the organiser to find out why his department does not work, ar
if he were a capable man he would know it.

But a kaffir can go away even under the Pass Law ?—Not if the Departmer
properly organised it.

In what possible way would you prevent desertion ?   The kaffir is registere
gets his pass, and then runs away with his pass in his pocket.   What ste
would you take to prevent this ?—Before he can pass out of a district he h
to produce his district pass.   Before he can get fresh employment he has
produce his own pass.   There is a complete system of checking provided by law, tl
letter of the law, but the working of the law provides no check at all.

But how will the pass officials know if the kaffir, perhaps when seeking wor
happens to have shown his pass to a fieldcornet ?—He has to get a special pass as so(
as he comes into the district.

Over that the officials have no control ?—But they ought to have.   That is ju
the point.   He has then to get a working pass.

Suppose now that the kaffir tears up the pass and goes away ?—Then he can l
imprisoned for not having a proper pass.

But how can you prevent a kaffir running away in the night ?   How can yo
prevent that ?—I will tell you how to prevent it.   There are here at different tim(
70,000 kaffirs, and—

See here, you are a mine director.   Why don't you prevent people stealing yo
amalgam ?—Well, we do our best.

And yet you come to the Government to complain ?—Yes.   It is just the same a
in the case of burglaries.   We lock up our houses, but that does not do away wit
the necessity for police.

You admit that you are incompetent to prevent it ?   What officials anywhere ca
cope with roguery ?—If there is to be an ideal state of affairs, no police are require
at all.

The police are placed there not to stop all the crime, but all they can.— Yes, wel
they might occasionally detect something.

But things often happen that should not, even in the most civilised countries, eve
in England ?—Certainly.   But in England they also have the best detective service i
the world.

And those at the head of the department can deal with crime ?—Yes.

But you can't put the crime down to the officials ?—I don't say that the poli(
steal the gold.

You can't take care of the gold yourself, and how do you expect the police to (
so ?   You have immense control over your employees ?—Yes; ordinary control, bu
we can't stop it altogether.

Yet you expect Government to do so ?   These things would happen under tl
best officials ?—Yes; you can't prevent crime altogether, but—

Neither can the Government ?—No, but the Government can make an effort i
that direction.

It is the duty of the Government to make the best laws possible for the commu
nity ?—Yes; *and* carry them out.

Under the best laws crime is done ?—Certainly.

And under the best officials you sometimes don't get detection ?—Sometimes !

But it doesn't often happen here ?—What, detection ? No.

Well, however good the pass officials may be, there will always be transgressors of the law ?—That may be so, but it should be the desire of the Government to make the transgressions as few as possible. If you thrust on individuals or companies the responsibilities and duties which are generally supposed to devolve on Government, you would give the directors of the mines the right to institute the compound system, to keep the boys on the property, and the searching system, so that amalgam thefts could be detected; but those are systems that we would never suggest, nor would the Government ever consent to such things.

I am a farmer. I work with cattle; the law on cattle thefts is strict, but still cattle are stolen. Now, if my cattle are stolen, can I blame the Government for it ?—You could certainly blame the Government if they made no efforts to check the thefts.

It is my duty to go to the Government after the theft and ask them to help me to trace my property ?—No; it is the duty of the Government to take steps to prevent thefts. The detection of one theft would prevent a recurrence. It is difficult to trace amalgam once it is stolen. You can trace a bullock. You cannot carry a bullock in your pocket, but you can carry a lot of amalgam in your pocket. Therefore, there is all the more necessity for detective measures.

But cattle thefts are often undetected. The thieves might kill and eat the ox.—I repeat you cannot spoor a piece of amalgam across the veld, but you can a bullock.

You accused the head of the pass department of being incompetent. I would like to have some facts. Now, can you give us any ?—You have the result. It shows faulty administration, because there have been no detections of desertions. I will put it this way. You would not take a clerk out of our office to drive your bullock wagon. You would take one who had experience in driving bullocks. Now, in a department of this nature, which is so very important to the mining industry, you want an experienced man at the head. You want a man of fine capacity for organisation, who has a special knowledge of the circumstances of the mines; who has a particular aptitude for carrying out the system; who has a knowledge of men. You would not select a man for the head of such a department who knew nothing about the work. Administration of Pass Law.

But you cannot expect a pass officer to act as a detective ?—Detection is a part of the department. I do not mean to say that the clerk who signs the passes should trace deserters, but that is a part of the department.

Is it not a matter for the head of the police to deal with ?—It is part of the department for the carrying out of the law. I don't mean that the gentleman who signs the pass ought to catch the kafir. But the head of the department must organise it. To give you another illustration. You have got a High Court, and they sentence a man, but the Chief Justice does not go and hang a murderer. The whole thing works together; one supplements the other, so that you get an efficient working system.

But somebody who has been hung does not go and lodge a complaint against the Chief Justice ?—He made his complaint beforehand, but it did not carry any weight.

The department is there to issue passes. Now, my kaffir obtains a pass to work for me, and he deserts. I would go to the police and ask them to help me to catch him.—But your case would be different. This Pass Law provides for a system of check to be carried out by that department. Say a boy obtains from the Pass Office a pass, and he goes to work on the Robinson Mine, and subsequently runs away and destroys his pass, as is often done. He should be captured and punished. If his time had expired he would be provided with a district or travelling pass. But with all the desertions I have mentioned, not one has been captured.

But could you not go to the Pass Office and get the number of the boys who ran away ?—That would not assist us. The one-half of the duty of the department is to issue passes, and the other half is to catch deserters. They are under one chief. The latter half·does not work, although the law makes every provision for it.

Why, if you had all these complaints against the department, did you never complain to me, as Minister of Mines, about the bad working of the law ?—It is a special department.

But it is a matter that concerns the mines, and the complaints cannot be put before the Government, excepting through me. The Pass Department is a sub-section of my department ?—Then you are responsible. The bad working of the law has been discussed over and over again, and last year a petition was sent in to the Government, and deputations waited on you. This year a petition is being sent in to the Volksraad.

But why did you not send the memorials through me ?—We thought we had the privilege of approaching the Volksraad. The Volksraad made the law.

You say the law is good ?—Yes, that is true. What we want is to have it carried out.

But the Volksraad put officers there to carry it out, and if these officers were negligent, why did you not report them to me ?—I think you would understand it better if I got a copy of the law, and took it point by point.

Never mind the copy of the law. I know it well; I helped to make it.—Yes, and you helped to make the department too. We hope that you will help to improve it.

I will. If you had approached me before there would have been no need for you to have come here to-day to complain of the bad working of the law.

Mr. *de Beer.*

The only complaint you made is that 1,600 boys deserted from the Robinson Mine and were never recaptured.—I did not give it as the only complaint, but as an illustration of what goes on. I presume that the Commission is about to call in the mine managers, who will relate their own experiences.

This is the only complaint before us yet. Have you any knowledge that passes have been issued to deserters ?—I believe that such has been done : in fact that must have been done, because the boys, after tearing up their passes, obtain fresh ones to go and work elsewhere.

Of any two presumptions you should always take the most probable. My idea is that they go to their kraals.—I believe that they remain in the district. Of course the district is divided into so many parts, and it is necessary for the department to see that the boys have their district passes when they go around from district to district. That is the check.

You have been such a long time in this country that you must know that it is exceedingly difficult to prevent anyone going or coming.—I know it is difficult with regard to single individuals, but where you have kaffirs going the same route year after year, it ought to be within the power of organisation to stop desertion.

You know the peculiarity of natives. During the night he travels, and during the daytime he lies *perdu* somewhere ?—Yes, but I cannot admit Mr. de Beer's deductions are the stronger, for this reason : in many cases the boys, after coming a long distance to obtain work, desert at the end of the first month. That cannot be because they want to go home again.

Is there not an agreement existing between the mines not to take niggers ~~~~nging to another mine ?—There is an honourable understanding, yes ; I have been ~~~~rmed. I happened to hear a conversation between some directors of the Primrose ~~~~the Simmer and Jack Mines, where they stated that their compound managers ~~~~rned deserters from one to another, whenever they could detect them.

That chance certainly exists in the Pass Law. From whom did the Pass Law ~~~~inate ?—It originated from the mines. Origin of Pass Law.

You know that the Pass Law is controlled by two departments—the pass depart-~~~~it and judicial department ?—Yes.

As to the desertion of niggers, under which department would you place them ? ~~~~he judicial department is separate from the executive department—the police.

I take the judicial department to mean police included.—I do not think it is ~~~~sible to answer that question exactly. It depends in particular instances where the ~~~~lt lay, whether it is in the issuing of passes at improper times, or the failure to ~~~~est deserters and vagrants. Inefficient administration of Pass Law.

Do you know the official who has charge of the Pass Office personally ?—No.

And, of course, it would be in the interest of the mines to assist the official if he ~~~~s incapable ?—Yes.

I know the official personally, and that he would do all in his power to assist the ~~~~ustry. He has made several journeys to Pretoria to try and make the law practical. ~~~~el it hard that he should now be exposed as an incompetent official.—I did not say ~~~~t he did not do his best ; but that his best was not good enough.

But your explanation is also not good enough, seeing that you are unable to place ~~~~ir finger on the defective spot.—Well, you have general and hopeless failure. What ~~~~re do you want ?

Mr. *Brakhan.*

Mr. Brakhan took the witness in hand, and in reply to that gentleman, Mr. ~~~~zpatrick said he thought in the cold weather there might be a falling off in native ~~~~our ; but the supply would really depend on the carrying out of the Pass Law and ~~~~Liquor Law. The Liquor Law affected the supply this way. When the liquor ~~~~s in full swing, about one-third of the kaffirs were incapable, and the deficiency had ~~~~be made up. If the Liquor Law were properly carried out there would be a sufficient ~~~~ply, if general facilities for bringing the boys in were granted by the railway. ~~~~ey might charge them nominal rates to come to work, and, say double, to go away ~~~~in. He wished to make no unreasonable suggestions to the N.Z.A.S.M., of course. ~~~~agreed with Mr. Albu that the action on the part of the Native Commissioners ~~~~dered the supply of native labour. Mr. de Beer had hauled him over the coals for ~~~~king a statement without details, and he did not wish to do the same again. If he ~~~~, he would be asked to mention the name of the companies which have to make ~~~~se special payments, and as a sole result they would then probably suffer by not ~~~~ting boys in future. Native labour. Liquor Law. Exactions by Native Commissioners for supply of native labour.

Can you give us any figures about dynamite ?—I quoted yesterday the price of ~~~~3 per ton in Germany at the beginning of the year. That works out at 21s. 6d. per ~~~~e exactly. Price of dynamite in foreign countries.

Can you give us another instance ?—I give you an adverse instance. In Corn-~~~~ll they pay 36s. a case, but there is a reason for that. Their consumption is not ~~~~ge enough to enable them to control the prices of the manufacturers. Dynamite, ~~~~you know, is a compound subject to very severe restrictions as to transport and ~~~~rage, &c. You must either get big supplies, charter a special ship, and make large ~~~~vision for storage, and so on, or you may get small supplies and pay heavily for

E

the risk. If a ship has 10 tons or 1,000 on board, in the case of an explosion, it ma
very little difference, except in the spectacular effect.

Prices for impor-
ted dynamite.
Yet, even taking the high prices in Cornwall, it would be considerably less th
the 85s. here. If we had free trade here, at what price could it be laid down here f
of duty, on the basis of 36s. in Cornwall ?—If we bought retail in Cornwall—actua
bought from the mines, which would have already paid profit, we could land
dynamite here at 47s. 1d. a case.

Against 85s. ?—Yes.

And on the basis of the German price of 21s. 6d., that would work at 32s. 6d.
Yes, 32. 7d.

Are you quite sure that 21s. 6d. is right ?—It was sold publicly at that price
Germany at the beginning of this year. My information is from a gentleman w
got the price there personally at the very time.

I ask because it would appear from your figures that the Dynamite Company
making an exorbitant profit here at present ?—I think it is one of the best busines
in the world.

About 52s. 6d. a case profit ?—It is difficult to get the exact figures. You see
is not called a monopoly but a Government agency, and the Commission can ma
them turn their affairs inside out ; can get the Government to put an auditor on
them and publish all their figures. It is very hard that we should be called on
prove a case which the Government can expose at will.

Consumption of
dynamite.
How much dynamite is consumed, and not manufactured here ?—That is anotl
point the Commission can ascertain shortly. Our information (I make it merely a
suggestion to put the Commission on the line of inquiry) is that not more th
20,000 cases are manufactured here per annum, and the March output of the facto
(I should say the agency) was stated at over 20,000.

Dynamite royal-
ties.
Now, is there any commission or special profit in this dynamite besides i
Government 5 per cent. ?—It is a very complicated affair. You see 182,500 shares
the agency were granted to the shareholders in the original concession, which w
cancelled for reasons explained by the President in language stronger than I care
quote. Then there were—

No, I don't mean the share transactions. I mean, is there any actual sum pa
able per case besides the charges mentioned ?—Yes. There was 6s. a case that had
be paid to Mr. Lippert, 2s. a case to Messrs. Lewis and Marks, and a special payme
of 2s. a case for three years to Mr. Lippert. That would be, altogether, 15s., includi
the 5s. But the 2s. was only for three years, and for an explanation of that I mu
refer to private inquiry. There have been so many statements made about it that
think it is for the Commission to investigate it more than anyone else.

Price for impor-
ted American
dynamite.
You said yesterday that your firm had an offer from American manufacture
that they would deliver dynamite here for 37s. 6d. ?—Well, I do not know if I sa
that exactly. What I meant to convey was that they quoted a price to us, delivered
Port Elizabeth, which at the known charges would have enabled us to bring dynami
here at that price, of course without any duty being paid in the Transvaal.

Are you quite sure that that dynamite is of the same quality as No. 1 ?—It
guaranteed so.

Manufacture of
dynamite.
Suppose there should be free trade in dynamite, are you not afraid, on behalf
the mining industry, that the ring in Europe would raise the price so much that n
Possible dyna-
mite "ring."
Mining industry
could defeat
d y n a m i t e
"ring."
much benefit would occur to the mining industry ?—Not in the least, because we ha
several courses open to us. We can either build a factory in Europe, for here v
have the biggest consumption in the world ; we could build a factory where ra
materials could be bought cheaply. We could buy a factory, or several factori

lready in existence, or we could go to the manufacturers and say to them : " We are
n a position to place orders for 250,000 cases a year. We want your prices, and will
ive you a ten years' contract." I am perfectly certain that capitalists would them-
elves build factories to get these orders, and then we should get dynamite at the
rice mentioned here, of 21s. 6d., and I believe if we put them in competition for
hese big orders, we should get it cheaper still.

Yes ; but in the meantime you would be at the mercy of the Americans or Mr.
Nobel?—Any ring they might form would fail. The different manufacturers are not so
ound together that they cannot compete. In the first place, the American people
nd Nobel would not combine against us, and before we needed to build a factory, we
ould buy factories already in existence.

Then it is your opinion that if free trade were established in this country in *Free trade in dy-namite.*
ynamite, then a very large reduction in the price of dynamite is assured?—Oh, yes. A
ery large reduction, and it can so easily be done. You see, it is really a matter of
dministration only. It is the same with all our grievances here. It can be remedied
y sound administration. The Government have the right to hold the dynamite
eople to their contract, but even if they did not cancel the monopoly, they could
llow us to import what the monopolists could not manufacture. If they can only
manufacture 20,000 or 50,000 cases a year, we should be allowed to import the other
00,000 for our benefit, or for the benefit of the State. The difference in price could
o either to the mines or to the State, as the Government in its wisdom thinks right,
ut it ought not to go as an improper profit to the monopolists. Surely that is not
n unreasonable request.

Then even if the Government were to impose a fairly good duty, yet the in-
ustry would be able to import it at considerably lower prices than now ?—Certainly;
f the Government put even £1 a case on we could get our dynamite very much
heaper, and we hope that if the Government took that £250,000 a year they would
ive us relief in some other direction. This is not a matter of antagonism to the
ynamite factory, or philanthropy. It would be a direct gain to us.

In regard to the railways. You mentioned yesterday one figure on the basis of *Expropriation of railway.*
895 that the cost of expropiation would be £1,700,000 ?—I said £1,785,000.

What would it be upon the basis of 1896 ?—In 1896 it would be £700,000 more,
nd the longer this expropriation is postponed the more opportunity they have of
ringing in larger dividends. In the long run, of course, the taxpayers will have to
nd the money ; that is why it concerns us so very much. If the thing goes on for
nother six years, we will have to pay £6,000,000 for 1,666,660 shares. I leave out
he loans because they are under Government guarantee, and the Government can
ake them over in that way, as they are practically responsible. If notice is given
his year, this session we will get the thing for three-and-a-half millions, but if it
oes on for another six years, we will have to pay £6,000,000 unless the Government
uts down the profits.

But this is on the whole share capital. Of course, the actual cost would not be *Government share in Netherlands Railway.*
o high, because the Government holds a great number of shares ?—I believe the
overnment owns 5,500 out of 14,000 shares.

But if the Government takes over the railway soon, do you think it would be a *Loan for expropriation of railway.*
urden on the industry ?—The industry would have to pay. Supposing they gave
otice this year, they would have to pay £3,250,000, that is, £2,000,000 more than the
ctual capital. We would have to pay the difference between 6 per cent. on the
riginal capital, and the rate of interest on which the State could raise this
3,250,000, and if the State took over the whole debt, which would then amount to
bout £9,000,000, including all the loans, the credit is quite good enough to actually

save the interest on it, and you would also save the huge profit that I have already pointed out, viz., £1,300,000 a year.

Profits of Cape and Natal Railways.

Then you stated that the Cape and Natal railways drew out of the earning £1,800,000 over and above the amount they ought to do ?—Yes.

On what basis do you arrive at that figure ?—First of all the Government railways are not commercial speculations, entitled to get as much as they can out of the country. They are meant to facilitate the development of the country. As regards the Cape, the Free State, and Natal, that refers, of course, to their internal trade. While they are developing the Transvaal for us, they are entitled to some extra

Colonial transit dues.

consideration. Well, now, they have their transit dues. They raise their money at 2 or 3 per cent., and on that calculation I allow them 4 per cent., but the Commission can go further and allow them 5 per cent., which will give each country a profit over and above its interest to give away to their own people, or build other railways for their own benefit; I think that with these and the transit dues they could very well afford to give us relief.

Will you imply that the mining industry will be relieved in various quarters in

Colonial railways.

the case of expropriation of the Railway Company. It would be relieved by this Government, and also by Natal and the Cape, therefore this country would not bear the burden alone ?—Certainly. But this country is the key to the whole position. It was the Netherlands Railway which stopped the cutting of rates in the

Netherlands Railway holds key of position

beginning. It is the Netherlands Railway we are told which makes the Cape Government keep on their transit dues. It is the Netherlands Railway which charges 7s. 7d per ton on rough goods from Vereeniging to Johannesburg, when they allow the Portuguese over the same distance, doing about the same amount of trade and carrying the same goods, only 2½d., and even less than that. We impress upon the Commission that the whole power is in the hands of the Netherlands Company, and they can be controlled by the Government, and, therefore, the whole power is in the hands of the Government—of course I am speaking subject to correction, but that is what we believe.

Railway report of Chamber of Mines.

You quoted just now from the report of the Chamber of Mines on railways ; I have read this report and I can only gather from it that the accusation is levelled against the Netherlands Railway. From what you say the Natal and Cape Government Railways should also have been mentioned ?—That report only deals with 1895 and there is a supplementary report promised.

As I read the report, the neighbouring railways can hardly draw the conclusion from it that their rates are too high, which, as you have shown by your figures of £1,800,000, they are ?—Well, I have given you exactly the basis. They might not accept 4 per cent. I do not think they would ; I think if we could get an independent commission from outside they would tell these people that they are all plundering the Transvaal. The other day we were told, " What is the good of a milch cow if the cow turns round and drinks all the milk." This cow's head is tied so tight it can't even graze. They are killing the industry the whole lot of them.

I think it would be well if the supplementary report of the Chamber of Mines were to lay it down in so many words that the neighbouring railways are just as much culprits as the Netherlands, because I do not think the present report conveys that impression ?—A report framed by a number of people will give the average of their opinion. I have given you my opinion, and I would be quite ready, if I were to

Cape and Natal railway rates excessive.

write a report, to tell the Cape and Natal Governments that they are taking too much out of us, and that it is a short-sighted policy.

Cement.

Now with reference to cement. You are a director, or your firm is very largely interested in the Cement Factory ?—Yes.

Can you give us figures showing the cost of cement in England free on board, and the price at which it sells here ?—Yes. I may say I am glad you have alluded to cement. The factory is often spoken of as the Cement Concession, whereas there is no such concession. If any other person is sanguine enough to erect another factory, he is perfectly at liberty to do so.

The difference in the prices is very large ?—Very large. The figures were Prices of imported cement. included in the papers I handed in yesterday. The prime cost of cement—this comes via Delagoa Bay—the prime cost of a shipment would be £54 14s. in Europe, ocean freight would also cost £54, railway carriage to Johannesburg costs £240, and the Transvaal duty is £117.

Don't you consider that the duty is abnormally high ?—Yes. I think the duty Duty on cement. too high, that is my private opinion.

Surely there is a special railway rate, or it could hardly be five times the cost in Europe ?—I could not exactly tell you what the railway rate is. I think the weight of such material is sufficient protection for it. I do not know that it can be manu- Cement factory. factured as cheaply in this country as it can be imported. Our factory spends £1,000 per month in the Pretoria District in getting limestone, coal, etc., and the raw material, the limestone put down at the mill, has cost us more than cement free on board at Hamburg and London.

But don't you think that the factory is too much protected ?—I think further Protection of cement factory. protection is unnecessary.

Yes, but I want your opinion as to whether it would be better to knock off some of the existing protection ?—Yes, I do think so. I don't know what my fellow directors on the Cement Company will say ; but this is an inquiry into the mining industry, and I do think that artificial protection is unnecessary. Besides, I think the quality of the local article is sufficiently good to compete with that imported. I must point out that when the factory was started, it was done with the idea that it would relieve the industry. Cement was then £5 10s. to £6 10s. per cask, and there was no arrangement with regard to the railway coming forward ; so that it was then considered not only good business, but for the benefit of the industry. It it cannot, however, hold it own as a good business, my opinion is that, like all others similarly situated, it has got to go under. We have spent £113,000 to equip the factory, and it has not paid a dividend yet.

Mr. *Pierce.*

Do you consider that the high railway rates make out the main grievance ?—I Railway rates. have given you the figures charged by all the different railways ; but you will get from the engineers the exact proportions that the carriage forms in the equipment of a mine. I was unable in the time to work out the proportion. It is a very intricate subject, and I asked Mr. Seymour, the engineer of the Rand Mines, to prepare a state- ment. He is preparing it now, and will submit it to you. Now, take a company like the Geldenhuis Deep. It has a capital of £350,000, but the shareholders put up a working capital of £410,000, which is very much more than what they got for their claims, which was under £300,000. In the expenditure the great thing is the large and expensive machinery and other plant, and railage plays a much more important part in the equipment than in the working cost. You will get from Mr. Seymour exactly how the railway rates affect the mines.

And you consider that if the railway rates were reduced a great grievance would be removed ?—Undoubtedly, if sufficiently reduced.

If the Netherlands Company reduced their rates on the Delagoa line, do you think Netherlands Railway control of South African railway rates. it would force the Cape and the Natal Railways to reduce their rates as well ?—Most certainly. If the Netherlands Company reduced their rates even from Vereeniging here, to the Cape level, it would mean an instant reduction of the rates on the oth lines by 18 per cent. all round. Look at the various conferences which take pla periodically both here and at Bloemfontein, between the controllers of the differe railways. These commissions only meet to congratulate each other, and now and th they talk about the reclassification of sugar and corrugated iron, putting them in higher class, and taxing us more. A man like the Minister of Public Works of Nat. said that this was merely a figure of speech. A nice figure of speech to put a heavi tax on us. I have nothing against the Netherlands Company. I say that as commercial proposition they are perfectly right to put on heavy rates and make much profit as possible, but I also say that the Government has a right to interfere ar see that there should be no undue taxation on the people. The Government cou exercise its right and bring pressure to bear on the Netherlands Railway Company ar compel them to lower their tariff; but the real solution is expropriation.

You think that the reduction would give great relief ?—It would be an immen relief, in fact it is the keystone to the whole thing.

If the Government were to take over the line and work it for the benefit of th State, it would greatly improve the condition of things ?—Yes, certainly.

Everything centres on the railway ?—Yes, it is almost a matter of life and deat We all hope that the Government will exercise its rights and take over the railwa We know that there probably would be difficulties in the way of administration, b we believe that the Government could benefit by the experience already gained, ar would find it wise to select the best possible men for the work.

Do you think that the necessary money for the expropriation of the line would l obtained at 3½ or 4 per cent. ?—With the greatest ease. If the Government were exercise its right in connection with the dynamite monopoly and railway, and provid for a sound administration, there would be a restoration of confidence in Europe, so th the Government could obtain any money it required for the expropriation of the lin and for other purposes.

Now, assuming that the cost of expropriating the line would be £9,000,000, th annual interest to be paid would be about £360,000 ?—Yes.

Is it a fact that £360,000 per annum is required to pay interest on the railwa debentures alone ?—I am not quite sure of the figures, but the amount would l between £320,000 and £360,000. The debenture issue is about £6,000,000, but there another £1,000,000 that was to be issued, although I am not sure whether it has bee

issued yet. There is one other thing I would like to bring to your notice now ; that i before the company gets at its profit, 10 per cent. is taken off the gross earnings an placed to the reserve fund, and last year you will find that this reserve deductic amounted to £290,000. Now, what is the reserve fund, and who is to get it at the time the expropriation ? I think that is a point that the Commission should bear in min and find out when the Netherlands Railway people are dealt with. That reminds me another point that the Commission would do well to inquire into. They should fin out whether there were any special conditions under which the Potchefstroom line w built, so that its inferior earnings could be excluded from the general calculations whe the railway is expropriated.

You think that the settlement of the railway and dynamite questions will go long way towards giving satisfaction ?—Certainly, but I do not say that they are a the reliefs that the Government ought to grant us. I do not want to look a gift hor

in the mouth, but I could not admit that any settlement could be satisfactory sufficient which did not deal with the unnecessary £3,000,000 in the general Stat revenue. Look at the sum that is paid out of the general revenue, which should reall me out of a capital account as it were. I consider this most unfair and unjust. I do not suggest that this is done in a hostile spirit, but consider that the Committee will agree with me that it is a mistake, I do not consider that most of the reforms I have mentioned will entail any loss on the Government—I mean the suppression of the illicit liquor traffic, the better administration of the Pass Law, and so on—and I would point out that the Government will have a distinct gain by cancelling the dynamite monopoly. If they only threw open the whole concern they would only lose 5s. per case, or £60,000 per annum, but then no one will complain if they put on a duty of 8s., or even 10s. per case. In the Netherlands Railway affair Government will certainly lose a portion, a large portion of their profits; but, on the other hand, there will be a distinct gain to the whole of the State. Of course, the real solution, to my mind, is not to take it as necessary that the Government must spend five millions a year, but to see what economies in that direction can be effected, and to what extent expenditure can be cut down, with a due regard to good and safe government. I think the Commission would be able to make some suggestions on that point. *[margin: Equalisation of budget.]*

Do you think that the expansion of trade would minimise the loss of revenue entailed by the reduction of tariffs?—Most certainly I do. I say that the present scale of taxation is crushing, and even if the Government faced a loss of revenue—I do not say a deficit—the expansion of trade will compensate for it.

Do you think that this is a good country for trade?—I certainly do. I think the Transvaal is the finest country in the world.

Mr. *Schmitz-Dumont.*

Mr. Schmitz-Dumont questioned Mr. Fitzpatrick as to whether over-capitalisation was not the chief cause of the depression, as pointed out by Mr. Labouchere in *Truth* recently. *[margin: Capitalisation of mines.]*

Witness said he had not seen Labouchere's statement, but he could not pretend to check it till he knew the method by which the results were arrived at. He would give an instance of the difficulty. At one time the Goldfields Consolidated held shares in the Rand Mines, the Rand Mines held shares in the Jumpers Deep, the Jumpers Deep held some claims to the Jupiter. All those shares were only figures, not separate sums really. It was impossible to say, except one knew every particular instance, whether a Goldfields share holds an interest in a claim or a share in the Rand Mines, which holds a Jumpers Deep share, which holds a Jupiter share.

That is my opinion, and Mr. Labouchere has the same amount three or four times over?—No doubt. I only took the amount once. May I give you an instance of another thing. I was at a meeting of Mr. Dieperink's the other day, and he pointed to the Robinson Company as being over-capitalised. I really think the best judge of whether a mine is over-capitalised or not is the man who buys the shares, and as long as a man will pay £8 for a £5 share in the Robinson, he does not, I presume, think it too highly capitalised. That was really a very bad instance to quote.

I have the capital of all the mines in the Transvaal—the nominal capital of 185 gold mining companies in existence in 1896. The total nominal capital is £54,000,000 for the 185 companies. On this capital they have paid a dividend of £1,700,000, that is about 3 per cent. I don't know whether your Chamber has figures for the whole industry.— It is difficult to answer your question whether over-capitalisation was not the chief cause of the depression in the form in which you put it. For instance, the Ferreira (I speak from memory) has a capital of £90,000, and the shares are at £15. It began with a capital of £25,000 or £30,000, and the people honestly thought it was worth that. They worked a little, and found it was worth a bit more. Then the shares were sold at £3 or £4. And so it went on. The year before last the people who held the *[margin: Capitalisation of Ferreira mine]* shares, nearly all of them, I believe, in Paris, themselves paid £12 or £15 a share to provide more working capital. The Ferreira pays a dividend of 275 per cent. on the original £1 shares, but the French people bought at £15. No one man makes the difference between £1 and £15. One hundred people have turned their money over before the £15 is arrived at. You must, in order to answer your question, reason according to what the public thinks. At one time, as Mr. Albu told you, in 1887 they thought that £10,000 was sufficient to equip a mine. To-day I will tell you what they Capital of Glen Deep. think. Take the Rand Mines subsidiary companies. The Glen Deep, with a capital Capital of Rose Deep. of £500,000, put up £329,000, and they have to pay more yet; the Rose Deep have Capital of Geldenhuis Deep. capital of £350,000, and they subscribed £523,000; the Geldenhuis Deep, with a capital Capital of Crown Deep. of £350,000, put up £410,000 in sovereigns; the Crown Deep, with a capital of £250,000, subscribed £630,000, and so on. Now, I say the shareholder is the judge regarding the capitalisation. Remember his position. He can buy the shares or leave them alone, just as he likes. If he buys them, he has the right to register them, and then he acquires the right to vote. With his vote he can turn out the Directors if they do not manage the business rightly. The Directors know that, and even if there were no honesty amongst them, it is good policy to manage the mine properly. They would be discredited if they were turned out of office, and shareholders in Paris, Berlin, or London, would never afterwards entrust them with any of their money. You can only judge of mining by results. Of course, if a man takes a claim on the Main Reef, out of which you know only £30,000 profit can be got, and puts up a capital of £500,000, I should call that a swindle where there is such absolute proof. But you must know that people will speculate. You can get a man in the street who will give 30s. for a £1 ticket in Phillips's sweep, because he likes the number or believes in his luck.

Development of mining industry.

Do you think the industry has reached its full bloom yet, or is only in a state of development?—Decidedly in a state of development. There are two possible courses of development. There are now a certain number of companies working, or trying to work. These were started under the belief that the conditions would enable them to work at a profit, or the conditions would be immediately so much improved as to give them a good margin. They are not developed yet. Then we know that there are great stretches of ground which we can't work now at a profit, but which we believe in some few years' time we shall be able to work at great profit to ourselves and the State when the artificial conditions are improved. The natural conditions on the Rand are almost the best in the world—regular reefs, good value in them, long extent, large enough to work, coal on top of them—you can't ask more from nature than that; but it is the artificial conditions that require to be improved. I think if we talk these over, and come to understand one another, the members of the Commission may be the means of instructing others, and showing them what our hopes are for the industry and for the State.

Over-capitalisation.

You think then that the question of the over-capitalisation of the industry cannot be decided while the mines are still in a state of development?—No.

Law to prevent bogus flotations.

It must, in your opinion, be left for the future to decide?—Yes, quite so. I have noticed that there has been a suggestion made to the effect that shareholders should be protected by Government. I think everybody would support that idea—that the public should be protected against deliberate swindles. I would also point out that in England the shareholders *are* protected. A man can go to the courts and prove that there was not sufficient grounds to justify flotation, that the promoter did not act in a *bona-fide* manner, and there are lots of cases in which men have suffered from their misdeeds in this direction. Even as the law stands now in this country, I believe a man could go to the High Court and obtain protection, and I say "Good luck to him."

Mr. *Joubert.*

Should not the Chamber of Mines co-operate with the Department of Mines to
 a law protecting European shareholders from being defrauded by swindlers ?—I
 't know if such a law could be framed without interfering with what, in other
 untries, is considered to be personal liberty. You have to come to the point whether
 e man intended to swindle, and that can only be settled by the Court, as a matter of
 rsonal judgment. If a good law could be devised, it would be beneficial.

Is there no possibility for the Chamber of Mines to work with the department for
 e passing of such a law ?—I don't know if laws exist in France, Germany, England,
 America, to that specific effect; but if so, I would be guided by the wisdom and
 mense experience of the law makers of those countries; otherwise we might be
 shing in where angels fear to tread.

Is it then impossible ? Are you not willing to discuss the matter with us ?—Oh,
 s ; but I do not think that is exactly what is wanted in order to restore confidence.
 ts of things combine to shake the confidence of investors. For instance, to deal Concessions.
 th some small and homely matters, I was told by a member of the Sanitary Board
 sterday that an application for the underground rights of the Market Square, had
 en made by Mr. Jan Meyer, a leading member of the Volksraad. That does not help
 restore confidence. The Sanitary Board applied for a portion of the Telephone
 wer Park, in order to erect a Town Hall. They were refused. Now, someone has
 de an application for the right to erect swimming baths. That does not restore
 nfidence. I hope the mere publication of these things will prevent them from suc-
 eding. The Sanitary Board applied for the Union Ground, also for public purposes,
 t it was granted to private applicants on the quiet. They have hawked it about
 d borrowed money on it. It was offered to many of the big capitalists here, but they
 uld not touch it. The Sanitary Board are told that a building is to be put up, in
 ich fifty rooms will be set aside for them, but they are not satisfied that the authori-
 s should do good by stealth, and blush to find it fame.

I cannot understand how mere applications can shake confidence.—Well, they do,
 ause they are only made when there is a chance of their being granted. But, if
 u want facts, I will tell you what shook the investor's confidence as much as any- Ferreira raid
 ng that has happened for years—that was the Ferreira claim jumping raid, which
 was sworn to in Court had been suggested by you yourself, Mr. Joubert.

Not " suggested " by me—

Chairman.

The Chairman said Mr. Fitzpatrick was straying away from the original question.

Witness said that the Minister of Mines had wanted examples of what shook con-
 ence, so he was obliged to give them. Continuing, he added that, so far as he knew Chamber of
 e feeling of the Chamber of Mines, he could assure the Commission the Chamber Mines willing
 uld make every effort to co-operate with Government for the protection of share- to co-operate
 ders. If they could find a practical means of protecting Shareholders, the Chamber with Govern-
 uld gladly assist. ment to pre-
 vent bogus flo-
 tations.

Mr. *Joubert.*

If the Chamber is willing and will assist, I am willing to propose such a law
 be added to the Gold Law, this session of the Raad.—You will, of course, address
 e Chamber on the subject ?

Yes.

Mr. *De Beer.*

You speak a good deal about what is wrong on the side of the Government. Management of
 e you now quite satisfied with the economical working of the mines: is there no mines.

mismanagement or waste of material; is there not too much money spent on manage
engineers, &c., &c.?   Are you so perfectly satisfied with yourselves?—Certainly no
We are never satisfied—always trying to improve, but if I knew now where a fau
lay on our side, I should start in to remedy it, and not wait to report it to the Con
mission.   We have been trying to reduce expenses.   We are trying, and we wi
always try, and if we were satisfied, we would stop trying.   I have not the slighte
doubt there must be faults on our side too.   I never intend to give the idea that w
claim to be perfect.   It is impossible and absurd.   Every year we find out somethir
fresh in the way of reducing some of our costs, and we hope to go on in that way.
can only speak in connection with the costs of those mines with which I am cor
cerned, and I can tell you that if we knew there was anything requiring improvemen
and capable of improvement at our hands, we would tackle that at once on our ow
account, and in our own interest.

But you not only know about the mines which you are a director, or are in
terested in, but have a general knowledge?—Yes.

You have a general knowledge of the whole business?—Yes, but necessarily a
imperfect one of others' business.

I only ask you for an explanation of this question in order to justify yoursel
There will afterwards be other evidence on this point.   That would only prove tha
you only suggest improvements on the side of the mines on one point, and that is th
black labour question.   That is why this question was repeated?—No, I do not sug
gest that.   We keep on at every directors' meeting as to costs.   We divided thes
things up into percentages long ago, before a Commission was ever thought of, so tha
we could know whether we could put our finger upon extravagances, or the spc
where economies could be made.

Reduction of working costs of mines.

You have chiefly drawn the attention of the Commission to the black labou
question?—I think the fact that we have made an effort to cut down the black labou
within the last fortnight shows you two things—the first, that we realise we cai
effect some economy ourselves—and there we may be to blame for not doing it before—
and the second thing we realise is, that this is a good opportunity of doing it.

The witness was then permitted to leave, being thanked by the Chairman fo
his statement.

Mr. Laurie Hamilton's evidence.

MR. W. LAURIE HAMILTON was called.   He stated he was a civil and minin
engineer.   He had been up to now connected with the Barnato Companie
He had been in Johannesburg since the end of 1888.

Chairman.

Mr. Barnato.

Will you please inform the Commission on what points you can give evidence?—
I may say first Mr. Barnato had intended to offer himself to give evidence, but had t
go down to the House of Assembly.   He asked me to assist you with any informatio

Barnato group.

I had.   I propose to lay before you a statement of the stamps working in the Barnat
group, and of the additional stamps which might now be started if the Commissio
can help us to further reduce the costs.   I will also lay before you the actual costs c
a paying mine and the actual costs of a non-paying mine; also an illustrative estimat
supposed to have been made in 1890, showing how we estimated possible reductior
and how these had been partly fulfilled and partly falsified by certain reforms w
anticipated being withheld.   Witness then handed in the following statements, whic

Stamps running.

the secretary read: In the Barnato Group (Rand and Klerksdorp) we have:—

Stamps hung up.

companies with 400 stamps running, 400 stamps; 90 stamps hung up on thes

Mills idle.

companies, 90 stamps; 7 mills idle, with 650 stamps ready to crush, 650.   The tot umber of stamps that might now be crushing under improved conditions of country, ,140. In these 13 companies we propose to add 220 stamps, 220; 3 companies that ere crushing with small mills, but are ready for heavy equipment, would run 480; that under improved economics of the country we could have (instead of 400) 1,840 ushing in 12 months. In addition to these, out of many large properties held by is group, we have mining properties sufficiently proved to promise dividends under nproved conditions that would require a further equipment of 1,350 stamps, making total in this group, that could be crushing by the year 1900, of 3,190 stamps. It is stimated that the different groups could have 9,000 stamps crushing by 1900. Of e six companies crushing, the nominal capital is over 1½ millions, and the hard cash ınk in opening and equipping these mines amounts to over 1½ millions. Of the seven mpanies with idle mills the nominal capital is over 2 millions, and the opening and quipping them has cost over 2 millions. So that over and above the money spent for nd on partly developed properties now waiting the promise of better conditions, and e large amounts paid to farm and estate owners for other properties, this group of nanciers has more than two millions lying idle in machinery, etc., in seven mines, at under improved conditions of country might now be producing wealth to the untry and dividends to the shareholders. This does not include money paid for ese properties, but only the hard cash spent on them in bringing them to the roducing stage. In the above statement no part of the many properties in which the arnato group hold large interests, but which are under the control of other groups of nanciers, is included.

Possible number of stamps under improved conditions.

Total estimated number of stamps in 1900. Capital of crushing mines in Barnato group Capital of seven non-crushing mines of Barnato group.

The comparative costs of the New Primrose Mine for 1890, 1893, and 1896, mining nd milling, are as follows:—

Comparative costs of New Primrose for 1890, 1893 and 1896.

COST PER TON (not including Tailings Treatment).

	Six months ending June 30th, 1890.	Reduction accomplished between 1890 and 1893.	Six months ending June 30th, 1893.	Six months ending Dec. 31st, 1896.	Total cost per ton including tailings treatment 6 months ending Dec. 31st, 1896.
Labour—	s. d.		s. d.	s. d.	s. d.
European	6 2	34 per cent.	4 0	4 9	5 4½
Native	7 10	12 "	7 0	5 9	6 5½
Total Labour...	14 0½	22 "	11 0	10 6	11 10
Stores—					
Natives' Food ...	1 6	34 "	1 0	1 5	1 7¾
Explosives	1 11¼	(4 % inc.)	2 0	2 6	2 6
Fuel	1 11¼	31 per cent.	1 4	1 8½	2 1¼
Lighting, tools, lubricants, etc. ...	2 2	41 "	1 3½	0 9¼	0 9¼
Cyanide and zinc ...	—	—	—	—	1 7½
Maintenance & general	2 1	24 "	1 7	1 4¼	1 9¼
Total Stores ...	9 7½	25 "	7 2½	7 9	10 5
Miscellaneous, offices, salaries, etc. ...	1 9	—	1 4¼	0 7	0 9
	25 5	23 per cent.	19 7	18 10	23 0

Redemption and Depreciation not included.

Column I. gives cost of mining and milling, June 30, 1890. Column III gives st of mining and milling, June 30, 1893. Column II. gives percentage of reduction complished by improvements in mining and appliances from 1890 to 1893. Column

IV. gives cost in mining and milling, December 31, 1896. Column V. gives cost mining, milling, and cyaniding, December 31, 1896.

Reduction of costs in labour and stores, 1890 to 1893.

I would call special attention to the following points in these actual costs :—(The reduction obtained between 1890 and 1893, 22 per cent. in labour and 25 per cer

Reduction of costs in labour and stores, 1893 to 1896.

in stores. (2) A further reduction in the total (19s. 7d. to 18s. 10d.) from 1893 1896, in the face of greatly increased hardness of ore depth of mine. It is noticeab that while by the introduction of machine drills, etc., we reduced the labour by 6 the stores were increased 6½d. by the increased consumption of coal and dynami (amounting to 10½d. between them). The food of natives also increasing 6d., co sequent on scarcity of mealies (through locusts) and the heavy railway charges fro coast and Free State for imported mealies. (3) The low cost to which we hav

Reduction of costs of administration.

brought administration, which includes mine office, town and London offices, co sulting engineer, manager, directors, etc. The reduction on this from 1s. 9d. in 189

Increase of cost of dynamite.

to 7d. in 1896, is equal to 70 per cent. (4) The heavy increase of cost per ton dynamite in face of all our efforts at economy. These charges are worse in mo other mines.

Langlaagte Royal working costs

The costs of mining, milling and cyaniding at the Langlaagte Royal Gold Minin Company were as follows :—

	5 months ending Nov. 30th, 1896.		1 month May 1—31, 1896:		Estimated cost, with reasonable reductions in railway rates, price of stores, and cost of kaffir labour.
	Cost per ton.		Cost per ton.		
	s. d.	s. d.	s. d.	s. d.	s. d.
Labour—					
European	7 6	...	6 7		
Native	6 11	...	6 7		
Total labour ...	...	14 5		13 2	9 0
Stores—					
Natives' food ...	1 0	...	1 7½		
Explosives	3 0	...	2 6		
Fuel	3 1½	...	2 9½		
Lighting, lubricants, timber, etc. ...	1 4	...	1 5½		
Cyanide and zinc ...	0 10	...	0 8½		
Maintenance and general	2 1	...	1 4		
Total Stores ...	...	11 4½		10 5	6 6
Water rent, etc. ...	0 11	0 11	...	0 8½	0 6
Miscellaneous offices, salaries, etc. ...	...	1 2	...	1 0	1 0
Total working costs ...	...	27 10½	...	25 3½	17 0
Cost of milling and mining	24 6	...	22 1	...	
Cost of cyaniding tailings	3 4½	27 10½	3 2½	25 3½	
Yield of gold per ton ...	...	...	...	25s. 2d.	

Column I. gives last five months before closing down. Column II. gives cost fc May, 1896, when boys were more plentiful and mill worked nearer full time. Durin the five months of column I. boys were scarce, and there was a strike at reduction c wages, drills having to be employed, raising costs of white labour, explosives, fue intenance, and general. Column II.—cost 25s. 3½d.—is somewhat above cost of :king with plenty of kafirs under present circumstances. Column III. gives mated cost under improved economic conditions of country. That is, with co-ration of Government; reasonable reductions being given in coal, dynamite, rail-y rates from coast, and assistance in reducing kaffirs' wages by:—*(a)* Inducing the nsvaal kaffirs to come to the Rand, and enforcing and improving the Pass and uor Laws; *(b)* Reducing cost of coal, dynamite, etc. The mining companies can n make the air drill a real live competitor with kaffir labour. These reforms, which *not the ultimate extent we hope for*, are reasonable, and will enable the Royal and er mines (of which the Royal is a sample) to re-start crushing at once. The uction in European labour will be brought about by getting sufficient kaffirs at low ges to supersede drills (air), in stoping and increased output. This mine, promising l in outcrop claims, has by reduction of yield in second and third rows, become ssed as a low grade mine: this was not anticipated; and although expected to be erage grade, its capitalisation is about the lowest on the Rand, the property ount standing in books at £760 per mining claim. The Balmoral stands at £1,230, Primrose at £2,084 per claim, and the three companies surrounding the Royal, ich are considered far from being over-capitalised, stand at £3,200, £5,200, and ,500 per mining claim respectively. The Royal is equipped in the most approved le, with 140 stamps and all accessories; the mine and equipment stand at £1,480 stamp, which will compare favourably with other mines on the Rand.

To show what we expected to do, and what has been done, I give the following strative estimate, showing reductions estimated:—(1) Reduction possible to the ning companies unaided by the introduction of improved management, machinery l appliances, reducing *amouut* of labour and stores necessary in producing and shing the ton. (2) Reduction possible with the assistance of the Government in ucing *price* of labour and stores.

[marginal notes: Reduction of costs desired from Government. Results of reductions of working costs. Capitalisation per claim of Langlaagte Royal, Balmoral and Primrose. Equipment of Langlaagte Royal. Reduction of working costs possible without and with Government aid.*]*

	Mining and Milling.		Cost per Ton.	
	Labour.	Stores.	Administration.	Total.
	s. d.	s. d.	s. d.	s. d.
Cost of a typical mine in 1890	16 0	14 0	2 0	32 0
1. Estimated reduction in amount of labour and stores by improved management, machinery, and appliances	4 0	4 3	1 0	9 3
Reducing cost to	12 0	9 9	1 0	22 9
2. Estimated further reduction from reduced price of labour and stores to be got by economic reforms of country	3 0	4 0	0 0	7 0
Reducing cost to	9 0	5 9	1 0	15 9

Langlaagte Royal mining and milling costs reduced from 32s. in 1891 to 22s. in 1896.

The cost of cyaniding tailings is not included in this estimate, not being commenced 1890. Since introducing treatment of tailings by cyanide, which at first cost from to 10s. per ton, the companies have reduced the cost of this process by 5s. per ton hope to get a further 2s. by improved economic conditions. The companies have s accomplished a reduction of 14s. 3d. per ton in mining, milling, and cyaniding, are hoping to be helped to at least another 9s. per ton.

[marginal notes: Costs of cyaniding. Reduction of working costs already accomplished by companies.*]*

Chairman :

Can you give the present average wage of a white man on the mines ?—I cannot e you the average actual wage; on a properly managed mine they vary from £15 £25.

[marginal note: Average of white wages.*]*

Is it not possible for you to state the average wage on the mines which you ha
been connected with ?—I cannot from memory.   I can send it to you.   I may say
agree with the evidence of Mr. Jennings, Mr. Way, and Mr. Fitzpatrick.

I would be very pleased if you would hand them in.

[*Supplied afterwards, according to the Chairman's request.* —In six mines
the Barnato group, taking the New Primrose, Ginsberg, Rietfontein, Roodepoort a
New Spes Bona, for the first three months of 1897, and Langlaagte Royal for the fi
months before it shut down, the average monthly pay was £15,737 to 640 m
equal to £24 11s. 7d. per man per month.   This includes managers and staffs].

Mr. *de Beer :*

Capital and costs
of develop-
ment of crush-
ing mines of
Barnato group

You say amongst your group there are six mines crushing ?—Yes.

The nominal capital of which is over a million and a half ?—Yes.

For the purpose of developing these it cost another million and a half ?—Yes.

The statement made by you is in connection with these six mines ?—I have tak
the New Primrose and the Langlaagte Royal, one being a paying mine and the oth
a non-paying mine.   The New Primrose is the paying mine.

Capital and costs
of develop-
ment of seven
non - crushing
mines of Bar-
nato group.
Meaning of in-
stallation.

The seven non-paying mines have a nominal capital of over two millions ?—Yes.

And opening up and installation another two millions ?—Yes.   That does n
include the unequipped properties.

What does opening up and installation mean ?—The sinking of shafts and t
equipping of them with machinery, and the erection of mill, cyanide works, and t.
erection of houses, etc., in connection with the mines.   In other words, the hard ca
we spent before we began to crush.

Development of
mines of Bar-
nato group.

Is it to be understood that the development of these mines is in such a way th
all of them have a certain quantity of ore on hand ?—Every one of them ; the lea
has nine months development ahead of the mill.   We have numbers of mines besid
these that are not equipped, which have a large amount of development.   May
suggest, in regard to over-capitalisation, you should look at these figures.   We ha
sunk over our nominal capital in every one of these mines, the money being found
Barnato Bros. putting it up at a premium.

I see in your expenses there is a reduction since June, 1890, between 12 and
per cent. ?—Yes, that is to 1893.

Comparative
cost of hand
and machine
drills.

I see in December, 1896, there is an increase again.   Can you tell the Commissi
to what reason do you ascribe the increase ?—You will notice the increase is in stor
6½d.   There is a decrease in labour, 6d.   We brought labour down from 11s. to 1
6d.   There is an increase in European labour of 9d., and a reduction in kaffir labo
of 1s. 3d.   During that period we put in machine drills and put in more Europe
labour.

Cost of native
food.

I see in your stores, native food was reduced by 34 per cent. in the three yea
from 1890 to 1893 ?—Yes ; but the locusts and other plagues raised the cost of meali
Since then, having to import them from America we have to pay so heavily for bringi
them from the coast up here.   We pay 8s. at the coast and 22s. here.

Cost of explos-
ives.

What is the reason of the increase of 4 per cent. in explosives ?—It resulted fro
the same cause, introducing drills instead of kaffir labour and the ore getting mu
harder, and that is why I ask you to reduce these items and enable us to make t
drills real live competitors with the kaffirs, and so enable us to reduce kaffir wag

Quality of dyna-
mite.

Since we have been obliged to buy dynamite from one man—I don't care whether
is Nobel or anyone else—we could not guarantee the best quality.   I myself repeated
applied to the Government to import other qualities of dynamite.   I was refused.   T
result is, I go and buy 100 cases, I take it home, and kill 100 kaffirs perhaps.   I

ck to the man I bought it from, and I say: "Your dynamite is bad. I am obliged buy it from you even if I kill another 100 kaffirs. I have been taken before the agistrates for manslaughter. I escaped scot free because witnesses for the prosecution proved that I had done all I could, and it was the fault of the dynamite." I had ne all I could according to the regulations—the fault lay with the dynamite. A oy was suffocated through the bad fumes. I may say this, I have put a shot in id fired it. A boy has put a drill in it and found a part of it left unexploded, hich injured him, and afterwards a third portion was unexploded in the bottom of e same hole. I don't say Transvaal dynamite is worse than any other, but if you re obliged to buy from one man, whether sugar, dynamite, or anything else, he arges his own price and supplies his own quality.

Can you tell me what was the price of the dynamite per case?—It was pretty uch what it is now. We were using such a small quantity that we could not buy to dvantage, and I believe there was a "ring" then.

But we understood from other witnesses that dynamite No. 1 standard was good? –I think the witnesses that said so only use gelatine. We did away with dynamite s much as possible, and the dynamite factory very readily made special cartridges for s so that we might use gelignite instead of dynamite.

Do you know No. 1 standard of dynamite?—Yes.

Do you know the percentage of nitro-glycerine in it?—No.

You have never analysed it?—No.

Have you used it? And is it the dynamite you complained about being in ifferent qualities?—I do not need to tell you how much there is in it. They take nis earth and they impregnate it with as much nitro-glycerine as it can carry.

With regard to the bad dynamite which exploded—from whom did you buy it? –We were obliged to buy it from the concessionaires.

And which was it?—No. 1.

Do you know any other company that is dissatisfied with the dynamite?—Yes. Vhen I was prosecuted I had evidence from nearly all the managers on the Rand. I ot workmen and had their opinion, and it was the almost unanimous opinion that it as inferior and irregular—just the biggest danger—in quality. The quality, as far s I hear to-day, is better than it was. But I say we are in continual danger so long s you compel us to buy from one man. We cannot complain of it; we must buy it.

With regard to fuel?—We reduced fuel 31 per cent. from 1890 to 1893, but uring the last three years it has increased on us, not because of increased price, but ecause of the introduction of labour-saving appliances which needed the consumpon of coal; causing the consumption to increase, so that we were between two ifficulties. Either we had to continue the expensive kaffir labour or we had to ipersede them by machinery, which would use expensive stores. We now say we ave reduced as far as we can the *amount* of labour, and the *amount* of stores by the troduction of the best of engineers, workmen, and machinery, and we cannot touch e *price* of these articles. Therefore we ask relief upon the prices. *Fuel.*

How are your mines situated?—They are very much separated. They are from ietfontein to the Balmoral and Kimberley Roodepoort. *Situation of mines of Barnato group.*

What mines have you got between here and Krugersdorp?—The Royal, Crœsus, nified, Aurora, and Kimberley Roodepoort.

Did the Crœsus exist in 1890?—It existed as a 20 stamp mill.

What was the price per ton of coal delivered at the Crœsus in 1890? –I cannot y, it was not in our hands then.

Or from the Aurora?—I can tell you from the Royal. At the Royal the cost in 890 was about 23s. or 24s. per ton. *Cost of fuel of Langlaagte Royal mine.*

Costs of stores.

After May, 1896 ?—We paid up to the time we stopped about 22s. 9d.; in fact, i the summer we could bring it as cheaply by ox-wagon as by rail.

With regard to lighting, tools, etc. ?—We have reduced that very largely, as yc see given in the case of lighting. Candles, paraffin, etc., we have superseded in great proportion by electricity, transferring some of that cost to fuel. Then the pri of candles and lubricants and other things has been reduced slightly, not because c the reduced rates so much, because we can import it ourselves without fear c the traffic being stopped. I mean merchants used to import large stocks in th summer, and they could charge us any price they liked. Take candles, for instanc The carriage from Durban amounted to about 6s. coming from the border by ox wagon. The present charge is 6s. 9d. But I gladly say that the convenience of th rail is in being able to buy anywhere we like, and we thus get these supplies at much lower rate than we did before. They are, of course, a very small proportion c the costs—under 3 per cent.

Costs of cyanid-ing.

With regard to cyanide and zinc, you have got nothing to say about that ?—No but we are very thankful for the help the Government has given us in the matter c cyanide. I did not show any reduction in the statement because we were not using i in 1890.

You have heard the evidence of some of the other witnesses ?—Yes.

Comparative costs of differ-ent mines.

Then you have noticed there is a great difference in the cost of your min compared with other mines ?—I think the costs given previously were average cost I may say I made up the average cost quite apart from those gentlemen, and cam out about the same.

We have never had such a satisfactory statement before us like this. Was th total cost of working 22s. ?—In the other estimates ?

Average working costs of most mines.

When the average was taken ?—29s. 6d. was given by Mr. Eckstein, and that i the basis of most. I made it 29s.

Working costs of New Primrose mine.

At present your mine works at 23s. ?—I would say yes, but you have to mak that 25s. to compare with the 29s. average.

You are still 4s. below the others. How much per cent. would that be ?—Tha would be about 15 per cent. It would not be fair for me to allow you to infer tha we manage better than the other mines.

The others can speak for themselves ?—This table which is before you is com piled on the Primrose, which has a large thick reef. It would not apply to all th others. Take, for instance, the Ginsberg, which is a much higher grade mine and ha a much smaller equipment. We cannot work there at the same cost as at th Primrose.

You have made a note that you gave the average for the six mines ?—No, that i for the New Primrose and Langlaagte Royal.

You say the Primrose works under very favourable circumstances ?—Yes, it doe Go to columns 4 and 5 of this table. Might I suggest one favourable circumstanc in the Primrose—that freight and coal is a good bit less than the mines on the oth side. It is not a large item, but it is a real one.

The total cost is about 4s. more when you include cyanide. That 1s 7½d. is fc cyanide, or cyanide and zinc ?—That is so.

So in order to work and treat, the cyanide will cost you 4s. per ton, What ar the returns ?—Well, I may say our profit is all in the cyanide. In most of our mill we are making a loss, so far as our milling is concerned. So that had we not at great cost introduced this cyanide process, or some other process, some of the ric mines would have been shut down.

Cyanide patent. Is the process a patent ?—No, not now.

Has it been a patent ?—It had a patent in this country. I may say I for one
used to pay the royalty for years before the matter was settled. I told them, " We
quite willing to pay you a reasonable royalty, because you have done something,
we will not and cannot pay you what you ask." For instance, they came to me
en I was on the Primrose. They wanted to take 15,000 tons to treat then, and to
e us a proportion of the gold. Then we were to take the works over at cost price.
said no, and we paid them their highest royalty, and out of this 15,000 tons we
de a profit of £8,500. They would have given us £2,500.

In the six mines are there any water-rights, or so ?—They are not kept separate.

Was water and material increased in cost ?—It may be in bringing water from a
ance, as we have to do on the Royal, it increases. Would you permit me to
attention to the last line on this page before you turn over. The item is miscel- **Reduction of salaries.**
eous—offices and salaries. You will notice we brought that down for mining and
ling, leaving the cyanide out, from 1s. 9d. to 7d., a reduction of 70 per cent. That
ludes directors' fees, managers' fees, consulting engineers, office expenses in London
l Johannesburg, and at the mine, and I don't think you can call it high.

Is this a true extract from the books of the Primrose Gold Mining Company ?—
. I can give you the actual certified figures, but I may say I have condensed them
as to compare them.

Mr. *Schmitz-Dumont* :

In the beginning you say you have 400 stamps at work ; is that right ?—Yes. **Number of stamps working.**
Do you know how many stamps are working in the whole of the mining
ustry ?—About 2,600 I think. I speak from memory.
Is it not 5,500 ?—Working this month ?
No, last year.—I am talking about to-day.
Are there 4,400 working to-day ?—No. I think in the Rand and Klerksdorp
re are about 3,000 working now.
Last December there were 5,500. Is it not 10 per cent. less to-day ?—I think
ı will find it is under 3,000 stamps to-day.
There were 5,500 last December, according to the statistics ?—Last March I think
ı will find there were 2,850 in Heidelberg, Klerksdorp, and Johannesburg.
[*Supplied afterwards.*—The number of stamps crushing in March last on the
Rand and Heidelberg districts were :—Chamber of Mines, 2,440 ; Association
of Mines, 835. Total, 3,275.]
I only want to make a comparison. In the year 1900 you will have about 3,200 **Estimated number of stamps in 1900.**
mps ?—We expect that.
So you multiply your present number by eight ?—We do not multiply our present
mp power by eight. Our present stamp power is 1,140. If you go back to 1896
ı will find we were working most of those stamps.
How many stamps had you at work in December, 1896 ?—I cannot tell you
ess you can give me a list.
According to your statement you have 400 at work, and in the other companies
00, and in the year 1900 you expect eight times as many stamps working, but for
other companies you only allow two-fold or double ?—I can only speak of our own
npanies, where I know the facts. As to the 9,000, it was an estimate made up by **Total estimated number of stamps in 1900**
n who can get at the books of most of the companies. I am careful to say it is an
imate.
With regard to the working of the 9,000 stamps, which would signify a great
rease in the development of the Goldfields, how are you going to get water to work
m ?—It would take at least two years to bring the water from the Vaal River to

F

here. I think you are rather premature in saying that in 1900 there will be t
many stamps on the fields. I do not think you will be able to provide water on
Rand for such a quantity of stamps ?—Take the Rand Mines dam, for instance, t
will supply an enormous number of stamps. It is already made and full, and th
are other large dams being made, and we are not going to run our heads into c
years without providing for all contingencies.

Native labour.   In place of 70,000 natives, 140,000 would be required if 9,000 stamps were wo
ing, would there not. Do you think it will be possible to provide that number
natives ?—I see no difficulty in doing so if the Government give us real solid as
tance in compelling or inducing the great native population of the Transvaal to wo
I will give you figures, and you can certify them yourselves. I believe you will fi
in the 3-mile radius, that out of about 30,000 kaffirs there are about 750 from
Transvaal. I say if we cannot make our 400,000 kaffirs work better than that, tl
I think we ought to be ashamed of ourselves.

Dividends of companies of Barnato group   About the dividends. You have six companies working. Which of them ha
paid dividends ?—I have not gone into that at all, but I believe all of them have.

I have a compilation of all dividend-paying mines. In the year 1896 none
your companies appear ?—I do not know as to that. But I may say the Primrose l
just paid up its 20 per cent. dividend, part, in fact all, of which belongs to 1896.

Yes, but it wasn't paid in 1896. What dividends have your companies paid
1896 ?—I cannot tell. I am an engineer and only take figures that I can prove. I c
go into that.

Comparison of dynamite and gelatine.   I will ask two technical questions. About the dynamite—which is the wor
the dynamite or the blasting gelatine ?—We find there are few complaints as to bla
ing gelatine.

Was the accident at the Langlaagte Royal caused by blasting gelatine or dy
mite ?—It was dynamite.

Fuel.   About the fuel—you said that you made great reduction in it. Did you ev
make a careful investigation of the matter with respect to the different machines ?
Yes.

What is your opinion ? I have made special enquiries of a boiler inspector, a
would you be surprised to hear that, with the same machinery, in one mine the c
was £50 per annum, while in another it was £200 ?—I should not be surprised. B
they must be very poor and badly managed mines.

And you say you have made great reductions. Formerly there must have be
a considerable waste in your companies ?—Undoubtedly. We had not the means
have now. We had, as you know, the old locomotive boilers.

At present great saving could be effected in most mines in regard to fuel ?–
daresay, and if you tell me where, in any of our mines, we burn too much, it will h
us very much.

Mr. *Brakhan :*

What tonnage did you crush in the last six months of 1896, and what was t
average per ton ?—We crushed 133,000 tons at the Primrose.

That is about 22,000 a month ?—A little over.

What was the quantity in the six months ending June, 1893 ?—66,400. That
11,000 a month—half the quantity.

Labour saving machines.   You mentioned that between 1893 and 1896 you introduced a good many labou
saving machines. Would you not consider, taking the tonnage crushed during t
period under consideration, that the reduction in cost, as stated here, is a very sm
one ?—It would be if the circumstances were the same. Put us, in 1893, into t

ame ore that we are now working, and you would have probably to add 6s. per ton
o the cost of 1893. In other words, we have reduced the cost in the face of greatly
ncreased hardness of quartz and deeper mines. When I left the Primrose one black-
mith sharpened drills for five times more tonnage than was done at the Royal when
 went there. In other words, after sinking a three-foot hole, we used five drills to
ne at the Primrose. The one was in the soft ground, the other was in the blue.

What difference do you estimate there has been between the mining of
he free milling ore and the mining of the present blue ore ?—I said I thought about
s.; but I may say this, that a kaffir used to drill two, and sometimes three holes,
vhere he now drills one.

And to that, and the dynamite, and other causes, you ascribe a difference of about
s. per ton ?—It's a rough estimate.

Reduction of working costs of New Primrose mine.

You also said that the cost of officers' salaries was in 1893 1s. 4½d., and now 7d.,
naking a saving of about 60 per cent. ?—Seventy per cent.

Bearing in mind the tonnage crushed, the percentage gained, or rather saved,
vould not appear to be so high, because these charges do not increase in proportion to
he tonnage ?—No. May I say, in connection with that, much has been said about
he salaries paid to officials. When one official—a consulting engineer for instance—
ooks after, say, 12 large companies, you cannot expect him to take the same salary as
f he was sitting down in one. So that, supposing you double his salary, you will
educe the cost per ton very largely. I want this point brought up. There are some
f us here because we are obliged to be here for our health. I could get as big
 salary at Home to-day as I do here, and there living is a third of what it is here;
o I think that managers and engineers are not paid, nor the officials of the Govern-
nent either, as much as they ought to be.

Salaries of mine officials.

You said that mealies at the coast cost 8s., while here they cost 22s. Isn't that
 slight mistake—14s. for railage and duty ?—We imported ourselves. There was
ne shipment that cost us 23s., and which cost 10s. in Durban. We can now buy it
or 8s. in Durban, and the price is pretty much about 22s. here.

Cost of mealies.

Would it surprise you to hear that our figures give the price at 9s. 7d. in Durban
nd 20s. here ?—That is my reckoning. It would not surprise me at all if you did.

With regard to the charges of the New Primrose for 1893 and 1896, does that
nclude any charge for mine development and redemption ?—No. During the last
eriod named we put on about 2s. for redemption, so that our cost for the six months
nding 1896, including redemption, was 25s. roughly.

Working costs of New Primrose mine.

Mine development is of course part of the working cost ?—This 2s. has nothing
o do with mine development.

Let us be clear. The cost is 23s., including any work for drives, winzes, etc. ?—
t includes all the work. In the Primrose for instance, where I increased the develop-
nent from 40,000 to 200,000 tons in sight, it was all charged against mine cost during
he period of the first three years mining here.

And is it still so ?—No, it is done in this way. If they develop 30,000 tons and
vork 20,000 tons they give the cost credit for something, or if they reverse that,
evelop 20,000 tons and work 30,000 tons, they charge 10,000 tons against the costs;
f course that is included in the 23s.

Mr. *Smit.*

What do you mean by improved state of economy ?—I mean the economics of
he country.

Which way ?—The last table explains that. We have reduced the costs you see
n No. 1 by 9s. 3d. by economising the *amount* of labour and stores. We now hope

State relief.

that you will help us to reduce a further 7s. in mining and milling by reducing the *price* of labour and stores. In other words, we see that you must reduce your charges so that our coal and other stores may be reduced in price. Taking the coal, for instance, if the Raad will permit the railway company to lay the south railway they ask for they will be able to give us all sidings. That will save us 1s. 3d. for bags, 8d. for bagging and handling, and 3s. for transport, making a very substantial saving without a penny being taken out of the railway company's pocket. In addition to that, instead of starting at 3d. per ton for the first ten miles, I will be reasonable in saying they will start at 2d., which will give us a further reduction of 3s., so, roughly speaking, it will give us a saving from 6s. to 7s. per ton in coal. I say the economics of the country are not right if the railway can charge so much above the actual costs. In the Old Country when we have been in the same position we could lay down a railway ourselves. I remember, in the case of a railway company charging us their maximum rates, we surveyed a connection to another line necessitating a two mile tunnel, and then went to the railway company and said "we will make this and send our traffic past your line," and they had to reduce their rates. We cannot do that here.

Burdens on the mining industry.   What do you mean by the "improved conditions of the country"?—I mean the heavy rates for everything imported—coal, dynamite, etc. I do not go into high politics at all, it is simply a question of hard cash with me—a question of political economy.

Increased revenue result of relief.   You say there are certain things on which you want the Government to meet you, and we want you to point out these things.—All I would say is that, speaking from experience, I can promise the railway and the Government greatly increased revenue if you grant these abatements.

Co-operation means that something is to be done from both sides—can the Government expect that co-operation from your side?—Gladly; we have already done a good bit on our side; we have reduced our costs 14s. 3d., and we are asking you to help us to reduce them another 9s.

Quality of dynamite.   Are the accidents from dynamite of recent date?—Accidents are quite frequent even now. I am anxious to say I have no objection to Transvaal dynamite. I, as a resident of the Transvaal, have made the Transvaal my home. I should buy Transvaal dynamite in preference to any other, all things being equal. If you turned around, and said "you have got to buy from England" I would kick against it just the same, because England would sell just as bad stuff as the Transvaal.

Was dynamite cheaper formerly than now?—I think practically it is about the same.

Price of coal.   Is the price of coal higher now, or lower?—It is lower, and we are thankful to the Government for it. The reduction in the coal rates helped them very little. If they got the coal for 2d. for first ten miles, they would get a large supply from Middelburg.

Netherlands railway rates.   Are the railway tariffs of such a nature, that, notwithstanding you buy cheaper at the Ports, still articles are dearer here than formerly?—No; they are cheaper because of competition. May I suggest a figure to you, and which will help you to see how we are placed? We imported two crushers from Chicago; the rate from Chicago to New York, which is considered very high in America, is £37 5s. 10d. for a distance of 1,000 miles, and from Vereeniging here it was £39 6s.—more for 50 miles than it cost for 1,000. I don't ask you to run it at the same cost, but it shows you what America is doing for the stranger in her State—not her own children—and we ask you to do for your children to-day as well as they do for strangers.

You say you can get the same salary there and live at a third of what it costs u in the Transvaal; does not that show that our railway rates should be somewhat gher?—I acknowledge that your rates ought to be higher, but when you charge ore for 50 miles than they do for a 1,000 then you come to this: That we pay you d. per ton per mile, while we pay the Cape and Natal 2½d. The difference is too eat, although I think you have a right to more than they get.

You know that Vereeniging is exceptionally high for certain reasons?—I say u have a right to more. But the point is that if you reduced the rate you would ake the Cape reduce it also. They are charging us too much. For instance they arged us £152 on the shipment I have referred to for 650 miles, while in America e charge was £37 for 1,000 miles. Both the Cape and Natal are sinners. You ve got the key, and you can go and tell them that they must reduce the rate.

Supposing they say they wont?—You say they have got to do it, and we will ck you up.

We must get the goods along their railway?—You simply tell us which Govern-ent won't do it, and we will simply say to them that we won't order a single ton of ods into their docks, whether it be Delagoa Bay, Capetown, or Durban. You can ly on co-operation from us.

What do you mean by a possible reduction by improved management—which anagement do you mean?—Mine management. Further reduction of working costs possible.

Are there any faults you can lay your hands on which can be improved?—This timate is made of 1890. It is what I call an ideal or illustrative estimate. We ve acomplished that saving of 9s. 3d. by the means shown. The second estimate reduction is what we want you to help us to do, to make it 20s. per ton, including laries. The estimate I have always had fixed before me of 20s. is what we must ing our costs down to. We have done what we can to the extent of 14s. towards at, and we ask you to help us towards getting a further 9s. What improvements can be effected.

In what way would you suggest that we can ensure a good supply of kaffir bour?—That is rather a difficult question for an engineer to answer. We have eat difficulties in getting Transvaal kaffirs. As an instance, I sent one man up to t a large number of boys, and he wired, saying he had got them ready, but that e official would not allow them to come out without payment of 10s. per head. My an wired: "Shall I pay it?" I replied: "No." And then he wired to say that a oclamation was at once put out, saying that owing to smallpox the boys would t be allowed to leave the district. That is a negative way in which you can help The positive way is to put on hut tax. The Dutch, who are more accustomed to orking the kaffirs than anyone else, are well able to devise means to make them ork. Supply of native labour. Native Commissioners; exaction by.

Where there is no complaint how can the Government interfere. It is just as fficult for the Government as it is for you?—I quite see that.

Chairman.

Have you been obliged lately to discharge white miners?—I am not now manager. e have been for the last six months on some of our mines reducing our staff. In t, in every possible way we are reducing costs. I myself am to-day without a ary from the company, and I may say, further, you think our expenses are charged the companies. My salary has never been charged to the companies as consulting gineer. Messrs. Barnato Brothers have paid that. We are now touching our own ckets, giving valuable time without remuneration. The directors are drawing rdly any fees. I am on about seven or eight companies, and I have got a small fee m one company this year—about £8—for directors' fees. I give that as a sample. Reduction of cost of white labour.

I am managing director and acting manager of the Langlaagte Royal, and th without a salary. The directors meet every week, and charge no fees. We a simply doing everything to reduce costs to the very lowest possible limit.

The Chairman said he wished to thank Mr. Hamilton for the statistics he h given. The way he had prepared his statement had saved a lot of time to the Cor mission, and he (the Chairman) was very pleased to hear from what Mr. Hamilt had got to say, that there would be co-operation from the group he represente The points he had brought under notice would have the best consideration.

Mr. Hamilton, in return, thanked the members of the Commission for the co sideration they had shown him.

In supplying the figures *re* European wages and stamps crushing on the Ran Mr. Hamilton added the following:—May I say that but for your preferring question me instead of my giving an opening statement, I had intended mentionir one or two important points in which the Government and Raad had helped u

Liquor, Pass and Purity laws. namely—the Native Liquor Law, the Native Pass Law, and the Public Purity Lav These are admirable laws, and I take the opportunity of heartily thanking th Government for them; and of pleading that the necessary staff may be provided adequately enforce them. Your Honourable Commission has only to enquire into th to find that considerably more money must be provided to do this, else they w become a dead letter or worse; in fact, the Pass Law is far from being a real he now. I desired also to call your attention to the terrible injury done to the count

Iron concession. and to the burghers thereof by the Iron Concession. Years ago, but for this co cession you would have had iron and steel works started. On the behalf of Europe capitalists, I approached the holders of this concession in 1889, for permission make and manufacture iron and steel, and the lowest terms they would give was royalty of 2d. per lb., or nearly £20 per ton, which was, of course, prohibitive. T iron and steel industry is a better industry for the permanent welfare of the count than gold, and if you consider the money sent out of the country since 1889 for ir and steel, that could have been manufactured here, you will see what this count has lost through a concession that has only blocked the way of progress.

Mr. Raleigh's evidence. Mr. FRANK RALEIGH stated he was secretary of the Rand Mines since t 1st January; previous to that he was business manager and secretary of t Rand Central Ore Reduction Company, and was seven years secretary the Crown Reef Gold Mining Company.

Chairman.

On what points can you give evidence?—I can give the Commission informatic regarding the railway charges on machinery. I can give the general working cos of the only mine that is producing in the Rand Mines Group—Geldenhuis Deep.

Mr. *Hugo.*

Will you be able to give information regarding the native labour question a labour generally?—No, I cannot give information on that.

Chairman.

Railway rates Begin with the Railway question.—I have prepared a statement showing t cost of importing machinery, taken from the Rand Mines' books, the statement shov the percentage of total importing charges. Railway charges vary from about 12 460 per cent., but that is an outside case.

Is that calculated on the cost ?—Yes. There is one item in connection with the Delivery charges on the Netherlands Railway. delivery of goods by the railway department that I would like to draw the Commission's attention to. The railway delivery is to take place free within 2½ miles radius. The Langlaagte Deep lies within a mile from the 2½ miles radius, and the charge for delivery is 3d. per 100 lbs; at that price delivery can be obtained direct from the goods station. The mine gets no consideration for the 2½ miles radius for free delivery. The charge for delivering heavy weights, say between 15,000 and 20,000 lbs. weight, is 1s. per 100 lbs. The same work we can get done for 6d. The working percentages of the Geldenhuis Deep are:—Native labour for the year 1896, exclusive Geldenhuis Deep working costs. of food, appears at 21·2 per cent.; food cost, 3·89 per cent.; white labour, 35·89 per cent.; coal, 8·45 per cent; dynamite, 10·7 per cent.; cyanide, 2·2 per cent.; and the balance is made up of sundry items.

Mention some of them.—Zinc, ·15 per cent.; oils and lubricants, 1 per cent.; candles, 1·36 per cent.; dies, quicksilver, and screening for the mill, 1 per cent.; sundry stores, assaying, chemicals, and machinery, 5·6 per cent.; insurances, licences, rents, printing and advertising, premium on natives, and sundry items, 5½ per cent.

Mr. *Smit*.

Is the delivery of coal charged in the 8 per cent. ?—Everything is included.

How much does it cost at the pit's mouth ?—Our price is for delivery at Elandsfontein. The price at the pit's mouth may be estimated.

Mr. *Hugo*.

In the 36 per cent. you put down for white labour, does that include office Salaries of mine officials. expenses, manager's salary, and directors' fees ?—Manager's salary is included, but directors' fees are not included; they only amount to £92 8s. for the year.

All office expenses are included in that, except directors' fees ?—I think the head office salaries are not included; they amount to £840 for the year.

Chairman.

You have not stipulated in that statement what the price of coal is, and how Railway rates on coal. much it costs for carrying it; would you specify how much of that 8½ per cent. is freight, and how much really is the cost of coal ?—That I only will be able to estimate.

You see there is a complaint about the high rate charged for coal, and I am anxious to fix the percentage of the freight on coal ?—I have not got the information, but I can obtain it.

You say the freight on machinery varies from 12 to 460 per cent. ? I notice Cement railway rate. there is one as low as 7 per cent.—The 460 per cent. is an outside case—it was the freight on Portland cement.

Mr. *De Beer*.

One would expect a far heavier expenditure on a deep level property than on an Economy of deep levels. outcrop mine. I see several of your expenses are less than the expenses handed in of several of the outcrop companies. Their working expenses come to 29s. 6d., and your expenses are shown at 25s. Can you adduce any reason for that ?—Probably better equipment; improved machinery might have a good deal to do with it. Some of the outcrop companies have not the most improved machinery; the deep levels are being equipped with the very best.

What is your yield per ton ?—For the year 1896 it was 6½ fine dwts. Annual yield of Geldenhuis Deep.

Including cyanide ?—Including the yield from all sources.

What is the value per ounce of fine gold ?—£4 4s.

So that your profit was about 3s. per ton ?—2s. 4d., exclusive of interest o:
debentures and advances.

Was the mine developed twelve months ago ?—It commenced milling in December
1895. But more than 6½ dwts. was not to be expected, and so far as I know the out
crop South Reef is estimated as being struck at 3,000 feet.

Is it not possible that the reef is faulty ?—6½ dwts. is the average for the twelv
months.

Bonanza assays. The Bonanza is a deep level, and it goes much more than 6½ dwts. ?—Very mucl
more. I believe the Bonanza goes 20 dwts.

Over an ounce ?—Yes; but the Bonanza is in a very rich area.

Ferreira, Worcester and Wemmer deep levels. Won't the Ferreira, the Worcester, and the Wemmer deep levels also be very
rich ?—We hope so.

So that you cannot take 6½ dwts. as an average yield ?—I don't think so.

Do you know a French engineer called Mr. F. Pollock, and have you read hi
report ?—No.

It is perhaps not quite fair to put these questions as you are not an engineer
At the same time I am pleased to get your statement; it is a true extract from you
books and disproves the report of Mr. Pollock, who says deep levels cannot pay, anc
that it is impossible for them to pay.

Mr. *Schmitz-Dumont.*

You say white labour on the Geldenhuis Deep costs 36 per cent. Is not that
very high compared with other mines, where the average is between 25 and 30 per
cent. ?—I know no reason why white labour on the Geldenhuis Deep should be greater
than other mines.

Salaries of directors and mine officials of Geldenhuis Deep. To what account do you charge directors' fees ?—General expenses.

In what way are they calculated ?—One guinea per meeting. Meetings are held
fortnightly, and the total amount paid in 1896 was £92.

There is no proportionate share of profits in the Geldenhuis Deep ?—No.

Can you give us what salaries are drawn by the mine secretary, workmen, and
managers—especially the officials charged with administration ?—The manager gets
£1,500 per annum; mines' secretary, £540 per annum; storekeeper, £300. I do not
remember what the compound manager is paid, but he is not a highly paid official
The assayer gets £480 per year.

Do you think other mines pay about the same to their officials, or do you know
of mines where they receive much higher pay ?—I don't know of a case, but I believe
there are cases where they are more highly paid.

RAND MINES. LIMITED.

Details of Importing, Cost of Machinery, Plant, etc., via East London.

Description of Goods.	Home Cost.	Sea Freight.	Colonial Charges, Duty, Agency, Landing, etc.	Railage.	Z.A.R. Duty.	Insurance an Commission.	Total Cost.	Total Importing Charges % on Home Cost.	Railage Charges % on Home Cost.
	£	£	£	£	£	£	£		
Copper Plates	413	13	2	53	7	14	502	21·55	12·59
Cast Iron Base Plates	114	53	8	201	2	4	382	235·09	176·31
Wrought Iron Pipe	285	46	9	214	5	11	570	100·00	75·09
Gate Valves	79	3	1	15	1	3	102	27·85	17·72
Battery Post Shoes	26	10	2	38	½	1	77	192·30	142·31
Boiler Breechings	127	79	12	63	2	4	287	126·77	48·82
Netherton Iron	268	46	9	227	24	9	583	119·79	84·33
Hex Black Nuts	60	9	5	35	6	2	117	93·33	56·66
Two Comet Crushers	880	108	15	265	16	30	1,314	49·20	30·11
Shoes and Dies	252	27	5	104	5	9	402	59·13	40·87
Mill Engine	3,656	325	48	806	66	126	5,027	37·47	22·04
Air Pump	223	5	2	16	4	8	258	14·79	7·17
Sheaves	184	33	5	44	3	7	276	49·45	23·37
Cornish Pumping Rig	1,227	131	20	402	22	41	1,843	50·28	32·76
Condenser	505	121	9	99	9	17	760	50·49	19·60
Amalgam Retorts	50	5	1	17	1	2	76	50·00	34·00
Anchor Bolts	109	16	2	61	2	4	194	77·97	55·05
Base Plates	249	114	15	433	5	9	825	231·32	173·90
Steel Stamp Heads	700	42	8	160	12	24	946	35·14	22·71
Two Cyanide Tanks	99	19	3	71	2	4	198	97·97	70·70
Steel Shaft	21	3	½	10	½	1	36	61·90	42·38
" Shafting and Fittings	277	30	5	111	5	10	438	58·12	40·08
One Corliss Engine	416	40	7	105	8	14	590	41·58	25·00
Angle Iron	185	49	9	240	3	7	493	166·48	129·19
Pump	51	4	½	7	1	2	65	29·41	13·73
Mill Parts	785	70	15	240	14	29	1,133	44·46	30·57
Cast Iron Capitals	20	7	2	34	½	½	54	220·00	165·00
Winding Engine and Hoisting Plant	2,414	151	29	396	43	82	3,115	29·08	16·40
Plunger Pump	230	23	4	87	4	8	356	54·35	37·83
Rope Fly Wheel	145	67	4	60	3	6	285	95·99	46·69
Bolts and Nuts	46	5	1	15	1	2	70	50·00	30·43
Two Cast Iron Pulleys	61	3	½	10	1	2	77	27·87	14·75
Bottom Balance Bob	18	1	1	5	½	1	26	44·44	27·78
Rubber Pump Valves	46	1	½	2	1	2	52	10·87	4·34
Steel Shafting and Pulleys	504	43	8	123	9	17	705	39·88	24·40
Stamp Mill Parts	864	49	9	155	15	32	1,124	30·09	17·94
" "	2,274	154	31	587	41	78	3,165	39·18	25·81
Three Tanks	266	43	8	207	5	9	538	102·63	77·82
4 8in. Plunger Pumps	230	24	4	90	4	8	360	56·09	39·13
Manilla Rope	91	5	6	13	8	3	126	38·46	13·18
Cast Steel Cams	780	31	8	118	14	27	978	25·26	15·00
Cornish Pumping Rig	1,057	88	31	258	19	36	1,489	41·06	24·40
Spur Wheel	195	16	3	56	3	6	279	43·08	28·72
Mortar Bodies	300	49	7	124	5	12	497	65·33	41·00
Steel Wire Rope	458	27	8	97	8	16	614	34·06	21·18
Pigs of Lead	12	2	1	8	32	½	55	358·33	65·00
Steam Winch	505	32	4	78	9	17	645	27·72	15·45
Whiting Hoist Plant	262	22	2	41	5	9	331	26·33	15·27
Cast Steel Pulleys	68	11	2	18	1	2	102	50·00	26·47
Stamp Mill Parts	797	87	14	246	14	30	1,188	49·06	30·74
Steel Chimneys	285	64	12	239	5	10	615	115·79	83·51
Machinery	811	87	14	226	14	29	1,181	45·87	27·86
Cam Shafts	340	26	4	100	6	12	488	43·56	29·41
Stamp Stems	1,150	104	15	394	21	39	1,723	49·65	34·10
Iron Piping and Fittings	403	60	7	143	7	14	634	54·34	35·23
Auxiliary Shaft	190	19	3	51	3	7	273	43·16	26·31
Mortar Boxes	2,800	376	37	975	50	104	4,342	55·10	34·46
Lathe	89	5	1	12	2	3	112	24·72	12·36
Steel Pipe Joints	2,085	249	36	1,238	38	77	3,723	78·60	59·35
Piping	180	26	4	133	3	7	353	94·44	71·66
"Knowles" Tank Pump	78	2	1	6	1	3	91	16·66	7·69
Portland Cement	82	83	13	385	180	3	756	819·51	469·50*
Liner Plates	130	7	1	23	2	5	168	29·23	17·69
Wrought Iron Pipe	412	66	9	314	7	15	823	99·75	76·23
Steel Crank Shaft	150	42	2	38	3	5	240	60·00	25·34
Boiler	355	82	7	112	6	12	574	61·69	31·55
24" Stroke Column Shaping Machinery	85	7	1	13	2	3	111	30·58	15·19
40 Steel Rails	80	26	5	130	1	3	245	206·25	162·50
Wrought Iron Pipe	886	189	20	732	16	33	1,876	111·74	82·62
Picking Table	200	24	4	78	4	7	316	58·00	39·00
Winding Engine	2,135	215	23	405	38	73	2,879	34·85	18·92
Six Steel Tanks	1,021	162	18	586	18	35	1,840	80·21	22·26
One 10' Boring and Turning Mill	759	94	8	169	14	28	1,072	41·24	22·26
Six Sets Cast Iron Columns	323	207	11	332	6	17	896	177·74	102·79
Angle Iron	243	74	9	335	22	9	692	184·77	137·86
Total of above items	38,156	4,628	671	14,034	941	1,351	59,748	6,298·45	3,891·44

* Special Transvaal Duty of 3/- per 100 lbs.

Details of Importing Cost of Timber, via Delagoa Bay.

Description.	Home Cost.	Sea Freight.	Delagoa Bay Charges 4/- per ton measure 4/- per ton weight 3% Duty.	Railage.	Commission and Transvaal Duty %.	Total.	Total Importing Charges % on Home Cost.	Railage Charges % on Home Cost.
	£	£	£	£	£	£		
Rough	1,700	3,363	801	6,150	82	12,096	611·53	361·76
"	44	59	22	112	2	239	442·95	254·54
"	16	28	11	55	1	111	593·75	343·75
Selected	65	100	23	202	3	393	504·62	310·77
Tongued and Grooved	317	335	72	512	28	1,264	298·74	161·51
Doors	86	27	7	30	8	158	83·72	44·18
Windows and Frames	181	59	14	60	16	330	82·32	33·15
	2,409	3,971	950	7,121	140	14,591	505·69	295·59

The material originally positioned here is too large for reproduction in this reissue. A PDF can be downloaded from the web address given on page iv of this book, by clicking on 'Resources Available'.

Mr. ROBERT MAYO CATLIN, who was next called, said he was mining engineer of the Jupiter, West Simmer, Simmer and Jack West, Simmer and Jack East, and Knight's Deep. He arrived in Johannesburg on the 9th November a year ago. Before that he was in America, and had been in mining business since 1874. He had been connected with various mines in America—the Grand Prize, Navajo, Belleisle, North Belleisle, Commonwealth, and others. These were gold and silver mines. *Mr. Catlin's evidence.*

Chairman.

On which point will you be able to speak to the Commission ?—Most particularly on the wages paid to employees.

Have you formulated any statement or statistics ?—No, I have not. I have not gone into the matter that has been so fully canvassed here. I may say I have read the testimony of most of the witnesses, and it would be unnecessary to occupy your time repeating the same. I have been informed that there was considerable criticism made upon the wages, or the money which we allowed our employees to obtain, particularly in relation to the so-called bonus system.

What do you call the bonus system ?—We pay our miners in addition to their regular wage, a bonus on a certain rate for every foot sunk above a certain distance. When I came here I was not familiar with the native labour, and adopted the system of bonus then in vogue, but since that time I have twice reduced the rate. I would, for illustration, take the most extreme case where we have paid the greatest amount of bonus. Last month, in the Catlin Shaft, we made 142 feet in the month by hand, and the same distance in the Howard Shaft on the Simmer and Jack West. The bonus amounted to £483, that is in addition to the wages of the miners, and I have claimed, and believe, and I think can demonstrate, that this system enables us to do more work at a less price than any other system that I know of. I believe it would be admitted by everyone, and in fact the record of the Rand and the world shows that, working only by daily wage without bonuses, a progress of 80 feet in one month has rarely been accomplished. For argument's sake, assume that the Catlin Shaft last month had paid no bonus, but had paid a daily wage, and had been able thereby to sink 80 feet, the result would have been we would have saved the bonus which we paid, and proportionately down through the different accounts, amounting to £829. As a result, we would have had 80 feet of shaft sunk at a cost of £24 1s. 1d. per foot. As a matter of fact we obtained 142 feet of shaft at a cost of £19 7s. 10d. per foot, resulting in a saving to us of £289 1s. 6d., besides giving us 62 feet more of shaft. Therefore I claim that the bonus system, which has been so much condemned in many quarters, is by long odds, the cheapest system in vogue. I take this instance as an extreme case. This is the largest bonus we have ever paid. *Bonus system* *Sinking of "Catlin" shaft.* *Economy of bonus system.*

Mr. Smit.

How are these bonuses paid—per man per foot, or do the men divide the sections? —All the men participating in the work participate in the bonus. *Division of bonuses.*

Kaffirs also ?—No, white men ; and it is divided among them in proportion to the burden they bear, so to speak—the work they have done.

Mr. Hugo.

Not according to the number ?—No, not according to the number. The miner below who directs the work of the kaffirs receives the most, while those of lesser importance receive proportionately.

Mr. Smit.

Now, what proportion of the total working costs of the mine do these wages

make, together with the bonus ?—I give the average now of nine shafts—the cost
Percentage of white and native wages on working costs on mineshafts. white labour averages 27·43 per cent., and of native labour 33 per cent.

Which percentage of the total working expenses of the mine is represente
in paying bonuses to white men ?—All the work we do in the mine is sinking shaft
we do no stopes, we are not yet on the reef, and these figures cover the entire cos
The percentage is as I said, 27½ and 33. The timber and the framing, 15 35-100tl
per cent.; lubricants, 56-100ths per cent.; fuel, 4 69-100ths; general stores, 7 48-100th
maintenance 1 15-100ths; office expenses, London office, and so on, 5 per cent.

What do you mean by fuel ?—Coal.

As it is put down in the mines, including carriage from the pit's mouth ?—Ye
including everything until put into the boiler.

Mr. *Brochon.*

You have said nothing about dynamite ?—Explosives 5¼ per cent.

Mr. *Hugo.*

What is the real objection raised to the bonus system you introduced ?—I don
claim to have introduced it. I work it. It is an old system, and used all over the worl
Pay of white miners. Well, what is the real objection ?—The objection I have heard is that it seemed a
anomaly that an ignorant miner should be able to receive £75, £80, or £100 for on
month's work. But my object is to get the shafts down as rapidly, and at the cheapes
possible cost; and I do not care whether I have to pay an ignorant man or an educate
man. I believe I work for the interest of my shareholders, and on this system woul
gladly pay a man £200.

Mr. *Schmitz-Dumont.*

You say that you have a Catlin shaft, in which you sank 142 feet in one montl
How many working days did they work ?—About 24.
Re speed of shaft sinking. That is sinking at the rate of 6 feet a day. Do you think that the work don
at such a rate would be safe in future ?—I do, and I invite inspection.

What is the distance between bearers, from 80 to 100 feet ?—72 feet or less i
most cases.

Of course that depends on the speed at which you want to haul ?—What depends

Say, for instance, you want to haul at 3,000 feet per minute.—Not at presen
Later on perhaps.

You have not calculated that ?—Yes. Our winding engines will be capable o
working at that rate.

You think that the timbering would be sufficient ?—Yes. We are timberin
very securely, because we realise that these shafts are to be the highways fo
enormous traffic at high speed, and our timber is far in excess of the strengt
required.

Mr. *Brakhan.*

Can you tell us how many men were employed last month in sinking the shaft
—I understand you to mean white men. There is only one white man at the bottor
of the shaft, and connected with the sinking of the shaft 12 white men.

In three shifts, I suppose ?—Yes, per day of 24 hours.

I suppose the kaffirs clean the shaft after blasting ?—Yes.
Amount of bonuses. Twelve men then divide the bonus of £483 ?—Yes.

That is £40 each ?—Yes.

What is their average pay per month ?—£1 per shift.

That would be about £24. In other words, these men have drawn about £66 pe
head. I have heard that in some of these deep level shafts £150 has been paid pe

l?—Each man does not get the same in the division. The white man in charge
he bottom being in the greatest danger receives the greatest amount.

What would he receive from this?—I cannot say from memory, but over £100.

Do you not think that is very large pay?—No; if I can increase my sinking 62 Economy of bonus system.
they can earn it. I believe that the progress of 80 feet in a 25 feet by 6 feet
t is far above the average, and not long ago it was considered a record. If we
me that shaft has gone down 80 feet, and we pay the required wage and no
us, it would have cost us £24 1s. 1d. per foot, and, as a matter of fact, it only cost
7s. 10d. per foot, and so it does not matter to me whether a man earns £100 or £200.

You say the cost per foot is less. But if you had only sunk 80 feet it would
e been less.—True, I take out the bonus and the cost of fuel, stores, lubricants,
I have also taken out the maintenance, although that is hardly fair.

But yet, surely, although the price per foot would be a large one, your expen-
re under that would be less; therefore, I don't see how you arrive at the saving
£289?—If I save 62 feet of timbering I save 62 times that number of pounds,
lings and pence, and so on through the list.

Do you consider that with contract work you could achieve the same result?—I
sider I could not. I have never been able to do it. I do not know that the men
the only men in the world who can do this, but I do know, so far as my
rmation goes, no other men ever have done it.

Of course the speed of sinking the shaft very considerably affects the price; Cost of rapid shaft sinking.
ess there are particular difficulties with regard to the ground, the price does not
n very cheap?—Bear in mind these shafts are not small ones, they are the largest
d shafts on the Rand.

I know a shaft of similar dimensions on the West Rand. It has been sunk,
rything included, for £15 per foot by contract work, and the speed was 90 feet a
ith; of course the speed was less, but the price compares very favourably with
h instances you give?—I quite believe that can be done, and we could do it. Of
rse, should the ground get more favourable, we could reduce that price very
erially.

Well, the main point is this, you establish the fact that it is advantageous to pay
r men £100, or even more, per month?—If they earn it I feel justified in paying
0 or £200.

On that point I daresay opinions are divided. The 27½ per cent. for white
ur includes the bonus?—Yes, and the manager's salary.

And yet the kaffir native wage comes to 33 per cent.?—Yes.

Now if in sinking a shaft 12 white men are employed, you have a certain
ber of white men on the surface. Can you tell me how many men there are?—
elve altogether—nine outside and three in the shaft.

And how many kaffirs?—It depends on circumstances how many we can get out.
sometimes have 45 on the shift.

How much do these kaffirs working in the shaft get a day?—Our black labour
rage in that shaft only comes to 2s. 7d. and a fraction.

Mr. *Brochon.*

Do these white men working in the shaft include carpenters, who put in the frame
he timbers?—The carpenters who frame the timbers are charged in the timbering.

Yes, but they are working in the shaft?—The timbers are framed by men who
nothing else.

So you have not only three men in the shaft; you have more?—We have the
bering men up in the shaft above.

You gave an illustration, which was a very exceptional one, of a man drawing £140 to £150 a month in the shaft?—Then I only gave the illustration because I thought it would be more in my favour.

What do you reckon the average sinking will be in your shaft?—I cannot say, off-hand. We have some very bad ones, but I think the average will be up to 80 feet or 90 feet a month.

Yon have nine shafts and 12 men for each shaft. That will make 108 white men. What is the average salary these 108 white men make?—There are certain shafts that make no bonus at all, and there are certain others that do make a bonus, and the average would depend entirely on the average footage. I have not the figures, but if you desire it I will send them to you.

The average salary would not be £100?—No, it would be far below £50. The peril is not so much from the ground; we have one or two shafts in which the ground is very good, but the progress is nominal owing to a great influx of water.

Mr. *Brakhan.*

Can you tell us what the average pay for six months would be of the man who might draw in one month £100?—It would depend entirely on the progress his shaft made.

His salary is bound to vary, hardness of rock might prevent him doing much one month, and it would be well to know what his average would be for six months?—I would not like to state it off-hand, but I will send you the figures.

SIMMER AND JACK EAST, LIMITED.

Statement of Average Wages earned by men working on the Shaft, including the bonus paid, for 12 months to 31st May, 1897.

1896.					£	s.	d.
June	...	...	...	...	37	0	0
July	...	...	...	...	61	8	7
August	...	...	...	...	60	14	3
September	...	...	...	...	54	18	9
October	...	...	...	...	39	10	7
November	...	...	...	...	46	8	2
December	...	...	...	...	48	3	3
1897.							
January	...	...	...	...	52	11	9
February	...	...	...	...	43	18	1
March	...	...	...	...	35	15	7
April	...	...	...	...	48	8	5
May	...	...	...	...	50	14	3
					£579	11	8
Average wage for the 12 months	...	...	...	£48	5	11

KNIGHTS DEEP, LIMITED.

Statement of Average Wages earned by men working on the shaft, including the bonus paid, for 12 months to 31st May, 1897.

1896.					£	s.	d.
June	...	...	...	...	31	2	8
July	...	...	...	...	28	10	0
August	...	...	...	...	35	0	0
September	...	...	...	...	33	5	6
October	...	...	...	...	34	13	5
November	...	...	...	...	31	9	3
December	...	...	...	...	29	0	6

					£	s.	d.
1897.							
January	...	...	...	...	22	6	1
February	...	...	...	...	26	3	4
March	...	...	...	...	26	1	1
April	...	...	...	...	28	14	6
May	...	...	...	...	31	16	5
					£358	2	9
Average wage for the 12 months ...		...	...	£29	16	10

MR. WM. DALRYMPLE was the next witness called. He made the following statement: Mr. William Dalrymple's evidence.

I have resided permanently in this country for nine years, and have been, during that period, more or less connected with the exploitation of the mineral resources of the country, and latterly, in the actual mining of gold on these fields. I have for the last five years permanently resided in Johannesburg, and during that period have been the representative of the Anglo-French Exploration Company, Limited, which company is a financial corporation, having its head offices in London and Paris. In the meantime, during the absence of Mr. George Farrar, I am the representative of the Anglo-French Farrar group of mines. These mines are situated in the Boksburg The Anglo-French-Farrar group of mines. district, commencing at the Driefontein Consolidated Mines, Limited, and finishing at the New Kleinfontein Company, Limited, a distance of approximately from eight to nine miles along the reef. During the time I have been in Johannesburg, we have been engaged on an entirely new section of the Rand, which has been opened up and exploited during the last five years. With one exception, none of these mines can be termed high grade mines, but are all considered highly-payable by the exercise of the strictest economy, and consequently the suggested reductions enlarged upon by previous witnesses have special importance with our group of mines. Following on the very exhaustive and lucid statements which have been made by the gentlemen preceding me in this enquiry, I feel in coming before this honourable Commission at this stage, that I can only bear further testimony, and affirm the evidence which has already been led up, setting forth the excessive taxation which this gold industry, in the past, has been called upon to bear; therefore I do not feel justified in wearying the honourable Commission by detailed recapitulation. I shall, therefore, be as concise as possible.

In the matter of white labour, I was, at one time, of opinion that material reduc- White wages. tions could be effected under this heading, which constitutes the heaviest charge in the working costs of these mines, but, after careful analysis of the cost of living at present on these fields, and making due allowance for the expense incurred in transporting oneself from Europe to the Witwatersrand, there is little margin left; and I consider that the evidence of Mr. Fitzpatrick on this point can be accepted as the absolute position, and, if it were not for the fact the various companies interest themselves in and provide suitable accommodation for their employees, and also see that they are properly and reasonably catered for, the margin between their wage-earning capacity and their expense of living would be indeed infinitesimal. The average pay of all whites on our properties, including charges for administration, works out at from £22 10s. to £24 14s. per month.

In the matter of native wages, it has recently been decided by the industry to Native wages. 30 per cent. reduction of native wages resolved upon. reduce the native wages by 30 per cent.—this is, of course, only as far as the actual wages are concerned. I would, however, point out to the Commission that the cost of bringing the labour to these fields, and the feeding of the natives, remain the same

Cost of transport
of natives to
East Rand Pro-
prietary Mines
during 1896
and to March,
1897.

therefore, the actual reduction is considerably less than what appears on the face of i
The item of expenditure by the companies in bringing native labour to these fields i
a very serious one, which you will fully recognise when I tell you that it cost the Eas
Rand Proprietary Mines, from the commencement of 1896 up to the end of March las
a sum of £8,204 5s. 3d. ; and I may say the greater portion of this was paid away i

Reduction re-
quired of cost
of transport of
natives by Ne-
therlands Rail-
way.

railway fares, and, bearing in mind the extremely poor accommodation provided b
the Railway Company, the charges are outrageous. I thoroughly endorse a previou
suggestion, that the Netherlands Railway Company should transport labour for thes
mines at a more or less nominal rate.

The Pass Law.

The Pass Law is an admirable law provided it is properly administered, but, althougl
we have had every assistance from Mr. Maré, the Landdrost, and Mr. Klynhans, th
Mining Commissioner of Boksburg, in trying to recover deserters, still the fact remain

Deserters from
New Kleinfon-
tein Company,
from Septem-
ber, 1895, to
March, 1896.

that, from September to March, we had 245 deserters from the New Kleinfontein
Company, and not one single native was recovered. I am perfectly convinced that i
was never the intention of the Government, nor did they anticipate, that such larg
amounts of money would be received through fines ; therefore I suggest that th

An advisory
board desir-
able to admin-
ister the Pass
Law.

carrying out of this important law should be entrusted to a local Advisory Committee
under a responsible Government official, which, in view of the past receipts, woul
absolutely be made self-supporting. The Advisory Committee would have access t
every mine on the Rand, and would thus be in a position to learn of the desertion
which take place, and how to counteract the same ; and would endeavour to make al
managers deem it a point of honour to refrain from engaging boys where there was
suspicion of desertion ; and in other ways would gradually perfect the administration
which can only be done by establishing a thorough co-operation amongst all the mines

Failure of actual
system of fines

I am not in a position to say how much these fines have amounted to since the law wa
promulgated, but I would point out that, whereas previous to these depressed times, th
fines of boys were readily paid, latterly, in our own district of Boksburg, the gao
has been overcrowded with deserters, who fail to procure the £3 fine, and, as ther
was no further prison accommodation, the Landdrost was obliged to reduce the fin
from £3 to as low as 3d., which clearly proves how unmanageable the present method
of administrating the law has become.

The Liquor Law

So unanimous has the evidence been on the desirability, nay, absolute necessity, in th
interests of the mining industry, of a strict enforcement of the liquor law, that furthe
testimony is unnecessary, but I must again refer to the assistance rendered us by
Messrs. Maré and Klynhans, which has gone greatly towards mitigating this pest ir
our district. It is hopeless to expect, however zealous the Landdrost is, to subdue thi

Kaffir eating
houses and
canteen licen-
ces.

evil whilst low kaffir eating houses and traders are licensed and permitted to trade ir
the mining areas. If all such licences were refused it would greatly facilitate th
duties of the authorities, and I would therefore suggest that all eating-houses and othe
than respectable stores be abolished, similarly to the low canteens. For example, there
are about ten disreputable stores or eating-houses on the boundaries of the East Rand
Proprietary Mines, and it is self-evident to any business man that it is impossible for

Percentage of
drunkenness
at the New
Kleinfontein
Company since
the extension
of the licenses.

them to live legitimately. At the New Kleinfontein Company, since the extension of
the licences, drunkenness amongst the natives has again become very serious, and from
10 per cent. to 13 per cent. of the native labour is incapable for work owing to the
effects of liquor.

Dynamite.
Expenditure of
and excess cost
to East Rand
Proprietary

In affirming the statements of Messrs. Albu and Fitzpatrick under the heading of
Dynamite, I will simply state that the East Rand Proprietary Mines spent £20,506, and
the New Kleinfontein Company £8,983 for dynamite respectively for 1896, which mean

at owing to this concession it has cost these two companies £10,000 and £5,000 respectively more than it would have done under reasonable circumstances.

The question of Railway Rates has also been very fully dealt with by Messrs. Albu and Fitzpatrick, and I simply give you a few examples of the difference in the European cost, and the cost as delivered at the mines here, analysing the various charges. (See Statements 1, 2 and 3.) I will now give you the details of actual cost of bringing machinery, &c., from England to Johannesburg. The statements given do not include any commission which has to be paid to an agent in London for buying and shipping, neither do they include any profit to the importer. I may add that my figures are based on actual data, and all the separate charges are detailed. Statement No. 1 (Compressor). This is for a compressor. The machine costs in England £1,269; by the time it reaches here the cost is £2,018 17s., or the charges come to 59 per cent. on the Home cost. The rail carriage in this case is the most important item, as it amounts to no less than £383 15s. 10d. By working out this consignment, I find that the Cape Government Railway charges 9s. 4½d. per mile for conveying 113,716 lbs. (which is the total weight of the compressor), and the Netherlands Railway charged £1 16s. 5½d. per mile, or £1 7s. 1d. per mile more than the Cape Government Railway. These figures speak for themselves, and I have the statement here showing all the percentages worked out in detail, and you will see that the rail carriage is in excess of all other charges. Statement No. 2 (Rails).—This is for rails used on the mines here. The rails cost in England f.o.b. £97 5s. 8d., and by the time they are delivered here the cost is £296 8s. 2d., or the charges come to 204 per cent. more than the Home cost of the rails. The rail carriage alone from East London to Johannesburg comes to £158 1s. 2d., or 62½ per cent. more than the original cost of the rails delivered on steamer. Take for example:—Supposing I were to purchase a ton (2,000 lbs.) of rails in England at a cost (for the sake of argument) of £5, I should have to pay £6 15s. for rail carriage only, from East London to Johannesburg; that is to say, the rail carriage only would cost £1 5s. more than the manufacturer charges for the rails, and sometimes rails can be bought cheaper than £5 per ton. Rails are in everyday use on the mines, and a very large quantity is used. Statement No. 3 (Carbon for retorting purposes).—A mine with which I am connected decided to import 10 tons of carbon for retorting, and the cost delivered free on board the steamer was £20 exactly, or £2 per long ton (2,240 lbs.) By the time the carbon was delivered at Johannesburg it had cost, with charges, £132 6s. 4d., or the charges were 561 per cent. more than the original Home cost. The rail carriage from East London to Johannesburg was alone £5 12s., or just over 3½ times as much as the manufacturer charges for the stuff itself. It is surely needless for me to add any remarks with regard to these figures, as, in my opinion, they speak for themselves only too strongly. I have given you an extract from three costs, and shall be pleased to hand the detailed statement over to you if you desire it, for publication or otherwise. You will notice that I have based all my calculations on goods coming *via* East London, as this is the cheapest port for these fields, with the exception of Delagoa Bay (Durban rates being equal with East London). In the case of Delagoa Bay, the railway rate to Johannesburg upon the goods I have already mentioned is £6 per ton, instead of £5 15s. per ton from East London, but against this saving in railway carriage the following have to be taken into consideration :—

Increase in sea freight.

Increase in receiving and forwarding charges on account of the great difficulties to be contended with at Delagoa Bay.

Delay in despatch. ... ...

Marginal notes:

and New Kleinfontein companies in dynamite. Railway rates.

Price of air compressor at English cost price, and when delivered in Johannesburg, with extracts of charges.

Cost of rails at English cost price, and when delivered in Johannesburg, with extracts of charges.

Cost of ten tons of carbon at home price and when delivered in Johannesburg, with extracts of charges.

Railway rates from Durban, East London, and Delagoa Bay to Johannesburg.

Drawbacks to Delagoa Bay route for imported goods.

Mr. W. Dalrymple's Evidence.

Elandsfontein and Boksburg rebates on Johannesburg port rates

In having goods brought from the Cape ports and Natal, should you take delivery at Elandsfontein, the Netherlands Railway allow you 4d. per 100 lbs., and for delivery at Boksburg, 2d. per 100 lbs., from the through rate to Johannesburg. But if you have goods brought from Delagoa Bay the Netherlands Railway will not allow you any rebate when goods are delivered at Elandsfontein or Boksburg. I understand the Netherlands Railway have been asked why this should be, but, as usual, no explanation is forthcoming. Leaving out of consideration the amount overcharged the principle is most decidedly a wrong one. Last year we thought it advisable

Cost of transport of mealies from Durban to New Comet Company.

owing to the rinderpest, to protect ourselves by importing mealies from America, and the companies we represent bought conjointly during 1896 25,000 bags, which, after having been sown, reaped, bagged, and landed in Durban, cost 9s. to 9s. 6d., and before they were delivered at our siding at the New Comet Company the cost had reached 21s. to 22s. per bag, the mileage from Durban being only 350 miles. Further comment

Reduction of railway rates.

is unnecessary. Assuming, for argument's sake, that owing to it being a new line the concessionaires might reasonably expect to make liberal charges during the earlier period of its existence, but now they have got the line well ballasted and everything is running satisfactorily, and further they have done exceedingly well, therefore it is only reasonable to expect that the Railway Company should make marked reductions on the rates of their own free will and accord without having pressure brought to bear, if only from the desire to encourage traffic over their line. In concluding my

Mining board recommended: its nature and advantages.

statement, I would strongly advocate the appointment of a Mining Board made up of a fair representation from the leading members of the industry, who, together with the necessary Government nominees, would constitute a permanent committee for the guidance of the Government in all matters connected with the administration of the various laws directly concerning the welfare of this industry. In other words, the Government should enlist the knowledge and experience of those who are not only experts but trustees of huge interests of the European investor. Such a course would relieve the Government of an immense amount of responsibility and detail work, and would promise faithful and honourable co-operation in all matters affecting the

Necessity of immediate reforms for the mining industry.

industry, and hence the progress of the State. A careful analysis of the figures already laid before this Commission will clearly prove that at least a half of the total number of companies at present existing are simply in the balance of profit and loss and substantial reforms, if granted, would immediately turn the scale, and place them on a sound footing, and, in addition, give an immense stimulus to the exploitation of idle gold-bearing ground.

STATEMENT NO. I.

Analyses of costs of air compressor, originally bought in England, when delivered in Johannesburg.

Actual cost of air compressor from England to Johannesburg *via* East London :—

	£	s.	d.	£	s.
Cost delivered free on board steamer	1,269	0	0	1,269	0
Insurance	21	13	2	1	3

Freight and primage to East London per steamer :—

				£	s.	d.
653ft. 8ins. at 71s. 3d. per ton 40c. ft.	...	...	...	64	0	10
95ft. 2ins. at 59s. 3d. per ton 40c. ft.	...	...	...	7	15	1
392ft. at 95s. per ton 40c. ft. ...	...	...	...	51	4	1
131ft. 5in. at 47s. 6d. per ton 40c. ft.	...	...	...	8	11	7
119ft 6in. at 37s. 6d. per ton 40c. ft.	...	...	...	6	3	0
13:13:2: 0 at 118s. 9d. per ton 2,240lbs.	...	...	...	89	6	4
6:14:3: 0 at 71s. 3d. per ton 2,240lbs.	...	...	...	26	8	1

	£	s.	d.	£	s.	d.
14:0: 0 at 59s. 3d. per ton 2,240lbs.	8	16	0			
:5:1: 8 at 47s. 6d. per ton 2,240lbs.	32	1	1			
2:19 at 37s. 6d. per ton 2,240lbs.	1	0	0			
				295	6	1
ntries and stamps at East London	0	10	6			
'harfage at East London, £1,269 ; add 5 per cent., £63 9s. ; total, £1,332 9s. ; 10s. per cent.	6	13	3			
anage at East London, 72 tons at 6d. per ton	1	16	0			
orwarding and receiving at East London, 72 tons at 2s. per ton	7	4	0			
				16	0	0
ail carriage from East London to Vereeniging : 113,716lbs. at 5s. 1d. per 100lbs.	289	0	7			
ail carriage from Vereeniging to Johannesburg : 113,716lbs. at 1s. 8d. per 100lbs., total 6s. 9d.	94	15	3			
				383	15	10
ransvaal duty : £1,269, add 20 per cent., £254, total £1,523, 1½ per cent.	22	16	11			
ransport to Mine : 80,500 (being over 3000lbs. each package) at 3d. per 100lbs.	10	1	3			
				32	18	2
				£2,018	17	0

The above does *not* include London agent's buying and shipping commission.

	£	s.	d.
otal cost delivered	£2,018	17	0
ome cost	1,269	0	0
otal charges	£749	17	0

Or 59 per cent. total charges on Home cost.

Percentages made up as follows :—

Percentages of charges on home cost of air compressor

Insurance	...	...	1¾ per cent.	
Freight by sea	...	...	23¼ ,,	
Coast charges	...	...	1¼ ,,	
C.G.R. rail carriage	...	22¾ ,,	} 30¼ per cent.
Netherlands do.	...	7½ ,,	
Transvaal duty	...	...	1¾ ,,	
Transport	...	...	¾ ,,	

59 per cent.

Rail carriage on whole consignment :—

				£	s.	d.	
er Cape Government Railway : 615 miles, at per mile	...	...	...	0	9	4½	Comparison of rates of Cape and Netherlands Railway for transport of an air compressor.
er Netherlands Railway : 52 miles, at per mile	...	...	...	1	16	5½	

howing that the Netherlands Railway charged £1 7s. 1d. per mile more than the Cape Government Railways. (This is calculated on total weight, viz., 113,716lbs.)

G

Analysis of cost
of rails origin-
ally purchased
in England,
when deliver-
ed in Johan-
nesburg.

STATEMENT NO II.

Actual cost of rails from England to Johannesburg *via* East London :—

	£	s.	d.	£	s.
Cost of rails delivered free on board steamer	97	5	8		
				97	5
Insurances	0	13	10		
				0	13
Freight and primage to East London per steamer	34	13	1		
				34	13
Entries and stamps at East London	0	10	6		
Wharfage at East London, £97 5s. 8d.: add 5 per cent., £4 17s. 3d. Total, £102 2s. 11d., 10s. per cent. ...	0	10	3		
Cranage, 23½ tons at 6d.	0	11	9		
Forwarding and receiving, 23½ tons at 2s.	2	7	0		
				3	19
Railway carriage from East London to Vereeniging, 46,832lbs. at 5s. 1d. per 100lbs.	119	0	7		
Railway carriage from Vereeniging to Johannesburg, 46,832lbs. at 1s. 8d. per 100lbs.	39	0	7		
				158	1

	£	s.	d.			
Transvaal duty	97	5	8			
Add 20 per cent.	19	9	2			

         116 14 10   1½ p.c. 1 14 11

                                                    1 14 1

                                       £296 8

	£	s.	d.
Total cost delivered	296	8	2
Home cost of rails	97	5	8

             199 2 6 or 204¾ per cent. total charges on Home cost

Percentage of
railway rates
on home cost
of rails.
The rail carriage in the case of rails is 62½ per cent. more than the Home cost of the goods themselves, delivered free on board.

	£	s.	d.
Rail carriage	158	1	2
Home cost of rails ...	97	5	8

         Difference ... ... £60 15 6 in excess of Home cost.

STATEMENT NO. III.

Analysis of cost
of importation
of carbon.
Actual cost of retort carbon from England to Johannesburg, *via* East London :—

	£	s.	d.	£	s.	d.
Cost of carbon delivered free on board steamer	20	0	0			
				20	0	0
Insurance	0	4	10			
				0	4	10
Freight and primage to East London per steamer, 10 tons at 60s. per ton	33	0	0			
				33	0	0
Entries and stamps at East London	0	10	6			
Duty at East London, £20 ; add 5 per cent., £1. Total, £21, 5 per cent.	1	1	0			

				£	s.	d.			
arfage at East London, 10s. per cent ...	...	...		0	2	1			
nage at East London, 11¼ tons at 6d. per ton	...	...		0	5	9			
warding and receiving 11½ tons at 2s. per ton	...	...		1	3	0			
							3	2	4

l carriage from East London to Vereeniging, 22,400lbs. at
5s. 1d. per 100lbs. 56 18 8
l carriage from Vereeniging to Johannesburg, 22,400lbs. at
1s. 8d. per 100lbs. 18 13 4

75 12 0

nsvaal duty £20 0 0
Add 20 per cent. 4 0 0

1½ per cent. £24 0 0 0 7 2

0 7 2

£132 6 4

The above does not include London agent's buying and shipping commission.

Total cost delivered £132 6 4
Home cost 20 0 0

£112 6 4

or 561½ per cent. total charges on Home cost.

The railway carriage in this case is the most important item, it being 278 per cent. more Comparison of home cost of ten tons of carbon and railway rates on the same consignment.
n the Home cost of the carbon itself delivered on board steamer.

Rail carriage ... ... £75 12 0 over 3¾ times as much as the carbon cost in England.
Home cost of carbon... ... 20 0 0

£55 12 0 in excess of Home cost.

Chairman.

How many white labourers have you had on the mines these last few years ?— Reduction of white labour on mines of Anglo-French-Farrar group.
o years ago they were about 500; now they are reduced to 250.
What is the reason for that ?—Principally on account of curtailing works,
ng to some of the companies having run short of money. I would just point out
t our district is a new one, and most of the mines are in the development stage.
So far as I can gather from your statement, all your mines are payable except Grade of Anglo-French-Farrar group of mines
?—No; what I do say is, they are all considered low grade mines except one.
How about your black labour? How many had you a couple of years ago, and Reduction of native labour.
y many have you now ?—About 8,000 previously, and this number is now reduced
4,500.
I understand that you do the same amount of work with less quantity of labour,
ause the mines have been opened up ?—No; there has been a curtailing of con-
uction work.

Mr. de Beer.

How long have these mines been in existence ?—Only for the last five years; of
rse, in the early days they had been prospected, but they were practically
mant.
What is your cost of production per ton ?—We have only two mines running Working costs of New Comet and Angelo.
t now in the shape of milling—the New Comet, the Angelo—and the Kleinfontein

started on 1st April. We have not got the costs from the Kleinfontein; for the oth
two the average is somewhere about 27s. 6d. to 30s. per ton.

Was this the price of labour in the year 1891?—These mines were not crushi
in 1891.

When did the mines begin crushing?—The Angelo only about a month ago; t
New Comet has been crushing regularly for about six months.

Wages in 1897 and 1891. Have wages gone up or down since 1891?—I should think they have gone up
little on the average.

You have got no figures here?—No; but I consider wages have gone up in th
way. Higher wages were paid higher officials. During the excess inflation of t
Wages in 1895 and 1897. years ago, there was a considerable demand for expert labour, and groups were
clined to compete for labour; but that, I think, is gradually coming down again.

Then two years ago labour was paid higher than now?—A little; though I thi
they are certainly attempting to reduce wages.

Labour in 1895 and 1897. Is not labour much more plentiful now than then?—I don't consider go
labour is.

Still it is more plentiful?—Yes.

Native labour in 1895 and 1897. As regards native labour; it is surely cheaper and more plentiful than two yea
ago?—Yes; and I think it is gradually being brought to a better quality. To
mind, the great trouble is due to the "bad" boys we have been getting.

Railway carriage and mine machinery in 1897 and in 1895. How about railway carriage; is that higher than two years ago?—A little less.

And machinery has been very much improved?—There is a very much better cla
of machinery.

So all these matters have changed in favour of the mines?—Yes; but the min
are being worked on a larger scale, in which case they require larger machiner
which has been perfected from time to time.

Working conditions of mines in 1897 and in 1895. Therefore, I may conclude from your evidence that the mines work under mo
favourable conditions than was the case two years ago?—Somewhat more favourabl

How is it that only several mines, and not all of them, are benefiting by bett
machinery and cheaper labour?—I think they are all benefiting by better machiner

How do you account for the circumstance that at the present moment sever
mines do not pay, whereas two years ago they did pay?—I think that two years a
mines were worked with the expectation of them being able to pay; but latterly th
have got rid of their working capitals, and naturally the only course open to them
to curtail work for the time being, and at the same time entertain the hope that th
will get facilities for cheaper working.

Over-valuation of mines in 1895. But how is it they were disappointed in these expectations where the circu
stances have been proved?—I think they over-valued the mines in those days, a
expected better returns than they have actually had.

Transit dues on machinery. What are the transit dues on machinery in Cape Colony?—There are no tran
dues on machinery to the best of my knowledge.

Not to your knowledge?—No; I don't think so.

All the figures given here by you, are they all charges in connection with t
machinery?—They are absolutely taken from shipments.

Purchase of machinery. Where do you buy your machinery?—It is bought in England from differe
people, and in America.

Do you get a free hand to order where you like?—The directors order all t
machinery.

Do you have a free hand?—Yes. The directors have full power, with the recom
mendation of their managers.

You say that the lodging-houses, or rather the eating-houses, interfere with the ⟨ca⟩rrying out of the Liquor Law ?—Yes.

Eating houses
and the Liquor
Law.

That liquor is smuggled into these houses and sold there ?—Yes. It must be ⟨ser⟩ved up in the shape of soup or some such thing.

You mean that in the vessels in which soup ought to be served, liquor is served ?—⟨Y⟩es. It is probably made up in some way.

Have you any suggestion to make in order to reduce this evil ?—Wipe them out ⟨of⟩ the place.

How do they get their licences ?—They get their licences through the officials. ⟨T⟩he Boards grant them.

What class of people usually keep these boarding-houses?—I should say Russians, ⟨as⟩ far as I know, but I do not have much to do with them.

As regards the Pass Law, I understand from you that it cannot be very well ⟨ca⟩rried out ?—No.

Administration
of the Pass Law

That one of your reasons is because the gaol is too small ?—The gaol is too small, ⟨bu⟩t there ought to be separate compounds for deserters, so that people could go in and ⟨se⟩e them.

Then you can go to the gaol and see the deserters there ?—I suppose so. But so ⟨fa⟩r as I am concerned, and most people, it is a very difficult thing.

It is probable that many of these deserters find their way to gaol ?—Quite ⟨po⟩ssible.

Then you say that the exacting of a fine of 3d.—less than the maximum of £3— ⟨by⟩ the magistrates has filled the gaols ?—That is so ; it has taken place. If the fine ⟨w⟩ere kept up to £3, it would not pay a boy to desert.

Chairman.

How do you reconcile these two facts—that out of 200 and odd deserters, not one ⟨ca⟩me back, and yet the *tronk* is full ?—Of course, we made the formal application to ⟨th⟩e officials, to the effect that we had lost these boys, but we never got them back. ⟨T⟩he fact is, I don't think the administration is defective in this way ; there are merely ⟨no⟩t sufficient officials to carry out the law. There appears to be a great deal of ⟨an⟩xiety amongst them in Boksburg to assist us, but there are too few to carry out ⟨th⟩e work.

Who should know the kaffir best—the police or the former master ?—Naturally, ⟨th⟩e compound manager.

Now, within your knowledge, has it ever been tried by the compound manager ⟨to⟩ go to the gaol and try to find the boys ?—Yes, they have, but could not recognise ⟨th⟩em.

Then your argument would fall to the ground.

Mr. Smit.

There is really very little reason for complaint when so many kaffirs get to gaol?— ⟨W⟩e take a great deal of trouble to get deserters ourselves. We get some back from ⟨ot⟩her mines. The probability is, very few get to prison at all.

You do not know, not having been to gaol to see ?—I have not been there, but ⟨ou⟩r compound manager has.

But you think that they don't know them individually ?—It is very difficult to ⟨kn⟩ow them individually where you employ thousands of kaffirs.

You get back some from other mines. Did you fetch them yourselves ?—Yes. ⟨W⟩e heard it from other boys.

Did you get any boys back through the efforts of the officials ?—No ; but I sa
they are very good.

It is quite possible that some of these boys of yours may be in gaol ?—Not at t
present time. It happened some time ago, but I don't think they ever reached ga
They may have got into other compounds.

How can you say that if you do not send someone to the gaol, and if you do,
does not know them. You said that, of all the deserters, you got none back ?—N
of the 245.

Mr. *Hay.*

Expenditure of East Rand Proprietary Mines Can you tell us how much money the East Rand Proprietary Mines have spent ?-
Since they started ? In everything ?

Yes ; in everything.—I should think it would run into a million and quarter
money.

Payment of dividends by East Rand Proprietary Mines. They have not paid any dividends ?—No. They have not reached that stage y
Is there no immediate prospect ?—Not immediately. Probably some time next yea

Mr. *de Beer.*

Grade of New Comet and Angelo Mines. How many dwts. do the various mines average ?—The Comet about $9\frac{1}{4}$; t
Angelo for the past two months would average about $12\frac{1}{2}$ or 13 dwts. It is what w
call our rich mine.

Mr. *Brakhan.*

Percentage of railway rates on expenditure of East Rand Proprietory Mines. Can you inform us how much of this money, the million and a quarter, has bee
spent on the various articles which have been brought here by the railway ?—I cou
get that for you. I have not got it here.

It would be interesting to get to the conclusion how much has been paid t
the Railway Company, in order to find out that if the rates had been lowered, sa
25 or 30 per cent., how much less working capital would have been required to do th
same work ?—I will get it for you.

Chairman.

White wages, As regards the labour, you here state it costs £24 or £25 per month. Do you ir
clude in that directors' fees ?—Yes, everything ; the charges of the London office as wel

Mr. C. S. Goldmann's evidence. Mr. CHARLES SYDNEY GOLDMANN was called. He said :—

I exceedingly regret having to say that the statement which I have in preparatio
is not complete for distribution, but I hope it will be to-morrow, in English as we
as in Dutch.

I beg to respectfully state that I came to the Witwatersrand in the first month
1888, and have more or less been on the Rand from that date. I have been connecte
in business associated with the mining industry from the date of my arrival. I hav
been connected with company work for a considerable time; I have been intereste
in the formation of gold-mining companies; I am chairman of 12 mining companies
I am a member of the Boards of numerous companies, including several dividenc
paying companies and a good many producing companies; I have been connected wit
financing, and claim to have gained experience during my sojourn in England; I am
member of the Executive Council of the Chamber of Mines, and also a member of th
Native Labour Association. I am the author of two issues of the history of thes
fields, and also the compiler of a map of the Witwatersrand and neighbouring group
of mines. I have been a witness of the prosperity as well as the vicissitudes of th
industry. My firm is representing very considerable interests in this State, includin
interests in mining properties, as also real estate. I therefore submit to your kin

sideration the evidence I am about to give, evidence which I feel is given entirely
biassed, inspired by wishes only calculated to benefit the mining industry collectively,
the interests I represent, individually. In trying to arrive at an explanation of
depression which has overtaken an industry which generally is acknowledged to
bine all the elements requisite for success and prosperity, with a view to bringing
ut relief it is necessary not only to examine the circumstances which led to the
nowledgment of its potentialities, but to cast a retrospect of the general conditions
ler which the industry sprang into existence, and the various vicissitudes which it
ce has undergone, and to investigate all the defects and disabilities which have
tributed to the present state of affairs. The reasons which, in my opinion, have Reasons for in-
flow of capital
into the Wit-
watersrand.
racted the attention of the public, as also the commercial mind to this country, as
the application of vast sums of capital to investments in it, or connected with its
ources, is directly attributable to :—(1) The discovery of the Witwatersrand Gold-
ds under circumstances hitherto unknown in the history of gold mining ; the gold
urring in unique deposits which, in their uniformity of character, resemble coal
ls ; (2) The exceptionally favourable conditions prevailing for mining, including
h as a salubrious, exhilarating climate, periodical rainfalls, easy approach from the
, and extensive coal deposits in close proximity ; (3) The world's scarcity of gold,
l the increasing production of gold in this country—the production for the years
34 to 1895, inclusive, yielding 9,749,170 ozs., having a value of £33,730,427 ; (4) The
bility of returns of some of the leading companies ; (5) The aggregate of dividends
d up to the end of 1895, which amounted to £7,408,371 ; (6) The confident and
uguine opinions expressed by geologists of highest repute, and mining authorities
ably eminent ; (7) The confirmation of their opinions by independent reports made
the instance and on behalf of foreign Governments ; (8) The complete record of
ults and the comparative facility of obtaining information and statistics, as also the
ility afforded of inspecting the mines. All these circumstances led to a considerable
centration of attention from outside, and an inflow of capital to these fields, which
minated during 1895 in an unequalled and unprecedented state of universal com-
rcial prosperity. This, however, was of comparatively short duration. An acute
ction set in, which did not fail to mark in manifesting itself most detrimentally,
only so far as the investing public was concerned, but also to the actual develop-
nts of the fields. This condition of depression, instead of abating, has become
entuated, and it is therefore necessary to enquire into the causes of the depression,
ich, in my opinion, are :—(1) Withdrawal of capital ; (2) Disappointment to inves- Causes of the
present de-
pression.
s ; (3) Over-estimated value of the richness of the reef ; (4) Under-estimated cost
equipment of mines ; (5) Unsatisfactory condition of the native labour market ;
Extreme taxation to which the mining industry has been subjected ; (7) Inefficient
ninistration of laws primarily designed for the benefit of the industry ; (8) Feeling
distrust and want of confidence on the part of the investing public ; (9) The relaxing
uence on the energies of those responsible for the maintenance of the industry, due
feelings of discouragement in failing to enlist the necessary co-operation of the
horities in matters frequently requiring immediate attention, relief, or assistance.
at the causes are real is manifested by the fact (1) That many developing and
mising companies are stopped for want of funds ; (2) That a change of sentiment
taken place in the minds of European capitalists, who, for the time being, are
isposed to embark any further capital in these fields ; (3) That the average yield
ore crushed during latter years as compared with former, has decreased ; (4) That
total equipment of mines is shown to be far in excess of original estimates,
iciently proved by the fact that the actual cash spent in mines exceeds, in many
tances, four times the total original capitalisation ; (5) That the companies have for

their requirements been obliged to purchase native labour at great cost and expe[n]
to themselves, outside of the high cost for actual work done; (6) That the industr[y]
subjected to unnecessary taxation, to which it is only necessary to refer to the taxati[on]
under the head of railway rates, dynamite, and duties; (7) That a universal compla[int]
has been raised by all mining companies and their representatives of the ineffici[ent]
administration of such vital laws as the Pass Law, Liquor Law, Gold Thefts La[w]
(8) Of the great depreciation in all values, and apparent apathy on the part of inv[es]
tors and capitalists in spite thereof—the acknowledged effect in Europe of the is[sue]
and settlement of the Bewaarplaatsen question; (9) By the difficulty experienced [in]
effecting united and energetic action in questions involving spirited co-operati[on.]
Having classified the causes which in my opinion have led to the depression in [the]
mining industry and its necessary reflex on trade, I will now refer to the reme[dy.]

Remedy for the
present de-
pression.
Government co-
operation
necessary. Restoring of confidence amongst European investors, for which purpose the loyal a[nd]
active co-operation of the Government is necessary. On the part of the Governm[ent]
suggestions for the better working, made on behalf of the industry, should in [my]
opinion have their friendly and prompt attention, and be considered as dictated in [the]
best interests of the industry and the country. Reference to the reports of t[he]
Chamber of Mines will sufficiently prove that in the past this has not been the ca[se.]

Relief required. Having gauged the conditions existing and required to make a commercial success [of]
mining on these fields, careful study of economy in every department is necessary, [in]
order to effect the largest possible margin between revenue and cost, with the use [of]
equipments of the highest class to assist in such economy. Granting of every facili[ty]
for introduction of native labour by providing cheap means of access and protecti[on]
on the way, and holding out inducements for the permanent residence of train[ed]
labour on these fields. Removal of disabilities in every case where it can be sho[wn]
that unnecessary burdens are placed on the industry. The proper administration [of]
all laws with the assistance and co-operation of the representatives of the indust[ry.]
To make every endeavour to justify every appreciation of values by actual results.

After this general statement I will now endeavour to enter into a more detail[ed]
statement of those burdens and disabilities which affect the industry, the removal [of]
which will afford speedy relief and redress. I will begin with the Pass Law. T[he]
Pass Law—reas-
ons for. necessity of having a control over the natives, the necessity, too, of insuring a bindi[ng]
contract between the mines employing native labour and such employees, the necessi[ty]
also of affording complete protection to the natives coming to and going from t[he]
goldfields, induced the heads of the mining industry to frame a law which was intend[ed]
to cover these conditions and requirements—a law which in their opinion was to gi[ve]
mutual satisfaction to the Government, the employer, and the employee. T[he]
necessity for this law dates back as far as 1893, when representations were made [to]
the Government to give effect to it. In spite of all the petitions and deputations, [it]
was not until October 3rd, 1895, that the proposed regulations became law, and it w[as]
Originated by
mining indus-
try. not until May, 1896, that it became actively operative. In connection with this la[w]
I wish to point out that it came into existence at the request of the mining industr[y;]
that the law was framed by certain persons connected with the mining industry; th[at]
it was the mining industry that solicited the Government to administer the law; [it]
was the mining industry that suggested to the Government to pay consideration f[or]
the proper carrying out of the law. As you are aware, prior to the passing of th[is]
Application of
pass fees, law the pass fee per month was 1s. It was increased in order to meet the requi[re]
ments of the proper administration of the law, and a further sum of 1s. per head w[as]
agreed upon by the Government Commission and the industry, which was to be a[p]
plied solely to the administration of this law, as will be observed from the draft la[w]
which was approved by the Government Commission. The law as passed does n[ot]

Mr. C. S. Goldmann's Evidence.

A.

Suggested Divisions into Pass Districts of that Section of the Witwatersrand Goldfields where the Pass Law is in force.

No. 1. Springs. 6 Officials.	No. 2. Benoni. 6 Officials.	No. 3. Boksburg. 6 Officials.	No. 4. Knights. 6 Officials.	No. 5. Elandsfontein. 6 Officials.	No. 6. New Heriot G. M. Co. 6 Officials.	No. 7. George Goch G. M. Co. 6 Officials.	No. 8. Johannesburg. 12 Officials.	No. 9. Langlaagte. 6 Officials.	No. 10. Maraisburg. 6 Officials.	No. 11. Roodepoort. 6 Officials.	No. 12. Krugersdorp. 6 Officials.	No. 13. Randfontein. 6 Officials.
1 Responsible Clerk 1 Clerk 2 Inspectors 2 Police	1 Responsible Clerk 1 Clerk 2 Inspectors 2 Police	1 Responsible Clerk 1 Clerk 2 Inspectors 2 Police	1 Responsible Clerk 1 Clerk 2 Inspectors 2 Police	1 Responsible Clerk 1 Clerk 2 Inspectors 2 Police	1 Responsible Clerk 1 Clerk 2 Inspectors 2 Police	1 Responsible Clerk 1 Clerk 2 Inspectors 2 Police	1 Administrator 1 Book-keeper 1 Secretary 1 Responsible Clerk 1 Clerk 1 Chief Inspector 2 Inspectors 4 Police	1 Responsible Clerk 1 Clerk 2 Inspectors 2 Police	1 Responsible Clerk 1 Clerk 2 Inspectors 2 Police	1 Responsible Clerk 1 Clerk 2 Inspectors 2 Police	1 Responsible Clerk 1 Clerk 2 Inspectors 2 Police	1 Responsible Clerk 1 Clerk 2 Inspectors 2 Police

One Man to be Resident at each Mine along the Reef.

EXPENDITURE.

SUB-OFFICES.

12 Responsible Clerks at £400	...	£4,800 0 0
12 Clerks „ 225	...	2,700 0 0
24 Inspectors „ 400	...	9,600 0 0
24 Police „ 200	...	4,800 0 0

HEAD OFFICE.

Administrator	...	650 0 0
Book-keeper	...	400 0 0
Secretary	...	400 0 0
Responsible Clerk	...	400 0 0
1 Chief Inspector	...	450 0 0
2 Inspectors at £400	...	800 0 0
4 Police „ 200	...	800 0 0
Maintenance of, say 30 horses at £120 each per annum	...	3,600 0 0
150 Men at Mines at £200 per annum each	...	30,000 0 0
Office Furniture, Stationery	...	5,600 0 0
Total per Annum		£65,000 0 0

INCOME.

Assuming that Boksburg employs	...	44,000
Assuming that Johannesburg employs	...	60,000
Assuming that Krugersdorp employs	...	18,000
		122,000 at 2s.
		£12,200 per month.
		or £146,400 per annum.
Difference in Income over Expenditure...	...	£81,400 0 0

The material originally positioned here is too large for reproduction in this reissue. A PDF can be downloaded from the web address given on page iv of this book, by clicking on 'Resources Available'.

arate the application of the 1s. per head, as originally understood, but simply
cts that a 2s. tax is to be imposed. It was understood that these pass fees were
e applied to the administration of the law, as instanced by interviews with the
ernment (*Chamber of Mines Annual Report*, 1894, *page* 51), and not to add to the
enue of the Budget, as stated by a member of the Government in the Volksraad on
ruary 2, 1897. I regret to say that the law has not been administered effectively. Maladministration of Pass Law
s not for me to say to whom the blame attaches, but it is only justice to the head
s officer of the Johannesburg department to state that, in my opinion, he is not at
lt, as stated by a previous witness. Continual complaints were being received by
Chamber of Mines of the ineffective administration and operation of the law, and
interview was arranged with Mr. Koch, who explained the impossibility of giving
sfactory effect to the law with the machinery which was placed at his disposal. Complaints of Chamber of Mines as to Pass Law
suggested, and it was agreed, to form a deputation to wait on the Minister of Mines
the Government, and to urge on them the necessity of increasing the staff
essary for the proper administration of the law, as also to alter some of the defec-
 clauses in the law. In making the statement which the Minister of Mines made
ore this Commission, in respect to any dereliction on our part in not having
sented matters to him, I think he must either be unaware of the circumstances or
y must have escaped his memory, inasmuch as I formed one of the deputation who
ited not only on the Acting Minister of Mines, Mr. Kleynhans and Mr. Liebenberg,
 we also meant to interview the Government, who, however, were unable to see us
t day. The Acting Minister of Mines suggested that we should send in a petition
our requirements in effecting the better working of the law, which we did, as per
 petition. To my knowledge, the only result of this petition was the fact that
 law was altered in the Volksraad in December, increasing the fines for Increase of fines under Pass Law.
ertion from 10s. to £3 ; the increase in the fine, it is true, was made at our
uest. I now propose dealing with this law. As you are aware, the only districts
which the pass law is proclaimed are Krugersdorp, Johannesburg, and Boksburg,
h of which is administered by a pass officer and his staff. I have statistics to Number of passes issued in Johannesburg from April, 1896, to March, 1897.
w that from April, 1896, to March, 1897, no less a number than 574,000 passes
e issued in Johannesburg, the average registration for March having been 63,000
ives. The revenue from these passes at 2s. per head per month I estimate as
ing £57,000. This sum is exclusive of fines which have accrued by reason of Average number of boys registered under Pass Law in Johannesburg district and revenue from passes.
ertion and arrear of passes. I will take the cost now of the administration of the
 in this district. I take my figures from the *Staats Almanak*, which show that,
lusive of the pass officer, there are three pass inspectors, one responsible clerk,
 eleven clerks to administer the law, at a total cost of £5,760. As near as I can
 it, the average number of boys employed in the Boksburg district is 44,000, giving Average number of boys registered under Pass Law in Boksburg district, and revenue from passes.
approximate revenue with " reis " passes of £52,800. The machinery to administer
 law in that district consists of one pass officer, two pass inspectors, one respon-
e clerk, and four clerks, at an annual expenditure of £3,350. In the Krugers-
p district I have ascertained that there are an average of 18,000 natives, giving an
roximate revenue of £1,800 per month, equal to £21,600 per annum, besides a sum Average number of boys registered under Pass Law in Krugersdorp district, and revenue from passes.
rom £300 to £400 per month derived from " reis " passes. This gives a total of
5,000. The staff in Krugersdorp consists of one pass officer, two inspectors, one
onsible clerk, and three clerks, at a total expenditure of £3,050. Therefore,
roximately, the number of registered natives at the mines, according to what I Total number of boys registered, and total revenue from passes, and total annual expenditure
e been able to ascertain, amounts to 120,000, with an approximate revenue to the
ntry of £150,000. Against this the total pass administration was £12,160.
tlemen, I should not raise this question for the sake of the money if the law were
ried out in the spirit in which it was intended. I may mention that the whole

intention of the law is to have a hold on the native whom we have brought down, it from the East Coast, South, or from the North, at a considerable outlay ourselves, but experience has shown that the law is broken with impunity, that boys desert, that the money spent in bringing down these boys is lost, and dectection of their desertion is effected. I have gone to the trouble of ascertain from 33 companies a statement (see Statement B), which I append, showing th since the Pass Law came into operation no less a number than 14,000 boys deser out of a total of 19,000 monthly employed by the companies, without a single one those deserting natives being brought back to the mine, or at least brought to justi

Now, I wish to point out to you that this pass fee is not the only amount which ad to the expense of native labour, but it is the cost of bringing these boys to the min which money is all lost if the boys desert. I will give you a few instances whi come under the category of companies I am interested in :—

WOLHUTER GOLD MINES.—Our total premiums for securing natives for the ye 1895 amounted to £2,520 13s. 4d. ; the boys refunded £234 6s. ; and the net loss this company upon premiums, owing to desertions, amounted to £2,286 7s. 4d. F 1896 the figures are much more alarming, though during that year the law w already in operation. The sum expended on procuring natives was £6,577 3s. 3 of which £1,129 12s. 7d. was refunded by boys, causing a loss to the mine £5,448 10s. 8d. The total number of boys employed averages 1,105 for 1895, against 1,641 for 1896.

TREASURY GOLD MINES.—We paid premiums for securing boys in 1896 to t amount of £3,116 11s. ; £453 18s. was refunded, and there was a net loss £2,662 13s. The average number engaged by this company was only 369.

BANTJES CONSOLIDATED MINES.—Premiums paid, £601 ; refunded, £72 ; net lo £528.

VOGELSTRUIS CONSOLIDATED DEEP.—£345 paid in premiums, £150 refund £195 lost, 194 boys employed.

I have a statement (see Statement C) from several companies, which shows t actual losses in premiums. Five companies in 1895 lost £4,531 ; in 1890 sixte companies lost £25,333 ; and four companies in 1897, £2,897.

These are examples of direct losses, actual losses which the companies susta without any means of recovery. I respectfully submit that the law is a good, thou intricate one, and a law that, under good administration, is easily operative. Bu think you will admit that in order to handle the inflow and outflow of 120,0 natives, and to have a control over them, requires more than 30 officials. I think is wrong to attach blame to one officer in particular, and I say that with the n chinery at his disposal it is impossible to administer the law satisfactorily.

The administration of the laws, such as the Pass Law, the Liquor Law, and Go Thefts Law, should, in my opinion, be vested in a Local Government Board assisted an Advisory Board of the representatives of this industry. It would certainly preferable if the Government have representatives of the mining industry constituti a section of this local incorporated Mine Board, which would bring them into clos touch with the officers of the Government, who would thereby more readily und stand the requirements of the industry.

After endless deputations, petitions and memorials, a Liquor Law was introduc and brought into operation which met with the approval of the mining industry, a which was expected to compensate for all the worry and trouble which had be undergone, and be a boon to the industry. Immediately after the introduction of the l the beneficial effects of it were largely felt, and satisfactory reports were forthcomi from various mine managers. This state of affairs, regretably, was of too sh

B.
RETURN SHOWING DESERTION OF NATIVES

From 33 Companies only, since the Pass Law came into force; Average Monthly Desertion, Number of Boys Engaged and Discharged, and average requirements for Month.

COMPANIES.	No. left during month February, 1897.	No. engaged past month.	Next month's require-ments.	Desertions since Pass Law.	Desertions monthly.
Aurora West	0	50	300	160	40
Bonanza	42	65	0	207	20
Chimes West	11	32	0	174	20
Champ d'Or	6	64	200	43	14
Crown Deep	62	277	0	120	10
Crown Reef	59	95	250	?	?
City and Suburban	65	238	200	1,328	147
Glencairn	43	165	300	272	23
Ginsberg	30	50	0	160	20
Grey's Mijnpacht	8	10	20	0	10
Geldenhuis Deep	91	220	400	270	90
Geldenhuis Main Reef ...	20	15	0	60	12
Glen Deep	25	72	100	?	?
Jubilee	26	38	50	?	20
Jumpers	44	206	0	500	35
Knight's Deep	31	31	0	35	5
Meyer and Charlton	14	116	0	667	66
Modderfontein Extn.	12	26	153	120	9
Minerva	44	57	0	118	20
New Unified	12	1	0	100	10
Nourse Deep	18	119	200	270	30
New Heriot	42	142	50	606	81
*New Florida	11	19	...	150	12
New Rietfontein	40	40	50	440	55
Roodepoort Central Deep ...	12	32	...	13	1
Robinson	72	447	...	1,600	100
Rose Deep	67	133	...	300	43
Simmer and Jack East	44	100	...	137	14
Simmer and Jack West	50	205	...	500	70
Treasury	94	151	...	1,924	190
Vogel. Consolidated Deep ...	10	111	...	515	40
Wolhuter	55	140	...	1,540	140
West Roodepoort Deep	11	49	...	26	9
	1,171	3,596	2,273	12,355	55 average

* No Pass Law in that district.

Average Total Desertion, 426 per Company ; Average Desertion Monthly, 55 per Company.

C.

NATIVE LABOUR—PREMIUMS PAID.

COMPANIES.	1895				1896				1896-7 TO DATE.			
	No. of Boys.	Gross Premium Paid.	Refunded.	Net Loss.	No. of Boys.	Gross Premium Paid.	Refunded.	Net Loss.	No. of Boys.	Gross Premium Paid.	Refunded.	Net Loss.
		£	£	£		£	£	£		£	£	£
Vogelstruis Con. Deep					194	345	150	195				
Bantjes Con. Mines	85	85	Nil.	85	457	601	73	529				
Knight Central					237	72	12	60				
Treasury Gold Mines	172	83	Nil.	83	369	3,116	453	2,662				
Wolhuter Gold Mines	1,105	2,520	234	2,286	1,641	6,578	1,129	5,448				
Agnes Munro					162	?	?	350				
New Comet	536	?	?	1,952	762	?	?	3,570				
Angelo					149	?	?	274				
Driefontein Company	168	?	?	124	313	?	?	1,816				
Marie Louise									240	727	553	173
New Midas Estate					385				450	1,418	1,281	137
York									190	219	90	129
Lancaster									500	340	106	234
Champ D'Or					1,320				266	309	234	75
Durban Roodepoort					1,167				1,233	Nil.	Nil.	Nil.
Roodepoort Deep									600	Nil.	Nil.	Nil.
Robinson G. M. Co.					1,606	2,160	553	1,587	2,090	4,219	468	3,751
New Kleinfontein	780	?	?	2,787	654	507	Nil.	507				
Benoni					150	371	Nil.	371				
Nourse Deep, Ltd.					?							
Geldenhuis Deep					?	?	?	3,427				
Crown Deep						738	199	539				
Worcester									420	764	383	380
Ferreira									2,041	6,648	3,026	3,621
Meyer and Charlton									1,092	564	171	393
Henry Nourse									1,654	612	143	468
Jumpers									1,450	4,013	1,630	2,383
Stanhope									350			
City and Suburban									2,393	1,883	825	1,057
Langlaagte Estate									1,790	12,120	530	11,589
Crown Reef									1,792	859	171	688
Paarl Central									685	3,035	153	2,881
Robinson Deep									400	1,021	711	309
New Heriot									1,068	3,316	339	2,976
				£7,317				£21,335		£42,067	£10,823	£31,823

In 1895 ... ... 6 Companies alone show a Loss of £7,317
In 1896 ... ... 14 " " " 21,335
In 1896/1897 to date 17 " " " 31,823
Which latter represents as near as possible 75 per cent. loss of their outlay.

D.

Particulars elicited from the Managers of 74 Companies in relation to the Illicit Trade and Sale of Liquor

Being carried on in Contravention of the Liquor Law which came into force 1st January, 1897, prohibiting the Sale of Intoxicating Drink to Natives.

The material originally positioned here is too large for reproduction in this reissue. A PDF can be downloaded from the web address given on page iv of this book, by clicking on 'Resources Available'.

ration, and, in the opinion of those best capable of judging, only a nominal improvement on the previous state of affairs exists. Whilst convictions undoubtedly have taken place, showing that infringements of the law are occurring, I am still of opinion that by far the greatest amount of the liquor traffic remains undetected. To show what the opinion of the mine managers is with regard to the operation of the liquor Law, we have had a table (see Statement D) prepared from 74 companies on the Rand which conclusively demonstrates the absolute necessity of a better administration of this otherwise excellent law. A summary of this table shows that all the managers of the 74 companies are unanimous in declaring that liquor is being sold freely to the natives. It further goes to prove that although in some cases the amount of drunkenness on some mines is small, still the overwhelming returns indicate that a large percentage of natives employed on the fields is rendered incapable for work owing to the effects of drink. A further perusal of the documents will show that while in some individual cases the police supervision has been fairly satisfactory, the bulk of the cases demonstrate that the supervision has been totally inadequate. It will also be seen from the statement, that while in some instances the mines have recently gone to the trouble of opposing applications for licences, in the bulk of cases they have refrained from doing so, owing to the ill-success which has attended previous efforts in that direction, and to the loss of time which is entailed by such matters. I wish to read one letter which I have received from Mr. Johns, manager of the Ferreira Company:—"In reply to your letter of yesterday's date respecting illicit liquor traffic, and asking why I did not protest against granting any licences in this neighbourhood, the reason why I did not protest is that I consider it would be quite useless to do so, previous protests having been of no avail." In my mind this liquor trade amongst the natives constitutes one of the great grievances under which the mining industry is labouring, and requires energetic and immediate suppression. The administration of the Liquor Law should be placed under the control of a Local Government Board, having for assistance as advisory members representatives of the mining industry.

I am convinced in my own mind that gold thefts have been and are still taking place on these fields, but to what extent it is impossible for me to say, and I would not like to venture an opinion. It is impossible to have a perfect check on all the gold won from the mill and cyanide works. The greatest security against thefts rests on the fact that the men engaged in this specific responsible work are regarded as men of honour and beyond suspicion, which, from an ethical point of view, is highly satisfactory, and cannot fail to raise the standard and the sense of their morality. The fact of a detective continually watching over them would, in my judgment, destroy the object it hopes to serve, and the men, if engaged under such conditions, would deteriorate, or tend to cause an exchange of honest men for such as would require close watching. However anxious one might be to have a perfect check system, this, as experience can prove to you, is hardly possible. I assume, guided herein by certain circumstances, that gold thefts are being practised to a large extent on the Rand. I think that the general opinion of mine managers and representatives of the industry is that the men employed in the reduction works are inherently honest, but it is the instigation which they receive from the outside which has such tempting and demoralising influences. The great necessity, according to my judgment, lies in detecting and bringing to justice the offender who illicitly buys the amalgam, and it is for this reason primarily that we require a special organisation of well trained men to apprehend such offenders against the law. Previous witnesses have already referred to its deficient administration, and we all know that many men in this place are nominally carrying on a trade which they are virtually not prac-

Marginal notes:
- Table of returns of 74 companies concerning administration of Liquor Law.
- Police supervision under Liquor Law inadequate.
- Mr. Johns' letter and the granting of licences.
- Local government board for administration of Liquor Law.
- Gold thefts.
- Best security against gold thefts.
- Special detective force necessary to bring to justice illicit gold buyers.

Legislation against gold thefts: its administration defective. tising. In order to effect apprehension and conviction it is necessary that laws shou exist which are applicable to these special circumstances. In view of past experienc I respectfully submit that the Law of Illict Gold Buying is defective, and that t. administration of the law is inefficient. I will apply my first remarks to the la itself, and will show to you where it is defective, and would further suggest tl Articles 145 and 146 of the Gold Law. greatest urgency in getting such law altered. Article 145 of the Gold law says th no person shall carry on trade in amalgam, &c., under which is included the purcha. or bartering, &c., of amalgam, &c., unless he possess a special licence to do so, fc which he must pay £10 per annum, with this proviso: that an individual digger company shall not be required to take out a licence for the sale of amalgam, &c. Tl fine for the infringement of this law is a sum not exceeding £100, or imprisonmer or both together for the first offence; for the second offence a fine not exceedir £200, or imprisonment, not exceeding 12 months, or both together; and for a furth. offence according to the judgment of the Court. Article 146 says that any persc found in the possession of amalgam, and who can give no proof of having obtained in a lawful manner, shall be punished with a fine not exceeding £500, or imprisonmer not to exceed two years, or both together, for the first offence; and for the secon offence with a fine not to exceed £1,000, or three years, or both together, and fc further offences, fines or imprisonment according to the judgment of the Court T my mind the defect of the present Gold Law with respect to illicit gold buying is thi it neither goes far enough nor is sufficiently explicit in its meaning as to what coi stitutes unlawful possession. Section 146 merely throws the onus of proof on th accused to show that he obtained gold found in his possession in a lawful manner, bt we are left in doubt as to what these words may mean. Purchase, sale, barter an exchange are in themselves lawful, and they are not necessarily rendered unlawful b the operation of Section 145. This section only provides that persons dealing i amalgam, &c., shall take out a licence to do so under certain comparatively sma penalties. Consequently the penal operation of Section 146 is rendered nugatory, fc under an indictment under this section the accused has only to prove purchase, barte or exchange to ensure his acquittal. The prosecution is then thrown back on Sectio 145, which, as already pointed out, does nothing more than provide a penalty for ne taking out a licence. This to my mind constitutes an ineffectual law which I thin Proofs of inefficient administration of legislation against gold thefts. should be altered. That the administration of the Gold Thefts Law is not an efficier one is sufficiently demonstrated by the fact that no convictions have taken place i the past, and that where there have been detections, and where after endless pain an trouble and expense have been incurred by the companies to effect detection, thos who have infringed the law have been able to escape. I suggest a Local Governmer Local government board for administration of laws against gold thefts. Board, who shall have the power to enrol a special detective force for administratio of the law, and that an advisory board of representatives of the mines be at th disposal of the permanent board.

Native labour.   It is needless for me to state that the mines have to go to considerable expens Supply of native labour. and trouble to effect an adequate supply of natives. The supply formerly has nc been so great as now due to the expansion of the industry, and for a considerabl time there has been a great shortfall. If you were to examine returns and reports c companies during the last year, as I have had the opportunity of doing, you woul see much of the decreased returns are due to the scarcity of native labour. The chic supply of natives is from the East Coast, equal to 50 per cent. The supply from th North is about 20 per cent. I feel convinced that the supply from the North can b considerably increased, seeing that the labour of these natives is regarded as efficien I may mention, in qualification of this, that the Wolhuter Company brought down 5C boys; they have stayed their full time with the manager and he has been we

ised with them. I say it is in the interests of the Government that they should us by every means possible to bring the labour from within the boundaries of Republic. Firstly, because of the less expense of bringing down natives to this tre; secondly, because it is more in the interests of the Government that the ney which the boys earn remain and be spent in this country, and not go out of it; thirdly, because the amount of money that is taken out of the country would ain here. I can further say that if the Government were to assist in the supply natives from within this country they would by these means be serving two poses. According to the native laws the actual tax per native in the native tricts amounts to about £2 10s.; the only exception to the liability of this pay-nt being natives residing as servants under white persons. Thus, if the dignity of our were impressed upon them by the enforcement of this law, we are likely to a larger supply. The other purpose served would be—that such boy coming to rk would earn money, and after completing his term of service he would have ficient funds to enable him on his return to his district, when called upon by the vernment, to pay all his taxes, which would be an additional revenue to the vernment. At present one-half of our supply comes from the East Coast, and the nstrous sum of 26s. 10d. is levied on each native for his passport by the Portu-se. It costs, on the average, 56s. 6d. to 60s. to bring down natives to this centre m this part of the country, which is only 300 miles off from here; which is, in my nion, an excessive burden on the industry, and necessarily increases the price of ive labour. In connection with this matter, I will refer to the rates for carrying se natives. I hold that it would be to the interests of the Government and this ustry to facilitate this traffic as much as possible, at the least possible expense the companies, and, if anything, sooner to put an increased rate of conveying them their return journey. My opinion is, that the rates of transport of natives are ogether too high. From Volksrust to Johannesburg is only 170 miles, and the rge is 20s. 6d. per head; from Indwe to here a distance of 543 miles, 25s. 3d. is rged; from Komatipoort to here, a distance of 351 miles, 18s. 9d. is charged, and the return journey 39s. is charged. The boys on their return to Indwe have the ion of engaging a truck; 25 and over can engage a truck, which works out at £1 ead. Now I argue that as a good many boys can go in trucks, and if boys are ught in trucks they should be carried on what I would consider a reasonable ck-load basis. On this basis boys would be brought from Indwe to here for about . From Volksrust to Johannesburg, 170 miles, the native would pay 7s. 6d., tead of as at present 20s. 6d.; from Komatipoort to here, 351 miles, the native uld pay 11s. 5½d. instead of the present amount of 18s. 9d. I will now go to show at the mining industry has done to try and facilitate the transport of natives from north where there is no railway. An organisation is in existence for the con-ance of natives. We have a staff of men in Pietersburg, who collect the natives l bring them to the depot there. Our next depot is at Potgieter's Rust, 20 miles ay, another depot at Vroom's Store, 30 miles distant, a depot at Kaufman's Store, miles from there, one at Pienaar's River, 25 miles from the latter, and one at uwkraal, 30 miles distant, and in Pretoria we had the use of Beckett's compound. from this you will observe that the journey is completed in eight days, and the s have shelter and protection at each stage, and there can be no cause for plaint in this respect. This route should be encouraged, and in my opinion the vernment should appoint additional commissioners in the Northern districts to ist in bringing the material to Pietersburg. I should like to point out to you what Cape Government has done in the supply of natives. They have given notice ough their kaffir chiefs to collect native labour, and the Government have brought

Marginal notes:

Government co-operation for supply of native labour from within the Republic required.

Taxation of natives.

Supply of native labour from East Coast.

Cost of transport of native labour.

Railway rates for transport of native labour.

Suggested reduction of railway rates for transport of native labour.

Government aid required for supply of native labour

Native Commissioners.

Cape Government and native labour.

it to Imvani Station, where we have taken delivery during the months of Janua
and February last of between 400 to 500 natives, and 2,797 during the eight mon
in 1896. The Cape Government have depots at Umtata. I can further show y
letters which we have received from the Commissioners of Natives in the C
Colony, telling us that their depots are full, and urging upon us to take the nativ
I merely wish to show, to illustrate by this, that we should not want to look for
supply from this quarter at all, but that we should get it from within the borders
this country. I would like to impress upon you also the necessity, as stated befc
of bringing down these natives at as low a rate as possible, and that if it is to c

Statement show-
ing losses of
companies on
unrecovered
premiums paid
for native la-
bour.
anything at all it could be put on in the return journey, inasmuch as we have t
large outlay in the beginning so uncertain of recovery. My statement, which i
complete one, shows the amount of premiums paid for obtaining native labour, whi
has not been recovered. In 1895, taking six companies only, the loss was £7,317 ;
1896 14 companies showed a loss of £21,335 ; in 1897 17 companies show a total l
of £31,823. The latter represents as nearly as possible a loss of 75 per cent. on t

Loss of Lang-
laagte Estate
Company on
unrecovered
premiums paid
for native la-
bour.
outlay. I should like to draw particular attention to one company, the Langlaag
Estate. The number of boys they employ is 1,790, and the gross premium
obtaining these boys was £12,120 ; they have only recovered from these boys £5:
leaving a loss of £11,589. I will take the case of the Bonanza Company ; they h

Loss of Bonanza
Company on
unrecovered
premiums paid
for native la-
bour.
paid £750 for obtaining boys, and they had not recovered 6d. I now wish to dr
your attention to a matter connected with the Pass Law, which I omitted yesterd:
namely a defect which also means a great expense for the company. The prese

Defective admin-
istration of
Pass Law.
offices at Boksburg, Johannesburg, and Krugersdorp are too far apart on t
distinctive mines for proper administration. As an instance I will take a gang
boys arriving at Elandsfontein Station for the Geldenhuis Estate. A boy is fi
walked off to the company's compound, and then he is walked off to Boksburg a:
back, eight miles each way, for the purpose of getting registered. This tak
altogether one day. The boys have to be provided with bread at 3s. per dozen, equ
to 3d. per man. At Boksburg he is delayed and has frequently to camp out ov
night, with the result that many desert. Another defect in the law is in the movi
of natives from one district to another. No transfer books exist whereby a boy wl
for instance, wishes to go from his district to Johannesburg, can go and get his distri
pass and his pass for the unexpired period of the month transferred to that distri
which in itself necessitates an unnecessary expenditure. An illustration will bett
explain the point. On the 18th January 600 boys were transferred from the Crœs
to the Rietfontein Mine. They were then in possession of a pass paid until the end
January. In order to pass they had to come to the Johannesburg Office, and the
take out a "reis" pass for the Boksburg district at 1s. per head. They then had
walk to Boksburg, arriving there on the 20th, for the purpose of taking out t
district pass and their new pass for the month, in that district 2s. per head, a distan
from there and back to the Rietfontein Mine of 27 miles. As the passes only r\
from the 1st to the 1st, the pass taken out on the 20th lapsed on the expiration of t\
month, and a new pass had to be taken out from the 1st of the month, so that t\
expenditure per boy in being transferred from one district to another amounted to '

White wages.
I would point out to you that, according to the evidence of a previous witness,
estimates the average cost of white labour at 28 per cent. on the total cost. /
argument took place as to whether white labour is not too highly paid. In r
opinion it is not. The opinion expressed was that the pay of European labour is t
high in this country and should go down. But in adducing these arguments, I thi\
one of the principal considerations is to ascertain whether the men employed on t
mines have only to look after themselves or to supply the wants of their families

ell. This I think is a very important question, which may throw a different complexion altogether on the pay of white labour. I have obtained statistics of the returns f European labour from about 53 companies (see Statement E), which goes to show lat they employ a total of 3,620 miners. Of these, 470 are married miners with families n their properties; 1,195 are married miners, but their families are away from here; nd 1,955 are single men. The number of miners who have left during the last six reeks are 827, of which number approximately 380 left the country and 480 remain 1 the country. This shows the following percentage: that 54 per cent. are single ien and 46 per cent. are married, of which 33.1 per cent. are absent. It therefore evolves upon them to support their families. I think it ought to be the desire of the fovernment to make it possible for these miners not to have to live apart from their imilies, but that the conditions should exist which would enable them to live in this puntry, which in itself would add to the revenue of the country. As regards white ibour in itself, I will acknowledge that the figures of Mr. Catlin would go to show hat by greater pay a greater amount of efficiency is to be obtained. Consequently I hink it should be the object of every mine manager to see that his labourer improves 1 efficiency, and does more work, which would mean a saving. A system which is ow being introduced, and which in my opinion is the only system which will work ut satisfactorily, is the contract system, whereby a man is told to do a certain amount f work for a certain sum of money. This expedites the work, and is found to be the heapest. I do not approve of the bonus system. I may mention one thing in regard o white wages, we have an instance in point of a man—a fitter on the Central Ore Reduction Company—receiving £30 a month. He got married, and the moment he ad an increase of family, he found the conditions did not enable him to keep his amily here, and he was obliged to send them away, the cost of living being too high.

According to the Chamber of Mines returns, I find that 53 producing companies n the Rand have returned an average of 11½ dwts. per ton. However, on analysis, it hows that the average is only brought up by a few companies. Of the 53 companies,]ur companies average 24.4 dwts., or 7.5 per cent. of the total producing companies; wo companies average 17 dwts., or 3.8 per cent.; 16 companies average equal to 30 per ent.; and 30 companies average 7.9 dwts, or 58 per cent. Gentlemen, I wish to npress upon you now that the backbone of the industry is not the four companies]hich average the high returns, nor the two; it is the 30 companies which are only eturning 7.9 dwts., and which are struggling unavailingly with the existing impedi- ients. I go very much further, and I say the condition of affairs ought to be such hat many of the companies which are to-day unable to work may be brought into life gain. I would draw your attention in reference to these 30 companies to the very nall margin on which they are working. I may say the results have been worked ut reliably, not from estimates taken from the Chamber of Mines, but figures taken rom the most careful investigation of the balance sheets of the companies, and in the iajority of cases checked by Mr. Jennings. The average of these 30 companies shows return of 30s. 0.4d. per ton, which leaves a profit per ton of 1s. 10d. This will show ou how very close these companies are working, and how little it would require to iake the average show no profit whatever. The companies I refer to include]mpanies which have been producing from the earliest days. In regard to the ividends, I should like to point out to you that 20 companies have only paid dividends uring 1896, the amounts paid being £1,523,581, (see statement F) showing a decrease 1 dividends over the previous year of over £540,000. That in itself is very significant. Vhilst these companies paid 23 3-8 per cent. on their issued capital, taking it at to- ays market value, they returned 10.38 per cent., but if you apply these total dividends ver 51 producing companies you will find that the total return of these companies

H

Statistics of European labour of 53 companies.

Number of married miners with families on their properties; number of married miners with families absent

Number of unmarried miners.

White wages.

Contract system.

The bonus system.

Chamber of Mines' gold returns of companies.

Percentages of 53 companies on total amount of gold produced.

Small margins of profits of 30 of the 53 producing companies.

Dividends of companies.

Average of total dividends on 51 producing companies.

E.   **RETURN OF EUROPEAN LABOUR,**

Shewing Number of Married and Single Miners, and Number which left during previous Six Weeks from 30th April, 1897.

COMPANIES.	Married Miners with Families on the Property.	Married Miners with Families Abroad.	Single Men.	Miners Left Mine during past Six Weeks.	Of which Left the Country Approximately.	Approximate Number Remaining in Country.
Banket	0	6	0	6	0	6
Bonanza	3	11	23	5	0	5
Champ d'Or	6	6	4	0	0	0
Cassel Colliery	10	5	30	20	10	10
City and Suburban	62	62	184	64	26	38
Durban Roodepoort	5	17	13	1	1	0
Ferreira Company	15	48	39	14	10	4
East Rand Proprietary	30	150	200	110	55	55
George Goch	6	33	22	8	2	6
Geldenhuis Main Reef	0	6	4	0	0	0
Geldenhuis Estate and G. M.	3	30	23	15	4	11
Geldenhuis Deep	5	96	193	28	8	20
Glen Deep	2	?	?	38	31	7
Henry Nourse	2	29	36	8	3	5
Horsham Monitor	1	9	2	1	0	1
Jumpers	5	23	33	9	1	8
Jubilee	5	12	22	8	7	1
May Consolidated	4	?	?	21	5	16
Meyer and Charlton	6	10	16	13	3	10
Modderfontein	2	24	?	83	40	43
New Heriot	23	52	114	9	3	6
New Primrose	16	9	52	32	3	29
New Spes Bona	0	7	2	0	0	0
New Kleinfontein	5	19	19	0	0	0
Nourse Deep	19	73	54	18	3	15
Princess Estate	2	17	22	7	3	4
Rand G. M. Company	2	1	1	0	0	0
Rietfontein A	0	8	13	3	2	1
Robinson Randfontein	1	15	9	15	3	12
Roodepoort G. M. Co.	1	0	15	7	3	4
Roodepoort United M. R.	3	6	9	13	7	6
Rose Deep	2	34	69	14	8	6
Salisbury	3	20	3	2	1	1
Stanhope	2	2	1	0	0	0
South Randfontein	2	8	25	16	16	0
Springs Colliery	18	4	49	17	0	17
Treasury	0	9	19	7	2	5
Transvaal Coal	3	6	14	8	2	6
Van Ryn Estate	2	33	22	14	10	4
Village Main Reef	45	17	82	12	2	10
Vogels. Estate	2	0	22	4	0	4
West Rand	4	?	?	12	12	0
Wemmer	2	25	21	3	2	1
West Roodepoort Deep	0	?	?	32	7	25
Wishaw Coal Co.	1	0	0	0	0	0
Windsor Co.	1	0	0	0	0	0
Wolhuter	17	19	34	12	4	8
Robinson Co.	7	63	29	7	1	6
Rietfontein Estate	1	10	15	14	1	13
Violet Consolidated	1	2	9	6	2	4
Roodepoort G. M. Co.	1	9	5	0	0	0
Simmer and Jack	97	116	322	63	60	3
Crown Deep, Ltd.	15	34	60	28	17	11
	470	1,195	1,955	827	380	447

RECAPITULATION.

Companies, 3620 total Miners :—

    12·9 % Married Men on the Properties with Families.
    33·1 % Married Men on the Properties without Families.
    54·0 % Single Men.

  7 Miners left during the past six weeks, of which 46% have left the country; 54% have remained in the country.

y comes to 4·3 per cent. of the money invested at present market rates. Now I nk that everyone connected with mining will admit that a 4½ return per cent. on one's ney in mining, equal to a railway return, is not what capitalists expect with all the ks appertaining to mining. I think all Governments will acknowledge, where mining arried on, that a certain amount of risk is attached to mining, and that therefore the ustry should be assisted, knowing full well that a liberal percentage on the capital lay is justified. A question I wish to bring before you as one of supreme ortance, is to see in which manner the better condition of affairs can be brought ut in the mining industry, so as to assist us in restoring the capital which has been lting away from us, and which is necessary for the development of a good many nes which are silent at the present moment. I feel this, that unless relief is given, will only rest on those few companies to bear the burdens of the industry. A good *Necessity of development of non-producing mines.* mber of companies which were on the list of working and developing companies, d which are all pillars on which the whole welfare of the country rests, will be pping away, throwing increased pressure on the remaining ones. It is therefore cessary, and this is now the critical moment, to bring about better conditions. I ll say that this refers in particular to the question of dynamite, railway freights, *Reliefs desired.* d general import dues, and also to the influence of the Government to see that the er neighbouring Colonies that derive benefits from this industry are reasonable. I ll not travel over the same ground. I agree perfectly with the previous evidence th reference to dynamite, but I will say that I am strongly in favour of seeing free *Dynamite.* de in this article, with a reasonable duty for the Government. As far as the *Free trade in dynamite.* lway concession is concerned, in my opinion, gentlemen, I believe that the *Reduction of railway rates and expropriation.* vernment should be determined to bring down the rates to a reasonable proportion, en probably we would find that the expropriation can be affected at a later date der better conditions than to-day, but that would absolutely depend on the termination of the Government now to see that the tariffs are considerably reduced, ling which, it is much the best that expropriation takes place now instead of at ch greater cost later on. I believe that in many respects a great reduction can be *Reduction of cost of living.* de, which will bring down living expenses to a reasonable basis. I also believe at in the question of coal rates that there could be more advantageous tariffs, so that *Coal railway rates.* ere we find mines to the west of Johannesburg, which are acknowledged to be orer than mines to the east, the railway freights to them ought not to differentiate *Differential railway rates on coal.* m those in the immediate proximity of Johannesburg. In my opinion the tariff m Johannesburg, going west, should not exceed the rates from Elandsfontein to hannesburg, or they should differentiate in their favour, so as to give these mpanies in the west a chance. I could mention that some of the coal bills in the est Rand exceed the amount of saving in railage to the mines to the east of hannesburg; or, in other words, the difference in the coal rates would cover the total penses of the coal bill of some West Rand mines. How the general relief can be ought about it is hardly for me to suggest, but I do believe, without going into *Maintenance of State revenue.* ures, that if we get considerable relief the revenue could still remain on a level. By ving greater facilities to the mines, gentlemen, you would indirectly derive great nefit, you will enable companies which at the present moment cannot work to work, *Compensation for reduction*

of State reven-
ue through re-
lief requested. and you will bring about an expansion of trade and vitality. I fully believe that could be brought about within the margin of the expenditure of the country.

F.

TABLE

SHOWING

1st. Amount of Dividends paid by 20 Rand Companies for 1896.

2nd. Interest percentage on Issued Capital.

3rd. Interest percentage on Market Value, May 1st, 1897.

Name of Company.	Total Share Capital.	Issued Share Capital.	Market Value of Issued Capital on May 1st.	Dividends in 1896.	Per Cent. on Issued Capital.	Per Cent on Market Value
	£	£	£	£		
1 City and Suburban	1,360,000	1,360,000	930,000	68,000	5	7·31
2 Crown Reef ...	120,000	120,000	1,230,000	132,000	110	10·73
3 Durban Roodepoort	135,000	125,000	656,250	56,250	45	8·57
4 Ferreira	90,000	90,000	1,440,000	247,500	275	17·18
5 Geldenhuis Estate ...	200,000	200,000	525,000	25,000	12½	4·76
6 Henry Nourse ...	125,000	125,000	656,250	37,500	30	5·71
7 Johannesb'g Pioneer	21,000	21,000	199,500	84,000	400	42·11
8 Jubilee	50,000	50,000	300,000	30,000	60	10·00
9 Jumpers	100,000	100,000	281,250	30,000	30	10·66
10 Langlaagte Estate...	500,000	470,000	1,586,250	141,000	30	8·89
11 May Consolidated ...	275,000	275,000	481,250	55,000	20	11·43
12 Meyer and Charlton	85,000	85,000	371,875	17,000	20	4·57
13 New Chimes ...	100,000	100,000	25,000	5,000	5	20·00
14 New Heriot ...	115,000	111,864	811,014	95,084	85	11·72
15 Robinson	275,000	2,750,000	3,645,750	330,000	12	9·05
16 Stanhope	35,000	34,000	23,375	1,700	5	7·27
17 United Main Reef ...	150,000	150,000	431,250	37,500	25	8·69
18 Van Ryn	200,000	177,000	273,375	32,000	20	11·70
19 Wemmer	80,000	80,000	460,000	47,500	75	10·33
20 Worcester	100,000	93,722	351,487	51,547	55	14·66
	6,591,000	6,517,586	14,678,876	1,523,581	23⅜%	10·38

Profits of 30 of
51 producing
companies. I now want to come back to the figures of yesterday in reference to the cost 30 companies which I mentioned. I wish to say that in re-checking the figures found a slight difference. The profit of these companies is 2s. 5d. per ton instead 1s. 10d., as I stated yesterday. I also wish to draw attention to the fact that doing this I wish to draw no comparisons of one company as against another. All

sh to demonstrate was that these 30 companies crushed during 15 months 3,000,000 as of rock, and that is the result. I may mention that I have taken 30 companies owing the lowest yield of the 53 producing companies, and I include in my list, of urse, companies showing good returns. For instance, 14 companies out of that 30 ve crushed 2,036,000 tons, which show profit, without depreciation, of 7s. 3·658d., d with depreciation, 4s. 5·01d. per ton. I further want to draw attention to the ct, taking the figures, for instance, of a witness who appeared to-day before you, as the benefit a reduction of 6s. a ton would mean to some of the companies I am terested in a company which has crushed 72,000 tons without making any profit. his company, with a reduction of 6s. per ton, would return a profit of £22,000. In ferring also to the railways, there is one thing that I should like to draw your rticular attention to, and that is the necessity of trying to bring about a reduction rates. Other Governments have shown a desire to do so, but they have been mewhat prevented from doing this.

Beneficial results of reduction of 6s. per ton on working costs.

Reduction of railway rates prevented by Netherlands Railway.

Mr. *Hugo.*

Who prevented them ?—The Netherlands Railway Company. I can give an stance. I have a letter here from the Cape Government, dated 24th July, which ates : " In consequence of representations made by the Netherlands Railway ompany it will be necessary to raise the rate for the conveyance of cement to the ransvaal for rough goods to third-class rate from the 1st September."

Increase of railway rate on cement.

Mr. *Albu.*

What year is that ?—1895. I have another letter of the 14th March, 1895, in ference to reduction of the rough goods rate. It was the intention of the Cape overnment to assist us in reducing tariffs—by rough goods I mean timber, rails, and l heavy goods. The Netherlands Company immediately thereon put on an increase their railway rates on rough goods from 1s. to 1s. 8d. per 100lbs., which to a rtain extent counteracted the intentions of the Cape Colony. At the same time the ape Colony felt that though the Netherlands Railway Company had increased their eight, they at least should not do it, and whatever the Netherlands Railway ompany increased they reduced. I will read a letter from Mr. Difford : " With ference to the Netherlands Railway Company's advertisement of an increase of 8d. r 100lbs. for the conveyance of rough goods from Mid-Vaal River to Johannesburg d other stations on and after 1st April next, I have the honour to state that the ape Government does not intend to disturb its through rates from the ports to either iljoensdrift or stations along the Vaal River, and that the existing through rates om the ports will therefore remain in operation. On traffic for intermediate stations additional 8d. levied by the Netherlands Company will be charged, the port rates, owever, being the maximum charge." I should like to mention transit dues, which, think, the other Governments are absolutely not entitled to, and I think should be moved in their entirety. The argument I have heard mentioned is that the ransvaal Government are maintaining the transit rate of 3 per cent. for any goods ssing through the Transvaal for the North. I think, for instance, if this transit ere removed, the other Governments would also be open to reason. We have to pay ties on produce coming from Basutoland. The Orange Free State, having free ade with Basutoland, take their produce from there. The Orange Free State have, owever, free trade with us again here, and what stands to their advantage are the eavy protective duties here for produce which is imported. The Orange Free State ke their grain free from Basutoland, and sell us their produce at increased prices der the protective duty. I merely wish to convey that we are paying more for our

Increase of rate on rough goods by the Netherlands Railway.

Transit dues.

G. CAPITALIZATION COMPARISON, SEPTEMBER, 1895—MAY, 1897.

Statement showing 105 Companies which had a Capital in SEPTEMBER, 1895, of £29,521,735, which, at ruling rates during the month, which was the height of the boom, meant a capitalization of £150,470,191 roughly.

These same Companies to-day have a Capital of £36,808,155, and at ruling rates show a capitalization of £53,262,535 roughly, or a difference of £97,364,402 compared with September, 1895.

There are only two Companies to-day which show a higher capitalization than in September, 1895, viz.:—BONANZA: Capital £200,000, which, at current rates, shows a difference of £210,000 in favour of to-day, and JOHANNESBURG PIONEER Co.: Capital £21,000, which shows £21,000.

Alexandra	250,000	27/6	343,750	250,000	4/6	56,250	287,500
Angelo	175,000	£6/12/6	1,159,375	225,000	55/-	618,750	540,625
Angelo Debentures ...						150,000	
Angle Tharsis	92,500	55/-	254,375	150,000 M. Reef.	13/-	97,500	156,875
Aurora	65,000	37/6	121,875	65,000	12/6	40,625	81,250
Aurora West, United ...	100,000	55/-	275,000	140,000	15/-	105,000	170,000
Balmoral	100,000	65/-	325,000	130,000	17/-	110,500	214,500
Banket	180,000	10/-	90,000	111,500	7/6	41,812	48,188
Bantjes	435,000	5/7/6	2,338,125	435,000	18/9	407,812	1,930,313
Benoni Gold	200,000	75/-	750,000	204,100	7/6	76,537	673,463
Block A Randfontein ...	480,000	20/-	480,000	480,000	7/-	168,000	312,000
Champ d'Or...	133,000	76/3	507,062	133,000	15/-	99,750	407,312
Chimes West	150,000	70/-	525,000	175,000	6/3	54,687	470,313
Consolidated Deep Levels...	187,250	7/2/6	1,334,156	187,250	57/6	538,343	795,813
Crown Deep	250,000	12½	3,125,000	250,000	9¼	2,312,500	812,500
Crown Reef...	120,000	11⅜	1,365,000	120,000	10⅛	1,215,000	150,000
City and Suburban ...	1,360,000 In £4 shares	6⅞	2,337,500	1,360,000 In £4 shares	66/3	1,126,250	1,211,250
Driefontein	175,000	81/3	710,938	175,000	26/3	229,687	481,251
Driefontein Debentures ...						100,000	
Durban Roodepoort ...	125,000	8¼	1,031,250	125,000	5¼	656,250	375,000
Durban Roodepoort Deep	290,000	5¾	1,667,500	290,000	37/6	543,750	1,123,750
East Rand Proprietary ...	650,000	12⅜	8,043,750	746,325	30/9	1,147,474	6,896,276
Ferreira	89,000	19½	1,735,500	89,000	16	1,424,000	311,500
French Rand	480,000	80/-	1,920,000	560,000	17/3	483,000	1,437,000
Geldenhuis Deep	280,000	10½	2,940,000	280,000	3⅛	875,000	2,065,000
Geldenhuis Deep Debent.						160,000	
Geldenhuis Estate... ...	200,000	6⅜	1,275,000	200,000	50/-	500,000	775,000
Geldenhuis Main	150,000	28/9	215,625	150,000	11/3	84,075	131,250
George Goch	160,000	65/-	520,000	325,000	20/-	325,000	195,000
Ginsberg	152,500	35/-	266,875	160,000	30/-	240,000	26,875
Glencairn	225,000	90/-	1,012,500	500,000	33/9	843,750	168,750
Goldfields' Deep	600,000	13¼	7,950,000	600,000	95/-	2,850,000	5,100,000
Goldfields' Deep Debent....							
Gordon Estate	175,000	20/-	175,000	197,500	3/9	37,031	137,969
Great Britain	60,100	60/-	180,300	60,100	20/-	60,100	120,200
Henry Nourse	125,000	7/1/3	882,812	125,000	5½	687,500	195,312
Horsham Monitor	190,000	40/-	380,000	190,000	2/6	23,750	356,250
Jubilee	50,000	9½	475,000	50,000	5¾	287,500	187,500
Jumpers	100,000	8/1/3	806,250	100,000	55/-	275,000	531,250
Kleinfontein Central ...	225,000	65/-	731,250	225,000	7/6	84,375	646,875
Knight's Deep	330,000	3⅞	1,278,750	330,000	15/-	247,500	1,031,250
Leeuwpoort...	95,000	13/3	62,937	95,000	2/3	10,687	52,250
Lancaster	234,500	46/3	542,281	234,500	33/9	395,718	146,563
Langlaagte Block B ...	535,000	61/3	1,638,437	535,000	13/9	367,812	1,273,625
Langlaagte Deep	75,000	40/-	150,000	75,000	13/-	48,750	101,250
Langlaagte Estate ..	470,000	6/16/3	3,201,875	470,000	70/-	1,645,000	1,556,875
Langlaagte Royal... ...	180,000	6⅝	1,192,500	180,000	6/3	56,250	1,136,250
Langlaagte Star	240,000	60/-	720,000	240,000	7/6	90,000	630,000
Luipaard's Vlei	350,000	40/-	700,000	350,000	15/-	262,500	437,500
Marievale Nigel	250,000	72/6	906,250	250,000	7/6	93,750	812,500
Main Reef	135,000	42/6	286,875	135,000	13/9	92,812	194,063
May Consolidated... ...	275,000	76/3	1,048,437	275,000	32/6	446,875	601,562

CAPITALIZATION COMPARISON, September, 1895—May, 1897.—*(continued.)*

Meyer and Charlton ...	85,000	£6/17/6	584,375	85,000	87/6	371,875	212,500
Minerva	150,000	67/6	506,250	150,000	2/6	18,750	487,500
Modderfontein	200,000	15/7/6	3,075,000	1,000,000	33/9	421,875	2,653,125
				£4 share.			
Modderfontein Extension	325,000	85/-	1,381,250	£325,000	8/9	142,187	1,239,063
Mijnpacht Randfontein ...	657,500	25/-	821,875	657,500	3/9	123,281	698,594
Molyneux Mines	220,000	58/9	646,250	220,000	10/-	110,000	536,250
Molyneux West	300,000	15/-	225,000	300,000	2/6	37,500	187,500
New Chimes	100,000	57/6	287,500	100,000	3/9	18,750	268,750
New Comet...	182,486	87/6	798,376	182,486	12/6	114,053	684,323
New Crœsus	500,000	61/3	1,537,500	500,000	6/6	162,500	1,375,000
New Florida	125,000	77/6	484,375	162,500	10/3	83,281	401,024
New Heidelberg Roodept.	125,000	51/-	318,750	160,000	6/3	50,000	268,750
New Heriot...	85,000	11½	977,500	111,864	7/7/6	824,997	152,503
New Midas Estate... ...	100,000	82/6	412,500	137,500	15/-	103,125	309,375
New Orion	160,000	95/-	760,000	160,000	1/3	10,000	750,000
New Primrose	280,000	7½	2,100,000	300,000	3 9-16ths	1,068,750	1,031,250
New Rietfontein	270,000	61/3	1,636,875	270,000	17/6	236,250	1,400,625
New Spes Bona	160,000	57/6	460,000	160,000	12/6	100,000	360,000
New Steyn Estate... ...	190,000	40/-	380,000	190,000	11/3	106,875	273,125
Nourse Deep	375,000	£9	3,375,000	375,000	£2⅛	796,875	2,578,125
North Randfontein ...	185,250	53/9	497,859	185,250	22/6	208,406	289,453
New Kleinfontein	185,000	6½	1,202,500	231,250	27/6	317,968	884,532
New Blue Sky	150,000	31/-	232,500	150,000	6/-	45,000	187,500
Nigel	199,300	7/8/9	1,482,293	199,300	31/3	311,406	1,171,887
Nigel Deep	500,000	77/6	1,937,500	500,000	10/-	250,000	1,687,500
Paarl Central	200,000	46/3	462,500	400,000	11/3	225,000	237,500
Porges Randfontein ...	437,500	£5	2,187,500	437,500	18/9	410,155	1,777,345
Princess Estate	160,000	85/-	680,000	160,000	27/6	220,000	460,000
Randfontein Estates ...	2,000,000	82/6	8,250,000	2,000,000	27/6	2,750,000	5,500,000
Rand Mines	332,708	£44¼	14,722,329	332,708	£16	5,323,328	9,339,001
Robinson	2,750,000	£11	6,050,000	2,750,000	£7	3,850,000	2,200,000
	£5 share.			£5 share.			
Robinson Deep	400,000	£9¼	3,700,000	400,000	6⅛	2,450,000	1,250,000
Robinson Randfontein ...	600,000	35/-	1,050,000	600,000	18/9	562,500	487,500
Roodepoort Central ...	220,000	65/-	715,000	220,000	20/-	220,000	495,000
Roodepoort Deep	175,000	92/6	809,375	175,000	12/6	109,375	700,000
Roodepoort U. M. R. ...	150,000	7/7/6	1,106,250	150,000	58/9	440,625	665,625
Roodepoort Kimberley ...	125,000	67/6	421,875	125,000	28/9	179,687	242,188
Rose Deep	355,000	£6¼	2,218,750	355,000	50/-	887,500	1,331,250
Ruby	23,114	£11	254,254				
Salisbury	93,000	95/-	441,750	100,000	27/6	137,500	304,250
Simmer & Jack	250,000	£27¼	6,812,500	4,940,000	50/-	2,470,000	4,342,500
				£5 share.			
Stanhope	34,000	18/9	31,875	34,000	12/6	21,250	10,625
Treasury	540,000	72/6	489,375	540,000	30/-	202,500	286,875
	£4 share.			£4 share.			
Van Ryn	160,000	£9	1,440,000	160,000	32/6	260,000	1,180,000
Van Ryn West	120,000	£5	600,000	120,000	17/6	105,000	495,000
Vesta	130,000	35/-	227,500	130,000	3/9	24,375	203,125
Village Main	180,000	£9	1,620,000	180,000	65/-	585,000	1,035,000
Vogelstruis Estates ...	200,000	£6¼	1,250,000	200,000	28/9	287,500	962,500
Vogelstruis Cons. Deep ...	327,500	80/-	1,310,000	327,500	10/-	163,750	1,146,250
Vulcan	90,000	12/-	54,000	90,000	3/3	14,625	39,375
Vogelstruisfontein... ...	41,800	7/-	14,630	41,000	2/9	5,747	8,883
Violet	600,000	15/-	450,000	800,000	8/9	262,500	187,500
West Rand Mines... ...	400,000	63/9	1,275,000	400,000	13/9	275,000	1,000,000
Wolhuter	215,000	12½	2,687,500	860,000	77/6	833,125	1,854,375
				In £4 shares			
Witwatersrand	250,000	10¼	2,562,500	250,000	55/-	687,500	1,875,000
Worcester	90,727	85/-	385,590	93,722	70/-	328,027	57,563
York...	90,000	20/-	90,000	90,000	9/6	42,750	47,250
	95,217,325		150,470,171	36,808,155		53,262,535	97,364,402

grain than we really should pay. This is a very important matter, seeing
consumption of mealies, for instance, of some companies—I will take one compa
the Modderfontein. They use 4,118 bags per year, at a cost of £5,560 last y
working out at 27s. per bag. 1,700 bags of these came from the Transvaal; 500 fi
the Orange Free State; and 1,700 came from America.

Coming back once more to the question of capitalisation of companies and
shrinkage of capital. I have drawn up a statement (see Statement G) showing
enormous depreciation of values of companies. I have taken 105 companies which sh

a capital of £36,000,000, which in 1895 showed a capitalisation of £150,000,000,
they to-day only show the valuation of £53,000,000, showing a depreciation
over £90,000,000. This is exclusive of another 115 companies which have an issu
capital of £29,000,000, and which, I should say, had also considerably appreciated
value during 1895 and since depreciated Regarding the companies referred to by
above, I would state that I spoke from memory. There were 105 companies
September, 1895, with an issued capital of 29 millions. At the ruling rates dur
the highest price of 1895, the valuation came out at 150 millions.

The share value was 150 millions?—Yes; the share value. These compar
show a valuation at to-day's price of £53,252,000, and show a difference
£97,000,000. The only two companies which have not depreciated in value are
Bonanza and Pioneer.

This concludes my statement, and I must thank the Commission for hav:
listened so patiently to the whole of my statement.

Chairman.

You tell us that this ground had a value of 150 millions, and that value is n
reduced to 53 millions. How is that?—I think the prices were inflated.

I am going to take the opposite view. I am going to presume that the value
the ground in reality is to-day much better and much more than when you capitali
in 1895, so there is no proof before us that the value has depreciated, but it is onl
proof that the capital has been put in the ground in excess of the value of i
ground.—I can explain. The value of 29 millions did not in 1895, nor does it nc
represent the intrinsic value of these properties. The public have placed their
value upon them. Some shares, even under the greatest times of depreciation, su
as now, show a premium. For instance, I will take the Ferreira. It has a capital
£90,000, and the shares are standing at £16 a share. The Robinson Company I
a capital of 2¾ millions, and the shares are standing to-day at a 40 per cent. premiu

Irrespective of speculation in shares, has the real value of the ground be
diminished?—Apart from disappointing development, the intrinsic value of so.
ground has, however, only diminished from a working point of view. I mean, y
have companies to-day which you know have a certain intrinsic value, but the cc
ditions are such that some of the companies cannot be worked at a profit.

According to your statement you say that there are burdens due to unnecessa
taxation. What do you mean by that?—That, at the present moment, all t
burdens are absolutely on the mining industry itself.

What do you mean by taxation forming all the burdens?—That is: heavy ra
way freights, monopolies, and imposts.

Do not the merchants of Potchefstroom and Pretoria pay the railway rates ;
They do.

Then why do you say it is only on the mines?—I do not say absolutely all; b
I say that nine-tenths of it is.

They pay the same taxation?—Yes.

What do you mean by monopolies ?—The dynamite monopoly, principally.

You said monopolies ?—Well, I mean monopoly.

You must not speak so generally.—I could speak of the cement concession, which ᴡas a concession, but is no longer so.

You have also said that the confidence of capitalists has been shaken ?—Yes, and Ⅰ can give you several reasons. One is that the incessant requests of the mining ɪndustry to the Government to assist the burdens have met with tardy and very often ꜰutile consideration. That, instead of facilitating the lowering of living expenses, ɴothing is done in that direction; that, speaking collectively, no desire is shown to ʀeally meet the industrial grievances of the mining industry, not even when most ᴜrgently required. Laws have been passed affecting mines which have been suffering ɢreat hardships, and on this I quote the *bewaarplaatsen* question. It was claimed by ᴄompanies who sunk into the ground over £9,000,000 that their claim should have ᴘreference. The Gold Law prescribes that the discoverer of gold must have the preꜰerence. The farm-owner is provided for under the Gold Law, and why give him an ᴀdditional consideration, and no consideration to the gold company.

[margin: Confidence of capitalists shaken: reasons for this.]
[margin: Past remissness of Government to assist mining industry.]
[margin: Industrial grievances of mining industry unsatisfied.]

I do not want an explanation of the Gold Law. It has been discussed in the ʟand. Now, the capitalists invested their money first of all when the same condiᴛions existed. How is it that they have lost confidence now? What has been done ᴛo shake confidence? When things were worse they invested their money; now ᴛhings have been improved, confidence is shaken.—In the first place I must dispute the ɪmprovement in the condition of things; secondly, the confidence increased as people ʀecognised and became more and more cognisant of the value of these goldfields. I ᴡill quote a geologist (a man of great repute), who states that within twenty miles ᴀlong the reef from Johannesburg, he estimates the gold contents to be £700,000,000. ᴛhat in itself is quite sufficient to inspire confidence in the value of the goldfields— ᴀssuming such statements to be trustworthy. The general belief also has been all ᴀlong that the existing industrial conditions will alter. We are now brought face to ꜰace with it, because we see that a good many companies that have been trying to ꜱtruggle all along are gradually giving way. We also find that it would require ᴍuch more for the equipment of the mines than was originally estimated. This ᴍoney was forthcoming. At the present moment it is lost.

[margin: Value of Witwatersrand gold fields.]
[margin: Industrial conditions of mining industry must be altered.]

Mr. Smit.

How do you reconcile the statements of experts who contend that there are £700,000,000 of gold in the fields, with that made by Mr. Albu, who has said that ᴜnfortunately there has been too great credence given to such reports, and that, thereꜰore, many have been misled. In the second place, there are proofs that so-called ɢold mines had been floated where there was never any gold. If such reports are so ʀeliable, as you say, why were not all the reports obtained before the companies were ꜰloated.—I cannot account for what certain people have done, nor have I knowledge, ɴor on the evidence of such opinion do I know that Mr. Albu for that matter made ᴛhe statement that these companies were formed, and the shares taken up at a high ᴘrice. I will admit and agree with Mr. Albu that in a time of excessive prosperity ɢreat advantage was taken by irresponsible people. But if you take the average ᴏf flotations here, and if you take the temptation that has been held out to make ᴍoney out of flotations, and that more advantage has not been taken of it, you will ᴄome to the conclusion that these cases are exceptional. I think the temptation is so ɢreat that to-day, if some firms of reputation wanted to float a company on the ᴍarket Square for instance, they would get the following to take up the shares. But ᴛhey have not taken any such advantage. I will admit that there have been flota-

[margin: Mr. Albu's evidence.]
[margin: Bogus flotations.]
[margin: Flotations.]

tions which, properly speaking, should never have come into existence, but they for a small percentage of the companies which have been honestly floated.

Now, do you not think that the flotation of such valueless companies goes muc farther to shaking confidence than a law which can be remedied?—I will admit this that it has added to the withdrawal of capital. But I say that these people are no justified in losing confidence for these reasons only, because for the good reason tha companies which, under normal conditions should work, cannot work at all now.

The Transvaal laws and the mining indus-try.

Suppose, now, you are a capitalist in Europe, and you invest £100,000 in th Free State, where the laws are bad, and £100,000 here, where the laws are goo Now, suppose you make money in the Free State, and you lose your £100,000 ir vested in the Transvaal, where would you put more money into?—What is a goo and what is a bad law? My reply would be, I would put my money into the countr where I knew that, under normal conditions, I would be able to make money.

But here the fact is established, that you can or you cannot make money?—I the laws had any bearing on insecurity of title, I should not put my money into tha country where I knew that I had no protection. I can give an instance where w went to the Government and asked for the alteration of a law to give title-protectio This Government gave our title, for instance, immediate protection in the constructio of the law regarding excess area.

You have never lost title to a property through defect in the law?—Yes, throug the interpretation of the law, in the case of the Modderfontein Company on proclama tion. We interpreted the law according to the opinions of the first lawyers her We took counsel's opinion on the interpretation of the law, and then we went an pegged out our claims. The result of it is that through litigation we lost 110 claim and we had to buy these back at an expense of £110,000.

Now, is that the fault of the law or the fault of arrogating to yourselves to much knowledge of the law? Did you ask the lawyers' opinion before you pegge off ground, or after?—We asked the lawyers' opinion before.

But about every law there are always two different opinions. Now, you canno possibly say that it is the fault of the law if the High Courts' decision goes agains you. The question I put to you was: Do you lose money through the defect of th law?—No. But there are instances, not speaking personally, but some in whic I am interested, where properties on questions of the reading of the law are still i dispute.

Bewaarplaatsen.

Has any law ever been made in this country where property you held is take away from you?—What do you call ownership under the *bewaarplaatsen?* I clai ownership because I have rights for which I pay licenses.

There you come again into the interpretation of the law, which is arranged b those interested?—What I say is, that the law exists, and under the Brickmaker Law the *bewaarplaatsen* is mentioned, and that states that we should be entitled t the underground rights, and therefore, rightly or wrongly, it is either the defect o the law or the interpretation of the law. I say it is a defect in the law, and tha under this law the companies had a claim of indisputable ownership.

The Gold Law nowhere gives underground rights, and the *bewaarplaatse* regulation says that when gold is discovered, that those on top shall have the pr ferent right, but that you shall pay licences according to those you work on th top?—I can only quote the Brickmakers' Law.

You mentioned a law the other day which you proposed to the Governmen which was once more adopted by the Government. Which one was that?—Th Pass Law.

Further, you said that, after endless petitions, the Liquor Law has been intro-
ed. Do you mean by that that it was the first time the Liquor Law was passed in
country ?—No ; I mean the prohibition of the sale of liquor.

But you said after endless memorials ?—That was the result of our memorials restricting the sale.

I may tell you that the Liquor Law was in existence in 1881.—I only knew that en I wanted to get liquor for my boys, I had previously only to give him a note to nearest canteen, and he would be supplied.

The law passed last year is only the amended law of 1881.—Do I understand t two laws exist—one prohibiting the sale of liquor in 1881, and another merely ricting the sale in 1896 ?

There is only one Liquor Law, but it has been amended from time to time.—That he perfection of 1881 culminated in the law of 1896.

The other day you stated that kaffirs had to pay £2 10s. ?—That is the native
. I have it to show that a native has to pay 10s. per hut, including one wife, and . for every additional wife per year, and that he has to pay £2 capitation fee apart m that.

The kaffir fee is 10s. per hut, and 2s. 6d. for road tax, and he may take as many es as he likes, and if he keeps all the women in one house, he has only to pay for hut, so that giving £2 10s. you allow each kaffir five wives. Is there no reducin kaffirs coming in parties of twenty-five through Komati ?—I am not aware of t.

If you take the trouble, you will find that a considerable reduction is made, if import them in lots of twenty-five ?—I only know we pay 18s. 9d. per head for m.

Why do you always look at the dark side of the question, and not at the light e ?—I must acknowledge that I did not know that I can engage a truck for firs from Komati at under 18s. 9d. I must say that if this is the case, I am prised that it is not done by the manager of the Native Labour Association.

I tell you it is so. You say that from Indwe you pay 18s. per head for travelling enses ?—25s. I said.

Do you not have anything to pay to get kaffirs ?—We get most of them from the e Government. They deliver them here when we pay.

You only pay the travelling expenses ?—Yes. An arrangement of this kind was e to between the manager of the Association and the Cape Colony.

You have said in your declaration that some mines must pay their dividends in
er to justify their capitalisation. What do you mean by that ?—What I meant to vey was that some of the outcrop companies have a longer life than others. It is essary to consider the gold contents in a company, which is practically your capital ; refore, you have to make provision for the amortisation of this capital, because this ital is represented by the gold you are taking out. Every investor would, I should k, take the life of a mine, or take the gold contents into consideration, and so find amount to be redeemed in a given time ; therefore, he will make the provision out he profits, because he knows that in the profits and corresponding price to-day is e included this amortisation fund.

Now, suppose the profits do not allow them to pay dividends, they do not take of the capital, and still they pay dividends, do you pay dividends out of the ital ?—That would be the case if you consider the contents of ground capital.

Do you suggest anything to meet the reductions to the revenue that would take
ce ?—My idea is this, as a witness explained to-day : You show a revenue to the te which could be curtailed without any harm. If these concessions are given to

relief re-
quested.
the industry, and to the population constituting the mining industry, this will br
new life into the industry. You must realise you have only got 53 producing c
panies, of which 20 are only paying dividends. We have over 158 mining compan
and I believe, and firmly believe, that if there is a reduction, not only of 2s. 8d.
coal and dynamite, but a considerable reduction, the vitality which will be given
the whole industry, the inflow of capital, the re-starting of companies, the increa
number of people coming to the country, will more than compensate the concessi
which we ask for now ; and that expenditure will be equalled by the revenue, provi
also that sums which, in my opinion, do not belong to the actual working of
administration, should come out of the revenue. For instance, mines have cap
expenditure and working expenditure—that is what I mean.

I quite agree with you, but at the same time the State as an institution must
stop and go backward.—I believe the change would be an immediate one. I go furth
I believe that a lot of companies would very soon start work, and I argue that if

*Worse depres-
sion will ensue
if relief is not
given.*
do not get industrial economics that the depression will become more acute. Thi
will become worse, and I think my suggestion will be the better remedy.

*Statistics of ex-
penditure of
companies.*
Can you show statistics as to how the expenditure of the companies is made u
—I have got them with me. There is the statement of the Henry Nourse (statem

*Expenditure of
Henry Nourse.*
handed in). I can give several more. Mr. Hennen Jennings will give you a compl
statement of the working expenses of many companies I am interested in.

*Reduction of
rates between
Port Elizabeth
and Vereenig-
ing in 1895.*
Do you know any reason why in 1895 the tariff between Port Elizabeth a
Vereeniging was considerably reduced ?—Representations were made by Commissic

Do you know why it was increased here at the same time ?—The impress
exists that it was in order to bring about no reduction, and then the Delagoa.

That is only an impression ; I will tell you the facts. Delagoa Bay railway v
just about being finished, and at the same time the Colony reduced its fares to such
extent that the administration of the railway asked for tenders to carry stuff fr
Vereeniging to Johannesburg ?—That was the object, to charge low rates from P
Elizabeth—to give no chance to earn money in carrying goods from Vereeniging
order to make them come by Delagoa Bay line if possible. If you judge that cas
would like you to take all these facts into consideration. I only want to explain
you because somehow you take a wrong view of matters. I don't want to excuse
Cape Government, they have also sinned.

*Transit dues of
Transvaal.*
You alluded to the transit rates of the Transvaal; what do you mean by tha
—If you want to bring mealies, for instance, to Matabeleland through the Transv
you will have to pay 3 per cent. duty as well.

*Transit dues in
Cape Colony
and Natal.*
What are the transit dues in the Cape Colony and Natal ?—It works out betwe
3 and 5 per cent.

*Increase and fall
of market
values of com-
panies in 1895.*
What do you adduce to be the reason for the value of the mines rising in 18
and coming down in the same way ?—The rise is due, as I have given in my stateme
to several conditions, and the reaction is due partly to over speculation and partly a
to disappointment.

One of the former witnesses declared that the shareholders ought to know
value of shares. You have already said that the public gives the value to the shar
—Market value.

Flotations.
The public living outside cannot form a correct value of the ground unless it
told by the promoters of the company ?—I think that touches on flotation. I
promoter floats a company, and asks the public to subscribe capital in other countr
it is done on the issue of a prospectus, and that prospectus gives the objects of flotati
and the reasons of flotation, and the promoters are responsible for what they say
that prospectus. But when companies are floated privately, and the public asks

ares, and they assume to have a certain knowledge, or good reasons for taking up e shares, how can it be prevented.

Can we assume for a moment that shareholders in Europe take up shares in such mpanies on the statements made in prospectuses ?—It is not done in this country. know of very few companies which have been floated on prospectuses ; in the early ys it was done.

If it should appear that the public put their money into valueless ground that n only be attributable to the promoters ?—I can only say this, that if a law does not ist, I think it would be a very good law if certain penalties were attached to promo-rs for misrepresentations in prospectuses.

I do not agree with you that the public give the market value to shares.—If I rm a company, and I bring out a new company, and the public wish to take these ares on the reputation of the firm, and take them to a high price, how can I revent it.

This morning I heard that the main reef does not pay so well, but there is a rich ader. Suppose you work the rich leader for two or three months, and the mine elds an average of 16 dwts., and you float a company, and put their shares on the arket, and people bid for these shares. Then you work the main reef, and bring wn the yield to 6 dwts., are the public then to blame for having put so much money it in the first instance ?—In the first instance I would say this, that most of the mpanies issue reports, and very lucid reports, from which the shareholders can get l the information they require. If a company works this very narrow leader for arket purposes they would be doing a wrong act.

I don't say it is done, but it is quite possible. Did your firm subscribe to the _{Subscription of Neumann and Co. to the Dynamite fund.} ynamite fund ?—Yes ; We subscribed £5,000

Did you take it from your companies ?—We did not take sixpence from the mpanies.

Chairman :

You give a long historical story of the whole matter ; but it is, shortly, reduced this, that what really the industry requires is lower railway rates, cheaper dyna-ite, and popular administration of the Pass Law and the Liquor Law ?—No ; I say at it is not going to satisfy the whole of the country.

Still that is what the industry requires from the Government ?—No, I want _{Import duties.} mething further ; what I suggest is the reduction of import duties ; and I want to _{Cost of living.} e that living expenses are reduced. A great drawback is the expense of living in e country.

How does the living here compare with other places in South Africa ?—Con-derably more if you compare the salaries given here with those in the Colony. Take _{House rents.} use rents alone. I know people who have got in Natal houses at £5 and £7 10s. r month, and here you have to pay £40 or £50. Take men living on a mine. At e Wolhuter there are 50 miners married, and they have to live in town or away om the mine. Their house costs them between £7 10s. and £9 per month. That nt is high I can understand, it is the question of capitalisation. A man builds a use and wants to get as large a percentage as he can on his capital outlay, because , as he assumes, the conditions alter and the freights come down, he knows that, _{House values and railway rates.} robably in three years time, the houses built to-day would cost considerably less. nsequently he wants amortisation of his money. That is why rents are so high.

Of course that would all be reduced if the railway rates were reduced ?—I should ke to give another instance. It concerns myself. I bought a house this year for 7,500, and it has been valued by the Sanitary Board at £22,500. I objected, and _{Sanitary board rates.}

the valuation was reduced to £17,500, in spite of the proof I brought that I had pu[r]chased the house *bona fide* for the sum named. I therefore have to pay taxes [on] £17,500, which is a hardship. I should like to say that in the £7,500 the sum [of] £1,400 is for the stands.

That is an entirely different question. You prove that the building cannot b[e] excessive ?—I say I am wrongly taxed. I have bought in the open market; this ma[n] sold me nothing cheap.

The Sanitary Board here represents the public, therefore you do not put this as [a] grievance against the Government ?—No, certainly not; I am only speaking about th[e] expenses of living here.

But that is a grievance against yourselves. Now, yesterday you suggested, [as] regards the execution of the Pass Law, and Liquor Law, that the Government shoul[d] form an Advisory Board here of persons largely interested in these fields. Can yo[u] suggest any scheme how such a Board would be constructed—what would be it[s] functions, duties, and its rights ?—I will take the Pass Law for instance. An incor[-] porated Government Board should be formed, who shall have powers vested in ther[e] to amend and alter that law from time, to time as they may consider fit. They shal[l] have funds—say, the result of passes—placed at their disposal. If it is possible, le[t] the Government make members of the mining industry members also, as in the Hos[-] pital and Sanitary Boards; then you can have this Board constituted by officials of th[e] Government and members of the industry. But if the Government cannot see thei[r] way to do it, then we must have an Advisory Board, and if there are any suggestion[s] for the alteration and the amendment of the law or its administration, the Board woul[d] consult with the advisory members of the Board.

I fear if we adopt that system, the kaffir, instead of having to pay 2s., would hav[e] to pay 5s., just on the same lines as in the case you have mentioned in regard to th[e] Sanitary Board. It will be a second Government within a Government. I conside[r] it an unhealthy system. The law must be properly made—and it can be mad[e] properly without that Board—as formerly by yourselves, and experience will teac[h] every time how we can amend and improve it. The Government must appoint suc[h] officials, and in sufficient number, and police for the carrying out of that law. S[o] long as there is a want of that the public have always the right and liberty to petitio[n] the Government about it. I think this would be much better than establishing [a] Board here to carry out the law.

Mr. de Beer:

You said yesterday that many of the mines were stopped for want of workin[g] capital ?—Yes.

Now, if the industry and Government together can effect a saving of 6s. per to[n] thereby creating a profit on the production of gold, do you think that money will b[e] available at once to re-open these mines ?—I certainly think that the effect on som[e] of the companies, which are just making a very small profit to-day, and to whom [a] profit of 6s. per ton would make great difference, would in itself bring about a grea[t] change in our favour. I don't say that even a reduction of 6s. would bring man[y] mines into life again.

Not the majority ?—No.

What do you think the reduction ought to be to bring the majority into lif[e] again ?—That is something I wish to bring before the Government. We ought to b[e] able to work here at from 15s. to 17s. 6d. per ton. If we were able to do that yo[u] would see a very different state of things very shortly from what we have to-day.

Local govern-ment board.

Advisory board.

Effects of a sav-ing of 6s. per ton on working costs of mines.

Reduction of working costs required to bring majority of mines into work at a pro-fit.

I understand from other witnesses that there is a large amount of ground which
be worked with profit in case the production costs can be reduced ?—Yes ; cer-
ly.

Are there many outcrop companies which give from 4 to 6 dwts ?—Yes.

And these give a profit if they are worked at 15s. 6d. ?—Yes ; very handsome.

At 4 dwts. ?—No, not in reduction ; 4 dwts. is not enough. There is an irreducible
it, and that is too low.

I take as a case the Geldenhuis Deep Level. This morning a diagram by Mr. Geldenhuis Deep
mour, splendidly executed, was handed in, in which it showed that deep level near
danger line.—We must make allowance for outcrop mines having greater facilities.

Now, what difference would there be between the outcrop mine and the deep
el to make the deep level pay ?—The case is a difficult one, because the Geldenhuis
p are working a very wide reef. If you go to the West Rand you find companies
working a very narrow reef, and the working expenses are consequently more.
ey have to work more ground for milling purposes, and it is only by sorting that Sorting.
y can bring up the average.

In the companies you mention is it a general method to sort ?—Yes, they all sort.

Now, about the Pass Law. You say the law was made by the industry, and that Pass Law: amendments required.
now find defective clauses in it ?—Yes.

Have these been altered ?—One has been altered in regard to the fines. One
ect I pointed out to-day.

You will agree that these defects only appear when you work the law ?—Yes.

Upon the improvement you say that the Government makes £75,000 out of passes State revenue from pass fees.
ne ?—I think I said about £54,000.

That gives a total of £150,000 in passes, Boksburg and Krugersdorp included.
u said that money goes to enrich the Treasury ?—The net result I think.

Are you a member of the Hospital Board ?—Yes.

Do you know how the Hospital was called into existence ?—I know exactly.
merly they got all the pass money ; now they don't get all the pass money, but
y get £26,000 grant from the Government instead. What we asked in the Pass
v is not to get the 2s., but I particularly laid stress on it yesterday by referring
he Draft Law. We do not ask for the 1s. the Government always used to get,
we ask for the additional 1s. we subscribe for administrative purposes.

HENRY NOURSE GOLD MINING COMPANY, LIMITED.

STATEMENT OF COSTS FROM 1st JANUARY, 1890, TO 31st DECEMBER, 1896.

Period.	Tons Milled.	White Labour.	Native Labour.	Coal.	Dynamite.	Stores, Gen. Expenses, Depreciation, &c.
6 Months from 1st January to 30th June, 1890	3,657	£2,538 1 11	£1,253 10 6	£1,104 7 6	£976 0 0	£3,433 0 0
12 ,, 1st July, '90, to 30th June, '91	8,259	5,015 10 6	2,848 6 10	2,599 13 0	1,934 12 6	4,585 10 2
6 ,, 1st July to 30th December, '91	4,494	3,512 17 10	2,015 9 3	1,772 3 6	2,359 10 6	2,424 14 4
6 ,, 1st January, '92, to 30th June, '92	5,267	4,391 0 4	3,597 16 11	2,120 7 3	2,225 17 6	4,517 19 5
6 ,, 1st July, '92, to 31st December, '92	6,675	5,346 11 3	5,058 14 0	2,540 15 0	2,551 0 0	3,340 11 8
6 ,, 1st January, '93, to 30th June, '93	8,122	6,997 12 9	8,169 10 6	3,529 9 1	5,312 2 6	7,512 13 1
12 ,, 1st July, '93, to 30th June, '94	23,417	16,549 7 9	20,408 14 3	7,489 1 5	8,947 4 6	16,675 15 10
12 ,, 1st July, '94, to 30th June, '95	29,366	26,338 17 0	31,493 10 11	8,903 17 5	15,318 15 0	18,317 11 2
12 ,, 1st July, '95, to 30th June, '96	72,095	40,358 13 9	48,514 9 7	10,421 18 9	18,934 17 6	34,616 19 7
6 ,, 1st July, '96, to 31st December, '96	51,563	22,131 13 3	26,520 10 8	4,494 1 8	10,212 10 0	24,826 3 7
Total ...	212,915	£133,180 6 4	£149,880 13 5	£44,975 15 7	£68,772 9 6	£120,250 18 10

	Cost per ton.	Percentage.
White Labour	12s. 6·14d.	25·75
Native Labour and Food ...	14s. 0·90d.	29·00
Coal	4s. 2·50d.	8·70
Dynamite	6s. 5·52d.	13·32
Stores, General Expenses, Depreciation, &c. ...	11s. 3·44d.	23·23
	48s. 6·50d.	100

NOTE.—In above Statement White Labour does not include the Manager's Salary, Directors' Fees, London and Johannesburg Office Expenses, which are included with the Stores, General Expenses, Depreciation, &c.

HENRY NOURSE GOLD MINING CO., LTD.

Details of Expenditure for Year ended the 31st December, 1896.

Heading.	Amount.			Cost per Ton.		Percentage.
	£	s.	d.	s.	d.	per cent.
ative Labour	48,241	13	0	10	5·448	29·332
ative Food	7,520	8	7	1	7·556	4·573
hite Labour, Salaries, &c. (see footnote)	45,295	4	9	9	9·786	27·540
al	11,130	16	5	2	4·944	6·767
ynamite...	18,884	15	0	4	1·108	11·476
anide	3,207	18	4	0	8·341	1·950
nc	285	4	5	0	·741	·173
ining Timber	2,155	5	10	0	5·604	1·310
mber, Deals, &c.	931	4	5	0	2·422	·566
eel	1,473	4	11	0	3·831	·895
ls, Greases, and Paraffin	1,877	16	7	0	4·879	1·142
ndles...	2,230	3	0	0	5·799	1·366
opes (Steel and Manilla)	308	5	11	0	·801	·187
orage, Chaff and Bran	1,010	4	8	0	2·627	·614
ectric Spares	196	1	7	0	·509	·120
ill Spares, Shoes, Dies, Cams, Cam Shafts, Stems, Mortar Boxes, and Screening, &c.	1,350	16	11	0	3·512	·821
rucks, Wheels, and Rails...	448	13	2	0	1·167	·273
pes and Pipe Fittings	884	6	1	0	2·299	·537
use and Detonators	1,043	17	6	0	2·714	·634
ar Iron, Nuts, Bolts, Assay Chemicals, Mercury, &c.	6,890	13	7	1	5·918	4·190
neral Charges (see footnote)	6,772	4	7	1	5·610	4·117
surances	1,131	7	7	0	2·942	0·690
censes and Rents	847	2	6	0	2·203	0·514
inting and Advertising	351	5	2	0	·913	0·213
Totals	164,468	14	6	35	7·674	100·000

OTE.—General Charges include the salaries of the Manager, Mine Office Staff, Engineer, London and Johannesburg Offices, and Directors' Fees.

MEMO. OF SUNDRY COSTS, &c.

Sundry costs of Henry Nourse G.M. Co.

Cost of Round Coal at present time is 20s. per ton, delivered to bunkers ; 5 years ago was 23s. per n, delivered to bunkers.

Cost of coal on Henry Nourse in 1892 and in 1897.

Cost of Dynamite (Gelatine) at present time is £5 7s. 6d. a case, plus 1s. for cartage ; 5 years ago ice was £5 12s. 6d. a case.

Cost of gelatine on Henry Nourse in 1892 and in 1897.

White Men and Natives.—At present the Company employs 170 White Men, 1,650 Natives. With ew exceptions, all White Men are housed by the Company free. Rates of white wages at present, s. 4·34d. per day ; 5 years ago, 16s. 7·02d. This includes salary paid to the Manager and all Mine ficials, but does not include Directors' fees, or London and Johannesburg Offices. Rates of Native ages at present, 2s. 2·84d. per day ; 5 years ago, 2s. 2·38d. per day.

White and native wages on Henry Nourse in 1892 and in 1897.

Waste Rock.—For 12 months, to 30th June, '96, sorted out 23 per cent. ; for 6 months, to 31st cember, '96, sorted out 19 per cent.

Sorting on Henry Nourse.

I

BONANZA, LIMITED.

Statement showing Details of the various Expenditure from September to December, 1896.

Specification.	Amount.			Cost per Ton.		Percentage.
	£	s.	d.	s.	d.	per cent.
Native Labour	2,920	10	5	3	7·4	11·1
Native Food	913	9	4	1	1·6	3·5
White Labour, Salaries, &c.	8,643	5	1	10	8·7	33·1
Coal	3,221	15	5	3	11·9	12.3
Dynamite	1,490	17	6	1	10·2	5·8
Cyanide	740	0	7		11·0	2·9
Zinc						
Mining Timber	326	17	9		4·8	1·2
Timber, Deals, &c.	1,354	8	11	1	8·1	5·2
Steel	103	0	1		1·5	·4
Oils, Grease, &c.	677	13	6		10·0	2·5
Candles	146	18	5		2·1	·5
Ropes (Steel and Manilla)						
Forage, &c.	84	19	7		1·2	·3
Electric Spares	260	18	7		3·8	1·1
Mill Spares, &c., &c., &c.	312	1	1		4·6	1·2
Trucks, &c.	80	4	8		1·1	·3
Pipes	175	3	9		2·6	·6
Fuse and Detonators	58	13	6		0·8	·3
Bar Iron, Nuts, Bolts, Assay Machinery, &c. ...	629	15	9		9·3	2·5
General Charges—Transfer Office, London Office, Mine Office, and Salaries	3,598	19	0	4	5·5	13·8
Insurances	310	16	10		4·6	1·2
Licences and Rents	42	0	0		0·62	·1
Printing and Advertising	23	4	9		0·3	·1
Total ...	£26,115	14	6	32	3·72	100·0

NEW MODDERFONTEIN G.M. CO., LTD.

Expenses from 1st May, 1896, to 31st March, 1897.

[Calculations based upon 81,935 Tons Milled.]

	WEST MINE.		
	Value.	Cost per Ton.	Per Cent.
	£ s. d.	s. d.	
Native Wages	34,524 11 6	8 5·13	29·196
Native Food	6,675 11 3	1 7·56	5·646
White Labour (Salaries)	35,564 0 9	7 8·45	26·689
Coal	6,987 14 1	1 8·47	5·910
Dynamite	9,096 2 6	2 2·64	7·693
Cyanide	1,135 10 2	3·32	·962
Zinc	212 0 0	·62	·177
Mining Timber	1,693 10 1	4·96	1·433
Timber, Deals, &c.	373 11 3	1·09	·317
Steel	1,547 18 3	4·53	1·310
Oils, Grease, Paraffin ...	978 15 5	2·89	·826
Candles	1,432 15 1	4·19	1·213
Ropes, Steel, Manilla ...	219 4 2	·64	·187
Forage, Chaff, and Bran ...	1,328 9 11	3·89	1·125
Electric Spares	137 13 3	·40	·118
Mill Spares	1,022 18 3	3·00	·866
Trucks, Wheels, Axles ...	642 0 0	1 88	·545
Pipes and Pipe Fittings	551 5 7	1·61	·468
Fuse and Detonators ...	784 0 8	2·30	·665
Sundry Stores and Machinery ...	7,174 7 6	1 9·01	6·067
General Charges	1,975 3 11	5·80	1·670
Licences and Rents	216 14 0	·63	·185
Printing and Advertising... ...	1,458 5 3	4·27	1·199
Town and London Offices ...	6,541 11 3	1 7·16	5·533
	118,273 14 1	28 10·44	100

TREASURY GOLD MINES. Ltd.

Statement showing Details of the various Expenditure during the Year ended March 31st, 1897.

Specification.	Amount.			Cost per Ton.		Percentage.
	£	s.	d.	s.	d.	Per cent.
European Wages	19,691	9	2	5	4·302	22·2
Native Wages	17,964	7	5	4	10·662	21·2
Contractors	3,849	14	5	1	0·571	4·3
Miscellaneous Cash	312	6	9	0	1·009	·3
General Charges	8,101	11	4	2	2·455	9·2
Native Labour Supply	3,532	14	4		11·536	3·9
Coal	9,850	19	1	2	8·168	11·1
Explosives	8,608	3	10	2	4·109	9·7
Native Food	4,287	2	5	1	1·999	4·9
Cyanide	2,840	14	0		9·286	3·2
Zinc Discs	261	17	9		0·855	·3
Candles	992	2	10		3·239	1·1
Oils and Grease	880	16	5		2·876	·9
Drill Steel	311	13	6		1·017	·3
Tools	202	15	5		0·662	·2
Chemicals	590	0	6		1·926	·6
Mercury	133	17	6		0·438	·1
General Stores	2,629	12	6		8·587	2·9
Battery Fittings	920	6	6		3·005	1·0
Packing and Waste	310	13	5		1·024	·3
Bolts, Nuts, Washers, Bar Iron, &c.	382	17	4		1·250	·4
Mining Poles	148	15	7		0·485	·1
Shoes and Dies	813	12	9		2·656	·8
Rock Drill Spares	369	0	2		1·204	·4
Boiler Tubes	555	2	8		1·812	·6
Total	£88,542	7	7	£1 4	1·133	100·0

Tonnage, 73,496.

THE WOLHUTER GOLD MINES, Ltd.

Statement showing Details of Working Expenditure for the Year ended December 31st, 1896.

Specifications.	Amount. £	s.	d.	Cost per Ton. s.	d.	Percentage on Total. per cent.
Native Labour (including Contractors and Redemption	54,402	6	3	7	9·8	28·4
White Labour do. do.	51,248	11	7	7	4·3	26·7
Charges, General Printing, &c.	1,998	2	7		3·5	1·04
London Office Expenses	891	2	6		1·5	0·5
Directors' & Financial Committee's Fees	1,250	0	0		2·1	0·7
Paris Agency	129	12	8		0·2	0·07
Committee of Investigation	533	6	8		0·9	0·3
Native Labour Expenses	4,312	7	11		7·5	2·2
Cyanide Royalty	5,360	16	5		9·3	2·8
Insurances	577	17	9		0·10	0·3
Claim Licenses	655	0	0		1·1	0·45
Stamps, Telegrams, and Cables	126	1	0		0·2	0·07
Stores (including Contractors)						
Coal	21,152	3	9	3	0·6	11·07
Gelatine	17,014	3	7	2	5·3	8·8
Cyanide	4,293	19	4		7·2	2·2
Zinc	234	18	3		0·3	0·1
Mining Timber	2,156	19	4		3·7	1·2
Timber, Deals, &c.	246	13	6		0·5	0·1
Steel (Drill)	2,503	3	4		4·3	1·3
Oils, Greases, and Paraffin	3,013	4	11		5·2	1·6
Candles	1,815	6	3		3·1	0·9
Forage, Chaff, and Bran	763	0	0		1·3	0·4
Electrical Spares	375	6	3		0·5	0·23
Mill Spares, Shoes, Dies, Cams, &c.	2,862	1	3		4·9	1·5
Truck Wheels, Rails, &c.	349	1	6		0·6	0·2
Pipes and Pipe Fittings	137	11	3		0·2	0·07
Fuse and Detonators	2,243	3	9		3·9	1·2
Bar Iron, Nuts, Bolts, &c.	279	4	9		0·6	0·1
Native Food	8,248	19	8	1 2·2		4·3
Sundry Stores	2,261	4	7		3·9	1·2
Total Working Expenses for Year	£191,435	11	6	£1 7	5·7	100·0

CROWN REEF G.M. Co., Ltd.

Statement showing details of the various Expenditure during the Year ended December 31st, 1896.

Specification.	Amount.	Cost per Ton.	Percentage.
	£ s. d.	s. d.	per cent.
Native Labour	63,902 6 1	6 5·365	24·146
Native Food	12,305 15 10	1 2·898	4·650
White Labour, Salaries, &c. ...	77,222 8 3	7 9·491	29·180
Coal	25,909 14 5	2 7·368	9·790
Dynamite	24,995 18 2	2 5·172	9·105
Cyanide	8,324 3 5	0 10·077	3·146
Zinc	578 8 8	0 0·700	2·219
Royalty	7,907 6 3	0 9·573	·989
Mining Timber	2,091 5 0	0 2·531	·789
Timber, Deals, &c.	2,003 8 10	0 2·425	1·759
Steel	3,491 4 9	0 4·226	·319
Oils, Greases and Paraffin... ...	2,300 9 10	0 2·785	·869
Candles	3,175 3 1	0 3·844	1·199
Ropes (Steel and Manilla) ...	805 11 1	0 0·975	·304
Forage, Chaff and Bran	1,549 13 3	0 1·876	·585
Electric Spares	2,915 0 4	0 3·529	1·001
Mill Spares, Shoes, Dies, Cams, Cam-shafts, Stems, Mortar Boxes, Screening, &c.	4,027 8 7	0 4·875	1·522
Trucks, Wheels and Rails... ...	1,830 5 5	0 2·215	·691
Pipes and Pipe Fittings	953 13 8	0 1·154	·360
Fuse and Detonators	1,516 17 10	0 1·836	·572
Bar Iron, Nuts, Bolts, Assay Chem-icals, Machinery, &c. ...	11,567 0 5	1 2·006	4·370
Insurances ... £1,449 7 0			
Gen. Charges, Sundries 1,412 0 5			
Licences and Rents 205 0 0			
Quartz Account... 1,187 6 1		dec. 7·463	
Printing & Advertising 1,913 16 3	6,167 9 9	dif. ·010 ...	2·330
Total	£264,640 12 11	£1 6 8·394	99·995

MEMO. OF SUNDRY STORES, ETC.

Sundry costs of Crown Reef G.M. Co.

Cost of coal on Crown Reef in 1892 and in 1897. COST OF ROUND COAL.—At present is 18s. 9d., delivered on Mine; 5 years ago was 21s., delivered on Mine.

Cost of dynamite in 1892 and of gelatine in 1897 on Crown Reef. COST OF DYNAMITE.—At present £5 7s. 6d. a case—Gelatine—carriage 1s. 9d. per case; 5 years ago, £5—No. 1 Dynamite.

White and native wages on Crown Reef in 1892 and in 1897. WHITE MEN AND NATIVES.—At present the Company employs 231 Whites and 1,695 Natives. About half the white men are housed by the Company, free. Rate of White Wages at present, £24 1s. 10·4d.; 5 years ago, £20 1s. 1d. This includes salary paid to the Manager and all Mine Officials, and also includes Directors' Fees, both London and Head Office and London Secretary, i.e., all, Rates of Native Wages at present, £2 12s. 7d. per month of 24 days; 5 years ago, £2 15s. 7d.

Sorting on Crown Reef. WASTE ROCK.—None Sorted.

Mr. Martin Lubeck was the next witness called. He read the following statement :—

As so many details have been given by competent men, I should like to refrain n giving further details, and restrict myself to general remarks. The question of day is focussed under that one point : "Is it possible to put an end to the prevailing ression, and to create prosperous times again?" My idea is that it is not alone sible, but that this is at the same time not so difficult at all. In reverting back to former times of the industry, we find that only reefs giving an ounce per ton were sidered payable, whereas, at the present time, reefs giving half that value, say dwts., over the stoping width, are giving reasonable profits. The principal reasons his are the great progress in the methods of extraction, and the great improvement the machinery. Without these improvements the industry would surely have ained pretty small, for there are very few propositions which yield an ounce. w, we all hope that further progress will be made in the methods of extraction as l as in machinery, but we cannot rely on that, and so at this moment we can better state of things only through a material reduction in the working expenses. We st not lose sight of the fact that, wherever large industries have sprung up, the rking costs of same are continually decreasing, and that, in anticipation of a similar cess here, enormous sums have been invested here in low grade propositions. These ns would be lost if that process of gradual reduction of the working costs should not on, and that would all the more be regrettable as the assumption under which the estment has been made was quite justified, and as, if this money should be lost, it uld act as a severe check upon fresh capital being introduced. In America and Australia, nes of much lower grade have been made payable, as I am told. My opinion is now t it is possible to reduce the working cost by at least 6s. per ton, and I am convinced t, in case we get to that, the actual depression would at once be superseded by a w era of prosperity. The dividends given by the mining companies in 1896 ounted to about £1,500,000. The amount of tons crushed monthly is at present ut 400,000, and a saving of 6s. on this quantity would amount to £120,000 per nth. That would mean £1,440,000 a year, or, in other words, through such a uction, the dividends paid by the mines of the Rand would at once become twice as ch as they are now, and this fact alone would, in my opinion, be quite sufficient to tore confidence in Europe, whereas, on the other hand, it would also allow a great nber of properties which do not pay at all now to be regarded as payable, and to be en in hand. How do we now come to the reduction of 6s. per ton? I think it not y difficult to obtain this. It requires nothing but honest work and energy on the t of the leaders of the industry, and a willingness on the part of the Government to p as far as possible. As regards the management of the mines, for which the leaders he industry are responsible, I am quite sure that most of these men are constantly ing to improve the administration of the mines, but I think that much can still be e in this respect, and that they ought to apply to that their utmost energy and ity. As regards the Government, I think that in case they give the industry sonable reductions in the railway rates and the price of dynamite, this would effect irect saving in the working costs of about 2s. per ton. The leaders of the industry now already trying to reduce the kafir wages by 30 per cent., and if they succeed hat, which, in my opinion, they can do if they can get the support of the Govern- nt, this means another saving of 2s. Now, I am quite sure that the reduction of railway rates and of the kaffir wages would cheapen the general conditions of ng to such an extent that it would be possible to save another 2s. by reducing the ite wages, the prices of stores, &c. As regards the general conditions of living here, v are, as everybody must confess, exceptionally high; and I think it is difficult to find any other country in the world where they are as high as here. What is

Causes of excessive cost of living. reason of this? In European countries the conditions of life depend to a great ext
on the wages which the day labourer gets. These wages are, so to say, the basis
the whole cost of living. In all greater works, as agriculture, construction of railwa
building of houses, transport of goods, the wages of the day labourer represent a
item, and, besides that, if you give a day labourer, say 3s. per day, you are compel
to give a skilled labourer something more, say 4s. or 5s. per day, a clerk perhaps
per day, etc.; and so the whole scale of wages, and further on, the whole construct
of national economy, is built upon the wages of the day labourer. Now, as rega
young countries whose industries are still in their infancy, and who have to imp
merchandise of every kind, the same principle prevails, with the addition that,
course, the freight rates play a most important part. I should, therefore, like

Reduction of native wages and railway rates necessary. point out that the whole conditions of life here depend on the wages of the kaffirs a
on the freight rates, and that, if we can succeed in reducing these two items, the c
of living will become cheaper, and the value of the mines far greater. As regards
reductions which the Government is requested to grant to the mining industry, i
quite clear, and it has been proved by former witnesses, that the railway rates
excessively high, in fact so high, that it is astonishing that they are still allowed
prevail. I understand very well that the Railway Company were allowed in th
concession to charge high rates, because in these times the traffic was not very lar
but now, as the traffic has become of an importance never dreamed of, a considera

The Government and the railway rates: right of expropriation. reduction is only too reasonable. It is true that the Railway Company is, so to say
private company; virtually, however, the Government is master of the railw
and can dictate the rates, because if the railway would not conform to them,
Government have the right to expropriate the railway, and the Government would,

Reduction of railway rates and the State revenue. this case, do a splendid business. There is only one point to be considered in this, a
that is the possibility that through a reduction of the rates the share of
Government in the profit would decrease in such a way that the Budget
the State would be endangered by it. Now, it is my firm opinion that
profits would not at all decrease, because a reduction of the rates wo
doubtless bring a far greater traffic, for the simple reason that it will bri
forth greater activity in mining, agriculture, etc. But in the unexpected c
of a material decrease, such could not at all endanger the Budget. T

The State budget and the surplus. Budget of this State is more splendid than the Budget of any other State in
world. The Budget for the current year leaves a certain surplus, though the hea
extraordinary expenses for different works and material have been brought ir
account as ordinary expenses, whereas anywhere else such kinds of expenditu
would figure as extraordinary items, and would not be covered by the curre
revenue. I estimate this extraordinary expenditure at about £1,000,000, and, bes
that, the profit of the Government in the railway business for 1896 has be
estimated at only £500,000, whereas it will probably amount to one million—that
£500,000 more. The real result of the Budget is therefore a surplus of £1,500,0
This is indeed a most marvellous thing, and the State may be congratulated on
Budget, for it is quite clear that other young countries are generally in wa
of great amounts of money, and have to raise big loans in order to develop
country. A great and very rich State like Great Britain has for the financial year
1896 a surplus of £1,500,000, and you have no doubt read in the papers what ext
ordinary pleasure this surplus causes. A surplus of £1,500,000 in the Transv
means £10 a head, as I take the white population to be 150,000, the black populat
not coming into consideration. If, for instance, Germany, with a population
52,000,000, could make a proportionate saving, this would mean £520,000,000, anc

ink that would be sufficient to repay the whole debts of the German States. It is nce quite clear that the consideration of the Budget need not hinder the Government from reducing the railway rates, provided the Government supports the mining dustry, from which the revenue of the State is drawn, and this support of the ining industry is just done by reducing the rates. Touching the question of namite, I think the erection in this country of a factory for such an article must be nsidered as an economic error, as the factory has to import all the raw materials, ese not being found in the Transvaal. I once saw a dynamite factory belonging to e Nobel Company, situated on the banks of the River Elbe. Of course, such a factory s, besides its cheap wages, cheap machinery, etc., the great facility of getting its aterial by water at a low rate, and of shipping its manufacture in the same manner. think if a factory in this country, with the big cost of everything, can sell dynamite o. 1 at 85s. with a profit, then that factory on the Elbe should be able to sell it at out one-fourth that price and make a nice profit still. Besides that, the factory here only producing a small part of the dynamite wanted in this country, whereas it ports the greater part and sells it at an enormously high price, which it ought only get for stuff manufactured here. This is clearly unjust, and I think it would not difficult for the Government to obtain for the industry a considerable reduction in e price through negotiations with the dynamite factory, unless the Government efer the cancellation of the monopoly. It is a known fact that all the goods manuctured on a large scale are bound to become cheaper from year to year through proved methods of working. As an example I would quote the case of cyanide: a monopoly for the manufacture of cyanide had been granted here, the industry ould have to pay a certain price, probably based on the price of the article which rmerly prevailed here, as is the case with the dynamite, whereas the consequence of e free competition in cyanide has brought the price down in a few years from 30d. 11d. a pound. I repeat that I refrain from details, and I think that these general marks are quite sufficient. I am firmly convinced that the Government in giving e above-mentioned facilities, and in working hand-in-hand with the men of the dustry, will effect an early restoration of confidence and prosperity. In conclusion, should like to refer to a suggestion which has already been made. In European untries the authorities generally consult financial, commercial, and industrial men all questions regarding freight rates, customs, construction of new railways, etc. rhaps it would suit the Government here to do the same. Amongst this large mmunity in Johannesburg there are men from every part of the world, and I think ere are a number of men who understand these questions very well. I think it uld not be difficult for the Government to select from these men a certain number persons in whom the Government could have entire confidence, and whose perience could be advantageously made use of by the Government.

Mr. Smit.

You are manager of a financial company?—Yes.
You remember the fund that was created for the dynamite disaster?—Yes.
Did you make a subscription to that fund on behalf of the company, or as anager personally?—Oh, no; on behalf the company.
Every person does not subscribe himself?—Sometimes they subscribe themselves; e directors of financial companies have the right to give certain sums for such rposes.
Can you give to charitable purposes without the consent of shareholders?—Yes, course, if it is not a big sum; the subscription must be within certain limits, hough a director of a company must have certain liberty.

Supposing I was the holder of 20,000 shares, and living in Europe, and in t[
absence of special instructions would you be justified in giving £2,000 ?—I would no
and I have not done it.

You can subscribe without the consent of the shareholders ?—As a director [
must have certain liberties.

As far as is wanted for business ?—Yes; but the shareholders, in electing me [
director of a company, must have sufficient confidence in me. I am responsible f[
what I do, because at the end of the year the books are audited, and if I have do[
anything to which I am not entitled, then I lose their confidence. My shareholde[
have great confidence in me; if I were to request a greater amount for investmen[
I would get it to-morrow. I have just received an application in that respect, and
have answered that I don't recommend investments in this country, because I cann[
see the prospect of good times until we get a material reduction in the workin[
expenses.

These are two entirely different matters ?—Oh, yes; but the directors have
certain right in spending certain sums of money; they cannot spend thousands an[
thousands. But they have this privilege everywhere. My bank in Berlin alway[
contributes certain sums to such purposes; you can see from the papers every da[
that all these companies do this.

The raid expenses and Mr. Lubeck's company.

At the time of the raid did you contribute to a syndicate for the expense[
incurred ?—No. My company had nothing to do with the raid at all.

Not for the expenses made in Johannesburg ?—What expenses ?

There was a relief fund in Johannesburg ?—No, we never contributed to tha[
I would not have given anything to it.

Mr. *Hugo.*

Reduction of the price of dynamite and of railway rates.

You say there would be a 4s. per ton saving if certain reductions were made i[
the price of dynamite and railway rates. Now, to what price must dynamite b[
reduced to bring about that ?—It is difficult to fix a price. People have already state[
that the price ought to be reduced to half the present price, but I don't know whethe[
it is possible. But I think if you reduce the price of dynamite by one third only, an[
if you reduce freight rates considerably, especially on the coal, and if the railwa[

The transport of coal.

transports coal in a more practical manner. I have never seen coal transported i[
bags. If the railway transports coal in a practical way, then I think about 2s. can b[
saved out of dynamite and freight rates. It is difficult to fix the amount of savin[
because these expenses are different on different mines, and depend on different cir[

The reduction of native wages. Reduction of 6s. per ton will restore confidence.

cumstances. The other 2s. would come out of a reduction in kafir labour.

If the reduction of 6s. per ton takes place, will a low grade proposition improve
—If there is only a prospect of getting the reduction of 6s., the whole situation wil[
alter at once. My opinion is that we can get back the confidence of European share[
holders—not through words, but through dividends. Such a reduction of 6s. woul[
increase dividends enormously, and such a state must restore confidence, there is n[
doubt about it. If I knew we could get this reduction, I would write my people a[
home to invest large sums here.

Reduction of white wages by reduction of costs of living.

It is very doubtful if you can get a reduction of white labour of 2s. per ton ?—
The third 2s. per ton represents more than white labour; it includes stores, timber, &[

And consequent on the reduction of the railway rates ?—My idea is that th[
whole cost of living will become cheaper. It is very high here. Of course it must b[
higher than in Europe, and even in other transatlantic countries. But here it [
exceptionally high. I at one time could not comprehend it, although I have seen [
great part of the world.

Mr. *Smit*.

Do you know the proposed south line from Elandsfontein to Roodepoort?—Yes. The proposed Elandsfontein-Roodepoort line and the coal traffic.
Don't you think if it is carried through it will do very much to reduce the freight
coals?—It is difficult to say. I have not studied it; but I think the principal
pose to be served by that line will be to secure a regular supply of coal for the
es. This supply has sometimes been irregular on account of the enormous traffic.

Mr. *Schmitz-Dumont*.

What is a fair dividend to expect a gold mining company to pay?—My idea as a Dividends of gold mines.
ncial man is that you must expect a high dividend. One day I heard a compari-
was made between a railway and a mining company, but I assure you that I have
a large experience in financial matters, and in Europe you make a great difference
ween a railway share and a mining share, and especially a gold mining share.
t is, a railway share is generally considered as a safe investment, and men who
e to live on the interest invest in railway shares. But such men would not invest
gold shares. Besides which, there is another point. A dividend-paying gold
ing company does not represent interest alone. A mine has a certain number of
rs of life only. If you take the dividend as interest, then after a certain number
years you will have seen that you have made a very nice interest, but that your
ital has disappeared. You must calculate a certain part as amortisation.

There are 54 companies on the Rand who altogether declare dividends amounting Dividends of Rand gold mining companies.
4½ per cent.?—But that is no dividend at all for mining companies. The whole
ation here is that big dividends are as yet only expected; but I think if we get
mal conditions here companies will make good dividends. For instance, take a
npany with a capital of £80,000. I know such a company. If you reduce kaffir Dividends and reduction of working costs.
ges by 30 per cent., as is proposed, it would mean for this company a saving of
2,000 per year—that is 15 per cent. dividend. If we get a reduction in freight and
amite, this would equally mean a saving of 15 per cent.; and if we get the other
uction in white labour, after having created normal conditions of life, it will make
ther 15 per cent. And so this company, the shares of which are now about £5,
which gave a dividend of 40 per cent. this year, would give after these reductions
ividend of 85 per cent. So you see what I say about the renewed prosperity
ld be fulfilled if the people in Europe see that the profits of mines increase in such
ay. They will get confidence at once, and I say this after having had great
ncial experience in every department in Europe and America.

A lot of people ascribe low dividends to the over capitalisation of the mines?— Over-speculation.
my opinion a great deal of over speculation has gone on here. But, of course, in
a new country as this and in such new industries, this is intelligible. After
0, when Germany came into possession of a great amount of money, there was an The "Vienna smash."
rmous period of flotation, and, at the same time, an enormous amount of over
ulation. Of course, a very big smash followed, known as the "Vienna smash."
, later on, after the recovery, many of these former flotations which had appeared
became good again, and I thought the recovery which had followed that smash
the cause of the great prosperity and success of German industry. For among a
t number of flotations, there were finally a certain number of good flotations, and
hat period of flotation had not existed we could not have got these good things.

You prefer people would call it over-speculation rather than over-capitalisation? Over-capitalisation.
think in mining companies it is very difficulty to say what is over-capitalisation.
see in floating a company you put in the ground at a certain price; sometimes
think you know the value of the ground from the returns of the adjoining claims,

but you never really know the value, which is only found after working a cert
time, so you see it is difficult to say anything about over-capitalisation. If the cos
working does not become cheaper, a certain number of mines will have to shut do
and the question with these mines is not whether they are over-capitalised or not,
that the monthly revenue in gold covers, at least, or exceeds the working expense
that is the question now.

You say the question of over-capitalisation can only be judged by the results
the mine?—If you speak of over-capitalisation, you can also speak of und
capitalisation. I know, for instance, a company with a capital of £85,000, and
spent £100,000 last year for machinery, &c. They put a big premium on their rese
shares; and so if you see on the one side over-capitalisation, you see here at the sa
time a good deal of under-capitalisation as regards the nominal capital.

Take the industry in general, could it be said there is over-capitalisation to a
extent?—It is very difficult to answer that question; you have to study ev
individual company in order to ascertain that.

Deep level cap-
itals. A lot of companies, especially the deep levels, still require money?—Yes, th
still require money. I think most of these deep levels are under-capitalised; th
have issued their shares at very high prices, otherwise they would have a nomi
capital of millions. Take, for instance, the Crown Deep; I think the whole capital
£400,000, but the value of the mine is such that the shares are in the market at £
and the value in the market, therefore, is £4,000,000. The capital being so small
in my opinion, the only reason that the shares have been issued at a very hi
premium.

Chairman.

Do I understand you that you say there must be a general reduction all roun
—That is my opinion.

Merchants' pri-
ces and reduc-
tion of price of
dynamite and
of railway
rates. It will not help much to make a reduction in railway rates and dynamite, becan
the working people on the fields are more dependent on the mercantile people—s
for instance, a reduction is made in railway rates and the mercantile people reta
their prices?—They cannot retain their prices; competition will bring them dov
There is great competition between commercial people here. I am connected with
large commercial firm, and I know that very well.

Merchants' trade
profits. What is the average profit put by merchants on their merchandise generally?-
think the profit is not very great; the reason of that is, expenses are so high a
there is really enormous competition.

Do you think the profit would be 100 per cent.?—No, that is impossible.

Can you give any idea of the average?—The company with which I am co
nected makes very small profits, sometimes 5 per cent., sometimes 10 per cent., and
some articles perhaps 20 per cent. Generally the profit is very small, and
expenses are enormous; expenses for horses, natives, for rent, &c., are very high.
know a great number of merchants have not succeeded on account of competitic
the competition, for instance, in corrugated iron is so great that I do not belie
merchants make any profit on it at all.

Reduction of
railway rates
and the State
revenue.
Hungarian rail-
way rates. Do you think a reduction in railway rates will cause an increase instead o
decrease in revenue?—I think so. That has been the case in one country in wh
industry has become splendid—that country is Hungary, where you have very che
railway rates. You can imagine what they are when a labourer can go from
boundary of the country to the other for a few shillings. I went from Pesth to
place named Deva, a distance of at least from 250 to 300 English miles, first-cla
fast train, for about 12s. The Government of that country is held in high esteem

ving succeeded in creating a very good state of affairs in the country; everybody nows that in Europe.

Conditions are different here because expenses are so high, and if you have rgely increased revenue it means largely increased expenditure?—Yes, but the penses never increase proportionately; if the traffic becomes greater the expenses come proportionately smaller.

Of course, if you get a reduction there never will be a bigger traffic than demand quires?—Yes, there will be a bigger traffic, because we will begin to work other ines.

You want a reduction in all branches of the industry in order to make it possible make the mines pay. You acknowledge some mines don't pay, and some mines y a dividend of 275 per cent. If a reduction is made on everything in order to ake non-paying mines paying mines, my conviction is that there must always main a certain number of mines that won't pay, and after all, the reduction would e made in favour of those mines that already pay big dividends. Do you consider at right, and what steps do you propose to level matters?—You cannot level up vidends. I think the more profits a mine makes, the better it will be for everyody. I think if you create such a condition as to make payable all the mines on the Vitwatersrand—and I think it is possible—then you will see development of business ere of which we have no idea at this moment.

Mr *de Beer.*

Can you give a more explicit reply to that question? In the first instance rich ines like the Ferreira, Worcester, Crown Reef, and Robinson, and such like mines ay large dividends, and if they share equally in the reductions they would benefit to great extent by-and-by. Can you suggest something to remedy that state of fairs?—You see in case you get these reductions the dividends of these rich mpanies will not increase very much. Take the Ferreira for instance. Say they ake a profit now of 30s. per ton, and later on they will make a profit of 36s. That ill not increase their dividends very much. If they give 275 per cent. now they ould then give 325 per cent. These reductions would make an enormous difference the poorer mines. A mine that can make 6s. profit per ton will afterwards make 2s., and in the case of a mine that can pay nothing at this moment it will afterwards y 6s. That is a big difference to the poor mine; for the rich mine it does not mean ery much.

That does not answer my question; it only reminds me of the good old saying, That unto him that has much more shall be given." Will not the rich mines under e altered conditions get enormous dividends?—No.

If everything is brought down will not the greatest benefit be derived by the ch mines?—No, I don't think they will benefit very much. Say we have a poor ine that employs 1,000 kaffirs and 200 white men. In case we shut down that mine e traffic which is caused by the 200 white men and 1,000 kaffirs will disappear, esides all the traffic of stores for the mines. The State gets a little out of this traffic customs and freight, and in other ways, and it would be a great disadvantage to e Government to shut down this mine. On the other hand, if you can work more ines, and if you have more white workmen and more kaffirs, then of course the affic will increase and the Government will get more revenue.

Mr. *Smit.*

What company do you speak about that carries so cheaply. Is it a private mpany?—No, it is a State railway.

Is it over the entire State, or over a certain distance in order to benefit a certa industry?—I think most railways belong to the State now.

And they all charge as cheaply as the one you quote?—Yes; they are all work on the same cheap basis, and I know that State has made enormous progress with the last few years.

Mr. Seymour's
  evidence.

LOUIS IRVING SEYMOUR was next called, and he stated:

I am a mechanical engineer, and have been resident in Johannesburg since Jul 1896. Before that time I lived in London.

Chairman.

On what points can you give the Commission evidence?—I can give you son evidence on railways, the transport of coal, and the equipment of deep level mines.

This evidence you have about coal and freight rates, is it the same as the oth evidence we have got?—I have given more carefully prepared statistics, and son suggestions with regard to the transport of coal.

About coal rates and freight we have got a lot of evidence. and if you will han in your statistics then you can give your information about deep level mines?

Railway rates on
coal.

Witness.] There is a little evidence about the transport of coal I would like give. I will refer first to American railways. In 1892 all the American railway

Rates on coal on
American rail-
ways.

carried 88,241,050,225 tons one mile, for which they received ·442 of a penn per ton per mile. The lowest rate was one farthing per ton per mile, and tl highest ·866 of a penny per ton per mile. To show how the industry and tl whole of South Africa, not alone in the Transvaal, is handicapped, I will quo some further figures. We have machinery in America at one half-penny per to

Railway rates on
machinery in
America, the
Cape, the Or-
ange Free
State, Natal,
Portuguese
territory, and
on the Nethe-
lands Railway.

per mile; in the Cape and Orange Free State it is 2⅓d. per ton per mile; in Nat it is over 3d.; in Portuguese territory more than 4d; in the Netherlands Railwa by the Cape it is 7 7-10ths. pence, which is 15 times the rate in America, an by the Rand Tram it is seven times. Especially the rate on coal is exceedingl heavy here. The standard rate for conveyance in America, over a mountaino journey in specially built trucks, which cannot be used on the return journey,

Railway rates
on coal in
America and
on the Rand.

one-third of a penny per ton per mile. The rate from Springs to Geldenhuis Dee is 10·80 times that amount. I think a great saving might be made in the transport coal. There could be a saving in bagging by the adoption of scientific trucks, whic

Price of coal at
pit's mouth.

will save us the total cost of off-loading coals. The average selling price of coal at th pit's mouth is 8s. per ton, and the average distance covered by rail is about 30 mil

Consumption of
coal by mines.
Suggested re-
duction of rail-
way rate on
coal.

on the Rand. The tons consumed by the mines, which were transported by rail fo last five months, were 83,080 tons per month. If the railway rate were reduced t 1¼d. per ton per mile all round, including terminal charges, this rate would be sti more than five times the rate in America, and the saving for the last five month

Costs of bagging
and off-loading

would be more than £18,000 per month in transport. Bagging costs 2s. per ton, an off-loading at the Jumpers Deep, for instance, where we have accurate accounts kep

Possible total re-
duction in cost
of transport of
coal.

costs 2s. ⅜d. per ton. These three items could be reduced in the following amounts- £18,173 for transport, £7,477 for bagging, £8,308 for off-loading, making a total £33,958 per month, equal to £407,500 per annum. The estimated costs for equipmer

Estimated cost
of equipment
and develop-
ment on deep
level mines of
100 and 200
stamps respec-
tively.

and development on an average for deep level mines having 100 stamps is:—For cor struction, £231,000; development, £197,000; total money actually required for equip ment, without paying for claims at all, is £428,000; so the average cost per stam erected is £4,280. For a mill having 200 stamps, construction will cost £315,000; de velopment, £236,000; total, £551,000; so that the average cost per stamp is £2,75 These amounts are found principally from actual costs, only the items yet remainin e constructed being estimated on. One reason for the high cost of the construction ·k is the large outlay necessary for cyanide and slimes plant, and the necessity of ing down such plant as will save as much labour as possible. Now with regard to points on which any saving can be made in deep level construction. We have on mine the sum of £93,788 spent for construction alone; £61,587 for material, or per cent., and £27,799, or 29⅔ per cent. for labour, and general expenses were 400, or 4·69 per cent. I do not think that this percentage for labour is too high, I find in large manufactory works in England that the average cost for labour was 7 per cent. on the average of the total cost of machinery manufactured. I have :en one mine, the Jumpers Deep, for instance, at which data are very carefully kept. to December 31st, 1896, we have spent for construction, £101,000; for development, 11,000; total cost, £212,653. The wages during that time amounted to £41,710 for ite labour, and £14,128 for kaffir labour, or £55,838, which comes out 26¼ per cent. our total expenditure. The items on which we hope to save are, for material, about per cent., and for labour, 25 per cent. So our chance for saving on machinery is ·ee times as much as on labour. In developing the deep level mines our total pay a white man is on an average 19s. 6 6-10d. per day. That is higher than is usual th mines which are stamping, since they have lower paid men than we have, during development and construction stage, as nearly all underground men are first-class ners, and for construction a large number of high-priced mechanics are employed. ave developing wages here for a few gold fields, of which I have got accurate infor- ·tion. These are new fields in the same sense as the Johannesburg fields are. ansport is so easily obtained all over the world that we are in competition with these lds to some extent for labour. We have on the Crown Reef 18s. 6d. paid per shift; the Jumpers Deep 19s 4d.; in Montana, in the northern part of America, we have s. 4d.; in Nevada, one of the Western States, we have 17s. 3d.; in British Columbia ;. 6d. So I do not think our wages are greatly in excess of those paid in other ·ts of the world. In my special department here I have a number of draughtsmen king plans, the four principal men receive £27 10s. per month. The four principal ·n in engineering works in England, with which I was connected, receive £21 2s. 6d. : month, so our wages are about 29 per cent. higher here. In England the cost of ing, bedroom, etc., is £8 12s. per month; here it is £11 a month for less accommoda- ·n. The extra cost of living here is 28 per cent., and the wages are 29 per cent. ·re. Such items as cab fare, railway tickets, going to the theatre, and other expenses ich men have to incur, are very much greater here, and I do not think that those ·ges can be reduced at all without sacrificing efficiency. I come now to the cost of ·chinery on board the steamer in England, America, or the Continent, and the cost ·erecting it in working order on the mines. I have only got a few items here, and average cost of all these items is £13,928; the cost of erecting on foundations, ·hout any buildings over them, is £34,079, so that machinery costs, erected at our ·es, two and a-half times more than its original value. From the Chamber of Mines' ·orts, it would appear that 5,135 stamps have been erected, and during the year ·6, 3,740 of these were running at some period or other. If we estimate the amount ·money which has been spent on stamps, and what we find it costs us at present, and ·ich I think is cheaper than the early mines were working upon, it would amount to ·ut £22,000,000 sterling spent upon construction and development of mines, not ·luding the payment for claims. Then that amount will be about £12,000,000 for ·struction and £10,000,000 for development. I have here a table which I need give at present; it contains the number of men employed on the mines per stamp.

Mr. de Beer.

What do you mean by 30 per cent. for sorting?—I mean, taking the case of the

Side notes (right margin): Expense of cyanide and slimes plant. Percentages of construction expenses. Percentage of cost of labour to total costs in English machinery manufactories. Statistics of expenses on Jumpers Deep mine. Percentage of cost of labour to total costs on Jumpers Deep mine. Expected economies on material and labour. Average daily wage of white miner on developing deep level mines on Rand. Average developing wage per shift of white miner on Crown Reef and Jumpers Deep mines, and in Montana, Nevada, and British Columbia. Average monthly wage of four principal draughtsmen on the Rand, and in England. Cost of living on the Rand and in England. Comparison of prime cost of machinery delivered on board ship and when erected on mines here. Total cost of construction and development of mines, not including payment for claims. Sorting.

Saving on Ferreira mine through sorting.

Ferreira, that for each 100 tons of mining done, 30 tons waste rock is sorted out—t… is, rock that has no gold in it.

What do you reckon is saved by that?—Mr. Johns has made a statement which he shows that the saving is £200,000 per annum.

Sorting at the Geldenhuis Deep and Crown Reef.

Is it a general principle adopted on all the mines?—It is being adopted. I m… say that at the Geldenhuis Deep we have commenced sorting, and for 7¾ per ce… allowed for this we have an increased value of the yield of 7·10ths. dwt. It does … pay to crush the rock that has no gold in it. At the Crown Reef also we have b… better results. We began sorting last month also.

Introduction of sorting.

Is it a new method?—No, it is not.

It has only just lately been applied?—It has been applied for more than three … four years by some companies.

It is now commencing to get general?—Yes.

The Ferreira mine carry this on with an average profit of £200,000 per annum … No; an average saving.

Economy of sorting.

Now, when sorting gets into general use, will it not revolutionize mining?—Ma… companies have too many stamps erected, and the manager likes to see all the stam… working. This sorting would prevent this, in other words, the rock containing t… gold can be crushed with fewer stamps than when crushing the waste as well.

Then there is proof when the Ferreira can save over £200,000 a year, others c… also save money?—You can save money by sorting rock, but where the leader and t… Main Reef come together you cannot sort at all.

Are there many mines where it happens that the Main Reef and the leader co… together?—A great many. At the Geldenhuis Deep we have the Main Reef, which … not very rich, while the Main Reef leader is very rich. If we sort out the interveni… waste rock we can crush more of the Main Reef, but the Main Reef being mu… poorer, we do not get a corresponding advantage. It means crushing rock which w… return perhaps 6 dwts., where the leader may run 2 or 3 ounces, so that the total ga… in sorting is not in proportion to the total amount crushed.

The mines to the west of Johannesburg have not the Main Reef and leader clo… together?—But they have a thin reef, which in order to crush, you must take out… large percentage of rock.

And this makes sorting necessary?—Entirely so, many mines could not be work… at a profit without sorting.

Mr. *Smit.*

Cost of living for a draughtsman in the United States and at Johannesburg.

How would you describe the cost of living on the mines?—Well, a draughtsma… in the States would pay for board, two rooms, and washing, £5 18s. a month; and … Johannesburg some of my draughtsmen, who occupy similar positions, pay from £… to £12 and have only one room.

Salaries of mine officials in Johannesburg, Australia, and the Western States of the United States.

How do the salaries of officials run?—They are less in Johannesburg than … Australia, and slightly higher than in the Western States of America.

What do you mean by mine officials?—The manager, engineer, mill manager, a… cyanide men.

And these are paid more in Australia than here?—Yes. I may state that I w… managing director of a large manufacturing firm of mine machinery in London, whi… also did business in America. We were constantly asked by mining companies … Australia, the Straits of Borneo, and South America, to send out managers, m… managers, and other skilled workers, and the average rates in Australia were mu… higher than here. We have had to pay as much as £3,000 per annum for a first-cla… underground foreman. The demand during the past two years has been very gre…

r managers, and this class for Australia, British Columbia, South America, Siam, d the Straits of Borneo.

How does the salary to miners here compare with those paid in Australia and merica ?—The salary to miners is about the same as in Australia, less than in British lumbia, and slightly more than in the Western States of America. I have given a ble about that. It is to say that these are new fields, which are in competition ith us.

Have you compared the salary of the miner in America with the salary of the iner here, and the expenses of living there with the expenses of living here ?—Yes. he expense of living would be 25 or 30 per cent. less than here.

On the salary he earns in America, how much per cent. ?—The salary, in some ses, would be slightly less—say as 17s. 3d. is to 20s.—that is 12 per cent.

You calculate the cost of mining per stamp ?—Yes. The total construction and evelopment is £4,280 per stamp for a 100-stamp mill, and for a 200-stamp mill it is 2,750 per stamp. That is to say you must have the same offices and the same shaft, d nearly the same general construction on the surface for the 100-stamp mill as for e 200-stamp mill. The larger mills are cheaper.

Mr. de Beer.

Can you explain why the Geldenhuis Estate Company is marked on this diagram being far nearer the danger-line than the Geldenhuis Deep ?—I think the value of e rock varies in diagonal chutes, and in certain parts of the Geldenhuis Deep, pecially the upper part, it is much poorer than the lower levels. At present the eldenhuis Estate is now working rock of less value than they did on some of the upper vels, so that certain levels are poor, and at another level you may find much better ck, and it is quite possible that below that you may find poor rock.

Can you tell us the average return per ton of the Geldenhuis Estate ?—The covery is given on the plan. I could not tell you exactly.

I know that the deep level is 6½ dwts ?—It is a little more just now.

I know that, but what is the average ?—In February the recovery was 7.42 wts., and the yield for the month of April was still more, but we are working now in tter levels and the rock is slightly better.

You do not know the yield of the outcrop company ?—I have a complete table, t unfortunately I have not got it by me.

The Chairman then thanked Mr. Seymour for the information supplied, and ked him to hand in the statistics about the yield.

The following Statistics and Diagrams were handed in by witness in the course his examination :—

K

OCEAN FREIGHTS.

(All per Ton of 2,240 Pounds.)

UNION, CLAN LINE, and AMERICAN and AFRICAN STEAMSHIP LINE.

(From New York to South Africa direct.)

FREIGHT RATES ON MACHINERY.

						Cape Town and Algoa Bay.	East London and Port Natal.
Not exceeding 2 tons in weight		...	...	...	...	32/6	40/-
,,	2½	,,	...	...	...	...	37/6	45/-
,,	3	,,	...	...	...	...	42/6	50/-
,,	3½	,,	...	...	...	...	47/6	55/-
,,	4	,,	...	...	...	...	52/6	60/-
,,	4½	,,	...	...	...	...	57/6	65/-
,,	5	,,	...	...	...	...	62/6	70/-
,,	6	,,	...	...	...	...	67/6	75/-
,,	7	,,	...	...	...	...	72/6	80/-
,,	8	,,	...	...	...	...	77/6	85/-
,,	9	,,	...	...	...	...	82/6	90/-
,,	10	,,	...	...	...	...	87/6	95/-
,,	11	,,	...	...	...	...	92/6	100/-
,,	12	,,	...	...	...	...	97/6	105/-

NOTE.—Ten per cent. primage is charged on all the above rates, returnable in the form of rebate. The latter is claimed on the 31st January and 31st July of each year, and is payable six months thereafter.

SAILING VESSELS—LONDON TO EAST LONDON, &C.

	East London.	Algoa Bay.
1. Mining Machinery and Cement (iron drums), up to 3 tons	18/9	17/3
2. Boilers, &c., 3 tons to 9 tons	23/-	22/3

All per ton weight or measurement (ship's option). Freight net. No primage.

STEAMER FREIGHTS.

(All up to 3 tons weight.)

From LONDON, LIVERPOOL, or GLASGOW to :—

Destination.		Name of Line.			I.	II.	III.	IV.
East London	...	Bucknall and Clan	...	...	51/3	38/9	32/6	30/
East London	...	Castle and Union (intermediate)			52/6	40/-	32/6	30/-
East London	...	Castle and Union (mail)		...	55/-	41/3	32/6	30/-
Algoa Bay	...	Bucknall and Clan	...	...	42/6	31/3	25/-	22/6
Algoa Bay	...	Castle and Union (intermediate)			45/-	32/6	25/-	22/6
Algoa Bay	...	Castle and Union (mail)		...	47/6	33/9	25/-	22/6

Class I.	...	...	...	Machinery, Boilers, &c.
„ II.	...	...	..	Trucks, Piping, &c.
„ III.	...	...	...	Rails, Soap, Earthen Pipes, &c.
„ IV.	...	...	...	Bar Iron and Steel, Cement.

On packages over Three Tons weight, 5/6 additional on every Ton or Half-Ton up to Five Tons.

From Five to Twelve Tons, 5/6 per ton additional. No charge for heavy lifts or heavy measurement.

SEA FREIGHT.

From New York to London ... ... 12/6 per long ton.

From Chicago to London on heavy boilers, *via* Kanawha Despatch (Railway, 1,000 miles; sea distance, about 3,300 miles), 50 cents. per 100 lbs., equals 40/6 per ton of 2,240 lbs.—(Weight or Measurement *not* at ship's option.)

SEA FREIGHT.

From New York to San Francisco, *via* Galveston by sea, thence by rail on South Pacific Road to San Francisco:—

| In Summer | ... | 1/5¼d. per 100 lbs. ; per ton, 2,240 lbs., £1 12s. 2d. |
| „ Winter | ... | ... ... „ „ £2 6s. 0d. |

RAILWAY RATES.

For comparison of Indian and other Railway Rates per mile, *Engineering*, Vol. 42, p. 214, says:—

CHARGES PER TON PER MILE IN PENCE.

Class of Goods.	India.	England.	Belgium.	Holland.	Germany.
Grain	0·85	1·54	0·79	0·96	1·13
Cotton	1·53	2·77	1·74	1·61	1·61
Cotton Goods	1·28	2·64	2·22	1·61	2·06
Sugar	0·85	1·12	1·60	0·96	1·32
Average ...	1·13	2·02	1·59	1·28	1·55

ENGLISH RAILWAY RATES IN 1893.

From *Engineering* (Vol., 65, p. 48 Jan., 1893.)

Name of Railway.	Old Maxima per Ton per Mile.	First 20 Miles.	Next 30 Miles.	Next 50 Miles.	Remainder of of Distance.
Great Eastern	2d.	1·80	1·50	1·20	0·70
Great Northern	2½d.	1·80	1·50	1·20	0·70
Great Western	2½d.	1·80	1·50	1·20	0·70
London and North Western ...	2½d.	1·80	1·50	1·20	0·70
London, Chatham, and Dover ...	3d.	1·80	1·50	1·20	0·70
North Eastern	2d.	2·0	1·75	1·50	1·25
South Eastern	2d. to 3d.	1·80	1·50	1·20	0·75
Taff Vale	2½d.	1·80	1·50	1·20	0·70
Lancashire and Yorkshire ...	2d.	1·80	1·50	1·20	0·70

THE COST PER TON PER MILE IN GERMANY HAS BEEN :—

Year.							Cost in Pence per Ton per Mile.
1868	...	...	...	...	..	...	1·063
1878	...	...	...	...	...	...	0·911
1880	...	...	...	...	...	...	0·852
1882	..	...	...	...	...	...	0.815
1884	...	...	...	...	...	...	0·792
1886	...	...	...	...	...	...	0·788
1888	...	...	...	...	...	...	0·753
1890	...	...	...	...	...	....	0·749

Ordinary recent rates for machinery over various roads in America per ton 2,000 lbs.

		Total charge.	Distance (Miles).	Rate per ton (per Mile).
Chicago to Atlanta, Georgia	...	47/7	1,500	0.3807d.
„ Syracuse, New York	...	18/10½	670	0.3381d.
„ Denver, Colorado	...	94/5	1,041	1.088d.
„ New York, New York	...	24/7½	960	0.3078d.
„ San Francisco, Cal.	...	90/3	2,416	0.4485d.

On the following named materials the rate from Chicago to New York in 189 and which practically governed all railway rates in the Eastern States, was per ton 2,000 lbs. in car-load lots :—

(Distance: 960 miles average).

	Cotton Goods.	Stores.	Coffee.	Starch.	Sugar.	Soap.	Machine
Material Rate in pence per ton per mile	0·513	0·257	0·257	0·257	0·257	0.2668	0·308

For American Railways the total actual cost of carriage to the Railwa themselves was as under :—

Railway.	1887.	Pence per ton per mile. 1888.	1889.	1890.
Main Line Branches ...	0·3298	0·3103	0·3053	0·2955
United Railroads of New Jersey	0·6303	0·6007	0·5761	0·5663
Philadelphia and Erie Railroad...	0·2659	0·2511	0·2709	0·2511
Lines East of Pittsburg and Erie	0·3595	0·3398	0·3348	0·3201

Transport of and rate for coal on American railways in 1892.

In 1892 all the American Railways combined carried 88,241,050,225 tons o mile, for which they received $799,316,042, or at an average rate of 0·898 cent equals 0·4422d. per ton per mile.

The lowest charge was on the Chesapeake and Ohio Railway, which was 0·2561 per ton per mile. The highest was the New York, New Haven, and Hartford, whi sent most of its heavy freight by steamer. Its railway rate was 0·866 per t per mile.

Dividends of American railways in 1892.

During this year the average rate of dividend paid by all the railway compani combined was 2·11%, and this amount was paid by 40% of all the lines. During t same time, 15% of all lines paid no interest on their debentures.

Comparing the various average rates above cited, we have

German (latest quoted)	...	0·749d. per ton per mile, State Railways.
English (average)	...	1·125d.	do.	Private	do.
American do.	...	0·4422d.	do.	do.	do.

Machinery, American	...	0.5126d. per ton per mile, 1·000 per cent.
do. Cape	...	2·34d.	do.	4·565	do.
do. Orange Free State	...	2·34d.	do.	4·565	do.
do. Natal	...	3·04d.	do.	5·931	do.
do. Portuguese	...	4·07d.	do.	7·940	do.
do. Netherlands-Cape	...	7·69d.	do.	15·000	do.
do. do. Natal	...	5·06d.	do.	9·871	do.
do. do. Delagoa	4·27d.	do.	8·330	do.
Actual cost coal, Rand Tram	...	3·58d.	do.	6·982	do.

The standard rate for conveyance of coal from Pennsylvania to New York over mountainous roads in specially built trucks for coal, which cannot be used on the return journey, is 0.3305d. per ton per mile.

The actual cost of coal from Springs Station to the Geldenhuis and Jumpers Deeps, in bulk, is 3·58 per ton per mile, or 10.83 times the rate in Eastern United States of America.

TRANSPORT AND HANDLING OF COAL.

The average selling price of coal at the pit's mouth in the Brakpan district is, roughly speaking, 8s. per ton, and the average distance hauled by rail, to the various mines, about 30 miles.

The average tons consumed by the mines, which was transported by rail for the last five months, was 83,080 tons per month.

I estimate the average value per ton delivered at the gold mines as 18s. per ton, say £74,772 per month.

Were the rate by rail reduced to 1¾d. per ton per mile, which is still 5·295 times the rate in Eastern United States, an economy in transport of 83,080 tons x 30 x ¾d., equals £18,173 1s. 6d. per month, would result.

Bagging costs on an average 2s. per ton of coal, or, allowing 90% of all coal delivered to the mines in bags, bagging costs £7,477 4s. per month.

Off-loading at the Jumpers Deep, Limited, at which mine accurate costs have been kept, is as under :—

Average monthly tons consumed	...	...	960
Average cost off-loading (white labour) ...	...	£15 0 0
do. do. (black labour) ...	...	82 10 0
Total cost per month off-loading coal	...	£97 10 0

Average cost for off-loading coal per ton 2s. 0·375d.

Monthly economy obtainable in off-loading by means of automatic wagons.

Were side-tipping railway wagons adopted, as used in America, and which wou suit existing sidings and bunkers, the saving in off-loading coal would be 2s. per to or £8,308 per month.

Possible total saving to the mining industry by reduction of expenses regarding coal.

Summed up, the total saving per month to the industry is as under, viz :—

	£	s.	d.
Railway transport	18,173	1	6
Bagging	7,477	4	0
Off-loading	8,308	0	0
	£33,958	5	6

or £407,500 per annum.

MACHINERY SHIPMENTS TO JOHANNESBURG—ACTUAL COST.

Cost per Ton of 2,000 lbs.	An average lot of Mining Machinery.			Percentage of Total Cost.	Cast Iron Mortar Bases, Cored & Planed, Columns, Girders, &c.			Percentage of Total Cost
	£	s.	d.		£	s.	d.	
F.O.B. London or Steamer... ...	31	5	0	75.64	4	1	10	29·75
Ocean freight (intermediate class) to Port Elizabeth	2	0	2	4·86	2	0	2	14·60
Landing	0	4	3	0·51	0	4	3	1·55
Wharfage 3/8% on home cost ...	0	2	4	0·28	0	0	3	0·09
Clearing and forwarding	0	3	9	0·45	0	3	9	1·36
Railage to Viljoen's Drift (3rd class)...	5	10	0	13·32	5	10	0	39·98
Viljoen's Drift transport to Johannesburg, including cartage ...	1	13	4	4·04	1	13	4	12·12
Transvaal duty, equals 1½% on home cost, plus 20%	0	7	6	0·90	0	1	6	0·55
Cost Delivery at Johannesburg ...	£41	6	4	100·00	£13	15	1	100·00
Difference between home cost and cost delivered Johannesburg ...	10	1	4		9	13	3	
If Carriage was 1·13d. per ton per mile, as was charged in India in 1886 on grain, sugar, cotton, and cotton goods, the railage would have been	3	7	3		3	7	3	
Leaving cost at Johannesburg ...	37	10	3		9	19	0	
Or difference between home cost and cost here per ton	6	5	3		5	17	2	
Saving per ton over present cost ...	£3	16	1	9·27%	£3	16	1	27·66%

Percentages of construction costs of a deep level mine.

Out of a total expenditure of £93,788 9s. 10d. for construction work at a Dee Level Mine, the proportionate amounts are :—

	£	s.	d.	Percentage.
Material	61,587	19	3	65·67
Labour	27,799	16	1	29·64
General expenses	4,400	14	6	4·69
	£93,788	9	10	100·00

The percentage of total cost paid for labour, viz :—29·64, is a close approximation he average cost of labour at a large machinery manufactory works in England, ipped with the most modern labour-saving appliances, at which factory the total ur was 31·7 per cent. of the total cost of the manufactured goods.

PROPORTION OF EXPENDITURE IN DEEP LEVEL COMPANIES.

Jumpers Deep, Limited.

From Commencement to December 31st, 1896.

			Percentage.	
Construction cost	...	...	£101,047 2 3	47·52
Development cost	...	...	111,606 15 7	52·48

Total cost (including all expenses except payment for claims) £212,653 17s. 10d.

Percentages of costs of Jumpers Deep from its commencement to 31st December, 1896.

During that time the total wages paid was :—

Whites,	43,032 shifts at 19s. 6·62d.	£41,710 9 2	19·62%	
Natives,	112,385 shifts at 2s. 6·17d.	14,128 1 0	6·64	
	Total wages	£55,838 10 2	26·26	of total Expenditure.

[No cost of native food included in native wages].

The development of a Deep Level Mine requires a heavy outlay for timber, amite, and coal, and during the development and construction stages, the average e per man per shift is higher than would obtain in the same mine when stamping, was stated by Mr. Sidney Jennings, whose figures are, for all white men, 18s. 6·4d. man per shift.

Cost of development of a deep level mine.

In the mines of Montana, the standard rate of pay is $3·50 per day for all underund men ; equals 14s. 4·3d.

Wages in the mines of Montana, U.S.A.

In the Comstock mines of Nevada, it is $4·00 per day ; equals 17s. 3d.

Wages in the Comstock mines, Nevada

In the British Columbia mines, the standard rate of wages is $5·00 per day ; als 20s. 6¼d. per shift.

Wages in the mines of British Columbia.

Tabulated, the rate per shift is :

			s.	d.	
Crown Reef	..	...	18	6·4	average.
Jumpers Deep	...	...	19	4·62	„
Montana	...	...	14	4·3	standard.
Nevada	...	...	17	3	„
British Columbia ...		...	20	6¼	„

Table of wages on the Crown Reef and Jumpers Deep mines, and in Montana, Nevada and British Columbia.

All above are new goldfields with which we are in competition. From consider experience in finding men for various responsible positions at mines for the Cape, tralia, the Straits, and South America, I think, generally, the salaries paid on the d are somewhat lower than are paid in the other districts mentioned above.

Lowness of salaries on the Rand.

In my own department of mechanical engineering the rate of wages paid at present he four principal draughtsmen is £27 10s. per month, while that paid to the first r similar men at Messrs. Fraser and Chalmers' Engineering Works, near London, £21 2s. 6d. per month, for similar work, so that the same man in Johannesburg

Wages of four principal draughtsmen at Johannesburg and in England.

receives 29·44 per cent. more wages than at London, while the cost of living is m
greater here than there, per month, as follows:

Comparative cost of living in Johannesburg, Erith, England, and Scranton, N. America.

Erith, England—Cost of bedroom, sitting room, fires, washing,
beer, gas, etc.   ...   .   8 12 0   1·

Scranton, North America—Bed and sitting room, with bath and
lavatory, fires, gas, washing, etc. ...   .   5 19 0   ·

Johannesburg—Bedroom, fire, candles, and washing   ...   11 0 0   1.

The above rates are given as the actual costs of living for a draughtsman or cle
All other items, such as clothes, cab fares, railway tickets, and pleasures, which go
make up the sum total of living expenses, are about double in Johannesburg to wl
similar things cost in England or America.

Reduction of clerks' wages not advisable.

I consider the rate of pay for this class of men cannot be reduced without
great sacrifice in the quality of talent.

Relative cost of machinery f.o.b. in England, on the Continent, or in America and on Witwatersrand mines.

RELATIVE COST OF MACHINERY f.o.b. ENGLAND, CONTINENT,
AMERICA, AND ERECTED ON THE MINES:

	Home Cost. £	Percentage.	Cost Erected. £ s. d.
Single drum hoisting engine ...	1,550	48	3,218 11 1
Double drum hoisting engine ...	1,612	42¼	3,802 14 8
Double drum hoisting engine ...	2,160	47¼	4,582 1 0
Cornish pumping plant ...	1,528	33	4,625 17 3
35-drill compressor, complete ...	4,000	54¾	7,312 0 11
8 boilers, 125 h.p. each ...	2,736	31¼	8,738 9 4
8½ft. x 135ft. chimney, complete	342	19	1,799 17 0
	£13,928	40¾%	£34,079 11 3

Generally speaking, the principal machinery at any mine will be found to c
erected, two-and-a-half times its home cost.

STAMPS ERECTED.

Total number of stamps erected and running on Witwatersrand gold fields in 1896.

From the Chamber of Mines reports, the total number of stamps erected on th
fields to the end of 1896 is 5135, of which 3,740, or 72·8 per cent., have been runni
some portion of the time in the past year.

Estimated total cost of equipment and development of Witwatersrand gold fields.

If we estimate the amount of money that has been spent in equipping a
developing for 5,135 stamps, the same as above noted for a 100-stamp mill, i.e., £4,2
per stamp, we have about 22 millions sterling spent to equip and develop the vari
mines on these fields, aside from the money spent for claims. I believe not less th
£5,000 per stamp has actually been spent.

Construction costs of mines of Witwatersrand gold fields and excess cost through high railway rates.

Of this 22 millions sterling about 55 per cent. (or say, twelve millions sterli
will have been spent on construction, of which amount I should say one mill
sterling might have been saved if the railway rates had been such as would have o
returned a good rate of interest to its shareholders.

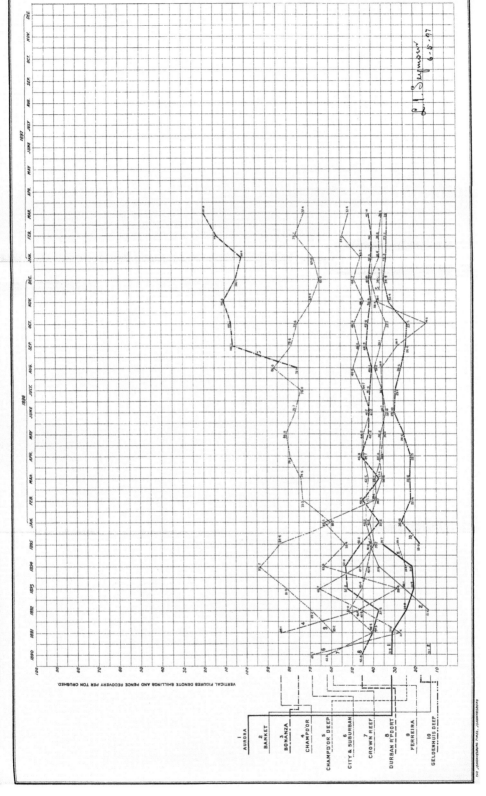

TABLE SHOWING RECOVERY OF GOLD PER TON OF ORE CRUSHED IN SHILLINGS AND PENCE OF 60 LEADING MINES OF THE WITWATERSRAND.—I.

159

The material originally positioned here is too large for reproduction in this reissue. A PDF can be downloaded from the web address given on page iv of this book, by clicking on 'Resources Available'.

TABLE SHOWING RECOVERY OF GOLD PER TON OF ORE CRUSHED IN SHILLINGS AND PENCE OF 60 LEADING MINES OF THE WITWATERSRAND.—II.

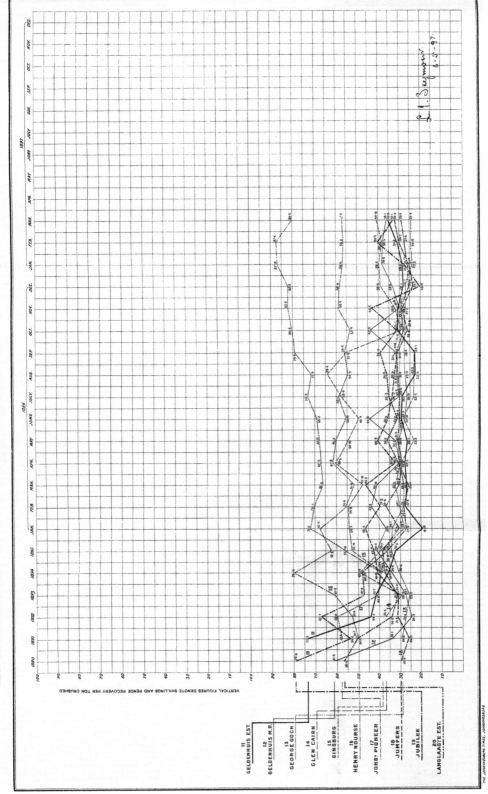

The material originally positioned here is too large for reproduction in this reissue. A PDF can be downloaded from the web address given on page iv of this book, by clicking on 'Resources Available'.

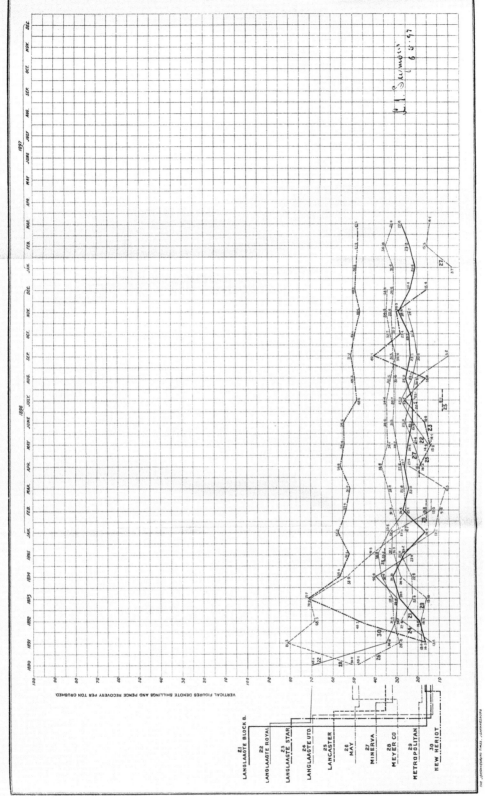

The material originally positioned here is too large for reproduction in this reissue. A PDF can be downloaded from the web address given on page iv of this book, by clicking on 'Resources Available'.

TABLE SHOWING RECOVERY OF GOLD PER TON OF ORE CRUSHED IN SHILLINGS AND PENCE OF 60 LEADING MINES OF THE WITWATERSRAND.—IV.

The material originally positioned here is too large for reproduction in this reissue. A PDF can be downloaded from the web address given on page iv of this book, by clicking on 'Resources Available'.

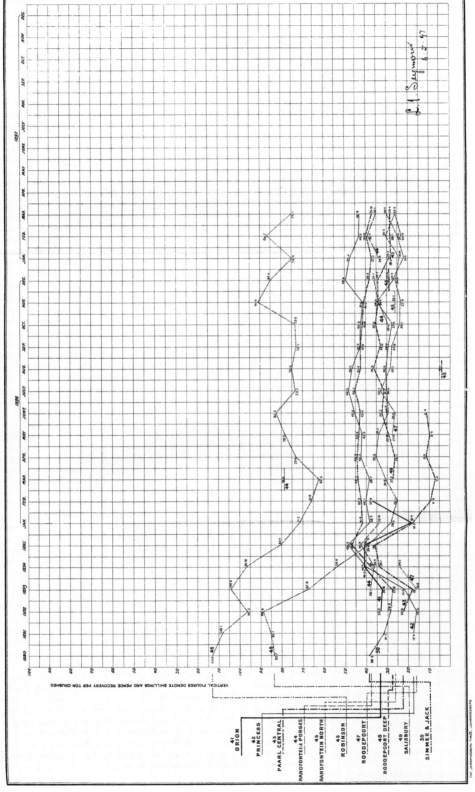

The material originally positioned here is too large for reproduction in this reissue. A PDF can be downloaded from the web address given on page iv of this book, by clicking on 'Resources Available'.

TABLE SHOWING RECOVERY OF GOLD PER TON OF ORE CRUSHED IN SHILLINGS AND PENCE OF 60 LEADING MINES OF THE WITWATERSRAND.—VI.

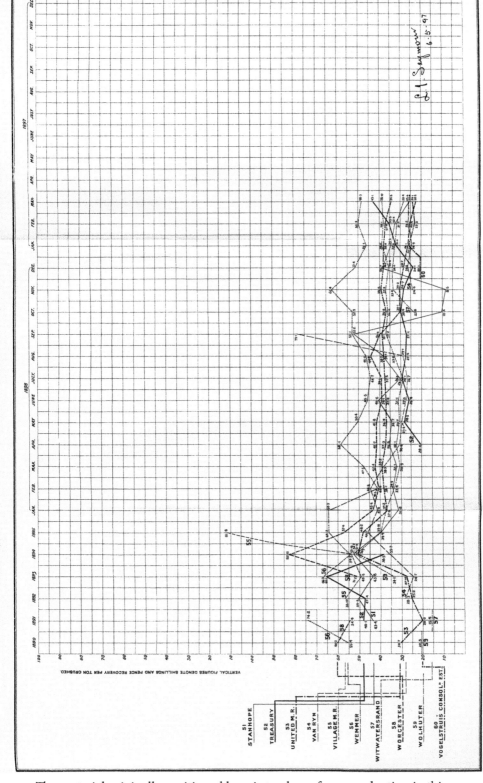

The material originally positioned here is too large for reproduction in this reissue. A PDF can be downloaded from the web address given on page iv of this book, by clicking on 'Resources Available'.

TABLE OF DISTRIBUTION OF LABOUR AT THE DIFFERENT DEEP LEVEL MINES.

Name of Company.	Construction. Whites.	Construction. Blacks.	Development. Whites.	Development. Blacks.	Total at Present. Whites.	Total at Present. Blacks.	Estimated No. when Stamping. Whites.	Estimated No. when Stamping. Blacks.
Glen Deep, 100 stamps	40	53	75	247	115	300		
Langlaagte Deep, 200 stamps ...	16	23	152	679	168	702	300	2,000
Crown Deep, 200 stamps ...	39	60	168	890	207	950	400	2,500 to 3,000
Nourse Deep, 100 stamps ...	37	137	111	560	148	697	140	1,200
Jumpers Deep, 200 stamps ...	42	160	138	740	180	900	150	2,000
Rose Deep, 200 stamps	75	310	145	565	220	875	260	1,500
Average ...	41·5	123·83	131·5	613·5	173	737·3	250	1,840

	Actual No. before Milling.	Estimated No. after Milling.	Average No. per Stamp.
Average number whites employed for 100-stamp plant	132	140	1·4
,, ,, ,, 200-stamp ,,	194	280	1·4
,, natives ,, 100-stamp ,,	498	1,200	12·0
,, ,, ,, 200-stamp ,,	857	2,060	10·3
Whites employed at Robinson mine (120 stamps)		280	2·33
Natives ,, ,, ,,		2,369	19·74
Whites employed at Geldenhuis Deep (155 stamps)		272	1·75
Natives ,, ,, ,,		1,316	8·49
Whites employed at Crown Reef (120 stamps)		246	2·05
Natives ,, ,, ,, ,,		1,749	14·60

Average number of white men when stamping, per stamp erected 1·79

    ,,   ,, natives ,,   ,,   ,, 13·03

Mr. ROBERT BARROW was the next witness called. He made the followin statement :—

I am a miner from the North Lancashire District of England, and have bee working underground for 26 years. At present I am mine foreman at the Jumper Deep, Limited, and have been in South Africa since the latter end of 1887. O arrival I worked for six months in Kimberley in the De Beers Mines ; since then have worked in the Transvaal. I have a wife and four children. When I came t South Africa I left my wife and family living in Dalton-in-Furness, Lancashir where they remained five years, when they came out here, and have been living her with me about four years. I have read the evidence submitted to this Commissio and, generally, agree with it, especially with the evidence given by Mr. Fitzpatrick I therefore intend to confine my statement to a simple analysis, and a comparison o cost of living in England with my family and the cost of living here, and th difficulties of coming out to this country.

The cost of living and the wage earned by a miner in Lancashire, England, wil be dealt with in order that a comparison of facts and figures leading up to the poin under notice, viz., cost of living in the Transvaal, may be arrived at.

A miner receives 5s. per day of eight hours, the month being composed of 2 working days. This totals up to £5 10s. per month.

The 22 working days are as follows, viz. :—

	Days.
First week—Monday, 6 a.m. till 2 p.m., and so on till Saturday, 12 p.m.	6,
Second week—Monday, 2 p.m. till 10 p.m., and so on till Friday . night, 10 p.m.	5

(Saturday being a half-holiday, he does not go down to work at 2 p.m., therefor no work is done from Friday night at 10 p.m. till Monday at 6 a.m.)

	Days.
Third week—Monday, 6 a.m. till 2 p.m., and so on till Saturday, 12 p.m.	6
Fourth week—Monday, 2 p.m. till 10 p.m., and so on till Friday night, 10 p.m.	5
	22

The balance of a month of 30 days being made up as follows :—

Sundays, non-working days, 4; two Saturdays, non-working, 2 ; Saturday, 12 p.m.—Monday, 2 p.m., no work, 2 ...	8
Total days	30

An ordinary miner's cottage of six rooms costs 3s. 6d. per week, or 16s. pe month, in England, leaving a balance of £4 14s. per month for food, clothing, &c.

In the Transvaal the same cottage would cost £8 per month, i.e., £7 4s. more.

The food consists principally of porridge, bread, butter, meat, vegetables, te coffee, milk, and eggs.

The following is a table of the approximate cost of these articles in England :—

TABLE I.

Butter, 10d. to 1s. per lb.
Flour, 1s. 8d. per st. (14 lbs.)
Bacon, 4d. per lb.
Tea, 1s, per lb.
Coffee, 1s. per lb.
Eggs, 9d. per doz.
Milk, 1d. per pint.
Potatoes, 3d. per 14 lbs. (stone).
Meat, 8d. per lb.
Oatmeal, about 1½d. per lb.

Clothing.—This in England is, at the very least, 43 per cent. cheaper than in the Transvaal. For example, a suit of clothes costing 20s. in England would, for the same quality and material, cost 35s. in the Transvaal.

A pair of ready-made miner's boots, costing 8s. 6d. in England, would, for the same quality, cost 17s. 6d. here.

A detailed estimate of the cost of living per week, for a miner's family of five, in England is given :—

Estimate of weekly cost of living of miner's family in England.

TABLE II.

	£	s.	d.	
Milk, 1 pint per day at 1d. per pint	0	0	7	per week.
Butter, 2 lbs. per week at 10d. per lb.	0	1	8	,,
Meat, 9 lbs. per week (three times per week) at 8d.	0	6	0	,,
Vegetables, per week	0	2	6	,,
Bread (a 4 lb. loaf and a half per day), at 6d. per loaf	0	5	3	,,
Groceries (tea, sugar, soap, coal, etc.)	0	5	6	,,
	£1	1	6	
			4	

	£	s.	d.
Per month	£4	6	0
Rent per month	0	16	0
Doctor's fees for whole family	0	1	0
Schooling (free)	0	0	0
	£5	3	0
Leaving balance for clothing of	0	7	0
	£5	10	0

Further, a miner generally belongs to one of the numerous benefit societies in England, by which for the payment of 2s. per month he is entitled to receive 12s. per week in case of sickness. In case of his death his wife receives from the society £14 down, and in case of his wife's death the husband receives £7 down. Numerous privileges are also enjoyed by a miner, for which he pays nothing, such as free reading rooms and free recreation grounds. The above expenditure per month enables a miner and his family to live in greater comfort and enjoyment than it is possible to do here at £1 per day. Leaving the cost of living in England for the moment, the expenses connected with a voyage to the Cape will now be noted. A third-class passage to the

English benefit societies.

Voyage expenses of miners.

Cape from any part of England costs sixteen guineas.   Add to this railway fare, th
class, from the Cape to Johannesburg (which is £4 8s. 9d.), the expenditure for
voyage amounts to £21 4s. 9d.   This does not include cost of food during the th
days occupied in the journey by train, which would bring the amount up to £
Further, the majority of miners arriving here have to allow for about a month
being out of employment, necessitating a further expenditure of £8 (or more)
living during this time.   Taking into consideration all these items, amounting
£30, and referring to Table II., by whcih it will be seen that he has only 7s. per mor
left over from the actual cost of living for himself and family, for clothing, etc., it
not difficult to judge of the length of time it would be necessary for him to save
sufficient money to bring him out to Johannesburg, and what sacrifices he and
family would have to undergo in order to enable him to do so.   As a matter of fact,
is impossible for him to collect enough out of his earnings for this purpose, and he b
to borrow the amount from his unmarried friends.   Bearing the above in mind, it
only natural to suppose that he undergoes these sacrifices in the hopes of obtaini
sufficient pay, once arrived here, and at work, to make up for these.

Average daily
wage of white
miner on the
Rand.

AVERAGE RATE OF WAGES FOR MINERS ON THE RAND.

75 per cent. rock-drill men at 20s. per day.

25 per cent. bossing boys in stopes at 12s. to 15s. per day, giving an avera
of £23 16s. 8d. per month of 26 days.

Monthly cost of
living of min-
er's family on
the Rand.

With this amount per month a married man with a family, say of five altogeth
has to pay the following.   The undernoted different amounts are the actual averag
for mine families.

TABLE III.

						£	s.	d.	
Rent ...	...	...	...	...	...	6	10	0	per month.
Butcher's account	...	...	...	...	...	2	10	0	,,
Baker's account	...	...	...	...	...	2	0	0	,,
Milk (1 bottle per day) ...	...	...	...	...	0	15	0	,,
Groceries	...	...	...	...	...	8	0	0	,,
Fuel ...	...	...	...	...	...	1	1	0	,,
			Total	...	...£20	6	0		,,

This amount is merely for absolute necessaries to sustain life and to give a shelt
for the head, placed at the lowest estimate.   It will be noticed that the amount do
not take into account the following absolute necessaries also:—

TABLE IV.

			£	s.	d.		
Clothing	...	...	4	0	0	per month.	
Schooling	...	...	1	10	0	,,	(not including books).
Doctor's fees	...	...	0	7	6	,,	
Kitchen boy	...	...	3	0	0	,,	
Railway fares	...	...	1	2	6	,,	(for children to school).
			£10	0	0		

Making the total £30 6s. per month for mere natural and compulsory wan
leaving out all consideration of such small items as reading matter, school boo

reation, and small comforts indispensable for comfort and enjoyment. It will be
en that in Table III., groceries exceed in cost all other items, taking them one by one,
d it would be as well to give here a table showing how this amount is made up.

TABLE V.

	£	s.	d.		
Butter, 2 lbs. per week, at 2s. 6d. per lb.	1	0	0	per month.	Monthly expenses of miner's family on the Rand in groceries.
Tea, 2 lbs. per week, at 2s. 6d. per lb.	1	0	0	„	
Sugar, 10 bs. per week, at 4d. per lb.	0	13	4	„	
Coffee, 2 lbs. per week, at 3s. per lb.	1	4	0	„	
Flour, 6 lb. per week, at 4d. per lb.	0	8	0	„	
Jams, three tins per week, at 9d. per tin	0	9	0	„	
Condensed milk, three tins per week, at 8d. per tin	0	8	0	„	
Cheese, 4 lbs. per month at 1s. 6d.	0	6	0	„	
Rice, 4 lbs. per week, about 3d. per lb.	0	4	0	„	
Soap	0	6	0	„	
Lights	0	10	0	„	
Small sundries (too numerous to mention) ...	1	11	8	„	
	£8	0	0		

In order to show more clearly the difference of cost of living in England and in
hannesburg, I will bring forward table No. 1 of cost of living of a miner and his
mily in England, and put beside it the cost of living in Johannesburg for exactly the
me articles :—

TABLE VI.

	England.			Transvaal.			
	£	s.	d.	£	s.	d.	
Milk	0	2	4	0	15	0	Comparative cost of living of miner's family in England and the Transvaal.
Butter	0	6	8	1	0	0	
Meat	1	4	0	2	10	0	
Vegetables	0	10	0		—		
Bread	1	1	0	2	0	0	
Groceries	1	2	0	8	0	0	
Rent	0	16	0	6	0	0	
Doctor's fees	0	1	0	0	7	6	
	£5	3	0	£20	12	6	

A difference in favour of England of no less than £15 9s. 6d. On looking through
able No. II. in this statement, it will be seen that a balance of only 7s. per month is
ft for clothing, and it will be asked : "How can a miner clothe himself and family
7s. per month?" The answer to this is that he cannot, but it must be remembered
at at home there are wealthy men in every district who help by their charity, to say
thing of different "Dorcas Societies," who make clothing and distribute it among
e poorer classes ; and there are philanthropists who found free institutions for the
nefit of workmen. In fact there are many things which help miners to tide over any
isfortune through sickness or otherwise. There is none of this in the Transvaal, and
ery man has to help himself or sink.

English aid societies.

Mr. *Smit.*

Have the mines never imported workmen and paid their expenses out ?—Not that
am aware of.

Importation of miners

Mr. *Brochon.*

White wages.   In this statement we see that you have white men working at 12s. and 15s. p
shift. Is that so?—Yes, we have got them at the Jumpers Deep. We have got
many at 12s. as at 15s.

Mr. *Albu.*

Do you consider them good men?—They are men new out from home, and the
have not had much experience and they are glad to work for almost anything.

They are not miners, but men who come out here and say they have learne
nothing?—Yes.

But these men would not get a shift at £5 10s. per month at home?—There is
probability that they might. We are not supposed to know what a man is until w
try him.

Miners wages in England.   What is the average pay in England for competent miners such as those you woul
engage as stoping men. What is the pay in coal mines or tin mines at home?—
worked in the iron ore mines, and the average pay was what my opening statemen
says—5s. per day. That was ten years ago.

Married miners' quarters.   I will admit that £20 won't go a very long way in the case of a married man
especially if he has to pay house rent; but is it not a fact that most married men ar
provided with a cottage on the mine?—No, there are not 10 per cent. who have go
cottages on the mine.

Board of single miners.   A single man on a mine pays about £5 or £5 10s. per month on the mine fo
board?—At the present day he pays £6.

I think £6 is an excessive amount.—I am speaking of the boarding-house at ou
mine.

I know of a boarding-house at a Pretoria factory and the charge is £3 10s. pe
month, and the men seem very well satisfied. A workman here who pays £6 per mont
gets his room, light, and his coal. Now, the average earning of the competent mine
Wages of single miners. is between £20 and £22 per month. If he pays £6 per month out of that he has £1
over. Don't you think he could save a good deal out of that?—Yes, I think th
single miner ought to save a little out of that, but he has got a much better chance tha
a married man.

In your statement I find that at home, a married man with a family of five, ha
9-lbs. of meat per week at 8d. per lb., that is 6s. In the table relating to this countr
the butcher's account is put down at £2 10s. Now meat does not cost as much here a
at home?—No, but it is much inferior, it has not the same substance and it takes s
much more to serve you.

Married miners' quarters.   Do you think a married miner's lot would be considerably improved if the min
companies were to erect cottages and charge a small rental for them, and that it woul
save the miner a lot?—If the companies could erect cottages and let them about £2,
think it would. Of course my figures refer to a miner who has to take a house in
place like Jeppestown.

All over the world if a man starts as a clerk or miner and is married, it is awkwar
to make both ends meet, is it not?—I am only speaking of England.

Do you think a man with three children is justified in taking a cottage at £8 pe
month?—Not at all. I am speaking of a man and wife with five children.

But you give us an exceptionally bad case. It must be very hard on a woma
and five children if the husband has got no further in life than a miner?—Yes, bu
you know we all make these mistakes.

The married miner with five children is badly off. What would you suggest to ..edy the evil. I want to be fair to the married as well as to the unmarried miner ? ..beg your pardon, I did not quite catch what you said.

I am giving the married and the unmarried an equal chance. You admit that £20 .22 is a good wage for an unmarried man. I admit that for a married man it is ..ing more than sufficient. What would you suggest to me to do. Can I give the ..ried man a higher wage than the unmarried because the former has got a wife and .. children, and is not a better labourer than the unmarried. How can you suggest ..et out of this difficulty, if his labour is not worth to me more than the unmarried ? ..he only thing I can suggest is to bring down the cost of provisions and house rent.

That is what we are all trying for, to get the Government to bring down the cost ..iving. The consequence would be that I would say to the unmarried man, " I can .. pay you £15 per month." I would like to see the man with five children get on ..ell as the other.—It is very hard to suggest anything, because one man is as good ..he other.

Well, what is the use of complaining if you cannot bring forward a remedy ?—The ..edy would be to bring down the cost of provisions and house rent.

Then the standard of wages will come down. It is a question which is troubling ..whole world. I don't call an unmarried miner getting £16 or £18 a poor man. It ..r the poor man I am speaking. I have been waiting for the answer for the last ..years.—I am afraid you will have to wait for another 10.

I can see that the married man cannot save anything out of £22. I admit that. ..dence is being taken for the purpose of trying to remedy the evil. But you have ..e forward with evidence showing the evil, but cannot suggest a remedy.—Well, I ..ow it is an evil.

Yes, I know. We know the price of dynamite is an evil, and the high freights .. an evil, and the gentlemen who have given evidence have suggested remedies ?— ..ll, that is the only one that I can suggest.

All I can say is that the man with five children, who has not been able to hold a ..ter position than the ordinary miner, is better to leave his wife and children at ..ae. If wherever he goes, to America or Australia, he is only able to earn the ..est standard wage, he cannot support them properly anywhere. I say it is a social ..stion, and you deserve the gratitude of mankind if you are able to solve this ..stion.

Mr. *Hay.*

In this Table IV., where you calculate out the cost of living in the Transvaal, you **Married miners'** ..e set down £3 a month for kitchen boy. In calculating the corresponding table **expenses.** .. England you don't put down anything for assistance in the shape of labour ?—No, ..ave made a slight mistake in that.

Of course it is quite apparent that in England it is a struggle for existence ..ording to the statement made, and the chances are that if a man, with a wife and .. children, would have to depend at times on charity for clothing, these people ..ald never need to have any assistance in the house work ?—No, that is quite right.

And in the corresponding position in this country they would not need to have ..stance. The woman would have to do the housework ?—Yes.

Mr. *Schmitz-Dumont.*

In this statement you reckon the family of five to be the man and wife and three ..dren ?—No. A wife and four children. That makes six with the husband.

In England have the married miners any advantage over the unmarried miners ? **Married and** ..ot at all. **single miners.**

I know in some districts unmarried miners have only a sleeping room, or t
sleep in barracks.—On some mines the companies build houses, so they live chea
than in the town.

So they have a great advantage over the unmarried men. Then the married m
has certain other advantages—he has got coal and light—but the unmarried ones
nothing. I know some in England and Germany where the companies try to give
married miners some advantage over the others. In that way something can be d
to assist the married miners here?—Yes.

MR. EDWARD BROCHON was then sworn, and made the following declaration:—

I have begged for the privilege to be heard by you. My object is certainly
to worry you with figures and statistics which several eminent members of the min
industry have already placed before you; I believe that now you have on th
different points of fact all desirable information. On the contrary, I have thought
might be interesting for you to possess certain indications of a more general order,
hear some explanations on the conditions of the gold mining industry of the Ra
compared with those of the same industry in other mines; also keeping in mind t
Views of large I represent here great French financiers, I have also thought that you would
French finan-
ciers. interested in knowing what advice these friends of the Transvaal could give you, h
they the privilege of speaking to you on certain points on which they are especia
Comparison of competent. I shall be as brief as possible. The Transvaal gold mines are of a pecul
Witwatersrand
and other gold nature. No mine in the world possesses in the same extent an industrial charact
mines. In all the gold mines of the world the production is subject to alternatives
weakness and importance very often considerable, and the average, even when bas
upon the returns of several years, is often upset by the most unforeseen results. It
that feeling of the unknown, the hope of a rich pocket, which in a few hours' wo
will return more than a whole year of labour may have given, which often cau
the shareholders to be patient by keeping up their courage, and causes them to acce
very heavy sacrifices. In the mines of the Rand there is nothing like this; fro
Regularity of the moment a mine is developed its average richness is known—it is a 12 dwts.,
yield of Wit-
watersrand dwts., 7 dwts. mine—and there is no chance for that value to be altered in a
mines. marked way; if you take the statistics of the mines from the beginning of th
existence up to this date, you will be surprised with the regularity of the yield p
ton; the working of a poor reef, such as the Main Reef in the central mines, m
cause this average to appear smaller; a more careful sorting of the ore may cause
to increase, but on the whole the ore has not appreciably changed in value. It is t
regularity which has made the fortune of the Transvaal, for, if at times capitalists a
found who accept to risk their money with a chance of a problematical profit, some a
always found who are disposed to open their purse when the business is a matter
certainty. This regularity, I have said, has made the greatness of the Transvaal;
has attracted to this country in a few years a heap of money which no other busin
Reduction of had ever obtained on the European financial markets. But it is also this regular
working costs
necessary. which, excluding all hope of a sudden stroke of fortune, compels us to strict accoun
and does not allow us to work our mines if the budget established in advance for t
working of them does not leave a margin for profit. It is this regularity whi
enables the mining industry to come and say to you: Help us to save 2s. per ton, a
50 mines now idle will then work; help us to reduce our expenses and new mi
will soon be started. I could mention to you the history of a silver mine in
country. The company working it was almost ruined, at least the capital w
exhausted, when one day, by one blast, a lump of precious metal, nearly half a ton

ight, was discovered. That lump was worth, I believe, £3,000. This gave a new urage to the shareholders; they reconstituted a new working capital which, in fact, s just as rapidly exhausted. Here, a similar instance is not possible—a mine proces 24s. worth of gold to the ton, there is no hope for a change, and if the directors nnot establish the working cost below that figure they are compelled to close the ne down. There is no getting out of it. You will forgive, gentlemen, the frankss with which I speak to you; I trust you will also forgive the details with which m worrying you. I do it because I believe that you wish to see things as they are, d because I think that, when a question is being argued, it is necessary to put it arly and avoid misunderstandings. Then, gentlemen, circumstances are such that a mber of mines on the Rand can only work at a higher cost than their returns, or, some cases, with an infinitesimal profit; the consequence is either the working cost 1st be lessened or these mines must close down. If they close, the sources of revenue the State would be lessened—its finances jeopardised. I have no need to insist on is to let you see, as well as I see it myself, the fearful consequences which will be und to follow. Allow me, in passing, to say that the time no longer exists when rghers of the South African Republic can say: "Let the mines perish, and let us go ck to our former poverty." The South African Republic has taken some engageents towards capitalists, who have opened their credit to the needs of its treasury, its railway companies. Numbers of officials have linked their lives to the osperity of the State. The Transvaal has contracted heavy engagements; it must lfil them; the honour, even the religion of its burghers, make it a sacred duty. It 1st not be said that the mines, into which the Creator has put gold in sufficient 1antity, are put in jeopardy through the fault of men. In order to render working ossible the cost must be reduced. This object can only be attained by two means: st, reduction of taxes; 2nd, economy in the work. Several gentlemen who have receded me on this seat have told you of the reduction of taxes which the mining idustry expects from your justice and your clear-sightedness. I am willing admit that to use the expression "taxation" with regard to the 56s. which the industry pays on dynamite, over and above the cost price may seem cruel we think that the Government only receives 5s. out of these 56s.; but still, as it emains with the Government to do away with these 56s. in the interests of the ountry, the Government has the right to reduce this charge to whatever proportion chooses, the expression "taxation" is sufficiently justified. Be it as it may, the overnment has in hand the possibility to reduce the working cost of the mines by s. per ton; that is the excess of expenses represented to-day by the exaggerated price f dynamite, and transport of coal, and other merchandise and material necessary for ur work. Now, gentlemen, you have been told that 2s. means life for many mines. is only 8 per cent. on the working expenses, but, as in many instances the working osts of a year reach and even exceed the nominal capital of a company, it may be per cent. on that very capital; in cases where there was nothing to give to the nareholders, it means a dividend of 8 per cent., justifying the par quotation of their nares. Where there was a small loss, it means salvation instead of bankruptcy. robably you will argue that the reduction in the cost of dynamite would not nstitute a loss to the State finances, but that such is not the case when we deal ith the railways, of which the State is a large shareholder, receiving 85 per cent. of e profits. Your objection, gentlemen, would not be right, and, as I have just xplained to you, unless a prompt remedy is applied to the situation of the mines it eans jeopardy for these, and, as a consequence, for the finances of the State. On e contrary, if you give life back to many enterprises which to-day are stopped or agging towards bankruptcy, you will see very soon an increase in all the branches

Necessity for working Transvaal gold mines

Means of reducing working costs.

Results of reduction of working costs by Government.

Advantage of reduction of working costs by Government.

L

of revenue of the State; not only these enterprises, so sickly to-day, will be able
pay their share of public expenditure, but new ones will be created and therefo
contribute to it. The State would therefore find on the whole of the revenue a
increase far superior to the amount of which it may be short in its receipts fro
railways, but I may even tell you that this loss on the railways will prompt
disappear; reduce the tariffs and you will see an increase in the transport. Co
timber, general goods, which to-day cannot reach the Rand, prevented as they are
the exaggerated expenses, will come to it, creating a wholesome competition, and th
contributing to better the conditions of existence of the mines; and the railwa
receipts will benefit by this transport which to-day being impossible, does not exi
Examples of similar facts which have taken place in Europe prove the absolu
correctness of this law of political economy. Reduce the tariffs of a public service
such as transport, by rail or water, postal or telegraphic service—very soon you g
an increase in the quantity carried sufficient to compensate the reduction in charge
and even to make the receipts larger than they were under the old tariff. I do n
hesitate in stating that should the Government grant us the reduction asked f
concerning transport, an immediate effect would be felt in the different sources
revenue, and before six months elapse the same receipts of the railways will equ
those before the reduction of tariffs. I have stated that the second way to lower tl
cost of production in the mines was the economies which these must introduce in the

Government aid in reduction of working costs indispensable. work. At first sight it would seem that the State has nothing to do with th
question, and that the mines alone should see to the reduction of their expenses. I
fact, this is not correct; and if it is true to say that the managing boards of tl
different mines should act with energy by themselves, it is not less true that the
efforts would be useless unless a moral and material action on the part of tl
Government comes to help and support them. The first moral action on the part
the Government must be to reduce the excessive price of things over which it has
control. What right would the Government have to advise moderation and econom

Excessive cost of dynamite. if it allows the Dynamite Company to take a profit of over 50s. per case without an
way justifying such exaggeration; and if it allows the Netherlands Railway Compan
Excessive railway rates. to apply tariffs, so high that, up to the time when rinderpest made transport by o
wagon impossible, it was to that last means of transport that merchants in Johanne
burg had recourse, as being more advantageous to bring their goods from Vereenigin
Let the Government give the example by suppressing these two abuses, then we sha
see, under pressure of public opinion in the whole world, the managements of th
different mines find their way to economise. Prodigality is one of the mo
contagious diseases in the world. If you find yourself amidst prodigal people yo
will soon lose the notion of the value of money; the pound sterling, which i
ordinary life you think twice before spending, will slip between your fingers withou
your noticing it. With regard to this, gold mining districts have always been th
seat of ideas and training ever to be regretted, and the Transvaal, like othe
auriferous districts has not escaped that disease. Let the Government be the first t
react against this tendency, let it set the example wherever it is possible to do s
and little by little we shall attain the object in view. I have just explained that tl
Suppression of abuses. Government should give the example by the suppression of two abuses; its wor
should not be limited to that, and I believe that a great deal can be done by th
introduction of regulations in many of the branches of the administration, chiefly tha
of the railways. It is with great reason that you have been told here that the fir
condition to reduce the salaries of white employees is to render their condition
Reforms required in railway administration existence more economical. Well, gentlemen, it is not only the reduction of tari
which should bring about cheapness of provisions on the Rand; it is also tl

anisation of a rapid and regular transport of these provisions. For instance, in present state of things would it ever come to a farmer's mind to send milk from delburg or Standerton to Johannesburg? Certainly not, for he knows that the x would only reach its destination after several days, and consequently be spoilt, still there is but one night's journey between these two points and the great annesburg market. But it is known that the railway company, six times out of would take several days to bring this produce to its destination. Do you know, tlemen, that if the railways of Europe showed the same diligence to carry ishable provisions, large agglomerations of people, such as are in London and Paris, se populations are respectively five millions and three millions, would die of vation; a bottle of milk, which is sold there for 3d., would reach a fabulous price. tead of this, each night special and rapid trains run from all parts of the country ards the capital. The milk obtained at night arrives there at daylight; the same g takes place for vegetables, fruit, eggs, and all perishable provisions. Farmers rich through it, and inhabitants of cities find therein the security of a wholesome cheap alimentation. Why does not a similar system exist here? Why does the ligence, the incapacity of the Netherlands Company, deprive your farmers of this ce of revenue and remuneration for their labour? Why should we be forced by o pay here fancy prices for provisions only when the sluggishness of the service caused them to lose all their freshness? Is not this a state of things all the more uitous, all the more deplorable, that it is the result of the dilatory ways of a ctive administration destroying the resources of producers, whose present fortunes, however, should deserve the greatest consideration? But, gentlemen, s not only in the administration of the Netherlands Railways that regulations and er should be introduced. You have been told here about the budget of the State. ormous figures have been put before you, and certainly if we take into con-eration the actual state of the different sources of revenue, that is to say, mining industry, it must be acknowledged that the amount is exagger-d. Permit a friend to tell you that here an error exists on the part of the vernment of the Republic. In my opinion the error is not to have spent 00,000 in public works; no, that is a useful expenditure of which the whole untry—industry in the first line—feels the benefit. The error is to have charged e special budget with this enormous amount. Why does not the Government take vantage of its credit to borrow money, which could easily be found at 3½ per cent.; another 2 per cent. be added to it as a sinking fund for a comparatively short iod, and instead of crushing us with £900,000 of expenditure in one year, about 0,000 per annum would be all that would be required from us. This system applied the £9,000,000, which at the present day the railways would cost, would constitute ighter charge than is at the present moment the service of its debentures, and in a iod comparatively short in the life of a nation, the railways themselves would ome the entire and free property of the State. This powerful instrument of tune and civilisation would require no other expense beyond that concerning nediately its maintenance and traffic expenses; I shall draw your attention to the t that the necessary period is in itself very inferior to that of the life of deep level nes—that is to say, the great mines of the future. I certainly do not pretend, tlemen, to supply you in a few lines with a financial plan, my object has been to your attention to the ways opened to your Government. At the beginning of s note I expressed my intention to inform you of the ideas of great financiers of country; I have now placed them before you. As you may see, they are dictated an absolute confidence in the stability of your institutions, in the future of your ntry; therefore, they deserve your consideration. There is no doubt that the

The food supply of great towns.

Public works.

The finance of railway expropriation.

projects which I have just mentioned require a serious study; on this subject al
me to 'tell you with a frankness, which may perhaps be considered rather straig
that your administration, whose financial experience is only a few years old, has
as yet acquired the knowledge of these questions as may have been done by spe
bodies of large European centres. Your right judgment, the good faith which
show in listening to, and weighing the arguments placed before you, cannot comp
sate this experience, only acquired by long years of labour. I am far from conclud
that you should relinquish in any proportion the management of the affairs of
Republic, but I believe that when you were advised to adjoin to your committ
some foreign members, the advice was good. I believe that if your Governme
Departmental committees. making the duties of the Executive Council lighter by appointing great committ
for each of the special branches of public administration, finances, legislation, railwa
mines, industry, agriculture—committees composed of burghers as voting member
I believe that these committees could, by studying, each one, the speciality devolv
upon them, prepare and greatly facilitate the task of the Executive Council.
Advisory boards. believe above all that if every one of these committees adjoined themselves consult
members, chosen among foreigners established in this country, you would obtain v
serious results. In the first place, you would draw to you specialists who would g
you the benefit of all the science acquired in their respective countries, where th
questions have been for centuries the subject of deep studies. In the second pla
these foreigners working with you and beside you, would learn to know you, an
mutual esteem would prevent in future any friction, and perhaps facilitate
harmony so desirable among the different inhabitants of this country. In the th
place, this mark of the greatness of your ideas, of your earnest desire to get at
truth, would give the old world the proof of the straightforwardness of your inte
tions, would reassure it in the future, and lastly would re-establish, to the great
benefit of the Republic, the confidence so necessary to its prosperity, its developme
and even security.

Chairman.

The Chairman said he would not put any questions to Mr. Brochon, as his sta
ment could be dealt with when the report was being prepared. If any of the otl
advisory members of the Commission thought it necessary to make a similar sta
ment, it would not be necessary to give it in evidence but to hand it in.

Mr. Brakhan.

Mr. Brakhan' statement. Mr. Brakhan, at the sitting of the Commission, asked if he would be allowed,
conformity with a few remarks made at last sitting, to hand in a statement.
statement was mostly on general lines, since very full particulars had been alrea
given. He had made a more especial point of it to show that if certain reductio
had been made in the railway rates, still very fair and even very good pro
would remain to the Netherlands Company, the Orange Free State, the Cape a
the Natal Railways. He then handed in the following statement:—

Mr. AMANDUS BRAKHAN, manager, for South Africa, of Ad. Goerz and Co., L
of Berlin, London, Paris, and Johannesburg.

Market inflation. The depression at present prevailing with regard to the mining industry of
South African Republic is attributable to some extent to the inflated market con
tions which prevailed about eighteen months ago; but there can be no doubt whate
about it that the principal cause has to be looked for in the various burdens wh
militate against favourable working costs. These burdens have to be divided i

two classes—firstly, those which the directors of mining companies have to remedy themselves through their managers, and secondly, those for an alleviation of which the community can reasonably look to the Government of this State.

There can be no doubt about it that the wages ruling on the mines of the Witwatersrand are high, and that they must come down in course of time, partly through an influx of skilled labour, and partly through a reduction in the cost of living, which is very high at present. There are many instances on these fields where reductions have already been effected, without causing any trouble where it has been pointed out to the men that it was quite impossible to go on paying the high wages which were ruling. I have no doubt that further savings can be made in this direction, but it seems to me that this can only be effected gradually. One might take the wages ruling at the present time on the Rand to be about 75 per cent. to 100 per cent. higher than those paid in California, but it must be borne in mind that there the cost of living is much lower than here. I am, however, of opinion that the value of white labour does to some extent not only depend upon the pay a man draws, but upon the value he gives for his remuneration. A man may be expensive at £15 per month if he does insufficient work and wastes the company's stores; while another's pay of £30, or even £40 per month for risky work, such as shaft-sinking, may result in work which is much cheaper, and which expedites the company's operations. Diligence and intelligence ought to be encouraged, and I, personally, am in favour of doing as much as possible by contract work, which puts the men on their mettle, and generally gives good results to the companies, if the contract price has been determined intelligently by the manager. Contracts which enabled a man to earn per month up to £100 or even more, can, to my mind, by no board of directors be defended. It is not alone dear, but also in many cases inefficient labour under which the mining industry has to suffer. White wages. Contract work.

The supply has generally not been sufficient for the demand, and it was heretofore very difficult to effect a reduction. In October last, the wages were reduced somewhat, and this measure having worked well, it has quite recently been resolved by the board of directors to effect a material reduction, which averages 30 per cent. on the wages ruling at present. It is to be hoped that this step will not result in too large a number of natives leaving work. It may, however, be reasonably expected that, if this should take place, and the supply become inadequate for a time, the natives will soon return or others take their place, if the mines remain firm in their determination. One point must, however, not be lost sight of: if the Government takes such steps as will tend to expand mining operations, the demand for native labour is bound to increase, and it behoves us to look around in time to fill this demand. I am afraid that private endeavours, even if they be in the hands of the industry itself, will prove unavailing to cope with the demand, and I think the Government ought to seriously consider what steps they are to take to assist the mining industry in its endeavours. Such taxes, I think, must be imposed on the native living in this Republic as will virtually compel him to work not alone for a short period, which is generally now the case, but for the best part of the year. The Government might also to advantage approach the adjoining States and Colonies to ensure their co-operation in securing an efficient supply of native labour to the gold industry, for they must be aware that any such facilities will redound to their advantage through the extended carrying trade on their railways and the spending power of their native population. It is especially in the direction of Delagoa Bay, where at present such conditions obtain, that the bringing of natives to these fields is most expensive. A tax of 27s. 6d. per head is levied by the Portuguese authorities, which, everyone will own, is exorbitant. Not alone is this excessive tax exacted, but Native labour. Reduction of native wages. Co-operation of Government necessary to supply native labour: means suggested.

the greatest difficulties are placed in the way of labour agents.   There are man
ways in which the Government can assist the mining industry in its endeavours t
procure a sufficient and cheap native labour supply.   I will only mention, th

Locations, Na-
tive Commis-
sioners, Pass
and Liquor
laws.

encouragement of locations not far from the Rand, the unselfish co-operation of th
Native Commissioners in sending down boys, and an adequate administration of th
Pass and Liquor Laws.

Board to admin-
ister Pass and
Liquor laws,
and to prevent
gold thefts.

I think that the suggestion to establish a special Government Board, which i
to confine its work to questions affecting the mining industry, is a most excellent one
The welfare of the State is so intimately connected with the prosperity or otherwise
of the industry, that it is of the greatest importance to have every phase studied by
Board which has an intimate knowledge of the requirements.   To attain this end
think it would be of the greatest importance to appoint to this Board also a certai
number of members who are leaders of the industry.   It would be well to give power
to this Board to administer, and, if necessary, amend, with the consent of th
Executive Council, the Pass and Liquor Laws, and to take such measures as will tenc
to decrease the gold and amalgam thefts.

Excessive price
of dynamite.

The price charged to the mines for dynamite is out of all proportion to the cost a
which the explosive is being laid down here by the monopolists, for everyone know
that the quantity actually manufactured here is only very small, and that, therefore
enormous profits accrue to the monopolists ; whilst the Government has to be satisfie
with a modest 5s. per case, and earns all the abuse for a state of affairs which certainly
ought not to exist.   Since it would appear that the manufacture of dynamite in thi
country has insurmountable obstacles placed in its way, as all the articles necessary for
the manufacture itself have to be imported, and are several times the bulk of dynamite
further, as the manufacture itself is here very expensive ; and, finally, as the bye-
products can hardly be utilised in this country, and might even be a source of danger
I think it entirely unreasonable that the industry should be made to pay 107s. 6d. for
a case of blasting gelatine, which can be placed free on board at Hamburg for about a

Free trade in
dynamite.

quarter of that amount.   I beg to give it as my humble opinion that once free trade
in dynamite is established in the Transvaal there would be no question of a ring in
in this article ; the large consumption in the Transvaal would create such competition
that no ring could come up against it.   Reasonable prices for dynamite would affect
mining costs most materially.   The expenditure per ton of ore crushed depends
naturally on the condition and width of the reefs in the various mines.   Whilst, for
instance, this item amounts to only 1s. 6d. in the Meyer and Charlton Gold Mining
Company, it continues to be 4s. 4d. per ton in the Princess Estate and Gold Mining
Company, or expressed on a percentage basis—6·325 per cent. as compared with 13·42
per cent. respectively of the total working costs.

Excessive rail-
way rates.

The railway rates paid, not only to the Netherlands Company, but also to the
lines feeding that company, are so preposterously high that they tend to make
gold mining in this country in most cases almost an impossibility.   When some years
ago the traffic was a limited one, those rates may have been perhaps justified.   But at
that time everyone was looking forward to very material all-round reductions, which
however, so far have in vain been waited for.   There can be no doubt about it, that
if these rates are not reduced, the expansion of the industry will be materially
checked, nay, that operations will even have to be materially curtailed, since a reduction in the price of dynamite and in the railway rates, in many cases, means turning
a loss into a profit.   I think the Government will grant that the industry can
reasonably look forward to their warm support in this matter, for the leaders of the
industry have shown that they use every endeavour to bring about such reforms in
the management of the mines as will tend to the highest possible economy.   I have

several tables worked out in order to show what the profits of the various rail-
~s during 1896 have been, and also what interest would have been secured in case
.ain reductions had been made in the rates.

STATEMENT No. I.

The Netherlands Company will pay on its ordinary share capital, after paying
.rest on bonds, redeeming bonds, placing £297,000 to reserve, and paying to the
.rd and staff £52,677, a dividend of 14·71 per cent. The profit to the Government
. amount to £895,475. These figures are approximate. Now, if the passenger
·s would be reduced by 15 per cent., and the goods' rates by 30 per cent., a saving
. the community of £801,900 would be effected, and the shareholders would still
·ive the respectable dividend of 8·52 per cent. The Government's profits would, of
.rse, be materially reduced, and would amount to £282,064. ^(margin note: Approximate returns of Netherlands Railway for 1896. Effect of 15 per cent. reduction on estimated returns for 1896.)

STATEMENT No. II.

This deals with the returns of the three systems of the Cape Government
.lways—both as regards local traffic and through traffic to the Transvaal. Here a
.uction of 10 per cent. has been taken for passenger rates, and 20 per cent. for
.ds rates, as the present rates are considerably lower than those of the Netherlands
.mpany. The interest earned in 1896 on all traffic on an invested capital of
.,218,580 for the Cape lines, or including Orange Free State line, of £20,790,288—
. been £8 19s. 7d. per cent., equal to £1,867,198 9s. 6d. This includes 50 per cent.
. the net receipts on traffic over the Orange Free State line, and 4 per cent. interest
. the invested capital of £2,571,702. With the above reductions on the rates, the
.rage interest of the three systems of the Cape would amount to 5·18 per cent.,
.al to £944,776. The Western would earn 4·44 per cent., the Midland 7·22 per cent.,
. the Eastern 3·06 per cent. It must be borne in mind that this is an average rate
. the whole system, and that certain lines pay even at present no interest, or only a
·y small one. I have shown in this statement a reduction on *all* receipts, whilst in
.tement No. VI. I have dealt with the benefits accruing in such a case to the
.nsvaal. ^(margin note: Returns of the three Cape railways for 1896 on an estimated reduction of rates of 10 per cent. for passenger, and 20 per cent. for goods traffic.)

STATEMENT No. III.

The same reductions in the rates as in the Cape operating on the Orange Free
.te Railway would still yield interest at the rate of 19·98 per cent., equal to
.3,567 to the Free State for 1897, when this line is worked by the Government.
.is is, of course, on the basis of the traffic during 1896. The rate of interest on the
.ested capital of £2,571,702 amounted during 1896 actually to 26·9 per cent., of
.ich half, after deducting 4 per cent. on the invested capital, went to the Govern-
.nt of the Orange Free State, amounting to £289,553. ^(margin note: Estimated returns of Orange Free State railways for 1897, with an estimated reduction of 10 per cent. on passenger, and 20 per cent. on goods traffic. Interest of Orange Free State Railways for 1896.)

STATEMENT No. IV.

During 1896 the Natal Government Railways yielded £11 9s. ½d. per cent. on an
.ested capital of £6,236,555, equal to £714,224. Had similar reductions of 10 per
.t. and 20 per cent. been made on the rates the interest would still have amounted
.8 18s. per cent., equal to £509,983. ^(margin note: Interest on Natal Railway for 1896.)

STATEMENT No. V.

Estimated economy to Transvaal population on Netherlands Railway, and through rates for 1896, with an estimated reduction of 10 per cent. on passenger, and 20 per cent. on goods rates.

This statement shows how much the Transvaal, *i.e.*, inhabitants and the mini industry, would have saved if the reduction in the railway rates, mentioned in previous statement, had been ruling. It must be well understood that I give h only the saving on the through traffic from the Cape, Orange Free State, and Na to the Transvaal, and on the entire traffic of the Netherlands Company. Unf tunately, no figures as regards the Portuguese line are in my possession. The savi to the Transvaal on this basis would have amounted to £1,195,201, of which nearly million would directly or indirectly have benefited the mining industry.

STATEMENT No. VI.

Estimated cost of expropriation of railway.

It is well to analyse what it would cost the Government to expropriate t Netherlands Railway Company if this course were decided upon now. I find that t price would be about 257 per cent., equal to £2,996,600 for the total issued capital £1,166,666 (of which £476,033, equal to 5,713 shares), are owned by the Governme Adding to this the issued debentures, the Government would have to provide a to of £8,424,633 (minus the value of their shares in the ordinary capital of t

Estimated profit on Netherlands Railway after expropriation.

Netherlands Railway Company.) Taking the safe figure of 4½ per cent., at which t Government could borrow, the reduced rates would still yield her £354,480, af paying all working costs, 10 per cent. of gross revenue for depreciation, and t interest on the loan.

I am, however, firmly convinced that the reduction in the rates would be follow by a material expansion of the traffic, thus increasing the profit.

STATEMENT No. VII.

Profits on English railways.

This statement shows the average yield in per cent. per annum of some of t leading English railways.

Working costs of Meyer & Charlton and Princess Estate G. M. Cos.

I append detailed cost sheets of the Meyer and Charlton Gold Mining Company a the Princess Estate and Gold Mining Company, numbered respectively VIII. and I The cost per ton crushed of the latter company is higher than on the Meyer a Charlton, caused through the thinness of the reef. The cost of the Princess Esta and Gold Mining Company, through lower prices for dynamite and a reduction in t railway rates, would be substantial, as the figures for dynamite and fuel per t crushed are 4s. 4·1d. and 3s. 7·7d. respectively. Both at the Meyer and Charlton a Princess every step has been taken to reduce expenditure as much as ever possib and consequently the cost of the latter company shows a marked decrease again that ruling during 1896. In the same way the working costs of the Meyer a Charlton have been reduced from 24s. in 1896 to 18s. 9d. for April last. This redu tion is partly owing to an increase in the stamping power.

STATEMENT No. I.

NETHERLANDS RAILWAY.

Average aggregate earnings for 1896 according to the Chamber of Mines Railw report, £2,970,000; of which 41 per cent. may be expected to cover working expense this would mean a dividend of 14·71 per cent. on the share capital and a profit £895,475 to Government.

According to the 1894 and 1895 returns, the revenue for passenger traffic w about 20 per cent. of the total traffic receipts.

Taking a reduction of 15 per cent. on the receipts from passenger traffic, and of 30 per cent. on goods, the receipts would have been as follows :—

REVENUE.

Passengers	£594,000	
Less 10 per cent.	89,100	
		£504,900
Goods, etc., ...	2,376,000	
Less 30 per cent.	712,800	
		1,663,200
		£2,168,100

EXPENDITURE.

Working costs (41 per cent. of £2,970,000 ...	£1,217,700	
Interest and redemption of loans... ...	335,500	
10 per cent. of gross revenue to reserve ...	216,810	
Guaranteed interest on shares	66,250	
		£1,836,260
		£331,840

Of which—

85 per cent. = £282,064, goes to Government.
10 per cent. = 33,184, goes to Shareholders.
5 per cent. = 16,592, goes to Directors.
The Shareholders get £66,250 guaranteed interest.
33,184 surplus dividend.

Total ... £99,434

Equal to 8·52 per cent. per annum on the capital of £1,166,666.

STATEMENT No. II.
CAPE GOVERNMENT RAILWAYS.

Basis : 1896 returns.
20 per cent. reduction on goods traffic receipts.
10 per cent. reduction on coaching receipts (passengers and parcels).

WESTERN SECTION.

Earnings :		
Coaching	£539,260	
Less 10 per cent.	53,930	
		£485,330
Goods, &c.	675,930	
Less 20 per cent.	135,186	
		540,740
Total		£1,026,070
Expenditure :		
Total		674,460
Net balance		£351,610

Capital entitled to interest, £7,918,394.

MIDLAND SYSTEM.

Earnings:

Coaching	£219,453	
Less 10 per cent.	21,950	
		£197,503
Goods, &c.	1,116,142	
Less 20 per cent.	223,228	
		892,914
		£1,090,417
Expenditure		608,232
Net Balance ...		£482,185

Capital entitled to interest, £6,674,890.

EASTERN SYSTEM.

Earnings:

Coaching	£98,770	
Less 10 per cent.	9,877	
		£88,893
Goods, &c.	£385,170	
Less 20 per cent.	77,030	
		308,140
		£397,033
Expenditure		286,072
Net Balance ...		£110,961

Capital entitled to interest, £3,625,300.

NET REVENUE AT REDUCED RATES.

System.		Capital entitled to Interest.	Net Balance.	Yield in per cent.
Western	...	£7,918,390	£351,610	4·44
Midland	...	6,674,890	482,185	7·22
Eastern	...	3,625,300	110,981	3·06
Total	...	£18,218,580	£944,776	5·18

STATEMENT No. III.

Orange Free State Railways.

Earnings:

Coaching ...	...	...	...	£315,618	
Less 10 per cent.	...	...	...	31,562	
					£284,056
Goods, &c. ...	...	...	...	£728,216	
Less 20 per cent.	...	...	...	145,643	
					582,573
					£866,629
Expenditure	...	...	...		353,062
	Net Balance	...			£513,567

Which is 19·98 per cent. on £2,571,702 (capital entitled to interest).

———

STATEMENT No. IV.

Natal Government Railways.

REVENUE.

Passenger and parcel	...	...	...	£230,018	
Less 10 per cent.	...	...	...	23,002	
					£207,016
Goods, &c. ...	...	...	...	£906,196	
Less 20 per cent.	...	...	...	181,239	
					724,957
					£931,973

EXPENDITURE.

Total ...	...	...	...	...	...		421,990
	Net balance	...			...		£509,983

Capital entitled to interest, £6,236,555. Yield, 8·18 per cent. per annum.

N.B.—Expenditure includes £20,284 3s. 8d. for compensation in connection with the Glencoe Railway Disaster.

STATEMENT No. V.

RECAPITULATION.

The gross earnings of through traffic to the Transvaal in 1896 are :—

CAPE GOVERNMENT (including O.F. State Line) RAILWAYS.
£1,592,898, of which

Taking the passenger traffic at 30 per cent. of the total	£477,867 ; 10 per cent.,	£47,787
Taking the goods traffic at 70 per cent. of the total	1,115,031 ; 20 per cent.,	223,006

NATAL GOVERNMENT RAILWAYS.
£680,600, of which

Taking the passenger traffic at 20 per cent. of the total	£136,120 ; 10 per cent.,	£13,612
Taking the goods traffic at 80 per cent. of the total	544,480 ; 20 per cent.,	108,896

NETHERLANDS RAILWAY.
£2,970,000, of which

Taking the passenger traffic at 20 per cent. of the total	£594,000 ; 15 per cent.,	£89,100
Taking the goods traffic at 80 per cent. of the total	£2,376,000 ; 30 per cent.,	712,800

Total saving	£1,195,201

(Exclusive of Portuguese Railway, report of which is not to hand.)

The maximum rate of the Netherlands Company, according to the Concession, is fixed at 6d. per ton per mile.

It would appear, however, that the Netherlands Company's share in through traffic from the Cape amounts to 7·7d. per ton per mile from Vaal River to Johannesburg.

STATEMENT No. VI.

NETHERLANDS RAILWAY.

Should the Government expropriate the railway at the rate of 12 per cent., *i.e.*, an average dividend on Netherlands shares on the basis of the following dividends :—

9 per cent. for 1895,
14 per cent. for 1896,
13 per cent. for 1897,

The amount to be paid by the Government would be—

	Per cent.
20 times 12 per cent.	240
Plus 17 per cent. (1 per cent. for each year 1897-1915) ...	17
	257

On a capital of £1,166,666 ... ... £2,996,600

The debenture debt of the Netherlands Railway Company at the end of 1896 amounted to 5,428,033

(Since then authorised, £1,100,000.)

Government would have to provide for £8,424,633

At the reduced basis of 1896, and assuming Government can raise money at the rate of 4½ per cent., its net revenue per annum would amount to—

Gross revenue £2,168,100

Expenditure :

Working cost	£1,217,700	
10 per cent. depreciation	216,810	
4½ per cent. interest on £8,424,633 ...	379,110	
		1,813,620

Net revenue £354,480

STATEMENT No. VII.

ENGLISH RAILWAYS.

Name of Railway Company.	Issued Share Capital.	Issued Loan Capital.	Average Yield on Total Capital per Annum.
			Per cent.
Great Eastern Railway	£32,858,519	£14,784,171	about 3
Great Northern Railway	37,204,305	12,972,763	„ 3·15
Great Western Railway	59,392,000	18,351,734	„ 4·32
Lancashire and Yorkshire Railway...	36,346,616	16,931,017	„ 3·59
London and North-Western Railway	78,782,555	37,532,804	„ 4·11
London and South-Western Railway	25,780,633	12,365,359	„ 3·59

Mr. A. Brakhan's Evidence.

STATEMENT No. VIII.

MEYER AND CHARLTON GOLD MINING CO., LTD.

Expenses for the year ending 31st December, 1896 :—Mill tonnage, 101,397.

	£ s. d.	Cost per Ton. s. d.	Per Cent. Total Cost.
Native labour } Native food }	39,630 9 9	7 9·803	32·549
White labour, salaries, &c., including manager's salary and all administration expenses at the mine	32,520 15 0	7 0·075	29·173
Coal	10,647 12 9	2 1·202	8·745
Dynamite	7,700 19 4	1 6·228	6·325
Cyanide	4,359 15 1	0 10·320	3·581
Zinc	290 2 2	0 0·687	0·238
Royalty	2,017 13 4	0 4·776	1·657
Mining timber	920 11 7	0 2·179	0·756
Timber, deals, &c.	213 7 10	0 0·505	0·175
Steel	777 15 1	0 1·841	0·639
Oils, grease, and paraffin	983 10 10	0 2·327	0·808
Candles	1,494 14 3	0 3·537	1·227
Ropes, steel and manilla	264 10 11	0 0·626	0·217
Forage, chaff, and bran	279 9 9	0 0·662	0·230
Electric spares	190 16 11	0 0·453	0·157
Mill spares, shoes, dies, cams, cam shafts, stems, mortar boxes, screening, &c. ...	711 14 11	0 1·685	0·585
Trucks, wheels, and rails (capital account)	...	...	...
Pipes and pipe fitting	260 0 0	0 0·616	0·214
Fuse and detonators	793 13 6	0 1·877	0·651
Sundry Stores — Bar iron, bolts and nuts, assay chemicals, machinery, &c.	6,894 6 5	1 4·318	5·662
General charges— Insurance and sundries £5,523 14 3 Licenses and rents ... 84 0 0 Printing and advertising ... ... 1,089 15 1 Directors' and committees' fees 1,108 0 0	7,805 9 4	1 6·474	6·411
	£121,757 8 9	24 0·192	100

STATEMENT No. IX.

PRINCESS ESTATE AND GOLD MINING CO., LTD.

Average Working Costs per Month.

Description.	Amount.			Cost per Ton.		Percentage of Costs.
	£	s.	d.	s.	d.	
Native wages	2,165	2	4	8	7·7	26·73
Native food	321	10	1	1	3·4	3·96
European wages, including contracts ...	2,058	14	2	8	2·6	25·40
Fuel	912	3	11	3	7·7	11·26
Dynamite and gelatine	1,087	15	6	4	4·1	13·42
Cyanide	99	18	9	0	4·8	1·24
Mine timber	31	5	0	0	1·5	0·38
Deals	28	13	9	0	1·3	0·36
Drill steel	82	18	11	0	4·0	1·02
Lubricants	113	10	6	0	5·4	1·39
Candles	130	14	6	0	6·3	1·61
Shoes and dies	55	10	0	0	2·6	0·68
Fuse and caps	96	3	11	0	4·6	1·19
Screening	11	14	9	0	0·6	0·15
Screws, nails, bolts, &c.	10	13	11	0	0·5	0·14
Sundry stores ... ... {	20	0	3	0	1·0	0·25
	517	13	1	2	0·8	6·38
Head office charges	209	3	4	0	10·0	2·58
Sundry expenses at mine	151	3	3	0	7·2	1·86
	£8,104	9	11	32	4·1	100

Mr. Jennings'
evidence. MR. HENNEN JENNINGS, Consulting Engineer to Messrs. H. Eckstein and Co.,
then called to give evidence.

Witness said: I have resided in Johannesburg since the latter part of 1889.

Chairman.

On what points do you wish to give evidence?

Witness.] I wish to give evidence in accordance with the Chairman's statem
in order to bring to light the actual state of the mining industry of the Witwatersr
goldfields, and the reasons for the same, and my candid opinion on the pres
condition of affairs. I have a statement to make which I wish to read.

Witness then read the following statement:

I wish to make a statement, more or less summing up, including and extend
the evidence of preceding witnesses, and to vitalise the facts and statistics set bef
you by a connected linking of these facts in a logical and orderly manner, and to g
you my candid ideas as to the actual state of the mining industry.

The magnitude and wealth of these goldfields have been examined, discussed, a
written upon by very many able men from all parts of the world, and they have
agreed in stating that this deposit is unique in its characteristics, and contains v
Extent and na- possibilities. These reefs, which are conglomerate beds, have been traced for so
ture of reefs 50 miles ; showing varying thickness and gold value, and in one point proved by
on Rand.
Estimated Bezuidenville borehole to a vertical depth of 3,130 feet. Mr. Hamilton Smith
wealth of reefs, happily described the fields by stating that the excellence of these mines is not due
their exceeding richness, but rather to the large continuous bodies of ore of
moderate grade, and has recognised the necessity for the best possible mechani
plants, and the most skilful and economical management. He, moreover, was of
belief that if the management were radically bad, not more than three or four mi
could have yielded considerable profit. He also estimated (January, 1893) that with
the then recognised paying area of the Witwatersrand goldfields, down to a verti
depth of 3,000 feet, there was probably 325 million pounds sterling worth of gold
be extracted. His statement has been corroborated by Mr. Schmeisser, a Germ
Government engineer, who estimated at the end of 1893 that down to a verti
depth of 3,900 feet, and for a lateral extent of eleven miles, there were possibilities
£349,367,000.

Professor Becker, of the United States Geological Survey Department, w
visited these fields in 1896, estimates the possibilities within twenty miles
Johannesburg, to a vertical depth of 5,000 feet, at about 700 million pounds sterli
Advantageous Hitherto, in all gold-mining regions of the world, gold mines have been consider
conditions of
Rand. highly speculative ventures, and liable at any time to give out; they have nowh
else such advantageous natural conditions as here for making a staple perman
industry, nor the same justification for the great expenditure of initial capital on th
equipment and development. Gold is here supplemented by coal in close proximi
ample water supply, and favourable climatic conditions. Of course there are fluctu
tions even here in the richness of the different mines, and there are unaccounta
rich, medium, and poor mines in juxtaposition or in distinct sections. There is
doubt there are sections of the Rand which can be continued to be worked at a go
profit at the present rate of costs ruling on these fields, but there is a far lar
amount of ground that will not be worked, or only tried and then abandoned, if
conditions prevailing as to costs are not lowered, and the predictions of the emin
authorities I have quoted can only be realised by all parties interested doing eve
thing in their power to obtain highly efficient working at low cost, and thus incre

the scope and possibilities of the whole fields. Take Professor Becker's estimate Estimated life of Rand. 700 millions sterling. At the present rate at which we are now taking out gold, ese fields would have a life of about 90 years, but the rate at which we extract this ld will be constantly increasing if the working conditions are rendered more vourable, and the life of the fields will become correspondingly shorter; this takes to no account the working of our southern low grade reefs, but only the Main Reef ries. Professor Becker's estimate, too, as well as Mr. Hamilton Smith's and Mr. hmeisser's, do not include the Klerksdorp, Potchefstroom, Heidelberg, Lydenburg, Percentage of gold from Barberton, Klerksdorp, Heidelberg, &c. arberton nor other districts, which, according to the figures for 1896, contributed proximately 9 per cent. to the total gold production of the South African Republic.

The State Mining Engineer, in the course of the proceedings of this Commission, Number and capital of gold companies in Transvaal. as stated that there were 185 gold mining companies in 1896 in this Republic, with nominal capital of £54,000,000.

On the Witwatersrand fields there have been about 5,500 stamps erected. The Number of stamps on Witwatersrand fields. nnual report of the Chamber of Mines shows that on an average 3,470 stamps were nning during 1896; consequently, it would appear as if 2,030 stamps had been opped; but this is not really so, as many have been dismantled, and new ones have placed them. But it is a fact that there are on the fields many companies with a rge number of stamps that have suspended operations, and there are several others hich, during this year, will probably follow suit.

The Chamber of Mines' report shows that in 1896 there were fifty-six companies Companies working in 1896 and now. operation: while the statements from the Chamber of Mines and the Association of ines for March show that there are now only forty-seven companies with 3,275 amps working. On the other hand, great energy is being shown by deep level Deep levels. d other companies in pushing forward work with the object of starting more amps, and it is estimated that about 1,000 new stamps will start during the current ear, if conditions are favourable. I have gone to considerable pains to obtain as far possible the last annual report of all principal mining companies working in 1896, d which have been working continuously during the periods covered by their last nual report, and to analyse these reports; the gold returns being according to e sworn statements of their managers, and the accounts being in each case signed y the auditors and secretaries. It should be noticed that, in dealing with these Analytical return of 29 gold companies. wenty-nine companies, the period covered is not necessarily the year 1896 only, but braces the actual period covered by each individual report, and often this is for art of 1895 and part of 1896, and in several cases includes periods longer than one ear. This table I consider most remarkable, in that it is compiled by a private dividual from published statements given freely to the world, and anybody can ake out the same table who obtains the same reports. In this connection I would ate that in discussing the matter of statistical information about these fields with ifferent eminent mining men from all parts of the world, the consensus of opinion is at more generous and accurate information is given on these fields of the working f the mines than is the case in any other part of the world. In addition to the mpanies' reports, we have also the vast amount of accurate information collected y the State Mining Engineer, the Chamber of Mines, and the individual enterprise f C. S. Goldmann, so that the investing public should certainly be cognisant of all tal facts here with such statistics before them; and if they exaggerate the possilities of the mines, we have nothing to reproach ourselves with. At the same time, is regrettable that more publicity has not been given to the work of the State State Mining Engineer's statistics. ining Engineer's Department as regards the statistics of the gold industry. The overnment should have been proud of this collection, and had it published in all nguages, and distributed to the world. They have, I think, been negligent in this

M

respect, for, although their information is most valuable, it is inaccessible to th[e] majority of investors in these fields.

Names of 29 companies shown in analytical return. Now, to return to my own statistics. The companies included in my list are a[s] follows :—City and Suburban, Crown Reef, Durban Roodepoort, Ferreira, Geldenhu[is] Deep, Geldenhuis Estate, Ginsberg, Glencairn, Henry Nourse, Johannesburg Pionee[r,] Jubilee, Jumpers, May Consolidated, New Comet, New Heriot, New Primrose, Robin[n]son, Salisbury, Simmer and Jack, Wolhuter, Worcester, George Goch, Langlaagt[e] Estate, Langlaagte Royal, Meyer and Charlton, New Midas Estate, Roodepoo[rt]

Explanation of analytical returns of 29 companies. United, Van Ryn Estate, Wemmer. It will be noticed that there are twenty com[-]panies omitted from the total now working; a large proportion of the reports of thes[e] do not cover a full year's work, while of others I was unable to obtain copies.

The only dividend companies of 1896 omitted from my list are :—

Stanhope	...	...	...	...	£1,700
Langlaagte Block B (preference shares)	...		...		6,500

The above twenty-nine companies I now divide into three groups, summing u[p] the yields, working costs, &c., under the heads of mining, milling, secondary treat[-]ment, &c., and also give the dividends paid during the period, the capitalisations, an[d] the interest per cent. on such capitalisations.

These three groups are :—

(a) Mines that have paid dividends during the period covered by their las[t] annual report.

(b) Mines that have shown a profit, but for various causes have paid n[o] dividends during the period of their last annual report.

(c) Mines that have worked at a loss during the period of their last annua[l] report.

The summary of this statement is as follows :—

ANALYSIS OF OPERATIONS OF 29 PRINCIPAL COMPANIES, AS SHEWN BY THEIR LAST PUBLISHED ANNUAL REPORTS.

	No. of Stamps	Tons Mined	Tons Steered	Per Cent. Steered	Tons Milled	Mill Returns Value	Mill Returns Yield per Ton	Secondary Treatment Sands and Concentrates Tons Treated	Value Yield	Waste Yield per Ton Treated	Waste Yield per Ton Milled	Total Recovery Per ton Milled	Total Recovery Value	Mining	Mine Development and Redemption	Total Mining	Transport	Milling	Secondary Treatment	General Charges not segregated	Total Cost per ton	Depreciation	Total Cost with Depreciation	Gold Produced Average Value on milled tonnage basis per ton	Gold Produced Value	Total Working Expenditure	Profit Total	Profit Per Ton	Loss Total	Loss Per Ton	Tonnage of Ore Developed	Dividends declared	Nominal Capital	Issued Capital	Value of Issued Capital at Market Rate	Dividends Paid Per Cent. on Issued Capital	Dividends Paid Per Cent. at Market Rate
Total:						£	s. d.		£	s. d.	s. d.	s. d.	£	s. d.	s. d.	s. d.	s. d.	s. d.	s. d.	s. d.	s. d.	s. d.	s. d.	s. d.	£	£	£	s. d.	£	s. d.		£	£	£	£	Per Cent.	Per Cent.
A. 18 Companies	1625	3,028,309	169,367	6·987	2,489,380	3,731,811	29 10·74	4,660,653	1,366,176	18 5·68	12 6·96	42 5·79	5,267,987	12 10·97	3 10·94	16 8·41	0 1·51	3 7·16	3 1·93	2 6·73	26 1·16	3 6·19	29 7·35	42 11·53	5,346,363	2,666,710	1,659,653	13 3·98	—	—	4,290,436	1,729,103	6,861,386	6,881,386	15,123,876	25·127	11·433
B. 7 do.	561	794,779	138,470	16·164	666,309	534,669	25 7·94	449,595	366,608	16 9·55	11 0·91	36 7·96	1,321,697	14 4·44	4 5·08	18 10·02	0 1·83	3 8·29	2 9·94	2 6·64	28 9·31	4 10·31	32 10·92	36 8·29	1,222,369	1,096,151	126,218	3 9·47	—	—	9,543,343	—	6,945,000	6,342,509	14,040,927	—	—
C. 4 do.	270	388,371	—	—	386,341	396,945	19 10·96	985,272	120,354	19 8·33	10 5·69	30 3·86	487,199	15 6·29	7 5·80	22 6·08	0 1·85	4 3·70	4 9·40	4 7·45	36 4·48	2 7·83	39 0·31	30 5·93	439,533	562,502	—	—	122,969	9 0·36	622,812	302,000	708,000	718,135	523,897	4·420	6·016
29 Companies	2456	3,743,559	307,777	7·86	3,444,482	4,663,445	28 2·86	2,836,139	2,685,638	17 2·65	12 1·81	40 4	6,946,483	13 4	4 3·12	17 7·12	0 2·96	3 8·98	3 2·24	2 8·90	27 4	3 8·44	31 0·44	40 9·31	7,008,363	5,345,363	1,660,982	9 7·87	—	—	7,406,481	1,761,103	14,691,989	14,140,259	29,686,710	12·446	9·970

Note.—The dividend paid by one of the companies in the group showing a loss during the financial year is explained by the fact that although it was declared in January, 1896, it referred partly to a preceding period. This company has also been written off heavily for depreciation of old plant and mine development, and has thus considerably increased its working expenditure on the basis of my analysis.

The material originally positioned here is too large for reproduction in this reissue. A PDF can be downloaded from the web address given on page iv of this book, by clicking on 'Resources Available'.

This statement shows that, even at present depressed prices, the public places a [va]lue on the shares of the twenty-nine companies, which is more than double the [am]ount at which they were originally capitalised, and that, taking the dividend [act]ually paid, the interest obtained by investors in the eighteen dividend-paying [com]panies alone is 12·4 per cent., and that, if these dividends be distributed over the [wh]ole twenty-nine companies in my list, the interest obtained is only about 6 per cent. [W]hat must it be for the whole fields? It appears to me that too much stress has been [lai]d by this Commission on company capitalisation. What, after all, does it mean to [th]e intrinsic investor what the capital of a company is, so long as he can buy into it [at] what he considers a profitable price? Are not the original capitals mere guesses to [est]ablish rates of division of interest, and if the guess is too small, may not as much [ha]rm be done as if the guess is too high? The conscientious engineer and examiner [of] a mine simply regard capitalisations as counters, on which he places value in accord[an]ce with the probabilities of its earning power. *Market values of companies.*

From this statement of yields and costs it is seen that the cost per ton of ore [mil]led is shown in two ways:—

(a) Cost per ton, with depreciation of plant.

(b) Cost per ton, without depreciation.

Depreciation is considered by many merely a book entry, and unfair to include in [leg]itimate working costs.

On the other hand, most companies do not include permanent main mine works in [th]eir running costs or current construction work; therefore I think the mean of these [tw]o costs a fair average for the fields, before any dividends are distributable, and we [th]us obtain for the total working costs of the fields, as shown by the twenty-nine [co]mpanies I have mentioned, 29s. 4d. per ton, and the total yield from all sources, [in]cluding mill, cyanide works, &c., 40s. 8·31d. per ton. The cost thus arrived at is seen [to] correspond with all reasonable degree of accuracy with the statement made by the [ch]airman at the Rand Mines Meeting, and I therefore beg to hand in as evidence that [po]rtion of his speech which deals with this subject. It will be noticed that there are [se]ven million tons of ore developed by these twenty-nine mines, which is equivalent to [a] cash asset of £1,750,000. *Speech of chairman at Rand Mines meeting*

Another interesting feature to be noticed from the tables is that the yield from [th]e secondary treatment is shown to be 12s. 1·14d. per ton on the basis of the tonnage [mi]lled, and working costs, 3s. 2·34d., the profit from this treatment therefore figuring [at] 8s. 10·8d. From this it is clearly evident that, of the total profit of 9s. 7·87d. [ob]tained by the combined treatments, no less than 8s. 10·8d., or 92 per cent., came from [th]e secondary treatment, without which obviously only an extremely small number of [th]e very richest mines here could ever have paid dividends. This is a strong illustra[tio]n of what intelligent metallurgical and engineering skill has done for the prosperity [of] these fields. *Secondary treatment.*

I also beg to submit a statement showing the analysis of the working expenditure [of] six prominent companies for the year 1896. In this sheet are given the details of [co]sts under labour and supplies of the following:—Crown Reef, Henry Nourse, City [an]d Suburban, Robinson, New Heriot, Geldenhuis Deep. *Analysis of working costs of Crown Reef, Henry Nourse, City and Suburban, Robinson, New Heriot, and Geldenhuis Deep.*

The summary of this statement is as follows :—

	Costs per ton. s. d.	Per cent. of total cost.
Native labour	6 9·62	23·73
Native food	1 2·24	4·14
White labour, salaries, etc.	8 7·78	30·18
Coal	2 4·35	8·24
Dynamite	2 10·13	9·92
Fuse and detonators...	0 1·97	0·57
Cyanide	0 8·12	2·36
Zinc	0 0·62	0·18
Mining timber	0 2·98	0·87
Timber, deals, etc.	0 4·05	1·18
Steel	0 4·21	1·22
Oils, grease, and paraffin	0 3·73	1·09
Candles	0 4·15	1·21
Ropes, steel and manilla	0 0·93	0·27
Electric spares	0 1·47	0·43
Mill spares, shoes, dies, cams, cam shafts, stems, mortar boxes, screening, etc....	0 4·59	1·34
Trucks, wheels, and rails	0 2·24	0·65
Sundry stores : bar iron, bolts and nuts, buildings, machinery, assay chemicals, pipes and pipe fittings, etc. ...	2 0·73	7·19
General charges : Insurance, licences and rent, printing and advertising, sundries	1 5·99	5·23
Totals	28 7·90	100·00

This again corresponds so closely with the statements made by the Chairman at the recent Rand Mines Meeting, that I beg again to put this portion of his speech in evidence. It will be noticed that on this sheet I submit, each Company's Secretary has placed his signature as a voucher for the accuracy of the statements.

Percentage of working costs of the whole Rand, from State Mining Engineer's report.

In support of these figures, as being a criterion for the whole Rand, I beg to state that the following statistics were compiled from the State Mining Engineer's report for 1895 :—

	£	Per cent of total cost.
White labour	2,400,000	34·3
Kaffir labour	2,000,000	28·6
Coal	700,000	10·0
Explosives, i.e., dynamite and gelatine...	600,000	8·6
Mining timber and sawn lumber ...	300,000	4·3
Cyanide	240,000	3·4
Meat, mealies and mealie meal (being for the most part food for kaffirs) ...	250,000	3·6
Iron	85,000	1·2
Candles and paraffin	95,000	1·4
Tools	70,000	1·0
Steel	65,000	0·9
Mercury, zinc, and other chemicals ...	45,000	0·6
Caps, safety fuse, ropes, cement, etc. ...	150,000	2·1
	£7,000,000	100·0

This is seen not to correspond exactly with the statement I have given; a simple ...lanation of which is that the State statistics are for a different period and cover an ...enditure of £7,000,000, which includes the non-producing as well as the producing ...es, while the figures in my statement only cover an expenditure of £1,300,524.

I again wish to put in evidence the State Mining Engineer's figures regarding ...ges paid on these fields to white labour, taken from the report of 1895, which ...w:

Occupation.				Number.	Average monthly wage. £	
Shift bosses	...	...	...	185	33	White wages in 1895.
Miners	...	...	...	1,430	23	
Rock-drill machine men		...	...	956	17	
Trammers	...	...	...	226	18	
Engine drivers	...	...	...	765	24	
Pump men	...	...	...	129	23	
Stokers ...	...	...	...	89	19	
Carpenters	...	...	...	1,058	26	
Smiths ...	...	...	...	638	26	
Mechanics and fitters		...	...	900	26	
Bricklayers	...	...	...	75	22	
Stonemasons	...	...	...	213	29	
Daily labourers	...	...	...	149	18	
Mine and store clerks		...	...	287	23	
Amalgamators	...	...	...	291	23	
Cyaniders	...	...	...	217	22	
Concentrators	...	...	...	35	22	
Vannermen	...	...	...	32	20	
Smelters ...	...	...	...	21	26	
Various workmen	...	...	...	472	21	
				8,168	£461	

...king an average of £23 7s. 10d. per man per month.

Average white wages.

This amount is seen to be somewhat lower than that given by the manager of ...e Crown Reef in his evidence, which figured out at £24 1s. 10d., and which is, I ...ieve, representative of the five other companies dealt with in this statement, but I ...uld prefer to deal with this subject from the State statistics basis, and if there are ...y errors in the statement as regards the State Mining Engineer's Department, I beg ...t he will correct them so that they can be put in this statement on their right ...is.

I also wish to vitalize all these statements by more or less culling from the ...tory of the six companies I have given, and whose workings I am in a position to ...te with accuracy, and to show how these yields and costs have been arrived at, and ...w these whole fields compare with some of the yields and costs of gold mining in ...er parts of the world.

We will take the Robinson Company as the typical rich mine, and follow a little of ...s history. It will be noticed from its published annual reports that it first figures ...a gold producer in the year 1888, and that it commenced with 10 stamps, which ...n up to 1889 before being superseded by 40 new ones; that the yield per ton for its ...st year's work was 272s. 7·04d., and that the working cost, which then only ...luded mining and milling, was 72s. 1·04d. per ton; that the extraction was 65 per

Early development of gold mines.

cent.; the machinery then erected was of a crude nature, and the mine worki
rather of a prospective than a permanent kind.

Go to any old prospector and ask him the method in which he looks for gold i
new region. He will tell you that he has no great geological knowledge, but that
knows gold when he sees it; that he goes over the surface and wherever he finds
outcrop he tries it with the pan. He goes over the whole extent of outcrop tha
open to him and naturally picks out the richest points at which to start work.
commences on a small scale and he works these rich parts, and as they give h
profit so he extends his operations. So started the Robinson, and so was the R;
developed.

The richest mines are started first, and the richest places in these mines
selected for a start. It would have been folly to have done anything else. In
early stages there was no need of a highly trained engineer. In fact, a conscienti
one would have told his principals that he had never seen any deposit like this, a
he would have to be guided by actual disclosures in order to intelligently advise the

With this digression let us return to the history of the Robinson Company.

Capital of Robinson G.M. Co.
ROBINSON G. M. Co., LTD.—The nominal capital of the Robinson was first £50,0
in £1 shares, of which £5,000 were working capital. This small original worki
capital was due to the insistance of the original owner of the ground. The origi
owner was bought out after a time, and on January 24th, 1889, the capital v
increased from £50,000 to £53,375, in order to acquire six claims leased to third part
before formation of Company. This again was changed on Feburary 16th, 1889, t
capitalisation of £2,750,000 in 550,000 £5 shares, to meet the public, who had place
value of £60 or £70 upon the original £1 share. All of this capital was issued
shareholders with the exception of 16,250 shares, held in reserve, the area of the g
bearing ground being equivalent to 106 claims, which has since been increased
purchase to 136 claims.

The financiers who controlled the workings of this mine realised the large capitali
tion, and their endeavour has been to justify it by actual returns from the mine, a
their success is demonstrated by the fact that, even on the present low market va
of to-day, viz., £6 14s. per share, the capitalisation of this company is held by
shareholders at £3,685,000, and it is considered in Europe one of the Consols of
1896 Profit.
industry. On this capitalisation the last year's profit shows 10·21 per cent.

Stamps.
Now, how was this brought about? The 10-stamp mill was replaced in 1889
40 stamps; the 40 were extended in 1891 to 60; the 60 extended in 1894 to 70, a
in 1895 the mill was further extended to 120 stamps.

Yield and working costs.
The yield and working costs during these periods were as follows:—

				Working cost per ton, including depreciation.		Yield per ton.	
				s.	d.	s.	d.
1888	...	...	...	72	1·042	272	7·04
1889	...	...	...	65	11·846	182	7·24
1890	...	...	...	65	1·865	113	2·94
1891	...	...	...	52	5·575	103	5·53
1892	...	...	...	46	5·997	95	6·78
1893	...	...	...	42	1·097	101	0·02
1894	...	...	...	41	4·736	97	4·94
1895	...	...	...	30	0·913	80	5·67
1896	...	...	...	30	11·096	69	10·20

Reefs.
Mining was carried on in three reefs in this mine, known as the South Reef, M
Reef Leader, and the Middle Reef. The latter was afterwards discovered to be sim
an overlap of the South Reef, and disappeared altogether at the third level.

The ore in the upper level, down to a depth of about 210 feet, was what is known "free milling." The dip was 42 degrees, but has gradually flattened, until, at the greatest depth, viz., 1,484 feet down on the incline, it is only 29 degrees. At a depth of 210 feet the matrix of the conglomerate pebble formation changed from an oxidised to a pyritic character, and the mining became somewhat more difficult and costly. Nature of ore.

The difficulties in obtaining satisfactory results by simple plate amalgamation then became greater, and one of the problems facing this company was to get an adequate return of gold from the ore, as tailings leaving the mill averaged as high as 14 dwts. per ton.

This company was the first on the Rand to successfully run frue vanners. It supplemented this work by the erection of a chlorination plant, which not only dealt with its own concentrates, but also those of other companies; and this chlorination plant has produced gold to the value of over £860,000 since it started. Chlorination plant.

This company was also the first to introduce on a large working scale the cyanide process. It replaced the first original works by larger ones, and has expended in connection with this branch of the industry, over £40,000. Cyanide works.

The treatment of slimes was also introduced on a large scale at this mine, and in connection with the Rand Central Ore Reduction Company, it has expended £60,000 to £70,000 in this direction. Slimes treatment

Outlay of Robinson G.M Co.

The total amount of money put into buildings, plant, improved processes, etc., by this Company has amounted to £426,736

Development 355,528

Making a total outlay of £782,264

and the reserve ore in sight in the mine is 441,506 tons. Reserve ore.

Granted that a large proportion of this money was obtained from the ground, it was put back into the ground, and it aided all other companies in improving their appliances, and in their own case has brought up the gold extraction from 65 per cent. in rich free milling rock to over 90 per cent. in the pyritic ore worked at the present day, and has thereby given encouragement and impetus to all mining on these fields. In dealing with the metallurgy of the ores on the Rand, the ordinary process of milling, concentration and chlorination, though adopted at this mine, did not prove as successful as in other parts of the world, owing to the way in which the gold was found in the rock, i.e., in very minute particles; and this great percentage has been obtained by the initiation of a comparatively new system in metallurgy which has had its growth and development on these fields, viz.: the treatment of tailings and slimes by the cyanide process, and the Robinson Company was one of the early pioneers in this direction. It will be noticed that a remarkable decrease in costs has taken place from the early stages of the mine to the present time. Cyanide treatment. Decreased working costs of Robinson G.M. Co.

Milling and tramming costs have been reduced from 18s. 8d. to 3s. 8d. per ton; mining costs 36s. 3d. to 17s., inclusive of development.

Cyanide costs started at 13s. 6d. per ton treated, including royalty, and were reduced to 3s. per ton treated last year. The total cost per ton on a milled basis was 72s. 1d. in 1888, and is now 30s. 11d., including two more metallurgical processes, working in harder ground, and all current capital expenditure as well as depreciation, showing a reduction in cost of 41s. 2d. per ton.

In comparing the cost of the Robinson with other mines, it must also be remembered that, although little sorting is done on the surface, a considerable quantity of waste is eliminated below. These are indeed startling reductions, and, from an engineer's point of view, I cannot see how the efficiency of this Company's works ca[n] be greatly increased.

Officials of Robinson G.M Co.

The Board have used every endeavour to obtain men of acknowledged excellenc[e] in their departments from all over the world.

The manager of the Alaska Treadwell, the working costs of which mine have [a] prominently figured before the public, was induced to take the management of th[e] Company in 1892, and, though not alone, a great deal of the credit of the reduction i[n] costs is due to his instrumentality and to his wonderful power of dealing with th[e] employees of the Company. His motto among his officers was to impress them wit[h] the idea that in each department they were to work as if the Company were the[ir] own; and with great firmness he combined great kindness, and was loved as well [as] respected.

The work done at the Robinson has had its effect on other mines, and without Robinson mine you would not have a Heriot, and without a Heriot you would not hav[e] a Geldenhuis Deep.

New Heriot.

NEW HERIOT.—The Heriot Company is an illustration of a not exceptionally hig[h] grade mine starting with inadequate working capital, poor and meagre equipment, an[d] being obliged to suspend operations owing to the fact that it could not be made to pa[y] with the appliances and funds at the disposal of the Company.

Capital and claims.

The Company was formed in August, 1887, with a capital of £50,000 in £1 share[s] the vendors receiving £4,000 as the price of the property, which consisted of twenty nine claims.

Initial yield and costs.

The battery commenced work in January, 1888; the initial yield after six month[s] was valued at £2 16s. per ton, and the actual expenditure £1 19s. 8d.

Increased capital

The capital was increased in October, 1888, by issuing to shareholders 10,00[0] shares at 30s., and three dividends of 5 per cent. were declared, but the Company agai[n] ran out of funds.

In December, 1889, the Board was authorised to increase the capital to £75,000 b[y] creating 15,000 new shares. But no tenders for these shares were received, and it wa[s] not until April, 1890, that they could sell even at par the small amount of 1,000 share[s] and these only on the condition that they were to be redeemable at 30s. within si[x] months. In the following month 5,000 shares were allotted to an applicant for £7,50[0]

Attempts were made to obtain loans, but these were fruitless owing to th[e] restricted borrowing powers of the Directors, which were limited by the trust deed t[o] £3,000; and, moreover, the bank not only refused to sanction an overdraft beyon[d] that amount, but expressed disapproval of the debt already incurred.

Development and history of New Heriot.

During the year ending July, 1890, the mill of twenty-five stamps crushe[d] 8,873 tons, yielding gold to the value of £3 1s. 4d. per ton, the working costs bein[g] 52s. 6d. for mining and milling only.

During 1891 the mill practically stopped work. Early in 1892 the New Heri[ot] Company was formed, the capital increased to £85,000, and the management an[d] finances put into strong hands.

The mine was developed and thoroughly equipped with the cardinal idea of centralisation of power. The cyanide process was introduced, and the new work[s] were started towards the end of 1893. The total working costs in 1894 wer[e] 32s. 11d.; in 1895, 27s. 4d.; in 1896, 26s. 10d.; and the extraction brought up to a tota[l] of 85·3 per cent.

This is now considered one of the model mines of the Rand, and the manager is [a] practical man who has grown up with the industry here.

Actual capital and claims of New Heriot.

The capital was increased in 1895 to £115,000, in order to acquire more groun[d] and the total number of reef-bearing claims is now fifty.

Henry Nourse G. M. Co., Ltd.—This Company was floated at Pretoria in ~~~cil, 1887, with a capital of £35,000, in £1 shares, of which 24,000 shares were ~~en for the property, and 11,000 shares were issued against £11,426 5s., which ~~stituted the original working capital. This sum was soon exhausted, and a special ~~eral meeting of shareholders was held in Pretoria on June 4, 1888, when the ~~ital was increased by 15,000 shares, which the Directors were instructed to issue ~~not less than 30s. each. At the first annual meeeting of shareholders held on ~~gust 14th, 1888, the Directors reported that owing to this limitation they had been ~~ble to dispose of these new issue shares, excepting 2,670 shares taken by Sandy- ~~ft's agent to settle an amount due to them and to pay for a new 15-stamp mill ~~ich had been ordered. The balance sheet to June 30, 1888, shows that 1,642 ozs. ~~lwts. of gold had been won, so that the original 15-stamp battery must have ~~rted about March of that year, but no record of the number of tons crushed ~~ears to have been kept. On June 30, 1888, the Company's cash was exhausted, ~~, there were on hand 12,330 out of the 15,000 reserve shares created in June, 1888.

At December 31st, 1888, the west shaft had been sunk to a depth of 103 feet, the ~~tral to 16 feet, and the eastern to 39 feet. The report to that date states that ~~30 of the reserve shares had been disposed of at 31s. per share, and the balance of ~~000 at 56s., thus placing the Company in funds ; and that an order for a 15-stamp ~~tery had been increased by 40 stamps, making 55 stamps in all, to make with the ~~stamp mill then running a battery of 70 heads. This battery was of too light a ~~tern, and was never erected, but was disposed of as an opportunity occurred.

At December 31st, 1889, the Company's indebtedness had increased to £24,905 ~~s. 9d., and at June 30, 1890, to £26,946 3s., and at a special general meeting of ~~reholders held on September 10, 1890, the capital, then £50,000, was increased by ~~ creation of 50,000 to £100,000. Of these 50,000 shares, 37,500 were offered to ~~reholders at 30s., but were not applied for. Eventually these shares were taken and came into strong hands.

The report of December 31, 1891, shows that it had been necessary to pledge the ~~mpany's assets as security for an overdraft at the Standard Bank, and the above ~~angement as to the issue of the reserve shares was the best the Directors were then ~~e to make.

At 30th June, 1892, the Company had paid off its liabilities and had a cash balance ~~£25,000. By 31st December, 1892, the 15-stamp battery hitherto running was ~~reased by 20 stamps, and on 12th December, 1892, a cyanide plant was erected ~~r the old battery and commenced work.

During the next half-year five more stamps were added to the battery, and ~~ensive additions were made to the pumping and hauling equipment, and at 30th ~~ne, 1893, the Company was again in debt about £17,000.

The mine was, however, opening up well, and showing such good returns that a ~~cial meeting held on the 7th March, 1894, sanctioned the increase of the capital to ~~25,000 by the creation of 25,000 shares, which were taken up by shareholders and ~~arantors at 40s. each. The capital thus raised, and profits accruing from mining ~~rations, were expended in the erection of a first-class plant on the basis of 60 ~~mps. The total expense incurred in the equipment and buildings amounting in all ~~£200,000.

The total number of claims in this property is about eighty.

The debt that was incurred in connection with the equipment was not wiped off ~~til the middle of 1896, and the first dividend was 30 per cent., declared in December, ~~6, and paid in February, 1897.

The yield from this Company has been fairly uniform, and shows an aver extraction from the start to the present day of about 82 per cent.

The costs have been reduced from their maximum of 56s. 3d., to the minim 35s. 7d., shown in my table of working costs.

Even the present costs are high, owing to the small lateral extent of the proper which has necessitated the working through three shafts, and also to the fact that the most part only one narrow reef has been worked, and 25 per cent. of the r hoisted from the mine sorted out as waste; the rock has also been exceptionally ha The small dip area for the major extent of the mine is due to the fact that, on starti the conglomerate beds showed a declination of about 80 degrees, which would all mining to be conducted at considerable depth before reaching the southern bounda

The beds, however, within a horizontal distance of 240 feet have gradua changed their dip to 46 and 50 degrees, thus permitting the deep level company commence mining operations at a comparatively shallow depth.

CITY AND SUBURBAN G. M. Co.—This Company was formed in 1887 with capital of £50,000 in £1 shares, of which the vendors received £30,000, and th certain other interests were acquired, reducing the working capital from £20,000 £8,900.

The capital was increased in

1888 by	1,000 shares, realising	...	...	...	£15,548
1889 by	5,000 "	"	...	...	...	62,950
1892 by	10,000 "	"	...	...	...	65,000
1893 by	10,000 "	"	..	...	...	86,250

So that the total working capital subscribed amounted to £238,648

It must also be added that in 1895 the capital, which then stood at £85,000 in shares, was transformed into 340,000 shares of £4 each.

The mining area of the Company is 150 claims (about), of which about 20 clai have been worked out up to end of 1896, including poor ground and pillars. T total tonnage crushed up to this period is 670,463 tons, and the gold bullion recover from same, 428,794 ounces.

The total cash receipts from all sources have been ... ... £1,838,4 and the total cash expenditure on property, development, equipment and working expenses to end of 1896 1,559,6

leaving a profit of ... £278,7 out of which £251,661 has been paid in dividends to shareholders, and the balance £27,128 is represented by cash, stores on hand, etc.

The equipment of the mine, the cost of which stands at £524,110, includes development of ore reserves, amounting to 375,895 tons.

The first 10-stamp mill started crushing in August 1887, to which was add another 10 stamps in June, 1888. In May, 1891, a new 30-stamp mill was started, which was added the first 20 stamps two months later. This 50-stamp mill work on till November, 1895, when it was finally closed down, having been replaced by improved plant of about 80 stamps started in July, 1894; 40 stamps were added the latter in July, 1895, and in September following a further 40 stamps, making 160 stamps at the new mill. The full plant, however, was not worked until Ju 1896, owing to inadequate supplies of native labour.

Cyanide works were started in 1893 to treat the product of the 50-stamp mill a the accumulation of tailings prior to that date. In July, 1894, a new cyanide dire ling plant in connection with the new milling plant was started, which has since en extended for the treatment of coarse sands and concentrates, and double treatment is been adopted.

As no systematic samples of the ore were recorded prior to 1892, figures are not *Increased extraction of.* hand to supply the percentage of recovery previous to that year. In 1892 the covery by amalgamation only was 59·596 per cent. of the value of the ore crushed, hich has been raised to 81·95 per cent. for 1896 by mill and cyanide, showing that ith improved methods the extraction has been increased by 22·36 per cent.

It will also be noted that the working expenses have been reduced from 60s. 4·56d. *Reduced working costs of.* r ton in 1887 to 26s. 3·91d. per ton in 1896, due to the improved method and pliances of mining and milling, and ore treatment, and working on a large scale, us now making it possible to work profitably lower grade ore than formerly.

CROWN REEF.—Taking this company next, which in early days was considered ly a low grade mine, though having two very regular reefs running through it with a average stoping width of 4ft. each.

Its history can be summarised as follows :— *History of Crown Reef.*

This company was formed on the 1st April, 1888, to acquire the lease of a ijnpacht on the farm Langlaagte from a private syndicate. It had an issued share pital of £100,000, in £1 shares, of which amount £14,000 was working capital. he share capital of the company was increased to £106,000, in 1890 ; to £110,000 in 892 ; and £120,000 in the latter half of 1892 ; the profit from the sale of shares eing utilised to equip the property.

The milling power of the company was 30 stamps at the start. This was *Equipment.* increased by a new mill of 40 stamps in 1890. To this mill a further 20 stamps was dded in 1892. These two mills were replaced by a new mill of 120 stamps, with implete cyanide works in 1894, and slimes plant in 1896.

Up to March 31st, 1895, the company had expended on capital account, buildings, *Capital expenditure.* machinery, and plant, dams and reservoirs, etc. ... £308,963 0 9
Purchase of freehold rights 26,009 0 0
Sinking main shafts and driving main cross cuts ... 62,521 7 3

£397,484 8 0

Besides this, mine development, charged to working
expenditure, cost 58,850 16 9

£456,335 4 9

Since that time all expenditure has been charged against revenue account, and *Revenue and expenditure.* pital account has ceased entirely. During the two years ending 31st March, the mpany has expended for :—
Sinking main shafts and driving cross-cuts ... £21,618 9 2
Mine development 64,674 10 10
Buildings and additions to plant 6,433 18 0

£92,726 18 0
Amount brought down from above 456,335 4 9

Making a total of £549,162 2 9

The amount expended on development and sinking main shafts brought 1,495,550 *Reserve ore.* ns of ore in sight, of which 442,859 tons are in reserve ready for stoping.

Increased ex-traction.
The company originally recovered only 57 per cent. of the value of gold in th ore, this value being arrived at by the addition of the assay value of the residues t the total gold recovered.

This percentage has been increased gradually up to 86 per cent., which is th extraction for the last half of the financial year ending March 31st, 1897, when slimes plant was added to the already existing equipment of mill, cyanide, and con centrating plants.

Working costs.
The company first got its rock from open trenches which was a cheap method f a time. During the second year of its existence it started actual underground work The total costs, exclusive of capital expenditure for that year, averaged £1 13s. 7 Last year with the additional cost of three separate secondary treatments, the cost inclusive of capital expenditure, were £1 8s. 5d. Although the mining costs hav shown no great reduction, the milling costs have been reduced from 11s. in 1890, to 3 in 1896. The position of the property in 1890 was most exhaustively dealt with in report by myself, which deals fully with the difficulties and imperfections of gol recovery on these fields.

Yield.
Leaving out of account the first year of the Company's returns, which wa abnormal, the yield per ton has been fairly constant, though slightly increasing durin; the last two years, and varies from £1 15s. 6d. during the second year to £2 7s. 2d. fo the last financial year.

Capitalisation of Geldenhuis Deep.
THE GELDENHUIS DEEP, LTD.—This Company was formed in January, 1893, with a capital of £350,000 in £1 shares. The vendors received 175,000 shares, while 90,00 shares were issued for working capital, realising £94,500, and 85,000 shares were kep in reserve.

Number of claims.
The property consisted of 212 claims, and work was commenced at once.

Debenture issue.
Cost of equip-ment.
In 1894, it was found advisable to issue debentures to the amount of £160,00 and in 1895 15,000 out of 85,000 reserve shares were sold, realising £103,474 15s., an further sums were gradually borrowed to complete the development and equipment, o which, altogether, about £410,000 will be spent. This is the cost of putting the min on a paying basis, and, after all the experience gained in former years there can be n doubt that the works here, as well as at other subsidiary companies of the Rand mine are of an extremely high order. The mistakes of early days have been avoided as fa as possible, and every effort has been made to introduce the latest improvements.

Initial yield.
The mill started crushing towards the end of 1895, and the early results were poo and unsatisfactory. During the last three months of that year the yield was onl 18s. 2d. per ton, while the costs were 26s.

Increased yield.
In 1896, the yield was raised to an average of 27s. 4d., with working costs of 25s while for April of the current year, the working costs, including sorting, wer 26s. 5d. per ton, the yield 37s. 3d., and the monthly profit, £9,018.

Rand Mines.
The Geldenhuis Deep is only one of the subsidiary companies of the Rand Mine Ltd., which, as shown by the last Annual Report, has seven other important companie already in course of development and equipment, and expects to require £3,630,065 t put them on their initial running basis of 710 stamps, with the intention of eventuall increasing them to 1,300.

The total nominal capital of the eight companies is £3,607,391, a sum almo identical with the amount of cash estimated to put them on an earning basis.

I trust that I have not wearied you with all the details I have given yo concerning the history of these mines; I have laid everything so fully before you i order to show you what has been the work of one group of capitalists on these field I do not for a moment wish to imply that our firm has been the only one to achiev

liant success, as you have been already, or will be, informed by the representatives
he other houses regarding the good work done by them.

You will have seen from the struggling history of many of these companies, that
er the early boom of 1889, there was a most serious depression, during which all the
ies suffered, but it was during this very depression that the foundations were laid,
means of hard, earnest and intelligent work, of the revival which followed in the
r 1895. We now again are experiencing a period of the most acute depression after
recent boom, but there is an enormous difference (which I cannot too strongly
press upon you) between the position and hopes of the industry at the present
ment, and during the preceding relapse. In 1890 the industry was still young, it
s undeveloped, and there was, as I have endeavoured to show, immense scope for
roving mining results, both as regards working costs and extraction of the gold.

Comparison of depression in 1890 and in 1897.

Now, in 1897, the class of machinery on these fields can be considered the most
fect of any gold fields in the world; the various processes dealing with the
raction of gold are rapidly approaching practical perfection, and our working costs
ve been decreased until we can scarcely reduce them further without the Govern-
nt's help; with this help however, we can still make great reductions.

Government co-operation necessary to reduce working costs.

I have tried, and I cannot too earnestly try, to impress upon you that the very
n who in the early days obtained their profits from rich mines like the Robinson
l Ferreira, freely put back this money into other mines, like the City and Suburban,
Henry Nourse, and the New Heriot, then struggling under the greatest difficulties,
l after reaping the fruit of their energy and intelligence here, again turned their
ources to gigantic enterprises like the Rand Mines.

Profits put back into mines.

Before pursuing further the investigations of these fields, I desire in a way to
npare the yield, cost, etc., shown in the foregoing statements, with those of other
d mines in the world.

It must be remembered that to make comparisons applicable, the conditions under
ich work is carried on must be taken into account. Even comparing the twenty-
e different mines in the foregoing list, it will be found that different conditions exist.
ne companies sort their ore, and others do not ; some work only one reef, others two or
ee, varying in thickness, hardness, etc. ; it is obviously unfair, for instance, to com-
e the costs of a company exploiting, for the most part, only one thin reef, and
ting out 40 per cent. of its rock, with a company which is not sorting and working
reefs averaging ten or twelve feet in thickness. The scale on which work is
ducted must also be taken into consideration, and it is presumable that companies
h large stamping power should have an advantage in working costs over those of
ch smaller power, and companies who are treating ore by two or three secondary
cesses should be under a disadvantage when comparing costs with those employing
y one or two. It will be noticed that the average stamping power of the twenty-
e companies is about eighty-five stamps per company.

Working conditions of different mines.

I will commence with the Alaska Treadwell Mine, the annual report of which
pany for 1896 I beg to put in evidence.

From this report the operating costs are seen to be as follows —

Operating costs on 263,670 tons (all construction charged directly to operating

	Dollars per ton of ore.	Shillings per ton of ore.
Mining	·5491	2·29
Milling	·3476	1·45
Chlorination	·1138	0·47
General Expenses (Douglas Island)	·0819	0·34
,, ,, (San Francisco)	·0218	0·09
London Office Expense	·0112	0·05
Bullion Charges, Freight, Insurance, &c. ...	·0372	0·15
Total operating costs	1·1632	4·85
Net profit for year	1·8862	7·86
Total Yield	3·0494	12·71

The Wages paid were as follows :—

	Per diem.	Per diem. s. d.
Miners, with board and lodging	2·50	10 5
Labourers ,, ,, ...	2·00	8 4
Drillmen, with bonuses and board and lodging (Summer)	2·50	10 5
Drillmen, with bonuses and board and lodging (Winter)	3·00	12 6
Indians (paid daily	2·00	8 4

MILLMEN.

	Dollars per month.	
Concentrators, with board and lodging	65·00 to 100·00	£13 10 0 to £20 16 8
Feeders ,, ,,	70·00 to 100·00	14 11 8 to 20 16 8
Amalgamators ,, ,,	90·00 to 100·00	18 15 0 to 20 16 8

CHLORINATION WORKS.

	Per diem.	Per diem. s. d.	s. d.
Roasters, with board and lodging	2·50	10 5	
Roasters (helpers) ,,	2·00	6 4	
Floormen ,,	2·00 and 2·25	8 4 and 9	4½

MACHINE SHOP,

	Per diem.	Per diem.
Mechanics, with board and lodging	2·00 to 6·00	8 4 to 25 0
Blacksmiths ,,	4·00	16 8
Blacksmiths' helpers ,,	2·00	8 4

The Alaska Treadwell Company, however, is situated on an island with a go
harbour. The mill is near the ocean, with the tailings running into the water, and
worked by water power for the greater part of the year; the lode varies in thickne
from 50 feet to 426 feet, and the mining is more or less quarry work. The numb
of stamps is 240. The mine is most favourably situated for obtaining supplies at lo
rates, as is shown by detailed account, which I beg the Commission will compare wi
the rates of similar supplies on these fields, especially dynamite.

The following table is roughly made out to show the relative prices paid f
stores at the Alaska Treadwell mine and at the Crown Reef here for 1896, on t
basis of the amount used at the former mine :—

ARTICLE.	AMOUNT USED.	ALASKA PRICE.	CROWN REEF PRICE.	
ynamite	200,089 lbs.	5,134 11 2	17,354 12 2	Comparative table of prices for stores at Crown Reef and Alaska Treadwell G. M. Cos.
ise	14,314 coils.	474 5 0	268 7 9	
ips	75,182	168 5 0	150 8 0	
mber	14,909 cubic ft.	482 0 0	3,168 2 0	
eel, Mining	25,519 lbs.	429 16 5	637 18 0	
ils	6,545 gallons.	428 3 5	1,309 0 0	
andles	272 boxes	177 15 0	145 0 0	
ortars	2	96 0 0	304 0 0	
ortar Liners...	58,058 lbs.	756 12 0	1,209 10 10	
im Shafts	3	59 4 0	52 10 0	
uide Blocks	120 pair	22 16 0	856 0 0	
noes and Dies	151,922 lbs.	2,178 17 3	2,278 16 8	
creens	1,300 sq. feet	109 6 0	97 10 0	
eads	12	49 16 3	78 0 0	
ilphuric Acid	328,000 lbs.	1,000 0 0	4,100 0 0	
ilt	455 tons	790 8 6	2,733 0 0	
ar Iron	63,503 lbs.	275 9 6	529 3 10	
ead	1,461 lbs.	18 4 6	52 11 6	
		12,651 10 0	35,324 10 9	

If the same proportion exists for the balance of the stores used by the Alaska readwell which are not classified above, and which amount to further £3,500 clusive of coal, these total stores costing £16,100 in Alaska on the above basis of ices, here amount to about £45,100, thus increasing their costs by £29,000, and the tal cost per ton at the Alaska Treadwell Mine by 2s. 2d. on the tonnage milled : 3,670 tons. *(margin: Cost of total stores per ton milled at Alaska Treadwell G. M. Co.)*

On the other hand, if the Crown Reef Company had been able to obtain its stores st year at the above prices ruling in Alaska, their supplies, exclusive of coal, which tually cost them £85,100, would only have cost £30,500, which would be a saving £54,600, or no less than 5s. 6d. per ton, on their tonnage of 198,236 tons. *(margin: Cost of total stores per ton milled at Crown Reef G. M. Co.)*

	CROWN REEF.	ALASKA TREADWELL.
		1 dol. = 4s.
Tons crushed	198,236	263,670
Pounds of Dynamite used per ton crushed ...	1·10	0·76
Tons mined and milled, secondary treatment and general expenses per man per day	0·31	4·14

Comparative working costs of Alaska Treadwell and Crown Reef G. M. Cos.

	CROWN REEF.		ALASKA TREADWELL 1 dollar—4s.	
	Cost per ton Milled.	Per cent. of total cost.	Cost per ton Milled.	Per cent of total cost.
	£ s. d.		£ s. d.	
Labour, total white and black, including food...	0 15 6	57·98	0 2 11	63·78
Coal	0 2 7	9·79	0 0 5	8·57
Dynamite	0 2 5	9·11	0 0 5	8·37
Cyanide Zinc and Royalty...	0 1 8	6·35	—	—
Timber	0 0 5	1·55	—	0·79
Steel, Mining	0 0 4	1·32	—	0·72
Oils	0 0 3	0·87	0 0 1	0·92
Candles...	0 0 4	1·20	—	0·23
Mill Spares	0 0 5	1·52	0 0 4	6·54
Fuse and Detonators	0 0 2	0·57	—	1·02
Trucks, Wheels, and Rails...	0 0 2	0·69	0 0 1	0·01
Pipes and Pipe fittings	0 0 1	0·36	—	0·50
Sundry Stores, General Expenses } Electric Light and Drill Spares }	0 2 4	8·79	0 0 2	3·46
Chlorination Supplies	—	—	0 0 3	5·09
Total cost per ton	1 6 8	100%	0 4 8	100%

This shows that the relative proportion of cost for labour at the Alaska Treadwell is somewhat higher on a percentage basis than at the Crown Reef, and also that the great lowness of cost is, in addition to the cheapness of supplies, due to the fact that the tons mined and milled per man per day are in a ratio of thirteen to one at the Crown Reef.

Working costs of Deadwood Terra G.M.Co.

The next comparison of cost I wish to make is that of the Deadwood Terra Gold Mining Company, Dakota, U.S.A., given me by the manager of the Geldenhuis Deep who, previously to coming out here, was manager of this property. It was on account of the remarkably low costs ruling there that we were induced to obtain his services here on the Rand.

The total Mining costs of this company in 1895 are shown to be 1·37 dollars made up of :—

    Mining   ...   .   88·539 cents = 3s. 8d.
    Milling   ...   .   48·861 cents = 2s.

Yield of Deadwood Terra G. M. Co.

The yield of the ore being 1·74 dollars — 7s. 3d. per ton.

If it interests you, further particulars can be obtained from the manager of the denhuis Deep. He informed me that the width of the lode varied from 25 to feet, the deepest shaft was 600 feet and no secondary treatment was used. The was coal obtained by rail, and ruling rates of wages were as follows :—

MILLHANDS.

Wages at the Deadwood Terra G.M. Co.

Engineer	...	...	...	2 at 3·00 per shift of 12 hours.				
Foreman	...	...	...	2 „ 2·50	„	„	„	„
Foreman helper	...	..	1 „ 2·00	„	„	10	„	
Amalgamators	...	...	2 „ 3·50	„	„	12	„	
Amalgamators	...	...	4 „ 3·00	„	„	„	„	
Feeders	...	...	2 „ 2·50	„	„	„	„	
Oilers	...	...	2 „ 2·50	„	„	„	„	
Carpenters	...	...	1 „ 3·50	„	„	10	„	
Carpenter helpers	...	...	1 „ 2·50	„	„	„	„	

Miners in Deadwood Terra mine received 3·00 per shift of 10 hours and shovellers).

Wages at Homestake and Highland mines and mills. In the Homestake and Highland mines and mills all of this labour is paid 50c. shift more.

The Deadwood Terra mine ran 160 stamps.

Working costs of Californian gold mines. Regarding the gold mines of California the total costs in some of the principal es vary from 10s. to 38s. per ton, depending on local conditions.

Mr. Leggett, a more recent arrival than myself, can give you fuller particulars.

The next comparison of cost I wish to put in evidence is taken from *Mineral dustry*, page 312, in which it states :—

Working costs of Mount Morgan mine. "Mount Morgan Mine reports for 1895, the cost of working last year was almost dollars a ton."

Working costs of Mysore Co. *Mine Industry*, 1895, same page :—" Mysore Company in India treated 60,654 s, and cyanided half the tailings; cost, 9·50 dollars per ton." *Mineral Industry*, 5, page 319 :—" Milling in four districts in U.S.A. is averaged by P. A. Richards as ler :—

Milling costs in some mines of the United States.

Black Hills	...	...	...	70 cents a ton.
Gilpin	...	...	...	75 „ „
Grass Valley	...	...	...	80 „ „
Amador	...	...	...	46 „ „ (soft ore)."

Taking the average of the first three districts, we get 75 cents a ton, or 3s. This ractically the same as the Crown Reef cost for the past two years, including stone shing.

Average milling costs in United States. From this it is seen that the average cost of milling in the Black Hills, Dakota, the Gilpin Country, Colorado, and Grass Valley and Amador Country, California, s. 10d. per ton, and the mining cost is not given, but varies with local conditions the width of the lodes.

El Callao mine. EL CALLAO.—The next comparison is a table of results showing the genera rations of the El Callao Company from its formation up to June, 1894.

Initial working and yield. Work was first started in 1870 on a small scale, and by people who had no vious experience in mining. The yield per ton is seen to have varied from 5·66 in 1884 to 0·6 ozs. in 1892, the average for the whole period being 2·03 ozs., or s. per ton.

N

Table showing the General Results of the operations on "EL CALLAO" Lode, since formation of the Company.

PERIODS.	Lode area worked on incline square metres.	Lode Average thickness metres	Ore Gross Yield in Tons.	Gold Gross Yield in Ozs.	Gold Yield per Ton Ozs.	Gold Gross Yield Value. £	Gold Yield per Ton Value. s. d.	Mining Costs per Ton. s. d.	Milling Costs per Ton. s. d.	Miscellaneous Costs per Ton. s. d.	Total Cost per Ton. s. d.	Total Dividends Paid. £ s. d.
1870 to March 11, 1881	22,102	1·52	91,046	318,855	3·50	1,218,115	267 7	...	...	...	...	313,433 13 5
Mar. 11, 1881, to Dec. 31, 1883	15,461	1·60	67,073	300,650	4·48	1,148,700	342 6	...	...	...	149 2	497,886 4 11
1884	7,513	1·54	31,261	177,055	5·66	677,569	433 5	86 7	29 10	5 10	122 3	383,300 15 0
1885	8,949	1·94	46,868	114,500	2·44	435,040	185 8	59 1	20 4	4 5	83 10	181,429 0 5
1886	13,867	2·00	74,399	181,300	2·40	685,860	184 4	43 9	14 8	1 5	59 10	436,962 17 1
1887	13,273	1·75	64,215	73,872	1·15	282,000	87 10	45 10	7 3	1 10	54 11	58,772 15 7
1888	13,528	1·45	54,438	52,598	0·97	199,994	73 5	51 9	7 11	2 0	61 8	5,110 13 7
1889	9,755	1·68	56,389	52,973	0·93	204,134	72 4	42 5	6 3	5 2	53 10	20,442 14 1
1890	13,113	1·52	53,977	49,432	0·93	189,829	70 3	46 8	6 3	1 9	54 8	20,442 14 1
1891	16,321	1·33	59,284	34,774	0·59	132,270	44 7	32 8	5 0	2 1	39 9	
1892	13,825	1·40	52,823	31,931	0·60	120,297	45 6	33 3	5 0	3 1	41 4	
1893	11,000	1·36	40,085	34,537	0·86	131,559	65 8	32 10	6 3	7 0	46 1	
Jan. 1 to June 30, 1894	3,048	1·40	11,607	8,417	0·73	32,063	55 2	45 9	6 3	1 8	53 8	12,607 6 8
TOTALS	161,755	1·54	703,465	1,430,894	2·03	5,457,432	155 2					1,940,478 14 10

The working expenses varied from 149s. 2d. per ton, which was the average for the first 13 years, to the minimum of 39s. 9d. in 1891, the total average being 53s. 8d. for the whole period.

Working expenses.

The total gross yield from this mine is shown at £5,457,432, while the dividends declared have only amounted to £1,940,478, in spite of the phenomenal richness of the ore. This, with the exception of the Mount Morgan mine, can be considered to have been at one time the richest gold mine in the world.

Yield and dividends.

The success of this mine induced capital to be invested freely in other lodes, which, however, were not of the same richness, though in many cases of as high a grade as that ruling on these fields, and 31 companies were started, which erected 758 stamps. At the present time the industry is almost dead; there are only ten stamps running on these fields, and these are working without a profit, and the celebrated El Callao mine was just closed down in debt to the extent of 150,000 dollars. Let us now enquire into the above high costs and final languishing of the fields. In the early history the discoverers worked on a very small scale with very little experience, and their immense costs are not to be wondered at considering the general political and climatic conditions. The Callao mine is situated about 150 miles south of the Orinoco River, in a latitude of about 7 degrees north of the equator, without railway communication, and with very bad roads, and in its early history was considered most unhealthy, so that high wages had to be offered to induce skilled men to come to the property.

Initial success and subsequent failure of El Callao mine.

In 1884 a new *regime* was started, and high grade machinery with increased stamping power, and high grade men put to work, the Company giving them a free hand and every encouragement to do their best, and expenses were lowered in eight years from £6 2s. 3d. to £1 19s. 9d. per ton. The cardinal feature in this reduction was the improvement in machinery and mining methods, but another was the encouragement of negro labour obtained from the West Indian Islands. At first this class of labour was considered hopelessly incompetent, but by patient training and judicious graduation of wages in proportion to work done, it was finally possible to run the mine with 11½ per cent. of the white men originally required, and the blacks were better able to stand the climate. The Government of Venezuela, which was not in sympathy with the alien mining population, believed in high and onerous tariffs, monopolies and concessions, and did very little to foster the industry, in fact tried in every way to extort as much as possible out of it. The present unfortunate condition of the mining industry there, is I think, in no small measure due to the attitude of the Government. The ruling rates of wages during late years, when good work has been done, are:—

Introduction of high-grade machinery.

Reduction of working costs on El Callao mine.

Negro labour.

White and black wages of El Callao mine.

White, average per month	£35
(This does not include the Superintendent).	
Blacks, per day	6s. 6d.

I would state in this connection that Mr. H. C. Perkins, late general manager of the Rand Mines, initiated in 1884 the better working and equipment of this mine. I succeeded him as superintendent in the latter part of 1887, and remained until the middle of of 1889. Mr. Webber, now general manager of the Rand Mines, succeeded me, and remained until he came here in 1891, and he in turn was succeeded by Mr. Searle, now manager of the Crown Deep, who remained until 1896. Mr. Searle, the most recent arrival from El Callao, will be best able to give you further details regarding the working of the mines and the Government of the country, should you desire them. Although now out of date as a treatise on the comparison of working costs, I wish to put in evidence an interesting little pamphlet published in 1886 by Mr. Hamilton Smith, who deals with the relative costs in the United States and Venezuela gold fields, and gives the relative conditions under which work is accomplished.

Mr. H. Jennings' Evidence.

The table herewith which I incorporate in my statement, gives the substance
the comparisons, and is as follows:—

Relative working costs of United States and Venezuela gold fields. MINE.	Period.	Average No. of Stamps.	Tons crushed in one year.	Average No. of Tons crushed by each stamp per month.	Costs of milling per ton in dollars.	Total costs per ton in dollars.	Costs of milling per ton in shillings.	Total cost per ton in shillings
Sierra Buttes ...	1885	76½	54,493	59	·56	5·83	2·33	24·2
Plumas Eureka...	1885	60	55,973	78	·61	5·57	2·54	23·1
Homestake ...	1882-3	200	170,074	75	1·17	4·03	4·87	16·7
" ...	1883-4	200	191,505	80	1·21	4·19	5·03	17·4
" ...	1884-5	200	213,190	89	1·01	3·25	4·20	13·5
Father De Smet	1883	100	104,100	85	—	2·49	—	10·3
" "	1885	100	106,855	89	—	2·12	—	8·8
Caledonia ...	1885-6	—	48,848	—	·88	2·95	3·66	12·2
El Callao ...	1882	60	22,405	31	11·19	45·34	46·55	188·6
" ...	1883	60	24,750	34	—	44·33	—	184·4
" ...	1884	60	30,936	43	7·25	35·17	30·16	146·3
" ...	1885	80	47,223	49	4·98	21·96	20·72	91·3
" new mill	May, 1886	40	—	83	ab't 3	ab't 15	12·50	62·5
New Potosi	11 m'ths 1884	25½	7,456	27	—	46·96	—	195·3

I regret that I cannot put in more details of the working costs in other countrie
compared with the elaborate details given by me for these fields, although I have gon
to considerable trouble to obtain further figures, but this is in accordance with th
statement already made by me that information is more generously given here tha
in any other mining district in the world.

Milling costs on Rand.

From the figures, however, that I have given it is evident that our average cos
of 3s. 8d. for milling (some companies running under 3s.) compares most favourabl
with the milling costs of other mines in the world, working under similar condition
and speaks eloquently for the excellence of our machinery and mill organisatio

n the high price of labour and supplies is taken into consideration, and when we
e to conserve and pump our mill water. These milling costs can still further be
aced, but only in items of labour and supplies. To show the improvement in
ing on the Rand since 1890, I would state that I had cause to examine a mill of 100
nps in that year, at which the milling costs were 10s. 2½d. per ton, not including cost of
es and dies, the number of white men employed being 29, and the number of black 188.

The number of men employed to-day at the Geldenhuis Deep mill (155 stamps) is
ut 20 white and about 20 black, including engine-men.

Cyanide costs of these fields are not comparable with any others at my disposal, Cyanide costs on
may safely be assumed to be the lowest in the world. The main costs are Rand.
a to be in mining, including mine development, the average amounting for the 29 Development
npanies to 17s. 7·12d. per ton. This is abnormally high, and is the department in costs on Rand.
ch our principal future reduction is to be made. This department has little to
ect from improved machinery, and the main hope of reduction lies in increasing
efficiency of labour or decreasing its wage, or both, and also in decreasing the cost
ll supplies, especially dynamite and coal.

Before leaving this subject I wish to state that a mere reduction in working costs Sorting.
not the only thing to be aimed at, as I believe there is still considerable scope for
ing the yield by extending and improving the system of sorting in vogue at some
the mines, and mining underground a minimum amount of waste. In this way an
arently higher cost per ton on the basis of the tonnage milled might be shown
ile actually cheaper work was being done, but larger profits would result. Mr.
ins, who is the pioneer of this system on these fields, can give you better informa-
a than I, though I also have been, and am introducing it at all the mines with which I
connected. I roughly estimate that now, for the 29 principal mines, not over 8
cent. of the ore is sorted, and I think in time this figure will be more than
bled. The only further improvement I see possible from an engineering point of
w, is the introduction of slimes treatment throughout the mines.

This will be an expensive matter with the freight rates, etc., ruling here, and will
bably cost for plant approximately between £120 and £200 per stamp, according
the size of the mill. The increase of yield and profit will depend on the grade of
slimes leaving the mill, which varies in the case of every mine, and in some cases
y not warrant the expenditure of erecting such a plant.

I have included in this portion of my statement an immense amount of figures
ich have been compiled with great care, but owing to the short space of time
ich I have had at my disposal in drawing this up, it is possible that a few small
ors may have occurred, and if so I hope I shall be informed of the fact by the
tlemen on the Commission, as I do not wish a few possible clerical errors to vitiate
y of the arguments I am advancing.

I have already explained that the engineer is about at the end of his tether as
ards further improvements under present conditions.

From the analysis of working costs on labour and supply basis, it is evident that
our is the most vital point of all, and the point towards which our chief attention
st be directed.

The summary of my statement for six companies shows that labour figures on a Cost of labour.
is of total costs per ton as follows :—

White labour	...	...	8s. 7·78d. per ton.	30·18 per cent.
Black „	...	...	6s. 9·62d. „	23·73 „
Kaffir food	...	...	1s. 2·24d. „	4·14 „
			16s. 7·64d. per ton.	58·05 per cent.

The State Mining Engineer for the year 1895 gives

White labour at	...	...	...	34·3 per cent.
Black „	...	...	...	28·6 „

                                                   62·9 per cent.

Taking the mean of these two estimates, we have, roughly speaking, 60 per c‹
of our working cost appearing under the item of labour.

Now, what have we to face in our labour problem? It is, first, that our lab‹
is accomplished in the proportion of, roughly, 1 white man to 8 or 10 black. Some
the white labour is the best that money can command, and is culled from all over
world. It is very highly paid when compared to labour in old-established count‹
where climatic and general conditions are favourable, but when compared to ‹
fields, to which men only go for high wages, it is not excessive, as shown by
statement made by Mr. Seymour with regard to the price of labour in Neva
Montana, and British Columbia, and also by the figures I have myself already gi‹
of wages in other districts.

I now give a tabulated statement showing the average daily wages paid to
employees in the older mining districts of various countries :—

Country.	Mines.	Average, Surface.	Average, Underground.	Reference.
Belgium,	Coal	2s. 3·8d. to	2s. 11·7d.	Engg., v. 20., 1888-9
Bilbao, Spain,	Iron	1s. 6d. to 2s. 6d.	2s. 6d. to 3s. 4d.	Engg., v. 44, p. 271
Durham, Eng.	Coal	2s. 6d.	3s. 8d.	Engg., v. 53, p. 413
France,	Coal	2s. 4d. to 2s. 10¼d.	3s. 1½d. to 3s. 11d.	Engg., v. 53, p. 413
Germany,	Coal	2s. 2d. to 3s. 0d.	2s. 4d. to 3s. 3d.	Engg., v. 53, p. 413
Hungary,	Coal	0s. 10d. to 1s. 2d.	2s. 0d. to 2s. 6d.	Engg., v. 54, p. 179
United States :				
California,	Gold	4s. 0d. to 8s. 0d.	10s. 0d. to 12s. 0d.	Approximation.
Georgia,	Coal	3s. 10d. to 4s. 0d.	6s. 0d.	Engg., v. 52, p. 582
Pennsylvania,	Coal	4s. 9d.	5s. 0d.	Engg., v. 53, p. 413

NOTE.—In Hungary and Spain the number of hours per week is, in summer,
high as 72; while in the other named countries the hours vary from 54 to 66.
the American coal mines, the average number of days worked in 1894 was only 2
but wages are based on the actual weekly payments, divided by six.

Mr. Goldmann's statement regarding 3,620 miners on the fifty-three compani
Witwatersrand goldfields, is food for serious reflection, showing that 54 per cent.
the men are single, 33 per cent. are married, with their families in other countr‹
and the small balance of only 13 per cent. consists of married men with th‹
families here.

What does this mean?—It means that the majority of the men have come ‹
here simply attracted by the high wages, and have not deemed it advisable owing
the condition of the country to make it their home. Other witnesses have sho‹
how wise they were in so doing owing to the great cost of living prevailing here.

What would it mean if we materially reduced these men's wages? Would it ‹
be that the best men for the industry and the Republic, and those whom we are m‹
anxious to keep, would leave, and we would be left with the improvident, and th‹
who could not command work in their own country?

Now, regarding the native labour, which comprises in numbers by far the grea‹
proportion of labour we are using. What has been the keynote of our troubl‹
Lack of supply in proportion to the demand, and inefficiency and ignorance of t‹
class of labour which is not trained to the intricate work demanded of it. Far m‹

ill is required of the kaffir on the Witwatersrand than is the case for the most part the diamond fields, or in any agricultural pursuit in South Africa. The boys me here raw, some very young, often with weak physique, and are all comprised the same classification. They are accustomed to their own simple ways, and desire return to them as soon as possible. They come, in fact, only in order to make ough money to return to their kraals with sufficient means to enable them to marry d live in indolence. There is much latent possibility in them for learning, but ey leave us often as soon as they become really useful, and by the various com- nies vieing with each other to obtain their services, they have become masters of e labour situation. If they had facilities for making their homes in this country, d if they could be induced to remain with us, I am satisfied that their efficiency uld be increased two-fold, and they could even be trained to do much higher grade ork than they are now employed at. This fact is illustrated in these fields by the ys who have worked long periods being able to finish their task in half the time at raw boys require, and this illustration is further strengthened by the well-known olution of the negro in America since the abolition of slavery, and also by my own perience in dealing with the West Indian negro in Venezuela.

The Pass Law and Liquor Law have been modified and strengthened, on the titions of the industry, to give more control to the mining companies in dealing ith this class of labour.

These laws, though not perfect, are good and useful if well administered.

But what is the testimony already brought before you in this regard ?

Witness after witness has testified to the unsatisfactory manner in which they ave been carried out, and the elaborate tabulated statement, brought in evidence of e seventy-four companies, is eloquent on the subject of the Liquor Law, whose aladministration is a great source of loss to the companies, danger of life to the atives, and discredit to the Republic.

If you should desire further evidence on this subject, I would ask you to call r. A. Grant, manager of the Nigel Mine, who can give, I believe, even stronger stimony than any before you.

Regarding the Pass Law, there has been, as far as I am aware, no witness yet efore the Commission who has stated that this law, as administered, had benefited is company, and Mr. Goldmann has informed you that out of thirty-three companies nploying 19,000 boys monthly, 14,000 have deserted since the new Pass Law me into operation, without one single one of these deserters having been brought ack into the mines and justice. In my opinion, the Pass Law, though good as a mporary expedient, is only the kindergarten of the native question, and before these elds can ever reach their maximum possibilities, the whole question of native labour ust be dealt with on broader and more liberal lines, and modifications and sugges- ons in regard to it must be constantly expected by the Government.

The medium and lower grades of white labour here have to a great extent been moralised by the black labour; and although there are exceptionally energetic and rnest white workers here, there is a lot of indolence and incapacity shown by many. he majority, although they may have skill in doing work themselves, lack the culty or interest in getting the best work out of the black labourer.

What we require from both black and white labour is greater efficiency, which, if ally obtained, renders rate of wages a secondary consideration, as shewn by the nus system in sinking deep level shafts. Of course, we desire to get the unit of age as low as is consistent with the contentment of the labourer.

What the management of the mines must aim at is to encourage in every way the ficient man, and give him every preference and advantage over the inefficient man, and to elevate the quality of native labour, which at the same time will justify a greater rat of wages being paid to the whites. Contracts, piece work, bonus systems, and uniformit in accounts should be encouraged, and the companies should not strive to mak statistical records of low wage rates, but rather accomplish cheap results judged b work actually done.

Co-operation of Government necessary to lower white wages. The Government on its part should endeavour to lessen the good workers' livin expenses, and make them interested in the welfare of this country, so that they wi be satisfied to remain here, and be contented with a lower wage.

Co-operation of Government necessary to encourage native labour. The Government should also do everything to bring about an abundant supply c black labour, and give the mines reasonable control of it through the prope administration of the Pass Law and all other laws connected with the native question and should encourage this labour to the utmost extent, realising its vast importance t the prosperity of these Fields and to this Republic.

Dynamite costs. The next item figuring on our expenditure sheet is dynamite, 2s. 10·3d. per tor and 9·92 per cent of the total cost. So much evidence has been already brought u by various witnesses on this subject that there is very little further to be said a **Price of imported dynamite.** regards the price at which dynamite can be landed here free of duty. I, however, ar in a position to state that in February last I had an offer from reliable people i America of dynamite (70 per cent. nitro-glycerine) to be delivered to any port i South Africa at 17 cents per lb., or 35s. 6d. per case of 50 lbs., in large quantitie With landing charges, agents' fees, railage, colonial duty, etc., the price would b raised to 42s. 7d. per case, delivered in Johannesburg free of Transvaal duty. Thi price would practically save 50 per cent. on the present price of dynamite No. 1, o **Concessions.** 1s. 5d. per ton on the basis of the tonnage milled. There is, however, a great mor to be said on the subject of the Dynamite Concession than mere £ s. d., and I believe am the first witness that has dealt with the subject from this standpoint; and, afte all, it is the main standpoint, as this concession, yea, and the principle of concessions, i one of the fundamental causes which have brought about the estrangement betwee the original population of this country and the uitlanders.

Take the Government Volksraad Dynamite Commission's report on the subjec of dynamite, and it is there stated that the main articles required for dynamit manufacture are not found in this country, and that the concessionaires have no adhered to the terms of their contract. What justification is there then in fosterin; such a manufactory, especially in the early struggling stages of the mines, which ar the main source of revenue to the whole country, and the essence of its prosperity Take the concessions as a whole, what justification, intrinsically, is there for them a all? What nations are the most prosperous, and which of them have concessions?

I speak feelingly and knowingly, as an American. Although we have protectiv tariffs to foster industries, we have the most complete internal system of free trade There is no such thing known as a trade concession in the United States of Americ **Evils of concessions.** What is there vitally wrong about a concession? It seems to me the crux of th whole thing is that it places the production of an article of necessity in the hands of few, who are given opportunity to profit by the necessities of the many. The man rebel against this principle, and the Government reaps inadequately, and derives littl benefit from the burden it imposes on its people. Vexations crop up on all sides excuses from managers and directors as regards working costs; excuses from director to shareholders, and general ill-feeling and destruction of confidence; these are th results of concessions.

In order to keep their concessions, concessionaires are tempted to use ever specious device of argument to the Government to continue their profits. It give opportunity to unscrupulous persons to play upon the best and worst motives o

r people, and it is wrong in principle and in practice. This general line of argu-
t can be applied to all the concessions in your country.

The Chairman's patriotic suggestion to manufacture machinery, etc., in this Manufacture of machinery.
ntry, and thus to give employment to a far greater number of people, is, I think,
ost dangerous one, though made with the best intention. It might be taken
antage of, and new burdens in the shape of concessions would then be imposed
n us. There is no doubt that if our population were such that we were ripe for
manufacture of machinery, it would be an excellent thing, but to produce at
rmous cost the raw materials, and to manufacture all the complex machinery now
uired, would take almost a larger number of white men than is now actually em-
yed at the mines, and the initial stages of such an industry could only be rendered
ufficient inducement to capital by heavy protective duties, and consequently
nense further taxation of the mines. Let us first get our full growth before
h a thing is earnestly considered, and then also allow every form of healthy
npetition.

Referring to the table of analysis which we have already dealt with, we find that Railway rates.
have dealt with about 68 per cent. of the mines' total costs. General charges
ire at 5·22 per cent., which cannot well be further detailed, so that we have then
81 per cent made up of supplies, exclusive of dynamite remaining.

It is then in this item of 26·81 per cent. of our total costs, as well as on the 4·14
cent. for kaffir food, already included under the heading of labour, that the rail-
y charges have the most direct bearing. Previous witnesses have gone into great Railway rates on coal.
ail with regard to this railway question, giving all manner of comparative figures
l suggestions, besides dealing with capitalisation, profits, etc. Mr. Fitzpatrick has
wn you that if the English rates of ½d. per ton per mile for coal had prevailed on
Netherlands line, 5s. 8½d. per ton. of coal, or about a 1s. of our total costs per ton
ore milled, would have been saved; while Mr. Seymour has shown that by reducing
present rates per ton per mile to 1¾d. without terminal charges—which rate
uld still be five times higher than in America, and by employing side discharge
cks, and so doing away with bagging—a yearly saving to the industry of £407,500
uld be effected. I would emphasise that this saving would be on coal alone; and
he rate per ton per mile for all other goods were reduced to the basis of other
ntries, and the Government used its influence with the other South African
lroads to effect a similar general reduction, our supplies (notably timber) could be
ained at an enormously cheaper rate, the reduction varying as shown by Mr. Albu
l other witnesses from 20 per cent. to 40 per cent.

I see no new facts that I can bring before the Commission in this matter, and I
l now simply touch upon it from the standpoint of an engineer, and take the
eral rates of transport per mile as given by Mr. Seymour, selecting machinery for
purposes of comparison, which is the most favourable for the Netherlands
lway. This shows:—

COST OF TRANSPORT BY RAIL IN PENCE.

Machinery—	American	...	...	0·51	pence per ton per mile	...	1·000	
,,	Cape Railways	...	2·34		,,	,,	...	4·565
.,	O. F. S. Railway	...	2·34		,,	,,	...	4·565
,,	Natal Railways	...	3·04		,,	,,	...	5·931
,,	Portuguese	...	...	4·07	,,	,,	...	7·940
,,	Netherlands (Cape)	...	7·69		,,	,,	...	15·000
,,	Netherlands (Natal)	...	5·06		,,	,,	...	9·871
,,	Netherlands (Delagoa)	4·27		,,	,,	...	8·330
"	English Railways	...	1·12		,,	,,	...	2·190

Comparative railway rates for machinery.

I find from Mr. Dawsey's "Comparison of English and American Railways," a the Chamber of Mines Report, the following information, which I tabulate :—

Cost to Build Railways (Open for Traffic).

<table>
<tr><td>Comparative cost of railway construction.</td><td>1883—England</td><td>...</td><td>Cost per mile, £41,846</td><td>0</td><td>0</td><td>Standard gauge.</td></tr>
<tr><td></td><td>1883—America</td><td>...</td><td>Do. 12,756</td><td>0</td><td>0</td><td>Do.</td></tr>
<tr><td></td><td>1895—Cape ...</td><td>...</td><td>Do. 9,056</td><td>9</td><td>1</td><td>Narrow gauge.</td></tr>
<tr><td></td><td>1895—Natal ...</td><td>...</td><td>Do. 15,254</td><td>17</td><td>9</td><td>Do.</td></tr>
<tr><td></td><td>1895—Netherlands</td><td>...</td><td>Do. 15,359</td><td>6</td><td>10</td><td>Do.</td></tr>
<tr><td></td><td>1896—Cape ...</td><td>...</td><td>Do. 9,406</td><td>15</td><td>0</td><td>Do.</td></tr>
<tr><td></td><td>1897—Orange Free State</td><td></td><td>Do. 7,479</td><td>4</td><td>6</td><td>Do.</td></tr>
</table>

From this it will be seen that the Netherlands Railway on their portion of t Cape Line charge fifteen times as much per ton per mile as the American railroa while their cost of equipment is only in the ratio of £15,359 per mile to £12,756 America, or a ratio of 1 in America to 1·247 on the Netherlands Line. I grant, as have shown for our operating costs in mines, that it is more expensive to work in t country than in America, but nothing like in the ratio of 15 to 1. Why then is permitted to keep up this ratio ?

Expropriation of railway. If the Government has no control of the detailed working of the railway wh the Netherlands Company has the management, by all means let it exercise its rig to take the railway out of the company's hands, and run it more in accordance wi the rates in other civilised countries. After all, a fair interest on the road-bed bas open for traffic, after deducting working costs, is, in a case like this, the rig standard for fixing its tariff. The cost of transport by rail ought to be moderate the Transvaal in view of the absence of heavy gradients, which would cause ext expenditure for tunnels, fills, etc., and of the lines having been laid to follow t natural levels and contour of the country, so that the length of railroads between tw stations is often considerably greater than the direct distance between them in *Railway rates for produce excessive.* straight line. These high rates are not only bad for the mining industry, but also f agriculture. The railroads in this country should form a potent factor in its develc ment, by enabling the farmer to sell his produce in the market in competition wi goods from other parts of South Africa, and if railroads and agriculture were both a sound basis here, we should no longer see such an anomaly as we now witness America, 10,000 miles away, supplying Johannesburg and the mines with meali Australia, Sweden and Switzerland sending butter and tinned milk, and ev California supplying a portion of the preserved fruit !

In this connection, I beg to put in evidence a table taken from the *Statistici and Economist*, 1893-94, showing the relative value in 1892 of the different produ of the State of California, where, as you know, gold mining which started in 18 was the pioneer industry :—

	Products.			Value in Dollars.	£
Relative value of Californian products.	1. Wheat	...	...	26,626,584	5,325,317
	2. Gold	...	...	9,361,486	1,872,297
	3. Wool	...	...	7,260,000	1,652,000
	4. Grapes	...	...	4,844,331	968,866
	5. Mealies	...	...	1,208,213	241,643
	6. Oats	...	...	794,956	158,991

Co-operation of Government required to prevent gold thefts. There is no doubt that the mines are suffering very serious loss in this directi and that it is the imperative duty of the Government to aid in putting a stop to it.

The Gold Theft Laws should be amended so that there is no possibility of Gold thefts legis-
lation. escaping justice through a mere technical quibble, and the police and detective department should be made more efficient; for it is certainly most discouraging that the Company which went to such expense and trouble in attempting to bring the insidious tempters of their tried and trusted men to justice should only reap as a fruit of its efforts the better advertisement of the business of illicit gold amalgam buying, illustrated by the escape of Hart, the lenient sentence of Hildebrandt, and the myathy of a certain class said by the newspapers to be circulating a petition for Hildebrandt's release.

Several witnesses have most ably gone into this matter, and shown the peril of Taxation. the Government and mining industry in this connection. It is a recognised fact that the mining industry is the chief source of wealth of the country, and through its development has made great demands upon the Government for facilities to work to the best advantage. It is therefore the duty of the industry to take upon itself the burden of taxation in proportion to the demands it makes upon the Government, and as there are a large number of mines working, this burden will be felt less than if only a few are kept running. I have endeavoured to show the vast natural resources of these goldfields, and how they differ from others in the world.

A great impetus has been given to mining here, through the success of some companies, and in their wake have followed all manner of new mining enterprises; money has been forthcoming on the supposition that this was a permanent industry which would be encouraged and fostered, and that, with time, a continually lower grade of ore would be payable. I believe that, although the limit for further mechanical and metallurgical improvements is very narrow, there is still immense scope for the management of the mines and for the Government to reduce working Future reduc-
tion of work-
ing costs of
mines. costs through the medium of labour and supplies, and if the mining community and the Government work energetically and harmoniously together, I see no reason why in course of time the present costs should not be reduced by one-third, or about 10s. on the average basis of 29s. per ton. But this cannot be accomplished at once. It will take time and earnest efforts on both sides. If we show that we are effecting this reduction, and that the Government is earnestly helping us, capital will again flow into the country, new mines will be opened up and old ones re-started, and the Government co-
operation re-
quired to re-
duce working
costs. revenue of the Government maintained and increased by renewed prosperity. But, if nothing is done by the Government, the comparatively few present working mines must directly or indirectly pay the whole or nearly the whole taxation of this country. The direct taxation is certainly small, but the indirect is extremely heavy; and it is obvious that these few mines are utterly unable to meet the enormous strain of supplying the Government with the necessary funds for its yearly expenditure, which in 1896 reached, according to the budget returns, the huge total of £4,500,000. The obvious result of this condition of affairs will be a deficit in the Government budget, and the strangulation of the mines. The evil day may be averted by loans, which the Government can only finance upon the assumed prosperity of the industry; and if the life is crushed out of the industry by oppressive direct or indirect taxation, it will be harder and harder for the Government to continue raising loans. If the industry has made mistakes in being over confident and launching out in a greater measure than was intrinsically justifiable, the Government has profited indirectly by this wrong and is party to it.

Now, this line of argument brings me to the main problem we both have to face, Lack of confi-
dence between
Government
and mining
industry. viz., lack of confidence. You may wish to call this a sentimental grievance, but it is to my mind the most vital with which we have to deal. It would appear to a great many who have read the statements in the press, memorials of grievances and their

method of acceptance and treatment, that you do not believe in us, that we do
believe in you or each other, and I fear the world will soon not believe in any of us,
the existing state of affairs continues. It is no use for the industry and t
Government to incriminate each other; this will only make matters worse.

Government has benefited by over-speculation.
Granted, on the one hand that there has been over speculation on these field
surely on the other hand the Government has been a partner to it by receiving emol
ments through fictitious values. It has made boom budgets if we have made boo
estimates; but I do not think there is any necessity to grant this to the world.

Duties of Government.
What I think the Government should do is to justify the policy of its Republ
and its main industry to the world, to show to the world that we have intrinsic meri
here; that we have the greatest gold fields in the world here; that there are mo
earnest workers here; that the world has been given most exhaustive and accura
statements by the State department and by the industry; that a great deal of th
troubles that we are subject to is made by the world, which has taken our good wor
as a basis for unjustifiable speculation, and made gambling tables of our mines. Th
argument we can bring to the world only in one way, and that is by being united ou
selves. How can we be united?

Government required to cancel dynamite and railway concessions.
Let the Government commence by abolishing the dynamite concession, taking ov
the railroads and reducing their rates. This must, however, only be considered as a
initial measure and an earnest of the Government's desire to conduct the governme
of this Republic on true, broad Republican principles.

Representation of the mining industry necessary.
What have I shown to be the main factor for us to deal with? Is it not th
labour question, involving all the vital principles of Republican government? We hav
not complained so much against the laws of this country as against their administra
tion. The Government must take us into its confidence. It must allow our traine
ability to bear upon the serious problems before us. We must be made partl
responsible for the administration of this Government, and to be made responsible w
must have representation. I would be a coward not to face this issue with my bia
towards you and Republicanism. I see no other way out of it.

Radical relief required.
If we are only granted the reliefs prayed for now, we will come back for othe
shortly, and there will be ill-feeling and heart-burning as of yore. Face the difficult
fairly and squarely. This country has now an opportunity in its history of showin
its true greatness, by giving freely what could not be forced from it. I have not bee
mealy-mouthed, and I leave it to the Government to devise how it can most safel
grant us a voice in its affairs. I think the workers on these fields care nothing for th
shaping of the foreign policy or the general government of this Republic. They d
not wish to deal with problems in districts in which they do not work or are n
interested. What they want is representation and a voice in things which concern th
economic problems that they have to deal with. How to do this I will not be
presumptuous as to suggest; all I ask is that the present burghers admit their ow
limitations, lack of experience and training for these problems, and ask the best an
wisest of all countries to aid them. Let them first believe in their hearts the necessit
and right of this demand, and the way will be made clear.

This statement is made by me as an individual, and one in sympathy wit
Republican principles, and not as one representing any body of men or corporation
this place.

MR. HENNEN JENNINGS on coming up for examination, expressed his wish to fir
substantiate the statement he had made as to dynamite. He proceeded:

Price of imported dynamite.
In my statement I say that dynamite can be obtained from America for 17 cen
a pound, at any South African port. I wish to put in evidence copies of cables sent t

erica, and the answer to the same, which show that, in large quantities, dynamite per cent. nitro-glycerine), can be delivered on the coast at 35s. 6d. per case of 50 lbs. cable I sent in February of this year, which was to a gentleman I knew in ifornia, who has been connected, to my knowledge, with the dynamite business for ething like 20 years, was as follows:—"Referring your letter, 23rd July, 1892, te present price afloat, South African port, dynamite, 70 per cent. nitro-glycerine, ge quantities, cases 50 lbs. Cable reply immediately. Wanting a comparison local ces." The answer received was—"17 cents." This cable I will put in evidence, and uld state that this tender was secured without even a reasonable prospect of business ng done, and without a guarantee of Government support in any way. You will I also made a statement that the landing charges, agents' fees, &c., would raise it 42s. 7d. per case, delivered in Johannesburg, free of Transvaal duties. You have evidence of other witnesses showing that landing charges are 6d. a case, agency 6d. ase, Colonial duty 2s. 1d., and railage 4s.; in addition to which, by taking the 17 ts a pound, and bringing it into English money, makes 35s. 6d. This offer means that can get dynamite here for 42s. 7d. per case, or just about half the present price, and an guarantee the reliability of the parties in America making this offer, as I have l long acquaintance with the gentleman who cabled the offer, and know that he can l will carry out what he agrees to do. I would also state that Mr. Pichoir, the atleman who has made the offer, has written to say that the three established dynamite npanies in California, by jointly contributing, could agree between them to increase ir plant so as to furnish 16,000 cases monthly, within two or three months after eiving a fixed order. Of course they would require a definite contract to increase ir factories to this extent, but arrangements could be made with them to guarantee s supply. I don't know the minimum length of contract they would demand, but I i't think it would be unreasonable. In this connection, I would also state that I ve received information from London to the effect that, since this Commission of quiry commenced its sittings, Nobel's Trust have used every influence and device to event other European manufacturers from making offers, but, in spite of this, a tain firm in Europe makes an offer to Wernher, Beit & Co., by which dynamite can delivered here, including all usual charges, to Johannesburg, excluding Transvaal ty, for not more than 40s. per case, and blasting gelatine for 56s. This offer is from e small manufacturer, and would only partially meet our consumption, but is very uable in this respect, that, in making the offer, the manufacturer states that he has n approached by a person describing himself as the agent of the Transvaal Govern- nt, ostensibly to ascertain at what price supplies of dynamite can be bought, but gesting that the selling price in the Transvaal is 85s., and that the manufacturer uld frame his offer accordingly. I have brought this matter to the notice of the mmission, not in the belief that the Government has anything to do with the so-called nt, but to put them on their guard against the ingenious devices of the dynamite nopolists, so thoroughly in accord with their past tactics. I take it the Government appointed this Commission in order to get the truth, and they will be judged before the world by what they do. It is our desire to assist them by all means in our power, l to protect the interests of ourselves and the Government, which are identical; and, t is the Government's intention to actually get cheap offers of dynamite, and break the present monopoly, I would suggest that they should throw the tenders open to whole world, giving *bona fide* competitors ample opportunity to make bids, by ing them reasonable time to extend their works and meet the demands of this ustry; and, in this way, I am satisfied that even lower figures than those I have ated would be obtained. A bid obtained through the agency of the monopolist, and short notice, would be wholly misleading, and would be an advertisement of bad

Free trade in dynamite.

faith on the part of the Government. Another point I wish to make; It is not
that the quotation is for 70 per cent. nitro-glycerine. They claim in California, h
ever, that this 70 per cent. nitro-glycerine dynamite is equal to 75 per cent. manu
tured from kieselguhr and nitro-glycerine. They claim also that, by using a diffe
absorbent, they obtained the same strength as obtained by using guhr alone with ni
glycerine; and they also claim, and state that, by test, through a mortar throwin
projectile, they have obtained the same distance as in the test for the 75 per cen
believe it is even a slightly greater distance. I think that is all.

Mr. *Albu.*

What absorbent do you use in America instead of kieselguhr?—There are var
absorbents used by the different factories in California. I don't know them all,
that in use at the factory I have just now quoted, is partially kieselguhr, nitrate
soda, and wood pulp.

You know the article principally used on these fields is gelatine, and the absorb
collodion cotton. They make the same in America don't they?—They make it,
their theory is somewhat different to ours. They don't believe in using such inten
powerful explosives as we do. They regulate their dynamite in accordance with
work, using a lower strength on softer ore; and they consider it more economica
use a lower grade of explosives than we do.

What is the proportion of strength of dynamite No. 1 and blasting gelatine?
believe that blasting gelatine has nitro glycerine something like 93 per cent.

Yes, but I mean the proportionate strength.—I believe the strength is about
portionate to the amount of nitro-glycerine used.

Are you aware that, in Cornwall for instance, dynamite is sold—containing 93
cent. of nitro-glycerine—at 30s. per case?—The only knowledge I have is obtai
through the evidence of other witnesses.

In the Cape Colony the duty is 12s. 6d. per case, is it not? I mean the dynan
imported into the Colony, not transhipped—I am not prepared to state that.

You don't think there would be any difficulty in getting dynamite if we had f
trade?—None, with proper notice to the manufacturers. I have shown from Mr. Pichc
statement that the dynamite works can be increased in two or three months to incre
their supply.

Would you advocate free trade in dynamite?—Most assuredly.

In other countries, is the manufacture and sale of dynamite carried on un
the supervision of the Government?—In the United States anyone can manufactu
but in Venezuela it is under Government control.

Are there any particular reasons why it should be carried on in Venezuela un
Government supervision. Was it not in order to procure an income to the Gove
ment?—Yes, and there I think it was particularly unfortunate, because the Nob
people had the same kind of contract as here. They put up two factories simply
put cartridges together, as at first done here, and, it being a very hot climate, they
two or three explosions at their works. The dynamite was very much worse th
here, and it was very dangerous to the lives of the workmen. We had no control in a
way, and had to use what they gave, and the price was even higher than here.

Supposing Nobel's, through their influence, were able to form a ring, do
think it would be possible for the mining industry to build their own factory?—Th
would be absolutely no danger whatever; I speak knowingly from the early histo
of California. Nobel's, more or less, had a monopoly in California, through pat
rights, and they regulated their prices just as they pleased. But another compa
was formed with a different absorbent, called the Vulcan Company, and it ma

ctured dynamite which suited the purpose of the mines just as well as theirs. They
d a lawsuit on the ground that the Vulcan Company was infringing their rights,
t the United States Courts of Law decided against Nobel's, and this company was
owed to manufacture dynamite; and in its train others came, and through the com-
tition the price of dynamite was reduced immensely, and anybody can manufacture
namite in America in any way they see fit. The only thing is that the established
mpanies have a start, and in building a new factory it requires capital.

Provided the industry procure the amount of capital required, there would be no
fficulty in establishing a factory in Germany, England, or America ?—No; and it is
own how quickly a factory can be built by the fact that after explosions, where the
uildings are swept away, a new factory springs up again very quickly, and continues
s trade. Dynamite factory could be built by industry.

Has sulphur or saltpetre ever been found in this country in large quantities ?—I
ve never heard of it, and I think the Dynamite Commission appointed by the
overnment made that statement. Importation of raw materials for dynamite.

Then a local dynamite factory would have to import sulphur, saltpetre, glycerine,
d guhr ?—Yes, and skilled labourers besides.

If the monopolists claim to manufacture dynamite after importing all the raw
aterials into the country, would it not be as just for us to claim that we manufacture
achinery and engines ?—You could certainly not claim that.

With regard to railways, is there any principle in America regulating the
uilding, management, and tariff of railways ?—Yes, and in America the system of
ilroads is the greatest in the world. I think there were 370,000 miles of railroads in
e world up to 1890, of which the United States—not the whole of North America—
ad 163,000 miles, or 44 per cent. of the whole railroads in the world, and nearly 4,000
excess of the mileage of the combined railroads of Europe, Asia, and Africa. The
stem of encouraging this immense railroad system in the United States is, in my
oinion, one of the features of the development of the United States. In the United
ates the Government allows—in the settled part of the country—private under-
kings to build railroads when they show their financial capacity to do so, and allows
em to expropriate private property, the indemnity being fixed by the Courts of
aw; but in return for this, reserves the right to control and fix rates— Regulations for railroad building in United States.

Control of railway rates i United State

Equal to the right held by the Board of Trade in England ?—I will explain how
ey control rates. In the United States there is a Federal or Central Government
d a States Government. In each State there are Commissioners appointed. A
aximum tariff is fixed by law in the States, but the Commissioners have power to
x rates under the maximum tariff declared by law on presenting good reasons for so
oing. In addition to the State Commissioners, there are appointed by the Federal
overnment Inter-State Commissioners, who are appointed with the object of pre-
enting railroad combinations which would be detrimental to the public, and impose
cal and exceptional impositions. These laws, thus briefly outlined, have wonderfully
xpanded internal trade. Take Mr. Seymour's testimony, in which he shows the total
llions of miles of haulage in the United States and the maximum rates on the main
ne to be lower than a penny, and the minimum a farthing per ton per mile. You
us see what wonderfully cheap and economical work can be done through competi-
on and judicious Government regulation.

Most of the railroads in America are private enterprises, are they not ?—Private
terprises for the most part, but in some of the unpopulated territories, in the early
mes, the Government gave certain bonuses to the railroads in Government lands, and
rtain aid; but in giving them this land they reserved to themselves the alternate

sections, and the Government thus shared half and half with the company in t
increased value of the land.

There is a maximum rate and a minimum rate, which the Government has g
the right to supervise?—Those rates are regulated by two Boards of Commissioners.

What policy is adopted generally by these railway companies on these lines whi
lead through new countries which have to be opened up. Will these companies charg
maximum rates, or such rates as would induce people to settle and cultivate the lanc
—They charge, in the sparsely populated districts in the United States, wonderfull
low rates for the amount of traffic they have, and in some cases they expect to lo
money in the initiation of railroad systems, hoping to get the loss back by opening u
the country, and, so to speak, stimulating and producing traffic.

They don't try to make big profits at first, but expect to make it when th
country opens up and is prosperous?—Yes, they try to make their main profit whe
the country has been developed.

What means, in your opinion, should be adopted by this Government to regula
our native supply of labour?—I think I have made a very forcible point in my state
ment about that. In this connection I first state "the Government should do every
thing to bring about an abundant supply of black labour and give the mines reasor
able control of it through the proper administration of the Pass Law and all othe
laws connected with the native question, and should encourage this labour to th
utmost extent, realising its vast importance to the prosperity of these fields and t
this Republic." Now I should like to amplify what I have shown in my statemen
that the labour is in the ratio of one white man to eight or ten kaffirs. I a
thoroughly satisfied that the kaffir is susceptible to training, and becomes far mor
useful to us after he has been with us for a length of time. My experience i
Venezuela, where we dealt with the negro, shows that, by staying a number of year
and giving them incentives to stay, a great deal more work, and more complicate
work, could be got from the negroes, and we could reduce the number of whit
employees by their instrumentality. I think what the Government should do here i
to aid us in trying to keep in every possible way the natives that show capacity i
special departments. I have enquired from compound and mine managers, and it i
noticeable that the East Coast kaffirs take better to mining than the higher clas
native—Zulus and Basutos. The Zulus and Basutos are not willing to work unde
ground to the same extent. Now, these peculiarities of the different tribes of kaffi
should be taken into consideration.

Do you think it would be to the advantage of the labour market if the railwa
authorities were to bring down natives from up country at a very low rate, and charg
the difference when they go back?—Certainly; I do not think the railway would los
anything by it.

It would induce natives to come down here, because it would give them a
opportunity of reaching this place with very little money?—Another thing strike
me, and I can say it with all candour to the Government—I do not think, considerin
the drafts we are making on the native labour supply, and considering the numbe
the farmers require for their own use, that there is sufficient native population her
You want natives here for agricultural purposes at as cheap, or even cheaper price, a
we do for mining purposes. We require kaffirs with good physique for the mine
and take the population of any country, a comparatively small number are fitted fc
miners. You want the mining and agricultural industries to work hand-in-hand wit
regard to the natives.

Chairman.

With regard to the last portion, that the Government ought to encourage kaffir
ur, all the witnesses insist on that point, but none of them, up to now, have shown
vhat way the Government can encourage native labour. The establishment of
tions would spoil the natives, and you would get very little service from them. *Objections to locations.*
t is my experience, and I have worked with them all my life. One way to encourage
n to come to the mines would be to give them facilities for coming here, to make
r lives as pleasant as possible, and to pay them as much as possible, even more than
present, and that you don't want to do; while to compel them, everybody
nowledges, is impossible. The Government can use its moral influence with the *Government influence on Transvaal natives.*
irs, as far as those who reside in the Republic are concerned, and give them every
ntive to go to work on the mines; but, if the kaffir does not feel inclined, and if
oes not lie in his nature to go, how can you get him to go? The same difficulty is
nd here as is found everywhere. The agriculturist feels it apart from the mines.
Volksraad, year after year, is stormed by memorials from the public asking them
levise some means to make the kaffir work. Notwithstanding all the laws that *Inability of Government to retain natives of other countries.*
e been made by the Government, we cannot keep them here, and the kaffir from
East Coast will not reside on the Rand or in any part of the Republic. His
ination is that he must reside in the district where he comes from. I think every
nber of the Commission is trying to solve the native question. I only say this to
w that if the Government, on their side, fail in their endeavour, that it is not *Good intentions of Government*
uuse they are not inclined to assist, but because it is an insurmountable difficulty.

Witness. I appreciate what the Chairman has said, and there is a great deal of
ee in his words. I say there are difficulties, but I do not think they are insur-
ntable.

Chairman.

Will you please say how the difficulties are to be surmounted ?—The reduction of
railway fare is a trifle. Suppose the railway brings them for nothing they will
ae, but to get them to work is another thing. I agree with the Chairman that this
ive labour question is the main question for the mines and the whole Republic. I
e had no experience as the early settlers in this country have had in subjugating
aboriginal race, and I admit I have no right compared with them to speak on this
tion of the subject, but I claim having been born in the Southern States of the
ited States, and having been connected with the working of negro labour in the
aezuela mines, that I have a right to speak on the kaffir labour question. The
gestion with regard to locations was a general one, but let us see how it worked in *Locations in Venezuela.*
aezuela. The aboriginal race was thoroughly unfitted for the mines. The white
e, owing to the heat and the climate, could not do all the work, so were driven to
labour from the West Indian Islands. The Government tolerated their importation.
ey came first without their women and their families. The mines paid immense
ges to induce them to come. Little by little they brought their families, and the
npanies who had ground rates encouraged them to have what they called *canucos* or
dens. They came from different islands, and they had these little locations. There
s a certain amount of rivalry between them, their wants increased, and that stimu-
d their ambition, and they were finally willing to do far more work than at first.
y remained long enough, satisfied with having their families in the country, to
ble them to become skilled. Now, in suggesting locations, I do not mean simply
great big location around the mines. I should think the farmers would, for their *Small allotments preferable to locations.*
interest, in the best agricultural parts of the country, try to get natives to come
offering some little inducements, and allowing them certain plots of land. The men

O

of the strongest physique could go to the mines, but the younger and older men
some of the women could work on the farms. If that is practicable—I know i
difficult—the agricultural population as much as the mining industry would ben
Something must be tried different to what we are doing at present. Now that I h

Difference be-
tween United
States negroes
and Kaffirs.

gone so far, I want to say that, of course, I know the negro of the Southern State
not the same as the kaffir; that from being in contact with the white race for so m
years he has developed more; but it shows you the latent possibilities of the bl
race. What these negroes are capable of doing in the Southern States, I do not m

Progress of ne-
groes in United
States.

it is possible to do here right off. In 1863 a proclamation was made by Presid
Lincoln, freeing all the negroes in the States. At that time there were about 4,000,
negroes in the States, and it was supposed that we would have immense trouble
controlling them, but the natural peacefulness of the race was such that they were
to speak, absorbed in the American Republic, and were granted full franchise rig
There is a social race distinction in America, as there should be, and in the South t
recognise their inferiority, though they have equal political rights, but even so we h
no trouble in keeping them in their place. In the Southern States the Government
demanded compulsory education; they have their own schools, their own colleg
training schools, and ministers. I am giving you this as an illustration of what
black race is capable of being brought to. We cannot do this in a day, but I am sim
pointing out to you the direction in which to work to develop the latent possibili
of the black race.

There is also a portion of South Africa where slaves have been freed, where t
have got their full franchise rights, and what has been the consequence? They w

Objections to
locations.

to be more bosses than the white men themselves. Experience here teaches that i
just those kaffirs who live in the locations of missionaries that you cannot get to w
when you put them on a farm to sow, etc. From that class you won't get one to w
on the mines. That would be the consequence of any locations that might
established here.—I don't wish you for a moment to suppose I advocate giving
native races equal rights with the white races at all, but I say you ought to do all t

Improvement of
native races
possible.

is possible to encourage them to come and not to lose heart by present failures h
but to feel that these races by judicious development are susceptible of imme
improvement. You want to give them a stimulus, and you also have to make the l

Taxation of na-
tives.

ones have the necessity of earning their livelihood by taxation.
They are already taxed higher than the white population, and it would
unreasonable to tax them much more than they are taxed.—There is one point I v

George Goch and
Buffelsdoorn
locations.

reading over in the testimony of other witnesses. It was stated that the little lo
tion at Buffelsdoorn is doing very well, and Mr. Way, of the George Goch, sp
favourably of his location.

Locations on
mining com-
panies' grounds

I will admit that where a mining company has got its own ground, and wh
the kaffir is given ground to work, the kaffir is entirely dependent upon the cc
pany for that ground, and there he does work. But where would you get a place

The Squatters'
Law.

put all those kaffirs. The Plakkers Wet provides that no more than six families s
occupy a farm, whereas you say there are not enough kaffirs in the Republic to sup
the wants of the mines.—I would try to induce them to come from the East Co

Sparsity of
Transvaal
population.

here. Come down to one of our main troubles here. It is the sparseness of
population, and the great demand made on the country from the sudden introduct
of this great mining industry. The population of the whole world averages ab
twenty-eight to the square mile. The population of this State in whites is less t
two and a half, and with white and black it is not over seven. That was one of
reasons I did not think we were ripe for manufacture. If you take the manufact
ing districts of the world, you will find the population very dense.

But not with blacks.—Well, blacks work in some of the Southern factories in *Employment of blacks in factories.*
America.

In America, but not in other countries.

Mr. *Brakhan.*

With regard to taxing the natives, it is your opinion that this tax can be in- *Taxation of natives.*
creased. Seeing that the whites pay, in direct taxation, very little, and yet pay a
good deal in indirect taxation—that is to say, in duties on the articles they consume—do you think for that reason the hut tax could be increased?—I would not
like to say it could or could not. I say it is a judicious mixture of encouragement
and necessity that will make them work. But I beg to differ from the Chairman as
regards the kaffir taxes here being greater than that of the whites. It may be so in
direct taxation, but indirect taxation has been so much written about and spoken *Indirect taxation of whites.*
about that I think the Government should really find out what that is. I have seen
statements in the paper where some one man figures out that it is £31 per head, and
others different sums, but it is certainly very great, and I would advise the Government to put their statisticians to get reliable statistics of all other countries in the
world, and compare them with the indirect taxation here.

If these figures given in regard to the indirect taxation of whites are anywhere *Increased native taxation.*
near the mark, then there is reasonable room for increasing the taxes of the kaffir.—
I don't see that connection, because you cannot tax the kaffir beyond what he is
capable of paying. They could not pay in proportion to a white tax of £31, or
even £10.

This taxing him more heavily would compel him to work—would force him to
work.—It would induce him to work, but you have to get him into the country first,
and you do not want to discourage him too much. Although I may be alone in the
idea, I think we have to graduate the wages of the kaffirs in our mines—that is to say,
try to induce the best kaffirs to work on piece or contract system, and pay them *Contract system for native labour.*
according to what they do. It is human nature to do better when encouragement is
given. We all want encouragement.

In regard to locating kaffirs on farms. The Plakkers Wet limits the number of *The Squatters' Law.*
families located on one farm to a very small number—six. Don't you think that law
would be in the way of bringing them to agricultural districts?—Is that the law?
Well, I think that is a small amount.

Chairman.

That does not prevent the Government from creating locations wherever they *Ownership of American railroads.*
might think fit. In America, is the railway chiefly owned by the State or by private
enterprise?—Private enterprise, under State control.

You say here in your report it would strengthen confidence if the Government
were to run the railways themselves.—Yes, that is a point I would like to speak
about. Although I believe in the private railroad system of America, I advocate, for
the best interests of the Government, that they expropriate these railroads here on *Expropriation of railway.*
the ground that they are neither private enterprises nor a Government enterprise, but
a mixture of both, and it is more or less the same principle that I mentioned with
regard to dynamite. It is a concession, and the curious part is—I may be mistaken
in this, and some gentleman connected with railway matters will perhaps correct
me—that, although the Government are such large stockholders in the railroad, they *Government has no voice in Netherlands Railway administration.*
have really no voice in the administration, and, although they guaranteed the whole
debt of the company, absolutely the only way they have of regulating the railway is
by expropriation. I understand that the Government have not even a director on the

board in Holland, and, although they have a great holding of shares, they have r more voice than a small holder. Mr. Middleberg, in his statement, has practical said that the company had the right to regulate the tariff, and the Government cor trol is only through expropriation. Now, how are you going to get the very be working for the industry and the Government under such a condition? M Middelberg, as the representative of this Corporation, tries to make the bigge dividends he can. He made a very clever statement, practically laughing in both of faces and throwing dust in our eyes. We are reduced to expropriation if we want t control the railway.

Reduction of Netherlands Railway rates, and expropriation. If the Government decide to expropriate it is very evident you cannot get a immediate reduction. Thus we get a difficult position, because all the witnesses sai it was the duty of the Government to insist on a reduction. Thus we get a difficul position, because all the witnesses said it was the duty of the Government to insist o a reduction, and also that it is the duty of the Government to expropriate the railway You want both at the same time.—I think it is not in the power of the Governmen to give us both at the same time, even if they want to. I don't know if I am righ or not.

How not? You admit the Government cannot give both at the same time. Wh was it given by all the witnesses that they wanted immediate reduction in tariff an expropriation?—According to my argument, that is impossible. Am I not right i my argument that the Government had no power to reduce the tariff withou expropriation?

I do not want to answer the question, but in your evidence you insist upo lowering the tariff and expropriation.

Reduction of Netherlands Railway rates to follow expropriation. I understand from you that you are asking for two things at the same time— reduction of tariff and expropriation?—What I want to make clear, and I am afraid did not do so this morning, is that if expropriation takes place, the reduction in tari will follow. Also, that, although I believe they have no legal right by which th tariff can be reduced before expropriation takes place, there is always the possibilit of making arrangements to take over the railway prior to the eighteen months b giving the company satisfactory equivalent. Therefore, it is not impossible that bot can take place, although it cannot be done by the exercising of legal rights alone.

Price of imported dynamite. I understand from your evidence that without Transvaal duty, dynamite can b landed here at 40s. per case?—42s. 7d. from America, and 40s. from the sma manufacturer I spoke of.

And that dynamite will be equivalent to No. 1 used here?—Yes.

Quality of imported dynamite. Have you any proof to that effect?—Simply from their statement—of tests tha have been made showing the number of feet a projectile was thrown; and th calculations were carefully made. In sending dynamite here they would b willing to subject their dynamite to a test, to prove it is of the same quality as the guarantee it.

White labour. As regards the latter part of your statement, you and many witnesses have sai before that white labour should be put on such a footing here that white peopl should feel at home here, and make their abode here, but that expenses of living kep them back from doing so. I understand that the wages paid here are proportionat to the expenses of living, and that should not be an obstacle. If I were in Europ earning £2, and living on £1 10s., then I would be on the same basis.—There i Married and unmarried miners. logic in that. I tried to point out that these high wages did induce single men t come here, but for married men the inducement is not sufficient to bring them her with the idea of settling. The statement of Mr. Goldmann shows the percentage o miners whose families are left behind; and, after all, the thing to get in a Republic i

people to cast their lot in with it, and the basis of that is, that the married popu-
on and their offspring, in the course of time, would feel most satisfied to live in the
ntry, and be genuinely satisfied with a lower wage.

In the latter part of your evidence, under the heading of "want of confidence," *Lack of confidence between Government and mining industry.* bring forward matters that are a political contemplation, and are not really a ject for discussion before the Commission, but still there are some remarks with ich I differ. This is not the time and place now to discuss the matter, because the rge of the Commission is only to see what is necessary to assist and foster the ustry, to take away the present depression as far as possible. There are a couple of tences which I do not quite understand, and I would like some enlightenment on subject. You say, "what have I shown to be the main factor for us to deal with? tling of the labour question involves all the vital principles of republican govern- it." I do not quite understand the meaning of that. Must I understand that it is duty of the Government and Republic to solve the labour question by supplying employer with workpeople?—That is a question I have endeavoured to touch on in light a manner as possible. I felt diffidence in doing so at all. If you notice, in last part of my statement, I said I will not be so presumptuous as to suggest any- g. I feel, with the Chairman, that the time and place is not propitious for a free ussion upon it, but, in considering the labour problem of the country, it is almost ossible to go down to the vital elements without touching on politics, and, if the irman gives me the invitation, with all sincerity, to discuss this matter, I am fectly willing to do so, but I do not care to do it unless he feels it is advisable for to do so. I have a good many arguments to bring up, and, if I attempted it at all, hould have to speak just as I feel—in a perfectly frank way, and it might give nce, but I would do it with all kindness of purpose. Now do you think it would wise for me to do it?

I only want that one sentence explained. I do not consider that a political *Duty of a Republic to provide labour.* stion. All I want to know from you is what you mean by that sentence: That it he duty of the Government, as a Republican Government, to provide the necessary our?—It says that in so many words. I believe it is the duty of the Government *Duty of Government to encourage labourers.* encourage all classes of labour in every way, to make men satisfied. It is also so as ards all these questions of Liquor Law, Pass Law, gold thefts, etc., because it olves itself into this; the only argument I can bring into such a case is that the ple most vitally interested in the carrying out of that law must have the power in selection of an overseer in the work of the people, and therefore it is necessary to ng in a certain amount of politics in speaking of local government. I do not want go into high politics. I merely want to state this: I am a mining engineer, and e never engaged in politics in this country or any other country, and I do not lerstand them very well, but I understand mine management, and I would bring s illustration forward. Take a general corporation as a simple illustration of a public; take the shareholders as the public at large; take the board of directors as main central Government; and take the mine manager as the local government. he board of directors say to the mine manager, we are sending you a man we know very good as mine or mill foreman, and we know he is so good that you shall have power to see he does his work, and the only thing you can do is to complain to us— t is the result? Perfect chaos in the management of the mine. The board of ctors must have confidence in their local government, so to speak, that is in their nager, otherwise he has not got the control of his employees, and the thing won't k. That is as far as I care to go into politics; I think you can draw your own clusions.

Still that is not a reply to my question, which is simply this—whether it is
duty of the Government to regulate the supply of workers for the employers ?—
absolutely directly, but indirectly, yes.

Means of attract-
ing labour.

On that point I should like to have some information, in order to give us so
guide.—The Government could make the cost of living low, to make the labou
satisfied, and give him political rights.

Political rights.

"Political rights" is out of the question. Of course the natives could not
political rights.—I am talking about white labour.

I am talking about black labour. In what way will it make the white labou
more contented to give him political privileges ?—In possession of these privileges
feels he has power to regulate his living expenses; also that he has the contro
educational advantages for his children, and can gratify his ambition in political l
I think these are three main reasons.

You say now if they got political rights, it would encourage them to live he
whereas in your statement you express it somewhat differently ?—I see there is son
thing rather like a contradiction. What I want to impress on you is that a n

Local self-gov-
ernment.

should have rights in local government and not necessarily in the central governme
I have been educated in the United States, where the keynote of the whole system
local rights. In the territories they have no voice in the central government,
they have perfect local rights to arrange things among themselves. Now in
territories I think it would be an interesting point for you to know that the cen
government appoint a governor and certain other officials with him. But the peo
have a right to their legislators in a similar manner as in States where they have
full franchise, and they regulate their own little circle of affairs without interfere
from the central government. They are not obliged to take the oath of allegiance
the central government, and they need only live three months in the place in
district in order to obtain a vote for their own affairs. Those are territorial rigl
and I wish you not to confuse them with State rights. And, after all, that is the k
note of American republicanism. There is another instance, in my native State
Kentucky, where there is no general prohibition of the sale of liquor—to show you
extent of local rights—any town can have its own liquor laws and prevent the sale
liquor within its own district.

You are going away from the subject. There is another point in your stateme
What do you mean when you say "If we are only granted the reliefs prayed for no
there will be other questions shortly, and there will be as much heart-burning and
feeling as of yore ?"—I mean this. If we are granted advisory boards, and have

Insufficiency of
advisory
boards.

control over the *personnel* of the people who minister to our local wants, we shall f
things won't work, and we still feel—rightly or wrongly, it may be our own fault—
we think it is the Government. Whereas if we have our rights in our own lo
affairs, and we make mistakes, and even make a mess of it, we are happy in having
finger in the pie."

That is not the question put to the Commission or Government, to erect your o
local board, which can tax the public according to its own ideas. The real question
to the Government was to give certain relief, and that is the only relief wh
Government can give, even if you have a local board, because the local board can
lower the railway tariff throughout the whole State, nor go into the dynam
concession or other questions you have quoted here.—Perhaps I have not gone even

Want of touch
between Gov-
ernment and
mining com-
munity.

enough; I feel that there wants to be a touch between this community and the cent
Government, and I feel that all things which are not thoroughly done will be heard
later on, and if we simply go into the question in a patch-work fashion without getti
at the fundamental cause, we don't cure the evil. What I mean to say is that I wou

seech the Government to take everything into consideration, and to take the point I
ve made into consideration, and, without giving us full rights, to see that it is to the
eatest good of this Republic to bring us into touch with each other, and to give us
e greatest possible rights at once.

You are now entering upon a point which is not open for discussion, and what
ou want to discuss is not what you have put down on your statement. What you *The relief asked for.*
k for really is the lessening of import duties, railway tariff, the cheapening of living,
id for cheaper dynamite. These are the reliefs asked from the Government. Now
ou say, even if you got all that, that within a short time you will still come up again,
id that the same feeling of unfriendliness will remain, and other questions will have
 be discussed. Now if they cause "unfriendly feelings and hatred," how can I
isume that if you get all these and come back with others, and they are granted, the
me feeling will not remain?—We feel we have in this Commission an exceptional
iance—the most exceptional I have known for seven years. We have the ear of the *Beneficial effect of Commission*
overnment and the kindly consideration of the Chairman. Are these Commissions
 be of all time? We want to feel that if we have now asked something that we
ay hereafter find inadequate when there is no Commission, we will still have the ear
: the Government.

But you say that if these reliefs are granted it will only foster unfriendly feelings
id hatred?—No; I do not say that. We will be satisfied now, but we may come
ick with other requests we don't know of now.

There was no unfriendly feeling or hatred?—I don't say that at all. If I have
orded the passage at all to give the Chairman that impression, it was not my
itention. After all, I mean to say, commencing as well as we have, we should have *Political status of uitlanders.*
certain political status by which we have a right to come to the Government. Now,
 don't think we have, and we appreciate the Government for appointing this
ommission.

We will leave this point alone. I only want you to understand that it would
ave been better left out of your report.—I regret if it has given any offence.

There is another sentence reflecting on the lack of experience of the Government
 deal with these problems. I do not want to discuss this point, but as a burgher of
ie State I feel aggrieved at the sentence, and it makes a bad impression on the
overnment.—I am not at liberty to discuss that question.

Coming back to the question of local boards. Is the Sanitary Board a success *Sanitary Board.*
ere—it is a Local Board?—I have not recommended Advisory Boards.

Do you think the Sanitary Board a success?—That is a difficult question. It is
 success in some ways and not in others. I do not, however, know the internal
orkings, and I am not in a position to discuss it.

I only put the question because it is a board established for the well-being of
ohannesburg. It is a local board, established by the inhabitants of Johannesburg—
 least under their government—and lately I have heard several complaints to the
fect that a heavy burden is imposed on the inhabitants of Johannesburg.—I am not
:epared to discuss that; I don't know anything about it.

Mr. Joubert.

Is it not possible for a mining company to put a proposal through the Minister *Inefficient administration.*
: Mines and the Superintendent of Native Affairs by which native labour could be
gulated? On the basis of civilised government, of course?—Well, I am not very
peful about making suggestions, unless we have some control in carrying them out.

You say in your statement, in regard to the laws, that you have nothing to
mplain about.—It is the administration we complain about.

But if the law is not properly carried out there is always somebody to whom you can attribute the maladministration ?—I think we must come back to my original contention that we must have some power over the *personnel* of the administration.

Then the law would not be good if there were not proper control established ?—It is easy to make good laws, and it is a different matter altogether controlling them

But if the law is not properly carried out there is somebody to whom you can attribute that non-carrying out ?—I have been brought up in a different country, so that I cannot discuss this in a way that Mr. Joubert would like. We don't consider in America that we can have the laws carried out unless in each district the inhabitant of that district have some control over the officials of the district.

That is also the case here.—Well, I am not aware of it.

I say so. I want you to go back now to the question of want of confidence. want to ask you, as a civilised man, if a stranger comes and lives on my farm, and give him every chance to make profit for himself, on whom does the first duty rest t create confidence—on the owner of the farm, or on the stranger who comes on th farm ? Who takes the first step towards creating confidence ?—Confidence has to b mutual.

Who has got the first duty in that respect to create confidence ?—Well, I would like to see the exact illustration you mean.

Supposing you have got a farm and a stranger comes ; you give him every facilit to live there, and to do well for himself. You want to create confidence. From which side should it come, from the stranger or the owner of the farm ?—From the side o the owner of the farm.

But he has given every confidence by giving all these privileges ?—But h demands work from the stranger in return.

Supposing somebody comes on my farm—a poor man. I give him every chance I say : "There is my farm ; you can make every profit you can." He has got his chanc and he makes every profit he can, but after having made his profit he comes to me an says " You don't regulate your own house properly. I want to instruct you how t put your house in order." Does that create confidence from his side ?—I think Mr Joubert is giving a very extraordinary case. He is practically giving something an exacting nothing. I don't see the bearing on our case here at all.

That has got a relation to mutual confidence.—But the mutual confidence we ar speaking of is where we are mutual workers. We don't take and not give. We giv as well as take.

And, according to that, the matter has to be regulated ?—Yes ; but then I say thi analogy is not applicable to our case.

I say it is applicable. You say " If you give us everything we want we still wil come back with some more questions. These will cause bad feeling and dissatisfac tion amongst us." How is it possible you can expect from the Government and th people that, in the first place, everything will be granted, when you already say i will not help you a bit—that you will still have grievances against us ? You wi still come back with further requests. That stands here in your declaration.—Yo are pushing me on to what the Chairman did not want me to do—to discuss politic

That is not politics.—I am not going to take an illustration which is no applicable to our case and give definite answers.

Now, do you think that sentence of yours here is conducive to establishing goo feeling between the old population and the new ?—If it is taken in the spirit I mea it, I think it should. It was not the intention of the writer to introduce ill-feeling a all. It was simply to show how, with whatever good intention the Governmen wished to deal with us now, and however they may smooth over the sore with a salve

il we heal that sore we cannot be thoroughly satisfied. It was done with the Radical remedy for uitlander grievances required.
atest kindness, to show the Government—and I spoke in the same statement that
s was a crisis in their history—that they should give freely and liberally, in order
make that cure permanent; and I feel, from the treatment witnesses have had
ore this Commission, and the statement of the Chairman, that they wanted the
th from the bottom of my heart, and that they don't want me to trick them into
ing temporary advantages, and tell them what I don't believe in my heart would
ult. And what I mean in this whole thing is that I have been brought up as a
ublican, and the great fundamental principle of republicanism in my country
qual rights; and, unless the Government is willing to make the uitlander popula- Incorporation of uitlander population.
n, which outnumbers the original population, eventually a part and parcel of this
ublic, it is my candid opinion that, with the very best intentions that you may
ve, you won't have the maximum peace and prosperity in this country. I may be
ong, and I think that I have taken a departure in this from other witnesses, but I
ve done it with the best intention and the kindliest feeling towards the original
pulation of this country. I want to show them the danger of patchwork, and it is
belief if they want the permanent peace and prosperity of this country they
st give trust to the uitlander, not unreasonable trust, but trust. In my own
siness I find that if I should attempt to run a property by distrusting everybody
it that was not of my little country or place, or whatever it might be, I would not
ke a success of that business.

I now speak as a burgher, not as a member of the Commission. According to my
nion those words put down there in your statement, in black and white, clearly to
read by the people, are not calculated to inspire that confidence.—I am only sorry
it the phraseology was different from my intention.

I quite understand that.

Mr. *Smit.*

Your declaration as far as concerns its practical side is of the greatest interest,
t I am sorry you opened up into politics. On the one page of your statement you
y you hope the Government will take the people into their confidence, and on the
lowing you say confidence cannot be established, because you have further requests
make. It is a great pity that should appear at the end of a very able declaration.
I hope I have in some way mitigated that by the explanation I have given. I hope
will in no way interfere with what the Government will do from the testimony of
ier witnesses. I gave it simply as an American individual, and with the best
entions and on my own responsibility.

Of course I take your declaration as one thing, and your political feeling as
other. Your political ideas cannot influence the good the Commission intends doing
the mining industry. On page 34 you say, " There is no use for the industry and
e Government to incriminate one another." What do you mean by that ?—I mean Antagonism of Government and mining industry.
I don't say the industry and the Government officially have done so—but I mean
it members on each side, more or less, have taken up antagonistic positions.

The complaints of the industry against the Government we have had fully, but
at accusations are there on the part of the Government against the industry ?—
ell, as I say, I don't think there is any official complaint on either side. It is
lirectly.

From what indirect complaint ?—It is written in newspapers. They get inter-
ws from your officials, who say the whole trouble here is all ours and that sort of
ng. I mean to say that a section of the Press say the whole trouble is on the

Government side, and the other section says it is on the uitlanders' side, and cert
prominent people on both sides talk about it. That is what I mean.

I would like to have a direct answer. You should not give an indirect answ
The complaint before us is that the railways are too expensive, dynamite is
expensive, the Government does not carry out the Gold and Pass Laws, and also t
Liquor Law. These are accusations directly against the Government. Now, you s
the Government has also made accusations. Now I want to know what accusatic
are made against the industry.—I say, directly and officially as a Government, no
but I say as far as I can learn from newspapers, some high officials of this Gove
ment have made statements against the mining industry and how it is carried o
This is a question I don't want to go into detail about.

I did not expect you to take notice of what is put in the newspapers of things
that description ?—Well, that is my meaning.

'Boom budgets" and over-flota-tions.   You have mentioned in your declaration " boom budgets " and " boom estimate
I want you to quote a boom budget ?—What I mean by a boom budget is a boc
amount of receipts and an immense expenditure, and I think that the last budget
that kind, as given in the Chamber of Mines' report, shows that. That is
excessively abnormal budget.

Now, do you mean to say that if the inhabitants of the State make false a
excessive flotations, by which means the income of the State itself is inflated a
increased, and when the State is ignorant of the over-capitalisation and over-flotatio
then the State ought to leave alone public works and public expenditure that may
necessary because there is a mismanagement of finance by their subjects without t
State's knowledge ?—I am not taking the motives of the Government, I am n
taking our own motives when I made that statement. What I mean to say is if the
has been an excessive amount of money invested in this country, the Government g
a share of it, and make their expenditure accordingly.

How can you say that the Government are accomplices, so to say, to ove
flotation, &c., when they did not know there was such a thing ?—I say they a
partners in it ; they share in it ; however it is brought about they share in it. Ho
has the revenue been increased except through this industry here ? I will tell one
the reasons that I wrote that. It was that at the time of the first evidence broug
before the Commission, Mr. Joubert spoke about wanting to get at the wron
flotations, and I did not know how far that policy would extend when I wrote the
I wanted to justify the industry. If there has been over-flotation here, the Gover
ment get their share of it in import duties, from prospecting licences, from railro
carriage, and everything in connection with the company. They are partners.
don't want to blame ourselves more than the Government. I am taking bo
together.

You really mean to say this much, that the Government was a partner, thou
not necessarily parties to it ?—That is what I have said here [*referring to h
declaration.*] " There has been a partner to it." That is what I say in English.

Expropriation of railway.   About the expropriation of the railway. Supposing the mines are met as mu
as possible through the lowering of the rates, off-loading facilities, and all that ki
of thing, would you even then still insist upon the expropriation of the railway ?
Well, there is this about the expropriation of the railway. Neither the Governme
nor any of us have any control over its workings, and the tables that I gave are
very much different from the rates of my own country that I think them abnormal.

That I can see for myself. It is unnecessary to go further into that. I kn
the Netherlands Company's rates are much more expensive. Of course, you know
cannot be brought down to the level of American railways ?—Not at once.

But supposing it was brought to the same basis *pro rata*, taking into consideration the cost of wages there and here ?—You have a constant factor which, I think,
is detrimental to the population and the Republic in that. If the railroad made a
little too much, and it all went to the Government, we should not feel it so much. If
the railway company were doing the thing at their own risk, it would be another
matter, but the Government have practically financed them, and yet do not have
control over the railway. Then, I don't see in what way the Government can have
control over these people except in keeping them within the maximum tariff, and the
company are not going to make any other arrangements with the Government unless
they make money by it.

That we don't know. If the railway was in the hands of any other factor, it
would be allowed to exist so long as the tariff was reasonable ?—I don't care in whose
hands it is. With its present constitution, I don't think it is in a position to give the
maximum benefit to the country or to get the lowest possible working expenses.

Would you approve of the constitution if the Government were to expropriate ?
—If the Government were to expropriate it would bring about a better state of
things. It gives all the profit back to the Government. The Government then, if it
sees the necessity of the community, has the power of lowering rates, which it has not
present.

The tariffs have already been lowered.—The whole thing comes back to the [Concessions and free trade.]
principle of concessions, and I say you cannot get the same good work out of a
concession as you can with free trade. That is my opinion.

You do not want to answer the question ? If the tariff is reduced you still want
the railway expropriated, and I make the deduction you only want it expropriated
because you do not want to see it in the hands of a company, and because in
America the railways are in the hands of the Government, and every railway [Construction and control of United States railways.]
company has a concession ?—No, they have no concession.

Can everybody make a railway who likes ?—Yes, they can go in competition
with other railways.

Supposing you want to construct a railway, have you got to get the consent of
the original railway company ?—If it is on Government property, of course they
would not have the right to run along the section of line already constructed, but they
can apply, and run a railway 50 or 100 miles from another point if they thought it
would pay.

Now, supposing the railway be constructed on Government ground, as well as on
private ground, from whom does the company obtain its right to construct the line ?—
The company, as I said before, applies to the Government, and they give them the
right, provided they show their *bona fides*, and their ability to build the line.

And the Government gets the right to control the line, and regulate its tariff ?—
Yes, but it does not prevent other people who apply to run a line close by. That is
the great difference here; if we were empowered to run a line parallel with the present
line, it would be another matter. I believe there is no other company except the
Netherlands allowed to build railways in this country. You see the whole principle
of American trade and the American railroad system is internal free trade—anybody can
build railways. There is no trade monopoly granted in America. If a tariff is put on
to protect any industry, any amount of other industries would spring up, and no one
manufacturer or company is given preference over another. That is the whole
difference; and it is a great difference.

Can anybody build a railroad parallel to an existing railroad ?—I do not know
exactly the distance they should be apart, but parallel lines in America have been very
close to each other.

You said this morning that Mr. Middelberg threw dust in the eyes of the Co
mission. I take that to mean he told an untruth. Can you point out anything in h
statement that is an untruth ?—I did not make the statement that Mr. Middelberg to
an untruth. I said it appeared to me he threw dust in our eyes.

In what portion of his declaration is there anything that appears to be incorre
or untrue ?—I have not made a careful study of his evidence; and I do not say I
stated any untruths; but, to me, what seemed a very curious thing was his starting
with the tenant and house business. I do not say that there was any untruth. Th
was a clever way of bringing out his point, but it did not seem to me logical
perfectly fair, and that is what I mean by throwing dust in our eyes. He left out
very important factor in the illustration of the tenant and the house. There are tw
principals engaged in it—the owners and the tenants, but the tenant was a force
tenant not a free tenant, and one of the so-called principals was only an agent, and w
as the poor tenant, can fall back on the Government for redress.

I only made the remark, because, if there were anything that was an untruth
the statement, I wanted to know it.—I do not say it was an untruth at all; I mean
was very cleverly put.

There were some other clever people before the Commission as well as M
Middelberg.

Chairman.

I feel myself called upon to thank you for your exhaustive evidence, and speciall
because you gave yourself the trouble to give the Commission a printed translatio
which made it very easy for the Commission to follow your evidence; and, as far as
can see, your statements with regard to the working of the mines, and the figures give
by you, are very exact. Your statement has given us a clearer insight into the workin
of the mines than all the previous statements. As regards the other part of you
evidence, about which we had a discussion this afternoon, I feel assured you hav
given your honest conviction and feeling; and I believe that the interchange of idea
will perhaps lead you to other thoughts, and will also give me thought for reflection
and perhaps it may be for the public good after all.—I wish to return my since
thanks to the Chairman and Members of the Commission for the patient and fa
manner in which my testimony has been received.

MR. THOMAS H. LEGGETT, Consulting Mining Engineer for S. Neumann & Co
was next called. He said he had been twenty months in the Transvaal, an
prior to that time in America. He proceeded :

In coming before you, it is not my purpose to go over the ground already well tr
versed by men who have been longer in this country, and are therefore more thorough
acquainted with its condition; but I am in hopes of presenting to your notice one c
two matters that have come within my experience, which have a direct bearing upc
the mining industry of the Rand. The matter of railway freights has been gone int
very completely, hence I have little to say about it other than to draw your attention to or
particular shipment of mining material recently received from San Francisco, whic
has, in fact, reached here during the past month, and upon which I have been able
get the different charges from the Pacific coast to Johannesburg. These are s
forth in the table marked "Exhibit A," which I hand to you for inspection. The tot
weight of the shipment was 9 tons, and you will note that the per-ton mile rate fro
San Francisco to New York, which is something over 3,000 miles, was 0·28d. ; t

n freight from New York to East London was 0·17d., being somewhat higher than
al on account of the bulky nature of the freight; the Cape Government and
nge Free State charges for haulages of 286 and 328 miles respectively, were
atical, namely, 2·27d., or exactly eight times the rate on the American railway for
-fifth of the haul; while the Netherlands Railway charge was 7·45d. per ton per mile,
early 27 times the rate in America, and for a haulage of only one-sixtieth the
ance! You are doubtless aware that, in this haulage across the Continent of
erica, there are hundreds of miles of country very similar to that traversed
the railroads of South Africa, while the altitudes to be surmounted exceed 8,000 ft.
ve sea level; and further, on many of the freight (or goods) trains, the engines
e to be doubled in order to surmount the heavy gradients. Even the lack of
way competition in this country can hardly be considered as accounting for this
nendous difference. In short, the Netherlands Railway charges are out of all
son, and can be considered as nothing short of absolute extortion. In reference to
particular shipment, the agent in Johannesburg informs me that one portion of
was delivered at the Johannesburg Goods Station, and the other portion, approxi-
ely half, at Elandsfontein. At Johannesburg Station he was charged 1½ per cent.
y, but at Elandsfontein he was forced to pay 7½ per cent. on exactly the same
ds. He naturally made a protest to the Elandsfontein agent, who in turn referred
Pretoria, receiving instructions in reply confirming his charge of 7½ per cent. It
ild seem as if a very substantial error had been made in this particular, and it
phasises the necessity which exists for the Government taking over the railway,
giving it that thorough and systematic administration which is so urgently

Mining claim licences.

ded. With respect to the direct taxation of the mining claims by the Government,
first sight these do not seem excessive. Nevertheless, a comparison with the
rges which are made in other republics in America may be worth making. For

Cost of title to mining claim in United States.

ance, what does it cost in the United States to obtain title to mining property?
expense of locating, i.e. pegging, the average-sized claim of 600 × 1,500 feet
ual in size to 15·62 Transvaal claims of 400 × 150 Cape feet), together with
order's fees, is approximately £10. Title in fee simple or freehold can be obtained
m the United States Government on payment of £100. To this must be added the
t of surveys, maps, and incidental expenses, increasing the amount by about £50
re. In other words, by a payment of £160 one obtains absolute title to 900,000
are feet of mining ground, which may be worked or allowed to lie fallow for years,
he option of the owner. Let us compare this with the cost of the licences paid by

Wolhuter claim licences.

h a property as the Wolhuter, consisting of a mining area of 171 claims. This
pany paid during 1896 the sum of £519 10s. in licences, which is about its average
ual payment. In the United States this amount of ground would be covered—
, of course, in actual area, but by virtue of the mining law of the apex—by two
00 foot claims. The cost of acquiring perpetual possession or the freehold of this
und would be £320, or only 61 per cent. of one year's payments on a mining

Mining claim licences in S. America.

perty of equal size in this country. The Spanish-American republics are equally
ourable to the development of the mining industry. Their claims are bounded by
tical planes, as is the case on the Rand, and the Government charges are very
ilar to those which prevail in the United States. I do not know that any com-
int has ever been made on the score of too heavy charges for mining licences, and
not make this comparison in any carping spirit, but merely to draw your atten-
to the policy pursued towards the mining industry by other republics, who
ept as an axiom the principle that the success of this industry conduces to their
prosperity to a greater degree perhaps than that of any other. The matter of

Native labour.

Pass Law has been thoroughly well ventilated. The question of the cost of

natives delivered at the mining properties, so to speak, is to my mind a serious it
In one mine that I am acquainted with, not a very large property, having a mill
40 stamps, the payments on this account during the past year, after deducting
amounts subsequently refunded by the "boys," totalled £2,663. Now, inasmuch as
average of about 390 natives were working at this property during the same peri
this comes out at a cost of over £6 16s. per "boy." This cost divided over the t
crushed for the year, gives a charge of 6s. 8d. per ton. At the Wolhuter Gold M
in 1896 the cost of procuring native labour, after deducting the amounts subsequen
refunded by the kaffirs, equals £5,448 10s. This works out at a cost per "boy"
£3 6s. 4·8d., there being 1,641 "boys" employed on the property. Spreading t
charge over the tons crushed for the year, the cost comes to 9s. 5d. per ton. I thi

Comparative working costs of Californian and Rand gold mines. you will admit that these charges constitute a very heavy burden upon the min
industry, and trust you will afford us your aid in remedying the matter. Wha
wish most to draw your attention to, however, is the cost of working in the Unit
States mines, which are similar to those of the Rand, more especially those of Ca
fornia, where the veins are of a width similar to the banket beds of this district, a
the mines are of even greater depth. The data contained in the sheet mark
"Exhibit B" will be of interest in this connection. The costs of working such mir
as these can, with all fairness, be compared with our own working costs on the Ra
inasmuch as the types of the ore deposits are similar, or rather, I should say, that t
methods of mining a quartz vein, 3 feet to 4 feet wide, and dipping at 40 degs. to
degs., are precisely similar to those employed in working the banket beds of the Ra
You will note that the poorest mine in this list, with a yield of only 23s. per ton, pa
a profit of 13s., when working at a depth of 800 feet to 1,000 feet; and the avera
grade ore of 27s. to 30s. gives profits of 9s. to 12s. per ton. The main items th
enter into the cost of mining operations may be summarised as follows:—(1) moti
power; (2) supplies or stores; (3) labour. These must be taken in connection wi
the character of the ore deposit, in which the hardness of the ground to be broken, t
width of the ore body, and the amount of water to be handled are the chief consider
tions. I have been unable to obtain the itemised working costs of the properti
mentioned in "Exhibit B," but from my experience of mining in California I a
largely familiar with the general features of the mining costs there. In regard to t
cost of motive power in this country, the item is considerably in excess of that
California, and this is largely due to the fact that water-powers are numerous in t
Sierra Nevadas, and are utilised either directly or by means of electricity. Whe
these powers do not exist timber is usually plentiful. In this respect I think that o
Rand mines will show up more favourably within the next year, inasmuch as I belie
that you are becoming convinced of the high cost of our coal, due to excessive freig
charges. In the matter of stores the same condition exists, namely, a highly increas
cost, due largely to excessive railway rates in the Cape Colony and here. In this cc
nection I would submit a statement showing the costs of the chief mining supplies
the extensive mining camp of Butte City, Montana, for the year 1894, and the cost
similar articles in the Transvaal at the present date. (See "Exhibit C.") Butte is
inland town, situated in the heart of the Rocky Mountains, 1,000 to 1,500 miles aw
from the sea coast, and over 2,000 miles from the source of supplies of drill ste
round iron, piping, etc. From this table you will note that dynamite costs
Johannesburg 3½ times as much as in Butte City, and even with equal percentages
nitro-glycerine, the proportion of cost would be about as three to one. Detonate
cost 1½ times as much in Johannesburg as in Butte City; and drill steel is 20 per ce
more expensive here. Common iron costs 44 per cent. more than in Butte, a
Norway iron 60 per cent. more; 3 inch pipe is 68 per cent. more costly in Johann

rg, and 5 inch pipe is one-third higher in cost. Timber can be obtained in Butte c one-seventh the price demanded here. Mining stulls cost us here three times as uch, while lagging poles are thirteen times more expensive. After a haulage of 450 les from Rocky Springs, Wyoming, to Butte City, coal costs slightly less than it es on the Rand with an average haulage of 28 miles. I have faith that in this also u will apply the proper remedy. The mining conditions are very comparable, shown by the width of the veins in the list of mines in "Exhibit B," and e depth at which they are being worked. In so far as the hardness of the ound is concerned, the Californian mines as a rule have a considerably softer aterial to work in. This, however, is largely offset, and in some cases *more* than unterbalanced by the much greater amount of water to be handled, and it is a rfectly fair conclusion therefore, that so far as the natural conditions of the deposits the two countries are concerned, a comparison of the costs incurred in working em is a fair one. The item of labour comes next, and here I think we shall have me instructive matter for consideration. You will note that the Plumas Eureka d the Sierra Buttes mines, having mills equal in capacity to but 30 and 40 stamps spectively of the Rand type, employ from 230 to 250 white men, or from six to eight en per stamp. This is three or four times the number of white men per stamp ployed on the Rand, the difference being offset by the use of kaffir labour. The ages paid to these men in California are $2\frac{1}{2}$ to 3 dollars per day, or roughly from)s. to 12s. This is a little more than half the average price paid for white labour the Rand, and considerably less than half where contract work is done, and it must remembered that contract work prevails here very largely. The salient feature is be found in the fact that, notwithstanding the employment of white labour at the oove rate of wages, mines which would just about pay operating expenses on the and are made to yield a large profit in California. We have found that the natural nditions of the ore deposits in the two countries are similar, and the disadvantages at exist about balance one another. The greatest differences in the cost of mining perations in the two countries lie in the cost of motive power, of dynamite, and other ores, and of labour. In the reduction of the first two items we count confidently pon your most necessary assistance. In the matter of labour we know that in alifornia we have largely the same class of miners as are to be found on the Rand -day, namely, Cornishmen. Why is it, then, that these men are willing in one untry to accept half the wages that they require in the other? I think the answer ill be found in the simple fact that in America these men go with the idea of settling ermanently. They become an integral part of the country. They say to themselves, This country is good enough for us and our children." Their margin of profit at the oove stated wage is almost equivalent to their margin of profit in this country, due iefly to the difference in the cost of living. But, above all, they realise the fact that ey have gone into a country in which they intend to stay and make their home. ere, on the contrary, the aim of nine miners out of ten is to accumulate sufficient oney to leave the country, which is not the country of their adoption, as in other publics. And, gentlemen, until it is made so, until the labouring man—who is the ack-bone and sinew of any industry—becomes an integral part of your country; ntil he feels that he can settle here and obtain for his family the necessaries and mfort of life, without this feeling of being obliged to save money in order to get vay—until this condition of affairs prevails, we cannot hope to reduce this item of st to a figure comparable to that which obtains in the United States. Mr. ennings has shown you what has been done with black labour in other countries, d has pointed out in a clear and forcible manner the latent possibilities of the kaffir, d what we may justly expect of him when properly trained. The point which I

White labour in California and on Rand.

Co-operation of
Government
necessary for
white and na-
tive labour
supply. wish to emphasise is, that in the matter both of white and black labour we a
dependent on your active co-operation ; in the matter of white labour to so alter tl
conditions surrounding the white workman that his wage may be reduced withov
impairing the margin of profit which he now receives, and which all acknowledge
be but a fair recompense to the efficient labourer ; in the matter of kaffir labour,
increase the supply so that it shall be adequate for the entire fields, and at the sam
time to so control it that we may succeed in increasing the kaffirs' efficiency, an

Development of
deep levels. extending the scope of his work. I do not know whether you quite realise the grea
importance of the development of the deep level mines of the Rand, and the bearin
which the successful outcome of this work will have on the future prosperity of tl
country. By deep level mines I do not mean such mines as the Geldenhuis Dee
where the shafts cut the reef under 1,000 feet in depth, but I refer rather to tho
properties where the reef lies at a depth of 2,000 to 3,000 feet from the surface, whic
properties require the expenditure of a large amount of capital, and the exercise o
the part of the shareholders of a great deal of patience before any return can t
expected from the outlay. Roughly speaking, in such deep level properties you hav
more than double the area of ground of the outcrop companies. It will readily l
seen, therefore, that if these deep level reefs can be brought to the productive stag
and made to yield a profit, not only will the original faith of those investing in thes
fields be verified, but the prosperity of the country will also be greatly enhanced.

Depths and dis-
tances from
outcrop of
deep levels. here submit a diagram of the deep level shafts now sinking upon these fields, showin
the depths at which they are estimated to cut the reefs, and the horizontal distance
south from the Main Reef outcrop at which they are located. This diagram show
that within the first 1,000 feet from the outcrop there are 8 shafts = 13%

1,000 to 2,000	„	„	„	„	25 shafts = 40%
2,000 to 3,000	„	„	„	„	12 shafts = 19½%
3,000 to 4,000	„	„	„	„	4 shafts = 6½%
4,000 to 5,000	„	„	„	„	8 shafts = 13%
5,000 to 6,000	„	„	„	„	4 shafts = 6½%
6,000	„	„	„	„	1 shaft = 1½%

The last shaft has to go through 3,318 feet of ground before reaching the reef. W
have a parallel instance of faith in the value of deep level mines in the case of th
Tamarack cop-
per mine. Tamarack Copper Mining Company of Michigan, which company sank a shaft o
2,300 feet deep before cutting the copper-bearing lode, spending thousands of pound
on that operation, and waiting nearly four years before the mine became a produce
History of Tam-
arack mine. This mine started crushing in 1886, and has been a steady producer ever since. It ha
to-day five deep level shafts, and their total depths in the early part of 1896 were a
follows :—No. 1 shaft, 3,232 feet ; No. 2 shaft, 3,535 feet ; No. 3 shaft, 4,450 feet ; N
4 shaft, 4,450 feet ; No. 5 shaft, 226 feet. This No. 5 shaft will be connected on th
27th level (3,920 vertical) with shaft No. 2. It will intersect the reef at 4,700 vertica
and is of five compartments. At present this mine has one stope, working at a dept
of 4,500 feet, according to the 1895 issue of the "Mineral Industry, its Statistic
Technology and Trade," to which publication I am indebted for many of my figure
Dividends and
working costs
of Tamarack
mine. The total dividends paid by this property to the close of 1895 were 4,700,000 dollar
or £900,000, with mining ore worth from 20s. to 22s. per ton at a depth of 2,200 t
3,200 feet. The working costs of this property figure at 16s. per ton, showing tha
even when mining at this depth the average profit in 1895 was 5s. 6d. per ton.
attach statements marked exhibits " E " and " F " showing the costs at this propert
Atlantic mine. for the years 1888 to 1894 inclusive, as also those of the Atlantic Mine, which is a
outcrop company in the same district, and working during the period mentioned at

th of 850 to 1,250 feet. This latter property is one of the best managed in the ld, as it is making a small profit on an extremely low-grade copper ore. The rage value of this ore for the year 1895 was 6s. 3d. per ton, upon which they ially made a profit of 1s. 4½d. This mine is, however, an exceptional instance of arkable economical management. It has also easier ground to mine in than the narack. I have drawn up a statement, which I here submit ("Exhibit G"), showing total mining, including surface expenses, of three outcrop mines in this copper district, rder to be able to make a comparison with the costs of the Deep Level Tamarack e for the same period of six to seven years. The mining costs of these outcrop es, namely, the Atlantic, Allouez, and Osceola, including surface expenses, average ½d. per ton; the same costs for the Tamarack Deep Level are 9s., showing an increase 3s. 9½d., which increase may be said to be due to the greater depth of mining. se costs exclude transportation and milling, inasmuch as the method of reduction opper ore differs from that of gold ores, and further, the reduction costs are not cted by the depth from which the ore is extracted. I have worked out the mining s (including development work) of 22 Rand companies, which show an average of . 7½d. Mr. Jennings has just submitted to you a statement, including a greater nber of companies, 29 in all, in which he shows this cost to be 17s. 7·12d., which is rly double the costs at the Tamarack mine, where they are stoping to-day at a th of over 3,000 ft. We, of course, have no mines working at such depths here h which we could make comparison with the Tamarack, and the question arises ether such comparison would be a fair one from a mining point of view. To this stion I answer, yes; inasmuch as every indication thus far goes to show that upon Rand the natural conditions will be quite as favourable as they are in the copper ricts of Michigan; in other words, that we shall have no disadvantageous increase temperature for several thousand feet in depth, no undue amount of water, and bably even less timbering to be done than is required in the deep level mines of t district. Hence, the mining conditions admit of comparison, but of course it st be borne in mind that in the Michigan mines they are working on a lode 12 ft. 15 ft. wide, which width is an important factor in the cheapening of mining costs. they are to-day extracting in the United States ore that is worth 21s. 6d. per ton, m a depth of over 3,000 ft., and making a profit of 5s. to 6s. upon it, I would ask— aot the same thing feasible here? Given proper conditions, it certainly is feasible; , under present conditions, we cannot even make an outcrop mine of that value of yield a profit. We have a number of deep level mines on the Rand to-day which unquestionably of much better grade of ore than this, and which will yield a fair rgin of profit. I wish, however, to direct your attention to the very large area of dium-grade reef which, if the local conditions are favourable, could be made to ld a profit. Experience gained in the deep mines of the copper district makes it sonable to expect that, when mining here at similar depths we shall have an reased cost, due to that depth, of approximately 4s. per ton. On the other hand, if the United States, in a district where the mining conditions are similar, ore can be aed at this depth and placed in the mill for 9s. per ton, is it not reasonable to ect that conditions may be so altered within the next few years in this country as enable us to do the same work here for 15s. to 16s. per ton, even with our rower ore bodies? It is true that the Tamarack crushes 392,000 tons per year, the Simmer and Jack Mine is to-day been equipped with a 280-stamp mill able of crushing over 400,000 tons annually, and it is certain that in handling lium-grade ores, if we would obtain a profit, we *must* crush in large quantities. If contrive to mine the deep levels in the near future at the figure stated, we can ke a reasonable profit on our medium-grade ores, and, in this event, will make

Marginal notes: Value and profit of Atlantic mine. — Comparative working costs of Allouez, Atlantic and Osceola outcrop, and Tamarack deep level mines. — Average working costs of 22 Rand companies. — Comparison of working conditions of Rand and Michigan mines. — Tonnage crushed at Tamarack and Simmer and Jack mines.

P

Mr. T. H. Leggett's Evidence.

productive an immense area of deep level ground, and the life of the industry wil[l] assured for many decades to come. This is the immediate and burning ques[tion] **Medium-grade outcrop mines.** to-day—how to make our medium-grade outcrop mines payable? But thi[s] inseparably connected with the future of the deep level mines. If we can obtain s[uch] reductions in working costs as to render mines yielding 25s. to 30s. per ton profita[ble] investments, we can then look forward confidently to obtaining profits on a sim[ilar] grade of ore in the deep levels. I appear before this honourable Commission a[s] citizen of a sister republic, and in so doing am animated by none but the friendl[iest] motives. I feel that I cannot more fittingly conclude my remarks than by remind[ing] **Incorporation of uitlanders — President Steyn's dictum** you of the memorable words of President Steyn, when, in his address to [the] Legislature of the Free State on March 11, 1896, he said :—" Here in the Free St[ate] where we have raised the banner of republicanism, where from all quarters strang[ers] are coming to us, is it not a glorious task to incorporate these strangers with us [and] amalgamate them in one republican people." Gentlemen, I cannot embellish so w[ise] and true a statement. I can only commend it, and the principle that underlies it [to] your kind and most earnest consideration. Finally, I beg to express the hope t[hat] the evidence which has been submitted here may convince you that the future of [this] country—not for the next 10 years, but for many times that period—lies in [the] economical and successful development of the deep level properties of these fields. [I] believe that a grasp to-day of the conditions that are essential to such developm[ent] will lead this country to a prosperous, and even brilliant future.

EXHIBIT A.

Tabular costs of imported mining material from San Francisco. Table showing cost of 9 tons of mining material (bulky) from San Francisco [laid] down in Johannesburg :—

	Total cost. £ s. d.	Cost per ton. £ s. d.	Percentage of total cost.	Percen[tage] of pr[ice] in S[an] Franc[isco]
Price in San Francisco, F.O.B. ...	166 9 5·2	18 9 11·2	44·99	100
Freight, San Francisco to New York	31 14 10·3	3 10 6·5	8·58	19
Cartage, insurance, fees	7 11 10·5	0 16 10·5	2·06	4
Freight, New York to East London	58 1 2·0	6 9 0·2	15·69	34
Port charges and landing ...	14 18 11·0	1 13 2·5	4·04	8
Freight, East London to Johannesburg	66 19 10·0	7 8 10·5	18·11	40
Transvaal duty	12 18 3·0	1 8 8·3	3·49	7
Cartage to mine	9 17 6·0	1 1 11·3	2·66	5
Exchange	1 9 0·0	0 3 2·7	0·38	
Total	370 0 10·0	41 2 3·7	100·00	222

ANALYSIS OF OCEAN AND R.R. CHARGES.

	Distance Transported. Miles.	Total Charges. £ s. d.	Percentage of total charge.	Rate p[er] ton per [mile] d.
R.R., San Francisco to New York ...	3,000	31 14 10·3	20·24	0·2[5]
Steamer, New York to East London ...	9,000	58 1 2·0	37·03	0·1[5]
Cape Government Railway	286	24 8 8·2	15·57	2·2
Orange Free State R.R.	328	28 0 5·3	17·88	2·2
N.Z.A.S.M.	52	14 10 8·5	9·28	7·4
Total	12,666	156 15 10·3	100·00	

Exhibit B.—Sierra Buttes Mine, Sierra County.—Depth of mine, 1,000ft.; 'erage dip, 45degs. Two mills, 50 and 60 stamps respectively, equal in capacity to out a 40-stamp mill on the Rand. Six months crushing, 29,243 tons, yielding 9,196dols.=6·47dols. per ton=£1 7s.; mining, 3·85dols.=16·04s.; milling, ·45dols.= 96s.; total costs, 18s.; profit per ton, 9s. The average yield of the ore for ten years as 7dols. per ton=£1 9s. 2d., yet they disbursed in dividends 1,360,288dols.= 272,000. The number of men employed in mine and mills averages 250.

Working costs of Sierra Buttes mine, U.S.A.

Plumas Eureka Mine, Plumas County.—Depth of mine over 1,500ft. Dip 'degs.; width of vein, 3½ft. (average); 60-stamp mill=30-stamp mill on the Rand, en employed, 229; in six months crushed, 27,789 tons; yield per ton, 7·27dols.= 1 10s. 3d.; cost mining and milling, 4·32dols.=18s.; profit per ton, 12s. 3d.

Working costs of Plumas Eureka mine, U.S.A.

Zeile Mine, Jackson, Amador County.—Ore yields 5·50dols.=£1 3s. per ton; sts, 10s. per ton; profit per ton, 13s.; depth, 800 to 1,000ft.; vein, 3 to 4ft. wide; ushing, 120 tons per day, 40 stamps.

Working costs of Zeile mine, U.S.A.

Plymouth Consolidated, Amador County.—Vertical depth of mine, 1,500ft.; 120 amps crush 250 tons per day; yield per ton, 13 dols.=£2 14s. 2d.; costs mining, 20dols.=13s. 4d.; milling, ·69dols.=2s. 10d.; total costs, 3·89dols.=16s. 2d.; profit r ton, £1 18s. The annual report shows—Gold bullion produced, 1,033,518·29 dols. £212,658; operating expenses, 331,163·84dols.=£68,141; profit, 702,354·45dols.= 144,517; twelve dividends paid, 600,000·00dols.=£123,456; surplus carried over, 2,354·45 dols.=£21,061. The management and general office expenses are not tainable for the above mines. They would increase the costs about 2s. per ton.

Working costs of Plymouth Consolidated mine U.S.A.

Exhibit C.—Table showing Prices of Supplies

At Butte, Montana, U.S.A., in 1894, and at Johannesburg, Z.A.R., in 1897.

Comparative prices of supplies at Butte, Montana, U.S.A., and Johannesburg, S.A.R.

Material.		Butte, 1894. £	s.	d.		Johannesburg, 1897. £	s.	d.
ynamite per case of 50 lbs.	(a)	1	3	11½	(b)	4	5	0
etonators per box		0	13	6½		1	0	0
ıse per coil of 25 feet		0	0	7 11/12		0	0	4⅝
ındles (16 ozs.) per box of 25 lbs.		0	12	4⅖		0	10	9
rill steel per lb.		0	0	4¼		0	0	5⅛
on (common) per lb....		0	0	1⅜		0	0	2
on (Norway) per lb....		0	0	2½		0	0	4
pe (3-inch) per foot		0	1	0½		0	1	9
pe (5-inch) per foot		0	2	1		0	2	10
mber per cubic foot		0	0	7⅕		0	4	1
ulls per inch of diam., and 1 foot of length ...		0	0	0 3/10		0	0	0 9/10
ıgging poles per foot of length		0	0	0¼		0	0	3⅓
ɔal per ton, 2,000 lbs.	(c)	0	19	9½	(d)	1	0	0

(a) 40 per cent. (c) Includes 450 miles of railage.

(b) 70 per cent. (d) Includes 28 miles of railage average.

EXHIBIT E.—ANALYSIS OF EXPENSES, 1888 TO 1894—ATLANTIC MINE.

Working costs of Atlantic mine, U.S.A., from 1888 to 1894.

	1894. Cents.	1893. Cents.	1892. Cents.	1891. Cents.	1890. Cents.	1889. Cents.	1888 Cent
Cost of air drills, etc. (a) ...	8	9	8	9	10	11	8
Cost of fuel for engines ...	7	7	7	6	6	5	5
Other underground expenses	51	53	57	67	69	60	58
Other surface expenses ...	10	10	12	12	19	13	12
Total running expenses at mine ...	75	79	84	95	104	88	84
	3/11½d.	3/3½d.	3/6d.	3/11½d.	4/4d.	3/8d.	3/6d
Transfer to mill and stamping ...	26	28	28	29	31	31	30
Total running expenses ...	102	108	112	125	135	119	114
	4/3d.	4/6d.	4/8d.	5/2½d.	5/7½d.	4/11½d.	4/9d
Construction	45	34	3	11	10	11	8
Total, including construction ...	146	142	115	136	145	133	122
Smelting, freight, and marketing ...	17	18	18	18	20	20	21
Total cost, less construction ...	119	126	130	143	156	139	135
Total expense to market ...	165	160	133	154	166	153	143
	6/10½d.	6/8d.	5/6½d.	6/5d.	6/9d.	6/4½d.	5/11½d
Thousand tons stamped ...	315	316	301	297	278	279	298
Estimated average depth ...	1250	1200	1150	1000	950	900	850

(a) Pumping also included.

TAMARACK MINE.

Working costs of Tamarack mine, U.S.A., from 1888 to 1894.

	1894. Cents.	1893. Cents.	1892. Cents.	1891. Cents.	1890. Cents.	1889. Cents.	1888 Cents
Cost of air drills, etc.	—	14	18	21	25	21	20
Cost of fuel for engines ...	—	19	24	22	31	33	23
Other underground expenses ...	—	130	134	142	165	151	140
Other surface expenses ...	—	28	26	26	25	30	30
Total running expenses at mine	—	191	202	209	246	235	213
		7/11½d.	8/5d.	8/8½d.	10/3d.	9/9½d.	8/10½d
Transfer to mill and stamping	—	46	49	47	59	64	72
Total running expenses ...	246	237	221	256	305-303	300	285
Construction	60	45	80	124	05	40	01
Total, including construction ...	306	282	301	380	310	340	286
Smelting, freight, and marketing	72	81	77	76	107	107	128
Total cost, less construction ...	318	323	298	332	412	307	413
Total expenses to market ...	378	368	378	456	417	447	414
Thousand tons broken ...	(a)	413	392	330	182	197	163
Thousand tons hoisted ...	—	369	363	301	163	179	152
Thousand tons stamped ...	350	346	339	283	155	169	144
Estimated average depth ...	3100	3000	2900	2800	2700	2600	2500

(a) Estimate not official, affecting all the figures in this column.

Tamarack and Atlantic mines

The expenses after stamping depend really on the amount of copper rather than on tons of rock. The cost of pumping is included in the cost of running the air drills in the Atlantic mine, but not in the Tamarack. The totals vary two or three cents sometimes, owing to neglected fractions, from the results of direct addition. The expense is per ton stamped in the Atlantic mine, per ton hoisted in the Tamarack.

(f) ATLANTIC MINE.—An outcrop mine. Average depth, 1,300ft. Width of vein, Working costs of Atlantic mine, U.S.A.
. The record of the output for 1895 was: Value of ore, 14·6lbs. copper per long equal to 0·73 p.c., equal to (at 10·52c. per lb.) 1·5352dols. or 6s. 3d. per ton; cost mining, selecting, and breaking, 0·7525dols. per ton; crushing and concentrating, 0dols. per ton; transportation (three miles) and surface charges, ·0408dols. per ton; ght, smelting, and marketing, ·1881dols. per ton; total costs, 1·2034dols.; profit per 1s. 4½d.=·3318dols.; tons milled, 313,058 tons; product, 4,832,497lbs. refined per, 508,252dols.=£104,578; average pay of contract miners in this mine for 10 rs, 1881-1891, 62·90dols.=£13; average pay of whole force for same period, 0dols.=£10 16s.

TAMARACK MINE.—Deep Level. Width of vein, 12 to 15 feet. Estimated Working costs of Tamarack mine, U.S.A.
rage depth of working, 3200ft.; one stope at 4,500ft. The record of output for 5 was: Value of ore, 49·72lbs. per ton, equal to 2·49 per cent., equal to (at 10·52c. lb.) 5dols. 23c. or £1 1s. 6d. Tons crushed and costs not published since 1894. ing an estimate on the figures for that year, tons crushed about 300,000. (Note: duction cut down 50,000 tons less than in 1894 by accident to the hoisting engine No. 1 shaft, and the encountering of poor ground in the territory tributary to No. haft.) Total operating expense at mine, including transportation and milling, ls. 50c., equal to 10s. 4d.; expense to market, including construction, freight, lting and marketing, 1dol. 36c., equal to 5s. 8d.—total costs per ton, 16s.; profit ton (approximate), 5s. 6d.

(g) Comparison of costs of outcrop and deep level mines in the Michigan copper Comparative working costs of outcrop and deep level mines, Michigan, U.S.A.
rict. Table showing mining and surface expenses per ton milled, over a period of to seven years. Does not include transportation and milling.—Width of ore body, to 15ft. Outcrop mines.—Atlantic: depth, 850ft. to 1,300ft., 3s. 8d.; Allouez, depth r 1,000ft., 5s. 10d.; Osceola, depth over 1,000ft., 6s. 2d. The average cost per ton was 2½d. Deep Level.—Tamarack, 2,500ft. to 3,100ft., 9s.; increased cost of mining chiefly to depth, 3s. 9½d. The Tamarack crushes 392,000 tons of 2,000lbs. per um. The Atlantic crushes 371,000 tons of 2,000lbs. per annum. The Allouez shes 115,000 tons of 2,000lbs. per annum. The Osceola crushes 229,000 tons of 0lbs. per annum.

Mr. *Smit.*

In quoting your railway rates from this Republic, did you only quote rates Railway rates from Vereeniging to Johannesburg.
ween Johannesburg and Vereeniging, or the whole of the Republic?—They are y from Vereeniging to Johannesburg.

Do you know the tariff charged between Vereeniging and Johannesburg is her, *pro rata*, than the money charged by the same company on other lines?—No.

In making a comparison, you say that workmen have to be paid higher here on Cost of living of white miners on Rand.
ount of the cost of living here; but does not the same apply to those working in manufacture of dynamite and on the railways?—But, in the matter of dynamite, ot a large quantity brought into the country—that is, there is not much labour ployed on it.

There is a very great staff of white men.—Is not that a misapplication of energy? y not put that labour in the countries where the materials and labour are cheaper.

You will, of course, make allowances that dynamite made in this country will t more money made here than the cost price of that imported?—Unquestionably. erefore I object to its being made here.

You have had a lot to do with mines in California?—Yes.

You say that circumstances are very much easier there than here?—I say so in Working conditions in California.
matter of motive power.

Mining pays better there because the motive power and the labour are cheaper
Yes.

This being so, why didn't you go back to California when you found that min
was so much cheaper than here?—Most engineers come out here under an engagem
entered into before leaving.

Incorporation of uitlander mining population in State. In which way do you propose to make workmen an integral part of the Repub
and offer them sufficient inducement to stay here?—I feel that is a question that is bet
answered by a statesman of the country. I feel it has a vital bearing upon
economic working of our deposits here. Deep levels are a matter for the future, a
I am trying to bring forward to your attention the immediate necessity of maki
workmen an integral part of the Republic, and that to work the deep lev
economically we must unite the bone and sinew in the interests of the country.

When did you frame your statement?—The latter part of last week.

Mr. Hennen Jennings' evidence Did you, more or less, co-operate with Mr. Jennings?—No; my statement
entirely independent of his.

Still you refer to Mr. Jennings' declaration in a couple of instances?—Yes.

You must have known last week what Mr. Jennings would say?—Mr. Jennir
read me a large portion of his statement yesterday afternoon.

And you have consulted him about your declaration?—No.

Mr. de Beer.

Cost of native labour supply. You have stated that it cost one of the mines £6 7s. to deliver a "boy" on to
mines. How do you arrive at that?—By dividing the total cost expended in proc
ing "boys" by the average number working.

How do you arrive at the total cost?—By the totals paid, less the amou
refunded.

But in what way is the money spent?—I do not know that.

How do you arrive at your figures?—I take them from the secretaries' sta
ments at the company's office.

The amount you quoted differs very largely from that by other managers. T
highest figure quoted up to the present is £2 to deliver "boys."—These are t
secretaries' statements taken from the annual report showing the amount charged
that account. I think you will find these figures agree with those given by
Goldmann.

Contract work. It is new to me that most of the work, as you have stated, is done un
contract?—"Largely prevails here," is the expression I used.

You think that miners earn much more working by contract than by shift
Many miners earn more, and I think Mr. Catlin's statement is in support of that.

That is the bonus system?—I mean the contract system in its broad sense.

I understand by contract work you mean piece-work?—Literally it does me
piece-work, but I used the term in its broad sense.

White wages. But is it not very difficult under these circumstances to give a correct average
wages earned by white miners?—Not necessarily. In any one mine you m
have a given number of contractors, and their pay must show on the pay rolls.
the same way you may take the number of men on day pay; then it is very easy
make an average on the total of men you employ.

But you still don't give the Commission a fair idea of the wages actually earn
when you say that a man in receipt of a salary of £18 a month may earn £50 or £
under the bonus system?—Well, I think these figures have been gone into with gre
detail by Mr. Sydney Jennings and Mr. Hennen Jennings, and if I remember righ
they gave the average at about £24.

Unfortunately they were not questioned on contract work.—Contract work does Contract and
time work. t greatly exceed that average pay, in my experience. You will never, in any part the world, get a miner or any other class of workman to work by contract for the me money exactly as he will work by day. A contractor expects to put in some of s own time. If he works overtime, that is his own personal investment in the work has in hand, and he expects to come out above the day-pay man, because he feels has devoted more time to his work.

Are there no miners' licences in America—that is, have the mine workmen to pay No miners' licen-
ses in United
States. y tax to the Government—say 7 dollars per month ?—They only pay their taxes as izens.

Are you certain there is no such licence as the one I refer to ?—Absolutely certain.

Chairman.

You have already stated, with many other witnesses, the wages paid and the cost Comparative
rate of wages
and cost of liv-
ing in United
States and on
Rand. living in California, compared with the wages and the cost of living here. I want know whether the rate of wages paid here is higher than the rate paid in America, mpared with the cost of living ?—I think so.

How do you reconcile that with your statement, if you say that most miners come re to make money, whereas in America they stay ?—From the fact that the majority ve not their wives and families with them here. If you refer to the married men ho settle here with their families, then I would say the cost of living here is cessive.

Here they must make more, for they have the cost of coming out and the expenses, e sending money home to their wives, and yet they save money here ?—Yes, un- arried men.

Still, as long as he works here he must send money home to his family, and also must have money to go home again.—I think that makes the point very clear, that en do not and cannot settle here.

What would be the comparison of the population of the goldfields here and the Comparative
population of
Rand and Cali-
fornian gold
fields. ldfields of California ?—The goldfields of California are much more scattered. u have camps there of from 1,000 to 3,000 people spread over a length of hundreds miles of mining ground.

And in these camps is there any other occupation besides gold mining?—On the estern slopes of the Sierra Nevada, immediately below the mining camps, there is fertile district.

When was the gold first discovered in California ?—In 1849. Discovery of gold
in California,

When did the United States come into existence ?—As the United States, in 1776.

Do you know how long this Republic has been in existence ?—In the neighbour- od of 50 years.

And the goldfields here ?—To put it roughly, about 11 years.

When was the first railway built in the United States ?—I do not know exactly ; First railway in
United States. think at the beginning of this century, 1820 to 1830.

I am very pleased to learn about all the other countries, and to take example om them. Other witnesses have given comparisons between other countries and this. think everyone will agree that, unless you can change the whole economical position the Republic in one day, it is impossible to make a just comparison between mining re and what it is in the old countries. The development and progress of the country arches with the times, and you may be convinced that the Commission will do every- Commission in
tends well to-
wards mining
industry. ing in their power for the industry. I am sorry that all who have given evidence ve only given the position of affairs, and how you desire them to be, without giving

a way out, still, I am in hopes that some of the other witnesses will point a prop
way out.—I do not wish to take up the position of a mentor. In alluding to oth
countries, I only point out what has been accomplished, though it is with the hope th
we may accomplish the same thing here, and I realise fully it will be a question
great difficulty, and I think a great deal depends on starting rightly. I fully belie
that the Mining Commission is ready to aid us in every way possible, and I belie
that the ways out of the difficulties are matters for serious consideration and thoroug
Advisory board. discussion. The only thing a witness can do is to make suggestions, and su
suggestions are only the opinions of one man, whereas if you had an advisory Boar
as has been suggested, to work in conjunction with the representatives of the industr
a way out will be clearly found.

Mr. Schmitz-Dumont.

Deep levels. When you. talk of deep levels you do not mean to comprise mines like th
Bonanza, which strikes the reef under 1,000 feet ?—Exactly.

Deep level mines
of 2,000 or 3,000
feet. What you call a deep level is a mine 2,000 or 3,000 feet deep ?—These are th
mines to which I wish to draw the attention of the Commission.

Have you not seen in the papers that the Bonanza and Geldenhuis Deep a
always mentioned as models or examples of deep level mines ?—An engineer pa
very little attention, as a rule, to the ordinary everyday expressions. He comes
his own conclusions.

I see it in all the papers. It is always the Geldenhuis Deep and the Bonanza
examples of deep level mines ?—Let me explain the distinction I wanted to draw.
is that some of the outcrop mines are to-day working at very nearly the same vertic
depth from the surface as these mines. When you are a few hundred feet more
less under the maximum of, say, 1,000 feet, it affects the working cost much les
Look at the working costs of the Geldenhuis Deep, and you will find they are work
ing about the same cost as the outcrop mines, which goes to show that at that poi
the depth is not a vital factor. But when you get to 2,000 or 3,000 feet then the dep
does become a vital factor, and that is the point I wish to draw your attention
for consideration.

You don't wish to judge the future deep levels by the Geldenhuis and th
Bonanza ?—Certainly not.

If the papers say the future of the deep levels depends on the future of th
Geldenhuis and Bonanza, you think they are wrong. You don't agree with the
opinion ?—Everyone has a right to his own opinion. I don't say they have not
marked influence. In deep level mining we go step by step as the industry pr
gresses. When a man finds he can work at 1,000 feet and make a profit, as the
are doing at the Geldenhuis Deep, then he thinks he will try 2,000 feet. That is a
index, and the Geldenhuis Deep is more of an index because it is a medium grade or
whereas the Bonanza is a very rich grade.

Don't you think the Robinson and the Ferreira Deep, or any of those, would be
far better index than the Geldenhuis of the future ?—Of the future of what ?

Of the future indications of deep levels—of the cost of working deep levels
the future.—Of the mines I am alluding to ; yes.

You said at the Tamarack Deep Level mine a ton of quartz cost 9s. to mine ?—
Comparative
working costs
of outcrop and
deep level
mine. The mining and surface work.

And for the outcrop of the Tamarack mine it only costs 5s. 6d. ?—What I sa
was that the average cost per ton of three outcrop mines was 5s. 2½d.

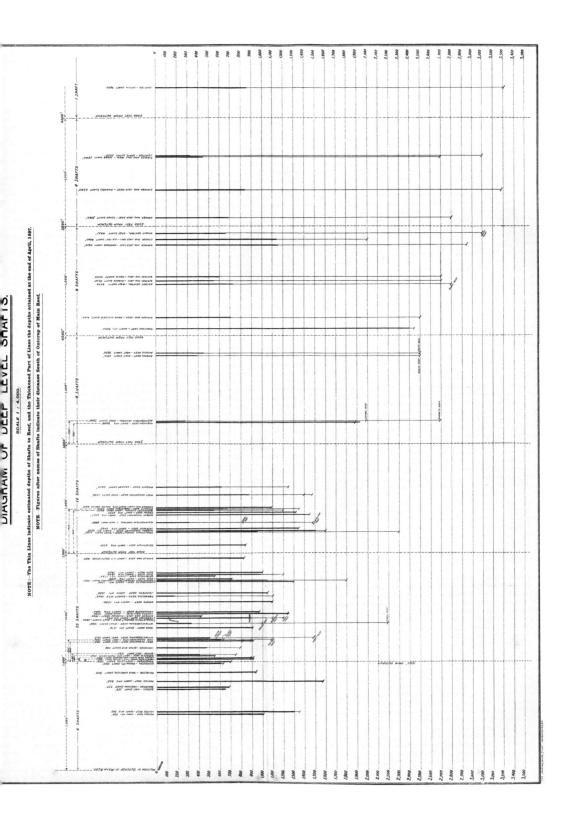

DIAGRAM OF DEEP LEVEL SHAFTS.

SCALE 1 : 4,000.

NOTE:—The Thin Lines indicate estimated depths of Shafts to Reef, and the Thickened Part of Lines the depths attained at the end of April, 1897.

NOTE.—Figures after names of Shafts indicate their distance South of Outcrop of Main Reef.

The material originally positioned here is too large for reproduction in this reissue. A PDF can be downloaded from the web address given on page iv of this book, by clicking on 'Resources Available'.

What do you think of the comparison here of the cost of the outcrop mine and the deep level?—I have stated in my testimony that I anticipated an increased cost 4s. per ton.

How do you arrive at that 4s.?—In the Tamarack there is about 60 per cent. difference between the cost of the deep level and outcrop—5s. 2d. and 9s.—the actual difference in cost is a direct factor of the extra depth in so far as the cost of hoisting is concerned. It does not cost any more to mine underground at a depth of 3000 feet; the actual cost of the amount of dynamite used, the number of men employed per ton of rock broken, the number of carmen and trammers employed will be the same. Therefore, it is a fair assumption that the actual difference in cost will approximate with what it is found to be in Michigan.

Don't you think in the deep level your ventilators, timber, etc., will cost you much more than in the outcrop mine?—No.

Mr. Pierce.

Abolition of dynamite monopoly and expropriation of railway.

In giving the comparison between the railway rates, dynamite charges, etc., do you suggest that a solution of the present difficulties would be found in the expropriation of the railways and the abolition of the dynamite monopoly?—I do.

You think if these two items were taken in hand and relief granted it would go a long way to remove all difficulties?—I think it would be a very long step in the right direction.

Mr. Johns' evidence.

MR. JOHN HENRY JOHNS, general manager of the Ferreira company, and consulting engineer of the Worcester company, was then sworn in, and stated that he had resided in Johannesburg for a little over eight years. He had been with the Ferreira company for eight years, and previous to that he was manager of gold mines in India for seven years, and was engaged for 12 years in the tin and copper mines of Cornwall.

Witness made the following statement:—

I am general manager of the Ferreira Gold Mining Company, Limited, consulting engineer to the Worcester Gold Mining Company, Limited, and chairman of the Association of Mine Managers. I have managed the Ferreira mine over eight years, was manager of gold mines in India seven years, and prior to that was engaged 12 years in the tin and copper mines of Cornwall. I hold the highest certificates granted by the Royal School of Mines, London, in mining and metallurgy. I agree with the evidence already given before this Commission, that what is chiefly needed by the mining industry to prevent the forced closing down of mines on which an immense amount of money has already been expended, and to bring prosperity to the industry and to the State, is a reduction of the abnormally high cost of dynamite, of railway rates, and of native labour; better administration of the Pass Law and the Liquor Law, and an earnest endeavour on the part of the Government to stamp out the nefarious illicit traffic in gold. The excessive cost of dynamite on these fields is one of the heaviest burdens the mining industry has to bear, while at the same time it adds comparatively little to the revenue of the State. The Ferreira company uses blasting gelatine at a cost of £5 7s. 6d. per case, plus 2s. for transport, or £5 9s. 6d. per case delivered. Last year this item cost the company £15,919 19s. 5d., or 8·08 per cent. of the actual working expenses. If the cost of this explosive were reduced by 50s. per case, the Ferreira company would be saved the expenditure of £7,302 per annum. The greater the reduction effected in cost of dynamite and coal, the greater will be the quantity consumed, not only on account

Reduction of railway rates, costs of native labour and dynamite, and better administration of Pass and Liquor laws and Government aid in suppressing gold thefts necessary.

Cost of blasting gelatine at Ferreira mine

Reduction of cost of dynamite would increase consumption. of the additional mines that would be worked in this State, but because a reduction would admit of a more extended use of air drills in actual mining work, which would necessitate increased consumption of both dynamite and coal. In mining with air drills, about double the quantity of dynamite is used per ton, extra coal is required for Cost of blasting gelatine at compressing air, and less kaffir labour needed. The average cost of blasting gelatine Ferreira mine. per foot driven by hand labour in developing the reef in the Ferreira mine is 7s. 5·9

	£	s.	
In driving 3,746 ft. by air drills, the average cost of gelatine per foot was	1	1	3
or about three times the quantity required by hand labour.			
In stoping 717 square fathoms of reef by hand labour, the average cost of gelatine per square fathom was	0	17	1
In stoping 899 square fathoms of reef by air drills, the average cost of gelatine per square fathom was	1	9	8
or 1·63 times the quantity used by hand labour.			

The cost of blasting gelatine per ton mined by the Ferreira company in 189 was 1s. 9·35d., or, calculated on the tonnage milled, 2s. 7·63d. With regard to the Railway rates. high railway rates on coal and other materials, which so adversely affect the mining industry in this State, I will avoid, as far as possible, going over ground already traversed by former witnesses, and merely state some of the rates charged by the Madras Railway Company in India. The distance from Madras to the Colar Gold Madras Railway rates for fuel. Fields in Mysore is about 170 miles, and the difference in elevation about 3,000 feet. Coal is carried to the gold fields at the rate of eight pies per long ton per mile, equal to 0·54d. per short ton per mile. Firewood is carried at ½d. per ton per mile, and machinery at 1d. per ton per mile, while for large quantities lower rates could be arranged. If coal were carried over the Netherlands Railway at the rate of 1d per Ferreira and Worcester coal expenses. ton per mile, the saving to the Ferreira and Worcester companies would be £5,70 per annum on the basis of last year's consumption, and if provision were made for delivering coal in bulk without bagging, a further 2s. 6d. per ton could be saved which would reduce the cost of coal delivered to those mines to 13s. 5d. per ton. agree with the statements made by Mr. Goldmann and others in connection with native labour. A native in the employ of a mining company is well fed, and the wage he is paid is almost as much as that of a white labourer in Europe, who has to feed, clothe, and house himself and family. The great difficulty experienced in reducing Reduction of native wages. the native wage, and keeping it down, is the frequent scarcity of native labourers and the high cost of bringing them to the mines. I am of opinion that the Government Government co-operation to supply native labour necessary. could greatly assist the mining industry in reducing the native wages to a normal standard, if it could find means to induce the natives in the North to work in the mines, and would see that the Native Commissioners should not charge mining companies, or their accredited agents, for natives procured from their "districts," by reducing the railway tariff for bringing natives to the mines to a minimum, and by doing all in their power to assist in bringing natives to the mines. A constant and ample supply of native labourers is necessary to fix and adhere to a low standard of native wages. Frequent reductions of pay tend to impair the quality of available native labour—a matter of no small importance to the mines. In affirming Mr. Gold Pass Law. mann's statements in relation to the Pass Law, I would mention that I was a member of the deputation that waited upon the Government in connection with the draft law before it was submitted to the Volksraad. After explaining to the Government the advantage of preventing the desertion of natives from the mines, the deputation stated that they did not propose to ask the Government to provide funds from its revenue for the administration of the Concept Law, but proposed that an extra tax of 1s. per d per month be levied on the natives for that purpose, and thought that the sum raised would be required for its efficient administration, and had inserted a clause the draft Concept Law, providing for the expenditure of the whole of the amount, ound necessary. To this the Government expressed their approval, but the clause erred to does not appear in the Pass Law, and I understand that at present little re than one-sixth of the revenue derived from the extra 1s. tax is expended in the ministration of this law. The Pass Law, if efficiently administered, would save a ge sum of money annually to the mining companies now lost through desertions, at present it not only affords us no protection against desertion, but actually ourages it. As an instance, a native found without a pass in the Johannesburg Maladministra-
tion of Pass
Law. trict is usually fined 60s., while in the Boksburg district the fine for a similar ence is usually 20s., and has been as low as 3d. If I get a fresh supply of natives m the East Coast, at a cost of 60s. per head, of which each native agrees to refund ., they find out within a few days that by deserting to the Boksburg district, and omitting to a fine of 20s. they save 35s., consequently many desert, and my company es the money advanced to bring them to the mine. The following returns from en companies, sent in to the Association of Mine Managers, show the number of serters from each company from the date of the Pass Law coming into operation to e end of March last :—

				Deserters.	
City and Suburban G. M. Co., Ltd.	...	...	...	1,323	Desertion re turns
Worcester Exploration and G. M. Co., Ltd.	...	...	223	
Minerva G. M. Co., Ltd.	...	...	...	116	
New Heriot G. M. Co., Ltd...	...	...	...	703	
French Rand G. M. Co., Ltd.	...	...	...	300	
Crown Reef G. M. Co., Ltd...	...	...	...	1,030	
Ferreira G. M. Co., Ltd.	...	...	...	1,480	
	Total	...	5,175		

These desertions would probably represent a loss to the seven companies of from ,000 to £7,000, as most of the desertions occur shortly after the natives arrive at the nes.

From the beginning of 1896 to the end of last month, the Ferreira company Loss of Ferreira mine through desertions. pended, in bringing natives to the mine, £6,648 9s., of which £3,026 17s. 6d. have en refunded, leaving a balance of £3,621 11s. 6d. not recovered, of which I estimate arly £2,000 is lost through desertions.

Of the 1,480 deserters from the Ferreira mine mentioned above, 19 only were covered; 12 of these were returned by compound managers of other companies, and ven were found by our private police in another company's compound, and were covered through the aid of the Pass Law officials. As administered, the Pass Law o bears heavily upon mining companies situated at a distance from the pass offices. ke the case of the Randfontein companies, who have to send their natives a distance Randfontein companies and Pass Law ad- ministration. about seven miles to Krugersdorp to get district passes and badges before they can ow them to work; and frequently, I am informed, a man with a gang of natives has return without passes or badges, owing to pressure of work in the pass office, and e journey has to be made a second time. This causes some of the natives to desert thout having worked a day for the company, and the cash advanced to bring them the mine is lost. The Association of Mine Managers, has, on several occasions, com- Complaint against Pass Law made by Association of Mine Manag- ers. ained to the chief pass official in Johannesburg and to the Mining Commissioner, rough whose office, I understand, communications from the pass officials have to pass reach the Minister of Mines. On the 10th September last, the Association of Mine

Managers was represented on the deputation that went to Pretoria, to lay
grievances of the industry, relative to this law, before the Minister of Mines and
Government. Not being able to meet the Government that day, and the Minister
Mines being absent, the deputation had an interview with the Assistant Minister

Petition of
Chamber of
Mines, Associa-
tion of Mines,
and Associa-
tion of Mine
Managers re-
garding Pass
Law.
Mines, Mr. Liebenberg, and discussed the matter with him. About the 15th Septem
last, the Chamber of Mines, Association of Mines and the Association of M
Managers, sent in a joint petition to the Government, pointing out the chief defects
the administration of the Pass Law, praying for certain alterations in its administ
tion, and for an increase in the fines imposed on natives found in the labour distri
without pass or badge. So far as I am aware, nothing was granted beyond t
increased fine, and that, which under good administration would have been of gr
assistance to the industry, now frequently operates against it, in encouraging t
desertion of natives as explained above. On 11th December last, the Assista
Minister of Mines, Mr. Liebenberg, came over to Johannesburg to discuss the worki

Further com-
plaints of As-
sociation of
Mine Manag-
ers regarding
administration
of Pass Law.
of the Pass Law with a committee of the Association of Mine Managers, with t
result that another petition to the Government, praying for more efficient administr
tion of this law, was being drafted by the managers, when we heard of the appointme
of this Commission, and the Association decided to wait and lay its grievances befc
you, in the hope that you will see fit to recommend to the Government the advisabili
of granting the wishes of the industry as expressed in the joint petition referred
above, and to see that the chief aim of the administration of the law shall be the p
vention of desertions, as intended by those who framed it. The inefficient administr

Maladministra-
tion of Liquor
Law.
tion of the Liquor Law increases the cost of native labour on the mines, because
have to feed and keep a great many natives that would be unnecessary if they we
unable to procure liquor, and frequently natives are rendered unfit for work throu
the effects of liquor shortly after they go into the mines, and are unable to do anythi
approaching their due amount of work.

The alterations in the Liquor Law, prohibiting the sale of liquor to natives, car
into force on the 1st of January last, and during the month of January comparative
few natives were off work, and but few cases of drunkenness were observable amo
them, but from the end of January the sale of liquor to natives has been on t

Ferreira Com-
pany's employ-
ees and Liquor
Law.
increase. During the month of December last, the average number of the Ferrei
company's native employees off work, chiefly through drunkenness, was 338.
January, when the alterations in the Liquor Law came into force, the number fell to 8
In February the number increased to 126, and in April the average number off wo
was 339, so that, as far as the Ferreira company is concerned, we have as mu
drunkenness among our natives now as prior to the amendment of the law prohibiti

Reduction of
white wages.
the sale of liquor to natives. The question of reducing the wages of white miners
these fields is one that must be approached with a great amount of caution. O
miners are not, for the most part, ordinary labourers, but men who have had mar
years' experience of mining work, the majority of them having gained experience
various countries. These men have mostly been trained to mining work almost fro
childhood, and cannot be replaced by men of little or no experience. With the mine
we endeavour to keep in our mines, it is not a question of drilling a hole and blasti
it, but of supervising the work done by the natives; and the miner who can direct h
holes so as to break the greatest quantity of reef with the least expenditure
explosives, is the least expensive man we can employ. To a layman it would hard

Value of exper-
ienced white
miners.
seem possible that there could be 30 per cent. difference in the amount of work do
by one miner of long experience with a gang of natives, more than by another
equally long experience working as many natives under precisely similar conditio
yet this is often the case, as the Ferreira Company's books will testify.

The conditions prevailing here differ from those of many other countries; the ate force required in mining we endeavour to get from the natives, while we aim to intelligence and energy in our white miners, and if we have to pay a little more it, it is, nevertheless, the cheapest labour we can employ. In 1890, we paid £10 foot for sinking one of the Ferreira shafts, then 200 ft. deep, while to-day we pay 5s. per foot for sinking the same shaft nearly 1,600 ft. deep, which shows the ference in the class of labour we employ to-day, and that we had available in 1890. reduction of 47½ per cent. in the cost of shaft sinking is comparatively an unimrtant item to a producing company—but a matter of vital importance to a deep level mpany, whose work consists chiefly of shaft-sinking, and where speed is the main ject until the reefs are reached and the mine developed sufficiently to supply a stamp ll. The most skilled miners obtainable are requisite for this work, and the extra ges they may make on either the contract or the bonus system, would be more than mpensated by the standing charges of the company if the exploratory work be concted slowly. In my opinion the standard wage paid to the white miners on these lds to-day will not admit of a reduction until the cost of living, house rent, etc., be nsiderably reduced. The acknowledged standard wage of a white labourer all the world er is the amount a man can live upon with a wife and family, and I think but few ners can do that on these fields on £4 10s. per week. The most skilled miners can ways earn more than an ordinary mine labourer if working on contract; and, after arly sixteen years' experience in managing gold mines, I am of the opinion that the ntract system for our mines is the best for securing the most efficient white labour, d keeping the mining expenses low. A more suicidal policy could not be adopted the present juncture than that of attempting to reduce white wages, after aiming r years to secure the most efficient labour, which, although more highly paid, is the ast expensive we can employ. In 1887 an attempt was made, on the Indian gold lds, to reduce working expenses by importing cheap labour, and a considerable mber of Italian mine labourers were brought out at about half the pay of the nglish miners employed. The attempt at reduction proved a failure, because, as in is State, the miners were required to supervise native labour, and it was found that telligence and energy were required, and proved the cheapest at double the price. 'ithin 18 months the low wage men had practically disappeared from the gold fields. we were to reduce white miners' wages under present conditions, we would drive e best miners away from these fields, because skilled miners are in demand in any ining country, and they know it, while we should be taking a step that would land nearer the working costs of 1890 than of the reduction we aim at. White labour nstitutes a very important item of expenditure on our mines, and if through a duction of railway rates, duties on food stuffs, etc., cost of living becomes sufficiently duced to enable our white employees to settle here with their families, much of the oney now being sent to other countries would be spent here. Some time ago I was formed, on reliable authority, that £10,000 per month was being sent from these ines into one mining district in England, to keep the wives and families of our iners. The question naturally arises, how much of the money thus sent out of the ate could be kept here by a liberal policy of the Government, and to what extent ould it affect the prosperity of the State? It has been suggested that if the overnment assist the mining industry by reducing railway rates, cost of dynamite, c., the leading members of the industry must also do something towards reducing penses. I would point out that the labours of the Chamber of Mines, Association Mines, Association of Mine Managers, and the Chemical and Metallurgical Society, ive all along been directed to that end. As an instance of the advance made by the ining industry during the past few years, the Ferreira Company's working expenses

[Marginal notes:]
White wages in contract work in 1890 and in 1897.

White wages not at present reducible.

Contract system in white labour

Failure of reduction of white miners' wages in India.

Results of reduction of white wages.

Cost of living of white miners reducible by Government action.

Reduction of working costs of Ferreira Company since 1892.

per ton mined in 1893 were 15·42 per cent. less than in 1892; in 1894, 15·82 per cent. less than in 1893; in 1895, 20·62 per cent. less than in 1894; and in 1896, 4·43 per cent. less than in 1895—making a total reduction in 1896 on the expenses per ton 1892 of 45·99 per cent. The reduction made is chiefly due to:—

Details of reductions.

(a.) Improved quality of labour.

(b.) Sorting the ore as it comes from the mine, by which means an average 35 per cent. of the rock mined since March, 1893, has been picked out and discarded as valueless, thereby increasing the value of the ore milled by an average of 56·19 per cent., saving the cost of transporting, milling, concentrating, and cyaniding 160,000 tons of waste rock, and increasing the value of the output by over £600,000.

(c.) Expenditure of large sums of money for equipping the mine, with the latest and most improved machinery.

(d.) Improvements in the methods of treating tailings by cyanide, whereby the cost of treating has been reduced from 11s. 1·32d. (exclusive of royalty on the process) in December, 1891, to 2s. 6·15d. in December, 1896.

Reductions in working costs made by mining industry.

These improvements in the working of our mines are due to the combined effort of those on whom the responsibilities of the mining industry have devolved, and should lead this Commission to see that those men have not been idle, that they do not now come to you and ask that the Government should make the first move in bringing about a reduction in working expenditure to enable the majority of mines on the Rand to continue operations, but having done their best in the matter, they feel justified in asking that the Government should do something in fulfilling its obligations to the industry, which is the mainstay of the State, and on which its prosperity chiefly depends.

Chairman.

Maladministration of Pass Law.

You stated in your evidence that the Pass Law, instead of assisting the industry assisted the kaffirs to run away?—Yes, as at present administered. As I pointed out if we pay 60s. per head to bring boys here, and they agree to refund us 55s., they go to Boksburg and pay a fine of 20s. per head, and save 35s. per head.

But a kaffir does not get anything out of that? He only owes 55s., he does not make a direct cash profit, he only gets rid of a debt.—He gets rid of a debt, and we incur a loss. It costs us 60s. to bring the boy, and we reckon that we advance him 55s., which he agrees to repay, but by leaving this district and going to the Boksburg district he gets rid of that liability by paying 20s.; so that after paying 60s. we get no labour out of the boy.

But the fine inflicted on the kaffir is only because he has no pass. But that does not do away with the fact that the boy can be brought back to the place he deserted from.—Yes, but if the Pass Law were properly administered it would prevent desertion.

That is the intention of the Law.—Yes, we don't complain of the Law, we complain of the administration.

The question is this. Suppose your kaffir runs away and is caught at Boksburg by the police, without a pass, the officials there can only punish him for being without a pass. But who is the person to give information to the officials there whose nigger this is they have caught without a pass?—The fact that the officials do not get information shows plainly that the administration is faulty.

If they catch a nigger at Boksburg without a pass they know he is a deserter and fine him, but how are the police to know whose nigger he is?—We give notice

he pass officials in our district when our natives desert. We hand to the pass
ials the district passes of the deserters, which give the general description
ach native, and the number on the badge worn by him. These particulars should
ent to the pass officials of the other districts. The Pass Law, in its operation, is
ded into three districts. If I manage a mine on the border of one district, and *District adminis-*
kaffirs desert and go to the adjoining mine in the other district, the pass officials *tration of Pass*
hat district will not help me to recover my boys. If the Pass Law in these fields *Law.*
in the hands of one administrator he would be able to regulate matters in the
ee districts.

Do I understand that there is a separate chief of the Pass Department for each
rict ?—There is one for each of the three districts.

That is one for Johannesburg, one for Boksburg, and one for Krugersdorp ?—Yes.
e fault that we have to find with the administration of this law is that the fines
not in proportion in the different districts, and that tends more than anything else
ards desertion. In our petition to the Government we asked for a Special Judicial
mmissioner for the three districts, who would regulate the fines so that they should
be more in favour of one district than another.

The fines are all the same, from £1 to £3, and it is in the discretion of the
erent judicial authorities to impose what fine they think fit ?—If we had one
cial Judicial Commissioner for the three districts he would impose the same fine
the same offence.

One of the officials met me and pointed out that when he fined the boys heavily
often happened that they could not pay the fines and had to go to prison. The
nk became full in consequence. These boys were never fetched, so that they could
urn to the mines, but had to remain in the tronk until their time was served, and
n when they came out they had to obtain a working pass. For that reason the
cial imposed lighter fines, so that they could return to the mines.—Yes, that is the
lt of bad administration of the Pass Law. If there were an efficient detective *Inefficiency of*
ff, who did their duty and looked up deserters, there would be no necessity to put *Pass Law offi-*
boys in prison. There is more than enough money provided to properly carry out *cials.*
Pass Law, but the money is lying idle. If it were expended the law could be
ried out.

Then, I understand from you, the law is a good one ?—Yes, I think it is. I do
complain of the law. The law, in itself, is a good one.

You think that more detectives should be appointed ?—Yes, and I think that if
Government appointed one able administrator to carry out the law in connection
h a general committee appointed from men who understand the requirements of
mines, I think the law could be successfully carried out, and would be a blessing
the community.

Mr. de Beer.

How do you arrive at your figures, when you say that you pay £3 per boy to be *Cost of native*
ivered here ?—I have not the figures by me, but I understand they have already *labour supply*
n placed before the Commission. I have paid as much as 70s. to get boys here, the
est figure paid for bringing natives from the East Coast being 57s. 6d. The East
ast natives make the best mine boys, as they stay longer, and get to do better
rk, and it is the better quality of labour that pays us best. *Remuneration*
                                                              demanded by
You say that the Native Commissioners charge for the natives in their districts. *Native Com-*
m which direction do these natives come which cost 60s. ?—From the East Coast. *missioners for*
                                                                               supply of na-
                                                                               tives.

The boys the Ferreira Company have had to pay for came from the north of Transvaal.

How much per head does the Native Commissioner charge?—Well, I will tell you what I know about it. Men were sent up to get natives, and I communicated with them. They informed me that they had to pay 10s. per head for every boy they got from the Native Commissioners. At any rate, the company had to pay that amount. I believe my agents, especially one I sent up as a test, but I cannot prove that it was the case. I only tell you that the company had to pay the money for every boy that got down.

Personally, you don't know?—No, I could not swear it is the case.

Reduction of
cost of explos-
ives. About explosives. Is it not too much to propose a reduction of 50s. per case? I was even then allowing the Government twice as much as they get now.

How do you bring it out you want to reduce the price of blasting gelatine 50s.?—I said that if it were reduced by 50s. we should save that much money.

But you proposed it as a feasible thing?—Yes.

What is the cost price here?—£5 7s. 6d.

What can it be landed for here?—I cannot give you the exact figures, but it has already been put before the Commission.

But no one has even yet proposed a reduction of 50s. per case?—Well, I cannot give you the exact cost of manufacturing it; still, judging from other countries and the price they pay, I think it could be delivered to us for that price, and a good profit made.

Gold thefts. Can you suggest any remedy against illicit gold buying?—Yes.

What percentage of amalgam is stolen, do you think?—That I could not say.

Can you suggest a remedy?—Well, I think an efficient detective department would greatly reduce the amount stolen.

Reduction of
working costs. In your statement you say that the working costs showed a reduction of 46 per cent. between 1892 and 1896. I must take it that the industry is working under far more favourable conditions. How do you account for the depression with the improvements for working under better conditions?—In 1892 there were not so many low-grade mines at work, and only the richer mines could pay at the high cost of working at that time.

Sorting. Is sorting in general use now?—It is becoming general.

That also improves the position 20 per cent. or 30 per cent?—No. I think the percentage sorted out by dividend-paying companies was given by Mr. Jennings yesterday as 6 per cent., whereas we have sorted out an average of 35 per cent. since 1892. I was the first to start systematic sorting on the fields, and have probably worked at it closer than they have done in any of the other mines.

Mr. *Smit.*

Remuneration
demanded by
Native Com-
missioners for
supply of na-
tives. You have got no other proof that the native commissioners take payment for boys except the statements of agents?—No, but many agents have been sent up to the various mining companies, and have made similar statements.

They never mentioned the names of those commissioners to you?—Not that I am aware of. I don't remember their doing so. Many other managers have told me they also have had to pay.

It is stated by the companies that money is spent in that way, but don't you require a receipt or some proof that the money is expended, for it is possible that the money may remain hanging somewhere on the road?—It is possible, but not probable. Many managers, I understand, have sent up special agents, and these agents have come back with the information that it was necessary to pay this money.

Do you think that gold thefts could be prevented by a better staff of detectives?— Gold thefts.
obably by a greater number of detectives, provided they are honest.   If you get
nest detectives, then I believe that the illicit traffic could be stopped to a very
eat extent.

You think that the detectives would be able to find it out after the occurrence,
t as a preventive measure, the managers should try to stop the thefts themselves.
u know you cannot expect the Government to place detectives on the mines to
tch them.   These precautions should be taken on the mines?—They are to a great
tent.   We do all we can, in the first place, by getting the best men we can.   We
t men of fairly good standing, who, we think, would be ashamed to do wrong.   I
ll give you an instance.   On the Ferreira, the mill manager is a Colonial Dutch-
n.   I suppose one-third of the men are Colonials, whose families are of good
nding at the Cape.   We have one or two Americans, one or two Englishmen, one
two Irishmen, and one or two Scotchmen.   We mix them up as much as we can
prevent, as far as possible, any collusion between them.

By whom are those thefts committed—by men on the mines or by outsiders?—
hink it is done, when it is done, by the amalgamators, because the amalgamators
e the only ones who could handle the amalgam.

Mr. *Hugo.*

I understand you to say that dynamite costs £5 7s. 6d. per case?—Gelatine (we Cost of gelatine.
n't use dynamite), plus 2s. carriage, costs £5 9s. 6d.

You suggest that it should be reduced by 50s. per case?—I don't make it as a
ggestion.   I thought the suggestion had already been made.   I simply take the 50s.
a basis for calculation.

Still, you seem to arrive at 50s. as a reasonable reduction?—Without being able
give you the details of the cost, I think, judging by prices in other countries, it
uld be delivered to us at that price.

Then you say that if this reduction were effected, the Government would still
ake a greater profit than they do now?—Yes, if, as I understand, the Government
ly gets 5s. per case now.

How do you arrive at this estimate that there would be so much profit to the
overnment?   At what price could gelatine be delivered here?   I suppose you
fer to the imported stuff?—Certainly.   I don't think that anyone would argue that
could be made here as cheaply as it could be imported.   Blasting gelatine now costs
£5 7s. 6d. per case.   If this could be reduced by 50s. per case, and another 10s. be
ken off for the Government, this would reduce the amount to 47s. 6d. per case, or
s. more than the price for which it has been stated dynamite can be delivered here,
d I think we would be able to get gelatine at that price.

MR. JOSEPH BENJAMIN ROBINSON was the next witness called, and said he had Mr. J. B. Robin-
been in Johannesburg ever since it was of any account. son's evidence.

He then made the following statement:—I wish to say that the gold industry
ay well be congratulated on the fact that the Government have appointed a
ommission for the purpose of investigating matters connected with both the mining Industrial Com-
d commercial enterprises which have done so much to build up the prosperity of mission of En
is State.   It is also a matter for congratulation that the Commission has gone so quiry.
lly into the various questions brought to their notice, and is exercising such patience
their enquiries into all those reforms which are so necessary to advance the interests
the South African Republic.   I am sure the Commission will realise that whilst the

Q

present misunderstanding exists on the gold industry, there will always be more
less a severe tension in the financial position of the State; and the Commission w
also no doubt consider well the circumstance that, whilst the Government and t
industry are not acting in conjunction, the prosperity of the State must be retarde
and every individual inhabitant of the country must, to a certain extent, suffer fro
this want of harmony. I am, therefore, very pleased to see that the Commission h
shown so keen an insight into the important matters to which their attention has bee
directed, and have, in a calm, impartial and judicial manner enquired into the wan
of the community. May I add that everyone who is carefully following the
proceedings from day to day feels gratified that there is evidently a determination c
the part of the Commission to do their utmost to bring about a better state
feeling, and a strong and permanent unity of the various interests concerne
in the prosperity of this Republic. The questions which are now before th
Commission have been fully enquired into, and a great deal of evidence has bee
given to show where the pressure comes from which is so seriously interferin
with the proper working of the mines, and is exercising such a baneful influenc
not only upon the community of the goldfields, but throughout the whol
State. The first matter to which I wish to refer is the railway. On this subjec
the Commission has elicited evidence which proves conclusively that the tari
is far too high, and that this high tariff is really injuring the welfare of th

Excessive Railway rates. State. Figures have been adduced by different witnesses to show that the existin
tariff is abnormally high, and that the oppressive rates which are being paid upon a
goods imported into this country, as well as the excessive coal rate, constitute a grea
injury to the gold industry. What we seriously want to arrive at is the exact amoun
to which we can reduce the working cost per ton of ore taken from this or that min
I have gone into figures, and I consider that if we can reduce the cost of each ton o

Five shillings per ton reduction in working costs required. ore by 5s., that will place the whole industry on a sound basis, and will remove th
disabilities under which the poorer mines labour at the present moment. I ma
mention that we are crushing in the aggregate at the rate of about five million tons o
ore per annum. If, therefore, a reduction in working cost of 5s. could be effected, i
would leave a profit of £1,250,000 over and above the results which are now obtaine
in milling the above quantity of ore.

Reduction of railway rates on coal.   It is, in my opinion, absolutely necessary that the coal tariff should be reduced
so that the companies would be able to effect a saving of 1s. on every ton of or
crushed at the present time. The mileage is 3d. per ton, the company is put to
further expense of 3s. a ton for bagging, and Langlaagte Estate, over and above thes
items, has to pay 3s. per ton for cartage from Johannesburg Station to its works. W
have repeatedly applied for a siding, but have not succeeded in getting one. Th
railway trucks stop at a platform, but only allow twenty minutes to off-load from 10(
to 150 tons of coal. For this purpose we require 150 natives, and they have bee
kept waiting on some occasions for a period of four hours, through the irregula
arrival of coal trains. This entails a very serious loss on the company, which is nov
compelled to cart the coal from Johannesburg Station at 3s. per ton to ensure regula
delivery. The south railway line, now under contemplation, would do away with thi
additional expense, but the coal tariff would have to be reduced to meet the require
ments of cheaper mining.

    I am now only dealing with the railways as belonging to a public company, i
which, of course, the Government of the country holds a certain interest. But I shoul
at the same time, prefer to view this matter in a far more comprehensive manner, an
Expropriation of railway. to state exactly the opinion as to the railways if owned by the Government of th
South African Republic. There is no doubt that the railway, if expropriated, woul

)me an asset of enormous value to the State; it would be the means of relieving
only the industry, but also all other interests surrounding that industry; it would
be the means of relieving the burdens now pressing so heavily upon the welfare
he country, and would bring back that prosperous condition of affairs which was
)yed by this State for a considerable period. In the hands of the Government the
way would be an important factor. In some countries railways are built and
ntained for the purpose of opening up these territories. They are run for
dreds and thousands of miles, and people as a rule follow the railway. They
chase and occupy land, and thus the territory traversed by the railway becomes
ductive, and eventually yields a large revenue. The railways of the South African
ublic, however, are not run upon those lines. The tariff is fixed at a very high
, and the outcome of that high tariff means a most disastrous hindrance to the
per development of the country. Whilst the railway is in the hands of a purely
mercial company, it stands to reason that their sole aim and object is to regard it
the light of a dividend-yielding enterprise which could be turned to the best
sible advantage to shareholders. In the hands of the Government far higher and
ater considerations would be the lever which should guide the Government in
ulating the tariff so as to make the railway a benefit to the whole State. It is a
taken policy to keep the tariff at a rate which not only prevents the mines working
profit, but also injures the whole trade of the country. By means of a cheap
way tariff we could bring about an expansion of trade, and whatever revenue
ht be lost in the first instance by reducing the tariff, would be more than com-
sated for by the facilities granted to every branch of enterprise, and the increase
rade which would follow the reduction in the railway rate.

I notice that a question was put to some of the witnesses as to whether there *Loan for railway expropriation offered.*
ld be any difficulty in the Government being able to borrow the money required
the expropriation of the railways at a low rate of interest. I may mention that
e eight months ago, when it was clearly foreseen that there would be difficulties to
ow a high tariff, a cable was despatched from London by a syndicate to the
ernment offering the requisite sum for the expropriation of the railways.

This offer on the part of the syndicate was made because they fully realised the
)ortance of the Government acquiring the railway, and I feel certain that if the
. the Volksraad decide during this session to take over the various lines, it would
e great satisfaction not only to the people of this country but to every person in
rope having an interest in the Republic. I can also assure the Commission that,
ler these circumstances, the money would be forthcoming at a very low rate of
erest. I need hardly say that the effect of so wise a measure would be such that it *Effects of railway expropriation.*
ld place the financial position of the Republic on a most solid and favourable
ting. It would be the means of restoring confidence in this country throughout
whole world. It would have a most marvellous effect upon the trade of the
ntry, as well as upon the mining industry. It would bring about a revulsion of
ling in favour of this Republic which would be far-reaching in its effects, not only
mercially and industrially, but politically as well. I know, of course, that the
ernment will have to give one year's notice, in accordance with the terms of the
way concession, but as long as that notice is given it would be sufficient to make
public understand that the Government really intended to expropriate, and we
uld, of course, expect that the Government would exercise its power to afford relief
the substantial reduction of the general tariff during the year's notice.

I now come to the question of dynamite. I think, gentlemen, you must be aware *The dynamite concession.*
t the Dynamite Concession has proved a great irritant from the very day it was
nted by the Government. I do not myself believe that the Government fully

realised the danger connected with the granting of such a concession, or the
advantages it was calculated to impose upon the profitable working of the mi
When the concession was first granted I publicly addressed the mining industry
the subject, and I distinctly remember pointing out the evils that would follow a c
cession of such a nature. What I then said has been fulfilled to the very letter, ane
long as this concession remains it will continue to be a cause of dissatisfaction to
mining community. To all business men it is incomprehensible that a burden of
nature should be placed upon the mines; that a company should have the right
send dynamite to this country at a fixed price; that we should be forced to take i
that price when dynamite is offered to us at a far lower rate; and when it has becc
absolutely necessary that every nerve should be strained to make the industry pro
able, and to keep the mines in working order. The concessionaires have not fulfi
their conditions; they have not built a factory, and although they have had 2½ ye

Excessive cost of dynamite. extended to them, still that factory will not be built. We are, therefore, forced to ;
£2 5s. per case more for dynamite than what we could purchase it for from ot
sources. What makes the matter more unintelligible is the fact that out of this hea
pecuniary burden which we have to endure, the Government only derive a profit of
a case, and the rest goes into the pockets of the concessionaires, which they cc
placently appropriate, whilst we are slaving to overcome the formidable difficult
which present themselves in all our mining operations. Dynamite, as you are awa
is one of the most requisite, as well as one of the most expensive items in mini
The figures which have been submitted to you show that its proportion of the cost
working the mines is 2s. 11d. per ton. You will fully understand, therefore, that
we could have our dynamite at 45s. a case we would save 1s. 4d. per ton. T
amount, in addition to the 1s. per ton on coal, comes to 2s. 4d. per ton of ore crush

General reduction of railway rates required. There should also be a general reduction of the railway tariff, so as to enable
mining material, merchandise, and stores to be brought to Johannesburg at less c
and thus bring down the cost of living.

Reduction of taxation. I think you must be convinced by this time that every effort should be made
the Legislature of the country to reduce taxation in every direction for the purpose
keeping the mines in full operation. The mining industry, as you are aware, is
backbone of the whole financial fabric of the South African Republic. In discussi
this matter with certain interested parties at Pretoria, I reminded them that
taxation of this country was like a horizontal weight representing five millic
sterling of revenue which the Government were receiving by taxation of the mini
industry and commercial undertakings, as well as all surrounding interests. I deme
strated that that weight of five millions was held up by a certain number of pilla
each of these pillars being a gold mine. Many of these pillars were giving way,
mines were shutting down, and the whole superstructure was weakening. I poin
out that the remaining pillars would not be strong enough to carry that weight
five millions, and the result would be that the whole fabric would topple over, w
terrible financial disaster to the entire State.

Mines must all be kept working I cannot too strongly impress upon you how imperative it is that we sho
endeavour to keep all the mines at work. By doing so we shall retain in this coun
a large population, whose wants must be satisfied. Trade developments must inev
ably follow, and thus there will be brought into circulation enormous sums of mon
The revenue of the country will thereby be augmented, and every burgher of
State will participate in the advantages which will accrue from the increased circu
tion of cash. From the calculation which I have made, I consider that if we succe
in reducing the cost of working by 5s. per ton, there will be very few mines inde
which will not resume operations, and although some of them may still sh

ly a slight profit under this reduction, yet there is no mine that would shut down long as a profit was made. It is only when the revenue falls below the expenditure at mines are compelled by force of circumstances to stop operations. But you must member that even those mines working at a cost of from £6,000 to £10,000 per nth spend the greater portion of that sum in wages, which is again circulated roughout the country. Another large proportion is expended in stores and other quisites for mining, which are supplied by the commercial element in the State. erefore the expenditure of money leads to a further inflow of capital, all of which ds to promote other industries and enterprises, which acts in promoting the welfare the country, and the Government itself derives therefrom a very large revenue.

Now, in connection with the railways, I have shown that a reduction in the rail-y tariff should be made on coal. Therefore, if the general reduction were made, en the tariff for machinery and stores would also cost the companies less, and this uld add a further reduction to the cost per ton. I have shown you what I think is fair the mining industry, and what we consider we can reasonably ask the Legislature do for us; but I may mention now that, while I consider it absolutely necessary to cure the reduction of 5s. per ton, which I have referred to, yet the mining community emselves should co-operate in bringing down the costs in working by reducing penditure. Co-operation of mining indus-try in reducing working costs necessary.

Now, gentlemen, with regard to the liquor question. The law which the Volks- Liquor Law. ad passed during the last session is as nearly as possible perfect, but I have to mplain greatly of the manner in which the law is administered. Many of my Maladministra-tion of Liquor Law. mpanies have suffered greatly through the illicit and unrestrained supply of strong ink to natives, and I hold in my hand correspondence which has passed between my-lf and the Government on this matter. I have also here copies of affidavits made by y managers showing conclusively the drawbacks we have to encounter in consequence the manner in which the Liquor Law is set at defiance. The beneficial effects of the w, as it was first promulgated, cannot be overrated, but, as the administration becomes x, the sale of liquor increases, and the evil effects are immediately felt by the industry. his is a matter of most serious moment, and the documents which I now submit will able you to realise the loss which the companies must sustain under the circumstances.

The Pass Law is another subject which I consider it my duty to bring before your Pass Law. tice, as requiring immediate attention. The provisions of this law are not observed, and many instances the companies have been placed in very difficult circumstances on count of the faulty administration of this law. I may mention an instance that Maladministra-tion of Pass Law. curred the other day on the Langlaagte Estate. No less than 270 natives packed up eir goods and chattels one morning and said they were leaving for home. The mpound manager told them that their period of service had not expired, and they uld not leave. However, they went off, and they were followed. Some police were et by the officials of the company, but they were too few to take so large a gang of tives in charge; but the boys were persuaded to go to the Charge Office, when a arge of desertion was lodged against them. While this was being done, the com-und manager states that one of the pass officers said the boys could not be charged, d it would cost the companies £5 a head for having taken such measures. The sult was that we lost three days' work of these boys, as well as the services of e company's officials for the same period, owing to their having to wait about the ourt to give their evidence. The case was decided in favour of the Langlaagte ompany, but at the same time a serious loss was sustained, especially as it must be rne in mind, that mining and milling operations should be carried on with regularity d without stoppages. It is such occurrences as these which cause not only annoy-ce but heavy loss to the industry. It is therefore a matter for the consideration of

this Commission, as to whether prompt steps should not be taken to place the administr
tion of the Pass Law on a proper footing. I may mention also that, out of the bo

Desertions at the Langlaagte Estate.
engaged at the Langlaagte Estate since the Pass Law has been in operation, a lar
number of desertions have taken place, of which large number not one boy has be

Losses to Langlaagte Estate G. M. Co. through desertions.
recovered. It has cost the Langlaagte Company, since the law was promulgate
£11,839, boys costing 55s. to 65s. each, out of which the company had to recover
from each boy for railway fare, but on account of the numerous desertions, on
£517 has been recovered, instead of about £4,000, leaving an absolute loss of abo
£3,500 on the railway fare alone to bring these boys here. You will thus reali
the enormous amount of money all the companies must expend in bringing labour
the mines; and you will further realise what a serious loss it is to the companies whe
boys can desert with impunity, after their employers have expended such enormo
sums to bring them from great distances to work here.

Gold thefts.
The gold thefts' question is also one of great importance, and should certainly
dealt with by the Legislature during the present session. I would suggest that a Prote

Protection board to prevent gold thefts.
tion Board be appointed, consisting of five members, some of whom should be Gover
ment nominees, and the others members of the mining industry. This board wou
adopt somewhat the same system as is adopted by the Diamond Protection Board
Griqualand West. From its members the detective department would receive ever
assistance and advice in carrying on their work; and the mining companies would al
be in a position to engage directly with the Board on any matter connected with go
thefts or suspicious characters. If this Board were properly constituted, it would be
great assistance in tracing stolen amalgam, and in suggesting methods to the detectiv
department for carrying out a proper system of prevention and detection of theft.
feel sure if this board were established we should be able to put a stop to a great de
of the stealing of amalgam and gold.

Customs dues.
In considering the reduction of the railway tariff, and also the extreme advisabilit
of dealing with the dynamite concession, I would like to mention that it is al

Customs abatements necessary.
necessary to consider the whole incidence of taxation. Customs duties should, there
fore, receive close attention, and abatements made without delay. What should
urgently remembered at the present moment is that the cost of living should
reduced as much as possible. A very large amount of money is absorbed in the pa
ment of wages, which is one of the largest items that has to be met by companies.
need not enlarge upon this matter, because I feel sure that the intelligence of th
Commission will enable the members clearly to see the bearing it has on the work
the mines, and I am equally convinced that they will do their utmost to cheapen th
cost of living, so as to secure the objects to which I have referred.

In conclusion, I would like to say that, as the Commission has been appointe
to enquire into the grievances of the Witwatersrand community, and also to mak
suggestions as to how reforms can best be brought about, I would take the liberty
referring to what I consider a very essential element in the establishment of a bett
state of feeling, and in relieving the unrest which is doing so much harm not only
this Republic but throughout the whole of South Africa. I venture to touch on th
subject because I know that during the four months I have been here it has been
most important factor in keeping that unrest alive, and in stirring up the objectionab
racial feeling which is working so much evil in our midst. It is my earnest desire
enlist the sympathy and gain the assistance of the Commission in carrying out th

Closer union between Government, Legislature and inhabitants of Rand required
views which I beg to lay before you. What I wish to impress upon the Commissio
is that we should do something to bring the Government, the Legislature, and th
people of this country into closer and more harmonious contact. I may mention tha
I have already expressed a desire to His Honour the President, that he, as well

bers of the Executive, should visit Johannesburg with the object of meeting the
le and establishing a more friendly feeling between the different races. The com-
ity of the Witwatersrand numbers about 120,000 people, who, therefore, form a
important element in the population of this country, and it is my heartfelt desire
; the Commission should use its influence with His Honour the President, members
he Executive and the Legislature to visit the goldfields, so that the mining
munity may have an opportunity of illustrating to the Government the actual
tion of affairs. I feel confident that unless we destroy the barriers which have
e or less separated the people from the Government, a feeling of unrest and dis-
tent will continue, and will keep alive an undesirable agitation, not only in the
ublic, but in the whole of South Africa as well as in Europe. I may say that Discontent of
watersrand is the defective spot, and from this spot all the discontent radiates, Witwatersrand
ers in strength, and brings about those strained relations which are retarding the
gress of the the whole country. Apart, therefore, from the practical good results
ch we expect to obtain from the investigations now being made by the Commission,
anticipate that their power and good services could not be utilised in a nobler work
a the bringing about a feeling of friendship and unity between the Government and
se that are governed. I am sure that the people on the Rand would be glad to meet
Honour and the Executive, and members of the Legislature, and so establish a bond
h the object of working together in harmony for the good of the State; the feeling
disquietude would die away, and we should find every section of the population
ving their utmost to advance the prosperity of the country. The good effect would
be confined to the Transvaal, but would extend throughout South Africa. It would
eed be a most pleasing result to investors in Europe if confidence could again be
ored, and there could be brought back to this country a permanent peace, with all
attendant blessings. I may refer to the monster petition which has only quite
ntly been brought out, but which has already been very numerously signed. The
ratories are most sincere in their desire to create unity and work hand in hand with
Government, the great aim and object of all right-thinking men being to foster and
elop the great resources of the South African Republic.

Mr. *de Beer.*

You have mentioned that in the beginning of this year a syndicate approached Loan offered for
Government for the purpose of advancing the necessary money for expropriating railway expro-
railway ?—Yes.   priation.
At what rate of interest ?—It was about eight months ago, and I cannot for the
nent give you the exact rate of interest which was intimated to the Government.
ink the chairman of the Commission will bear me out in my statement, because it
; submitted to the Executive.
You say it is not likely that the dynamite factory will be built.   What reason Dynamite fac-
e you for saying so ?—I mean it will not be built within the time.   tory.
When you refer to dynamite here, what class do you refer to—the usual No. 1 Dynamite.
idard ?—Yes, of the same character and strength as is in use now.
Is that number the standard ?—Yes; equal in strength to what we get now.
Are you of opinion that if the working costs are reduced by 5s. per ton most of Effect of five
mines would start working again ?—Yes.   shillings re-
                                                                                  duction in
With a profit ?—Yes, with a profit.   working costs
Do you know any other open reefs that have not been worked which could be   of mines.
ked if working costs were reduced by 5s. per ton ?—You mean reef that has not
a touched. I cannot remember for the moment if there is any such ground, but
es which are now shut down would be re-opened.

Past reduction of
working costs.
We have been told by a previous witness that the labour question has been v
much improved within the last few years. Mr. Johns, the chairman of the Asso
tion of Mine Managers, and who is a man of great experience in the gold-fields h
has declared that his working expenses in the mine are now 46 per cent. less than
1892 ?—I am not quite sure about that.

Improved work-
ing conditions
In any case you will admit that the conditions are now better and more favo
able than formerly for working expenses ?—Yes, as far as machinery is concern
but our labour is still a very serious item indeed.

Here we have got the evidence of a practical miner, who says that the labou
four years ago has now reached a higher degree of efficiency, and that they can w
so much cheaper now than then ?—In what respect ?

That is what I wish to elicit from you ?—We may have more skilled labo
But in what respect is the question put ? Does it refer to skilled labour or exper
ture. If it is to skilled labour it is better.

Can you not admit that the condition under which the work is now done
better than within the last two years ?—Well, I can't say that so far as my compan
are concerned.

For instance, machinery has reached a higher degree of perfection, and is m
efficient ?—Yes, there have been improvements in machinery.

Labour of all kinds is very easily procurable ?—Yes.

Now that labour forms about 50 per cent. of the average working expenses
the mines, and that machinery has reduced the cost of labour, and also that co
panies have taken to sorting ore, don't you think, taking all these circumstan
into consideration, that the conditions are better than they were three years ago
With some mines, yes. Sorting is a good principle on some mines, but on the La
laagte it is not so.

Reason for pres-
ent depression
To what do you ascribe the alleged depression ?—Do you mean as rega
shutting down ?

No. To what do you ascribe the present depression ?—To the cost of worki
and, unless we can reduce the expenditure, many of these mines that have shut do
will remain shut down, but others will shut down. That is why I have said in t
statement before you, that we must reduce the costs of working by 5s. per ton. St
the companies must also do their share to bring down the costs of working to 5s.
ton. If we can get that, many of the companies that are working now, and perh
just keeping a balance with regard to revenue and expenditure, will be able to ma
a slight profit. If these companies continue their operations, others that have b
shut down will, when the working cost is reduced by 5s. per ton, come into operati
again.

Those same conditions prevailed three years ago, yet there was no depression
You must remember that mining is deeper now, and of course the cost of worki
increases as you go down. Our labour question was not such a serious one in th
days, and I think labour is much higher than three years ago.

Is it not really the cause of the closing down of some mines that they have co
to the end of their tether, so far as money is concerned, that they have got no furth
capital ?—Of course, many mines have been re-constructed. Unless we reduce
cost of working, some more mines will shut down.

Mr. *Smit.*

There are no other reasons for the expropriation than those already stated
you ?—The general burden of expenditure.

How many companies have you floated here on the gold fields ?—Langlaagte Mr. Robinson's
flotations. state, that is the only one of the companies that I floated myself. When I speak of e Langlaagte, I mean Robinson and Langlaagte, in conjunction with the Rand- ntein Estate.

Do any companies which you floated not pay, or have they been shut down ?— e Langlaagte mine will by no means be shut down, and I am making myself great orts to reduce expenditure. I am talking of Randfontein and also Block B at esent.

Of your companies none have been shut down ?—No, none have been shut down, ith the exception of one company on Randfontein. On account of the drinking of ffirs we have been obliged to shut down. It will be re-opened.

Are there any grounds you originally floated into a syndicate or company not veloped yet—lying unprospected ?—No. There are some grounds prospected and ady for flotation.

The Robinson mine has a capital of $2\frac{3}{4}$ millions ?—$3\frac{3}{4}$ millions. The Robinson
mine.

The property of the Robinson Company simply consists of mining claims ?—I ve no further interest in the Robinson Company.

You are aware that some mines have closed down on the Rand on account of the pression ?—Yes.

How do you account for it that some of the mines have closed down and ex- Increased out-
put. nses are exorbitant, and still the output for the last two months has been fairly ogressive—better than ever before ?—The mines that are productive, and in active orking, have, in some instances, increased their machinery, and some new mines ve also been opened.

Mr. *Joubert.*

Mr. Joubert remarked that Mr. Robinson had given important evidence in regard a great number of points, and he would like to have an opportunity of considering e evidence and asking questions afterwards.

Mr. *Hugo.*

Do you think if the reductions now asked for are brought about, the influx of Results of reduc-
tion of work-
ing costs. pital will come again, which is checked now for the present ?—Yes, certainly.

If there is 5s. per ton reduction ?—It will restore confidence over the whole orld, and will make a marvellous change in this country.

You say Government can borrow money at a low rate of interest to expropriate Loan for railway
expropriation. e railway. What do you think it could be borrowed at now ?—That is a question e cannot very well answer here ; but I am sure, more especially if it is known that e Government wanted to take over the railway, they could get it at a very low rate interest.

You think this reduction of 5s. per ton will enable low-grade mines to be worked Effect of five
shillings per
ton reduction
in working
costs : yably ?—The majority, I don't say all, would be able to work. A great many uld work with 5s. reduction per ton of ore. To give you an instance. Langlaagte sts 17s. 3d. per ton. That includes milling, mining, and all office expenditure.

Is it working at that now ?—It is working at that now. If we get 5s. per ton on Langlaagte
Estate ; duction it would make it 12s. per ton.

But that would be exceptional ?—Well, Block B Langlaagte works at 20s. per ton on Block B
Langlaagte. l told. If we could bring it down by 5s., to 15s., it would be a very valuable operty. That applies to other companies on the Rand. I reckon, if the Govern- ent give 3s. out of the 5s., the companies ought to find the other 2s.

Method of making a five shillings reduction in working costs.

Other witnesses have stated they would be satisfied if the Government could onl
bring about a reduction of about 2s. per ton ?—Yes; of course one must accept th
statements made. I have gone into calculations very carefully, and if we could ge
coal and dynamite brought down 3s., and the companies also reduced the expenses 2.
—they might reduce 2s. 3d.—there is no doubt that between both the companies an
the Government a reduction of 5s. could be made. I adhere to my statement that tha
reduction would bring about a marvellous change in this country, confidence woul
come back in great force, there would be a great inflow of capital, and all th
depression we now see would be swept away. I consider greater prosperity woul
come back to the State than ever we had before.

Chairman.

Reasons for expropriation of railway.

I see you urge the expropriation of the railway, but it is quite possible to get th
company to make the necessary reductions without expropriation, and then you coul
have nothing to complain of—would not that be equally beneficial ?—If you will jus
follow me I will explain why I suggest expropriation. I consider the company in th
hands of the Government would be a very valuable asset; not only a valuable asset
but it would give a marvellous standing to the whole position of the State.

Supposing the Government expropriated, would the mere fact of expropriation
without going into the question of reducing the rates, materially influence matters a

Effect of expropriation of railway.

regards the outside world ?—Certainly, of course, one would naturally expect if th
railway were in the hands of the Government, the Government would then have th
power to regulate the traffic to meet the requirements of the industry.

Of course the tariff would have to be regulated according to revenue and expendi
ture, and taking also into consideration the prime cost to the Government ?—Th
railway, of course, in the hands of the Government, would be a powerful lever to brin
about great changes in this country; it would have a very far-reaching effect, an
would have a marvellous effect on the prosperity of the country. I look upon the railway as the moving lever to the whole prosperity of the State.

Formerly the Cape Colony had a railway, and that railway could not have made
the Cape Colony what it is to-day but for the transit carriage to the Transvaal.—Exactly,
and that is why I want the Government to have equal advantages with the adjoining
States, and then they could get the reduction on the Cape lines and Natal lines. The
enormous dividend which the Cape line has made is mostly on account of the great
traffic to this Republic.

Of course the question of expropriation is not a matter that falls within the
province of this Commission; that will be dealt with by the Government.—Of course,
I am only putting facts before the Commission.

Importance of expropriation of railway.

We must simply confine ourselves to the point of the reduction of taxes; that is
the point that comes within the province of this Commission; and to see whether the
Government can get for the companies such reductions in tariffs as will meet their
requirements; and then, if that can be done, and if the Government can agree with the
Railway Company to give the gold mining companies such reductions as they require
the expropriation of railways won't matter so much.—I take a more comprehensive
view. If you were to expropriate the railway, the Government could obtain such
reduction, that it stands to reason that it would be of great advantage to the industry
and the whole State.

Price of dynamite.

As regards dynamite—other witnesses have complained about the expense of
dynamite, and I will take it for granted that dynamite can be delivered here cheaper
but no proof has been submitted to the Commission to show that, supposing the concession were cancelled to-day, the industry would be enabled to get dynamite landed her

per.—There is proof, Mr. Chairman, that we were offered dynamite at a very much
rate than what we are paying.

That has been stated, but I would like proof positive of it.—Has not that been
ed before the Commission?

No.—The question has not been put before us in that form. All we know is that
were offered dynamite at a certain price which is considerably less than what we
for it.

It would be very important if the Commission could obtain proof on that point
ore the close of the evidence.—That we would be able to obtain dynamite cheaper
he event of this concession being cancelled?

Not that; that you get a firm offering to deliver dynamite cheaper in Johannes-
g. The Commission would like you to submit a proposal for a draft contract, made
some responsible contractor, by which he agrees to deliver to the industry a given
ntity at a certain price.—I suppose that can be done.

You say in your evidence that confidence has been shaken, and that it will be more
less restored if the President, and Executive, and Members of the Raad were to pay a
t to Johannesburg. I want to know do you mean that confidence has been shaken
account of his absence?—More or less, since the unfortunate occurrences that took
ce here. I think myself, if the President and Members of the Raad, now, whilst
y are in session, were induced to come over here and meet the people here, and the
sident was to address them publicly, as the head of the State, and exchange senti-
nts with them, it would have a very good effect. We want to see the head of the
vernment here.

Lack of confi
dence between
Government
and mining in-
dustry —
means of re-
storing this.

That is not yet proof to me that confidence in the gold fields has been shaken
ause the President has not been here.—I am not speaking of any proof. I say, if
1 want to bring about confidence, there must be a certain unanimity. There is a
tain feeling which is known throughout the world to exist, and that feeling must be
ed down; and if the President was to come here and address the people it would
ve a marvellous effect in restoring confidence. I suggest that the Commission should
their kindly offices to bring that about.

You will agree with me that after the unfortunate occurrences you refer to, the
vernment, even more than before, were always ready to meet the industry where
sible?—But the world does not know that.

It is quite enough as long as the gold fields know it and find it out.—That could
demonstrated by the action of the President mingling with the people and talking
hem.

I know that the President would not be unwilling to come here, but you must
ee with me that things have happened here formerly which would keep the
sident away. I do not know that from this side proof has been given that he
ght not have the same experience again.—No, I am sure he won't.

You are convinced. You can hardly be sure?—As far as I know, from those I
ve spoken to, I am sure of it.

Witness said he would like to say that, when that morning he had been asked
ich of the mines he was connected with were closed down he had mentioned one,
also the Langlaagte Star was closed down for the purposes of development.

Langlaagte Star
mine.

You stated this morning that if the railway rates are lowered, the price of
namite lowered, import duties lowered, a general reduction in the cost of everything
l take place; you even went so far as to say that you thought expropriation of the
way was necessary, and that then the railway will truly be a benefit to the public.
er witnesses have stated other burdens which are pressing on the mines, and other
es which might be reduced. How do you propose to remedy the loss in revenue

which will ensue if these reductions should be made?—In the first place, I sugge
that the Government, as far as public works are concerned, should raise a loan, a
that would relieve the revenue considerably. At the present moment we are payi
for all these public works out of the revenue of the country, and I dare say the Co
mission are well aware that if the Government would take up a loan to deal wi
public works, the expenditure would be considerably lightened—we would be in a f
better position. Apart from that consideration, I maintain that if the mines could
kept in working order, as set forth in the statement which I placed before you th
morning, there would be a very great expansion of trade, and you would find that t
revenue of the country would increase in proportion.

Admitting that if the Government were to undertake any important public pe
manent works money should be borrowed, how about general management a
administration. I will make it plainer. The main object of getting a reduction
everything is to make payable these mines which at present do not pay or hardl
pay ; as against that there are mines which, under present conditions, pay han
somely, and yield very large dividends—say the Ferreira, which pays 270 per cen

I want you to make a suggestion by which these richer mines should be taxed in pr
portion to what the poorer mines would be relieved by taxation. Read this artic
from *Machinery* :—" To compensate for the remission of taxation on necessaries
life, and loss of revenue from the railway expropriation, we would suggest a duty c

all the gold won from the mines, say five shillings an ounce. This would bring
approximately £750,000 per annum, as we estimate the output for 1897, with caref
management, will be equal to 3,000,000 ozs. It may be argued that to tax the go
won is taxing the industry more than ever. This may appear so at first sight, but
is a right principle to tax the finished article, not the raw materials : the taxation
the present time is borne by the producers of the gold, in the shape of heavy railwa
rates and dear labour, etc. In taxing the gold won the consumer will pay the ta
and as the world at large is the consumer in this case, it follows that a great portio
of our taxation would be borne by the population diffused over the whole worl
Therefore, although the mining companies producing the gold would pay the tax i
the first place (while the companies not producing would pay no tax at all), they wou
recover it by charging 5s. per ounce extra to the consumers, and the consumers cou
not refuse to pay this extra charge, because they must have the gold." What is you
opinion of that ?—Well, I don't agree with the article.

In which way do you differ from that article ?—Because I maintain the positic
would be worse if this principle was carried out. If you impose a tax upon gold
will have a disastrous effect throughout the world. It is a very typical proble
that the Chairman has just now propounded. I don't see how you can make any di
tinction. If richer companies possess rich ground—the Ferreira or Robinson fc
instance—it is a fortunate circumstance which attended that particular holdin
belonging to shareholders, and we cannot take away from their profits and handica
them to feed the poorer mines. The same principle applies to rich and poor.

I still think that, supposing this reduction were made, it would benefit the rich
mines more than the poorer mines, and that, therefore, to be quite fair and just
taxation, a tax on the richer mines should be proportionately heavier compared wit
the tax on the earnings of the poorer mines.—I maintain, Mr. Chairman, that a cours

of imposing further taxation would have a very disastrous effect. I am quite su
that if such a course is pursued, and you make that suggestion to the Governme
and it was acted upon, then instead of the work of this Commission being a blessin
to the mining industry and the whole of the community, it will have the opposi
effect.

I want to try and evenly balance taxation.—I have suggested that if this idea, which no doubt you have thought over, that the dynamite and railway can be arranged and a public works fund provided for them, so that the revenue of the country was not burdened with that serious item, I feel confident, in my own mind, instead of the revenue decreasing, it would increase, and the Government would have difficulty in balancing its budget.

How is it there are very few complaints from the mercantile community? A merchant, if he sells £1,000 worth of goods, is taxed on that amount; if he sells 10,000 he is taxed on that sum. Now, then, if you produce an ounce of gold, it is proposed that you should be taxed on that, and if 10,000 ounces taxed on that. Comparing the merchant with the gold producer, where is the unfairness of the suggested taxation?—It would be very unsound legislation indeed. If you begin to tax your gold in this country a more suicidal measure it is impossible to conceive.

These questions are only put to elicit your opinions, of course, and due weight will be given at the time the report is drawn up. It is not suggested to make this alteration; the question is put to elicit the fullest information possible. You and *White wages.* several other witnesses have stated that white labour is one of the chief items in the working expenses of the mines. Supposing you can effect a saving in the wages of the whites as well as the blacks, don't you think you will have a falling off in white labour?—No; we must consider the conditions here. In the first instance, they are desirous that the Government should lessen taxation so that living will be cheaper, and of course the reduction of wages follows.

I understand that last week you introduced a reduction of wages on your mines? *Reduction of white wages on Randfontein mines.* On some of them.

How do you reconcile your being able to effect that saving in face of the statement of several witnesses that it would not be possible to reduce the wage of the white miner until reductions have taken place?—I cannot answer what other men are influenced by. It is impossible to say. I have made that reduction on my mines and they are working to-day.

The effect of your having been able to successfully reduce white labour wages seems to speak directly against some of the evidence which has been submitted to the Commission, where they state it would be absolutely impossible under present conditions to reduce white wages. Facts like these speak.—Yes, I have read the statements.

Mr. *Joubert*.

In the beginning of your statement you say you have got hopes that the labours of the Commission will be fruitful of much good for the industry. Do you think that is the general opinion of the public in Europe and the mining industry?—Yes.

Therefore you attribute the present depression greatly to a misunderstanding?— *Reason of the present depression.* No, but it is a drawback when there is no confidence in the people.

Do you think the impartial dealings of this Commission will be able to remove such *Effect of Commission's action in Europe* misunderstandings, or can you suggest any other way out of the difficulty?—I think the impartial action of the Commission up to now has inspired great confidence, not only here but in Europe as well. I have cables to that effect.

You think if the Commission continues in the same spirit as it started much of the feeling will be removed?—Yes.

Do you think it will be in the interest, not only of the gold industry, but also the *Expropriation of railway desirable for general population as well as for mining industry.* general population of the republic, if the railway be expropriated?—Yes.

Can you adduce any argument in support of your opinion? Of course the decision on that point will remain with the Volksraad. I should like to hear your arguments in favour of expropriation as one of the public at large, also your economic

reasons as a financier, with a view to showing how it will benefit the public as
whole ?—I stated this morning that if the Government expropriated the railway th
that would be the groundwork of a very strong financial position of the Sou
African Republic. This railway in the hands of the Government immediately becom
a very valuable asset. I said this morning that the railway is the moving lever
this State's prosperity. If the railway belonged to the Government of this count
they would have power to regulate its working and tariff to meet the requirements
the whole country. The advantages would not be confined only to the mini
industry, but every inhabitant of the State would derive the advantages which wo
accrue to the country under these circumstances. That, I think, every person wl
follows events as they stand at the present moment in this country would grasp wit
out the least difficulty. The very moral effect of it being announced that the railwa
belonged to the Government would be marvellous throughout the world, the financi
position of the State would become much stronger and the confidence in the Sta
would increase. And I mean to say not only that, but it would lead to a furth
inflow of capital into this country. When capital is brought into the country it
not circulated only among a certain section or body, but every inhabitant of th
country participates, more or less, in the circulation of that money. I consider
would be a very wise policy indeed—a policy so far-reaching in its effects that no
of us seated at this table to-day can possibly conceive the marvellous results th
would follow the expropriation of the railway once it had become a Governme
asset.

So you are of opinion that the heavy taxes do not only press on the industr
alone, but also on the mercantile community, agriculturists, and in fact everybody ?-
Exactly.

And then you are of opinion that in case the Government could have the enti
control of the railways, they would have it in their own hands to remedy this ?-
Materially.

And that is your reason for saying that you think the Government ought to tal
it over ?—I think so.

In favour of everybody in the republic, not only for the gold industry ?—Yes, fc
the whole country.

But supposing the Government can get the Railway Company to make all th
required reductions, would not that meet your purpose just as well ?—I am taking, a
I said this morning, a more comprehensive view. I know what a great effect it wou
have if the State acquired that railway, as far as the industry is concerned, but I da
say, trade generally, if those reductions were made which we are desirous should t
made and the State would also benefit. But I maintain not to that extent as if th
State expropriated the railway, and the State owned it as a property.

If the State takes it over, of course it takes it over with all its burdens an
responsibilities ?—Yes.

Would the mining industry in any way be prepared, do you think, to assist th
Government in getting the required capital at a reasonable rate ?—Oh, yes.

Now we get to dynamite. Do you not think it is desirable that the Governmen
of the republic should have its own manufactory of dynamite in its own country ?-
Well, I would certainly have no objection to the Government having it, but then w
would like to have dynamite at a certain price and of a certain quality.

Is it possible that, with the co-operation of the industry, the Government ca
devise means by which dynamite can be manufactured in this country, so as to l
delivered here as cheaply as that exported. Is it feasible ?—Well, I am in doul
about that.

Beneficial effects of expropriation of railway

Expropriation of railway more beneficial than reduction of railway rates alone.

Mining industry and railway expropriation loan.

Dynamite.

What would be the objection. Why could you not make dynamite to deliver : to the mines as cheaply as to import it?—I don't think you could make it as ʋply here.

You will agree, of course, that every man, and every company, and every State, ʌes to be as independent as possible from importation from outside. If a factory ʌd be started here which can produce dynamite as cheaply, or nearly as cheap, as ʌ can import it, it would be a desirable thing?—Certainly.

And don't you think it would be the duty of the industry to assist the Govern-ʌt as much as possible towards attaining that object?—I am certain the mining ʌstry would not hesitate for one moment.

Is there no possibility of establishing a dynamite factory in this conntry which ʌd manufacture dynamite at a cost nearly equal, or lower in cost, than imported ʌamite?—I am in doubt about it, but still, if a position of that kind is to be ʌidered, I am quite sure the representatives of the mining industry will only be too ʌ to meet the Government on the subject.

I am not going on the present basis at all. Do away with the present contract; ʌ, could not a scheme be devised in which a dynamite factory can be started in this ʌtry, under Government control, and with the assistance of the industry, which will ʌble to deliver dynamite at about the cost of imported dynamite?—Certainly.

Mr. *Hugo.*

But do you think there is a chance of establishing such a factory? Is there a ʌibility of such a factory?—Assuming that dynamite can be manufactured here at ʌething like the price we can import it, I am quite sure there wonld be no difficulty.

Mr. *Joubert.*

It is not the intention of the Government in the least to oppress the mines, pro-ʌd there be co-operation from the side of the mines, and to back up the Government ʌhat they can be as much as possible independent from foreign importation.—Quite ʌt.

Then, of course, you can depend on co-operation in return from the side of the ʌernment.—Certainly.

Is it impossible to have such a factory?—That is the difficulty. I cannot answer ʌ at the moment. If such a thing is feasible there would not be a moment's ʌitation.

Within your knowledge, is any dynamite made in this country out of materials ʌnd in this country?—Not so far as I am aware.

Have you anything to say against the quality of the dynamite made here?—No, ʌink it is fair.

Do you know any mines in other countries?—Not intimately.

Have you heard of so many people ever being killed by a mining explosion at one ʌe as happened here the other day?—Yes, often.

Then, I suppose that is not attributable to the quality of the dynamite?—That is ʌossible to say.

Now we will get on to the Pass Law. Do you suggest any means by which the ʌs Law can be improved, so as to prevent the running away of natives?—The only ʌy is to appoint competent officials to undertake the duties.

Do you know of any special faults or mistakes made by any officials of which ʌplaint can be made?—It seems a very difficult matter. For instance, when the ʌive comes to this country, he has what is called a "reis" pass; then he afterwards ʌ a district pass; then he gets a monthly pass. The district pass is held by the

Marginal notes: Comparative cost of dynamite manufactured in the Transvaal and imported dynamite. Establishment of dynamite factory in Transvaal under Government control. Composition and quality of dynamite in use on Rand. Pass Law. Competent officials needed. Maladministration of Pass Law.

employer, and the native has in his own possession the monthly pass. Still, un
those circumstances the natives disappear, and it seems an extraordinary thing t
they cannot be traced, and that there is no power in the country here to intercept th
natives, to stop them, or to deal with them in a manner justifiable under
circumstances.

There is no fault in the law; it is in the administration of the law ?—The law
an excellent one. It is a first-class law.

Can you suggest any way to administer the law ?—I can suggest ways, but I
not think it would be advisable to mention what is in my mind at the moment, as
hinges on the officials who administer the law at present.

The administration is laid down by the law.—Yes, I mean to say it is the carry
out of the law.

An official is the servant of the public, and, if he should not do his duty, there
a way to complain about it; because it is not only natives of this country, there
officials who don't do their duty everywhere.—Quite right.

Government not to blame for maladminis-tration of Pass Law. You cannot blame the Government. There is no real grievance against the Gove
ment. It is really the fault of the people who allow such things to continue with
lodging a complaint to the Government.—We don't blame the Government.
approach the Government through this Commission.

I only want to point out to you that some neglect is attributable to the mana
ment of the mines. If officials do not do their duty, it is incumbent on the mines
Liquor Law. complain of such officials. We will turn to the Liquor Law. That is not carried
Maladministra-tion of Liquor Law. properly ?—No.

Remedy for mal-administration of Liquor Law. What remedy can you suggest to get it better exercised ?—I think a body sho
be constituted to follow up the lines of the law, and I mean to say it is very eas
done. I see in the papers lately that the Government have been appointi
Commandant Schutte for the getting of detectives for following that matter
clusively. I think if that idea was followed out we should be able to enforce
provisions of that law pretty well.

Supposing there is any connivance from the side of the mine manager in
transgression of the law ?—That would be a very serious offence if a mine mana
defeated the object of the law.

Is it not possible ?—It is possible, but very improbable.

What is your idea ?—Do you not think there is a single mine manager w
transgresses the law ?—I can only speak of my managers that they don't transgr
the law. All I can say is, if a mine manager is not worthy of his position he sho
certainly be cleared out at once.

Gold thefts. It is very difficult to find it out. Now the gold thefts. Don't you think
Protection Board to pre-vent gold thefts. law on gold thefts is stringent enough ?—I suggested that a board should
appointed on the same lines as they have at Kimberley with regard to diamc
dealing. The members should consist of Government nominees and members of
mining industry, and I believe if that Board was properly constituted it would b
very great assistance in tracing amalgam thefts on the Rand here. They have
mines in communication with the detectives, and it would lead to the discovery
amalgam thefts. The conditions of this were that when any suspicion existed
mine was directly placed in communication with that Board.

Reduction of import duties. What reduction on import duties can you suggest ?—I am not prepared to s
what reduction on import duties should be made, but the Commission should consi
that a great deal hinges on this in this country. Our object is to cheapen things h
as much as possible, and the more we cheapen things, provided we keep up
revenue of the country, I am assured that it would be of great benefit to the whole

e State. It is impossible, off-hand, to say what reduction should be made. It is a estion to be gone into very carefully, and all the points have to be considered, and proper scale has to be marked out before you can say what reduction should be de.

Still you think it is highly necessary for the progress of the mining industry that reduction should be made ?—Yes, certainly.

You see, I ask the question because the people pay these import duties too ?—I not speaking for a reduction for the industry alone; it would benefit the whole ate.

Now I am coming to the point; there should be a better understanding between e people and the Government. I quite agree with that; there should be more aternising, more closer union ?—I am glad to hear it. *Closer union required between people and Government.*

I want to hear first from you, what are the people here prepared to do, and what they expect from the Government, the Executive, and the Volksraad in order to ing about that fraternising ?—All I want is the Commission to use its influence ith the President, the Executive, and the Volksraad, that they should come over to hannesburg and that we should shake hands all round, and that the President ould address the people here, and that the people should have the opportunity of changing ideas with the President and the Executive. The moral effect of this on the world would be simply marvellous. It would show that all our differences d been dropped and that we had come together again as a united people to work nd in hand for the welfare of the State.

That cannot come from the State to the Government ?—No. I only throw out at suggestion to the Commission, and if the Commission would see that the resident, the Executive, and the Volksraad members would come here we would ake the necessary arrangements to receive them.

Before the Commission can undertake to put any such suggestion to the resident and the Government, it is their duty to inform the mining industry what the ommission considers to be their duty, and the first duty of the mining industry and e new population is to make friends with the true people of the Republic, and to low that there is no feeling of enmity against them; that they are really in earnest trying to co-operate with the old population in furthering the interests of the untry. Then the people of the country will see that the Government will do their ity by the mining industry. I will be very pleased when the day will break when e new population will join hands with the old one in order to further the common terests of our rich country, and in order to develop our rich gold mines; so that even ere will be a living for the poorest man, because the country is good enough. If it is ot it is our fault. If the population will only join hands together, I repeat the country good enough, and I hope that everything that has passed will be left behind, that om this day co-operation will exist, and that the new population will support the overnment, and they will see that the Government are prepared to take their terests to heart, and I feel that I am only expressing the feeling of all members of is Commission, and on that basis we will make our recommendations to the Government. There is another question that occurs in your declaration. What is your idea the effect of the development of the deep levels? Do you think the deep levels e of such a value that their development will be good for the mining industry? It ands to reason the longer the mines last the greater benefit it will be for the State. ave you got any idea about the payable capacity of the deep levels?—They will be ke the outcrop mines. *Duty of mining industry towards the burgher population.* *Value of deep levels.*

What do you think of the Gold Law; as it exists at present does it meet the quirements of the situation?—I think it is a good law. *Gold Law.*

R

Mr. Brakhan.

Illicit sale of li-
quor.

I see in your statement that you say you consider many of your companies ha~
suffered greatly through the illicit and unrestrained supply of strong drink to native
Where principally are these canteens situated which have done this harm to th
industry ?—At Randfontein.

Are some of these canteens situated on mining areas ?—Some are situated c
stands on claims, and I think all the claims adjoin' the mijnpacht.

Liquor licences.

The law as it was promulgated some time ago provided that no canteen licenc
shall be permitted on mining areas ?—Mr. Langermann, my representative at th
time, brought on action before the Court with regard to the decision arrived at by th
Licensing Court. The Court gave judgment the other day reversing the decision
the Licensing Board. To show how matters are complicated, there is a licensing cas
pending the decision of the Court, and the Licensing Board granted these men
licence.

Undesirability of
canteens on
mining areas.

Then you hold that it would be a good thing for the natives that no licence
should be issued on mining areas ?—Certainly, it would be good for them. Of course
if the industry is unhampered with such drawbacks as the sale of liquor to natives, i
stands to reason that the whole State must benefit by it. I certainly say that n
licences should be granted on mining areas.

Then you hold that these canteens on mining areas, although they are now onl
permitted to sell to white people, yet there is a great deal of likelihood that they wil
also sell liquor to natives ?—Oh, yes. The natives are seen carrying any number o
bottles of brandy.

You think the argument of the Licensed Victuallers' Association, that these
people can only sell to white people, does not hold good ?—Certainly. I am sure i
does not hold good.

Taxation of gold.

You have given your opinion with regard to the article which appeared in
Machinery. Now I take it that this article will lead people to believe that the gol
produced is really the last product of the company. Now, don't you hold that th
last product of a company is the dividend which it pays ?—Yes.

Don't you think that if this suggestion would be followed upon, that these poo
mines would be very much handicapped in comparison to the rich ones ?—In wha
way ?

Because I take it, the poor mines would have to pay the same amount of thei
production, although their profit is minimum ?—Certainly. It is a dangerous policy
to introduce such a thing. It will have a very injurious effect if you tax gold.

Taxation of divi-
dends.

Don't you think it is much more advisable to introduce a tax on dividends ?—I
object to that also. I don't say that for any personal reason. But I say this : that
if instead of reducing taxation the Commission is going to impose further taxation
I foresee that no good will result. That I say in plain English. The forecast I made
to-day is right. You don't want further taxation ; you ought to lessen it. The
balance of the budget will not be disturbed.

We do not anticipate, if these reductions are made, that in the long run th
Government will be on the wrong side with the budget. Yet it may be necessary.—

Loan for public
works desir-
able.

They won't be on the wrong side. They want to raise a million to-morrow for publi
works, and then it is off the revenue of the country. It is easily adjusted. There i
no danger of the balance getting on the wrong side.

Taxation of gold
or dividends
reprehensible.

If it came to a question of whether the gold product or dividends should be taxed
would you not prefer that dividends rather than gold be taxed ?—I don't prefer any
thing of the kind, because I think you are starting a dangerous theory. You hav

dea what you are doing. If the outcome of the Commission's work is to tax
dends or gold I should be sorry you have been appointed on the Commission,
that tax you are not going to benefit this country. You should wait until cir-
stances arise before you raise this question. You should not start this question
, moment like this. You should see whether you can reduce taxation, and how to
ore confidence and bring back the prosperity of the country; you should not seek
outlet of this nature. Why, you will completely frighten people at home.

It has been started in the papers, and I want to point out the danger Yet are
re not other countries where they have an income tax?—Yes; but I prefer a
ntry where there is no income tax.

But the question is—if the occasion should arise whether there should be a tax on *Income tax un-desirable in Transvaal.*
l or on income, which would you prefer?—I don't admit either. It is suicidal so
as the industry is concerned.

I don't think we can argue that way, as in well established countries an income
does exist.—In well established countries you have a great many industries. Here
are dependent entirely upon the industry—the mining industry, which is the back-
e of the country. If, as in Germany or England, there were all kinds of industries
heir own, of course the position would be different, but here the whole position
ends upon the profitable working of the mines, upon inspiring people in Europe
h confidence so that they will invest in the country and assist us in developing the
ources of this country. If you once begin to tax gold or tax dividends, you will
ainly do an immense amount of harm. You will stop that good which we all
icipate will follow the action of this Commission.

I personally hold that it would be better for the welfare of the mining industry,
t it should get every possible facility from a reduction of railway rates and other
rces. In that case the revenue of the State would be curtailed, and ways and means
uld be devised to balance the budget. But it should not be a tax on the production *Taxation of gold undesirable.*
gold if other means can be found.—There should not be a tax on gold or dividends.
er ways can be found.

I have previously referred another witness to a certain point in the Gold Law, *Taxation of gold produced on mynpachts.*
nely, where the Gold Law provides that in the case of mijnpachts Government have
ght to 2½ per cent. on the gold produced. Do you consider that a good or a bad
position?—It is a very bad one. I have often discussed that with high officials,
, they themselves knew that if they imposed that tax it would have a very bad
ct.

Now, the Government not having imposed the tax heretofore, is not that a
rantee that Government is not going to impose a tax on production or dividends,
ch is likely to be injurious to the industry.—I am quite sure the Government won't
such a thing.

Do you consider that the Gold Law in other respects, say, as regards the tax im- *Claim licences.*
ed on claim licences, is reasonable, and not oppressive?—I think so, more especially
they have made the alteration with the Mining Commissioner's department, who
e got power, according to the Gold Law, to regulate what amount shall be paid as
m licences and what as prospectors' licences.

You think, then, that diggers' licences should only be asked for on claims actually *Distinction of claim and prospectors' licences.*
ked?—That is a matter for consideration. It is a point I have not thought of.

Mr. Smit.

You said this morning, in reply to a question, that you would expect a bigger *Increased output*
put when more mines were working?—Yes, in those mines with improved
chinery and increased steam power.

The initial expenses of a mine, the development, etc., are much heavier than expenses when it is started and in full swing?—Yes, much heavier.

These new mines which are started, are they so good that they will pay expen[...] seeing that some old mines had to close down on account of not being able to [...] expenses?—Yes.

Reason for good effect of expropriation in Europe. You think the expropriation would create a good impression not only here bu[...] Europe?—Yes.

But why?—Because the impression is only to be formed that when the Gove[...] ment holds the railway it will alter the position, and they could regulate the tariff they liked, to meet the wants of the country. Apart from that, the railw[...] would be regarded as a valuable asset in the hands of the Government.

Have they got such a lot of interest in our Government that they are anxious [...] Government should have good assets?—I am taking up the position that this railw[...] is a very important factor in the welfare of the country, and when I come to consi[...] that we look towards Europe for our support in making this country what it actua[...] is at the present time, and what I maintain it will be through the inflow of furt[...] capital, I say to bring about that desirable object the Government should be posses[...] of the railway to restore that confidence, and make the investing public at Ho[...] realise that the asset is the property of the Government, and they can do with it they think fit.

Expropriation of railway preferable to reduction of railway rates alone. But supposing tariffs are put on an equitable basis in order to meet all the requi[...] ments of the Commission, does it then concern you much whether it is run by a priv[...] company or by the Government?—I have answered that already. It would be a ve[...] good thing if the tariffs were brought down. It would be of great assistance to t[...] people of this Republic. But I am taking a higher and more comprehensive view. [...] is a question of very high finance. It will have a moral and financial effect throug[...] out Europe, and would have a great effect on the future progress of this country.

This concluded Mr. Robinson's evidence, for which he was thanked by t[...] Chairman.

Mr. H. F. E. Pistorius' evidence. Mr. H. F. E. Pistorius submitted the following statement from the Joint Co[...] mittee of the Chamber of Commerce and Mercantile Association:—

This committee, representing the merchants and traders of Johannesburg, mak[...] the following statement regarding the present position of the mining industry, alwa[...] **Mining industry is financial and industrial mainstay of country.** bearing in mind that that industry is the financial and industrial mainstay of t[...] country. Without the market afforded by the mines other industries could not ex[...] in the Transvaal, and this economic fact is so far-reaching in its effect on lo[...] industries that even agriculture comes under the same rule. The successful worki[...] of the mines affords a basis for industrial, agricultural and commercial developme[...] in many other ways. Admitting this fact then, the first necessity for the prosperi[...] of the country from an industrial standpoint is to ensure the success of the min[...] **Unjust burdens on mines.** We are of opinion that at present the mines have to carry many heavy and indefe[...] sible burdens. The chief of these are the monopolies for railways and for explosiv[...] We ask the favour of your careful consideration of the following burdens that can readily removed:—

Railway monopoly. Railways being necessarily a monopoly, and in all countries superseding the hig[...] ways of the country, are consequently under different economic and administrati[...] conditions to other industrial enterprises. The public have to be guarded against t[...] possibilities of such a monopoly as that afforded by a railway, being used to t[...] general disadvantage. In England and America the average dividends paid by t[...]

ways amount to between 3 and 4 per cent. per annum. In view of these facts the Netherlands Railway rates.
es charged and profits secured by the Netherlands railway cannot be justified.
e rates obtaining on the Netherlands Railway are far in excess of those ruling on
other lines in South Africa. The very great differences are shown in the following
les:—

				Normal per ton per mile. d.	Intermediate per ton per mile. d.	Rough per ton per mile. d.	
Cape	...	...	...	2·34	2	1·3	Comparative table of South African railway rates.
Orange Free State	...	...		2·34	2	1·3	
Natal	...	...	...	3·04	3·04	1·94	
Portuguese	...	...	...	4·07	3·53	2·44	
Netherlands, *via* Cape	...	...		7·7	7·7	7·7	
" " Natal	...		...	5·06	3·82	3·26	
" " Delagoa	...			4·27	3·69	2·54	

AGRICULTURAL PRODUCE.

					Per ton per mile plus terminals.
Cape, for 23 miles	...	...	...	...	½d.
Orange Free State, for 23 miles	...		...	...	½d.
Natal, for 13 miles	...	...	...	...	1¾d.
Portuguese	...	...	...	...	2·2d.
Netherlands, *via* Cape and Orange Free State				...	3·1d.
" " Natal	...		...	...	3·26d.
" " Delagoa Bay	...		...	...	2·3d.

The mines mainly consume heavy goods that have a low prime cost in the Railway rates on heavy goods,
ntries from which they are brought. The following table will illustrate the
sition:—

		Prime cost. £ s. d.	Rail charge. £ s. d.
Cargo of Swedish deal	...	1,484 10 5	2,658 13 9
" Pitch pine	...	2,379 7 1	7,361 8 6
300 casks cement	...	80 16 10	405 0 0
1,000 cases paraffin	...	207 0 8	306 13 4
1,000 boxes candles	...	347 11 9	104 12 6
120 drums grease	...	19 9 1	25 15 2
100 shoes and dies	...	170 15 8	64 11 2
Steel rails	...	69 3 11	118 12 8

In the United States of America the railway lines cost about £12,000 a mile to Cost of equipment and rates of railways in the United States.
ild and equip, and the average rate charged on all goods is 2·5 of one penny per
n per mile. The high rate charged by the Netherlands Company for coal traffic is an Netherlands Railway coal rate.
pecial hardship on the mines. The bulk of the coal traffic is carried on the Rand
am. The rates vary according to distance from 2·08d. per ton per mile to 2·92d.
Natal the rate is ¼d. per ton of 2,240lbs. per mile. In the Free State the rate is Natal Railway coal rate. Free State Railway coal rate.
. per ton of 2,000lbs. The coal mines produced 1,437,297 tons during 1896. It is
timated that the railway received £350,000 for transport of the coal. If the Free
ate rate were adopted there would be a saving to the mines of over £200,000, and
ample margin would still be left for the railway. The management and general Netherlands Railway administration.
rking of the railway also leaves much to be desired. Most of the staff appear to
without railway experience and administer the railway with all the disadvantages
the general public that an unchecked monopoly will allow. The higher adminis-

tration is also inefficient. This is conclusively shown by such facts as the Lingha contract—a document so loosely drawn as to have cost the railway £60,000 to get cancelled—and the dynamite disaster. Competent administration would have avoid both these evils. Dynamite is another monopoly that bears heavily on the industr

Dynamite mon-
opoly.

The present lowest price of No. 1 dynamite is 85s. at the factory, plus 2s. 6d. per ca for delivery. We are informed that No. 1 dynamite is selling in Germany at 21s. 6 per case. It would cost 11s. 3d. per case to land it here, making the landed co 32s. 9d. For the purpose of comparison, we will take the price at which Nobels co tracted with the mines in 1893. That was 40s. a case. To that add 5s. a case, as no received by the Government in lieu of duty, bringing the price to 45s. a case. Tl Government agent sells at 85s., and thus has a margin of profit of 40s. a case. Tl consumption is equal to 250,000 cases a year, and the mines therefore pay £500,000 year more than the market value of the article. Amongst the excessive charg making up this enormous sum are the agency charges levied by Mr. Lippert and tl royalties in favour of Messrs. Lewis and Marks. Cement furnishes another burde for the mines, increases the cost of building dwelling-houses, and generally has bee to the great disadvantage of the community. First-class cement costs in Euroj 5s. 6d. per cask of 400lbs. gross weight. It costs 44s. a cask to bring here. The con sumer is not only burdened with the heavy cost in freight and railage in bringing tl cement to this market, but has to pay a protective duty of 12s. a cask, so as to bolste up the local factory. The protection given the local factory is 12s. a cask throug the Customs and 7s. 8d. through excessive railway charges. The local factory pr duces equal to 30,000 casks per annum, and is, therefore, subsidised by the State t the extent of £28,000 per annum. We submit that such an anomaly as this subsid to a small industrial company (which is only a parasite on the main industry of th country) should be swept away.

— European
and Transvaal
prices.

Dynamite agen-
cy and royalty
charges.

Cement.

European and
Transvaal pri-
ces for cement

Duty on cement.

Cement factory.

The evidence herein already adduced regarding the disastrous experience gaine in supporting the dynamite and cement concessions indicates the evils springing from such a policy. The concession to manufacture bricks is another that bears heavily o this community, and should be abolished, and so also should the heavy duty o printed matter.

Brick-making
concession.

The incidence of taxation, by which the necessaries of life carry such a heav share of the burden, should be amended. It is not only an economic mistake, but, i our opinion, a positive wrong to tax the bread of the people. During 1896 grain an flour to the value of £1,000,000 were imported. Although the special duties wer suspended the amount paid in ordinary *ad valorem* duties amounted to fully £60,00(and this heavy burden was mainly contributed by the wage-earning portion of th community. The Customs charges are altogether excessive and require materia reduction. In all other South African States and Colonies machinery is importe free, but here we have to pay £1 16s. per cent. This charge directly bears on th mines and should be removed. Amongst general questions that have already com under enquiry by the Commission, are white labour, native labour, over-capitalisatio and merchants profits.

Incidence of tax-
ation.

Grain and flour
duties.

Import dues.

Import duty on
machinery.

We are of opinion that no material reduction of white wages will be possibl until the cost of living has been reduced. The present policy of high tariffs undul enhances the cost of necessaries, checks enterprise, and produces such a high cost c living that a workman earning £20 a month can but barely maintain his wife an family. Native labour is an equally important factor to the mines. We are confiden that if native labourers were afforded facilities and due protection in coming to thes fields, the supply would be so great and continuous as to enable wages to be reduce to an average of 35s. a month. The ill-treatment and hardships of natives whils

White wages.

Native labour.

ing to and travelling from these fields, the injustice with which they are treated
er the Pass Law, and the oppressive regulations imposed on them cost in extra
es alone fully 25s. a month. Estimating for 70,000 natives working for wages in
district, that shows a loss of over one million per annum. To illustrate the
ressive working of the Pass Law we adduce the following recent incident:—A *Maladministra-tion of Pass Law.*
ding contractor absconded from Jeppestown and left 25 natives without a
night's wages and without their passes. The chief contractor on the job decided
arry on the work, and arranged with the natives for them to continue at work.
went to the Pass Office, reported the case, and asked for new passes for the boys.
was promptly refused, and told that the whole lot would be arrested and fined or
risoned for being without passes. Such administration can only have one result,
that is to drive away labour, and, as a reflex result, increase the cost of what
ft.

Over-capitalisation is a point that appears to have occasioned some misunder- *Over-capitalisation of mines.*
ding. Whether a mine is over or under capitalised does not in any way affect
working charges. It is purely a market question, and affects the price of shares,
industrial question for the mines is whether or no they can produce 20s. worth
old at below a cost of 20s., and therefore at a profit. How the mine is capitalised
s not affect the industrial problem either way.

Merchant's profits in Johannesburg are on a narrower margin than in any *Johannesburg merchants' profits.*
ing camp in the world. The leading lines used in quantities by the mines are
tracted for at a margin of the barest possible profit, and we will submit proofs of
statement.

Chairman.

As Chairman of the Chamber, I should have expected you to have given some *Commerce and agriculture.*
ication of the measures required to facilitate commerce and agriculture. In your
ement there is very little on that point. You practically go over the same ground
traversed by mine managers. I can understand that the prosperity of the mines
great measure influences the prosperity of commerce and agriculture. But still
annot be denied that commerce and agriculture are separated from mining, and for
prosperity of the country generally agriculture and commerce should go hand in
d. Your report suggests no redress or measures to be taken to relieve the
essities of commerce and agriculture. Now, what can be done by commerce to
st agriculture? The only point I find in your statement on agriculture is this—
t the only thing done by the Government in order to protect the agriculture of
country is that the commercial people want to take away—that is, the import
y on food stuffs.—In the first place, I should like to point out that my report *Import duty on foodstuffs.*
rs to the price of labour, which would materially assist commerce and agriculture, *Cost of labour.*
in order to get commerce and agriculture to flourish in this country, the mining *Commerce and agriculture de-*
ustry, which is the backbone of this country, should flourish. That is why we say *pendent on mining indus-*
t the tax levied by the railways, dynamite, and native wages should be reduced. *try.*
shown in the question of dynamite alone, £500,000 could be saved in the way of *Free trade in dy-namite.*
trade in dynamite. Take railway statistics. For instance, on a load of coke of a *Railway rates*
ne cost of £68 10s., the railway carriage was £294. The two Colonies took 293
cent. of the cost, and the Netherlands Railway for carrying from Vereeniging to
annesburg got 136 per cent., the entire cost being from Europe to Johannesburg
per cent. on the prime cost. So the load which originally cost £68 10s., cost
led here £455 10s. In the matter of pig iron, a lot which cost in England £149,
to pay £294 for transport. The Free State and Cape Colony drew 134 per cent.
carrying, and the Netherlands for a distance of 52 miles got 63 per cent. The

cost of laying down a quantity of pig iron costing in Europe £149 1s. 3d. increases the time of delivery here to £514 1s. 8d. That shows that those heavy railw charges made it so expensive that it must be a heavy burden on the mining indust Then you say that the Chamber of Commerce tries to take away the only protect granted to agriculture in this country by suggesting the removal of the tax

Import duty on foodstuffs. foodstuffs. If you take the tax on foodstuffs, you will find that not alone is the the usual nine per cent. *ad valorem,* but also a special tax in many cases 100 per ce Notwithstanding the expense of this heavy tax very little is coming into the count and up to the present that has not improved the position · of agriculture in country

Agriculture. It has not been shown what we have to do to assist agriculture. Pig-iron a dynamite, which you speak about, do not concern agriculture; they concern mini I want to speak exclusively about agriculture. I think you will agree with me th it is desirable that agriculture, as well as the mines, should be developed in t country. Foodstuffs, which to-day are brought into the country, might be produced the country itself, and that would also be a great support to commerce. There hardly any necessity to travel over the same ground as has already been gone over other witnesses. What the Commission would like to know from the Chamber Commerce is, what are their requirements, and what can be done to foster agricultu the importation of machinery, etc. As long as we can import sheep here it appears me that Mr. Pistorius does not mind what becomes of the agriculture of the count I take it that the prosperity and advancement of the goldfields is a big factor in t country, but the backbone—the sinews of the country—is agriculture. That is w we would have liked very much some opinion on those points. You have shown how agriculture and commerce can go hand in hand. There is another question I wa

Importation of iron. to speak about—the importation of iron. It is stated that this Republic contains ir as good as any other country. Don't you think there is a chance of getting iron o of this country—that is, instead of importing it at a high cost? Would it not another development of industry, providing work for thousands of people, and whi

Agriculture. would keep the money in our own country?—In reply, I would like to say to t Chairman, regarding the prosperity and advancement of agriculture, that I acknowled it is the backbone of every country. But in this country, so far, agriculture has n provided for the wants of the population. The prosperity of agriculture at the prese moment is dependent on the prosperity of the mining industry, and although there a big market here and good prices for all produce, agriculture has only advanc very little. How can you then say that the Chamber of Commerce or the populati

Amount of food-stuffs import-ed. want to take away the only protection of the country? The market shows that mo of the produce on the market here comes from the Free State and outside. Regardi iron, I believe there is lots of iron in the country, but up to the present I cannot s

Working of Transvaal iron ore. how it would be possible to get iron out under present conditions. If transport we easy and cheap, and wages to get ore out of the ground were cheap, then I would sa "Yes, let us get the iron out of our own country." Until such times as the conditio are altered in such a manner that it can be worked cheaply, it would be impossible compete with Europe.

Mr. Joubert.

Commerce and the mining in-dustry. I want to know in what way is the prosperity of commerce dependent on t prosperity of the mining industry.—Here in Johannesburg they are so close connected that the prosperity of trade or commerce entirely depends upon t prosperity of the mines.

And the prosperity of the mines and commerce chiefly depends on the prosperi

agriculture?—The prosperity of the country depends upon the prosperity of the
nes.

The country cannot exist for mines and commerce without agriculture. Don't
u consider that the regulations which press on the mines and commerce also press on
riculture. The commercial men do not pay import duties; the farmer pays that.—
at indirect taxation is paid by the whole population. The reduction in railway rates
es not only affect the mines and commerce, but also the farmer.

Mr. *Brakhan.*

All the matters which have been laid before the Commission so far are very clear on
me points, except dynamite. The dynamite question seems to be shrouded in a good
al of mystery. We cannot arrive at any particulars as to how much of it is really
nufactured here, and in order to arrive at some conclusion about the question I
ould like to ask you certain things. Can you inform us how much nitrate and how
ch sulphur has been imported into this Republic by the various railways?—I don't Importation of
ink that the Customs returns show how much of these goods are separately materials for
ported. And then, besides, sulphur is largely imported in connection with the Scab manufacture.
t, for the purpose of sheep dipping.

You think it is difficult to find out how much sulphur has actually found its way
re into the Transvaal?—There would be no difficulty, provided the Customs
thorities took a separate account of it.

I should like to put a suggestion to the Chamber of Commerce and Mercantile
sociation to try to find out what the quantity has been, and also what quantity of guhr
s been imported, and what quantity of ready-made dynamite and nitro-gelatine. I
ink the latter points should not be so difficult to answer, as the data could no doubt be
t from the ports. Nearly all the dynamite which comes into South Africa is used in this
public.—I don't think that will help you. The quantity of dynamite imported into
is country the Government have the statistics of, and guhr also. The dynamite
ctory could produce that to the Commission, and therefore there would be no
casion to see that specially through the Customs. These matters are all in the hands
the Government.

I think it would be wise if some evidence came from outside quarters.—You mean
this question. I don't see that would help you at all, because the whole of the
namite consumed on the fields must come through the dynamite factory, and there-
re the whole information is at the factory, and in the hands of the Government, and
available, I suppose, for this Commission. The Government can call upon the factory
thorities to say what quantity of these goods has been imported.

With regard to the revenue derived from the importation of dynamite, I was glad State revenue
see that you take a broad view of the case. I think everyone must know the from dynamite
overnment is quite entitled to make a profit out of it, and I hold that your opinion monopoly.
that the monopoly make too much profit on this very necessary article?—Far too
uch.

And you hold, as a mercantile man of experience, that there would be no
fficulty in importing dynamite at a reasonable rate, and in ample quantities to
pply the demand; and if the Government were to receive a duty of 10s. a case, it
uld mean about £125,000 per annum, and yet you think the mining industry would
ve enormous benefit?—Certainly.

I see under taxation with regard to the duty which is imposed on machinery, Import duty on
u do not say it is exactly high, but that it should be removed; don't you think, machinery
king other taxation into consideration and the general conditions which prevail here,
at this duty of 1½ per cent. is a low one?—In comparison with others it is.

I hardly think the mining industry has raised the question of this duty being burden ?—I think they have not, but seeing you wish to develop the resources of t country, therefore you must give the people who undertake this particular dut every opportunity to lay down machinery as cheaply as possible.

I think it is much more important that the railway rates should be cut down to reasonable extent, and this would make an infinitely bigger amount than this duty $1\frac{1}{2}$ per cent., which I understand is levied on the cost of machinery in Europe, plu 20 per cent. ?—Yes, making it 36s. per cent. I agree with you that this does n affect the question very materially, but taking into consideration the development the country, and a new country, particularly where you have many mineral resourc to be developed, you want your machinery brought into the country not only for th mining industry, but for agricultural purposes, as cheaply as possible ; therefore, th import duties should be taken off and railway rates should be brought down to reasonably profit-paying basis.

I take it your remark in your statement refers to mining machinery ?—In thi particular instance it does, but, we take it, the prosperity of the mines means also th prosperity and development of other industries in the country. We take it th mining industry is the first point with us. Every other industry is dependent on i and if you develop the mining industry you develop agriculture and the othe manufactures in the country.

All Transvaal industries dependent on mining industry.

I personally hold we ought to be fair in our demands. We ought not to ask th Government to cut down everywhere.—That is quite right. If the price of dynamit is reduced, and if you reduce the rates charged by the railway to a fair profit-payin basis, you will help the country forward to such an extent there will be no reason complaint.

On the other hand, I do not think anyone connected with the minin industry will grumble if they have to pay the rate charged on the cost of machiner in Europe ?—I do not say so either. The object of bringing forward this question the enormous charges of the railway is to bring indirectly forward the question of th desirability of the Government taking over the railway, and working the railway fo the benefit and development of the country. The railway, then coming into th hands of the Government, will be managed by the Government, and then the profit which will be made will be merely sufficient to pay interest on capital and sinkin fund. Then the railway rates will be reduced to such an extent that all industrie whether they are mines, manufactures, or agriculture, will be stimulated, and will a benefit to such an extent that they will work hand in hand for the general develop ment of the country. There are many reasons why the public wish to see th railway in the hands of the Government—not only to do away with the enormou charges, but to have the railways as an integral part of the institutions of the countr Then we can expect that railway rates and general management of the railway wil be subject to public opinion and the direct control of the Government. We do no say that the general management of the railways should be altered so far as th interior *personnel* is concerned, but as regards the higher officials, and that thes should all be controlled by a Government department. Then, of course, we ca expect redress, and it will tend to the development of the country.

Expropriation of Netherlands Railway.

Native labour.

Now, with regard to native labour. You refer to the ill-treatment and hardship which the natives have had to undergo in coming to and travelling from these fields there is no doubt that from the reports we get, the boys are really under ver great difficulties whilst coming to the fields—if they come on foot—and also whe they go away. Your experience is also in that direction ?—In our business we d not employ the class of natives who come to work on the mines ; the majority of th s we employ, for instance, in our works, are boys who come from Natal, Cape ony, or Basutoland, and they come by railway.

But does it come within your knowledge, irrespective of your business, that the s are subject to ill-treatment?—That is another reason why the railways should *Transport of native labour.* n the hands of the Government: that they will grant facilities to bring boys from r homes and back again in perfect safety, and in a short space of time.

And also that the rates might be lowered, still leaving a profit to the railway?— tainly. In connection with native labour, I would like to say that at a meeting *Illicit liquor traffic.* he committees of the Chamber of Commerce and Mercantile Association yesterday, solution was passed that I should inform the Commission in connection with the ve labour question, one of the greatest difficulties which the mines experience with question of the illicit liquor traffic along the line of reef, whereby a very large aber of natives are incapacitated from performing their work for perhaps a third he week. Provided this liquor traffic was under better control, the miners would e the services of the boys for full time. As a remedy in connection with this ter, they suggest that, instead of a fine, imprisonment should be substituted, and ich were adopted, they feel that a great deal of the present illicit liquor traffic, ch is a source of annoyance and inconvenience to the mines, would be removed.

Do you think that the illicit trade to natives is such a remunerative one that the s are readily forthcoming?—I do not know that for certain, but I have heard that tles of brandy are sold for 5s. and 6s. which cost 1s.

Under these circumstances, it would certainly appear that imprisonment would be ary much more severe remedy than a fine?—My own opinion was that it was a very stic resolution, but when other members gave their experience and said that these it dealers were fined once, twice, and three or four times, and it did not prevent m from carrying on the business, I came to the conclusion that, under these circum-aces, nothing but very drastic measures would prevent the continuance of this iness, and cause an improvement in the natives in physique, and an advantage to employers and mines.

Mr. de Beer.

There are two institutions in Johannesburg of the same kind, the Mercantile *Johannesburg Mercantile Association and Johannesburg Chamber of Commerce.* ociation and the Chamber of Commerce—have they got the same object in view? es.

Then why should there be two?—It is difficult to give an explanation to that. work harmoniously together for the prosperity and advancement of commerce.

Would it not be better to have amalgamation instead of harmonious working?— ppose it is a case of "many people many minds."

Witness said that no bricks could be made by machinery because there was a con- *Brick - making concession.* sion given. The quantity of bricks made certainly did not improve the quality. at is the price of machine-made bricks?—About £4 10s. per 1,000. *Price of bricks.*

It is a very high price.—Yes, under ordinary circumstances it should be about per 1,000. That would be a good price if brick-making was open to the public.

Now, take the same class of bricks, hand-made; what could they be made for?— are is a difference between the two. A hard-pressed brick, made by machinery, is y much better than a soft-pressed one made by hand. There is no comparison.

You say that there is a heavy tax on food-stuffs. It is not an *ad valorem* duty of *Import duty on foodstuffs.* er cent. only?—Oh, no. There is an *ad valorem* duty of 7½ per cent., with the ition of 20 per cent.; or, in other words, we have to pay 7½ per cent. on £120, and t brings the duty up to 9 per cent. In addition, there is a special duty on different cles of commerce.

Does the 9 per cent. not include the special duty ?—No.

Maladministra-
tion of Pass
Law.

Now, with regard to the Pass Law. You give an instance of a kaffir being treated. Do you know of any other cases ?—No, I am not intimately acquainted w the law. Other witnesses will doubtless be able to give you many instances.

Are you personally acquainted with the case you cited?—No, it was reported to

Cost of native
labour.

How do you make out the 25s. extra wages required to be paid to the boys ?— have to pay them 25s. more than we ought, owing to the stringent laws, and the lac protection afforded to them on the roads. If they were better protected, and could brought here cheaper, I think we could get them to work for 35s. Take a contrac on the Natal Railways employing a number of boys. While they are in Natal ter tory they pay the natives 30s. a month, but the moment the boys cross the border Volksrust, they want higher wages, because they are taken up and fined for smallest offence. Therefore they must be paid at a higher rate to compensate them

Over-capitalisa-
tion of mines.

You refer to over-capitalisation of the mines. Do not you think that ov capitalisation affects the credit of the country as well as the mines ?—No, not country so much. It affects the shareholders, not initially, but when they find out t their mine has been over-capitalised ; but that is not the question. The question whether the mine can be worked at a profit.

We are well aware of that, but we consider that, eventually, over-capitalisation mines will cause the credit of the country to suffer.—It may eventually, but it impossible to find out whether the mine has been over-capitalised. When a prope is floated, a large sum is sunk in the mine, and, as development proceeds, it may necessary to increase the capital, and yet after all the mine might be found unpayal

Do not you think too much money is invested in the properties ?—No, besides importation of money would not detrimentally affect any country.

Look at Capetown. It is an old-established town. It has its port, and extens commerce attends it. No one has thought of putting up such extensive buildings Perhaps, but the buildings in Johannesburg are erected in many cases out of mon made on share transactions in Europe.

The Lingham
contract.

You refer to the Lingham contract. What do you mean by the contract?—I contract entered into between Lingham and the Netherlands Railway Company carry wood from Delagoa Bay at a lower rate than the ordinary tariff. It was fou that it did not pay the Railway Company, and they cancelled it ; and it is said th paid Lingham £60,000 to get out of it.

Mr. Smit.

Do you know it for a fact ?—No.

Do you know that the contract was entered into ?—I cannot swear that it v signed.

You should not make such damaging statements unless you are sure of them.- know that there was such a contract, but it was given to me in such a manner as preclude me from referring to it in detail. The Chamber of Commerce has the cop

The Pass Law.

Do you think that the Pass Law, even if properly carried out, would be a bad la —I think that the law, if properly carried out, will prove a very good law, and it v prevent desertion, because the boys deserting will be brought back to the mines fr where they ran away, by the administration. If the kaffirs once knew that they co not easily escape, desertions would be minimised.

I think so myself.—Yes, perhaps not one in a hundred would desert. I consi the fine of £3 a heavy one.

It was fixed for the purpose of deterring boys from deserting.—Yes, but still i a heavy one. If there was an efficient and sufficient staff, the boys would not des frequently. They never like to be brought back to the mines from which they ᵓert, and if they know that they will almost certainly be recaptured should they ᵓert, they will not run away.

But it is difficult to recognise a kaffir.—I don't know if you are acquainted with ᵓ togt law in force in Natal. There they have headmen, who are appointed over ᵓ kaffirs. He knows his boys, and it is his duty to bring back runaways. But ᵓt, again, is simply an administrative matter.

You say that it does not matter whether a mine is over-capitalised or not, it ᵓuld not affect the working costs. It will affect the dividends, though?—Yes; I ᵓeat it might affect the shareholders, but it has nothing to do with the working ᵓts.

It speaks for itself that it affects the payability of the mine. If a mine with a ᵓital of one million sterling paid 5 per cent., the same mine with two millions capital ᵓuld pay only 2½ per cent.?—Yes, but you cannot find out whether a mine is over-ᵓitalised or not until the capital is exhausted.

Over-capitalisation of mines.

Mr. *Hugo.*

When you referred to dynamite, what did you mean by agents' charges?—It is ᵓmitted that Messrs. Lippert, and Lewis and Marks, both get a royalty on dynamite.

Agents' charges on dynamite.

But you refer to agents' charges?—Yes; but dynamite is sold only by Lippert or ᵓ agents.

Do you know the amount of royalty?—No; but I know that the price charged—ᵓat is, 85s. per case—leaves about 40s. per case for dividends.

Chairman.

You are the Chairman of the Chamber of Commerce?—Yes.

Mr. A. A. NOBLE was next examined, and stated that he was a merchant residing in Johannesburg, and Chairman of the Mercantile Association.

Mr. A. A. Noble's evidence.

He said he confirmed the evidence of Mr. Pistorius, and he had made a few ᵓtes in addition which he would give. Proceeding, he said:—Under the heading of ᵓilways, I would give one instance in addition to what has already been given to ᵓow the very high rate charged by the Netherlands Company on South African ᵓoduce. The rate from Winburg Road to Mid-Vaal, a distance of 150 miles, is 6s. 8d. ᵓr ton for the whole distance. The rate from Mid-Vaal to Johannesburg—52 miles—ᵓ 13s. 4d., or double the amount for one-third the distance. Bearing on the lack of ᵓcouragement given by the railway in favour of the Transvaal farmer, I have at ᵓesent a consignment of hay from Standerton, which left that village on the 27th ᵓpril. The hay was delivered this morning after three applications to the railway ᵓation to see what had become of it. No explanation of the delay is given, and as ᵓis was a trial consignment, it is quite possible that had it come within reasonable ᵓne two or three further consignments would have been here now. There is another ᵓint we desire to bring out, namely, the manner in which the Netherlands Railway ᵓake use of the clause referring to goods carried at owner's risk. There is an instance ᵓ a consignment—a truck load of grain bags—being despatched from Delagoa Bay in ᵓne last year. It has not yet been delivered, and the railway department repudiates ᵓ liability under the clause that the goods were carried at owner's risk, and as they ᵓre lost the company was not responsible. The matter of expropriation of railways ᵓving been dealt with very fully by preceding witnesses, I desire merely to convey ᵓ you that the feeling of the commercial community is entirely in accord with expro-

Produce rates on Netherlands Railway.

Maladministration of Netherlands Railway.

Expropriation of railway.

priation.   The commercial community would hail with much satisfaction th
nationalisation of the railway, and is strongly of opinion if the railway were und
competent Government officers many of the complaints which have been justly ma
against the Netherlands Company would he done away with, and the railway cou
be in many ways of much more service to the community.   To reduce the cost
living so as to enable a reduction of wages to be made, I would suggest that the who

Special duties on
foodstuffs. of the special duties on foodstuffs now in force, and those held in abeyance by th
Government, be abolished entirely.   As an illustration, take a case of jam which cos
in Europe 18s. 6d.   It pays to the Government of this State 12s. special duty, an
1s. 7d. *ad valorem* duty.   In 1896 jams and confectionery, weighing 1,278,130 lbs
valued at £26,393, were imported, and upon these items alone the special duty wa
£15,976 12s. 6d., and ordinary duties, £2,375.   Thus there was £18,350 taxation in on
year upon articles which from a regular portion of diet among the poorer portions c
the community.   Milk, which costs the same in Europe, bears no special duty, and
sold in Johannesburg at 28s. per case, whereas the price of jam is 42s.   It is needles
to give any further details on this point.   The removal of special duties will invar
ably cause larger consumption.   As an instance, during 1895, when special duties wer
on, pork was imported weighing 432,980 lbs., and valued at £17,015.   In 1896, whi
the special duty was suspended, the import amounted to 1,529,310 lbs., valued a
£51,943.   As a further relief to the commercial community, I would suggest that th

Transfer duty on
landed proper-
ty. transfer duty on landed property be reduced.   This, of course, will bear also on minin,
properties, and we think should be reduced.   Regarding the Pass Law, much has bee

The Pass Law. said before this Commission for and against this Law, and I may venture also to sa

Amendments re-
quired to Pass
Law. that, in my opinion, the law is a good one in the main.   But it requires amendmen
in some clauses.   The clause which stipulates that a pass should be renewed on th
first of every month is unworkable, and frequently causes innocent natives to b
arrested and fined before their employers have had time to get a renewal of the pas
An instance came to my notice in which a van-driver was arrested on his master's va
on the 1st April, at 11 o'clock in the morning.   This arrest took place in spite of th
fact that the man was in possession of his pass and badge for the month of March
It is acts such as these which make natives from other States afraid to come here i
search of work, and when they come they demand higher wages to cover such risk
It would be a good thing if the passes could be taken for a longer period than on
month.   In Kimberley, where I formerly lived, it was possible to take out a native
pass for twelve months, all payments for that time being paid when the pass wa
taken out.   A point which I have been asked to bring forward specially is tha

Sweepstakes and
lotteries. relating to sweepstakes and lotteries.   We feel that the evil is growing so rapidly tha
something should be done to put a stop to it.   It is reported to me on good authorit
that during the last race meeting over £100,000 was spent over these lotteries an
sweepstakes.   It is in the experience of many traders that they cannot obtain pay
ment during the currency of these sweepstakes.   We also feel it is a cause of dis
honesty.   An instance was brought to my notice this morning.   I cannot say it is
positive fact, but I believe it is true that recently a youth took three tickets and pai
for them in postage stamps.   I think your recommendations might do something i
that respect.

Mr. *de Beer*

Why was not the matter of sweepstakes referred to in the statement of th
Chamber of Mines?   Should it not have been referred to by the joint associations?—
I can only explain its omission as being an oversight.

I have seen the crowd so large on race days that you could not get throug

missioner Street, and I feel that the Commission is quite prepared to act in this
ter.—We can, if the Commission desires it, bring further evidence on that point.

Do you mean by taxation that some of the duties are so high as to put the goods Import duties.
of the reach of poor people?—Yes; to a certain extent, certainly.

And if the duties should be reduced the poor people would be able to buy
per?—Certainly.

Mr. *Smit.*

In the evidence before the Commission, it has been suggested to take the duty off
article and off another. Don't you think it is desirable to chuck the whole lot at
?—No; I don't think so. You must let me explain. I think the Government
nue is very large; it can stand reductions. But, in the case of some reductions, if
Government had possession of the railways, they would make them pay.

Mr. *Joubert.*

You consider the expropriation of the railway desirable?—Certainly. Expropriation of railway.

Supposing the company are prepared to make reductions—the main point is the
stion of reductions—that would also satisfy?—It might satisfy temporarily, but
permanently.

But why not?—Because the Government can control it better.

What you are really asking for is !reasonable reductions in everything. After
se have been made it really matters very little who is in management?—I think it
ters a good deal. I might explain we are constantly hearing of incivility.

You see the Commission has to report; that is why they want to go into details
he matter.—I quite understand the reason of the question. I would only say I
e frequently heard complaints of incivility and lack of attention, and these com·
nts, in my own opinion, do not apply to the regular Government officials to the
e extent.

MR. KARE ROOD was the next witness called. He said: Mr. Kare Rood's evidence.

I want to give evidence with regard to the enormously high taxes levied by the Sanitary Board rates.
itary Board of Johannesburg. I have only a short declaration to make. I have
proofs to show that the charges come to about 20 per cent. of the revenue of
d property, which, of course, makes living in Johannesburg very expensive, and
sequently affects the mining industry. I hand in a number of receipts which speak
themselves. My place is bringing in a revenue of £4,000 a year, and taxation
es to £800. That includes taxes in general.

Mr. *de Beer.*

Do you consider the water rates as taxes?—I don't refer to the Sanitary Board Taxation of fixed property in Johannesburg.
1e. I refer to all taxation on fixed property in Johannesburg.

Do you also include stand licences?—-Yes, but that is a very small part of the
le.

What are the stand licences per month?—I think it is 10s. per month.

Do you consider the stand licences too high?—No.

It is the only Government tax?—Yes. I gave £15,000 for my stands in the boom
es, and the Sanitary Board have assessed them now at £16,000.

Why do you not work in the matter?—If I were elected a member of the Sanitary
rd I certainly would work in the matter. I have an agent, and he told me he i_s

not treated with ordinary courtesy when he goes to make objections. I consider
high taxation is one of the reasons which make living so very expensive. I
want to express my surprise that the people of Johannesburg always talk about ot
taxes and never refer to these.

Chairman.

That is not really a matter that comes within the province of the Commiss
The authority of the Commission does not include a recommendation to mix th
selves up in the local administration of Johannesburg. I always understood
matter to be entirely in the hands of the people of Johannesburg, and it is for th
to look after their own interests. Unless the Government gives special instr
tions we cannot possibly go into this matter. We will go into the evidence and
if any of it comes within our scope.

Mr. Kock's evidence.

FRANS W. KOCK, chief of the Pass Department of Johannesburg, was then call
He handed in a statement, of which the following is a translation :—

The Pass Law.

I have the honour to state, with due respect, that I have read the differe
declarations with attention, dealing with the Pass Law, being Law No. 31, 1897,
given by the different witnesses before the hon. Commission. To make any rema

Administration of Pass Law.

to that portion which reflects on my defective administration, I consider unnecessa
as comment would be superfluous; but still, the evidence of Mr. C. S. Goldma

Pass Law good but requires amendment.

on that point is worthy of consideration. That the Pass Law is an exceedingly go
law for the control and regulation of the native labour on the goldfields in this St
must be acknowledged; it requires, however, some modifications and improveme
to make it better and more complete. And although most of the witnesses who w
before the Commission, wished strongly to impress this upon the Commission, I ha
not yet learned that one of them has made a definite and practicable proposal how
effect these improvements, and I will now try to give your Commission an idea
what would be necessary for the proper administration of the Pass Law, and will th
place my report under two heads, namely—*(a)* Administration and *(b)* Amendme
of the existing Pass Law.

Administration of Pass Law.

(A). Administration.—I. According to a proclamation in the *Staats Courant,* t
Witwatersrand goldfields were proclaimed in three divisions, namely—Johannesbu

Proclamation of Johannesburg, Boksburg, and Krugersdorp districts.

Krugersdorp, and Boksburg. First under Law No. 23, 1895, and, later, under La
No. 31, 1896 (at present in force). In each of which divisions the Government a
pointed a staff of officials.

II. Since the Pass Law Regulations were put into force, it appears that, in ord
to ensure good and efficient administration of the Pass Law, it is necessary, and
the greatest importance to the mining industry, that further appointments should

Appointment of chief administrator.

made under the Pass Law, namely—(1) a chief administrator, or head of the depa
ment over the three labour districts on the Witwatersrand goldfields, and ov
such other goldfields, public diggings, and private unproclaimed fields of this Sta
as the President, from time to time, by virtue of Article 2, Law No. 31, 1896, m

Duties of chief administrator.

proclaim. Such chief administrator shall stand under and be responsible to t
Minister of Mines, and under such instructions and regulations as the Minister
Mines shall draw up and submit to the Government for approval; (2) a special pa

Appointment of special pass commissioner.

commissioner for the Johannesburg labour area, where the circumstances are peculi
and such other labour areas where circumstances demand it; (3) a force of twenty

Special police force instituted for districts under Pass Law.

more mounted police, and as many for the other labour districts as may be fou
necessary; (4) one chief warder, with six or more under-warders, for the Johannesbu
labour district, and as many for the other districts as may be deemed necessary. Th
appointments are *inter alia* necessary.

(*a*). Chief administrator or head of the department, to conformably regulate the A chief adminis-trator and identical ad-ministration in all districts un-der Pass Law necessary. different Pass Offices under his jurisdiction, so that the Pass Law may be administered the same way wherever proclaimed; for instance, it is administered in a different way in each of the present proclaimed areas, whereby the objects of the Pass Law become frustrated and useless. A head who would take an interest in the working of the department, and who would have the time and opportunity at his disposal to represent and lay before the Government the difficulties and requirements, in this respect, of the mining industry.

(*b*). A Pass Commissioner, who shall have the same jurisdiction and powers as a A pass commis-sioner with criminal juris-diction neces-sary. criminal Landdrost, and who shall stand in direct connection with the pass offices, so as to expedite matters, to adjudicate upon all cases falling under the provisions of the Pass Law.

Attached to the pass offices must be a charge office, where natives who have Special charge office required for carrying out Pass Law. transgressed the provisions of the law, especially arrested deserters, can be kept for about twelve hours, for identification by their employers, after which they could immediately be dealt with according to the law, or ordered back to their employers, as circumstances may demand.

(*c*). For the assistance of the pass issuer, and the detection of deserters, a Special staff of police required for carrying out Pass Law. complete staff of police is necessary; and

(*d*). For the proper control of the charge office, and assistance to the pass issuer, a A staff of ward-ers required. staff of warders, as above specified.

The probable revenue from this office for the year 1897 will be £67,500, and about Estimated rev-enue of pass office. 15,000 in fines, while, if a staff, as suggested by me, were appointed, the expenditure Estimated ex-penditure of pass office through re-organisation. would hardly be £15,000 per annum.

(B). Modification of the present Pass Law.—Since Law No. 31, 1897, was put into force it appears that certain regulations thereof are incomplete, and to make it more Amendments necessary in Pass Law. practicable further amendments are necessary, namely :

Art. 4. 2nd par., 4th line, to erase the words "without unreasonable delay," and Article 4. insert therein, "within 4 days."

Art. 5 (*a*)., 7th line, to erase the words, "Irrespective whether the same be Article 5. from within the Republic or from beyond the borders thereof," and to insert therein, "obtained in accordance with Art. 4 of Law No. 22, 1895, or Art. 11 of these regulations."

(*b*). To add a new sentence as follows :—"And the pass official shall destroy the travelling pass immediately after registration."

Art. 7. To add, "contraventions of this article shall be punishable with a fine Article 7. of not less or higher than £3, or not more or less than three weeks' imprisonment with or without hard labour, or lashes not to exceed 25."

Art. 13. New par. to add the following. (*a*) "The pass issuer is empowered, in Article 13. the event of registered natives going to work temporarily in another labour district, to issue a certificate granting leave that natives may be moved to another labour district on travelling passes; provided that their employer made proper application to the pass official, such certificate must mention the name and registered number of each native, the time for which it is granted (not to extend, however, beyond two months), what sort of work has to be executed, and the name of the employer. A copy of this certificate must be sent to the pass officials, for information, in the other district. Such natives must be provided with (*a*) a monthly pass of the district in which they are registered.

(*b*). When natives are transferred for good from the one labour area to another, or wish to leave in accordance with Art. 11 of these regulations, in order to work

S

there, their monthly passes shall remain in force for the new labour district, to the end of the current month, provided they are endorsed by the proper official.

Article 14.

Art. 14 to read as follows : " Any native found in the labour district without the district pass of form 'A' and metal badge of that labour district, or without travelling pass or any contravener under Art. 9, shall be punishable on conviction with a fine of not less or exceeding £5, or imprisonment for not less than six weeks or more than two months, with or without hard labour, or lashes not exceeding 25.

New par.—Any native sent by his employer, or who, with the consent of his employer, wishes to go anywhere within the labour district wherein he is residing, must be provided by his employer with a special permit, describing the circumstances of his mission, the date of issue, and period for which the permit is granted, but in no case shall such a permit be granted for longer than three consecutive days.

Any native found in the labour district without this permit shall be punishable in accordance with the punishment as laid down in the above-mentioned article.

Article 16.

Art. 16, 15th line, after the figure £5, to insert the word "or."

Article 18.

Art. 18 to be replaced by the following—" Any native leaving one labour district for another, not provided with the proper travelling pass of form 'C,' shall, when arrested, be immediately handed over for punishment to the authorities in the labour district from where he came in the first instance ; and, in the event of having deserted after punishment to be sent back to his employer. Contraventions of this article shall be punishable in accordance with the punishment as laid down in Art. 14 of these regulations."

Article 18A.

Art. 18A. It shall not be lawful for any native within a labour area to be a master of natives. Punishment for transgression of this article to be in accordance with the punishment as laid down in Art. 14 of these regulations.

Second Art. 18 to be altered to Art. 19.

Article 21.

Art. 21. To add a new par. to Art. 21, as follows :—" Whenever a native is hired by the week or month, either the native or employer shall be held to give one another one week or one month's notice. In all other cases, if the engagement is for a longer period, one month's notice shall be required. In case of misbehaviour or dereliction of duty on the part of the native, the master shall not be obliged to give this notice if he wishes to discharge the native."

Article 22.

Art. 22 (a), first line, to insert after the word " employer," the following " agent, mediator (bemiddelaar), or person."

Article 23.

Art. 23. To add a new par.—" The district passes of all deserted natives shall be sent in, together with the returns of form 'E,' to the pass official, and a note shall be made in the registers kept in the Pass Office of such desertions, and the district passes destroyed."

Article 27.

Art. 27, fifth line, to insert after the words " labour inspector," the following :— " Clerks, police, warders, and other subordinate officials under the jurisdiction of the pass issuer.

Article 32.

Art. 32. To add a new par. :—" The Sanitary Board shall not issue any travelling ('togt') or other licence to natives unless permission first be granted by the pass issuer."

Article 32A.

New Art. 32A. All contraventions committed by natives, against which no provision for punishment is made in this law, shall be punishable by a fine not exceeding £3, or imprisonment not exceeding three weeks, with or without hard labour or lashes; and contraventions committed by whites shall be punishable in the same manner, with the exception of lashes.

The whole object of the Pass Law is the control and regulation of native labour on the goldfields, and if the desertion of natives can be prevented, the mining ustry would be fostered, and the object of the law attained. Should the above Control of natives on gold fields and throughout the Republic obtainable. gested proposals therefore be approved of and accepted, I have no doubt that ; would to a large extent be the result, and with some further modifications the s Law might be made to operate throughout the entire Republic, so that this trol and regulation will be exercised not only over the natives on the various dfields, but also over those going to and from them, and over all of those in the public. It is, of course, well known to me that large numbers of natives desert Desertion. m the mines, and also that not many of them are again brought back to their ployers; I do not, however, admit, as several of the witnesses stated before the Some deserters arrested. mmission, that *no* deserted natives have been arrested and returned to the mines. sides, it is by no means certain that natives deserting are not punished, as no native obtain a travelling pass, district pass, or badge, or be re-registered unless he has plied with the one or other regulation of the Pass Law. It thus speaks for itself t, perhaps with a few exceptions, deserting natives are punished. It has to be nowledged that when a native throws away his passes and badge, he cannot again Identification of deserters difficult. ily be identified by any of the pass officials, and I challenge anyone to describe a ive, and register him in such a way that he would be able to identify him without aid of his passes and badge, out of 60,000 other natives.

This is the case with every native registered, but should they still be in possession Means for identification of deserters. any of their passes or badge, identification becomes easy enough. Identification uld, therefore, be easier by the officials of the different mines, and in order to meet s I have suggested a charge office, with a large yard, where all natives arrested ld be kept for a certain time to ensure identification by their employers.

According to my opinion, the question is not so much the detection and apprehen- Means for preventing desertion. n of deserters, but the prevention of desertion. Prevention is always better than e, and this may be accomplished only by taking away the inducement to desert, ich may be done in two ways:—

(1) By mine managers and other employers of natives; that is, by acting strictly conformity with the provisions of the law by not engaging deserted natives and se who have not fulfilled the requirements of the Pass Law, such as was and is the e at the present day.

It is unreasonable to expect that the Pass Law can be carried out with proper ct if only a small portion of the public act up to it.

(2) By making the punishment for desertion so severe that no native will venture leave his employer illegally, and for this offence I have accordingly suggested a nishment to meet the case.

Finally, I may state that I am the first Pass Issuer appointed under the Pass w, and the above remarks and suggestions have been made from facts gained by perience, and I believe I have had a better opportunity than anyone else to become roughly acquainted with the different requirements and discrepancies of the Law, l that I am therefore in a position to give a sound opinion on the matter; being at times willing to give any further information or explanation.

If these proposals were adopted it would be greatly in the interest of Administration of Pass Law. mining industry. I thought the mines had approached the Government them- ves regarding the faulty working of the Pass Law, and being under that impres- n I waited the outcome before carrying out my intention of approaching the vernment personally on the matter. There was a meeting of mine managers called, l before it was held some of the managers called on me for an expression of my ws. I agreed, and they then asked for my views in writing. I complied, and the ument is still in the hands of Mr. De Roos and Mr. Johns. The managers then

asked me if I was willing to submit my statement to the Government if they agr
to the provisions, and I said I was quite prepared to go to Pretoria and explain
matter to the head of the Mines Department. Nothing, however, came of th
Subsequently I saw in the paper that the mines were taking up quite a different p
posal to the one I had submitted, and that is the reason why I have delayed plac
the matter before the Government. I got no report from the managers what th
opinion was, although the mine managers were going to petition the Government.
cannot quite see if the law were altered that it would interfere with the administ

Re - organisation
of pass office. tion of the three departments—Judicial, Minister of Mines, and Native—and
suggestion is that the head of the Pass Department would still be under the Minis
of Mines.

Mr. Joubert observed that if the law was altered as proposed it would create
new department of administration.

Witness said there would be another landdrost, and he would sit on these spec
cases. Continuing, he said : What I want to see is one head regulating equally t
work on these fields.

Mr. *Hay.*

The proposal regarding the appointment of a special judicial officer practical
means another landdrost?—It would only be a special department for a spec
judgment.

He would be dealing with the Native Department?—Yes. Government mu
appoint a third or fourth landdrost whose work is to deal with the Pass Law.

Mastership of
natives. There is one clause, or a suggested new article, referring to the question that
native is to be a master of natives. Don't you think that in laying down a hard ar
fast rule of that kind the law would work very awkwardly sometimes?—There is
correspondence pending on the point. I formally proposed to the Superintendent
Natives, that if special free passes were asked for, the applicants should be registere
But a Volksraad resolution has been taken, and it now happens that natives, exce
in the case of missionaries, ask for free passes, and then they lure a lot of native
The Pass Law says every native must have a master, and that is the reason why
make this proposal regarding native masters. As an alternative I have asked for
limit to place on the number of kaffirs a native can hire.

Would it not be wiser to include in this law a provision that in the case of
"native" man hiring natives that he has the authority of the head of the pass admini
tration.—It is a difficult question.

These pass regulations, as drawn up, apply particularly to kaffirs?—Yes.

Cape boys and
bastards. Then the difficulty arises with the people known as Cape boys and bastards.
That is the reason I made the proposals, in order to give the Government an oppo
tunity of drawing the line.

Don't you think it would be better to separate the two classes of peop
altogether—that is, make a distinction between the native who works on the mi
and what is known as a bastard?—I think it would be difficult to draw the lin
You cannot make two laws, and the same law must apply to all natives, just as t
same law applies to all whites.

But you have got the question of white people, you have got the mixed bree
and you have got the pure kaffir. Don't you think it would be better to make
regulation to enable this middle class people to register, and give them a certificate f
a year?—My recommendation to the Superintendent of Natives was that the li

ld be drawn between kaffirs and those who depended on themselves for a liveli-
od, and that they should pay a different tax.

Yes. As illustrating the difficulty, I will give you a case which happened to my-
f. I have a man in my employ and he is very dark, but his father is an English-
n, who is married to a woman who is descended from a St. Helena woman and a
ite man. Out of nine children this man is the dark one ; all the others are white.
Was the case before the court ?

Yes.—And the Landdrost gave judgment ?

Yes. I am not finding fault, as originally I made the man take out a pass. But
uld it not simplify the law very much if these people were made to pay a separate
arge—a reasonable amount, and give them licences.—That is being dealt with at the
esent moment.

There are some of these amendments which, if I may suggest it, I should like to Suggestions for Mine Managers Association.
nd to the mine managers. I think if the amendments were put before the Mine
anagers' Committee, asking them to send a reply in writing whether they approved
disapproved of these alterations, that could be handed to Mr. Kock for his considera-
n. I understand Mr. Kock to say in his report that the pass regulations taken as a
ole are good, and that the fault of the law not being properly administered is
inly because of the pass office having been undermanned.—The law is a good one,
hough several articles require modification.

Replying to the Chairman, witness said the registration of kaffirs was good enough
the present moment. One of the objects of his suggestion regarding hiring natives
s that nobody should be able to hire kaffirs who were not in possession of district
sses, and he hoped that would stop desertion to a great extent.

MR. ALEXANDER BUCHAN FYFFE was called, and being duly sworn in, said that he Mr. Fyffe's evidence.
wished to give evidence on the working man's wages on the Rand. He said:

Mr. Chairman and gentlemen, in the first place allow me to apologise for not being
esent this morning when I was first called. I only knew yesterday that I had to
pear before the Commission this morning, and I was in the Orange Free State. I
en left by the first possible train last night, and arrived here this morning. I have
thank you, on behalf of the working men of the Rand, for allowing me to give in a
atement with regard to the working man's wages on the Rand. In the first place, I
sh to point out that the wages of white men generally, working on the Witwaters- White wages.
nd goldfields, are none too high, considering the cost of living. That has been
iply proved by those who have already appeared before the Commission—
Mr. George Albu and Mr. Fitzpatrick. Let me say that the average wage of a
rpenter, the trade to which I belong, is £1 per day. On the average that
mes to about £27 per month, and the expenses are made up in much
e following fashion :—Food comes to £6 per month at a mine boarding house. Some
the mines again charge 10s. per month for a room. Then you have to provide for
ur wife and family, who are generally not provided with a house on the property on
ich you work. That house rent in the district of Krugersdorp, costs at least £7 per
onth. Then you have to provide food for your wife and family, and this costs about
per month, and that leaves you with about £6 with which to buy clothing and
educate your children, and to make provision for a rainy day, doctor's fees, and such
tle odds and ends as clothing for yourself, and tobacco, and some little enjoyment.
ost of us now present on the Rand left our homes in Britain and America because of
e view put before us by the capitalists that wages were high on the Rand, and the
st of living not exorbitant. We left our comfortable homes and the pleasures of life,

and we came out here in the hope of making a little money, and at some future da
of going home to see our friends and the place of our childhood.   Now, I hold that
living wage is what a working married man can live on in peace and comfort.   Accor
ing to the evidence given you by Mr. Barrow, you will see that the working ma
unless he gets a house provided on the mine on which he works, cannot keep a wi
and family in this country out of the wage he at present receives, because, gentleme
the majority of men in this country are not carpenters but are miners, and their wag
do not rise as high as £27, but who have, gentlemen, on an average, £20 per mont

White wages and mine officials' and directors' salaries.
Now, sir, in estimating the cost of white labour on these fields, all divisions of whi
labour, from the general manager downwards to the lowest working man on the min
have been thrown into one lump sum, and this has been taken as the average expens
of white labour on these mines.   No witness as yet examined has stated in detail ho
these wages are paid.   I would suggest that the Commission have a public audit
appointed to enquire into the various items which figure as white labour on the
mines.   Gentlemen, it is unfair to saddle the working man with the entire cost
working these mines.   I should suggest that a statement be got from the leading com
panies giving in detail the following :—The London and Johannesburg directors' fee
the London and Johannesburg secretaries' fees, then the consulting engineer's salar
the general manager's salary, the mine secretary's salary, the total clerical staff
salaries.   Put these down and get the cost per ton, and in another column get the co
of the qualified working man's wages.   In regard to the question of rent, I see tha

Rents of miners' quarters.
some companies adopt a very unjust line.   Take the following instance : a compan
puts up 12 single men's rooms on their property.   This costs at the outside £80
They charge you on an average £1 per room per month ; therefore they draw fro
these 12 rooms the sum of £144 per annum, and the return on their outlay of £800
about 16 per cent.   Now, gentlemen, if the mine directors and the mine manage
grumble about the extortionate charges of the Netherlands Railway, they ought also, i
the first instance, to make their own house clean, so that if we have to pay rent fo
rooms let it be a fair return on their outlay.   Let me here state that all mines do n
charge for rooms ; some mines provide good married men's houses, and also good sing
men's quarters, without charging anything for them from employees.   Again, I wis
to point out another item on which the Commission ought to get some informatio
from mine managers and directors.   If I am rightly informed, the cost of dynamite

Cost of gelatine and fuse to contract work men.
about £4 5s. per case.   How does it come about that on certain mines they charge me
who are working under contract from £5 10s. to as high as £6 per case.   I saw thi
from the bill of a contractor on the Randfontein Estates for 25 cases of gelatine.
think, according to the statement of the manager of the Crown Reef, that gelatine cost
£5 2s. 6d., while Mr. J. B. Robinson charges £6 for a case of gelatine.   How do the
charge so much more to contractors than the actual cost of the article.   Take anothe
item, perhaps small in its way, but still important, namely, fuse.   That costs, at th
very outside, in Johannesburg, 5d. per coil.   In Randfontein, contractors are charge
6d. per coil.   Now, Mr. Chairman and gentlemen, I wish to point out another thin
which has a very important bearing on the wages of working men on these mine

Comfort of miners on mines.
In the first place, on many mines—I don't say on all mines, of course there a
exceptions—there is simply no provision made for enjoyment or pleasure of any kin
for employees.   A man is supposed to rise in the morning, take his breakfast and go
work ; work till dinner time, take his dinner, and go to work again till tea time, an
then there is nothing left for him to do but to go to his room—which, in some cases
hardly fit for a kaffir—to spend the rest of the evening.   We have no enjoyment wha
ever, and I hold that unless you can make the lives of the employees of the min
happy and comfortable, the best men at present working in the country will find

not pay to work here, and will go home to their own country, where they can
y life, and have the pleasures and comforts of a home life. Another point I wish
ring before the Commission. is the question of dismissing men on short notice. **Dismissal of miners.**
en a man comes to a mine and gets work, he is told first of all to go down to
office and sign an agreement, whereby he gives or takes 24 hours' notice.
v, gentlemen, this is not optional, because they don't compel you in the strict
e of the word to sign this document; you are compelled by the exigencies of the
to do so. If you don't do so, you are not employed. Another thing which the
king men on the mines are much against is this compulsory signing of an
rance coupon. The man when received on to a mine must agree to take a **Miners' insur-**
ulated sum in the case of receiving an accident on that mine when in the **ances.**
pany's employ. The outside limit on the mines I have worked on is £300.
v, gentlemen, I claim if a man, through the culpability of a manager or the
ials of a mine, in which he is working, sustains an injury whereby he is disabled
life, he is entitled to a little more than £300. I would urge the Commission to
roach the Government with a view to introducing an amendment to those two
s in regard to employment on the mines. I consider in this country we ought to
e an Employers' Liability Bill, framed on somewhat similar lines as the Employers' **Employers' lia-**
bility Bill in Great Britain, whereby an employee is not allowed to contract **bility.**
self out of the benefits of the Employers' Liability Bill. At Home if a man
ains injury when in the employment of the company, although he has signed an
ement that he will take a certain sum, he has the right to sue that company for
providing sufficient means for safe working on that company's property. As I
at the commencement, gentlemen, the living wage I laid down as an irrefutable
im, is what a married man can exist upon. Now everyone agrees that unless
e is a home life in a country, that country has not the elements of success and
ility in it. Is there any inducement in this country at the present moment for a
to settle down and make it his home? You want to make the conditions of life
e pleasant enough to induce married men to settle instead of coming here for a
years and going back again. Some talk has been going on about the mines
ing down in the event of no reduction being made in the burdens resting on the
ustry, namely, the cost of labour and dynamite. I wish to point out that if the
ernment allow the mines to close down they are exposing themselves to a great **Dangers of clos-**
grave danger. If the mines are closed down a large number of men will be **ing down**
wn out of work. These have not enough money to take them out of the country, **mines.**
they will be compelled to live in the country, although starving. Unrest will
ue, and the consequences will be that the Government of this country will be in
ger. This is no fanciful picture, gentlemen, and I would like to point out that in
tralia, in the Victorian Colony, when the managers closed down the mines, and
ew a large number of men out of employment, the Government of the country
ped in and gave them a fortnight's notice to open the mines, with the option of
ing them confiscated. Now, I don't know that I have much more to say, because I
e not been able to place before you the written statement which I had prepared,
I have had to speak entirely from memory, and I hope the Commission will
use my disjointed remarks. I shall be pleased to give any further information. I
ild again impress upon the Government the necessity for making the life in the
ntry such, that married men can settle down and become citizens of the country.
you want to make this a healthy, happy, prosperous country, you have got to keep
the standard rate of wage, and induce the best men to come here, because in the
g run it will come to this—that good men will not come here, and the rag-tag and

bobtail will; and even the companies will be the losers by their policy. As the [Burns said :—

> Go make a happy fireside clime for weans and wife
> Is the true pathos and sublime of human life.

That is all I have to say, and I have only to thank the Commission for having patiently listened to my rambling remarks.

Mr. Smit.

Have you been employed by one of the mines ?—Yes, on the Violet Consolidat Krugersdorp.

To whom did that mine belong ?—Mr. J. F. Henderson, I think, is the princi shareholder.

What salary did you get there ?—£1 per day. We were paid monthly, but are liable to dismissal at 24 hours' notice.

You say that the average of white labour is calculated on the basis of lumpi together all the big salaries and the workmen's salaries, and then the average struck. I quite agree that the men getting the smaller wages must suffer; can y

Mine officials'
salaries. give an instance of any big salary paid to officials ?—I cannot give informati: because I have not seen the books. The report is that the manager on the mine was working on received £2,000 per year, and one of the witnesses before Commission stated there were instances of mine managers receiving as high as £3,(a year.

You say that the Government must adopt such means as to make it a good pl

Dismissal of min-
ers. to live for married people; what do you mean by that ?—I mean that the Gove ment should interfere in the instance I have mentioned. A man being dismissed 24 hours' notice, where he is paid monthly, is putting the men in a wrong positic because it places him at the mercy of the company, and I would ask the Commissi and through them the Government, to make a regulation that if a man is p monthly he should get a month's notice. I may say that the kaffirs on these fie receive a month's notice, and the white workmen on the Randfontein Estates, wh the reduction took place, only got three hours' notice. The Government can put white workmen on the same basis as the kaffirs, and give them at least a mont notice.

You are entitled to a month's notice unless you make a special contract by whi you bind yourself voluntarily to accept 24 hours, and how can the Government st in ?—If you don't take work on these conditions, you won't get work at all. It impossible for a man to refuse, because if he does he is turned adrift. There is union amongst the men sufficiently strong yet to take up the case of the men.

Supposing the mine managers and the directors think that the wages must co

A good living
wage. down, how could the Government meet you there ?—The only way to make possible to live here is by giving the men a good living wage. Most of the witness including Mr. Albu and Mr. Johns, stated that the wages of white labour cannot reduced under present conditions. It is absurd for the companies to throw the wh blame of the mines not paying at the door of the Government and at the door of white men's wages. There are mines on the Rand which will never pay even thou the cost is reduced to 15s. per ton.

Supposing the Government improve the conditions, and the mining men will

Cost of living of
white miners
reducible by
Government
action. pay you good wages, how can the Government help you ?—Well, for one thing, they c reduce the cost of living materially, and bring it down to the same level as in t Cape Colony, where a man can live for at least £1 2s. 6d. per week.

The expenses of living cannot be the same here as in the Cape Colony, as, for stance, grain has to be brought by transport 1,200 miles?—What is to hinder this untry producing all the grain it requires?

Mr. *Hugo.*

Witness.] I came to Johannesburg in November, 1895. I was employed at the andfontein Mines, not directly but through a contractor.

There has been some agitation there recently in connection with the reduction of ages?—Yes.

Reduction of white wages on Randfontein mines.

You took a rather active part in it?—Yes.

What has been the result of the reduction?—Well, the effect of the reduction has en something like this: Mr. Robinson threatened to reduce wages of carpenters om £1 to 16s. 8d. per day. The men refused to work, and the company has been mpelled to get the whole or at least the bulk of the carpentering work done by ntract. The contractor got most of the men who were formerly working on the andfontein Estates, and he gives them £1 2s. 6d. for nine hours, and Mr. J. B. obinson was only going to give 16s. 8d. for 10 hours.

Are any of the men going back to the Randfontein Mines to work who left on count of the reduction of wages?—I left Randfontein on Saturday, and up to that me no carpenters had gone back to work. A drill sharpener took work by contract, d instead of earning 18s. 4d. per day as proposed, he earned £1 7s. 6d. That is the stimony of some of the men at present working by contract.

Have you any experience on other fields?—No.

You think the life of white workmen in this country is not very favourable?— o.

Is it not a fact that they are able to participate very liberally in subscription lists d sweepstakes?—I cannot say that they have gone in for sweepstakes; I have not en able to go in for sweepstakes myself. I was seven months on the Violet, and no bscriptions were got up during that time. I worked till March, 1896, and then I ok typhoid fever. I was off for sixteen weeks, and that sickness cost me at least 200—over £100 in expenses. I am also counting the money I would have received d I been working. It takes all my money to pay my current expenses.

Sweepstakes.

You appear to make a strong point of the fact that companies invest £800 in uilding rooms, and charge £1 per month; is it not a fact that buildings of that escription depreciate very considerably?—I think the charge is exorbitant. If a uilding is properly put up it lasts as long again as a mine.

Rents of miners' quarters.

Do I understand that the Robinson group charge contractors £6 for blasting elatine?—I saw the account of one man who came out on strike; he was not affected y the reduction of workmen's wages, and he was charged for 25 cases of gelatine, 150.

Cost of gelatine to contract workmen.

You say the price of gelatine delivered at the mine is £5 2s. 6d. I think that is mistake; the charge is about £5 9s. 6d.?—I might have made a mistake. They sell contractors, and pay no licence for stores at all.

Mr. *Hay.*

In your statement, where you calculate how much miners receive, and then how uch they pay out, you made a statement there that they sometimes paid a rent of Js. per month for a room?—I made the statement that single men paid 10s. on some roperties, and that married men, in the majority of cases, cannot get rooms on the ines.

Rents of miners quarters.

Subsequently you went into a calculation, and said that on some mines the
charged unfairly. You calculated that a charge of £1 per room per month, on a
outlay of £800, would return 16 per cent.—Yes ; but you are forgetting the fact th
in single men's quarters on the mines there are always two occupants in a room, an
they have to pay 10s. each.

Do you think the charge for a room is universal on the mines ?—No, I don't sa
so ; but there are mines that do.

Practically you don't know anything at all about it, except the mines you hav
been on ?—I may say that on the mine I was on I was not charged.

Practically it is only what you have heard. You can only answer for son
mines ?—Yes ; but why should it be on some mines ?

Uniform rate on
mines for white
wages. But you would not expect people to be paid at the same rate on every mine ? I
that what you are arguing, and, irrespective whether a man is competent or a me
" botch," he should be paid at the same rate ?—I argue that the same rate shoul
obtain on the East Rand as on the West Rand.

Your argument is that every man who is a carpenter, wherever he lives—whethe
at Modderfontein or Randfontein—should get exactly the same rate always, competen
or not.—No, decidedly not. If a man is incompetent he should be kicked off the pro
perty, but I hold that a competent man deserves £1 per day.

White wages. The question is whether a mine can pay or not. It appears that a man must b
paid £1 per day. Now, if a mine cannot afford to pay £1 a day, what are th
managers to do ?—Well, they should approach the Government and try to get suc
concessions as to make the mines not paying, pay, Speaking for myself and the res
of the working men, if the cost of living be reduced they will be quite prepared t
take a good deal less than £1 per day.

You recommend, or warn the Government in a way, that the mines will be close
down ?—Yes.

Supposing a mine does not pay to work then, what is to become of that mine
Is it to be closed down or go on ?—I hardly follow you.

Supposing there is a mine which does not pay to work—and you have said ther
are mines on this Rand which will never pay—then what do you propose to do ; i
that mine to be closed down or go on ?—Well, if it is proved that nothing will mak
that mine pay they must close it down. But there are plenty of mines which wer
paying which will be shut down, I suppose, if the white man's wages are not reduced
and concessions are not granted the industry by the Government. If the Governmen
does this these mines will be compelled to keep open.

What authority have you for making the statement that mines will be closed
down if the concessions are not granted by this Commission ?—If you judge from th
companies which have shut down which were paying, you can easily see that othe
companies will follow suit.

Closing down of
North Rand-
fontein. Will you name a company that has closed down which paid to work ?—Th
North Randfontein was paying, and it closed down for several months.

Why was it closed down ?—I don't know what reason it had for closing dow
It had a good output, and it was closed for several months ; and Mr. J. B. Robinso
said that, if he did not get white labour reduced to the rate he wanted, he would clos
down Porges Randfontein, which is a paying mine.

Then you mean to say Mr. Robinson made that statement ?—Yes. I mean to sa
that Mr. Robinson made a statement to the effect that if he could not get white labou
reduced, and other concessions, he would close down the Porges mine.

The North Randfontein was re-started again ?—It stood about a fortnight durin
the lock-out ; now, I believe, it is at work again.

Therefore, as far as you know, the closing down of the mine may have been for ∣e very good reason ?—It may have been.

Is it not a fact that the mine was closed down because the natives were drunk, ∣ that no native labour could be got ?—No; I don't think so. I will give you an ∣ance. I was speaking to an official of Block A, which is presently to be closed ∣n, and he told me that on that mine they never had any scarcity of boys, even ∣en the difficulty of getting native labour was at its worst; and the common belief ∣hat Block A was closed down because there was no reef there.

That was inevitable if there was no reef there ?—No; and I don't think capitalists ∣ float mines unless the reef is there, and then saddle the Government and the ∣rking man with the blame if these mines are not paying.

You refer to the question of blasting gelatine. The price at the factory at Cost of gelatine ∣dderfontein is £5 7s. 6d. per case, and it costs practically 2s. 6d. to bring it to ∣annesburg. That would bring it up to £5 10s., and to that there is the carriage ∣ Randfontein.—I can produce evidence in confirmation of what I have stated ∣arding the price dynamite was sold at to a contractor.

You seem to complain because the companies insure men's lives against accident. Miners' insurances. ∣t is a grievance to me that a man is compelled to insure, and if he is injured he gets ∣s than he would in a court of law.

If a man works on a property, and the injury he receives is the result of his own ∣elessness, he has no claim on his employer. Is that a fact or not ?—Yes, that is a ∣t.

Not only here, but elsewhere, the same conditions exist ?—Not only here, but all ∣er the world.

If I employ a man to work for me, and he sustains an injury through his cwn ∣lt, am I liable for that or not ?—In a court of law you are not.

You say that £300 is the limit of compensation a company pays in the case of ∣al disablement ?—I am speaking from the agreement I signed myself. The agree-∣nt on the mines here is that, if a man is killed, the company pays a year's wages, ∣th the limit of £500. That is, those who earn more than £500 are limited to £500. ∣at is the universal custom on these fields. On the mine on which I worked, if a ∣n were totally disabled he got a year's pay.

With the limit of £300 ?—I did not say the limit was £300.

Yes, you did.—I don't know whether he was alluding to the secretary or not.

It is a year's pay with the limit of £300 ?—Is there a working man in any branch ∣ trade getting more than £300 ?

Yes, there is. I am speaking from knowledge. I know that during last year we ∣ve paid a lot in compensation.—Do you hold that £300 is sufficient for a man totally ∣abled ?

Most of the accidents which occur are the men's fault.—I don't say that, because ∣least nine-tenths of the accidents on these mines are the fault of the company, as ∣ as my experience goes.

These things were talked over long before you came into this country, and the ∣nditions have been considered fair and equitable.—I don't think so. I know the case ∣ a man with a broken arm who has lost more than the company have paid him.

How much do you think a man ought to get ? You ask the Government to step ∣ and help you. What sum do you think the Government ought to fix ?—I think it ∣uld be presumptuous for me to fix a sum for the Government. It ought to be left ∣ a court of law to settle, and I am quite confident that the working man would get ∣re than he receives in compensation.

Do you think it would be best to give one, two, or ten years' wages?—I do
think I should express anything of the kind; that ought to be left to a court of l

The question is do you think that £300 is too small.   What do you think wo
be fair?—I don't think it would be a fair question to ask at all.

When you say the amount is too small, the question is a fair one.—At home, i
man is injured, he can go to the law courts.   He can't contract out of the benefits of
Employers' Liability Bill.

Mine officials' salaries.   You say in the first part that you think many managers' salaries are too hi
You think a man with £2,000 a year is overpaid?—In some cases I think he is.
don't consider any man on these fields, whatever is his experience, is worth £3,000
year.

Still you think a man ought to get more in this country than in Europe?—Y

In the same way you would get here £1 a day; how much did you get
Europe?—When I was in Glasgow I was in receipt of £1 18s. 6d. a week.

Then you get in this country three times as much as you got in Glasgow?—Y
have to bear in mind that a manager's salary is not only two or three thousand poun
he has, in many instances, a carriage and pair, servants, coal and light.   All these p
quisites count up to about £1,000 a year.   A working man only gets his bare £6
week.

A man with a manager's appointment is supposed to be a man who has been w
trained?—I have undergone a training also, and have have had as much training
any man here.   The fact remains that there has been no attempt to reduce the
officials' salaries; it is always the working man.   In Mr. J. B. Robinson's circular the
was nothing about reducing the consulting engineer's salary, or the manager's sala

Chairman.

Miners' insurance.   What premium have you to pay for insurance; or do the mines pay it?—On so
mines you pay it, and and on some mines you don't pay anything.   I did not pay an
thing on the Violet for insuring my life.   If it had been optional I would not have i
sured my life, but I was compelled to sign the agreements of 24 hours' notice a
insurance, or lose the prospect of work, which is none too plentiful at the prese
time.   On some mines I believe they do pay a small sum per month for insuran
doctor's fees, and other things of that description.

Mr. *Hay.*

The insurance is not mixed up with the doctors' fees; they are quite different.

Chairman.

Your objection is that there is an obligation to sign these agreements?—It
practically compulsory, because, if he does not sign, he would not get a job on the min

What premium have you to pay in the accident companies for £300?—I cann
say as to this country at all.   I was insured for £300 at home, and my premium w
£2 5s. a year.   That was against accident.

You object, because, having signed that agreement, you have no action against t
company?—Yes, you have to accept a sum, in most cases, totally inadequate to t
injuries received.

Comparative wages and cost of living in Scotland and on the Rand.   Now, as regard wages.   Here wages are £1 a day, in Scotland £1 18s. 6d. p
week.   Now, what is the comparison between the two countries in the matter of wag
and the cost of living?—Well, my board and lodging, mending, washing, and ironi
in Glasgow came to 13s. per week.   That included a comfortable room, well furnishe

addition. Washing and mending comes to a pretty sum here when they charge 4s. r dozen articles. Plenty of men live in Glasgow and other parts of Scotland as low 8s. per week. Here in Johannesburg if you work, as I did, in town, they charge £6 d £7 per month for food; £3 per month for your room. My washing bill came to out 10s. per month on an average. Clothes cost three times as much as they do at me, and the quality is very much lower; and boots last about a third of the time ey do at home, and cost about twice as much.

So you agree with the mine managers that it is impossible to reduce white labour present?—Under present conditions it is impossible. If the cost of living is duced to a reasonable rate, there is no workman who would not be willing to cept a good reduction in wages, and be prepared to accept 16s. per day if the cost of ving was proportionately reduced. We have no desire to keep up the £1 per day r good, bad, and indifferent men, but so long as living continues as high as at esent, it is absolutely impossible for a workman to live in a decent manner under 1 per day. *Reduction of white wages.*

What is the object of your evidence?—I may say that I was appointed by the wly-formed Mineworkers' Union, which takes in all branches of employment on the ines—miners, carpenters, blacksmiths, drill-sharpeners, handy men, and all others— represent before this Commission the fact that wages could not be reduced from rrent rates unless living was proportionately reduced. I am not representing yself alone, and I have no desire to come here, as I am losing time. I was asked by is union to appear before you and give their views on these questions of wages and st of living.

You said we must try and get a statement from the different mine managers owing the salaries and wages paid from the highest to the lowest?—Why should ot mine companies be compelled to properly audit their books to show exactly how e money is spent. *Comparative amounts of mine officials' salaries and white wages.*

The average given us of the percentage of cost of white labour ranges between 23 and £28 per month. Now, if we were to get the wages of all, that average ould be reduced?—Most decidedly it would be. A mine manager drawing £3,000 er annum would pay, and will pay, the salaries of a good many workmen. One of e witnesses examined before the Commission would lead the public to believe that e working men were getting the vast bulk of that percentage. I hold that a very rge proportion of it goes in salaries, of which there is no mention of reducing at all. don't mean to say that mine managers' salaries should be reduced, because, as a mine anager said to me, "If my salary is reduced, yours will have to come down also." hat we want is a living wage for ourselves. That is what we are fighting for, and e will allow the mine managers to look after themselves. I don't care if a mine anager gets £3,000 a year, so long—

Do I understand that, with reference to the closing down of these mines of Mr. obinson's, that after the work had been stopped through the proposal to reduce ages, the work was given out to contract?—Yes, on Porges Randfontein; where they re putting up large workshops, and the work was practically begun, the foundations aving been laid, and it was intended to be completed by the company. This has en let out to a contractor who is employing a good few of the men who were locked t, at the rate of 22s. 6d. per day. *Contract work and time wage.*

So you think that at the present moment the work will cost more than it would ave done at the original rate of wages?—Of course it will cost more, as far as I can e. The contractor will do the work quicker no doubt, but it will cost more than if e wages had not been reduced below £1 per day.

Mr. *Smit.*

Miners' insurances.

You say you did not pay your accident insurance ?—I did not pay it on the Violet.

Why are you against it ?—Because I am compelled to receive a lower sum than would receive if I put it before a Court of law.

The contract you sign there prevents your going to a Court in case of accident ?—Yes.

It does not prevent further insurance of your life ?—Certainly not; it does no control your private actions.

Mr. *Brakhan.*

White wages.

You stated that the wages of miners are inferior to those of carpenters, and yo give us a figure of £20 per month. Isn't it a fact that a competent miner earns £4 £50, and even more per month ?—I don't know what the average wage is per mont for miners. I know that the wages on the Randfontein Estates were reduced t £4 10s. per week.

You speak of Randfontein Estates. Why don't you speak of the Rand generall I know for a fact, and it has been stated before the Commission, that the averag wage is considerably more than £20 per month ?—I quite agree that where a man i working by contract he can earn more than £20 per month; but the fact remains tha where a man is not working by contract, and I take it the majority of miners don work by contract, their wages are not above £20 per month.

Is it not a fact that most miners prefer to work by contract than by the day? speak of mining in the mine, not surface work ?—There are some parts of work tha cannot be let out by contract. A stope cannot be let by contract, and the stope is paid 8s. 6d. per day.

I know one mine which does not work by contract, and the average pay o miners last month was somewhat over £29. Some did better, some worse, on accoun of working better ?—Yes; you have got a number of these men who get big pay, wh

Sunday work on mines.

work on Saturdays and Sundays.

Do you mean to say there is any work done on Sundays ?—Most certainly.

On the mine to which I refer there was no work on Sundays except in th milling. Therefore, it shows clearly that a competent workman is able to earn a ver good wage on the Rand, and that those who don't earn such good money are not suc good men, and are not taken on by the contractors. I don't say in all cases, but in a

Overtime.

good many.—I have seen it stated in the papers that on one of the mines, contractors after the beginning of June, would not be allowed to make more than £26 per month I know plenty of mines where there are no contracts given out. If I were allowe overtime I could make considerably more than £1 per day.

Experience is not in favour of overtime, as it is found that work is done durin overtime in three hours which takes four hours by day work ?—That is the fault o the foreman.

It is to be regretted that intelligent men have to be watched ?—If any of th companies had men of the class referred to they ought to be put off the mines, as ther are plenty of men to do a fair day's work for a fair day's wage.

White wages.

The point is this: a competent miner is not confined to £20, his pay, in mos cases, averages much more. There may be some who only get £15 per month, bu companies would be much more ready to pay them £30 by contract if good work i done, than pay at a smaller rate and yet be to the good. There is no endeavour her to cut down miners' wages if they do good work. It is not correct to say that th

ge of miners is £20 per month.—I hold it is not above £20. It has not been
ved before this Commission or anywhere else. The average of any mine should
be taken, you should take the average for the whole Rand.

Some men are earning nearly £100 per month?—Yes, I saw where the manager
he Simmer and Jack gave £140, but you must point out the opposite at Rand-
tein. How many men at the Simmer and Jack get £140 per month?

There is one statement you made that capitalists had told the workmen that high
ges were earned on the Rand; can you gave any names?—That is a general state-
nt. What I mean is that there are men going round about at Home, I do not know
ether they are in the pay of capitalists or in the pay of steamship companies, or
ose pay they are in, but the fact remains that these men lecture at Home about
big wages paid, indirectly inducing men to come out here without their having a
e knowledge of the state of affairs.

Can you substantiate the statement with regard to the capitalists?—I say it lies
er with the capitalists of the mines or the capitalists of the steamship companies.

I want to elicit where capitalists who control the mines have been spreading these
orts with the consequences you name?—I say that last year there was a letter sent
by the Master Builders' Association enlarging on the rate of wages on the Rand,
contrasting the high rate of wages here with the low rate of wages, as they call
at Home. I take it you would call them capitalists because they are directly
ponsible to the mining industry; without the mining industry Johannesburg would
last six months.

You do not accuse any of the mining houses spreading about such reports?—No,
nnot give you the names of any mining houses, but I know there are men going
ut lecturing for this purpose, and they do not do it for love, and it follows that
n who pay them will reap the benefit of the men coming to this country.

Now about the short notice. Cannot the man just as well give 24 hours' notice
leave as the company?—Yes. Most decidedly. I think I said so in my statement.

So it is a hardship on the company also if a man gives 24 hours' notice. It cuts
h ways.—You won't find a man who will throw up a good job to take the chance
getting work in another place.

I know two years ago, carpenters have thrown up and left in 24 hours' notice,
ause they could get 2s. 6d. more at another mine.—I know a man who got a job
a mine not far from Krugersdorp, a married man, who took his wife and family to
district. He was only there three or four days, and he had all the expense of taking
belongings, and furniture out, and because he was at the mercy of the consulting
ineer he was thrown out.

Anyhow, it cuts both ways. In the case of the men the chance is the men are
competent, and the company is justified in dismissing them?—If they are going
dismiss them, they ought to get a month's notice, as they pay them monthly. If
y are going to dismiss a man by the day they ought to pay him daily. I don't
tend they ought to be paid daily. In the case of clerks, secretaries, and amal-
nators, they get a month's notice and they are paid monthly. If a secretary is
missed at a day's notice, he claims a month's pay.

Chairman.

I understand you have a written declaration, but, being called at short notice, you
ld not bring it with you?—Yes, I had a statement written out, but owing to the
t that I was in the Free State yesterday, and I had to appear to-day, I was unable
bring it with me.

Where is it ?—In Krugersdorp.   I can send it in.

I shall be glad to have it.—Then I shall only be too pleased to hand it in to
Commission.

Mr. G. A. A. Mid-
delberg's evi-
dence. Mr. G. A. A. MIDDELBERG, after being duly sworn, said:

Before proceeding to answer the questions which will be put to me, I should li
to have the opportunity of supplying certain information, in consequence of t
interrogatory of witnesses which has already taken place.   The most important po
Netherlands of the accusation laid against the tariffs of the Netherlands Railway consists in t
Railway share
in through share of the carriage obtained by us in the traffic from the seaports to Johannesbu
rates. The accusation that the tariffs from the ports to Johannesburg should be higher
our taking a greater share of the profits, than they would be if we accepted a low
share, is devoid of foundation.   Let us commence with an illustration, which w
make the situation and position clear.   When two individuals decide to build a hou
and provide the necessary funds therefor, and when the rental of that house has be
fixed, then it is certainly a matter of indifference to the tenants of the house wh
share of the rent each of the two owners receives.   This is exactly the same in t
case of the share of carriage received by each of the administrations in the traf
with the ports.   Let me now return to the history of the present existing tariffs.   Wh
History of pre- the railway from the Cape ports to Johannesburg was completed, the Cape Gover
sent railway
rates. ment had obtained the right, by the so-called Sivewright Convention, to raise t
tariffs entirely at their pleasure, only binding themselves to pay out a certain share
the N.Z.A.S.M.   These tariffs exist at present, although since then reductions ha
been introduced here and there.   So far as I know, prior to six months ago, no obje
tion was uttered against these rates, and the agitation which has arisen during t
past few months has certainly surprised both you and me not a little.   When t
Delagoa Bay line was opened for traffic, we asked ourselves, as any railway manag
ment would have done, what rates must be introduced on that line, so that that li
should have a share of the traffic in accordance with the forwarding capacity of t
Difference of line.   The difference in rates from Delagoa Bay with East London was fixed on a
rates on Dela-
goa Bay and average of 15s. per ton.   Again, somewhat later, the construction and opening of
East London line with Natal was negotiated, and again the question was asked, what tariffs sha
routes.
Through railway be recognised on that line, so that also that railway connection should obtain a pr
rates on Natal
line. portionate share in the traffic.   As you are aware, and as appeared later from exper
ence, the rates from East London to Johannesburg have assured also to Durban
sufficient share in the traffic.   The rates from the ports to Johannesburg thus in th
Shares of differ- way stood firm with the most sound railway principles.   What share each of t
ent railway ad-
ministrations administrations should receive therefrom has nothing to do with these rates, but
in through the result of agreement; or, if you will, of struggle between those different admini
rates are inde-
pendent of the trations.   When, therefore, a limit was placed thereon, by the Cape manageme
amount of the
rates. taking measures to prejudice the railways from Delagoa Bay and Natal, by deman
ing from us a higher share of the rates, there was no mention of increase of tarif
but alone of the ceding of a greater share by the Cape administration to us.   T
correspondence having reference to this is to be found in Green Book No. 1, 1895.
is surprising that these so simple facts are not grasped in Johannesburg.   This is t
more to be wondered at, because by a comparison of the so-called rates from Mid-Va
River with those from Vereeniging, an elucidation of the fact could so easily
arrived at.   But this is still more surprising, for when some time back a di
agreement arose between the Free State and Cape administrations regardi
the share of rates which each should enjoy in the through traffic, and when t

[Ca]pe administration threatened to extort a greater share for itself, no cry of [ind]ignation sprang up in Johannesburg that the tariffs would be raised, because [the]y then fully understood that a higher share for the Cape administration was [equ]ivalent with a lower share for the Free State. I do not here contend that the [rat]es from the ports to Johannesburg are high, or low, or just; I merely wish to [de]monstrate that the share which the N.Z.A.S.M. has obtained has nothing to do with [the] tariffs from the ports. Certainly the N.Z.A.S.M. could have induced a tariff war, [ins]tead of warding it off; but I consider myself fortunate that hitherto the tariff war [ha]s been avoided. Many in Johannesburg would have rubbed their hands in ecstasy [ha]d the three competing railway lines to the ports commenced a tariff war in the [gen]uine American manner. It requires no demonstration that this would have been [gr]eatly to the detriment of the whole of South Africa and its Governments. With [res]pect to this State, the important fact should not be forgotten that it receives 85 [per] cent. of those higher tariff shares, and of those greater receipts, and over and [ab]ove this, as a large shareholder, about another 5 per cent. In place of which it [mi]ght have been expected it would have been said, "Thou, good servant, thou hast, in [ac]cordance with genuine commercial principles, assured thyself of the largest share of [the] general revenue by which this State has been placed in a position to cover the [inc]reasing expenditure,"—a cry of indignation is uttered, which, taken at its least, is [un]just. Permit me now to subject the direct tariffs to a closer examination. In the [fir]st place, people have distorted the shares of rates of the N.Z.A.S.M., and made them [to] appear as tariffs; and they have compared them with those in other countries of the [wo]rld. It is astonishing that they have forgotten to make a comparison of the tariffs [fro]m the ports to Johannesburg, with the tariffs from the ports to other places in [So]uth Africa, namely, to stations of the Cape Colony, Free State, and Natal. Had [th]ey done that, they would have arrived at the surprising result that not alone had [Jo]hannesburg reason to pity itself, but all the other places, for instance, in the Free [St]ate and Cape Colony. I attach hereto a statement of the tariffs per ton and per [mi]le in the Cape Colony, Free State, and Natal, and I find that, far from the rates [fro]m the seaports to Johannesburg being high, when compared with those to other [pla]ces, they may be called exceptionally low.

[margin note: Share of State in Netherlands Railway shares of through rates.]

[margin note: Comparative railway rates from ports to Johannesburg and from ports to other South African places.]

[CO]MPARISON OF THE TARIFFS PER TON AND PER MILE ON THE CAPE AND NATAL RAILWAYS AND FROM THE PORTS TO JOHANNESBURG :—

[margin note: Comparative table of railway rates per ton per mile on Cape and Natal railways, and from ports to Johannesburg.]

	Normal Goods.	Medium Class.	Timber (Rough Goods).
[Ca]pe Railway (local traffic)—			
50 miles, delivery fee not included	6d.	2·80	4·80
100 ,, ,, ,, ,, ...	5·40	2·40	3·60
200 ,, ,, ,, ,, ...	4·90	2·20	3·30
[fo]r long distances, such as Port Elizabeth, Johannesburg	4	1·71	2·68
[Ac]tual rate to Johannesburg—			
From Port Elizabeth, delivery fee included ...	2·70	2·41	1·75
,, East London ,, ,, ...	2·76	2·43	1·77
,, Cape Town ,, ,, ...	2·56	2·17	1·67
,, Durban ,, ,, ...	3·79	3·34	2·43
,, Delagoa Bay ,, ,, ...	4·24	3·64	2·52

T

					Normal Goods.	Medium Class.	Tim (Ro Goo
Rate from Port Elizabeth—							
To Bloemfontein	...	...	...	...	3·90	1·78	2·
„ Kroonstad	...	...	...	...	3·18	1·97	2·
„ Viljoen's Drift	...	...	...	...	2·85	2	2·
„ Kimberley	...	...	...	...	4·01	1·82	2·
„ Mochuli ...	...	...	...	...	3·53	1·97	2·
Natal Railways (local traffic)—							
25 miles	...	...	...	...	8	6	5·
50 „	...	...	...	...	4·50	3·70	3·
100 „ and more	...	...	...	...	4	3·25	2·
Netherlands South African Railway Company—							
For all distances without terminals			...	...	6	4·50	3

Thus for instance, where the 2nd class goods are forwarded from Port Elizabet
to Johannesburg for 2·7d. per ton and per mile, the rate to Bloemfontein amounts
3s. 9d., to Kroonstad 3·18d., to Kimberley slightly over 4d. ; and we see that th
inhabitants at Viljoen's Drift have to pay almost the same rate for oversea goods as
Johannesburg, certainly a proof that a share of the rates from the Vaal river
Johannesburg has no effect thereon. But the differences come out strongly when w
compare the rate for timber to Johannesburg with that in the Cape Colony and th
Free State over similar distances. There we find that timber from Port Elizabeth t
Johannesburg is rated at 1·75d. per ton per mile, to Bloemfontein 2·60d., Kroonsta
2·87d., Kimberley 2·72d. The same applies to the Natal line, though in a somewha
lesser degree. We now go a step further, and ask under what rates the mining industr

Through railway
rates to Rho-
desian mines. in Rhodesia will have to come for development. People have fixed all hopes on th
development of the mines in Rhodesia. Nowhere have I heard it asserted that thes
mines are richer than those on the Rand. Well, now, the rate from Port Elizabeth t
Mochuli in transit to Rhodesia amounts, for normal goods, 9·4d. per 100 lbs., agains
8·1d. to Johannesburg, and the rate for timber 5·8d., against 5·3d. to Johannesbur
To this rate there must still be added the rate over the great distance from Mochuli t
the gold fields. Is it not marvellous how anyone can think of the possibility of eve
developing these fields, when it would appear, with the existing rates to Johannesbur
already to be impossible. We see from the foregoing that, when anyone in Sout
Africa has to complain regarding the high railway rates, it can certainly not, in th
first instance, be Johannesburg, but nearly all the other places in the Free State, th
Cape Colony, and Natal which are deprived of the results of the privilege of lyin
nearer the sea. And when the great wish, recently expressed, that the endeavours c
all must be that all whites south of the Zambesi shall have equal rights is realised, the
important reductions in the matter of railway tariffs will have to be introduced for th

State railway
principles un-
suitable for
South Africa. benefit of these other places. It is just because the principle of a State railway so littl
suits the railways in South Africa, and the railways are rather managed on commercia
principles, that this more satisfactory result is obtained for Johannesburg. If the tru
State railway principles whereby privileges for one standard or class above another ar
excluded, were recognised here in South Africa, then this certainly would not come i
the interests of of Johannesburg tariffs. I now come to the second great grievance : th

Railway rates for
coal on English
railways. coal rates in conjunction with the working costs. What has not been told regardin
the coal tariffs ? In the manifesto of Mr. Leonard, it was already contended, and
myself was mentioned as authority, that the profit from the coal rates for the minin

stry along the Rand would be sufficient to cover the expenditure over the entire
to Delagoa Bay. This was repeated almost recently in the report of the Chamber
lines, and by Mr. Eckstein. Mr. Fitzpatrick, with a dexterously chosen example,
ch is really an exception, has attempted to give an illustration in the case of the
lenhuis Deep, of the weighty burdens which rest on the mining industry through
coal rates. Another went so far as to quote the tariffs for coal on certain English
roads, and it was even said that because the Free State Railway charges the Cape
way ¼d. per ton per mile for the coal on behalf of the Cape Railways, this tariff
d be suitably introduced on the Rand. Why did they not go a step further,
wing that the N.Z.A.S.M. does not charge anything for the coal for its own use on
own line, no more than the Cape Railways for theirs, and declare that thereby the
of was furnished that the coal for the mining industry could be forwarded for
ing? The basis for the compilation of all tariffs is the calculation of the working
s, as well as of the interest and further necessary and actual expenditure. There
t two ways by which the working cost can be calculated. Let me, by an example,
ke both these modes of calculation clear. Suppose a railway forwarded 100,000
of goods per annum, and receives as carriage £1 for each ton, and let us allow
the cost of working, say thus: the costs for the maintenance of roads and build-
, the actual cost for motor power, the cost of stations and traffic *personnel*.
ther, the general expenses, the interest, and the writings-off amount to £100,000,
the costs are covered, and it can be said that the actual cost for the forwarding
ne ton amounts to £1. Suppose now that that railway, which has there not
hed the limit of its forwarding capacity, gets an offer to forward 10,000 tons
e, and must do this at such a reduced price that it can make no profit, or, at least,
little. To estimate the actual cost, which is necessary to forward these 10,000
, over and above the already existing 100,000, we go to work as follows: we say
railroad is there, and is maintained. By the increased transport of 10,000 tons
interest of a railway is not increased, any more than the cost of maintenance.
personnel of the stations remain the same, whether one or more trains have to
through. The only thing that costs more is the *personnel* and the fuel of the
ns which have to travel more. Suppose now we arrive at a figure of 5s. per ton,
which these extra 10,000 tons could be forwarded, then we find at the end of the
r an income of £102,500, as against an expenditure of £102,500. That railway has
s remained in the same condition. Then, however, the forwarders of the first
,000 tons say: "You can, and you admit that you can, forward 10,000 tons for
500. How can you then ask us to pay £1 for each ton?" And yet what a
erence in the account. In the example thus far quoted the returns for 110,000
s are £102,500. Should, however, the whole 110,000 be forwarded for 5s. per ton,
returns would amount to £27,500, or, in other words, a loss be entailed of £75,000.
e, in Africa, far too much is already forwarded for prices which do not cover the
according to the first account. It is not long since the Commissioner of Railways
he Cape Colony assured me that the net cost of a ton of goods per mile on the
e Railways, bearing in mind all the cost and expenditure for maintenance,
unted to between 1½d. and 2d. I could not believe that then, but recently I have
vinced myself of it by the following calculation, which, as all the data were not at
service, cannot lay claim to entire exactness, but is certainly sufficient for our
pose. I estimated the average revenue per ton of goods per mile on the
e and Natal Railways. I said, were those estimated average prices reduced to
l., how much would be the loss sustained by the Cape and Natal Railways, and
und that the smaller income represented a larger sum than the whole net returns
he Cape and Natal railways, after the subtraction of the interest of the construc-

[margin notes:] Basis of compilation of railway rates on coal. Methods of calculating railway working costs.

[margin note:] Net cost of a ton of goods per mile on the Cape railways.

tion capital. From it appears that, by a general application of a tariff of 1½d. per
per mile, these railways would not be in a position to cover the interest and expen
For our railway, ampler data are at my disposal, and applying the same method
our returns, I come to the conclusion that the loss for the railway, after the paym
of all remaining costs, amounts to over £150,000 ; 1½d. per ton per mile is thus be

Working costs of
Netherlands
Railway.

our actual cost. It has been said that our working expenses must be exceptiona
low. The argument of the influence of low grades, so attractive for the layman
always brought forward. Did our working costs amount to less than those of
other railways in South Africa, then it certainly would be the only thing in
Republic that is cheap. I have never heard it stated that we pay extravagantly h
salaries to the *personnel*, or that our *personnel* is too extensive, and yet I can ass
you that the working costs amount to considerably more than on the other lines.
this respect we are proceeding by degrees ; each year the working expenses beco
less, but it will be long before we reach the figure of the other railways. It wo
take me too far to sum up all the reasons for this, and point out the facts which pl
these reasons beyond any doubt. Should the Commission be interested therein

Railway rates
lower than ac-
tual cost.

shall certainly give information later with regard to it. Now, it has not been
intention in the above to contend that it is unsound policy to fix tariffs lower than
actual cost, by which all expenditure is taken into consideration. We are quite
guilty as the other railways thereto. The cattle traffic, for instance, is done at a mu
lower rate than the so-called actual cost, and demonstrates clearly how far we can
with the lowering of the tariffs in South Africa. Where, for instance, a truck w
eight oxen is forwarded on our line at a rate of one or one and a half tons ordina
normal goods, the Cape and Natal Railways forward this wagon as if it was o
loaded with one ton of goods. When we bear in mind that the average load of
wagon is eight tons, then this cattle traffic, which certainly belongs to the m
difficult class of traffic, and to which delay can do so much mischief, takes place
one-eighth of the tariff for ordinary goods. The forwarding of coal to the ports ta
place on all South African lines at ½d. per ton per mile, more or less. These examp
go to show how far we are already below the average actual cost of traffic. W

Railway rates on
coal along the
Rand.

respect to the rate of coal along the Rand, I shall certainly not contend that t
cannot be lower. The returns are somewhat greater than the actual cost, but assure
not so much as people think. Let us closely examine the returns of the coal tra
Here follows a list of the quantities of coal which have been forwarded on the
called south line, from Pretoria to Vereeniging, and Springs to Potchefstroom.

Table of coal
tonnage trans-
ported.

TABLE OF COAL—IN TONS—FORWARDED ON THE SOUTH LINE AND RAND TR
(INCLUSIVE) TRANSPORT FROM BRUGSPRUIT AND BALMORAL TO STATIC
SITUATED PAST PRETORIA :

1896.

November	...	...	...	...	76,589 tons.
December	...	...	...	...	89,676 „
1897.					
January	...	...	...	...	81,898 „
February	...	...	...	...	76,528 „
March	...	...	...	...	90,735 „
April	...	...	...	...	88,847 „

February coal
returns.
March coal re-
turns.

In February the returns from the coal traffic amounted, including costs for sidi
and platforms, all in all to £25,362 15s., or an average of 6s. 7d. per ton. In Ma
the returns amounted to £29,567 3s. 6d., or an average of 6s. 6d. per ton. In A

returns amounted to £28,411 4s., or an average of 6s. 5d. per ton. This was the l required for all purposes—mining industry, trades, and household use. The whole enue of this traffic, including the high cost for sidings so enlarged upon by Mr. zpatrick, amounted in February to £25,362 15s., or an average per ton of 6s. 7d. March the returns amounted to £29,569 3s. 6d., or 6s. 6d. per ton. In April 8,411 4s., or 6s. 5d. per ton. Well, now, in these returns of less than £30,000 per nth, people seek for the covering of the expenses and the interest of the whole pital of the railway. Were this coal forwarded for nothing, then the loss in the urns of the railway, and almost the profit of the mining industry, would amount to 00,000 or £360,000. Should your Commission come to the conviction that the dy mining industry could be practically assisted by a reduction of the coal tariffs, d if the opportunity were given us by a lengthened term of existence, then I do not lieve that this would receive any preponderating objection from us. We could omise, for instance, that for three years all mines which pay no dividend should ve considerable restitution of the sum paid out by them for coal transport. This nner of helping a poor industry was, *inter alia*, applied on the railways in Dutch dia during the crisis of the sugar industry; and we thus avoid that to the rich even re riches would be added. But, to proceed, we will now examine the actual profits d surplus of our railway, and also those of the Cape Colony and Natal. With gard to our railway, imagination has unfolded its wings, and as though we were on e market, where people bid against each other, these profits have been mentioned as bulously high. People have spoken of 1¼ million, and I know not what besides. r. Chairman, there is nothing of the kind; these figures exist solely in the imagina- n of accountants, who had no facts at their disposal. I attach hereto a list of the tual surplus on our railway during the years 1895 and 1896:

TABLE OF SURPLUS—1895 AND 1896.

	1895.			1896. (Rough).		
	£	s.	d.	£	s.	d.
rplus after payment of the guaranteed interest, redemption of loans, deposit in the Reserve Fund for extensions, truck hire, extraordinary losses, &c.	379,209	0	4	890,000	0	0
f which the shareholders and the company receive...	56,881	7	0	133,500	0	0
nd the State as shareholder	14,282	10	0	36,000	0	0
e share of the surplus for the State (85 per cent.) amounts to	322,327	13	4	756,500	0	0
hile in import duties was raised by the railway	137,337	2	3	242,200	0	0
that after subtraction of the import dues, the share of the State in the surplus amounts to...	184,990	11	1	514,300	0	0
rplus of the Natal railways—						
rcentage on the construction capital ...	4	1	0	11	9	0½
rplus of the Cape railways—						
rcentage on the construction capital ...	7	9	10	8	19	7
rplus of the Netherlands South African Railway Company—						
ter subtraction of the share of the State, in percentage on the construction capital ...	5	8	2	about 6	2	0

The surplus in the year 1896, after payment of the guaranteed interest, redemp- n of loans, deposits in the reserve fund for extensions, wagon hire, extraordinary losses, etc., etc., amounts roundly to about £890,000, for the figures have not yet bee

Division of Neth-
erlands Rail-
way surplus of
1896.
stipulated by the Government Commissioner in the Netherlands. Of this the shar
holders and the company receive £1,335,000, and the State, as shareholder, £36,00
The share of the surplus for the State. amounts to £756,500, according to th
concession, while £242,200 was raised by the railway in import dues, so that, aft
deducting the import dues, the share in the surplus for the State amounts to £514,30
Well, then, Mr. Chairman, the whole surplus amounts thus to £514,300, plus £133,50
This amount could thus be thrown into the lap of the poor mining industry. In ho
far this is necessary, in how far the State will give up its income, is not for me
decide. I can only speak of the share which the company receives, and I for myse
can declare that, should the Government consider that we, by continuance, served t
work the line, and should the assurance be obtained, we would have no objection

Profits of Cape
and Natal rail-
ways.
meet the wishes of the Government. I do not here need to repeat what surplus th
Cape and Natal railways could deposit in the lap of the mining industry in the sam
manner. This is a matter which does not lie in my path. I would only remark th
the profits made by the owners of the railways in the Cape Colony and Natal, a
considerably higher than those of our railway, and hence I come to the important fac
that the surplus, according to the percentage, make a greater share of the genera
returns, and also of the returns of the goods traffic in particular. Should this appea
strange to you, and the desire be entertained to have further data, I shall be willingl
prepared to answer your questions. Before concluding, I must return to a couple o

Railway divi-
dends.
general points. It has been declared that the railways must be satisfied with a
interest of $2\frac{1}{2}$ to $3\frac{1}{2}$ per cent., even when the market rate of the money should be s
low. While this at the present moment amounts to 4 per cent., I can declare tha
although I have seen many railways in my life which only paid out $2\frac{1}{2}$ to $3\frac{1}{2}$ per cen
dividend, I have never seen one that was satisfied therewith. On the contrary, I se
that even big railways in Europe, in the most populated countries, carry thei
dissatisfaction so far that they pay out dividends which are considerably higher—eve
as high as those of the mining industry in Europe. It is also said that the minin
industry is an uncertain industry, and must therefore make bigger profits. We mus
consider, in this connection, what another witness has said here before your Com
mission, that the railway and the mining industry are subject to the sam

Uncertainty of
Netherlands
Railway pro-
fits.
risks. If the mining industry deteriorates, he says, the railway does also in a lik
degree. Well, now, if that is so, then the uncertainty of the mining industry
decidedly a reason for the railway industry to desire higher sums for profit, and fc
the rapid redemption of the capital when it stands and falls with the industry whic
is declared to be uncertain, and which, in the natural course of circumstances, wi
one day come to an end. It has been said that our railway has the key of the situa
tion in its hands. I will admit this for a moment, and declare myself satisfied th
up to the present the possession of that key has been the reason for the prevention c
a tariff war to the detriment of this State, and of very brief benefit to certai

Possible reduc-
tion of railway
rates in con-
junction with
Government
and other S.
African rail-
ways.
merchants and the mining industry. I repeat that when we are further placed in
position to work for the benefit of the State and the industry—and no attention
given to the desire of many in Johannesburg to expropriate the line at any pric
when that cannot be done for other reasons—then certainly a way will be found
deal with the reduction of tariffs in conjunction with the Government and the parti
concerned. But this is certain, that the remaining railways in the other countries
South Africa can never thereby be lost sight of. Which portion of the returns of th
various railways in South Africa should be yielded for the profit of the minin
industry, and perhaps also of other whites south of the Zambesi, now labouring und
prejudicial conditions, can only be fixed in conjunction with the allied administration

with an eye to the general welfare; and not by the use, or rather misuse, of the ~~ession~~ of the key to the situation. I have now come to the conclusion, but I ~~t~~ not omit to touch on a couple of minor points, which by declarations made ~~re~~ you might have brought about an entirely wrong impression. It has been ~~le~~ to appear as if we are opposed to the construction of sidings, and as if it were *Construction of sidings.* fault that the coal is still always forwarded in bags. Nothing is more unjust ~~1~~ that. We have frequently insisted, and are still insisting, that the mines make ~~ags~~, and when it is at all possible, we meet their wishes in the matter. For several *Traffic of coal in bags.* ~~rs~~ we have gone to much trouble not to forward coal in bags. For instance, we ~~ays~~ do it for our own service, and it has always been a puzzle to me how, on ~~unt~~ of the not inconsiderable cost, the traffic in bags is not given up. I have ~~atedly~~ asked thereanent, but have never got a definite answer, and now at this ~~nent~~ it is pleasant for me to be able to say that one of the mines between Elands- ~~ein~~ and Johannesburg, even without having a siding, will make a fair trial of the ~~fic~~ without bags. The other points are of too subordinate interest, but perhaps I ~~l~~ find opportunity to bring these forward during examination. I thank you, Chairman, for having listened to this declaration, and hope that you and the ~~nbers~~ of the committee will give me opportunity to further elucidate any points, ~~iciple~~, or meanings contained therein, which may not be clear to you. After the ~~going~~ was prepared, I received the tariffs on the Beira Railway. This railway *Beira railway rates.* ~~n~~ Beira to Chimoio is the property of, and is worked by the same company which to develop the mining industry in Rhodesia. The length is about a third of that ~~n~~ Delagoa Bay to Pretoria, and the rates are :—Machinery, corrugated iron, ~~ent~~, provisions, liquors, and general merchandise, 7s. per 100 lbs.; furniture, ~~inery~~, beds, &c., from 7s. to 20s. per 100 lbs.; grain, 3s. 6d. per 100 lbs.; horses, ~~es~~, cattle, £3 10s. each. Before declaring the tariffs of the N.Z.A.S.M. the highest in world, a comparison with that railway in our immediate neighbourhood should be out of place.

Mr. *de Beer.*

According to the estimate you made in your statement, it carries about a million *Estimated coal traffic of Netherlands Railway.* ~~s~~ of coal per annum ?—Yes.

This is at an average charge of 5s. 6d. per ton ?—Yes. *Average rate per ton of coal on Netherlands Railway.*

Can you state to me the percentage of profit per ton ?—You cannot possibly take *Percentage of profit per ton of coal on Netherlands Railway.* class of goods individually in estimating profits. As I have said, the real ex- ~~ses~~ of one ton per mile is averaged on the entire traffic, and is 1½d. per ton per ~~e~~. The carrying of coal on the Rand is certainly not the cheapest traffic we have

The cheapest traffic we have got is across the Free State, where the train is ~~en~~ over the boundary without any shunting. The carrying of coal on the Rand is ~~der~~ slightly more difficult circumstances.

The suggestion has been made to the Commission that the carriage price of coal *Suggested 30 per cent. reduction of railway rate on coal.* ~~ld~~ be reduced 30 per cent. Can you tell me the actual cost of coal ?—I cannot say distance it is carried.

It is said to be 28 miles ?—It is wrong to say it is 28 miles, because at the *Distance of coal transport.* ~~sent~~ moment 500 tons of coal are sent daily from Brugspruit and Balmoral.

You cannot give us what the price per ton per mile is ?—No, I cannot do it. I have it done for a month to get the average, but it would take a lot of time to do ~~t~~.

You have made use of the expression "the key of the situation." Who has got *The key of the railway situation.* key of the situation ?—We have got it.

It has been declared that way before the Commission, and witnesses have furt
stated that if tariffs are lowered, that, as a natural consequence, the Colony and of
neighbouring States will have to follow suit, and if they don't do it we could get
goods through Delagoa Bay ?—That is quite right. Assuming that the tariff fi
Delagoa Bay was lowered considerably, Natal will have to follow suit, and the C
will put the question to itself as to whether its traffic will still pay, because
difference between the freight to Johannesburg and the tariff in the Colony will be
great that opposition will arise from the side of the inhabitants of Cape Colo
unless the local tariffs are lowered, and the Government will see it is better to d
the traffic.

Railway rate on coal from Springs to Krugersdorp.
Can you carry coal at 3s. 6d. per ton from Springs to Krugersdorp without lo
—I must again point out to you the different ways of calculating. If one takes
charges to the other traffic—maintenance, expenses, interest, amortisation of loa
reserve fund, and so forth—and coal has to bear its share of general expenses
could not be done, but you could carry coal cheaper if you only have to charge
hauling power.

Mr. *Schmitz-Dumont.*

Differential railway rates for dividend paying and non-paying mines.
You have said in your statement that the directors would have no objection
granting a restitution of freight pay to mines which did not pay a dividend for th
years ?—That is an idea I have thrown out, and I am quite prepared to abide by i
the Government desire it.

You have not gone into details yet ?—I have worked it out in my mind.
course, if the idea were adopted, it might not become a permanent institution.

And for those mines that pay very low dividends ?—We could make a slid
scale from 10 per cent. up to 50 per cent.; so that mines paying three per cent. wo
get a reduction of ten per cent.

Proportion of profits to capital of Netherlands Railway.
The real railway surplus is £647,000 ?—Yes.

What proportion would that be on the share capital of the company ?—Fi
per cent.

Do you know any railway which makes a profit of 50 per cent. ?—You must be
in mind there are very few railway companies where the share capital is so sm
compared with the total amount expended. If the share capital were the whole c
of building, the dividend would be nothing out of the way.

There are debentures ?—You put the question whether I don't consider
surplus. If certain capitalists say we want good security for capital, with I
interest, that has nothing to do with the economical position of the railway.
have always carried out the wishes of the Government, and also carried them out
this instance.

You propose that the Government must lose about £500,000 ?—Excuse me, I
not. It is a question of how much you can give, and return nothing. I don't
you must do it.

If the Government gave £500,000 and the company £133,000, how would it
possible and how would you bring about a reduction ?—We could reduce machin
to a lower rate on an average of two or three months taking the same quantity
Apportionment of surplus following reduc tion of railway rates.
traffic as exists at present. We should have to see how much less revenue we sho
get. Say we give £200,000 out of the surplus we should have to distribute that s
in such a manner that the mining industry gets a share and agriculture as well.
can give you every facility for getting an estimate.

30 per cent. reduction of railway rates on
The mining industry wants rates lowered by 30 per cent. on foodstuffs, mac
nery, etc. ?—In one month the revenue of the entire goods' traffic is about £200,(

d a third of that would be £70,000. That would mean a loss of £840,000 to the **entire goods** ilway, and that would be a bigger figure than could possibly be given according **traffic exces-** the surplus of last year. **sive.**

Mr. *Albu.*

May I ask you again what the gross receipts were in 1896 ?—There will probably · a lot of questions asked me about figures of last year, but I must state that they ave not been fixed by the Railway Commissioner at Home, consequently I cannot be :act. Within a few weeks, the whole statement will be published.

It is a pity that we cannot have the figures approximately to-day.—If you put a 1estion, I will give the figures as near as possible.

What were the actual receipts of the Netherlands Railway for 1896 ?—I will **Netherlands** ve the figures approximately, and I shall be open to correction. [On referring to **Railway re-** s portfolio, Mr. Middelberg could not find his data, and said he had omitted to bring **ceipts for 1896.** 1e figures.]

Now, would it be correct to estimate the receipts at £2,970,000 for last year ?—I 1nnot give you a reply with certainty, but the figures you name seem familiar to me, 1d may be correct, but I am not certain.

I would like to know how you arrive at a surplus of £500,000, as, according to y figures here, we arrive at much higher ?—I don't know. The report will be very 1ortly published, but I cannot give you details.

It will be published before the Commission publishes its report ?—Yes.

When I was examined I gave figures, and I think they are pretty reliable, that **Working costs** 1e actual receipts of the Netherlands Railway were £2,970,000, and the working **of Netherlands** xpenses £1,237,000.—1 don't think that last figure is correct. What is your source **Railway for** : information with regard to working expenses ? **1896.**

I would rather not mention that. From these figures I said that, if the Govern-1ent were to expropriate the railway, and take last year's figures as a basis, and allow · per cent. on the debentures, and on the expropriation capital—We pay 4 per cent.

I say, if you allow 6 per cent., you get, in excess of actual receipts, £1,298,000.— 'ou must have made a mistake somewhere.

It is a pity we have not got the figures before us. Now, you have pointed out to · member of the Commission that the capital of the Netherlands Company is in itself 1ut very small, but you have debentures which, to a great extent, cover the cost of the 1aterial and building the railway line.—Yes, to a great extent.

But you must not forget to point out that it is owing to the fact that the interest **State guarantee** 1 those debentures is guaranteed by the Government that you are able to have such **of Netherlands** 1 enormous proportion of debentures on the share capital. I could float a gold mine **Railway de-** 'ith a small capital if the expenses of machinery and equipment, and the development **bentures.** f the mine, is guaranteed by the Government in the shape of interest on debentures. 'he credit of this Government is so good that we would be quite satisfied if the Govern-1uaranteed our debentures at 4, 5, or 6 per cent. That's a difference.—That is so 1anifest that it it is unnecessary to argue it. You see the position is this : you must ever forget that, on account of the Government guarantee of the entire amount of ebenture interest, the Government also gets 85 per cent. of the surplus ; and the **Government** lovernment gets nearly six times as much as shareholders. **share in Nether-**
lands Railway
What I wanted to point out is that the Netherlands Company claim a special **profits.** 1erit for having so small a share capital, and a larger debenture capital since the lovernment of the Transvaal has guaranteed the debentures—I don't claim any merit.

I want simply to point out that, had these debentures not existed, your dividends 'ould be infinitesimally small, and the big profits over which we are shouting about would be nowhere.—I don't think you understood my reply to Mr. Dumont. He aske me how much was the capital and dividend, and I said so much. There was no prid in it, and we take no special merit.

Estimated bonus
to *personnel*
of Netherlands
Railway for
1896.
Bonus to *person-
nel* of Nether-
lands Railway
in 1895.

May I ask you—I hope I am not indiscreet in putting the question—what do yo estimate the bonus to the *personnel* to be ?—Two-ninths of £133,500.

It was in 1895, £18,500 ?—Two-ninths of £56,000.

You think this time it will be about £35,000. Now, the capital of the Nether lands Railway is £1,166,000. In the event of the Government expropriating th railway, considering that the Government has got 400,000 shares, this will leave abou £700,000 to pay dividends at 4 per cent., and interest on debentures. Of course w must assume, in case of expropriation, that the shares would have to be expropriate at least at 150 per cent. premium.—I don't quite follow you.

I wish to show in case of expropriation very little more would be required in th shape of premium on guaranteed interest than the *personnel* alone receives here.—I you take it for granted that the bonus to the *personnel* is simply a present; you see even the mines give a bonus to their employees, which is a voluntary action.

Quite so; for services rendered. These services would have to be rendered in th case of the railway, even in the event of the Government taking over the railways.— In some other way you would have to pay it, unless you go from the standpoint that the wages are too high.

I would be induced to put that question because I do not know how much the directors at Home get out of it ?—I can say a considerable portion of that is retained for a pension fund.

We maintain that the rates charged by the Netherlands Railway are too high.— Do you speak about local tariff or the tariff from the ports ?

Excessive Neth-
erlands Rail-
way rates from
ports.

The tariff on the Netherlands line portion.—Such a tariff does not exist. In my declaration I hold such a separate tariff does not exist; it is only the portion of the whole traffic charged from the port to Johannesburg that the N.Z.A.S.M. receives. I maintain you have got very little to do with what the railway receives out of it ; you must go on the broad basis and deal with the tariff from the port to Johannesburg.

We must go on the basis that we must not take into account how much the Netherlands get out of the traffic, or how much the Cape Colony gets, but we must be satisfied to pay and look pleasant, and not mind who gets the profit.—No, you can say that the whole of the tariff charged from the port to Johannesburg is too high, but it is a mistake to say that that portion of the tariff is too high. It is simply an arrangement between the two administrations.

I say that the whole tariff to Johannesburg is too high.—This discovery has been made within the last six months; it is a marvel that it had not been discovered within the four previous years. I wrote a long letter six months ago, expressing my surprise that the mining industry had not long ago objected to the high tariff levied from the port to Johannesburg.

Only for argument's sake I will put the question, is not the tariff from the port to Johannesburg too high ? For instance, the tariff from Port Elizabeth to Viljoen's Drift is, for third-class goods, 2d. per mile per ton, but from the Drift to Johannesburg

Through and
local railway
rates.

is 7d.—You forget to mention that in the through tariff there is a transit tariff and a local tariff. The transit tariff is a fighting tariff. The one you quote is the transit tariff, and I will give you the local tariff to Viljoen's Drift. The local tariff from East London to Viljoen's Drift is 6s. 6d. per 100 lbs., and from East London to Johannes burg is 4s. 11d. From Port Elizabeth the local tariff is 5s. 3d. to Johannesburg, and to Viljoen's Drift 7s. 1d. It would look, according to your argument, as if the N.Z.A.S.M. paid 2s. towards carrying the goods.

I don't quite understand it. You charge 7s. 7d. ?—No.

That is what we pay; who gets it ?—The Netherlands get it from the Cape.

If you get it from the Cape, who pays the Cape ?—You pay 10s., and out of that Netherlands gets its share. The charge on timber from Port Elizabeth to Johanburg is 5s. 3d., and out of that we get 20d. May I say one word with regard to t ? 20d. from Mid-Vaal to Johannesbusg looks extreme, but it is really a fighting ff. We get the lion's share, but you must not forget that the expense of hauling a in from Mid-Vaal River to Johannesburg is not higher than the expense in ₁annesburg for the station, kazerne, and delivery. I did not like to put it in my laration, because I might have given the impression it was the tariff I wanted to end. That is not the tariff, it is our share of the total tariff from the port to ₁annesburg.

Who gets the lion's share; I have got the statement of 1896, and it shows an ₁rmous income. I have also got a table of the Cape Government Railway, and it ws an enormous income; it is generally stated you are the stumbling block of the ₁ole of South Africa.—There is a lot of calumny scattered about it.

Is it not a fact that at a conference at Maritzburg you and Mr. Hunter, of the ₁tal Railways, proposed that galvanised iron and flour should be removed from a ₁er to a higher class, and that the Cape Government, as represented by Mr. Elliott, ₁osed it ?—No; it was an indiscretion on the part of Sir James Sivewright to assert t, and he is plainly answered by Mr. Murray of Natal and Mr. Brounger of the ₁e State. The question was raised casually at Pietermaritzburg whether it was not ₁sible to do away with that special class, but they thought it better to ignore it, as ₁he goods in that class were put into a higher class it would make a bad impression. ₁ matter was not even mentioned in the minute.

There was no definite proposal made ?—No.

Then you absolutely deny that you have been the cause of the railway rates not ₁ng reduced right through South Africa ?—Of course, I absolutely deny it. The ₁pe has never made a single proposal for the reduction of the tariff. It is only since ₁s Commission has been appointed that Sir James Sivewright, in an unofficial ₁nner moved for a commission to look into railway matters. I have not yet ₁eived an invitation to attend such a commission, nor has the Government.

In other words, there is a good deal of protestation and assumed fighting going ₁, but there is no earnest desire to see in what way the rates could be reduced ?—I ₁'t want to say that. Now that matters have taken this course, conferences will be ₁d to seriously consider the question.

The mining industry is in this position. We find that under present circum₁nces it is impossible to work the majority of our mines at a profit. We have got ₁se burdens—high railway rates, dynamite, and minor legislative measures. We ₁proached the Netherlands Railway and the dynamite people to help us by lessening ₁se burdens. Our feeling is that where a surplus has been obtained during one ₁r of over £1,000,000 in the railway department, a further £2,000,000 have been ₁ained from us in the Cape Colony, the dynamite people made a profit of £500,000 ₁more out of us, it is natural we should think these are the spots which we can ₁ch. These various industries can help the big mining industry, which, after all, ₁ports everything. If the Netherlands Railway Company could not be expropriated ₁the Government, then they would be quite right to make as much as they could, ₁ the Government has the right to expropriate, and has not the Government the ₁ht to dictate the tariff to you ?—I have never found that in the concession. We ₁e the right to fix the tariffs, and the State has the right of expropriation.

I have always thought if the mining industry and the various other industries in this country could come more often toge' er and discuss matters, we would be able

Original local
rates of Neth-
erlands Rail-
way.
settle this difficulty. In the first instar ⸱, you take the tariff four or five years a
when you started your railway, it was ⸱amed on a very small traffic?—Are you ⸱
cussing local or otherwise?

When I am speaking about five or six years ago it must be local; but althou
the traffic has increased enormously you have not seen fit to reduce the tariffs to ⸱

20 per cent. re-
duction of rail-
way rates on
coal.
same extent at all?—You got a reduction in coal. You call it a small reduction
don't. It was a reduction of at least 20 per cent.

It was a small reduction, the traffic was very limited in the early days. In y⸱
supposition in your declaration about the carriage of coal, would it not
better to reduce the tariff to an average of 18s. 6d. Is it not a fact that y

Possible increase
of rates
against Cape
railways.
dictate this 7·7d. to the Cape? If the Cape were to reduce their rates would you ⸱
immediately raise your rates so that the Cape would not be a competitor of Delag
Bay and Natal?—I do not know what I would do.

But you have done it?—No.

Sir James Sivewright said in his speech the other day that whatever the Ca
reduced their rates by, the mining industry would not benefit by it?—Sir James Si⸱
wright spoke as a prophet and not as a man who quotes facts.

Alleged raising
of rates
against Cape
railways.
But have you not done it before?—No; there is a Green Book for 1895 whi⸱
contains the whole of the correspondence on the subject, and since that time there k
been no further correspondence on the subject.

Komati Poort
line not to be
used to reduce
port rates.
Now your line from Komati Poort to Johannesburg in conjunction with t
Delagoa Bay line can act, if you so wish it, as a lever upon the Natal and Ca
Government lines. What prevents you from reducing these rates considerably
order to make the Cape reduce its rates?—Because our policy is not to exercise
leverage, but to act in conjunction with the railways of the Colony and the neig
bouring States.

Your sentiments are to bring our goods as cheap as possible?—Why not?

Your actions have not proved it?—Because our motives are higher.

Are these motives higher dividends?—No, they are to keep pace with the ra
ways in South Africa. You must not forget these tariffs have been fixed yea
before by the Government, when nobody knew of the surplus, such as we had l⸱
year or this year.

Just so; that brings me down to the question I put before. These tariffs we
fixed some years ago, when the extent of the gold mining industry in the Transva
was not certain, but for the last two or three years the traffic has increased enc
mously, and so far we have not seen that you have paid any consideration to this a⸱
reduced the rates?—Why should the railway company take the initiative? V
always heard, until a short time ago, of the enormous profits of the mining indust⸱
and the poorer mines have only been discovered quite recently. Why did not t'
initiative come from the side of the industry?

I can answer that by saying that the mining industry, or rather the leaders
the mining industry, had found out that the industry—and you must not take one
two mines—was not as rich as we anticipated, and we have also become convinc
that our working expenses, compared with those in other countries, are abnorma⸱
high, owing to the concessions given by the Government.—If the mining indust⸱
discovered that lately, how could you expect the railway company to have fou
it out?

Past representa-
tions of min-
ing industry
against Neth-
erlands Rail-
way rates.
It is not lately that we have discovered it. We have urged upon the Gover
ment, the dynamite people, and the railway, the necessity of reducing tariffs.—Wb
there was a question about the reduction in coal tariff—a reduction which I consic

portant—was made, do not forget that the reduction in the coal tariff was the result of a conference at which the member for the First Raad for Johannesburg was present, and the coal mining industry was represented, and they were quite satisfied. *Reduction of railway rates on coal in 1896.*

When did this reduction in the coal tariff take place ?—1st July, 1896, and it was temporary at the request of the industry.

Since then you have opened your Charlestown and Delagoa Bay lines ; of course what we had to see how these lines would work, but when they had a large margin of profit we expected you would reduce your rates.—We do not go on the question of sentiment, but on business. *Opening of Charlestown and Delagoa Bay lines.*

I have no sentiment in the matter. As I have told you, if the Netherlands Railway Company were a private company with a concession, they would be perfectly right to make as much profit as possible, but the industry looks to the Government for protection, and if the Railway Company is stubborn, and says we won't reduce the rates, then we are perfectly justified in requesting the Government to nationalise the railway, in order that we should get cheaper rates.—I don't dispute your right to ask it. *Netherlands Railway and Government right of expropriation.*

I am not bringing sentiment into the question. I simply appeal to the Government, and say that the Netherlands Company are making this enormous profit, and don't reduce their rates ; and the mining industry finds this burden too heavy. There have been many deep levels which have stopped work for want of funds, and from the fact that capitalists say they will not put another 6d. until the conditions on the fields are such as to make our work profitable, we do not want to work for the railway or the dynamite people. It is a matter of dire necessity that something must be done. The mining industry has to do its portion, and everybody else has to do their portion. I am surprised in your very able statement to find you draw a comparison between the Beira Railway and the Netherlands Railway in the matter of tariffs. Do you not think this railway will reduce its rates 50 and 75 per cent. when the traffic justifies it ? I do not indulge in prophecies. *Necessity of reforms for mining industry.*

I will make a bet they will reduce them 60 per cent.

Witness said that when an industry was in its infancy, imposing killing tariffs was not the way to foster the industry.

It is a matter of opinion, Mr. Middleberg. If I had the administration of this country, I would run cheap railways to develop the country. It might be useful to show you a few comparisons between actual rates in the Transvaal and the maximum rates in Holland, also in England. From Vereeniging to Johannesburg we know it is 54 miles, from Volksrust it is 178 miles, and from Komaati Poort 341 miles. In the Transvaal, for mining machinery, it costs from the port 104s. to bring to Johannesburg ; in Holland the maximum rate over the same distance, and on the same kind of goods, the cost is 11s. 3d. In England it is 31s. 8d. On iron and steel in South Africa it is 72s. 2d. ; in Holland 11s., thus showing the great discrepancy between the railway rates in England, Holland, and South Africa.—If you will only go one step further, and apply the tariff of Holland and England to our tariff, not only will surplus interest disappear, but the State would have to pay a large sum into the railway. *Comparative railway rates in England, Holland, and South Africa.*

I am only showing you the difference. I don't say it can be done.—What leads you to your conclusion ?

I will give you the results of the earnings of certain railways. The revenue of the Transvaal is £4,775 per mile.—I cannot contradict it, because I have not the figures. *Revenue per mile of Netherlands Railway.*

I am checking these figures by Mr. Gregson's book.—As regards the railway, that book has incorrect figures as a rule, and has to be taken with the greatest care. If you take our report you can depend upon it.

The revenue per mile in the Transvaal is £4,775; in Natal, £2,825; in the Ca £1,810; in India, £685; and in the United Kingdom, £3,844.—Everything is ve cheap in Holland, and the circumstances are altogether different.

We must make an allowance for these things. I want to show you the en mously high rate charged here. Do you think it is necessary for the Commission point that out to you—that your rates are very high?—I don't want to show the p centage. I want to show the surplus of profit, and that is the only sum which can taken into account in a reduction of tariffs.

You say the Government gets 85 per cent. of the profits.—The Government a the Company together get a certain amount of surplus, and that is the basis on whi you must go if you want to reduce the tariff.

That is quite so. But the Government get 85 per cent. You say the railw company shows a comparatively small income.—I refer to the amount of surplus th is available for the reduction of rates.

But if the Government expropriate the railway?—They would have the sa surplus as now.

Supposing the Government expropriate the railway, and paid you out?—Then t Government, unless wages are reduced, and they find material cheaper, cannot ea more than we are earning.

If the Government were to expropriate and issue debentures at 6 per cent., th would mean £435,000 interest on the working expenses for 1896, which we £1,237,000.—That is not correct.

In 1895, the total expense on the revenue was 43 per cent.; in 1894 it was 48 p cent. Is that correct?—I don't know for 1894, but for 1895 it is correct.

Very well, then, your revenue has increased, but your expenditure does not increa in proportion, so we can take 40 per cent.—From the figures here, I cannot say t exact amount of working expenses; but you have got the sum of £890,000 as surpl

You see, it is somewhat difficult for me, as you have one set of figures and I ha another. I base my figures on the expropriation of the railway by seeing how muc the profit would be for last year. You have not got your figures, which is an u fortunate thing. With regard to the collection of customs at Delagoa Bay; does th amount go into the railway revenue? I understand that, according to the concessio you have got the right to charge 5 per cent. commission for collecting, and that t whole amount you collect goes as income to the railway?—Yes.

Eighty-five per cent. goes to the Government. You take out your reserve fun and you pay your shareholders a proportionate profit. It is not in the concession, arrangement with the Government, that you should collect customs dues at Koma and then charge 5 per cent. for collection fees. You simply take this as railwa revenue?—I will read you the article in the concession.

Yes, please.—This is the portion of article 17: "Import, export, and transit duti on the Portuguese boundary, due for all goods transported by railway, including coa are collected by and on behalf of the concessionaire, according to rules and regulatio to be fixed in conjunction with the Railway Commissioner, or on instructions fro the Government."

What instructions were given?—They are exactly the same instructions as a given to other collectors of customs at Komati Poort.

You have an income of £20,000 per month from this source alone?—The first co cession was exactly the same as that between the Cape Colony and the Free Sta The original concession between the Netherlands and the Government was that of t net profits, 50 per cent., having to go to the Government, and 50 per cent. to the co pany. When, in 1886, it became necessary, for financial reasons, to have bett

rity than the Netherlands guaranteed the State, which at that time was not rich, History of concession of Netherlands Railway to collect customs.
the interest should be increased from 50 per cent. to 85 per cent. At that time
collecting of import duty cost about 10 per cent.

You say that you know the cost per ton per mile on the Cape Railway is 1½d. or Cost of transport of goods per ton per mile on Cape railways.
May I ask you when that was?—You will find it in the Cape Blue Book for 1892.
as in consequence of the tariff charged by the Cape Colony Government on rails
sleepers. I wanted 1½d. per ton, and the Commissioner told me the cost was 1·07d.
rwards there was a Parliamentary Committee, and the cost was based by the Com-
ee as 1·07d. as the net cost.

It would have been cheaper to-day.—I have made the statement, and the cost in
e Colony is not far from 1½d.

Do you make concessions with regard to your railway tariffs to merchants here in Privileges for large consignments.
shape of bonuses?—No; at the last conference in Pietermaritzburg we agreed that
e of the railway companies should give any privileges for large consignments.
Cape Colony did for the transport of coal up to a short time ago, but it is now
ished. There is no privilege of any kind on our company.

You did not give Lingham privileges, for instance?—In the year 1894 we made a The "Lingham" contract.
ract with Lingham, and I have often explained the circumstances. We were then
ut opening the Delagoa Bay line without knowing the attitude of the other rail-
s, and without knowing whether we should get any traffic. Then we assisted
Lingham in the transport of really very large wood consignments for Delagoa
. We attained our object, and in March, 1896, that contract lapsed.

Since then he has paid the same rate as anybody else?—There was a lot of The "Davies" privilege.
ilege to Davies, whose wood the railway companies agreed to take at 40 lbs. the
ic feet instead of 52 lbs. Since then it has been increased to the usual rate. With
rd to the Lingham contract, it has been said that the Netherlands Company have
£60,000 to make the contract null and void. There is not a word of truth in
statement. The bonus got by Mr. Lingham according to contract did not by any
ns reach that figure, and no sum has been paid in order to cancel the contract.
in conjunction with the English firm, have found a re-arrangement which has
sfied both parties.

Is it true that the Netherlands Company forces the Cape to keep up transit dues Transit dues on Cape railways.
certain articles?—No; I would not know how to do it. In the Green Book you
find an interchange of telegrams at the beginning of 1894. During negotiations,
sit duties were lowered by the Minister of Finance without any communication
g made to me, upon which I asked information by telegraph whether such was
. But he must have made a mistake if he was under the impression that I should
e any observation on the subject, and so far we have never used any pressure.

You cannot tell us what was the approximate profit on your coal traffic?—I have Profit on coal traffic.
ed to Mr. de Beer that I cannot give the exact revenue per ton per mile.

Is there any objection to the coal companies having their own trucks?—Under Special railway wagons.
ain cases you might have special wagons, if these are used between two fixed
its. I know in England it is not customary to allow special wagons unless
ween fixed points.

Chairman.

Must I understand, if we agree with the company to make a reduction in the Reduction of railway rates.
ting tariff, that it would not be desirable to make such reductions until you have
a conference with the other States and Colonies?—If the Government should Co-operative action of South African railways desirable
h that we should break the amicable relations with the other States, I certainly
ld not take up politics myself.

I think it desirable that a conference should be held on that point.—That is personal conviction.

Mr. *Brakhan.*

So far, the argument seems to me to be confined to the profit which the Neth lands Railway have been able to make out of the rates ruling from the traffic to coast. Now, what I want to bring forward is this—that not alone the Netherla

Reduction of railway rates of all South African lines necessary.

Railway Company, but also the adjoining railways have to cut down their rates, that, therefore, the benefit would, directly or indirectly, come to the mining indus In connection with this, I would ask you whether, in case the Netherlands Compa were to reduce their rates on the Delagoa line, whether in that case the other railw

The Netherlands Railway can compel reduction of rates on all South African lines.

companies, to maintain the traffic, would also not be compelled to reduce their rate —Certainly.

Therefore, if the Netherlands Railway Company were to call a conference of railways in South Africa, and would insist on the rates being reduced, then the Na and the Cape, which principally come into consideration, would also follow suit. want to bring this out, and particularly to lay stress on it, that it is not alone the c rates in which a reduction would benefit the mining industry, but principally

Reduction of through railway rates from ports necessary.

coast rates, because, if we don't have a reduction in rates from the coast, it seems me almost excluded that any amelioration in the cost of living, not alone in Johann burg, but in the whole of the Transvaal, would follow. As I have already said, all round reduction on these coast rates, the amount which will be saved directly the mining industry, and indirectly again by cheaper living, would accrue through reduction in the revenue of the adjoining railways. Now, if you will allow me point out the Cape never asked you to get a reduction, may I ask if the Netherla asked the Cape or Natal for a reduction?—No ; I gave a reason for that just no There was no reason for it.

I express the opinion generally held, and, if I may be allowed to, give my p sonal opinion. Of course we know that in the coal rates some reductions have be made, but not on the coast rates, which is after all the material thing. You refer to the rates which are ruling on the section from Viljoen's Drift to Johannesburg

"Fighting rates" from Viljoen's Drift to Johannesburg.

"fighting rates." I should like an explanation why you call these "fighting rates." When the tariff for the Delagoa line was about to be fixed, we had a conference Capetown, where a difference in Port Elizabeth and East London rates had be made, and to be secured of a certain guarantee of traffic, for the Delagoa line wished to have a large difference. The Cape Administration wished the difference be a very small one, in order to retain the bulk of the traffic from the Cape por Then I carried, against the wish of the Cape Administration, that the difference of t freight by Delagoa Bay should be about 15s. per ton, whereas the Cape wished fo much greater sum. If we were to place merit, then we might claim we are the peop who made Delagoa Bay rates as light as they are. The Cape Administration th threatened to lower the tariff to such an extent, to come so low that under any c cumstances they would have secured half of the traffic ; the moment had arrived us to take up our defence, and what the Cape had never thought, that one of points of defence would be, and what would compel our share of the traffic fr Viljoen's Drift, we established these fighting rates. Don't forget one point that y should not lose at all. The time when these tariffs were in existence there was reason for creating opposition for us, and we then made them so that Delagoa B should secure for Delagoa Bay a fair share of the traffic.

Increased traffic and reduction of railway rates.

That may be so, but at the same time the general trade of the Transvaal v very much smaller than at the present time. Therefore, when the rates were qu

led for at that time, there is quite room for a material reduction which would yet
ve the company such a profit on its capital, and a share of the profit to the Govern-
nt, which would be about on a par with the railway results at that time, say 2¼
rs ago.—I have put that in my declaration very plainly.

I only wanted to bring out again that there is certainly room for bringing the
es down to a lower level,—Yes.

Then you brought some examples as regards timber. You mentioned that the *Railway rates from ports to Orange Free State.*
e from Cape ports to Viljoen's Drift, for consumption in the Orange Free State, as
gher than those rates paid on the timber traffic to Johannesburg. Now, don't you
nk that this is quite justified, or more than justified, in so far that the timber traffic
om the coast to Johannesburg is infinitely larger than that up to Viljoen's Drift.—
at also explains the carriage to Kimberley.

I take it the Kimberley people themselves will look after this, also that the *Kimberley railway rates.*
mands in this respect are not to be compared to Johannesburg.—Don't you forget
at there is a great deal of wood used for the mines in Kimberley. Still, for the
ilding of houses, why should people in Bloemfontein pay a higher rate than those
Kimberley?

Then people in Bloemfontein must bring pressure to bear on their Government,
d the people in Cape Colony too. The argument hardly holds good in our case.
is a fact that the Rand here is an enormous customer of the railways in South
rica, and on that account they are entitled to consideration. Now, Mr. Middleberg, *1896-1897 returns of Netherlands Railway.*
u have told us you have not the exact figures with you, but I should like to know,
a kind of calculating from the surplus, and by taking the receipts which you have
id this morning were about £2,970,000, how to arrive at the various items which
ake up the difference. In taking the receipts at £2,970,000 we have to make the
llowing reductions: The interest on bonds and redemptions I take to be £335,500.
out it in this way. Of course it is somewhat a smaller item, and some bonds are
t redeemed. The guaranteed interest to shareholders is £66,000, that is 6 per cent.
11,000,000 florins. That would be a total of £698,750. This, deducted from the
,970,000, leaves £2,271,250. Now, you mention that the interest on the bonds
ich were issued for the Natal line—or, I ought to put it differently—for the Natal
ction, would increase the item to £335,000. Can you tell me about how much that
ould be?—I don't wish to commit myself to figures, which are at present being
inted, and I would not speak from memory.

In other points you give us figures, but do not give us the basis on which you
rive at them. It is possible for us, in discussing the whole matter, to arrive at a
rtain conclusion?—You can only compare the figures.

Then you cannot give us the basis on which you arrive at the £800,000 surplus? *£800,000 Netherlands Railway surplus.*
No.

We can only gather from the figures you submit to us, that the shareholders of the *Dividend of Netherlands Railway for 1896.*
mpany for the year 1896 received 13⅓ per cent.?—I cannot say whether the figures
e correct, but it is about that.

I have mentioned it, because I have not had any contradiction so far that the
areholders got 13⅓ per cent. That means that they got over and above the
uaranteed interest of £66,250 another £89,000. The concession provides that one-third *Bonus to *personnel* of Netherlands Railway*
rplus which remains after the Government has received its share, shall be
vided amongst the employees. That would come to about £44,500. You take then
o-thirds for the directors and one-third for the remainder, that is about £15,000 and
0,000. Now I much regret I have not the basis to work, as regards the actual
orking expenses, because the figures before me, which I submitted to the Commission
evidence, show that if certain reductions took place in the rates, yet the shareholders

Estimated divi-
dend of Neth-
erlands Rail-
way on reduc-
tion of rates. would receive an $8\frac{1}{2}$ per cent. dividend, which anyhow, in my opinion and general
is considered a very good rate of interest.—If your figures are just and correct,
would be a very agreeable surprise, not alone to us, because that would show me th
the figures would be too low and that agreeable surprise would show that the figur
would be available to effect reductions, so that I really must express the hope that t
figures prove to be correct, though I don't believe they are.

I have since found some inaccuracies so far as the rates in goods and passenge
are concerned, as the duty has been included, but taking this into consideration, t
figures are improved. But from the figures we now have before us, and which it is
be regretted, are incomplete, it would prove that yet a substantial surplus does exi
and these figures would also prove that the working expenses have not decreased in t
ratio of the extension of the traffic, for whilst the proportion of the reduction of t
working expenses in 1895 is about 43 per cent., they are most likely more for 189

Netherlands
Railway holds
key of position Now, as regards the adjoining companies, if, as I hold, the Netherlands Railway calls
railway conference, and declares that they are going to lower their rates on the Delag
Bay line, in consequence of the matter which has been brought before the Commissio
and from the Commission to the Government, then the Cape Government as well as th
Natal will be compelled to also lower the rates in order to maintain their shares of th
traffic. Now is there any agreement between the railway companies which prevent

Agreements of
Netherlands
Railway with
other railways. the Netherlands Company taking this step?—There is an agreement with the Nat
Government published, and public property; there is an agreement with the Fre
State Government about an amicable arrangement of the tariff; and further, with th
Portuguese Government regulating the shares and the freight; beyond that there is n
fixed agreement.

It would appear that this agreement does not prevent the Netherlands Compan
from coming forward with these proposals.—A proposal anyone can make, bu
whether such proposal be accepted is another question. There may be serious an
weighty arguments for not accepting the proposal by the other party; I cannot sa
before the time comes.

The only reason I can see is that they would want to make an unjustifiabl
profit out of the traffic to the Rand.—You see the different railway administration

Government con-
trol of South
African Col-
onial railways. are entirely under the control of the different governments, consequently it is th
governments of these different companies and their parliaments to say how far they wi
co-operate, or what pressure, in the other direction, to this Government they will giv

Netherlands
Railway holds
key of position It would appear that the Netherlands Railway holds the key in their hands, an
if they have the earnest will to help the mining industry here, not alone to maintai
a great number of mines which at the present moment everyone knows cannot pa
but also to further the interests of the mining industry—if this desire exists on th
part of the Netherlands, the situation can be materially altered. Then I have als

South African
railway sit-
uation. read that semi-official declarations have been made in Capetown that, as far as th
Cape is concerned, they are anxious to reduce the rates in order not to jeopardise th
industry in this part. Therefore, you acknowledge the company could do a great dea
in the matter.—If that should be, the Cape Government Railway is a philanthropi
institution. There may be another explanation, that they are not satisfied with thei
share in the traffic. That, reading between the lines, I take to be a threat held out b
the Cape Colony in the correspondence which is contained in the agreement, namely, i
the declaration by Commissioner Laing.

That was in 1892.—The end of 1894; a couple of months before the opening o
the Delagoa Bay line.

Don't you think the situation has greatly changed since then. At that time
would appear from your remarks that the Cape tried to do everything to stifle th

herlands Railway Company on its Delagoa Bay line, but now it has to reckon it as an accomplished fact.—I would reply to that by a fact that has happened ly. When the Free State Railway was taken over by the Government of the e State, the Cape seriously threatened to stop the entire traffic to this Republic, to pel the Free State to concede their demands. So that to think that the Cape ernment administration would be ready to sacrifice everything for its philanpical feelings towards this Republic or Johannesburg, is not borne out by the s of later times. Dispute between
the Orange
Free State and
Cape railways.

I should say the Cape is less stimulated by philanthropic motives than by the on that they see very well if these high rates are maintained they will be a much ter loser than by reducing the rates. If the traffic were to lose by about one-half vhat it is at present, they would—having all their lines opened and having their ney invested in them—lose much more than by reducing their rates materially. I k the same argument also holds in regard to the Netherlands.—I don't know t is in the minds of the Cape administration, but I only refer to the fact that a rt time ago the Cape administration threatened to stop all traffic sooner than give o the demands of the Free State. The object was to raise the share of the Cape inistration to such an extent that there would be very little chance of traffic with Transvaal unless the Free State gave in.

Yes, but they would have injured themselves, and I suppose it was only a little of bluff. The result has shown that the Free State got its own way.—Yes.

Mr. *Pierce.*

Are the railways in Holland owned by the State or by private companies?— -half of the railways are owned by private companies and one-half are owned by State, but exploited, or worked, by private companies. Ownership of
Dutch rail
ways.

Were the half now belonging to the State originally State railways, or belonging rivate companies?—They were built by the State.

And afterwards leased?—And afterwards leased to the company who worked it.

Are the railways generally on the continent owned by the State?—I cannot say greater portion, but a considerable portion; the French only a small proportion, German a greater proportion, and the Austrian a small proportion. Ownership of
continental
railways.

Do the railways play an important part in those countries?—Like in this ntry, of course.

They are very useful in developing the country?—As you see here.

And the country and people are entitled to the railway for assistance?—As they ays get.

We have been told that certain railways in Germany carry coal at rates which ely cover expenses. Is that in order to encourage mining in certain districts ough which the railway passes?—The reason is more to be able to compete with sign coal. In Hamburg and North Germany they only get a very low tariff for l, in order to exclude English coal. Railway rates on
coal in Ger
many.

Can you tell us if goods are carried in Holland at special rates in order to foster ustries?—Only small rates to ports, in order to get the through transport from ts. Dutch special
railway rates.

Still they do carry goods at very low rates in order to assist?—They carry at a e which pays expenses and a certain interest. The great element in all railway ffs is how much the population can carry.

It is not the object to get as much out of the industry as they can?—Well, in English railway
rates.

England it is that way. The only object is high dividends. That they do succeed in making high dividends is not their fault.

Do you know that in England complaints have been made from time to t\[about the high rates of railways, and those rates have formed the subject of enqu\[by the Board of Trade, with the result that the railway has been compelled to red\[them ?—I don't know whether they were obliged to do so. I know about passenger rates on the so-called Parliamentary trains, but that was a rate granted their concessions by the companies to the Government. I don't know that Government have compelled the railway companies to lower the rates on goods, whether they are allowed by law to do so.

Status of Nether-
lands Railway. Well, it is a fact that they have done so. Do you consider the Netherla\[Railway a private company ?—It is a quarrel about the name. You know the c\[cession, and you know the articles of association.

Can you give any other instance of a so-called private company in which \[Government is the largest shareholder, and whose debentures are guaranteed by \[Government ?—I cannot recall one just at the moment.

The position is a rather anomalous one. It is an unusual one, is it not ?—N\[don't think the Italian railways differ very much from our system. Take \[railways in the Netherlands, where the railway is the property of the State. T\[company who work the railway have a very small capital and consequently a ve\[small risk.

Netherlands
Railway and
Transvaal
commerce and
agriculture. They are the lessees of the railways, not the owners. Do you consider \[Netherlands Railway has, through its rates an important influence on the devel\[ment of the trade or industries of this country generally, agriculture as well mining ?—That is very probable, although I have not got an absolute certainty that in my mind. I have noticed on repeated occasions that when taxes or railw\[rates have been reduced, no reduction takes place in the price of foodstuffs or goods the retail trade. Is has repeatedly occurred that the lowering of taxes or tari\[simply puts more profit into the pockets of the middlemen, without a profit to t\[consumer.

That has not been the experience in other countries. From some instances gi\[of the railways in other parts of the world, it appears that the rates charged Holland are very low.—We have already discussed that this morning.

Low and high
railway rates. Do you consider low rates or high rates best calculated to assist the industry \[That question is not capable of a direct reply at once. I can imagine that a cert\[tariff existing gives a certain development to an industry, but the lowering of t\[railway tariff would not assist in any material way to foster such an industry agriculture, because the only reason of the development is certainly not to be soug\[alone in railway rates.

Still it helps it. If the lowering of rates does not assist an industry, why is that manufacturers and others are so anxious to get low rates ?—I don't think order to foster the industry, but for their own benefit.

Effects of a rail-
way rates war You say in your statement, in speaking of the tariff war, that this wo\[have been greatly to the detriment of the whole of South Africa and its Governmen\[Would you give us an explanation of that. How would the Government suffer \[For instance, the mining industry is in a flourishing condition, as it has been up \[the last six months—as it appears to have been up till the last six months.

Now, is it possible that, with a lower tariff, a great surplus might be p\[out in the shape of dividends and bonuses, and a great deal might be sent England ?—The higher railway tariff gives the Cape Colony, Free State, Natal, a\[

is Republic the means to develop the country by the building of railways, the isting of railways which do not pay, improving harbours, etc., etc. Then certainly e question is what is best for the entire community.

You say you could have induced a tariff war instead of stalling it off? It is ident that if the rates had been lowered, and so brought on a tariff war, somebody ust have benefited. It could only have been the people here in this country. erefore, by not bringing on this tariff war, and so getting reduced rates per- anently, you have done the people of this country a very bad turn?—I don't agree ith you there. I have never heard that the railway tariff war would have been any permanent benefit to the people of this country. It would only have been of nefit to a few.

As a matter of fact, where a tariff war has taken place, rates have never returned their old level?—I would ask, is that a benefit or is it a disadvantage? You only fer to the benefit to one particular industry. I argue from the broad standpoint of hat is best for the whole community. I don't admit that the low tariff of railway tes is under every circumstance best for the whole Republic.

Well, many people think differently.—But I believe that many people are wrong.

Has the Netherlands Railway approached Natal and Cape Colony with a view reducing rates?—No. *Reduction of through railway rates from ports.*

If the Netherlands Railway were agreeable to reduce their rates from Vereenig- g to Johannesburg—You see, I don't admit that the rate of 7·7d. is the tariff from ereeniging to here. That was fully discussed this morning.

It might not be the tariff, but it is not denied that the Netherlands Railway ceive it.—That has been already discussed this morning.

You do get it. There is no doubt about that.—I don't say yes or no. I simply fer to the discussion this morning.

Well, we will take it as a fact that they do get it. If the Netherlands were illing to reduce the rates to assist the industry, would it be open to them to reduce at charge?—That is only a matter of arrangement between the Cape Colonial overnment and the Netherlands Railway. You can only mention the question of e reduction of tariff.

Yes, but I want to mention the tariff received by the Netherlands Company.— he only question you have to do with is the tariff you have to pay for carrying your ods. What the division is you have nothing to do with.

Well, as we have to pay for it, I think it does matter.—You don't pay it.

You don't deny that you get the proportion of that charge for through rates?— o, I don't deny that. That you will find in any tariff book.

If the Netherlands Company were willing to help the industry, could they not ive up a portion of that?—I don't see why you should always come back to that int. I am prepared, as I said this morning, to co-operate towards a reduction. *Netherlands Railway willing to co-operate to reduce way rates from ports.*

Well, that is satisfactory at any rate. You have heard that the Cape Government solved to make a reduction of 6s. 8d. in the carriage of cement, and that the Nether- nds Company induced them to withdraw the reduction by threatening to put on the ifference at this end. Is there any truth in that?—I have been trying to get at the uth of that assertion. I have even asked Mr. Goldmann by letter, to put me on the ace of that rumour, but he has refused to give me the name of the informer. But know I cannot trace a particle of truth in that statement. I know nothing of it. *Increase of railway rate on cement.*

Is the rate charged on goods the same to all towns or points in the Transvaal; I ve heard that the rate charged on goods to Heidelberg is the same as the rate arged to Johannesburg?—No, that is not a fact. *Differential railway rates on goods.*

Overcharges. It is also stated that in certain cases where goods are carried to places beyon the actual destination, the consignees are charged an overcharge. The Jumpers an Heriot had to pay carriage on goods to Johannesburg and back?—That might be true, because, perhaps, these goods had to be cleared for Customs in Johannesburg But it is just as easy to consign the goods to Elandsfontein, and send them from there to the Jumpers. It might, too, be the fault of the agent at the port, who simply consigns to Johannesburg.

It is the fault of the consignors then?—In very many cases it would be.

Railway rates for bulky goods. What justification is there for charging the same rate for large tanks and boiler which occupy much cubic space, as for rails and girders, which occupy a small space —That remark is very just. We have got in our tariffs an increased rate for bulk goods, but we have had to waive that because the other administrations have not go a similar charge. It ought to be done, but it is never done. We, for a long tim persisted in following a similar calculation for furniture, which is very light, bu bulky, but have had to abandon it because the other administrations have not got a similar charge.

Has an effort been made to try and reduce them?—Discussion has taken plac but never a serious effort. The fear to introduce any novelty in the existing tariffs ha kept them back.

Is it true that in Holland the rates for truck loads are very much smaller tha the rates for lots?—There are cases where it happens.

What could the mining companies do to assist the railway to reduce expenses an make it possible to carry goods at lower rates?—I believe very little. I think in tha way the railway has to look after itself.

"Fighting rates" What do you mean by fighting rates?—A fighting rate is, for instance, a rate tha is far below the real cost, and also the rate to places where competition exists. Fo instance, from Johannesburg to the Free State or Cape Colony.

Differential railway rates on goods. There is no railway competition in the Transvaal?—No, but the tariff here i lower than to Bloemfontein, Kimberley, etc.

The fact that the rate to Kimberley is higher than the rate to here has bee explained in another way.—And Bloemfontein?

I don't know about Bloemfontein. That concerns the Free State. It is a smal community in Bloemfontein.—There is no reason to charge burghers more in a smal place than in a big one.

Advantages to mines of reduction of railway rates. You refer to the saving that would be effected. Do you consider, if the railway rates were lowered, that is all the benefit the mining industry would get?—That is al the State and the railway company would get.

Yes, but that is not all the mining industry expects to get. That is a very hand some sum itself, but, if the railway rates were reduced all round, including the Colonia rates, the mining industry would benefit to the extent of about three times that sum Evidence has been given of the average pay of white miners. Can you tell me th

Wages of European railway employees. average pay of European employees on the railway?—I cannot give you the average The lower officials are paid about the same as in the mining industry. I also take int consideration that the railway has a surer income, and enjoys greater advantages tha the mining industry.

You think, then, the rate of pay to the railway employees is just about the sam as paid to the mining industry?—Yes.

About what pay would these men get in Holland?—A man who gets £20 a montl here would get in Holland from £100 to £125 per annum at the outside.

Differential railway rates on goods. In reference to a question as to the rates to a place with a small population bein higher than to a large town, witness said the question of population was no reaso living should cost more in a small place. So far as he knew, that was not done ∗ngland. That was against every principle of a railway as a public institution. ∗ry ratepayer would protest most earnestly to his representatives in Parliament ∗nst any privileges being granted in that manner to any large centres.

In other countries it generally happens there is competition in railways, but we ∗e none here ?—In some countries it is so, and in some it is not. In France and ∗many there is no competition. They are all State railways, or big groups, which do compete with one another.

The fact that there is no competition in some countries, Germany for instance, ∗ one of the reasons the Government took over the railway ?—I don't think that is ∗ of the reasons.

It may not have been the sole reason, but it was one of them.—That is quite new ∗ne.

Railway competition.

Mr. *Albu.*

You say fighting rates are those which leave a very small margin to those running *"Fighting rates"* railways ?—I don't say that is in all circumstances a decided definition of fighting ∗s.

The Netherlands Railway is employing fighting rates at the present moment ?— ∗are.

And when I look at the balance sheet, and find that you have got a million and a ∗ revenue over your expenditure or working expenses, I think your fighting rates very stiff.—And still leaves the opposition very healthy.

Yes, unfortunately, there is no opposition here. The unfortunate thing is that ∗ industry pays these fighting rates.—Only within the last few months you have ∗e to the conclusion there is something unhealthy about the industry.

Not for the last few months, but for the last five years. You have not seen that? ∗o.

The industry is so healthy that 185 companies have invested at par fully 85 ∗lions, but a lot had been subscribed for at a high premium. I think the industry ∗d last year about a million and a half in dividends. Do you consider it healthy *Dividends of mines and Netherlands Railway profits.* ∗t the Netherlands railway, with a capital of one million, makes a profit of nearly a ∗lion. You have said our industry is a healthy one. I am proving it is not, and that ∗rs is much more healthy than ours is.—I cannot say whether the situation is ∗lthy or not. It is in the hands of the Commission.

You have the key of the situation in your hands in Delagoa Bay. What prevents *Netherlands Railway holds key of position Rates of Delagoa Bay line.* ∗ from reducing the rates to such an extent that the traffic from Natal and Cape ∗ony would be threatened, and they would be thereby compelled to reduce too. ∗at prevents you from doing that ?—I just gave a very plain explanation of that to ∗ Pierce. If there was only one consideration in South Africa, namely, the industry ∗ Johannesburg, then it would be quite easy, but other industries have also a right to ∗ heard in the lowering of the tariffs.

I have lived 21 years in South Africa, and there is only one consideration and one ∗ustry in South Africa, and that is the Transvaal gold mines. There is nothing else ∗ the whole of South Africa so far.—Then I suppose Natal and the Cape Colony ∗uld also appreciate that fact.

Yes, but so long as you keep the Delagoa Bay rate so high, just a little lower than ∗ others, they won't lower it. Finding you have the key of the position you must ∗uce the tariff to such an extent that the Cape traffic is endangered and they will at ∗e acquiesce.—Then the consequence will be certainly to your benefit, but to the ∗riment of whom ?

Nobody.—If there was no agriculture or anything else but the mining indust[
then certainly you are right.

Agriculture would profit immensely if the produce could be brought to the mark[
which is Johannesburg, and no other town. I don't see why you don't force t[
situation. By doing this you would support the whole industry, the industry of So[
Africa.—And if we do as we do at present we support the State. The Commission[
here to give a reply to that. I have already said the result of that reply will certai[
not excite any opposition from me.

As I have the honour to be a member of this Commission, although I may not[
asked to be present when the report is handed in, I should like to know what preve[
the Netherlands Railway from making use of the key which they have in their powe[

Chairman.

You simply all go round the one point, and do not go any further.

Mr. *Albu.*

Yes, because I don't get a satisfactory answer.

Chairman.

Position and pro-
fits of Nether-
lands Railway.
 The question is—what is the position of the railway, and what are the prof[
to-day ?

Mr. *Albu.*

Then I cannot get even what the profits are.

Chairman.

We want to find out in what way the mines are oppressed, and to take [
particulars. Then it is for the Commission to come together to discuss the differe[
points and frame their report.

Mr. *Albu.*

Yes, but I have not been able to find out what the profits are.

Chairman.

Mr. Middelberg has promised us this morning that before the report is made up [
the Commission, he will hand in the official report for 1896, which is not yet in [
hands.

Witness.] I have given the profits. The only things I cannot supply are tho[
particulars which are not yet fixed.

Mr. *Albu.*

Thank you very much.

Mr. *Hay.*

Conditions for
reduction of
railway rates.
 As far as I understand, the position is this : a reduction in the tariff depen[
upon practically the extension or alteration of the concession which you have.—N[
that is not correct.

Do I understand that means an extension of time ?—It means that, supposing t[
Volksraad this session resolved to expropriate the railway, then we could not possib[
give a lower tariff.

If the Government agreed to take it over, according to the agreement, they wou[
have to give a year's notice, and the tariff would remain as it is ?—Up to the end [
next year.

If we go to the Netherlands Railway as a company, and ask them to reduce the ~~iff~~, would they want an alteration in their concession?—No, the concession fixes the ~~ximum~~ tariffs.

The question is, here there is a surplus which, Mr. Middelberg says, would be given ~~ay~~ by the Government, of £500,000. But if the tariff was reduced—the passengers ~~d~~ goods exactly the same—then the revenue would be reduced, and therefore the ~~fit~~ accruing to the shareholder would be naturally less. Do I understand that Mr. ~~ddelberg~~ would be agreeable, as far as he can speak, to a general reduction?—Yes. *(margin: Mr. Middelberg agreeable to a general reduction of railway rates.)*

Then the point put us by the different people who have given evidence is that a ~~all~~ proportion of the mining companies pay dividends, and a large proportion of ~~m~~ pay nothing, and if many of them cannot effect a reduction in the cost of work~~,~~ then they must close down the mines. If that occurs, then the revenue of the ~~lway~~ would be reduced. Therefore, it is to the interest of the railway to have as ~~ny~~ companies at work as possible, and, therefore, if the reduction of the tariff would ~~sure~~ the working of the whole of the mines and the opening of mines which are not ~~work, it might probably make up the profit which they gave away by the reduction~~ tariff.—That is a thing which theoretically seems to be quite correct, but to which *(margin: Increased receipts of Netherlands Railway.)* ~~are~~ not accustomed yet in South Africa. Here there has always been an increase, ~~en~~ in this last month of so-called depression. We have always had an increase in ~~e~~ receipts, so the subject for me—that is, during the last year—has never been what ~~ad~~ to do supposing traffic should diminish, but always what I had to do to cope ~~th~~ the increase. So I never trouble very much about the dark future or the ~~ought~~ that in case it were realised there would be a great retrocession of business.

The evidence we have had is that a large number of mines must close down ~~less~~ they can work at a profit.—I cannot see the result of that yet within my ~~rrow~~ horizon.

But Mr. Middelberg must see that it must come about.—It is quite possible.

The gold produced last year is only worth seven millions, and the profits of the ~~therlands~~, the Cape, and Natal Railways comes to nearly half that.—So the result *(margin: Profits of Cape, Natal, and Netherlands railways.)* that the Cape Colony, Free State, Natal, and this Republic get a good share of the ~~ld~~, which I think is a very happy sign.

If the railway people are to get all the profit, how can the mines live?—I have ~~en~~ asking myself that question for the last two or three years.

One question in regard to the carrying of coal in bulk. What are the charges *(margin: Sidings.)* ~~r~~ a siding?—The charges for sidings are that the company pays for the construction, ~~d~~ for every truck or wagon used on the siding, 4s.

Then the responsibility of the engine rests with the company that makes the ~~ling~~ whether an accident be the fault of the Netherlands or not?—That has to be ~~oved~~ first.

The question of the railway tariff is simply that the Netherlands must decide to *(margin: Netherlands Railway holds key of position)* ~~duce~~ their tariff, and the Cape and Natal lines are compelled to do so. You, Mr. ~~iddelberg~~, are a man of long experience, and we have only a superficial knowledge. ~~rhaps~~ you will be able to advise us on what points reductions can be made. I have ~~re~~ a number of questions which I wish to put, and these I can hand to Mr. Middel~~rg~~, and also a copy to the Commission, and this will save going through them, as ~~at~~ would take too long.

This arrangement was agreed upon.

Mr. *Brakhan.*

I should like to have a little information about the following passage, which ~~pears~~ in your statement:—"I can only speak of the share which the company receives, and I, for myself, can declare that, should the Government consider that by continuance served to work the line, and should the assurance be obtained, would have no objection to meet the wishes of the Government."   Are we to unde

Conditions for reduction of railway rates. stand from this that the Netherlands Railway Company will make a reduction rates in case the State foregoes for a certain period the right to expropriate t railway ?—That would be a matter for negotiation with the Government.   What wanted to express is that if the railway company, according to the desire of t Johannesburg mining industry, is expropriated this year—and one cannot expect th without compensation—the amount for expropriation would be considerably lower.

If the Government think it wise to enter into this arrangement, the Governme would deprive itself of or forego the benefits which would accrue to it from expropri tion until such time as is decided upon ?—Certainly.

I was desirous of having this point clear, because I think it is a very importa matter for the welfare of the State in throwing light on the question of expropri tion.   Because if this arrangement, as suggested, were to be entered into, the Nethe lands Railway Company would have absolute power later on.—I cannot agree wit your last conclusion.   I do not see how the Railway Company can at any time acqui power to do what they like.

I do not mean to convey that in a very broad sense.—Within a narrow sense would not apply.

It would in so far that the Government would never be satisfied with the prof they get out of it, whereas if expropriation should take place at any time with or Expropriation of railway. year's notice, the benefits might be much larger ?—It is for the Government to judg of the benefits of immediate expropriation, or if expropriation be postponed.

Notice of expropriation of railway. I read in Article 27 that notice of expropriation can be given at any time.— Notice can be given at any time, but it must run for a calendar year.

Is it so expressed in the concession ?—No, there is a correspondence settling th point.

Mr. *Brochon.*

Railway rates. Yesterday you said that in case of a mine not paying dividends for three yea you would be willing to meet them by a restitution of rates.   Is that correct ?—Yes.

By acting so it will be a rather late remedy.—It is for this Commission to mak a recommendation on that point.

Still I am pleased to learn of the disposition on the part of the Railway to mak this reduction.

Mr. *Hugo.*

Cost of expropriation of railway. Yesterday, in reply to a question put by Mr. Albu, you stated that if the Gover ment went in for expropriation that about 150 per cent. would have to be paid.—N 150 per cent. above par.

It would mean about £250 per share.—The calculation is very easy to mak Let us estimate that the extraordinary dividend above the guaranteed interest taken on a three years' average at 6 per cent.   Then take it that all shares are 6 p cent. shares ; then average the dividend for the last three years, and that would be per cent.   Twelve times 20 is 240, and add to that 1 per cent. for each year fro 1898 to 1915, *i.e.* 17 per cent., then you get the figure of 257 per cent.

That is if the Government expropriate the railway at the end of 1898 ?—Yes.

Railway rates on coal. With reference to the coal, the average cost of transport is about 3d. per ton p mile ?—From Springs to Johannesburg a little over 2d. is charged.   It is a slidi

in conjunction with the coal mine to give the Brugspruit and Balmoral collieries
ance to carry their coal.

May I ask what you would suggest as a reduction on that tariff?—As to the
tion of how much coal rates can be reduced, it would depend on other tariffs. By
luction of 1s. per ton, the loss, reckoned on last month's returns, would be £4,400,
you always have to make the reduction in such a manner that the difference
een the price of carriage between Springs remains what it is at present, otherwise
ould be a great disadvantage, and a great injustice to mines brought into life
er the present arrangement.

Reduction of railway rates on coal.

The mining industry complain that they have to carry their coal in bags, and not
ulk.—I cannot understand where the accusation comes from. We do everything
ur power to encourage carrying coal in bulk. As I have said, at the present
ent one of the mines that has not got a siding is trying to carry its coal in bulk.

Traffic of coal in bags.

What is the local tariff between here and Vereeniging?—It is 6d. for ordinary
ls, and 3d. per ton for rough goods.

Vereeniging and Johannesburg local railway rates.

The industry has promised us, and if the Government will assist us in getting
reduction they will endeavour to reduce their expenses. Isn't it possible for the
vay company to reduce your working expenses, or are the present expenses as low
hey can possibly be?—The present working expenses are as low as they can be
er present circumstances.

Reduction of Netherlands Railway working costs.

Mr. *Smit.*

You mean to say that if the profits of the railway remain as at present the cost
xpropriation would be less every year?—One per cent. less every year.

Cost of expropriation of railway.

And the concession has still got to run eighteen years?—Yes.

Mr. Fitzpatrick has stated that several lines have had to wait on account of the
s having had to go to Holland?—That statement is entirely incorrect. No plan
ever been sent to Holland to be judged upon, the only exception to this being the
vay station here, which was worked out by an architect in Europe.

Length of Netherlands Railway concession.

Dutch control of Netherlands Railway works

It was stated by Mr. Fitzpatrick that there was a profit of £1,300,000?—It will
y soon be seen from the printed report that the figure I have given is the correct

Profits of Netherlands Railway for 1896.

The reserve fund is £290,000; the public would like to know what became of
-The reserve fund fund goes to building stations, laying double lines, buying rolling
k, and, further, the expenses of each line—as laid down by the concession—is not
ited to capital account, but is taken from the reserve fund, which is fed from the
enue. This is a sound stipulation in the concession, as under it the Government,
expropriation, gets value which is far and above the original cost of the railway
improvements. Take, for instance, that in ten years that every year £300,000—
quote round figures—is taken, that is £3,000,000. This is used to improve the
way and for doubling lines, so that the railway gets a larger value, and the
tion of the £3,000,000 not being used for that purpose remains in the reserve
d and goes back to the Government without any reduction.

Reserve fund of Netherlands Railway.

Was the reserve fund last year sufficient?—It was sufficient for the rail ex-
sion in South Africa, but it has not been sufficient for the large increase of rolling
k. Therefore, the Volksraad have approved of a loan which will have to be
aid by the reserve fund itself.

Mr. Robinson has stated here that he has taken a lot of trouble to get a siding at
of his mines and could not get it.—I have tried to find out which is alluded to.
Robinson has many mines and I don't know of any refusal to give him a siding.
now of a case where, after a long correspondence and a lot of trouble being taken,

Sidings.

the idea was relinquished. Perhaps Mr. Robinson refers to the correspondence
couple of years ago to make sidings for a group of mines—the Langlaagte Royal
Block B—where bigger efforts would be made to put coal in trucks to allow
wagons to go up to the mines. But that was dropped by these mines.

Pretoria railway conference — Cape railways' proposals. At the Railway Conference at Pretoria a little time ago, can you tell me why
arrangement was come to about the tariff, etc. ?—The reason was that, notw
standing the promise of the Premier of the Cape Ministry, the delegates from
Cape Railway asked for a much bigger share of the traffic for themselves than an
the other railway companies were prepared to give. The Cape Railways wanted
of the traffic oversea to come over the Cape lines, and besides that the Cape
should get a bigger share of the traffic between the port and Johannesburg—*pro r*
to the length of their line. That proposal, worked out, came to this, that the C
would have half of the oversea traffic, and that the goods would have to be carr
from Mid-Vaal River to Johannesburg free of charge. It was clear that the prop
was made because the delegates did not wish to go home without making se
proposal.

Is it a fact the Cape wanted three-fifths, and wanted to give the other railw
two-fifths ?—The Cape has tried to get everything. I know that some time ago
Laing, Commissioner, thought he would be satisfied with half, but he afterwa
thought he went too far.

The railway administrations could not agree to take two-fifths between them
It was ridiculous.

Mr. *Joubert.*

Conditions of expropriation of railway. In the concession it is left to the Government to expropriate the railway wh
ever they think fit ?—Yes.

Under what conditions can the Government expropriate ?—The railway is to
liquidated, has to pay all its liabilities and receive all its assets, must pay all its los
and the money wanted for that purpose must be handed over by the State, and
shareholders will receive 20 times the average dividend for the last three years, p
1 per cent. for each year that the expropriation takes place before 1915.

What constitutes the dividend ?—The dividend is formed as follows : Interest
guaranteed on the shares at 6 and $4\frac{1}{2}$ per cent., and there is an extra dividend of
per cent. out of the surplus, but that has never been paid except in 1895, when it v
3 per cent.

The dividend comes out of the revenue ?—Of course.

If reductions were made in the tariff, and the railway was expropriated, wo
not the reduction be far more than 1 per cent. ?—Undoubtedly, if the revenue g
less, the expropriation price is less.

Mr. *Pierce.*

Off - loading of coal in bulk. You said your company is now trying experiments to have coal off-loaded
bulk. What company is it ?—The George Goch.

How long have you been trying the experiments ?—Works are being construc
which will make it possible.

Then you have not tried experiments yet ?—Not yet.

Questions for Netherlands South African Railway Company,

Handed to Mr. MIDDELBERG by Mr. HAY, with the answers thereto.

---

1. Have the regulations of your company, on the strength of which you accept ╵ds for forwarding, been passed by the Volksraad or only by a Committee of the ╵ecutive appointed for that purpose ? *Authority for Netherlands Railway Regulations.*

I consider that the regulations are authorised by the Honourable Volksraad.

2. Is it a fact that on the strength of these regulations you repudiate liability ╵ total loss of goods which you carry at a reduced rate, such as deals, iron, etc. ? *Liability of Netherlands Railway for loss of Goods.*

No.

3. Is it not a fact that your regulations endeavour to contract you out of all ╵bility for damage and loss ?

No.

4. Has this position of yours ever been contested in a court of law in the ╵ansvaal ?

Yes.

5. Are you aware that in all other civilised countries, innumerable cases for loss ╵ve been decided against the Railway Companies, notwithstanding clauses having ╵n inserted to the effect of exempting the Railway ?

No ; our case stands wholly on the basis of sound legislation.

6 (a). Do you invariably shield yourself under the " Owner's Risk " clause, ╵when unable to trace or deliver goods handed to you for transit under that clause ? *" Owners' Risk on Netherlands Railway.*

(b). Have you lost whole truck loads of goods and refused to pay compensation for such loss ?

(c). Do you contemplate any alteration in the conditions under which you ╵carry goods at the so-called " Owner's Risk " rates ?

(d). How do you account for the frequent losses of goods carried at the so-called " Owner's Risk " rates ?

(a—b). No, certainly not.

(c). I intend when eventually altering the tariff to abolish " Owner's Risk."

(d). I know nothing about it.

7. It is a fact that your regulations shield you from claims for loss for any value ╵yond 1s. per pound ? *Liability of Netherlands Railway for loss of Goods.*

When classifying for rates does not the higher rate cover such risk, and therefore ╵u should be liable for losses ?

Yes, but everyone is free to insure for a higher value.

8. Are there not constant complaints of the delay given by your Company in ╵ciding on claims for loss and damage ? *Delay in deciding Claims for Loss and Damage.*

No more than of any other railway.

9. Does your Company refund the railage, if paid in advance, on goods lost ╵hilst in transit ? *Refund of Railage on Lost Goods.*

N.B.—The Company fails to deliver the goods ; declines to admit claims for such goods, but yet retains the amount paid for carriage.

Yes.

10. Do you not think that this part of your regulations is manifestly unfair to ╵e public, who are thereby placed absolutely at the mercy of the Railway Company ?

No.

Refusal of Trucks at Delagoa Bay.

11. Is it not a fact that trucks have been refused to forwarding agents Delagoa Bay, unless they signed the clause exempting the Railway from shortage a damage?

It is a mattter that concerns the Portuguese authorities. I do not, however, belie that the statement is correct.

Inspection of Consignments by Consignee before Signature of Receipt

12. Do you consider it fair to the consignee that he should sign for consignmen to be delivered to sidings, before having had an opportunity of checking the goods?

This does not occur. There is always an opportunity of seeing the goods. On on private sidings this can cause difficulties. I see no help for it.

Liability of Netherlands Railway for loss of Goods.

13. Is it not a fact that in cases where a discrepancy is discovered, that you pr duce the clear receipt and shield yourself under this and repudiate liability for t deficiency?

Naturally.

Receipts for consignments.

14. When consignments of a truck load and more are being delivered Johannesburg station, do you decline to give receipts for the separate trolley load. Merchants report that you decline to give such receipts and will only sign after t consignment is completed. Evidence can be produced that the Company declines give receipts for each trolley load and afterwards disputes the total quantity.

No, we sign for receipt of portions of consignments.

Receipts for small consignmegts.

15. Does not your Company refuse to give proper receipts for small consig ments? It is stated that instances can be given where several parcels have been se to the station at the same time and the Company make a jotting of the charges on or delivery note only, initial that note, and positively decline to give any other recei Is not this a contrast to your practice in taking receipts?

Whenever a receipt is asked for we sign one.

Charges for demurrage.

16. Do you consider it a fair charge for demurrage to levy double the ra charged you by the Cape Railway Department? [*Vide* Chamber of Mines Report, p. 9 No.

Use of the Dutch language on the Netherlands Railway.

17. Are you aware of the disadvantage to the mercantile community in cor ducting your business in the Dutch language?

18. Are you aware that only a very small minority of the mercantile firms wh are members of the Chamber of Commerce and Mercantile Association, understan Dutch, and the majority have to employ translators to enable them to understand yo letters and notices?

19. Are you aware that the staff at Johannesburg is at a constant disadvantag in carrying on its work through not being able to understand the mercantile languag of the community?

(To 17, 18, 19). Yes. One cannot insist too much on the importance of learn ing foreign languages and especially the vernacular.

Refusal of initialled cheques as payment for Railage. Payment of Railage in Coin.

20. Did you refuse initialed cheques in payment of railage charges?
No.

21. Did you insist on payment of railage in coin at the Johannesburg station?

22. Was not this a serious difficulty to the consignees and to your department?

23. Was not this regulation to insist upon payments in coin a serious risk, bot to consignees and the Company?

(To 21, 22, 23). No. It does not exist.

Netherlands Railway rates.

24. Note.—Refer to Chamber of Mines Railway Report, p. 2, *re* rates per variou systems. What justification is there for the excessive rates charged by you administration?

Refer to p. 5 of Chamber of Mines Report, Cape Railways carry South Africa produce at ½d. per ton per mile.

Cape Railways carry	South African produce at ...		...	...	½d.
„ „	„ imported	„	...	...	1d.
O. F. S. „	„ South African	„	...	...	½d.
„ „	„ imported	„	...	...	2d.
N. Z. A. S. M.	„ all produce at	...	...	...	$3\frac{1}{13}$d.

—What reason has your Company for charging the extra rate?
The report of the Chamber of Mines errs altogether as has been fully shown, and
this respect quite inaccurate.

25. The delivery charges on packages over 3,000 lbs. weight is 3d. per 100 lbs. **Delivery charges**
y is a rebate not allowed for the 3,000 lbs. which is already paid for in the railage,
the charge only levied on the weight over and above the 3,000 lbs. maximum
rding to the regulations?
It is my intention to extend considerably the limits of the delivery service.

26. Did you have a special contract with Mr. F. R. Lingham, by which he had a **The "Lingham" contract.**
erence of 20 per cent. in rate over other importers? What amount was paid in
pensation to Mr. Lingham to secure the cancellation of the contract?

27. Had you a similar contract with Mr. Davies? Did you transport "karri" **Mr. Davies' contract.**
ber at over 30 per cent. under the actual weight?

28. What was the reason for giving the parties named preference over other
ber importers?
(To 26, 27, 28). The questions were fully dealt with before the Commission.

29. Do you consider your employees are experienced railway men? **Experience of employees.**
Naturally, if the circumstances are taken into consideration.

30. Have they had previous railway experience or have they only gained
ere?
All the *personnel?* No. A large portion? Yes.

31. Importers of produce suffer considerable loss through shortage. Recently, **Shortage of goods.**
of your head officials was charged before the Landdrost with having taken certain
ntities of produce, but was acquitted on the ground that these were *sweepings*. Do
r regulations permit your officials to remove goods in this manner belonging to
signees?
No.

32. Drapers and similar traders complain of your Company taking from 10 to 12 **Delay in delivery of goods.**
rs to deliver goods, after the truck has arrived at station here. Cannot you expe-
such deliveries?
Incorrect.

33. There are serious complaints regarding the delays in transit and delivery of **Delay in transit and delivery of live-stock.**
stock, causing these to arrive here in a deplorable condition.
The fault lies almost exclusively with the consignors.
It is reported that poultry consignments are treated in a similar fashion, and a
happened the other day where some crates of fowls were put on the delivery
gon over-night, left out in the cold and wet, and in consequence between 20 and 30
e dead next morning. Can you not make some arrangements by which such cruelty
loss could be avoided?
The statements are completely incorrect.
You compared rail rates to Johannesburg with those to Kimberley for dyna- **Kimberley Railway rates.**
e—the Cape charge is 2nd class rate. Does not Kimberley submit to the high

rates to Kimberley on all goods and also the high duty on dynamite of 12s.
per case as a set off against any tax on diamonds, and also supports Colonial coal mi[]
for the same reason, and therefore is not comparison quite upon different condition[]

Rates to Mochudi—normal goods, distance from Port Elizabeth, 832 miles, []
9s. 4d. per 100 lbs.; Port Elizabeth to Johannesburg, 714 miles, rate 8s. 1d. per 100 l[]
timber 5s. 8d. against 5s. 3d. per 100 lbs.; reasonable difference for extra distance [ ]
the fact that all coal has to be carried such long distances, and again the tonn[]
carried is infinitesimal as compared with that to Johannesburg.

The rate to Mochudi has nothing to do with the argument that I have advan[]
in reference thereto.

Rates of Nether-
lands and
Beira Railways Is not the comparison of N.Z.A.S.M. rates with those on the Beira Railw[]
altogether on different local conditions?

Mr. W C. Thom
son's evidence. MR. W. C. THOMSON, merchant, then made the following statement:

My object in offering evidence before this honourable Commission is to show t[]
the economic conditions of mining would be materially enhanced were the Gove[]
Blasting mater-
ials.
The Transvaal
dynamite mon-
opoly. ment to realise and legislatively recognise the fact that forms of blasting mater[]
other than composed of nitro-glycerine, are in successful use in other mining cent[]
throughout the world. The Transvaal dynamite monopoly, which has practica[]
been in existence for eight years, is responsible for retarding the introduction o[]
class of explosives that would have performed a large proportion of the work done on []
Rand and elsewhere within the State, in an economical and satisfactory manner wi[]
out the faintest shadow of risk from accidental explosions. It may be said that t[]
enquiry is only concerned with the pounds, shillings and pence aspect of the questi[]
It must, however, without doubt, be acknowledged that economical conditions []
working are influenced by considerations quite apart from mere cost price. The l[]
to the country from the dynamite monopoly is far beyond any figures that have be[]
Deaths and losses
through dyna-
mite. laid before your honourable body. When we take into account the thousands of liv[]
that have been sacrificed, and the enormous value of property destroyed; when []
reckon the loss of time caused by these constantly recurring accidents from dynami[]
or gelatine cartridges left unexploded in drill holes, and the daily delays from noxio[]
fumes—and all in spite of the most stringent regulations that the mining authorit[]
can devise—it will be found that the loss resulting from the employment of nit[]
glycerine compounds has to be reckoned, not by hundreds of thousands, but []
millions of pounds sterling. I do not for one moment mean to say that the quality[]
Quality of Trans-
vaal dynamite. the dynamite and gelatine supplied by the Government contractors is not as good []
can be bought in any other part of the world; but I do urge the honest recognition []
our industrial legislation of the unquestionable fact that all nitro-glycerine explosiv[]
Disadvantages of
dynamite mon-
opoly. are intrinsically dangerous. My contention is, briefly, that had there been []
monopoly, the Rand, and other mining centres within the State, might have be[]
supplied with the best and cheapest and safest blasting material procurable. N[]
inventions, if worthy of encouragement, would have had a chance of being adopt[]
Inventors in the region of chemistry would have been stimulated to fresh discover[]
for the benefit of the industry, and consequently of the State; and with t[]
healthy competition that would have ensued, there might have been a reasona[]
chance of preventing the growth, to its present dangerous dimensions, of th[]
"Nobel's dyna-
mite trust." greater monopoly or ring, known by the name of "Nobel's Dynamite Trus[]
in whose hands the Transvaal monopoly practically now is. The object of t[]
ring is well known to be the strangling of all competition in whatever part []
the world it can exercise its influence; not so much the competition arising fr[]
the makers of dynamite outside the ring (who are easily reduced to submissio[]

the suppression, by every means possible, of such improved modes of blasting threaten to interfere with their interests. In spite, however, of this powerful ~agonism, there is an explosive, or rather a blasting compound (for it is not itself explosible, like powder, dynamite or gelatine), that has made very con-~erable headway in many parts of the world, notably in Germany, Spain, England, ~nada, British Columbia, Australia, India, and the Cape Colony. The material is ~led roburite, and since its first introduction, before the granting of the Lippert ~ncession, not one life has been lost by its accidental explosion, for the reason that ~h a thing is impossible. The proved safety of this class of blasting material has ~n wisely recognised in South Africa by the Government of the Cape Colony, by the ~nicipal authorities of Port Elizabeth, and by the Harbour Boards of the more ~portant seaports. It is manufactured without restriction in Port Elizabeth, carried ~ the Cape Railways as ordinary merchandise, and shipped from one port to another ~ ordinary freight. These privileges were not obtained until the most searching test ~d been made, and reported upon by the Government chemist and analyst, and con-~ncing proofs afforded by demonstrations in presence of practical experts as to ~solute safety. Patent rights for roburite were granted at Pretoria in 1890, but up ~l now the terms of the dynamite monoply have prevented either the manufacture or ~ sale within the Transvaal of any blasting materials of this class. Besides assuring ~ incalculable advantages of safety and the innocuousness of its fumes, roburite ~uld be sold at from one-half to two-thirds of the present prices of the explosives ~w in use. The employment of blasting materials of this class, by doing away with ~cidents, would naturally have the effect of inspiring native boys, as well as white ~ners, with more confidence in their work ; and the withdrawal of labour by reason of ~s of life and limb of hundreds of workers being put an end to, labour would necessarily ~come the more plentiful, and by so much the cheaper. One of the most serious ~stacles to the increase in the number of native labourers for the mines, is the ~vincible repugnance of all the Zulu speaking races and of many of the most intelli-~nt and industrious Basuto races to work underground. Those familiar with ~ native character and modes of thought will agree that this repugnance has its ~igin primarily in the deleterious fumes and in the terrible accidents inseparable ~om the use of nitro-glycerine explosives; and the majority of them unite in thinking ~at the elimination of these two serious drawbacks to underground work would ~questionably, within a short time, tempt thousands of natives (who are now so ~rmly prejudiced against this most important department of labour) to abandon their ~t unnatural attitude. It must, therefore, be clear to minds of the meanest capacity ~at the cancellation of the present dynamite monopoly—or at least the removal of all ~gal obstacles to the importation and use of other classes of blasting materials—would ~nefit the mining industry, not only by the certain prevention of accidents in those ~ines which decided to abandon the use of nitro-glycerine explosives, and by the great ~ving of time assured by the absence of noxious fumes after blasting, but also by the ~rtain large increase in the number of natives willing to work underground, and by ~e reduction of wages naturally following such competition. There is no doubt ~at, for some purposes, many miners would still prefer gelatine, and there is no ~estion whatever as to its efficacy ; but wherever any blasting material less ~ghly concentrated is considered suitable, such as dynamite or black powder ~e class represented by roburite would undoubtedly be at once preferred. Possibly ~e-half of the work performed in gold and coal mining, and certainly all the work ~ prospecting and quarrying, could be better performed in safety than by dangerous ~plosives, and at infinitely less cost; and no doubt when prejudice has been overcome, ~d experience has been gained by continual practice, it will be found that all blasting

[Marginal notes:] Roburite. — Safety of roburite. — Manufacture and transport of roburite. — Roburite patent. — Price of roburite. — Advantages of employment of roburite. — Free trade in blasting materials. — Low-power explosives. — Safe and dangerous explosives.

W

operations may be carried out without the employment of dangerous explosives.

Casualties through nitro-glycerine ex-plosives. will hardly be necessary to dwell long upon the havoc that has been wrought to li limb, and property by explosives of the nitro-glycerine class. Every gentleman on th Commission is familiar with the terrible calamity that occurred here 15 months ag which cost the country hundreds of lives and hundreds of thousands of pounds; wi the destruction of the town of Santander in Spain a year or two ago, when over thousand lives were sacrificed; with the many disastrous explosions in Kimberley years past; with the recent Langlaagte Deep calamity (which proved the dead) nature of nitro-glycerince fumes, by 'causing the death of 32 human beings in a fe minutes), and with the tale of victims furnished us by the newspapers with sickenir regularity. Rules and regulations cannot possibly be framed to prevent suc occurrences. Only a few weeks ago in one of the most rigidly regulated dynami factories in the world (Nobel's, at Ardeer, in Scotland), five men, including the resider chemist, were blown to atoms, the only trace of remains recovered being a shirt-cu adhering to a piece of human flesh. I have endeavoured to obtain statistics from th books of the mining inspectors, but have been informed that because of official instruc tions received from Pretoria, they were debarred from affording any information tha had not already been published. The report for last year not being as yet in print, had therefore to fall back on the report for 1895, by which it appears that 78 me were killed and 113 more or less injured. Judging by the casualties recorded in th Boksburg district inspector's book for 1896 (the only one to which access was obtain able), viz., 44 killed and 59 wounded last year, it may safely be assumed that th deaths and injuries on the Rand mines from this preventible cause, will be quite doubl what they were in 1895. Nearly three-fourths of the recorded accidents were cause by natives drilling into or close to holes in which unexploded cartridges still lay. Th casualties of the present year bid fair to exceed those of any previous one, for, durin the week of the Langlaagte Deep accident, according to newspaper reports, about 4 deaths, to say nothing of mutilations, were recorded. With whatever fault stranger may tax our legislators, I do not think that the charge of inhumanity can be laid a their door; and I feel certain that it is only necessary to bring the facts I have state prominently before their notice, in order that they may take steps to thoroughl investigate this matter, with the aid and advice of others than those interested in th

Introduction of safe explosives maintenance of the dynamite monopoly. By permission to allow fair trade in blastin materials which do not contain nitro-glycerine, the lot of those who form the mainsta of the country's prosperity may be ameliorated at an actual financial gain to the State At the same time the additional safety of the lives and property of the inhabitants wi be assured by abolishing the monopoly in dynamite, or, at least, by providing for th introduction of the class of safety blasting materials to which I have referred. If can afford this honourable Commission any further information on the subject I sha be glad to answer such questions as may be put.

Chairman.

Invention of ro-burite. When did roburite become known?—It was invented in 1886.

Why roburite is not more used. If it is so very good, why should it not be used instead of dynamite?—I canno answer for the mines. As I have mentioned in my declaration, Nobel's Dynamite Trus is a very widespread organisation. I believe their capital is something like te millions, and this dynamite trust has prevented anything of a new nature coming int the market that would injure the interests of this monopoly. Another reason that it i not generally used is that miners are very conservative in regard to explosives. I took about 12 or 13 years from the introduction of dynamite before miners would tak to it. They used to employ black powder, and then there was no ring or monopoly t

ent the introduction of dynamite as there is now to hinder the adoption of newer
hods of blasting. In various parts of the world where mining is carried on I can
luce documentary evidence to prove that, in spite of this opposition, roburite has
i preferred. Of course in many places where there is a large consumption of
losives, the tactics of Nobel's Trust is sufficient to wreck anything but a strong
pany. The principal reason why miners in the Transvaal know very little about
irite is simply because they have been forbidden to import it, even in small
ntities. Five years ago I had a small quantity, and I was trying experiments at
e of the mines. A complaint was sent by the concessionaires to Pretoria that I was
orting this against the law, and I was ordered to appear before the Chief of the Government
toms to give an explanation. If the Government would permit trials to take place, trials of robur-
n perfectly certain that I would convince not only the Government, but also those ite suggested.
were more directly interested, of the many advantages of roburite. I have met
es of miners here who have used roburite in England, Australia, and other parts
he world. If the Commission wished, I could give the names of managers and
ers who might be called as witnesses.

Is it better and more harmless than dynamite?—It is absolutely harmless. Safety of robur-
il a detonator is added, which is different in composition to a dynamite detonator, ite.
ill not explode at all. Neither fire, concussion, lighting, or other agency which would
lode powder or dynamite could explode roburite. It is a well-known fact among
ers and mine managers that roburite would be a very good substitute for dynamite.

Why have you not made it better known here?—What is the use of advertising
naking known an article which I am not allowed to sell or import?

Is it forbidden to make roburite in Europe and use it?—No, there is no monopoly
e.

Is it well known in Europe?—Yes. It is known in Germany, Australia, Spain, Use of roburite
it is largely used in England, Wales, and Scotland. in Europe.

Do the mine managers here, and contractors and merchants, know of the
tence of roburite?—Many of them do.

Many gentlemen connected with the mines, including the Chairman of the
mber of Mines, have given evidence before the Commission regarding explosives,
they have only referred to the dynamite monopoly, and asked for free trade in The dynamite
amite, but not a single one has mentioned roburite.—Of course, they don't mention monopoly and
explosives; they want free trade. If there is free trade and free importation, roburite.
n miners and mine managers will have an opportunity of using whatever explosive
y please. Of course, I may mention, it has never been to the interest of the con-
sionaires to say anything in favour of any other explosive.

You see the dynamite monopoly is for the importation of all explosives; so, con-
uently, when it is proved that for the mines roburite is better, that can be arranged,
ugh the Government, to import roburite instead of dynamite.—About two
a half years ago, the Chamber of Mines sent a memorial to the
ksraad asking for amelioration with regard to the dynamite monopoly.
was brought before the Raad, and it was stated by Mr. Vorstman that
oon as an explosive could be manufactured at a price lower than the present
e of dynamite, the Explosives Company was wholly prepared to treat with the
ders of such patents with regard to the manufacture and sale of such explosive, so that
mines should have the benefits accruing from such invention. Acting on this, I in-
viewed Mr. Vorstman, and asked in what way he would allow us to import roburite.
manager promised to bring the matter before his directors, and on Sept. 5, 1895,
lied that his directors had decided that my offer could not be taken into considera-
. I replied, expressing surprise at this decision in view of the assurance given

to the Volksraad, pointing out that roburite was quite as effective for most min
purposes as dynamite, and much more suitable for coal mining and quarrying, to
nothing of its valuable properties of safety, and stating that as under similar c
ditions as those which the Explosives Company enjoyed from Government, robur
could be manufactured and sold in the Transvaal at much less than the present pr
of dynamite—even after providing the Explosives Company with an adequ
consideration for the privilege of working under their rights—I should be glad
know in what manner the Company was "wholly prepared" to treat with the hold
of the roburite patent.   To that communication a formal acknowledgment w
received, stating that the directors saw no reason to depart from the resoluti
already come to.   My firm had been trying for seven years, without success, to get
fair trial for roburite in the Transvaal.

Roburite and No-
bel's.   I understand that the Nobel's people are trying to suppress roburite?—Y
they are trying to suppress the manufacture of all articles that interfere with nit
glycerine explosives, not only here, but all over the world.

Suppose the dynamite monopoly is taken away and free trade is given?—Th
would allow the mines to select their own explosive.   I mentioned in my stateme
that the Cape Government, in 1890, in view of the many accidents which h
taken place in the Colony, submitted a sample of roburite to a chemical expert, wl
after many trials, has given a certificate to the Government guaranteeing its perf
safety.   The Cape Government has allowed us to manufacture roburite in Pe
Elizabeth, and it is sold and conveyed through the country without any restriction
Safety of robur-
ite. to the observance of the Act that applies to dynamite.   I need hardly point out th
this is a great boon to prospectors and quarrymen, as they can keep the roburi
about their work or in their houses without the slightest danger.

I am very pleased with the evidence and your declaration, because it is the fi
duty to protect life and property, and this evidence will give great assistance in co
sidering the dynamite question.   People ought to look after the lives and property
the mines, and this is one of the reasons for considering the doing away with t
dynamite monopoly.

Mr. Smit.

Experimental-
ists in robur-
ite.   Can you give us names of people here who have had practical experience
roburite?—Yes.   Mr. Howard Harris, of the Tyne Valley Colliery; Mr. J. M. Dona
of the Bantjes Consolidated.

Mr. Hugo.

Power of robur-
ite.   Is it as powerful as dynamite?—It is a better explosive than most classes
dynamite, but it is not as powerful as blasting gelatine.   For coal mines it
invaluable, not only because it brings out the coal in a more marketable conditic
but because there is no risk should unexploded cartridges happen to be shovelled in
a furnace with the coal, as sometimes occurs, with disastrous results, in the case
dynamite cartridges.   If an opportunity were given in the Transvaal to use roburi
there is little doubt that with the assistance of chemical science, means would
found to make roburite as strong as blasting gelatine, so that it could be used for t
very hard rocks in deep level mines.

Mr. Joubert.

Information re-
garding min-
ing disasters.   You say you cannot get information about the mining disasters last year.   If y
wanted information you should have gone to the head of the department and not
subordinates?—I would have done so if I had had time.   I cast no reflections on t

cials, but merely state the fact in explanation of my inability to furnish fuller
ails as to accidents.

Roburite has been receiving my attention for some months, and from the informa-
n I have on the subject, and which it is my intention to lay before the Commission,
elieve it is far safer and less costly than dynamite. *Price and safety of roburite.*

Mr. *Brochon.*

I was induced some years ago to use roburite, and it was fairly satisfactory. You *Roburite fumes.*
ak of the noxiousness of the gas of dynamite; what is the gas of roburite?—I am
a chemical expert, but I know that the gas roburite emits does not contain carbon-
noxide, which is the poisonous gas in dynamite. There are, of course, fumes from
ery explosive, but gases emitted from roburite are not harmful like those emitted
m nitro-glycerine explosives. I may mention that, in the first inception of roburite,
bel tried every means to damage its reputation, and it so happened that a miner had *Roburite and Nobel's.*
d from the effects of an accident, and it was said that he had been poisoned with
fumes of roburite. Nobel industriously circulated this to his agents all over the
rld. The directors of roburite instituted a searching medical investigation, with the
ult that it was stated on the best authority that the man did not die from the fumes
roburite.

How do you use it?—By the aid of a special detonator. The detonator for exploding *Manner of exploding roburite.*
atine and dynamite is not of the same character. It is very small. It has been
ved that dynamite cartridges left in a hole may be exploded with a strike of a drill,
t, with roburite, you may strike it with a sledge hammer and it will not explode.

Can you tell us anything about its composition?—It is composed of the same in- *Composition of roburite.*
edients as the Sprengel class of explosives. Dr. Roth was the inventor of this
rticular explosive. It is composed of nitrate of ammonia, with the addition of an
tract of coal-tar, commonly called tar salts. The chemical name is chloro-di-nitro-
nzole.

How if you put fire to it?—If you place it in a fire it simply burns away. *Comparative safety of dynamite and roburite.*
If you take a dynamite cartridge it will burn too, though part of it when hot
ough will explode. Now, does roburite burn right through, or will part of it ex-
de?—You cannot ignite it, hence another reason of its being a very good explosive
mines. It does not sustain combustion. Supposing you take a bucket full of
burite and plunge into it a red hot iron rod, it would simply blaze up, but, im-
diately the iron is withdrawn, the flame disappears; hence it is not liable, like
namite, to ignition when, as sometimes happens, the detonator in the priming cart-
ge is pushed in too far, and the dynamite becomes ignited and sends off poisonous
mes.

Can you tell us something about the price of roburite, as many witnesses here *Price of roburite*
ve stated that the actual cost of dynamite is 37s? What would be the price of
burite without duty? What is the price at home?—It is sold at home at £2 1s. 6d.
r case.

That is very expensive. We can get dynamite at 21s. 6d. a case, that is, £43 per
n.—I may mention that the power of roburite is greater than dynamite. A smaller *Proportionate power of dynamite and roburite.*
antity does the same amount of work in proportion of three cases of roburite to four
dynamite.

Do you mean that the roburite is as strong as dynamite? It is stronger.

What is the density of roburite?—It is a little more bulky than dynamite.
here you would use 4 ozs. of dynamite in a hole, 3 ozs. of roburite would occupy the
ne space, and do equal work.

Mr. Schmitz-Dumont.

You say yourself that in many cases the mine manager gives the preference
gelatine ?—Undoubtedly.

Last year the mines used about 40,000 cases of dynamite and 110,000 cases
Roburite and blasting gelatine. You only mean to substitute roburite for dynamite, not for blastin
gelatine. gelatine ?—I don't imagine that were roburite permitted to be introduced everyboc
would run and buy it. It would naturally take some time before the mine manage
fully realised the advantages of using roburite.

Have you got any idea of the cost of using roburite instead of blasting gelatin
for the same work ?—Well, we could sell roburite here for something under £3 per cas

In the one case you take roburite, and in the other gelatine. Which would co
most ?—Roburite would cost a great deal less, the one against the other, to give th
same power.

Extensive trials have been made at Home and it has been found that for th
hard class of work you have here roburite would cost about 30 per cent. more tha
blasting gelatine ?—I daresay 30 per cent. more than the low price at which you g
blasting gelatine in America and Europe. I quite agree that roburite cannot be mae
as cheap as some of those nitro-glycerine compounds, for the reason that the enti:
cartridge of roburite is chemical. There is no earth or kieselguhr employed in i
manufacture.

Witness thanked the members of the Commission for the manner in which the
had heard him.

Mr. Samuel
Foote's evi-
dence.   Mr. SAMUEL FOOTE, Chairman of the Licensed Victuallers' Association, was ne:
called. He read a statement in Dutch, of which the following is a tran
lation :—

It affords me great pleasure to be permitted to offer some information to yo
honourable Commission upon the old vexed liquor question, especially with regard
its bearing upon the mining industry. I must, however, admit that I feel the weig
of the heavy responsibility thus imposed upon me in the face of the formidab
opposition and grave indictments laid against the liquor traffic, not only by the hea
of the mining community, but also by the Mercantile Association and Chamber
Commerce, as well as by the various other sections of the community at large.
pray, therefore, for your kind indulgence. I may be considered, perhaps, as goin
somewhat beyond the sphere of this enquiry, upon touching upon that portion of th
Liquor trade de-
pendent on
gold industry. trade which at first glance may not seem to have any direct bearing upon the minir
industry, but I may venture the opinion that all branches of commerce, of which the liqu
trade is one of the most important in this State, must be considered equally depende:
upon the success or failure of the gold industry. The liquor question is one whic
has exercised civilised nations for many decades past, and the manufacture and sale
wines, spirits, etc., have a considerable influence upon the revenue, I may say, of th
whole world, and may consequently be looked upon as a huge commercial item. F
some considerable time, I regret to say, the dealers in liquors generally in th
Republic have been looked upon as desirous of working in opposition to the interests
the State industry ; and in their desire to work on the most economical basis, tl
mining community agitated what may be termed a hasty drastic legislation, of whic
extremists in our midst took immediate advantage, the consequence thereof beir
Liquor Law No.
17 of 1896. Law 17, 1896, which will and must, in its operation, bring about a state of financi
collapse of those engaged in the trade, as well as enormous loss to the revenue of th

e, the extent of which I cannot believe the most honest protectors of the industry
d ever even have contemplated. I shall endeavour to point out roundly the
equences of the operation of some of the most important clauses in the present
or Law, brought about entirely by the said agitation of the mining community,
after having stated the various grievances in connection therewith, I shall take
liberty of offering a few suggestions for the improvement of legislation on this
ect, and especially with reference to its relations to mining interests and to the
nunity at large. Article 3 provides that—"No licence for the sale of spirituous *Article 3 of Law 17 of 1896.*
rs by retail or wholesale shall be granted except in established and acknow-
ed towns, villages, and diggings under Government control." This provision, *Abolition of roadside hotels*
h means the abolition of all roadside hotels, was agreed upon by the hon. Second
sraad, and upon strong opposition being shown by a large number of the popula-
the operation of the clause was suspended until next month, when it must come into
. It is hardly necessary for me to point out how severely the operation of this Article *Effects of article 3.*
affect the interests of many burghers and others throughout the Republic who are
r proprietors or tenants of such establishments, as well as the great inconvenience
will be occasioned to the travelling public. The non-existence of convenient
nmodation along the various roads of the country must also be specially and
usly felt by those members of the mining community employed in prospecting,
I shall now, with your permission, make reference to two of the most important
ses in the law so far as the mining interests are concerned, namely, Articles 5 and *Articles 5 and 6 of Law 17, 1896*
hich prohibit the sale or gift of any kind of liquor to any coloured persons. This
not only apply to natives, but to other coloured races, including Colonials, among *Sale of liquor to coloured persons.*
m will be found many honest tradesmen, and in fact many well-to-do people. I
e to be able to show you that those governing the mining interests were hardly
re in their agitation for the passing of the measure, and that they did not
ust the means at their command for lessening the evils they complain of before
g instrumental in obtaining legislation which will bring disastrous consequences
it. It was the mining people themselves who encouraged the sale of liquor to
ves, powerfully assisted by those in their employment. In order to place the
er clearly before you, I hope your hon. body will permit me to give a slight
mé of the liquor agitation. For some considerable period it was found that
ves were illegally served with adulterated and injurious liquor, especially by un-
cipled and unlicensed dealers, and from time to time my association made strong
esentations to the Licensing Board not to increase "kleurling licences," and even *Kleurling licences.*
to grant any new licences in town unless actually required for the convenience of
public. Then, again, for a long time past, extremists have agitated for the
sion of the Liquor Laws, and, for a considerable curtailment of licences generally.
these culminated in a resolution of the hon. the Second Volksraad on the 5th
ember, 1895 (Minutes, page 645, Article 1571). See Dutch copy enclosed, trans-
n as follows : "The Second Volksraad, having regard to the report of the Com- *Appointment of commission of enquiry into liquor question, Sept., 1895.*
ion appointed by Art. 49 of 13th May, to take the Liquor Law under revision,
lves to refer all petitions and documents in reference thereto to the hon. the
ernment, with instructions to appoint a Commission of Enquiry during the recess,
a view to investigate the liquor traffic in the S.A.R., to consider the various
tions, to obtain information, take evidence, and to draw up as soon as possible a
plete and adequate new law ; and, further, to publish same for treatment by the
the Second Volksraad. The Volksraad further resolves that the said Commission
l have the power to summon witnesses if necessary, and to give memorialists copy *History of commission of enquiry into liquor question.*
his resolution." Unfortunately, owing to the late crisis, the Commission appointed
sisting of the Criminal Landdrost of Johannesburg, the State Attorney, and the

Landdrost of Pretoria, did not commence its labours till about May, 1896, and the
in question was never published in accordance with above resolution, the people
large being therefore debarred from considering the same. The Commission sat
Pretoria for only one week or two, and I venture to submit that it was impossibl
so short a time to investigate to the full extent all matters in connection with
important branch of commerce as intended by the Volksraad resolution. I wish r
to point to the practical encouragement given by the mining community, as well as

Liquor conces-
sions by min-
ing companies. its employees, in the sale of liquor to natives. It is a well known fact that m
concessions for the sale of strong drink have been granted by mining companies.
is difficult for many obvious reasons to give accurate details in all instances. In m
cases tenders were publicly called for in the newspapers for the right to sup
natives, and the following are a few examples. When Mr. Cowie's right to sell liqu
on the Geldenhuis Estate had expired (for which, by the way, he paid the company
per month), advertisements appeared asking for new tenders, and Messrs. Sack a
Lediker were successful in obtaining these privileges from the company on lease at
rate of £1,800 per annum. In the case of the New Crœsus Gold Mining Compa
Limited, Mr. F. W. Smith got the preference at a rental of £1,500 per annum, with
proviso that he should build suitable premises, which cost about £1,500. Then on
New Primrose a similar concession was granted on payment of £1,200 per ann
Other instances could perhaps have been given, if the lessees were not so reticen

Compound man-
agers and the
liquor ques-
tion. giving details. Then, again, considerable impetus was given to unnecessary drinking
employees engaged in the mining industry, and notably so by some compound manag
Last year, when I had the honour of interviewing the Government on the matter, I pla
in their hands a number of permits for the purchase of quantities of liquor signed
compound managers, and which are doubtless in their possession. Of course it is m
difficult to prove conclusively the guilty knowledge of contravention of the liquor la
by the white employees of various companies, because it is impossible to obtain a
assistance from those in league with them. It would, however, be interesting to qu
two or three instances which have been publicly reported and which I think you v
consider somewhat bear out my statement. I see a report in the *Star* of the 1
April, 1896, headed "15 gallons of brandy." It was a case wherein seven nat
policemen employed at the City and Suburban Gold Mining Company, Limited, w
brought before Mr. Van den Berg, charged with being in possession of 15 gallons
brandy. Mr. Clarke, the compound manager, gave evidence for the defence,, and sta
that he depended on the prisoners to keep order in the compound. The Landdr
stated that he was surprised there was no union amongst the managers on the Ra
The accused were discharged. A little time since a white employee on the Rip G
Mining Company, Limited, was fined £50 for supplying natives with liquor, and on
30th April last, W. R. Polithon, described in the *Star* as the compound manager of
Pioneer Gold Mining Company, Limited, was fined £75 for selling liquor to a nati
I further learn that an employee of the Oceana Coal Company, Limited, in the distr
of Heidelberg, was likewise fined for the sale of liquor to natives on the 12th inst.
beg to produce a few permits, signed by a compound manager in his capacity as su
for the supply of liquor. It is true that the quantities asked for are small, but the f
remains. I am aware that, unfortunately, illicit trade is rampant, and that ma
witnesses before your honourable Commission have declared that the illegal tra
emanates chiefly from unlicensed dealers, such as stores and kaffir eating houses wit
the precincts of the mines, and I can assure you that no one regrets this state of affa
more than the respectable licensed victuallers, especially when one sees that the pol
seem powerless to discover the origin of this unlawful traffic ; and while on this subj
I must again state that it appears to me that compound managers do not use their b

rts to suppress this excessive and injurious drinking. It has been stated that great
antities of liquor find their way into the compounds, and I should say diligent
ocution of the compound manager's duties on going his rounds, at certain periods of
: day and evening, should lead him to discover the existence of such liquor. I am
newhat borne out in this contention by a remark that fell from the criminal land-
ast, Mr. Van den Berg, on the 23rd July, 1896, where, in a case emanating from
uor before him, he stated that the compound managers were responsible for rows
ling in death very frequently, as they did not sufficiently supervise the compounds
 night. It has been urged that the existence of canteens along the reef have
ilitated the thefts of gold. Messrs. Sack and Finestone, canteen-keepers, along the
w Primrose Gold Mining Company, Limited, were actually instrumental in tracing and
taining a conviction for gold thefts from the company. I beg most respectfully and
mbly to submit that the introduction of total prohibition to natives has defeated its
n object. It is clear that there exists more illegal traffic than ever, and it is only
 regulating the system upon a thoroughly sound basis that this illegal trade can be
t a stop to. I would like to be permitted to point out to you that the Liquor Laws
the United Kingdom are perhaps the most severe, and yet it has been conclusively
oved that the more stringent the prohibition introduced the greater the secret
inking and the more huge the illicit traffic. Especially was this the case in Wales,
ere prohibition was introduced on a large scale, and it was afterwards discovered
at there were in existence more shebeens than there were ever licensed houses pre-
ously. Without desiring to cast any reflection upon our Scottish brethren, it is
etty well known that, notwithstanding the Sunday restrictions, liquor in Scotland
 that day is easily obtainable, to say the least of it. I mention all this to prove the
tility of so-called prohibition. But that I do not desire to occupy your time at any
 great a length, I could give you many more logical proofs. Still, however, the
uor question generally is of such vast importance that I may claim your indulgence
r occupying your time longer than I had desired; but I would just like to draw
ur attention to the fact that in Holland, Belgium, France, Germany, Italy, etc.,
here huge industries exist, and where the liquor trade is comparatively free, much
s drunkenness is visible than in countries where the severest restrictions obtain.
. order to make the working of the prohibition more complete in this State, Article
3 was introduced, which enacts that the granting of licences for the sale of any kind
 liquor on any ground given out as a claim, mijnpacht, bewaarplaats, etc., etc., is
tally prohibited. Under this law fall some excellent hotels in districts where
ndreds of white men are employed, and in all these places food is supplied to the
ine workers at a price leaving little or no profit. These establishments are supplied
th reading-rooms, billiard-rooms, etc., and the operation of this clause means the aboli-
on of all conveniences to the detriment of the working men, who, requiring their
ants fulfilled, would leave the works, not only to obtain their glass of beer, but in
arch of social intercourse and recreation, now to be denied them. The effect of this
easure will not only be felt in the district of Johannesburg, but also in the important
stricts of Boksburg, Klerksdorp, Krugersdorp, Heidelberg, Lydenburg, etc. The
rther disastrous effects of the working of this article will bring about the demolition
 valuable premises and good-wills, and the throwing out of employment of many
ousands of people. I now beg to draw your attention to Article 17, which provides
r the number of licences in proportion to the white male adult population. Now,
e number in the Johannesburg district alone is about as follows:—(a) Wholesale,
; (b) bottle-stores, 56; (c) retail, 305; (d) roadside, 3; beerhalls, 23—total, 436.
e revenue from licences and billiards may be taken approximately, in this jurisdic-
on alone, to amount to not far short of £40,000. It has been computed that in order

to give effect to Article 17 about 70 licences in all could be granted. Seeing that t
above totals include about 112 hotels, 56 bottle-stores, 27 restaurants, 49 wholes
houses, considerable difficulty must ensue in apportioning these licences. And furth
the effect of the operation of this clause would occasion much suffering, in fact ru
and bankruptcy, to an extent not easily contemplated. In Johannesburg alone,
believe, the losses in the forfeiture of stocks, good-wills, and decrease in value
buildings would reach, I may say, millions, and to whom are the sufferers to lo
for compensation? I would further deem it my duty to point out to y

Liquor Law 17, 1896, and the State revenue. that the enforcement of this Liquor Law 17, 1896, would affect the reven
of the country to a serious extent. The general revenue of Customs for t
past six years has been as follows:— 1892, £441,436; 1893, £692,831; 189

Contribution of liquor trade to State revenue. £812,173; 1895, £1,085,419; 1896, £1,355,486. I may say that at least on
third of the whole of these customs receipts is contributed by the liquor trade, and
huge reduction of that income would have to be made good from other sources.

English customs liquor and excise duties for 1895. would probably interest you to know the total of customs and excise duties deriv
from the manufacture and sale of alcoholic liquors in England during 1896. Th
amount is £30,886,129, being 32·62 of the total exchequer receipts for that year, an
this does not include local taxation, such as licence money, etc. The example set i
England, where, as I have already stated, the law is very severe, may possibly be som

English royal commission on liquor laws. guidance in the framing of the new legislation. In that country a Royal Commissio
has been sitting for nearly two years to thoroughly investigate the liquor laws i
every town and village, and its effect upon the morals and intelligence of the peopl
The latest report gives a *resumé* of the evidence of Captain Nott Bower, Chief Constable
Liverpool, one of the most important shipping ports in the world. This officer, a gentleme
who is believed to be a great authority, states, among other things, that a large proportio

Drunkenness and crime. of the crimes of violence were due to drunkenness, but by no means all; and the sam
applied to cases of neglect of children; but, when they came to cases of house-breakin
and larceny, or what may be called professional crimes, they were rarely due to drink
in fact the professional criminal must almost necessarily be an abstemious person; b
could not possibly carry on his trade if he were not. Offences of indecency were ver
seldom due to drink, and as to embezzlement, forgery, and crimes of that characte
drunkenness was very often the result of crime, rather than crime the result c
drink. It was said in some quarters, and often said, that if there was n
drunkenness there could be no crime, but he did not think that was correct. Facto
in the decrease of drunkenness were the demolition of insanitary property; increase
facilities for football and cycling; the general improvement in the tone of the workin
classes, and the doing away with unlicensed drinking places. I earnestly hope that

Liquor traffic and the mining industry. may not be deemed as desirous to advocate anything that can in the least be construe
as antagonistic to the mining industry. On the contrary, I should esteem it a privileg
to be allowed, in my humble capacity, to render every assistance in removing any im
pediment to the progress of that industry; but I cannot refrain from contrasting th
opinions expressed by so important an authority as Captain Nott Bower with th
action of Mr. J. B. Robinson in his orders prohibiting men on Randfontein from in
dulging in those very manly sports which are recommended by the captain as a speci
means for the prevention of drunkenness. Prohibition in any direction, as well as undu
interference with the liberty of the subject, always creates ill feeling and revolt. I ventur
further to submit that a great deal of this agitation in reference to the liquor traffic ha
been greatly accelerated by the desire to introduce the compound system. This measur
was advocated especially by Mr. George Farrar, when he suggested at the Simmer and Jac
that Mr. Rhodes had offered to build a second Kenilworth for the men, and subsequentl
emphasised this at a meeting of the Mine Managers' Association. I may here mentio

I am more than surprised at the attitude of the Mercantile Association, especially l branches of legitimate commerce should work side by side. Seeing that it has generally acknowledged that a huge illicit traffic emanates from the storekeepers kaffir eating-houses along the reef, it is astonishing that, if that body is so sincere s desire to alleviate the troubles of the mining community, that the Association not advocate the removal of all stores as well as canteens from the immediate hbourhood of the mines. From this side of Krugersdorp to the border of Boks- , a distance of over 30 miles, only 17 licensed canteens, including well-appointed ls, exist along the line of reef, and surely these 17 licensed houses can hardly be responsible for the huge illegal traffic now extant. In view of the suggestions I ld venture to make, I would say that at the time I had the honour of appearing re the Commission at Pretoria, in May, 1896, referred to in the earlier of this statement, Mr. Jas. Hay, Chairman of the Chamber of Mines, and ad practically offered similar proposals, especially with reference to the ir liquor traffic. Mr. Hay then contended that the native will, and should have drink, but that it should only be meted out to him in State defined and stamped sures, but that the toleration of drunkenness, the supply of liquor in any quantity consumption off the premises, or sale of adulterated or injurious stuff, should be ished in the severest possible form, and I am bold enough to believe, without pre- ing to dictate to the mining community, that, so far as natives are concerned, method, combined with honest supervision, is the one most likely to prove ient. In conclusion, I earnestly trust that your honourable Commission will pardon length of this statement. There are many more minor details in connection with Liquor Law generally which are open to improvement, but with which I will not trouble you. Let me assure you that it is my earnest desire to be permitted to perate with the mining community and the authorities in bringing about such ges and improvements as shall tend to the alleviation of the grievances of the industry, and especially to contribute to the comfort, welfare and happiness of mine workers. The following are just a few suggestions that I respectfully sub- for your earnest consideration :—

(1) That every applicant for a liquor licence must be armed with a certificate of good character, countersigned by the higher officials.

(2) That the house for which the licence is asked must be of a certain normal value, and have proper sanitary arrangements.

(3) That the house, and not the man, be licensed. This would obviate the possibility of underhand transfers. This, and the previous conditions, would be the best security for good and lawful conduct, as loss of licence upon contraven- tion would mean enormous decrease in the value of the property.

(4) Improved and efficient police supervision, and the abolition of any share of the fines. This system places a premium upon crime and often imposes hard- ship upon men, who, perhaps, had no desire to contravene the law.

(5) Proper and equal administration of the law, and the carrying out thereof to be enforced upon *all* licensed dealers. It is the larger and more important houses that should set an example of obedience to the law.

(6) Thorough supervision of the quality of liquors, under severe penalties for the sale of adulterated or deleterious stuff.

(7) A firm licensing board.

(8) Imprisonment *only* on conviction of unlicensed dealers.

(9) That natives be allowed to obtain, under strict regulations, a certain quantity of sound liquor, to be served in a stamped State measure, under severest penalties for serving larger quantities than prescribed by law, the toleration of

drunkenness, or the sale of any quantity no matter how small, for consump
off the premises. I may mention that if the native wages be reduced as posed, it will leave very little margin for excessive drinking.

(10) Thorough supervision of the stores in the vicinity of the mines, improvement in the general condition of the eating-houses, for which lice
should only be granted to responsible and respectable men.

(11) The abolition of all licensed insanitary shanties.

In my humble opinion, if these conditions were acted upon, Articles 3, 5, 6, 16 :
17 might well be deleted, and I venture to believe that the Liquor Law, with s
minor but still important additions would be workable, and ultimately give satisfact
all round, while the irresponsible illegal licensed dealer would soon be weeded out.

MR. S. FOOTE on examination said :

Vested interests
of liquor trade.
I would like to say a few words more with reference to Articles 16 and 17,
given in my statement. With reference to my statement, I would like to point
several things in the Liquor Law as it stands. The huge vested interests in conr
tion with this trade amount to immense sums. Take, for example, the wholes
houses here are perhaps the largest in the trade in South Africa, when I tell you t
the duties paid by Messrs. Rolfes, Nebel amounted to something like £110,000 for
year. Their business and stock is about a third of a million of money. These who
sale houses labour under considerable difficulty on account of having to apply for th
licences every quarter, and not alone is it a very great and serious inconvenience
may be considered that it is almost unfair to these firms that have such large ves
interests. Of course I do not advocate the cause of Messrs. Rolfes, Nebel alone.
only give them for example ; the other firms are in the same position, and therefor
would like to suggest that this Commission would be kind enough to consider in th
Wholesale and
commercial li-
censes.
report the advisability of recommending to the Government that these wholesale licen
should be considered as commercial licences. Further, I should prefer to say noth:
until you have examined me.

Mr. de Beer.

Mine officials and
sale of liquor
to natives.
You say here that the mine managers—that is mining people—encourage the s
of liquor to natives ?—Yes. In the first place, on many occasions when the Licens
Board sat there had appeared very many recommendations from mine manag
advocating the sale of liquor. Then again on many occasions, as I have shown in :
statement, advertisements have appeared in the papers calling for tenders for
right to sell liquor to natives on certain mines, and in each of these instances
successful tenderer had to pay a very large amount of rental for the preferen
right. I have given you several instances in my statement, and I think that is dir
encouragement for the sale of liquor, actuated by the mine people themselves.

Quality of liquor
sold to natives
You say that natives are supplied with bad and spurious liquor. Do you kn
where it comes from ?—The largest amount of liquor, as far as importations are c
cerned, comes from Delagoa Bay. Whether that liquor was originally injurious a
deleterious, I am not prepared to say. No doubt in many instances that liq
was seriously adulterated. At present the enormous sale of so-called whisky amon
kaffirs is, of course, illicitly sold. You would be surprised at the enormous quantit
Quantity and
price of liquor
sold to natives
which are on the market. This so-called whisky is sold to-day at 13s. 6d. per case
12 bottles. There are about 13,000 cases a month sold.

Importation of
liquor sold to
natives.
The liquor you mention is usually called Delagoa spirit ?—It is made of the sp
chiefly imported from Germany.

Originally made in Germany from potatoes ?—The liquor comes from Dela
Bay, without tax, as a product of Portugal. That whisky was brought in at 96 :

t. strength, and reduced here to half, and adulterated and mixed up, and sold in tles at 13s. 6d. per case.

Have you also included licences for billiards?—I have not. They were difficult Billiard licenses. obtain in Pretoria.

You speak about canteens on the mines; that is a great grievance for the trade. hink there are only 70 licensed houses on the whole line.—What I wished to show, Number of licen- sed houses on reef. appeared in my statement, the 17 who have fallen under the Article 17, can hardly held entirely responsible for all the illicit traffic going on. You will find from the Contravention of Liquor Law on reef. January to the 25th May, that four-fifths of the convictions for contravention of liquor law emanated from individual illicit-dealers, unlicensed men, and keepers of res and kaffir eating-houses.

According to the evidence put before the Commission, the greatest evil is the Kaffir eating- houses. ffir eating-house?—There is no doubt about it. With reference to the eating- uses, I may at once tell you that I was approached by an official of the Sanitary ard on the same question, and I considered then, as I do now, that the supervision uld be placed in the hands of the Licensing Board; that in each case the applicant uld satisfy the Board, either by writing or otherwise, that he is a respectable man, d convince the Board that his house is of normal value, properly situated, and that should enter into a bail bond for the legal performance of his business, and, in the ent of any illicit traffic, so far as liquor is concerned his bail is forfeited.

Mr. *Brakhan.*

In your statement you have thrown out various insinuations that the mining mpanies were furthering the sale of liquor?—I have done so.

Can you tell me or do you know the exact terms of the lease entered into Geldenhuis Es- tate and Cowie contract. tween the Geldenhuis Estate and Cowie?—I do not know the details of the con- ct, but as I understand, their lease has still one year and a half to run.

You are wrong there. The lease has expired. This lease you have left out is ry important in the details. The lease provides that no native should be served thout a written authority of the manager, and this proves clearly that the company s desirous of having the control over the sale of liquor to natives; in other words, limit it?—That means that they must have given a large number of permits to ffirs, as he would not be prepared to pay £150 a month. I speak of the Cowie se.

He has not got it now?—He had it.

Yes. He paid for the first year, £30 per month; for the second year, £430; d £500 for the last year; and that is much less than £80 per month.—The next rty undertook to pay £150 per month.

The company is not desirous of having this lease, as will appear from the follow- g: Mr. Sacke had to pay £1,800 a year. The company had reduced this to half the ount since the sale of liquor to natives has been prohibited. The terms of the se empower the company to take the whole from Mr. Sacke. That is clear proof at the company does not want the lease for the sole object of making money. I ink the terms of the lease are so stringent that the contract could have been can- lled any moment if the lessee did not comply with the terms of the agreement.—I n only say that, in that particular case, the company was extremely lenient and nd to the man.

What reason have you for saying that?—You yourself state that the company, eing that since the 1st January a considerable amount of trade must fall off on the eldenhuis Estate, were very kind, when they could enforce £1,800 a year, to reduce at by a half.

It was not a matter of enforcing; it was in terms of the contract.—I understa
you to say they had reduced the amount; therefore, it was very kind of them, und
the circumstances.

Then that proves their wish was not that of making money?—Well, I thi
£1,800 to sell only to whites on the property is very high.

It was not only for that. It was for a kaffir eating-house, hotel and boardir
house. You hinted in the same statement with regard to a certain company—
suppose you do not want the name mentioned?—No; I think it better not.

Permits of compound managers to purchase liquor. You mentioned permits being brought to some canteen. For what purpose w
this liquor used, do you think?—In my opinion, I have no hesitation in saying th
this must have been drink required for natives.

Forged permits. Still, I have enquired into this matter, and I find some of these things must ha
been forgeries. There are, for instance, on certain days, permits signed by a certa
man as compound manager. That man has never been in the employ of the cor
pany, and the compound manager is quite a different man.—I shall be pleased to gi
you privately the name of the individual from whom I received those permits, a
my object in putting them before you was not with a desire to injure any man, b
knowing and feeling convinced in my own mind that in a great many instances co
pound managers were instrumental in the purchase of liquor for natives, and that
is extremely difficult to obtain absolute proof, even as it is difficult for you to obta
proof of your gold thefts. I thought when those permits were offered to me th
might, if genuine—I never dreamt for one moment they would not be genuine
assist me and you in getting at the bottom of this illicit traffic.

I don't want to insinuate that those permits were handed in not *bona fide*, b
enquiries have proved they are not right, because on many of the names given
those permits the initials are wrong, or the individuals are not in the employ of tl
company.—I shall be very pleased to give you every facility to get at the bottom
it, and shall take the earliest opportunity to gauge the thing for myself.

Mine directorates and the sale of liquor to natives. You mention that compound managers have been instrumental in selling liqu
to natives. I don't deny that might have been the case, and perhaps is yet the ca
but that does not prove that the directors of the companies would further, or we
cognisant of any such fact. In fact, the directors would be pleased if they could g
information about it, and I should guarantee that those compound managers, or oth
servants of the company, would be at once dismissed, because the directors, fro
personal supervision, found out that if the natives do not get any liquor at all—goc
bad, or indifferent, whatever it may be—the amount of labour they can get out
them, and the discipline is far better than if they were supplied with liquor. Als
their own physique and health is greatly improved. If, formerly, the opinion migl
have been that the kaffir must have his liquor, yet, from experience, that opinion ha
been altered, and that is just where the mining industry insists that the Liquor La
should not be altered, so that kaffirs should not have any chance whatever to g
liquor. Can you inform me if Mr. John Judellsohn is a member of the License
Victuallers' Association?—He was, but he is not now a contributing member.

He has resigned then?—He is not a contributing member. He failed to pay u
and is no longer a member.

But he was a member?—Yes, originally.

License of Old Park Bar, Jeppestown. I want to draw attention to the manner in which matters about licences sometim
are managed. There is a certain Old Park Bar in Jeppestown. The man who had tl
bar, or, perhaps still has it, has been convicted for contravention of the law in Ma
1896, and January, 1897, and since then has been several times trapped, but no convi
tion could be got. At the December sitting of the Licensing Commission, a ma

on, was refused a licence. At the March sitting, another man, who is connected
Mr. Cotson, applied for the licence for the same place, but was also refused. Now,
Judellsohn, on the 3rd April, 1897, acquired a transfer of the licence from Mr. H.
Iordon, of a certain bar in Alexander Street, Ferreirasdorp, and this was at once
sferred to the Old Park Bar. This shows how the ramifications of licences are
aged.—I know the circumstances full well. In the first place, I should like to tell
that even if a man is a member of the association, I should never try to defend him
ny shape or form against an improper action. This question of this transfer is not *Transfer of licen-ses.*
y a question of this individual transfer, but it opens up a much wider field. I have
r and over again protested against these interim transfers. If you will look to the
d suggestion in my statement, you will see I there said that the licensing of the
se would obviate anything of the kind again. According to the present law, the
irman of the Licensing Board, in cases of unforeseen circumstances, such as fire, etc.,
the right to transfer, *ad interim*, any licence from place to place, subject to con-
ation by the Board at its next sitting. But, unfortunately, these transfers have
n granted from time to time, and not with the wish or countenance of the most
ectable dealers of the Licensed Victuallers' Association.

I am very pleased to hear you, as charman of the Association, with the full
port of the other members, advocate this alteration. It brings out my desire that
hands of the Licensing Commission should be strengthened in order to bring about
alteration, because if a certain canteen, or a certain man who holds a canteen, is
victed continually or several times, and yet is able to carry on this trade, then it is
h time an alteration in this law should be made.

Mr. *de Beer.*

These are not facts you have stated, Mr. Brakhan.

Mr. *Brakhan.*

They are facts.

Mr. *de Beer.*

What you quote are not facts.

Mr. *Brakhan.*

I received them for facts.

Mr. *de Beer.*

When you say people have been convicted repeatedly, and can still get licences,
a are wrong.

Mr. *Brakhan.*

I beg pardon. That was a slip of the tongue. I mean they are able to get trans-
of licences. Of course, this licence which he now holds by transfer is subject to
firmation by the next Licensing Board, and I have no doubt this licence will not be
firmed.

[*Addressing witness*]. Now with regard to one point in the suggestion you make, *Punishments for licensed and unlicensed li-quor dealers.*
on't quite see why you suggest in No. 8 that imprisonment should only take place
conviction of unlicensed dealers.—I don't know whether you quite understand.
at I mean to convey is this: I say imprisonment only. I don't mean imprisonment
uld be inflicted upon unlicensed dealers only. I mean imprisonment only. That
uld be the only punishment.

Why not also for licensed dealers ?—That is easily answered.   In the first pl
you must bear in mind the majority of licensed victuallers are men who have b
established for many years in this country, and who have large vested interests
their stocks, buildings, and goodwills.   I do not say that a continuance of infrin
ment of the law shall not be followed by punishment by imprisonment, but if you v
take notice of my proposition that the house shall be licensed and not the man, :
that after one or two convictions that that man will lose his licence and the value
his house and the value of his good-will, then I consider that that man is sufficien
punished.   Then, again, that man contributed, and is contributing largely to *
revenue of the State for years, whereas the unlicensed man is an illegal dealer, w
defrauds the Government of its just dues.   Then, again, I would like to point out th
you have probably no idea of this so-called trapping system in vogue.   Of cou
you have heard of these cases and you read of them, and you see remarkable puni
ments meted out, but the licensed victualler must be protected against this wholes.
trapping, because I undertake to say that the very largest and most important hou
in the liquor trade, including even the largest wholesale houses, can be as eas
trapped as the small canteen keeper who serves to the kaffir.   And we have had ve
many instances of that nature, and I consider, therefore, that the man who has vest
interests in his trade should have a certain amount of protection, and not be open
that awful drastic punishment the same as the man who defrauds the State of its j
dues.

There might be another view of that.   A man in whom the Government pla
trust, which it really does by conferring on him a licence, ought all the more to
jealous of this trust, and punished for betraying it.—Exactly, but I don't think th
that man should be so severely punished, because if you give that man a certain tr
and repose confidence in him, I venture to think, and it has been proved in ot
parts of the world, that the respectable licence-holder, with interests at stake, will
the best possible detective for the prevention of the contravention of the Liquor La
generally, and you must not give too much latitude to the officials to ensnare th
The   trapping people into the commission of crime.   That is all that the trapping system mea
system, to-day.   I have seen instances where large hotels here—it is not necessary to give t
names, but I can give them to you privately—two of the largest hotels in Johann
burg—have been ensnared into the commission of a crime by the trapping system, a
not long since.   I should say the combined value of their two properties would
over £100,000.   These people being ensnared into the commission of this crime
think it would be very unfair that men of such position should be subject to imprise
ment.

I suppose it is a case, as you put it, of ensnaring people ; in that case the mag
trate would not bring about any conviction.—I am sorry to think you perhaps ha
little knowledge—and perhaps you ought to be pleased of it—with the meth
adopted in the Criminal Landdrost's Court, or else you would not have made th
remark.

Stamped liquor   Now, you say natives should be allowed under certain restri .ions to be suppli
measures   for with a certain State measure, a stamped measure.   How can you prevent that ka
natives. from returning again with a measure he might get from somewhere else, and gettin
third or fourth dose ?—It is possible I have not made myself clear.   First of :
everything will depend upon the quality of the people to whom the licence should
granted.   For that purpose I have made certain recommendations earlier in *
Security for ob- declarations.   I should like to go further by suggesting that the security bond for t
taining liquor due performance and the legal performance of business on the premises where a ka
licenses. may get liquor should be increased to about £1,000.   Then, coming back to yo

estion, my suggestion was intended to convey this : that the houses which are Stamped liquor measures for natives. ensed to sell to kaffirs shall be supplied with State stamped measures, that these asures should be under the supervision of an Inspector of Weights and Measures, at in the event of any measure not being quite perfect the owner should be nished. The kaffir should not, under that regulation, be allowed to come with a asure at all. He goes to the house and calls for his liquor, which should be meted t to him in that State measure.

Yes, and then he goes and gets another lot.—Yes; I am coming to that directly. ae quality of that liquor should be thoroughly supervised by excise officers, and that .y man who gave more than measure—that is to say, he might give it in a larger ass for sake of competition—shall forfeit his licence and lose his surety bond. With ference to another lot which you have mentioned, that could be easily controlled by e mine management itself.

It is hardly possible for a mine manager to run after every kaffir, you know. hen they are off shift kaffirs go about as they like. There is, unfortunately, no mpound system here.—It has not been difficult in the past to get as many permits were required. Under a regulation of this nature, I don't say my suggestion is an tirely perfect one, but I certainly believe that it would be beneficial to all parties ncerned. You must bear in mind this, and I am really sorry to say it, that the od people to-day are suffering very severely on account of the bad. The illicit affic to-day is larger than it has ever been. It is a fact that nearly 10,000 cases of Extent of illicit liquor traffic. hisky were sold last month. This means 120,000 bottles. Say that the average ice at which it was sold was 5s., the product was £30,000. I want to point out to u that the Mercantile Association strongly favoured the movement of the mining The Johannesburg Mercantile Association and the liquor traffic. dustry in regard to the liquor business. They were afraid, and perhaps justly so, at if the kaffir could get his liquor *ad lib.* the storekeeper would materially suffer; d, on the other hand, that the abolition of drink would improve their business aterially. Now, it was only last week that I was in communication with one of the aportant members of the Mercantile Association, and what do we find? That the aopkeepers' returns to-day are very much less than hitherto. I say, therefore, if you ake further restrictions that there will be a greater illicit sale of liquor, and that the affirs will pay not 5s., but, on account of the risk these people run, 10s., and the orekeeper will have nothing at all left.

But if imprisonment was made the punishment for an infringement of the law Possibility of abolishing illicit liquor traffic. is illicit traffic would soon be put a stop to.—I don't think you will thoroughly root t the illicit traffic. In every part of the world the greater the restriction in any rection the greater the illicit trade. It has been proved very largely in England of te years, where the liquor laws are perhaps more severe than in any part of the orld. In certain parts of Wales was introduced what was practically total pro- bition, and very shortly after that they found there were more illicit dealers than ere had been licensed houses.

I don't think we can draw a parallel between Wales and this case. There are, so speak, no aboriginal races in England.—I will give you an illustration nearer me. In the Orange Free State there is supposed to exist total prohibition. In 395 there was imported into the Transvaal Republic something like 180,000 gallons Cape kaffir brandy. In the same year there was imported into the Orange Free tate—which is, of course, a much smaller country than this, and has a much smaller pulation—something like 130,000 gallons.

I don't think that is any proof of your contention.—I will go nearer, then. In atal there is a prohibitive law. Of course there is no labour required there. Yet it as only very recently that five of the most important hotels in Maritzburg were

x

convicted for having sold to natives, and the magistrate, in fining them, stated h
regret that he believed this illicit traffic had been going on for years. I may tell y
that on appeal they won their case, and the conviction was quashed.

Repeal of Liquor Law inadvisable.

If this law is repealed we shall revert to the old state of affairs, and very litt
work could be got out of the kaffirs.—I am quite of your opinion. But I don't thin
that state of things would be brought about if the mining industry would exe
themselves to assist the honest licensed victualler to bring about a better state
things. There is no doubt that several people hold licences who never ought to ha
held them. We cannot deny the fact that in many instances mine managers, or mi
employees, have encouraged, by recommendations and otherwise, the granting
licences to certain people, and I think if you can accept a compromise of this natur
and try for three months, I feel you would have less trouble with regard to illic
traffic, and when the men to whom these licences are entrusted are under stron
securities, they will assist in the abolishing of this filthy illicit traffic now existing.

Mr. Albu.

You are the chairman of the Transvaal Licensed Victuallers' Association ?—Ye
The object of this Association is to protect their members, who are license
victuallers ?—Not against illicit traffic.

I regret I cannot possibly ask you any questions on the subject at all, for yo
well advocate, in your capacity as chairman of this Association, that the law again
serving natives with liquor should not be abolished as far as it concerns license
victuallers.—Yes.

And my experience is that it should be abolished; and that to supply nativ
with drink in fair measures or indiscriminately, as during the past eight years,
simply a dark blot on humanity. I shall ever advocate the total abolition of the sa
of drink to natives. Your duty as chairman of this Association dictates a differer
policy, therefore it is quite useless for me to ask you any questions on the subjec
It is quite true, as you say, that no matter what happens you can never reduce th
illicit traffic, but there is no law yet strong enough that has prevented men fro
committing crime such as theft, murder, or any other crime. If the decision of th
Volksraad be upheld that natives should not be served with strong drink, and n
matter how heavy the punishment of those who commit the crime, you will never b
able to stamp it out altogether, but that should not be the reason why the Raa
should not, in the interest of the industry, and for the welfare of the natives, be aske
to uphold their decision.—It is unnecessary to answer you, as it would only lead to
controversy as to individual opinions. There are, however, one or two things I woul
like to mention. Of course, as you say, although you have severe laws, there ar
crimes which will always be committed. Still, in other countries where strong law
are in existence, the system of improving matters is regulated by Act of Parliamen
But I would like to point out this to you. Assuming for the moment that you ar
right in your contention as to the abolition of drink with reference to kaffirs, yo
must not forget that the law, as it stands at present, is very far-reaching in it
calamitous results. Under Article 16 of the present law, it is provided that no ma
shall be allowed to retain his licence on certain prohibited areas. Now it must b
borne in mind that the collective vested interests in these houses falling under Artic
16 are really enormous, and not only would the people then according to you
argument be deprived of selling to kaffirs, but also from following their business s
far as the whites are concerned. I can assure you that the values sunk in propertie
are very large indeed, and most of these people have held their licences for a con
siderable period of time.

I don't want to ask you any questions but you talk of these vested interests and
e of them under the guise of respectability are not ashamed to import the vilest of
f they get from Delagoa Bay. You talk about their value, but what about the
1e of the interests of the mining industry here?—If you had been here earlier you
1ld have heard my opinion of this adulterated stuff. I maintain that these values
a matter which should be considered. I know some houses that have been offered,
1roperties, £9,000 and £10,000. The mining industry must be supported, and no
1t-minded man would do anything that would hinder its progress. But I say this,
t licence-holders, as subjects of this land, must have their trading liberties respected;
1, while giving the mining industry the whole of its due, I am positive that this
1ernment will take into consideration the interests of the masses generally. When
1oke about these laws I touched upon Article 16; but it must not be forgotten that
1 agitation brought about Article 17, which, I say, does not mean the abolition
1 demolition of millions of pounds of vested interests. The property owners have *Vested interests*
yet begun to feel the shoe pinch, but eventually, if this law comes into force, they *of owners of*
1 find the huge amount of rental they have lost. A law of this nature—which, I *licensed prem-*
1tend, encroaches on the liberty of the subject—is guarded against in the Grondwet, *ises.*
1 I ask who is going to compensate these people for their loss.

Chairman.

Do I understand from your evidence that the law does not apply equally to all *Unequal admin-*
1nsed dealers?—I am sorry to say, in my opinion, it does not. I have found very *istration of Li-*
1ny instances where unlicensed dealers wilfully and illegally selling liquor to kaffirs *quor Law.*
1whites in contravention of the law have been fined much less in a good many
1tances than the licensed victualler who has been trapped in the commission of a
1ht offence. Then, again, I mean that the officials take a great deal of trouble with
1 smaller dealers and hotel-keepers, and so forth, while the more important houses,
1ich should set an example of good conduct, are entirely left alone, and are fre-
1ntly known—not, perhaps, intentionally—to break the law, perhaps in a higher
1ree than some of those smaller men who are trapped.

That is almost a direct accusation against the officials that they have not been
1lying the law properly. The judge decides each case according to the evidence.—
1ould be very sorry to cast any reflection upon any official in Johannesburg.

Your regret is too late, you have already done the evil.—I was going to explain.

I understand you do not approve of the present Licensing Board?—I might have *The Licencing*
1de the inference, but I did not say so. *Board*

What is your idea with regard to the Licensing Board?—I mean to say that the
1ensing Board should be resolute and firm, and should have under its control all
1tters in connection with licences. We have on many occasions seen that the
1ensing Board have been too lenient, and what is wanted is a resolute Board that
1l carry out its duties, and only grant licences where necessary. My object in
1ntioning this question of a firm Licensing Board was that I have, on one or two
1asions, protested very strongly against the granting or renewal of a number of
1nces, and I have been met with the taunt that my protest was only entered on
1ount of trade jealousy, whereas, in fact, what we want to see is the trade in the
1st respectable hands.

That is also a question of opinion, of course. That is another accusation against
1 Licensing Board. One always wants a change, but whether the change would be
1 the better is another matter. Take this Board away, which is perhaps too kind
1 too lenient, and you may get another one in its stead which, perhaps, would be
1 severe against you and too kind to somebody else. Now, touching the case

generally; you are only dealing with large vested interests of licensed victuallers, a

you have even gone so far as to make an appeal to the Grondwet, which protects

portance of li-
quor and min-
ing interests.

liberty and possession of every individual. My view of the matter is this, that if general interests of the gold industry and the working power of the kaffir is sap by liquor and injured, the lesser interest must give way to the greater. It is an disputable fact that the liquor traffic saps the working power of the kaffir, so tha is impossible to keep control over them. You want to protect the large dealers liquor, and you want to put the blame on the small retailers, but it was not th who imported the bad liquor, and the people whose chairman you are should wat the importation of bad liquor.

Mr. *Hay.*

of enquiry into
the liquor
question, May,
1896.

In your statement you refer to what took place in Pretoria in May, 1896. Y wrote that from memory?—Will you kindly refer me to the point to which you allu "I had the honour of appearing before the Commission in May, 1896, and I James Hay, the Chamber of Mines, and I, offered similar proposals, especially wi reference to the kaffir liquor traffic. Mr. Hay pointed out the kaffir should have drink, but it ought to be only meted out to him in State defined and stamp measures." I don't think that is correct. I will state what took place. Whe appeared before the Commission I pointed out that the law, as it stood, was good if were carried out. The native was prohibited from getting drink, except with t permission of his master. Therefore, if the master carried out his duty, he had regulation of the law in his hands. I then pointed out that in the law there wa certain anomaly; it provided that a native could not be proceeded against if he had his possession half a bottle of brandy, and the consequence was this, that althou natives were found in possession of liquor they could not be prosecuted as long they had not more than half a bottle, and by that means liquor was taken into t compounds in considerable quantities, and evil arose. I suggested that that sho be expunged from the law. Mr. Van den Berg, who presided over that Commissic asked me whether I was in favour of total prohibition to natives, and I said yes, if could be properly carried out. Is not that what took place?—It is only a question memory. I am certainly under the impression that you advocated what I said in n declaration.

That is what took place.

Brown's evi-
dence.

MR. W. R. BROWN, representing Barberton Chamber of Mines, was called a duly sworn. He said:

hannesburg
witnesses.
Price of dyna-
mite at Bar-
berton.
Quality of dyna-
mite.
Accidents
through bad
packing of dy-
namite.

I have little to add, gentlemen, to what has been said by the Johannesbu witnesses, as they have dealt with the various matters very thoroughly, and I, representing the De Kaap district, fully endorse what they have said. Dynamite Barberton costs £5 to £5 1s. per case, and the price has been recently raised 5s. case, for which action we have received no satisfactory explanation. Mine manag in my district were almost unanimous in stating that the quality of dynamite is r equal to that of the early days, and consequently, in our hard ground, many of t mines use blasting gelatine, which costs, delivered on the mines, £6 5s. Being so ne to the port we do not understand why we are charged a higher price for dynam than is paid by mines on the Rand. Miners complain bitterly of the manner in whi dynamite is packed. Many cartridges arrive so much out of shape that the min are compelled to cut the cartridges down the centre in order to get them into d holes, and this practice has resulted in many accidents. On the Sheba there was

ident two months ago. Dynamite can be laid down in Barberton *via* Delagoa at Possible price of dynamite at Barberton.
. per case. The average cost of driving and sinking on our mines amounts to 18
cent. of the total cost. This question of coal is becoming a serious matter with us.
many instances mines would put up milling plant, provided coal could be laid
vn at a reasonable rate. At present the price is too high for us to use it for Price of coal at Barberton.
ving our batteries. It costs about 30s. per ton. I may mention these mines are
hly prolific. We are desirous of sending our concentrates to Johannesburg for Railway rates.
atment, but the railway rate of £4 per ton is prohibitive. We prefer to ship them
Delagoa Bay to Europe for treatment. The next question I would refer to is the
lage to the port. I do not wish to bring any statistics, but I will give one instance.
small parcel of wagon wood costs in Cape Town £5 13s. 9d., and the railage from
pe Town to Barberton was £10 2s. Another instance is in connection with the
rberton Waterworks. I have not the exact figures, but I have them approxi-
tely. The railage, cartage in England, and ocean freight came, roughly, to £500,
d from Delagoa Bay to Barberton it cost about £2,000—and that for public works. Maladministration of Netherlands Railway.
have not been able to get any remission of railage rates. There are bitter com-
ints from merchants with regard to claims for loss in shortage. Proof can be pro-
ced, if necessary, that claims for damage and shortage, even when certified by the
f at Barberton, are seldom, if ever, recognised by the head office in Pretoria. It is
most difficult thing to get these matters settled with the railway company, and
ple, unless the sum is considerable, prefer to lose their money rather than go to
etoria to sue the company. We feel it would be only fair and right if we were
owed to sue the railway company up to a certain amount in our local Court. It
nes very hard on people to have to lose their goods and to have to incur the expense
coming to Pretoria to sue the railway company. Another point is the right of the
lway company to impose fines. There is one instance I will name. A parcel of
alie meal of 50 bags arrived from Delagoa Bay about a fortnight ago; the invoice
s lost through no fault of the consignor or consignee; it was lost in the post, and
fore another invoice could be obtained, a charge of £8 10s. for storage was imposed
the consignee, although the meal had been stored in a warehouse he had rented
m the railway company at the railway station. The question of native labour is Native labour difficulty at Barberton.
coming a very serious matter with us in Barberton. Up to quite recently we never
d any difficulty in getting the number of natives required. It is a difficult
ing to talk about, because the best heads in Johannesburg have apparently not been
le to deal with the matter satisfactorily. I do not think we would have any diffi-
lty in getting the small number of natives we require if it were not for the fact
at natives who are travelling, and intend to come to work in Barberton, are taken
ay against their will by touts to Johannesburg. We would like to have some
thod adopted by the Government to put an end to this interference with natives. Government surveys.
lo not know that I am in order in dealing with the matter of Government surveys.

Chairman.

Yes; if you have anything to say we will be pleased to hear it.—It is merely
s, that in a district like ours, where claims are taken up, as a rule, by poor pros-
ctors, the new law with regard to Government survey presses very hard on them. I
n quite understand it is not the same in Johannesburg; the conditions are quite
ferent. In our district it has absolutely put a stop to prospecting. There is a small
tter of purely local interest I would like to mention, and that is the question of
ilities for inter-communication between the different mines. As the Chairman is Barberton roads.
are, ours is a very rough country, and we are very badly off for roads. That has
en brought before the Government by memorial. If it is within the province of

this Commission we would be very glad if some recommendation were made that t
Government should assist us in this matter; more especially a road that would conne
Barberton with the goldfields, which would be extended later on to Swazieland, a
tap the tin mines in that district.

Quality of dyna-mite.
I want to examine you with regard to the dynamite monopoly, more especially
it affects Barberton. You not only complain, I understand, of the expense, but also
the quality ?—Yes, more especially because of the bad state in which the dynami
reaches us.

Price of dyna-mite.
You say you can lay down dynamite at Barberton for 53s. ?—Yes, we import it
Delagoa Bay.

Railway rates on coal.
Then with reference to coal. Can you say what you would consider a reasonab
price to pay on coal from Brugspruit to Barberton ?—Well, my idea of a reasonab
price for that would be about ½d. per mile.

You would be satisfied with that ?—Well, yes.

Maladministra-tion of Nether-lands Railway.
Now with reference to the other complaints about the fines imposed by t
railway, and invoices being lost. Can you not hand in some documents bearing
this matter ?—Yes, I have a letter here. I have a letter from the person who ma
the complaint in question.

Will you be able to let the Commission have the documents in this case; cou
you send them in to the secretary ?—Yes. I can let you have the documents, as we
as sworn declarations. This is only one case. There are many others of a simil
nature.

Native labour.
With respect to native labour. I understand that the only complaint is th
while boys are coming to Barberton they are caught by Johannesburg touts ?—Y
that is the only complaint we have in the matter of native labour. I can gi
instances. I have boys on two of the mines with which I am connected, who ba
walked to Swazieland, knowing that if they went by Komatie Poort they would
caught by the touts.

Government sur-veys.
Now, regarding the survey of claims. This matter does not, I think, lie with
the scope of this enquiry, but as it is in the interests of the industry, I would advi
you to bring the matter to the notice of the Barberton Chamber of Mines, who cou
work through the Minister of Mines to the Government.—Thanks, Mr. Chairman.
brought it to the notice of the Commission in the interests of the industry.

Mr. *Joubert.*

Coal—quality.
I only wish to ask if the coal from Belfast is worse for mining purposes tha
that from Brugspruit ?—Oh, no ! I only gave Brugspruit as an instance, because
the distance.

What I want to know is if there is any difference in the quality of the coal ?-
That I cannot say say ; I have not gone into the matter.

Mr. *Schmitz-Dumont.*

Gelatine.
Do you know whether the managers are satisfied with the blasting of t
blasting gelatine ?—Yes, they are, so far as I know, satisfied with it. They on
complain that they have to use it in place of dynamite. The blasting gelati
certainly does heavier work than dynamite, but if the dynamite was as good as it w
in the old days, they would not need the gelatine.

Mr. *Hugo.*

White labour—supply and wages.
With respect to the question of white labour, is there any difficulty in yo
district ?—We have no difficulty in that matter. We get as many good men as w
require at fair wages.

How do these compare with Johannesburg?—I do not know what the rate is at
nnesburg. We pay a miner from £18 to £22, or even up to £25 per month.
enters get £5 10s. to £6 a week, while for native labour we pay at the rate of
t 50s. per month.

What is the cost of living? Do the white men complain of the cost of living?—I
r heard of any complaints. Cost of living at Barberton.

How does the cost of living compare with Johannesburg?—That I cannot say.
y of the men get free quarters, and then feed themselves. Since the special
es have been taken off, I should say that they have no complaint in our district. In
old days, when the old duties were in force, they had cause to complain, for then
e were many things which a miner could do with which he could not have. Under
present conditions, however, they had no cause for complaint.

Mr. *Brochon.*

What is the charge for living at the boarding houses?—Well, there are no
ding houses.

But big mines like the Sheba have boarding houses on the property; is that not
—Yes, there are boarding houses on some of them, but the men do not use them
h. On the Sheba mine, I believe, the men pay about £6 10s. a month. Sheba mine boarding hou-ses.

Have you read the evidence given with regard to married men at Johannesburg?
o, I have not read that specially.

Do you think the married men can live on £20 or £22 per month?—Well, with
ried men there is a difference. I should think that a married man could ust live
hat and little more; that is, after he has paid his household expenses, food for his
ily, etc.

Mr. *Brakhan.*

Is it usual to give the married men quarters?—Well, that depends to a great Married miners' quarters.
nt on the managers.

For the single as well as the married men?—No.

Mr. *Albu.*

How do you arrive at the cost of dynamite to be 53s.; is that from merchants? Price of dyna-mite.
es; in Johannesburg.

Mr. *de Beer.*

What is the cost of production per ton?—I have no statistics on that point.

You say that Johannesburg employs touts for the kaffir labour. You have the Native labour.
t to do the same thing.—Yes, but we have not the wealth. We complain of boys
ing their homes to come to Barberton and being intercepted, and practically
ed to go to Johannesburg.

Mr. WILLIAM SHANKS was next called and duly sworn. He said: Mr. W. Shank's evidence.

I am the manager of the Barberton Consolidated Mine. I have not made any
ement, as all the questions have been so thoroughly thrashed out by the Johannes-
g witnesses; but I will hand in a table of figures showing in detail the cost of the
e for the last four months so as to give you an idea of the various items. I have
w remarks to make on native labour. You will notice from the statement that Native labour—
native labour is by far the largest item of the cost. To begin with, these costs supply and cost.
for developing and not for the mines running in full operation. It is not the
unt we pay the kaffir per month that runs up that cost; it is the fact that we

have no guarantee whatever that we can keep up the supply. To-day probably
may be fully supplied, and next week we may be many natives short. The boys c
out without giving notice. This is a matter which affects the whole of the gold min
industry of the Transvaal, and, in my opinion, it has to be dealt with chiefly by
mining community of Johannesburg and the Government. The question of efficie
is one which must be dealt with. I think they should get the boys to work fo
fixed time, say with a minimum of 8 or 12 months. Then we should get much hig
efficiency out of them than we do at the present time. By far the dearest natives
those who get paid the lowest wage, these being the green and untrained boys. T
the largest percentage of those who are getting used to the work leave. Nov
should think that if there were a committee appointed in Johannesburg to deal w
this question, consisting of representatives of the Government and representatives
the mining industry, and if they legislated in the direction I have indicated to
kaffirs to bind themselves for 8 or 12 months, I think we should derive much ben
This same unreliableness of the natives also affects the cost of our white labour.
have always to keep a full supply of white labour whether there are sufficient nati
or not, because if we are short we may always get others from time to time. To
anything in this matter the whole mining community must be unanimous. T
Reduction of native wages.
Want of unanimity among mine managers. have lately reduced the kaffir wages, and it is a well-known fact that many of
mines have not stuck to the agreement. They have been very unanimous at
Mine Managers' meetings, and afterwards many have paid the natives just what t
pleased. Of course the chief cause of this want of co-operation is due to the fact t
it is rarely ever that the native supply is equal to the demand. But I think if
companies were unanimous, not only on the wages question, but on other points, s
as the making of some arrangements binding them to work for a fixed time, that
Co-operation of Government required to lower white wages. mining community in general would greatly benefit by it. But, as before stated,
must have the co-operation of the Government in carrying out any scheme we n
formulate as regards the price of white labour. I have read some of the evide
given before the Commission, and, under present conditions, I agree that we can
reduce the cost. Taking the mines in this country, we find that they are in a tota
different position to what they are in Europe, where they have to do the work the
selves. In this country they are more in the position of foremen to look after
many natives, and for this reason we have to select the best men for this purpose,
therefore many miners who come to this country are not suitable, and they can
get employment unless there is a scarcity. The cost of dynamite has been fully de
with by other witnesses, and I myself use only the blasting gelatine. If you look
Cost of gelatine. the cost of that as before you, you will see that is very heavy. It is something i
£6 per case, buying 50 cases at a time. If we could get it for about half the price t
reduction would materially assist us. With regard to the railway rates, I had a sn
Railway rates. consignment of goods from Johannesburg, and it cost me at the rate of £8 or £10
ton, and this seems to me to be out of all proportion.

Mr. *de Beer.*

Percentage of costs of labour at Barberton to total working costs. From the statement before me it would appear that the labour ranges from
per cent. to 70 per cent. of the total cost, and then you must allow about 7 per ce
for food. Can you explain why Barberton is so much higher than the Witwatersra
which is only from 50 per cent. to 60 per cent. ?—The reason I have pointed out
that these figures are for development, and at present we have no machinery at we
as is the case in Johannesburg. Therefore our percentage of expenditure on labou
less.

THE BARBERTON CONSOLIDATED GOLDFIELDS, LIMITED.

Statement showing Costs per Foot, with corresponding Percentages, on the various items of Expenditure from December, 1896 to March, 1897.

(Handed in by Mr. W. Shanks as an annexure to his statement.)

"PIONEER" DEVELOPMENT.

	December Cost per foot (s. d.)	January (s. d.)	February (s. d.)	March (s. d.)	Average (s. d.)	Percentage
European wages	16 6·099	15 8·521	20 7·687	20 3·418	18 3·431	25·262
Native wages	28 11·306	26 3·169	32 8·508	27 8·327	28 10·828	39·928
Explosives	15 7·298	12 0·986	14 3·970	14 3·365	14 0·905	19·445
Lighting	1 8·628	0 5·240	1 5·127	1 8·400	1 6·849	2·170
Lubricants	0 0·843	0 0·423	0 0·671	...	0 0·484	0·055
Food	4 5·554	5 1·774	4 11·015	5 4·109	4 11·613	6·863
Fuel	0 6·099	0 5·887	0 5·776	0 4·945	0 5·677	0·653
Tools	0 8·545	1 10·500	1 0·918	0 2·182	1 5·536	2·019
Stable	0 2·579	0 3·634	0 4·075	0 8·109	0 4·599	0·530
Small stores	0 2·256	0 0·972	0 2·298	0 2·400	0 1·981	0·228
Miscellaneous	2 2·281	1 9·000	2 0·224	2 3·418	2 0·731	2·847
Totals	71 1·488	65 2·106	78 2·269	75 0·673	72 4·634	100·000
Footage	121 ft.	142 ft.	134 ft.	165 ft.	140 ft. 6 in.	

"UNION" EXPLORATION.

	December Cost per foot (s. d.)	January (s. d.)	February (s. d.)	March (s. d.)	Average (s. d.)	Percentage
European wages	35 8·000	30 9·643	33 0·364	25 4·200	31 2·552	38·705
Native wages	27 0·000	29 2·143	23 9·091	12 5·640	23 1·218	28·646
Explosives	9 11·166	15 1·929	8 11·970	8 10·000	10 8·766	13·306
Lighting	0 10·400	1 4·393	0 9·273	0 9·720	1 11·447	1·183
Lubricants	...	0 2·143	...	...	0 0·586	0·055
Food	5 8·400	5 4·500	4 11·818	6 1·320	5 6·509	6·873
Fuel	0 6·567	0 10·536	0 8·727	0 2·400	0 10·058	1·040
Tools	...	4 4·178	0 5·636	4 9·720	2 4·883	2·985
Stable	4 4·178	1 9·643	1 11·273	0 5·160	1 9·019	2·172
Small stores	1 10·000	...	...	0 3·480	0 0·870	0·090
Miscellaneous	2 5·000	3 9·214	4 10·727	4 10·500	3 11·860	4·945
Totals	83 11·533	92 10·322	79 6·879	66 2·140	80 7·718	100·000
Footage	30 ft.	28 ft.	33 ft.	50 ft.	35 ft. 3 in.	

"PIONEER" SHAFT SINKING AND STATIONS.

Size of shaft 14 ft. × 6 ft.

	December Cost per foot (s. d.)	January (s. d.)	February (s. d.)	March (s. d.)	Average (s. d.)	Percentage
European wages	35 6·568	62 9·908	59 9·699	61 8·636	54 11·703	30·527
Native wages	39 8·432	55 6·646	72 1·808	73 6·000	60 2·721	33·443
Explosives	10 11·757	31 6·615	21 3·726	30 10·909	23 8·252	13·153
Lighting	2 10·216	4 3·785	3 5·918	4 10·909	3 10·707	2·161
Lubricants	0 2·757	0 1·846	0 2·466	...	0 1·767	0·082
Food	7 6·811	15 2·585	13 6·247	17 1·091	13 4·183	7·412
Fuel	0 11·946	1 4·677	1 1·151	1 3·273	1 2·262	0·660
Tools	3 6·108	5 11·723	3 0·082	3 11·864	5 7·444	3·121
Timber	3 6·243	4 9·784	4 1·068	3 6·364	3 11·865	2·215
Stable	0 7·378	1 1·108	0 11·918	2 9·818	1 4·556	0·766
Small stores	0 6·892	0 1·385	0 6·082	0 6·818	0 5·294	0·245
Miscellaneous	12 9·622	9 8·769	10 6·630	11 8·182	11 2·301	6·215
Totals	116 10·730	192 8·831	190 8·795	219 11·864	180 1·055	100·000
Footage	37 ft.	32 ft. 6 in.	36 ft. 6 in.	22 ft.	32 ft.	

"PIONEER IVY" PROSPECTING.

	December Cost per foot (s. d.)	January (s. d.)	February (s. d.)	March (s. d.)	Average (s. d.)	Percentage
European wages	17 10·369	10 10·857	21 6·085	20 1·350	20 1·165	45·150
Native wages	10 11·301	8 11·714	11 8·282	12 7·050	11 0·587	24·823
Explosives	6 1·068	5 5·476	4 0·282	13 0·500	7 1·832	16·069
Lighting	1 10·136	1 3·679	2 2·155	3 8·550	2 4·353	0·815
Food	0 2·874	0 1·178	0 2·704	0 6·300	0 2·589	5·695
Fuel	...	0 0·107	0 1·268	0 3·600	0 3·125	0·485
Tools	...	0 7·679	0 0·253	1 1·125	0 1·717	0·585
Stable	1 1·786	...	...	1 9·150	...	2·508
Miscellaneous	1 2·330	1 7·572	1 7·986	2 3·525	1 8·352	3·810
Totals	39 6·893	30 7·762	43 4·761	64 5·150	44 6·141	100·000
Footage	51 ft. 6 in.	84 ft.	71 ft.	40 ft.	61 ft. 7½ in.	

NOTE.—These Costs include all General Expenses with the exception of Claim Licences and London Office Expenses.

The material originally positioned here is too large for reproduction in this reissue. A PDF can be downloaded from the web address given on page iv of this book, by clicking on Resources Available.

There is a charge of 13 per cent. to 19 per cent. for explosives ; that is also higher Comparative cost of explosives at Barberton and on the Rand.
in Johannesburg ?—I suppose it is because our rocks are so hard.

Mr. *Schmitz-Dumont.*

Can you tell us the cost per ton for dynamite ?—In the main shaft the average
per foot is 23s.—that would be about 3s. 4d. per ton.
I know mines in the Rand who spend 6s.—That is probably due to drilling with
drills—explosives for that are always very much higher.
On the Rand it varies from 6d. to 6s. per ton.

Mr. *Brakhan.*

Can you give us the size of the shaft ?—The inside dimensions are 14 feet by
et. It is a vertical shaft of three compartments.
Well, the cost does not seem to be excessive. Do you timber the shafts ?—We
not divided the cageway yet. It is only partially timbered on account of the
lness of the rock.

Mr. *Brochon.*

What do you think about the quality of dynamite used on the Rand?—I really do Quality of dynamite and blasting gelatine.
know much about dynamite. I have tried it on several occasions. I tried it at the
ropolitan five or six years ago, but the fumes were so bad, and I did not get the
iency I considered necessary, so I turned to using blasting gelatine. I think there
ery little to complain about blasting gelatine. What I complain about is the cost.

Mr. G. A. DENNY made the following statement :— Mr. G. A. Denny's evidence.

I have been asked by the combined Klerksdorp Chamber to represent them
re this Commission. I was lately resident in Klerksdorp as general manager of
Klerksdorp Proprietary Mines, Limited, and consulting engineer to the Buffels-
rn Consolidated and Southern Klerksdorp Companies, and was elected vice-
sident of the Chamber of Mines. I am an Australian, and was educated in Victoria
mining engineer, and have practised as a consulting engineer in London, and have
professional capacity examined mines in many countries of the world, including
gary, Canada, U.S.A., Central America, Australia, and Tasmania. I came to the
nsvaal in 1893, and have since been actively engaged in the pursuit of my pro-
ion. The combined Klerksdorp Chambers have themselves drawn up a statement,
ich they wish me to present to this Commission. Before doing so, however, I Personal statement.
ild like to make a personal statement dealing with the present condition of the
rict. I have carefully read through the evidence given, and the statements made
previous witnesses, who have, however, confined the applicability of their remarks
re especially to the Witwatersrand district. It is obvious, if the evidence which
been adduced in support of the contention that the mining industry of the
nsvaal is labouring under extraordinary burdens be a true reflection of the con-
ons which have conduced to its present low vitality, that the Klerksdorp district Klerksdorp district—its burdens.
burdened more heavily than that of Witwatersrand, for the following primary
sons : (1) The average lowness of grade of its reefs ; (2) Its outlying position. It
n axiom throughout gold-producing countries that a mine of proved richness, and
n of only moderate payability, will directly influence the prospective value of the
nediately adjoining properties, and indirectly affect that of a whole area within
sonable distance. Such being the case, it follows that, as long as the postulated
ie is producing gold profitably, there is some reason to hope that intelligently

directed prospecting of other areas within the stated reasonable distance, will deve
an equally profitable ore deposit, and hence the district is regarded as one
possibility, and enterprising companies can always be found to work therein. Giv
however, on the other hand, that a district is one which has only a record of failu
to show, which can only keep one or two mines running along precariously in a h
to mouth manner, and what is the result? There is no room for hope of possibil
based upon an actual successful mine; the district suffers in times of in:
tion from the machinations of the wild-cat promoter, who, without thou
of intrinsic values, saddles the public with useless properties at exorbit
rates, and when the bubble bursts, saddles the district with a name wh
spells "fraud" to the minds of the investing public. The latter description
eloquent of the condition of Klerksdorp to-day. Boomed with extravagant repo
and estimates in the excited months of June and July, 1895, the punctures in
armour caused by the suspension of operations of company after company, have o
too surely reduced it to utter collapse. It has now clearly been shown that

Reefs of Klerksdorp district. characteristic feature of the district's auriferous resources is bodies of banket
averaging about 20s. per ton in money value, in many instances 20 ft. or more
width. The output of the Robinson, Wemmer, and other rich mines in the Witwate
rand district, prove that the wealth of their ores is more than competent to balance
evil of excessive dynamite costs, railway rates, etc., which have been so fully ventila
before this Commission, and the effect of such a demonstration is two-fold. Firstly
maintains the commercial status and credit of the towns which in parasitic grow
cluster around them; secondly—and, if possible, more important still—it maintains
courage of directors and shareholders in mines which are not certain from month
month on which side the balance of profit and loss will fall, and stimulates aga
indirectly, commercial development. In the Klerksdorp district, there is, unfortunate

Companies of Klerksdorp district. Failures. no such stimulus. Company after company has initiated work with great anticipati
of success, and without exception the companies which have reached the milling sta
have proved either unprofitable or only profitable enough to show a very slight amou
above the working costs. The district as a whole, then, gentlemen, is reduced to tl
basis: (1), reduction of working costs; (2), abandonment of operations. Of 25 co

Working companies in Klerksdorp district. panies holding property in the district, only seven are working; namely, two, t
Buffelsdoorn Estate and Gold Mining Company, Limited, and the Eastleigh Min
Limited, are producing; one, the Klerksdorp Gold and Diamond Company, engaged
mill erection; and three, the Eastleigh Deep, Eastleigh "A," and Buffelsdoorn Conso
dated Gold Mining Company, engaged in prospecting their holdings; and one, Arist
working on tribute. The remaining companies and scores of syndicates are lyi

Improved working conditions required. dormant, awaiting the advent of conditions more in keeping with the average grade
their ores, before attempting to re-start work. The whole vitality of the distri
therefore, is contingent upon the provision of such conditions as shall make t
exploiting of the Klerksdorp low grade ores a commercially successful venture. A

Common interests of Government and mining industry. here the mining industry and the Government of the country meet upon comm
ground, for in the death of the one is involved firstly, heavy losses to the pastoral a
agricultural industries of the district; and secondly, and more directly, a serious loss
revenue. The industry and the Government have therefore to contend against comm
conditions, which are inimical to their progress, and the question arises in what way
the common danger to be avoided, and the languishing industry rehabilitated a
re-vitalised. The voluminous expert evidence already given before this Commissi

Reduction of railway rates and abolition of dynamite concession. makes it superfluous to again illustrate the facts that have been adduced under t
heads of dynamite, railway rates, etc. It has been shown that a reduction of rat
and the abolition of the dynamite concessions will secure the first step in the

eliorating conditions which are absolutely essential for the vitality of a district like rksdorp. Given low rates of transport and taxation only of such articles as the ntry can itself legitimately produce, and the now distressful burdens of living will reduced, and in direct proportion will it be possible to reduce the costs to the mining ustry, under the heading of white labour. The pay of the kaffir should be reduced nearly one-half its present rate. I may state in passing that in the mines of ngary, the white miners under my control were paid at the rate of from 10d. to 1s. 10 hours' work; mechanics, such as carpenters, smiths, fitters, etc., at the rate of 1s. to 1s. 6d. per day. In all cases these men housed and fed themselves. The climate of country is extreme. Contrast with this the condition of the kaffir. From his earliest ancy his wants are practically supplied by nature. The desire for comfort, and the bition to occupy any particular social distinction, requiring luxurious display, is solutely unknown. He lives in a climate which is one continuous sunshine. hence then the necessity for paying him coin in the quantity which he demands, a antity which is perfectly fictitious, and only arises from the fact that he has a tural aversion for work, and therefore the demand for his labour exceeding the pply which spontaneously offers, creates a competitive market, of which he is not w to take advantage. It seems to me that the one final method of reducing kaffir y rests with the Government. It has the power to create laws which shall compel ery able-bodied kaffir to perform a given amount of work per annum. A system mewhat of this kind was put into practice by the Government of the Republic of atemala. The Government watched with growing anxiety the gradual shrinkage the country's revenue, and decided to make a bold step for the purpose of aug- nting it. In pursuance of this, they enacted a law that every able-bodied resident the country should sow a certain area of ground with coffee, or, failing personal per- rmance, should pay the Government an assessed amount of coin for the provision of substitute to do the work. The plan proved a perfect success. Guatemala is to-day e most prosperous of the Central American Republics. The institution of a modified heme to meet the special conditions of this country, would, I believe, be of great assist- ce to the mining industry, and through that to the State. Under such compulsory ethods the hordes of idle, and, at present, useless kaffirs, who reside within the terri- ry of the South African Republic, would become a factor of economical importance the staple industry of the State, and the question of want of native labour would nish from the horizon of practical work. From a manufacturing standpoint, the ntral American Republics may fairly be classed with the Transvaal. I had occasion import certain machinery and supplies from the United States, and from England, the carrying out of mining operations in the Republic of Honduras. The Govern- ent notified me that absolutely no import dues would be charged on goods of any ass whatsoever, so long as it could be proved that they were *bona fide* for use in the eration of my company, or for the company's employees. It was further stated that e Government was so anxious to foster the mining industry in their country that ey would assist in every possible way to meet the wishes of its responsible represen- tives. In consequence of these concessions there is a growing feeling of confidence the status of the Republic; and its mineral resources are under exploitation by ny wealthy London corporations. A modification of such policy on the part of the vernment of this country would undoubtedly lead to a cheapening of the necessaries life; and specially the treatment of the industry with more confidence and republican irit, would inevitably result in an activity that would be for the lasting benefit of e State. In Victoria, Australia, not only does the Government do all in its power, in administrative capacity, to assist the mining industry, but it actually votes from 00,000 to £300,000 each year for the purpose of assisting prospectors to develop their holdings; the course being for the Government, upon approved opinion, advance £1 for every £1 spent by the prospector. In the event of the find provi valuable the money is repaid ; in the reverse case no claim for repayment is made, t view being that, in stimulating the mining industry, good use is made of the money.

Agricultulture and pastoral interests dependent on mining industry.

It is not necessary to point out, gentlemen, that a flourishing condition of t mining industry is a direct specific to agricultural and pastoral depression. Mini populations require all the produce of the farmers' gardens and fields, and l surplus stock. At present, and until the cost of gold winning can be reduce Witwatersrand is the only profitable market, and only farmers fortunate enou; to be within reasonable distance of Johannesburg can expect to derive a material benefit. Should, however, costs be reduced by the concerted acti of the Government and the leaders of the mining industry, then such ou lying districts as Klerksdorp, Heidelberg, etc., will revive, and the farming communit at points embracing the whole territory, will participate in the gener

Klerksdorp prices.

prosperity. I have before stated that one strong reason why Klerksdorp shou suffer in a greater measure from the imposition of heavy burdens than Witwatersran is because of its outlying position. The centre of the mining industry of this republ is Johannesburg. There centre all the depots of supply for the ordinary requisites every-day work. An article costs in Johannesburg a certain sum, in Klerksdorp th amount is enhanced by the transport rates between the two points, therefore tl

Labour supply at Klerksdorp.

working costs are higher. In the matter of labour, also, locality has a very gre influence. Johannesburg being the seat of industry, it is quite natural that men search of employment seek that as their objective point, consequently the majority men in the outer districts are mere stragglers, whose competency may always be call in question. Precisely the same may be said in connection with the native labou The most efficient working kaffirs are those obtained from the north and north-east this republic. The Witwatersrand mines have always been able. to take more kaffi than were forthcoming, hence, again, Klerksdorp is only able to secure some few th filter through the main centre. These are seldom the best class of workers, and ther fore their performance is poor and expensive in comparison with the average train Rand kaffir. Klerksdorp indubitably is on the high road traversed by the Ca; Colony and Basuto kaffirs, but for some months past these have been denied this rou owing to the rinderpest regulations in vogue in the Orange Free State. In any ca; however, as before indicated, the southern kaffir, as a workman, is distinctly inferi to the northern, and, moreover, entertains great prejudices against underground wor I have shown, therefore, that both in the matter of white and black labour, and cos of supplies, Klerksdorp suffers under greater disabilities than the Rand.

Dynamite.

The expenditure under the head of dynamite is likewise very seriously increased i

Price of dynamite and transport charge at Klerksdorp.

Klerksdorp. The present price of dynamite at the magazine is 95s. per box of 50lt The transport rate per case from the dynamite factory to the Klerksdorp magazine 5s. 6d., therefore the company not only makes an enormous profit on the factory sa price, but makes a further 4s. 6d. per case profit on the transport. Other witness have shown that it would be possible to lay dynamite down here, exclusive of Tran

Australian price of dynamite.

vaal duties, at 42s. 7d. per case. The ruling rate for dynamite in Australia is abo 35s. per case in Sydney, Melbourne, Adelaide, or Brisbane ; that dynamite has to transported from Europe, a distance of 12,000 miles, and is then sold at a figure abo two and a half times less than the price at the Transvaal factory. The cost of blas

Cost of gelatine.

ing gelatine is 107s. 6d. per case, the concessionaires again taking a profit of 4s. 6

Concessions.

per case on transport. Mr. Hennen Jennings has clearly shown the evils of concession granting, and I entirely endorse his views. With the abolition of the dynamite co cession a free market is opened, and if treated by the Government with that liberalit

h the industry claims and deserves there is no reason why dynamite should not
ld in this republic at 50s. per case. Finally, gentlemen, the case of the Klerks-
district is one which it is hoped will be proportionately weighed in your delibera-
regarding the recommendations you may see fit to make to the Government.
liberal concessions made, the district will live and expand; without them, it
ot exist excepting in name.

Mr. Denny then handed in the following statement:—

Mr. Chairman and Gentlemen,—We the Klerksdorp Chamber of Mines and the Klerks- Statement of Klerksdorp Chamber of Mines and Klerksdorp Chamber of Commerce.
Chamber of Commerce, representing the following mining companies: The Klerks-
Gold and Diamond Company, Limited, Wolverand Gold Estate and Mining Company,
ted, Buffelsdoorn Estate and Gold Mining Company, Limited, Eastleigh Mines,
ted, Westleigh Mines, Limited, Klerksdorp Proprietary, Limited, Niekerk (Klerks- Names of Klerksdorp memorialists.
) Gold Mining Company, Limited, Rietkuil Gold Mining Company, Limited,
xander Gold Mining Company, Limited, Elandslaagte Gold Mining Company, Ltd.,
elsdoorn "A" Gold Mining Company; and merchants: T. Leask & Co., Teengs
, A. Chittenden, Aldred, Lombard, James A. Taylor, J. Levenson, H. and J. Israel,
Morton & Co., Gordon, Mitchell, J. Groth, Percival H. Read, Mackenzie & Co., E.
tt, H. Brown, Hamilton & Co., in acknowledging your circular of the 14th inst.,
esting evidence in respect to grievances and burdens of the mining industry,
ectfully beg to point out that in this district there are 25 mining companies, with Number, capital and actual condition of Klerksdorp mining companies.
tals amounting to over £5,000,000, of these but two are crushing and two develop-
the remainder having closed down; and should no prompt and substantial relief be
ined from the disabilities under which the mining industry is now suffering, more Necessity of immediate reforms for mining industry.
cially those hereinafter enumerated, it is the firm opinion of these Chambers that
mining industry will entirely collapse. On the other hand, should such relief be
ined through your advice and influence, we consider capital would be found, not
sufficient for the restarting of the closed mines, but for still further exploration.
object to be obtained is a working cost of from 12s. to 18s. per ton of ore mined
milled, to allow 5 dwt. or 6 dwt. mines to become payable propositions. To Relief asked for
mplish this, substantial reductions are necessary in the cost of explosives, trans-
, European and native wages. The cost of No. 1 dynamite at the factory for 50
s and upwards is 85s. per case, at Klerksdorp 95s. per case; whilst the cost of
sport from the factory to Klerksdorp is but 5s. 6d. per case, showing that the con- Price of dynamite and transport charge at Klerksdorp.
ionaires not only receive their large profits from the sale of dynamite, but also
e a considerable further profit on the transport from the factory to their Klerks-
magazine. The cost of No. 1 A gelatine is 107s. 6d. per case at the Gelatine — cost and transport charge at Klerksdorp.
ory; this is retailed at 117s. 6d. per case, transport being at the same rate
for No. 1 dynamite, consequently the same advantages accrue to the con-
ionaires as from the sale of dynamite. The above are the only explosives used
hese goldfields in quantities. Some of the softer rocks of surface workings would,
ever, allow of the use of blasting powder at a cheaper cost than dynamite, if
ter facilities were given for obtaining the same than at present. We would also
attention in relation to the foregoing charges that in the Orange Free State, 13 Comparative price of dynamite in Transvaal, Orange Free State, and at Kimberley.
s from our mines, the cost of dynamite is £1 10s. per case less than in the Trans-
, while the Free State Mining interests are, as your Commission is aware, infinite-
l as compared to those of this country. No. 1 dynamite is also delivered at
iberley at 52s. 6d. per case. We consider that the best way to alleviate the above
ld be to allow of competition in the import of explosives, but should you not see Free trade in explosives.
r way to advise this course, as an alternative, relative to these goldfields only, we

would suggest that the concessionaires be instructed to allow explosives to be impo

Suggested im-
portation of
dynamite for
Klerksdorp via
Kroonstad. direct to their Klerksdorp magazine *via* Kroonstad, Orange Free State; the mine
this district to have any advantages obtained from the more direct transit, over
above any reduction of the present price at the factory, which may be contempla
Should this latter alternative be conceded, the following would be the transport f
Port Elizabeth:—

Railway Rate to Kroonstad	...	...	4s. 9d. per 100 lbs.	
Agent's Charges	...	...	...	0s. 4d. „
Wagon Transport	...	...	...	2s. 6d. „

7s. 7d. per 100 lbs.

This would allow a saving to the mines of 10s. per case on the present Kler
dorp price, and a difference of 2d. per 100lbs. only in favour of the factory, as the rail
rate to Cyrfontein is 7s. 2d. per 100lbs. transport to factory, say 3d., making a t
of 7s. 5d. per 100lbs. This 2d. per 100lbs., however, is not material, as it would o
make about 1¼d. per case difference in the cost.

Railway rates. Railway rates.—These should be made with more consideration to the min
districts still developing, and farmers' produce such as mealies, forage, etc., and st
Reductions in
railway rates
required for
agricultural
produce and
stock. such as cattle, horses, and mules, should be carried at a mere nominal rate betw
the agricultural districts and the mines, and we consider it a matter for y
consideration that, notwithstanding the large profits of the railway during the
twelve months, the present depression has brought with it no corresponding reduct
in the railway charges for mining material, nor have matters otherwise b
facilitated. Take for instance the rough goods' rate from Port Elizabeth. The o
point of entry open to Klerksdorp during the first rinderpest regulations of
Railway rate
from Port Eliz-
abeth to
Klerksdorp via
Vereeniging. Orange Free State was Vereeniging. The rate from Port Elizabeth to the middl
the Vaal River Bridge was 3s. 7d. per 100lbs., mileage 664·42. Netherlands char
from the middle of the bridge to Vereeniging, 1s., for a distance of only one m
Customs and forwarding charges, 5d. per 100lbs.; mule wagon transport fr
Vereeniging to Klerksdorp, 6s. 6d. per 100lbs.; making a total of 11s. 6d. per 100
Railway rate
from Port
Elizabeth to
Klerksdorp via
Johannesburg. Had the same goods been taken on to Johannesburg, the railway rate would ha
been 5s. 3d. per 100lbs.; passing Customs and forwarding, 5d. per 100lbs.; m
transport from Johannesburg to Klerksdorp, 7s. 6d. per 100lbs.; making a total
Railway rate
from Delagoa
Bay to Klerks-
dorp. 13s. 2d., or 1s. 8d. in favour of Vereeniging. From Delagoa Bay to Johannesburg
railway rate would have been 4s. 2d. per 100lbs.; forwarding, etc., 5d. per 100l
mule transport to Klerksdorp, 7s. 6d. per 100lbs.; making a total of 12s. 1d.
100lbs., showing a difference of 7d. in favour of Vereeniging. We may here ment
that the Chamber of Commerce, when the Orange Free State proclamations were f
issued, approached the Government and Netherlands Railway to assist us, as fa
Request to Gov-
ernment to re-
duce railway
rate on rough
goods across
Vaal river. possible, in reducing the heavy charge on this class of goods across the Vaal Ri
and to allow us to clear our goods as before in Klerksdorp; but both these propositi
were coldly received, and met with no support whatsoever. We would also like
point out the difference in mileage rates to the nearest railway stations to Klerksd
Railway mileage
rates on rough
and third class
goods to sta-
tions nearest
to Klerksdorp. on rough and third-class goods:—Rough goods' rate from Port Elizabeth to Kroons
(577·49 miles) at 3s. 7d. per 100lbs.; rough goods' rate from Durban to Potchefstro
(672 miles) at 5s. 11d. per 100lbs., equal to 40 per cent. over Port Elizabeth-Kroons
rate on the mileage of 577·49 miles only; rough goods' rate from Delagoa E
to Potchefstroom (428 miles) 5s. 3d. per 100lbs., equals 97 per cent. over P
Elizabeth-Kroonstad rate on the mileage of 577·49. Rail carriage from Port Elizab
to Kroonstad (577·49) 4s. 9d. per 100 lbs. Rail carriage from Durban to Potch
stroom (672 miles) 8s. 11d. per 100lbs., equals 36 per cent. over Port Elizabe

oonstad rate on the mileage of 577·49. Rail carriage from Delagoa Bay to tchefstroom (428 miles) 7s. 9d. per 100lbs., equals 120 per cent. over Port Elizabeth-oonstad rate on the mileage of 577·49. From this you will see the rough goods' e from Durban is 40 per cent. higher than the Cape tariff, and Delagoa Bay per cent. On the third-class goods, Durban is 26 per cent., and Delagoa Bay 0 per cent. more than the Cape, taking the average mileage at 577·49, which we isider gives ample margin for large reductions on the Netherlands' charges. The ange Free State concessionaires are now surveying the new railway line from oonstad to the Vaal River, and should your Government at once decide to connect with the present terminus of the Netherlands Railway in Klerksdorp, it would eatly facilitate the transport of general goods, but more especially coal, which ould on the completion of such a railway line, be delivered at our mines at from s. to 15s. per ton, instead of from 20s. to 40s. as at present. The ox and mule agon transport between the Free State coalfields and these mines is also greatly peded by the bad repair in which both the main transport road and the roads to e mines are kept. The drift at the Vaal River is also in an almost impassable state. ae mines in this district being scattered over an area of 500 square miles, the vantage of the general up-keep of the roads is a matter of great necessity. In rther reference to this, we would mention that while the State has received from is district of an estimated population of 2,500 (whites) a revenue for the year of 62,000, besides the extra expenditure upon the official staff, amounting but to a few ousand pounds, very little has been expended upon public works, and we are of the inion that in common fairness more of the district's revenue should be spent in the strict itself, and less retained by the Central Government.

European wages are eight per cent. higher than in Johannesburg, though the actual st per ton of ore mined is less, which is to be accounted for by the comparative rgeness of the lodes worked. Miners and millmen are employed in this district at om 15s. to 20s. per shift, but notwithstanding the expense gone to in providing orkmens' quarters, &c., by the companies, the mine managers are of the unanimous inion no substantial reduction can be anticipated in wages until the cost of living n be correspondingly reduced, and that is to be arrived at only by an all-round duction of the customs and railway charges on the commodities of life.

The Chamber consider in time the present native wages may be reduced, owing to e Free State rinderpest regulations being again relaxed so far as to allow natives to ss through their territory from Basutoland and the Cape Colony to this country. ae charges of the Netherlands railway are, however, still prohibitive for the importa- n of natives from Mozambique and Natal, and to further the supply of natives, and assist towards a further reduction in their wages, we would suggest that natives ould be encouraged to come to this district by a minimum railway fare being arged, any loss resulting from such a reduction to be made up by an extra charge the natives when returning. It is also remarkable that, notwithstanding the very rge number of natives resident in this State, they are conspicuous by their absence om employers of labour, and we consider it would be beneficial if native taxes ere increased, and natives that could show certificates of having worked six months the year be allowed a reduction of 25 per cent., besides which all Fieldcornets and hers engaged in the collection of native taxes, should discourage the system of the tives selling their cattle to meet the tax, and by their paying only in coin, there ould be a greater necessity for them to come out and work.

We consider this law in itself is beneficial, but in this district it has not been put to force, and should it be enforced, this Chamber consider a competent body of ficials would have to be established to carry out its provisions. The reason of the

Margin notes

Comparative railway mileage rates on rough and third class goods on the Natal, Cape and Delagoa Bay routes.

Suggested connection between Klerksdorp and the proposed new line from Kroonstad to Vaal river.

Klerksdorp roads.

White wages.

Reduction of native wages.

Railway rates for transport of natives.

Taxation of natives.

Pass Law.

Chambers not having requested the enforcement of the law was, from the unanimo
opinion received from the districts where it was in operation, because of the unsati
factory manner in which the provisions of this law were being carried out.

Liquor Law.

We consider this law also good in itself, but not carried out. Could an addition
Maladministration of Liquor Law. made, to the effect that no white man be allowed to obtain liquor either by writing
otherwise through the medium of natives, it would greatly facilitate the object of th
Suggested amendments to Liquor Law. law, and that offenders should be imprisoned without the option of a fine, the profits
the trade being too large for the present fines inflicted to lessen the evil. We al
Native locations. think that the introduction of a law establishing large native locations in the vicinity
the mining camps would be a great advantage in keeping up the permanent supply of labo
and hereby beg to place before you a report on the Buffelsdoorn location in this district.-

On account of the isolated position of the Buffelsdoorn Gold Mine and th
attendant difficulty found in the procuring and retention of an efficient supply
native labour to carry on mining operations, a part of the policy of the company t
Buffelsdoorn location. overcome this impediment has been to always make the surroundings of the nativ
as comfortable and pleasant as possible. In pursuance of this, five years ago a loca
tion, situated on the smaller mijnpacht, and one mile from the works, was establishe
At the time of the formation of this, and on the same spot, there were then resider
17 natives. At the present time there are now living there 253 souls (100 men, 6
women, and 86 children), who occupy 94 huts, built by themselves and at their ow
cost. In addition to these places of living, the natives have subscribed among then
selves, and with the assistance of a little extraneous aid have built for themselves
commodious church and schoolroom, presided over by a native missionary and teache
Order is maintained, and the interests of the company guarded by two police; thes
in case of necessity, can easily get assistance, as the major portion of the company
police reside in the location. Of the numerous nationalities employed by the Buffel
doorn Company (some 13) there is a marked partiality by some tribes for huts in th
location; Zambesis, practically the whole of whom are drill-men, show this desire to
great degree, and to accommodate those who have gone to their countries to fetc
their families, there are now in course of erection 25 huts which will shortly be almos
doubled to shelter the families of other natives and their belongings from other par
of the country. From the experience gained here, there seems good ground fo
assuming that if locations were established in the proximity of the mines, there wou
be a base formed for a working force more permanent and steady in character tha
exists at present. In order to render police patrolling as easy and efficacious a
possible, great care should be taken in the first instance in the granting of plots o
ground for building purposes. Since the establishment of the location on the propert
of the Buffelsdoorn Estate and Gold Mining Company such a thing as the interferenc
with the members of one tribe by men of another nationality has not been known
sickness, crime, and other disturbing influences being at a minimum. The Fieldcorne
of the district, Mr. Andries Cronje, is personally acquainted with the location, i
situation, supervision, and the general behaviour of the inhabitants; and in no wa
does he consider its establishment as detrimental to the public peace or moralit
Another location recommended. From the results obtained by the introduction of the location here there is ever
reason to warrant the establishment of such another in districts more thickly popu
lated by natives working on the mines, and where the whole system would be brough
more prominently under the notice of the public. In conclusion, we trust from th
statements and suggestions we have been able to place before you at so short a notic
your committee will be of opinion, if only what is due to us is granted, that minin
costs will be so reduced as to enable the mines in this district to work on a profitabl
basis, and so increase the general prosperity of the district.

THE BUFFELSDOORN ESTATE AND G. M. CO.

SCHEDULE OF EUROPEAN WAGES.—MARCH AND APRIL, 1897.

	March.			April.			Total.			Cost per ton.		P.c. of total cost.
	£	s.	d.	£	s.	d.	£	s.	d.	s.	d.	
Miners	1,039	19	3	1,208	10	6	2,248	9	9	1	7·48	6·89
Fitters	257	18	3	206	0	8	463	18	11	0	4·03	1·42
Hauling engine-drivers	122	6	6	129	0	4	251	6	10	0	2·18	·77
Mill firemen ...	50	0	0	50	0	0	100	0	0	0	·87	·31
Compressor drivers	43	11	0	42	6	4	85	17	4	0	·74	·2
Electricians ...	43	13	4	48	13	4	92	6	8	0	·8	·28
Surface trams ...	21	7	6	5	3	4	26	10	10	0	·23	·08
Blacksmiths ...	136	17	11	141	4	7	278	2	6	0	2·41	·85
Drillsmiths ...	291	8	5	315	9	10	606	18	3	0	5·26	1·86
Masons	86	16	0	40	0	0	126	16	0	0	1·1	·39
Carpenters ...	168	7	1	170	9	7	338	16	8	0	2·93	1·04
Cyaniders... ...	133	4	0	131	10	0	264	14	0	0	2·29	·81
Millmen	220	12	0	205	7	6	425	19	6	0	3·69	1·31
Crusher engine-drivers	35	16	8	30	0	0	65	16	8	0	·57	·20
Mill engine-drivers	76	12	2	93	0	0	169	12	2	0	1·47	·52
Sundry	86	3	1	70	16	10	156	19	11	0	1·36	·48
Compound and watch	56	3	3	57	11	6	113	14	9	0	·97	·35
Time and store keeping and secretary ...	237	8	6	233	1	0	470	9	6	0	4·07	1·44
Totals ...	£3,108	4	11	£3,178	5	4	£6,286	10	3	4	6·45	19·2

Y

THE BUFFELSDOORN ESTATE AND G. M. CO.

SCHEDULE OF STORES CONSUMED.—MARCH AND APRIL, 1897.

	March.			April.			Total.			Cost per ton.		P.c. of total cost.
	£	s.	d.	£	s.	d.	£	s.	d.	s.	d.	
Candles	317	4	8	319	0	8	636	5	4	0	5·51	1·95
Cyanide	628	13	4	377	8	9	1,006	2	1	0	8·72	3·09
Explosives ...	1,667	4	8	2,031	11	2	3,698	15	10	2	8·04	11·33
Fuel	2,293	10	6	1,938	2	7	4,231	13	1	3	0·66	12·96
General	778	8	10	646	8	11	1,424	17	9	1	0·34	4·37
Lubricants ...	331	14	0	276	8	5	608	2	5	0	5·27	1·87
Mercury	18	7	4	—			18	17	4	0	·16	·05
Mealies	693	8	2	489	1	2	1,182	9	4	0	10·24	3·63
Oxen	133	5	10	178	1	0	311	8	10	0	2·7	·95
Steel	220	1	8	155	1	0	375	2	8	0	3·25	1·15
Shoes and dies ...	273	12	2	140	0	0	413	17	2	0	3·58	1·27
Tools	55	6	6	38	8	2	93	14	8	0	·81	·29
Timber	87	5	4	108	16	7	186	1	11	0	1·7	·6
Zinc	48	4	3	40	1	7	88	5	10	0	·77	·27
Forage	29	4	10	22	5	8	51	10	6	0	·45	·16
Crusher spares ...	125	9	2	83	12	10	209	2	0	0	1·81	·64
Rails and sleepers	14	11	7	0	6	7	14	18	2	0	·13	·04
Stationery ...	59	8	2	39	0	10	98	9	0	0	·85	·3
Totals ...	£7,775	11	0	£6,884	2	11	£14,659	13	11	10	6·99	44·92

EASTLEIGH MINES, LIMITED.

WORKING COSTS, MARCH AND APRIL, 1897.

	Cost per ton.		Per cent. of total cost.	
	March.	April.	March.	April.
	s. d.	s. d.		
White wages	7 0·3	6 2·7	23·20	22·78
Kaffir ,, ...	9 5·9	8 10·9	31·67	32·57
Coal	5 6·2	4 10·4	18·22	17·81
Dynamite	1 10·7	1 6·3	6·23	5·64
Cyanide	2 3·2	1 8·6	7·49	6·27
Sundry stores	3 3·4	3 4·5	10·86	12·46
Licences	6·7	4·9	1·86	1·52
Sundry expenses	2·8	3·1	0·77	0·95
Total	30 3·2	27 3·4		

BUFFELSDOORN ESTATE AND GOLD MINING COMPANY. LIMITED.

Table of Operating Costs, March and April, inclusive of Mine Redemption and Johannesburg Office Charges.

	Cost. £ s. d.	Tons.	Cost per ton. s. d.	Per cent. of total cost.	Cost. £ s. d.	Tons.	Cost per ton. s. d.	Per cent. of total cost.	Cost. £ s. d.	Tons.	Cost per ton. s. d.	Per cent. of total cost.
European wages...	3,108 4 11	13,414	4 7·61	18·2	3,178 5 4	14,292	4 5·37	20·44	6,286 10 3	27,706	4 6·45	19·26
Native Wages ...	5,037 11 6	13,414	7 6·13	29·48	4,705 6 2	14,292	6 7·01	30·25	9,742 17 8	27,706	7 0·39	29·85
Stores	7,775 11 0	13,414	11 7·12	45·51	6,884 2 11	14,292	9 7·6	44·26	14,659 13 11	27,706	10 6·99	44·92
Contractors and general	1,164 0 9	13,414	1 8·88	6·81	785 10 6	14,292	1 1·2	5·05	1,949 11 3	27,706	1 4·89	5·97
Totals ...	17,085 8 2	13,414	25 5·68	100·00	15,553 4 11	14,292	21 9·18	100·00	32,638 13 1	27,706	23 6·72	100·00

Mr. ALBERT PHILLIP, director of the South African Company of Explosives was called. He stated :—

In compliance with the request of this honourable Commission to give evidence ll matters known to us concerning certain grievances complained of by the ng industry, as well as on other matters connected therewith, I beg to submit following statement to this honourable Commission :—

The sole object of this statement is to prove to this Commission that different rtions which have been made during the sitting of this Commission, and materially ting the interests of the company I represent, are void of any foundation. It has urther object, as I am not acquainted with any grievances resting on the mining stry, which affect us as an industrial concern. The present company, the Zuid caansche Fabrieken voor Ontplofbare Stoffen, Beperkt, was formed and registered uch in the South African Republic in June, 1894. Its capital is £450,000. Since formation of the company we have erected a factory in this republic, which is largest dynamite factory in the world. Our capital outlay on the factories alone, out stock, is about £600,000. We commenced manufacturing in October, 1896. factories would have been ready before this time had it not been for causes ond our control, such as the Jameson raid and the rinderpest. At the commence- t the factories are worked very slowly, in view of the dangers attending the ufacture of explosives, and of the difficulty of drilling a large staff, including y hundreds of blacks, in the observance of all precautions necessary in so gerous a manufacture, when carried on on so large a scale, and it was thought rable that the actual production should be limited to about 80,000 cases per um, a rate which should subsequently be gradually increased as considerations of ty may admit. Under our contract with the Government the maximum prices wed to be charged for dynamite No. 1, containing 75 per cent. of nitro-glycerine, 0s. per case, and for other kinds in proportion. We charge 85s. per case for amite No. 1, *ex* magazine. Statements have been made before this Commission, to effect that dynamite No. 1 could be imported at a price of, I think it was, 35s. per , free of duty, laid down in Johannesburg. These statements have been of the test interest to us, as we were not aware of it before. At the last session of the ksraad, a Volksraad Commission was appointed, who brought out a report on dynamite question. This report has not been treated to its full extent by the ksraad, and until this is done, moreover, as it is the intention of the Honourable ksraad to specially enquire about European prices, I will refrain from comment- on above statements. All I can say for the moment is, that, as far as I know, amite No. 1 is being sold at the following prices in other countries :—

Australian Ports—From 79s. 2d. to 83s. 4d. per case.

British India—110s. per case.

Cape Colony—Port Elizabeth, 67s. per case ; Kimberley, 72s. 6d. per case ; De rs, 65s. per case.

Rhodesia—Bulawayo, 110s. per case, ; Victoria, 115s. per case ; Salisbury, 120s. case.

Natal—87s. 6d. per case.

Further, I wish to add that, according to an official report of El Callao and La umbia mines, both in South America, and of which Mr. Hamilton Smith, the well- wn authority on mining matters on the Rand, was consulting engineer, it appears t the price there for dynamite is 108s. 9¾d. per case, against 85s. in Johannesburg. many statements have been made about this company making 40s., and I do not w how much more, profit per case, I am very sorry to say that this is not the case.

Mr. A. Phillip's evidence.

South African Explosives Company—capital and formation.

Cost of erecting dynamite factory.

Annual production of dynamite.

Prices chargeable for dynamite under Government contract.

Actual price of dynamite.

Price of imported dynamite.

Volksraad Dynamite Commission.

Price of No. 1 dynamite in Australia, British India, Cape Colony, Rhodesia and Natal.

Price of dynamite at El Callao and La Columbia mines, South America.

Without going into the details of this company's business, which would be unprecedented action on the part of any trading concern, and which the direc[t] have not the right to do without the sanction of a general meeting of sharehold[ers]

Dividend of South African Explosives Company for 1895.

we may only refer this honourable Commission to this company's last balance sh[eet] for 1895, which produced a dividend at the rate of 8 per cent. per annum, so that profits of our company cannot be so abnormal as people try to make out. As to Government's share, it does not seem to be known that the State received dur[ing]

State's share of profits of South African Explosives Company.

1896 £44,000 as a royalty. Besides this, the State gets a certain share in the pro[fits] of this company, so that statements to the effect that this company derives all profits to the detriment of the State, are quite incorrect. This point has also b[een] raised by statements before the Commission, referring to accidents arising thro[ugh]

Dynamite accidents.

the alleged bad quality of our explosives. I may mention that all complaints com[e] to our notice have been thoroughly investigated, and all the accidents have b[een] traced to either bad ventilation of the respective mines, or to the careless tamp[ing] of drill holes. Another great factor which plays an important part in [the] prevention of accidents at mines, is the use of proper detonators and fu[se] but all these defects, we hope, will be abolished as soon as the new dy[na]mite or explosives' law comes into operation, which we trust will soon ta[ke] place. I may add that all the explosives, as soon as they are ready to lea[ve] our factory, are submitted to the so-called British test, and if they do [not] stand the test they are kept back and re-worked. I think it is hardly recogni[sed] amongst the industrial community in this republic that our undertaking is as good [an]

Industrial advantages derived by the Transvaal from the South African Explosives Company.

industry as the gold industry on the Witwatersrand. It would lead me too far [to] dwell on the advantages this country is deriving from an established industry such [as] ours. Suffice it to say that we have paid during the year of 1896 about £118,000 [to] contractors for building up houses, water dams, etc. And goods bought locally [in] Pretoria and Johannesburg amount to about £57,000, for coal, timber, corrugated ir[on] etc., and about £12,500 for kaffir food, and £104,000 as railage; not taking into c[on]sideration the money spent in the country by our staff and work-people, consisting [of]

Roburite — unsatisfactory experiments.

700 white people and 1,300 natives. A statement has been made to this honoura[ble] Commission recommending the use of roburite instead of nitro-glycerine compoun[d] Without going into the details of this statement, I may draw the attention of [the] honourable Commission to the following fact, viz., that in the year 1893 the Gove[rn]ment, on the request of the roburite people, bought 300 cases of roburite as a tri[al] of which we have still got 167 cases in stock. The balance was sent to several mi[nes] for trial, and we received reports to the effect that the roburite did not answer [the]

American dynamite—unsatisfactory experiments.

purpose. As to American dynamite I may state that this company also bought a tr[ial] shipment some time ago (1894) which resulted in a complete failure, and according [to] the four years' experience I personally had in Mexico, I should consider it my duty [to] recommend the Government not to import this stuff, the quality being quite unsuita[ble] for the work required in this country, and the danger connected with the use of th[e] defective article being too great. I should like to say that we are obliged, accordi[ng] to our contract with the Government, to give certain information to the Governme[nt.] This information we are at present, and will always be, anxious and eager to gi[ve] but, of course, always in terms of our contract. This company is most anxious to [do] everything in its power to assist the Commission in showing the magnitude of t[his] industrial undertaking of the company, and would, therefore, be pleased if the Co[m]mission would examine what is being done at the large factories which have be[en]

Price of dynamite in Kimberley, at De Beers, and in Natal.

erected by the company.

Chairman.

In Kimberley is the price 67s. 6d. per case ?—72s. 6d; De Beers get a reducti[on] live per cent., because they have a large contract ; and in Natal 87s. 6d.

Can you tell us who delivers that dynamite in Kimberley and Natal at that ce ?—The Nobel Trust Company.

Mr. *Hugo.*

I see you deny the statement that dynamite can be delivered here at 40s. ?—I am aware of it.

<aside>Price of imported dynamite.</aside>

It has been stated that at Hamburg dynamite is sold at 18s. 6d. ?—I don't know thing about European prices.

<aside>European price of dynamite.</aside>

You cannot say whether that is correct or not ?—No.

Mr. *Hay.*

In the first paragraph of your report you say that you are not acquainted with y grievances resting on the mining industry. Now, the contention all through this mmission has been that one of the industry's burdens is the high price of dynamite, l that if there were free trade in dynamite it could be imported at a very much ver rate. Can you tell us the quantity which you imported into the country last r ?—I may say this company does not import dynamite ; it is the Government who ports it.

<aside>Government the importer of dynamite.</aside>

Will you tell us how much dynamite the Government imported last year and d through their agents ?—The Government imported from 18th June, 1894, to the nd October, 1896, 466,000 cases of materials required for the manufacture of namite and blasting gelatine.

<aside>Importation of dynamite and gelatine materials.</aside>

When you say 466,000 cases of materials, will you explain what you mean, or, her, perhaps you will explain how you make dynamite—tell us the ingredients that required ?—It is very difficult for me to say how to make dynamite—if you say a tain kind of dynamite I will tell you.

You say 466,000 cases of material were imported between June, 1894, and tober, 1896. That means nothing to us unless you explain what you mean by the rd " material."—The material is called " gühr impregné," which is a sort of pre-ation of nitro-glycerine, in order to make it safer for transport.

Practically you are importing dynamite in bulk.—That is not exactly right. It ite depends on the kind of dynamite you want to produce. For instance, without ing into the technical question of dynamite, No. 1 is prepared quite differently from . 2, and blasting gelatine is quite different from No. 2.

I quite understand that. The difference between No. 1 and No. 2 is the strength the explosive. Practically you take gühr impregné as dynamite ?—You cannot call dynamite, because you cannot use it as it is.

It will explode the same as the other if used with a detonator ?—Nitro-glycerine itself does that.

You use the words " gühr impregné " when I ask you about " material," and I low that up and ask you what that is, and you give some other explanation which es not lead us any further. Guhr is earth and clay that absorbs the nitro-glycerine it is done in that way to carry the nitro-glycerine, and therefore when you import in block it is really dynamite ?—The difference in the questions and the replies is t we call the explosive that which can be used in a mine, so that if you ask me ether gühr impregné is dynamite I say not.

Does it not simply mean the difference between gunpowder in bulk and in tridge ?—No.

When you got these 466,000 cases, what did you do with them ?—We have to ry it through a certain process.

It will simplify matters, perhaps, if you tell us how many of these 466,000 ca
were gühr impregné ?—I have not got the information with me.

Gühr impregné is one way in which it is imported; how do you import it wh
it is for blasting gelatine ?—Blasting gelatine is introduced in a similar way to gü
impregné, also in block; but that does not say you can use the blocks as they are.

They could be used if you made the hole large enough to put them in ?—Y
that is why I say if you put nitro-glycerine in pure you can use it ?

The question I really want to get at is this : How much of this is import
already made, and how much of it has to be manufactured here ?—Well, these 466,0
cases were materials required for the manufacture of dynamite.

Report of Volks- In the report of the Commission, which sat last year, it said, if I remember rig
raad Dynamite that the factory was not able to make the quantity of dynamite required, and th
Commission. the stuff was imported practically already made ?—That is not correct.

In paragraph 8 it says: "This point arises in connection with the question wheth
the Government agent shall be allowed to import explosives, gelatine, and gü
impregné, which is, in fact, nothing but dynamite not yet made into cartridges." Yo
Commission gathers from the accounts placed in their hands by the honourable t
Profits of South State Secretary that the "profit of the company on blasting gelatine and gü
African Ex- impregné imported by the State amounts to almost £2 per case, of which t
plosives Com- Government only gets 5s. per case." The question comes to this—Is that correct
pany on im-
ported gela- not ?—May I ask what report that is ?
tine and "gühr
impregné." This is the report presented by the Volksraad Dynamite Commission to t
honourable the First Volksraad on the 22nd February, 1897.—I say that is n
correct. It is rather hard on me to examine me on a question which is still befo
the Volksraad.

This Commission has been appointed by the Government to enquire into t
grievances of the mining industry, and the price of dynamite forms one of the ve
important questions.—I do not deny that in the least, but I want to say I do n
think it is quite fair to examine me on a matter which is before the Volksraad, a
which has not been decided yet.

When this was before the Raad a resolution of the Raad was taken, and t
Government was then authorised to proceed with a further Commission, and out
that I understand this Commission has been appointed.—I think you are mistake
The Volksraad appointed a separate Commission to enquire into the European pric
This Commission was only appointed to enquire into the grievances of the mines.

If I understand you rightly, this Commission, by enquiring into the question
dynamite, is exceeding its powers.—I won't say exceeding its powers, because I do n
know the powers of the Commission; but I would like to mention that the dynami
question is before the Volksraad, and I do not think it is fair to examine me on t
same point until the Volksraad has decided upon it.

But surely you can state to us exactly what you stated to the Volksraad Cor
mission.—That is what I am doing; but you ask me whether the statement made
he report is correct.

Imported dyna- If I put the questions one by one perhaps you will answer. In paragraph
mite materials. clause 8, it states: "This explosive gelatine and gühr impregné imported is nothi
else, but No. 1 not yet made into cartridges." Is that correct ?—I am quite prepar
to give you all the information; but on this the Volksraad Commission has reporte
and I would prefer not to reply.

Government the The fact is that on this gühr impregné you pay the same duty in the Cape Color
importer of as you pay on dynamite ?—As we do not import it, of course it is the Governme
dynamite. pays the import duty.

The Cape Colony treats it as dynamite ?—That may be, but as the Government never imported ready-made dynamite up to the present, I cannot say if the Cape is the same.

I don't understand your position. You are here as the representative of the ~ry which manufactures the dynamite ?—Yes.

Then the question is: Has the Government imported this dynamite? Have you ~hing to do with that at all ?—That is rather a difficult question.

What I mean to say is, when I ask the question whether you import the dyna~ you fence by saying: "No, we don't; the Government does."—Yes, the Govern~ imports it.

Then who is the Government agent ?—Mr. Vorstman.

The question is, who is going to give us this information. In paragraph 9 it is ~ed : "The importation of this yields a very large profit, which has nothing to do ~ the profit on the explosive itself." Is that correct or not—that this importation ~ds a great profit to the company, which has nothing to do with the explosives ~ufactured by themselves. Is this true ?—The only thing I can say is that the pany makes profits.

The company makes profits out of this material, which is imported by the Govern~t agent. The question is, in respect to this gühr imported by the Government ~t, from whom it is bought ?—From whom does the Government buy it ?

Yes.—Of course this is in the Commission report. They buy it from Nobel's ~amite Trust.

It is fair to assume that these people make a profit, and that Nobel's Trust make ~ofit on the other side ?—That, of course, I cannot say. It is supposed to be so, but ~nnot swear to it.

It is fair to assume they do make profit on it ?—If you like. I would not like to ~ar to it.

In paragraph 10, the reply is that the approximate profit on this material ~orted leaves a profit of nearly £2 a case. Is that correct ?—No; it is not correct. ~y in my statement I cannot go into details as to the company, and how much ~t they make. It would be quite an unprecedented case in any trading company.

If I asked you how much profit you made on the manufactured article— ~uinely manufactured at the factory—that might be a fair reply to give. But this ~ question here whether the Government import the dynamite not made in the ~ntry and sold to us. Now, the question is simply a fair question: How much ~fit is made out of that ?—The only thing I can say is, that I only refer to the ~ance-sheet of our company for 1895, from the time that we got the sale of the stuff ~oduced by the Government. This shows only a dividend of 8 per cent.

Do you mean Nobel's Trust or this company ?—This company.

How does this Volksraad Commission arrive at the conclusion that almost £2 a ~ profit is made ?—That is a question I cannot answer. I was not present when ~ Commission made up their report.

Because £2 a case on 466,000 cases would be nearly a million of money ?—Yes, we have not got it.

Then who gets it ?—I don't know. The only thing I can say is, I don't believe it.

Then this paragraph in the Volksraad Commission's report is not true ?—There ~ put questions. I cannot say that the things the Commission state are not true. ~ I can say is, we don't make that profit.

Then can you say who made it ?

Chairman.

Mr. Hay must understand that Mr. Phillip is only the representative of factory, and that he is not the Government agent for the sale of dynamite.

Mr. Hay.

I must simply say that in the report of the Commission they use the wo「 " the profit of the company," and then Mr. Phillip says he represents the compa Therefore it is fair to assume that the profit went into his hands.

Witness.] Mr. Chairman, what I object to is, that Mr. Hay asked me whet this report was true.

Chairman.

I don't think it is reasonable to ask such a question, because we don't kn ourselves from where the Volksraad Commission got their information.

Mr. Hay.

They say the accounts were placed in their hands by the State Secretary. ` think, at any rate, supposing that was correct—that £2 a case was made out imported stuff—that would be very large profit ?—It would be a very large profit, `

And it would be a reasonable ground for the industry to have a grievance. ` say you don't know anything at all about European prices, and, therefore, on question of Nobel's Trust agreeing to sell dynamite down to 40s. in bond in Johann

Price of Nobel's
dynamite in
the Transvaal
in 1893. burg, you don't know whether that would leave them a profit or not ?—That ` before my time.

I suppose you are aware of the fact that Nobel's people sold dynamite here 75s. a case, and paid the Government 37s. 6d. duty ?—At what time was that ?

That was in November, 1893.—I don't know about those times.

Composition of
" g ü h r im-
pregné." and
dynamite.

Mr. Brochon.

What is the composition of gühr impregné ?—Gühr is kiesel gühr and nit glycerine.

What proportion of nitro-glycerine ?—It differs materially from 65 to 75 per ce

What is the composition of the dynamite No. 1 ?—Dynamite No. 1 is nit glycerine and gühr—75 per cent. and 25 per cent.

And No. 2 ?—No. 2 consists of nitro-glycerine, kiesel gühr, nitrate of soda, cha ochre. I think that is all.

What quantity of nitro-glycerine ?—If I am not mistaken it is about 60 per ce —between 58 and 60 per cent.

And of kiesel gühr what is the proportion ?—That depends upon the nitrate

Composition of
gelatine. of soda, ochre, and all those things you mix together.

Yes, but how much kiesel gühr ?—I should say about 34 per cent.

What is the proportion of nitro-glycerine in blasting gelatine ?—We make between 91 and 93.

Importation of
gelatine mat-
erials. By these figures we see it is very easy for you to make dynamite 1 and 2 you have gühr impregné ?—I don't deny it.

Do you receive the gelatine all ready as gelatine ?—No, we receive it in blocks

Do you take this nitro-glycerine off your gühr impregné, or receive it already gelatine ?—In order to explain to you I would have to go into the whole dynam nufacture from the beginning. I am not up in the technical manufacture of namite. I know, of course, a good deal about it. The only thing I can tell you is .t there are a lot of things in making dynamite, which people have hardly any a about.

I only ask you from where you take the gelatine that is in the nitro-glycerine?— ose 466,000 cases ? They served to manufacture the dynamite here.

So all those 466,000 cases are gühr impregné ?—That I cannot say.

What are you making now at the factory—only dynamite, or gelatine too ?—We *Articles made at* ke all sorts of dynamite. *dynamite factory.*

They are really manufacturing blasting gelatine at the factory—nitro-glycerine d everything ?—Yes.

In your statement you seem to consider it impossible that dynamite can be *European prices* livered at 43s. Other witnesses have said that they are quite certain it can ; but *of dynamite.* you think it possible to do so without the dynamite being of an inferior quality?— 1ave said already that I do not know anything about European prices.

Do you think there can be much difference in two kinds of dynamite which only *Composition and* rry 75 per cent. of nitro-glycerine ?—Yes ; there can be some difference. *quality of dynamite.*

Do you think nitro-glycerine could make a great difference in the cost price ?—It not exactly the quality of nitro-glycerine, but it is the material you put into it.

We will take dynamite No. 1 ; with 75 per cent. of nitro-glycerine, do you use esel gühr ?—Not always.

You would have to have good kiesel gühr to carry 75 per cent. of nitro-glycerine, all the difference is in the nitro-glycerine?—That is where I don't agree with you.

Why ?—Because you can use as an absorbent material—say, wood, meal, nitrate soda.

I don't admit that this can carry 75 per cent. of nitro-glycerine.—I quite agree th you.

So that all the difference in the price must arise in the quality of nitro-ycerine ?—Yes.

How much water can nitro-glycerine carry ?—There you are going into technical estions again.

We can say that the dynamite offered in Hamburg at £43 per ton and £1 1s. 6d. r case, when it contains 75 per cent. of nitro-glycerine, must be equivalent to obel's dynamite. Do you admit that ?—I admit what you say, but I don't know tything about European prices.

You admit that the dynamite containing an average of 75 per cent. of nitro-ycerine is good dynamite ?—Yes.

Mr. *Albu.*

You have been a director of this company for some time, have you not?—Since ovember, 1895.

Have you acted in a like capacity for Nobel's in any other country ?—Not in the *Mr. Phillip and* me capacity. *Nobel's.*

But you have been connected with the dynamite business for a good many ars ?—Oh, yes.

I gather that from the ability with which you give prices in Australian rts, in British India, in the Cape Colony, in Rhodesia, and in Natal. But is somewhat strange, with all this experience, that you could be totally norant of the prices which are ruling in England and France. You simply deny l knowledge of that?—I don't see the connection of one point with the other.

You see, it is strange that we should know the prices at which it is sold at ustralian ports, and you, who have been connected with the dynamite business for so many years, don't know : your father is chairman of Nobel's Trust, and you, as director of Nobel's Trust, should not know the price at which dynamite is sold England or on the Continent. Of course, I only express my surprise at this ; I do expect you to know.—First of all, if my father is a director of the Nobel Tr Company that does not imply that I know anything about it. Consequently, you a me whether I had any connection with the Nobel Dynamite Trust for a long peric You don't ask me in what capacity. I have been acting as agent for the Nobel Dyn mite Trust Company in Mexico, and, as agent, I have no right to enquire about t cost price. The only thing I know, as agent, is the selling price.

How do you know the selling price in Australia and British India ? It is stran you do not know it in Austria and Germany. I cannot help being astonished at it. In that case you may be surprised that I don't know the price in Holland, Ind China, and Japan.

In China, no ; but wherever Nobel's Trust is I should expect you to know t prices ruling there.—If I had known you would want the price I would have got for you.

I know the price, and I always make it my business, as a purchaser, to kno what an article costs.—It is my business to sell, not to buy.

But surely, as a director of Nobel's Agency here, and knowing the grievances the mining industry, and knowing the clamour for cheaper dynamite, you hav inquired of Nobel's : " What are you selling dynamite for at Home ? "—Allow me express my surprise, Mr. Albu, that you should make such a remark. You know have got a contract in this country to sell at a certain price, and whether you hav got grievances or not is no business of mine.

And you, as supplier of an article, make no attempt to find out whether it is or not.—You may tell me what you like ; I stick to my contract.

Quite so. Will you contradict me when I say that dynamite is sold at De Beer Kimberley, not for 72s. 6d. but 57s. 6d. —Yes, I flatly contradict you. Dynamite sold to De Beers at 65s.

Under the new contract it is 57s. 6d And my authority for my statement Mr. Francis Oates, director of the De Beers Company.—You had better call him witness.

I am chairman of a diamond mining company in Kimberley. I don't buy m dynamite from Nobel's " ring ;" I buy it in France, and get it delivered on my min in Kimberley at 55s. per case.—What quality ?

Seventy per cent.—I have been talking about No. 1.

That is 75 per cent. Out of that 55s. the Cape Government get 12s. 6d. dut against the magnificent sum which the Transvaal Government receives. I get delivered in any quantity I like, and the quantity used by the company of which am chairman, is 300 cases a year. Another addition is the heavy rail charges t Kimberley mentioned by Mr. Middelberg. Take off the 12s. 6d. the Government get and it would cost the company of which I am chairman 42s. 6d. per case.—I can onl compliment the company on having a chairman like you.

What we want is that our shareholders should have the money they hav invested used to the best advantage.—To the detriment of the dynamite company the Transvaal.

I don't wish to tell you at the present moment to whose detriment.—You a always accusing this company.

I am simply going to prove that we are paying too much for dynamite.

Chairman.

You must not have arguments.

Mr. *Albu.*

My idea is to prove that we have paid too much for dynamite, and in trying to Cornish and former Transvaal prices for dynamite. this I shall only adopt fair means. Mr. Francis Oates, who is a director of the Beers Company, was director of a dynamite factory in Cornwall called the Cosmos, ch sold dynamite delivered on the mines in Cornwall at 30s. per case. We have, her, bought dynamite three or four years ago, at the time the Government gave ous merchants permits here, as low as 75s. a case, Government receiving, I think, per case duty. Isn't that so?—I don't know.

You stated this morning that from 1894 to 1896 you, or the Government, Importation of dynamite and gelatine materials. orted 460,000 cases of material. You don't mean machinery for the erection of dynamite factory, do you?—I stated quite clearly gühr impregné.

How is that possible? We only use the gühr impregné dynamite to about the nt of 10 per cent. We mostly use here blasting gelatine, which has as an absorbent el gühr. Now, if you have imported 460,000 cases of kiesel gühr impregné, how ny cases of blasting gelatine have you imported?—I have replied to Mr. Hay and Mr. Brochon. I said that gühr impregné and blasting gelatine were both included, latter in lumps.

What process do these lumps undergo after you receive them, to make them ready Preparation of imported dynamite and gelatine materials at factory. use on the mines?—The best way to explain it would be to do as I have said. I ll be pleased if the Commission comes to the factory, and if they do that I will w you. Of course, I could give you a very long explanation now.

I don't want a technical explanation. What I wish to arrive at is whether sting gelatine, imported in lumps, is ready prepared for use—in a word, all the k you do here is to make cartridges of it?—That is where you are mistaken.

And your gühr impregné is dynamite, and all you do is to make cartridges of it? f you say so.

It is a well-known fact. What inducements did you hold out to the Government The dynamite concession. the time they gave you this concession?—I think that is a trying question.

I only want to know what *quid pro quo* you gave the Government for the conion.—What do you mean?

The Netherlands Railway, for instance, has a concession to build railways. What e you done, or what are you doing?—If you have read my statement——

Yes, I have.—I think I said quite plainly that since the formation of the comy took place, it has erected this factory in this republic.

You cannot tell me what are the manufactured prices of dynamite at Home. If Prices of manufactured dynamite in Europe and the Transvaal. u don't wish to answer me, don't. I refer to dynamite, 75 per cent.—I don't know.

Can you tell me what it is here?—I could.

Of course, I cannot expect you to.—Certainly not.

Have you found the necessary ingredients in this country that you can use for Dynamite ingredients—where found. namite?—Oh, yes; I have found sulphur.

Have you found saltpetre?—Yes, there is some saltpetre, and kiesel gühr also.

I mean, have you found any quantities that would justify your using them in the nufacture of dynamite?—Yes, sulphur.

How much have you found already, may I ask?—Of course, I cannot tell to a tainty, but I know that sulphur was found in sufficient quantities for us to use it.

To make 1,000 or 2,000 cases?—Yes.

I must tell you that answer is very trying to me. I want to put a practical estion. Have you found sulphur and saltpetre in this country in sufficient antities to make 5,000 cases in the month?—I have found sufficient sulphur in is country to make about 200,000 cases in the year.

Why don't you make them then ?—Who tells you I don't ?

I tell you. You have told us you imported 466,000 cases in 1894 and 1896.—are now in 1897.

I am sorry if I have to contradict you. You cannot have found sulphur in country, or saltpetre, in sufficient quantities to make 200,000 cases a year. Befor go any further, Mr. Vorstman is the purchaser of the dynamite ?—He is the Gove ment's agent.

He is not here ?—No.

Is he a director of the dynamite company ?—Yes.

Who is his alternate ?—Mr. Jorissen.

That is the gentleman close by you who is prompting you ?—That is the gen man, but that he is prompting me I do not know.

Capitalisation of
the South Af-
rican Explos-
ives Company. The capital of the dynamite company is £450,000 ?—Yes.

What portion of this was fully paid up ?—I can tell you, but I do not see w this has got to do with the case.

I am sorry to see you cannot see it. I only ask the question in the same way members of the Commission asked how much was paid for machinery.—If you dra comparison——

No, no, I wish I could; I wish mining was as profitable as dynamite. Can y tell me what the paid up-capital was ?—No, I won't tell you that either.

What was the consumption of explosives in the Transvaal in March ?—It v about 16,000 cases.

Profit and divi-
dend for 1895
of South Afric-
an Explosives
Company. You say your company is only making eight per cent ?—I said, up to 1895 have distributed a dividend of eight per cent.

May I ask, according to the balance of 1896, what your profit was ?—The bala sheet is not out yet.

It is a similar case to the Netherlands railway.—If you read the *Staatscoura* you would see that the general meeting of this company will be held on the 28 June, and on the 29th June I will be most happy to tell you what the company going to pay in dividends.

The Government
agent and the
purchase of dy-
namite. Your company does not send orders Home to Nobel's ?—No.

And you don't make remittances in payment ?—It is the Government's agent w does it.

Now, the new contract says: "The said company from the date of its formati will take the place of the said L. G. Vorstman in this contract, and will carry out his obligations as regards the Government in connection therewith." From this appears that Mr. Vorstman has nothing more to do with it ?—You can take it as y like. I maintain what I say.

This is in the *Government Gazette*, signed by both the State Secretary and N Vorstman. How can you explain this article ?—I cannot explain it at all. I mainta Mr. Vorstman is the Government's agent. You have been asking me about the buyi of material and importing of material, and I maintain that the Government, throu their agent, Mr. Vorstman, do it.

The Government
royalty on dy-
namite. You said in your statement that the Government received in 1896, £44,000 royalty ? Now, if you have not published your balance sheet, and do not know wh the profit is approximately, how can the Government receive £44,000 as royalty ? Because we pay royalty every three months. I do not know what that has got to with the question.

You mean the duty of 5s. per case ?—I mean royalty.

There is a difference between royalty and import duty. What do you call th per case that the Government magnanimously receives ? The Cape Government ‚eives 12s. 6d., and they call it duty.—I think the Cape Colony charges 2s. 1d.

That is for transit. Do you call that 5s. royalty ?—If the Government imports it ‚annot call it duty.

Then the Government gets no duty on dynamite ?—The Government imports it.

Is that royalty in order to permit the Government of the Transvaal to import),000 cases ?—I do not know what the object is.

Ah, now, you do know. It reads very peculiarly by talking about your profits. I your profits are only 8 per cent. for 1895, but if this agency company were to float ‚ther little agency company they could make the profit show two per cent. or none ‚all.—That is a very good idea.

We would do very well together; only I would not get anything. Now you ‚ke a point of this in your statement, that the Government's share does not seem to known. Well, it is pretty well known that the sale of explosives amounted to ‚ut 176,000 cases, and 5s. per case on that comes to about £44,000. It is known ‚y receive 5s. per case, and you most innocently say it does not seem to be known. ‚is known that the Government of the Transvaal receives a very small royalty, as ‚u call it. If the Government does not require that income, the price of explosives ‚ght to be reduced. You buy the pulp of the dynamite off Nobel's ?—No; I buy it ‚m the Government here.

The purchase of dynamite pulp

From whom does the Government buy it ?—That is no business of mine.

From whom is the stuff bought ?—Nobel's Trust Company.

Nobel's sell it to the Government, and the Government sell it to the dynamite ‚tory in Pretoria, and the dynamite factory makes its payments to Nobel's.—Well, if ‚u like it so.

The Government agent sells it again to the dynamite factory; the factory makes ‚t the accounts for the gold mining companies. Now, does it not strike you that I ‚ justified in putting these questions to you, because the whole thing seems to be ‚volved.—What that has got to do with your grievances I do not see.

No, no; we have no grievances. Nobel's have a large interest in the dynamite ‚tory of the Transvaal ?—I do not think I am quite entitled to reply to that ‚estion. Are you a shareholder in our company ?

Connection of Nobel's and the Transvaal dynamite factory

I sincerely regret I am not.—In that case I am not going to give you any ‚formation.

It has been proved beyond any doubt that Nobel's has underwritten 220,000 ‚lly paid-up shares of £1.—Have you got it officially ?

Yes.—May I ask where you got it from ?

Your own people have supplied these figures.—Before you proceed, as long as ‚u do not say whether it is official or where you got your information from, I ‚nnot vouch for all the figures you are going to quote.

The capital of the company is £450,000, 220,000 shares were fully paid up by ‚bel's, and there remained 230,000 shares. Can you tell me how your company ‚alt with these 230,000 shares ? I do not wish to pry into your company's affairs, ‚t it would help us very much if you answer my question.—I think it is unfair on ‚ur part to examine me, when I have never had a chance to examine you on the ‚ivate affairs of your companies.

Partition of the shares of the South African Explosives Company.

I have sat in the witness chair for two days, and the members of the Commission ‚amined me. I want to show you what a funny business it seems to laymen like ‚rselves. Your dynamite factory is nothing else but an offspring of Nobel's ‚mpany. So that Nobel's sells dynamite to the Government, the Government sells ‚ the dynamite factory, practically selling it back again to Nobel's; so that Nobel's

Nobel's and the South African Explosives Company

sells to Nobel's, and they try to make a profit on both sides.—If you want to prove to the Commission you don't require me.

If you do not wish to be questioned, I will give it up, and there was no necessi for your appearing here.—I certainly did not appear to tell you all the ins and ou of the company.

That I believe. I think the Commission kindly appointed me to try and fi out.—I wish to give all information to the Government.

If you give it to the Commision you give it to the Government. You wo answer who received the 230,000 shares ?—I am not entitled to tell it.

Do all these shares rank equally ?—Yes.

For voting purposes ?—More or less. There is a small difference.

Is it not a fact that Nobel's have the controlling power in your company ?—cannot reply to that question.

Have you any reason to believe that Nobel's are not interested in your facto here ?—I have no reason to believe one thing or the other.

Cost of erecting dynamite factory. May I ask you what this factory cost at Modderfontein ?—We have spent abou £600,000 on it.

Is that on building; or does that include the ten months of material on hand ?-Only the buildings.

I think you said £900,000 included ten months' material; was it not so ?—I sa our capital outlay on the factory alone, without stock, is about £600,000.

Quite so. On page four, the Government agent informed the Commission of th Raad that the cost of the factory to date, including the supply of material for te Cost of materials for dynamite. months, was £900,000. If the building cost you £600,000, as you say, then we ma reasonably conclude that ten months' supply cost you £300,000 ?—It all depends o what you call stock.

Would you call stock the materials for ten months ? I would call it material fo ten months' supply of dynamite. I would call it gühr impregné, or blasting gelatin in lump.—That is where you are mistaken. In this report, by material is meant sal petre, sulphur, glycerine, and timber.

That is not alone gühr impregné. That is material for ten months. That is th article for which we would have to pay £800,000 or £900,000.—If you want to bu the factory.

No, I don't want to buy the factory. I mean the stock of materials in your book for ten months' supply. Ten months' supply of dynamite to the mining industr amounts to about that. Is that saltpetre and sulphur found in the Transvaal, or im ported ?—Not yet.

Oh, it will be found, but it has not been found yet ?—You asked me whether thi was sulphur found in the Transvaal, and I say it has not yet been found.

No, it is imported stuff ?—Yes.

Has the local company—your company—ever protested against the high price charged by Nobel's Trust ? Have you ever protested against those prices ?—We hav not got anything to do with it.

Oh, it is the Government that buys it ?—That is what I said before.

Transvaal Government buys its dynamite materials of Nobel's. Have you reported the matter to the Government, and told the Government tha they are paying too high a price to Nobel's Trust ?—No.

You have not. Is the Government bound to buy this stuff from Nobel's ?-Certainly not. They can buy it wherever they like.

But you are bound to buy it from the Government ?—Yes, according to contrac

If you were not compelled, according to contract, to buy your material from th

ernment, could you manufacture dynamite cheaper here ?—That is a question I
⸗ not gone into.

It has not interested you. You don't find it necessary to see whether you could The South African Explosives
Company and
the mining in-
dustry.
⸗to the mining industry the same article at a cheaper rate ?—The mining industry
dealt very kindly with us up to the present. We would have done anything for
⸗.

In which way has the mining industry treated you badly ?—"Kindly " was the
⸗d I used.

Oh, kindly! But that is a paradox.—You perfectly understand that the mining
⸗stry has been fighting this company from the beginning.

No, I beg to differ from you.—Since I have been in this country they have been.

And you think that is the reason you must get your pound of flesh ?—Well, that
⸗t quite correct, because you know perfectly well we are entitled, according to our
⸗ract, to charge 95s. per case of dynamite No. 1, and we only charge 85s.

May I ask why is this kindness done ?—To tell you frankly, that is no business
⸗ours. That is a question for us to decide. I only want to mention we have done
⸗e for the mining industry than they have done for us.

But I am surprised. You are a director of the dynamite factory ; and you com-
⸗n of the small profits you are making.—I beg your pardon. I never complained
⸗he small profit.

But I beg your pardon—

Chairman.

I have already made the remark that Mr. Albu's questions, and Mr. Phillip's Mr. Albu's inter-
rogation of Mr.
Phillip.
⸗ies do not bring us an inch further in the direction of solving the question. I
⸗k it is better for Mr. Albu to confine himself to the case itself. Our only object
⸗ find out whether dynamite can be supplied here cheaper, and any questions that
⸗put as to the factory here, might be whether, under the present contract, there is a
⸗ibility of getting a reduction from the factory ; what their mode of importation
⸗ what is the mode of working or preparing the stuff here ; what is the consumption
⸗uired ; does the factory supply the demand ; is the dynamite delivered of good
⸗lity. If, through the said means, it can be shown that the dynamite can be
⸗vered here cheaper, everybody will agree that it is not a question for us to solve
⸗e. What is to be done in future with the company and the factory will be dealt
⸗h in committee before we make our report to the Government. I think Mr. Albu
⸗ntering upon matters which only concern the company themselves. Supposing
⸗ry question is answered which Mr. Albu has asked, it does not help us a bit further.

Mr. Albu.

Well, Mr. Phillip, you have heard the statements made by various witnesses as European prices
of dynamite.
⸗he price of dynamite at Home, offers received, and so forth. You would say, of
⸗rse, it is impossible ; these gentlemen are mistaken ; or what would you answer ?—
⸗at I have said before : I don't know anything about European prices.

You only know about the prices in Australia, British India, and Rhodesia. I
⸗ly don't know what more questions I can ask you. Mr. Chairman, it is impossible
⸗ou stop me. Statements have been made to the Commission by so many witnesses
⸗t dynamite can be imported cheaper. I can show to the Commission that a certain
⸗pany, of which I am chairman, paid 55s. per case, and paid to the Government
⸗ 6d. duty, so it would be a fallacy on my part, or on the Commission's part, to try
⸗elicit a statement from Mr. Phillip whether dynamite can be made cheaper, or
⸗orted cheaper than he does it. He would say no ; his article is the cheapest.

z

Chairman.

It is a question for the Commission to decide later on. It is not for us to sa[y]
the present moment what we can exact, or what we cannot exact. The Commiss[ion]
must decide in committee.

Mr. Albu.

The task, I mean, is quite useless, because I do not expect for one moment
Phillip will prove to me he can import dynamite at 35s. per case.

Mr. Smit.

To come to conclusions can only be done by the Commission, when they are
committee.

Mr. Albu.

But, Mr. Chairman, is it not necessary for me to elicit certain facts, so that
members of the Commission can weigh the various questions and answers, and ded[uce]
from them their conclusions.

Mr. Smit.

I don't object to your questions. They are very good, but no argument sho[uld]
follow. The time has not come for argument yet.

Mr. Albu.

The South African Explosives Company and the cost of dynamite materials.

There is one question as to the royalty to Government. This is 5s. per c[ase.]
You say in your statement, Mr. Phillip, with regard to the profit, " The balance-sh[eet]
for 1895 produced a dividend of 8 per cent. per annum, so that the profits of our co[m-]
pany cannot be so abnormal as people try to make out." You see this is a di[rect]
accusation against the people who try to make out that they are paying too much [for]
their dynamite. You tell us, in fact, this deplorable state of things exists, that [you]
only make 8 per cent. for 1895, and yet you, as a director, have not tried to induce [the]
Government to buy the supply elsewhere. It is quite possible. As a director, wo[uld]
you not try to induce the people who supply you with the ingredients to buy them [in]
a cheaper market so that you might increase your dividends or meet your custom[ers]
by a reduction of price ?—You know perfectly well dynamite is not like sugar-ca[ne]
for instance. If you want a good quality of dynamite you must get it at the b[est]
place. That is the case with us.

And Nobel's is the best place ?—As far as I know.

And the cheapest place ?—I tell you that is no business of mine.

I ask you as a director of the dynamite factory. I know it is no business [of]
yours.—I am a director of the Dynamite Company in the Transvaal.

American dynamite.

You say you bought American dynamite in 1894 ?—Yes.

And it resulted in a complete failure ?—Yes.

May I ask where the test was made ?—At our factory.

At your factory. But you did not test it in the mines here ?—It was too danger[ous]
to send it out of the factory; the nitro-glycerine was exuding.

America is a big mining country too, is it not ?—I think so.

Quartz mines mostly ? And they get along with their dynamite, don't they [?]
They have to, because they have got such heavy protective duty, nobody else can [sell]
their's in there.

But they manufacture their dynamite themselves ?—If they cannot import [it]
they have to make it.

They have got large saltpetre beds, have they not? Where do they get their ~~ phur from?—I have never been in the States.

You acted in a like capacity as you do here in Mexico?—No; I told you no. I ~~ ve told you I have been an agent in Mexico.

A dynamite agent?—Yes, in Mexico.

And here in what capacity do you act?—Here I am director of the company ~~ led the South African Fabrieken.

You deny that dynamite is supplied to De Beers at 57s. 6d.?—I have said so.

Price of dynamite at De Beers.

If I were to bring it to you in writing from De Beers Company, would you still ~~ tradict it?—I think we can get along much better if you explain for what kind of ~~ namite they pay that price.

It is for 75 per cent. dynamite.—Then the only thing I can say is that I am very ~~ dly informed.

And the directors of De Beers told me they could get it for less.—All you people ~~ Johannesburg say the same thing.

Is it not sufficient if we get it for 37s. 6d., and pay the Government 12s. 6d.? We ~~ uld be quite content if we get it even down so far.—As the Chairman said, that is ~~ question for the Commission to resolve.

Well, I thought you might know these things.—According to my contract, I can ~~ arge up to that price. If I do that, no one can blame me.

The Government dynamite contract.

Of course not. But the concession was granted on the condition that you ~~ anufacture the dynamite here?—That is what we do.

~~ at is what you don't do.—How not? Have you read the contract I made with the ~~ vernment?

Who has got it—Mr. Vorstman or yourself?—Mr. Vorstman got the contract.

To manufacture or to sell?—That is where the point comes in. The contract ~~ as "for the carrying out of the State monopoly for the making, selling, negotiating ~~ , and the importation and exportation of powder, ammunition, dynamite, and all ~~ her explosives." This contract was transferred to the company now existing.

Before Mr. Vorstman had this contract who had it?—I don't know. That is not ~~ question for me.

Mr. Vorstman got this contract?—

Chairman.

We have got nothing to do with who had the contract before the present ~~ ntract.—This contract was transferred to the present company for the execution of ~~ e State monopoly for the manufacture and selling of explosives here, and the ~~ tying was given to the Government's agent, Mr. Vorstman.

Mr. Vorstman, Government buyer.

Mr. Albu.

The buying?—Yes. It was given to Mr. Vorstman, and he transferred it to the ~~ mpany.

Now, you state that your factory is large enough to manufacture 80,000 cases a ~~ ear?—And more.

Quantity of dynamite manufactured per annum.

Since when has the factory been completed?—We commenced the factory in ~~ ctober, 1896.

How much have you manufactured since October, 1896?—About 40,000 cases.

And the requirements would be about 136,000. And the gühr impregné?—We ~~ ve manufactured out of our own nitro-glycerine we make here.

Quantity of dynamite required annually Manufacture of dynamite materials in Transvaal.

Do you make the sulphuric acid here?—Everything. We make the nitric acid, ~~ e nitro-glycerine, the dynamite, and blasting gelatine here.

Importation of dynamite materials.
You make the nitro-glycerine and sulphuric acid here. You import sulphur? Yes.

You import the saltpetre?—Yes.

You import the glycerine?—Yes.

You import the gühr?—Yes.

You import the cotton?—Yes.

Then, what on earth do you make here?—I make the dynamite.

Now, you admit you import all these things. You have to pay freight on sulphur, on saltpetre, on glycerine, on gühr, and on the cotton. You have to pay your workmen about three or four times as much as you pay them at Home. Now you import all these articles. Where does the advantage come in to the country. What advantage has the country got?—What is the advantage to a country of an industry?

We don't want to go in for political economy. You might answer the question. Have not engineering firms the same right to say that they manufacture engines here. They import all the parts, and only put them together here. What I wish to show the Commission is that, with the very best intentions, what you have executed lately, of making 40,000 cases, surely must have been made at a much higher cost than that

Comparative expense of importing and manufacturing dynamite.
at which you could import them? May I ask you what it costs to make blasting gelatine here?—Well, I am certainly not going to reply to that. I am not going to ask you what your cost price is, if you manufactured anything here.

But if someone has got to buy an article, he will know what it costs at home and here. I assert that dynamite No. 1A, 75 per cent., costs at the factory at Home, 18s. 6d. per case.—May I ask you what you know about dynamite.

Well, I have never manufactured any.—Because you are talking of dynamite No. 1 and No. 1A.

I am talking of No. 1.—Then you must not talk of No. 1A.

I mean 75 per cent. dynamite, costing 18s. 6d. at Home. I say if you manufacture it here it costs you over 60s. Blasting gelatine costs at Home 50 per cent. more than

Comparative expense of importing and manufacturing gelatine.
the manufacture of 75 per cent. dynamite, and it will cost you more than 50 per cent. here to manufacture gelatine. But you say you have not manufactured blasting gelatine here?—Oh yes; we make it.

Will it surprise you to hear that one of the leading chemists here says that, with the appliances which you have got at the factory, it is absolutely impossible to make blasting gelatine here at anything like a reasonable price?—I suppose that is one of the chemists we discharged.

That must have been a misleading chemist. I am speaking of a leading chemist —Is he an expert in dynamite?

Yes, he is.—Would you mind telling me his name?

I don't know whether I am at liberty to tell you his name.—In those circumstances, I maintain he does not know much about dynamite.

But it appeals to the common-sense of everybody. You have to import all the ingredients and all your workmen, so that it must cost you very much more than they

Manufacture of powder by South African Explosives Company.
can make it for at Home. You also manufacture powder?—Yes.

In large quantities?—It depends on what you call large quantities.

Is there any sale for powder in this country?—What sort of powder do you mean?

Gunpowder.—There is a pretty good demand for it.

Do you supply the Transvaal Government with gunpowder?—Yes; I do.

Why is it then that they import all their cartridges?—You had better ask the Government.

They cannot make cartridges here, can they ?—Well, I make them.

Manufacture of cartridges by South African Explosives Company.

You import detonators ?—Well, you can't call them detonators. You mean the
?

Yes. And you import the bullets ?—Sometimes.

Then you fill them with powder ?—That is the principal part of it.

Then why does not the Government buy their supply off you ?—You had better
the Government.

It is strange to say these cartridges are manufactured here.

Chairman.

That has nothing to do with the mining industry.

Mr. Albu.

Where do you procure your raw material for powder ?—Partly in this country and
ly elsewhere.

Manufacture and importation of materials for powder.

Which Transvaal product do you use for the powder ?—Charcoal. We make it
selves.

Do you sell your cartridges to the burghers ?—I do.

Chairman.

That has nothing to do with the mining community.

Mr. Albu.

It affects the question so much that when the concession was granted it was
ated out what enormous advantages they would have through it in the case of war.
w we find the Government is even importing powder too.

Chairman.

I suppose the Government has its own wise reasons for that.

Mr. Albu.

Oh, yes! You are the sole agent for selling detonators ?—Yes.

The price of detonators.

You cannot tell what they cost in Europe ? We pay 4s. a case.—No.

When we had an open market for detonators we paid 3s.—I don't know the price
cannot tell you.

Can you tell us why Lewis and Marks draw this royalty on dynamite ?—I think
had better ask Lewis and Marks about it.

I know I should get the information from them, but I thought you might know
a director of the dynamite company.—I am a director of the present dynamite
pany.

Chairman.

The question of cheap dynamite is considered by the mines to be a vital question,
therefore we must try and find out as much as possible, to see how far it is possible
meet the mines and give them cheap dynamite. Several questions Mr. Albu put to
you have not replied to. In several cases you have said that the case rests with
Government. I have myself found that Mr. Albu has, perhaps, put some questions
you, which you were under no obligation to reply to. But there is one question
n which I want to have an answer from you. You say the Government purchased,
not the company. The Government of course have a person who conducts the

Mr. Phillip's replies to Indus trial Commis sion.

sale for them, though I thought it was done through the company, and since you
a director of the company I thought that you were the person to give us
information on this point. Now I only want to know from you who is the per
who buys for the Government ?—It is the Government agent, Mr. Vorstman.

So consequently I must draw the deduction that the company has not yet ta
the position that Mr. Vorstman had in the original contract ?—It is so difficul
explain. I know that Mr. Vorstman has always been entrusted with the buying
the material. Of course it is practically the company, so there is some difference,
how this originated I really cannot say. Mr. Vorstman is the Government agent
buying.

Then you further said that you could not state the price in Europe, and at w
price it could be delivered here. It does not concern you very much, because, as lo
as you remain within the terms of your contract you consider you have fulfilled y
obligations. In the contract there is a maximum price of 95s. per case, and if you
at 85s. you mean you are within the boundaries of your contract ? I must say on t
point that I am astonished that the company here, which has to import, is not aw
of the price at the place from whence it imports dynamite. The contract does
fix a minimum price, and you will agree if you sell at a lower price, and still make
same profit as at present, that will then be in favour of the consumer. And I h
always thought that any man of business should study the interests of the consum
I, therefore, think that you ought to be cognisant—although you buy for
Government—that you at any time can advise the Government when the Governm
ask for advice, and I hope you will still be able to do it when called upon, and to
whether you can deliver it cheaper here and sell it cheaper, for against you we h
got very strong evidence from the other side, which I must take to be true, which s
dynamite can be landed here for so much less than at present.—May I make
remark. It must not be lost sight of that the Government is importing for us, a
during the time we had to build factories, and the contract stipulates that as soon
the factories are ready and cover the whole of the requirements of the country, t
the importation would stop, except in case of accidents which are beyond our contr
That is the reason why the company has not fixed their attention on the Europe
price so much. Its importation period will soon be ended, and then all the dynam
or explosives will be made in this country.

That does not throw light on the case from my point of view. In October, 18
your factory was finished, and you say you now make dynamite here ; I now und
stand from you that the time will arrive that the importation of the materials fr
which dynamite is manufactured will stop.—Yes, and I think I can promise in abc
a year or a year and a half, if the consumption remains as it is to-day, I will be a
to produce the whole requirements of the country.

By material found in the country ?—Ah, that is another question.

That is the point I put to you. If all the material has to be imported it does
bring us any further ?—As soon as I am able to produce the whole requirements of t
country, then gühr impregné does not play any part in the importation. Then the on
thing I will import will be saltpetre, sulphur, glycerine, a little gühr, and a few artic
which I cannot find in this country in sufficient quantities. I am making experimen
and I think I can get the whole of the sulphur in the country. Of course I mu
import a certain quantity of sulphur to have a reserve. As to saltpetre, I cannot fi
sufficient quantities in this country.

To come back to the question with reference to the importation of the materi
required for dynamite. Is the company bound to buy that stuff from Nobel's, or a

free to buy it from any other manufacturer?—I suppose you refer to the raw material?

Yes, the 466,000 cases.—That, of course, the Government buys. In connection therewith, I would like to say, and could not before explain, or did not recollect at the moment, how it was that Mr. Vorstman was Government agent for buying these raw materials. I have remembered since that there exists a letter from the Government appointing Mr. Vorstman and Mr. Klimke together as agents to buy the raw materials. I cannot remember the date. It must have been before the time I became a director of the company.

So you cannot answer the question?—No.

Can you tell how many cases of dynamite were manufactured at the factory out of the 466,000 cases of raw material?—I find that during the period from June, 1894 October, 1896, we sold 340,000 cases.

Can you state the cost price of one of those 466,000 cases?—Well, of course the Government keeps the invoices, and I cannot tell.

You are wrong there, Mr. Phillip. The Government does not buy and does not sell. The Government have the right to do so, but they do it through other people. The Government buy nothing, sell nothing, and keep no books.—I really do not know the cost price.

I have no more questions to put, but I wish to point out that in dealing with this question you must not lose sight of several facts—in the first place, that it is to the interest of the country certainly to keep manufactories going here. The dynamite factory, for its origin and existence, depends upon the mining industry, and so we have to try to regulate it in such a manner that through the existence of the dynamite factory in our country the mining industry may not be injured, but should be benefited. And in this case you must keep the interests of the company itself in view; and if now it really appears to us that it may be through the fault on the part of the Government in granting such a concession, or it may be the fault of the company that they cannot carry out the concession on a cheaper basis, then it is our duty to try that the Government or company should find a way by which dynamite can be delivered cheaper at the mines here?—May I add that I can ask the Government to give all the prices required. I have not got them.

Mr. Brakhan.

What commission does Mr. Lippert draw on detonators?—I think it is 5 per cent. Is it not 7 per cent.?—It may be 7. I am not quite certain.

Do you manufacture detonators in the Transvaal?—No. We have made a proposition to the Government, but we have found that the climatic conditions of this country would render the manufacture of detonators too dangerous.

Then you import all the supplies of detonators?—No, I don't import them.

Well, who imports them?—The company imports, but not all supplies. There were permits given out some time ago by the Government. It must be about three years ago, and on these permits they are still importing detonators into this country. That is, merchants are importing.

Now, what do detonators cost in quantities in Europe?—I really cannot tell you. I mean I did not prepare myself for detonators in the least.

Well, it goes very closely hand-in-hand with dynamite?—In some respects it does; in others it does not.

What is your selling price here for No. 6 detonators?—I can get you these figures in the afternoon.

Marginal notes:

Mr. Vorstman and the State Mining Engineer the Government Agents.

Quantity of dynamite manufactured from imported materials, from June, 1894, to October, 1896.

The dynamite factory and the mining industry.

Mr. Lippert's commission on detonators.

Manufacture of detonators.

Importation of detonators.

Price of detonators.

Is it not 4s? That is what I gather from an account I saw.—I have not got t
figures.

If the market was open, as it was formerly, we could buy detonators at 3s., No.
and that has no doubt left a good profit to the merchant. In that case the mini
industry would save on detonators alone £72,000 a year?—The only thing I can s:
is that this company does not sell all the requirements of detonators for the reason
explained, so in accusing the company of charging too much for detonators I do
think there is much foundation for that. We have tried to stop the permit syste
The permits are valid as long as the total amount for which the permit is given is n
written off. Under the permit they are allowed to import so many cases. Eve
time the cases are imported they are written off, and until the whole amount
written off the permit holders are still allowed to import.

But the biggest quantity is supplied by the company?—I am sorry to say no.
don't think so. I have not got the figures of the detonators supplied during 189
but I can give you them in the afternoon.

European prices of dynamite.   I say from the evidence brought before the Commission as to dynamite suppli
to De Beers, that the price paid leaves a large profit in Europe. Yet there is :
doubt that this surplus might be materially increased if there was free trade :
dynamite?—You will get all the information from the Government as soon as tl
Commission, which has been appointed to investigate specially this question, ha
handed in their report.

Personally, I cannot help saying that I am very surprised that the compan
should not be able to give to the Commission the cost price which they, in terms (
the contract with the Government, pay in Europe for the dynamite which the
import, and for the raw material.—All the members of the Commission hav
expressed their surprise that I don't know the European price. I have given you
declaration under oath, and I am sorry to say I don't know the European price.

Mr. *Pierce.*

Price of imported raw materials for dynamite.   Can you tell the price at which the Government agent brings in the ra
material here?—The Government agent imports the materials for the Governmen
He keeps all the invoices, with freight expenses, etc. The invoices he hands in to tl
Government.

Then the Government hands over the stuff to you as it arrives?—Yes.

The Government and the South African Explosives Company   You get a certain amount of raw material at the factory. Whom do you pay fo
that?—According to the contract we have to hand in the product of the sales to tl
Government. We do not pay for the raw material delivered to us by the Governmer
agent. The product of the sales is handed to the Government, who retains the origin:
amount and returns us our expenses, and so on. It is mentioned in the contract wha
the Government retains—that is 5s. each case, and 20 per cent. of the surplus profi
while the Government relieves the agent of any special tax.

You invoice No. 1 dynamite at 85s. Do I understand you hand over the who)
of that to the Government?—Well, practically we do, and receive a certain amour
back. We do not carry that arrangement out to the letter, because it would be to
complicated. We render an account every three months of what we have sold.

Then you do not know how much you receive?—No.

The Government receive 5s. a case. Then I take it you receive the remainin
80s. per case, less, of course, the original cost of the raw material?—I refer you t
our last balance-sheet for 1895. There we have made a profit at the rate of 8 pe
cent. per annum. I may tell you that from the formation of the company in 1894 u

he end of 1895 we paid to the Government about £48,000 royalty. We made a profit of £58,000.

I want to know what the raw material costs delivered here ?—I don't get the European account. The Government tells us, through the Government agent, so many cases have arrived. The Government agent says, "You owe so much for this." *Price of imported raw materials for dynamite.*

Yes, that is what I want to know. How much do you pay for it, including freight, and everything, delivered at the factory through the Government agent ?—I have not got those figures.

You referred to the balance-sheet of 1895. Can you put in a copy of that at —Yes, but I have not got it with me. I can send it to the Commission. You have the report of the Volksraad Commission.

But we are investigating the matter now.

Mr. *Brochon.*

Where is the head office of your company ?—At Pretoria.

You do not know anything about the profits of 1896 ?—That I did not say. I said to Mr. Albu yesterday that our general shareholders' meeting will be held on the June, and on the 29th June I will be at liberty to tell you what profits we have. *Profits of South African Explosives Company for 1896.*

I do not ask what your profit was, but you have made your payments to the Government, and I do not see how the holding of your general meeting of shareholders can alter these figures ?—I do not say we are going to alter figures.

How many pounds, shillings, and pence have you given to the Government last year ?—I can send you these figures from Pretoria.

You said yesterday that you expected to find the materials in this country for the manufacture of dynamite ?—I do not remember having said that I was going to find all the raw material in this country. I have said that, according to my ideas, there is sufficient sulphur in the country, but not saltpetre. *Importation of raw materials for dynamite.*

Now you are importing all these raw materials ?—Yes.

Can you tell me what is the weight of raw material you import for making, say, a ton of dynamite ?—You know about the manufacture of dynamite. There is saltpetre, sulphur, glycerine, then you have all the bye-products, nitrate of potash, soda, chalk, ochre, and then your boxes, nails, etc.

What do you reckon, about, is the weight of these materials that go to the manufacture of a ton of dynamite— do you think it is six tons ?—For argument's sake I will accept your figure of six tons as true.

That is a very important point, because, if we make a calculation of the transport have to pay on about six tons instead of one ton of dynamite if it were imported prepared, you will see it is a wrong speculation.—If you take any dynamite industry in Europe, it has to import most of the raw materials. In England don't you import saltpetre, sulphur, and glycerine ? In Germany where do you find saltpetre ? Even in France you import glycerine. *Cost of importing materials for dynamite in bulk.*

Transport by sea is not heavy ; we all know you must import saltpetre, but what very expensive is the transport from Delagoa Bay to the factory.—Don't you say it is wrong speculation ?

In Germany and France we pay 20 and 25 sous per day to girls we employ, and pay ten times as much here ?—No, we employ kaffirs and machinery.

You told us you expected to find some sulphur here ; will you kindly tell us whether it is free sulphur, or sulphur in pyrites ?—At present it is only in pyrites ; we have got pyrites containing between 38 and 40 per cent. of sulphur. *Quality of Transvaal sulphur.*

When the pyrites contain less than 45 per cent. it is not a mercantile one ? We know that if you burn pyrites which carry less than 45 per cent. of sulphur you have

a lot of difficulties to contend with ?—I am not a chemist. I have not studied dyna[...]
technically, and I go by what my chemist tells me. Our general works' manager [...]
man of very great experience in dynamite and everything connected with it, an[...]
has told me that, as long as pyrites contain 38 or 40 per cent. of sulphur, he is q[...]
satisfied to take all the pyrites you can bring to the factory.

Have you practical proof, or is it only laboratory experiments ?—Practical p[...]
on a large scale.

Well, I am very much surprised at it. Where in this country do you get pyr[...]
with 38 per cent. of sulphur ? It must be very pure ?—Well, I get it f[...]
Johannesburg.

If you get it in Johannesburg it must be an exception, because we know v[...]
well what kind of concentrates we are treating, and we know we cannot get [...]
centrates which carry 75 per cent. of pyrites. You must have a very small quanti[...]
—We are promised any amount.

Mr. *Albu.*

You say your head office is in Pretoria ?—Yes.

Nobel's and the South African Explosives Company. You keep your share register there ?—Yes.

You do not know whether my allegations were correct, that Nobel's h[...]
220,000 shares in your company ?—I did not say whether I knew it or not, I [...]
it has nothing to do with the case, and prefer not to reply to it.

Don't you think that the deduction which people will make on hearing t[...]
answer will be very disadvantageous to yourself ?—Mr. Albu, whatever I may say [...]
this Commission, as soon as the public gets hold of it they are going to draw all s[...]
of conclusions, whether I reply or whether I do not reply. Public opinion is agai[...]
me, I know.

Transvaal sulphur. Your statement that you find sufficient sulphur in this country to make two [...]
three hundred thousand cases of dynamite, might lead people to think they [...]
listening to stories of Jules Verne.—I do not say this in order to show that I care w[...]
the public thinks of it. The question was asked, and I replied to it. If ot[...]
questions do not suit me on account of my private interest in the company, I am [...]
going to reply.

Nobel's and the South African Explosives Company. You prefer not to answer whether Nobel's are registered for a large amount [...]
shares in your property ?—About the share register I simply deny any information.

The purchase of dynamite materials. You see the question is very important. The Government agent buys [...]
material, etc., from Nobel's ; the dynamite factory buys it from the Governmer[...]
agent, who happens to be, practically speaking, the same man ; and my contention [...]
that this dynamite factory is nobody's but Nobel's, and the mining industry buys [...]
an enormously high figure. You do not know the profits for 1896, or at least y[...]
do not want to tell us ?—You are under a wrong impression. I said [...]

The Government and the South African Explosives Company. Government sold us material. I expressed myself wrongly. I think you gather [...]
from the replies I have given of how the transactions are made, that the Governm[...]
sold us the material. The Government does not make any profit on the transacti[...]
it transfers the materials to the company.

You know the whole thing would be a very good subject for Gilbert, the auth[...]
For this Commission it is sufficient to know that dynamite is sold at Home at 23s., a[...]
that this enormous interest is to pay 85s. Where does the difference go to ? Son[...]
body must make the profit.—I do not know what European prices are. I have not se[...]
the offers the mining industry has been bragging about for the last six months. I ha[...]
seen by the evidence given by Mr. Jennings the other day, he gives prices of Americ[...]
dynamite, and works it out at certain prices laid down in Johannesburg. If I take [...]

res, I arrive at a much higher figure in Johannesburg. With the incidental charges European and Rand prices for dynamite. will find it eventually will cost twice as much.

If you take the figures of Mr. Jennings, and you add your factory charges and er little leakages, then you might have a higher price than now. We recognise Nobel's Dynamite Trust and the price of dynamite. t Nobel's Trust is a very strong corporation, and it may be interesting to you if I d an extract from a letter I have received from Vienna, where the mining industry rying to get dynamite reduced, not from 85s. per case, but from 26s. per case. ey tried to get a reduction, and Nobel's ring would not entertain the proposal. The ult was that the gentlemen concerned combined to form a company and to build ir own factory. They were backed by two of the most eminent bankers on the ntinent, and it was agreed that only cost price would be charged, and that any profit sing should be returned to those interested in the mines. Their grievances are not . per case, but only 26s.—What is the consumption of that country ?

I have no idea ; but Austria is one of the largest mining countries in the world.— you think you can run a dynamite factory without making a profit ?

This is quite a mutual arrangement, and one I suggested to this country five years . But, in the case I have mentioned, the interesting portion is contained in a letter ead, dated April 23, to the effect that Nobel's, in order to prevent the erection of a w factory, have made considerable concessions to the mining industry. Now, if you ld manufacture dynamite which could reasonably compete with that manufactured Home, or if you had imported dynamite and sold it to the industry at a reasonable ure, I for one would never have taken up this position. But to be squeezed, as it re, to pay 85s. for an article sold at Home for 23s., that is more than the mining lustry can stand.—What do you call reasonable prices ?

That is a thing I cannot go into.

Mr. *Hay.*

Prior to the dynamite explosion you admitted that the price of dynamite was Transport charges on dynamite from factory. ed at the magazine at 85s., and that the delivery to the companies is about 6d. per se. What did it cost you to transport the dynamite from your factory to the gazine in Johannesburg?—At that time we had to transport the dynamite from the l factory by rail, and I think the cost of transport came out at about 5s. per case.

The conclusion arrived at is that, since the explosion dynamite has been increased the mines by a shilling per case, and that is additional profit. What is the cost of ur magazines ?—Magazines as we build them, underground, cost £250 each.

What is the interest on £250 ?—About 6 per cent, £15 per year.

How many cases of dynamite can be stored in the magazine ?—Say about 2,000 ses.

It would, therefore, be fair to assume, if you take it for 12 months, that 12,000 ses of dynamite pass through that factory, and you save £600.—You start from a :ong principle. You say this belongs to you, and I say it belongs to me.

I want to get a straightforward answer to a straightforward question. Since the plosion your company has profited 1s. per case more than they did prior to the plosion ?—Not exactly. We have to carry our stock from Leeuwfontein to our new :tory. After the explosion we were ordered to clear the magazines, and in order to close to the mining industry we established magazines on our factory. We had erefore to transport the stock from Leeuwfontein to our old factory, which means e same as if we had brought it to Johannesburg.

Your contract is 85s. at the magazine, and since the explosion you have made us y 1s. more. The 1s. you save you do not give to us. As managing director of this mpany it is your duty to make the best possible profit you can for your share-

holders. You also see that the profit is made as much as possible, because 20 per
cent. goes to the Government, after 8 per cent. has been paid, as well as sundry

Cost price of imported dyna-mite materials reductions. Is it not your duty to see that the material required is bought in the
cheapest possible market?—What do you mean by the cheapest market?

The question is simple enough. The terms of the contract are that you erect the
factory, and the Government gets 20 per cent. of the profits, and that the books are
kept in a proper mercantile manner, and the Government shall have the right at
times to look into them, so that they have some control over the manufacture, and so
that the Government may see that they get the 20 per cent. Now, as managing
director of this company, should you not see that the goods are bought at the cheapest
possible price?—I don't quite agree with you.

Then will you explain your duty as managing director?—Yes. My duties are
first to look after the safety of the people in the factory and then to turn out a first
rate explosive. It is the duty of the Government's agent to buy the material in the
best market.

No, no. I don't want the Government agent, I will come to that by-and-by.
You are in charge of this factory, and you have to get the material from the

The quality of imported dy-namite mater-ials. Government agent. Is it not your duty then, as the head of this institution, to see
that you get good articles at the best possible price?—Yes.

Then can you tell me whether you get good quality?—Yes.

The cost price of imported dy-namite mater-ials. Can you tell me the price it has been supplied at?—I can tell you the cost price
at the factory, and I don't feel entitled to give that price away.

The Government is entitled to 20 per cent., and, representing the Government, I
want to see that they are getting the right amount.—I would suggest that a special
commission be appointed by the Government.

That is the best thing we could have. Can you tell us now whether you get the
goods at the best possible price? Are you satisfied, as managing director, that the
materials are bought in the best possible market, having regard to quality?—Yes ; I
am quite satisfied.

Do you pay the Government or the Government agent when the material is
delivered at your factory? Does the Government agent furnish you with the invoice?
—Yes.

The agent pays expenses of transit and insurances and cost of the material, and
you pay him ; therefore, you must know the cost of the material in Europe approximately?—Yes ; approximately.

Then you do not know whether the Goverment agent supplies you with the
goods at the cost price?—He has to.

How do you know?—According to the contract.

How do you know whether he is fulfilling it?—I have good faith in him.

You test the quality when you get it?—Not exactly. Dynamite is an article
that you can buy to-day and to-morrow. During our building period the Government imported large quantities,—I mean larger quantities than any factory in Europe
could supply.

You don't exercise any control over the 466,000 cases of material brought in
during the past 18 months. You don't exercise any check over anything whatever?
—It is no business of mine.

The purchase of dynamite mat-erials and No-bel's Dynamite trust. These goods are bought through Nobel's Dynamite Trust, and if they charge
twice as much for anything, you pay it and reduce the profit of the company, and the
profit due to the Government is also reduced. Therefore, the factory is Nobel and
Company. That does not show that the goods are bought in the best possible market.

he profit may have been made larger than 80 per cent.?—What is the best et?

The best market is where you can get the best goods at the cheapest price.—I know the price in Europe.

You should see, in your position of managing director, that the State is protected, uying in the best possible way. The fact is, you have to buy from Nobel's and charge e highest possible price. Now, suppose the Government agent delivers goods of value of £350: Do you give him £350?—We pay it to the account of the rnment.

First of all you buy the material from the Government agent. Does he give you voice?—I credit the Government with the amount received, and then I hand in ccount for the sales I have made, and after deducting my expenses the Govern- t gets 5s.

Now, I have a few simple questions. If you will give me simple answers we soon get through. Who is the Government agent?—Mr. Vorstman.

Where is Mr. Vorstman now?—In Europe.

How long has he been in Europe?—He left on the 31st March.

Who acts for him now?—Well, to tell the truth, I don't know. I was not here n he left. I don't think there is an acting Government agent, because Mr. tman intends to return very soon.

Then how does this thing work now? You have told us that the Government t orders the goods and hands them over to you. Who does that when Mr. tman is away?—The company does it.

Which company?—The dynamite company—the company I am representing.

Therefore, all this talk which we have had before, that it is sometimes the agent sometimes the company, all comes back to the fact that it is the company?—In special case it is so, as to the duty of the Government agent.

You are the Government agent now?—No.

Well, acting Government agent?—I have not got the appointment.

Will you tell us then under which thimble the pea is?—I tell you the company it now.

How long has the company been agent for the Government?—Since April.

The question at the present moment is, that the company orders the goods from ope from Nobel's Trust, brings them out, hands them over to you; you sell them, you hand over to the Government what you like?—What I like? No.

How much do you hand over to the Government?—I hand over the statement, rding to my contract—5s. per case.

And you adjudge the payments in Europe as it suits your company?—Yes.

How many cases do you anticipate you will make out of the raw product this r?—I said, since the month of October up to the end of April we manufactured 00 cases.

How many cases do you expect to make now onwards per month?—It is very cult to say, because we have to take advantage of the cold weather. But we ufacture now at the rate of 80,000 cases per year.

The consumption here is probably about 180,000 cases a year?—More or less.

How has the remaining 100,000 cases to be got?—It has to be imported.

In the same manner?—According to Volksraad resolution.

In importing that gühr as it is, and the glycerine in lump, would it be cheaper to ort it already made up in cartridges?—That would be going into the European e.

Which you don't know anything about?—No.

In your opinion, would it be cheaper to bring 120,000 cases, all ready as blas
gelatine or as dynamite, or to bring it out in bulk, and then manipulate it here,
put it into cartridges?—That is a question of calculation for which, of course, I m
have European prices. The only thing I can tell you is that we started to manufac
in this country. It costs us about the same as the goods prepared out of gühr impre
in those places. I cannot say whether it is cheaper to introduce the finished art
because then I ought to have the European price of the manufactured article an
the half-finished article.

You don't know the prices of the half-finished article and the finished article
No. The only thing I can say is this : The cost of the cartridge explosive made in

Comparative
cost of dyna-
mite manufac-
tured in Trans-
vaal, and of dy-
namite made,
of imported
half-finished
goods.
country, and the cost of the cartridge explosive made of the imported half-finis
goods would be about the same.

Now, we have got something at last. Then the question comes to this. If
statement made before the Volksraad Commission, that the profit on the manipulat
of imported stuff leaves a profit of about £2 per case, then the manufacture of
dynamite out of the imported ingredients would be about the same price ?—Assum
that the report is true and correct.

Estimated profit
of dynamite
factory.
Therefore, the profit of the factory, if the output is 180,000 cases, would
£360,000 a year ?—Yes, if you take £2 as correct, for argument's sake.

We have got one definite statement—that the cost of making the raw mate
and making it from gühr impregné and lump gelatine would be the same. Theref
the capital of your company is £450,000, and the profit, at that rate would
£360,000 ?—Well, I cannot follow the calculation.

It is very simple.—Yes, if you take £2 to be correct. But I said it was

Profits of South
African Ex-
plosives Com-
pany for 1895.
correct. I have said we only made £58,000 profit for the year 1895.

The point is, you have got shareholders, and have to hold meetings. Now, wl
is the use of talking about ancient history. We might as well talk about the anci
Romans as what occurred in 1894. Surely you can give us something more reas

Returns of South
African Ex-
plosives Com-
pany for 1896.
able. We want the figures for 1896.—I am not entitled to give out figures before
balance-sheet is accepted by the shareholders.

It is a very curious thing. You say the figures are not correct, and then, whe
ask you in how far they are not correct, you decline to answer ?—I have given
the reasons and I think they are very good.

Will the balance-sheet show how much profit you make per case ?—Yes ; you
figure it out very easily.

You cannot remember what these figures are ?—Well, of course, I can say, m
or less, but I do not see any reason for telling you the figures now.

Partition of
shares of South
African Ex-
plosives Com-
pany.
When the question was put as to how the capital was made up you declined
answer. Mr. Bourne, the secretary of the Transvaal Dynamite Factory, when he v
here, gave me those figures when the contract was entered into. 182,500 shares of
each were paid to the previous concessionaires, whose concession had been cancell
25,000 fully-paid-up shares were issued to Mr. Lippert; 22,500 shares were issued
persons unknown ; and 220,000 were issued to Nobel's Trust against payment in
cash. What did the company get for £230,000 ?—You say Mr. Bourne told
182,500 were issued to the old company in exchange for all the assets and propert
in this country ?

The assets were not worth £182,500.—But perhaps the property was—the
farm and the buildings.

Would you say the farm and the buildings thereon were worth £182,500
They may have been worth that to our company at the time.

Does the agent, who buys for the factory, get remunerated?—As the Govern- Remuneration of the Government buyer.
nt agent, he gets nothing.

Does he do it for goodwill, or for love?—As Government agent, yes.

Why does Mr. Vorstman do it; he is the only man I know who serves the
vernment for nothing?—I don't think I am entitled to reply for Mr. Vorstman's
vate affairs.

Do your company pay him anything?—Yes, because he is a director.

Does he get commission for buying?—No.

Is it a fixed remuneration, or does it depend on the profit that is made?—He
:s a fixed remuneration, and a bonus at the end of the year.

If you import this large quantity of raw material, assuming that it takes six tons Railway rates and the importation of raw materials for dynamite.
raw material to make one ton of dynamite, then if there is a reduction in railway
;es, there would be a large saving on the cost of transport?—Yes.

If these reductions are made by the railway, is your company prepared to take
the profit, or are they prepared to reduce the price of dynamite?—We are quite
:pared to reduce the price then.

I will only say I regret having had to put these questions to Mr. Phillip. I am
:ry that Mr. Vorstman, or someone who is intimately connected with the retaining
this concession, is not here to answer the questions.—I may remark, Mr. Chairman,
at all the information Mr. Hay requires, if I, as a representative of the company,
: an order from the Government, I shall be very pleased to give the information.

Mr. *Smit.*

What is the weight of the blocks of gühr impregné?—They vary from 5 to
'bs., and up to 10 lbs. each.

What is the price of a block delivered at your factory?—I cannot tell you
actly; we never calculate on blocks.

How many of these blocks does it take to make a case of dynamite?—Five or
ven, according to weight.

What does it cost to manufacture cartridges, then, out of such a block?—We Cost of manufacture of dynamite cartridges
lculate it about 21s. or 22s. per case, without general expenses.

Chairman.

With regard to the last arguments of Mr. Hay and Mr. Phillip, I feel obliged to Mr. Phillip and information concerning the importation of dynamite.
y this. Mr. Phillip stated in the beginning, and maintained, that he could not give
some information because Mr. Vorstman was the agent. I thought the informa-
n was not in his possession, and, therefore, I came to the conclusion to call Mr.
orstman later on, or his representative here. Now, Mr. Phillip states that he can
ve such information when the Government gives him instructions to do so. I must
ll him that we are a Commission appointed by the Government to enquire into
ery matter connected with the case, and to hear all the witnesses necessary; and, if
r. Phillip can give this information on behalf of Mr. Vorstman, I do not want to go
ck and get instructions from the Government. I have got instructions, and if you
ve the information, you ought to give it.—When I said I was willing to give the
formation on the instructions of the Government, I did not say I had the informa-
n with me. I will have to get it from the Government, as the Government keep
 the papers referring to importation, so that, if this Commission asks me to produce
 I have to get it from the Government.

Mr. *Smit.*

I do not understand why you should go to the Government to get the informa-

tion, because you stated the agent had all the information, and the agent had all
papers. The Chairman has stated that all the work is done by the agent, and
Government do nothing themselves. Consequently, the papers are all in the hands
the agent, and you are the agent at the present moment, and now you want to go
the Government for information.—As I have said, all the invoices have to go to t
Treasurer-General.

You would do better to say that you won't answer the questions, as at prese
you leave the impression that you won't answer.—I am sorry this impression
created, as I am willing to answer anything I know.

Cost of imported dynamite materials.
You have stated that you don't know the cost of gühr impregné here; how
you pay for it—per pound, per ton, or per case?—The Government gets the invoi
and it is made out per case or per ton.

You say you get the invoices, and after you have deducted the charges you c
find out what it costs in Europe?—If I deduct the charges—yes. If the Governme
ask me for the invoices, I will ask for them and produce them.

I shall be very pleased if you will get those papers and give the informatic

The purchase of dynamite.
You said in your statement that, practically, the company buys the material. T
Government are practically intermediaries, and as the company are really the peop
who buy, they must be able to give all the information.—Yes. As I said, the Gover

The Government buyer.
ment agent is separate from the company, so far as buying is concerned. I sa
later I had refreshed my memory, and I remembered that a letter had been writt
from the Government appointing Mr. Vorstman and Mr. Klimke Government offici:
for buying raw material.

Was that before the new contract was entered into?—The letter must have be
written somewhere about the same time.

I understood from you, when Mr. Brochon questioned you, that six tons of ra
material are necessary to manufacture one ton of dynamite.—I admitted it for arg
ment's sake. I am not a technical man, and I have not got the figures, so I ca
tell you exactly.

Comparative cost of imported and Transvaal manufactured dynamite.
Seeing that so much raw material is required in bulk for the manufacture
dynamite, it follows—seeing that some of the material disappears during the course
manufacture—that dynamite must be far more expensive here. It cannot be made
be profitable, or delivered at competing prices, because you have to pay for such a l
of waste weight?—I daresay.

You would lose such a lot in freight that you could not possibly manufactu
here at competing prices with imported dynamite?—I do not think I could do it, n
only on account of freight, but on account of local conditions, such as wages, livin
expenses, and native labour. All these items must always make the manufactur
article here somewhat more expensive than the imported.

Mr. *Hugo.*

Pretoria directors of the South African Explosives Company.
Who are the directors of the company at Pretoria?—Mr. Wolmarans, Mr. Vors
man, Mr. Wolff, and myself.

Managing director.
You are the managing director?—Yes.

Directors of Nobel's Dynamite Trust.
Who are the directors of Nobel's Trust Company?—My father is a director, M
Reid, of Glasgow; Mr. Beckett, of Glasgow; Mr. Johnson, of Glasgow; and, I thin
Dr. Aufschlaeger, of Hamburg.

Chairman of South African Explosives Company.
Who is chairman of this company here?—My father.

And a director of Nobel's in Hamburg?—Yes.

Nobel's head office.
Where is the European head office of the company?—In Hamburg.

Was it not formerly in London?—No.

Who is general manager of the company ?—Mr. Bourne.

And the same Mr. Bourne is secretary of the Transvaal Dynamite Company ?—

In reply to Mr. Albu, you flatly contradicted the statement that dynamite was *Nobel's and Mr.* to De Beers in Kimberley for 57s. 6d., and then you added " We sell to them at *Phillip.* Whom do you mean by " we " ?—Of course that was a slip of the tongue.

But whom do you mean by " we " ?—I mean the Nobel Dynamite Company.

Are you agent for Nobel's ?—No ; therefore I say it was a slip of the tongue.

Coming back to the question of the directorate of the company. I believe you *The directorate* the names of the gentlemen who are on the Board in Europe. Dr. Aufschlaeger *of the South African Ex-* is a director of this company ?—Yes. *plosives Co.*

He is also a director of Nobel's ?—Yes.

Similarly Mr. Beckett, of Glasgow ?—Yes.

Also a director of Nobel's ?—Yes.

Mr. Heydemann is a director of your company ?—Yes.

Also a director of Nobel's ?—That I cannot say.

And Mr. James Johnson ?—Yes.

Also a director of Nobel's ?— Yes.

Similarly, your father, Mr. Max Phillip ?—Yes.

Mr. Levy ?—Yes.

Mr. Taylor is also a director of your company ?—Yes.

Also of Nobel's ?—Yes.

At anyrate, you are sure that about six of the directors in Europe of this *Nobel's director-* pany are also directors of Nobel's ?—Yes. *ate.*

As a matter of fact, is not the duty of this company simply to act as agent of the *The Government* svaal Government, in accordance with Article 3 ?—I understand a letter has been *agency and the South African* ten, but that was before my time, appointing Mr. Vorstman and Mr. Klimke for *Explosives* buying of materials. *Company.*

It must have been written a long time before the new contract ?—No ; because new contract, as far as I can remember, was signed in 1894. I am connected with Dynamite Company since 1895.

The nominal capital of the company is 450,000 shares of £1 each ?—Yes. *The share capital* And 220,000 shares were issued against cash ?—Yes. *of the South African Ex-*

Is it not a fact that only 45 per cent. of that was paid-up ?—No; the shares are *plosives Co.* paid-up.

That is not an answer to my question. Was £220,000 paid in cash ?—Yes.

Mr. Hay gave us the information that 25,000 shares, ranking as fully-paid-up *Mr. Lippert's* es, were issued to Mr. Lippert ?—Yes. *shares in the South African*

What for do you know ? Was it not on account of an agreement entered into by *Explosives Co.* with the old company ?—That I do not know.

I think in your statement to the Commission you stated it is the intention of the *European prices* sraad to enquire into European prices, which you tell us you know nothing *for dynamite* it ?—Yes.

How do you know it is the intention of the Volksraad ?—Of course the Volks- took a resolution to that effect.

Do you also know through whom this enquiry will be made ?—As far as I know, Dr. Leyds and Mr. Klimke.

Are you interesting yourself in the matter ?—Not in the least.

You stated in reply to Mr. Albu you would be surprised if dynamite could be vered here at 40s. I am going to ask you a question. Supposing a firm offer e made you, satisfactorily guaranteed, to deliver to you in Johannesburg dynamite

A 2

equal to No. 1, approved of by the State Mining Engineer, at 40s. per case, would y
company accept that offer ?—I think so.

Cost price of raw materials for dynamite.

I am sorry to have to come back to the cost price of these articles, and I mu
also express my surprise that you do not know the cost price of material, consideri
you order and pay for it. I will put it this way : You pay the Government the co
price delivered at your factory, plus 5s. royalty ?—Yes.

You also know the cost of freight, landing, transport duty, etc., about 11s. 1d. ?
About that.

Well, it is very easy to find out the cost of the raw material free on board
Hamburg ?—I never denied I could find it out. I really never have taken the troub
to find it out.

The office of the Government agent and your office are in the same building
Pretoria ?—Yes.

All the invoices pass through that office ?—Yes.

It certainly is surprising you do not know what the Government's agent pays fr
on board at Hamburg. From the reply you gave just now, I infer you can get t
information through your office in Pretoria ?—I can get the information by the syste
you explain. As I told the Commission, I am quite willing to put all these documen
in their possession.

Will you supply the Commission with the price of the raw material free on boa
at Hamburg ?—Yes.

Profits of South African Explosives Company on imported materials for dynamite.

Now, you remember that the Special Commission appointed by the Volksra
reported that a profit of £2 per case is made by your company. You would not sa
that that was correct or incorrect, but later you said it was incorrect ?—I said,
reply to Mr. Hay, that it was not correct, but Mr. Hay asked me was it true, and
could not say that the Commission stated a truth or an untruth.

It is not a question of truth or untruth. According to the accounts submitted
the Commission by the State Secretary, there is a profit of £2 per case made by t
company.—I cannot say what the State Secretary submitted to the Commission.

It must have been those invoices you told us about, which are in the hands of t
Government.—The only thing I can say is that £2 is not correct.

Sale price of dynamite.

You sell dynamite at 85s. that is correct ?—Yes.

Royalties and charges on dynamite.

And give the Government 5s. ?—Yes.

The charges are 11s. 1d. ?—Yes.

And Mr. Lippert gets 6s. per case, more or less ?—Yes.

Then what is actually paid per case to people other than the Government ?—
comes out to about 1s. 2d.

The total charge, therefore, is £1 3s. 3d.—say 24s. Deduct that from 85s, an
there remains 61s. That must be profit after deducting expenses. Where does th
profit go to ?—Where do you put in the cost of the raw material ?

Working costs of dynamite manufacture.

Well, say 21s. for the raw material ?—No, I said 21s. for working expenses.

We have got information that the stuff can be bought in Hamburg for 18s. Eve

Profits of South African Explosives Company on dynamite.

making it 20s., there still remains 40s. profit ?—I don't see how you figure that ou
Take the cost of working expenses at 21s., that leaves 40s. Now, we make a divider
of 8 per cent.; that figures out at about 6s. 2d. per case net profit.

But there still remains a good profit after that ?—But you must take into co
sideration the risk on the money invested.

Maximum price for gelatine.

Then you have your sinking fund. Is it a fact that the company recently appli
for the right to raise the price of blasting gelatine ?—Not exactly to raise the pric
but to stipulate for the maximum price we could charge for blasting gelatine.

What was that price ?—127s. I think.

I think you applied for the maximum price to be fixed at 133s. ?—I tell you I am quite sure whether it was 127s. or 133s.

What do you sell it for now ?—£5 7s. 6d.

Cost of gelatine.

Mr. *Albu.*

You stated that dynamite in Buluwayo sold for 110s. per case. I, to-day, saw a tleman who is largely interested in Mashonaland, and on reading your statement told me they paid 90s. per case for Nobel's No. I. Out of that they have to pay . extra transport from the last railway station to Buluwayo. That is included in 90s., and, after deduction, would leave the price 64s. Then the railway to Palapye much further than that to the Transvaal. So you are wrong in this statement that y pay 110s.—You can say I am wrong. Of course you don't know where I got information from. I have the information from a gentleman in Port Elizabeth; I know this gentleman I trust him.

Price of dynamite in Buluwayo.

It is not from your own knowledge. Have you had the other prices you men-n also from agents in British India and Australian ports ?—Yes.

Well, I have heard, on unquestionable authority, that in Buluwayo they only y 90s. On the Tati goldfields they pay 80s.?—I have as good reason to doubt your tement as you have to doubt mine.

I don't doubt yours, because if I did doubt it, I would say you make the statement owing it to be incorrect. You only get your information in the same way as I do., m not selling any dynamite in Buluwayo. You said it would not cost much more manufacture dynamite here than in England or Germany. Is that correct ?—I d that a case of cartridge explosives made in this country amounted to almost the ne as a case of cartridge explosives manufactured of imported half-finished goods.

Cost of local manufacture of dynamite.

Then how is it possible that packing and cartridging cost you 21s. a case here, en the whole article ready for shipment does not exceed that price at Home ?—ere is another item you don't take into consideration. Mr. Hugo enumerated all e expenses we have. One thing he did not mention was the amortisation of the pital spent in this country, our capital outlay.

Expenses of amortisation of capital outlay of South African Explosives Company.

Would that amortisation increase the expenditure considerably ?—I think so.

I have got here a cutting from one of the financial papers. I only read it cause it may be interesting. It is a Stock Exchange paper, and appears in Berlin. ey are discussing the dividends of the Nobel Dynamite Trust Company. The t of it is as follows :—" The management of the Nobel Dynamite Trust Company s decided to propose, at the next general meeting, the payment of a dividend of' per cent., against 13 per cent. in the previous year. This dividend does not come to expectations which have been entertained during the last few months, in con-quence of the result of business not coming up in the Transvaal to the expectations ich they were justified to entertain." And the reason given in this article is that e position and conditions prevailing in the Transvaal, with regard to the dynamite nopoly, do not look so favourable as they had reason to believe. Now, it shows u what a great factor your Transvaal business plays in the whole Nobel Dynamite ust ring.—You cannot make me responsible.

Connection of Nobel's dynamite trust, with the Transvaal dynamite business.

Oh, no. It is only an interesting article. I would not go so far as to make you sponsible for articles that appear in European papers. I only want to show what enormous factor the industry here plays in your business.—You put such a lot of portance on all these articles.

Well, if such a reason is given for reducing the dividend by 1 per cent., though e profits have not been reduced, it shows that the position is a little more shaky, if

I may use that word.—Because it suits you, therefore you believe in it.   If there h
been an article quite to the contrary you would not have brought it.

I have not written that article, Mr. Phillip.—No; but you have read it.

Mr. *Schmitz-Dumont.*

The price of dynamite and railway rates. You say you would be very glad to reduce the price, in case the railway tariff
lowered, and thereby lower wages, cost of living, etc. ?—Yes.

I think it would be of very great value to the Commission to know to wh
extent you could reduce it.   In order to arrive at that, we must have an insight ir
the working expenses of the manufactory.   It is as well to point out that, before
Future price of the dynamite factory. condemn a factory like this, and confiscate £600,000, the Commission must investiga
whether there is a future before the factory—to deliver dynamite cheaper in t
future.   To do this it will be necessary for the Commission to learn something abo
the working expenses ?—Certainly, you can do so.   I have not got the data here, b
I can get them for you.   May I make a remark on Mr. Brakhan's statement abo
Detonators. detonators.   I have got the figures for 1896.   I think I understood Mr. Brakhan
say that if detonators were imported in free trade, the mining industry could sa
£72,000 per year.   I can make out for 1896 the mining industry in the who
republic have drawn the supply of detonators from us, amounting to a sum of £7,36
I do not see, even putting the figures at £10,000 for argument's sake, where t
mining industry could save £72,000.

Mr. *Brakhan.*

Those were figures I compiled, so I will look into the matter.

Mr. *Smit.*

Mr. Phillip and the European prices of dynamite. Since Mr. Vorstman has been to Europe, has any material been ordered
received here ?—I left in April, and am only here about a month.   Since then the
has been only one shipment received.

Who received it ?—It has arrived at Port Elizabeth recently, and there is anoth
ship on the way out.

It has not yet been delivered here ?—Partly.

Who received it ?—It was sent to the factory.

Who received the invoices for the load ?—They were addressed to Mr. Vorstma
and when he is away the company opens them.

Do they call the directors together to open the letters, or does Mr. Vorstman
representative open them ?—The representative.

And that is you ?—Yes, I open the letters.

And yet you don't know the price of the stuff ?—It did not take my attention.

Chairman.

Visit of the Industrial Commission to the dynamite factory. You have failed to put us in possession of several details, and you have invite
the Commission to pay a visit to the factory.   We will discuss that, and the Commi
sion will reply to the invitation later on.   There are some points remaining, in whic
we must have information, and which we should get from you.   This we will tak
into consideration, to consider which will be the best way in order to get informatio
I thank you for your evidence.

Mr. W. H. Hall's evidence.
Nature of statement. MR. WILLIAM HALL was called.   In reply to a question, he said :

I am a civil engineer, residing in San Francisco, California, and have prepared
statement relating more especially to the water supply of the mines, the labour pr

as arisen here, and to the general advancement of the agriculture of this country, nding to make living cheaper, and mining cheaper. I have nothing to say on the ect of dynamite or railway transportation, for these have been exhaustively dealt . I must first apologise to the Commission for making this statement in English , as I did not know what was required. I have put it in the hands of a translator ay, and will remedy that omission as soon as possible. I suppose the Commission's is limited, and I will therefore wait, if the Commission desires, and read only opening and closing paragraphs, and then I will attend the Commission, whenever ted, for cross-examination.

Chairman.

As you say, the Commission's time is limited. You have handed this in as your rn declaration, but I will expect your Dutch translation all the same. When the mission think it necessary for you to come to answer questions the time will be l.

Mr. Hall's statement was as follows:—

Gentlemen,—Complying with your invitation to me, addressed under date of the a May, I submit this memorandum of my views concerning the condition of the l mining industry in this State, together with some remarks and suggestions as to Governmental problem springing therefrom, and which you are to report upon. I roach the subject in the same sympathetic spirit for both Government and ustry, which your honourable Chairman, speaking for yourselves, representing the ernment, expressed for the industry in his opening statement; and I accept, as my tation, the declaration of one of your members, made on the same occasion—that "desired the widest evidence" you "could possibly get with regard to the ject" of your enquiry.

In deference to your requirement of those who have thus far given evidence re you, I first record some facts as to my experience which may entitle my statement our attention. I occupied for 10 years the office of State Engineer of the State of Mr. Hall's engineering experience. fornia, United States of America, and, subsequently, was supervising engineer in United States Geological Survey for several years, and, in these capacities, was ged with duties relating to mining and agricultural industries over a very wide of country, and thus have had favourable opportunity for insight upon those nomic questions which have sprung out of agricultural and mining developments railway transport practice in the United States of America.

I have no interests whatever in the South African Republic, and do not expect to e. My mission here is absolutely disassociated with all industrial controversy or s grievance. I came under engagement to examine and report upon matters of er supply for deep-level mining of the future, should the industry be permitted to and. I soon go away, probably not to return, except, it may be, for another ally brief business trip. The professional work I have undertaken has brought arely before me this question: what is to be the extent of mining on the Rand, much of which I am asked to plan a water supplying system? And with this Possibilities of mining developments on Rand. come the corellative question: what population immediately dependent upon ing will have to be provided for in water supply estimates?

As the firms and companies to whom I am to report, control or represent the ership of about seven-eighths of the deep-level mining ground and half of the crop mining area, within the central 15 miles of the Witwatersrand Goldfields, des much other mining property lying east and west of this focus of mining ivity and prospects, it may be seen that I have had to look broadly at the future

possibilities of mining developments. You will hence appreciate the fact that
study has, incidentally, been of some matters which enter into the problem r
before yourselves. I propose, later in this paper, giving you some results incide
to this study. The general fact is thus mentioned at the opening of my statement
way of showing, I hope, that though a comparatively recent comer to the Ran
have been thrown into practical contact with the industrial question of the day, a
may thus be qualified, as well by some special local knowledge as by previ
experience, to speak earnestly on the subject.

It only remains to be added that I have been entirely free and' unhampered,
suggestion even, in my examinations; that my work has been done and judgm
formed, without the slightest idea of presenting any of its results or incide
thoughts to your Commission or your Government; and that I now do so, on y
invitation, without the knowledge even of those for whom I am professiona
engaged, and so far as I know, to the knowledge of several personal friends only.

A problem of national economics.

The problem before you seems to me to be one of national economics, and not
merely of class grievance. Every rapidly advancing country has had frequent
to remodel its fiscal system and administrative laws, not only to meet the requi
ments of its growing Government, but to satisfy the strenuous demands and imp
ative necessities of its expanding or languishing industries. The present case in t
South African Republic is not exceptional in the mere fact of clamorous demand
reform and abolition of industrial burdens. It is singular only as to the form in wh
it has appeared, and in that it has become so acute as to cut its way into internatio
politics.

If the local mining industry were in the hands of burghers of the South Afric
Republic, the clamour for relief would be regarded as merely an internal industr
agitation, paralleled by industrial upheavals in other countries, though possibly
equalled by them. In other words, there exists here a great governmental probl
outside of any particular complication made by the presence of a more or l
troublesome *uitlander* population. This problem is primarily a fiscal one—
problem of how to derive a sufficient governmental income, not only witho
strangling the industries on which it rests, but so as to permit those industries
expand. But, immediately this question is considered, it leads into politics—
partly politics; not Uitlander *vs.* Boer politics, but social politics, in that it is
question of people—of labour.

A problem of social politics: its solution.

You may expropriate the railways, and operate them at the most reasonable ra
which will return a fair interest for a government to receive for the use of a pub
work; you may throw the dynamite business open to competition and admit t
article from the outside world free of duty; you may reduce annual burdens
productive industry by reducing Governmental expenditures in some directions; a
you may still further lighten present burdens on industry by raising money for rea
necessary permanent public works by issue of long term debentures. By the last t

Reduction of import duties.

steps you may be enabled to very materially reduce Customs tariffs on artic
necessary to development of the staple industry, and for the use of those who li
upon wages and moderate salaries; and you may do other things which will ma
living here comfortable, safe and comparatively inexpensive to the burgher, mi
worker, and the merchant.

Maintenance of State revenue. Compensation for reduction of State revenue through reliefs requested.

All these can be done while still providing sufficient revenue for your Gover
ment. They will stimulate the gold industry, it will expand, more money will co
into the country, a far greater demand for labour will ensue, and then will come t
acute stage of the labour problem, which is present in a mild form to-day. If y
start on the right principle with that problem now, you will be able to handle it la

If you take the wrong course with it now, it will be very much more difficult to ...dle then. This problem is altogether aside from any complication as between ...r Government and any other, or as between your people and any other nationality.

There is not only gold in these reefs in immense quantities, which nature put ...re, but, what is more, there are tens on tens of millions sterling in and on these ...ds, which men have put there. The problem is to get it out, and it requires a vast ...y of labour to do so. Where labour abnormally congregates, formidable political ...stions arise, whether that labour be black or white, free or slave. This is the ...ater part of the question before you—the labour part. It will bear more discus... ...n than all the rest put together. It is the problem of life on the goldfields, which ...he problem of revenue for your Government, and of return of capital invested, and ...be invested, here.

The very first result of the existence of your Commission, and following close ...n the publication of evidence taken before it, will be the discussion of this pro... ...m—your problem—on its merits, all over the civilised world. Those peoples who ...interested financially here, will, of course, be most concerned; but, now that the ...ts have been made authoritatively available, strong thinkers everywhere will take ...the topic. The day of outside discussion of Transvaal affairs from the standpoint ...prejudice only, if there has been such a day, will now rapidly pass away, and, ...derstandingly, the intelligent world will await the result of the internal handling ...the problem you are to report upon.

The crucial question here is one of *cost* of mining. Capitalisation, too great or ...small, has nothing to do with it. The problem is to get the gold out of the ...und at the least possible cost. Your Government is more interested in effecting ...desired result than any other party concerned. The cheaper mining is made here, ...greater may be the Government revenue, from the people engaged in it, without ...pressing the industry. Make the cost of mining such that three times the popula... ...n will be thereby justified on the Rand, and the proper basis for Governmental ...venue has immediately been trebled. The Government's dividend, so to speak, ...nes first, the shareholders' afterwards.

That it is desirable to stop wild speculation in good shares and wild promotion ...bad schemes, is perfectly true; but such wild speculation and promotion have not, ...d do not, keep, 23s. ores from paying the cost of working them on the Rand, and ...ve not produced the present depression. Disappointment in genuine enterprise is ...e cause of this trouble, and this disappointment has been brought about by unanti... ...ated burdens now resting on gold production, and by some other causes which have ...en brought to your notice in statements already before you. A company may have ...en capitalised for ten times its proper value, but the cost of mining its property, ...r se, is not made a whit greater thereby. Dividends will, of course, be a less per ...it. on nominal values, but costs of production are not affected.

For the purpose of judgment as to what should be the cost of winning the gold ...om the reefs of the Rand, the natural conditions and circumstances under which this ...ning is prosecuted may well be compared with those surrounding and affecting the ...st of working auriferous lodes, veins, or ledges in the Rocky Mountains and Pacific ...ope States of America. The methods of mining and reducing the banket ores here ...e practically the same as those followed in American quartz-mining.

Having made such comparisons, from my own personal knowledge I have no ...sitation in saying that the conditions—so far as nature has made them—under ...ich the industry is here developing, viewing the Witwatersrand fields as a whole, ...e decidedly more favourable than those present, and affecting the cost of similar ...ning, as a general thing, in America.

Marginal notes:

The labour problem.

Value of Witwatersrand reefs and fields

Nature of labour problem.

Working costs of mines.

Working costs of mines and the State revenue.

Reasons for the present depression.

Over-capitalisation.

Comparative working conditions of Witwatersrand mines, and American mines in Rocky Mountains and in Pacific Slope States.

There are, of course, exceptions; I state this as a predominating, not the ~~i~~ varying, rule. Not only is gold easier to get out of the ground here, but man sho~~w~~ be able to live as cheaply, in as healthful and vigorous a condition, and as contente~~d~~ here as in the American mining districts spoken of. The unavoidable conclusion that this gold should be obtained at less cost, and if it is not so obtained, the reas~~on~~ is to be found in the shortcomings of man, not the obduracy or unkindness of natu~~re~~.

Comparative working costs of Witwaters- rand mines and of quartz lodes of American fields. As a matter of fact, it costs from 20 to 25 per cent. more to win the gold of t~~he~~ Witwatersrand reefs than it does to gain that of the quartz lodes of Americ~~an~~ fields, in cases where circumstances justify direct comparison.

Reduction of working costs on Rand pos- sible. I do not mean to say it is in the power of man to at once bring about su~~ch~~ changes here as would reduce the cost of this mining to its legitimate minimum, n~~or~~ do I imply that any men are yet to blame for the full extent of the difference betwe~~en~~ the cost as it is and the cost as it might be. But I do mean to say that men alo~~ne~~ will be to blame if, within a very few years, this cost is not brought to near its low~~est~~ possibility, in the present state of human knowledge. Moreover, the way is clear f~~or~~ very material reducing of costs at once, and very much blame will find its legitima~~te~~ resting-place, in the judgment of the world, should this initial reduction be not ma~~de~~ and thereafter promptly followed by such other ameliorations as will bring the c~~ost~~ of Rand mining to where it should be.

Dryness of mines on Rand: To make altogether clear, and I hope convincing, that which I have said in ~~a~~ general way above, I ask your attention to several points. On the Rand, as a ru~~le~~ there is very little water to contend with in mining, and the cost of pumping or othe~~r~~ wise raising water out of the shafts is, by comparison, an insignificant item of the co~~st~~ of gaining the ores. Data, which have been collected under my direction, for the ~~i~~ miles of Central Rand especially, show that, as a rule:—1, The outcrop ground yiel~~ds~~ in outcrop mines an average of about 50,000 gallons per shaft per day—the range of amount being fro~~m~~ 10,000 to 90,000 gallons, and there being three or four exceptional cases where t~~he~~ amount runs materially higher; 2, that the first row of deep-levels, as a rule, yields ~~an~~ in deep levels, first row. average of about 45,000 gallons per shaft per day—the range of amount being fro~~m~~ 8,000 to 80,000 gallons, and there being two or three cases of very material high~~er~~ in deep levels, second row. water output; 3, that the second row of deep levels, with one exception, yiel~~ds~~ from 2,500 to 5,000 gallons per shaft per day only. There is an annual variation ~~in~~ amount of water yield, due to alternation of rainy and dry seasons; and cases whe~~re~~ decidedly larger flows, by comparison, exist, are of short life—the amounts soon dr~~awn~~ away to parity with other shafts in the range. These amounts of water, leavi~~ng~~ aside the few exceptional cases, which in a short time will probably run down to t~~he~~ normal, are all small.

Water in Amer- ican lode mines Most of the mine managers and engineers here think that, by comparison wi~~th~~ their experience elsewhere, they have no water in their shafts at all, and my ow~~n~~ observation confirms this view. In American lode or vein mining the rule is the oth~~er~~ way. The pumping plant is almost always a prominent item of initial cost. T~~he~~ volumes of water encountered are seldom insignificant, as here. The cost of operati~~on~~ and maintenance of the pumps is a material and notable item in the cost of gainin~~g~~ the ores.

Comparative timbering in Rand and Am- erican mines. On the Rand, the "ground" or rock over stopes and drives, as a rule, stands safel~~y~~ without timbering—blocking up with waste rock being found all sufficient to preve~~nt~~ subsidence or dropping masses. In this, also, nature has peculiarly favoured t~~he~~ Witwatersrand miner, and those who are familiar with mine workings in Americ~~a~~ cannot but be struck by this fact in going underground along the reefs in Johanne~~s~~ burg. For in American lode or vein mining, it frequently happens that the workin~~g~~

me vast labyrinths of heavy timbers, necessarily used to support the overhead,
eping " ground, or to prevent rock masses from falling.

As a rule, in American mining for gold, mine timbering is a heavy item of
nse. Huge piles of immense logs from 1 to 2½ feet in diameter, and covering an
or more of land, are collected alongside of mine openings, and are dropped
rground for the purpose stated. These logs are frequently hauled on wagons
points half a day's journey away, for the country is often so extremely rugged
precipitous that the cost of railway construction from the mine to the timber belt
ohibitive. The Rand miner is spared this logging and timbering expense, by
parison, almost entirely.

On the Rand the banket ore and the rocks which enclose it, are, as a rule, more *Easy working ores on Rand. Comparative hardness of American ores.*
ly drilled than the gold bearing quartz veins and their enclosing rocks in American
kings. Less labour and less steel should accomplish equal results here. Although
Rand advantage in this respect is doubtless less marked and material than on the
ts of mine water and timbering, it is an advantage which should tell in costs.

On the Rand there is practically no local heat in the rocks. In a matter of *Absence of ground heat in mines on Rand. Heat in American mines.*
perature a Rand mine should be, and generally is, an ideal place for underground
labour, and artificial ventilation is not an item of cost. In American mining
erground temperature is not infrequently a consideration not to be overlooked,
artificial ventilation of mines often constitutes a material class of running costs.

Here, then, I have enumerated four points incident to underground mining
ditions proper, wherein the Rand miner has material advantage over his *confrère*
America. If we consider conditions not incident to the gold mine itself, we find
the Witwatersrand miner is even yet peculiarly favoured. Within 23 miles of
very *centre* of Rand mining operations, within five miles of some of its extensive
kings—and a practically level country intervening—lie vast beds of fairly good *Cheapness of fuel on Rand.*
, as easily worked as almost any in the world.

This coal is actually so abundant, and so easily won that, under any possible
ree of gold mining expansion and consequent coal demand on the Rand, yet ought
er here to be cheap—very cheap. I have personally inspected some of these
beds and mines, and I am familiar with the working of the coalmining industry.
conditions here are such that these gold mines ought to have as cheap fuel as
ost any ore mines in the world. For American gold mining, fuel is often brought *Comparative expense of fuel on American mines.*
dreds of miles by rail, and, over portions, at least, of such distances, climbing heavy
dients and rounding obstructive curvatures of track alignment. Or, in other cases,
sting, milling, pumping and other machinery is driven by the burning of wood as
m-making fuel, and this wood is hauled by wagons over steep and rough mountain
ds, from points further from the mines than the coal output is from the centre of
gold industry on the Johannesburg Rand.

As in the case of mine timber hauling, the cost of railway construction to meet
fuel transport demand is often prohibitive in America, so that hauling has often
e done by wagon. There are, of course, exceptions to the rule I have stated for
erican workings. Some few mines are fairly well situated with respect to fuel
ply, but no gold mines are nearly so well favoured as those of this Johannesburg
ge. Some American mines, too, are operated with power derived from water
ssure, obtained at more or less, but often immense, outlay of capital in bringing
er, by means of canals, ditches or pipes, to advantageous points for the mine
ply; and operative power is delivered at still other mines by electric currents
ducted from points where cheap water power generates it. But, as a general thing,
erican ore mining is prosecuted by the use of power generated as steam on the
of application, and by consumption of fuel brought from afar.

In this respect the American cases would be paralleled on the Rand if the
had to be brought from over the Drakensberg Range in Natal, from some poin
Portuguese territory, or even from Rhodesia, were there rail communication f
Buluwayo to this point.

Climate of Rand.   Again, the climate on the Rand is an ideal one for mining industry—never
Comparison of climate on Rand and American gold fields. cold nor excessively hot, and free from snowfall.   There are very material items of
from which the Rand miner is exempt, but which the American miner is obligec
meet.   There are no heavy snows to shovel off from about the Rand surface wo
there are such snows about many American mine openings, and for several month
some years.   The Rand miner does not have to lay in a great stock of fuel for wi
use; he can get it as well one time as another throughout the year; but the Amer
miner not infrequently has to lay in a four or five months' fuel stock, and someti
he has to house it to make it available for handling under heavy snows.

The mine worker on the Rand does not have to burn much fuel to warm his h
in winter.   With the American mine workman this fuel item is often a very mate
element of living expense.   This Rand climate is at times invigorating without be
rigorous is at other times relaxing without being enervating, and is always favc
able to vigorous exertion.

Sanitary condition of Rand.   Men should live here as healthfully as in almost any American mining reg
and decidedly more so than in many of them.   There is typhoid fever here for nea
half the year, but that is man's fault, not nature's, and is almost wholly preventi
by man.   There is pneumonia here for much of the other half year, but that als
largely man's fault, and is in no small degree preventible.

Proper sanitation in matters of sewerage, water supply, and municipal and prem
cleanliness, and proper supply of water in, and health regulation about, the mines,
prevent typhoid fever; and, with such street and road improvement and maintena
as would keep down the poisonous, irritating dusts of winter, that class of colds wh
result in pneumonia here would be much less frequent.   At its worst, though, pn
monia is not as prevalent here as it is every winter in the famed Cripple-Creek min
region of America, or as it has been, and is, at Bodie and other districts of t
country; and there it is due to the extreme cutting cold, which man cannot amelior

While the white man should be able to live here in health and vigour, and be
efficient worker, on a wage comparable to that which he receives for a like serv
elsewhere, nature has provided in adjacent parts of South Africa a vast and rese
Native labour supply. labour crop in the native negro population.   If more highly civilised man does
reap on the goldfields a full benefit from this provision of nature, while at the sa
time benefiting the kaffir, it is the white man's fault.   American mining enterp
has the benefit of no such bountiful labour supply, which, by all rules of reas
should be cheap, and in the exercise of good judgment, should be made efficient
well.

Natural advantages of Rand.   I have now called your attention to four marked advantages—the small amo
of ground water, freedom from heavy timbering costs, tractability of ores, and freed
from oppressive ground heat—which the mining field itself affords here; and I h
also presented three points wherein nature seemingly has intended to favour min
industry on the Rand—namely, an abundant fuel supply close at hand, an abund
labour supply at no great distance, and a good working climate.

Agriculture.   There is one other point worthy of note in this connection.   The climate and s
of the Transvaal are favourable to agriculture, and the cost of living ought to be
most, moderate on the Witwatersrand fields to those who are content to live, or
their earnings do live, on ordinary plain food, such as the country should produce.

By comparison with the American miner, the Witwatersrand worker should be Cost of living for miners in America and on the Witwatersrand.
e to live as well and as cheaply, and would be able to do so, were the agricultural
ources of this country brought to the stage of development they might be. I know
re are peculiar drawbacks here, and special ones recently or at the present time—
usts and the rinderpest. But the American pioneer agriculturist has had, and has,
urges to contend with also, and very often in the neighbourhood of mining regions
has not nearly such favourable conditions to work under as the Transvaal presents.

The development of the Transvaal goldfields can never reach the stage which in The mining industry and agriculture.
human reason it should reach, until the agriculture of the Transvaal is measurably
vanced beyond where it is to-day. I do not say this lightly or with intent to dis-
rage the farmers or people of the Transvaal, and certainly not with the intent to
little the praiseworthy result which they have brought about in making a civilised
untry out of a most savage and barbarous one within the span of one generation's
e. But it is a material point in the economic problem which the present condition
the mining industry has brought to your doors—that the cost of mining is largely
1at the cost of living makes it, and the cost of living is in the greatest degree
pendent upon local agricultural production.

The miner has brought into your country the most perfect mining machinery and
pliances, the most refined methods of work, and some of the best trained and
perienced experts on earth, and he has by these means brought his industry from
e crudest to the most advanced stage, within little more than half a decade. Has
e local agriculturist kept pace with him? For, mark you, they must go abreast
r the best results.

If it were not for the exceptional perfection of mining and reduction machinery
d plant, if it were not for perfection of method and process, in the present state of
1man knowledge which have been brought to your doors, and if it were not that
any of the best men in various departments of mining work have been called from
her countries to the advantage of the Witwatersrand, there would not be a dozen
orking mines upon it to-day, and there would be no prospect of increase in the
1mber.

By these means has the miner attained a certain success, which has made a
arket for the produce of the farmer. Has the farmer, meanwhile, brought his
ethods to a comparable degree of perfection, enabling him to supply the miner at
west profitable price, so that he may make still other mines pay for their joint
nefit and the advancement of the country?

I am professionally and practically familiar with the agricultural resources and Agriculture.
orkings of vast American regions adjacent to or supplying mining districts. I have
oked into this matter in the Transvaal, and I regret to say that for myself I answer
1e last above query in the negative.

The Transvaal agriculture is crude, its methods are wasteful, the farming results
e poor, and the market price of produce is excessively high. How is it possible,
1der such conditions, to bring the cost of mining on the Rand down to what it should
? ? The point is a vital one in the economic problem before you, if it is to be treated
her than in the most superficial manner. At least, it should be considered, when a
ll is made by those representing the farmer on the miner, to still more perfect his
ethods, to yet further improve his machinery and to cut down the salaries of those
ho have virtually made these mines and the past prosperity, or else, as an alterna-
ve, not ask for relief from your Government.

It is no purpose of mine to invidiously reflect on the farmers of the Transvaal.
could have no possible object in so doing; and to criticise them unjustly or un-

necessarily would be repugnant to me.   I have found much to admire in them.   B
this is a case wherein the truth should be pressed home to the minds of all.

The mining industry and agriculture. You cannot have the best development of the mining industry here in the mid
of a woefully backward agricultural development, except you make such free at
open communication with, and cheap transport from, the outside world as will enab
it to supply the wants of these mining people almost as cheaply as they could b
supplied by home-raised produce under good agricultural practice.

You cannot expect the mining industry to pluck the mote out of its industri
eye until your farming population removes some, at least, of the beam in its industri
eye, except your Government, representing your people, come to the rescue.   It is ju
Causes of grievances on Rand this state of things which has made the trouble on the Rand.   The deficiencies cause
by these conditions, under the circumstances, it is the province of the Government t
fill.   It is for this reason there are and have been " grievances " here; and it is fo
the same reason that they will continue until very substantial relief is granted, an
the cost of living is brought to a reasonable figure.

Conditions are such here that the mining industry cannot work out its ow
salvation; and, just as it would be asking too much of the Transvaal farmers t
immediately change their methods, as a whole, and at once step into the first rank c
agricultural economists—bringing living expenses down to old country rates—so is
The mining industry and the Government. asking too much of the mining industry to try to go materially further in reducin
its running costs until it has had such relief as the Government, representing th
exceedingly backward agricultural industry, can grant.

Cost of living an index to wages The cost of living must ever be a fair index of the wage to be paid, in order tha
the workman remain contented in whatever capacity he may be serving.   Those wh
labour only with their hands receive but small margins over living rates, while thos
who have some specially valuable professional or managerial ability demand and ge
wide margins.   Nevertheless, living expense is an index to the wage or salary in eac
grade of service, separately, for each locality.

Being familiar with wage rates and salaries and the cost of living in some of th
mining regions and towns and cities of the Pacific Slope States of America, I hav
Comparative cost of living for miners, mine officials, and engineers, on the Rand and in California. enquired into the subject here, with this result (I give you comparisons in percen
ages, and not actual rates, because I can thus more briefly convey the lesson which th
figures would show):—

The ordinary miner, single, and living at a boarding house, pays 13 to 17 per cen
more here for his board and bunk and other necessaries of life than at California mine
If he is married and attempts to keep house, his expenses will be 22 to 27 per cen
greater here to support himself and family than in Californian mining districts.   I
the case of the mechanic, receiving better wages and desiring better food and accommo
dation generally, I place the differences at 18 to 25 per cent. if single, and 28 to 32 pe
cent. if married.

And so on, as we mount the scale of wage and salary earners, the cost of livin
here, as compared to California mining towns and cities, increases alarmingly, unti
when we reach the highest paid consulting engineers, general managers, and managin
directors, I am satisfied that it costs them from 150 to 200 per cent.—from two to thre
times as much as it would cost to live in the same style in the city of San Francisc
California.

Take a few items of which I know.   House rents are from two to four time
greater here than in San Francisco, or in any mining district in California.   Wate
costs four to 10 times as much as in San Francisco and Californian mining regions.
have compared the rates per volume supplied, and also a number of monthly wate
bills here, with my knowledge of what similar service would be rendered for in Sa

cisco, or in any mining region in California, where there is an independent company ng water). To keep a stable of two to six horses, costs three to four times as much ohannesburg as in San Francisco, or as it would in any mining district in fornia.

I might enumerate other items of expense which make drafts on the salary and e-earner's purse—all showing costs ranging at 50 to 200 per cent. higher here than merican mining districts and neighbouring cities, but the above are enough to trate the point I seek to make.

The following table shows in a general way the result of my enquiry. The figures ot, of course, purport to accurately represent the facts, but I venture to say that if a iled enquiry were made on the subject its results would not much differ from my tration.

LE SHOWING APPROXIMATELY, THE PERCENTAGES OF HIGHER COST OF LIVING ON THE RAND AS COMPARED TO LIVING COSTS IN PACIFIC COAST MINING DISTRICTS AND CITIES :—

AMERICA.

Class of Employment, graded from Least to Greatest Pay.				Percentage of Excess of Cost of Living on the Rand over Costs in American Mining Camps and Cities.	
				Single Man.	Man with Family.
Miner ...	...	...	...	13 to 17	22 to 27
Mechanic ...	...	...	...	18 „ 23	28 „ 32
Foreman ...	...	...	...	25 „ 30	35 „ 40
Captain ...	...	..	...	30 „ 35	45 „ 50
Clerks ...	...	...	...	40 „ 45	55 „ 60
Surveyor ...	...	...	...	—	60 „ 70
Accountants ...	...	...	...	—	80 „ 90
Managers and engineers	...	...		—	100 „ 120
General managers and consulting engineers		...		—	150 „ 200

Percentages of excess of cost of living on Rand over cost of living in American mining camps and cities.

Two points are prominently apparent from this tabulation :—(1) The comparative ess in cost of living on the Rand falls more heavily on the employees of the higher n the lower grades; (2) The percentage of excess is far greater for married men h families attempting to keep house, than for single men living at boarding houses n rooms.

Comparative greater cost of living of higher than lower grade employ- ees. Comparative higher cost of living of mar- ried than un- married min- ers.

I submit that this exhibit strikingly illustrates the reason for the point made by Goldmann in evidence before you, as to the remarkably small proportionate part of e white employees on the Rand who are married, and the still more remarkably ll number who have their wives and families here with them.

But, if the results of my enquiry are near the truth, the above exhibit illustrates ther point, namely, a greater proportion of the highly-paid employees having ilies resident here with them, than of those of lower pay. Those of higher pay, as ass, unless their salaries are proportionately very much in advance of those of er, are the greatest suffers financially by the burdens of Transvaal living costs. d this I believe to be the case.

I turn to the rates of pay for the employees of various grades on the Rand, as put vidence by several witnesses—commencing with the cheapest white miner at £14 month, and advancing through the roll to mine managers at £1,500 to £3,000 pe r—and I find that, whereas the wages of the lowest grades of white mine employee 15 to 30 per cent. higher here than in the older and more settled mine regions in stern America, the employees of highest grades, up to the managers and engineers,

Comparative sal- aries and wages on Rand and in Western America of higher grade and lower grade mine employees.

receive salaries not more than the same 15 to 30 per cent. higher than they wo
command in the same American mine centres for like services.

If we compare these latter percentages, as to wages and salaries, with those of
illustration just given you, as to relative cost of living, and remember the rule—that
of living must be an index of the wage—we find that it is not the higher paid w
employees on the Rand who are reaping the harvest, if one is being garnered at pres
rates. I take up the more direct application of the foregoing to the problem wh
you have in hand.

You have in evidence, so far as I have observed, the cost of mining and reduct
of ores on the Rand, varying from about 24s. to about 29s. per ton milled. I h
collected some data, which show a higher range, namely, up to 32s. per ton ; and
result of my enquiry is rather to the point that there is more ore mined and redu
on the Rand at costs over 29s., than under that figure. Next, it appears that the p
portionate part due to white labour, of the total cost, ranges from 28 to 35 per c
And, again, I assume, upon the basis of my own enquiry and comparisons, that
average cost of living of all white mine employees is 25 to 35 per cent. greater h
than in the American mining countries spoken of.

If, upon these rates and ratios, we estimate how far wages might, without affecti
the employees' profits, be cut down, and how much cost of production would thus
lowered, if the cost of living here were reduced to the American standard, and
wages proportionately lowered, we would have a result somewhat as follows :—Cost
mining and reduction, 24s. to 32s. ; part due to labour, say 32 per cent., 7·68-10·2
part due to excess cost of living; if rates here are 35 per cent. higher, 2·69-3·58s.
rates here are 30 per cent. higher, 2·30-3·07s. ; if rates here are 25 per cent. high
1·92-2·56s. From this it appears that the difference in cost of living here, as compa
to American mining regions, may account for between, say 2s. as a minimum, and 3·5
as a maximum ; that is, if cost of living for the white man were reduced here to w
might be considered a reasonable basis, all wages and salaries could be cut, with
diminishing the workers' profits, so as to reduce the cost of producing the gold from
to 3·58s.

This reasoning is based, you will observe, upon the assumption that the cost
living, at the mean of the wage scale, is a correct index of the fair average wage r

If, now, we consider the application of this conclusion to the present wage rate,
have an interesting result, and that is, that the higher cost of white labour of
kinds, engaged in mining and for the mining companies, is accounted for, or son
what more than accounted for, by the difference in the cost of the necessaries, and
amounts of expenditure, of life.

And, now, I come to a matter as to which I speak with confidence, because
personal experience in the management of labour, both skilled and unskilled, and o
wide opportunity to observe and hear the results of different systems of handli
labour. This is the bonus system of rewarding extra exertion on the part of mine
There appears to be here a leaning towards an opinion that the system is unfair a
extravagant. I desire to testify, not only to its equability and economy, but to
wisdom for other reasons, and to illustrate my testimony by some facts I ha
collected here, and by results of experience elsewhere. At the outset I desire
explain that I use the words "bonus system" as expressive of all forms of grad
payment, whereunder a premium is set upon extra exertion, as evidenced by excess
results over the normal, due to simple day-wage results. In this category would co
the graded-rate contract system, as well as the bonus system proper.

The higher grade American contractors on heavy engineering constructions,
well as managers of great manufacturing works, have long recognised the justice

underlying principle and the value to them of its application in management of ir labour forces. Special rewards, extra pay, advances of rates of pay, made untarily to those men who prove specially active on arduous and dangerous duty, to the more orderly bonus system, which is quite common in some branches of gineering construction, and in great iron and steel working establishments, to my n personal knowledge. Certainly, high-grade contractors and managers whose rk is systematised, and the costs and relative costs known to a penny, would not pt a system which did not pay them. If it would pay a contractor to follow that tem in driving great tunnels, as I know from experience it does, it would pay him adopt it in sinking a shaft. And if it would pay him to adopt it in shaft work, it uld equally pay a mining company to do the same. That it does pay here you ve had illustrated to you in the testimony of Mr. Catlin.

I endeavour to give some further illustration of its advantages, not alone on count of the direct benefits to be derived from the working of the system itself, but cause there are very important correlative benefits which have not been brought to ur notice, and because it embodies a principle whose application is indispensable to solving of your entire labour problem—the great problem for the Rand and for South African Republic.

Bonus system beneficial.

The mining industry has appealed to Government for relief of burdens. Repretatives of Government say that there is a desire on the part of Government to ter the industry: It only wants to see its way clear to that end. And they ask at the industry proposes to do to help itself. Members of the industry's staff point t that one way is to extend the bonus system. Whereupon, there are those in ominent positions who imply or say, that the system, so far from being economical, extravagant. To entertain this latter assertion, to adopt its idea, would be a fatal stake for your Commission to fall into, for the reason above given.

I therefore ask your indulgence to present the matter somewhat more fully than r. Catlin could do, owing to his being on the eve of going away on vacation, when appeared before you. First: Completing Mr. Catlin's figures as to the Catlin aft. Passing over the first two or three months, when the work was not yet nning regularly, there came two months, whose average rate was 60 feet per month, a cost of £21 15s. 8d. per foot. Then the next five months, during which work as regular, the mean monthly progress was 128·3 feet, at an average cost of 9 5s. 6d. per foot. Now, it is well-known that such shafts had never before been nk by the ungraded day-wage system, at a faster rate than 80 feet per month, or a wer cost than about £24 per foot. The far better result attained in the Catlin shaft running the cost down in one month as low as £18 6s. and, in another month, the te of speed up to 142 feet—is due to the incentive of the premium on extra ertion. It does seem that there can be no disputing the lesson taught by such ures.

Bonus system and the Catlin shaft.

I ask your attention to a business simile pointing this lesson. If a mercantile use makes a shipment of goods over a long voyage route, its manager considers st, cost, interest, insurance, meeting of demand, and profit. A question with him is to whether he will order shipment by sailing vessel or by steamship, which will ke less than half the time, but whose freight rates are greater. The world's exrience shows that it pays the merchant to employ the quicker mode of transit at the gher freighting cost. The story is told by figures of the capital account in his oks. An exactly similar story, only with far more favourable results, would be told the capital account of a mining company engaged in sinking or developing work, ere the books kept so that the point might be brought out, and if the bonus stem were operated as the fast-rate steamship line against the one-grade-wage

Economy of bonus system.

system representing the comparatively slow line of sailing packets. Sinking a dee
level shaft is, in this way, an exact counterpart of freighting over a long voyage.
attempt to illustrate upon a basis of the experience on the Rand.

The Simmer and Jack East Company has a working capital of £186,000 su
scribed for the purpose of putting down to the reefs three shafts, with probable dept
estimated at 2,400, 2,500, and 2,700 ft. As these are nearly the same, we may s
that £62,000, one-third of the above total working capital for them, may be charg
against each in capital account, and against that amount interest at, we will say, 6 p
cent. should be charged in such account. If, now, the shafts are put down at the ra
of 60 ft. per month, it will take 40, 41$\frac{2}{3}$, and 45 months respectively to sink them, a
the amounts of interest which the capital account will show against the cost for ea
will be £12,400, £12,916, and £13,950 respectively. Adding these amounts to t
principal in each case, the shafts will have cost the shareholders who put up the
money originally and waited for return, £74,400, £74,916, and £75,950 respectivel
But if the shafts are driven at double the rate of speed (120 ft. per month) the wo
would be accomplished in half the time, and half the above amounts of interest wou
be saved to the shareholders, because the mine could be brought into paying conditio
with the saving of that amount of time to which that amount of interest on sha
working capital would be due.

In the above instance the saving to the Simmer and Jack East capital accoun
and to shareholders, would amount to £19,633—a very handsome amount, you mu
admit, to be saved by good management. That this is an actual saving, ever
business man who keeps a capital account, will testify. And, be it remembered, it
entirely aside from the saving in actual cost of the shafts themselves, due to the low
rate of cost per foot attained, with the higher rate of speed in driving. The hig
speed bonus system is thus seen to operate both ways.

I next note what the total saving might be by it in the above illustrative cas
Sunk by day labour, unencouraged, and at the rate Mr. Catlin found it cost to sin
similar shafts in the same neighbourhood—say, £24 per foot—the 7,600 fee
aggregate footage in depth of these three shafts, would cost £182,400—a small margi
only, less than the working capital £186,000, provided for them. Sunk under th
bonus system at, say, £20 per foot (which is nearly 10s. more than Mr. Catlin's lea
rate under it) the cost would be £152,000. The direct saving in money would l
£30,400; which with the saving of £19,633 to the Company's capital account and th
shareholders, makes £60,033, which amount is nearly 40 per cent. on the actual co
of the shafts, or 33 per cent. of the working capital provided for them.

But this is not all; there would be a saving of 20 to 22$\frac{1}{2}$ months' time; and th
time in the full development of the enterprise is worth money to the shareholders i
other ways than in saving interest on the working capital provided for the shaft
For instance, to shareholders who hold their shares, say, for the 20 to 22$\frac{1}{2}$ months aft
the mine commences to produce, the saving of that length of time in the shaft sinkin
is worth their *pro rata* of all the net product in that time.

It may be said that I have calculated interest on a capital which is greater than
required for the shafts. And so it would, in such a case, prove to be, but the estimat
of capital required for the shafts was based on previous experience and rates for wor
here. That it is possible to do the work for a less sum, and thereby save, not only th
interest on the whole sum for a very material length of time, but also a good part c
the capital itself, is due to the operation of the bonus system. For constructions, a
uncertain in incidental difficulties as shaft sinking, a liberal margin of capital must b
provided in the estimates.

The above case is a hypothetical one, and no deep-level shaft has been completel

: at as great an average rate of speed as 120 feet per month, with as low an
age cost as £20 per foot.　But experience thus far warrants my using these
res for the purpose of illustrating a principle.　Mr. Catlin's best speed was even
h higher, 142 feet per month; his average for five months was 128·3 feet, at a
n cost of £19 5s. 6d., as we have seen.　The actual costs of, and rates in, the
mer and Jack East shafts themselves show figures ranging from different groups
onths, as follows:—

| Shaft Depth. | Mean depths of two months each. | | Total times at rates. | Total costs at rates. | Total interest on costs. |
	Feet.	Costs.	Months.		
2,400	90	£23 14 2	26¾	£56,900	£7,681
2,400	112	20 9 3	22	49,120	5,403
2,500	82	23 13 2	30	59,146	8,872
2,500	98	22 4 1	26	55,510	7,216
2,700	62	28 1 0	43	75,735	16,288
2,700	84	25 3 8	32	67,994	10,878

Cost of, and rates of speed in sinking of Simmer and Jack shafts.

The figures which I use in this statement were made up by the resident secretary
he company, Mr. Roberts, and have been furnished to me by Mr. Webb, consulting
ineer to the company, arranged at my suggestion, so as to illustrate the point I
ke, namely, that with increased speed comes decreased cost per foot, decreased time
essary to sink the shaft, decreased cost of the work as a whole, and, of course,
portionately less interest to be charged in the capital account.　Examination of
h couplet—one for each of the three shafts, separately—tells the story.　The cases
fairly selected.　The incentive of the bonus produced the favourable result in
ry case.

I beg to submit another illustration of the economy to be attained by rapid
king of deep-level shafts.　The nominal capital of the Simmer and Jack Proprietary
es, Limited, is £5,000,000.　The shares have actually been taken by the public and
vendors at rates up to £7 10s., but to be entirely conservative, I adopt the nominal
of £5, which produces the capitalisation above quoted.　Now, the shareholders
waiting for returns on their investments; the outcrop part of the property is
ng worked, and paying, but three deep-level shafts are being sunk, upon the com-
tion of which the opening of fully one-third of the property necessarily depends.
en these are producing ore, it is expected that the monthly returns will be doubled.
ese shafts, to open one-third of the producing area of the property, properly repre-
t one-third of the company's capital, or £1,666,667, which, running at 6 per cent. per
r (not a high rate for mining capital), properly has charged against it £100,000
rest per year in the capital accounts of those who hold the shares.　This is at the
of £8,333 per month.

Economy of rapid shaft sinking in deep levels, particularly in Simmer and Jack Proprietary Mines' three deep level shafts.

If the three shafts are driven at the rate of 80 feet per month each, the maximum
ained without bonus rewards (or 240 feet total), the interest being consumed is £38.
hey were driven at an average of 110 feet each month (a rate which it is believed
ld be maintained over considerable periods, or until some untoward circumstance,
a temporary inburst of water, should happen), the total footage per month would
330 feet, and the interest running would be, say, £25 per foot.　This more rapid
of driving, hence, would save to the shareholders, in interest on their investments
ar, £13 per foot of shaft, which is materially more than 50 per cent. of the cost of
work thus far done on these particular shafts, and is over 60 per cent. of the least
t per foot attained in them.

B 2

This is a conservative example, which may well find its counterpart in practic matters in future run smoothly, and the bonus system is operated to best advant. The data for this illustration were furnished me through Mr. Webb, consult engineer to the company, by Mr. Watson, manager, who has made some even stron deductions in the same line of argument, showing economy and advantage of bonus system in shaft-sinking. I submit these figures as illustrating, locally, advantages of a system, which I have proven in the construction of canals and driv of tunnels in other countries.

Bonus system cheaper than time wage system.
I now ask your attention to a point as to actual comparative costs. You may told that some shaft or shafts, wherein labour was paid by the day, without the ex incentive of a bonus, have been put down at less rates per foot than those where bonus system was adopted. Having enquired into this matter, I suggest that, be you hesitate to fully appreciate and accept the advantages of the bonus system : its underlying principle, you make enquiry: First—As to the comparative size : character of the shaft or shafts alleged to have been put down more cheaply; Sec —As to the nature of the material through which sunk; Third—As to whether it v not an incline shaft sunk on a mine already operative, and from which drifts or le were at the same time being driven either way on the reef.

You will see immediately that in the case of a company sinking deep-level sha only, *all* the hoisting expense on surface work, and all the office, management, prof sional and other costs, have to be charged proportionately against each foot of sh sunk. There is no other work being done to charge part of them to. But in the c of a shaft being dropped down the reef on an operative mine, all this is quite differe In the first place, there is charged to that shaft, or incline, only its proportionate p of all the general expense of the mine—the mine office, the Johannesburg office, a London office expense, the management, professional service; and such items as their entirety went against the shaft or shafts alone in the deep-level instance, are the operative outcrop mine instance, divided and charged against a number of fa being driven in developing the mine, and against the stoping for ore output throu other inclines. Then, again, as soon as drives commence to be made from the n incline, the general expenses and hoisting costs are again distributed against footage made on all these faces for each month.

Thus, I think you will find, on careful and complete enquiry, that there are cases where nearly as cheap work has been done in shaft-sinking by day labour wi out the incentive of a bonus, as has been done under influence of rewards for ex exertion.

Objections to bonus system.
And now we have seen that the bonus system operates greatly to the sha holders' benefit, what are the objections to it? That it enables common miners make very much higher wages than miners usually do or should; and that it has a may again enable a common miner to draw from a company as much money in month as high-grade professional men can earn in like time. This is alleged to be e travagant waste of company money. In the face of the facts and deductions wh have been shown you, this ground of objection is untenable.

The primary conclusion from the facts must be that the company saves mon and the shareholders make money under the operation of the bonus system. N withstanding the miner receives a higher wage, taking time and work done i consideration, the bonus system is the cheapest. Even if the cost per foot, or oth unit of work, were as much under the bonus system as by the day wage, yet it wou save the time and the interest and the mine profit due to the time, which are ve handsome considerations for the shareholder.

But beyond this, even, there is the benefit to the entire force on a property, ·ich reward of merit on fair competition among members of that force produces; ·l the bonus system, properly applied, is not only a money maker to the shareholder, · a reward of merit to the miner. Where labour is graded in classes by mere ·ming of trade, and all individuals in each class or trade are paid alike a standard ·ge for that class—as all carpenters, all miners, the same for each in each calling— ·re is absolutely no reward for industry, extra intelligence, or special skill.

It is nonsense to say: "If a man does not come up to the mark, discharge him." ·hat mark is meant? Men in all callings are graded, as to result they will produce, ·m very bad, bad, indifferent, fairly good, good, better, best, and extra. What is · standard? The mediocre? That would be an injustice to all above, and when graded in reward, the best men drop to that plane, while those below, being paid much as any, have no incentive to do better than their ordinary inefficient doing.

The true way, therefore, is to grade men on the pay-roll according to their ·serts—their industry, good faith, and skill. This makes active-brained, industrious ·n of them, and none but the stupid dolts or the incorrigible loafers will fail to be ·nefited by recognition of special merit in some members of their class. The result ·he greater amount and better quality of work all round. If some men are chosen · reason of their ability or push, and are given a job where they may win a very ·bstantial bonus, all the fairly good men in that force will strive to merit the same ·vour at the hands of the manager.

Moreover—and this is a point which I desire to bring specially to your atten- Principle of bonus system, a republican principle. ·n—the principle of this bonus system is that which goes by the common name in ·merica, and probably elsewhere, of "Let the best man win." That is the principle ·derlying the republican form of Government. It works as well in industrial ·tters as in national affairs, and no republic can long stand which resolutely turns · back upon it, either as applied to national affairs or to industrial affairs within its ·rders.

The very reverse of this principle is that which dictates the grading of men's ·ges simply by trade. One trade, one wage, results in classifications of men which ·eed discontent and uprisings, such as monarchical forms of Government can best ·pe with. The principle of this grading is an autocratic one, not a republican one.

I respectfully submit that, whatever action this Government takes with relation · mine labour matters, it should do so with the idea of encouraging application of ·is principle of "Let the best man win."

Nor should this idea stop with the handling of the white labour problem. It Principle of bonus system desirable in native as in white labour. ·ould be carried into the management of kaffirs as well. There should be some ·stem of grading according to skill or proficiency, or some system of bonus reward · amount of work done, and with this should go some gradation of pay due to ·ngth of service in one employ. The boy coming anew to a mine should not be per- ·itted, no matter what his skill, to take pay equal to those of the same grade who ·d been working on the property for, say, three months or six months.

If this idea could be carried out—if the good boys knew that, on deserting from ·e mine they could not under three or six months get an equal wage on another— ·ey would not desert. It may be said that this is human nature, but is not kaffir Native labour. ·ture. I simply submit that the kaffir is working for money, and it would not take ·m long to become altogether "human" in this point if it were faithfully enforced. ·nd this, in my opinion, is the key to the kaffir labour problem on these mines. It · said that the kaffir is by nature a child, and must be treated as such. Well, there · vast families of these children here, and they have as many fathers and mothers ·king out for them as there are mine managements. Each such pair of parents

spoils these children for all the other fathers and mothers, by taking the wayw?
runaways into their mine families on application, on an equal footing to that held
the family they left. If the deserting boys could not get into other mine famil
without sacrifice of standing, they would not desert.

Close organisa-
tion of mine
managements
necessary.

In short, the mine managements must work together in this matter. For t?
purpose they must be organised as one institution, and every mine management m?
be in it. This could only be effected under a law of the Republic. The details of ?
law should be presented by the representative Chambers of Mines. The operation
it should be wholly in the hands of the organisation created by it, under gene?
supervision—not absolute dictation—of the Government. By some such means on
can I see the way at all clear to handle the kaffir labour problem of the future of t
Rand.

Possible expan-
sion of mining
industry under
favourable
conditions.

For purposes of my water supply study here I have, with several consulti?
engineers of the large mining managements, made a study in detail of the possib
extent to which mining may be developed on the Rand, should the industry
relieved of undue burdens, and be permitted to expand under entirely favoural
conditions.

Possible number
of stamps on
central Rand.

The general result is that within the fifteen miles of the Central Ra?
somewhat over 6,000 stamps could advantageously be supplied with ore and broug
into operation.

This estimate takes into consideration the development of the two tiers of dee
levels, an increase of stamps on some outcrop properties, as well as the entire worki?

Actual number
of stamps on
central Rand.

out of other outcrop properties. There are now within this fifteen miles of territo?
2,550 stamps, of which 2,330 are believed to be working. The study has been ve?
carefully entered into for this central part of the Rand, and an approximation h
been made for the extension west to and including Randfontein, and east to a?
including Modderfontein.

I conclude that the population directly dependent on mine work, and alm?
wholly living on or closely adjacent to mine properties, for operating, not constructi?
work, might be expected to reach, under the most favourable conditions, for the fifte?

Possible popula-
tion of central
Rand.

miles of Central Road, 12,000 whites and 100,000 kaffirs, and as many more for t
two extensions combined. On top of these figures would go the general mercant?
and business population, and some labour yet employed on surface constructio?
though most of this latter would, by time of full stamp development, have be?
finished.

Aside from the city of Johannesburg, under these most favourable condition
there is a possibility for employing, therefore, say 30,000 whites and 250,000 blac?
on the Rand. It is not, for purposes of my point, necessary to assume the full figur?
We might accept 25,000 whites and 200,000 blacks outside of the city population as
not unreasonable probability if very substantial reliefs are granted ; and this, with
10 years : always provided that the black population can be made to come, stay a?
work faithfully at the lower wage necessary for development of this state of thing
Besides all this population, there would be the city.

Government sys-
tem of admin-
istration re-
quires to be
reformed.

If the present system of administering Government affairs should be kept up,
would then take a very large proportion of able-bodied burghers of the Republ
simply to administer the laws. This could not be, and at the same time establish
revenue system which would relieve the mining industry and permit the developme?
contemplated. The expense of administration would advance proportionately to t?
development, and that would at once arrest all progress. Moreover, the advanc?
agriculture necessary to advance the mining industry, could not itself be accomplish?
were the burghers nearly all occupied in public service.

The conclusions are unavoidable—(1) the burgher population must increase, pro- *Burgher population must be increased.* ‐ionately, even more rapidly than the mining population; (2) the administration ‐aws on the Rand must be greatly changed; or (3) there can be no very great *Administration of laws on Rand must be altered.* ‐ance, no matter what reliefs be granted in the way of cheaper dynamite and ‐per transportation, and grievances will continue to exist.

The administration of kaffir labour, and of all mine labour matters at the very ‐t, will have to be left to the mine managements under some Government law, ‐ch would make all of them come in and stay in it for their own good and that ‐he country. The anomalous condition of 50,000 to 70,000 white people and ‐000 blacks, including city populations, massed in a limited area, and wholly ‐erned and kept in order, even as to local matters, by guards and administrative ‐ers drawn from a sparse agricultural population, cannot be made to work. It ‐ld be in every way unnatural and repugnant as a condition within a republic.

I refer to this merely as a labour question; not a political one outside of that *The labour problem.* ‐ediate connection. It is facing this inevitable condition, gradually growing more ‐e,—no matter how good-natured and well-disposed all the people, burghers, ‐anders, and kaffirs may be—which presents the real problem of your country ‐ay, a problem which will come up for solution as a fiscal one—one of revenue. It ‐d not come up in any other form to force you to solve it effectually, and you cannot ‐ibly do so without the close co-operation in public affairs of those who are ‐anders to your land, but producers of its wealth.

The problem can only be solved by making the *uitlander* feel at home here, as a *Incorporation of uitlanders.* ‐a fide resident, under, and participant in Government, at least of some sort, local ‐istrict. As to the kaffir, he cannot be made to become a progressive and efficient ‐er and reliable employee under the unnatural condition in which he is now held. ‐t he should have at least a temporary home within no great distance of the mine *Native locations.* ‐tre, to which he could inexpensively retire after his engagements on mine service ‐over, and with the view of returning to mine work, seems to me to be absolutely ‐ntial to the end in view; or else he must be carried by rail, at a merely nominal ‐, practically, to and from the country of his home. As I have tried to impress ‐n you, your problem is a very serious one, altogether aside from the political and ‐ander grievance form, in which it has heretofore come up. This mining, for ‐sons which already appear in evidence before you, is to be ranked in matters of ‐ernmental economy, with the staple industries in other countries.

It has been said in evidence that there is no competition in gold mining. This is *Competition in gold mining: Transvaal and foreign fields.* ‐e in a sense; but not true as applied to the gold mining of the Transvaal at the ‐sent time. It is yet a question of capitalisation for the deep-level mines and those ‐ers not already advanced to near the paying stage, and the Transvaal fields, in the ‐ley markets of the world, must compete for that capital as against other regions, ‐ speculative venture. Moreover, there is and must be competition among cliques ‐ financiers to secure for their properties the capital which is willing to come here, ‐ the most successful and best managements will command the strongest financial ‐port.

Thus all the elements of great industrial problems are here present, and your ‐stion is an industrial one of the highest order and most intricate complications, and ‐e dealt with accordingly.

The sanitary condition of Johannesburg and the mines, and the system of water *Sanitary reform necessary.* ‐ply and refuse disposal, are not such as will admit expansion of the industry as ‐einbefore estimated. There will be disaster here if these subjects are not taken ‐ngly in hand for the public good. You only have to look at what is happening in certain parts of your country now, in the way of disease, destruction, and death form a small idea of what will happen here if matters are not speedily corrected.

The way to effect this correction is not to grant concessions which will m speculative monopolies of sewerage and municipal water supplying. These matt above all things, must be conducted honestly and faithfully for the public good, :

Johannesburg water supply. not as speculations. You never will bring mining to a reasonably low figure of until you have a cheap and abundant city water supply for all purposes. This ma of water rates is, the world over, an index to industrial conditions. It will be b and you cannot prevent it. Dear water, dear living, dear mining; it is always case.

To relieve this water supply and sewerage situation there are enough ear people interested on the Rand to supply the capital out of hand, to place first-c works at the disposal of the city of Johannesburg at lowest possible cost price, w lowest rates of interest. And I venture to say that such an arrangement could made if your Government would do its part and enable public-spirited capital accomplish such an end without having to meet the demands of Government con sionaires.

Concessions. From the standpoint of industrial economy the granting of exclusive c cessions is a bad feature of Transvaal affairs. It finds no counterpart in United States, and never did. Although it may have been necessary here the past, it certainly is not so now. This country is at a stage where o competition on republican principles can make it great for the burghers; but is also at a stage where a failure to recognise the principle, " Let the best man w may ruin it for them through the working of natural laws in industrial developm

Agriculture. While the crucial question, as directly affecting the mines, is, in my judgment, labour question, there goes with it the problem of agricultural development. Thi an agricultural country, some of it as good as any in the world. If the Governm would actively and earnestly take steps to advance agriculture, in the light of t examples and practice the world over, and in a way suited to the people and

Cost of living. country itself, the longest possible step would be taken to permanently settle problem of cheap mining by settling the problem of cheap living.

Mr. W. Hosken's evidence. MR. WILLIAM HOSKEN called, said :

I am a merchant resident in Johannesburg since 1889, and represent the Cham

Confirmation of Mr. Pistorius' statement. of Commerce. I affirm that the statement of Mr. Pistorius is true. The Chamber Commerce requested me to attend to give further evidence, especially with regard railway questions. When this Industrial Commission was appointed, the represen tives of the Chamber of Commerce and Mercantile Association held special meeti

Reasons for pre-sent depression to consider the position and formulate a statement affirming that the causes of present depression were effected as follows :—(a) The Netherlands Railway admin tration. Such as the differential and excessive rates, and lack of capable administ tion. (b) The excessive cost of dynamite. (c) Excessive taxation. (d) The industr and trading monopolies, such as are being used for the development of industr enterprise. (e) As shown by the insecurity evidenced by the withdrawal of cap by investors from the Transvaal, and the difficulty of arranging financial transactic and the want of firm legal measures to suppress gambling, especially in the form

South African industries, in-cluding agri-culture, depen-dent on mining industry. sweeps.

I will endeavour in my evidence to avoid going over the same ground traver by previous witnesses. Before taking up the definite points referred to, I shall the attention of the Commission to the industrial and economic fact that South Afr a mining country, and all other industries are dependent on the mining industry, excepting agriculture. In proof of this, I have a table which shows that in 1896 the imports through the Cape and Natal amounted in value to £23,372,000, and the exports totalled £17,878,000. Of the minerals, gold showed a value of £8,355,000; diamonds, £4,640,000. Agricultural products exported include grain, flowers, grass (to the extent from the Cape of £20,000), spirits, wine, bark, oathay, feathers, wool, hides, skins, hair, and horns, totalling in all about £4,166,000. For other agricultural products the markets are found in this country through the mining industry. The markets are the mining towns, and the places through which the traffic for the mines passes. I don't wish to minimise the value and importance of the primary industry—namely, agriculture—but in this country the mining industry is pre-eminently the backbone and support of the whole country. The crops I have referred to are sold in the mining towns, and at the ports where the traffic for the mines passes through. The economic question outlined by these figures has in the past not received sufficient attention by even the people or the Governments in South Africa. I wish to put forward as a practical proposition to the Commission: If an acre of ground is cultivated for minerals, it should produce say £10,000 during a certain period. Is it not an equal advantage to the State and community to make the production through the mineral kingdom, as it would be for the same return to be made through the vegetable kingdom. The experience gained in other countries also assures us that the successful working of the mining industry brings success for all other industries with it, and especially success for agriculture. For examples, we can look California, and Australia, and New Zealand. These countries were, in the first instance, exploited for minerals, and success in mineral work has enabled them to become foremost in agriculture. Therefore, the true policy for South Africa, and especially for the Transvaal, is to aid the mining industry in every possible way. I will now proceed to give definite evidence regarding the various points that the Chamber of Commerce considered so important. In the first place, there is the Netherlands Railway. In this connection the Chamber of Commerce wishes me to make some remarks on Mr. Middelberg's statement, laid before this Commission. Mr. Middelberg commences by correctly stating the accusation made against the Netherlands Railway, that it is taking an undue share of the transport dues from the ports to Johannesburg. He then proceeds to illustrate and defend his action in exacting this undue share by the analogy of a tenant with a house having to pay certain rent to the two or more joint-owners. Mr. Middelberg says it would be a matter of indifference to the tenant as to how the rent was divided amongst the owners. We accept the illustration as showing the position we are in as regards the South African railways. But Mr. Middelberg overlooks a most important point. He assumes that a tenant is satisfied with the rent. We are not satisfied. That entirely alters the proposition put forward by Mr. Middelberg. In pursuing the analogy further: Say the house consists of six rooms, all equally essential to the comfort and well-being of the tenant. The rent is £4 18s. 4d. per month—I take that sum as it represents the rough goods' rate per ton from Durban to Johannesburg. The tenant learns that the joint proprietors own the property in rooms, and that four rooms belong to one of the owners, and two to the other, but that the owner of the two rooms claims half the rent for his share. The tenant wants his rent reduced, and first calls on the owner of the two rooms to reduce his rent to the same standard as that of the owner of four rooms. Having secured that reduction, the tenant will proceed to press both owners for a further reduction. That is the position in the Transvaal to-day. The owner of the four rooms can be likened to Natal, which has 309 miles of railway on the line we have under consideration, and the two rooms the Netherlands, who have 178 miles.

Value and nature of imports and exports through Cape Colony and Natal in 1896.

Agriculture dependent on mining industry.

The Netherlands Railway.

Mr. Middelberg's statement.

The total rate is £4 18s. 4d. Natal gets. £2 10s. and the Netherlands get £2 8s. 4
We, therefore, think that, taking Mr. Middelberg's own analogy, it is a most defini
proof of our case for a demand for a reduction. I then follow some special pleadin
by Mr. Middelberg that are even more fallacious than the house analogy, until
come to the statement that people have distorted the share rates of the Netherlan
Railway, and made them appear as tariffs, and compared them with those in oth

Netherlands Railway share in through rate. countries in the world. The amount shared by the Netherlands is not a share of t
through-rate, but a definite tariff charged for that portion of the line under t
Netherlands administration. The Cape and Free State sections show in all the
tariff and railway debits separate entries for their portions of the line to Mid-Va
River. I hope I have made this clear to the Commission. Mr. Middelberg made
strong point of this through-rate from the port to Johannesburg, and said that we a
only interested in the through-rate, and that we are not interested in the question
how that rate was apportioned by the different owners, and pointed out that th
through-rate had been arranged for, with the help and assistance of the Netherlan
Railway, on a low basis. My endeavour will be to show that whatever benefits w
get in the way of a low rate, are not due in any measure to the Netherlands Railwa
but have come, in fact, in spite of it, and that the rates as quoted by the differer
administrations are rates to the border, and the Netherlands Railway have levelle
the different rates up to the point that suits their idea of what they should be.

Chairman.

Mr. Middelberg's evidence. You are now quoting something which has been fully discussed by Mr. Middelbe
and the members of the Commission, and it has been argued over and over agai
The Commission does not want to go over the same ground again, and we cannot ca
Mr. Middelberg to reply to you. The cross-examination was of the same tenour
your statement, and if you follow Mr. Middelberg's examination, you will see that th
same questions which you are now touching upon were gone into.—The figures I wante
to put in could not have been before you.

Mr. Smit.

The Commission don't want you to come and plead your cause. We want evidenc
and not argument, especially so in the absence of a former witness.—But statemen
have been made and not controverted.

Chairman.

If you read the evidence of Mr. Middelberg, you will see it has been controverte
in cross-examination.

Mr. Smit.

You do not contradict; you simply argue and plead your case like an advocate.—
I wanted to explain my position up to the point—or how can I otherwise make clea
my standing in the matter? Mr. Middelberg, for instance, has repudiated a telegra
Increase of railway rate on cement. which was filed here by Mr. Goldmann, regarding a change in the price of cemen
The telegram was sent to the Chamber of Commerce, and put in evidence by M
Goldmann, from the general manager of the Cape Railways, saying that in consequenc
of representations made by the Netherlands Railway, the rate on cement had bee
raised. Mr. Middelberg referred to this previous evidence and repudiated it. Nov
on behalf of the Chamber of Commerce, I will, if you will permit me, and I am to giv
proper evidence, put in the letter, dated the 6th August, 1895. It is from th
Johannesburg Chamber of Commerce to Mr. Middelberg, and quotes this same telegra

he body of the letter, which charges the Netherlands Railway with having raised rates; and we ask for an explanation as to whether the Netherlands Railway have ed the rates. I have, further a copy of the telegram from Mr. Elliott to Mr. delberg, which, if I am to give evidence, I must read, saying that, " in consequence he conversation we had in Pretoria last Monday, I have issued a notice that the rate ement will be advanced one month hence." I have, further, a copy of a letter from general manager of railways, Capetown, to the East London Chamber of Commerce, ing the same statement, all about the same date. I think the only use of my lence about railways would be to traverse some of the statements made by Mr. delberg, so I leave it to the Commission to say whether I shall go on.

Chairman.

I don't want to hear any further arguments about it. We have got complete lence about the high tariff charged by the railway, and against this we have got evidence of Mr. Middelberg, and I find enough in all that evidence for the purpose ny report. If you have got any special grievances against the railway, or any new lence, I shall be pleased to hear it.

Further evidence as to railway rates inadmissable.

Mr. Smit.

I want to add, if you can prove there is anything wrong or misleading in Mr. delberg's statement, then the Commission will hear it.—The committee of the mber of Commerce examined this statement of Mr. Middelberg's critically, with a w to offering rebutting evidence.

Mr. Middelberg evidence.

Mr. de Beer.

We don't want criticisms. Of course, we will hear with pleasure any facts. The nbers of the Commission, as well as the Chamber of Commerce can use their retion in criticising Mr. Middelberg's statement.—Of course if the statistical comative reports that have been prepared with great care are not wanted, we must ply leave that and go on.

We want you to say where you differ from Mr. Middelberg and produce the proof.— it is what I wish to do. I would point out the fallacy of that table produced Mr. Middelberg. Then there is another table which we say is entirely wrong—it the tabulated statement of comparisons of tariffs. Mr. Middelberg endeavours to w that the Netherlands local rates are below the Natal rates. With one exception t is entirely wrong. Natal has a tariff for under 25 miles, which is above the Nether-ds rate; but when we come to 50 miles the Natal rate works out as follows:—For three classes 4·50d., as against the Netherlands 6d.; 3·70d as against Netherlands 0d, and 3·10d as against 3d. Practically the whole traffic in the Transvaal is for more n 50 miles, therefore the only reasonable comparison to make is for 50 miles and vards. Taking it for 100 miles for the three classes, the comparison is: Natal, Netherlands, 6d; Natal, 3·25d, Netherlands, 4·50d; Natal, 2·75d; Netherlands, 3d. the Railway Congress in Capetown two years ago, at which each of the Chambers Commerce in South Africa, from Capetown to Pretoria, and right away to luwayo, were represented, the representatives from Bloemfontein raised this question railway rates, and in the opinion of the members present, it was agreed that it was reasonable that the tonnage of traffic to Bloemfontein should come in the mileage e in comparison with the traffic for Johannesburg. Such a table, when put forward, iable to mislead public opinion. Mr. Middelberg compares the rate to Mochudi for tance, with the rate to Johannesburg. The comparison of traffic is five tons to chudi for every 1,000 tons to Johannesburg. So it is impossible to make a compari-

Local railway rates.

Differential rail-way rates.

Transvaal and Bechuanaland extension railway rates.

son on anything like equal conditions. Then follows a statement comparing the r charged on other lines, and it especially says that the rates inland on the exten through Bechuanaland are greater than they are in the Transvaal. The plainest r to that is the notice given in the Cape Colony about three days ago, that food sup will be carried at ½d per ton per mile. When we get in the Transvaal a rate o

Maladministration of the Netherlands Railway.

per ton per mile we will not complain. We say that the Netherlands managen of the railways is most expensive and inefficient.

Chairman.

Are there no reasons why it should be more expensive than the Natal man ment ?—On the contrary, we think it should be cheaper.

Have you tried to find out why it is more expensive ?—Yes. In the gen statement put in by the Chamber of Commerce it is put down to lack of capa administration. We say the Netherlands Railway should be run at a much less r because it runs mainly on the table-land ; it is in the midst of the coal coun and the traffic is concentrated, enabling the lines to be worked to their utm carrying capacity. To show how important that point is, we have a most useful obj lesson in the Cape Colony. We find that the returns on the different systems are follows :—Western, £6 17s 6d ; Midland, £10 17s 11d ; Eastern, £5 19s. 2d ; North £15 12s. ; which shows that the traffic concentrates on the northern line, and the pro jump up.

As regards the different statistics, cost per mile, and working expenses, I th they should get it direct from the different administrations, which would be prefera to getting it from third parties.—I should like to go into detail as to the earnin

Profits of South African railways.

The different railway administrations in South Africa make enormous profits. Cape administration show by their published accounts that they made a profit l year of £1,356,000 ; the Natal Railway, £456,000 ; and, we assume, the Netherla made a profit of 1,330,000. The Netherlands Railway Company has been credi with 6 per cent. on its capital, debentures, etc. : Natal has been credited with 4 cent., and the Cape 4 per cent., the amount over and above these charges is equal t tax of 15s 6d per ton on the companies' crushings last year. But, of course, a gr portion of the charge is borne by the deep-level and development companies.

We have had all that information from the Chamber of Mines, the Association Mines, etc. I wish you to confine yourself, as representing the Chamber of Commer to the interests of commerce and trade, and to show what can be done to assist co merce and trade. All the other points have been already dealt with by the mi managers and other people.—You see we are all so interested in the mining questio

I think the information the Commission have on the mining question is comple so we will thank you to confine yourself to what belongs to your department—t Chamber of Commerce. It is the same point that I mentioned to Mr. Pistorius.- would like to point out that Mr. Pistorius specially assisted in getting up the figu

Questions of Johannesburg Chamber of Commerce to Mr. Middelberg

I have given to you. I would like to file a series of questions prepared by Chamber of Commerce, with a view to Mr. Middelberg's examination. The Chaml of Commerce requested that it might be represented directly on the Commission, a that request not having been acceded to, the only opportunity to examine Mr. Mid berg was to prepare this series of questions. We understand they were handed to I Middelberg by a member of the Commission, but no reply has ever been received. have been requested by the Chamber of Commerce to present these questions, and ask the Commission if they will be good enough to get a reply from Mr. Middelbe

e questions themselves were so framed with the intention of showing the especial evances under which the commercial people suffer.

Mr. *Smit.*

You ask the Commission to forward these to Mr. Middelberg?—Yes.

You mean this Commission ought to make itself a special commission on behalf the Chamber of Commerce?—We thought, seeing the important interests the amber of Commerce represents, we hoped the Government would——

You consider the Chamber of Commerce is really a little Government of its own, ich wants to see this Commission put a special investigation against the N.Z.A.S.M. these grounds?—Certainly not. The thing seems too absurd to reply to almost. e Chamber of Commerce is there to look after the interests of the community. To ce that as a question to be considered seriously—that the Chamber of Commerce is iovernment in itself—approaches almost to the ridiculous.

But I say it is equally ridiculous to put in a lot of questions for the Commission put to someone else, whereas the Commission is sitting here, and knows how to iduct the enquiry. You have heard that the Chamber of Commerce has had the ne chance as everybody else to expose their grievances, and point out faults, but w the Chamber of Commerce comes, standing above the Chamber of Mines, above e Mercantile Association, and charging the Commission to begin, specially on behalf the Chamber of Commerce, an investigation against the railway company, against ich you have seen fit to adduce attorneys' arguments.—I think the member of the mmission who has just spoken is entirely mistaking his position. In the first place, e Chamber of Commerce does not arrogate to itself any position of superiority. at series of questions, instead of being arranged by the Chamber of Commerce elf, as Mr. Smit has stated, is the joint product of the Chamber of Commerce and e Mercantile Association. They had no opportunity whatever of getting infor-ation on these important points contained in the enquiries except through this mmission, and they therefore approached the Commission with the hope that such formation would be elicited. For the purposes of this enquiry, I am willing to assert ese statements instead of putting them in the form of questions, but our desire was be perfectly fair, and not make assertions until we were sure of our position, and, erefore, we asked the questions first before we made a protest against what we under-ood would be the answer. Surely, I submit, that was a respectful way in which to proach the Commission. It will be necessary for me, if I go on with my evidence, refer to these questions. I have overwhelming proof in regard to some points ferred to in these questions. For instance, we ask why the Netherlands Railway elters itself behind owners' risk to endeavour to entirely contract itself out of loss, ien the loss is so flagrant that it loses whole truckloads of goods at a time. I have idence to show that truckload after truckload, not merely solitary instances, has en absolutely lost, and the Netherlands Railway refuse to entertain any claim, eltering themselves under their regulations, which have been approved by the cecutive Council, and therefore, they say, are in force. They refuse to pay for the ods which they have never delivered, and refuse to refund even the money they ceived for the carriage of these goods.

"Owners' risk" on Nether-lands Railway.

Chairman.

Have any of these cases been taken into Court?—They have not been taken into urt.

It does not lie with the Commission to clear up this matter.—No, but this shows e mismanagement of the Netherlands Railway, and how it tells on the industry.

That is our point in the matter. Even the very fact of these cases not being broug
into Court is one proof of the mismanagement of the railway. Every firm reports
the Chamber of Commerce after their loss, and each firm is afraid of taking the on

Difficulty of legal
action against
the Nether-
lands Railway. of responsibility of taking the case into Court against the railway company, becau
of the master position of the Netherlands Railway, by which we are compelled
bring the whole of our goods through their administration. I think the Commissi
will see what a difficult position any firm would be in that takes up a case to fig
under such conditions.

You have mentioned several instances of goods having been lost through t
fault of the railway, and that the company shielded itself behind the regulation, th
they are not responsible for goods carried on their line. I have asked you wheth
you have already brought one case into Court where it has been decided that t
company in that manner allowed goods to get lost without compensation.—As far
the Chamber of Commerce has been aware no case has been decided. At the la
meeting a firm in town appealed to us for assistance to go on with the case, and su
mitted counsel's opinion showing that under the regulations, if they were uphel

The regulations
of the Nether-
lands Railway
unconstitu-
tional. there was no claim against the railway, but, the opinion went on to say, they we
ultra vires and beyond the powers of the Executive to grant, as overriding tl
common law of the country, and, therefore raised the very important point as
whether the Executive Council had power to make regulations beyond the laws, an
also raised the very constitutional question which has created such a difficulty recentl
with the judges. I am glad to have the opportunity to make this explanation,
show how difficult it is for any single firm to fight a claim through the Court
The regulations, as published by the Netherlands Railway, and approved by tl
Executive Council, permit them to disclaim responsibility. I have been requested
state to the Commission definite cases of whole truckloads of goods of various kinds-
grain, bags, timber, &c.—where they have actually been lost, and the Netherlands repl
that they shield themselves under the "owner's risk" regulation, and refuse to entei
tain the claim for the goods, or even refund the carriage they have collected on them

Merchants and
the Railway
Commissioner Have you made any complaints about that to the Government Commissioner
Railways?—During my absence in England I am advised that the Chamber of Com
merce and Mercantile Association had an appointment with the Railway Commission
to discuss this and other points in Pretoria, and deputations attended in Pretoria, b
the Railway Comissioner did not meet them, and they thought it impossible to go c
further in that direction.

Does a man usually address himself to the Chamber of Commerce?—The Chambe
of Commerce exists to assist traders.

Then, if a merchant finds himself in difficulty, why does he not apply to the Rai
way Commissioner?—The Railway Commissioner has not put himself in touch wit
the people in this town. The Railway Commissioner, for instance, has never attended
meeting of the Chamber of Commerce, or in any way put himself in touch with th
people who provide the traffic, and, in this particular instance, eight representativ
merchants went over to Pretoria by appointment, and, when they arrived there, th
Commissioner could not be found, and, therefore, the merchants of this town consid
it useless to appeal to the Commissioner.

That is not a reply to my question. I want to know whether it is imperative, if
merchant or trader gets into difficulties with the railway company, to first addre
himself to the Chamber of Commerce?—No; but two cases now pending have bee
submitted to the Chamber for advice. Beyond that, the Chamber could not assi
them.

You have made another remark I don't agree with, when you say that merchan d be afraid to bring their cases before the Court, owing to the regulations passed approved of by the Executive, and because they would be on the same basis as the of the judges. You also said the railway was such a mighty faction, and had such nfluence, that it is very hard to bring a case into Court. Now, I deny this, and ny case where I thought I was wronged by a railway official, or the company, I d not fear their power to go into Court. Beyond that I have got nothing to say.

Mr. Smit explained that the appointment referred to by Mr. Hosken was not kept ccount of the merchants making the arrangement to meet in his office without con- ng him or giving him details of complaints which had been made in a general . He, moreover, wired to them that Government business would take him to nnesburg that day. With regard to the regulations being contrary to the laws of country; if that were so, it was contrary to the protection of the rights of the ublic, and it would be the Commission's duty to alter that. Could Mr. Hosken e any of these regulations which were against the law of the land.

Witness said he had only given counsel's opinion, which he would be very glad to in. In this opinion the different regulations were enumerated.

Mr. *Albu.*

You were formerly agent of the Glasgow Dynamite Trust?

Witness said he had one or two other points regarding railway matters he would to submit, and he proceeded to detail cases of goods being lost, and of the company diating any liability whatever.

Won't the regulations allow you to sue them?—No.

You were formerly agent of Nobel's Glasgow Dynamite Company?—Then I am to go on with the railway case. I would like to state, on behalf of the Chamber, ; this letter I have put in, shows definitely the difficulties we are under, under these ner's risk" laws. This refers to a consignment of 50 boxes of candles, six dozen rels, and 8cwt. of nails consigned to the Nigel Company. The candles and shovels e under railway risk, and the nails under owners' risk. The railway delivered the dles and shovels, and lost the nails, and absolutely declined any claim, because they e under owners' risk. The merchants, and the town particularly, protest that er the "owners' risk" laws goods are constantly missing, and the railway refuse to sider any claims. This is a typical instance. The only one item in the whole con- ment under owners' risk is lost. They did not deliver a pound of it, and declined onsider any claim. That was a thing the merchants, as a body, said was so hard them. There are two resolutions I was instructed to submit to the Commission, ch were passed at the meeting on 28th May. The first is to this effect: " That Chamber protests against the short notice given from time to time of the rail- y company's special rates for food supplies coming from over the sea." Bearing in d the important question of food supplies for this large community, the Commis- will see the importance of the matter. The ordinary rate from Durban is 6s. 9d. 100lbs. on mealies. In view of the urgent necessity for supplies from oversea, a cial rate was provided by the Netherlands Railway of 4s. 4d.—a difference of 10d. a bag less in the cost of bringing the grain here. Therefore, it is evident t an important question it was. The special rate expired at the end of March. ry possible endeavour was made to get the Netherlands Railway to declare ether it would continue during April. The Natal Government did all it could, and red us, as traders in Johannesburg, to take goods up to the last day in March if Netherlands Railway would carry them forward. The Netherlands Railway ld not give a reply, and it was only on the 3rd April that we had a notice—not lished even then by the Netherlands Railway, but by the Natal Government Rail-

way—saying that the rate would be continued during April. It was only a notice
the month. At the end of April we, as dealers, wanted again to know our posi
We again could not get a reply from the Netherlands Railway, and the Natal Rail
published a notice on the 29th April, that the rate would be continued during M
The same thing happened in May, only not quite so flagrant a case. The Cape E
way published a notice on the 17th May, saying the rate would be continued du
June, and we think such an important question as this shows the utter wan
management, when the food supplies of a great community such as this are ta
into account. The next resolution passed by the Chamber of Commerce is also on
food supply. It states that the special rate for the food supplies should include flou
other products of wheat. Perhaps I might explain that the regulations only provide
grain, including wheat, but do not provide for the products of grain. Therefore,
have this extraordinary position, that wheat is paying 4s. 4d. per 100lbs., but fl
which is the food of the working men of the country, is paying 6s. 3d., and we th
it is an unreasonable position. With regard to the questions of the Chamber

Questions of Jo-
hannesburg
Chamber of
Commerce to
Mr. Middelberg Commerce, at the express instructions of that Chamber, I am requested to file tl
with the Commission. I would like the Commission to instruct me what repl
have to take to the Chamber of Commerce, as a representative, regarding tl
particular enquiries.

Mr. de Beer.

Mr. Hay informed me that Mr. Middelberg has those questions.—Yes, is he go
to reply to them?

We have not heard from him yet.—Might I say to the Chamber that they n
expect a reply from the Commission?

Chairman.

No, the Commission cannot give any special reply. They will make a gene
The Johannes-
burg Chamber
of Commerce
and railway
expropriation. report.—On the Chamber of Commerce questions, it is absolutely necessary to po
out that for three years past we petitioned the Raad for expropriation of the railw
We have been consistent in our policy from the first. The merchants are more
touch with the Railway Department than the mines are, and better able, therefore
judge of the management and general working. Surely that is best indicated by
fact of these petitions, which we have year after year sent in to the Raad.

I think this is just the question which the Chamber of Commerce cannot ju
about, and it is not their business to tell the Government to expropriate the railw
The Government was wise, without the Chamber of Commerce, to get the clause
the concession altered. It first of all read that the Government could only expropri
after ten years, and if it was not then expropriated they would have to wait anot
ten years. The Government has taken care that the clause is put so that they
expropriate at any time. The Government will also be wise to see when it is to
interest of the country, and when it agrees with the views of the Government
expropriate.—The Chamber of Commerce recognised that improvement, and direc
the Government made that improvement as to expropriation, they immediat
approached the Government, in a constitutional manner, through petition from
Raad, and asked them to exercise their right.

I repeat, it does not lie in your way. It is a matter entirely within the jurisd
tion of the Government.

Mr. Albu.

Mr. Hosken and
Nobel's Glas-
gow Dynamite
Factory. You have been agent or director of Nobel's Glasgow Dynamite factory?—I v
agent for sale.

Have you had any experience with the sale of dynamite elsewhere ?—I was ~ector of the Transvaal Company.

This Transvaal Company ?—Yes.

If I remember rightly, some years ago you were a great opponent of Lippert's. the face of that it seems somewhat strange to me that you became a director of the ~ansvaal Dynamite Company. I mean it would appear strange to anybody.—I don't ~ink so.

Mr. Hosken and the Transvaal Dynamite Co.

Well, you have been opposing Lippert as a monopolist. He is the monopolist ~-day, or rather Nobel's, for it is all the same, and you became a director. For ~hat? For opposing him at first? Was it a particular feeling of gratitude they ~owed to you ?—I may explain the position in a sentence. At the time we were in ~tive opposition—I am not speaking personally, but as a representative of Nobel's— ~e position regarding the monopoly as it then existed was that it was assailable— ~e original contract of Lippert's was assailable. It was contrary to the London ~nvention; it was contrary to the Treaty of Commerce with Germany. Nobel's, as ~ing manufacturers in both England and Germany, represented the case to both ~ese Governments, and both these Governments protested against the position.

Nobel's and Mr. Lippert's first dynamite contract.

But what does that matter ?—The new regulation comes within the provisions of ~e Transvaal Convention and their treaties of commerce, and we were absolutely ~barred from further opposition.

Nobel's and the present dynamite concession.

Who was ?—Nobel's. The position is entirely changed. Previously the regula-~on was wrong and could be attacked. Now, it could not be attacked, and that ~aterially altered the position. The only chance, therefore, as Nobel's agent, to get ~to this market was to make arrangements with the man who held the key of the ~or, and Mr. Lippert held the key of the door.

I suspected at the time that Nobel's was playing up to all three parties—to ~ippert, the mining industry, and the Government. Whichever party was winning, ~obel's was sure to slip in somehow.—I say you are entirely wrong. We were in ~na fide opposition, and as long as there was a chance to get into this market—the ~iggest in the world for explosives—we were prepared to fight the case. But when ~e Transvaal Government shut the door and gave the key to Mr. Lippert, our only ~ance to get in was to make an arrangement with Mr. Lippert. I think that replies ~ you fairly.

Yes, it clears up the reason why you have been a director of the Transvaal Com-~any.—Certainly, we had to make an arrangement with Mr. Lippert. You have ~roduced evidence to show that Nobel's provided the £220,000 to found the factory.

But Mr. Phillip would not admit it.—Well, if Mr. Phillip would not admit it, you ~roduced evidence yourself showing it. Nobel's selected men they had on the spot to ~present them on the Board. I say the position is perfectly straightforward and ~pright.

Oh, yes. I don't say anything against that. Did you offer to supply the mines ~ith dynamite, at a price very much lower than the present ?—You will find my name ~ on that contract we offered to all the mines, by which we offered to supply dynamite ~ 40s. per case, and retained the option to supply it at less than 40s. if it suited us.

Nobel's offer to sell dynamite free in bond at 40s. per case.

That was No. 1 dynamite, 75 per cent. ?—Yes ; delivered here *ex* magazine.

How about duty ?—40s. *ex* magazine duty.

You are absolutely certain you offered to do that ?—Yes. You were not a party ~ the contract. You at that time took the opposite side unfortunately for us.

I took the opposite side when Lippert was a monopolist; and the manipulation ~vas to get rid of Lippert, and somebody else would come in. I was afraid of that ~omebody else. That was Nobel's.—The offer was fully reported at the time. We said we would supply the dynamite at 40s. for 14 years if they liked. The Governme[nt] imposed a duty of 37s. 8d. per case on No. 1 dynamite.

Price of Nobel's blasting gela-tine. Blasting gelatine I suppose you offered to supply in proportion ?—To the 40s. [we] add 35 per cent. for blasting gelatine, plus the duty, which amounts to about £2 per ca[se]

And you think Nobel's would be willing to supply it for less ?—I don't know. [I] am simply agent for sale.

But, as agent for sale, had you the power to do so ?—We offered to supply it [at] 40s. for 14 years, and we retained the option, if it suited us, to go below 40s. I ha[ve] no experience in manufacturing. I am simply agent for sale.

Have you got any experience as to the sale of dynamite in any other countri[es] such as British India, California, etc. ?—I only know as a mercantile man would w[ho] takes an interest in his business what similar articles are sold for in other parts of th[e] world.

Price of No. 1 dynamite in England.
The dynamite trade. Do you know what dynamite No. 1, 75 per cent., sells at in England ?—Th[e] dynamite business, it might be necessary to explain, is different to almost any othe[r] The immense power of the explosive puts it under special regulations in every civilis[ed] country, and, therefore, there is not the same free trade in the manufacture and sale [of] dynamite as there would be, say, in candles or soap. Local conditions as to compet[i-] tion greatly influence the price. You cannot take a cargo of dynamite into a port, fo[r] instance, and sell it as you could any other article.

Cornish prices for dynamite. We are aware of these facts. What is the price dynamite has been sold for durin[g] the last two years in Cornwall, or any other part of England ?—In Cornwall to-da[y] the price, so far as I am informed, is £65 to £68 a ton. That is from 32s. 6d. to 34[s.] per case.

That is delivered on the mines in small quantities as required ? The min[es] generally have no magazine there ?—That is so.

While agent for Nobel's Glasgow Trust, did you ascertain at what dynamite sol[d] in Germany ?—I never inquired as to Germany.

Transvaal price of dynamite. As a business man you would think, if dynamite sold in small quantities i[n] Cornwall at 32s. 6d., a place like the Transvaal should have special facilities for i[t.] There is hardly a consumer in the world like the Transvaal.—Certainly. This [is] certainly the biggest market for explosives in the world.

Price of detona-tors. And that is why we pay the biggest price, I suppose. Do you know at wha[t] price detonators are sold at all ?—Now you come to that question, I think it is no[t] fair and reasonable I should be asked to give the information. I am an ex-director o[f] the local explosives company. You have had the managing director before you. H[e] is acquainted with the whole of those figures ; and you should have got it from hi[m]

He always said he was not acquainted with them. I don't want to ask yo[u] anything which might put you in an unpleasant position. Detonators are a thing o[f] which anyone can find out the price, and I don't think you will reveal any secrets b[y] telling us. We used to pay 3s. a box, and we now pay 4s. I would like to know th[e] Profits on sale of detonators. price at Home ?—It is evident the 3s. leaves a profit.

Do you know anything about the building of the dynamite factory ?—I don[t] know the ultimate cost. I retired from the company about eighteen months since.

But any factory capable of coping with the demand here ?—It is a very difficu[lt] question to estimate.

Had you, formerly, experience in the dynamite business, or only since you hav[e] been connected with Nobel's ? Had you any experience at Home ?—No, I have bee[n] in South Africa most of my life.

Mr. *Hay.*

Sale of detona-tors in Johan-nesburg. Is it within your knowledge, as a business man, that detonators are for sale i[n] nnesburg at any place except at the agent's dynamite factory ?—As far as I know are only procurable at the one place.

At one time permits were granted for the importation of detonators ; do you know ther these permits have expired ?—I think they are all exhausted.

The representative of the factory stated these permits were still running ?— representative of the company ought to be better acquainted with the facts than . I tell you what I think.

When you were a director of this company what was the method of procedure for importation of explosives into this country ?—I think it is hardly a fair question ut to me ; you have had a representative of the company here, and I have retired the company. It would be an invidious position for me to take up.

You say the first concession was contrary to the Convention, and to the treaty Germany, but you have given the opinion now, that the present concession is in rdance with the Convention. In what way do you explain that ?—You may be . we did not abandon the position until we found it was hopeless, and that is lenced by the fact that such a large sum was paid to get into the market.

Nobel's people came into this country to assist us in getting the first concession :elled because it was contrary to the Convention, and then they assisted to get the contract passed.—They did no such thing.

Well, it is a curious thing that since the new contract was passed it is not contrary he Convention.—Mr. Hay mistakes the position. It is evident that Nobel's offer to :ract for 14 years at 40s. assisted the mines to get the original contract cancelled.

Then the question is, if somebody else came in and offered dynamite at 40s., it ld be reasonable to expect that this concession should be cancelled —I think you find that this concession is on stronger grounds than the other. I have already .ted out the original contract was assailable.

And Nobel's have put the rope around our neck tighter than it was before ?— tainly not. The Transvaal Government closed this market absolutely to every- y except Mr. Lippert, and the only way to get in was to make an arrangement h Mr. Lippert.

The dynamite was sold at 80s., and now the same people supply us with dynamite .5s.—That is a subject for criticism.

Nobel's have offered to supply all the stuff which is brought into the country, and it at 40s. in bond; surely to-day there must be a handsome profit on selling the .e article at 80s. under the same conditions.—A previous witness before the Com- sion pointed out that the concession has a limited period to run, and they must vide an amortisation fund to wipe off the cost of the works, which runs to a very ;e sum indeed.

That all comes if they start making. I am talking about the imported stuff; ch is imported under the same conditions as it was before.—They have to provide the commission to Mr. Lippert, and the royalty to Lewis and Marks, and other rges. It is only reasonable for them to take the ordinary business precautions.

Did they buy over the old concession, or did they give this as a bonus on the new :cession ?—They gave nothing to Mr. Lippert, you may be sure about that. The rernment had a contract with Mr. Lippert, and they could only get in under Mr. .pert's contract.

Nobel's people put up £220,000 in cash out of £450,000, which left £230,000 as ital, for which interest is to be paid before the Government get any share of the fit at all. Can you give us any explanation why that £230,000 should exist ?—You rlook the fact that Nobel's had nothing to do with getting this monopoly, and when company was formed these shares were given to the old concessionaires. You have

Nobel's and the subscribed capital of the South African Explosives Company.

got the whole particulars as to how it was made up.   Nobel's came in as subscriber the company.

In other words, if Nobel's had not come in and found that amount of cash, guaranteed a large amount of debenture capital, it would have been impossible to ca the company through ?—It is not fair to assume such a position, because it is q: evident, as competent business men, that Nobel's would never have found all the wc ing capital unless they saw that that was the best possible opportunity to arrange supplying the market.

Nobel's and the French Dyna-mite Company in Paris for the Transvaal.

The concessionaires of the company that was floated in Paris amalgamated w Nobel's Trust ?—No ; as a promoter of companies yourself you can see the position

The old company that existed in Paris for supplying this place with dynan became absorbed in Nobel's Trust ?—It was a separate company altogether.

It was a separate company, connected with the French Trust.—The old comp: was a French company.   Europe is divided into two great trusts.

Yes, and when this was absorbed by Nobel's, it was practically taken into trust ?—That is not entirely so.   I have already stated to you that Nobel's arrange provide the working capital.

Mr. *Albu.*

Nobel's offer to supply No. 1 dynamite at 40s. per case to any part of the Transvaal Barberton price of dynamite.

The fact remains you were willing to supply dynamite at 40s., for which we n pay 85s.—We issued a printed document to every mine in the Transvaal.   We did confine ourselves to the Rand, but offered it also to Barberton.

What do they pay in Barberton to-day for what we pay 85s. ?—They have to for transport to Barberton, and the business charges for handling it there.

We cannot assume that the price of 40s. would have left a loss ?—The dynamite tr. is a trade that has been described in civilised countries as a sort of business with foot in the police court and the other in the grave, and, therefore, assuming it is such sort of business, we look for a decent profit.   It is possible we went down to a lov figure than we would under ordinary conditions.

So 40s. was a fighting tariff ?—Yes.

It is wonderful that all fighting tariffs mean millions of profit to others.

Mr. *de Beer.*

The by-products of dynamite manufacture.

During the time that you were director of the company here, was any money m: out of by-products ?—We were not manufacturing up to the time I retired.

Can the by-products be used for vegetation ?—Chemists say it is possible, but I of opinion that every experiment so far has been unsuccessful.   I was also instruct

Import duties.

to complain to you about general taxation and import duties.

That is in the statement of the Chamber before the Commission.—I would like put in a table showing the freight, after allowing for Government imports, railw imports, and specie brought into the country, because none of these pay duties.   I a allowing the 1½ per cent. paid on machinery, and the *ad valorem* duty paid on impo coming into the Transvaal, works out at £12 15s. 11d. per cent.

Chairman.

I wish to say a few words on this point, but I do not want to cause an argume You said before that if a reduction is made on railway rates it will be to the det

Reduction of im-port duties.

ment of the merchants.   You say now, what has been stated several times before t Commission, that the import duties should be reduced.   I would be in favour of th as soon as I am convinced that it would be to the benefit of the public in general the consumer.   I have already asked Mr. Pistorius what proof have we if we ma se recommendations to the Government that the consumer will get the profit reof. I have been answered that competition will bring that about, but I do not lieve that, because I have now found out that instead of competition, a combination ists, and consequently what the Government will lose in import duties, and what e railway will lose by giving a reduction in rates will go into the pockets of the mbination, and not to the benefit of the consumer.—I think it is only fair to the trade at I should be given a chance of replying to the statement. In the first instance the Chamber of Commerce there are over one hundred wholesale firms represented, d the competition amongst them is of the keenest nature, and I will say positively, an active member and vice-president of the Chamber of Commerce, that there is no mbination whatever for any one article or any combination of articles. The total mber of merchants' licences issued during the previous year was 1,400, and it must be ident that it is impossible to make a combination, and, further, if the Chairman uld be good enough to enquire from some of the members of the Commission he uld find that not only are we in competition with ourselves here, but the keenest mpetition also exists between ourselves and the merchants of Port Elizabeth, East ndon, Durban, and Delagoa Bay. It is absolutely impossible to have a combination, d the Chairman has been misinformed, and, therefore, as a merchant myself engaged in siness, I will assure him, and furnish him with a list of prices which can easily be ecked, showing that the main items now supplied to the mines are being sold for tual cost price or below it. *(Trade combination of merchants and competition.)*

Mr. *Albu.*

I admit that competition is very keen, not only here, but among Home merchants ding for this market.—Competition for every article is very keen.

Then what do you think you could get dynamite for if you had free trade ?—I nk I must be like the other dynamite witness, and say I don't know. *(Free trade and the price of dynamite.)*

Chairman.

I thank Mr. Hosken for attending.

The Commission then concluded its public sitting, the Chairman making a closing eech, as follows :—

Gentlemen, I have heard from the secretary, with pleasure, that there are no ore witnesses. I think everybody will be pleased, with me, that our labours, so far the hearing of witnesses goes, are finished, and I think we have obtained sufficient idence to enable us to work out satisfactorily the duty we have before us. *(Sufficiency of evidence.)* rhaps it has been thought that our work has been difficult and troublesome ; and, rhaps, it is true, at times, monotonous, but, as for myself, I can say I have carried this work with pleasure and ambition, because I feel, and I think the other mem- rs of the Commission feel with me, that it is a work for the good of the Republic in neral. It is my duty to thank the members for their co-operation so far in public, d for the support given me as Chairman of this Commission, and I hope when we ther have the several testimonies before us to draft our report and recommendations, *(Report of Commission.)* at we shall co-operate together harmoniously, and keep in view the interests of the ning industry, and especially those of the Republic in general. I think everybody els with me that we have a difficult task resting upon our shoulders, if we are to alise what is expected of us. I know our work will probably be submitted to ticism, but that will not prevent us acting in accordance with our honest con- ctions in making our report and recommendations on the work for which the vernment has placed us here. It is also my duty to thank Mr. Bosch, the inter- eter, with whose work I may say I am satisfied. I think it is also my duty to take

this opportunity to mention the reporters of the different newspapers, who, from t
first day to the last, have attended our meetings, for the quiet way in which th
have done their work, and for the faithful application they have shown. I think t
public in general, both inside and outside this country, owes a great debt of gratitu
for the reports given by them, and I may say their chiefs ought to give them
holiday and a bonus.

Mr. *Joubert.*

Chairman of
Commission
thanked.

I only want to thank our Chairman for the able manner in which he h
conducted our meetings, and I hope the result of this Commission will be a weight
the scale in which many questions will be solved. For myself, as Minister of Min
I have obtained very useful information during the session. I myself have perus
the newspapers, and, as far as I have seen, the reporters have done their wo

Unanimous re-
port desirable.

impartially and well. I hope that as the result of the Commission our report will
unanimous, and that it will do good for the mining industry.

EPORT OF THE COMMISSION.

His Honour the State President and the Honourable Members of the Executive Council of the South African Republic :—

Letter of the Commission to the State President and Executive Council.

In submitting the joint report of the Commission, the undersigned desire to draw ntion to the following :

As advisory members, the Government appointed Messrs. EDMOND BROCHON, RAKHAN, and J. M. PIERCE, but your Commission deemed it advisable, with the tion of the Government, to add Messrs. JAMES HAY and GEORGE ALBU to the ve list.

All these gentlemen kindly consented to assist us in our onerous duties, and un- rvedly placed their services at our command. Your Commission would be failing ourtesy were they to neglect this opportunity of expressing their keen apprecia- . of the services rendered by the Advisory Committee.

As men of ability and experience, their advice on matters local and technical erially assisted your Commission to grasp the situation, and it is with great sfaction that we commend the zeal and interest displayed by them throughout the eedings.—We have the honour to be, honoured sirs, your obedient servants, ned) SCHALK W. BURGER (Chairman), CHRISTIAAN J. JOUBERT, J. S. SMIT, THOS. 0, J. F. DE BEER, A. SCHMITZ-DUMONT.

His Honour the State President and the Honourable Members of the Executive Council, South African Republic.

Report of the Commission.

HONOURABLE SIRS,—In accordance with your instructions contained in your ers addressed to the members of this Commission, dated April 5, 1897, your Com- sion have the honour to report as follows :—

On April 13th last your Commission initiated proceedings at Pretoria, and, after ing been engaged there for a few days in arranging preliminary matters in con- tion with the inquiry, your Commission decided to proceed to Johannesburg to sue their investigations. On April 20th the inquiry commenced at Johannesburg, ! your Commission deemed it to the interest of all concerned that the proceedings uld be public, and to give the same the widest publicity.

Primarily, your Commission set themselves the task of instituting minute and eful investigation with regard to the depression in matters connected with the ing industry, and ascertained that during the year 1896 there were one hundred eighty-three mines within the State, whereof seventy-nine produced gold to an unt and value of £8,603,831.

The present depression.

The remaining one hundred and four mines yielded no gold, most of this number ng in a state of development and equipment, while only twenty-five companies lared dividends—to an amount of £1,718,781.

For various reasons some mines have temporarily ceased operations. The ca
of so many mines not paying dividends is principally ascribed to the high rate
production.

There are various other causes that have contributed to the existing condition
things, but, though mistakes have been made in the past, your Commission are plea
to state that at present there exist all the indications of an honest administration, ;
the State, as well as the mining industry, must be congratulated upon the fact t
most of the mines are controlled and directed by financial and practical men, v
devote their time, energy, and knowledge to the mining industry, and who have
only introduced the most up-to-date machinery and mining appliances, but also
greatest perfection of method and process known to science. But for these, a g
many of the mines now producing gold would not have reached that stage.

The extensive and voluminous evidence, as also the carefully-prepared statis
in connection therewith annexed to this Report, prove the colossal extent of
mining industry within the State. The figures, plans, calculations, specifications, e
are very interesting and exhaustive, and calculated to provide the thoughtful rea
with much material for contemplation. And it will further be patent from that t
the financial, economical, and political relations are very intricate.

Your Commission therefore feel the weight and responsibility of the great t
imposed upon them, but, strengthened by a sense of confidence that their efforts
arrive at a satisfactory solution of the different problems may meet with your appro
and support, they have undertaken that duty agreeably at your request by carefu
entering into all the details of the position and investigating the same.

The problem cannot be solved by probing the past of some mines. We kn
that there are some mines where the gold reefs only exist in the imagination of 1
promoters, and it can safely be submitted that these mines will not pay, even w
coal and dynamite delivered free of charge at the mines. Neither does the questi
of over-speculation or over-capitalisation affect the case.

As has already been shown, there are only twenty-five companies which h;
declared a dividend out of their profits. The rest work with a very small profit, a;
in many cases, do not cover the cost of production. The problem to be solved
What must be done to reduce the cost of production, so as to leave a margin of pr
upon the article produced? And this is a problem apart from any complicatio
between the Government and nationalities. A company might be over-capitalis
but the cost of mining property is in no way affected thereby.

It is within the knowledge of your Commission that the costs of working a m
may be averaged at £10,000 per month, and equipment and development fr
£200,000 to £500,000 per mine. Taking this average of £10,000 per month, a
considering that under existing conditions 100 mines will have to close down, in tl
case an annual amount of £12,000,000 will be taken out of circulation, with resu
too disastrous to contemplate. To avoid such a calamity your Commission are
opinion that it is the duty of the Government to co-operate with the mining indus
and to devise means in order to make it possible for lower-grade mines to work a
profit, and generally to lighten the burdens of the mining industry. This and 1
development and equipment of new mines are a few examples among many oth
where it is desirable that the Government shall take an active part; especially wb
the fact is taken into consideration that up till now the mining industry must be h
as the financial basis, support and mainstay of the State.

The question, therefore, becoming one of national economy, it is incumbent up
the Government, considering the rapid growth and progress of the country, to so al

fiscal laws and systems of administration as to meet the requirements of its ~ncipal industry.

A close scrutiny of the combined report of the Chamber of Mines and Mercantile ~ociation proves that the commercial interests and those of the mining industry are interwoven that it is hardly possible to separate the one from the other, and all ~nomical measures with regard to taxation, freight, etc., apply to both. *Commerce dependent on mining industry.*

Your Commission think that, with the natural facilities for agriculture, that ~ustry ought to be greatly encouraged. The consequence would be that the ~elopment of this industry would materially reduce the cost of living, which would ~ve an immediate and beneficial effect on the price of labour. *Agriculture.*

It is a fact much to be regretted that the advance of agriculture is not pro- ~tionate with that of the mining industry and the general growth and progress of ~ country, and it is therefore very necessary to establish an Agricultural Depart- ~nt, and for the Government to take active measures to promote the interests of the ~ustry by assisting where such is feasible, and to have it conducted on the most ~proved modern principles as practised in other parts of the world. *An agricultural department.*

In submitting to the Government a scheme for reducing the burdens of the mining ~ustry, it is naturally to be expected that the latter will also practise economy in ~ry department. Judging from the recent events and by the persistent manner in ~ich the mines have reduced, and are further trying to reduce, the working costs, ~ur Commission have no doubt that the mines, after so far having taken the initia- ~e, will act responsively to any economic measure the Government may think ~per to introduce.

Your Commission entirely disapprove of concessions, through which the indus- ~al prosperity of the country is hampered. Such might have been expedient in the ~st, but the country has now arrived at a state of development that will only admit ~ free competition according to republican principles. This applies more especially ~ the gold industry, that has to face its own economical problems without being ~rther burdened with concessions that are irksome and injurious to the industry, and ~ll always remain a source of irritation and dissatisfaction. *Concessions.*

Throughout the inquiry, it was clear to your Commission that the question of ~our was a most vital one for the mines, and, seeing that the cost of labour ~ounted to from 50 to 60 per cent. of the production cost, your Commission are of ~inion that the labour question ought to take precedence in their report. Not only ~ this Republic, but in most countries all over the world, the labour question is a most ~fficult one to deal with. It still remains a subject for discussion, notwithstanding ~at the most renowned and eminent politicians and statesmen have tried to solve the ~estion. A universal combination of circumstances in this country renders the ~tution still more difficult, and from the evidence to be laid before you it will be ~parent how complicated the question is. *Labour.*

To begin with white labour, your Commission would strongly recommend that ~ measures should be taken by which the cost of living at the mines may be reduced ~ much as possible. Judging superficially, and taking into consideration the wages ~id by the mining companies in other parts of the world, and the evidence on the ~bject submitted to your Commission, it would appear as if wages paid here are too ~gh, but, taking all the circumstances into consideration, the contrary is apparent. It ~ust be taken as a fact that no skilled labourer can or will work for a salary or ~age less than will enable him to support himself and his family. *White labour. Reduction of cost of living. White wages.*

According to evidence, a miner earns from £18 to £30 sterling per month, accord- ~g to ability, and your Commission are of opinion that these wages are not excessive, ~king into consideration the high cost of living at the mines. In fact, they are only sufficient to satisfy daily wants, and, consequently, it cannot be expected that wh labourers will establish their permanent abode in this Republic unless conditions a made by which their position will be ameliorated.

Wages, salaries, and directors' fees.
Your Commission wish to recommend that in future all companies shall ke their accounts in such a manner that it will clearly appear what proportion of wag salaries and remuneration is paid to white labourers, and what to directors, secretari clerks, engineers, etc., because at present all these are brought into one account, and would consequently appear as if the average wage paid to miners is higher than rea is the case.

Miners' quarters.
Your Commission further wish to recommend that the companies should bui dwelling-houses for white labourers, which is already done by some of the compani and should let those at a rental equivalent to a reasonable interest on capital expende This would mean a considerable improvement in the condition of living of thc miners.

The Master and Servants Act.
Your Commission further recommend that the law with regard to master a servant, as existing at present, be modified so that all contracts entered into in Euro and elsewhere, between employers and employees, would be legalised here by simp registration, and would not, as hitherto, require a confirmation of the contract parties before a Landdrost or Mining Commissioner before becoming of effect here. would be necessary to provide that such a contract must be reasonable as regards t

Employers' liability.
labourer. Further, this law ought to define the responsibility of the master to servant in case of accident, and, further, that neither master nor servant can make contract contrary to any provision of such law.

Import duty on foodstuffs.
Your Commission are of opinion that as long as the cost of living is not conside ably reduced it would be almost impossible to reduce the wages of white labourers; a they would strongly recommend that, as far as possible, necessaries of life should imported free of import duty and conveyed to the mines as cheaply as possible.

Encouragement of industries.
Your Commission further consider that it will be desirable to encourage oth industries besides the mining industry, which will also tend to procure employment f white labourers.

Native labour.
Native labour is one of the most difficult questions before your Commission. will be necessary to discuss three points, viz:—

From where must the industry draw its supply?
What supply can be obtained?
And at what wages?

In reply to the first point, it appears to your Commission, that the chief supp must come from the East Coast (Portuguese territory), and it is desirable to recommen to the Government to enter into correspondence with the Portuguese authorities, order to facilitate the supply as much as possible. Further, a great many natives ca be got from within the boundaries of the Republic if sufficient inducement be offere and your Commission propose that the inducement will be best offered by payi premiums to kaffir chiefs for the supply of labourers, and by the reduction of the fa

Reduction of cost of transport of natives.
for kaffirs per railway to one-third of that now charged, the difference to be recovere from them on the return journey. It must be borne in mind that the present requir ment of the Witwatersrand mines is 70,000 black labourers, while within the next thr years this number will be increased to at least 100,000, on account of the developme of the deep-level mines.

While mentioning the subject of correspondence with the Portuguese governmen your Commission are of opinion that correspondence with all South African Stat would be desirable, in order once and for all to place the question of black labour on sound basis. Should the Government be successful in coming to an understanding wi ifferent Colonies and States on this point, the question of reduction of wages will natural consequence.

As regards the supply of natives from within the boundaries of this Republic, your mission recommend that the Native Commissioners should receive extra payment ses where they are obliged to undertake journeys to interview kaffir chiefs to n labourers from them; that such kaffirs be conducted to the mines under super- n, and that it would be desirable to erect along the roads at distances of 18 miles t, except where there is a railway, compounds, where the kaffirs can sleep and n food. Your Commission recommend that the latter measure should be entirely r Government control. *(margin: Government co-operation for supply of native labour from within the Republic required.)*

Your Commission cannot recommend any measure which would be equivalent to d labour, neither can they recommend the imposition of a higher tax upon the rs.

Much has been said about the desirability of establishing locations for kaffirs close e Rand, but your Commission cannot at all recommend this course. Experience taught that the establishment of locations does not improve the kaffirs in any way, only tends to their deterioration. As soon as the kaffir with his family lives in a tion, his highest aim in life is to see his wife and children work while he himself s on. *(margin: Locations.)*

Your Commission has thought it desirable to consider the liquor traffic also in their ort, because they are of opinion that it directly affects the mining industry. It must emembered that the liquor traffic, together with the import duties and licences in ection with the same, contributes to the revenue of the State. *(margin: The liquor traffic)*

It has been proved to your Commission that the Liquor Law, No. 17, 1896, is not ied out properly, and that the mining industry has real grievances in connection ewith, owing to the illicit sale of strong drink to the natives at the mines, and they especially and strongly to insist that the stipulations of Article 16 of the law shall trictly enforced. The evidence given on this point proves that a miserable state of rs exists, and a much stronger application of the law is required. *(margin: Maladministration of Liquor Law.)*

Your Commission recommend:

    (a) That all licences for boarding houses for white people at the mines shall in future be only issued by the Commission for liquor licences and licensing boards. *(margin: Suggestions for better regulation of the liquor traffic.)*

    (b) More police, and a better system of supervision at the mines.

    (c) That, where any unlicensed person is convicted of selling strong drink to natives, at the mines or elsewhere, the only punishment to be inflicted shall be imprisonment.

Your Commission are in favour of the strict carrying out of this law, but have d that it is in some respects too drastic.

For instance, Article 17 of the law stipulates that four licences will be granted population of 500 persons, and, for every additional 400, only one more licence. der this Article is meant 500 male persons over sixteen years of age). There would o objection against such a stipulation, as such is more or less the system in other lised countries, but such a stipulation ought to have been initiated when the towns villages close to the mines were originally established.

It appears from statistics submitted that at present there are in Johannesburg following licensed liquor dealers:—*(a)* wholesale dealers, 49; *(b)* bottle stores, 56; canteens (bars), 305; *(d)* roadside inns, 5; *(e)* beer halls, 23; total 438. *(margin: Liquor licences in the Johannesburg district.)*

Letter " *c* " includes 112 hotel licences. Supposing that Article 17 were to be tly applied, and assuming that Johannesburg and mines in the neighbourhood have a male population over sixteen years of age of 35,500, the Licensing Board only issue 88 licences ; and 350 licences will have to be refused.

From a financial point of view this would entail very serious consequences for State, because the liquor licences, and the large amount paid for import duties of liq which form a large proportion of the revenue of the State, might then be considera diminished. But leaving this out of the question, and assuming that the Governm would accept this loss, trade would be seriously affected by the closing of 350 pla of business ; and large numbers of people who are interested in the trade, and have invested their entire capital in the liquor business, under the law then exist would be entirely ruined.

It is certainly desirable that the number of licences shall be reduced, but should not be done in such a peremptory manner : gradually, and as opportunity off these reductions can be effected. Article 17 of said law stipulates that licences wil granted according to the population of any ward.

Suburbs such as Doornfontein, Hillbrow, Hospital Hill, etc., are only used residential purposes, and up to the present the inhabitants have been able to succ fully oppose the opening of canteens there, by protesting and other means. inhabitants of these suburbs generally have their places of business in the city, remain there during the day—hence the many bars in Commissioner Street, wl street must be considered as the centre of the town, from a business, as well as fro geographical point of view. It must also be remembered that, when the bars at mines are closed, numbers of people living there will make use of the bars in town.

Notwithstanding the Second Volksraad resolution, Article 122, D.D. 14, 597, First Volksraad resolution, Article 112 D.D. 17, 597, your Commission consider t wholesale licences for the sale of liquor, as well as licences for bottle stores, can considered as usual trade licences, although under the control of the Licensing Bo

Generally, whenever a licensed liquor dealer is convicted for breaking the l he transfers his licence to somebody else, who continues the illicit sale of liquor. is, consequently, desirable that in future a licence for the sale of liquor shall granted to a particular house, and not to any individual. Permits for the keep open of bars after nine p.m. ought to be issued only by the Licensing Board, beca this is one of the duties of that body, and does not fall under the jurisdiction of judicial official.

No licence ought to be granted for kaffir eating-houses at the mines, because necessity for them does not exist, and they only afford the opportunity to cert persons to continue the iniquitous sale of liquor to natives at the mines.

Your Commission disapprove of the payment of a portion of the fines to the former, policeman or detective, because this not only puts a premium on crime, the informer, influenced by greed, puts the accused in a position which, without tr ping, he would not have occupied. It is not the intention of your Commission deal with the Liquor Law in its entirety, and they have consequently only refer to certain points which, in their opinion, require modification in the interests of trade and the mining industry.

Your Commission further recommend that all excise officials shall be under control of the Licensing Boards of the different districts, and that the Licensing Boa shall have special detectives and inspectors under their control.

The transit duties are unfair, and ought to be abolished. Yearly, an amoun £600,000 is paid by this Republic to the neighbouring States (Orange Free State cepted). It may be argued from the other side that heavy expenses have been m to construct docks and warehouses, but against this can be urged that the consign and consignees are charged heavy dock fees, which, if carefully calculated, am

ay the expenses. The authority of your Commission for the figures quoted is Mr.
ener, member of the Cape Parliament and chairman of the United Chambers of
mmerce of South Africa, and your Commission are of opinion that statistics from
h a source can be taken to be reliable. Your Commission recommend that negotia-
ns shall be entered into with the interested colonies to have those transit duties
lished, but before doing so wish to recommend that the Government of this
public shall abolish the transit duties on goods to the North, as at present levied.

With reference to the importation of foodstuffs, your Commission can only re-
mend that, if possible, foodstuffs ought to be entirely free from taxation, as at *Import duty on foodstuffs.*
present moment it is impossible to supply the population of the Republic from
products of local agriculture, and consequently importation is absolutely
cessary.

Before entering on the subject of explosives, we wish to put on record our dis-
pointment with the evidence tendered on behalf of the South African Explosives *South African Explosives Company.*
., Limited. We expected, and we think not unreasonably, that they would be able
give reliable information for our guidance respecting the cost of importation, as
ll as of local manufacture, of the principal explosives used for mining purposes; but,
ough persistently questioned on these points, few facts were elicited, and we regret
say they entirely failed to satisfy us in this important respect.

The importance of a cheap supply of all necessaries required for mining purposes,
order to ensure success, is perhaps too obvious to need repeating, but we may
ention that the one item most frequently referred to by witnesses in this connection
as the cost of the explosives.

It has, we consider, been clearly proved that the price paid by the mines for *Cost of explosives.*
plosives of all kinds is unreasonably high, having due regard to original cost and
penses of delivery in the South African Republic, and in our opinion a considerable
duction should be made.

In making recommendations with this object in view, it must be stated, at the
tset, that the main difficulty in dealing with the question arises from the existence
the contract, by means of which the monopolists are able to maintain the high
ice, in spite of the fact that the manufactured article is mostly obtained by them in
urope at a very much lower cost. Consequently, the advantages which the Govern-
ent intended to confer upon the country by establishing a new industry here, have
t been realised, whilst the monopoly has proved a serious burden on the mining
dustry.

That the principal explosives used here (blasting gelatine, and, to a small extent,
namite) can be purchased in Europe, and delivered here at a price far below the
esent cost to the mines, has been proved to us by the evidence of many witnesses
mpetent to speak on the subject, and when we bear in mind that the excess charge
40s. to 45s. per case does not benefit the State, but serves to enrich individuals for
e most part resident in Europe, the injustice of such a tax on the staple industry
comes more apparent, and demands immediate removal.

It has been proved that the South African Republic is one of the largest, if not the
rgest, consumer of explosives in the world, and, according to the rule of commerce in
ch cases, it is reasonable to suppose that the most advantageous terms would be
cured for so large a consumer. This, no doubt, would be the case were it not for
e monopoly now in the hands of the South African Explosives Company, whereby
ey and their friends make enormous profits at the expense of the mining industry. *Profits on present price of dynamite.*
hese profits have been estimated by the Volksraad Dynamite Commission at no less
an £580,000 for the years 1897 and 1898, being £2 per case on 290,000 cases, the *Report of Volksraad Dynamite Commission.*
mber which it is estimated would have to be imported to meet the demands for

those years. It is thus clear that the hope of establishing a factory capable supplying the requirements of the mines, within a reasonable time, from the produc of the country, is far from being realised.

From the evidence of witnesses other than the Explosives Company, we a bound to believe that dynamite No. 1, containing 75 per cent. of nitro-glycerine, ca

be delivered free on board at Hamburg at 23s. 6d. per case of 50 lbs., the costs bringing it to Johannesburg being about 14s. additional. The managing director the company, however, has since stated that Nobel's invoice it to them at 29s. 6d. fr on board in Hamburg, but the difference is not essential to the point we have to de with here.

This explosive, whether costing 23s. 6d. or 29s. 6d. in Hamburg, is supplied to th mines at 85s. per case, showing a profit of 47s. 6d. in one case, and 41s. 6d. in th other, of which this Government receives 5s. per case. That this is a reasonable estima is supported by the report of the Volksraad Dynamite Commission, who state that th company makes a profit of £2 per case on imported dynamite, and further by th evidence of a former agent of Nobel's Dynamite Trust, whose statement was to th

effect that he made an offer on behalf of Nobel's to deliver dynamite *ex* magazine on th Rand at 40s. per case, of 50 lbs., excluding duty, and this at a time when it had to b brought a considerable distance by ox-wagons.

In the case of blasting gelatine, which is now more largely used than No.

dynamite, the margin of profit made by the company at the expense of the mines far greater. The evidence led in favour of the company is that the cost is 43s. 6d. p case free on board in Hamburg, the freight, etc., to Johannesburg being about 14s. p case. Therefore, by the company's own showing, the difference in price in Europ between blasting gelatine and dynamite No. 1 is 14s. per case (43s. 6d. and 29s. 6d. whilst the charges for bringing the articles into the South African Republic are th same. Seeing that the company charges the mines for blasting gelatine 22s. 6d. ove and above the price of dynamite No. 1 (namely, 107s. 6d. as against 85s.), it is eviden that the profit falling to the company is still larger. Other evidence laid before you Commission gives the difference in cost of blasting gelatine and dynamite at only 7 to 10s. per case.

The mining industry has thus to bear a burden which does not enrich the Stat or bring any benefit in return, and this fact must always prove a source of irritatio and annoyance to those who, while willing to contribute to just taxation for th general good, cannot acquiesce in an impost of the nature complained of. Th importance of this to the mining industry may be gathered from the fact tha

explosives have been shown to average 9 per cent. of the total working cost, but fo the development work the percentage is a higher one.

On June 4, 1897, your Commission inspected the factory at Modderfontein, and i must be admitted that the construction of the works and general equipment are i many respects admirable, and it appeared to us greatly to be regretted that so muc money should have been invested in an undertaking for the manufacture of an article whereof the ingredients have to be imported at a great cost, four tons of raw material being required to produce one ton of the manufactured article.

It has been proved to our satisfaction that none of the raw material used i found in this country, or only in such small quantities as to make it practicall valueless for the purpose required; and the coal consumed, although obtained here, i 40 to 50 per cent. dearer than that delivered at factories in Europe. We understan experiments have been made with the object of manufacturing sulphuric acid fro materials produced here, but these efforts to use the products of the country are sti in the experimental stage. Labour of the kind required is three or four times mor ensive than, for instance, labour in Germany, while the excessive cost of transport pels the use of materials unnecessarily dear. There is also no market here for the products, which in Europe have considerable commercial value, thus further easing the cost of the manufactured articles. All these drawbacks, which make lmost impossible to establish a *bona fide* industry, fall on the mines, and render r task, especially that of the low-grade mines, extremely difficult and disraging. The desirability of establishing industries of all kinds within the Relic cannot for a moment be doubted; but when it is proposed to establish an ficial industry, whose only chance of success lies in the extent to which it may be wed to unduly profit from, instead of benefiting a natural and more important erprise, the economic fallacy of the proposition becomes sufficiently clear to need e further demonstration. Another point that has been brought to the notice of r Commission is the prejudicial effect exercised by this monopoly in practically luding from the country all new inventions in connection with explosives, and, in w of the numerous dynamite accidents that have taken place from time to time, it o be regretted that it is not possible to make satisfactory trials of other and less gerous explosives for the working of mines. These questions have received the eful consideration of your Commission, who are forced to the conclusion that the tory has not attained the object for which it was established, and that there is no sonable prospect of its doing so. Further, that there are good grounds for ieving that the contractors have failed to comply with the conditions of their tract, which require them to establish, complete, and bring into operation, on or ore April 24, 1896, one or more factories for the manufacture of dynamite and er explosives, of such nature and quality, and of such quantity, as the requirements demands within the South African Republic shall necessitate.

For the aforesaid reasons, and in view of the opinion expressed by the Volksraad namite Commission, that the legal position of the Government against the contract- is undoubtedly strong, your Commission desire to recommend that the case be ced in the hands of the legal advisers of the State, with a view to ascertaining ether the contract can be cancelled.

Cancellation of the dynamite monopoly.

Meanwhile, your Commission recommend that the Government avail itself forth- h of its right, under Article 15 of the Regulations, namely:—

Free trade in explosives.

> The Government will reserve for itself the right, when the interests of the State render it necessary, to take away the agency of trading in gunpowder, dynamite, cartridges, and other explosive stuffs from the above-mentioned persons, etc., and at once take into its own hands the importation of dynamite and other explosives for the benefit of the mining industry, subject to a duty of not more than 20s. per case or such other less sum as may be determined on from time to time.

This protective duty, while considerably increasing the revenue of the State, uld at the same time afford ample protection to any industry of this description in Republic. In the event of cancellation being advised to be possible, free trade in losives to be at once established, subject to a duty of 20s. per case, or such other duty as may be determined upon from time to time, and manufacturing of other losives in the Republic to be allowed, and also to be protected by the same import y.

Your Commission are of opinion that effective free trade will be in no wise pardised by the existence of any "ring" or combination for the sale of explosives in rope.

Your Commission further wish to recommend the free importation of detonators.

State's share of profits of South African Explosives Company

Your Commission desire further to observe that it is not clear to them, judg from the published accounts of the South African Explosives Company for 1895 1896, that the Government receives the proportion of surplus profit secured to it un the contract, namely, 20 per cent., and would strongly recommend, in accordance w Article 6 of the contract, an immediate investigation of the company's accounts qualified accountants, in conjunction with the financial adviser of the Commission order to find out what amount is still due to the Government under this head, further to cause inquiry to be made about the quantity of cases of blasting mater gelatine and dynamite imported during 1896-97.

Railway rates.

Your Commission have followed, with great attention and interest, the evidence statistics submitted under the head of railway rates. From those it appears that not o are the tariffs charged by the N.Z.A.S.M. such that, in the event of their being reduced industry would be considerably benefited, while such a reduction would not only fair, but necessitate that the neighbouring States and Colonies would have to red their tariffs considerably. It does not lie within the scope of the labours of t Commission to enter into the application of the tariffs at present existing a charged by the N.Z.A.S.M., because this would require a technical knowledge railway matters which your Commission had neither the power nor opportunity gain.

Reduction of railway rates.

Your Commission have come to the conclusion that, taking into consideration evidence submitted to them, and taking the gross revenue of traffic of goods at abc £2,000,000 (as in 1896), it would be desirable to recommend so to regulate the ta for the carriage of goods that the gross revenue for goods traffic for 1896, would ha been reduced by £500,000, equivalent to an average reduction of 25 per cent.

Further, your Commission deem it desirable that the Government shall make su an arrangement as will secure to them in the future a voice in the fixing of the tari of the N.Z.A.S.M., and express their confidence that, as soon as prosperous times sh warrant such a course, a further reduction in tariffs shall be effected.

Your Commission wish to recommend that the reduction shall be chiefly appli to the carriage of coal, timber, mining machinery, and foodstuffs, according to a sca to be agreed upon between the Government and the N.Z.A.S.M.

Your Commission are of opinion that in this manner the industry will be met a very fair way.

Your Commission wish to express their opinion that it is absolutely necessa that the reduction in all tariffs shall be brought about as speedily as possible, wh they express the hope that, where the co-operation of the neighbouring States a Colonies is required, negotiations will be initiated and carried out so speedily that t reduction to be so initiated shall come into force not later than the 1st of Janua next.

Expropriation of railway.

Several witnesses and some of the members of the Commission have urged t expropriation of the N.Z.A.S.M. by the Government. Your Commission, however, several reasons known to them, and after the same have been communicated to th members of the Commission who wished to urge expropriation of the N.Z.A.S.M., not at the present moment desire to urge expropriation, provided by other mea terms can be secured from the company, so as to obtain the reduction at prese urgently required, on the basis as above set forth.

Your Commission have been informed that the company have promised to t Government to adopt the dividend of the three years—1895, 1896, and 1897—as t basis for the expropriation price, and your Commission can agree to such a propos The expropriation price being fixed, the company will have all the more reason to operate towards the lowering of the tariffs.

Further, it appears from the evidence of the managing director of the N.Z.A.S.M. ...t, in consideration of the reduction of tariffs, he wished to have secured to the ...pany a certain period of existence. Your Commission cannot recommend this ...rse, because they do not deem the same to be in the interests of the State, and it ...uld be contrary to the wishes of the public.

Your Commission further wish to recommend that the Government shall take **Reduction of railway rates on all South African lines.** ...asures to effect an alteration as speedily as possible in the railway tariffs of the ...ghbouring States and Colonies, so as to place them on a reasonable basis. From ... evidence and statistics submitted to your Commission, it appears that the neigh- ...uring States and Colonies have made very large profits out of their railway traffic, ...d it is only fair to expect that they will understand the desirability of a consider- ...le reduction.

Before leaving the subject of the reduction of tariffs, your Commission want to **Railway rates on coal.** ...mark that the tariff for coal traffic ought to command the largest reduction. Your ...mmission have further found that the mining industry have real complaints about ...e few facilities given by the company in delivery of coal and goods in general, and **Delivery of goods on Nether- lands Railway.** ...ur Commission are of opinion that every measure ought to be taken in order to ...cilitate such delivery.

Your Commission recommend that a line of railway shall be constructed to the **Elandsfontein- Roodepoort line.** ...uth of the main reef, between Boksburg and Krugersdorp, specially intended for the ...rrying of coal, and that to the different companies leave should be granted to con- ...ruct sidings from that line and other lines to their mines, with permission to employ ...eam power, after approval of the plans by the Government Commissioner of Rail- ...ys. This will do away with the objection at present existing against the payment ...r the detention of coal trucks, and the expenses connected therewith.

Your Commission further wish to recommend that it will be desirable to relieve **Charges for de- murrage, shunting, &c.** ...riffs for coal traffic of every and any petty charges which are at present charged for ...ck-hire, shunting, detention, etc.

Your Commission further recommend that the company shall, as soon as possible, **Special railway wagons.** ...ovide a quantity of proper coal trucks, by which coal can be carried in bulk, and by ...hich the unnecessary expense of bags will be obviated.

Finally, your Commission are of opinion that the greatest facilities ought to be **Agriculture.** ...anted for the transport of all agricultural produce at lowest prices, and, if required, by ...ght trains to the principal markets of the Republic. It cannot be questioned that ...erything ought to be done to encourage agriculture and stock-breeding in the ...epublic. There is no reason why milk and other perishable articles cannot be loaded ... night at any station of the N.Z.A.S.M., and delivered in time for the markets. As ... argument against this it might be said that, at the present moment, a very small ...antity of such produce would be offered for transport; but your Commission consider ...at, if the opportunity were afforded, probably an important industry in these articles ...uld be created.

Your Commission wish to refer to what has already been said about the carrying **Transport of natives.** ... rail of kaffir labourers, whereby it is proposed to charge for kaffir or coloured ...bour travelling to the mines one-third of the usual fare, and to recover the balance ...om them on the return journey.

Further, your Commission deem it of the greatest importance that measures should ... taken by which all South African railway companies shall carry passengers and ...ods throughout South Africa under uniform conditions.

According to the evidence submitted to your Commission, gold thefts are on the **Gold thefts.** ...crease, and, although the Volksraad have given the matter their favourable considera- ...n, and have, at the instance of the mining industry, so amended the Gold Law as to provide for punishment for the sale, and the being in possession of, raw gold, still, has been stated to your Commission in evidence that the gold thefts amount to abc 10 per cent. of the output, equivalent to an amount of £750,000 per annum. It follo that the administration of the law must be faulty, because there are only a very f instances where the crime has been detected and punished. If these figures are exaggerated, and your Commission have no reason to suppose so, then this matt deserves the serious consideration of the Government.

Remedies for gold thefts.

The suppression of this crime can be considered as a real saving to the indust and this amount of three-quarters of a million would, especially in times of depressio exercise a large influence on the yield and financial position of the mines. T industry ask that the penal clauses regarding this matter shall be eliminated from th Gold Law, and that a separate law be passed, more or less on the basis of the I.D. Law of Kimberley, Cape Colony; and that measures shall be taken by which t injured parties shall be enabled to exercise control, and have supervision over a department to be established for the detection and suppression of thefts of raw gol Your Commission are of opinion that the Government could grant this reque without injuring their dignity, on the basis hereafter mentioned; on the contrary, would remove the blame from the present administration, viz., that these thefts can l practically carried on with impunity.

Pass Law.

As regards the Pass Law, your Commission have obtained very important eviden from Mr. Kock, the Chief of the Johannesburg Pass Department, and they desire refer you to his report, from which it appears that certain alterations are desirabl although what is really required with regard to this law is that it should be appli more stringently.

Administration of Pass Law to be given to Superintendent of Natives.

The Honourable Government will find later on in this report, a recommendatio in which it is suggested that the carrying out of the Pass Law be placed under th control of a local Board on the Goldfields, and your Commission desire further to r commend that the whole of the administration of this law be placed under the contr of the Superintendent of Natives, instead of the Minister of Mines, as is at present th case.

It is far from the Commission to, in any way, blame the Mining Department fo the inferior carrying out of the law until now. But should Government take int consideration the suggestions made by your Commission with regard to the supply native labour, mentioned under that head in this report, the object of your Commissio in making this suggestion will be obvious, and it is also impossible for two depart ments to be engaged with the carrying out of one law.

Local Board.

The evidence given before your Commission has suggested the advisability appointing a Board or Commission in Johannesburg, to be composed of member appointed by the Government, representatives of the mining industry, and commerci firms of the Witwatersrand, in order that the Government members may benefit b the experience of men who are daily occupied in the careful consideration of a matters appertaining to mining. Your Commission are of opinion that it is advisabl that effect should be given to this recommendation. The objects of this Commissio would be the supervision of the administration of the following laws: Liquor Lav as far as the proclaimed goldfields are concerned; the Pass Law, and law regard ing gold thefts; and, further, they would have an advisory vote as regards the suppl of natives to the mines, concerning which your Commission have already advised th Government as to what steps should be taken. The districts under the supervision this Board or Commission ought to include Heidelberg, the Witwatersrand, Klerks dorp and other goldfields, as may appear essential.

Your Commission suggest that this Board or Commission shall consist of five Special detective
force. bers to be appointed by the Government, and of four members to be deputed by ollowing bodies, subject to the approval of the Government, namely, one delegate the Chamber of Mines, one from the Association of Mines, or, in the event of two bodies amalgamating, two delegates from the joint Chamber, one delegate the Mine Managers' Association, and one delegate from the merchants of nnesburg.

Your Commission would recommend that a special detective force be placed under department, the duties of the members of which shall be the tracing of con- eners of the above-mentioned laws, and then the prosecution of them in the usual ner. It shall also be within the province of this Board or Commission to report he Government any neglect on the part of the officials who are charged with the ying out of the above-mentioned laws. The Board or Commission shall also rt to the Executive Council upon the good or bad working of the above laws, and mmend alterations if necessary. It shall naturally be clearly stipulated that the er to be given to the Board or Commission shall in no way encroach upon the king of the Mining Department or of the Licensing Boards, but they shall work in on with them.

We would also advance as another reason in favour of the establishment of such ard that the Government will be able to depute to them the reception of deputa- s regarding mining complaints, for them to hear and investigate such complaints submit them to the Government, together with their opinions upon them. eby much time would be saved.

Your Commission would suggest to the Government that this Board be brought existence as soon as possible, and that they should draw up regulations and nit them to the Government for ratification.

Under the heading of the duty on cement, your Commission merely desire to Duty on cement. e that the import duty of 12s. 6d. per cask appears to be altogether too high. rt from this, the heavy transport rate on such a heavy article as cement causes self the price to be so high that it ought to be exceedingly easy for any local stry to compete.

Your Commission recommends, therefore, that the special duty on cement should bolished as soon as possible.

It has been clearly proven to your Commission that the concession granted for Brick-making
concession. supply of machine-made bricks is generally injurious to the inhabitants of the ublic. For this reason, your Commission recommend that steps be taken, as soon ossible, to relieve the inhabitants of the Republic from this undesirable monopoly.

Evidence has been given before your Commission that the sweepstakes and other Sweepstakes. as of betting held in the betting circles in the Republic have a very injurious effect n trade, and are especially injurious to the youth of this Republic.

Your Commission are aware that this question is already before the Raad for con- ration, and can, therefore, only give expression to the hope that that body will eed to alter the law in such a manner that the holding of all sweepstakes and r forms of betting will be prohibited.

Before concluding their report, your Commission must express the greatest satisfac- Witnesses
thanked. at the manner in which witnesses have appeared at the request of your Commission. ould be invidious to mention some names when there are so many who, at a great ifice of time, have devoted themselves to a careful compilation of facts and figures, which no more interesting or exhaustive statements of the local mining industry e ever been laid before the public.

At the request of your Commission, representatives from Barberton and Klerks-

D 2

dorp came to Pretoria to give evidence, and the public spirit displayed by these ge⟩ men in coming all that distance to represent the interests of their respective c⟩ munities deserves the greatest praise.

It must be mentioned here that the interests of the aforesaid mining commun⟩ are identical with those of the Witwatersrand goldfields, and any benefits resul⟩ from the enquiry must necessarily extend to those fields.

Recommendation for publication of the report and evidence, Your Commission respectfully suggest that, for the purposes of general refere⟩ and to be taken up in the official archives, the report with all the evidence statistics and further addenda, be printed and published in book form. It will serve a useful purpose in illustrating to foreign investors the conditions under wh⟩ the mines exist and are worked, the richness of the reefs and the regularity of the deposits.

Results of adoption of report. Credit will be restored, as it will be obvious to all who take an interest in matter, that the bogus companies, mostly floated in Europe by unscrupulous promot⟩ do not come within the pale of legitimate enterprise connected with the mining indus⟩ The establishment of a local Mining Board has been strongly urged by witnes⟩ From an industrial and financial point of view this country must be considered as ⟩ in its infancy, and without loss of dignity and prestige the Government may acc⟩ to the above request. Experience in these matters can only be attained after the la⟩ of long years, and by coming into contact with experts from other countries the S⟩ will reap the benefit of the knowledge obtained in their countries, where these probl⟩ have for decades exercised the minds of their leading citizens. In conclusion, y⟩ Commission fervently hope that they have truly and faithfully interpreted the obj⟩ of the inquiry, and that their suggestions and recommendations, if acted upon, ⟩ confer a lasting benefit on "Land en Volk."

The above Report was signed by all the Official and Advis⟩ Members of the Commission.

APPENDIX.

——

LETTER OF WITWATERSRAND CHAMBER OF MINES TO THE COMMISSION.

Witwatersrand Chamber of Mines
Johannesburg, 20th May, 1897.

To the Honourable the Chairman and Members of the Industrial Commission of Enquiry.

Gentlemen,—We have the honour to forward you herewith answers to the various questions put in writing to the Chairman of the Chamber, and in response to the request of the Government to all persons interested, to render assistance to your Commission by placing before it all possible information connected with the burdens and grievances of the mining industry, and to your confirmation of that request, beg to submit the main points of the more important questions which have formed the subject matter of the Chamber of Mines' memorials to the Volksraad, and of its memorials and communications to the Government.

The subjects referred to are: Dynamite, Native Labour and Pass Law, Liquor Law, Railway Administration and Rates, Gold Thefts, Bewaarplaatsen Mining Rights, Cement Duty; which will be taken in the order named.

DYNAMITE.*

As far back as 1890 the Chamber suggested that a commission should be appointed to enquire into various questions connected with the dynamite monopoly, and that it was of the first importance that a certain number of those connected with the actual working of the mines (the number proposed was three) should be nominated by the Government as additional official members. A commission was eventually appointed, but the mines were not accorded the representation on it which had been asked for, though at a later stage Dr. Simon was appointed to represent the Chamber.

In 1891, in its memorial to the Volksraad, the Chamber pointed out (1) that numerous complaints of the dynamite being of inferior quality had been received; (2) that the concessionaires were not manufacturing dynamite, but importing it under another name; and, (3) that the price charged was excessive; and asked that leave might be given to import direct from Europe, subject to the payment of a reasonable royalty either to the Government or the concessionaires. The import duty at this time was 7s. per case. The Volksraad resolved: "To answer the memorialists that nothing can be done with reference to their prayers; and further, to instruct the

---

* Throughout in speaking of dynamite, dynamite No. 1, containing 75 per cent. of nitro-glycerine is intended; this quality having been taken as the basis of the contract between the Government and the Government agent.

Government to see that the concession is strictly carried out, and that as quickly as possible the dynamite must be manufactured from materials found in the South African Republic."

The year following, the Chamber's memorial to the Volksraad stated that the mines were being charged by the concessionaires 40s. per case for dynamite, in excess of the price at which it could be imported; that while the mining industry was heavily burdened, the State was losing the revenue which ordinary importers would have to pay; that the terms of the concession were being ignored by the concessionaires, and that the concession ought to be cancelled; but that if the Volksraad were unwilling to proceed to cancellation at once, then that the mining companies should be allowed to import the same explosive and put it into cartridges in the same manner as that adopted by the concessionaires. At about this time, through information supplied by the Chamber, and at its request, the Volksraad Dynamite Commission ordered the seizure of a quantity of stuff which the concessionaires declared to be gühr impregné, but which, by the public firing tests, and the chemical tests of Drs. Schlesinger and Simon, was proved to be dynamite pure and simple. The Chamber thereupon at once asked that permits might be issued for the importation of dynamite. In August, on consideration of the revision of the tariff, various proposals were made for increasing the import duty on dynamite and other explosives. Strenuous endeavours were put forth by the Chamber to protect the industry against such additional taxation, but nevertheless the duty was raised to 3d. per lb. and $7\frac{1}{2}$d. per cent. ad valorem, equal to about 17s. 6d. per case. In the same month the Government cancelled the concession, and in due course the concessionaires claimed in terms of their concession that the matter should be submitted to arbitration. The Chamber then addressed a letter to the State President and members of the Executive Council, thanking them for their action in the matter. Great difficulty was, however, experienced in getting permits issued for the importation of explosives, and, when issued, they were not for a sufficient quantity.

In 1893, the Chamber's memorial to the Volksraad referred to the increase of revenue, which had resulted from the cancellation of the concession, and, after giving figures showing that dynamite could be laid down in Johannesburg, inclusive of 17s. per case duty, at about 66s. 7d. per case, prayed that provision might be made for the issue of permits, on application, to all duly licensed persons wishing to import. The doling out of permits had already, and was still, causing great inconvenience to the mines, and frequent complaints were sent to the Chamber, which duly made representations to Government on the subject.

But the trouble in connection with the question of issue of permits was overshadowed early in August, by information which reached the Chamber that the Government contemplated establishing a State Dynamite Monopoly. Immediate steps were taken to ascertain whether the information was accurate, and on the 8th of August, at a special meeting of the Chamber, a resolution was passed, of which the following is an extract:—

"The Chamber views the present unsatisfactory method of regulating the importation of dynamite with alarm, as it leaves the mining industry constantly confronted with the danger of an absolute dearth of explosives, and deprives it of the advantage of trade competition; and would urge upon the Government the desirability of expediting the arbitration on the points submitted for decision, and of establishing free importation of dynamite under permits. The Chamber also desires to protest most emphatically against the substitution of a State monopoly for the cancelled concession, regarding such a system as no less pernicious than the one it would replace."

A deputation, consisting of the Acting President of the Chamber of Mines, Messrs. G. H. Goch, J. B. Taylor, E. H. Dunning, S. B. Joel, C. E. Nind, and F. Lowrey, handed a copy of the resolution to the President, who, however, refused to accept it, on the plea of other more urgent business, and asked for a simple outline of the industry's grievance, saying that his policy must not be questioned, and that he must be left to look after his mines as he thought best.

At the ordinary monthly meeting of the Chamber, held on the 10th August, after the Chairman had reported on behalf of the deputation, the following resolutions were unanimously passed :—

"The Chamber hereby records its dissatisfaction at the extremely inconsiderate and hostile attitude of the Government towards the mining industry, as shown by its proposals to establish a dynamite monopoly, ostensibly as a State monopoly, but in reality as a monopoly in favour of an agent, to whom the industry will be handed over for spoliation."

"That the foregoing resolution be translated into Dutch and forwarded to all members of the Government, also to all members of the Volksraad, praying these to vote solidly against the iniquitous proposals of the Government *re* State Monopoly, and, if possible, to pass a resolution establishing free trade in dynamite."

Copies of the resolutions were dispatched to the Government and to the Volksraad members with, in the case of the latter, the request set forth in the second resolution. A resolution was also passed, thanking the Minister of Mines for his reception of the Chamber's deputation and for the promise of support which he had given them.

Within a few days the Government submitted its dynamite proposals to the Volksraad. In spite of the manner in which its deputation had been received, the Chamber determined not to remit its endeavours to work amicably with the Government, and at the same time protect the mining industry as fully as possible. Taking the view that the object of the Government was : 1. To provide a way out of the dispute between the concessionaires and itself, and avoid the possibility of damages being awarded against the State; and 2. To ensure the erection of a real factory and the *bonâ fide* manufacture of explosives within the State, the Chamber, while remaining of opinion that the best solution of the dynamite question was the granting of free trade in explosives, was nevertheless willing to assist the Government in seeking to attain its wishes. The following proposals were accordingly submitted by Mr. Jeppe, M.F.V., to the Government and to the Volksraad Commission, which had been appointed to deal with the Government scheme :—

1. The dispute between the Government and the concessionaires to be pushed to a settlement by means of arbitration.

2. The mining industry, if the Chamber is consulted by the Government as to the naming of an arbitrator by the Government, will be willing to pay the damages, if any are awarded, by means of a rate to be levied on each case of dynamite ; the Chamber reserving to itself the right to avoid the payment of additional dues by making one payment for the full amount.

3. That in order to ensure the establishment of a factory in the country, the Government should offer an annual bonus to anyone establishing such a factory. The Chamber of Mines will also contribute a bonus, say of equal amount ; and to make its success certain the Government to arrange for a joint control with the Chamber over such factory.

4. Pending the establishment of the factory and the supply of dynamite therefrom, companies to be allowed to import, under permits from Government, according to their requirements.

Nothing came of this, and on the 5th of September the dynamite regulations submitted by the Government were, with certain amendments, adopted by the Volksraad, and the State Monopoly was duly established by law. The day following the Chamber addressed the State Secretary asking Government not to close with any offer that might be made, before the Chamber had had an opportunity of submitting proposals having for their object the thorough carrying out of the dynamite regulations as passed, and adding: "The mines are so greatly interested, as large consumers of dynamite, that it is to their interest to make such proposals as will completely comply with the wishes of the Government, and on terms which will be far more advantageous to the Government than those provided in the regulations." Though no reply was received, and no acknowledgment was made of the attempts of the Chamber to assist the Government, on the 15th September the Chamber submitted the following offer to the Government on behalf of the mining industry:—

1. To erect a factory within two and a half years; security for the carrying out of this arrangement, to be given to the Government.

2. To pay to Government on every manufactured case of dynamite sold 5s. a case, and 50 per cent. of the profits.

3. To take over the powder factory as provided in the Volksraad regulations.

4. To arrange with the Government the details of a plan by which there shall be a joint control (Government and Chamber) over both dynamite and gunpowder factories.

5. Pending the completion of the factory, to import dynamite and such other explosives as may be required, for the account of the Government, and to arrange the sale and distribution thereof to consumers, subject to such terms and conditions as may be arranged.

Or in the alternative:—

To lend the money required for the erection of the factory to the Government at a rate not exceeding 5 per cent. per annum, provided that the Chamber shall be allowed joint control with the Government of the dynamite and gunpowder factories; details of such joint control to be mutually agreed upon.

This also was left unacknowledged.

It may be remarked that under the State Monopoly the duty payable on explosives imported under permit was fixed at $8\frac{1}{2}$d. per lb. above the ordinary *ad valorem* duty. The contract with the agent appointed by the Government to carry the monopoly out was signed on the 25th October, the term of agency being 15 years.

On the 9th November the Chamber discussed a draft contract with Nobel's; the consideration of the details occupying them three days. The contract, as amended, was then passed. The chief features in the contract were that Nobel's bound themselves to supply at 62s. 6d. per case in bond;[*] to charge the same price as is charged by the Government Agent unless the agent reduces the price to such an extent that less than 40s. nett, would be received, when they reserved the right to suspend deliveries; and that in the event of their erecting a factory for the manufacture of dynamite and other explosives, a Transvaal joint stock company would be formed, towards the capital of which the mining companies would be entitled to subscribe to the extent of one-third in the aggregate; the selling price of such Transvaal manufactured dynamite to be 80s. per case. As a result of the competition between the Government Agent and Nobel's, the price of dynamite was in November brought down to 75s. per case, inclusive in the case of Nobel's of the heavy import duty of $8\frac{1}{2}$d. per lb., and $7\frac{1}{2}$ per cent. *ad valorem*, equal to about 37s. 6d. per case. But the

---

[*] No. 1 dynamite is referred to.

next month, though application was made, permits were refused, and the price was again raised to 85s. per case.

With the opening of the year 1894 complaints were made to the Chamber by mining companies : (1) that the explosives supplied by the Government Agent were of inferior quality ; (2) that the particular kinds required were not procurable. On the 25th January, and on the 6th February, letters were sent to the Government covering copies of the complaints received from companies. Owing to the constant representations of the Chamber the Government was induced from time to time to issue permits, which were then used for the importation of explosives of good quality. In March a delegate of Nobel's Company submitted a scheme for securing the mines an opportunity of becoming shareholders in the company, which the agent intended to form for carrying out the monopoly, and embodying particulars with regard to the price of explosives and other matters. It was rejected on the ground that it " appears to be vicious to public policy as well as inimical to the vital interests of the mining industry," and a deputation interviewed the State President and Executive Council on the subject, as a result of which details of the proposal for the formation of a company to take over the working of the monopoly, which had come to the knowledge of the Chamber, were furnished to the State Secretary. The capital of the proposed company was to be as follows :—

> 182,500 shares of £1 each, to be issued fully-paid to the previous concessionaires, whose concession had been cancelled ;
> 25,000 fully-paid £1 shares to be issued to Mr. Lippert ;
> 22,500 fully-paid £1 shares to be issued to persons unknown ;
> 220,000 fully-paid £1 shares to be issued to Nobel's against payment in full in cash ; with the following charges :—
>
> 5s. on each case of explosives to Mr. Lippert for 15 years ;
> 2s. on each case of explosives to Messrs. Lewis and Marks for 15 years ;
> 2s. on each case of explosives to Mr. Lippert for 3 years ;

and Nobel's also undertook, in the event of further capital being required, to take up 8 per cent. debentures to the amount of £150,000, if the money could not be obtained by public subscription on more favourable terms. The payments to be made to the Government were fixed at 5s. per case, and 20 per cent. of the nett profits, after deducting 8 per cent. as interest on the share capital and the usual allowances for wear and tear, etc.; also £3,750 per annum as rent for the powder factory. In their memorial to the Volksraad, presented in the ordinary session, the Chamber recited the particulars connected with the proposed company, and pointed out that if the Government received its share of profits as well as the 5s. per case, the loss to the State, on a consumption of only 100,000 cases of dynamite per annum, would be £141,350 per annum, as compared with the revenue obtainable from importation under permits. And the Volksraad was asked to limit the maximum capital of any company formed for working to the actual amount of cash paid up; to prohibit the special commissions or royalties proposed to be imposed for the benefit of individuals and companies at the expense of the State ; and in view of the protection afforded to the factory by the import duty of 37s. 6d. per case, to provide that permits should be freely issued, unless, as an extreme case, for high reasons of State such issue be deemed inadvisable.

In May it was ascertained that a coalition had been concluded between Nobel's Company and the Government Agent, and that a company was to be formed on practically the same lines as those referred to above, with the exception that the question of royalties was to be left to the new company. Information was also received that the Government had made an arrangement with the agent, allowing him an extension of time for the erection of the factories. In September the Government resolution, varying the terms of the contract, came before the Volksraad for consideration, and the following resolution was passed: Article 1711—"The First Volksraad having considered the letter of the Government, dated 6th September, 1894, now on the Order, asking for confirmation of the Executive Council resolution, Article 457, dated September 6th, 1894, accompanying the said letter; having considered the memorials and the Commission's report, according to the conclusions based thereon:

RESOLVES :—" Not to confirm the Executive Council resolution, and not to grant the desired authority for alteration of the instructions, and to instruct the Government to act strictly in conformity with the regulations confirmed by the Volksraad." (Nevertheless the Government, as will be seen later, did alter the instructions.)

To memorialists the Volksraad replied that their " request cannot, be granted, as the matter was decided by the Volksraad last year."

In 1895 the Chamber again memorialised the Volksraad, pointing out that on an annual consumption of 100,000 cases of dynamite, the loss to the State from the monopoly exceeded £140,000 a year; this being the difference between the amount paid to the Government, and that which otherwise would accrue from customs dues on importations under permits; that the monopoly prevented the importation and testing of new explosives alleged to be as effective and much cheaper than dynamite; and praying that the Volksraad would consider the advisability of steps being taken for the purchase of the rights of the agent before further expenditure had been incurred in connection with the factory, so that the Government may recover its freedom of action, and be able to allow the mining companies to buy in the cheapest markets such explosives as may be most suitable for the work to be done. As reply, the Volksraad forwarded the following copy of its Memorial Commission's report :—

" The Commission taking into consideration the numerous discussions in the First Volksraad on this subject; taking into consideration Article 7 and Article 13 of the regulations referring thereto; considering that, in accordance with Article 6, maximum prices are fixed for the term of eight years, cannot recommend your House to have the rights of the agent purchased by the Government, as suggested in the memorial of the Witwatersrand Chamber of Mines."

In 1896 it was deemed futile to send in a memorial to the Volksraad, as the reply to that of the previous year indicated the determination of the Legislature not to consent to the purchase of the agent's rights.

During the special session of the Volksraad, held at the beginning of this year, a commission was appointed to enquire into the working of the monopoly, and their report was presented on the 19th February last. In this report the commission *inter alia* drew attention to the following facts :—

1. That the agent has failed to carry out his contract with the Government to establish factories for the manufacture of explosives in accordance with the requirements of the country within the time fixed, and that even within the further $2\frac{1}{2}$ years which the Government have allowed him, he will still be unable to do so.

2. That irrespective of the profit on explosives made at the factory, a profit of £2 per case is made on explosives imported at the cost of the State, of which the agent takes 35s. and the Government 5s. per case.

3. That during the four years, 1897 to 1900 inclusive, it is estimated that at least 430,000 cases of explosives will have to be imported, which, if imported by the State

direct, would benefit the Treasury to the extent of £860,000, and if dealt with as at present, would give the State only £107,500; a difference to the detriment of the State of £752,000.

4. That there is no prospect that the production of explosives will be independent of the importation of some of the raw materials.

5. That the Commission also expresses a doubt as to the possibility of reconciling the Executive resolution, varying the terms of the contract, with the Volksraad resolution Art. 1711, and Art. 16, Par. A, of the contract with the Government Agent. Thus it is clear that the object which the Government had in view when advocating the establishment of a State monopoly, viz., that the State should be rendered independent of foreign sources for the supply of explosives has not been and cannot be attained; and that the mines have been and still are seriously burdened, and the State is deprived of a lucrative means of revenue, simply for the maintenance of a factory which has to import raw materials in any case, and for the most part imports the already made explosive, and for the benefit of the shareholders and other persons having an interest in the South African Explosives Company. The more salient features of the commission's report have been set forth in the memorial presented by the Chamber to the Volksraad, in which also the statement is made that in 1893 Nobel's undertook to deliver in Johannesburg, free of duty, down to 40s. per case, and that there is reason to believe that it can be imported now at about that price.

The Chamber has, hitherto, endeavoured, though fruitlessly, to induce the Government and the Legislature to allow the mines to purchase dynamite in the cheapest markets. Were this allowed, dynamite could be obtained, inclusive of 5s. per case duty, the amount paid by the agent to the Government, at about 45s. per case, which on the present consumption would mean a saving of about £400,000 a year to the mining industry, and would leave the State revenue from explosives undisturbed. In conclusion it may be pointed out that, according to the published statements of State revenue and expenditure, the only payment made by the company has been 5s. per case, and that though large profits must have been made, the Government has so far received nothing on account of its 20 per cent. share in the nett profits.

NATIVE LABOUR AND PASS LAW.

With the development of the mining industry and the consequent increase in the demand for labour, the question of supply became a matter of considerable concern to the companies. In the beginning of 1890 a scarcity of supply was experienced, and from that time forward, the subject of native labour has engaged the almost unintermittent attention of the Chamber. The first communication to the Government was sent on the 23rd January, when it was pointed out that private enterprise had failed to maintain an equilibrium of supply and demand, and the authorities were asked to render assistance by inducing the natives of the thickly populated native districts to come to the fields. The Government merely acknowledged receipt of the letter.

The subject was also brought to the notice of the Minister of Mines, who promised assistance, and to that of the State President personally, on the occasion of his visit to Johannesburg, but without result. Still, owing to the efforts of the Chamber and the mining companies, the supply was brought nearly up to the demand, and later in the year, by the combined action of the industry, under direction of the Chamber, the rate of wages was reduced to from 41s. 6d. to 44s. per month.

In the winter of 1891 the supply again fell short, and numerous complaints were received of the want of shelter on the main routes, and of the ill-treatment to which the natives were subjected by farmers while coming to the fields. The Chamber accordingly asked the Volksraad to provide shelters on the principal roads, and to secure protection for travelling natives; while a letter was addressed to the First Volksraad member for Johannesburg, in which it was stated that there was a serious want of native labour, and the hope was expressed that during the session some measure to afford relief would be passed. The letter closed as follows :—" The mining community has made a strong endeavour to relieve itself of this unreasonable burden, but standing alone, little can be done, and it is to be feared that the efforts of the mines cannot be much longer sustained if the Volksraad and Government do nothing to assist them." Still nothing seems to have been done during the session.

As in 1892 the Government did not take any special action, the Chamber approached agents in the neighbouring States, who expressed their willingness to co-operate, the Cape Government offering to reduce railway fares for natives. It was then decided to organise and carry out the supply of native labour.

Early in 1893 the Chamber introduced labour from the Cape Colony which, however, failed to give satisfaction, owing to the natives objecting to work underground. In March, a deputation went to Pretoria to discuss the matter with the Government, and, in especial, to ask for the appointment of a Government Commissioner, whose duty it would be to communicate with the native chiefs, to provide shelter and protection for travelling natives, and to work in conjunction with the Chamber in all matters relating to native labour. The deputation also informed the Government that it was the desire of the Chamber to appoint an officer to organise the labour supply ; to give his official sanction to contracts between the employers and the natives ; to be the medium of communication between the mining companies and the Chamber, in relation to native labour ; and generally to perform the functions devolving on a special Government officer, appointed in countries where State-aided immigration obtains. The Government, in reply, asked that the matter might be laid more fully before the Superintendent of Natives and the State Attorney. The claim of the Chamber to receive support was admitted; but though the proposals were submitted in detail to General Joubert, Superintendent of Natives, on the 28th March, no reply was received. On the 16th May, a letter was accordingly sent to the General, drawing his attention to the previous communication. Again no reply ; but during June he intimated verbally that he had handed the communication to the Government, and that he was in favour of the scheme and would support it. After waiting a month, on the 10th July the Chamber addressed the State Secretary, referring to the interview in March and detailing the action of the Chamber since, and asking the Government to give its moral support to the Chamber's scheme. No reply was, however, received. The Chamber waited another month, hoping that a favourable answer to its representations might still come to hand from the Government, and none then being forthcoming, decided to proceed at once with the establishment of a Native Labour Department, as, owing to the prevalence of small-pox, the supply of labour from the north fell off, and the necessity for exceptional efforts became manifest. In view of the objection of the Government to the introduction of labour from the Cape Colony, arrangements were made to obtain a supply from the East Coast, but to ensure success the help of the Government was necessary ; in particular to obtain the consent of the Governor-General of the Province of Mozambique to the emigration of natives to this State. The deputation that waited on the Government on this subject received satisfactory assurances. But in November the Acting State Secretary informed the Chamber that its action would only be supported if the natives from the East Coast were brought overland *via* Delagoa Bay. The Chamber's lately-appointed Native Labour Commissioner went to Pretoria and saw the State Secretary, giving him assurances that the wishes of the Government would be complied with, though the Natal route was the cheaper.   This settled the matter so far, but the State Secretary stated that under no circumstances must natives be brought in until the Government had received a reply to the communication on the subject addressed to the Governor-General of Mozambique.   At the opening of the session a memorial was presented to the Volksraad, in which legislation, with the object of securing a more regular supply of labour, was asked for.   A Native Labour Commission, appointed by the Volksraad, reported that the complaints of the Chamber were well founded, and recommended that the instructions already given to the Government to frame an act dealing with the subject should be repeated and emphasised.   At the same time, suggestions were made by the commission |for the adoption of certain provisional measures calculated to induce the natives to come out to work, the chief object being to secure labourers for the farmers.   The Volksraad approved the report, but instructed the Government, in consequence of the prevalence of infectious diseases, to prohibit the natives from travelling.   General Joubert and Commandant Erasmus met the Chamber on the 30th November, when it was suggested to them : (1) that proper protection should be afforded to travelling natives ; (2) that the Pass Law should be so amended as to afford facilities for natives to travel in search of work ; (3) that provision should be made for the registration and numbering of, and the issue of distinctive badges to, the natives on their arrival at their destination ; (4) that the hut tax should be increased as an incentive to the natives to work ; and (5) that permission should be granted to mining companies to establish locations.   Suggestions 1, 2, and 3 received general assent, but the other two evoked differences of opinion.   However, General Joubert stated that he was convinced that the supply of labour was inadequate, and promised his support in inducing Government to legislate in the right direction as soon as possible.   Commandant Erasmus expressed concurrence with the General's views.

In 1894 the necessary permission having been obtained from the Portuguese authorities, the Chamber considered various schemes for the importation of labour from the East Coast, as well as from the north of the Transvaal.   The chief difficulties to be encountered were the want of adequate protection for travelling natives, and the impossibility of enforcing labour contracts with natives owing to defects of the Pass Law.   With regard to the first, representations were made to the Government complaining how natives travelling to these fields were frequently harassed and robbed.   The Government replied that instructions had been issued to all officials to afford protection to natives ; but as no good results were obtained from the action of the Government, the Chamber decided to erect depots where travelling natives could get shelter and food, and where they would find persons who would investigate any complaints of illtreatment on the road.   Respecting the second, the Chamber undertook to draw up regulations dealing with the issue of passes, registration of natives, provision for identification, etc.   After having obtained advice from the Department of Native Affairs in Natal, regulations were drawn up which were adopted by the Chamber and Association of Mine Managers.   They were afterwards submitted to the Mining Commissioner and Assistant Landdrost, and upon their advice forwarded on the 28th March to the Government.   The State President and the Executive Council expressed their complete concurrence with the principle of the regulations, and recognised that such a measure was urgently needed.   However, they were not at the time gazetted, and upon inquiry being made, the Chamber learned from the State Secretary that there was no immediate prospect of the Government taking action in the matter. Several interviews then took place between the Superintendent of Natives and a committee of the Chamber, but no progress was made.   The Chamber being anxious to have the regulations promulgated by the beginning of the next year, sent another deputation, accompanied by the Mining Commissioner, to Pretoria, on the 22nd November. The President agreed with the views expressed by the deputation, and the matter was referred to a committee consisting of the Superintendent of Natives and the State Attorney. This committee, after having made one or two unimportant alterations, recommended the regulations to the Government for adoption, with the suggestion that, if adopted by the Government, they were to be gazetted for one month for public information, and to afford an opportunity for objections to be sent in; and if no objections were sent in, they were to be put in force temporarily, pending confirmation by the Volksraad. The presentation of the committee's report was, however, delayed by the departure of the President; but it was expected that the regulations would be gazetted early in the coming year.

In the early part of 1895 the labour supply was plentiful, and then it began steadily to decrease; and, in May, owing to several native wars then in progress, the stream to the fields practically stopped: not only the natives ceased to come down from the North, but of those that were working on these fields large numbers left for their homes, while the commandeering of 4,000 natives from the northern districts utterly disorganised all attempts at improving the supply. Towards the end of June the war was over, and the Chamber learnt that General Joubert was on his way back with about 5,000 natives, whom he intended to locate in the Warm Baths district. The Chamber's native commissioner made written application for the allotment of 1,000 to 1,500 for service at the mines, to alleviate the great scarcity of labour, but a reply was given that the proposal could not be entertained, as, according to rights established by precedent, the burghers were entitled to the men. However, from this time the supply from the North somewhat improved, although continuing far below the demand. The Chamber devoted considerable attention to the question of importation of labour from the East Coast, but the cost to be incurred was so high that companies did not care to undertake this on a large scale, as long as the pass regulations were not proclaimed, and enforcement of contracts was impossible. As nothing further had been heard from the Government concerning the report of their own committee, which, at the end of the previous year, had advised the adoption of the regulations, a memorial was sent to the Raad at the opening of the session, asking that body to pass the regulations, and the Chamber did everything possible to get them pressed forward for adoption. After considerable delay they were passed on the 3rd October by the Raad, substantially, as drafted by the Chamber. In view of the scarcity of labour on the fields, it was decided to impress upon the Government the desirability of proclaiming them without delay. Letters were forwarded on the 11th and 21st October to the Government, dwelling upon the fact that the matter of proclamation was an urgent one. No reply was received; but on the 18th December, the Rand and De Kaap districts were proclaimed as falling under the regulations, which were to come into force on 1st January, 1896. Considering the urgency of the question, the various delays experienced caused great dissatisfaction. The regulations were handed to the Government in March, 1894, and although the Government expressed approval of them, they were not submitted to the Raad until the 1895 session; and then were only passed at the beginning of October, the districts coming under them being proclaimed two and a half months later, while no provision appeared to have been made for the appointment of officials for their administration.

In 1896 assistance was again asked from the Government to secure an adequate supply of labour, and the Chamber was informed in February, that in terms of the proclamation of the State President the Government would formulate plans to help the mining industry, and that further information would be given within a few days.

The Minister of Mines also wrote that the Chamber would soon be made acquainted with the scheme formulated by himself and the Superintendent of Natives, and with the Government's decision upon it. Nothing further was heard about the scheme; all that appears to have been done by the Government was to instruct the Native Commissioners to render all possible assistance in improving the supply, and to offer to give mine managers letters of introduction to the Native Commissioners. Great expectations were formed of the benefits that would accrue from this Pass Law, but at the very outset it was found there had been omissions of so important a nature as to make the regulations practically inoperative. The object of the new law was to bring the natives under effective control and reduce the risk of desertion to a minimum; but as the districts of the Witwatersrand, Boksburg, and Krugersdorp form one continuous goldfield, and only the central portion, Witwatersrand, had been proclaimed under the new Pass Law, desertion remained as easy as ever, and, in addition to this drawback, which was absolutely fatal to the working of the regulations, the department established for carrying out the law was wholly inadequate for dealing with even the one district placed under it. In March the Chamber urged upon the Government the absolute necessity of proclaiming the districts of Boksburg and Krugersdorp, and after a long delay this was done. The regulations under the new law were now put to the test, and the weak points, apart from the inadequate departmental arrangements, were soon discovered. The entire law was then considered by the Chamber of Mines, the Association of Mines, and the Association of Mine Managers, and a joint memorial was presented to the Government, in which the deficiencies and defects were pointed out, and remedies suggested. On the 23rd December, the present amended law was published, with a provision that it should come into operation at once.

By the new law the old one was repealed, and the proclamations under it, therefore, fell to the ground. But, though it consequently became necessary to proclaim the areas under the law afresh, no such proclamation appeared in the *Government Gazette*. The Chamber accordingly brought the matter to the notice of the Government by letter, on the 9th January, and asked that the districts of Witwatersrand, Krugersdorp, and Boksburg should be proclaimed, and the operation of the regulations be thereby legalised. No reply was received from the Government, but the Minister of Mines, who had also been communicated with on the subject, in acknowledging receipt of the letter, stated that the matter was receiving his attention. Nothing was, however, done until the 6th February, when, in consequence of the magistrate acquitting a number of natives charged with contravention of the regulations, on the ground that these were not in force, the districts above referred to were proclaimed in accordance with the law, in a special issue of the *Government Gazette*.

From the very beginning of this year it was found that even the new Pass Law regulations were utterly ineffective on account of the inefficient administration of the law. The law, as has been said, had been passed with two main objects: Firstly, of establishing thorough Governmental control over the natives employed in the mining districts; and, secondly, of protecting the companies as far as possible against their native labourers deserting; but neither of these objects has been attained. There was no thorough Governmental control, and the companies were in no way protected against their natives deserting; in fact the desertions took place on as large a scale and in as open a way as ever. A memorial was therefore presented to the Volksraad at the opening of the present session praying for an increase of the staff of the Pass Department, and for more police to assist in carrying out and enforcing the regulations; for special judicial commissioners to be appointed to deal with the offenders, and for assistance in other ways to make the Pass Law effective and beneficial.

NATIVE LIQUOR TRADE.

As early as 1890 the question of the sale of intoxicating liquor to natives at the mines engaged the earnest attention of the Chamber. Repeated complaints were sent in by the companies to the Chamber, and after many applications on the part of the Chamber to the Government officials, the Assistant Landdrost, Mr. Van den Berg, discussed the question in detail with the Executive Committee, and several amendments in the law were suggested and embodied in a memorial to the Government praying that a severe check be placed upon the sale of liquor to natives.

In 1891 another memorial was presented to the Volksraad reciting the baneful effects of the sale of drink on the work at the mines, and requesting that no liquor should be sold to any coloured person without a permit from his employer; any contravention to be punished by fine and immediate cancellation of licence.

A law which was intended to limit the sale of liquor was then passed by the Raad, but it had such grave flaws that its working proved an utter failure. It was, in fact, rendered absolutely nugatory by the clause which allowed unemployed natives to obtain one drink, at any canteen, without a permit. Another cardinal defect was the broadcast manner in which licences were issued to practically every applicant, so that the number of canteens was increased out of all proportion to the requirements of the population.

In 1892, therefore, a memorial was presented to the Volksraad, pointing out the evils existing under the law of 1891, praying for its amendment, and either the total prohibition of the sale of liquor to natives or the most stringent restriction of sale.

In other memorials and communications reference was made to the alarming proportions attained by the sale of liquor to natives, the fact being instanced that on a particular Sunday 466 natives had been counted leaving two canteens on a mining company's property. The chief cause of the evil was the indiscriminate manner in which canteen licences were issued by the Pretoria Licensing Board, no less than 572 having been granted for the Witwatersrand goldfields alone. The position was somewhat improved by an amendment to the Liquor Law, under which provision was made for the appointment of local Boards, the Chairman of the Chamber being eventually nominated a member of the Johannesburg Board: but in spite of the Chamber's representation to Government, no representatives of the mining industry were appointed to the Boksburg and Krugersdorp Boards.

It having come to the knowledge of the Chamber, in 1893, that petitions would be presented to the Legislature asking for modification of the constitution of the Licensing Boards, and for the right of appeal against their decisions, the Chamber sent in an opposing memorial, and the law was maintained unaltered. During this year there was a notable improvement in the Johannesburg district, but numerous and serious complaints were received by the Chamber from mining companies in the neighbouring districts of Boksburg and Krugersdorp, where like care in the issue of licences had not been exercised.

In January, 1894, the Executive Committee of the Chamber met the Minister of Mines, to whom they fully explained the unsatisfactory state of affairs in connection with the native liquor trade in the Boksburg and Krugersdorp districts, and asked him to support the Chamber in endeavouring to secure representation of the mining industry on the Licensing Boards of those districts. In consequence of the grave complaints which continued to reach the Chamber from those quarters, on the 7th April a memorial was sent to the State President and Executive Council, in which the evils caused in those districts, by the practically unchecked supply of liquor to natives, were set forth in detail, and the request for representation of the mining industry on the Licensing Boards was repeated.   Exactly a month later the State Secretary replied that the Government, having obtained the advice of the officials concerned, could not accede to the request.   Towards the end of the year frequent complaints were again received, and the Chamber again addressed the Government on the seriousness of the position, and once more asked for the appointment of mining representatives to the Licensing Boards.   In March, 1895, the reply came, stating that the Government could not alter its previous decision.

The mining companies of the fields generally were greatly hampered in their operations by the prevalence of drunkenness among their native employees, a large percentage of whom were, from this cause, constantly incapacitated for work.   This was due to the facilities to obtain liquor offered alike by licensed houses and by illicit dealers.   As it was considered most important that badly conducted places should be closed, and the number of licences in general reduced, the Chamber recommended the companies to instruct their managers to submit to the Licensing Boards any valid complaints that they might have, and to appear in person in support thereof, and to object to the granting of the licence.

In 1896 the Chamber addressed the Government, and presented a memorial to the Volksraad on the increase of the illicit liquor trade, and asked for a strict enforcement of the provisions of the Liquor Law, and for closer supervision of the canteens.   The Volksraad, in response to these representations, having appointed a commission to consider certain proposed amendments of the Law, the Chamber availed itself of the opportunity to pass a resolution strongly advocating the total prohibition of the sale of liquor to natives, and sent a copy to every member of that body.   To the great satisfaction of the Chamber a prohibition clause was embodied in the law.

On the amended law coming into force on the 1st January, 1897, there was an immediate and marked improvement in the condition of the mine natives, and during the first month of the year there was almost a total disappearance of drunkenness among them.   The relief, however, did not last long.   Illicit selling soon became rampant, and to-day the state of things is worse than ever.   This year the Chamber's memorial to the Volksraad laid special stress on the illicit liquor trade, and on the inability of the police to cope with it, asking, as a remedy, that a Government Board might be established, with a body of special detectives under its control ; and also praying the Legislature to maintain the prohibition clause, and the exclusion of canteens from the mining areas.

Letters, in some cases three and four, complaining of the revival of drunkenness among the natives have, since about the end of January, been received from the following companies :—

Salisbury, City and Suburban, East Rand Proprietary Mines, Robinson Deep, Knight's Deep, Henry Nourse Deep, Henry Nourse, West Roodepoort Deep, Bonanza, Treasury, Paarl Central, New Heriot, Robinson, Wolhuter, Minerva, Balmoral, Orion, Vesta, Geldenhuis, Rietfontein A, Worcester, Jumpers, and Nigel.

From these the following have been selected as illustrative of the magnitude of the evil :—

Henry Nourse Gold Mining Company, Limited,

Johannesburg, 29th April, 1897.

THE SECRETARY,

Witwatersrand Chamber of Mines,

Johannesburg.

DEAR SIR,—Upon the instructions of my Board, I beg to hand you the enclosed copy of a letter from our manager, with reference to a disturbance between the native employees of the Henry Nourse and Nourse Deep Companies on Sunday, the 25th inst., which is attributed entirely to the illicit liquor traffic carried on in the vicinity of the above mines.

Yours faithfully,

(Signed), W. M. TUDHOPE,

Secretary.

[*Copy of Letter received from the Manager, dated 26th April, 1897.*]

W. M. TUDHOPE, ESQ.,

Secretary, Henry Nourse Gold Mining Company, Limited.

DEAR SIR,—Yesterday afternoon there was a fight between our natives and those of the Nourse Deep, Limited. They have smashed nearly all the windows in the place, both here and at the Nourse Deep, and knocked up things generally. I would very much like one of the directors to see the damage so that it could be brought before the Commission. It all started through them being drunk, and, of course, the police were not to be found. The Heriot Bar and the kaffir location were the places from which they got the liquor.

Yours truly,

(Signed), J. WHITBURN,

Manager.

[*Copy of Letter received from Manager re Illicit Liquor Traffic.*]

W. M. TUDHOPE, ESQ., *Secretary.*

DEAR SIR,—Would you kindly forward this to the directors as soon as possible. I have again to complain of the selling of liquor to kaffirs. Almost everywhere along the reef it is being carried on to a far greater extent than it ever was before, and the police seem to be of no use whatever in suppressing it.

During Saturday night and yesterday the place was full of drunken kaffirs. The boys state that the liquor was got from the following places:—

Canteen at the New Heriot.

Kaffir location on Louis D'Or G.M. Co., Ltd.

Shops around the Penzance Hotel.

Store at the back of our battery manager's house on the Kimberley Main Reef ground.

Henry Nourse Hotel.

Our compound manager sent boys who bought liquor from a white man standing at the corner of the verandah of the Henry Nourse Hotel. This man, as fast as he sold one bottle, would enter the store and bring out another. Boys were also sent to the store at the back of the battery manager's house, and liquor was again purchased there. Some kaffirs who were drunk stated that they bought four bottles from the Heriot Bar, two of which they finished in the place, and the other two along the road. They say they are able to get any quantity they want, but the price has been raised to 7s. per bottle. The police were about here yesterday afternoon, sergeants I believe, as they wore stripes. Everything was quiet during their stay, and for a quarter of an hour before their arrival, but within ten minutes of their departure the trade was

E 2

carried on as briskly as ever. To-day there are several drunken kaffirs about, and a very great number unable to work.

I trust that every influence will be used to bring about the suppression of this curse.

Yours faithfully,

(Signed), J. WHITBURN,

Manager.

Worcester Exploration and Gold Mining Co., Ltd.,

Johannesburg, 10th February, 1897.

COMMANDANT VAN DAM.

DEAR SIR,—I beg to bring to your notice the continued sale of liquor to natives, which is carried on so largely that we are fast returning to the old condition of things prior to the new Liquor Law coming into force.

The Wiltshire Bar, just below Ferreira G.M. Co., and Princess Bar, near our mine, do a roaring trade. The latter has been frequently reported, but no conviction has been obtained.

Kaffir eating-houses swarm in this neighbourhood, and most, if not all, of them sell liquor—one in particular, near Oliver's Mill, on Booysen's Road, is doing an extensive illicit business, and so are the bars situated at Ophirton.

I shall be pleased to render any assistance in trapping offenders, but think it will be better to employ your own traps, but just as you please, and I confidently hope that you will give this matter your serious and early attention, as our work is greatly hindered by the drunkenness of our kaffirs.

Yours truly,

(Signed), J. L. DE ROOS,

Manager.

Worcester Exploration and Gold Mining Co., Ltd.,

Local Office, P.O. Box 75,

Johannesburg, March 16th, 1897.

The *Secretary,*

Chamber of Mines,

Johannesburg.

DEAR SIR,—I beg to hand you copy of a letter addressed to Commandant Van Dam, but nothing has been done to check the illicit liquor traffic—in fact it is more rampant than ever, and boys in squads can be seen openly carrying and drinking liquor *ad. lib.*

On the 8th inst. upwards of 300 of our natives were drunk and incapable.

In addition to the bars mentioned in my letter to the Commandant, the Good Luck Bar, situated close to the Robinson Co.'s boundary, is notorious, and it may safely be said that all bars, directly or indirectly through the eating-houses, are contravening the law.

I am of opinion that the Sanitary Board should be addressed on the matter of licensing kaffir eating-houses, which are a principal channel of supply of liquor to natives, and while they are allowed to carry on this nefarious business it is hopeless to attempt to keep the natives sober.

I remain, yours truly,

(Signed), JOHN L. DE ROOS,

Manager.

The Nigel Gold Mining Co., Ltd.,

Head Office, Pietermaritzburg, Natal,

29th April, 1897.

To the LANDDROST,

Heidelberg, Z.A.R.,

SIR,—I am desired by my board of directors to again bring to your notice the fact that although the Liquor Law in the Transvaal provides that no drink shall be supplied to natives, yet at this company's property drunkenness amongst these people is as rife as ever.

The authorities have, for reasons best known to themselves, withdrawn the licence of the only canteen situated on this company's property, but have re-granted licences to seven hotels and canteens, all within a distance of a few hundred yards from our boundary, and it speaks for itself that these seven liquor houses cannot be made to pay by serving white people only, and the consequence is an enormous native trade and attendant demoralisation of our boys.

The gravest feature of this matter is that this pernicious trade is carried on right under the noses of the police and local authorities, and although information has been given and witnesses sent to prove violation of the law, yet in no case whatever has conviction followed.

It is unnecessary to go into details—this evil is one that is too well known—and it only comes to this, that the board of directors of this company plainly see that it will not pay the company to resume crushing until some assurance is forthcoming that our native labour can be used to the best advantage, and this assurance can only be had by the Government strictly carrying out the law, or closing altogether the whole of the canteens in the neighbourhood of our property.

I am, Sir,

Yours obediently,

F. WEIGHTON,

Secretary.

ROBINSON DEEP—STATEMENT.

On Wednesday, the 7th April, at 6 p.m., an employee of the Robinson Deep, Limited, named Henry Kempster, accompanied by two witnesses not employees of that company, and a kaffir in the employ of the Robinson Deep, Limited, proceeded to the Hanover Bar, Ophirton, where he suspected liquor was being sold to natives.

The kaffir was given 5s., and on presentation of that amount the proprietor of the Hanovar Bar, C. Beiles, handed him a bottle of liquor, which the kaffir at once handed to Mr. Kempster.

Mr. Kempster at once took the bottle to the Charge Office, Johannesburg, in order to lay a charge against the bar proprietor, but the Charge Office officials refused to receive the charge, and directed him to the Detective Department, who in turn re-directed him to the Charge Office, informing him that they did not receive any complaint of that nature. Returning to the Charge Office, Mr. Kempster was instructed to proceed to the mounted police, who, however, told him they knew nothing of the matter, and could only refer him to the Charge Office again.

Mr. Kempster then returned with the bottle and deposited it, sealed, in the mine office of the Robinson Deep, Limited, where it is at present.

Paarl Central Gold Mining and Exploration
Company, Limited,
Mine Office, 1st March, 1897.

SPECIAL LANDDROST,
Johannesburg.

LIQUOR LAW.

SIR,—I beg to inform you that on Saturday night about ten o'clock, a cart drawn by four oxen was standing on the dam-wall of this company, near Langlaagte Village, selling liquor to natives.

Also during the whole of yesterday (Sunday) liquor was being sold wholesale to the natives at some canteens in the village, and, as a result, during Saturday night, Sunday and Sunday night, a large number of my boys were drunk and unfit for work to-day.

Trusting that this matter will receive your prompt attention.

I have the honour to be,
Sir,

Your obedient servant,
(Signed)   JAMES B. LITTLE,

General Manager.

RAILWAYS.

In 1889 the Chamber urged upon the Government the absolute importance of speedy railway connection with the sea, in the interest of the gold mining industry and of the State in general. Several endeavours were made to induce the Government to receive a deputation on the subject, but without avail. And it was not till the visit of the President to Johannesburg in March, 1890, that a definite official announcement was made that early steps would be taken to make the railway to the coast. In 1891 the Chamber wrote to the Government objecting earnestly to the proposed postponement of construction work, owing to financial considerations on the part of the Netherlands Company; and at the close of the year arrangements were made which gave promise of an early completion of the line. In September, 1892, the first through-train arrived in Johannesburg; but great as have been the advantages derived from the railway, especially in rendering transport independent of seasons, they have been largely neutralised by the high tariff imposed by the company.

The rates charged are not only inordinately high as compared with those of other countries, but are greatly in excess of those of the Cape Colony, Natal, and the Free State, which nevertheless secure an exceptionally large return on their several railway systems.

The following table of through-rates shows the difference in charges, and in this connection attention may be drawn to the fact that, while the Cape and Natal railways have to raise their traffic to an altitude of 3,988 feet and 5,433 feet respectively, the Netherlands Railway proceeds from the termini of these systems along a practically level course :—

	NORMAL. Per ton per mile.	INTERMEDIATE. Per ton per mile.	ROUGH. Per ton per mile.
Cape	2·34	2	1·3
Orange Free State	2·34	2	1·3
Natal	3·04	3·04	1·94
Portuguese...	4·07	3·53	2·44
Netherlands, *via* Cape ...	7·7	7·7	7·7
„ „ Natal ...	5·06	3·82	3·26
„ „ Delagoa Bay	4·27	3·69	2·54

And even for the carriage of South African agricultural produce the other systems offer greater facilities than the Netherlands Company, as follows :—

Cape, for 23 miles	½d. per ton per mile plus terminals.				
Orange Free State, for 23 miles	„	„	„	„	
Natal, for 13 miles	1¾d.	„	„	„	„
Portuguese...	2·2d.	„	„	„	„
Netherlands, *via* Cape and O.F.S.	3·1d.	„	„	„	„
„ „ Natal ...	3·26d.	„	„	„	„
„ „ Delagoa Bay ...	2·2d.	„	„	„	„

It is unnecessary to give specific examples of the actual railway charge in money on goods from the coast, as this has been fully dealt with in the evidence of many of the witnesses who have appeared before you; and the comparative tables, given above, afford eloquent testimony of the abnormal rates levied on the Transvaal lines.

As early as 1890 the Chamber found it necessary to complain alike of the administration of the Rand Tramway, as the coal line from Boksburg to the gold mines was called, and of the exorbitant rates charged for the carriage of coal. In May the Mining Commissioner was addresed on the subject, and in October a communication was sent to the Government. In the letter to the Government the Chamber asked to be allowed to send a deputation to discuss matters in detail, and the following grievances were set forth:—That the rates charged between Brakpan and Boksburg were irregular; that differential rates were charged; that, while the tariff was stated not to exceed 2½d. per ton, per kilometre, a much heavier charge was made between Boksburg and Johannesburg; that, though the Netherlands Company had engaged to construct sidings, they had not done so, and that this failure to carry out the engagement caused considerable extra expense to the companies for delivery of coal. In November the State Secretary replied that Mr. Verwey, general manager of the Netherlands Railway Company, was travelling in Natal, and that, as it was desirable he should be present at the proposed interview, an appointment would be made on his return. After Mr. Verwey's return another letter was sent to the State Secretary pressing for an appointment, and referring to the letter sent in November, but to this no reply was received. In 1891 a memorial was presented to the Volksraad detailing the administrative shortcomings of the Netherlands Company, and the high rates for transport of coal; finally asking for relief. The company evinced a better disposition to meet the requirements of the mines by slightly reducing rates, and by making arrangements for the construction of some sidings. In June, 1892, Mr. Middelberg, who expressed a desire to meet the wishes of the industry, had an interview with the Executive Committee, when the insufficiency of rolling-stock, difficulties with regard to sidings, and the high transport rates were referred to. The contracts for sidings were amended, and it was stated that additional trucks were on the way from Europe ; but, though it was admitted that the rates were high, no prospect of an early reduction was held out. The proposal for a line to the south of the main reef was submitted, and was favourably entertained, but no active steps were taken to carry it out till last year, when the Volksraad refused to sanction construction, on the ground that the information before them was insufficient. This year it is hoped the necessary authority will be granted, and the Chamber has memorialised the Volksraad with regard thereto.

Early in 1893 companies complained to the Chamber of scarcity of coal, and in some cases operations had to be suspended. The Chamber entered into telegraphic communication with the Government, urging that the strongest pressure should be brought to bear on the Netherlands Railway Company to compel it to fulfil its obligations to the mining companies. No replies were, however, received. In May complaints against the company were renewed, and a telegram was again sent to Government asking it to give its earnest attention to the matter. This time a reply was received stating that the telegram *re* coal transport had been referred to the Government Commissioner for Railways, to whom in future communications on railway matters should be addressed. The Chamber thereupon telegraphed to the Railway Commissioner pointing out the urgency of the case, but failed to elicit a reply. About a fortnight later the Chamber wrote to the Commissioner informing him that since the last communication further complaints had been received with respect to the Netherlands Railway Company failing to deliver coal to the mines, owing to an insufficiency of trucks, and pointing out that the company should be compelled to provide an adequate number of trucks for coal transport, or allow the companies to do so. Again there was no reply. In the middle of June the Chamber telegraphed to the Commissioner on the same subject, and at last, through the Assistant Commissioner, an answer was obtained, but it amounted mainly to an excuse for the negligence shown by the railway company, adding, however, that, if the Chamber could obtain the loan of trucks from the Cape Government Railways, the Netherlands Company would pay for them. In July, in response to the repeated representations of the Chamber, the Commissioner came to Johannesburg to hear complaints, when the Chamber's deputation laid stress on the fact that the railway company should not only secure sufficient trucks for transport of coal, but should grant greater facilities for the construction of sidings to the mines ; the desirability of a line to the south of the main reef was also urged. After this, owing to the arrival of trucks from Europe, the transport service improved.

In June, 1895, owing again to insufficiency of trucks, the coal transport service of the Netherlands Railway broke down, and the danger of mines having to suspend operations became imminent. In these circumstances the Chamber appealed to the Cape Government Railways to lend the Netherlands Company as many trucks as they required, and the appeal was at once fully responded to. The prompt action of the Cape Railways averted what would have been a serious industrial crisis ; but a letter to the Netherlands Railway Company, sent a few days later by the Chamber, asking them to expedite the return to the Cape of trucks bringing up goods, so that there might be no necessity for sending back those lent for coal transport, was not even replied to.

In May, 1896, the old condition of things recurred. Once again the railway company was unable to deliver coal to the mines in sufficient quantity. The Netherlands Company was addressed on the subject, and a copy of the letter forwarded to the Government, with a request that they would use their influence to induce the company to provide sufficient trucks for coal transport. No reply was received from Government.

The present rates for transport of coal on the Rand Tram, according to the sliding mileage scale for coal, vary from a maximum of 3d. per ton per mile to a minimum of 2d. per ton per mile; the average for distances up to 40 miles being 2½d. per ton; the charge from Springs to Johannesburg being £3 4s. 2d. per 10-ton truck, for which on the Natal system for the same distance only 12s. 11d. would be paid; while the same company's rate to Delagoa Bay is ·54d. per ton per mile; in the Cape the coastward rate is ½d. per ton per mile; the inland rate 1d. per ton per mile; in the Orange Free State the rate is ½d. per ton per mile; all on the basis of a 2,000 lb. ton; in Natal the rate is ½d. per ton per mile for the 2,240 lb. ton. This comparison shows that the rate for carrying coal from the collieries in the vicinity of the Rand to the gold mining companies cannot be described as other than extortionate.

To sum up the position we may draw attention to the fact that the Netherlands Railway Company earned last year, over and above the working expenses and guaranteed interest on loans and capital, the sum of £1,330,000. They also enabled —we might fairly say forced—the Cape and Natal lines to earn £1,801,000 profit, besides 4 per cent. interest on their capital. That is, the Transvaal consumers were taxed to the extent of £3,131,000 for the benefit of these three railway administrations.

The Chamber recently presented a memorial to the Volksraad asking that provision may be made for the expropriation of the Netherlands Company's railways; and, in its opinion, this will prove the only effectual means of preventing the system of overcharges, which, it must be presumed, will always be attempted by a purely commercial monopolist enterprise, and for utilising the railway system to the fullest extent for the development of the mining industry and the advancement of the general interests and prosperity of the country.

GOLD THEFTS.

In 1891, in its memorial to the Volksraad, asking for amendment of the Gold Law, the Chamber also urged the necessity of provision being made for the detection and punishment of thieves and receivers of gold. And it may at once be stated that the Volksraad has favourably received and given effect to the suggestions of the Chamber with regard to amendments to the Gold Law, imposing restrictions on the purchase and possession of raw gold, etc., and providing penalties for breaches of the law. But the failure to provide adequate protection to the mines has been, and still is, due to faults of administration. The law provides for the punishment of offenders, but no efficient machinery exists for bringing them to justice. Thefts have, therefore, gone on practically uninterruptedly since the early days of gold mining here, though the companies have endeavoured to protect themselves by all the means in their power; and except for an occasional prosecution the receivers have been able to prey on the industry with virtual impunity.

In 1892 in their memorial to the Volksraad on gold thefts, the Chamber asked that the Government should be authorised and requested to make regulations for the establishment of some public body or institution, or other systematic means or machinery for detecting thefts and illicit dealings in gold and other precious metals.

In 1893 in their memorial the Chamber asked the Volksraad to make provision for the appointment of a Government Board at Johannesburg, with a special detective force attached thereto; working under regulations best calculated to minimise the thefts of gold and illicit dealings therein. The subject was referred to a special commission, which reported as follows: " The Commission recommends that the petition be referred to the Government with instructions (1) to draw up, in conjunction with the Minister of Mines, such regulations as they may consider to be in the interest of the gold mining industry; to publish same, and lay them before the Volksraad next session; and (2) to instruct the Government provisionally to take such special measures as may be deemed necessary to suppress thefts of gold and amalgam. The necessity of the above recommendation has appeared to us, not only from the petition itself, but also from the information given by the Minister of Mines and members of the Chamber of Mines." After a three days' debate, the Volksraad resolved to disapprove their commission's report, and refer the petition to Government.

In 1894 the Chamber spent £1,070 in getting evidence in connection with the thefts of, and illicit dealings in, gold; and on the 10th April of that year a deputation went to Pretoria and interviewed the State President and Executive Council. The State President stated that he was satisfied that something ought to be done to diminish thefts of gold, but would not bind himself to establish a special detective department; he, however, favourably entertained a proposal for placing a sum on the estimates for the maintenance of extra police, and asked the Chamber to submit their proposal in writing. This was done; the proposal being as follows: (1) The Chamber engages to provide a sum equal to that set apart by the Government; (2) the police referred to shall be employed solely in connection with the detection of thefts of, and illicit dealings in, raw gold, amalgam, etc., and in taking measures for the suppression of these crimes; (3) the proceeds of all raw gold, amalgam, etc., that may be received shall, after the deduction of rewards or bounties to the police, and of the cost of maintenance of the force, be passed to credit of account, and such balance as may be to credit at the close of the year shall be divided equally between the Government and the Chamber, for the reduction of the respective contributions which may have been made; (4) the police referred to to be appointed by and be under the control of the Government; details to be arranged later; (5) this arrangement shall be in force for one year. The Government replied " that a sum of £6,000 had been placed on the estimates for detectives. On confirmation of this item by the Volksraad, the Government will be prepared to set aside therefrom a sum of £2,000 as soon as your Chamber contributes a like amount. This combined sum of £4,000 will be applied to the purposes described by your Chamber, under the express condition stated at the interview relating thereto, of absolute Government control and direction." The Chamber thereupon resolved that the action of the Executive Committee be confirmed, and that the sum of £2,000 be contributed to the maintenance of special detectives, as recommended. In July the Government were informed that the Chamber was prepared to contribute £2,000, subject to the Government providing a similar amount, for the purposes detailed in the letters exchanged, whenever required to do so.

In February, 1895, the Chamber wrote to the State Attorney with reference to gold thefts, and asked that the arrangement with the Government for the appointment of detectives to be engaged solely in the suppression of gold thefts, should be carried out, the Chamber having undertaken to contribute £2,000 for the purpose; and in conclusion said: " The Chamber hopes that you will at the earliest opportunity bring the matter under the notice of the Government, and point out that strong measures are needed, not only for the protection of legitimate industry, but also for the removal of the scandal occasioned by crime being carried on on a large scale with practically absolute impunity." The receipt of the letter was acknowledged. The difficulty in connection with carrying out the arrangement was that Government would not appoint a special gold thefts detective force. In 1895 amendments were asked for in the gold thefts section of the Gold Law and were adopted by the Volksraad.

This year the Chamber has in a memorial appealed to the Volksraad to make provision for the appointment of a Government Board at Johannesburg, with a force of special detectives under its control, for the suppression of thefts of, and illicit dealings in, gold.

It will be noticed that since 1892, the Chamber has been endeavouring to secure this necessary measure for the protection of the gold mining industry.

BEWAARPLAATSEN MINING RIGHTS.

In 1891 the companies found it necessary to acquire ground at some distance from the mines for the carrying on of their operations. This they did by taking areas under ordinary claim licence, but as this licence gave no title to use of the surface, bewaarplaatsen licences were also obtained. They were then advised to stop paying claim licence, as the bewaarplaats licence fully secured their rights, the Volksraad having that year passed an amendment to the Gold Law, by which digging under bewaarplaatsen was prohibited; and at the same time an annexure was attached to the Gold Law, containing certain regulations, providing that the holder of a bewaarplaats licence should have a preferent right to the minerals.

In 1892, at the instance of the Government, the Volksraad again amended the law, authorising the Government, subject to certain conditions, to grant permission to mine under bewaarplaatsen and other reserved areas. The Chamber thereupon endeavoured to get a rider attached to this amendment, giving the holder of the surface rights a three months' preferent right to take out mining rights, but did not succeed. It was currently reported that a group of speculators, cognisant of the contemplated alteration of the law, had already applied to Government for the mining rights under bewaarplaatsen, and the companies in self-protection also lodged applications. An announcement was then made that no application sent in prior to the 1st September would be entertained, and that in dealing with applications the question of preference would be matter of careful consideration. Both the State President and the Minister of Mines gave verbal assurances that no injustice to the mining companies would be permitted. On the 1st September the companies accordingly filed new applications, but up till now their receipt has not been acknowledged, nor within our knowledge have they ever been considered.

In 1893 the Chamber presented a memorial to the Volksraad on this subject. It was then referred to a special commission, which recommended certain further amendments to the law; one, in accordance with the Chamber's request, providing that the owner or occupier of bewaarplaatsen should have a preferent right to the mining rights in question over all other applicants. The Volksraad, however, decided to defer consideration of these amendments till the next session, and to have the law with the proposed amendments published as a draft law.

In 1894 the Chamber memorialised the Legislature again, and the Second Volksraad, after a protracted debate, adopted the draft law virtually as published, Article 21c providing that " such rights (mining rights) shall be granted to holders of machine stands, water rights, etc." An effort was made by the Government to induce that body to reconsider its decision, which, however, only drew forth a resolution not to alter the law as already passed.

The First Volksraad adopted the law in principle without making any alteration; but the bewaarplaatsen articles could not come into operation until the regulations controlling mining in these areas had been approved by the Second Volksraad; and, as the Government failed to submit the regulations before the close of the session, the whole matter was shelved for another year.

In 1895 the Chamber sent in another memorial. The Gold Law had, at the request of the Chamber, been codified, and in this form it came before the Second Volksraad for confirmation. The articles referring to bewaarplaatsen mining rights were passed with some minor alterations, but the provision that these rights should be given to the surface-holders, was left unchanged. In the First Volksraad the Government tried to secure an important amendment, providing that mining, except by or in the name of the State, should be prohibited under certain areas, and that the Government should be allowed to grant these rights to others when it was not intended to exercise the State's privilege. The chief alteration suggested was that affecting the preferent right of the surface-holder, which had already been confirmed by the Second Volksraad and approved in principle by the First, by substituting a new article, stating that " for the obtaining of these rights, etc., shall be taken into consideration," in place of the existing article which laid down that "these rights shall be granted to, etc." The First Volksraad, however, would not go further than referring the articles back to the Government, with instructions to print the Gold Law as amended by the Second Volksraad, and include in it any further amendments which they wished to submit to the Legislature. A few days later the draft law including the Government's amendments, was printed and laid before the House, and that body was asked by the State President to depart from the Order and at once to consider the amendments. This was done, and a two days' debate ensued. In its course it was pointed out that the articles under discussion had been passed by the Second Volksraad, on whom the duty of framing the Gold Law had been specially devolved, and had been confirmed by the First Volksraad. A resolution was finally passed, not to accept the Government's proposals, but to suspend the articles referring to undermining rights for a year, instructing the Government meanwhile to obtain further information.

In 1896 the Chamber presented a memorial to the First Volksraad, asking them to confirm the articles as passed by the Second Volksraad, but although no fresh information was submitted by the Government, the First Volksraad overrode the decision of the Lower Chamber, and stultified their own action of the two previous sessions by affirming the principle that mining rights under bewaarplaatsen, water rights, etc., shall be sold by public auction, one-half of the proceeds going to the Government and the other half to the owners of the farm.

This year the Chamber has again memorialised the Second Volksraad, pointing out that the mining companies are of opinion that they have been deprived of their equitable and legal claim to the mining rights under bewaarplaatsen, etc., by the First Volksraad, and asking that the amended articles as adopted in 1894, may be restored in the law.

CEMENT DUTY.

In July, 1892, the Chamber was informed that an application had been made to Government to impose an import duty of £1 per cask on cement. A memorial was thereupon sent to the State President and members of the Executive Council, pointing out that, in the opinion of the Chamber, sufficient protection was already afforded to the local factory by (1) the then existing import duty of 5 per cent.; (2) the heavy expense of importation from Europe, which amounted to £2 per cask; and (3) that the burden which would be imposed upon the industry by such extra duty would be a constantly increasing one, as cement was being used in large and steadily growing quantities; and a request was made that any attempt to increase the duty should be opposed. Mr. Jan Meyer, M.F.V., for Witwatersrand, was also asked to offer strenuous.

opposition to the proposal, and replied that he would do his best. Nevertheless the duty was raised to £1 per cask.

In 1893, the Chamber presented a memorial to the Volksraad, setting forth that cement was largely used in mining works and in the erection of buildings generally; that the English cost was 5s. 6d. per cask, and the cost of importation 34s. per cask, and that the tax was unduly burdensome on the mines and the general public, finally praying that the duty might be reduced to 5 per cent., at which it had stood till the previous year. But the memorial to the Volksraad was as fruitless as the one to the Government had been, though at the time the manufacture of cement in the Transvaal had practically come to a standstill. In 1894, the Chamber again addressed a memorial to the Volksraad, repeating its former arguments; stating further that the cement factory was not working, and asking for the repeal of the £1 duty. This time a measure of success was attained, the special duty being reduced to 12s. per cask, at which, *plus* 7½ per cent. *ad valorem*, it now stands. Last year, according to returns furnished to the Chamber, 22,165 casks of cement were used by 81 companies, and it is evident how undue a proportion of the total cost is attributable to the heavy import duty.

CONCLUSION.

In the foregoing statement, the chief burdens and grievances of the mining industry have been briefly touched upon, but others, in some cases of a serious nature, have been omitted, from a desire not to produce too lengthy a document. In this category we may cite the import duties on food-stuffs, which largely increase the cost of white and native labour, and which as far back as 1890 the Chamber tried to get repealed; and the constant vigilance which it has been absolutely necessary to exercise to prevent articles used in mining from being artificially increased in price through privileges to be granted to individuals under concessions, factory contracts, or, as in the case of cyanide, a State cyanide monopoly; while the endeavour to interfere with the High Court, by means of an amendment to the Patent Law, and so render nugatory any judgment in favour of the mines which it might give in the cyanide case, was only defeated by the barest majority. Fortunately, the action of the Chamber backed by the support of a majority in the Legislature, was successful in these particular cases; but the fact that year after year the mines have been threatened with the laying on of additional burdens, in some form or other, constitutes a real and solid grievance.

The appointment of your Commission may, it is to be hoped, be taken as an earnest that the value of the mining industry as the mainstay of the country is now appreciated, and that it is the intention of the Government and the Legislature to afford it relief from the intolerable burdens which at present render mining operations in many cases utterly unprofitable.

The memorials which the Chamber has presented to the Volksraad this year are attached hereto in the expectation that they will receive your support.

We have the honour to be,
Hon. Sir and Gentlemen,
Your obedient servants,

JAMES HAY, *President.*

G. ROULIOT, } *Members of*
H. F. STRANGE, } *Executive Committee.*

A. R. GOLDRING, *Secretary.*

Memorials of the Witwatersrand Chamber of Mines to the Volksraad.

Presented 3rd May, 1897.

PATENT LAW.

To the Honourable the Chairman and Members of the Honourable Volksraad:

The Humble Memorial of the Witwatersrand Chamber of Mines:

Sheweth :—

That a Concept Patent Law has been published in the *Staatscourant,* and will be submitted to your Honourable House to be dealt with.

That a number of amendments to the existing law are contained in the Concept Law.

That your memorialists respectfully desire to point out that the following proposed amendments will be against the interests of the State and the mining industry :—

(*a*) Article 4a provides that the term " new invention " shall include every invention that before the aforementioned time was not generally and with practical result in use in the branches of trade and industry to which the invention has reference. This portion of the article your memorialists wish to oppose on the ground that a new invention may be made by a person who does not desire to derive any financial advantage from his discovery, but places it freely and fully at the disposal of the whole world content with having added to the sum of knowledge and benefited mankind. This invention may, however, not be applied practically to trade and industry; and later someone may claim to have arrived independently at it and apply for a patent. The granting of such a patent would obviously deprive the world of the benefit conferred upon it by the disinterested action of the first inventor, and would allow another person to reap the fruits which have voluntarily been foregone by him.

(*b*) Article 8.—The amendment to this article makes it permissive for an applicant to lodge a description in his own language, in addition to the compulsory translated description in the language of the country. The translations by sworn translators, especially in the case of specifications involving the use of technical terms and dealing with complex chemical processes, have, within the experience of your memorialists, frequently been found to be unintelligible, and have proved a great difficulty to persons having an interest in ascertaining the nature of the invention for which the granting of a patent is requested. It is therefore desirable that the applicant should be compelled, as at present, to lodge one description in his own and one in the official language.

(c) Article 25a.—This article, which it is proposed to insert in the existing law, is, in the opinion of your memorialists, wrong in principle, and in practice will prove impracticable. For, in the first instance, it limits the duration of a lawsuit, a matter which rests with the discretion and judgment of the Court before which the case is brought; and in the second it is retrospective. In a recent important patent case the time occupied was, through the necessity of allowing the appointment of commissions to take evidence in distant parts of the world, extended far beyond the period mentioned in the above article, and it is clear that in future actions a similar procedure may have to be followed. Thus if this article were passed it would involve an encroachment on the powers and privileges of the High Court, and would probably be the means of justice being denied to litigants.

That having stated their objections to certain proposed alterations to the law, your memorialists would respectfully submit that it is desirable that the provisions of the 5th paragraph of Article 13 should be applied to applicants as well as to objectors. That is, that when an applicant is resident abroad, or possesses no fixed property within the State, an objector shall be entitled to claim that such applicant shall lodge security for the payment of costs to the satisfaction of the Commissioner, and that if such security be not lodged, the Commissioner shall refuse to consider the application. In support, your memorialists would submit that they have opposed the granting of many patents in the interest of the State and the inhabitants, and that in nearly every case they have succeeded. But, though in refusing the applications the State Attorney has given costs against the applicant, your memorialists have seldom been able to recover them from persons residing abroad and not having fixed property within the State. The course pursued by your memorialists proves that persons constantly apply for patents to which they are not entitled, and in many cases evade the payment of the costs given against them, thus imposing a heavy burden on your memorialists and others who may take steps to protect the public against the encroachments of individuals.

Your memorialists therefore pray that for the foregoing reasons your Honourable House will reject the proposed amendments :—

Article 4a.—So far as regards the second portion of the first paragraph.

Article 8.—Regarding the substitution of permissive for compulsory lodging of a description in the language of the applicant.

Article 25a.—In its entirety : and will amend Article 13 in the manner asked for in the memorial.

And your memorialists will ever pray.

GOLD THEFTS.

To the Honourable the Chairman and Members of the Honourable Volksraad

The Humble Memorial of the Witwatersrand Chamber of Mines:

Sheweth :—

That the mining companies of the Witwatersrand Goldfields sustain very heavy loss through thefts of amalgam and other metallic and chemical combinations of gold.

That from cases which have occasionally come before the Courts and from other information which from time to time has been laid before your memorialists, it has been clearly shown that this plundering of the mining industry is carried on in an organised and systematic manner, and that a combination exists between dishonest employees engaged in and about the works of the companies and the illicit buyers outside, who, for the most part, carry on a legitimate business, but use it mainly as a cover for their nefarious transactions.

That the mining companies have in the past, and do still, exercise all possible vigilance to prevent these thefts, but, so far, have been, and still are, unable wholly to do so, owing to the temptations placed in the way of their employees by the illicit buyers.

That there is reason to believe that with the expansion of the mining industry thefts and illicit purchases of gold have increased in volume.

That the provisions of the Gold Law and the efforts of the detective force have proved insufficient, either for suppressing these crimes or, to any appreciable extent, for bringing the criminals to justice.

That experience has demonstrated that the ordinary detective force is not adequate for the due protection of the mining companies, but that it is necessary that special means should be provided for the detection of the thieves and receivers and for bringing them to justice.

Wherefore your memorialists humbly pray your Honourable House to make provision for the appointment of a Government Board at Johannesburg, with a force of special detectives under its direct control, working under regulations the best calculated to suppress the crimes referred to in this memorial, and so afford the industry efficient protection from the criminal classes now preying on it.

And your memorialists will ever pray.

DYNAMITE.

To the Honourable the Chairman and Members of the Honourable Volksraad:

The Humble Memorial of the Witwatersrand Chamber of Mines:

Sheweth :—

That in the report of the Dynamite Commission appointed by your Honourable House last session, it is *inter alia* pointed out :—

1. That the agent has failed to carry out his contract with the Government to establish factories adequate for the manufacture of explosives in accordance with the requirements of the country within the time fixed, and that even within the further $2\frac{1}{2}$ years which the Government have allowed him, he will still be unable to do so.

2. That irrespective of the profit on explosives made at the factory, a profit of £2 per case is made on explosives imported at the cost of the State, of which the agent takes 35s. and the Government 5s. per case.

3. That during the four years 1897 to 1900 inclusive, it is estimated that at least 430,000 cases of explosives will have to be imported, which, if imported by the State direct would benefit the Treasury to the extent of £860,000, and, if dealt with as at present would give the State only £107,500, a difference to the detriment of the State of £752,500.

4. That there is no prospect that the production of explosives will be independent of the importation of some of the raw materials.

That from the foregoing it is perfectly clear that the State monopoly has not resulted in rendering the Republic independent of the importation of raw materials, or even of manufactured explosives, and that there is no prospect, at anyrate with regard· to raw materials, that it ever will do so ; and that moreover while the State finds the money for the importation of explosives the agent takes most of the profit, so that the mining industry is heavily burdened in order not that the State but that the agent shall benefit.

That Nobel's offered in 1893 to supply dynamite No. 1 in Johannesburg, down to 40s. per case free of duty, and if 5s. per case duty be added, which is the amount the agent pays to the Government, the cost would still be only 45s. per case ; while at present your memorialists are paying the agent 85s. per case.

That the Chamber has good grounds for stating that dynamite can to-day be delivered at the price quoted above ; that your memorialists have in their possession reliable information to that effect, and are prepared to place this information at the disposal of the Government, and in other respects to give all the assistance in their power.

That the Volksraad Commission state in their report that, according to returns given them by the Government Agent, the present demand for the whole country is 200,000 cases per annum.

That the difference between the price paid to the agent and that at which dynamite can be imported being 45s. per case, and the consumption for the year 200,000 cases, the burden laid on the mines for the current year in respect of dynamite amounts to £450,000, of which the Government will receive only £50,000, being at the rate of 5s. per case.

That, under the circumstances, viz.: that the agent has not fulfilled the terms of his contract ; that the State monopoly has failed, and must necessarily fail, to realise the aims for which it was established ; and that the high charge for dynamite imposes a heavy burden on the mining industry, it is desirable, in the best interests of the country, that the industry shall be relieved from any longer paying excessive prices for explosives.

Wherefore your memorialists will ever pray that your Honourable House may be pleased to take such steps as will relieve the mining industry from the burden which the present high prices of dynamite impose on it.

And your memorialists will ever pray.

LIQUOR LAW.

To the Honourable the Chairman and Members of the Honourable Volksraad :

The Humble Memorial of the Witwatersrand Chamber of Mines :

SHEWETH :—

That the provision made in Law 17 of 1896, absolutely prohibiting the sale or barter of wine, strong drinks, or malt liquor to any coloured person is calculated to greatly and permanently benefit the mining industry, and to decrease accidents and crime among the natives employed at the mines.

That when the law came into force at the beginning of the year, there was a marked decrease of crime, and an almost total disappearance of drunkenness among the mine natives, and your memorialists received most encouraging reports of the improvement in the efficiency of native labour, and of the greater quiet and orderliness prevailing along the line of the main reef.

That latterly, however, there has been a revival of drunkenness among the natives at some of the mines, particularly in the immediate neighbourhood of Johannesburg.

That this is due to the illicit sellers, who make large profits by supplying the natives with liquor in defiance of the law, and can only be remedied by the exercise of greater vigilance and activity on the part of the police.

That notwithstanding this revival of drunkenness at some of the mines, the prohibition of the sale of liquor to natives has proved of real and substantial benefit to the mining industry as a whole.

That Article 16 is equally necessary for the protection of the mining industry, and for the prevention of drunkenness among the natives.

Wherefore your memorialists pray your Honourable House to uphold Article 5, of Law 17, of 1896, prohibiting the sale or barter of strong liquor to natives, and Article 16 of the same Law, which prohibits the granting of liquor licences within mining areas, and to afford such relief with regard to the illicit trade in liquor as your Honourable House may deem fit, and for this purpose to provide for a Government Board at Johannesburg, with a special force of detectives under its control, working under regulations the best calculated to attain the end desired.

And your memorialists will ever pray.

DISPOSAL OF TAILINGS AND SLIMES.

To the Honourable the Chairman and Members of the Honourable Volksraad:

The Humble Memorial of the Witwatersrand Chamber of Mines:

Sheweth :—

That your Honourable House postponed the operation of Article 10 of the Mining Regulations for one year.

That your memorialists would now respectfully point out that the adoption of this article would cause great inconvenience and loss to mining companies, and would interfere with the operations of the mining industry.

That for purposes of convenience or trade, a portion of the township of Johannesburg, and the villages along the line of main reef, have been built in close proximity to the mining companies, and that such difficulty as has arisen is attributable, not to the mining companies, but to those persons who have built in the immediate vicinity of the mines.

That the mining companies are, however, desirous of preventing, if possible, or, at least, minimising the inconvenience with which Article 10 aforesaid is intended to deal.

Wherefore your memorialists pray your Honourable House to again postpone the operation of this article until the matter has been fully considered, and means found, if possible, for overcoming the difficulty without unduly hampering mining work.

And your memorialists will ever pray.

PASS LAW.

To the Honourable the Chairman and Members of the Honourable Volksraad:

The Humble Memorial of the Witwatersrand Chamber of Mines:

Sheweth :—

That great difficulties have been experienced in connection with the working of the Pass Law, Law 31, 1896, and considerable trouble, inconvenience, and loss of money have been caused to the mining companies thereby.

That the regulations contained in this law were passed with the twofold object:—(1). Of establishing thorough Governmental control over the natives employed in the mining districts. (2) Of protecting the companies as far as possible against their native labourers deserting.

That neither of these objects can be said to have been attained; and, in especial, desertions constantly occur without employers being able to obtain redress, to the very serious loss of the mining companies which pay large sums to have natives brought to these fields.

That this is chiefly to be attributed to the inefficient administration of the law.

That while an ample revenue for all administrative and other purposes in connection with this law is provided by a Pass Tax of two shillings per month, levied on each native employed in a proclaimed district, the staff of officials entrusted with the carrying out of the law is inadequate, and, moreover, there is no special police force for the service of the department for tracing and following up deserters.

That the facilities afforded for the taking out of passes and badges are insufficient, and the arrangements for dealing with cases under the Pass Regulations cause unnecessary loss of time and money to the mining companies.

That as a consequence of these shortcomings, while the companies are harassed and their work is impeded by such measures as the inspection of passes and badges, and by their officials having to attend Courts held at a considerable distance from the mines, they do not receive the protection and assistance contemplated by the regulations, but endure the inconvenience without deriving the benefit expected from the new law.

Wherefore your memorialists pray :—

1. That the three districts of the Witwatersrand may be placed under the control of a chief administrator acting under a Government Board, of which he shall be a member, and working under regulations the best calculated to secure the proper carrying out of the law, and who shall have authority over the Pass officials in charge of the different districts and receive periodical reports from them, so that there may be effective supervision and united action.
2. That the staff of the Pass Department may be increased sufficiently to enable it to successfully cope with the work devolving on it.
3. That a special body of police may be appointed to assist the Pass Department in carrying out and enforcing the regulations.
4. That sub-offices for the issue of passes and badges may be established along the mines.
5. That special judicial commissioners may be appointed at convenient places to deal with offenders under the Pass Law; so that the great loss of time and money involved in the officials and the native employees of the companies having to attend a Court at a great distance from the mines, and in which delays are frequent owing to pressure of other work, may be avoided.

F 2

6. That a new article may be inserted in the law providing that natives arrested, after having left a proclaimed field, for not having a travelling pass, shall be taken back to the district from which they came, so that they may be punished by the authorities of that district, and, if shown to have deserted from a company or other employer, after having undergone the punishment, be returned to such company or other employer to complete their term of contract.

And your memorialists will ever pray.

MINING UNDER BEWAARPLAATSEN, ETC.

To the Honourable the Chairman and Members of the Honourable Volksraad:

The Humble Memorial of the Witwatersrand Chamber of Mines:

Sheweth :—

That last year the Honourable First Volksraad resolved to maintain the prohibitive provisions of Article 121 of the Gold Law of 1893, till such time as the First Volksraad and the Government are satisfied of the necessity of removing the prohibition, and that in such case, subject to certain conditions, the undermining rights shall be sold by public auction to the highest bidder.

That your memorialists are of opinion that they have sustained injury by this decision; for in the annexure to the Gold Law of 1891, concerning brickmakers, &c., the principle is laid down that the holder of a bewaarplaats or dwelling-site licence shall, in the event of the presence of gold or silver or one of the precious metals or stones being suspected or discovered on the ground covered by such licence, enjoy the preference to obtain, in addition to the ordinary licence, a licence to prospect or dig on such ground; and so far back as 1892 the mining companies of the Witwatersrand, in conformity with the provisions of the then-existing law, made formal application for the mining rights under bewaarplaatsen, water rights, &c.

That the Honourable Second Volksraad in its amendments to the Gold Law, provided that the holder or possessor, under the Gold Law, of *bona fide* stands on which buildings are erected, machine stands, and water rights, shall be preferred before all others in the grant of the undermining rights in respect of such building stands, machine stands, and water rights.

That the mining companies which have developed the reefs of the Witwatersrand, and thereby demonstrated the value of the ground lying below the localities mentioned, are of opinion they have been deprived of their equitable rights, and also of the legal rights conferred under the annexure to the Gold Law of 1891, above referred to; whereby areas which, through them or their agency, might be profitably worked are kept unproductive.

Wherefore your memorialists pray your Honourable House to recommend that the prohibitive provision shall not be enforced in accordance with the amendment of last year, but that the articles referring to undermining rights as published in Law 19 of 1895, shall be restored with the addition in Article 124 of the word " bewaarplaatsen," after the words " machine stands."

And your memorialists will ever pray.

ACQUISITION OF THE RAILWAYS BY THE STATE.

To the Honourable the Chairman and Members of the Honourable Volksraad:

The Humble Memorial of the Witwatersrand Chamber of Mines:

Sheweth:—

That the Netherlands South African Railway Company charges exorbitant rates for the carriage of goods—rates far in excess of those charged in the Free State and the neighbouring colonies, where there is State ownership of railways, and where, too, greater travelling facilities are offered to the public in connection with special events, such as agricultural shows, etc.

That while the Cape Colony and the Colony of Natal make on their working system about £1,500 per mile, the Netherlands South African Railway makes £3,291 per mile.

That these heavy charges hinder the development of industries and commerce within the Republic and impose a grievous burden on the whole country.

That under the present system no material change can be expected, for the Netherlands Railway Company is a purely commercial enterprise, and a body of shareholders possessed of powers such as those conferred by the Railway Concession will not be content with a fair return upon their investment, but will naturally seek to obtain the maximum possible profit, irrespective of the mischief to the general weal caused by such a policy.

That under these conditions it is desirable in the best interests of the State and its inhabitants that the railway system should be owned and worked by the State, so that it may be made to conduce to the furtherance of the progress and prosperity of the country, and afford cheap means of travelling for the people.

That provision has been made for the expropriation of the railways by the State.

That one of the terms of expropriation, so far as known to your memorialists, being a sum equal to twenty times the average dividends declared during the three years preceding expropriation, it is evident, owing to the increased profits which will be earned from year to year, that the longer the delay in acquiring the railways, the greater will be the amount to be paid to the Netherlands South African Railway Company.

Wherefore your memorialists respectfully pray your Honourable House to take such measures as you may deem advisable for the immediate acquisition by the State of the railways owned by the Netherlands South African Railway Company.

And your memorialists will ever pray.

ROADS TO THE MINES.

To the Honourable the Chairman and Members of the Honourable Volksraad:

The Humble Memorial of the Witwatersrand Chamber of Mines:

Sheweth:—

That great inconvenience and loss are caused to the mining companies by the bad state of the roads leading to the mines.

That the traffic to the mines is considerable.

That it is desirable that every possible facility should be afforded for the conduct of such traffic.

That *kurveyors* and other persons who undertake the delivery of goods to the mines are liable to sustain bodily injury and to have their draught animals hurt and their wagons damaged through accidents which, from the dangerous condition of the roads, can at times hardly be avoided.

Wherefore your memorialists pray that your Honourable House may provide for the construction of a new road to the mines, or afford such other relief as you may deem fit.

And your memorialists will ever pray.

REPORT OF WITWATERSRAND CHAMBER OF MINES COMMITTEE ON RAILWAYS.

To the Executive Committee of the Chamber of Mines:

The committee appointed to investigate the relative positions of the various railways in South Africa has now completed its work. The following statements have been prepared with care, and accurately reflect the general disadvantages under which the industry suffers at the hands of the railways. The spirit of the Government to assist the mining industry is interpreted by the admission of all gold mining machinery and materials used for gold mining at 1½ per cent. of the value. This policy, however, is defeated by the railway carriage rates exacted over the Netherlands Railway lines for conveyance, the rates over which section are considered to be phenomenally high.

The comparisons per ton per mile will sufficiently demonstrate this so far as South Africa is concerned; but nowhere in the world is such a highly remunerative tariff permitted. The rates applied to the several divisions, more particularly from the Cape Colony, for the section Vereeniging-Johannesburg-Pretoria, etc., appear to be in conflict with the amended concession granted to the Netherlands Company by the Government, and confirmed by resolution of the Honourable Volksraad on the 25th June, 1890.

An effort has been made to ascertain whether any further amendments or alterations have been accorded to the company which would justify it in levying the rates at present charged, but without success. It is presumed that no authority is competent to amend the provisions of the concession unless the alterations or additions suggested are ratified by the Volksraad, which does not appear to have been done. The following are the clauses under the concession referred to which govern the tariff, namely:—

PART 4. TARIFFS FOR CONVEYANCE—

Article 17.—The concessionary may demand payment to be fixed by him for the conveyance of persons, goods, cattle, etc., and also for the unloading, loading, delivery, and all similar services for wagon hire, etc.

The tariff for the conveyance of persons and goods shall, however, without the previous consent of the Government, never exceed—

For persons, first class, threepence per mile (1⅞d. per kilometre); lowest class, twopence per mile (1¼d. per kilometre).

For ordinary freight goods, sixpence per ton per mile (3¾d. per kilometre), with a minimum of £1 per consignment.

For rough goods (coal, ores of not geater value than £45 per ton, stones, unsawn wood, etc., in quantities of at least five tons), threepence per ton per mile ($1\frac{7}{8}$d. per kilometre), with a minimum of £1 per consignment.

Article 18.—To all tariffs, and amendments thereto, the necessary publicity shall be given before they are carried into effect, and no tariff shall be amended before it shall have been in operation at least three months.

Article 19.—The concessionary shall be bound to convey, without distinction and without partiality, whatever shall be offered for conveyance, subject to the general exceptions provided for.

The following figures, per ton per mile, illustrate what each railway system derives upon the through traffic to Johannesburg, namely:—

	Normal. 1st and 2nd Class C. G. R. Per ton per mile. d.	Intermediate. 3rd Class C. G. R. Per ton per mile. d.	Rough. Per ton per mile. d.
Cape	2·34	2.	1·3
Orange Free State	2·34	2	1·3
Natal	3·04	3·04	1·94
Portuguese	4·07	3·53	2·44
Netherlands, via Cape ...	7·7	7·7	7·7
„ „ Natal ...	5·06	3·82	3·26
„ „ Delagoa ...	4·27	3·69	2·54

These rates include terminals and cartage.

From this table it will be noticed that, of all the railway systems, the Netherlands Company secure the highest rates out of the traffic. The only physical difficulties encountered by the company in the haulage of its traffic on the Eastern line is between Waterval Onder and Waterval Boven.

The connections from the Cape and Natal are practically flat tracts, and thereby place great advantages within the power of the company for economical exploitation.

The Cape and Natal convey the goods over the longest mileage and varying grades, and, naturally these railways should have a reasonably higher rate, as compared with the Netherlands, to compensate for the additional expense involved in working.

So far as can be ascertained, the company, in fixing the rates from Delagoa Bay and Durban, have taken as the basis the rate from East London, and, after allowing the Portuguese and the Natal Railways their respective local rates, the Netherlands Company appear to acquire the whole balance. An extraordinary dissimilarity appears to exist in the principle of the proportional receipts due to each railway. The Portuguese section, from Lourenco Marques to the frontier, is 55 miles, as compared with 52 miles on the Cape side from Mid-Vaal River to Johannesburg, whereas, from the table annexed hereto, it will be observed that the Netherlands Company only pay the Portuguese at the rate of 4·07d. per ton per mile for normal goods, 3·53d. for intermediate, and 2·44 for rough goods, while for the 52 mile section from Mid-Vaal River to Johannesburg they demand, for all classes of traffic, 7·7d. per ton per mile. If this is done to secure to the company profit on account of the shorter mileage by the Cape, then it would appear that the Portuguese are entitled, on that principle, to the largest amount of revenue per ton per mile, as their line is the shortest, and they secure the smallest aggregate receipts. The table further reveals the existence of a sliding scale of the most unique character, namely:—

On traffic from Lourenco Marques to Komatie Poort, a distance of 58 miles, the Netherlands allow the Portuguese 1s. 7d. per 100 lbs., but gradually, according to mileage, the apportionment of the Portuguese Railway diminishes, until on Johannesburg traffic they only receive 11·2d. for normal goods, 9·7d. for intermediate, and 6·7d. for rough goods for the whole distance, as compared with the all-round rate of 1s. 8d. per 100 lbs. over the 52 mile section, Mid-Vaal River to Johannesburg, by the Cape.

It has been necessary to examine these figures closely in order to appreciate the fact that the Netherlands are following a principle which cannot be equitably substantiated, and which, in business phraseology, is nothing more than appropriating the unwarrantable balances on the rates by each route, based on the longest mileage rate, namely, from East London to Mid-Vaal River.

The argument of the committee is not that the Cape or Natal are taxed too much, and the Portuguese too little, but that the basis of rates is not just to the industry, which already, in other ways, is too heavily burdened. After full and mature consideration, we come to the conclusion that the Netherlands Company has acted beyond its province in regard to rates, and that measures should be taken to remedy the unequal and preposterous charges which are generally being levied on over-sea goods destined to Johannesburg, which is the chief centre of consumption.

If a comparison is drawn between the Netherlands Company's through and local rates, the following result is obtained :—

NETHERLANDS COMPANY'S LOCAL RATES :

	Normal. 1st and 2nd class, C. G. R. Per ton per mile. d.	Intermediate. 3rd class, C. G. R. Per ton per mile. d.	Rough. Per ton per mile. d.
Vereeniging to Johannesburg ...	6·6	5·1	3·1
Pretoria to Komatie Poort	6·1	4·6	3
Elandsfontein to Volksrust	6·3	4·7	3

This comparison conclusively determines two principles :—

(1) That the local rate is considerably less, particularly in the case of rough goods, than the through rate from the Cape and Orange Free State, but more than the rates applied on goods from either Natal or Delagoa Bay; and

(2) That the local rates per ton per mile are practically based upon the same mileage principle, in accordance with Article 17 of the concession, which requires that the same rate must operate throughout the railways, and that no partiality shall be accorded. The Netherlands apply the differential rates only on over-sea goods imported through the respective frontier stations.

It is desirable, in considering these differential through rates which are applied to over-sea traffic, as compared with the uniform local rate in operation throughout all lines within the Transvaal, to refer to Article 13 of the London Convention of 1884, which reads :—

Except in pursuance of any treaty or engagement made, as provided in Article 4 of this convention, no other or higher duties shall be imposed on the importation into the South African Republic on any article coming from any part of Her Majesty's dominions than are or may be imposed on the like article coming from any other place or country, nor will any prohibition be maintained or imposed on the importation into the South African Republic of any article coming from any part of Her Majesty's dominions which shall not equally extend to the like article coming from any other place or country. And in like manner the same terms shall be given to any article coming to Great Britain from the South African Republic as to the like article coming from any other place or country.

These provisions do not preclude the consideration of special arrangements as to import duties and commercial relations between the South African Republic and any of Her Majesty's Colonies or Possessions.

COAL TRAFFIC.

To draw a comparison of the rates for coal traffic by the various lines will also prove of interest, namely :—

						Per ton per mile.
Cape (coastwards)	...	...	...	...	...	$\frac{1}{2}$d.
Cape (inland)	...	...	...	...	...	1d.
Orange Free State	...	...	...	...	...	$\frac{1}{2}$d.
Natal	...	...	...	...	...	$\frac{1}{2}$d. (2,240 lbs.)

Netherlands sliding mileage scale (maximum), 3d. per ton per mile; (minimum,) 0·686d. per ton per mile.

Netherlands to Delagoa Bay, 0·54d.

These rates are station to station.

The above comparison indicates that the Netherlands Company secure the largest revenue from coal as compared with any other railway system. The rate on the Rand Tram varies from 2·92d. to 2·08d. per ton per mile, while from the coal stations on the Eastern line to Johannesburg the rates per ton per mile vary from 1·56d. down to 1d., according to distance. This sliding scale for coal continues to diminish according to distance, until the minimum, ·686d. per ton per mile, is arrived at. A special rate of ·54d. per ton per mile is, however, extended for the conveyance of coal traffic from the Eastern coal stations to Delagoa Bay.

As the coal measures of Brakpan and Springs are adjacent to the gold mines, which are fed principally from these stations, the scale, which begins at the rough goods rate of 3d. per ton per mile, and diminishes according to distance, operates heavily against the mines. The Rand Tram presents no difficulties for exploitation, and the close proximity of the mines to Johannesburg is so much in the interests of the company, as the short distance enables the company to secure a comparatively handsome revenue with a minimum number of trucks, the line being well adapted for the expeditious conveyance and delivery of this traffic, and greater receipts per truck are consequently obtained. It is always a source of regret that this coal traffic is not conveyed in bulk, which would thereby reduce the first cost to the mines. The graduated scale operates, therefore, in the opinion of the committee, detrimentally to the interests and progress of the mines, upon the development of which the prosperity of the railway so much depends. The additional expenditure involved in working the deep-level properties necessitates the strictest mine economy, and we think the time has arrived when a further reduction on coal should be obtained. The cost of coal and its conveyance have a large influence in preventing the development of low-grade mines. It is considered that a rate of $\frac{1}{2}$d. per ton per mile would amply compensate the company for its service; the increase in volume of the coal traffic conveyed per month at the reduced rate of $\frac{1}{2}$d. per ton per mile would still maintain the Rand Tram as the premier earning section of the company.

A further comparison of the rates for agricultural produce in through traffic to Johannesburg charged over the various railways is given.

AGRICULTURAL PRODUCE—SOUTH AFRICAN.

Cape, for 23 miles...	½d. per ton per mile, plus terminals.	
Orange Free State, for 23 miles	½d. " " "
Natal, for 13 miles	1¾d. " "
Portuguese	2·2d. " "
Netherlands, *via* Cape and Orange Free State...	3·1d. " "
Netherlands, *via* Natal	3·26d. " "
Netherlands, *via* Delagoa Bay	2·3d. " "

It will be observed that while every encouragement is given on all the railways for the transport of South African produce, the Netherlands again derive the greatest benefit.

GENERAL RAILWAY STATISTICS.

We have considered the figures stated in the railway reports for 1895, and generally have based our conclusions upon the results of that year. No information is obtainable for 1896.

Particular attention is directed to the earnings of the various railways per open mile, viz. :—

Cape	...	...	... ...	£1,504 14 0
Natal	...	...	... ...	1,312 19 0
Netherlands...	...	...	...	3,291 0 0

The earnings per train mile are :—

					s. d.
Cape	...	...	...	...	8 4
Natal	...	...	...	...	7 11·53
Netherlands	...	...	...	...	14 7·36

It would be impossible to pass these results without comment. The Cape and Natal Railways earn roughly £1,500 per open mile, based upon rates which are generally considered to be fairly reasonable, while the Netherlands Railway derives £3,291 per open mile, or over 100 per cent. more than the leading railways in South Africa. No one, who is acquainted with the natural advantages enjoyed by the company for economical exploitation, will be able to justify the extraordinary profits obtained, as compared with the other and older railways. The advantages and facilities afforded to the Netherlands Company should enable them to work at a much lower cost than any other line. For instance, the Cape and Natal Railways not only have to encounter extreme physical difficulties (and in each case the railways raise the traffic to an altitude of 3,988 feet and 5,433 feet respectively, after which the Netherlands Railway pursues practically, a level course), but the coal for working has to be obtained from private sources. The Netherlands Company enjoy the advantage of their own coal mine at the Springs. The Cape and Natal Railways obtain their coal supplies from private mines. In the former case the fuel has to be conveyed over the Free State lines at a certain cost per ton before it can be secured by the Colony for ultimate distribution to its various stations. The only comparison, therefore, lies between the Cape and the Netherlands. In the first place, several of the Cape lines are non-paying. The Cape rate is the lowest; the mileage is the longest, and consequently the working expenses heavy. The Cape open mileage is recorded as 2,253 miles, as compared with the Netherlands 471 miles in 1895. The latter railway enjoys a highly remunerative tariff, and the advantage of all its lines being concentrated and payable. The tonnage conveyed during the year mentioned is the last and best argument which can be employed to convince anyone, who will devote himself to a careful study of the facts. The Cape tonnage on goods conveyed is recorded at 1,158,614 tons of all descriptions of traffic, on which the Cape Government obtains £1,504 14s. per open mile. The Netherlands goods tonnage for the same year is set down as 1,121,226 tons, rather less than the Cape, but the company's earnings are £3,291 per open mile. In each case, it should be noted, both railways practically convey the same tonnage, but the Netherlands receipts exceed those of the Cape by 100 per cent. Further, to work 2,253 miles of line the Cape expends 47·1 per cent. of its total earnings; Natal 52·94 per cent. for 401 miles, and the Netherlands 48·49 per cent. for 471 miles. A consideration of the expenditure per cent. of the earnings, taking the Cape mileage, tonnage, coal supply, grades, etc., will surely prove that the railway best adapted to produce the most economical results, is the Netherlands, yet the working expenses exceed those of the Cape by 1·50 per cent. The profit on coal traffic conveyed over the Rand Tram would cover the whole expenses of the company.

Having followed the interesting results of the working expenses of each railway, the committee would be guilty of a serious omission were not prominent attention directed to one more table. There is no Natal proportion for 1895, as the Natal railway was not open, but in due time the attention of the Chamber will be directed to the figures for 1896.

MILEAGES.

Capetown to Mid-Orange River (Norval's Pont) ...	629 miles.
Port Elizabeth „ „ „ ...	329 „
East London „ „ (Bethulie)	286 „
Mid-Orange River (Norval's Pont) to Mid-Vaal River	333 „
„ „ (Bethulie)	329 „
Mid-Vaal River to Johannesburg	52 „
Durban to Natal Border...	309 „
Natal Border to Johannesburg	178 „
Ressano Garcia to Johannesburg	341 „
Delagoa Bay to Ressano Garcia (Portuguese Railway)	55 „

The Cape General Managers' report for 1895 indicates that the gross receipts on their traffic (all descriptions) to and from the Transvaal amount to :—

Proportion to Cape Railways	£1,416,307
Proportion to Netherlands Railways	458,256
Total	£1,874,563

which includes passenger receipts.

This table demonstrates that of the total revenue derived, the Cape secures 75·56 per cent., and the Netherlands 24·44 per cent. As the Johannesburg trade predominates, and the passenger receipts only represent a little over one-third of the goods trade, it will be a fair conclusion to take the mean distance to that point from Port Elizabeth and East London, namely :—

Port Elizabeth to Mid-Vaal River	662 miles
East London to Mid-Vaal River	615 „
	2)1277
Mean distance	638·5 miles
Mid-Vaal to Johannesburg	52 „

or the Cape 92·5 per cent. of the total mean distance as compared with the Netherlands 7·5 per cent.

A further illustration in support of this statement is that for 1896, the goods tonnage exchanged between the Cape and the Netherlands Railway Company was 240,063 tons, or equal to a goods revenue of £388,323, or an average of £1 12s. 4d. per ton. The Johannesburg through Netherlands rate, Mid-Vaal River to Kazerne is 33s. 4d. per ton.

The average cost per mile open on the respective railways is:—

						£	s.	d.
1895.	Cape	...	...	...	...	9,056	9	1
„	Natal	...	...	...	...	15,254	17	9
„	Netherlands	...	...	...	...	15,359	6	10
1897.	Orange Free State...	...	...	...	...	7,479	4	6

The cost "per ton mile" cannot be determined from the statistics available, as the division of the train miles, passenger, mixed, and goods, are not distinguished; this would probably have been the best comparative table.

1896.—The average aggregate Netherlands earnings for 1896 may be calculated as equal to £3,250,000, of which 50 per cent. may be expected to cover working expenses, leaving a profit of £1,625,000 for division amongst the various interests.

It should not be overlooked that a considerable profit in this case accrues to the Government, but this profit does not anything like represent what could be obtained if the railways were exploited under Government control and supervision. The figures are based upon low averages; it is quite likely the revenue will exceed the amount named. During this year the Natal and Potchefstroom extensions have been opened for traffic.

The Cape Government Railway results for 1896 are :—

Open mileage ...	...	...	...	...	2,253 miles
Capital	...	...	...	...	£21,193,417
Cost per mile open	...	...	...	...	£9,406 15s.
Net earnings per cent. to capital, exclusive of Orange Free State share	...	...	...	...	£8 19s. 7d.

GENERAL MATTERS.

Apart altogether from the accepted and general manner under which every form of operation in the Transvaal is handicapped by exorbitant railway rates, monopolies and concessions, there are some disabilities to which attention is directed. Several of the principal firms have therefore been interviewed; there is entire unanimity of opinion in regard to the complaints.

PASSENGER FINES.

The system of permitting guards and other railway officials to fine passengers who may, unfortunately, be necessitated to join a train without having an opportunity of securing tickets, is generally condemned as an arbitrary proceeding. The imposition of fines is a matter which should only come within the power of the Judiciary, by whom punishment is administered. The company practically places a premium upon fraud, as all that is at stake is a fine of £1 in the event of the delinquent being discovered. The system, however, is a distinct hardship upon those who have no wish to defraud the company.

PASSENGER REDUCTIONS FOR SPECIAL EVENTS.

The periodical reductions granted by the company are not sufficiently liberal. As an instance, all Governments in South Africa afford better terms to visitors to the Johannesburg Agricultural Show than the Netherlands Company. The secretary of the show announces that the passenger facilities over the railways are:—

Natal	.. ...	...	Single fare for double journey.
Orange Free State	...	...	Half single fare for double journey.
Cape	... ...	...	„ „ „
Netherlands	...	...	{ Single fare plus 10 per cent., first and second classes.

DEMURRAGE.

Specific details have been received of instances where demurrage has been charged on trucks which have arrived at Elandsfontein and other stations in the vicinity, but were detained pending the issue of Customs permits, which in each case had been duly applied for—in some instances before the trucks had actually arrived. The demurrage for detention to these trucks awaiting permits is demanded by the Netherlands Company from the consignee. No period of time is allowed during which goods must be taken delivery of, the charge having effect from the moment the truck reaches the siding. Demurrage has not only to be paid to the owning railway, but 100 per cent., in addition, is demanded by the Netherlands Company as their proportion, for which no service is rendered.

SIGNATURES FOR CONSIGNMENTS.

With the extension of the mines, Johannesburg-Kazerne Station has ceased to be the point of distribution for many of the more distant mines. Consignments forwarded to sidings at which no stationmaster is appointed must be signed for before delivery is offered, no opportunity being given the consignees to check or otherwise examine the goods prior to signing for them. Any damage or loss afterwards ascertained is repudiated by the company on the grounds of a clean receipt. If signatures are not given as demanded, the goods are taken forward to the next station and there off-loaded, additional charges of every description being incurred, as well as the expenses of delivery back to the point to which the consignment was originally destined.

SHUNTING AND SIDING CHARGES.

Many of the larger mining companies have their own sidings, or make use of sidings provided by the company, but in each case a heavy charge is demanded by the company for shunting, &c., which is considered to be exorbitant.

COMPENSATION FOR LOSS OR DAMAGE.

In the matter of claims, numerous instances have come under notice where consignees have been compelled to accept payment on the basis of 1s. per lb. weight in full settlement of their claims for short delivery and damage. Instances have also been ascertained where claims have been settled in full. This diversity of system should be enquired into, as well as whether the regulations affecting the public have the force of law, as these regulations, although duly published in the Government Gazette, have only the approval of the Executive Council. The company is more than liberally treated by the Government in regard to means of revenue. In the matter of compensation they should be treated precisely as common carriers.

CRANEAGE.

A tariff governing the charges for the use of cranes at the smaller stations is in operation, although the off-loading appears to be clearly the duty of the railway.

PAYMENT OF CUSTOMS.

There is a difference of practice in the payment of duties, but the question is one which does not quite concern the merchant, and has drawn forth no complaint. It is immaterial whether the Customs are paid at the port or upon arrival of the goods. In the case of traffic *via* Delagoa Bay, the Transvaal duties may be either paid at Delagoa Bay, Johannesburg, or Pretoria, whereas duty on goods from Natal or the Cape can only be paid on arrival of the goods at destination.

PAYMENT FOR HEAVY LIFTS.

The rates to Johannesburg and Pretoria include delivery within a $2\frac{1}{2}$ mile radius; a special charge, however, is applied to all articles which exceed 3,000 lbs. weight. This tariff for packages delivered in Johannesburg within the radius is 6d. per 100 lbs.

The statistics compiled point to the necessity for redress and relief from the burdens of heavy railway transport and other concession monopolies under which the mining industry is expected to prosper. The question of railway tariffs for goods from the seaboard requires complete revision, so that each railway shall receive only a fair return for the capital invested, and no railway system enjoys greater freedom and opportunity for assisting the Transvaal in the development of all its mining industries than the Netherlands Company.

The following annexures are forwarded for the information of the Chamber, viz :—

Netherlands Report, 1895,
Netherlands General Regulations,
Natal Tariff Agreement.

JAMES HAY.
GEORGE FARRAR.
J. PERCY FITZPATRICK.

Chamber of Mines,
      1st April, 1897.

TABLE OF RATES PER TON PER MILE TO JOHANNESBURG.

"THROUGH" vs. "LOCAL."

NORMAL CLASS.

		Per ton per mile.	
Through Netherlands rate *via* Delagoa Bay	...	4·27d.	
" " Natal	...	5·06d.	Includes Cartage and Terminals.
" " Cape and Orange Free State	...	7·7d.	
Local Netherlands Rates ...	...	6·6d.	

INTERMEDIATE CLASS.

		Per ton per mile.	
Through Netherlands rate *via* Delagoa Bay	...	3·69d.	
" " Natal	...	3·82d.	Includes Cartage and Terminals.
" " Cape and Orange Free State	...	7·7d.	
Local Netherlands rates	...	5·1d.	

ROUGH GOODS CLASS.

		Per ton per mile.	
Through Netherlands rate *via* Delagoa Bay	...	2·54d.	
" " Natal	...	3·26d.	Includes Cartage and Terminals.
" " Cape and Orange Free State	...	7·7d.	
Local Netherlands rates ...	...	3·1d.	

TABLE SHEWING COMPARATIVE RATES PER TON PER MILE

FROM

THE PORTS TO JOHANNESBURG.

PORTS.	PORTUGUESE.		NETHERLANDS.		CAPE RAILWAYS.		O.F.S. RAILWAYS.		NATAL.	
	Miles.	Per ton per mile.	Miles.	Per ton per mile.	Miles.	Per ton per mile.	Miles.	Per ton per mile.	Miles.	Per ton per mile.
NORMAL CLASS (1st and 2nd Class C. G. Railways).										
		d.		d.		d.		d.		d.
DELAGOA BAY ...	55	4·07	341	4·27	...	...	...	...	...	...
PORT ELIZABETH ...	...	...	52	7·7	329	2·33	333	2·33	...	...
EAST LONDON ...	...	...	52	7·7	286	2·35	328	2·35	...	...
DURBAN	...	...	178	5·06	...	...	...	...	309	3·04
INTERMEDIATE CLASS (3rd Class C. G. Railways.)										
DELAGOA BAY ...	55	3·53	341	3·69	...	...	...	...	...	...
PORT ELIZABETH ...	...	...	52	7·7	329	2	333	2	...	...
EAST LONDON ...	...	...	52	7·7	286	2	328	2	...	...
DURBAN	...	...	178	3·82	...	...	...	...	309	3·04
ROUGH GOODS CLASS.										
DELAGOA BAY ...	55	2·44	341	2·54	...	...	...	...	...	...
PORT ELIZABETH ...	...	...	52	7·7	329	1·3	333	1·3	...	...
EAST LONDON ...	...	...	52	7·7	286	1·27	328	1·27	...	...
DURBAN	...	...	178	3·26	...	...	...	...	309	1·94

SUMMARY.

RATE PER TON (2,000 Lbs.), INCLUDING CARTAGE AT JOHANNESBURG AND PRETORIA.

To JOHANNESBURG.	PORT ELIZABETH.	EAST LONDON.	DURBAN.	LOURENCO. MARQUES.
1st Class ⎫ Normal	£9 6 0	£8 16 8 ⎫	7 13 4	£7 0 0
2nd Class ⎭ Normal	8 1 8	7 13 4 ⎭		6 0 0
3rd Class, Intermediate	7 3 4	6 15 0	6 15 0	6 0 0
Rough Goods (5 ton lots)	5 5 0	4 18 4	4 18 4	4 3 4
MILEAGE.	714	667	487	396

To PRETORIA.				
1st Class ⎫ Normal	£9 16 8	£9 6 8 ⎫	£8 3 4	7 0 0
2nd Class ⎭ Normal	8 11 8	8 3 4 ⎭		6 0 0
3rd Class, Intermediate	7 13 4	7 5 0	7 5 0	6 0 0
Rough Goods (5 ton lots)	5 13 4	5 6 8	5 6 8	4 3 4
MILEAGE.	741	692	513	349

Netherlands Railway Company's Local Coal Traffic Rates.

RATE FOR COAL—RAND TRAM DIVISION.

To	FROM BRAKPAN.			To	FROM SPRINGS.		
	Miles.	Per ton.	Per ton per mile.		Miles.	Per ton.	Per ton per mile.
		s. d.	d.			s. d.	d.
ELANDSFQNTEIN ...	13	3 2	2·92	ELANDSFONTEIN	21	4 9	2·71
JOHANNESBURG ...	24	5 3	2·62	JOHANNESBURG...	32	6 6	2·44
ROODEPOORT ...	34	6 9	2·38	ROODEPOORT ...	43	7 11	2·21
KRUGERSDORP ...	43	7 11	2·21	KRUGERSDORP ...	51	8 10	2·08

RATES FOR COAL TO DELAGOA BAY AND JOHANNESBURG.

From	TO DELAGOA BAY.			From	TO JOHANNESBURG.		
	Miles.	Per ton.	Per ton per mile.		Miles.	Per ton.	Per ton per mile.
		s. d.	d.			s. d.	d.
BRONKHORSTSPR'IT	309	14 0	0·54	BRONKHORSTSPR'T	88	11 5	1·56
BALMORAL ...	293	13 3	0·54	BALMORAL ...	104	12 1	1·39
BRUIGSPRUIT ..	282	12 9	0.54	BRUGSPRUIT ...	115	12 6	1·30
OLIFANT'S RIVER	269	12 3	0·54	OLIFANT'S RIVER	128	13 1	1·23
MIDDELBURG ...	254	11 6	0·54	MIDDELBURG ...	142	13 8	1·15
PAN	241	11 0	0·54	PAN	156	14 3	1·10
WONDERFONTEIN	226	10 6	0·55	WONDERFONTEIN	171	14 10	1·04
BELFAST	213	10 0	0·56	BELFAST ...	184	15 5	1·00

Natal Government Railways rate for coal (South African) ½d. per ton (2,240 lbs.) per mile.

Orange Free State Railways rate for coal ½d. per ton (2,000 lbs.) per mile in truckloads, station to station.

Cape Government Railways rate for coal, coastwards, ½d. per ton (2,000 lbs.) per mile in truckloads, station to station.

Cape Government Railways rate for coal, inland, 1st 100 miles, 1d. per ton (2,000 lbs.) per mile in truckloads, station to station.

Cape Government Railways rate for coal, extra distance over 100 miles, ¾d. per ton (2,000 lbs.) per mile in truckloads, station to station.

G 2

Netherlands Railway Company's Local Traffic,

Per 100 lbs.

LOCAL RATES IN THE DIRECTION OF THE ORANGE FREE STATE.

From VEREENIGING.	Miles.	NORMAL (1st & 2nd Class, C.G.R.)		INTERMEDIATE (3rd Class, C.G.R.)		ROUGH GOODS.	
		Per 100 lbs.	Per ton per mile.	Per 100 lbs.	Per ton per mile.	Per 100 lbs.	Per ton per mile.
		s. d.	d.	s. d.	d.	s. d.	d.
To ELANDSFONTEIN	40	1 2	7	0 11	5·5	0 6	3
„ BRAKPAN ...	53	1 6	6·80	1 2	5·3	0 8	3
„ SPRINGS ...	61	1 8	6·55	1 4	5·2	0 9	3
„ KRUGERSDORP...	70	1 11	6·60	1 6	5·14	0 11	3·1
„ RANDFONTEIN...	77	2 2	6·70	1 8	5·2	1 0	3·1
„ POTCHEFSTROOM	138	3 7	6·20	2 9	4·06	1 9	3·04
„ KLERKSDORP ...	167	4 4	6·20	3 4	4·8	2 2	3·1
„ PRETORIA ...	77	2 1	6·50	1 7	4·9	1 0	3·1
„ JOHANNESBURG	51	1 5	6·60	1 1	5·1	0 8	3·1

LOCAL RATES IN THE DIRECTION OF DELAGOA BAY.

From PRETORIA.	Miles.	NORMAL.		INTERMEDIATE.		ROUGH GOODS.	
		Per 100 lbs.	Per ton per mile.	Per 100 lbs.	Per ton per mile.	Per 100 lbs.	Per ton per mile.
		s. d.	d.	s. d.	d.	s. d.	d.
To MIDDELBURG ...	95	2 7	6·5	1 11	4·8	1 2	3
„ BARBERTON ...	283	7 3	6·2	5 6	4·6	3 6	2·9
„ KOMATI POORT	291	7 5	6·1	5 7	4·6	3 8	3

LOCAL RATES IN THE DIRECTION OF NATAL.

From ELANDSFONTEIN.	Miles.	NORMAL.		INTERMEDIATE.		ROUGH GOODS.	
		Per 100 lbs.	Per ton per mile.	Per 100 lbs.	Per ton per mile.	Per 100 lbs.	Per ton per mile.
		s. d.	d.	s. d.	d.	s. d.	d.
To HEIDELBURG ...	34	1 0	7	0 10	5·9	0 5	3
„ STANDERTON ...	105	2 10	6·5	2 2	5·1	1 4	3
„ VOLKSRUST ...	166	4 4	6·3	3 3	4·7	2 1	3

Comparative Statement of Rates charged for South African Produce.

Cape and Orange Free State Railways, 1 to 22 miles, 1½d. per ton per mile.
23 miles and over, ½d. " plus 1s. 8d. per ton terminals.

Natal Government Railways ... ... Inland ... ... 2d. per ton per mile.
Coastwards, 1 to 6 miles ... 4·16d. "
7 " 12 " ... 2½d. "
13 miles and over... 1¾d. "

Netherlands Company's Proportional Rates on Produce ex Cape, Natal, and Portuguese Railways.

To	Ex CAPE AND ORANGE FREE STATE.			Ex NATAL.			Ex DELAGOA BAY.		
	Miles.	Per 100 lbs.	Per ton per mile.	Miles.	Per 100 lbs.	Per ton per mile.	Miles.	Per 100 lbs.	Per ton per mile.
		d.	d.		s. d.	d.		s. d.	d.
JOHANNESBURG	52	8	3·1	178	2 5	3·26	341	3 3	2·3
PRETORIA	78	11	2·82	204	2 9	3·23	294	2 10·6	2·4

Portuguese Railway Company's Rates to Border, on Johannesburg and Pretoria Traffic.

	Miles.	Per 100 lbs.	Per ton per mile.
		d.	d.
To BORDER on Johannesburg Traffic	55	6	2·2
To BORDER on Pretoria Traffic	55	5·4	2

General Railway Goods Statistics.—1895.

	Miles Open.	Tonnage of Goods.	Train Miles run.	Earnings per open mile.			Earnings per Train Mile.		Expenses per Open Mile.			Earnings per Train Mile.		Expenses % of Earnings.
		Tons.	Miles.	£	s.	d.	s.	d.	£	s.	d.	s.	d.	
CAPE ...	2,253	1,158,614	8,135,550	1,504	14	0	8	4	708	7	11	3	11·1	47·1
NATAL	401	393,379	1,322,664	1,312	19	0	7	11·53	695	3	1	4	2·58	52·94
NETHERLANDS ...	471	1,121,226	2,120,970	3,291	0	0	14	7·36	1,418	17	10	6	3·52	48·49

	Miles Open.	Capital Invested.	Nett Receipts % of Capital.			Capital Cost per Open Mile.			Total Earnings.	Total Expenditure.	Balance.	REMARKS.
		£	£	s.	d.	£	s.	d.	£	£	£	
CAPE ...	2,253	20,404,195	*7	9	10	9,056	9	1	3,390,093	1,596,013	1,794,080	*Exclusive of O.F.S. share.
NATAL ...	401	6,117,211	4	1	0	15,254	17	9	526,494	278,758	247,736	
NETHERLANDS	471	7,234,250	12	3	9	15,359	6	10	1,550,072	668,298	881,774	

Comparison of Through Rates per 100 lbs. for Normal, Intermediate, and Rough Goods Traffic to the South African Republic.

OVER THE RAILWAYS OF THE

CAPE, NATAL, ORANGE FREE STATE, NETHERLANDS, AND PORTUGUESE DIVISIONS.

The material originally positioned here is too large for reproduction in this reissue. A PDF can be downloaded from the web address given on page iv of this book, by clicking on 'Resources Available'.

REPORT

OF THE

NETHERLANDS SOUTH AFRICAN RAILWAY CO.,

FOR THE YEAR 1895.

Although we are in a position to commence our report of the preceding year with the information that the railway from the Portuguese border to Pretoria, Johannesburg, and the Vaal River was completed, and that thereby the principal desire of our company had been accomplished, we must, in the first place, mention the princely manner in which the Government of the Republic celebrated this event. On the 8th, 9th, and 10th July, Pretoria was *en fete*. From all the States and Colonies in South Africa, and from all foreign countries, representatives of Governments and railway administrations had come together at the invitation of the Government of the South African Republic, and the most hearty proofs of sympathy were then exchanged. Several special trains were run for the convenience of the guests and burghers to Lourenço Marques, in order to give them an opportunity of becoming acquainted with the new line. His Honour the State President also visited the harbour so well situated for this Republic. Some European Powers, amongst which was Holland, were represented by one or more warships, in order to give proof of their interest in the celebrations of the Republic. With a view to giving a national character to the festivities, and to afford an opportunity to the burghers of the Republic to inspect the national line, each burgher, on application, was granted, between the months of June and September, a trip to Lourenço Marques at the expense of the State, and this was much availed of.

Shortly after the opening of the new line we experienced a great disappointment, when in February, consequent on a large bridge over the Kaap River being washed away, the traffic by Delagoa Bay had to be stopped. It seemed at one time as if we would have to discontinue the working of the line for a considerable time. Although in the unfavourable time of the year in this most unhealthy part of the country, work had to be done, and we were enabled to complete a temporary bridge and resume the traffic within a month after the disaster. Although the special trains in connection with the festivities had to go over the temporary bridge, yet, in a short time afterwards, the permanent bridge was completed and ready for traffic. Notwithstanding this calamity and the slackness in co-operation on the part of our Portuguese neighbours, the results of the working of the traffic over the new line are not beneath our expectations.

When at the end of the year the crisis at Johannesburg took place, and troops of the British South Africa Company made a raid into the Republic, it was found how useful the railway line could be in the defence of the State when it is in trusted hands. With satisfaction we may mention the position taken up by our staff, which was of such a nature in these troubled days and peculiar circumstances, that the

Government deemed it fit to express its thanks openly. In connection with the political troubles, the Government made use on the 31st December of its right, as set forth in Article 22 of our concession, to utilise the railway for the conveyance of troops.

In consequence of the decisive attitude adopted by the Government and burghers, the hostile attack upon the independence of the Republic was promptly defeated, and the uproar so soon suppressed, that the extremely undesirable warlike condition of the country lasted only a few days. On the 11th January, the eastern line was handed back to us by the Government, and the other sections of our lines conditionally. During the crisis the ordinary traffic was only stopped for two days, and that between the points Krugersdorp and Johannesburg.

We have every reason to be satisfied with the results of the working of our lines, which have been amalgamated this year.

Notwithstanding the competition by Delagoa Bay, the traffic from the Cape lines has not only maintained itself, but has increased to an important degree, in consequence of the extraordinary increase in the traffic for Johannesburg and the gold-fields.

Since the 2nd January, the port of Durban also claims a portion of traffic to Johannesburg and Pretoria at the cost of principally the Cape ports, but through the temporary block of goods traffic during the political disturbances and the colossal importation of goods during the latter months of the year, all the ports were so blocked with goods that until now each of the competing lines has had more than sufficient work. The future will show how the traffic will divide itself over the three routes, and much will depend upon the proper working and the facilities at the harbours.

25th June, 1890. Approval by the Executive Council of the amended concession for the railway line from the Portuguese border to Pretoria, Barberton, Johannesburg and Vaal River.

AGREEMENTS WITH OTHER RAILWAY ADMINISTRATIONS.

No alteration was made in our connection with the Cape Government Railways after the agreement mentioned in our previous annual report. The through rates between the Cape ports and stations in the Republic remained the same as when the Cape Government worked the traffic at Johannesburg and Pretoria, while' the rates proportion of both administrations remain as fixed in April of this year.

At the invitation of the Cape Government, a conference of representatives of South African lines was held in April, in Capetown, with a view to discussing railway matters. As the Cape railway administration claimed the right of two-fifths of the traffic to the South African Republic, no arrangement could be agreed upon regarding the rates at the different harbours, and the question was postponed for further treatment, until more particulars had been obtained and the Natal line opened for traffic. The conference had, however, the beneficial result that, by all present the desire was distinctly shown to obtain a unity in the system of the working of railways through South Africa, technically as well as administratively. Some points were submitted for study, the same to be dealt with at the next conference.

In the meantime the ox-wagon traffic between the Vaal River and Johannesburg and Pretoria continued until the commencement of the winter, but through want of forage for the cattle, the transport of traffic from the pont was temporarily suspended. As the Government of the Republic could well see that the ox-wagon traffic, supported by the Cape Government, was only a way to try and compel us to reduce our rate, it decided to impede this traffic by, when the summer commenced, limiting the clearance of goods at the drift to goods 'which had only come oversea.

At the same time the rate reduction, which had been allowed by us on agricultural products of the Transvaal, was also granted to products coming from the Orange Free State and the Cape Colony.

The closing of the drifts.—The action of the Government, known by this name, caused in the Cape Colony great dissatisfaction. This step was not only considered as an unfriendly one, but also as an unjust act, and contrary to the existing Convention. Whatever the case may be, the unfriendly feeling caused by this act made it advisable to arrive at an amicable settlement by which in future such a step would become unnecessary.

At the invitation of the Government of the Republic, representatives of the five interested Governments, viz., the Cape Government, Natal, Mozambique, Orange Free State and the South African Republic, met at Pretoria to discuss various railway questions. The Government of the Republic was represented by its Commissioner of Railways, Mr. J. S. Smit, the State Attorney, E. Esselen, and our Director, Middelberg. With the view of facilitating the conference, the Government had temporarily withdrawn the closing of the drifts. A circumstance, however, led that it was not put into working again.

Although the correspondence and discussions which had previously taken place, led us to expect the contrary, it appeared that the representatives of the Cape Colony still upheld the idea declared in April in regard to the dividing of the oversea traffic, by which the Cape railways should be assured of two-fifths during ten years. In consequence of this, all chances of an agreement being come to fell through, and after a long discussion, the effort to arrive at an arrangement had to be postponed, until a further knowledge was obtained in regard to the results of the traffic conveyed via Natal and Delagoa Bay. The existing condition of things, therefore, remained temporarily, and after the conference we had no cause for complaint in regard to our relationship with the other railway administrations.

The events in the Republic at the end of the year did not cause any alteration in our relationship to the Cape Government Railways. Through friendly co-operation every effort was made to overcome the difficulties of the traffic caused by the block of goods, consequent on the temporary stoppage of traffic.

In order to confer with our directors in regard to the steps to be taken, the newly appointed Minister of Crown Lands and Public Works, Sir James Sivewright, went personally to Pretoria in January, and we had the pleasure to receive from him the assurance, on that occasion, that we might count on his friendly co-operation.

PORTUGUESE RAILWAY.

The mutual arrangements arrived at between the administrations regarding through traffic, still remain without the approval of the Portuguese Government. The traffic was worked, however, without great difficulty in accordance with arrangements made. Repeated discussions took place in respect to small alterations or amendments in the tariffs, the results of the meetings generally being satisfactory, although in each case the approval of the Government at Lisbon had to be obtained. On the 15th November, an agreement was entered into at Pretoria with the Director of the Portuguese Railway for the use of our pier at Lourenço Marques for general trade, the pier then coming entirely under the control and management of the Portuguese railway authorities, but we reserved the right of preference for the unloading of our own goods.

For every ton of goods unloaded at the pier we receive a fixed compensation. This agreement was very soon afterwards approved of by the representative of the Government at Lourenço Marques, and remains in force until the 15th November, 1896.

NATAL GOVERNMENT RAILWAYS.

In view of the connection with Natal being completed before the end of the year, various conferences took place for the fixing of tariffs, and to arrange the service. As the preliminary matter for this had been fixed in the agreements of February and April, 1894, the conference only dealt with the details of the case, which gave rise to no particular difficulty, so that everything was properly arranged when the line was opened for traffic.

EXPLOITATION.

On the 1st January, 1895, the following lines were in working order :—

	Length.	
	Kilo.	Miles.
Krugersdorp-Johannesburg	32	20
Johannesburg-Elandsfontein (double line) ...	16	10
Elandsfontein-Springs	34	21
Mid-Vaal Bridge-Elandsfontein	66	41
Elandsfontein-Pretoria	59	37
Portuguese border-Pretoria	472	295
Total	679	424

During the year 1895, the following sections were brought into working order:—

	Length.	
	Kilo.	Miles.
Kaapmuiden-Avoca	28	18
Natal Border-Aansluiting	256	160
So that on the 31st December, 1895, ...	963	602

were in working order.

On the 1st April, 1896, the section Avoca-Barberton was opened for traffic, length, 28 kilo. or 18 miles, so that 991 kilo. or 620 miles are now in working order.

TRAFFIC.

The staff had to work under great pressure, on account of many alterations and the continued increase in traffic.

On the 1st January, 1895, it was necessary to re-organise our goods service to Johannesburg and Pretoria, on account of the discontinuation of the running power contract of the Cape Government, while, at the same time, the traffic on the newly-opened eastern line required every attention.

This was, however, not the cause of the complaints which arose in regard to the working of the traffic during the year.

Through the continued increase of traffic, more especially from the southern ports, our arrangements at Johannesburg could not keep pace with the traffic coming forward, and this was especially the case during the first half of the year. Our cartage contractors at Johannesburg were also not sufficiently equipped for the amount of traffic.

In August and September we feared there would be a serious block at Johannesburg, and only for the great exertions of our staff and the co-operation of the cartage contractors, who were continually extending their plant, we would have been unable to cope with the condition of affairs.

On the eastern line the miserable forwarding of traffic by the Portuguese interfered with the regular working of goods traffic, and the time taken between the unloading of the ships and the arrival of goods at destination is still too long.

In order to give the traffic on that line a fair chance, not only are many improvements necessary at Lourenço Marques, but the Portuguese line requires also to be taken in hand. Locomotive power at the disposal of the railway authorities should be considerably increased. It has already been pointed out in this report that we have been again disappointed this year in our expectations by the Portuguese Government in regard to the harbour railway organisation, and the working of the traffic.

On the 27th August we took over the management of the south-eastern line from the border to Standerton, and that section was opened for traffic. On the 15th November the section Standerton to Heidelberg was opened, and at the same time the goods traffic from the border to Heidelberg was started, although originally it was intended to open the line entirely on the 15th November to the south line, but heavy rains at the commencement of November compelled us to postpone the opening.

On the 15th December the entire line was opened for traffic, passengers, parcels, baggage, and perishables, while on the 2nd January, 1896, the ordinary goods traffic was allowed.

Since the 15th December a mail train, first and second class, has run daily in each direction, and a mixed train for passengers, first and second class, natives and perishables, and since the 2nd January a fixed goods train has also run, while additional goods trains were worked as required.

From the nature of the circumstances the traffic of 1895 was not of much consequence, but the large increase during the early part of 1896 gives great expectations of the traffic over this line for the future, both passengers and goods.

On the Barberton siding, of which the section Kaapmiuden-Avoca was opened on the 1st March, the traffic was satisfactory.

The increase in the local traffic as well as the traffic with the ports compelled us to considerably increase our locomotive and rolling stock. Although important orders for rolling stock had been sent, so that each month 7 locomotives and 100 goods trucks were being put in running, it was not easy for us to satisfy the reasonable demands with the stock at our disposal.

In consequence of the Kaap River bridge being washed away by a flood on the 7th February, a block took place. In another part of this report full particulars of this accident are recorded.

At the end of the winter the scarcity of water greatly impeded the favourable working of traffic forward. No other irregularities of any consequence have to be recorded, and the regular working of our service was satisfactory.

TRAFFIC STATEMENTS.

Of the results of working, of which details are in the enclosures of this report, the following figures give a rough statement :—

	1895.	1894.
Mean length in working	754 kilos.	445 kilos.
Number of day kilo.	275,210 „	162,333 „
„ „ Train „	3,395,553 „	1,608,557 „
„ „ Passengers 1st	296,614	137,462
„ „ „ 2nd	371,979	327,002
„ „ „ (coloured)	399,732	232,991
„ „ „ travelling on Govt. authority	2,273	901
Baggage (English lbs.)	3,056,258	1,562,885
Parcels „ „	4,691,351	2,915,333
Smalls „ „	22,204,004	6,228,825
Ordinary goods „ „	542,468,639	403,003,351
Rough goods „ „ ...	1,677,778,727	1,145,144,513

The receipts were as follows :—

	1895.			1894.			1893.		
Passengers and baggage	£329,562	13	5	£152,415	3	3	£124,919	6	10
Goods and live-stock ...	1,031,626	0	4	523,966	6	5	398,378	15	0
Telegraph	3,813	19	3	2,263	15	11	904	13	6
Import duties ...	137,337	2	3	56,536	9	5	47,370	2	11
Sundries	47,731	18	0	62,200	7	0	38,840	1	8
Totals	£1,550,071	13	3	£797,382	2	0	£610,412	19	11

The sundries include the monies earned by letting of refreshment rooms, book-stalls, etc., rent of house, storage, rolling stock in use by contractors, and compensation for the use of our pier at Lourenco Marques.

Cost of Working in 1895	...	...	£668,297	15	2
„ „ „ 1894	...	...	388,239	15	10
„ „ „ 1893	...	...	255,918	0	7

Finally we give here a comparative statement of the principal traffic figures.

	1895.			1894.			1893.		
Receipts per kilo. length ...	£2,055	15	11	£1,791	17	5	£1,811	6	3
„ „ day kilo.	5	12	8	4	18	3	4	19	4
„ „ train kilo.... ...	0	9	$1\frac{1}{5}$	0	9	11	0	10	$5\frac{4}{5}$
Cost per train kilo.	0	3	$11\frac{1}{4}$	0	4	10	0	4	$4\frac{1}{4}$
Traffic cost in percentage to receipts	48·49 per cent.			48·68 per cent.			41·92 per cent.		

When comparing the above it must not be lost sight of that the larger portions of the line were irregularly brought into working, as the sections were from time to time opened for traffic; this greatly influenced the eastern line in 1893 and 1894, and the south eastern line in 1895.

TARIFFS.

Our principal rates have met with no alteration except a small classification alteration, and the reduction on South African agricultural products.

Some special rates for the conveyance of some goods in local traffic, and for the exportation of some products came into operation this year, together with the tariffs fixed in the past year for through traffic with the Natal Government Railways.

FINANCIAL STATEMENT.

As mentioned in our previous report, the expenditure for the railway line from Charlestown to the connecting point on the southern line near Elsburg, was estimated at £1,250,000, of which an amount of £760,000 would be covered by the Natal Government, £800,000 four per cent. obligation to be sold at 95 per cent.

Of the loan £1,250,000 remained in portfolio £450,000

When in September an offer was made to purchase the obligations in hand in portfolio for more than 100 per cent., the same was accepted and approved of by the Government, and it was decided to discharge a similar amount at 5 per cent. obligation.

When compiling our building account it was found that the means on hand allowed us to increase the amount to £450,000 (5,400,000 guilders) and 6,873,500 guilders in order to reduce the rent.

Therefore, on the 31st December, 1895, the balance of 5 per cent. debentures was paid up, being 3,874,500 guilders and 3,000,000 guilders of the 5 per cent. loan of 1891, which are shown on the balance sheet, representing an amount of 8,940,000 guilders in accordance with the conditions of the loan were disposed of by ballot.

The obligation set aside for payment was disposed of by ballot in November.

The entire loan of £1,250,000 is now shown on the balance sheet.

In regard to some of the headings on the balance sheet, the following information may be useful:—

The construction (railway) account was increased by 2,888,034·905 guilders (£240,669 11s. 6d.). The increase is due partially to the expenditure on the siding for Barberton, which was not completed on the 31st December. Also through the heavy cost of ballasting, and having the main line in working order on the 1st January, 1895, and lastly in consequence of the important extension of works, of which an amount of 1,094,309·90 guilders (£91,192 9s. 10d.) was expended in 1895, and paid from the money in the reserve fund.

This construction account was reduced by the value of the articles of goods mentioned in the inventory statement, which was brought over to a separate account.

The construction account of the tramway is increased by 158,412·55 guilders (£13,201 0s. 11d.) on account of the extension of works, the cost of which was paid out of the reserve fund.

The Natal line has cost in 1895, 7,419,393·96 guilders (£618,282 16s. 8d.), and the money expended on the railway, Krugersdorp to Klerksdorp, was 557,430·73 guilders (£46,452 11s. 3d.).

Through the placing in working order of 29 engines, the value of our locomotive stock has been increased by 887,000 guilders (£73,916 13s. 4d.), and on the 31st December we had 119 engines in working order.

Our rolling stock was also largely increased in number, and the value increased by 1,402,877·885 guilders (£116,906 9s. 10d.).

Additional sheet No. 6 gives a specification of 152 engines, and 2,676 of other vehicles. Of this number, however, 33 engines and 663 other vehicles were not used on the 31st December.

After the dissolution of the contract with Mr. Watkins, the building of the

Barberton line was taken into our own hands, the payment of which was made by the sale loan of £330,000 to the Delginsfonds. The amount of the obligations in the portfolio was reduced thereby by 1,191,600 guilders (£99,300).

The new heading shown as " Mail Transfers from South Africa " showing the amounts which were on the road as remittances on the 31st December from Africa to Europe.

In consequence of the issue of the 4 per cent. obligation loan amounting to £1,250,000, the heading "Currency," difference is increased, notwithstanding the currency difference of the loan, was deducted on the payment of a portion of the 5 per cent loan.

The allotment, which was deducted from the balance to the exploitation account, amounted in 1895 to 236,000 guilders (£19,666 13s. 4d.).

In the reserve fund of the tramway of this year has been placed 214,839·63 guilders (£17,903 6s. 0d.) of which, however, an amount of 158,412·55 guilders (£13,201 0s. 11d.) was expended for extensions, and 5,694·15 guilders (£474 10s. 3d.) for extraordinary repairs. The fund has been increased, as well as by the loan, by 50,732·93 guilders (£4,227 14s. 10d.)

Be it hereby noted that the decision of the Executive Council of the 7th January, 1891, allowed us to accept, as a basis for stipulation, the annual payment into the reserve fund of the proceeds of 1894 on the tramway line, and, therefore, the separate booking of such proceeds was cancelled.

In the reserve fund of the railway has been placed a balance of 241,733·85 guilders (£20,144 9s. 9d.) viz: the difference between the amount of 1,650,120·80 guilders (£137,510 1s. 4d.), and what has been paid for extensions 1,094,309·90 guilders (£91,192 9s. 10d.), and for repairs 314,077·05 guilders (£26,173 1s. 9d.).

The latter also includes the cost caused by the destruction of the Kaap River bridge amounting to 125,019·30 guilders (£16,251 12s. 2d.).

Enclosure No. 2 shows the condition of the reserve fund.

The amount shown under the heading of " Superannuation Fund," represents the balance not invested of the extraordinary receipts collected on account of the fund.

The Delginsfonds shall be increased this year by an amount of 257,350 guilders (£21,445 16s. 8d.). The purpose of this fund has been fully described in our previous report.

After deducting from the clear account of the exploitation account the rental and amortisation loan, and the assured dividend, there remains an amount of 4,350,508·205 guilders (£379,299 0s. 4d.).

According to Article 34 of the concession, 90 per cent. is to be paid out, or 4,095,457·385 guilders (£341,288 2s. 4d.) so that as an extra profit remains the sum of 455,050·82 guilders (£37,920 18s. 0d.).

We would advise to issue thereof an amount of 420,000 guilders for payment of 30 guilders or 3 per cent. super-dividend on all shares in accordance with Article 38 of our Statutes, so that after the payment on the 2nd January of 22·50 guilders (£1 17s. 6d.) on the shares of the second series, and of 30 guilders (£2 10s.) on all other shares, on the 1st July a dividend of 52·50 guilders (£4 7s. 6d.) on the shares of the second series, and of 60 guilders (£5) on all other shares will be paid out.

The receipts for the year 1895 have greatly exceeded our expectations; they testify to an unknown flourishing condition, not only for the gold industry, but also to other sources of prosperity. Although Johannesburg proves to be the most important station for goods traffic, nevertheless we see that other stations contributed to an important degree to the receipts.

The year now commenced will prove the influence of the opening of the Natal line. The harbour of Durban has already drawn a considerable amount of traffic, and it is expected that each of the three routes will claim a sufficient paying portion of the importation and exportation, so that a killing competition will be obviated if none of the competing railway administrations try to master too large a proportion of the traffic at the cost of the others. Next to the different rates for traffic, the geographical position, and the institution of various harbours will remain of great importance in regard to the portion of traffic claimed by the three routes.

The prospects of the newly commenced year are favourable. From the under-mentioned comparative statement it will be observed that during the first four months the receipts have considerably increased.

It must not be lost sight of, however, that the length of line in working order was during four months in 1895 about 693 kilo., and at the commencement of 1896, 963 kilo.

According to the telegraphic statements the receipts for the first four months are as follows :—

1896.	January.	February.	March.	April.
Railway receipts	£135,100	£195,100	£194,500	£206,500
Import duties	13,900	16,100	18,300	15,900
Coal Mine—Springs ...	3,100	4,500	4,700	4,900
Totals	£172,100	£215,700	£217,500	£227,300
1895.				
Railway receipts	74,900	60,330	85,150	96,300
Import duties	6,500	3,870	8,100	8,700
Coal Mine—Springs ...	4,100	4,100	3,890	3,900
Totals	£85,500	£68,300	£97,140	£108,900

NETHERLANDS RAILWAY COMPANY.

GENERAL REGULATIONS.

ARTICLE 1.—Whenever the words "administration" and "manager" occur in these rules and regulations, they apply respectively to the administration and the manager of a railway or steam tramway.

ARTICLE 2.—A copy of the time-tables regulating the running of trains is posted up in the waiting-rooms in a conspicuous place.

ARTICLE 3.—The waiting-rooms are opened to the public at least half an hour before the departure of every train, and remain open until the train has left the station.

ARTICLE 4.—Whenever the traffic is interrupted, or when the usual means of conveyance are insufficient, conveyance cannot be claimed by any particular train.

ARTICLE 5.—The name of every station and stopping-place is exhibited so as to be readily and distinctly seen from the train.

ARTICLE 6.—All payments are made in currency recognised by the Government of the South African Republic.

The administration is not compelled to accept in payment any foreign coin or bank-note which may be refused in Government offices.

ARTICLE 7.—In relation to the conveyance of goods or any other articles on railways or steam tramways, the consignor is held to be—as long as no advice of the arrival of the consignment has been given—the person who has entrusted the goods for conveyance ; and, as soon as such advice of arrival has taken place, the consignee is held to be the person to whom the goods were invoiced (or addressed).

In this respect the administration is not bound to follow any other instructions than those given by the consignor.

When, however, the consignee has been advised of the arrival, the railway or tramway officials must act according to his directions.*

ARTICLE 8.—All papers, documents, permits, etc., which in conformity with the laws, regulations, and prescriptions of the Government of the South African Republic, in respect of import duties, taxes, or any other subject, are required for the conveyance of goods, must be provided by the consignor, and—according to the conditions of consignment—joined either to the consignment note or to the address label, on which

---

* Explanatory remark of the Neth. S. A. Railway Co. : The consignor has the right to request either the return of his goods, or their delivery to another person than the consignee mentioned in the consignment note.

The station officials are bound to give effect to his request whenever they receive it, either by letter or telegram, before the consignee has been advised of the arrival of the consignment ; provided : (1) That the forwarding station is requested by the consignor to authorise the station of destination to follow his instructions ; or (2) that the necessary instructions are given directly to the station of destination, without interference from the forwarding station.

In case of urgency, it is at first sufficient for the consignor to request the station of destination not to deliver the goods, stating at the same time that the authorisation of the forwarding station will follow ; he must subsequently act as above prescribed. The forwarding station, in such cases, is bound to see that the duplicate invoices or goods receipts eventually delivered are returned.

they have to be clearly mentioned. When no such mention occurs, the administration is not responsible for those papers, documents, etc., etc.

The consignor is and remains, as long as the consignee has not taken his place, responsible for the validity of those documents, and all costs arising from his neglect to observe any prescription of the law, the regulations, or the Government, are on his account.

ARTICLE 9.—The consignor, during the time of loading and conveying, and the consignee, at the time of unloading, are responsible for any damage caused to the rolling stock and plant of the administration by animals, goods, or things of any kind whatever.

ARTICLE 10.—Goods, live-stock, and vehicles cannot be taken for conveyance except from and to the stations mentioned in the tariffs as open for such traffic.

ARTICLE 11.—All articles which, at the expiration of one month after arrival of the train on which they were placed for conveyance, have not reached their place of destination, are considered as lost or missing.

ARTICLE 12.—All articles not of a perishable nature found on a train or at a station are temporarily taken in charge by the stationmaster, who, after having registered them, hands them over to the police, with the formalities prescribed by the administration with the Government's sanction.

Articles of a perishable nature, or which seem to be spoiling whilst being in charge, are sold by the railway or steam tramway officials in whose custody they are, the amount realised by the sale being then held to be " goods found," and disposed of as such.

ARTICLE 13.—A consignment note filled up on a printed form, signed legibly by the consignor, and bearing the stamp of the administration, must accompany all goods (excepting luggage and parcels), live-stock, vehicles, and corpses taken for conveyance.*

ARTICLE 14.—The delivery of goods (excepting luggage and parcels), live-stock, vehicles, and corpses, takes place when the consignment note is returned to the railway or steam tramway officials, and the stamp is cancelled as evidence of delivery; or when the goods are otherwise duly receipted for by the persons who receive them; and, if they were not forwarded " carriage paid," the amount due for freight and all incidental charges is to be paid before delivery. All hired covering sheets have to be returned.

ARTICLE 15.—Goods imported into the territory of the South African Republic, and sent to stations where there is a Custom House, are unloaded there and placed in charge of the revenue officers.

All freight and other charges due to the railway have to be paid before goods can be deposited in a bonded warehouse, in the name of the consignee.

The consignee has himself to provide, on his own account and at his own risk, for the removal of the goods from the Custom House under the supervision of the revenue officer.

Charges according to tariff are made for goods kept at the Custom House, where, however, they cannot be left longer than three days.

ARTICLE 16.—Whenever the freight and other railway charges are not paid within three days, the goods are deposited in the Government or railway warehouse, in the name of the railway, but on account and at the risk of the consignee.

---

* Explanatory remark of the Neth. S. A. Railway Co. : Station officials are bound not to accept wholly or partly sealed consignment notes.

In that case the consignee is bound to pay to the administration—besides the amount due for storage at the Custom House and removal to the warehouse—a sum equal, as a maximum, to twice the amount of the warehouse charges incurred ; one-half of that sum going to the warehouse in settlement of dues, and one-half to the railway as compensation for rent and administrative expenditure.

ARTICLE 17.—Whether the goods are cleared at their place of destination or at an intermediate station, the consignee is bound to provide for the proper declaration of goods which have arrived under Government's seal, or about which formalities are required.

Before goods, with the documents relating thereto (for which documents a separate receipt is obtained) are delivered to him, the consignee must see that all necessary formalities are complied with, that the goods, if required, are produced for inspection, and that all permits and other documents are cleared in due time. By neglecting to do so, he renders himself liable to all the consequences of his omission.

At the request of the consignee, the administration may, directly or through the intervention of another person chosen by itself, undertake, under the responsibility of the consignee, the fulfilment of the formalities and the clearance of the goods and of the documents, upon payment by the consignee of the tariff charges. The administration is not, however, bound to do so.

ARTICLE 18.—Should the consignee either refuse to receive the consignment or refuse or neglect to pay the freight and other charges arising therefrom, the administration wires to the consignor a request for instructions as to the steps which he may wish to be taken ; and if no satisfactory reply or no reply at all is received within twenty-four hours, then the administration may either :

(*a*) Return the consignment to the forwarding station at the disposal of the consignor, who can obtain delivery of the same on payment of the freight for the double journey and of all incidental charges, such as demurrage, storage, etc. ;

Or (*b*) cause, on account and under the responsibility of the consignee, the consignment to be unloaded, deposited in the goods shed or elsewhere, and wholly or partly sold, with or without the consignee's knowledge. From the proceeds of the sale the administration is authorised to retain the amount due for freight and other incidental charges ; and the balance, if any, or the unsold portion of the consignment is, on application to that effect, handed over to the person entitled to receive it.

A refusal to receive the consignment or to pay all dues entails the forfeiture of the consignee's and consignor's rights against the administration.

ARTICLE 19.—The prescriptions of Article 18 (*a* and *b*) are applicable in the case that the consignee cannot be found at the place of destination of the consignment. Should anything have been delivered to a consignee and no payment of dues have followed the delivery, the administration has the right to act according to Article 18 (*b*), in regard of other things intended for the consignee, and which are or may come into its possession.

ARTICLE 20.—The administration may claim, according to tariff :

(*a*) Compensation for blank forms and eventually for copying, filling up, and stamping consignment notes ; for the use of weighing machines, cranes, and other unusual appliances ; for the fulfilment of the Custom House formalities ; for the return freight of goods which could not be delivered or the acceptance of which was refused ; for the detention of trucks and the use of its grounds, sheds, or store-houses; for receipts given by the administration; and for meeting advances and reimbursements;

(b) Smart money and conventional fines in consequence of wrong declarations as to the kind, description, and weight of goods.

SECTION II.

RESPONSIBILITY.

ARTICLE 21.—Save the provisions of Articles 24 and 25, the administration is generally responsible for loss of or damage to goods entrusted to it for conveyance, occurring through the fault of its manager, officers, or servants.

ARTICLE 22.—The responsibility of the administration in respect of goods entrusted to it for conveyance, ceases as soon as their delivery has taken place. If the administration has undertaken the cartage of the consignment, its responsibility ceases as soon as the goods have been brought before the residence or storehouse of the consignee.

ARTICLE 23.—In connection with the foregoing provision, the administration undertakes the conveyance of goods, at the choice of the consignor, under the following conditions, viz. :

(a) The administration binds itself to deliver the goods received for conveyance, in outwardly good condition, at their place of destination, and is responsible for the non-fulfilment of this obligation, inasmuch as it cannot prove that this was the result of circumstances for which it could not reasonably be held accountable.

Such circumstances are, among others:

Higher might or greater might, fault of consignor or consignee, defective condition, nature or properties of the goods, etc.

(b) Conveyance at lower rates than under the foregoing provision, is undertaken on the principle of an agreement for the performance of a service, in virtue of which the administration is bound, merely and only, to convey the consignment, on its railway or tramway lines, to the appointed place of destination; but does not hold itself responsible for any loss or damage to which the consignment may be subjected by reason or in consequence of its being thus conveyed; the consignor taking upon himself all the risk of the conveyance.

ARTICLE 24.—The administration is not responsible :

(a) for loss of or damage to:

1. Goods or articles of any kind, in consequence of fire, war, internal disturbance, storm, violence, and in general higher might or greater might;

2. Packages or parcels conveyed at luggage, parcels, or goods rates, the insured value of which does not exceed £10, and which contain such valuable articles as : precious metals and precious stones either rough or polished; jewels, pearls, and jewellery; gold and silver coin; banknotes or other papers of a nominal money value; title-deeds or other valuable documents; maps, prints, engravings or paintings; costly articles, substances, ornaments, and valuable things of any kind;

3. Goods conveyed in open, uncovered trucks, whenever the loss or damage might have been prevented by proper and sufficient covering;

4. Goods not properly packed or not sufficiently secured;

H 2

5. Carriages or other vehicles, unless their value is insured according to Article 30; velocipedes conveyed as luggage or parcels;
6. Goods or vehicles placed, with or without covering, on open ground, either through want of sheds and covered places or of sufficient space therein, with or without the consent of the consignor or consignee;
7. Goods warehoused, according to Article 16, on account of non-payment of freight and other charges resulting from their conveyance;
8. Luggage conveyed without charge, not booked, badly packed up, or having old labels attached to it;
9. Empties returned at reduced rates, such as casks, cases, boxes, etc., and what may be secreted therein;
10. Smalls or packages of goods not properly packed up, marked, addressed or declared, or having old labels attached thereto;
11. Explosives or dangerous substances and goods, the conveyance of which is authorised by the "Rules and Regulations for the conveyance of dangerous substances" or by resolution of the Government.

(b) For damage to:
1. Packages, the contents of which are so different from each other that there is danger of breakage;
2. Goods of a fragile nature, such as glasswares, slight delicate articles of furniture, cast-iron wares, jars or bottles filled up or empty, bells, clocks, pasteboard works musical instruments, stuffed animals, barometers, thermometers, medicines, articles made of bamboo, straw or other brittle material;

(c) For goods sent to a station till further order or till called for, or deposited in the goods shed for the convenience of the consignee;

(d) For ordinary leakage or spilling of liquids through joints, sutures or other openings without visible signs of damage, and for leakage resulting from defective casks, tincases, or other vessels;

(e) For meat, fish, vegetables, fruit, game, eggs, bread, cheese, butter, ice, plants, and flowers, spoiled or decreased in weight;

(f) For the spoiling of liquids or wares apt to ferment or deteriorate through the action of frost or heat.

(g) For metals getting rusty.

ARTICLE 25.—The administration is not responsible:

(a) For luggage, parcels, goods or vehicles the consignor of which offers to pay the insurance premium but will allow no inquiry as to the value of the consignment;

(b) For damage resulting:
1. From insufficient fastening of covering sheets by the consignor;
2. In loading and in transit, from improper loading by the consignor; and, in off-loading, from improper off-loading by the consignee;
3. From loading or off-loading bulky or weighty articles, loaded or off-loaded by railway servants by request on the consignment note;

(c) For loading and off-loading and for return or further conveyance and storage (in case the consignment was neither off-loaded nor accepted by the consignee), of explosives, the conveyance of which is authorised in terms of the "Rules and Regulations for the conveyance of dangerous substances" or by Resolution of the Government;

(*d*) For goods, live-stock or vehicles :
1. Which, not having been off-loaded and taken away, are either sent back by the administration or off-loaded by the railway servants and placed and put up on the grounds or in the goods-sheds of the railway, or temporarily elsewhere ;
2. Which are stored in the goods-sheds or placed temporarily elsewhere, when the consignee cannot be found or refuses to pay the freight and incidental charges ;
3. Which have been left on the grounds, in the storerooms or on the trucks of the administration, on account of the consignor's or the consignee's want of attention to the prescriptions relative to the time of loading, off-loading, and taking away ;

(*e*) For live-stock lost or injured in transit :
1. Through jumping away, falling, being pushed or thrown out, or frightened, hurting each other, choking, and similar causes, whenever the loss or injury occurs whilst loading and tying, or untying, and off-loading, whilst in transit, or whilst stopping at a station ;
2. In consequence of the special dangers to which the conveyance exposes the animals, and for the prevention of which the presence of attendants is necessary.
3. Resulting from the off-loading and stabling, in case that the animals are not off-loaded and taken away by the consignee ;

(*f*) For the arrival in good condition of live-stock, when the animals are :
1. Sick ;
2. Savage, wild or vicious ;
3. Of small size, such as monkeys, dogs, cats rabbits, fowls, pigeons, birds, etc., forwarded in boxes, cages, baskets or bags ;

(*g*) For articles put upon carriages or other vehicles loaded on railway trucks ; for loading or off-loading carriages or other vehicles—whether without or by request—with the help of railway servants ; and for off-loading, if the consignee does not off-load and take away the vehicles.

SECTION III.

INSURANCE AND COMPENSATION.

ARTICLE 26.—For luggage, parcels, goods, or live-stock lost or damaged, the administration, whenever in duty bound to do so in terms of these Rules and Regulations, grants to the interested parties, as compensation for the loss or damage actually sustained, a sum not exceeding the amount fixed by the special tariffs established for every class of goods.

In cases of damage, the amount of damage sustained must be proved by the interested person, and the value of the undamaged portion is deducted from the whole value.

ARTICLE 27.—In such cases, none can claim compensation in excess of the amount fixed by the tariffs mentioned in Article 26, unless the value of the consignment has been stated, and the luggage, parcels, goods, or live-stock have been insured by the administration, on payment of a fixed premium according to the insurance tariffs.

ARTICLE 28.—Any request for insurance of luggage, parcels or goods must be accompanied by a declaration stating the contents of the packages.

The insured goods must be so packed up that nothing can be abstracted therefrom without destroying the packing case or wrapper.

ARTICLE 29.—Railway or tramway officials have the right to ascertain whether the declared value of insured luggage, parcels, or goods is correct, and, for that purpose, to request the opening of the packages. If their request is denied, no insurance takes place.

ARTICLE 30.—For vehicles lost or damaged, the administration is bound only to give compensation when the value has been declared and the vehicles have been insured by the administration, on payment of the premium fixed by the insurance tariffs.

ARTICLE 31.—The insurance premium must always be prepaid.

ARTICLE 32.—The administration and the person obtaining the insurance give each other a declaration stating the value covered by the insurance.

ARTICLE 33.—The administration, upon discharge of its liability, gives to the person entitled to it, as compensation for the loss or damage actually sustained, an amount not exceeding the insured value.

ARTICLE 34.—Whenever the consignee claims compensation for damage or loss, he is bound:

(a) In case of damage, to have the damage verified immediately on his taking over the goods, in presence of the stationmaster or any other qualified official, and to hand over his claim for compensation to the stationmaster, in writing and clearly specified, within three days from the arrival or delivery of the damaged consignment.

(b). In case of goods lost or missing, to hand over his claim for compensation to the stationmaster, within fourteen days, from the day on which the goods lost or missing should have arrived and been delivered, or from the day on which he is advised of their non-arrival.

A specified statement of the missing goods must, in every case, be joined to the claim.

SECTION IV.

CONVEYANCE OF PASSENGERS.

ARTICLE 35.—Passengers are conveyed exclusively by the trains appointed for their conveyance.

ARTICLE 36.—For the convenience of the public, passengers may, however, be allowed to travel by goods train not indicated in the time-tables as open to passenger traffic, if, in the opinion of the administration, there is occasion for it, upon payment of a second class ticket for place in a goods wagon. These tickets can only be obtained at stations or sidings where goods trains stop and where railway officials are stationed.

Such conveyance takes place in every respect without any responsibility for the administration.

ARTICLE 37.—Passenger tickets are obtained at the stations of departure and from the guards in the train, and they are available only for the train for which they are issued.

Passengers may be requested to hand over the price of their tickets in money requiring no return of change.

ARTICLE 38.—In ordinary passenger trains there are at least two classes for white people, and a distinct class for kafirs and coloured people.

No native or coloured person can sit in a compartment intended for white people.

ARTICLE 39.—In mixed trains and in express trains there may be only one class of carriages for white passengers.

ARTICLE 40.—When a train, for any cause whatever, stops on the line anywhere else than at a station, siding, or stopping place, no passenger is allowed to step out of the carriages without permission from the head guard.

ARTICLE 41.—At the arrival of a train at a station or stopping place, to prevent accidents, the passengers are not allowed to leave the carriages before the doors have been opened by railway servants. At intermediate stations, sidings, or stopping places, the carriage doors are not opened except at the passengers' request.

ARTICLE 42.—Besides the penalty to which they render themselves liable according to the police laws for railways and steam tramways, travellers attempting to evade payment for their conveyance are expelled from the train.

ARTICLE 43.—Passengers who take place on a train at a stopping place not mentioned on the tariff tables, have to pay the price of a ticket from the preceding station mentioned on the tariff tables.

ARTICLE 44.—Passengers who leave the train at a stopping place not mentioned on the tariff tables, have to pay the price of a ticket to the next station mentioned on the tariff tables.

ARTICLE 45.—Passengers who wish to pass from the second to the first class must take an additional ticket of the lower class next to the second class, from the station or stopping place where the change has taken place.

If the change of place occurs between two stations, the guard must at once be informed of it, and the additional ticket be taken from the next station or stopping place mentioned on the tariff tables in the direction wherefrom the train is coming.

SECTION V.

CONVEYANCE OF LUGGAGE, PARCELS, AND ARTICLES OF VALUE.

ARTICLE 46.—Luggage includes all the travelling requisites taken by a passenger for himself and those who accompany him, such as trunks, portmanteaus, travelling bags, hat boxes, and such other articles.

ARTICLE 47.—The railway or steam tramway official, whose duty it is to receive luggage for conveyance, decides, in disputed cases, whether the articles taken by the passengers may or not be held as luggage.

ARTICLE 48.—Luggage, for the conveyance of which no payment is required, is conveyed in the luggage-van, or, if there is room enough, and the luggage consists of small, easily portable articles, which in the judgment of the guard may without hindrance be placed under the passenger's seat or in the luggage net above it—in the carriage wherein the passenger takes his place.

The passenger must himself attend to the proper labelling, loading and off-loading of his luggage.

ARTICLE 49.—Passengers are at liberty to leave their luggage in the carriages in which they have taken a seat, provided that nothing in this matter be done in contravention of the prescriptions of the law relative to import duties and taxes.

ARTICLE 50.—Conveyance may be refused for luggage which in the opinion of railway officials is not properly packed or has old labels still attached to it.

ARTICLE 51.—Luggage which may be conveyed without payment is not booked unless at the passenger's request, who then has to pay according to the tariff rates.

In case of excess luggage, the whole luggage must be booked and freight paid for the excess weight, according to the tariff rates.

Exhibition of the passenger's ticket may be requested before the luggage is booked.

ARTICLE 52.—Booked luggage cannot be taken by a passenger in his carriage, but must be put into the luggage-van.

A receipt of booked luggage is given to the passenger, on presentation of which the delivery takes place, without any occasion for inquiry as to the identity of the receipt-holder.

ARTICLE 53.—Booked luggage not taken away within 24 hours after arrival, is, on account and at the risk of the passenger, taken in custody and delivered on payment of storage according to tariff rates.

ARTICLE 54.—Every passenger must himself see to it:

(a) That his booked luggage is duly loaded and off-loaded at the place of destination.

(b) That it is properly labelled with his name and the name of the place of destination.

(c) That no old address or label is attached to it.

ARTICLE 55.—Should there be eventually no available room left, the administration has the right to convey excess luggage by one of the next trains following that by which the passenger is or should be taken ; and, in that case, the passenger may, without any additional charge, have his ticket exchanged for another allowing him to take the train by which his luggage is conveyed.

ARTICLE 56.—Luggage not called for by the owner within one month after arrival, is, in terms of Article 12, handed over to the police.

ARTICLE 57.—Consignments of or under a certain weight are always conveyed as parcels, unless the conveyance as normal goods is positively requested.

Consignments exceeding either the maximum weight or corresponding number of cubic feet in dimension, are not necessarily taken for conveyance as parcels. Should, however, the address label contain a request to that effect, they may be conveyed as parcels, if the service permits of its being done.

ARTICLE 58.—Every consignment consists of a single package. If several packages (*colli*) are taken for conveyance to the same address, every package is held to be singly consigned.

ARTICLE 59.—Packages are charged for freight according to tariff rates.

The freight charge is increased 50 per cent. and levelled up to sixpence for:

(a) All bulky packages.

(b) Packages the contents of which are taken for conveyance at owner's risk, as mentioned in Article 24 (b2).

(c) Packages the contents of which are such as not to allow of any other article being placed upon them without causing damage. To that category belong paintings, engravings, baskets containing victuals, etc.

ARTICLE 60.—Consignments consisting of gold and silver coins, banknotes and other valuable papers, precious metals and precious stones (rough or otherwise), jewels, jewellery and pearls, as well as other sorts of goods, substances, or articles, of which the value exceeds £3, are taken for conveyance as parcels only, on payment of the tariff rates, and after having been insured by the administration.

ARTICLE 61.—The administration may refuse to convey parcels not properly or sufficiently packed up or containing goods or things of a perishable nature, which, in terms of Art. 24 (*a* 4, *e* and *f*), are conveyed without responsibility for the administration.

ARTICLE 62.—The consignee is advised—by post if expedient—of the arrival of a package, and, on calling for it, must produce the advice note and give a receipt.

ARTICLE 63.—If the consignee thinks that the package is damaged or not in good order, he has the right to have its condition examined at once by the railway official in presence of two witnesses.

ARTICLE 64.—Whenever the consignee refuses to receive a package, or when a package has not been called for within one month after arrival:

1. The administration must immediately inform the consignor, in writing, of the circumstance; the costs of that information are charged to the consignment.
2. The package is returned to the forwarding station, and placed there at the order of the consignor, who can obtain its delivery on payment of freight for the return journey, and of all incidental charges.

ARTICLE 65.—Should the consignor refuse to take back the package and pay for the return freight and other charges, the package is sold—with or without his being informed of it—the amount due being then deducted from the proceeds of the sale, and the balance, if any, handed, at his request, to the person entitled to receive it.

The refusal of receiving the package entails the forfeiture of all claim of consignor and consignee against the administration.

ARTICLE 66.—Packages containing goods or things of a highly perishable nature such as fresh fruit and vegetables, meat, fish, yeast, etc., which, according to circumstances, are not called for and taken over within from three to six hours, may be sold by the administration in any way it chooses; the proceeds of the sale, after deduction of all dues, are placed at the disposal of the person who has the right to claim them.

If the consignee is unknown, or either cannot be found or refuses to receive the package, it may be sold in the same way and within the above-mentioned time.

ARTICLE 67.—The freight of luggage and parcels must be prepaid.

ARTICLE 68.—Goods or substances, the conveyance of which by railways or steam tramways is forbidden or only conditionally permitted (see Articles 69*b* and 70*b*), explosives, and dangerous substances which, in terms of the "Rules and Regulations for the conveyance of dangerous goods by railways and steam tramways," are considered as "goods for conveyance," can neither be taken by passengers into their carriages nor be offered or taken for conveyance as luggage or parcels.

Railway and steam tramway officials have competent authority to make inquiry in that respect.

Anyone offering for conveyance, either as luggage or parcels, or under a false description, goods or substances of the above-mentioned kind, renders himself responsible for all the consequences, losses, and damages which may result therefrom.

SECTION VI.

CONVEYANCE OF GOODS.

ARTICLE 69.—No conveyance can be obtained for:

(*a*) Articles which, on account of form, bulk, weight, or other circumstances connected with the traffic arrangements of a railway or steam tramway, are not transportable.

(b) Substances or articles liable to explosion, with the exception of those of which the conveyance either is allowed in terms of the "Rules and Regulations for the conveyance of dangerous goods by railways or steam tramways," or may hereafter be allowed by Government proclamation.

ARTICLE 70.—Are conditionally accepted for conveyance:
(a) Goods which:
1. On account of their different nature cannot be loaded up with other goods.
2. Are not properly packed up.
3. Can damage the trucks.
4. Are to be described, with a statement of the conditions attached to the conveyance of every particular description.

The railway or steam tramway officials decide which goods are or are not included in one of the above-mentioned categories.

(b) Highly inflammable and self-inflammable substances and dangerous goods, described in the "Rules and Regulations for the conveyance of dangerous goods on railways and steam tramways," or which may hereafter be proclaimed as such by the Government.

ARTICLE 71.—The administration is not compelled:
1. To take goods for conveyance when the available rolling stock is insufficient to convey the proffered consignments within the usually required time.
2. To find shelter, shed, storehouse, or magazine for deposit and storage of goods not duly attended to, left behind, or not taken over.

ARTICLE 72.—When there is danger of the regular traffic being hindered by a considerable accumulation of goods at the place of destination, the administration is authorised—as long as the accumulation lasts—to increase its charges for storage, demurrage, and truck hire, and to shorten the time allowed for loading, off-loading, delivering, and keeping goods under its care.

ARTICLE 73.—Goods may be conveyed:
(a) As parcels by passenger trains (see Section V).
(b) As *colli* or consignments of small dimensions, exclusively by goods trains (see Article 76).
(c) As normal goods at the consignor's risk.
(d) As normal goods at the risk of the administration (see Article 74 and Article 75).
(e) As rough goods (see Article 88).

ARTICLE 74.—With due regard to the prescriptions of Articles 21, 22 and 23, normal goods—at the consignor's request entered on the consignment note—may be forwarded at reduced rates at the consignor's risk, in which case the freight is charged according to the reduced tariff rates for the conveyance of normal goods at consignor's risk.

ARTICLE 75.—Whenever the value of goods exceeds the amounts specified in the various tariffs (see Article 26), in addition to the freight charges according to tariff rates for normal goods conveyed at the risk of the administration, the consignment must be insured in terms of Article 27.

Should such goods be lost or damaged, compensation is given according to Article 33.

ARTICLE 76.—Consignments not exceeding a minimum weight are conveyed as parcels, unless the consignor positively requests their conveyance as normal goods; consignments exceeding that minimum weight are invariably conveyed as normal goods, unless the consignor requests their conveyance as parcels, and provided it can be done in terms of Article 57.

Consignments, in respect of which the distance to be run over, or the weight does not correspond to the minimum freight, are conveyed by goods trains as " consignments of small dimensions," and charged according to the tariff rates fixed therefor.

A consignment means either one or more than one package of goods, or a lot of loose goods addressed together by one consignor to one consignee. The conveyance of aggregated goods received from several consignors, or consigned to different persons, is not allowed. Agents are not held to be either consignors or consignees.

ARTICLE 77.—On the consignment note the date and place must be properly stated; it must contain an accurate description of the goods with mention of marks, numbers, quantity, kind of package, contents and gross weight of every package separately, as well as the correct address of the consignee, and the place of destination. Erasures and alterations on the consignment note ought to be initialed by the consignor.

All papers and documents accompanying the consignment have to be mentioned in the consignment note.

ARTICLE 78.—By truckload conveyance the consignor may be requested to make a separate consignment note for every truck.

ARTICLE 79.—Goods are held to be taken for conveyance, and the contract to be binding, as soon as the consignment note is stamped.

Should the consignor require a receipt for goods entrusted to the officers and servants of the administration, he must hand over with the goods and the original consignment note a true copy of this note marked " duplicate," and which is returned to him. Such duplicate serves only to show that the goods were taken over, but has not the validity of the original sent with the goods.

ARTICLE 80.—Whenever goods are loaded by the consignor and off-loaded by the consignee, according to the prescription of these " Rules and Regulations," to the tariff, or the terms of a special agreement, the mention on the consignment note of the weight and quantity of goods cannot be taken as evidence against the administration, inasmuch as no re-weighing of the goods of which the consignment consists has taken place, and as long as the number of packages (*colli*) or their weight as shown by the weight stamp of the forwarding station, is not mentioned on the consignment note.

ARTICLE 81.—Whenever no statement of weight occurs on the consignment note, the goods are weighed before conveyance, and a weighing charge is made according to tariff.

ARTICLE 82.—Should there be any doubt as to the accuracy of the weights stated on the consignment note, the goods may be re-weighed before conveyance.

If, by re-weighing, the stated weights are shown to be inaccurate, the consignment is liable to the weighing charge mentioned in Article 81, as well as to extra freight in terms of Article 84.

ARTICLE 83.—No weighing charge is reckoned :

(*a*) When the weight of a consignment under 100 lbs. is not stated.
(*b*) When the re-weighing shows the accuracy of the stated weight.

ARTICLE 84.—Upon discovering, either at the time of forwarding or later, that the actual weight of a consignment exceeds the stated weight, extra freight is charged for the excess weight at three times the amount of the tariff rate, always under reservation, as well of the prescriptions of Article 95, as of the right of claiming compensation for costs and damages, if the carrying power of a truck is exceeded.

ARTICLE 85.— At the consignor's request, the administration is bound to take an accurate account of the number of packages (*colli*) or of the weight of the goods, if this can be done without causing any detrimental delay, and the station is provided with the required weighing appliances.

The consignor, in that case, incurs the weighing charge mentioned in Article 81.

ARTICLE 86.—When the account of the number and weight of packages (*colli*) is not taken by the administration—which appears from the fact that the consignment note bears no weight stamp—the number and weight require no other evidence of their accuracy than a reference to their consignment note.

ARTICLE 87.—Piece goods, if not of such kind as to render this prescription impracticable, must have attached to them by the consignor the name of the consignee and of the station of destination, besides distinct particular marks or numbers, which must also be mentioned on the consignment note.

ARTICLE 88.—Rough goods mentioned as such in the tariffs are charged for freight according to the rates of the tariff for rough goods, when the weight of the consignment is not less than 10,000 lbs.

They are, as a rule, conveyed in open trucks; and, to prevent any damage arising therefrom, the consignor may, at his own cost and his own risk, protect them with covering sheets.

Lime cannot be conveyed otherwise than covered with sheets, provided either by the consignor or by the administration at the consignor's expense.

ARTICLE 89.—Goods are freighted according to weight or dimension, 1 cubic foot being held to be equivalent to 25 lbs.

ARTICLE 90.—The freight charge is reckoned upon twice the actual weight for goods which, on account of their nature, form, weight, etc., or in consequence of the way they are packed up, it is difficult to handle; and for goods, such as glassware, fruit in baskets, etc., upon which no other goods can be placed without damaging them.

ARTICLE 91.—By "loading" is understood the transfer of goods from the loading place of the administration to the railway trucks; and, by "off-loading," the transfer of goods from the railway trucks to the loading place of the administration.

ARTICLE 92.—Explosives of which the conveyance is allowed, either by the " Rules and Regulations for the conveyance of dangerous goods on railways and steam tramways," or by Government's Resolution, must be loaded and off-loaded on the most distant siding, as far as possible from all buildings and all objects susceptible to catch fire, and on places where there is no danger of collision with trains or vehicles.

ARTICLE 93.—The consignors of such goods must, at least 24 hours beforehand, inform the stationmaster (at the forwarding station) of the intended consignment.

Those goods can only be brought over to the station within two hours before the departure of the train by which they are to be conveyed; and they must, on their reaching the station, be at once loaded, by the consignor or by his direction, in the truck destined to their conveyance.

ARTICLE 94.—The consignee is bound to off-load and take away those goods as soon as they arrive. If he is not there at the time and nobody else has come in his name, the consignment is at once conveyed to a distant place where, on his account and under his responsibility, it is left at the disposal of the consignee, who is advised of it by the administration.

ARTICLE 95.—Whenever it is found that the consignor has overloaded a truck, he must pay for every overloaded truck an extra charge of £3 per distance of 50 miles or part thereof, besides the charges for excess weight and compensation for damage mentioned in Article 84.

ARTICLE 96.—Goods are conveyed "carriage paid" or "to pay," at the consignor's choice; if necessary, however, the administration has the right to exact payment beforehand of freight and other charges.

Prepayment is always required in the case of goods or substances:

(*a*) Mentioned in the "Rules and Regulations for the conveyance of dangerous goods on railways and steam tramways."

(*b*) Which, in the judgment of the railway official, are likely to get spoiled within a short time.

(*c*) The value of which is inferior to the freight charge.

ARTICLE 97.—Goods are received for conveyance, and delivered to consignees every day—Sundays excepted—at certain hours, which are later to be made known.

The administration is not, however, compelled to receive goods for the conveyance of which there are no wagons available.

ARTICLE 98.—The consignee whose name appears on the consignment note, is advised, by post if necessary, of the goods' arrival at the place of destination, the costs thereof being charged to the consignment.

ARTICLE 99.—The consignor is bound to give the consignee timely information as to the time of forwarding, and the expected time of arrival of goods which, if not duly called for, would be liable to damage, spoiling, or decrease of weight.

ARTICLE 100.—The delivery of the consignment takes place when the consignment note is returned and the delivery stamp affixed to it; or when a receipt or discharge is given for the goods, the freight and other charges are paid for (if their payment was not made at the forwarding station), and the covered sheets eventually hired are returned.

ARTICLE 101.—Whenever the Administration:

(*a*) Sends a wagon to fetch goods from the premises of the consignor, this is done at his own cost and his own risk.

(*b*) Sends a wagon to deliver goods to the premises of the consignee, the off-loading from the wagon and the storing of the goods in cellars or store-houses take place at the cost and risk of the consignee.

ARTICLE 102.—If the consignee thinks that the consignment is damaged or does not agree with the consignment note, he has the right to require its condition to be verified at once by the railway official in presence of two witnesses.

ARTICLE 103.—If the goods are loaded by the consignor or his agent, he is himself responsible for damage done, through the goods, to the rolling stock and plant, during the time of loading and in transit; and the consignee assumes the same responsibility during the time of off-loading, if the goods are off-loaded by him or his agent.

SECTION VII.

CONVEYANCE OF LIVE-STOCK, CORPSES, AND VEHICLES.

ARTICLE 104.—Horses, mules, and cattle are conveyed in open trucks, upon prepayment of the freight charges according to tariff rates.

The administration decides how many animals can be conveyed by a train, and by what train the conveyance is to take place.

For consignments at intermediate stations, previous arrangements are to be made by the stationmaster.

ARTICLE 105.—Live-stock is not taken for conveyance, unless under the care of an attendant. If the consignment freight is equivalent to 4,000 lbs. normal goods at consignor's risk, the attendant is conveyed without cost on the truck loaded with the animals.

This prescription does not apply to consignments of either the small-sized animals named in Article 110 or of animals consigned singly.

ARTICLE 106.—With due regard to the prescriptions of Article 25 e, (1 and 3), the loading and tying of live stock is left to the care and responsibility of the consignor, and the untying and off-loading to the care and responsibility of the consignee.

ARTICLE 107.—The consignor is responsible for damage done by animals to the rolling-stock or plant of the administration, while loading and tying, unless the damage result from the bad or unsatisfactory condition of the rolling-stock or plant; and the same responsibility attaches to the consignee, while untying and off-loading.

ARTICLE 108.—Animals which have died in transit, or before delivery, must, nevertheless, be taken over by the consignee, save his right, if he has any, of claiming compensation. The circumstance is stated on the consignment stamped for delivery, or a separate statement in writing is given to him.

Article 109.—The administration may refuse to convey:—
(a) Sick animals.
(b) Savage, wild, or vicious animals.

Should, however, animals of this description be taken for conveyance, they are conveyed altogether under the whole responsibility of the consignor, on prepayment of the freight charges, provided that such animals as are mentioned under b, are placed in sufficiently strong cages.

ARTICLE 110.—Live animals of small size, such as monkeys, dogs, cats, fowls, rabbits, small birds, etc., are, under the responsibility of the consignor and on prepayment of the freight charges, taken for conveyance in boxes, cages, crates, or bags.

ARTICLE 111.—The consignor of live-stock is bound to give the consignee timely notification of the time of forwarding the consignment and the expected time of arrival.

ARTICLE 112.—If it can be done conveniently, the administration may place goods in trucks wherein live-stock is being conveyed.

ARTICLE 113.—Corpses may be conveyed by all trains upon prepayment of the tariff charges, if properly inclosed in coffins so as to cause no hindrance to the passengers.

ARTICLE 114.—Any corpse not taken away within three hours after arrival of the train at the place of destination, is placed at the disposal of the police.

ARTICLE 115.—Goods may be loaded, on account and at the risk of the consignor, in vehicles forwarded on railway or steam-tramways.

The aggregate weight of the vehicle and its contents must not exceed the carrying power of the railway or steam-tramway truck on which they are conveyed.

The freight charges for goods so conveyed are calculated at the rates of the tariff for normal goods at consignor's risk.

ARTICLE 116.—In connection with the prescriptions of Article 25 g, vehicles are loaded by and under the responsibility of the consignor, and they are off-loaded by and under the responsibility of the consignee.

It is the duty of the consignor to see that the vehicle stands fast on the railway or steam-tramway truck, and to provide the required wedges, spikes and rope—all this to the satisfaction of the railway official whom it may concern.

ARTICLE 117.—Whenever in loading live-stock and vehicles, help is asked for and can be given, the railway or steam-tramway servants will lend gratuitous assistance to the consignor in loading, and to the consignee in off-loading.

Proposed, at Pretoria, the 14th December, 1892.

The Railway Commissioner,

J. S. SMIT.

Sanctioned at Pretoria, the 10th January, 1893.
    In the name of the Government,

DR. W. J. LEYDS,

State Secretary.

NATAL-NETHERLANDS AGREEMENT.

AGREEMENT DATED THIRD DAY OF FEBRUARY, 1894, between the Natal Government and the Transvaal Government:—

WHEREAS the Government of the South African Republic and the Government of the Colony of Natal are mutually desirous of immediately extending railway communication, now terminating at Charlestown, in the Colony of Natal, to Johannesburg and Pretoria, in the South African Republic,

AND WHEREAS an agreement was, on the 25th day of November, 1892, entered into between the Government of the South African Republic and the Government of the Colony of Natal, providing for the survey of the said railway extension,

AND WHEREAS the detail survey of the said railway extension has been completed,

AND WHEREAS the Honourable the First Volksraad of the South African Republic did, by resolution, on the 25th day of August, 1893, approve of the building and construction of the said railway extension, and authorised the Government with the advice and consent of the Executive Council to take steps for the carrying out of the said resolution,

AND WHEREAS the Government of the South African Republic with the advice and consent of the Executive Council, as aforesaid, did on the 4th day of January, 1894, finally decide upon the construction of the said railway extension,

Now FURTHER, it is hereby agreed as follows:—

ARTICLE 1.—That the Government of the Colony of Natal shall immediately extend its line of railway from Charlestown, at the border of the Colony of Natal and the South African Republic.

ARTICLE 2.—That the Government of the South African Republic shall with all possible speed construct, equip and work or cause to be constructed, equipped, and worked, a line of railway from the terminus of the Natal Government Railways on the border *via* the towns of Volksrust, Standerton, and Heidelberg, to the station at Elsburg, or such other point of the line of railway between Vereeniging and Elandsfontein as may be chosen by the Government of the South African Republic, *provided always* that the through distance to Johannesburg and Pretoria, as already surveyed shall not be materially increased.

ARTICLE 3.—That the construction and equipment of the lines of railway referred to in Articles 1 and 2 shall be in all respects of equality as regards stability and efficiency with the best constructed lines of railway in the Colony of Natal and the South African Republic, and serviceable for the conveyance of heavy and fast traffic.

ARTICLE 4.—That the work of constructing the line of railway referred to in Article 2 shall be commenced from the Natal and Johannesburg ends immediately, and that in order to accelerate the completion of the work the line of railway from Delagoa Bay shall be utilised to convey the rails and other materials for the construction from Delagoa Bay to the point of junction on the line from Charlestown to Elandsfontein as soon as such line of railway is sufficiently completed to permit of this being done. And it is hereby further agreed that the aforesaid line of railway from Charlestown shall be completed and opened for public traffic to Johannesburg and Pretoria if possible by the 31st July, 1895, but not later than the 31st December, 1895, and that as soon as the line can possibly be made fit for traffic it shall be opened in sections from Charlestown to Standerton and Heidelberg respectively in anticipation of the opening of the line throughout.

ARTICLE 5.—That the Government of the Colony of Natal binds itself not to construct or work any extension of the line of railway from Ladysmith to Harrismith which joins on any point to the north of Kroonstad to the now existing line of railway through the Orange Free State.

ARTICLE 6.—That near the boundary there shall be provided a joint station, where the services of the Natal Railway administration shall terminate and the services of the South African Government Railway administration shall commence. The site of this station to be at the option of the South African Republic, and the buildings to be designed by one or other of the administrations, as may be arranged in conjunction with the other.

ARTICLE 7.—That the two contracting Governments bind themselves to promote in every way the practical and expeditious working of the through traffic from places in the Colony of Natal to places in the South African Republic, and from places in the South African Republic to places in the Colony of Natal, and to grant to each other all usual and useful facilities for the interchange, development, and satisfactory working of the traffic.

ARTICLE 8.—That in order to promote efficient co-operation, an agreement shall be entered into between the two railway administrations, subject to the approval of the respective Governments, having regard to the following points :—

A. The conditions for the use by the one administration of the line of railway from the boundary to the joint station near the boundary, and for the common use of the said station.

B. Regulations for the interchange of rolling-stock and goods in through traffic, payment for hire of rolling-stock, the through traffic in passengers, goods, animals, articles, and the facilities for loading and unloading, collection and delivery of goods, the system for dividing and accounting for the proportions of fares and freights due to the respective administrations, and all other particular details which are necessary to secure efficient and economical working.

C. The harmonising of the systems whereby the rolling-stock of the respective administrations, with their " continuous brake " and other appliances may conveniently couple and interchange with each other.

D. The mutual assistance to be rendered by the one administration to the other, in the matter of stock, labour, and other matters in which such mutual assistance would be possible and beneficial.

ARTICLE 9.—That the running of the trains of both lines of railway shall be so regulated as to avoid unnecessary delay, and so as to effect the best possible through service.

ARTICLE 10.—That the consignment notes for through traffics shall be drawn up by both railway administrations in conjunction with one another, and shall be drawn up in both English and Dutch.

ARTICLE 11.—That the railway administration of each Government shall fix the rates applicable to its own line, and in the case of the route *via* Volksrust the through charges for goods traffic from Port Natal to Johannesburg and Pretoria shall be the sum of the two administration rates, *provided always :* that the rates for ordinary goods per mile and per ton of 2,000 lbs. shall not exceed 6d. per mile and per ton, and shall not be lower than 3d. per mile and per ton; and the rates for rough goods (*i.e.* coal, quartz of a less value than £45 per ton, unmanufactured wood in quantities of at least five tons) shall not exceed 3d. per mile and per ton, and shall not be lower than 1½d. per mile and per ton.

ARTICLE 12.—That if the through rates from Port Natal to Johannesburg and Pretoria upon the aforesaid basis shall become higher than the rates from Delagoa Bay to Johannesburg and Pretoria in proportion to the mileage of the lines of both administrations, then the through rates from Port Natal to these places shall, after consultation between the two railway administrations, be reduced to the proper proportions, but neither of the two administrations shall be bound to accept lower rates than the minimum rates specified in Article 11; but the rates from Port Natal to Johannesburg shall not, in any case, be more than 20 per cent. higher than the corresponding rates from Delagoa Bay to Johannesburg, and the rates from Port Natal to Pretoria shall not, in any case, be more than 40 per cent. higher than the rates from Delagoa Bay to Pretoria.

ARTICLE 13.—That should any circumstances arise which may necessitate the re-consideration of the rates and other arrangements herein set forth in connection with the promotion of the traffic, either administration may at any time call upon the other administration for consultation, with the view of making the necessary alterations.

ARTICLE 14.—That the Government of Natal binds itself to fix the rates to be charged on its lines in the Colony of Natal (subject always to its existing obligations), and on railways worked by it in other States, in such manner that the sum of the rates charged by the railway administrations of Natal and the South African Republic shall not be lower than the rates per mile and per ton of the traffic from Delagoa Bay to Johannesburg and Pretoria.

ARTICLE 15.—That the rates for the conveyance of passengers over the lines of both administrations shall not exceed the following:—First class, 3d. per mile; lowest class, 2d. per mile.

ARTICLE 16.—That the Government of the Colony of Natal binds itself to charge on goods from foreign ports, and destined for places in the South African Republic, dues which are not higher than the transit duties which are now in force or lower than the transit duties at Delagoa Bay; and the Government of the South African Republic shall afford to the Government of Natal all trade facilities which may have been or may be granted to any other Government.

ARTICLE 17.— That the two contracting parties bind themselves to co-operate in every way for the substantial and expeditious and speedy construction of the line of railway referred to in Article 2, and the Government of the Colony of Natal shall convey over its existing lines all materials, goods and things necessary for the construction and working of the aforesaid railway, with the least possible delay, at the rate of 1½d. per ton per mile, and shall admit all such materials free of customs and transit duties.

ARTICLE 18.—That in the event of it being found that either of the routes by Delagoa Bay or Charlestown is carrying a share of the gross goods traffic from the seaboard to Johannesburg and Pretoria, which shall exceed one-half or be less than one-third of such gross goods traffic, the two contracting Governments agree that, upon the application of either, a further conference shall take place for the purpose of re-considering the rates and making such re-adjustment thereof as shall be calculated, to a more equitable division of the traffic carried by both routes.

ARTICLE 19.—That it shall be understood between the two contracting Governments that they shall work together in a spirit of amity and friendship, for the promotion of the traffic between the South African Republic and the ports of Delagoa Bay and Natal, and all the provisions of this agreement shall be construed in the sense of the said understanding.

ARTICLE 20.—That any dispute or question arising out of this agreement shall be referred to arbitration, each Government to appoint one arbitrator, and the two arbitrators so appointed to appoint a third, and if the said two arbitrators shall not agree upon the selection of the third arbitrator, then the Chief Justice of the South African Republic, upon application made by either party, shall appoint a third such arbitrator, and the award of the majority shall be final.

ARTICLE 21.—This agreement is subject to the approval of the Government of the South African Republic.

ARTICLE 22.—This agreement is subject to the approval of the Government of the Colony of Natal on or before the 20th day of February, 1894.

I 2

IV.

Mr. Dougall's Letter on the Netherlands Railway Company.

Pretoria, 29th May, 1897.

The *Chairman*,

    The Industrial Commission of Inquiry,

        Johannesburg.

Hon. Sir,—Let me first state that I would not have ventured upon writing to you had I not realised, after receiving a letter from the Secretary of your Hon. Commission, reading as follows :

    "Naar aanleiding van uw schrijven d.d. 24sten Mei is mij opgedragen UEd. te informeeren dat ingevolge publicaties in de couranten gemaakt, de tijd voor applicaties ten einde getuigenis te geven, reeds verstreken is"—

that I had no alternative now but to do so; and, further, had I not keenly felt that, while the Government is sincerely desirous to get at the root cause of all these complaints and dissatisfaction with the Netherlands Railway Company, and a great deal of light has been thrown on the general question, yet the real first cause has not been got at and laid bare to all.

I now beg to lay before your Honourable Commission a table showing heavy overcharges by the Netherlands Railway Company for the carriage of through goods from the ports, from the Mid-Vaal River Bridge to Elandsfontein, Boksburg, Johannesburg, Krugersdorp, and Pretoria, as follows :—

	Normal Goods.	Intermediate Goods.	Rough Goods.
To Elandsfontein ...	5s. 8d. per ton.	10s. 11d. per ton.	19s. 6d. per ton.
„ Boksburg	6s. 0d. „ „	12s. 0d. „ „	18s. 0d. „ „
„ Johannesburg ..	7s. 4d. „ „	13s. 10d. „ „	20s. 4d. „ „
„ Krugersdorp ...	6s. 2d. „ „	15s. 0d. „ „	18s. 11d. „ „
„ Pretoria	4s. 4d. „ „	14s. 1d. „ „	22s. 2d. „ „

To make the position plain it will be needful that we should go back to June, 1890, when the railway concession, granted to the Netherlands Company by the Government, was confirmed by the Hon. Volksraad of this State. In granting the concessires, beyond the natural and legitimate desire to have railway communication with Delagoa Bay, no ulterior motive prompted the Government and Volksraad, and they insisted on the perfectly fair principle of equitable tariffs for the transport of persons and goods. The *maximum* rates were specified, and Article 19 distinctly bound the concessionaire

" to convey, without distinction and without partiality, whatever shall be offered for conveyance, subject to the general exceptions provided for." There was no distinction made in the concession as between the " through traffic from the ports" and the "local traffic." Transport-riding with the ox-wagon was done for, and the Government and Volksraad took good care that the railway company, while having a monopoly of the transport business in the land should carry it on on strictly fair terms, and within certain clearly defined limits. The farmers, mining companies, and merchants in the southern, central, and western districts were to have their through goods carried over the railway from Viljoen's Drift at the same or equivalent rates per ton per mile as the farmers and merchants in Standerton, Ermelo, Heidelberg, and Pretoria from Volksrust, and the mining companies and farmers in Barberton, Lydenburg, Middel-burg, and Zoutpansberg from Komatie Poort.

The Netherlands Railway Company had got a very good thing. From Delagoa Bay to Johannesburg did not exceed 400 miles, as against, say 500 miles from Durban, 670 miles from East London, and 720 miles from Port Elizabeth. What was there to fear from competition by the Colonial lines, once the Netherlands Railway was in complete working order from Delagoa Bay?

But, in time the competition became keen and still keener, more so than the Netherlands Company cared to meet on fair terms within the four corners of their concession. And so it was, because of the company's inability to run their railway satisfactorily on fair terms to all, or because of their insensate greed, which would not let them act fairly and secure their position with the good-will and assistance of all in the State, they misled the Government and secured the closing of the Vaal River drifts, that first act in the woeful chapter of sad events which has brought about the present strained position in South Africa.

I should like to make reference here to one or two statements made by Mr. Middelberg to your Honourable Commission.

1. He stated that " The accusation, that the tariffs from the ports to Johannesburg are higher by our taking a greater share of the profits than they would be if we accepted a lower share, is *devoid of foundation*." And he attempted to make this clear by the illustration of two individuals deciding to build a house, and providing the necessary funds therefor. And when the rental of that house has been fixed it is certainly a matter of indifference to the tenants of the house what shares of the rent each of the two owners receives.

And Mr. Middelberg alleged that
" This is exactly the same in the case of the shares of carriage received by each of the administrations in the traffic with the ports."

In reply to Mr. Albu, Mr. Middelberg maintained that the consignees or owners of the goods had very little to do with what the Netherlands Company got as its share of the carriage from the ports to Johannesburg.

Now, it is just on this vitally important point that the whole matter depends. Mr. Middelberg's illustration is not complete. In the event of complaints preferred and enquiry made thereinto, the Netherlands Railway Company is bound to make answer and give account to the Government in fullest detail of its dealings with the farmers, mining companies, and merchants in the Republic. Your Honourable Commission has been appointed for this very purpose. And *it does* concern the Government and ourselves *very much* to know what the Netherlands Railway Company receives as its share for carriage of the through traffic from the ports. And I maintain that under cover of the agreement with the Cape Railway administration in respect of the through traffic from the ports to Johannesburg and elsewhere, the Netherlands Railway Company receives and appropriates a larger share than it is entitled or authorised to receive under the concession. As for example in respect of the carriage to Pretoria, they receive on:—

Normal goods	...	£2 3s. 4d. instead of £1 19s. 0d. per ton.		
Intermediate goods	...	2 3 4 „	„ 1 9 3	„
Rough goods...	...	2 1 8 „	„ 0 19 6	„

2. When Mr. Middelberg stated under oath to your Honourable Commission that the actual rates to Johannesburg (delivery free included) were :—

	Normal Goods.	Interm. Goods.	Rough Goods.
From Port Elizabeth	2·70	2·41	1·75 per ton per mile.
„ East London	2·76	2·43	1·77 „ „
„ Capetown	2·56	2·17	1·67 „ „

he uttered nine distinct misstatements, on his part quite inexcusable, and which must have proved very misleading to the members of your Commission. The actual rates levied and appropriated by the Cape and Netherlands administrations, paid by consignees of goods to Johannesburg, are as follows:—

	1st Class Goods.	2nd Class Goods.	3rd Class Goods.	Gal'v'd Iron.	Rough Goods.
From Port Elizabeth to Mid-Vaal	2·77	2·32	2·0	1·80	1·30 per ton per mile
„ East London „ „	2·80	2·34	2·0	1·80	1·27 „ „
„ Capetown „ „	2·74	2·26	1·87	1·80	1·35 „ „
„ Mid-Vaal to Johannesburg	7·70	7·70	7·70	7·70	7·70 „ „

And it is a very extraordinary thing that, while the Netherlands Company under their arrangement with the Portuguese administration allow only about 11s. 2d. for the carriage of 1 ton of rough goods over the 58 miles from Lourenço Marques to Komatie Poort, and are authorised under the concession to charge a *maximum* sum of only 13s. for the carriage of 1 ton of the like goods over the 52 miles from Mid-Vaal River Bridge to Johannesburg, they demand no less a sum than £1 13s. 4d. for this 1 ton over the shorter distance and through a much healthier district.

It is in this way, as more fully shown in the accompanying table, that the fair and righteous principle of equitable rates for the transport of goods, on which the concession is based, has been departed from and its conditions broken. And the farmers, mining companies and merchants in the southern, central and western districts are made to pay much higher rates to the Netherlands Company for the carriage of their through goods from Viljoen's Drift, than the mining companies and farmers in the Barberton, Lydenburg and Middelburg districts are required to pay for theirs from Komatie Poort.

3. I have been somewhat puzzled over the replies made by Mr. Middelberg to Mr. Albu, as follows :—

Mr. Albu : You charge 7·7d. from Viljoen's Drift to Johannesburg.

Mr. Middelberg : No, no !

Mr. Albu : We pay it then. We don't know who gets it.

Mr. Middelberg : We get it from the Cape.

Mr. Albu : If you get it from the Cape, who pays the Cape ?

Mr. Middelberg : You don't pay 7·7d. You pay about 10s., and so much per ton, and out of it we claim so much.

It is a pity Mr. Middelberg is not more explicit in his explanations and willing to tell the whole truth. He is very misleading. As a matter of fact the Netherlands Railway Company collect all carriage in Johannesburg, Pretoria, Elandsfontein,

Boksburg, and Krugersdorp from the consignees on delivery of the goods, and accounts through the *Pretoria* Railway Clearing Office for amounts so collected which may be due and payable to the Cape Railway administration. And the share credited to and held by the Netherlands Railway Company for carriage of all through goods from the Cape ports *is equal to 7·7d. per ton per mile* from Mid-Vaal River to the above-named five stations.

4. On another very important point, Mr. Middelberg must have seriously misled your Hon. Commission. He has stated that he had convinced himself, that the net cost for working expenses and interest on construction capital on the Cape Railways amounted to 1½d. to 2d. per ton per mile. These figures are not correct, and from three points I am able to refute his statement:

a. The share which the Cape Railway receives for carriage of rough through goods from East London, Port Elizabeth and Capetown to Mid-Vaal River amounts to only 1·27d. to 1·35d. per ton per mile.

b. According to Mr. Middelberg's own figures, in spite of these low through rates, the Cape surplus from railways in 1896 amounts to £8 19s. 7d. per cent. on the construction capital.

c. Two years ago, if I remember rightly, a committee report was presented to the Cape Parliament showing that the working expenses with interest on capital, on the Cape lines from Port Elizabeth and East London to Mid-Vaal River, were as follows:—

Port Elizabeth to Norval's Pont, 328 miles, ⅝d. per ton per mile.

Norval's Pont to Mid-Vaal, 334 miles, ½d. per ton per mile.

East London to Bethulie, 290 miles, ¾d. per ton per mile.

Bethulie to Mid-Vaal, 325 miles, ½d. per ton per mile.

5. Mr. Middelberg claims praise as " a good servant " to his master, " for assuring himself of the largest share of the general revenue for the State, etc." I believe his master to be a just man, who, in spite of many difficulties, tries to be fair and upright in all his dealings. But in this very important business the servant has acted very wickedly. Unable or unwilling to carry out his master's commission on the terms laid down for him to work upon, he determines to make good his position and show large returns and good profits by disregarding his master's instructions and defrauding his master's customers and subjects. Thereby, he causes very grievous dissension in the house, and through his meddling propensities this extends to the neighbours in the adjoining houses, and even beyond, amongst his master's friends at a distance, so that they begin to speak reproachfully of each other, and are like to come to blows. But what cares this wicked servant about the widespread mischief he has made, the grievous troubles and great expenses he has brought upon his master and his master's friends, so long as he can come scatheless out of the evil situation he has created, and escape with large sums of money improperly obtained?

I have not made any close examination into the figures for carriage appropriated under the agreements with the Natal and Portuguese administrations. Nor have I made any inquiry into the appropriation of the customs duties collected by the Netherlands Railway Company. But these will require to be looked into most searchingly. Thus far, should my contention and figures be found correct, the consideration of this vitally important matter makes it clear :

1. That the consignees of goods have a good case against the shareholders of the Netherlands Railway Company for repayment of all amounts so overcharged and paid by them.

2. That the directors of the Netherlands Railway Company should be charged by

the Government to hold in suspense all these monies so obtained, pending a searching inquiry into the matter.

The monies so obtained should not have been included in the revenue, and carried into the Netherlands Railway Company's profits account for division among their shareholders : In the first place, because the railway company has no right to these amounts, and sooner or later they will have to be refunded in some way or other to the parties from whom they were received : And, secondly, because the inclusion of these improperly obtained sums into the railway company's profits affects to a very material extent the basis on which the expropriation of the Netherlands Railway is, to be effected. If the Government does not compel the Netherlands Railway Company to have their accounts re-opened and re-adjusted, and the amounts in question carefully ascertained and put aside for refund to parties, the South African Republic will be overcharged and deprived of a large sum of money when the expropriation of the Netherlands railway is brought about.

In conclusion, as one earnestly desirous for the peace and prosperity of the Republic, and the promotion of goodwill amongst all within our borders, I would state that if the Government will cause the most careful inquiry to be made into this, very serious matter, they will soon find themselves in a pre-eminently good position for ameliorating the conditions which now press so heavily upon the mining and other industries in the State. And, at the same time, this will afford the finest possible opportunity for the powerful financial houses in Johannesburg, acting in conjunction with the Nationale Bank and the other banks in the Republic to rally round the Government and help to remedy and improve the situation. The Netherlands Railway Company and the Dynamite Agency Company will of necessity require to be bought out, and loans must be raised for these purposes.

And, further, permit me to say, that the present seems to me to be a favourable juncture for arrangements to be entered into whereby the administration of the Portuguese Province of Lourenço Marques, the Delagoa Bay harbour, and the Portuguese Railway might be undertaken in a manner and on terms equally satisfactory and profitable to Portugal, the South African Republic, and Great Britain. And for this end all should lend their best counsel and help for bringing about this so-much-to-be-desired beneficial result. It is a perfectly feasible project, and, to begin with, only requires Great Britain to be as considerate and helpful towards Portugal and the South African Republic as she is to her own Colonies.

I have the honour to remain, Hon. Sir,

Your obedient servant,

JOHN DOUGALL.

TABLE SHOWING THE HEAVY OVERCHARGES AND EXTRA CHARGES MADE BY THE NETHERLANDS RAILWAY COMPANY ON THROUGH GOODS WITH THE CAPE RAILWAYS' ADMINISTRATION, BY THE NETHERLANDS RAILWAY COMPANY ON THROUGH GOODS FROM THE PORTS, FOR CARRIAGE FROM MID-VAAL RIVER TO ELANDSFONTEIN, BOKSBURG, JOHANNESBURG, KRUGERSDORP, AND PRETORIA, AND APPLIED, IN LIKE MANNER, TO ALL THROUGH GOODS CARRIED FROM MID-VAAL RIVER TO ALL STATIONS IN THE TRANSVAAL.:—

TO ELANDSFONTEIN—42 MILES FROM MID-VAAL RIVER.

MAXIMUM LEGAL CHARGES PER CONCESSION.	CHARGES LEVIED.	OVERCHARGES MADE.
Normal goods, 6d. per ton per mile...21s. 0d. per ton or 12·6d. per 100 lbs.	16d. per 100 lbs. or 26s. 8d. per ton.	3·4d. per 100 lbs. or 5s. 8d. per ton.
Intermediate do., 4½d. ,, ,, ...15s. 9d. ,, ,, 9·45d.	16d. ,, ,, 26s. 8d. ,,	6·55d. ,, ,, 10s. 11d. ,,
Rough do., 3d. ,, ,, ...10s. 6d. ,, ,, 6·3d.	18d. ,, ,, 30s. 0d. ,,	11·7d. ,, ,, 19s. 6d. ,,

TO BOKSBURG—48 MILES FROM MID-VAAL RIVER.

MAXIMUM LEGAL CHARGES PER CONCESSION.	CHARGES LEVIED.	OVERCHARGES MADE.
Normal goods, 6d. per ton per mile...24s. 0d. per ton or 14·4d. per 100 lbs.	18d. per 100 lbs. or 30s. 0d. per ton.	3·6d. per 100 lbs. or 6s. 0d. per ton.
Intermediate do., 4½d. ,, ,, ...18s. 0d. ,, ,, 10·8d.	18d. ,, ,, 30s. 0d. ,,	7·2d. ,, ,, 12s. 0d. ,,
Rough do., 3d. ,, ,, ...12s. 0d. ,, ,, 7·2d.	18d. ,, ,, 30s. 0d. ,,	10·8d. ,, ,, 18s. 0d. ,,

TO JOHANNESBURG—52 MILES FROM MID-VAAL RIVER.

MAXIMUM LEGAL CHARGES PER CONCESSION.	CHARGES LEVIED.	OVERCHARGES MADE.
Normal goods, 6d. per ton per mile...26s. 0d. per ton or 15·6d. per 100 lbs.	20d. per 100 lbs. or 33s. 4d. per ton.	4·4d. per 100 lbs. or 7s. 4d. per ton.
Intermediate do., 4½d. ,, ,, ...19s. 6d. ,, ,, 11·7d.	20d. ,, ,, 33s. 4d. ,,	8·3d. ,, ,, 13s. 10d. ,,
Rough do., 3d. ,, ,, ...13s. 0d. ,, ,, 7·8d.	20d. ,, ,, 33s. 4d. ,,	12·2d. ,, ,, 20s. 4d. ,,

TO KRUGERSDORP—71 MILES FROM MID-VAAL RIVER.

MAXIMUM LEGAL CHARGES PER CONCESSION.	CHARGES LEVIED.	OVERCHARGES MADE.
Normal goods, 6d. per ton per mile...35s. 6d. per ton or 21·3d. per 100 lbs.	25d. per 100 lbs. or 41s. 8d. per ton.	3·7d. per 100 lbs. or 6s. 2d. per ton.
Intermediate do., 4½d. ,, ,, ...26s. 7½d. ,, ,, 16·0d.	25d. ,, ,, 41s. 8d. ,,	9·0d. ,, ,, 15s. 0d. ,,
Rough do., 3d. ,, ,, ...17s. 9d. ,, ,, 10·65d.	22d. ,, ,, 36s. 8d. ,,	11·35d. ,, ,, 18s. 11d. ,,

TO PRETORIA—78 MILES FROM MID-VAAL RIVER.

MAXIMUM LEGAL CHARGES PER CONCESSION.	CHARGES LEVIED.	OVERCHARGES MADE.
Normal goods, 6d. per ton per mile...39s. 0d. per ton or 23·4d. per 100 lbs.	26d. per 100 lbs. or 43s. 4d. per ton.	2·6d. per 100 lbs. or 4s. 4d. per ton.
Intermediate do., 4½d. ,, ,, ...29s. 3d. ,, ,, 17·55d.	26d. ,, ,, 43s. 4d. ,,	8·45d. ,, ,, 14s. 1d. ,,
Rough do., 3d. ,, ,, ...19s. 6d. ,, ,, 11·7d.	25d. ,, ,, 41s. 8d. ,,	13·3d. ,, ,, 22s. 2d. ,,

MEMORANDUM.—It is to be noted here that the Netherlands Railway Company is, in addition to carriage, entitled to make a charge for unloading and delivery (including cartage), say, within certain areas; but this should not exceed 3s. to 3s. 6d. per ton at the very most. For comparison, we note the rates ruling in the Cape Colony, as follows:—

1st Class traffic—is free of charge within certain areas.

2nd, 3rd, and agricultural traffic—are subject, in Capetown to 1s. 3d., Port Elizabeth 1s. 3d., East London 1s. 8d., Kingwilliamstown 1s. 8d., Simonstown 2s. 6d., Graaff Reinet 2s. 6d., Kimberley 3s. 4d., and Dordrecht 3s. 4d. per ton.

But a rebate of a portion of such charges is allowed to persons, wherever residing, who prefer to enter into an agreement with the traffic managers, to bring to or take away from the station the whole of their traffic. These rebates are given as follows:—Capetown 9d., Port Elizabeth and East London 10d., Kingwilliamstown 9d., Simonstown and Graaff Reinet 1s., Kimberley 1s. 6d., and Dordrecht 1s. 8d. per ton.

V.

Netherlands Railway Concession.

CONDITIONS of the Concession granted by the Transvaal Government for the construction and working of a railway in the South African Republic from the Portuguese frontier to Pretoria, Barberton, Johannesburg, and the Vaal River.

PART I.

THE LINE TO BE CONSTRUCTED.

ARTICLE 1.

This Concession comprises the construction and working :—

(a). Of a railway commencing from the termination of the line from Delagoa Bay on the frontier of the Portuguese territory, and running thence in the direction of the Crocodile River to Nelspruit.

(b). Of a railway joining the line mentioned in (a) to Pretoria, Johannesburg, and the Vaal River.

(c). Of a railway from Barberton joining the railway mentioned in (a).

ARTICLE 2.

The exclusive right is granted to the Concessionary to construct the work on the conditions of this Concession, when the Volksraad resolves that such shall or may be constructed, railways or steam tramways, in the South African Republic, which either join foreign railways or steam tramways, navigable rivers, or the sea, and which may be deemed to compete with the lines already conceded to the company or portions thereof.

This right is forfeited in the case of those railways or steam tram lines the construction and working of which shall be undertaken by the State.

If the Government, during the existence of this Concession, should decide to entrust the working of such a railway line to others, the Concessionary shall be charged therewith on the conditions of this Concession, unless it shall be otherwise mutually agreed. The Concessionary shall be bound, within three months after the resolution shall have been passed by the Volksraad, to declare whether he will avail himself of his right.

ARTICLE 3.

The gauge shall be 1·067m. (3ft. 6in. English measure).

If, however, another gauge be adopted for the railway or tramway on Portuguese territory, then the same shall be compulsory for the line herein referred to.

ARTICLE 4.

With the exception of necessary sidings with double rails, the railway and the earthworks and artificial works belonging thereto shall be built as for a single line.

ARTICLE 5.

The direction of the railway between the points mentioned in Article 1 and the places where the stations and stopping places shall be built, and also the works required for the free flow of water, and the free passage of traffic on the existing roads, shall be determined by the Concessionary in consultation with the Commissioner of the Government. Where the Concessionary deems it advisable or necessary, in the interests of the undertaking, he may construct the line entirely or partly on existing roads and streets, provided he leaves sufficient space for ordinary traffic, to the satisfaction of the Government Commissioner.

ARTICLE 6.

All land required for the railway, the stations, stopping places, platelayers' cottages, dwellings and premises for the staff, and other appurtenances, or establishments ; for obtaining ballast, stones and limestones, or other similar materials ; for cutting wood ; the removal of materials and earth ; for the deviation of roads, rivers, spruits and water-leadings ; and, generally, for the construction and working of the railway, shall be placed at the disposal of the Concessionary gratis and timely by the Government, but the Concessionary shall compensate it for the price paid by it in those cases in which expropriation may be unavoidable ; and while the Concession is in existence, this land shall be conceded to the Concessionary for temporary use, with the exception of such land as is not required for the working of the line.

In determining the limits of this land, the necessary space for constructing a double line and for other extensions, and also for the prevention of grass and forest fires, shall at that time be taken into consideration.

ARTICLE 7.

The Concessionary shall be exempt from paying customs dues on all material, machinery, raw material, &c., required for the construction and working of the railway.

ARTICLE 8.

If the Government orders or permits the construction of roads, canals, etc., which intersect or join the railway referred to in the Concession, the same cannot be prohibited by the Concessionary.

All necessary arrangements shall be made by the Government in consultation with the Concessionary, in order that thereby no impediment resulting in extra cost to the Concessionary may be caused to the traffic or railway service.

If the extra cost is unavoidable, as also in case of permanent increase of expenditure for the maintenance of the line or the railway service, a lump sum of equal amount shall be paid to the Concessionary.

ARTICLE 9.

The railway works shall be commenced within one year after the acceptance of the Concession by the Concessionary, or so much later as the necessary land shall have been placed at the disposal of the Concessionary, and the line from Delagoa Bay to the frontier of the Portuguese territory shall have been so far completed that it is possible to commence carrying materials over that line for the railway referred to in this Concession.

The railway mentioned in Article 1 *(a)* shall be completed and in working order within the period of four years after the commencement of the works.

If the provisions contained in the two preceding paragraphs of this article, as regards the commencement and completion of this railway are not complied with, the Government shall have the right to seize all the property of the Concessionary, on payment to the company of the sum required for the complete liquidation of the company, and on returning 90 per cent. of the paid-up capital of the company.

ARTICLE 10.

If notice has been given by the Concessionary of the intention to extend the railway to Pretoria, this extension and also the whole line to the Vaal River shall be completed and in working order within the period of ten years after the completion of the railway to Nelspruit.

If this latter obligation is not fulfilled, or if the extension of the railway is not commenced within a period of five years after the completion of the railway to Nelspruit, the Government shall have the right to seize all the property of the Concessionary on payment to the company of the sum required for the complete liquidation of the company, and on re-paying the paid-up capital of the company.

The Concessionary undertakes speedily to complete the railways mentioned in Article 1, and unless unforeseen circumstances occur, they shall be opened for traffic on or before the 31st December, 1894, with the exception of the section which connects Pretoria and Johannesburg with the Vaal River, upon which traffic shall commence six months after it shall be possible that traffic on the Free State Railway to and beyond the Vaal River can take place, or six months after the traffic on the railway from Delagoa Bay to Pretoria shall have commenced. If this should occur at an earlier date, and for each day's delay a fine will be incurred, in the first case, of fifty pounds and in the second case of twenty-five pounds.

The railway company shall be charged in its books with the amount of these fines.

PART II.

SUPERVISION OF THE WORKS.

ARTICLE 11.

The Government has the right to cause the construction of the works and the working of the line to be supervised.

For this purpose it may, at all times, have the condition of the works and the material inspected.

Its officers charged with such inspection shall have access to all premises intended for the public and the service.

ARTICLE 12.

The existing laws, or those still to be framed, on the railway policy in the South African Republic, are applicable to the railway referred to in this Concession, but the

Government shall not thereby prejudice the rights granted by this Concession to the Concessionary.

PART III.

THE. WORKING OF THE LINE AND THE MATERIALS.

ARTICLE 13.

Steam shall be the locomotive power employed.

ARTICLE 14.

The Concessionary is bound, during the existence of the Concession, to maintain the railway and everything belonging to it in good order, and not to discontinue the service, except when compelled to do so by sheer force of circumstances.

ARTICLE 15.

The carriages shall be fitted up for at least two classes of travellers.

ARTICLE 16.

The Concessionary is bound to lay down regulations for his service, and to submit these for the approval of the local Government Commissioner, in order that the latter may convince himself that nothing occurs therein which is in conflict with the conditions of this Concession, and with the common law of the country.

These regulations are also binding on third parties.

The service shall not be commenced before these regulations have been approved of.

If, within three months after they have been submitted to him, the Government Commissioner has not dealt therewith, he shall be considered to have approved thereof.

PART IV.

TARIFFS AND CONVEYANCE.

ARTICLE 17.

The Concessionary may demand payment to be fixed by him for the conveyance of persons, goods, cattle, etc., and also for unloading, loading, delivery, and all similar services, for wagon hire, etc.

The import, export, and transit duties due to the Portuguese Government for the goods conveyed by the railway (and also for cattle), shall be collected by and on behalf of the Concessionary, according to rules to be laid down in consultation with the Government Commissioner in accordance with the instructions of the Government.

The tariff for the conveyance of persons and goods, shall, however, without previous consent of the Government, never exceed :—

For persons, first class, 3d. per mile (1⅞d. per kilometer); lowest class, 2d. per mile (1¼d. per kilometer).

For ordinary freight goods, 6d. per ton per mile (3¾d. per kilometer), with a minimum of £1 per consignment.

For rough goods (coal, ores of not greater value than £45 per ton, stones, unsawn wood, etc.) in quantities of at least five tons, 3d. per ton per mile (1⅝d. per kilometer), with a minimum of £1 per consignment.

ARTICLE 18.

To all tariffs and amendments thereto, the necessary publicity shall be given before they are carried into effect, and no tariff shall be amended before it shall have been in operation at least three months.

ARTICLE 19.

The Concessionary shall be bound to convey, without distinction and without partiality, whatever shall be offered for conveyance, subject to the general exceptions provided for.

ARTICLE 20.

The Concessionary shall be bound to convey gratis all sealed post parcels which may be delivered at the station by the postal administration.

For the conveyance of State post carriages, 8d. per mile (5d. per kilometer) shall be paid to the company.

ARTICLE 21.

The Concessionary is also bound to undertake the telegraph service along the railway line, gratis for the Government, and on payment from the public.

ARTICLE 22.

When there is danger of war, in time of war, or in cases of internal troubles, the Government may, in the interests of defence or of the public peace, dispose of the railway and of everything required for the use thereof, and may cause the ordinary traffic to be discontinued entirely or partly, and may order all measures to be taken which to it appear necessary, subject to compensation to the Concessionary.

ARTICLE 23.

The Concessionary is bound at all times to grant free access to the rooms in the station intended for the public and the service, and, if necessary, to the railway, to the officers of the police and of the customs department, and in the discharge of their duties.

PART V.

THE ACCEPTANCE AND LAPSE OF THE CONCESSION.

ARTICLE 24.

The Concession is accepted by the Concessionary as soon as a capital of five million guilders shall have been obtained in shares and debentures, and the conveyance over the Portuguese territory shall have been arranged to the satisfaction of the Concessionary.

ARTICLE 25.

The Concession may be withdrawn :—

(a) If the guaranteed capital mentioned in Article 36 shall not have been placed at the disposal of the Government within the stipulated time by the Concessionary.

(b) If the Concessionary does not comply with the provisions of Article 28.

The Government is, moreover, competent to withdraw the Concession if it shall not have been accepted within six months after the Concessionary has received notice to do so, referring to this Article.

ARTICLE 26.

The provisions contained in Articles 9, 10, and 25 shall not apply if the Concessionary shows that the delay or neglect was caused by main force or by acts or neglect of the Government or its officers.

The Government is, moreover, competent to extend all the periods fixed in this Concession at the request of the Concessionary.

The Concessionary shall be considered to be in default, simply by the expiration of the periods fixed, and without it being necessary that this should appear by any act.

ARTICLE 27.

The Government has the right to appropriate the railway, provided it also appropriates all the property of the Concessionary, twenty years after the railway shall have been brought into working order, and thereafter at the expiration of every ten years, provided that at least one year previously notice be given to the company in Holland of the intention to appropriate.

The Government shall then pay the amount required for the complete liquidation of the company, together with a sum equal to twenty times the average dividend which has been paid out to the shareholders during the three last years of the working of the line, with a minimum of twenty times the interest guaranteed to each of the shareholders, and at least at par, after the deduction of the fine mentioned in Article 10.

(Modified Article 27, as per First Volksraad " besluit" Article 1333, dated 7th September, 1893.)

" ARTICLE 27."

" The Government has at all times the right to nationalise the railway, and " all the properties of the grantee, but not until it shall have previously given a " year's notice to the company in Holland of its intention to do so.

" If the nationalisation takes place on 1st January, 1915, or at intervals of a " period of ten years later, then the Government shall pay the money required " for the whole liquidation of the company, besides a sum equivalent to twenty " times the dividend that was paid out on an average to the shareholders " during the last three years of the exploitation, with a minimum of twenty " times the guaranteed annual interest to those upon whose shares an annual " interest of 5 per cent. or higher, and the full nominal amount of those shares " upon which a lower annual interest has been guaranteed. From this amount " will be deducted any eventual fines due by the company by virtue of Article 10.

" If the nationalisation should take place before the 1st of January, 1915, or " before the expiration of the next period of ten years, it shall take place upon

" the same basis as laid down in the second paragraph of this article, yet, in
" addition, the nationalisation price shall be increased by one per cent. of the
" nominal share capital for every year that the nationalisation takes place before
" the 1st of January, 1915, or after the 1st of January, 1915, or the next follow-
" ing stipulated period."

PART VI.

GENERAL AND FINANCIAL PROVISIONS.

ARTICLE 28.

The Concessionary is bound within six months after the Concession shall have
been accepted by him, to establish a " Joint Stock Mercantile Company " in Holland,
named the " Netherlands South African Railway Company," and to make over to
this company the Concession gratis, *in toto*, and without reservation, and at least half
of the number of directors of this company shall be Hollanders.

ARTICLE 29.

The company shall not deal with any undertakings other than those mentioned
in this Concession, except with the consent of the Government of the Republic.

This consent is now given for the construction and working, or the working of a
railway or tramway on Portuguese territory, from Delagoa Bay to the frontier of the
Republic, which, according to Article 1, must be conjoined by the railway mentioned
in this Concession.

ARTICLE 30.

The company is bound to liquidate in case the Government avails itself of the
right of appropriation reserved to it in this Concession.
(*Modified Article 30, as per First Volksraad " besluit," Article 1333, dated 7th
    September, 1893.*)

" ARTICLE 30."

" When the Government avails itself of the right to nationalise the railway
" from the Portuguese boundary to Pretoria, Barberton, Johannesburg and Vaal
" River, this agreement shall be deemed to be cancelled, and the tramways and
" line (herein referred to) within the meaning of this agreement, with everything
" pertaining thereto, shall become the property of the Republic."

ARTICLE 31.

For constructing and bringing into working order the railways mentioned in
Article 1, and whatever belongs thereto, including the cost of acquiring, if necessary,
the Concession for the line Delagoa Bay—Transvaal frontier, all additional costs of
construction, temporary works, management, obtaining or making over money, and
also paying for account of the Republic, of the redemption and interest guaranteed by
it on behalf of those railways, the company shall be entitled, subject to the provisions
hereinafter contained, to issue to an amount of £9,600 per mile (£6,000 or 72,000
guilders per kilometer), shares and debentures bearing the counter-signature of the
Government Commissioner in Holland, and which are thereby, by virtue of Article 32,
directly guaranteed by the South African Republic.

Of this amount, one-fourth at most shall be obtained by issue of shares. The rate of interest of the debentures shall, in future, not amount to more than 4 per cent. (amended by resolution of the Hon. Volksraad, May 8th, 1891. See appendix A.).

The company may exceed the amount of £9,600 per mile, if under control, and with the cognizance of the Government Commissioner, with the consent of the Government, with advice and consent of the Executive Council, if this shall appear to be necessary for the completion of the railways under construction.

The rate of interest, the currency, the time, and the further conditions of issue or sale by the company of the shares and debentures mentioned in this Article, and also the proportion of the amount of the shares to that of the debentures, shall be determined by the company in consultation with the Government Commissioner in Holland, who, on instruction of the Government, shall countersign the documents in proof also of this consultation having taken place.

If this consultation has not led to agreement, the issue shall take place on the conditions desired by the Government Commissioner in Holland, in accordance with his instructions, but the shares or debentures not placed shall then be taken by the Government.

The Government shall have the right of option when the shares are issued on fixed conditions.

For the issue of shares or debentures, for purposes other than the above-mentioned, the express consent of the Government of the South African Republic, with advice and consent of the Executive Council is also required.

ARTICLE 32.

The South African Republic guarantees directly to the holders of all shares countersigned by the Government Commissioner in Holland, the interest therein expressed, calculated on the nominal amount of the company's capital paid up by them, and to the holders of all debentures, countersigned by the Government Commissioner in Holland, the redemption and interest, in accordance with the conditions of issue.

In the meantime the company binds itself, while any line or part of a line, the construction of which the company is bound to commence has not yet been brought into working order, and it has sufficient means for the purpose at its disposal, to advance to the Republic what it, for the reasons aforesaid, shall appear to owe in interest during that time to the holders of shares and debentures issued for the construction of that line, or of any section of that line.

The amount of this advance, for which the Republic shall be charged in the books of the company, may be called up when the Republic avails itself of its right to appropriate or when the company is in liquidation for other reasons.

ARTICLE 33.

In order to ascertain what the Republic, by virtue of the preceding Article, may become indebted for, or may have to pay in any year, the company shall open an account which shall be closed on the 31st December of each year, on which account are brought as assets all receipts without distinction belonging to the revenue account, and as liabilities:—

(1). All expenditure, except such as belongs to the construction and capital account, and except such as has been incurred for the guaranteed interest and redemption.

(2). Ten per cent. of the gross receipts of the working of the line, for the reserve fund mentioned in Article 35.

This account shall be framed in consultation with the Commissioner of the Government of the South African Republic in Holland.

The amount of the redemption and interest guaranteed in the first section of the preceding Article, reduced by the balance of this account, shall be the amount which the Republic, in accordance with the provisions of the second section of Article 32, shall have to pay annually to the company in Holland, within three months, at the latest, after the account has been tendered to the Commissioner. The amount which the company may receive from this source from the Republic, the company shall not be liable to refund to the Republic.

If the company neglects to pay out the redemption and interest guaranteed to the share and debenture holders by Article 32, and the Republic is compelled to pay this directly to the share and debenture holders, the amount of this payment shall be deducted from the first payment above-mentioned, due to the company by the Republic.

ARTICLE 34.

If the balance of the account mentioned in the preceding article amounts to more than the guaranteed interest and redemption, 85 per cent. of the surplus shall be paid to the Republic and five per cent. to the management and staff of the company.

The payment to the South African Republic shall take place at the office of the company in that country, within three months at the latest after the account shall have been tendered to the Commissioner of the Government of the South African Republic in Holland.

ARTICLE 35.

The reserve fund mentioned in Article 33, shall serve as far as possible to defray costs of repairs of extraordinary damage done to the line, works and rolling material, and generally the costs of all necessary renovations and extensions of the railways worked by the company. This fund shall be administered and invested separately, the interest being annually added to the capital.

As soon as, and as long as, a sum equal to forty-two hundred guilders (£350) per kilometer of £560 per mile in working order, has been reached, then the contributions otherwise destined for it shall be used for the redemption of loans.

This fund shall be considered to belong to the property of the company mentioned in Articles 9, 10 and 27.

ARTICLE 36.

As guarantee for the observance of the conditions of this Concession, the Concessionary, on accepting this Concession, shall pay to the Treasury of the South African Republic the sum of 100,000 guilders, which shall be refunded to the company one year after the railway shall have been brought into working order to Nelspruit, or, if the Concessionary constructs the extension line to Pretoria, as soon as the line shall be in working order to that place, or so much longer previously, as the Republic shall avail itself of its rights to appropriate.

On the guarantee fund 5 per cent. interest shall be annually paid to the company from the date of payment to the date of re-payment, payable in Holland on or before the 15th of January in each year.

ARTICLE 37.

The Government of the South African Republic shall appoint a Commissioner and a deputy in the South African Republic, and also with the company in Holland.

The Government Commissioners, or in the event of their inability, their deputies, shall have the right to be present at all the meetings of the company, the local Commissioner or his deputy, in the case of the Transvaal Republic, and the Government Commissioner, or his deputy in the case of meetings of the shareholders in Holland, and shall have the right to an advising voice in these meetings. They shall exercise an unlimited control over and superintend all matters pertaining to, and transactions of the company, and shall also have the right of access to the offices, to inspect the books, and to verify the accounts.

ARTICLE 38.

All disputes about the provisions of the Concession, and the way in which it is carried into effect, between the Government of the South African Republic or its officers, and the company or its officers, which cannot be settled amicably, shall be decided by two arbitrators, and when these do not agree in their award, by an umpire, who shall, as good men, without formality, pronounce judgment in the last resort. Each of the parties shall appoint one of these arbitrators, and these two arbitrators shall, before proceeding to deal with the dispute, appoint a third, who shall be umpire on all points upon which the two arbitrators cannot agree.

If the two arbitrators cannot agree on the selection of an umpire, the appointment of that umpire shall be made by the High Court of the South African Republic, if a local matter is the subject of dispute, and otherwise by the Court of Justice in Amsterdam.

ARTICLE 39.

In all cases in which consultation between the company and the Government of the South African Republic or its Commissioner is required, dispute shall be considered to have arisen if an agreement cannot be arrived at between them.

This Concession was approved of by resolution of the Honourable Volksraad on 26th June, 1890, and serves to replace the concession granted by the Government of the South African Republic, empowered thereto by the Honourable Volksraad by resolution of 27th May, 1895, with the amendment introduced therein by resolution of the Honourable Volksraad of 12th July, 1888.

APPENDIX A.

NETHERLANDS RAILWAY CONCESSION.

Article 31, third paragraph, amended by Article 32 of the Volksraad besluiten, dated May 8th, 1891 (minutes page 13), as follows :—
"The rate of interest of the debentures shall in future not amount to more than 4 per cent. without the consent of the Executive Council."

K 2

VI

REPORT OF THE VOLKSRAAD DYNAMITE COMMISSION.

Presented to the Honourable the First Volksraad on the 22nd February, 1897. The following translation of the Commission's Report was made by the Chamber of Mines and circulated among its members.

Pretoria, 19th February, 1897.

HONOURABLE CHAIRMAN AND MEMBERS OF THE FIRST VOLKSRAAD, PRETORIA.

Honourable Sir,

Honourable Gentlemen,

Your Commission, appointed by First Volksraad resolution, Article 46, dated 4th February, 1897, completed by First Volksraad resolution, Article 187, dated 8th February, 1897, has, in the short time placed at its disposal, in consultation with the Government, instituted as thorough an enquiry into the matters upon which it was instructed as has been possible, and has now the honour to submit the following report to your Honourable Assembly for its favourable consideration.

1. The State monopoly for the manufacture, import and sale of powder, ammunition, dynamite and other explosives, was established by the Honourable Raad by its resolutions, Articles 1,266 to 1,301, 1,303 to 1,305, dated 1st to 5th September, 1893.

2. According to Article 4 of the said regulations the Government was authorised to entrust the carrying out of the monopoly conferred on it to other persons.

3. In accordance with the aforesaid authority, the Government, on the 24th May, 1894, entered into a contract with Mr. L. G. Vorstman, copy of which is attached to this report.

4. In Article 10 of the regulations, the Government was empowered to give instructions within the shortest possible time, but at the outside, within a period of $2\frac{1}{2}$ years, to establish, complete, and bring into operation one or more factories for the manufacture of dynamite and other explosives of such nature and quality, and in such quantity, as the requirements and demand within the South African Republic shall demand and require.

5. In Article 6 of the contract, the agent undertook to establish a factory referred to in the aforesaid paragraph, at the outside, within $2\frac{1}{2}$ years, after the 25th October, 1894,* thus on the 24th April, 1896.

6. The Government agent has, under Article 1 of the contract for the purposes thereof, the right to form a company in the South African Republic, which was done by him, the said company being entitled "The South African Explosives Company Limited."

---

* The date should be 25th October, 1893.

7. It has appeared to your Commission that the said company is now working two factories, one for the manufacture of powder, and the other for dynamite and other explosives. For reasons afterwards to be mentioned, your Commission occupied itself more especially with the last mentioned factory.

8. This factory was established and commenced working on the 22nd October, 1896, thus, after the expiry of the period fixed in the contract. Your Commission is, however, of opinion that with reference to this neglect, the occurrences during December, 1895, and January, 1896, ought fairly to be taken into consideration.

9. On Friday, 14th September, 1894, the Government, in accordance with a note to Article 6 of the contract, made a request to the Volksraad for an extension of the time for the establishment of the factories, whereupon the following resolution was passed by this body :—" Article 1711. The First Volksraad having considered the letter of the Government, dated 6th September, 1894, B.B. 1979/94, now on the Order, asking for agreement with the Executive Council resolution, Article 457, dated 6th September, 1894, submitted by the above-mentioned letter having considered the memorials and the report of the Commission taken with reference thereto, resolves not to agree with the Executive Council resolution, and not to grant the authority requested for the alteration of the instructions, and instructs the Government to act strictly in accordance with the regulations, and to reply to memorialists that their request cannot be complied with as the matter was decided last year by the Volksraad."

10. The Government agent has informed your Commission that the productive capacity of the said factory, which is now completed, does not at present exceed 80,000 cases per annum.

11. On 14th October, with reference to an application from the managers of the company, an Executive Council resolution was passed, which reads as follows :— Article 893. On the order, Minute R. 1480/96, letter sent in by the managers of the South African factories for explosives, stating that their factories are completed, and that they are now in a position to manufacture 80,000 cases of explosives per annum, and, further, after giving reasons, requesting that instructions may be given them for the building of further factories, which, if acceded to, they will complete within two-and-a-half years. The Executive Council having considered that request; having considered Article 10 of the regulations concerning the same, as well as Article 16 of the contract referring thereto; recognising the necessity, that within the borders of the country establishments should exist which are fully capable of manufacturing in accordance with the demand for explosives of the mining industry, etc. ; resolves to comply with the request of the company, as contained in this letter aforesaid, and in accordance therewith and limited thereto to continue in force for a new period, at the outside, of two-and-a-half years, the provisions made in accordance with Article 10 relating thereto, and in connection with the aforesaid, to continue the stipulations of the company's contract of the 24th May in force for the purpose, and in so far as is needful to enable the company, in that interval to provide for the requirements of the country.

12. It appears to your Commission that this Executive Council resolution cannot be brought into agreement with the already quoted Volksraad resolution, Article 1711 of 1894. The Government agent has informed your Commission that since the passing of the said Executive Council resolution, the company has decided, and is now making preparations, to extend the workshops of the said establishment, and that it proposes within the two-and-a-half years provided in the Executive Council resolution to double the productive capacity, thus bringing it up to 160,000 cases per annum which number of cases by extreme effort can be increased to 200,000 cases per annum Your Commission will return to this subject later.

II.—THE FACTORY.

1. Your Commission regarded it as their duty to visit the factory for dynamite and explosives on the farms Modderfontein and Klipfontein, to satisfy themselves as far as possible of the condition of things there.

2. By anticipation, your Commission may say that they were not only favourably impressed by the factory, but also that the Government agent and the officials with great willingness, submitted its plant and arrangements for inspection, and also in other respects afforded your Commission the fullest information.

3. The factory is divided into two chief divisions, viz., that for the manufacture of explosives, and that for the preparation of non-dangerous materials.

4. The arrangements for the preparation of non-explosives, include a factory for the manufacture of nitric acid; two factories for the manufacture of sulphuric acid; two for the concentration of already used acids (for which a third is in course of erection) and the necessary smithies, carpenters' shops, pump stations, cooling places, and the mechanical arrangements belonging thereto.

5. The factory for the manufacture of the actual explosives, such as from nitroglycerine and the manufacture of explosive gelatine, gühr, dynamite, etc., is divided into four compartments, in each of which in fact the same work is carried on, but which are separated from one another to diminish the effects of an explosion; also in each of these compartments the work is carried on in separate compartments or rooms, which are divided from each other by high earthen walls, and are protected in other ways. Although your Commission, not being experts, cannot pass a conclusive judgment on these arrangements, they desire to state as their opinion that, according to their judgment, all measures of precaution are taken to prevent avoidable danger.

6. Generally, your Commission again repeat that, so far as they can judge, the factory is arranged with the utmost efficiency, and excels in neatness and in constant vigilance.

7. There are at present 2,000 working men employed, of whom about one-fourth are whites.

8. The Government agent has informed your Commission that the cost of the factory to date, including the stock of materials calculated for 10 months, amounts to more than £900,000.

III.—MATERIALS.

1. Seeing that under Article 13, Division A, of the regulations, it is laid down that all the required materials which are found within the South African Republic, and the quantity, quality, or other properties of which do not prevent their being made use of, shall be used in the manufacture of explosives, your Commission regarded it as its duty to institute a strict inquiry with regard thereto. In the manufacture of nitroglycerine, which, in combination with other substances, makes blasting gelatine, dynamite, etc., nitric acid, sulphuric acid, and glycerine are required.

2. Nitric acid is now made in the factory from imported saltpetre. To the regret of your Commission, it appears that at present there is no prospect of being able to obtain sufficient saltpetre within this country.

3. Sulphuric acid is also made of imported sulphur now. The company, however, expect shortly to be able to produce sulphur from sulphuric ores, and they have already erected a furnace in which they have begun to test this. With regard to both the foregoing substances, your Commission has been informed that neither trouble nor expense has been spared to make their production from local materials possible.

4. Glycerine is a bye-product from candle and soap factories, and there is no prospect of this product being obtained locally.

5. Your Commission thus (without desiring to accuse the company of any want of zeal) cannot cherish the hope that the production of explosives will be independent of the importation of some of the materials.

6. Dynamite is made of nitro-glycerine and gühr; kieselgühr is found in this country, but, notwithstanding many attempts, the company has not yet succeeded in discovering it in sufficient quantity; there is, however, every chance that this will be done, but your Commission attach little importance to this, as the cost of locally prepared gühr exceeds that of imported, and also because from year to year the use of dynamite is superseded by that of blasting gelatine—a relatively cheaper, safer, and more suitable explosive. Cellulose is required for blasting gelatine, and this will not in the near future be produced here.

IV.—IMPORTED EXPLOSIVES.

1. As will be shown later by your Commission, explosives are still imported for the purpose of meeting the requirements of the local demand. This is done on the order of the Government agent.

2. These explosives, to wit, blasting gelatine and gühr impregné, are worked up in the factory. For the manufacture of blasting gelatine, as required for trade purposes, dynamite No. 1, the preparation is merely a making-up into cartridges, a very simple process. For dynamite No. 2 and other explosives, which, however, are relatively little used, other ingredients of little value are added.

V—DEMAND AND PRODUCTION.

1. According to returns given to us by the Government agent, the demand for the whole country now amounts to about 200,000 cases per annum; this agrees pretty well with the return sent to us by the Chamber of Mines at Johannesburg, which gives the present requirements there as 186,000 cases per annum. The difference of 14,000 cases, therefore, represents the demands of the other mining districts and the remaining consumers of the Republic.

2. It is difficult to arrive at an estimate for the future. Your Commission, however, think—judging from the best information placed at their disposal—that an estimate of the demand for 1898, 1899, and 1900 is not calculated too high at 250,000 cases per annum.

3. As we have already stated, the company can now produce 80,000 cases. In 1899 it hopes to be able to double this production, or let us take it to increase it to 180,000 cases.

4. There will thus be a shortage as follows:—

1897	...	...	...	...	120,000	cases.
1898	...	...	...	...	170,000	„
1899	...	...	...	...	70,000	„
1900	...	...	...	...	70,000	„
			Total	...	430,000	

This estimate is put low, and most favourably for the company, as any trouble at the factory that perhaps may occur, or any increased demand which, judging from the past, will probably take place, will considerably raise this shortage.

5. It is thus plain that the Government agent has not complied with the obligation which he undertook in the contract, viz., to produce dynamite and other explosives in such quantity as the needs and demands within the South African Republic may require and demand (see Article 10 of the regulations), and even though it should be possible to reconcile the Executive Council resolution of the 14th October, 1896, with the First Volksraad resolution, Article 1711, of 1894, and Article 16, paragraph A, of the contract of the Government agent; yet even then the last-mentioned obviously cannot satisfy his obligations, seeing that the Executive Council resolution says that the same has been passed to place the company in a position to meet the requirements of the country in that interval.

6. Nevertheless your Commission does not wish now to propose the cancellation of the contract or the suspension of the Government monopoly. The Volksraad has repeatedly declared the desirability of the trade and importation of powder, dynamite, and other explosives being in the hands of the State. Your Commission is also convinced of the benefits which are derived from the production of explosives in this country; and, further, your Commission is of opinion that the undoubtedly earnest efforts of the company to establish a local industry render it undesirable that the provisions of the contract should be applied too strictly.

7. For other purposes, however, the undoubtedly strong position in law of the State against the contractor should not be lost sight of.

8. Principally this point arises in connection with the question whether the Government agent shall still be allowed to import blasting gelatine and gühr impregné (which, in fact, is nothing but dynamite No. 1 not yet made into cartridges).

9. This importation yields very great profits to the company, which have nothing to do with the profits of the explosives produced by itself.

10. Your Commission gather from the accounts placed in their hands by the Honourable the State Secretary that the profit of the company on blasting gelatine and gühr impregné imported and paid for by the State amounts almost to £2 per case, of which only 5s. comes to the State.

11. Applying the above calculations to the 430,000 cases, the minimum which must be imported during the first four years, one arrives at this result, that, if the State itself imported, the national treasury would benefit to the extent of £860,000, while, if the company imports, the benefit to the State would be only £107,500, a difference thus of £752,500 loss to the State.

12. The benefit that the State should derive from itself importing would after 1900 be further increased through the augmented demand.

13. The only reason that makes your Commission hesitate to recommend that the importation of dynamite and other explosives, with all the benefits connected therewith, should be at once placed in the hands of the State, is a doubt whether the Government would be able to purchase these explosives equally cheaply as the company. The doubt arises from the fact that many of the greatest dynamite factories in Europe are important shareholders in the company, and thus possibly supply it with explosives on more favourable terms.

14. The Johannesburg Chamber of Mines asserts that the dynamite No. 1 (containing 75 per cent. nitro-glycerine) can be delivered in open market at 45s. per case. This price would give the Government a still larger profit, as this dynamite is now sold by the Government agent at 98s. 6d. per case.

15. Your Commission is, however, of opinion that in view of the question suggested in Artlcíe 13, it would be more prudent to institute a thorough inquiry (for which time failed this Commission) for the purpose of establishing beyond doubt at

what price, and in what quantities the Government itself will be able to purchase explosives.

16. Your Commission therefore recommends your Honourable Assembly to institute an inquiry into this subject on the part of the Government through its official experts, who must obtain all information with regard to the question, where and under what conditions the required explosives can best be obtained.

17. A complete report of this inquiry ought then to be laid before your Honourable Assembly at its next ordinary sitting, when a final decision can then be taken on this subject.

18. Your Commission suggests further, that if the data obtained by them are correct, the Government, even if selling at much greater profit than it now gets, will be able to reduce the price of dynamite, and thereby meet the mining industry. It must, however, be kept in mind that the local factory ought not to be opposed by unfair competition.

19. Your Commission also thinks this a suitable time, having regard to all the foregoing, to enter into negotiation with the company for the raising of the State dues (5s. per case), and the reduction of its selling price for explosives, in which way perhaps a solution of all the foregoing problems will be reached, to the satisfaction of all the parties concerned.

VI.—ADVANCES.

1. Now coming to the point that specially gave rise to the appointment of your Commission, we wish to make the following observations :—

   (a). That the imported explosives are purchased by the Government agent, who sends the accounts in to the Government, by whom they are settled.

   (b). The explosives themselves, blasting gelatine, etc., do not come into the hands of the Government.

   (c). When the agent sells, he repays the amount advanced by the Government increased by 5s. per case.

   (d). A large quantity of explosives is kept in reserve (at the moment 60,000 cases), which reserve is more or less maintained, so that the advance is thus not repaid to the Government. The Government agent often repays the Government in excess of his sales.

   (e) While the explosives are in the hands of the agent, they are properly insured at the cost of the company.

2. In view of the proposed inquiry, and in expectation of the decision of the question, who shall import in the future, your Commission proposes to place a sum of £350,000 provisionally on the estimates, instead of the proposed amount of £500,000.

VII.—POWDER AND AMMUNITION.

Although the question that led to the appointment of the Commission, was not in direct connection with powder and ammunition, and your Commission did not therefore consider it necessary, in view of the restricted time at their disposal to visit the powder factory, yet in the course of their work they made some observations which they think it serviceable to lay before the Honourable Assembly.

1. The manufacture of powder is limited in this factory to the making of gunpowder.

2. No attempts are made to manufacture the so-named new (smokeless) powder there.

3. The manufacture of this last-named article stands in close connection with that of nitro-glycerine, and would consequently very suitably constitute a subsidiary part of the manufacturing at the factory at Modderfontein.

4. The contract with the Government agent includes this (see Article 1.)

5. Your Commission has been informed on competent authority that, especially from a military point of view, the manufacture of such smokeless powder fully deserves the attention of your Assembly.

6. Your Commission intends thus to recommend that the Government be instructed to lay a full report on this subject before your Honourable Body at the coming May Session.

And herewith, honourable gentlemen, your Commission deem that they have fulfilled the task imposed on them, and have the honour to be

Your obedient servants,

CARL JEPPE, *Chairman.*

J. de CLERCQ, *Azn.*

J. du P. de BEER.

Members.

Chamber of Mines,
  26th February, 1897.

VII.

BALANCE-SHEET OF THE SOUTH AFRICAN EXPLOSIVES CO., LTD.

31st December, 1896.

Dr.

To Share Capital ...	£450,000	0	0
(450,000 Shares at £1, fully-paid, issued in accordance with the Articles of Association.)			
Debentures—			
10,000 Five per Cent. Debentures of 500 francs each, repayable 31st January, 1900—5,000,000 francs ...	198,500	0	0
„ Creditors ...	487,349	4	6
„ Reserve ...	64,000	0	0
„ Explosion Fund ...	20,000	0	0
„ Insurance Fund ...	286	17	8
„ Profit and Loss—			
Balance as per last statement, 31st December, 1895 ... £58,623 13 2			
Less Dividend declared 29th June, 1896 ... 56,250 0 0			
£2,373 13 2			
Balance of Profit and Loss Statement for 1896 ... 56,965 1 10	59,338	15	0
	£1,279,474	17	2

Cr.

By Capital Outlay, Pursuant to agreement of 6th February, 1894, with the Zuid Afrikaansche Maatschappy van ontplofbare Stoffen, Beperkt, in liquidation.			
Amount as per last statement ...£141,424 0 4			
Transfer to Leeuwfontein Factory Cost account ... £17,000 0 0			
Sundry realisations ... 2,469 1 7			
19,469 1 7			
£121,954 18 9			
Written off ... 121,954 18 9	£0	0	0
„ Leeuwfontein Factory Cost ... £23,826 10 6			
Written off ... 3,826 10 6	20,000	0	0
„ Modderfontein Factory Cost ...	556,484	19	0
„ Baviaanspoort Factory—Sundry buildings, plant, &c., cost ... (After writing off £335 8s. 5d. for depreciation; 1895, £336 17s. 7d.)	1,000	0	0
„ Pretoria Office Furniture ...	280	0	0
„ European Office Furniture ...	600	0	0
„ Debtors, Cash, and Bankers' Balances ...	69,278	4	1
„ Modderfontein Shop ...	2,439	7	10
„ Difference between issue price and nominal value of Debentures and Commission and Expenses on Debenture Issue (to be written off in four instalments) ... £16,121 18 5			
Less One-fourth, carried to Profit and Loss ... 4,030 9 7	12,091	8	10
„ Stocks and Value of Current Policies, &c....	617,300	17	5
	£1,279,474	17	2

PROFIT AND LOSS ACCOUNT.

For the Year ending 31st December, 1896.

Dr.

	£	s.	d.
To Rent	3,750	0	0
(For Powder Factory at Baviaanspoort.)			
,, Government of the South African Republic	46,157	16	4
,, General Charges and Board Fees ...	34,500	4	11
,, Duties and Tax on Share Warrants and Debentures	2,888	9	1
,, Interest on Debentures ...	9,075	0	0
(5 per cent. Debenture Interest for 11 months, 1896.)			
,, Interest, Exchange, and Bank Charges ...	1,388	10	3
,, Difference between issue price and nominal value of Debentures and commission and expenses on debenture issue—			
One-fourth written off	4,034	9	7
,, Johannesburg Explosion	22,727	16	0
,, Amounts written off—			
Capital Outlay £121,954 18 9			
Baviaanspoort Factory ... 335 8 5			
Pretoria Office Buildings and Furniture ... 276 19 6			
European Office Furniture ... 74 10 1			
Leeuwfontein Factory ... 3,826 10 6			
	126,468	7	3
,, Balance, carried to Balance-Sheet ...	56,965	1	10
	£307,951	**15**	**3**

Cr.

	£	s.	d.
By General Manufacturing and Trading Account	307,851	18	9
,, Sundry Fees	99	16	6
	£307,951	**15**	**3**

Examined with the Books, Accounts, and Vouchers of the Company and found correct.

C. W. C. KRAUSE, *Auditor.*

HAMBURG, 10th May, 1897.

VIII.

THE STATE DYNAMITE MONOPOLY.

Contract between the Government of the South African Republic and Lambertus Gerardus Vorstman, of Pretoria, concerning the carrying out of the State monopoly for the manufacture, sale, trade, and import and export of gunpowder, ammunition, dynamite, and all other explosives.

The Government of the South African Republic, acting with advice and consent of the Executive Council, in accordance with resolution dated 9th October, 1893, Article 573, being truly and lawfully represented by the Honourable the Acting State Secretary, Mr. Cornelis van Boeschoten, who in its name subscribes the same, and has been authorised to conclude this agreement, by resolution of the Hon. the First Volksraad, dated September, 1893, hereafter to be named the Government, of the one part, and Lambertus Gerardus Vorstman, of Pretoria, of the other part, have agreed as follows:—

ARTICLE 1. The Government appoints the second undersigned, to the exclusion of all other persons, as the sole agent for the carrying out of the monopoly for the manufacture, the importation and exportation, the trade in and the sale of gunpowder, fireworks, ammunition, dynamite, and other explosives of whatsoever nature. The agent shall have the right to establish a company for that purpose.

ARTICLE 2. The duration of this agency shall be for fifteen years from the date of this agreement.

Where nothing is said in this agreement, the regulations laid down by the resolutions of the Hon. the First Volksraad, dated 1st to 5th September, 1893, above-mentioned, and copy of which is annexed, shall be binding.

ARTICLE 3. The Government undertakes that, if it issues permits to persons, as mentioned in Article 2 of the regulations, the following conditions shall be of force:—

(*a.*) Permits shall only be issued to persons or companies who have given a declaration in writing that they require the explosives only for their own use, and the quantity shall in no case be greater than for a consumption of three months.

(*b.*) No permit shall be of force longer than four months from the day of issue.

(*c.*) All explosives under such permits will be subject to a special import duty of 8½d. (eightpence half-penny) per lb. above the ordinary *ad valorem* duty.

(*d.*) The Government shall, on application concerning same, nominate to the agent an official who will give him monthly information how many and to whom permits for the importation of dynamite, etc., have been granted, and whether and when such dynamite has been imported, in order to be able to take measures with respect to the quantities required for consumption.

ARTICLE 4. The rent of the gunpowder manufactory, as mentioned in Article 5 of the regulations, is hereby fixed at £3,750 per year.

The Government shall have the right to take back the gunpowder manufactory at any time during the continuance of this contract against payment to the agent for the extraordinary improvements that have been effected, and which have been approved of by the Government, provided these are serviceable, and at the value they have at the moment of taking over, wear and tear, etc., being taken into consideration.

In this case the payment of the rent shall only take place to the day of taking over.

ARTICLE 5. The maximum prices, as mentioned in Article 6 of the regulations, which the agent shall be allowed to charge, shall be reckoned as follows :—

For dynamite known as No. 1	...	...	...	£4	15	0
Do.	do.	No. 2	...	...	...	4	5	0
Do.	do.	No. 3	...	...	...	3	15	0

The agent shall, in supplying cartridges to the Government, be held and be obliged to charge no higher price than that for which the same can be imported from Europe, not including the import duties, and the Government reserves to itself the right to supply the burghers of this Republic with such cartridges as it may deem fit, but only for own consumption.

ARTICLE 6. The agent undertakes to erect the manufactories mentioned in Article 10 of the regulations, at such spots or places as the agent shall appoint in consultation with the Government, at the outside within two years and a half from the date of the signing of this contract.

The agent undertakes to pay the rent fixed in Article 11 of the regulations, and the sum of 5s. on each case of dynamite sold, every three months, accompanied by duly certified statements, as well as an amount not exceeding 20 per cent of the surplus. By surplus is understood the balance which remains after deductions of all cost, wear and tear, the usual writings off, and an interest of 8 per cent. (eight per cent.) on the capital.

The agent shall be bound to keep proper books, in commercial style, as is customary in institutions of this nature, and the Government shall have the right at all times to cause these books to be inspected by an official, or person, or a commission of officials or persons to be appointed thereto.

A proper balance sheet shall be made up annually, whereby, in terms of this Article, the surplus shall be shown. Thereafter a certified copy shall be sent to the Government, and the amount due to it shall be paid.

ARTICLE 7. The Government undertakes, with respect to the letters patent mentioned in Article 12 of the regulations, that the following stipulations shall be of force :—

In the event of the Government granting letters patent for any explosive, such letters of patent shall, however, not give the right to anybody else than to the agent, to whom the carrying out of these instructions is entrusted by the Government, to manufacture the material therein mentioned, and to sell the same within the boundaries of the South African Republic.

Should the Government or the agent deem it desirable to apply or bring into use the said invention, and should the Government in that case not be able to come to terms with the owner of, or the person entitled to, that invention with regard to the application of the same, then the parties, (Government and patentee) shall each nominate an arbitrator, whilst the third arbitrator, or umpire, if necessary, shall be appointed by the Chief Justice, whose decision shall be final.

ARTICLE 8. This agreement shall be of force within the territory of the South African Republic, in so far as it now extends or eventually may be extended.

If the territory of the South African Republic should in the future contain districts or provinces in which provision already has been made with respect to the materials or substances which form the subject of the agreement, it will depend upon the Government whether these instructions will also be applied to the new districts or provinces.

ARTICLE 9. Should the agent of the Government, during a defined period, not be able to satisfy the requirements for explosives within the Republic, in consequence of explosions, accidents, calamities, or other superior force and causes arising beyond the control or fault of the agent, the Government may import these materials until the agent shall be able to supply the required materials. In that case the Government gives to the agent the preference for the carrying out of the same. The agent shall be obliged, after any accident, as mentioned in this Article, to place the manufactories again in working order within the shortest possible time.

ARTICLE 10. If the Government imports any explosive, as mentioned in Article 13 of the regulations, it gives the preference to the agent to do such in its name.

ARTICLE 11. All persons employed by the agent are hereby freed from personal military service on commando or in the field, provided their contracts are drawn up with the condition that the Government shall have the right at any time, if deemed necessary, to take over the contracts, and they bind themselves to serve the period of service with the Government.

ARTICLE 12. Should the Government avail itself of Article 15a of the regulations, it shall be bound to buy the explosives required in the country in terms of this contract from the agent, costs of trade deducted.

The period in Article 15f of the regulations is hereby fixed at six months.

Should the agent, by his own interference, fault, negligence, or default, fail to carry out the conditions of this agreement, after having been required in writing to do so, and after having been allowed at the outside a period of six weeks to do so, the Government will have the right to cancel this agreement; if the default or neglect is to be attributed to malice, the Government will have the right to cancel this contract without any notice.

ARTICLE 13.—The agent is entitled to entrust the sale of the articles mentioned in this agreement to one or more persons.

ARTICLE 14.—The agent of the Government is obliged to pay import duties on the machinery and tools required in the carrying out of this agreement.

ARTICLE 15.—The Government may prescribe measures of precaution or safety with reference to the transport and storage of the said materials.

The Government shall not hinder the export of these materials, except for reasons of danger to the State, or other weighty reasons.

ARTICLE 16.—With reference to Article 17 of the regulations, the Government makes the following arrangement with the agent to the exclusion of everybody else :—

(a). During the time that the manufactories to be erected by the agent are not completed, the Government itself shall import all materials and substances required for the manufacture of dynamite and other explosives in the magazines of the agent, and, according to a tariff of prices, quality and quantity to be approved of by the Government, with this understanding, that this importation shall only continue during the time that the manufactory or manufactories shall not have been completed, and in any case not longer than during a period of two and a half years.

(*b*). The Government shall place the said materials and substances at the disposal of the agent for manufacture, trade and sale, according to the conditions above mentioned, and the agent shall manufacture, trade in and sell on the order and for account of Government, under the conditions above mentioned, in so far as they apply here.

(*c*). The agent shall send statements to the Government every month, detailing the manufacture, trade and sale, and shall pay to it all moneys received for the sale thereof, from which, after deduction of five shillings per case, and the moneys paid by the Government for the materials imported, the balance shall be handed to the agent.

ARTICLE 17.—The agent shall be obliged, within eight days after the signing of this contract, to give proper security for the due performance of the obligation to erect the manufactories mentioned herein, and the carrying out of the contract until the manufactories shall have been erected and shall be in working order, to an amount of £30,000, for which all his assets in this country shall be available, and proper deeds of hypothecation shall be passed.

ARTICLE 18.—All disputes as to the meaning or reading of this agreement that may arise between the parties shall be decided, to the exclusion of the ordinary judges, by arbitrators as in highest instance, and shall be finally binding on the parties.

Should the parties not be able to come to an amicable arrangement with regard to the interpretation of this agreement, the one party shall give notice in writing to the other, and whatever the questions of dispute arising out of this agreement, they shall submit the same to the decision of the arbitrators.

The parties then shall each nominate an arbitrator, who, together, shall nominate a third. Decisions shall be given at the outside within three months. If one of the parties should not in good time appoint an arbitrator, or in the event of the two arbitrators not agreeing in the choice of a third, then the Chief Justice, or his substitute in the Supreme Court of this Republic, shall make a nomination, the parties having been heard or summoned.

Thus done and contracted at Pretoria, this 25th day of the month of October, 1893, in the presence of the subscribed witnesses.

(Signed) C. VAN BOESCHOTEN,
Acting State Secretary.

(Signed) L. G. VORSTMAN.

Witnesses:

(Signed) W. E. HOLLARD.

(Signed) P. L. A. GOLDMAN.

Budget Statements of the South African Republic for the years 1882-96 *(inclusive.)*

RECEIPTS.

The material originally positioned here is too large for reproduction in this reissue. A PDF can be downloaded from the web address given on page iv of this book, by clicking on 'Resources Available'.

Budget Statements of the South African Republic for the years 1882-96 (Inclusive).

EXPENDITURE.

Year	Pensions	Collecting Public Revenue	Administration Justice	Education	Hospitals	Police and Defence	Rent	Transport	Post Office Expenses	Telegraph Office Expenses	Public Works	Sundry Services Account	Refund Licences	Interest	Repayment Loans	Salaries	War Department Expenses	Purchase of Properties	Special Expenditure	Swaziland Expenditure	Pipeline Expenditure	Fixed Deposits	Total	Withdrawn Deposits	Advances	Total	Balance not Deposited	TOTAL.

* Includes cost of expedition against Mphefu and Magoeba.

† Include bonus £389,000 for shares in the Pretoria-Pietersburg Railway Company, Limited.

X.

LIST OF ELECTORS

According to Returns from Field-Cornets throughout the S. A. R.

(Taken from the " State Almanac," for 1897.)

DISTRICTS.	MALES between 18 and 34 years of age.	MALES between 34 and 50 years of age.	MALES under 18 and over 50 years of age.
Bloemhof	467	311	124
Carolina ...	182	329	50
Ermelo ...	390	228	147
Heidelberg	915	471	192
Krugersdorp	—	900	—
Lichtenburg	580	268	157
Lydenburg	507	218	125
Marico ...	547	418	200
Middelburg	1,067	592	396
Piet-Retief	200	85	78
Potchefstroom	1,966	941	693
Pretoria ...	2,095	866	513
Rustenburg	1,352	499	436
Standerton	696	268	116
Utrecht ...	381	146	82
Vryheid ...	484	214	182
Wakkerstroom	560	265	179
Waterberg	455	184	93
Wolmaranstad	328	111	94
Zoutpansberg	626	347	210
Goldfields	511	331	122
Grand Total	14,259	8,152	4,089

XI.

STATISTICS OF WHITE POPULATION OF THE SOUTH AFRICAN REPUBLIC.

According to the latest Returns obtained.
(Taken from the State Almanac for 1897).

DISTRICTS AND DIGGINGS.	Males.	Females.	Total.
Barberton	3,500	2,900	6,400
Bloemhof...	2,000	1,600	3,600
Boksburg	3,200	2,100	5,300
Carolina	2,500	1,200	3,700
Ermelo	2,700	1,850	4,550
Heidelberg	5,770	2,050	7,820
Johannesburg (town)	32,387	18,520	50,907
„ (neighbourhood)	4,000	2,500	6,500
Krugersdorp	10,500	9,950	20,450
Lichtenburg	3,500	3,000	6,500
Lydenburg	1,500	1,250	2,750
Marico	3,500	3,000	6,500
Middelburg	5,500	4,000	9,500
Piet-Retief	600	560	1,160
Potchefstroom	12,600	12,300	24,900
Pretoria	15,700	14,600	30,300
Rustenburg	5,600	5,000	10,600
Standerton	3,800	3,750	7,550
Utrecht	1,750	1,100	2,850
Vrijheid	2,640	2,520	5,160
Wakkerstroom	6,000	5,700	11,700
Waterberg	2,600	2,300	4,900
Wolmaranstad	1,600	1,500	3,100
Zoutpansberg	4,500	4,200	8,700
Total	137,947	107,450	245,397

The area of the Transvaal is given at 120,000 square miles, which makes an average of 2·04 whites to the square mile and the average of the native population 5·18 to the square mile, and of whites and blacks 7·22 to the square mile.

XII.

STATISTICS AND CENSUS OF THE NATIVE POPULA-
TION OF THE S.A. REPUBLIC.

According to statements received.

(Taken from the State Almanac for 1897.)

DISTRICTS.	Number of Men.	Number of Women.	Number of Children.
Zoutpansberg (Klipdam, Kalkbank and Spelonken)	17,877	22,551	48,169
Waterberg	5,598	8,828	29,287
Lydenburg	6,591	9,332	8,706
Utrecht*	—	—	—
Marico	3,030	1,796	2,704
Piet-Retief	4,583	5,488	11,800
Middelburg	6,335	8,325	17,690
Rustenburg	5,484	5,466	13,173
Bloemhof, wijk Vaalrivier	359	367	915
Standerton	1,181	1,431	3,395
Ermelo	1,313	2,132	4,819
Vrijheid	5,984	9,066	13,753
Wakkerstroom, wijk No. 3.	1,081	1,541	2,920
Pretoria, wijken Krok. rivier and Witwatersrand	2,132	2,466	5,584
Lichtenburg	1,357	1,494	3,080
Heidelberg	1,622	1,561	2,612
Potchefstroom	2,687	2,523	7,830
Carolina	1,028	1,420	2,528
Krugersdorp	387	373	1,034
	68,629	86,160	180,099
Further estimate of population in Zoutpansberg	59,691	73,806	154,159
Total	128,320	159,966	334,258

*No Returns.

Total Native Population 622,544

κ 2

XIII.

THE PASS LAW.

LAW NO. 31, 1896.

Being amendment of Law No. 23, 1895.

Declared valid by the Hon. First Volksraad by Article 2289 of their minutes, dated 10th September, 1896, until the First Volksraad decides more particularly with regard to them in their next ordinary session.

WHEREAS it is deemed necessary to amend Law No. 23, 1895, so it is hereby enacted as follows:—

Regulations in terms of Article 88 of the Gold Law. For the purpose of facilitating and promoting the supply of native labour on the public diggings of this Republic, and for the better controlling and regulating of the natives employed, and the relations of employer and native labourer.

IT IS ENACTED:—

1. These regulations shall only after proclamation, as in Clause 2 provided, be of force and effect within the boundary of the proclaimed public diggings of this State, and shall, therefore, in no way be taken to interfere with Law No. 13 of 1880, 3 of 1876, and 6 of 1880, or with Law No. 22 of 1895 (Native Pass Law), which laws shall remain in full force and effect within the proclaimed gold fields, in so far as they do not conflict with the provisions of these regulations, these regulations being regarded as special additional laws for the area proclaimed. The area mentioned in the third clause of Article 153 of Law No. 21, 1896, shall also be regarded as coming under these regulations.

2. These regulations shall come into force and effect for such public diggings and private unproclaimed ground of this State as the State President, with the advice and consent of the Executive Council, shall from time to time determine, and shall by proclamation in the *Staatscourant* proclaim as coming under the operation thereof.

3. Such public diggings shall simultaneously with the proclamation of the above effect be deemed, for the purposes of these regulations, to be divided into as many labour districts as there shall for the time being be Mining Commissioners and judicial officers on such goldfields, and the labour district will have the same boundaries and be coterminous with the district of the jurisdiction of such Mining Commissioner or judicial officer; provided always that the Government shall have the right to declare any town within the proclaimed area as a separate labour district.

4. In these regulations the word "native" shall be deemed to apply to males of all the native and coloured races of South Africa.

Every native, on entering any district governed by these regulations, and being in possession of the pass required by existing pass law, shall, without unreasonable delay, repair to the district office and get a pass and a badge as hereinafter provided for, and in proceeding thither he shall be protected by the pass he holds.

Any servant travelling within his labour district on his employer's service will be protected if he, in addition to the pass and badge required by these regulations, has a free written pass in terms of Article 1 of Law 22 of 1895 (Native Pass Law).

5. Upon entering the boundaries of a proclaimed goldfield and private unproclaimed area falling within the operation of these regulations, a native shall be bound, before engaging himself to any employer, to repair to the office of the Mining Commissioner or to the office of the officer or officers appointed for the district, and there exchange his travelling pass, whether same be from within the Republic or from beyond the borders thereof, for a district pass of the form on schedule A.

6. The Mining Commissioner or pass officer appointed for the district shall enter in a register to be kept for the purpose, of the form of schedule B hereto, the name of the native, his tribe, chief, father, district or country, stature and marks, if any, etc., and he shall also number each native consecutively. Such registered number shall thereafter be the native's official mark so long as he remains within the district. All these particulars shall likewise be entered on the district pass, form schedule A.

7. In addition to the district pass to form A, the pass officer shall at the same time issue to each native a metal ticket or badge, on which shall be clearly stamped or impressed at the time of issue the native's registered number, the initial letters of the labour district, and year of issue. This ticket or badge shall be attached to a strong leather strap or buckle, and must be worn by the native round his left arm above the elbow, so as always to be clearly visible. Such district pass and badge shall be issued free of charge.

8. Such district pass and metal badge shall enable and authorise the native to whom it is issued, to seek employment within the labour district for which it is issued for a period of three days from the date of issue.

9. If the native fails to find employment within the prescribed three days from the date of issue of district pass, or after discharge by his last employer, he shall return to the Mining Commissioner or pass officer who issued the pass and badge, and may have an extension of a further three days endorsed thereon by the pass officer, on payment of a fee of two shillings; failing to find employment within the further three days, he shall return to the pass officer, and it shall be in the discretion of the pass officer or officers charged with the administration of these regulations to require from such native his district pass and metal badge, and in return issue to him an exit or travelling pass, in terms of Articles 8 and 9, and the native shall pass on to another district or return to his home.

10. The district pass and metal badge will hold good so long as the native remains in the labour district.

11. A native working on a proclaimed goldfield, and wishing to remove from one labour district to another, on such or any other proclaimed goldfields, or to his home, or to any part of the Republic, if beyond the labour district, shall first apply for leave to do so from the Mining Commissioner or other appointed pass officer in his district, and such leave shall be granted him, provided he then holds a district pass, in clear order, with metal badge, and that his last employer, if any, shall have filled in the full discharge required on the district pass, form A. Thereupon the Mining Commissioner or pass officer shall issue a travelling pass of the form set out in schedule C, in exchange for the district pass and the metal badge held by such native, on the payment by the native of a fee of one shilling.

12. The Mining Commissioner or pass officer shall register the date, number, and particulars of such travelling pass against the native's name and number in the

register, form schedule B, and shall immediately destroy the district pass and metal badge received from such native.

13. Upon arriving in any new labour district of a proclaimed goldfield, a native travelling under the pass above described shall be bound immediately to repair to the Mining Commissioner thereof, or other officer appointed for the purpose, and there obtain a district pass and metal badge in manner and of form above described.

14. Any native found in the labour district without the district pass of form A and metal badge, or without a travelling pass, or any defaulter under Article 9, shall be punishable by a fine of not exceeding £3, or not more than three weeks' imprisonment with hard labour for first offence, and for second offence a fine not exceeding £5, or not more than four weeks' imprisonment with hard labour and lashes, and at the discretion of the Court before whom he shall be convicted for every offence thereafter.

15. Any native who has lost his district pass or metal badge, or both, may apply to the district officer who issues the same for a new pass or badge in substitution for the one lost, and the district officer shall issue a new district pass or badge if he is satisfied of the identity and *bona fides* of the applicant by means of a letter from the last employer, if any : provided that the applicant shall pre-pay for such new pass or badge a fine of 5s.

16. Any native being in possession of, or using or counterfeiting a district pass, employer's pass, travelling or exit pass, or metal badge, or falsely stating that he has not previously been registered, or making any other false statement, or doing any act for the purpose of deceiving the pass officers or evading these regulations, and any native who shall transfer any of the passes or metal badges hereinbefore described to any other person, and any native who shall accept transfer, or make use, or be in possession of any pass or metal badge belonging to any other native, shall be deemed to be guilty of contravening these regulations, and shall, upon conviction, be punished by a fine of not exceeding £5, with imprisonment of not exceeding one month and lashes not exceeding 25.

17. The Government shall make arrangements as it may deem desirable, so that each labour district in a proclaimed goldfield shall use and issue a pass distinctive in colour from those of the other labour districts, and metal badges with initial letters of each district, in order to facilitate the detection of vagrants or natives moving in any labour district without a pass and badge for that district.

18. Any native leaving a labour district without the proper travelling pass of form C shall be liable to a fine not exceeding £3, or one month's imprisonment with hard labour, with or without lashes. Should it appear to the satisfaction of the Court that the native has left his last or any employer in breach of his contract, then the said fine may be increased to £5, and the said imprisonment to two months.

19. It shall not be lawful for any person within the proclaimed public diggings:—

   (a). To engage or employ any native unless he is provided with a clear district pass and corresponding metal badge at the time such native seeks employment.
   (b). To engage or employ any native unless his district pass shall show that he has been duly discharged by his last employer, if any.
   (c). To provide a monthly pass for a native labourer who is not *bona fide* in his service.
   (d). To act as agent or intermediary with regard to the issue and obtaining of passes and metal badges for native labourers according to this law.

20. Immediately after engagement the employer shall enter upon the district pass of such native engaged all the particulars as required on the face of the district pass,

form A.　And shall take from the native such district pass and issue instead thereof an employer's pass of form D.　This employer's pass shall be renewed monthly on the first day of each month, and for the first pass and each renewal thereof the native shall pay the sum of 2s. per month.　And the employer shall be liable to Government for such amounts of pass moneys on every native in his employ, and he shall further be responsible for and issue the passes monthly to each and every native employed, such passes to be supplied by and purchased from the Government.

21. The employer shall take possession of and be responsible for the safe-keeping of all district passes so long as the native remains in his or their employ, and on the termination of the native's service the employer shall enter upon the said district pass the particulars of such native's discharge as are required by the pass form, and then return the pass to the rightful owner thereof.

22. Any employer who shall be convicted of a breach or failure to comply with any of the provisions of Clauses 19 to 21, or illegally withholding district pass from, or coercing any native, shall, upon conviction, be punished with a fine of not less than five pounds, and not exceeding one hundred pounds for each and every breach or failure in respect of every native employed, or in default with imprisonment not exceeding six months, with hard labour.　In the event of the employer being a company or syndicate, then, and in such case, the manager shall be responsible.

23. Every employer employing more than twenty native labourers shall be obliged to keep a register according to schedule form F, and shall at the end of each month, and not later than the fifteenth day of the month following, fill in and send in a return to the Mining Commissioner, or pass officer of his district, of form F schedule, giving the registered numbers of badges and district passes, with name, etc., of all and every native engaged and discharged during that month.　Such returns shall be filed and kept by the pass officer for record and reference.

24. Every employer failing to comply with the foregoing regulations, or making false or fraudulent returns, shall be liable to a fine of not less than £5, and not exceeding £100.

25. Any person making use of the provisions of these regulations for the purpose of imposing on and defrauding a native labourer of the wages, rations, or advantages due to him, shall, upon conviction of such offence, be liable to a fine not exceeding £100, or three months' imprisonment, with or without hard labour.

26. Any person found guilty of forging, counterfeiting, or imitating any of the passes or metal badges issued under these regulations, or forging, counterfeiting, or imitating any stamp, seal, or signature, or any such stamps, seals, or passes orges, which may have been issued in terms thereof, and not being the employer described in such employer's pass or form, or any pass, or not being by the employer authorised so to do, but making or writing on such pass or badges any entry, name, or mark intended to defraud the Government officials, whose duty it shall be to issue or inspect such pass or badge, or to deprive the employer, if any, of the services of such native, or in any other way to defeat the provisions of these regulations, shall, on conviction of each and every or any such offence, be punishable by a fine not exceeding £100, or by imprisonment not exceeding three months, with or without hard labour.

27. The Government shall appoint such officers in each district as may from time to time be found necessary for the due and proper administration of these regulations. And shall further appoint special labour inspectors for each labour district, with power to summarily arrest all natives contravening these regulations.

The duties of such special labour inspectors shall *inter alia* be:—

    (a). To make regular and frequent inspections of registers of native labour kept by employers, to inspect all natives employed, to ensure that their badges are worn and in order, and, if need be, compare any or all such natives with the district pass filed by the employer.

(*b*) Inspect monthly passes of all such natives.

(*c*) To inspect employers' passes or district passes, and metal badges of all natives when and wherever met.

(*d*) Generally to see that the provisions of the law and these regulations are carried out.

(*e*) To make a proper report to the pass officer of their district of every inspection held by them in accordance with the above regulations, and to keep a proper diary of their work.

28. Any native found by the police or special labour inspectors without his proper badge, and either district, travelling, or employer's pass, or being a defaulter under Article 9, shall at once be arrested, and fined or punished by any qualified Court having jurisdiction in terms of these regulations.

29. All complaints by employers as to desertion of natives shall be communicated to the district officer, or the inspectors, whose duty it shall be to take the badge and pass numbers, names, etc., of such deserters, and do whatever may be necessary to arrest the deserters for punishment in terms of these regulations.

30. All complaints by natives against employers shall be made to the inspectors, who shall at once report to the district officer appointed for that purpose, whose duty it shall be to make a full and proper investigation into the cause of complaint without delay; and, if need be, submit the matter to the Public Prosecutor, who shall at once proceed against the employer under the provisions of these regulations.

31. All fines imposed under these regulations shall be paid to the Government of the South African Republic.

32. All contraventions of these regulations and of any of the provisions thereof shall be cognisable by any Court having jurisdiction under the Master and Servants' Law, No. 13 of 1880, and under Law No. 22 of 1895 (Native Pass Law), and in whose jurisdiction the offender may be found. And such Courts are authorised to adjudicate on all such contraventions, and to impose the fines and penalties in these regulations and the schedules thereof provided for. All complaints under the regulations shall be brought to trial within 48 hours after arrest; the Court, however, having the right to direct postponements.

These regulations shall not affect the validity of the Supplementary Regulations of the Johannesburg Sanitary Committee, published under Government Notice, No. 385, on the 8th November, 1893, but, on the contrary, such Supplementary Regulations shall remain in full force and effect, and natives licensed thereunder shall be exempt from the provisions of these regulations with regard to district passes, metal badges, and employers' passes, so long as they remain under the said regulations of the Sanitary Board.

33. All pass issuers appointed in terms of this law to the various labour districts shall be *ex officio* Justices of the Peace.

34. Law No. 23, 1895, is repealed.

35. This amended law comes into operation immediately after publication in the *Staatscourant.*

The various passes A, B, C, D, and E, published in the 1895 Report of the Chamber of Mines, are unaltered. Schedule F had not been drawn up at the end of the year.

XIV.

Schedule of Native Wages Witwatersrand.

Agreed to at a combined meeting of Mining Companies, May, 1897.

Mine.	s.	d.	Mill.	s.	d.
Machine helpers	1	8	Elevator boys	2	0
Hammer boys	1	6	Vanner boys	2	0
Shovel boys	1	3	Mill boys (12 hours) ...	2	0
Tram boys (10 feet trucks) ...	1	2	Mill boys (eight hours) ...	1	4
Tram boys (16 feet trucks) ...	1	6	Blanket and sluice boys ...	2	0
Dry shaft and winze boys ...	1	8	Crusher boys	1	4
Wet shaft boys	2	0	Surface trammers	1	9
Wet shaft boys (when developing only)	2	6	Mule drivers	2	6
Boys cutting hitches for timber	1	6	**Cyanide.**		
Timber boys	1	2			
Stope gangers' assistants ...	2	0	Solution shed boys	1	4
Station boys (where white man employed)	1	2	Boys (filling and discharging)	1	9
			Zinc cutters	1	6
Station boys (where no white man employed)	2	6	Tramming residues... ...	1	4
Air hoist drivers	2	0			
Pumpman's assistants ...	1	8	**General.**		
Platelayer's assistants ...	1	6	Fitters' boys	1	6
Pipeman's assistants ...	1	6	Blacksmiths' boys (strikers) ...	2	6
			Blacksmiths' boys (helpers) ...	1	4
Surface.			Carpenters' boys	1	2
			Masons' boys	1	4
Stokers (12 hours)	2	6	Police	2	6
Stokers (eight hours) ...	1	8	Compound cooks	2	0
Engine cleaners	1	6	Drill packers	1	0
Sorting boys	2	0	Drill sorters	1	6
Head-gear boys (where white man employed)	1	4	Surface labourers	1	2
			Office and store boys ...	2	6
Head-gear boys (where no white man employed)	2	6	Assay office boys	2	6
			Coal boys (off-loading) ...	1	6

Notes.—Timber boys assisting in timbering shafts, to be paid at the rate of wet and dry shaft boys.

Seven and one-half per cent. of the natives employed may be paid special rates.

Month to be reckoned as consisting of at least 30 working days.

XV.

THE LIQUOR LAW

OF THE SOUTH AFRICAN REPUBLIC.

ACT No. 17, of 1896.

Being an amendment of Act No. 13, of 1892.

As amended and revised by Acts No. 12 of 1893, No. 21 of 1894, and No. 18 1895, defining the manner in which wines and spirituous or malt liquors includi? kaffir beer may be sold.

Approved of by resolution of the Honourable the Second Volksraad, Article 8? dated 22nd July, 1896, and accepted as notice by the Honourable the First Volksraa? under Article 1150 of its minutes, dated the 7th of August, 1896.

No liquor to be sold without a licence.
1. No one may sell, dispose of, or trade in wines, malt or spirituous liquo? including kaffir beer, without being duly provided with a special licence, as hereinaft? set forth.

Fines and penalties.
Any person contravening this Article, shall, on the first offence, be punished wi? a fine of not less than £36, and not exceeding £75, or, failing payment, with impriso? ment, with or without hard labour, not exceeding six months for the first offence ; ? a second offence with a fine of not less than £150, or, failing payment, with impriso? ment, with or without hard labour, for not less than twelve months ; on a third offen? with a fine of not less than £300, or, failing payment, with imprisonment, with ? without hard labour, for not less than 18 months.

Growers and producers require no licence.
The owner or tenant of a farm or piece of ground, or the person authorised ? him to convert the produce thereof into wine or spirituous liquor, may, however, ? that farm or piece of ground, sell the produce thereof, but then in quantities of n? less than one bottle.

They may remove and sell.
2. The person referred to in the last paragraph of Article 1 shall further also ? permitted to remove and sell his wines or other spirituous liquors in the above-me? tioned quantity without licence, except on premises, or within the limits of villag? or stand townships, or within three miles of any mining works.

Such person will, however, be permitted to sell without licence by wholesale o? public markets, and also to licensed liquor dealers, provided he is provided with ? certificate from the Fieldcornet of his ward, or Landdrost of his district, showing th? the wines or spirituous liquors were manufactured on the farm or piece of groun? mentioned in the last paragraph of Article 1.

Licences where granted.
3. No licence for the sale of spirituous liquors, by retail or wholesale, shall ? granted, except in established and acknowledged towns and villages, and digging? under Government control.

[By resolution of the Second Volksraad on the 22nd July, 1896, the operation of this Article w? suspended for 12 months, in order to give the public an opportunity of expressing their views.]

4. The licences referred to in Article 1 shall be the following:— Licences.

(a) Licence for the sale by wholesale. Under this licence not less than two Wholesale. gallons in vessels, or twelve bottles may be sold.

(b) Licence for a bottle store. Under this licence no sale by smaller measure than Bottle store. by the half-bottle shall be permitted, and always with the understanding that the liquor sold under this licence shall not be consumed on the premises for which licence is granted.

(c) Licences to sell by retail. Any quantity of liquor may be sold under this Retail. licence, and be consumed on the premises for which licence is granted.

(d) Licences for roadside hotels. This licence is only granted for roadside hotels. Roadside hotels. These hotels shall be at least six miles distant from any town, village, or stand-township, seat of a Landdrost, Mining Commissioner, or resident Justice of the Peace.

(e) Licence for the sale of malt liquors by retail. This applies to beer-halls Malt liquors. where only malt liquors are sold. Said liquors may be sold under this licence in quantities of less than a bottle, and may be consumed on the premises for which the licence is granted.

(f) Licensed liquor dealers contravening the conditions stipulated in their licence, Penalties. shall be punished with the penalties laid down in Article 19 of this Act.

5. Anyone exchanging or selling wines, spirituous or malt liquors to any coloured Selling to coloured persons. on, shall be subject to the penalties laid down in Article 1 of this Act.

6. It is prohibited to give wine, spirituous or malt liquors, including kaffir beer, Giving to coloured persons. oloured persons on diggings under Government control. Any person contravening stipulation in this Article shall be punished with a fine not exceeding £500, or, ng payment, with imprisonment, with or without hard labour, not exceeding one .

7. The licences are issued for not longer than one year, ending with the official Term of licence. , that is the 31st December. Licences may be issued for one or more quarters. The payment for licences shall be as follows :—

(a) Licence for selling by wholesale, £25 per annum ; £9 per quarter. Licence fees.
(b) Licence for a bottle store, £40 per annum ; £12 per quarter.
(c) Licence for selling by retail, £75 per annum ; £22 10s. per quarter.
(d) Licence for a roadside hotel, £35 per annum ; £10 per quarter.
(e) Licence for selling malt liquors, £25 per annum ; £9 per quarter.
(f) The Government shall have power to authorise the reduction of the amount for retail licences granted by the local Commissioner in small villages of not more than 100 white male inhabitants above 16 years, to the sum of £40 per annum and £12 per quarter, provided the applicant has proper lodging for six persons, and stabling for eight horses, mules, or donkeys.

8. No licence is required for the brewing of malt liquors or distilling of liquor ; but No licence required for brewing and distilling, but wholesale licence to sell liquor. wers, distillers, or others, excepting persons mentioned in the third paragraph of icle 1, who sell such brewed or distilled liquors, shall take out a wholesale licence the sale of such liquor, or be subject to a fine for the sale of liquor without licence erms of Article 1 of this Act. To obtain this licence no application need be made he commission mentioned in Article 9 of this Act.

9. There shall be a commission in each district and on every public digging to Licensing Commission. sider the applications for liquor licences, which commission shall be styled " The mission for Liquor Licences."

10. This commission shall be constituted as follows :—On the public diggings the Constitution of Commission. cial Landdrost, and where there is no Special Landdrost the Mining Commissioner,

In the districts, the Landdrost of the district, who shall also be *ex officio* chairma
the commission, and who shall be assisted by four members to be appointed by

Term of office.
Government, after consultation with the State Attorney. This commission shall
appointed for a period not exceeding two years with this understanding
regardless of the date of their appointment, the Government and the State Attor
shall, on or before the 1st December of every two years, appoint new members.
retiring members may be re-appointed.

Secretary of Commission.
The chairman shall recommend someone to the Government to act as secretary

Town Council to appoint two members.
Where there is a town council on any proclaimed goldfield or stand-township
in any other town or village, such town council shall have the right to nominate
to appoint two members out of their number, who shall be added to the Commiss
for Liquor Licences.

Three members a quorum.
11. Three members of this commission shall form a quorum. When the v
are equal the chairman shall have a casting vote, and in the event of there being

Casting vote.
quorum on the day and at the hour appointed by the chairman, the chairman s
have the right to adjourn the commission till a day appointed by him, of whicl
fresh notice must be given by him to the members.

Commission to sit quarterly.
The commission shall sit on the second Monday in the months of March, Ju
September, and December, or as soon as possible thereafter, to deal with applicati
for licences, etc.

No special sittings.
No special sittings of the commission shall be held.

Remuneration.
12. The members of the liquor commission shall receive a remuneration of
each for each day of sitting, and the secretary of the said commission £2 for each
of sitting and 2s. 6d. for each application.

Who shall not sit on Commission
13. The following persons shall not be eligible to be chosen or appointed, o
elected or appointed as such, shall not be able to remain acting as members of
Commission for Liquor Licences :—

(a) The holder of any licence for the sale of intoxicating liquors.
(b) Any brewer or distiller.
(c) Any person connected with or interested in a partnership with any holder
such licence as aforesaid, or with any brewer or distiller.
(d) Any person employed either directly or indirectly as an agent for
purpose of applying for a licence for any other person, for any partner
for any person thus employed as an agent.
(e) No person, the proprietor of a place for which a liquor licence has alrea
been granted, or for which application for a licence is being made.
(f) No police officer.
(g) No person, either the proprietor or holder of any property, or the agent
manager of, or a partner in, any trade or business carried on upon a
property in possession of a liquor licence, or who has made application fo
liquor licence, or the holder of any bond on such property, shall take part
the discussion or consideration of any application for or concerning a
licence upon such property.
(h) An un-rehabilitated insolvent.
(i) A person who, here or elsewhere, has had judgment against him of more th
six months' imprisonment. Any person who accepts or continues in t
appointment as member of a Commission for Liquor Licences, contrary to tl
Article, shall be punished with a fine not exceeding £500, and imprisonme
not exceeding three years with or without hard labour.

Procedure *re* application for licence.
14. For the obtaining of a licence legalizing the sale of wines, spirituous or m

ors within this Republic, the applicant must for that purpose first send in an
lication to the secretary of the Commission for Liquor Licences of the district or
diggings in which he desires to carry on his business. The secretary shall at once
ster the same in a book kept for the purpose, and have the same published as set
h in Article 15, and lay the same before the commission at its first sitting.

The application must be accompanied by an amount sufficient to cover the costs
ublication, and carry a stamp of 12s. 6d.

15. The application for the abovementioned purposes, shall, at least six weeks *When applica-*
ore the sitting of the commission, be handed in to the secretary of the commission *tion must be sent in.*
liquor licenses for the district or diggings in which the place is situate, for which
lication has been made. The secretary shall further cause the application to be
ted on the office door of the official entrusted with the criminal jurisdiction, as also *Publication.*
the *erf* or on the house or room for which licences are asked, and shall cause it to be
lished once at least in one of the local newspapers, if there are such, in the Dutch
guage, and once in the *Staatscourant*, to appear at least a month before the sitting
he commission.

All objections and protests against the granting of any application must be sent *Objections and*
n writing to the secretary, and notice of the same must be given to the applicant *protests.*
the person or persons objecting. This must be done personally or by registered
er at least five days before the sitting of the commission.

This stipulation shall not apply to objections made by officials of the State, or
cials of any town council.

Applicants for liquor licences must appear personally before the Commission for *Applicants must*
uor Licences. *apply person-ally.*

It shall be permitted to any applicant to be represented before the commission,
only by advocates, attorneys, or law-agents, duly licensed and admitted according
the laws of the land.

16. The granting of licences for the sale of any kinds of liquors on any ground *Where licences*
en out as a mynpacht, claim, bewaarplaats, machine-stand, or water-right; or on *prohibited.*
nds situate on any of the said localities; or on ground reserved in terms of Article
of Law No. 19 of 1895 (Gold Law); or in any compound, is totally prohibited.

17. No liquor licences shall be granted to— *Licences refused to*

(*a*) A person who has had judgment against him, here or elsewhere, of more than
    six months' imprisonment.
(*b*) Any person who is not residing in the South African Republic.
(*c*) An un-rehabilitated insolvent.
(*d*) Any person below 21 years of age.

Should it afterwards transpire that a licence has been granted to, or transferred *Licences null and*
any person incapacitated as above set forth, the licence shall be considered as null *void.*
d void, and the building in which the business was carried on shall be closed
thwith upon instructions of the Landdrost or official entrusted with the criminal
isdiction. Any licence-money paid therefor shall not be refunded by the
vernment. To a person whose application for a liquor licence has been refused by *Licences refused*
commission, because of contravention of the Liquor Law, no licence shall be
nted within two years after such refusal. In the event of any licence being
celled by judicial sentence, no licence shall be granted for the same premises for the *Licences can-*
e of wines, spirituous or malt liquors for a period of two years from the date of such *celled.*
gment.

When a licence is, in terms of this Article, declared forfeited, and the licence-
der notes an appeal, the licence shall, notwithstanding the appeal, be considered

forfeited until the High Court shall decide thereon, and the building or buildings sh
be closed immediately, and the sale of wines and spirituous or malt liquors prohibit

No licence to coloured person. No liquor licence whatsoever shall be granted to coloured persons.

Complaints of police. The commission shall, in the hearing of the applications for liquor licences, ta
into consideration the complaints of the police and the detectives, as also
complaints of the Inspector of Mines on the diggings, and limit the number of licen

Licences in proportion to population. in proportion to the population of an area, so that no more than four licences shall
granted to a community ranging from one to 500 persons, and not more than o
licence for every 400 above the 500 white male persons over 16 years of age.

No reasons given for refusing applications. The commission shall have the right to refuse new licences, or the renewal
existing licences, without stating any reasons. The commission may grant a licer
under such conditions as they shall stipulate, which conditions must be stated
the licence. When the commission consider it necessary, they shall have the right

Applicants examined under oath. examine any person under oath, and if it is discovered that the witness has mad
false declaration, he shall be held to have committed the crime of perjury and
punished according to law.

[The operation of Article 17, was suspended by resolution of the First Volksraad on 29th Septemb
1896, in terms of the following minute of the Executive Council].

RESOLUTION OF THE EXECUTIVE COUNCIL, ARTICLE 808,
DATED 22ND SEPTEMBER, 1896.

"Under discussion: Minute R 12376, 1896, containing a letter from t
chairman of the Liquor Commission at Johannesburg and a petition of wholesa
dealers in spirituous liquors, both in reference to Article 17 of the Liquor La
further, four memorials from burghers of Pretoria and Zoutpansberg in relation
the application of the Liquor Law;

"The Executive Council *considering* the petition of several firms
Johannesburg, that have for some years been engaged in the wholesale traffic
spirituous liquors, in reference to the application of Law No. 17 of 1896 (t
Liquor Law) and especially Article 17 of this Law;

"*Considering* that according to the petition sent in, a strict application
Article 17 of said Law on 1st January, 1897, the date on which the Law is to cor
into force, will cause great losses to several *bona fide* dealers, to their employe
and to other persons, who stand in relation to them;

"*Considering* that it is the desire of the Executive Council to devote
attention as much as possible to the alleged facts, and if possible to meet them;

"*Considering* that it is desirable to make transition regulations, previous
strict application of the letter of the Law;

"*Considering* the contents of the memorials mentioned above in reference
the enforcement of the Law;

"*Considering* that Article 17 of the said Law, as amended, has not been la
before the people for approval in the usual way;

"*Considering*, in conclusion, that according to the resolution on this matt
Article 876, dated 22nd July, 1896, the Honourable Second Volksraad h
suspended the clause relating to the granting of licences to hotels along the roa
in order to have it laid before the people for approval, while on the other hand
was explicitly resolved that the prohibition of the sale of liquor to natives shou

in any case be applied, but no special resolution was taken in reference to Article 17 of the Liquor Law;

"*Resolves:* to request the Honourable First Volksraad,

"1. To authorise the Executive Council to suspend the enforcement of Article 17 of the Liquor Law (Law No. 17, of 1896).

"2. To instruct the Executive Council to draw up as soon as possible according to circumstances, transition regulations in reference to the licences that are to be issued and all matters in relation thereto, with power to enforce these transition regulations immediately, in so far as may seem necessary even in the course of this year.

"3. To instruct the Executive Council to offer at the next session of the Honourable Second Volksraad after proper publication in the *Staats Courant*, according to law, definite draft regulations in reference to the granting of licences."

18. The chairman shall have the right, subject to Article 17 of this Act, to trans- *Transfer of licences.* icences from one person to another for the same premises where such business is ed on.

For each such transfer, a fee of ten shillings shall be charged, to be affixed in *Transfer fee.* ps to the application.

The commission shall have the right to transfer previously-granted licences from place to another, on payment of ten shillings in stamps as above set forth.

Of this application for transfer, six weeks' notice shall be given as set forth in cle 15 of this Act.

When through fire or other unforeseen circumstances, such is urgently required, *Transfer in case of fire.* chairman of the Liquor Licensing Commission shall have the right, subject to sub- ent decision of the commission, to transfer a licence from one place to another e, building, or room.

In special cases, the chairman of the Liquor Licensing Commission, has the right *Special licences for short periods.* rant permission to licensed liquor dealers on application, to sell liquor also at other es for a period not exceeding six days, on payment of £1 per day in stamps affixed ie permit.

19. Any person holding a licence for the sale of wines, spirituous or malt liquors, *Selling contrary to licence.* carrying on his business in a manner or at a place contrary to his licence, shall be ished for the first offence with a fine not exceeding £50; for the second offence a fine not exceeding £100: and for the third offence with a fine not exceeding 0; and failing payment of these fines, the penalty shall be imprisonment, with or out hard labour, not exceeding three, six and twelve months respectively. No sfer of a licence shall be granted within six months after the conviction of the er of the licence for contravention of one of the stipulations of this Act.

20. The decisions of the commission regarding the approval or otherwise of *Decisions of Commission.* ces, transfer thereof, etc., shall be communicated as speedily as possible to the ial entrusted with the issuing of the licences, and to the officials of the prosecution in the limits of whose jurisdiction the licence shall be granted, who shall then act ccordance with the decisions of the commission.

21. As soon as a retail licence, or a licence for roadside hotel shall have been *Surety bond.* ited to any person who has applied for the same, such person shall pass a surety- l before the official empowered to issue licences, and who is hereby authorised to pt such surety-bond for the sum of £200 sterling, with two good sureties who l be jointly responsible.

Form of surety bond in term of schedule A.

Must affix sign board in conspicuous place

22. Any person having obtained any licence, either for wholesale or retail aforementioned, shall place or affix in a conspicuous place to the wall on the out of the building where such wines, spirituous or malt liquors are sold, a signboard which, in large, visible and legible letters of at least two inches long, shall be pai his full name, or in case of partnerships, the name or title of the firm or partners and underneath this name or title, the words " Licensed Dealer " or " Dealer in wi spirituous or malt liquors, by wholesale or retail," as the case may be, and shall l such signboard in good repair during the continuance of such licence, and in def of affixing such signboard, or of keeping the same in a good state as aforesaid, he s be liable to and incur a fine not exceeding £5 ; and in case the full amount of the : imposed, together with the costs, be not paid within three days of the decision of judge, then to imprisonment not exceeding one month, unless the fines and cost previously paid. But nothing in the law contained shall be construed as if any si board were required to be affixed and placed on an hotel, boarding or lodging-ho or club.

Penalty for illegally affixing signboard.

23. Anyone who has obtained no such licence as aforesaid, and who shall a any such signboard on front of his house, shop, or store, or any other place, shall punished with a fine not exceeding £50, and in default of payment, imprisonm not exceeding three months.

No coloured person can be employed to sell or give.

24. A licensed liquor dealer shall not be permitted to employ a coloured per behind any bar, to sell, give, or dispose of wines, spirituous or malt liquors to : customer.

Upon a contravention of the above regulation, the holder of the licence will punished with a fine not exceeding £25, and in default of payment, imprisonm with or without hard labour, not exceeding three months.

No back or side door to be used as entrances or exits.

25. A licensed canteen, bar, or beer-hall keeper in a town, village, stand-tov ship, or diggings, shall not allow any customers to enter or leave his apartment aside for the sale of drink by a back or side door, or through a door which conn with a shop or business, under penalty for the first offence of a fine not exceeding £ or, in default of payment, imprisonment not exceeding one month ; for a sec offence a fine of £20, or, in default of payment, imprisonment not exceeding th months ; for a third offence, a fine not exceeding £50 sterling, or, in default of p ment, imprisonment not exceeding six months, with forfeiture of licence.

No other business on licensed premises.

26. It shall not be lawful for a licensed liquor dealer to carry on any business the same room, other than the sale of liquors under this law, and tobacco, cigars, : cigarettes by retail.

It is prohibited to serve liquor, either for money or otherwise, on the sa premises where a shop business is being carried on.

On a contravention, the holder of the licence shall be punished with a fine : exceeding £25, and, in default of payment, imprisonment not exceeding two month

Written permission required to allow another person to manage.

27. In case of a licensed dealer in liquors under the provisions of this Act, alle ing another person to manage or supervise the building or buildings for which, or which, he holds a licence to sell spirituous or malt liquors, during his absence or any other way, for more than 28 consecutive days, without previous written pern sion of the Landdrost or official of the criminal jurisdiction, he shall be liable to a 1 not exceeding £50, and, in default of payment, imprisonment not exceeding th months.

Temporary transfer of licence.

28. Upon written request of both parties, signed in the presence of two witnes the Landdrost or official of the criminal jurisdiction shall have the right to temporai

...sfer any licence under this Law to another person to manage the said business as ...resaid for the licensed dealer in liquors, for a period to be fixed by him. During ...h period, such manager shall be responsible for all contraventions of this Law, or ... subsequent laws, regulating the sale of liquor, in a similar manner as set forth in ...icle 49 of this Law.

29. No licence-holder under this Act will be permitted to sell liquor or keep open ... rooms or apartments in his building or buildings for the sale of such liquors as ...resaid, or permit liquor to be drunk or used therein during any part of the Sunday, ...d Friday, Easter Monday, Whit Monday, Dingaan's Day, and Christmas Day, or ...ween the hours of nine in the evening and six in the morning of any other day, ...ept in the hotels, boarding and eating-houses approved by the commission, wherein ...1or may be supplied to lodgers and boarders at meals as required by them; with ... understanding that nothing contained in this Article shall have reference to the ...e of liquor in clubs approved by the Government. *No liquor to be sold on Sundays, &c., or between 9 p.m. and 6 a.m.*

Contraventions of the above stipulations will be punished with a fine not ...eeding £25, or, in default of payment, imprisonment with or without hard labour ... exceeding two months.

30. The Landdrost or official entrusted with the criminal jurisdiction shall have ... right to grant to licensed retail liquor dealers, permission to keep open after 9 ...1. until 12 p.m. on working days. This permission may be granted for a period not ...eeding one month, with right of withdrawal. The permit shall carry a stamp ...culated at 2s. 6d. per day. Any person keeping open without permission as above-...ntioned, shall be punished with a fine not exceeding £25, or, in default of payment, ...prisonment with or without hard labour not exceeding two months. *Permit to keep open till 12 p.m. on working days.*

31. Any coloured person found in possession of wine, spirituous or malt liquors, ...vided he is not lawfully carrying such wine, spirituous or malt liquors for his ...ster, shall be punished with imprisonment, with or without hard labour, not ...eeding three months; lashes may also be imposed, not exceeding twenty-five. The ...uor found in his possession shall be declared forfeited for the benefit of the public ...enue. *Coloured persons in possession of wine, &c.*

32. Any person who issues a written consent or a permit to any native not in his ...ploy, or who falsifies any written consent or permit, or any native who issues such ...rmit either for himself or for others, shall be punished with a fine not exceeding ...00, or imprisonment, with or without hard labour, not exceeding six months. In ...e case of natives, lashes may also be added, not exceeding twenty-five. *Permits to natives prohibited*

33. No person shall, with or without a licence, sell, give, exchange, or in any ...1er way dispose of, wines, spirituous or malt liquors, to any child under 16 years, or ... any person already under the influence of strong or intoxicating liquor, under ...nalty of a fine not exceeding £50, and, in default of payment, imprisonment, with or ...thout hard labour, not exceeding six months. *Persons under 16 years of age cannot be supplied with wines, &c., or persons under influence of liquor.*

34. No person shall, with or without licence, give or in any other way dispose ... or hand out wine, spirituous or malt liquors to any person after being warned by ...e Landdrost or official entrusted with the criminal jurisdiction, or by the husband or ...fe or any other relation of such person, or by any other person interested in ...m, that he or she is in the habit of getting intoxicated, and after being requested by ...ch Landdrost or official entrusted with the criminal jurisdiction, relation or other ...terested person, not to sell or dispose of wine or any other intoxicating liquor to ...ch person as aforesaid. Any contravention of the stipulations of this Article or ...y portion thereof, shall be punished for the first offence with a fine not exceeding *No liquor to person habitually intoxicated.*

£15, or imprisonment, with or without hard labour, not exceeding three months ; a
for every subsequent offence, imprisonment not exceeding six months, with or with
hard labour ; and shall be liable in addition to pay compensation for fines or any ot
injury to the person to whom he shall have sold or handed such drink as afores:
and which such person may have incurred in consequence thereof ; as also to]
compensation for all damages which such person, acting under the influence of liqu
has occasioned or caused to any other person, or to the property of any other person.
case of any sale of wines, spirituous or malt liquors in any case as aforementioned
credit, the purchase amount shall not be recoverable in any Court of Law.

Accomodation to be provided by roadside hotels 34A. In future no licence for roadside hotels shall be renewed, unless the ap{
cant produces a certificate from the Fieldcornet of his ward, or Landdrost of
district, declaring that on the place for which the renewal is desired, there is pro{
accommodation for six persons and stabling for eight horses, mules or donkeys.

In case of new applications, the party to whom a roadside hotel licence has b{
grante1, shall be bound to provide proper accommodation for people and animals
above set forth within two months from the date of the granting of such licence.

Failing compliance with the stipulations contained in section 1 of this article, t
licence shall be refused by the commission.

Failing compliance with section 2 of this article, the licence shall be withdra\
by the commission or Landdrost.

Hotel, boarding or lodging house licences. 35. No hotel, boarding or lodging house licence, in terms of Act No. 13 of 18{
will be issued in towns, villages, or public diggings, for buildings in which wines a
spirituous or malt liquors are sold, without the consent of the commission, who sh:
first satisfy themselves that the buildings are suitable for that purpose, and that t
business conducted therein is that of a *bona fide* hotel, boarding or lodging house.

Right of entry in premises in cases of breach of the peace. 36. For the better maintenance of public peace and order, it shall be lawful f
any Landdrost, Justice of the Peace, Fieldcornet, or police officer, at all times to ent
upon any building, *erf*, place or stand within his jurisdiction, belonging to any licens
liquor dealer where any uproar or breach of the peace is taking or has taken pla{
or whenever persons may be found there at hours and on days forbidden by the la
or which may be found to be frequented by men and women of acknowledged b:
character, in order to remove or to arrest, or take into safe custody, any uproario{
peace-disturbing, or drinking persons found there, not being *bona fide* residents therei
and should the holder of the licence of any such house or his representative or su
ordinate refuse to allow any of the above-mentioned officials to enter, or hinder
resist them in the execution of their duty, he shall be punished with a fine n
exceeding £50, or in default of payment, imprisonment with or without hard labo{
not exceeding six months.

It is further understood that in case of refusal to allow the officials aforemention{
to enter, they shall have the right to enter the place by force.

Right to close licensed house in case of breach of the peace. 37. The Landdrost or official entrusted with the criminal jurisdiction, or a{
Justice of the Peace, Fieldcornet, or Assistant Fieldcornet, shall have the right, wh{
any disturbance or breach of the peace takes place, or has taken place, to close up,
to have any places where liquor is sold closed up, for a period not exceeding one mont
and should any person keep open against the order of the said official, he shall ?
punished with a fine not exceeding £50, and, in default of payment, imprisonment wi{
or without hard labour, not exceeding three months, and his licence may be declar{
forfeited.

The official above-mentioned shall in such case within three days send a full
t, accompanied by all the documents, to the State Attorney, who is hereby
prised, should he think fit to reduce the above stipulated period.

38. Any person found by the Landdrost, Fieldcornet, Justice of the Peace, or *Drunken persons may be arrested without a warrant.*
e officer, in a state of drunkenness, or drunk and incapable, or drunk and disturb-
he peace, whether in a street, road or lane, or in a public building, store, shop,
or anywhere else, may be arrested without a warrant, and should this occur in
vening, be locked up in gaol or in a reformatory, and shall in any case without
be brought before the Landdrost or Justice of the Peace the following day or as
as possible thereafter, provided it is not a Sunday or public holiday. Every such
n shall, if found guilty, be fined a sum not exceeding £1 for the first offence and,
fault of payment, imprisonment with or without hard labour, and with or without
diet, not exceeding fourteen days ; and in case of repeated contraventions with a
not exceeding £5, and in default of payment, imprisonment with or without hard
r and with or without spare diet, not exceeding one month. In cases of natives
arrested, lashes may also be added, not exceeding fifteen for the first offence, and not
ding twenty-five for subsequent offences.

39. Any Landdrost or official having similar jurisdiction, Public Prosecutor, *Search warrants may be issued if well grounded suspicion exists.*
dent Justice of the Peace, Justice of the Peace or Fieldcornet, shall, if satisfied by
ffidavit that there exists a well-grounded suspicion that at any place in any build-
room, or in any vehicle whatsoever, wine, spirituous or malt liquors are sold or
with the intent to sell, without the owner, occupier, or caretaker holding a
ce under this Law, be authorised to issue a warrant to search the house. The
n or persons executing this search warrant shall have the right if necessary to
the house or place, or vehicle mentioned in the warrant by force, and to seize
wines, spirituous or malt liquors, together with the casks or bottles and cases
h contain the liquors, and to take into lawful custody the person or persons
hose possession such liquors are found.

The owner, occupier or assignee as abovementioned, if found guilty, shall be
shed in terms of Article 1 of this Act, and everything which has been seized shall
orfeited for the benefit of the public revenue, with the understanding however, that
easonable expenses of seizure shall be compensated out of the proceeds of the goods
d.

40. Whenever any person shall give information under oath to the Landdrost, Resi- *Procedure in cases of suspected persons*
Justice of the Peace, or official having similar jurisdiction, and shall show reasonable
nds why he suspects anyone of selling any of the liquor aforementioned without
ence, it shall be lawful for such Landdrost, Resident Justice of the Peace, or official
similar jurisdiction, within his jurisdiction to summon such suspected person
re him, as also any other person whom such official may consider able to give good
ence in such case to be examined before him, on the complaints against such a
ected person, and should such persons thus summoned as witnesses refuse to
ear or refuse to be examined under oath and give evidence as aforesaid, it shall be
ful for the said Landdrost, Resident Justice of the Peace, or other official as afore-
tioned, to place every such offender in custody for a term not exceeding one month,
ill such time as he shall no longer refuse to give evidence as aforesaid.

41. Any Landdrost or official having similar jurisdiction and any Resident Justice *Dealing contrary to provisions of this act.*
he Peace shall be authorised if reasonable grounds of suspicion are brought to his
ce that any person is dealing in liquor contrary to the provisions of this Act, to
t a search warrant to search any shop or other premises where it is suspected
or is kept.

L 2

42. Any Landdrost or official having similar jurisdiction, Resident Justice of Peace, Justice of the Peace, Fieldcornet or Public Prosecutor, Chief of the Police Chief of the Detective Department, or any police officer authorised by then writing, shall have the right to enter any house or room where wine, spirituous malt liquors are sold, and demand inspection of the licence. When this is not duced and no just reasons are given for the non-production thereof, the licensed li seller shall be punished with a fine not exceeding £10, or with imprisonment not ceeding one month.

43. Whenever any licensed dealer shall be tried for any contravention of this he shall hand his licence into court. This document shall be sufficient proof that b the licensed liquor seller meant in the case in question. Should he be found gu the Court shall endorse the judgment at the back thereof, but in case the judgment quashed on appeal, such shall be endorsed on the back thereof by the Lower Co Should the accused not produce his licence or give no valid reasons, he shall at same trial and without the necessity of any further proceedings be punished wit fine not exceeding £10, and, in default of payment, imprisonment not exceeding month.

When a licensed liquor dealer shall be summoned for a contravention of regulation of this Act or any subsequent Acts regulating the sale of strong or n liquors, and the messenger of the Court is not able to serve the summons persona he may leave a copy of the same in the building where the liquor was sold. should the licensed liquor dealer not report himself within fourteen days thereafter the Court of the Landdrost or official of the criminal jurisdiction mentioned in summons, the Public Prosecutor shall apply to the Court to have the said building buildings closed forthwith for the sale of strong or malt liquors. The Court s then have the right to order, without any further process, that the request be comp with and to cancel the licence. The registrar of the Court after having endorsed licence shall inform the secretary of the Commission for Liquor Licences of st person.

44. When any steps are taken against any dealer, seller or owner of liquor v sells liquor without a licence or contrary to the terms of his licence, such person st be considered as unlicensed, or not to hold the licence under which he is accused having traded, until at the trial of the case he produces his licence or proves that has one.

45. Should any licensed liquor dealer permit any of his premises or rooms to used for immoral purposes, the Landdrost or official entrusted with the criminal ju diction shall have the right, after satisfactory proof, to declare the licence forfeit and to close the said premises or room for the further sale of liquors under this Act

46. It shall not be lawful for anyone to institute any proceedings or bring action at law for recovery of any sum of money for or on account of any wir spirituous or malt liquors sold on credit in any quantities less than the quant allowed to be sold under a licence mentioned under " b " of Article 4 of this law ; a in case any person shall take or receive from anyone any pledge by way of secur for the payment of any sum or sums of money for such liquors thus due, or in pa ment thereof take or receive any article whatever in place of money, he shall liable to a fine not exceeding £20 for each pledge so received and accepted by him, a the person or persons to whom such pledge may belong shall have the same right the recovery of such pledge or the value thereof, as if it had not been given as pledge.

47. When any one who has no licence to sell by retail, gives to any other person or for which he receives a consideration, although he represents it as though the sideration received is for something else, he shall, notwithstanding that such con- ration is indeed and actually partly given for something else, be convicted for the of liquor without a licence, and be punished with the punishment laid down for contravention.

Unlicensed person giving liquor for which he receives a consideration.

48. Public Prosecutors of the different Courts shall be bound in all cases where ives are brought up for drunkenness to institute a most searching enquiry as to the se of the drunkenness, and the place where and the person by whom liquor has n supplied them, for the purpose of prosecuting such person for illicit liquor trade

Searching enquiry when natives are found drunk.

In the event of the native charged with drunkenness refusing to give the name the person who supplied him with liquor, or to point out the place where he ained the liquor, he shall be punished with a fine not exceeding £5, or imprison- nt with or without hard labour not exceeding one month, and with or without hes not exceeding twenty-five.

49. Every licensed liquor dealer shall be responsible for any and every contraven- n of this Act which may take place on his premises, even should such contravention caused by his servants, subordinates, or representatives, or any other person. ould it however clearly appear that such contravention was caused with the intent injure such dealer in liquor as aforesaid, or to have him punished, such liquor dealer ll not be responsible for such contravention.

Dealer personally responsible

50. It is prohibited for any licensed dealer in liquors to give, sell, barter, or pose of in any other manner, any wines, spirituous or malt liquors to any police icial or turnkey during the time he is on duty or on guard, under penalty of a fine t exceeding £10, or imprisonment not exceeding one month.

No policeman or turnkey to be supplied with liquor while on duty.

51. A police officer shall neither directly nor indirectly have any interest in any siness where wines, spirituous or malt liquors are sold, neither shall he be entitled receive, either directly or indirectly, any gift or favour from any licensed liquor aler. In case of a contravention, the convicted police officer will be punished with fine not exceeding £500, and imprisonment not exceeding twelve months, with or thout hard labour.

No police officer can have any interest in a licensed house.

52. All contraventions of this Act may be brought before and decided by the anddrost or official with similar jurisdiction, or Resident Justice of the Peace within hose jurisdiction the same may occur.

53. Nothing contained in this Act shall be taken to mean or be construed to quire a licence to be taken out for the sale of any of the liquors aforementioned by Sheriff or other official acting under authority of any Court, Judge, or Landdrost, or trustees in insolvent estates, or executors testamentary and dative.

Sheriffs do not require licence

54. The regulations with regard to public diggings are also applicable to such eces of ground as have been either by law or by Government resolution placed der the jurisdiction of the official on the diggings.

Ground under jurisdiction.

55. The Government may allow a part, but not more than one-third, of the posed and paid fines to go to the informer.

Fines to informants.

56. All previous Acts and Regulations for the sale of wines, spirituous or malt quors hitherto having force at law, are hereby repealed.

Previous acts repealed.

57. This Act comes into operation on the 1st of January, 1897.

The following Articles retain force of law in accordance with a resolution of the Second Volksraad:—Article 875, dated 22nd July, 1896; Article 4, letter d; Article 7, letter d; and Article 34a.

(Signed)   S. J. P. KRUGER,

State President.

DR. W. J. LEYDS,

State Secretary.

Government Office,
    Pretoria, 17th August, 1896.

INDEX.

XVI.

THE GOLD LAW.

(S. H. BARBER's EDITION.)

LAW No. 21 of 1896.

DIFFERENT GOLD LAWS.

LAW 2 of 1872.
  „ 7 of 1874.
  „ 6 of 1875.
  „ 8 of 1885.
MODIFICATION OF LAW 8 of 1885 (29th July, 1886)
APPENDIX TO LAW 8 of 1885 (7th March, 1887).
LAW 10 of 1887.
  „   9 of 1888.
  „   8 of 1889.
  „   8 of 1890.
  „ 10 of 1891.
  „ 18 of 1892.
  „ 14 of 1894.
  „ 19 of 1895.
  „ 21 of 1896.

LIST OF CASES.

LAW NO. 21 OF 1896,

THE DIGGING FOR AND DEALING IN PRECIOUS METALS AND PRECIOUS STONES WITHIN THE SOUTH AFRICAN REPUBLIC.

---

*As amended and approved of by the Second Volksraad Resolution, Article 1358,
ust 24th, 1896, and accepted for notice by the Honourable the First Volksraad
er Article 1554, September 14th, 1896.*

CHAPTER I.

GENERAL PROVISIONS.

1. The right of mining for and disposal of all precious stones and precious metals
ngs to the State.

2. This law is applicable to diamonds, rubies, gold, and such other precious stones
precious metals as the State President, with the advice and consent of the
cutive Council, with reference to this article of this law, shall make known.

3. The words " public diggings " shall signify a proclaimed area thrown open by
ful authority for prospecting, digging, and mining. The word " claim " shall
ify either that portion of the fields on which a person or persons or companies
e obtained a legal right to dig or to prospect, or the right to dig or prospect on
a piece of ground. " Private ground " shall signify the ground belonging to
ate persons or companies, as shown by the title deed or deed of transfer.

" Government ground " shall signify all ground belonging to the State.

The words " coloured person " shall signify every African, Asiatic native, or
ured American person, Coolie or Chinese.

" Unwrought gold " or " unwrought precious metal " shall signify gold or precious
al in whatever form, which, although smelted, is not manufactured or made up
any article fit for trade. It includes also raw gold or other precious metal,
lgam, and slimes.

Further, all words shall be understood in the sense in which they are ordinarily
d.

In the case of *Donovan* vs. *The Turffontein Estate* (decided 16th September, 1895, Off. Rep., Vol. II.,
3, p. 298), the question was whether the plaintiff was entitled to dig for clay for the purpose of
ing bricks, etc., on a certain piece of ground leased to him by agreement of 12th December, 1891.
cle 7 of the agreement of lease gave the lessee the right " tot alle mineralen, edelgesteenten, metalen,
ndere delfstoffen, met het recht om daarvoor te prospecteeren en te delven " ; that is, " to all minerals,
ious stones, metals, or other minerals, with the right to prospect and dig for the same." It was held
the word " delfstoffen " must be taken in its ordinary sense as understood in South Africa, and that
was not as ordinarily understood a " delfstof," and that therefore the plaintiff was not entitled to
for clay.

4. The State President shall have power, with the advice and consent of the
cutive Council, to take measures for the establishment of a police force, and,
her, to take such steps in conformity with this law as he may consider necessary

[marginal notes:]
The right of disposal of precious stones, &c., belongs to the State.

This law applicable to diamonds, &c.

Meaning of "public diggings."

Claim.

Private ground.

Government ground.

Coloured person.

Unwrought gold

Words to be understood in the sense in which they are ordinarily used.

Establishment of a police force.

for the general welfare and the good order of the fields. The said police force s
stand under the orders of the official charged with the criminal jurisdiction.

Power of State President to draw up regulations. 5. The State President shall also have power, with the advice and consent of
Executive Council, to make provisions and regulations, whether general or special
instance, for one or more fields), for the regulation of matters mentioned in this
or connected therewith, provided they are not in conflict with this law, as, for insta
regulations with regard to the method of digging and mining, taking measures
safety, the registration of the quantity of gold won, and such other subjects as s
appear to him to require further regulation, under which may also be included
registration of and the issue of passes to coloured people. Under the provisions
regulations mentioned in this article are also included provisions for penalties
taxes. These provisions and regulations shall have the force of law from the date
publication in the *Staatscourant*; they shall be submitted at the first ensuing ses
of the Volksraad. Special provisions and regulations shall be of force on every
claimed field immediately after proclamation in the *Staatscourant*.

Alterations and additions. The State President shall have the power, with the advice and consent of
Executive Council, to make any alterations in or additions to the said special pr
sions on the propositions of the Mining Commissioner, in consultation with the H
of the Mining Department.

Such alterations or amendments shall be of force fourteen days after publicat
in the *Staatscourant*.

Repeal of conflicting laws. 6. All former laws, resolutions of the Volksraad, and regulations with regard
diggings, in conflict with this law, are hereby repealed.

Vested rights not interfered with The rights obtained to claims under Article 16 of the appendix to Law No. 1
1883 shall remain in force under this law.

Expropriation on payment of compensation. 7. Whenever it may be found necessary in the general interest for public p
poses, such as for railways, large water-courses, etc., to take away, wholly or in pa
rights once granted, the Government shall have the right to do so on compensation
be mutually agreed upon between the interested parties and the Government. In
event of such an agreement being impossible, the amount of compensation shall
Arbitration. fixed by way of arbitration by one or more persons appointed by both sides, w
reference to an umpire chosen by the arbitrators and named beforehand, who, if
arbitrators cannot agree on one or more points in dispute, shall decide on such poin

Right of tunnelling through another's ground in the Kaap diggings 7a. The Head of the Mining Department, in conjunction with the State Min
Engineer, shall have the right, when such is necessary for the more adequate exploi
tion of a mine, to grant permission to tunnel through another's claim or mine
ground, but under the condition always that this tunnelling does not hinder or obstr
the working of such mineral ground; that the obtainer of the right to such tunnelli
is answerable for all damage caused thereby; and, further, that all minerals fou
thereby in the mining ground of others shall be returned free of cost to the possesso
with this understanding, that this article shall only be applicable for the present
the Kaap diggings.

Imprisonment on default of payment of fine. 8. When according to this law a person is sentenced to a money fine, on defa
of payment this fine shall be replaced by imprisonment. The duration of this imp
sonment shall be fixed when judgment is given as far as possible in proportion to
fine inflicted, with this understanding, however, that such imprisonment may r
exceed the period of one month in case the fine inflicted amounts to £5 or less,
three months if the fine amounts to from £5 to £20, of six months if the fine amou

from £20 to £100, and of one year if the fine amounts to more than £100. It may stipulated when judgment is given that such imprisonment shall be coupled with rd labour.

CHAPTER II.

Of the Department of Mines.

9. There exists a Department of Mines in this Republic. At the head of this partment shall be someone with the title of Head of the Mining Department, ho shall at the same time have to possess the qualifications laid down in Article 4, Law No. 6, of 1890, and is responsible according to the instructions framed by the onourable Volksraad, in resolutions Articles 939-944, 946 and 947, dated 9th and th July, 1888. *Head of the mining department. Qualifications of.*

The Head of the Mining Department shall be assisted by a properly qualified xpert, to be appointed by the Government after consultation with the Head of the ining Department, with the title of State Mining Engineer, whose duty it shall be every district, to make investigations concerning, and to report fully upon, the inerals there present, and, further, to give advice and be of assistance to the Govern- ent, in all matters relating to mines and the development of the mineral resources of is land, under such regulations as the Government, subject to the later confirmation the people's representatives, may determine. *State Mining Engineer. Duties of.*

The State Mining Engineer shall be assisted by Mining Inspectors and Boiler spectors on the diggings. *Mining Inspector and Boiler Inspectors.*

10. The Government has the right, from time to time, to appoint one or more mmissions of trustworthy and competent persons to investigate any question relat- g to mines, and to report to it thereon. *Commissions — appointment of.*

11. For each prospecting and proclaimed field, a competent person shall be ppointed, if necessary, by the Government, as Mining Commissioner, whose salary all be fixed by the Executive Council, until later resolution thereanent by the First olksraad. The Government shall, moreover, have the right to appoint, if necessary, r every prospecting or proclaimed field, a special judical official, with the title of pecial Landdrost, with criminal and civil jurisdiction equal to that of the Landdrost. *Mining Commissioner. Salary. Special Landdrost — jurisdiction of.*

On the appointment of such judical official, the boundaries within which he shall ave jurisdiction shall have to be accurately defined by the Government. Within hese boundaries the Landdrost of the respective district shall no longer have criminal nd civil jurisdiction. *Limits of jurisdiction. Landdrost has no civil or criminal jurisdiction within these limits.*

In the exercise of jurisdiction by this Special Landdrost, the Laws and customs in se in Landdrost Courts shall be applied. The same rules shall also apply with regard appeals to a higher court. This Special Landdrost shall have, within the boundaries f the field over which he has jurisdiction, the same powers with regard to marriages s are given to a Landdrost by the Marriage Ordinance. The Government shall also ave the right to appoint, besides the Special Landdrost, other judical officials with he jurisdiction of a Landdrost in criminal and civil cases, and power to hold prelimi- ary examinations, and further to lay down instructions for such officials. With egard to the salary of these officials, the same regulations as above-mentioned shall pply. *Laws and customs applicable. Appeals. Powers with regard to marriages. Other judicial officials. Salary.*

Mining Commissioner's clerk.

12. The Mining Commissioner shall be given a clerk, who, if there be no Speci[al] Landdrost, shall also be Public Prosecutor and Registrar of the Lower Court.

Further clerks.

13. If required, the Government shall assign one or more clerks to the depar[t]ment of the Mining Commissioner.

Claim Inspectors

14. The Government has the power, if necessary, to appoint for every field one [or] more Claim Inspectors, and to make such regulations with regard to their duties as may consider necessary.

With regard to the salary of all the above-mentioned officials, the same provisio[n] as that in the first paragraph of Article 11 applies.

Powers of Mining Commissioner.

15. The Mining Commissioner shall have the supervision of the field, or field[s] over which he is appointed. He shall also be clothed with authority to regulate an[d] direct all matters relative to the diggings in accordance with this law, and all regul[a]tions which may by virtue of this law be published by the Government.

He will also have regard to the grievances of the diggers, and do all that may [be] conducive to the general interest, to the promotion of the prosperity of the digging[s] and the sanitary condition of their population, he shall define the places where n[o]

As to where digging may not be carried on.

digging or prospecting may be carried on, the keeping open of roadways, under whic[h] are also included roads, or paths from the claims to the batteries and places suitab[le] for waterrights, and such other places concerning which the Government may giv[e] instructions from time to time. He shall regulate the issue of stand licences, an[d] define the places which may or may not be built on.

Where more than five stands adjoin.

Where, however, more than five stands would adjoin or be near each other, h[e] must first, through the Head of the Mining Department, obtain the consent of th[e] Government, before issuing licences for stands in excess of that number.

Collection of personal taxes.

The Government shall have the power to depute to him, or another person unde[r] him, the collection of personal taxes within the boundaries of his field, under suc[h] regulations as the Government, after consultation with the Head of the Minin[g] Department, shall deem necessary to make. If no Special Landdrost has bee[n]

Jurisdiction.

appointed, he shall have criminal and civil jurisdiction equal to that of the Landdros[t]

Ex officio Justice of the Peace.

He shall, *ex-officio*, be a Justice of the Peace for the whole Republic.

Laws and customs applicable.

With regard to the exercise of civil and criminal jurisdiction by the Minin[g] Commissioner, the laws and customs in use in Landdrost Courts shall be applied.

Appeal.

The same rules shall also apply with regard to appeal to a Higher Court.

Powers with regard to marriages.

If no Special Landdrost has been appointed the Mining Commissioner, withi[n] the boundaries of the field over which he is appointed, shall have the same power[s] with regard to marriages as are granted to a Landdrost by the Marriage Ordinance.

Article 28 of Law 18 of 1892 does not give the Mining Commissioner of Johannesburg the right t[o] refuse to issue licences to peg off claims on portion of a proclaimed area within his jurisdiction on th[e] ground that he wished to reserve the said ground for stands in view of the probable extension of Johan[-] nesburg.—*J. Nicolls* vs. *W. J. Leyds, N.O., C.L.J., vol. X. p.* 337; decided 13 July, 1893, *coram* Kotz[é] C.J., De Korte and Ameshoff, J.J.

Article 28 of Law 18 of 1892 confers on the Mining Commissioner the power to reserve what he con[-] siders the most suitable portions of a farm, about to be proclaimed a public gold-fields, for the purpose[s] of water-rights, and to refuse to allow any pegging on such portions.

The Court will not interfere with the discretion of the Mining Commissioner when he acts *bona fid[e]* and does not exceed the powers conferred on him by law. *Kempin* vs. *The Modderfontein G.M. Coy., Ltd[.] and the Mining Commissioner of Boksburg.* C.L.J. vol. xii; p. 153 decided 2 December 1895, *coram* Kotz[é] C.J., and Jorissen, J.

a) In Kempin's case the Court read the words "en op plekkin geschikt voor waterrechten" as gh the word "op" did not appear, the chief justice saying "we should place too narrow an interpre-
n on the words of the article if we construed it as simply and solely referring to roads over places
ble for water-rights, and not as conferring on the Mining Commissioner the power to decide what
ons of the farm are most suitable for water-rights, and then to define these water-rights accordingly."
Court also pointed out the distinction between *Kempin's* case and *Nicolls's* case. The word "op" is
ut in Article 15 of this law.

With regard to Article 28 see further the remarks of Kotzé, C.J., on pages 81 and 82 of the C.L.J.
x. in the case of *The Witwatersrand G.M. Coy. Ltd.* vs. *R. Young,* decided 12 January, 1893, *coram*
é, C.J. and De Korte and Morice, J.J. It was there held that, where the plaintiffs with the know-
e and tacit consent of the Government had for four years occupied a portion of ground proclaimed a
ic gold-diggings, outside but in the vicinity of their "mijnpacht," and had erected buildings thereon,
laid a tramway for the better working of their mine and battery, such portion of ground was not
ground, and no third party was entitled to peg off the portion of ground so occupied, under pros-
rs' licences, or otherwise interfere with plaintiffs' occupation.

Article 15 of Law 19 of 1895 corresponds with Article 15 of this Law.

Cf. also *Ginsberg* vs. *The Gauf Syndicate and the Mining Commissioner of Boksburg* (C.L.J. August 1896)
n in Appendix C.

16. The grounds reserved, according to Article 54, for houses, buildings, water- **Limits of Mining Commissioner's jurisdiction.**
rows, gardens or lands, as also those under Article 28 for "mijnpachten," and further
pieces of ground which are wholly enclosed by a public digging or prospecting field,
ll be under the jurisdiction of the Mining Commissioner, or, if there be such, of
special judicial officials of that digging or prospecting field. The Government
ll also have the right, by proclamation, to bring under the jurisdiction of the
cials on the public diggings, farms or portions of ground adjoining such public
gings or situated in the neighbourhood thereof.

17. All admitted advocates, attorneys, notaries, agents, conveyancers, and sworn **Legal practition-ers.**
nslators, who, according to the law of the land, are entitled to practise in the civil
rts of the land and to carry out their profession, shall be allowed to practise on the
ds. The tariff of licences required to enable the carrying out of one of these pro- **Licences of.**
sions on the fields shall be according to established ordinances. No unadmitted and
icensed person shall have the right to conduct cases in any court for others or to
ry on the business falling under the professions of the aforementioned practitioners.
hall however be free to any person, should he so desire, to conduct his case in **Anybody may appear in per-son.**
son before a court on the fields or to transfer in person any stand, claim or any
tion thereof, as otherwise being his lawful property. He shall, however, not have **Bills of costs.**
right to draw up bills of costs of the defence of his case or to claim costs for any
d of cession, transfer or otherwise, except for witnesses' expenses, court fees,
mons or stamp dues.

18. From the decision of the Mining Commissioner or of the Special Landdrost, **Appeal from Mining Commissioner or Special Land-drost.**
there be such, there shall be an appeal to the Circuit Court, the judge sitting
Camera at Pretoria, or the High Court.

19. The Mining Commissioners shall be obliged to keep proper books of all **Registers to be kept by Mining Commissioners**
renue and expenditure. He shall also keep proper registers of all licences and
hts granted by him to persons or companies and such other registers as the head of
e Mining Department may from time to time prescribe.

Inspection of these registers shall be granted to the public, but it must be **Inspection of Registers.**
viously stated by the parties interested whereof information is required. For
ple inspection the sum of 1s. 6d. shall be paid for each inspection. For written
formation the sum of 5s. in each instance must be paid, consisting of stamps, which
ust be attached to the document and cancelled.

Monthly statements to Treasurer-General. 20. The Mining Commissioners shall further be bound to send their statem[e]nts monthly to the Treasurer-General, and to pay in monthly into his office the pu[blic] moneys in their possession.

Responsible clerks. 21. The Government, after consultation with the head of the Mining Departm[ent] shall, on such fields as it may deem desirable and necessary, appoint one or more of clerks of the Mining Department as responsible clerk or clerks.

Assignment of stands to. The Government, after consultation with the head of the Mining Departm[ent] shall have the right to assign to such responsible clerks, separate stands on differ[ent] portions of the proclaimed field. The responsibility of the Mining Commissioner is **Responsibility of Mining Commissioner.** removed by the responsibility of such a clerk serving in the head office of the Min[ing] Commissioner himself.

Powers of responsible clerks A responsible clerk may issue all licences falling under his division; he may a[lso] receive transfer dues (a) auction dues, fines, market fees, rents and other spe[cial] revenue; he may also do such other work as may be given to him from time to t[ime] by the Mining Commissioner.

Issue of licences. Licences signed and issued by such a clerk shall confer the same rights as if t[hey] had been signed and issued by the Mining Commissioner himself.

Registers to be kept by responsible clerks Responsible clerks having their own division, shall be obliged to keep pro[per] registers of all licences issued by them, and shall as soon as possible deposit with [the] Mining Commissioner all moneys received by them, and within four days after the [end] **Monthly statements.** of each month send in their reports and monthly statements to the Min[ing] Commissioner.

May be invested with powers of Justice of the Peace. The Government shall have the power to invest such a responsible clerk with [the] powers and jurisdiction of a Resident Justice of the Peace within such limits as [the] Government shall determine.

(a) Transfer dues on transfer of claims paid through mistake of *law* cannot be recovered. *Rooth* *vs. The State*, decided 2 October, 1888, *coram* Kotzé, C. J., and Esselen and De Korte, J. J. C.L[.] vol. v., p. 304. Under Law 8, of 1885, there was no transfer duty payable on the transfer of claims. was introduced by Law 9, of 1888, § 33. In the case of *Dell vs. The State*, decided prior to the passin[g of] Law 9, of 1888, it was held that the transfer of claims was not subject to the payment of transfer dues.

Duties of Mining Commissioner and responsible clerk. 22. Strict attention shall be paid to the following by the Mining Commissio[ner] and responsible clerks :—

Licences to be taken out. (a) That no one shall carry on any calling or trade, or shall dig or prospect wi[th]out a proper licence.

Proper records to be kept of all cases. (b) That their clerk or clerks keep proper records and minutes of all cases de[alt] with or decided in their Court, and that their subaltern and subordin[ate] officials fulfil their duties and render account of everything deputed to th[em] or of monies entrusted to them.

Care of Government buildings (c) That all Government offices, buildings and gaols, tents, goods, etc., etc., [are] kept in good order.

Import duties—collection of. (d) That all import duties according to tariff on goods imported from abroad, a[nd] on which no duty has yet been paid, are carefully collected.

Stamp and transfer duties — payment of. (e) That the stamp duties and transfer duties due to the Government on all tra[ns]fers of claims (a) and stands are properly paid.

Fees — payment of to State. (f) That all fees or other monies payable to the State in pursuance of this law [and] later laws and regulations are promptly paid and that all official docume[nts] are subject to stamp duty.

Fines and court fees—payment of. (g) All fines and Court fees received at the office of the special Landdrosts, m[ust] be paid monthly to the Mining Commissioners, together with a specifi[ed] statement of the persons fined.

a) The Paarl Ophir G.M. Coy. ceded three claims to the Pioneer G.M. Coy. The latter company ~~l~~oyed one Gutman as agent to receive transfer of the claims. The transfer was in Gutman's name. ~~T~~hen fraudulently transferred to Graham. It was held that the transfer in the first instance was to ~~Gut~~man *as agent*, and that therefore neither he nor Graham had any title, but that the claims belonged to ~~the~~ Pioneer G.M. Coy.

The Pioneer G.M. Coy., Limited and the Paarl Ophir G.M. Coy., Limited vs. *Gutman and Graham.*

23. The Mining Commissioner shall take the same oath as the Landdrost. All ~~offi~~cials, on whatever diggings appointed, shall be duly sworn on taking office. Oath to be taken by Mining Commissioner.

24. The head of the Mining Department and the officials of his department, as also Officials prohibited from holding claims, &c. ~~spe~~cial Landdrosts and Assistant Landdrosts, Judicial Commissioners and the officials ~~of~~ their department on a prospecting and proclaimed field, are not permitted, directly ~~or~~ indirectly, to hold claims, to carry on any business, to conduct any kind of agency ~~wh~~atever, or to have any share in a mining company, or in any syndicate or partner-~~shi~~p relating to mining matters. Landdrosts, head officials, and their subordinates are ~~als~~o prohibited from being connected with a mining company as directors, advisers, ~~con~~trollers or as officials. Should it be discovered that the above-mentioned officials ~~are~~ guilty of contravening the provisions contained in this Article they may be, accord-~~ing~~ to the nature of the case, suspended from office by the Government for a certain ~~tim~~e or dismissed.

Where plaintiff had sued defendants on a contract relating to certain gold claims, and an exception ~~tak~~en by them to the summons on the ground that plaintiff being State Mining Engineer, was disqualified ~~by~~ Article 29 of Law 18 of 1892 from suing on such a contract, was upheld by the Court, and plaintiff then ~~peti~~tioned the Volksraad, which, while accepting the decision of the Court, removed the disability for the ~~pur~~poses of this particular action, by passing a resolution granting him dispensation from the provisions of ~~the~~ said Article 29 :—Held, that it was competent for the Volksraad to pass such a resolution, and that, ~~pro~~vided it was in order, the Court was bound to give effect to it ; Held, further, that the merits of the ~~cas~~e had not been touched upon in the first exception, and plaintiff could therefore institute the action ~~afre~~sh now that the disability had been removed.

Joseph Klimke vs. *Ludwig Pogge, Frans Zboril and Herman Seelig ; C.L.J. Vol. XI., p. 65,* decided ~~N~~ov., 1893, *coram* Kotzé, C. J., and Jorissen and Morice, J.J.

Article 29 of Law 18 of 1892 corresponds with Article 24 of this Law.

The resolution of the Volksraad referred to is First Volksraad Besluit of the 8th of August, 1893, ~~Art~~icle 1,029.

CHAPTER III.

Concerning Searching, Digging, and Mining.

Section 1. *Prospecting by, or with permission of, the owner.*

25. It shall be free to every landowner (after having given notice of his inten-Right of owner to prospect on his own property without licence. ~~tio~~n to the Landdrost of his district or to the nearest Mining Commissioner or ~~Re~~sponsible Clerk) to search for precious stones and precious metals within the ~~bo~~undaries of his property without a licence, and to employ for that purpose, besides ~~co~~loured persons, not more than four white persons drawing wages, and to exploit ~~mi~~nes on his ground or cause the same to be exploited under the conditions herein-~~af~~ter described. No one, except the State President, with the advice and consent of Only the State President, with advice of Executive Council, can throw open property. ~~th~~e Executive Council, shall be allowed to throw open his ground to the public as ~~pu~~blic diggings. The Government shall always have the right to cause an investiga-~~tio~~n to be made of the prospecting.

On the discovery of precious metals and precious stones on private ground, the Notice of discovery of precious metals within 7 days. ~~ow~~ner shall be obliged to give notice thereof, within seven days after the discovery, ~~to~~ the nearest Mining Commissioner, Responsible Clerk, or Landdrost, as also of the ~~pa~~rticulars thereof, under penalty of a fine not exceeding £5 on neglecting to do so.

Written permis-
sion from ow-
ner to prospect
under licence.   26. Anyone having written permission from the owner of a private farm or pi of ground to search on his property shall be able to obtain the necessary prospecti licence, on payment of the licence money, from the Landdrost of the district where desires to search, or from such other officials as shall be appointed by the Gover ment, for the period mentioned in such written permission, not exceeding a period six months.

When, however, the said permission is granted for a longer term than six mont the Landdrost or such other official as shall be appointed by the Government sh after the expiration of the first six months, have the right, after proper investigatic to extend the term for which the licence was granted in accordance with the perm sion, as long as such extension does not exceed a further period of six months.

Where the Modderfontein G. M. Coy. granted "vergunningen" to a certain Dettalbach to peg 1,110 claims on the farm Modderfontein, on the understanding that the said claims were to belong to Company, and not to Dettelbach, and the Mining Commissioner of Boksburg, on the strength of "vergunningen" granted to Dettelbach, issued licences for 1,110 claims to the representative of Company before issuing licences to the plaintiff Gauf, notwithstanding that the latter had been the fi to apply for 110 licences on the morning of proclamation, and the Mining Commissioner subsequen refused to renew the licences for the 110 claims claimed by Gauf on the ground that these 110 claims w included in the 1,110 claims pegged off by the Company, Held (De Korte, J., diss.), in an action by t plaintiff Gauf to have the 110 claims declared his property, that he was entitled to succeed.

The owner of a farm is entitled to certain defined rights as owner under the Gold Law, and he cann grant "vergunningen" to a mere "dummy" to peg off claims on the understanding that such clai shall belong to him and not to the "dummy," as this is a way of getting possession, by indirect mea of a greater number of claims than he would be entitled to directly as owner, and is therefore *in fraud* of the Gold Law. *Gauf* vs. *The Modderfontein G. M. Coy. Ltd. and the Mining Commissioner of Boksbu C.L.J. vol. xii. p.* 217 ; decided 12th January, 1895, *coram* Kotzé, C.J. and De Korte and Ameshoff, J.J Article 8 of Law 18 of 1892 corresponds with Article 26 of this Law.

The plaintiffs obtained leave to prospect on the unproclaimed farm Rhenosterspruit from the owne and pegged off 62 claims. The defendants got the right to prospect on the claims, and undertook to·p the monthly licence moneys for six months. They found no payable quartz, and ceased to pay licen money, in consequence of which the claims lapsed to the owners. The plaintiffs instituted an action damages. The Court found it very difficult to assess the damages, seeing that the claims were of ve little value, and eventually awarded £37 4s. to the plaintiffs, this being 12s. per claim for the 62 clai for one month. *Stow and others* vs. *Chester and Gibb*, decided on the 17th February, 1890, *coram* Kot: C.J. and Esselen and De Korte, J.J. (unreported).

The plaintiff, on the 27th of June, 1894, the day when the farm Modderfontein was proclaimed public goldfields, pegged off one claim on the aforesaid farm under prospector's licence, and the defenda Company, the owner of the farm, also pegged off the same claim on the same day under prospecto: licence ; but the Company obtained its licence before the plaintiff obtained his, on account of the fa that it was the holder of "vergunningen" granted *in fraudem legis* to its "dummy," a certain Dettalbac Held,—on the authority of *Gauf* vs. *The Modderfontein G. M. Coy.*, that the plaintiff was entitled to t claim in dispute as against the defendant Company. The plaintiff, on the 6th of December, 1894, al pegged off 71 claims, and on the 3rd January, 1895, 150 claims under prospector's licences on the sar farm. These claims had previously, on the 27th of June, 1894, been pegged off by the defendant Cor pany in the same way as the one claim above-mentioned. Held,—that the defendant Company w entitled to these claims on the ground that the "vergunningen" had expired long before the date of t plaintiff's pegging, at which date the claims in dispute were being held by the Company under ordina prospector's licences which had already been renewed several times, and on the ground that the plaint was aware that the said claims were being held by the Company.

Held, further, that there is nothing in the Gold Law to prevent an owner of a proclaimed farm fro pegging off claims on such farm as an ordinary member of the public, notwithstanding the fact that is entitled to certain privileges in his capacity as owner of the farm.

Held, further, that a Company can lawfully employ a representative to peg·off claims for it, notwit standing the personal nature of Article 61 (c) of Law 18 of 1892, seeing that there is no direct prohibiti of such action in the Gold Law. *Frische* vs. *The Modderfontein G. M. Coy. Ltd. and the Mining Commi sioner of Boksburg.* C.L.J., Vol. xiii., p. 76, decided 2nd of December, 1895, *coram* Kotzé, C.J. an Jorissen J.

Article 61 (c) of Law 18 of 1892 speaks of "every white *person*," as also does Article 61 of Law 18 1892. *Cf.* Article 63 of this Law.

Section 2. Judgment as to Payableness.

27. The State Mining Engineer, or such other experts nominated by him, dele- *State Mining Engineer judge of payableness.* by the head of the Mining Department, either separately or as a commission, be the competent judges of the payableness of precious metals or precious stones.

Section 3. Exploitation under "Mijnpacht" or Concession.

28. The owner of a farm or piece of ground on which precious metals or precious *Owner may obtain mijnpacht-brief.* have been found by the owner himself, or, in accordance with Article 26, by a ctor, who desires to possess the right to open and exploit mines on such farm or of ground, must be in possession of a "mijnpachtbrief," to be obtained from the rnment. Of the private grounds or farms published for setting open for a public *Extent of ground under mijnpacht-brief.* ing, the "mijnpachtbrief" must be issued for one-tenth portion of the area of that or piece of ground.

In the measuring of ground for "mijnpachtbrieven," the reef may not be taken in *Ground for mijnpacht—how to be measured.* ngth only, but the proportion of its breadth to length must be at the most as one vo.

In no case shall the Government have the right to refuse a "mijnpacht," even if the *Government cannot refuse mijnpacht.* rnment should decide not to proclaim the ground as a public diggings or pecting field.

Where, in accordance with Article 54, homestead grounds are reserved by the *Mijnpacht on homestead grounds.* er before the proclamation of the farm, he shall be entitled to a "mijnpacht" on grounds, and over the whole surface thereof.

The Government shall not have the right to refuse such "mijnpacht."

Where certain "mijnpachts" were intended to be reserved to the owners of ground about to be pro- ed as a public gold diggings, and everything necessary for the granting of such "mijnpachts" had done before the proclamation, except that the "mijnpachtbrieven" had not been actually signed till weeks after such proclamation, but the Government considered the grant as complete; Held, that informality was immaterial in an action instituted years later for portion of the ground pegged off n the "mijnpacht." *James Parker Rothwell* vs. *The New Rietfontein Estates Gold Mines, Ltd.,* and *V. J. Leyds, N.O., C.L.J., Vol. XI., p.* 48, decided on the 22nd July, 1893, *coram* Kotzé, C.J., and orte and Morice, J.J.

In the case of the *Jewel G.M. Co.* vs. *Oosthuizen* (decided on the 13th of June, 1890, *coram* Kotzé, C.J., Esselen and De Korte, J.J., unreported) the plaintiff claimed to be declared the owner of certain s of claims on the farm Sterkfontein, on which the defendant was alleged to have trespassed. The ce was that the claims had been wrongfully pegged off by the plaintiff on ground which had been reserved by the defendant as a "mijnpacht" before the proclamation of the farm. The Court gave ment for the plaintiff on the ground that in the proclamation of the farm Sterkfontein no portion had reserved as a "mijnpacht," and that the defendant had failed to prove that a "mijnpacht" had been oned off.

Cf also *Cathcart* vs. *The Main Reef G.M. Coy.* in Appendix C. Also the case of the *Nabob G.M. Coy.* he *Phœnix G.M. Coy.* in Appendix C.

29. The "mijnpachtbrief" referred to in Article 28 shall be granted for a period *Duration of mijnpacht-brief.* ot less than five, and not more than twenty years. The holder of such "mijnpacht- f" shall, however, be at liberty to renew the said "mijnpacht" for another term of nty years or less, subject to the provisions of the law then existing. This right of *Renewal for 20 years.* ewal shall also be given to holders of "mijnpachten" already granted, after the iration of the term for which the "mijnpachtbrief" was granted.

M 2

10s. per morgen per annum payable on mijnpacht-brief.

The sum of 10s. per morgen per annum shall have to be paid on the "mijnpa brief," payable in advance to the official under whose administration the "mijnpa is situated, while the holder of such "mijnpachtbrief" is subject to the follo conditions:—

Proper account of finds to be kept.

(1) He shall keep proper account of all finds, and use such forms for that pur as the Government may find necessary to prescribe.

Inspection of books.

(2) Inspection of the books shall at all times have to be granted to the Mi Commissioner or official under whose administration the "mijnpacht situated, or to any other official appointed for that purpose.

2½ per cent. of the value of all finds in lieu of 10s. per morgen.

(3) The Government shall at all times have the right to demand, instead of payment of 10s. per morgen, payment of 2½ per cent. of the value of the f during the past year, as indicated by the books or other means.

Accuracy of returns to be verified.

(4) If such is demanded by the Government officials, the accuracy of the retu in the books shall have to be verified on oath by the owner or his b keeper.

Further conditions.

(5) Such other conditions as the Government shall consider desirable, not, h ever, in conflict with the spirit or the provisions of this law.

When payment for mijnpacht-brief is 6 months in arrear.

When the payment for the "mijnpachtbrief" for such "mijnpachten" is months in arrear, the Mining Commissioner or official under whose administration "mijnpacht" is situated shall call for payment of the same in the *Staatscourant*, by notice in writing to the owner.

Demand immediately after expiration of 6 months.

The Mining Commissioner or official under whose administration the "mijnpac is situated shall be obliged to make this demand immediately after expiration of six months.

When mijnpacht-brief lapses.

If within three months after the date of the publication of such demand paym of all monies due has not been made, the Government shall have the right to dec the "mijnpachtbrief" to have lapsed.

Angles of mijnpacht indicated by stone beacons.

30. All angles of a "mijnpacht" must be indicated by stone beacons of maso as stated in Article 43, and bear the inscription: "Mijnpacht" No..........(being number of the "mijnpachtbrief"), as also the official beacon number, to be given the Claim Inspector, while the sides must be indicated as stated in Article 44.

Holder of mijnpacht-brief responsible for maintenance of beacons.

For the proper maintenance of these beacons to the satisfaction of the Min Commissioner the holder of the "mijnpachtbrief" shall be responsible, according Article 3 of Law No. 3, 1864, as approved by the resolution of the Volksraad, Art 519, dated 22nd of March, 1866. These beacons shall, on neglect, be erected maintained by the Government at the expense of those entitled to the "mijnpac after notice has been given in accordance with Article 45.

The absence or the imperfect condition of the beacons can never give rise t dispute as to the size of the "mijnpacht," according to the approved diagram, according to the "mijnpachtbrief" granted.

See the case of the *Nabob G.M. Coy.* vs. *Phœnix G.M. Coy.* in Appendix C.

Lessee of mineral rights entitled to mijnpacht-brief. Lease notarially drawn and registered.

31. Anyone hiring a portion of a farm or of a piece of ground from the ow thereof for the purpose of exploiting mines thereon can, in the same way and on same conditions as the owner, obtain a "mijnpachtbrief." provided he causes his le to be drawn up notarially and registered. This "mijnpacht" shall be renewable long as he remains the lessee.

The Langlaagte Estate G.M. Coy, owner of the farm Langlaagte, leased the mineral rights on a ~~tion~~ of the farm to the Crown Reef G.M. Coy. When the farm was proclaimed the Crown Reef G.M. . obtained a "mijnpacht" and owners' claims on the said portion. Then that portion of the farm was ~~ed~~ by the Government with the exception of the "mijnpacht."

The Langlaagte Estate G.M. Coy. then laid out a township on the said portion which was closed. ~~Crown~~ Reef G.M. Coy. began making a tram line through the township from the "mijnpacht" to railway line for the carriage of coal, alleging it had a right of passage over the said ground. The ~~glaagte~~ Estate G.M. Coy. obtained a provisional interdict against the making of the tram line. The ~~rt~~ confirmed the provisional interdict, holding that if the Crown Reef G.M. Coy. had a right of ~~sage~~, such right should be exercised *civiliter* and the Langlaagte Estate G.M. Coy. should be consulted ~~o~~ where the tram line should run. *The Langlaagte Estate G.M. Coy., Ltd.*, vs. *The Crown Reef G.M. ., Ltd.* (decided on the 23rd February, 1892, *coram* Kotzé, C.J. and De Korte and Morice, J.J., ~~eported~~).

See also the cases of *Kraft* vs. *Bok, N.O., and the Witwatersrand Gold Mining Company* and *Du Preez ~~others~~* vs. *Meyer and Van der Walt* and *Taylor and Claridge* vs. *Van Jaarsveld and Nellmapius* referred ~~under~~ Article 51.

32. "Mijnpachten" and leased grounds with licences or "mijnpachten" thereon ~~iy~~ be transferred wholly or in part from one person to another, subject to the ~~gulation~~ laid down in Article 14, Law No. 7 of 1883.

Mijnpachten may be transferred.

On the division of a "mijnpacht" the holders of the portions render themselves ~~sponsible~~, jointly and severally, to the Government from the date on which the ~~gistration~~ of the transfer of the portions accruing to them took place, for the ~~yment~~ in full of all moneys due according to the original "mijnpachtbrief," and for ~~e~~ strict carrying out of the legal regulations applicable to "mijnpachten."

On division of mijnpacht holders of the portions are jointly and severally liable.

These regulations, shall as regards division, also be applicable to "mijnpachten" ~~ready~~ granted.

Every deed of transfer shall have to bear a stamp according to Law No. 5 of ~~82~~, Schedule A.

Deed of transfer to be stamped.

In the case of a sale in execution of "mijnpachten" and leased grounds the same ~~gulations~~ shall be applicable as in the case of a similar sale of immovable property.

Sale in execution of mijnpacht.

33. In regard to the renewal of "mijnpachten" under Articles 31 and 32, the ~~llowing~~ rules shall be applicable :—

Renewal of mijnpacht.

(1) That no "mijnpachten" shall be renewed except in the name of the persons or companies in whose favour they were last registered unless transfer has previously been made in the name of the new applicant.

Renewal in name of registered holder.

(2) That the renewal of a "mijnpacht" to a lessee according to Article 31 of this law shall take place only when it appears from the contract to be produced by him and notarially registered that the lease is still unexpired or has been properly renewed.

In favour of lessee when lease unexpired.

(3) That when a person was formerly a lessee, but since that time has also become owner of the ground on which the "mijnpacht" is situated, and it appears that he has in consequence the owner's rights as well as the mineral rights in his possession, the renewal may take place.

Merger of rights of owner and lessee.

(4) That in case a "mijnpacht" term has expired and it is desired, on renewal of this "mijnpachtbrief," to divide the "mijnpacht" in accordance with Article 32, then this shall be effected for as many parts as application for renewal is made for, in which divided "mijnpachtbrieven" the obligations mentioned in Article 32 must appear, and provided that with each such divided "mijnpachtbrief" proper surveyor's diagrams in quadruple are produced.

Division of mijnpacht on renewal after expiry.

When at the renewal of a "mijnpachtbrief" it appears that t "mijnpacht" belongs to more than one owner and that some or any of the owners do not desire to renew their portion or portions, the portion wher fore application is made can be renewed provided that at each such parti renewing proper surveyor's diagrams in quadruple are produced, and in cas of undivided "mijnpachten" such applicant or applicants shall be entitled take out their accruing portion of the "mijnpacht," in terms of paragraph of article 28, while the Government must then, within six months after t day of expiration, proclaim the remaining portion of the original "mij pacht" public diggings.

(5) That the extension or renewal may be effected for from five to twenty year as in the case of a new "mijnpachtbrief," in conformity with Article 29 this law.

(6) That the "mijnpachtbrief" shall be granted on the payment and on t conditions now laid down by law or to be laid down later.

(7) That in case of the division of an unexpired "mijnpachtbrief" of the portic to be sold a new "mijnpachtbrief" shall be issued by virtue of a notari cession, with proper diagrams, and that on application the original "mijr pachtbrief" must also be sent in, in order that a note of the division may b made thereon by the Registrar of Deeds, which shall also have to be don when a portion of a "mijnpacht" is afterwards subdivided.

34. No concessions on Government ground shall in future be granted. Whe however, localities are discovered where the working of claims by individual digger

is not sufficiently payable, or where the ground, after having been worked as claim has been abandoned, such localities may be given out under "mijnpacht" to a digge or diggers for a fixed number of years, for the purpose of working them by machiner or otherwise, on the following conditions:—

(a) The extent of pieces of ground given out under "mijnpacht" shall not be les than 150 by 150 yards or greater than 500 by 500 yards.

(b) Every application shall be posted for one month at the office of the Landdros of the respective district, or should the ground be under a Mining Com missioner, at his office, and also on the gronnd applied for, and shall contai a full description of the ground as to extent, situation, and whether it ha been already worked or not.

(c) Anyone concerned has the right to raise objections to the granting unde "mijnpacht" of a piece of ground, which must be done in writing giving th grounds of his objections, the validity of which the Landdrost or Minin Commissioner shall enquire into.

(d) Immediately after the expiration of the time of notice, the Landdrost, or th Mining Commissioner, shall send in the application to the Head of th Mining Department, with his report. If the Government, after consultatio with the Head of the Mining Dnpartment, approves of it, then th "mijnpacht" shall be granted, according to the form appearing in th schedules of this law.

(e) For this "mijnpacht" a yearly rental, always payable in advance, shall b paid, calculated at 10s. per morgen yearly. The "mijnpachtbrief" shall hav to bear a stamp of the value of £2 10s.

(f) " Mijnpachten " may be transferred in the same manner and under the same *Transfer of mijn-pacht.* conditions as claims and other mining rights.

(g) If the ground for which a " mijnpachtbrief " has been granted is not worked, *If ground not worked, mijn-pacht - brief shall not be renewed.* the " mijnpachtbrief " shall not be renewed except with the express written consent of the Government.

(h) Such other conditions as the Government shall consider desirable. *Further conditions.*

See the cases of *Boyne and Nightingale* vs. *The Spitzkop G.M. Company,* and *the Spitzkop G. M. ~~~any* vs. *Stanley and Tate,* referred to under Article 62.

See also the cases of *Gilbaud and Co.* vs. *Walker and others ; Cohen, Goldschmidt and Co.* vs. *Stanley Tate ; Stanley* vs. *Goldschmidt and Co.* in Appendix C.

35. When, within private ground which has been proclaimed as public diggings, *Localities, where working by individual diggers is not payable, within private ground may be given out under mijnpacht.* ~~~lities are discovered where the working of claims by individual diggers is not ~~~ciently payable, or where the ground, after having been worked as claims, has ~~~n abandoned, the Government, after consultation with the Head of the Mining ~~~artment, shall have the right to give out " mijnpachten " on such localities, in ~~~rdance with the provisions contained in Articles 28, 29, and 31 of this Law.

36. Persons or companies holding concessions or " mijnpachten " on private or on *Holders of con-cessions or mijnpachten may permit others to dig.* ~~~vernment ground, shall be at liberty, without violating the concessions or " mijn-~~~hten," to permit persons to dig on their own behalf on such grounds under conces-~~~n or " mijnpacht," under such lawful agreements as the said concessionaries or ~~~ijnpacht " holders and persons may mutually enter into ; provided that each ~~~son so digging takes out a licence from the official under whose administration the *Such digger must take out a licence.* ~~~und is situated. On such a licence it shall be clearly stated on which "mijnpacht" ~~~concession the same is granted, while the payment shall be the ordinary licence ~~~ney per claim.

The regulations regarding claims are applicable here, excepting those relating to *Regulations re-garding claims are applicable with certain exceptions.* ~~~ reversion to the Government in case of non-payment of the licence monies, while ~~~ther the extra licence monies, according to Article 86, second paragraph, need not ~~~paid. The $2\frac{1}{2}$ per cent. mentioned in Section 3 of Article 29 shall not be levied on ~~~se claimholders.

The concession or " mijnpacht " holder is obliged to give notice to the official *Notice of per-mission granted* ~~~ler whose administration the said ground is situated, of every permission granted. ~~~ery contravention shall be punished with a fine of not more than £10, or, in default *Penalty.* ~~~payment, with imprisonment as laid down in Article 8.

37. Diggers on ground under a concession or " mijnpacht " shall be under the *Diggers on ground under mijnpacht un-der jurisdic-tion of the Mining Com-missioner.* ~~~ning Commissioner under whose administration such ground falls, or the nearest ~~~ning Commissioner or the Landdrost of their district, according to the decision of ~~~ Government.

38. The concessionaire or " mijnpacht " holder who allows diggers to dig on the *Concessionaire or mijnpacht-holder shall receive three-fourths of the licence money.* ~~~ound which he holds under a concession or " mijnpacht," in accordance with Article ~~~, shall be entitled at the end of every month to receive from the Government three-~~~rths of the money paid for licences.

Section 4. Proclamation and Throwing Open as Public Diggings.

39. The State President has the power, with the advice and consent of the Execu- *State President has power to proclaim and throw open ground.* ~~~e Council, to proclaim and throw open as public diggings Government ground ~~~d, after consultation, if possible, with the owner, also private ground, or to ~~~ach the same to an already proclaimed field, whereby it must be kept in view that

-Proclamation after 6 weeks' notice in *Staatscourant*
no ground shall be proclaimed that is not necessarily required for the diggings. issuing of such a proclamation of Government and private ground shall, however, take place except after publication of notice during six weeks in the *Staatscoura*

Notice to be posted at office of Mining Commissioner.
such notice shall further be posted up either at the office of the Mining Commissio within whose jurisdiction the said ground is situated, or at the office of the nea Landdrost.

Proclamation to be published in *Staatscourant* at least 30 days
The proclamations of Government and private ground shall, howe after the expiration of the notice above-mentioned, have to be published in the *Sta courant* at least 30 (thirty) days previously, stating day and date of throwing open

In future no private or Government ground, declared a public diggings by clamation, shall be available for the pegging off of claims, before that the proclamat has been read by the official under whose jurisdiction such ground is situated in fr

No pegging of claims before reading of proclamation.
of his office, and where also the licences shall be issued for the first time. No per shall have the right to peg off claims before he or his deputy is on the ground intends to peg, with his licences.

If owner does not prospect or allow others to do so, his ground cannot be proclaimed.
40. So long as the owner himself does not prospect, or has not given permiss to others to do so, the State President, with the advice and consent of Executive Council, shall have no power to proclaim his ground as a public diggings prospecting field, nor shall anyone else be able to force him to allow his ground to prospected.

Three months' notice shall be given to the owner of intended proclamation.
41. The Government shall give notice of its intention in the *Staatscourant* to owner of the farm or piece of ground which it wishes to throw open as a pub diggings or prospecting field, three months before the proclamation of the throwi open takes place, so as to enable the owner to peg off his owner's claims accordi to Article 48, and to take out his "mijnpachtbrief" and to define his homeste building, and arable lands according to Article 54.

The Government must observe the law from which it derives its power.

The Government cannot decide whether or not a person has forfeited his rights.

The Government is bound to give the owner notice, in the way prescribed by law, of the inten proclamation of the farm as a public gold diggings.

It is for the Court to decide whether or not the Government has exceeded the power given it by la

The receipt of the owner's share of the licence money for claims pegged off on "mijnpacht" grou is not sufficient to empower the Government of its own accord to deprive such an owner of his " mi pacht " right.

Possessors of claims on ground wrongfully proclaimed have no *locus standi* or right to intervene in action to set aside such a proclamation instituted by the real owner against the Government, and m endeavour to maintain their right by way of a separate action. *The United Langlaagte G.M. Co., Ltd. The State and the Langlaagte Royal and the Rand G.M. Co., Ltd. Official Reports. Vol. I., Part 1, p.* (decided on the 10th February, 1894), *coram* Kotzé, C.J., and Ameshoff and Morice, J.J.

-Before proclamation private grounds must be surveyed.
42. Before the proclamation of a public diggings takes place all private groun shall be properly surveyed and diagrams thereof shall be made, which diagrams mu be approved of according to law. The lines between the beacons shall also beaconed off, according to Article 44, by a duly admitted land surveyor.

Likewise Government ground.
All Government grounds to be proclaimed as public diggings shall in like mann be surveyed and put into diagram, where possible, previous to proclamation. T lines between the beacons shall, however, in every case be beaconed off, according Article 44, by an admitted land surveyor.

If private grounds to be proclaimed are not surveyed by or on behalf of the ner of such grounds within three months after the date of the notice to do so, and diagrams sent in to the office of the Surveyor-General, the Government shall have right to cause the survey to be done at the expense of the owner.

If private grounds not surveyed within 3 months of notice Government shall cause survey to be made.

43. All angles of all surveyed proclaimed grounds shall be indicated by square cons of solid masonry, four feet high, bearing a notice in which the name and the mber of the farm, agreeing with the registers of the Registrar of Deeds, besides the cial number of the beacon, shall appear.

All angles of proclaimed grounds shall be indicated by square beacons

44. The sides of all surveyed proclaimed grounds, farms, portions of farms, being isions of proclaimed public diggings, shall, except where natural boundaries exist, indicated at clearly visible distances by round intermediate beacons of masonry, ee feet high, and also, should the Head of the Mining Department, after consulta-n with the Surveyor-General, consider it necessary, where the nature of the ground mits such, by a trench at least six inches deep. The distances of such beacons from h other shall not be less than one thousand (1,000) yards.

Sides indicated by round beacons.

Sometimes by trench also.

45. The erection of the beacons referred to in Articles 43 and 44 shall, on State und, be effected by the Government at the expense of the State after calling for oper tenders. In the case of private grounds, written notice shall be given to the ner by the Government within seven days after the State President has decided to oclaim such grounds under this law, to erect the beacons; should the owner not mply therewith within six weeks after the date of this notice the Government shall, er calling for proper tenders, cause the beacons to be erected at the expense of the ner.

Beacons on State ground erected at expense of State.

In case of private grounds, written notice must be given to the owner to erect beacons.

46. A number of claims, not exceeding sixty, may be granted by an owner of a rm of 2,000 morgen or less as "vergunning" claims to other persons and allotted ior to the proclamation of such farm or piece of ground subject to the ordinary ence after proclamation. For every hundred morgen that the farm or the piece of ound consists of in excess of 2,000 morgen the owner has the right to give out two ims more under the same conditions as laid down in the foregoing paragraph.

Number of "vergunning" claims.

See the cases of *Gauf* vs. *The Modderfontein G.M. Co., Ltd., and The Mining Commissioner of Boks-g; Frische* vs. *The Modderfontein G.M. Co. and the Mining Commissioner of Boksburg;* and *Stow and ers* vs. *Chester and Gibb*, referred to under Article 26 of this law.

The limitation of the number of "vergunning" claims was introduced by Law 14 of 1894, Article 10.

47. The discoverer of precious metals or precious stones in payable quantities on ivate farms or Government grounds, at least six miles distant from an already orked locality, shall, on the proclamation of such farm or ground, be entitled to tain and beacon off six claims, whether they be reef or alluvial, which shall be called d registered as prospector's or searcher's claims. Moreover, he may work thereon ithout licence as long as he remains owner thereof.

Discoverer of precious metals at least 6 miles distant from already worked locality may beacon off 6 claims.
May work them without licence.

48. Should the State President, with the advice and consent of the Executive uncil, desire to proclaim or throw open a farm or piece of ground, or a portion ereof, the owner shall have the right to peg off his owner's claims for himself before ggers (the searcher or prospector who discovered the precious metal or precious ones excepted).

Owner may peg off his owner's claims before other diggers.

The owner or owners of a proclaimed farm or farms shall be entitled to peg off r himself or themselves a number of claims, whether they be reef or alluvial, which all be called owner's claims, viz., for a piece of ground of 50 morgen or less, one aim; for a piece of ground of from 50 to 200 morgen, two claims; and for every

Number of owner's claims.

The discoverer of precious metal has the first right to peg off claims. 250 morgen in addition, one claim more, with a maximum of ten claims for a far and to hold these claims under licence, after the prospector, who discovered t precious metal or precious stones in payable quantities, has pegged off his prospecto claims. After this pegging off of prospector's "vergunnings" and owner's clai diggers may peg off claims for themselves according to law.

See *Gauf* vs. *The Modderfontein G.M. Co., Ltd.* and *Frische* vs. *The Modderfontein G.M. Co., L* referred to under Article 26 of this law. With Article 48 of this Law compare Articles 14 and of Law 18 of 1892.

Discoverer of precious metal shall not lose his rights through the unwillingness of Government to proclaim the ground. 49. The prospector who, in accordance with Articles 26 and 47 of this law, d covers precious metals or precious stones in payable quantities, shall not lose t rights through the unwillingness of the Government to proclaim the ground a publ diggings or to attach the same by proclamation to an already proclaimed farm diggings.

Discoverer shall have all the rights of an ordinary digger. 50. The holder of a prospecting licence shall, immediately after investigation h been made on his report, and the Government has decided as to the payableness the precious metal or precious stones in the grounds discovered by him, as is provid **On private ground he shall have these rights, even though ground not proclaimed.** in the foregoing article, enjoy all the rights of an ordinary digger, over and above h special right as prospector, and he shall have these rights on private ground ev though the same be not proclaimed as a public diggings. He shall in that case, **Use of water by such discoverer** order to be able to work his claims, be entitled to such use of the water on the far as may be agreed upon in writing between him and the owner of the farm.

When this article not applicable. This article shall not be applicable when a landowner specially hires someboc to prospect for him, or when a separate agreement is made before the granting of tl written permission mentioned in Article 26, whereby the prospector, in order to obtai the written permission, waives his claim in writing to the benefits under this article.

Owner to get half of licence money. 51. The owner of the private proclaimed ground, on which digger's and pro pecting licences are issued, shall receive half of the proceeds of the digger's an prospecting licences monthly.

Owner gets three-fourths of proceeds of stand licences. Of the proceeds of stand licences the owner shall receive three-fourths and tl Government one-fourth. This provision is not applicable in cases where contrac between the Government and the owner already exist.

Accounts to be made out in name of owner. The accounts for all these monies shall always be made out in the name of tl owner, and the monies, even in case of lease *(a)*, shall be paid out to the owner or h authoritised representative only.

In the case of *Kraft* vs. *Bok, N.O., and the Witwatersrand Gold Mining Company* (decided on the 20 of June, 1887, *coram* Esselen and Jorissen, J.J. C.L.J., Vol. V., p. 14), the question was whether tl lessee of the mineral rights on a farm obtained thereby the right that would otherwise, under Article 15 the Gold Law of 1885, belong to the owner, of receiving half of the monies paid to the Government f prospecting and digger's licences on such farm after it had been proclaimed a public goldfie under Article 10 of the Gold Law. The plaintiff in the case, who was the owner of the farm Driefontei had before the proclamation of the farm entered into a contract with H. W. Struben, by which the form leased to the latter " all the mineral rights of whatever sort accruing to the first undersigned (Kraft) ownei of the farm ; and the action arose through Kraft's claiming from the Government the half of tl licence monies paid to the Government for claims pegged out on the farm after it was proclaimed, whic monies the Government had been proceeding to pay to the Witwatersrand Gold Mining Company, cessionary from H. W. Struben of the lease. The decision of the Court was that the owner of the farm the plaintiff, was entitled to the half of the licence monies, as the right to receive such monies was not right to minerals, and was, therefore, not included under the words "all the mineral rights of whateve sort accruing to the first undersigned (the lessor) as owner of the farm " used to describe the right passing to the lessee.

must be noted that when this case was decided (20th of June, 1887) Law 10 of 1887 had not come
orce. The words "the accounts of all these monies shall always be made out in the name of the
, and the monies, even in case of lease, shall be paid out to the owner or his authorised representa-
ly" do not appear in Article 15 of Law 8 of 1885. They were introduced by Article 5 of Law 10 of
This, as is remarked by Mr. Morice (now Mr. Justice Morice) in his article in the "Cape Law
al," Vol. V., p. 15, would seem to indicate that the judgment was in accordance with the intention
legislature.

n the case of *Du Preez and others* vs. *Meyer and Van der Walt* (decided on the 23rd of February, 1887,
Kotzé, C.J. and Esselen, J., C.L.J., Vol. V., p. 15) it was held that under the Gold Law the lessee
rm on an ordinary, *i.e.*, an agricultural lease, obtains no rights as regards the precious metals or
ng out claims, though the owner cannot exercise his mining rights to the prejudice of the lessee in
njoyment of his rights under the lease. The same case also decided that it is not necessary to make
overnment a party to an action for setting aside a "mijnpacht."

n the case of *Taylor and Claridge* vs. *Van Jaarsveld and Nellmapius* (Feb. 26th, 1887, *coram* Kotzé, C.J.
sselen, J., C.L.J., Vol. V., p. 18) the plaintiffs sued for specific performance of a verbal contract by
the first defendant bound himself to give the plaintiffs the exclusive right of prospecting for six
hs, with the right, if they had found payable minerals, to take out a lease of the mining rights of the
which subsequent lease was to be executed according to law. It was argued for the defendants that
verbal contract was void in virtue of Article 14 of Law 7 of 1883 (upon transfer dues), which states
"no cession of a right to minerals assumed to be present or actually present on a farm, shall be
unless embodied in a notarial document and duly registered in the office of the Registrar of Deeds,"
oes on to enact that transfer dues must be paid, such cessions specially referring to leases. The
decided that the contract of the first defendant was not a cession or lease, but merely gave the
n of taking a lease at a future time ; and, therefore, did not require to be notarially drawn and
tered. Whether the contract could be described as *an agreement as to* the cession of mineral rights,
therefore, included in the words of the Volksraad resolution of August 12th, 1886, was expressly left
en question by the Court, the contract being prior to the date of such resolution. The resolution
mentioned is to the effect that all agreements *as to* the cession (*omtrent den afstand*) of rights to
rals shall be void, unless notarially drawn and registered in the Deeds Office.

ee also *Pearce* vs. *Olivier and others* in Appendix C, and *Steyn* vs. *Bezuidenhout* in Appendix C.

52. When a desire is expressed by way of memorial by inhabitants or by **[*Throwing open of town commonages and native locations.*]** piers of a location that town commonages or native locations be thrown open er wholly or in part, and such appears to the State President desirable and ticable, he shall have the power, with the advice and consent of the Executive ncil, after consultation with the head of the Mining Department, to throw open se grounds, either wholly or in part, for prospectors, or to declare them public ;ings under the provisions laid down in this law for Government ground, provided, ever :

That no right to prospect or to dig on the town commonage shall be granted **[*Application by at least two-thirds of inhabitants.*]** ss application therefor is made by at least two-thirds of the burghers and abitants of a town.

That no right as above shall be granted unless the town commonage of any town **[*Not to interfere with cattle grazing.*]** f sufficient size to cause no interference in that respect with the requirements of le-grazing.

That all roads and pathways leading to the town shall remain unobstructed. **[*Roads not to be obstructed.*]**

That no trees or other wood shall be used or removed for carrying into effect the **[*No trees to be removed.*]** ts to be granted.

That no encroachment shall be made on any existing rights to the leading and **[*No encroachment on rights to water.*]** use of water, whether it be for public or private purposes, and such encroachment ll be punished in accordance with the penalty clauses of Article 146.

That all rules and regulations with regard to public diggings on Government **[*Rules with regard to public diggings on Government ground applicable.*]** unds, as laid down in the now amended Law No. 8 of 1885, as far as the same are patible with prospecting and digging on town commonages, shall be observed.

Portion of revenue to be used for improvement of town.

That a certain portion of the nett revenue of the diggings, to be fixed later the State President, with the advice and consent of the Executive Council, shal applied for the benefit and for the improvement of the town.

Further regulations.

The State President shall be empowered, with the advice and consent of Executive Council, after consultation with the head of the Mining Department make such further provisions as may be necessary for the regulation of affairs, vided they are not in conflict with the above rules or principles.

Search for precious metals on locations.

53. When a chief, with the advice of his council, desires that investigati should be made as to the presence of precious stones and precious metals on location which he occupies with his people, he may request the Government to ca such to be done by white persons.

Preference given to persons whose farms were expropriated for extension of location

The persons proposed by the chief and his council shall enjoy the considera of the Government in the first place. Should the Government consider it desir to authorise other persons, this can be done without reasons being given; th persons excepted whose farms were expropriated by the Government for the purpo of the extention of the location, to whom the preference shall be given. The Gove ment shall cause to be pointed out to the person or the persons authorised by it w portion of the location is made available for prospecting.

Throwing open of locations.

When it appears through prospecting that precious stones or precious metals found in payable quantities within such locations the State President shall have right, with the advice and consent of the Executive Council, to declare these grou either wholly or in part, public diggings, under the regulations laid down in this for government grounds, provided, however:

Reservation of grazing rights. "Kraals" not to be interfered with.

(1) That grazing rights shall be left to the chief and his people.

(2) That their "kraals" (cattle pens) and lands shall be excluded and shall not disturbed except with their consent.

Water.

(3) That sufficient water shall be left for their domestic use and for their cattl

Mijnpacht may be granted.

(4) That a "mijnpacht" may be granted to the person or persons authorised the Government to prospect, when they give sufficient proof of the payal ness of the grounds, under the provisions of this law, the size to be fixed consultation with the Superintendent of Natives and with the head of Mining Department, but in no case greater than the maximum fixed private grounds by Article 28, par. 2 and 3 of this law, computed accordi to the number of morgen to be thrown open.

Compensation to chiefs and their people.

(5) That compensation, computed at a fourth of the proceeds of the licence a "mijnpacht" monies, shall be granted to those chiefs and their people w have received the locations gratis from the Government.

(6) That compensation, computed at a third of such proceeds, shall be granted those chiefs and their people who have acquired the location grounds, who or in part, at their own expense.

(7) The Government is empowered to make such regulations as it may deem with regard to the portion of licence and "mijnpacht" monies to be award to Moshette and the kaffir chiefs standing on an equality with him.

Where prospecting and digging shall be forbidden.

54. Where private grounds are proclaimed public diggings, or are attached proclamation to already proclaimed fields, or are made available for prospectors, Government shall first consult with the owner, if possible, to determine on what pl of ground, such as plots which are built on, homestead ground, gardens, bui

nds, "kraals," lands, and watercourses in the neighbourhood thereof, it shall be
ibited to prospect and to dig. On unworked farms or portions of ground, where
e is no occupation, the owners in conjunction with the Government, the Mining
mmissioner or the Landdrost of the district, may beacon off a "werf" (homestead **Right of owners to beacon off "werven" on unworked ground.**
nd) which shall be reserved for homestead, building and cultivation lands. The
ulations of Article 28 par. 3 shall be applicable to these "werven" (homestead
nd).

See the case of the *Witwatersrand G.M. Coy. Ltd*, vs. *Young*, referred to under Article 15 of this law.

55. Under any circumstances sufficient water shall remain free for the use of the **Water for use of owners.**
er, his family, his cattle, and for the watering of all gardens and lands existing at
time of the proclamation, and for the working of "mijnpachten" granted under
provisions of this law.

The quantity of the water required for these purposes shall, before the proclama- **Gauging of quantity of water required.**
a as public diggings, by order of the head of the Mining Department be gauged
determined by him. This water, so gauged, may afterwards be used by the owner
other purposes or disposed of by him.

The rest of the water and the water that is not so used shall at all times be **Surplus water to flow unobstructed.**
wed to flow away unobstructed. The use thereof shall be regulated by the lawful
horities, according to the provisions of this law. Lessees, servitude-holders, or
ers entitled to water, retain the right to such water in so far as they make use **Water for lessees and servitude holders.**
reof at the time of the proclamation for the purposes mentioned in the first para-
ph, and after the quantity thereof shall have been fixed by the head of the Mining
partment, which shall take place before proclamation. In this respect the pro-
ions of the second paragraph of this article apply.

The farm Zandrivier (Zoutpansburg) was proclaimed a public gold-fields on October the 6th, 1887, but
rtion of the farm containing the dwelling-house and lands of the plaintiff was reserved. The plaintiff
ained his water supply from a spruit running through the farm. The defendant company secured a
er-right higher up on the same spruit. The plaintiff instituted an action against the defendant com-
y for a declaration of rights to have it declared that the company was not entitled to take water from
spruit for its battery. He also sought a perpetual interdict against the company preventing it from
ng the water and from allowing its tailings to run into the spruit and thence into his dam, maintaining
t owing to the reservation of his dwelling and lands no water-right could be granted under the Gold
w so as to affect his rights. It was held by the full Court (De Korte, Ameshoff and Morice, J.J.) that
der Section 30 of Law 10 of 1887, the water-right was rightly granted to the company, although it
cted the rights of the plaintiff.

Held, further, that § 47 of Law of Law 8 of 1885 must be interpreted strictly, and does not permit
filling up of furrows or other watercourses with tailings.

An interdict was accordingly granted, restraining the Company from allowing its tailings to run into
spruit, and it was further ordered to remove such tailings as had run into it, and to pay the plaintiff
0 as compensation. *J. J. Maré* vs. *Mount Maré G. M. Coy., Ltd.*, decided on the 2nd of February,
2 (unreported).

§ 30 of Law 10 of 1887 gave to the old Digger's Committee the right to frame regulations with regard
the division and use of water.

Cf. § 126 of this Law.

§ 47 of Law 8 of 1885 is replaced by § 125 of this Law.

In the case of *Steyn* vs. *Johnson and the Diggers' Committee of the Witwatersand Goldfields* (11th Nov.,
7, C.L.J., Vol. V., p. 15), an application was made by Steyn as owner of a farm to set aside a grant of
ater-right on his farm by the Diggers' Committee on the ground that it had been granted contrary to
Gold Law. The judge refused to decide the matter on affidavits, but, giving the owner the advantage
being regarded as in possession, decided that the digger who had obtained the grant of the right from
Diggers' Committee must make good his right by action.

56. The Government shall further have the right to require from the owner or **Grounds occupied by owner mus be properly enclosed.**
s representative that these grounds for occupation be properly enclosed, and that a
agram thereof be made within a time to be fixed by the Government, which time,
wever, shall not be shorter than three months.

If within the time fixed this be not complied with the Government shall h
the right to do the said work at the expense of the owner or his representative.

Government may use portions of proclaimed private ground for public purposes.

57. On the private grounds referred to in this article the Government shall h
the right, as long as the proclamation continues, to occupy and to build there
without payment, such pieces of ground as shall be necessary for offices and ot
public buildings, for the deposit of rubbish, for burial grounds, and for other gene
purposes. Such pieces of ground shall, if possible, after consultation with the ow
be beaconed off by the Mining Commissioner at the expense of the State, an
diagram thereof shall be drawn up by a qualified surveyor, and these places may
be pegged off.

The buildings referred to in the previous paragraph shall remain the property
the State.

When ground on private proclaimed farms may be given out for gardens and plantations.

58. On private proclaimed farms, two years after the proclamation of the sa
pieces of ground may be given out for gardens and plantations, on places where
appears that there are no gold-bearing reefs or alluvial deposits present, under
following conditions:

(1) The issue of such grounds is effected by the Government, on the request
the owner, under such conditions as it may determine, after investigation
the Mining Commissioner concerned, and on the proposition of the head
the Mining Department.

What if gold-bearing reefs be discovered.

Compensation for damage fixed by arbitration.

(2) If it should afterwards appear that gold-bearing reefs do exist there, th
portion which such reefs pass through shall be given out in the ordina
way, with this proviso, however, that if damage is done to gardens or plan
tions, such damage shall be paid for by the licence holder or holders acco
ing to assessment to be fixed by arbitrators.

Such ground may not be used for any other purpose.

59. When pieces of ground are given out, according to the foregoing article,
gardens and plantations, such pieces of ground may not be used for any oth
purpose.

Dams.

Pipes.

Roadways.

60. Where, on the various proclaimed diggings, a person or company, holder
claims or a "mijtpacht," desires to make a dam for the collecting of tailings (a) or ra
water (provided it be not from an existing water-course or fountain), to lay down
tube, pipe, or other conductor, for the bringing of water to his or its machine stand,
to construct a roadway for the conveyance of quartz or material from the claims
"mijnpacht" to the machine stand, whether it be for ordinary wagons drawn
draught animals, or for so-called trucks conveyed along rails, provided such trucks

Permission by Mining Commissioner.

not propelled by steam or electricity, the Mining Commissioner may grant permissi
for that purpose.

If such water-races, ordinary roads, or truck rails go over claims, "mijnpacht
water-courses, streets, railways, tramways, or stands of other persons, the applica
in order to obtain the necessary permission for the construction and exploitation
the same, shall have to make a written application therefore to the Mini

Commissioner concerned. This application shall be published for a month in t
Staatcourant, and in one of the local papers, by and at the expense of the applica
for the information of parties, who must within that time send in their objections a
claims to compensation to the Mining Commissioner concerned. Any person co

Compensation and objections

structing such water-races, dams, roads, etc., over claims, "mijnpachts," etc., witho
having obtained the permission of the Mining Commissioner to do so, shall

punished with a fine not exceeding £10, or on default of payment, with imprisonme
for a period not exceeding six weeks, without prejudice, however, to the right of t

r or the owners of the surface to compensation. The amount of such compensa- Compensation fixed by arbitration.
shall be determined by two arbitrators. One of them shall be chosen by the
cant and the other by the interested party. Should the arbitrators differ, the Mining Commissioner referee.
ng Commissioner shall act as referee, from whose decision there shall be an Appeal from Mining Commissioner to head of Mining Department.
al to the Head of the Mining Department, whose decision shall be final.

ee the case of *The Langlaagte Estate G.M Coy., Ltd.*, vs. *The Crown Reef G.M. Coy., Ltd.*, referred
der Article 31 of this law.

). The plaintiff company allowed its tailings for two years to run down a creek and took no steps
vent their being entirely washed away. The defendants afterwards pegged off the ground on which
ilings had been washed. The company in an action claimed the tailings, but the Court held that
had been total abandonment, and gave judgment for the defendants.

eba G.M. Company Ltd. vs. *Vautin, Millbourne and Steers*, decided on the 5th of March 1889,
Esselen, Jorissen and De Korte, J.J. (unreported).

61. The Government may, by special agreement, grant permission for the laying Permission to lay conductors for electrical currents.
nductors for the transmission of electrical currents for the use of the mines and
ng works.

62. An area once declared a public diggings or portion thereof may not be closed When a proclaimed area may be closed.
r wholly or in part, except in the single case when the number of diggers within
boundaries of such portion which it is requested or proposed should be closed is
than a number computed at one digger for every twenty morgen, provided always
the closing of such proclaimed ground shall not affect the rights and claims to
nine stands, tailing deposit sites, water-rights, or other possessory rights already
ined. In the event of the closing of a public diggings or portion thereof six Six months' notice.
ths' previous notice thereof shall be given in the *Staatscourant*, and at least once
onth in a local paper, should there be one, in the latter case at the expense of the
icant. A diagram of the digging or farm or portion thereof, the closing of which Diagram shall lie for inspection.
been requested, shall lie for inspection at the office of the Mining Commissioner
ng the period of the said six months. All objections filed during the said six
ths shall be heard on the last day of such term, or, if this day fall on a Sunday or Hearing of objections.
liday, the day after. Moreover proper provision shall be made for the continuance
he work of those whose claims have not yet been exhausted, or compensation shall Compensation.
ranted. The amount of such compensation shall be fixed by mutual agreement Arbitration.
ween the Government and interested parties and, in case they cannot agree, by
of arbitration.

The farm Elandsfontein was proclaimed a public gold diggings. Subsequently the defendant
any prevailed on the Government to close a certain portion of the proclaimed farm under § 60 of Law
1890. The plaintiff went and pegged off claims on the portion thus closed, maintaining that the
ng was illegal, on the ground that the number of claimholders on *the proclaimed area* exceeded one
very 20 morgen of ground. The defendant company ordered the plaintiff to remove his pegs and
ed to allow him to peg off claims on the abovementioned portion. The plaintiff sought the confirma-
of a provisional interdict restraining the defendant company from interfering with his pegging. The
pany maintained that the words " zoodanige delverij," appearing in § 60 of Law 8 of 1890, referred to
ortion closed and not to the *area proclaimed*, and alleged that there was not one claimholder to every
orgen of ground on the portion closed.

Held (per Kotzé, C.J., De Korte, and Morice, J.J.), that the interdict must be confirmed.

Held (per De Korte and Morice, J.J. ; Kotzé, C.J., reserving his opinion until action brought) that
cle 60 lays down the condition under which alone the Government has the right to close any public
ings, and that the words " zoodanige delverij " refer to the whole *area proclaimed* and not to the
ion closed only.

Williams vs. *The Geldenhuis Estate Gold Mining Coy., Ltd., and Dr. W. J. Leyds, N.O.*, decided on the
of November, 1893 (unreported). N.B.—The application for confirmation of the interdict is not
rted, but the subsequent action is (*vide infra*).

Held, by the majority of the Court (Kotzé, C.J., diss.), that the correct construction of Article 60 of
Gold Law of 1890 is that the Government can only close a portion of any proclaimed area when the
ber of diggers on the *entire proclaimed* area average less than one digger to every 20 morgen.

Held, also, that where the Court has placed an interpretation on a point of law, and the reading of the Volksraad differs therefrom, the Volksraad should not assign to it a construction conflicting with the decision of the Court, but the proper course would be for the Volksraad to modify the terms of the law to accord with its (the Volksraad's) view, while accepting the Court's decision.

Semble, the number of licences issued is no test of the number of diggers present. *Williams* vs. *The Geldenhuis Estate and Gold Mining Coy., Ltd., and Dr. W. J. Leyds, N.O.* (C.L.J Vol. XI., p. 128.)

See First Volksraad Besluit of the 13th June, 1893, which alters section 60 of the Gold Law, and speaks of one digger to every 20 morgen of the portion to be closed.

In 1889 a portion of the proclaimed farm Doornfontein was given to Fawcus by the Government for the purposes of a township, and notice given thereof in the *Staatscourant*. In November, 1891, the agreement between the Government and Fawcus was cancelled and the cancellation duly notified in the *Staatscourant* of the 25th November, 1891. On the 27th November, 1891, the plaintiff pegged off certain claims on the abovementioned portion. In December, 1891, the Mining Commissioner refused to renew the licences for these claims. Held, in an action for damages for wrongful refusal, that the plaintiff was entitled to a renewal of his licences. Held, further, that when the Mining Commissioner definitely refuses to renew the licences, it is unnecessary to tender powers of attorney, etc. Held, further, that, when a proclaimed area *is* closed by proclamation or notice in the *Staatscourant*, the same means (*i.e.*, proclamation or notice in the *Staatscourant*) ought to be adopted when it is again thrown open to diggers. *Van Diggelen* vs. *Leyds, N.O.*, decided on the 13th April, 1895, *coram* De Korte, Jorissen, and Morice, J.J.

See all the remarks of Kotzé, C.J., on the last point in *Blomfield* vs. *The Mining Commissioner of Johannesburg and F. J. Bezuidenhout, Jr.* (Official Reports) I., 1, p.p. 135-136.

See also *The Langtaagte Estate G.M. Coy., Ltd.,* vs. *The Crown Reef G.M. Coy., Ltd.,* referred to under section 31 of this law.

In July, 1888, Braamfontein was proclaimed a public goldfields. In January, 1889, the plaintiffs pegged off certain claims there. In February, 1890, a portion of Braamfontein was closed by the Government. In an action by the plaintiffs it was held that they were entitled to the money spent in purchase of claims, as also to the licence monies paid. Money paid in exploiting the ground, to find out whether it contained gold in payable quantities could not be claimed, as it was too vague and remote a claim. The value of certain buildings erected on the ground was allowed, but not the cost of erecting the beacons, because the obligation to erect them was imposed by the law. *Berea Syndicate* vs. *Leyds, N.O.*, decided on the 30th of June, 1891, *coram* Kotzé, C.J. and De Korte and Jorissen, J.J. (unreported).

In the case of *Boyne and Nightingale* vs. *The Spitzkop Gold Mining Company* (C.L.J., Vol. IV., p. 71, decided on December 4, 1886), *Coram* Kotzé, C.J., and De Korte and Jorissen, J.J., it was held that the concessionaires of the sole right to dig for gold on a farm which had been deproclaimed were answerable only for direct damage caused by the granting of the concession, and not for damage not directly resulting from the granting of the concession, but from the withdrawal of the proclamation and the refusal to issue licences.

See also the case of *The Spitzkop Gold Mining Company* vs. *Stanley and Tate* (decided in August, 1885, and referred to in Cape L.J., Vol. IV., p. 72.).

Also the cases of *Gilbaud aad Co.* vs. *Walker and others ; Cohen, Goldschmidt and Co.* vs. *Stanley and Tate ;* and *Stanley* vs. *Goldschmidt and Co.* in Appendix C.

In the case of *Eloff* vs. *Dr. Loyds, N.O.* (decided by Kotzé, C.J., in Chambers, on the 29th November, 1895, (Off. Rep. Vol. 2, part 3), the applicant (Eloff) alleged in his petition that a proclamation dated the 5th of June, 1888, was published in the *Staatscourant*, of the 13th of June, 1888, by which a certain portion of Braamfontein, in the district of Heidelberg, was thrown open to prospectors ; that on the 22nd of July, 1895, a proclaimation was issued to the effect that the above-mentioned ground would be closed from the 24th of August, 1895 ; that on the 16th of August, 1895, and therefore before the closing took place, he applied for licences to peg off certain claims on the said ground, and that the Mining Commissioner of Johannesburg refused to issue the licences, notwithstanding the fact that everything necessary had been done according to law ; that he (the applicant) thereupon pegged off the claims which, on being surveyed, were found to be 90 in number. He therefore asked for an order to compel the Mining Commissioner to issue the licences.

The Mining Commissioner answered that on the 22nd of June, 1889, he received a telegram from the State Secretary ordering him to issue no further licences on Braamfontein, and that on the 3rd of February, 1890, notice was given in *The Mining Argus* that no further licences would be issued on the said ground, and that, therefore, when the applicant pegged in August, 1895, the ground was not open ground.

Kotzé, C.J., delivered the following judgment :

" The Court is of opinion that a proclamation published in the *Staatscourant* can only be withdrawn by a later proclamation (with a reservation of rights aiready acquired) unless the Law prescribes otherwise in any particular case. The instructions from the Government and the notice published by the Mining Commissioner in *The Mining Argus* cannot therefore set aside the proclamation of 1888. The later proclamation of the 22nd of July, 1895, first came into force on the 24th of August, 1895, therefore,

re the 24th of August, a person could make application for, and obtain prospecting licences, accord-
to law. The Mining Commissioner did not, therefore, act according to law. The applicant is
tled to prospecting licences for 90 claims. The Court must consider the application and deal with
nc pro tunc. The Mining Commissioner is ordered to issue the licences, and applicant is entitled to
:osts."

Section 5. Exploitation of Claims under Licence.

63. Every white person of full age, of the male sex, who submits to the laws of
land and produces (*a*) to the official charged with the issue of the licences referred
n this Article, the receipt or the certificate that he has paid his personal tax
ording to law for the current year, shall be entitled to twelve digger's licences to
or to mine on a public field for precious metals or precious stones; on one claim
every licence obtainable on payment of twenty shillings per month per licence.
is licence of twenty shillings may, however, only be demanded for claims on which
chinery has already been erected, and is in working order; or if, no matter where,
e is already made of machinery for the crushing of quartz coming from these
ims. Where, in other cases, the Mining Commissioner orders the taking out of a
ger's licence, only fifteen shillings per month need be paid for it. Every person as
ove-mentioned, provided he complies with the same conditions, is also entitled to
tain twelve prospecting licences, which shall give him the right to search on
vernment ground, situated within the jurisdiction of the official who issues the
ences, and made available for prospecting by the Government, or on private ground,
accordance with the provisions of this law. For every licence to prospect on
ivate ground, five shillings per month must be paid, and on Government ground
o shillings and six pence per month, besides a stamp of 1s. 6d. per claim for the
st month in every case of pegging off or taking out of claim licences.

Marginal notes: Every whit male person of full age entitled to twelve digger's licences. When 20s. payable. When 15s. Twelve prospecting licences. 5s. for prospecting licence on private ground and 2s. 6d. on Government ground.

A male married person may, besides those for himself, also peg off as many
ims as laid down in paragraph 4 of letter *b*, Article 65, for his wife and children in
own name, without power of attorney, provided that a certificate from the Field-
rnet is produced showing that he is married, and actually has as many children as
states in the certificate, which must be sworn to before the Field-Cornet concerned
a Justice of the Peace.

Marginal note: Married man may peg off claims in his own name for wife and children on producing certificate from Fieldcornet or Justice of the Peace.

No advantage could be taken of an incorrect description in the licence, where there was clear proof
the identity of the claim, and the intention always existed to acquire the same, and to hold it under
der the Gold Law. *Cohen* vs. *The Johannesburg Pioneer G.M. Company*, decided on the 15th of Novem-
r, 1889, *coram* Kotzé, C.J., and Esselen and De Korte, J.J. (unreported).

Prospecting licences were taken out to peg claims on the farm "Elandsfontein, Simmer and Jack's
rtion," and claims pegged in January or February, 1889, for the plaintiff's predecessor. The farm was
vided into two portions, the Simmer and Jack and the Geldenhuis. The peggers did not know exactly
ere the dividing line was. They pegged on the Geldenhuis portion. These claims were amalgamated
d licences were paid. In September, 1889, Ballott found out the mistake, and in November, 1889,
gged off the claims, knowing they belonged to the plaintiff. Held :—The Court will not allow a person,
o, knowing better and being fully acquainted with the circumstances, disturbs another in his occupa-
n or possession of claims, simply because there is an informality or wrong description in the licences,
take advantage of such informality or wrong description, where it appears that the person in posses-
n has acted *bona fide*. The claims was therefore adjudged to the plaintiff.

S. Syndicate vs. *John Ballott G.M. Company, Ltd.*; decided on the 15th of January, 1891, *coram*
otzé, C.J., and De Korte and Ameshoff, J.J., (unreported).

(*a*) The text is clearly wrong here. It reads " en aan den ambtenaar belast met de uitreiking van
in dit artikel bedoelde licentien, *en* de kwitantie, etc." The second *en* ought not to be there. See the
marks of Kotzé. C.J., in the case of *Kempin* vs. *Leyds, N.O., and the Modderfontein G.M. Company,*
ferred to under Article 15, with regard to the preposition " op."
See also the case of the *Paarl Pretoria G.M.Company* vs. *Donovan and Wolff, N.O.*, in Appendix C.

Persons who have pegged off prospector's claims before proclamation shall be entitled to remain in possession of them after proclamation.

64. If under this law an area is declared a public diggings by proclamation, person, or the persons, who has or have pegged off for themselves prospector's clai on that area under prospecting licences, shall be entitled to remain in possession such claims, provided this law be complied with.

See *Gauf* vs. *The Modderfontein G.M. Company, Ltd., and The Mining Commissioner of Boksbu* referred to under Article 26 of this law.

Pegging claims by means of a holder of power of attorney.

65. With regard to causing the pegging off, and thereafter the holding of digge or prospector's claims, by means of a holder of a power of attorney, the followi rules apply :—

Male and female persons residing in the country.
Married women to be assisted by husbands.

(a) Male and female persons, residing within the country, may cause digger's prospector's claims to be pegged off, and thereafter held, by a holder of power of attorney, provided, in case they are married women, they a assisted by their husband.

Male persons of full age must produce power and certificate.

Male persons of full age, acting for themselves or as husband, shall ha to produce, with their power of attorney, the receipt or the certifica mentioned in Article 63.

Power to be certified by Field-cornet.

(b) Every person who wishes to peg off or cause to be pegged off a claim or clai under power of attorney, must have the said power of attorney certified the Field-Cornet or Assistant Field-Cornet of his ward, and must produce t receipt for the tax paid for the current year.

Fieldcornet must certify that the holder of the power is entered on his list.
Powers for wife.

This official must further certify that the holder of the power of attorne is entered on his Field-Cornet's list, is known to him as an inhabitant of h ward, and is obedient to the laws of the land.

In case such a person also takes out powers of attorney for his wife, t Field-Cornet or Assistant Field-Cornet must certify that the statements the holder are correct. Should he doubt the truth of the statements of t holder of the powers of attorney, he can demand that the truth of t powers of attorney should be confirmed under oath.

Verification of powers under oath.

Not more than twelve claims may be pegged under power from one person.

On no power of attorney from one person shall more than twelve clain be pegged off.

Every male person of sixteen years and upwards can peg twelve claims.

Every male child of sixteen years or more has the right to peg off, cause to be pegged off, twelve claims, provided the Field-Cornet or Assistar Field-Cornet of his ward certifies that he is entered on his Field-Cornet list, is known to him as a resident of his ward, and obedient to the laws the land.

Unmarried female persons of full age, and widows may peg off twelve claims.
Persons who do not pay personal taxes must produce certificate that their father, guardian, or husband has paid his.
Certificate to be produced by persons who do not pay taxes and are not assisted by father, &c.

Unmarried female persons of full age and widows shall also have th right to peg or cause to be pegged off twelve claims. All persons mentione in this article who do not pay any personal taxes under the laws of the lan shall have to produce a certificate that their father, guardian, or husband ha paid his personal taxes for the current year. Persons mentioned in th article who are not subject to personal taxes, and are also not assisted b father, guardian, or husband, shall have to produce a certificate to that effec from their Field-Cornet or Assistant Field-Cornet for the purposes of th article.

The Field-Cornet or Assistant Field-Cornet shall for the signing of the certificate and the inspection of his books attach a shilling stamp on each certificate, to be paid by the holder of the power of attorney, whereof 6d. shall be returned to him monthly by the Government for each certificate. The Field-Cornet or Assistant Field-Cornet must keep a proper register of the certificates issued, and shall render monthly to the official of his district concerned a certified list with his account. The Field-Cornet or Assistant Field-Cornet who renders incorrect statements or accounts, certified as correct and true, shall be punished with a fine of not less than £5, and no more than £25, and in default with imprisonment not exceeding three months, with or without hard labour. *[margin: Stamp of 1s. on Field-cornet's certificate. Field-cornet wilfully certifying falsely.]*

(c) Male persons of full age residing outside the country may cause to be pegged off, and thereafter hold, one digger's or prospecting claim, by means of a holder of a power of attorney, provided the power of attorney be notarially drawn up and duly legalised, and this power of attorney, in addition to the ordinary stamp of 1s. 6d. per claim, carry a stamp of this Republic of one pound (£1) sterling. *[margin: Male persons of full age residing outside the country may peg a claim by means of power-holder. Power to be notarially drawn and legalised. Stamp of £1.]*

This stamp shall have to be renewed yearly, and is valid for that year for every power of attorney used by the same person on any goldfield of this Republic. *[margin: To be renewed yearly.]*

The holder of the power of attorney can obtain a receipt or duplicate receipt for the same from the official who cancelled the stamp on the first power of attorney of that power given for that year. *[margin: Receipt.]*

No women or minors residing outside the country shall be able to cause digger's or prospecting claims to be pegged off by a holder of a power of attorney. *[margin: Women and minors residing outside the country cannot peg claims by means of power-holders.]*

An error in amalgamating, *i.e.* a *bona fide* mistake made with the advice of the Mining Commissioner amalgamating 36 claims in three blocks of 12 each, for which the same 12 names were used in each case, as there were really 36 powers of attorney, did not deprive the syndicate of its right.

Madeline Reef Syndicate vs. *Coetzee and others* (C.L.J., Vol. V., p. 16; Official Reports, I. 1. pp. 134, decided on the 13th January, 1888, *coram* Kotzé, C.J., and Esselen and Jorissen, J.J.

If the powers of attorney by virtue of which a man obtains licences to peg off claims are false, the licences are invalid, and the pegging gives no title. It was proved that the powers of attorney relied on by the defendant Croft were not signed in the presence of the witnesses, and that some had not been signed by the alleged principals at all. Held, that the licences granted to Croft were invalid, and that he had no title to the claims. The powers of attorney ought to be signed by the principals in the presence of the witnesses, or the principals ought to acknowledge their signatures to the witnesses. *Nigel Coy.* vs. *and the Beatrice Syndicate*, decided on the 12th of April, 1890, *coram* Esselen, De Korte, and Ameshoff, (unreported).

Where, in pegging off claims, a certain number of them are pegged off under invalid powers of attorney, a third person, hearing of this, pegs off afresh a number of such claims, equal to the number of the invalid powers, the Court will not grant such second pegger a rule *nisi* preventing the first pegger from alienating claims pegged off afresh, on which licence monies are being regularly paid by the latter, pending an application for declaration of rights, unless he can show that the claims thus pegged off again by him are precisely those which were originally pegged off under the faulty powers. *Sylvester* vs. *Jacobs* (official Reports, I. 2. p.20), decided on the 26th of April, 1894, *coram* Ameshoff, J.

66. Articles 63 to and including 65 shall not be applicable as regards powers of attorney to alluvial goldfields, where a person shall not be able to peg off more than three claims in his own name. *[margin: Articles 63 to 65 not applicable to alluvial goldfields. One claim in person's own name.]*

N 2

67. Every licenced digger shall be entitled to hold under his licences on
proclaimed farm three alluvial claims and as many reef claims as provided in Art
63, 64 and 65 of this law. He shall also be at liberty to purchase a number of cl
from other licensed claimholders : he shall in that case have to hold a digger's lic

for each claim, unless the Mining Commissioner considers a prospecting lic
sufficient for the time being.

When the joint claimholders of an amalgamated block have had their respec
shares registered for the purpose of this article with the Mining Commissione
responsible clerk concerned on payment of five pounds (£5) sterling, each one of t
shall be allowed to peg off afresh one claim or to give a power of attorney afresh
that purpose.

The same power of attorney may be used only once and shall be returned
issuing the licences to the licence holder, after cancellation of the stamps, noting
number of first licence granted thereon, as also the number of the register
registration, and noting on the power of attorney that it may not be used for
other claim.

To the discoverer of payable gold reefs on and in proclaimed public diggings
on prospecting fields twelve claims shall be awarded without powers of attorney o
and above the twelve claims allowed him in subsection b of Article 65, but subjec
an impost of 6s. 6d. per claim for the first month and after that the ordinary licenc

68. If on a quartz reef claim alluvial gold or *vice versa* on an alluvial cl
quartz reef gold is also found and worked, a double amount of licence money sha
paid for such a claim.

69. The registration of one or more searcher's (prospector's) claims shall
effected by a Mining Commissioner when the discovered precious metal or preci
stone-bearing ground is situated within the boundaries of his field, or otherwise
Landdrost of the district wherein the said ground is situated.

70. Diggers or prospectors, being holders of adjoining claims to the number
not more than twelve, who wish to amalgamate their claims, may cause the s
claims to be registered as amalgamated, with all the water-rights belonging to s
claims, on application at the office of the Mining Commissioner or responsible cl
concerned.

On registration the share of each digger or prospector must be clearly
distinctly described.

On the granting of the certificate of such amalgamation, under a stamp of t
pounds (£2) sterling, the holders of the amalgamated claims shall enjoy the us
privileges as per regulations thereanent on the fields where they are situated.

The amalgamation of claims does not lapse through licences being changed.

See the case of the *Madeline Reef Syndicate* vs. *Coetzee and Others*, referred to under Article 65.

71. Every application for a "mijnpacht," right to lead water, protecti
amalgamation of claims, and other similar applications, must bear a stamp of
value of five shillings.

72. Pegging off claims between sunset and sunrise is forbidden, as also peggi
off on Sundays and Christian holidays recognised by law.

Pegging off at such forbidden times shall be considered illegal, shall not
recognised and shall give no rights whatever.

The plaintiff alleged that the defendant pegged off certain claims between sunset and sunrise,
that he, believing the defendant to have no legal title, pegged off the claims on a subsequent date.
Court granted absolution from the instance. *Tinling* vs. *Lang*, decided on the 26th of November, 18
coram Ameshoff, Jorissen and Morice, J.J. (unreported).

73. Every owner of a reef claim, or of an amalgamated block of reef claims, or a digger's claim or block of claims shall be obliged to deposit with the Mining Commissioner, Responsible Clerk or Landdrost concerned, within one month after the date of the first licence, a surveyor's diagram, or if there be no surveyor, a sketch plan of the situation of the claims or blocks, and signed by the person who made the survey. Such claims may not be transferred without a proper land surveyor's diagram. For alluvial digger's claims it shall be sufficient to deposit a sketch plan only so long as they are not transferred, in which case a surveyor's diagram is obligatory. The stipulations of the foregoing paragraph shall not be applicable to the unhealthy gold localities.

74. Every holder of a reef claim or an amalgamated block of reef claims under digger's licence shall be obliged within six months after the date of the first licence to deposit with the Mining Commissioner, Responsible Clerk or Landdrost concerned approved surveyor's diagrams in triplicate of a survey of his ground, made by a surveyor, and compiled on such a scale as shall be fixed by the Surveyor-General.

Such survey must show all works, buildings, tramlines, roads, footpaths, machine stands and the local conditions of the ground, and must be connected by trigonometrical or other survey with such fixed points or permanent beacons of another survey as the Surveyor-General shall determine, or in such other way as the Surveyor-General shall deem sufficient to define the place accurately. These diagrams shall be examined and approved at the office of the Surveyor-General. The Surveyor-General shall, before the diagrams are signed by him, make known by a notice in the *Staatscourant* that these diagrams have been sent in and that they will be signed by him if within the time of one month from the date of publication no protest is lodged against the same.

When a protest is lodged the same must be proceeded with within the period of one month, failing which the diagram shall be signed by the Surveyor-General just as though no protest had come in against the same.

Regarding diagrams already approved under this article and hereafter to be approved, the same regulations regarding legality and cancellation of faulty diagrams shall apply as enacted in Article 109. Before a surveyor may survey claims or ground, the beacons thereof must be shown by the owner or his representative with the claim inspector of the respective fields.

The defendant syndicate sent in a diagram of claims to the Surveyor-General for his approval in accordance with the Gold Law. The plaintiff syndicate filed a protest, alleging that the said diagram comprised more than the defendant was entitled to in that it included sixteen claims belonging to it (the plaintiff). Held, that the plaintiff had not succeeding in making good its protest, and that the defendant had a better title to the said claims inasmuch as it had pegged the claims in February, 1892, while the plaintiff had pegged only in July, 1892. *Chums Syndicate* vs. *The Rand Exploring Syndicate* (C.L.J. vol. XIII. s. 165), decided on the 7th February, 1896, *coram* De Korte and Ameshoff, J.J.

In an action for renewal of licenses for certain claims, the defendants excepted to the summons on the ground that the diagram attached to it was vague, and did not indicate the exact position of the claims. It was held that it was not necessary to attach a diagram to the summons at all, but even if it were necessary, the diagram attached was sufficiently clear. *Doyle* vs. *Leyds, N. O. and the Rand Exploring Syndicate* and *Nonpariel Syndicate* vs. *Leyds, N. O. and the Rand Exploring Syndicate*, decided on the 6th August, 1895, *coram* Kotzé, C. J. and Jorissen, J. (unreported).

75. The provision of Article 74 shall also apply with respect to diggers' claims pegged off before the taking effect of this provision, and for these claims the period for sending in the diagrams shall be six months after the taking effect thereof.

76. The period for sending in the diagram referred to in Article 74 may for well-founded reasons be extended by the Head of the Mining Department.

77. When a person has more ground than he holds a licence for, anyone provided with the proper number of licences shall be at liberty to peg off afresh within the

---

Margin notes:

Diagram or sketch of situation of claims to be deposited with Mining Commissioner within one month.

Transfer of claims cannot take place without surveyor's diagram.

Sketch sufficient for alluvial claims unless transferred.

Deposit within six months with Mining Commissioner of diagrams of claims under digger's licence.

Nature of such diagrams.

Approval of by Surveyor-General.

Notice of.

Protest against.

Art. 74 shall apply to digger's claims pegged before taking effect of this law.

Extension of time for sending in diagram.

Re-pegging of surplus ground

pegs or beacons of that person, the excess number of claims pegged off, with t
understanding, however, that such newly pegged out claims must lie together and
one of the sides of the block or portion of ground, but in no case on worked places
to the obstruction of the other claim holder.

Notices to be given by re-pegger to Mining Commissioner and to holder of claims. The second pegger is obliged, within 24 hours of such pegging off, to give writt
notice thereof to the Mining Commissioner or Responsible Clerk of the field cc
cerned, as well as to the holder or holders of the claims, and he must further, with
14 days thereafter, send in to the official concerned a surveyor's diagram of the whc
block of claims, showing not only the claims pegged off by him, but also the exa
situation of the other claim holder, after which the Mining Commissioner may gra

Appeal from Mining Commissioner to Head of Mining Department. the excess of ground pegged to the re-pegger. From the decision of the Mining Cor
missioner, appeal may be entered within 14 days after judgment, to the Head of t
Mining Department, whose decision shall be final.

Penalty for re-pegging ground lawfully held. Should it appear that the second pegger has pegged out within the beacons a
pegs of the holder of the claims, without these being open ground, then shall t
second pegger be punished with a money fine of £100 to £500, or in default, wit
imprisonment according to Article 8.

Surveyors may enter on ground belonging to others. 78. Surveyors, who are engaged in surveying claims, shall have the right to ent
for that purpose on another's ground, after giving notice to those entitled to sue
ground or their representatives, if they are on such ground, and to place there th
necessary instruments, flags, etc., for the survey.

Penalty for obstructing. Everyone who prevents them or obstructs them therein, or puts difficulties in th
way of the operations for the survey, shall be punished with a fine not exceeding £25

Surveyors must supply Head of Mining Department with copies of diagrams. 79. All surveyors shall be obliged to supply the Head of the Mining Departmen
through the Surveyor-General, with a copy of all diagrams which they have frame
for Companies, Syndicates, or private persons, in so far as they refer to publ
diggings.

Penalty for not depositing diagrams. 80. (1) He who does not comply with the depositing of diagrams and sketche
prescribed in Articles 73, 74, and 75 within the time fixed shall be punished with
fine not exceeding £15.

When renewal of licence postponed. (2) If this fine be not paid within the time fixed for the purpose, the renewal
the licence shall be postponed until the fine shall be paid.

Fixing time for deposit. (3) In the sentence a time may be fixed within which the deposit shall have t
be made.

Extent of alluvial claims. 81 An alluvial claim for digging for precious metals shall be in extent 150 b
150 feet, and shall be beaconed off with clearly visible pegs and trenches at righ
angles in the direction of the sides.

Extent of claim for digging for precious stones A claim for digging for precious stones shall be in extent 30 by 30 feet square.

Extent of quartz reef claim. A quartz reef claim shall be in length 150 feet (*i.e.*, in the direction of the reef
and 400 feet in breadth, in such a way that each claim, if possible, forms a rectangl
the breadth to be taken on one or both sides of the reef, as desired.

Two central pegs In respect of a quartz reef claim two central pegs shall· be sufficient pegs for th
first seven days.

Corner pegs after seven days. After the expiration of that time, four corner pegs shall have to be substitutec
and the direction indicated by beacons as prescribed by law.

Corner pegs for amalgamated claims. In the case of quartz reef blocks of amalgamated claims four corner pegs shall b
sufficient for each block, but the names of the respective claimholders in the bloc
must be legibly marked on each peg, with the date of amalgamation.

Permission to fence in claims Nobody shall have the right to fence in his claim or "mijnpacht" without th
previous written consent of the Head of the Mining Department, who shall decid

consultation with the Government, and in no case shall a larger portion of the
nd be fenced in than is necessary to protect the works, and to guard against
ructions and trouble with the workmen.

The use of barbed wire for fences or for other purposes is forbidden on pro- **Barbed wire forbidden.**
ned or prospecting fields, as also on grounds surrounded by public diggings.

All fences made or to be made without permission as aforesaid shall be removed **Removal of fences put up without permission.**
hose entitled to the ground thus fenced in, and in default of this the Government
l cause the same to be removed at their expense. Contraventions of this article
l be punished with a fine not exceeding £25, or, on default of payment, with im-
onment according to Article 8 of this law.

See the case of the *Berriman Syndicate* vs. *Simpson* in Appendix C.

82, The corner pegs or beacons of a claim shall be not less than three feet above **Height of corner pegs.**
ground.

These corner pegs or beacons shall be not less than three inches in diameter.

Where the nature of the ground permits, at each peg or beacon two trenches **Trenches for claims.**
st be dug, which shall form a right angle at the peg or beacon, three feet long,
-a-foot wide, and one foot deep, which trenches must indicate the direction of the
ndaries; moreover, the sides of a claim or amalgamated block of claims shall be
wn in a clear manner by trenches or piles of stones at least one half-foot high and
e feet long, and boundary beacons placed at distinct mutually visible distances,
ther marks.

When there is a surveyor's diagram of claims, or of amalgamated blocks of
ms, it shall be sufficient to erect the corner beacons, and to dig the furrows round
claims.

All claims and amalgamated blocks of claims must have on each corner beacon a **Notice board on corner pegs.**
rd at least nine inches square, on which shall be clearly and legibly written,
ated, or painted, the official number to be given by the Claim Inspector, the names
the mining property and the claimholder or the claimholders, the date of the
nce and the date of the pegging off.

When the Claim Inspector finds that any of the provisions in this Article have not **Non-compliance with this provision.**
n complied with, he shall have the right to inflict a fine therefor of at least two
llings and sixpence and at the highest five shillings per claim. He shall give notice **Duty of Claim Inspector.**
reof to the owner or his representative and he shall at the same time inform the
ning Commissioner thereof.

The person fined has the right to appeal within eight days to the Special Land- **Appeal.**
st, should there be one, or otherwise to the Mining Commissioner; if after expiration
this period fixed for the appeal, no appeal has been noted and the fine has not been
d at the office of the Mining Commissioner and the beacons not brought into order,
Mining Commissioner shall issue no further licence for the claims in respect of **Suspension of licence.**
ich the law has been contravened, till such time as the fine shall have been paid and
beacons brought into order. Article 86 shall apply in this case.

83. When on a public field a digger wishes to abandon his claim or claims in order **Abandonment of claims.**
peg off for himself a new claim or claims, he shall have the right to do so provided
pulls out the pegs of the claims which he wishes to abandon, and puts up a notice
a week on the ground to the effect that it has been abandoned, and also gives notice **Week's notice.**
the same effect to the Mining Commissioner or responsible clerk, in default of which
shall be liable to a fine not exceeding £10 or imprisonment for from fourteen days
three months, with or without hard labour.

On receipt of such notice the Mining Commissioner or responsible clerk shall c: such claim or claims to be sold by public auction in accordance with Article 86.

He may, before giving out such claims, first institute an inquiry, and sha▶ entitled to refuse to give out such claims and to cause them to be sold by auction the benefit of the State.

The renewal of a prospecting or digger's licence shall be refused by the Min Commissioner or responsible clerk when claims have been pegged off on places wł according to Articles 117 and 15 of this Law it is forbidden to search or to dig, anc places which in the opinion of the Mining Commissioner or responsible clerk are indisputable lawful possession of others.

See the cases of the *Witwatersrand G. M. Coy.* vs. *Young, Kempin* vs. *The Mining Commissioner of ł burg and The Modderfontein G.M. Co. and Nicolls* vs. *Leyds N.O.*, referred to under Article 15.

See also the case of *Ginsberg* vs. *The Gauf Syndicate and the Mining Commissioner of Boksbur* Appendix C.

When damages are claimed on the ground of the refusal to issue licences for ceded claims, the dee cession must be attached to the summons. *Chumleigh Syndicate* vs. *The State and Rand Exploring Synd* (Official Reports I., 1, p. 45), decided on the 2nd of February, 1894, *Coram* Kotzé, C. J. and Ameshoff Morice, J. J.

84. No holder of a reef claim situated higher up shall have the right to allow débris from his claim to be a nuisance to another or to obstruct him who is work lower down.

In case holders of claims require ground for depositing tailings or other dé▶ from the batteries, for placing sumps or pans, dams instead of pans or reservoirs, or storing quartz, such ground may be given to them on their own claims, after writ application has been made therefor by the Claim Inspector and a surveyor's diagr has been handed in at the office of the Mining Commissioner or responsible clerk c cerned, which officials may grant this application if there are no well-founc objections thereto. For this no extra licence need be paid. This provision shall : apply to those storage stands which have already been given out under licen at 2s. 6d.

The regulations laid down in Article 102 with regard to the non-payment witł the proper time of the licences on specially registered claims are also applicable to t Article. Applicants must, within a month after award, hand in plans in triplicate the said officials, framed as indicated in Article 73 of this Law.

85. On proclaimed fields the Mining Commissioner may determine where prospe ing can be carried on under prospecting licences, and also determine on which pla digger's licences must be taken out.

The Mining Commissioner shall have the right, if application be made theref to change the digger's licences, under which claims are held, to prospecting licenc after due investigation, and after having received the report of the claim inspec thereanent.

On finding that anyone is holding ground under prospecting licence, and is ı properly working the same to the satisfaction of the Mining Commissioner, with ▶ object of finding precious metals or precious stones, the Mining Commissioner sb have the right to order him to take out a digger's licence.

The Mining Commissioner shall in this matter have to take into considerati that when claims have been amalgamated, the working of one of the thus am gamated claims at a time must be considered as sufficient, which regulation, howev shall not be applicable to claims which were previously held under digger's licence.

The licence holders may, in case they are dissatisfied with such decision of the **Appeal to the Government.** ing Commissioner, appeal within thirty days to the Government, through the head he Mining Department, after which the Government shall finally decide on the er's report. Every Landdrost may, except on the proclaimed fields and the specting fields where a Mining Commissioner has been appointed or assigned, issue **When Landdrost may issue prospecting licences.** specting licences within the boundaries of his district.

See the case of the *Henry Nourse Gold Mining Coy.* vs. *Eland* in Appendix C.

86. If a digger's or prospecting licence expires without being renewed on or **When claims lapse to Government.** ore the day of expiry, the claim for which the licence was issued may not be ged off by another person, but lapses to the Government, and such claims shall be lt with as follows :—

During three months after such day of expiration the former holder of such **Former holder can recover rights within three months.** ms shall be entitled to recover his rights on these claims by taking out new nces therefor, on payment of extra licence monies equal to the amounts of the ear licence monies. If, however, the new licence be taken out by the former **If licence renewed within fourteen days.** imholder within fourteen days after the day of expiration, only the licence monies these days need be paid. After the expiration of the said term of three months, **Claims sold after three months.** head of the Mining Department must sell or cause these claims to be sold by lic auction. The head of the Mining Department shall, however, be obliged, before **Restoration of claims before sale to original holders on payment of arrears and expenses.** h sale takes place, to give back the claims concerned to the original holders reof, if no further questions exist, on the additional payment of all arrear licence nies, besides the expenses incurred therewith.

If the claims are not sold by public auction, the head of the Mining Department **If not sold within one month after lapse of said period of three months, they may be pegged off again.** ll be obliged to declare 30 days after date of the sale such claims open ground, en the ground may be pegged off by the public. Of such public sale a notice shall published in the *Staatscourant* at least 14 days previously.

These regulations shall be applicable to all claims which have lapsed at the time the taking effect of this law.

On the 2nd of September, 1887, the plaintiff pegged off certain claims. In October, 1887, these claims sed to the Government. On the 14th of January, 1890, the plaintiff bought the claims from the rernment under Article 61*b* of Law 10 of 1887. Between October, 1887, and January, 1890, the ndants pegged off the claims and got their licences renewed from time to time. Held (per De Korte, eshoff and Jorissen, J.J.) that the Government was not bound to sell the claims, but could allow them be re-pegged as open ground ; that therefore the defendant's title was better than the plaintiff's, the endant's pegging being prior to the plaintiff's purchase. *Edwards* vs. *The Britannia Coy.*, decided on 1st of September, 1890 (unreported).

N.B. Article 61*b* of Law 10 of 1887 is spoken of, but it is really Article 37 of Law 10 of 1887, which difies Law 8 of 1885 by the insertion of Articles 61*a* and 61*b* between Articles 61 and 62.

In the case of *Doyle and others* vs. *Leyds, N.O., and The Rand Exploring Syndicate* (C.L.J. Vol. XIII., 157) decided on March 19th, 1896.

Ameshoff, J., with whom Jorissen, J. concurred, said " Article 25 of Law 9 of 1888 is imperativ It pels the Government to sell claims in such a way as it pleases it is true, when the licences paid for the e have lapsed without being renewed." Now Article 25 of Law 9 of 1888 is the article which modifies ome unimportant details Article 61*b*, as laid down by Article 37 of Law 10 of 1887, referred to above. remarks, therefore, of Ameshoff, J. in *Doyle's* case are hardly consistent with the judgment in the e of *Edwards* vs. *the Britannia Coy.*, abovementioned.

The plaintiffs alleged that they pegged off certain four claims on the 22nd of June, 1889, that the nces were renewed on the 22nd of July, but that renewal was wrongfully refused on the 22nd of gust, though licence monies had been properly tendered. The second defendant alleged that the und in question was pegged by one Gebhardt on behalf of Schweizer in June, 1889, before the pegging the plaintiffs took place ; that subsequently Schweizer obtained the right to lay out all the ground ich he held as claims, including the ground in dispute, as a township, and that it (*i.e.*, the second endant) obtained all Schweizer's rights by cession. The second defendant further alleged that the plain- s had abandoned their claim to the claims, and that they were estopped by their long silence of four or e years from asserting any claim to the ground. Held, by the majority of the Court (Morice J. diss.), t the plaintiffs must succeed.

The Gold Law.

That the plaintiffs pegged on open ground in June, 1889, and that the renewal of the licences wrongfully refused by the Mining Commissioner in August.

That as the Mining Commissioner renewed the licences in July and refused the renewal in Aug the onus of proving the legality of the refusal lay on him, and that in this he had failed.

That no *animus relinquendi* on the part of the plaintiffs had been proved and that they were estopped from asserting their claim. The cases of *Walker* vs. *Leyds, N.O., and the Rand Explor Syndicate* and *Judd* vs. *Leyds, N.O. and the Rand Exploring Syndicate* were distinguished. Held (Morice, J. diss.), that the defendants ought to succeed. That when a person, who lays claim to clai for a long period of years neither tenders licence monies nor takes legal steps, and when others are ther prejudiced, the presumption is that such person has abandoned his right to the claims. That t presumption arises in this case and has not been rebutted. *Doyle and others* vs. *Leyds, N.O., and Rand Exploring Syndicate* (C.L.J., Vol. XIII., p. 157), decided on the 19th March, 1896, *coram* Amesh Jorissen and Morice, J.J.

See also the case of *Schweizer's Claimholders Rights Syndicate* vs. *Rand Exploring Syndicate* in Appen C.

With reference to the lapsing of claims to Government on non-payment of licence monies the case *Moolman and Coetzee* vs. *Schaffe and Drury* (decided on the 2nd of March, 1887, *coram* Kotzé, C.J., a Esselen, J. ; see C.L.J., Vol. V., p. 13) is of historical interest. It was there decided that under the G Law of 1885 the right to a claim lapsed on the expiry of the licence through non-payment of the licer monies, and that the ground on which the claim had subsisted could be pegged off as a claim by a th party. The law was, however, altered by a Volksraad Besluit, followed by Article 61b of the Gold Law, amended by Law 10 of 1887, Article 37, which distinctly says that lapsed claims may not be pegged again by a third party.

See also the case of *Underwood* vs. *Barnato Bros. and the Mining Commissioner of Boksburg* Appendix C.

Protection for reef or alluvial claims during commando. 87. He who is on commando or has personally responded to a call to mainta order and peace shall *ipso facto* have protection for his claim or claims (whether re or alluvial) during the time that he is on commando or such special service, and, the case of commando, also for thirty days after his release from such command without its being necessary for such protection to be especially granted, provided **Notice.** gives notice of such call to the Mining Commissioner concerned.

No licence monies to be paid. During the time of this protection no licence monies on the claims need be paid.

Exemption from payment of claim licences in case of unhealthiness of district 88. Provisional exemption from the payment of claim licence monies (wheth reef or alluvial) may be granted in case of sickness or owing to the unhealthiness the district, provided that work be done on such claims before and at the time of t application for protection, such as in the opinion of the Mining Commissioner may considered sufficient to justify the granting of exemption. Every such case of exem tion shall be sent as soon as possible by the Mining Commissioners, with a full repo to the Head of the Mining Department, for final approval or rejection by the Gover ment, who may grant or refuse confirmation of the exemption.

Duration. The duration of the time of exemption shall be fixed according to the nature each case, while nothing shall be charged for granting the same.

Claims belonging to estate of deceased person. 89. Claims belonging to the estate of a deceased person shall not lapse unless t executor fails to comply with the provisions of the law for thirty days after receipt his appointment or the confirmation thereof by the Orphan Master.

Assets of the estate. On further regular compliance with the provisions of the law such claims sha be considered as assets of the estate, and as such be dealt with according to the prov sions of the Orphan Law.

Licence holder cannot dispose of surface of ground. 90. The possession of a licence for a claim does not include the right of disposi of the surface of the ground, which right of disposal the Government reserves f itself for the purpose of defining roads and other works, etc., without, howeve obstructing the working of the claim.

Licence to dig to be produced on demand. 91. Any person who digs for gold, precious stones, according to Article 2 of th law, be it on his own, be it on another's account, must, if such is desired by an offici

fied thereto by the law or the Government, produce his licence, in default whereof
hall be punished with a fine of £1 to £3, and in default of payment with impri-
ent not exceeding fourteen days.

92. Every licenced digger or prospector shall be entitled to have a stand on his
as for his dwelling, for which stand he need pay no licence.

93. Each white person who desires to erect a store, or houses, or dwelling on a
aimed or prospecting field shall make application to the Mining Commissioner for
or more stand licences, Where five stands are already given out next or near
other, the Mining Commissioner shall not have the right to give out stands
in a distance of 300 yards.

Each licence shall give the right to a piece of ground 50 by 50 feet in a locality
oved of by the Mining Commissioner, but not so as to interfere with mining
ations on a locality known to contain precious metals or precious stones.

The Head of the Mining Department, in conjunction with the Government, shall,
ever, have the right to give out under a licence stands of greater dimensions
re he considers such necessary.

Such stand licence, whether monthly or yearly at the option of the applicant
t be renewed either monthly or yearly.

The price for a stand licence on proclaimed ground of 50 by 50 feet shall be 7s. 6d.
month.

When the payment of stand licences on proclaimed ground is three months in
ar, the Mining Commissioner shall demand payment thereof in the *Staatscourant*
in a local paper, if one exists. If one month after publication of the demand,
pliance therewith is not made, the Head of the Mining Department shall have the
t to declare such stands lapsed.

The price of a stand licence on approved stand townships on Government ground
l be: For stands of 50 by 50 feet, 7s. 6d.; and for stands 50 by 100 feet, 11s. 3d.
month.

In case a stand licence is not renewed at the proper time, the holder of the stand
ce shall have the right within a period of three months thereafter, to get his
d back under a new licence on the additional payment of all arrear licence monies
as a fine a sum of money equal to the arrear licence monies.

See the case of *Curtis N.O.* vs. *The Mining Commissioner of Johannesburg and the Johannesburg Town-
Co.* in Appendix C.

94. Where on private proclaimed farms stands adjoining each other are given out
er licence, so that they together in the opinion of the Government form a town,
nall have the right to impose a special tax of two shillings and sixpence per month
stand. The payment thereof shall take place at the same time as that of the
ies due for stand licences, on which the receipt thereof must be noted.

If this tax on a stand is in arrear, the renewal of the licences may be refused for
t stand.

95. Transfer and registration of portions of stands may take place provided an
roved surveyor's diagram of such portion be deposited in the office, where the
stration must take place. Such a portion of a stand shall be considered and
istered as a separate stand, for which a separate stand licence shall be due as
ows: For portions of stands 50 by 50 feet, 2s. 6d. per month; and for portions of
ds of 50 by 100 feet, 3s. 9d. per month. On such a portion of a stand the full tax
s. 6d., mentioned in Article 94, must be paid.

Registration of transfer of portions of claims at office. Registration of transfer of portions of claims may take place, provided approved surveyor's diagram of such a portion is deposited in the office where registration is to take place. Such a portion of a claim shall be regarded registered as a separate claim.

Registration of transfer of claims and stands at office of Mining Commissioner. 96. The registration of transfer of claims and stands and portions of claims portions of stands shall take place at the office of the Mining Commissioner Responsible Clerk concerned, while the same stamp dues shall be levied as in terms Law No. 5, 1882.

Stamp dues. Machine stands obtainable on claims gratis, and on ground not containing precious metals, &c., on payment of 2s. 6d. per month. 97. The company or the person who imports machinery for the purpose working one or more claims shall, over and above his ordinary stand, have the ri to acquire stands in extent 150 feet square on his claims (free of cost) and on a loca which is not known to contain precious metals or precious stones under licence 2s. 6d. per month, for the purpose of erecting the machinery on, where, that is to this is practicable without encroaching on the rights of others.

Coloured person may not be licence-holder. 98. No coloured person may be a licence-holder or in any way be connected w the working of the diggings, except as a workman in the service of whites.

Section 6. Special Registration.

Special registration of claims. 99. Each digger's claim or each amalgamated block of digger's claims may specially registered in the manner hereunder set forth.

Application for special registration. 100. Persons who desire to have their claim or block of claims speci registered must make application therefor to the Mining Commissioner concerned far as possible in the form hereafter prescribed.

Diagram. This application must be stamped as provided by Article 71, and must accompanied by a diagram framed by an admitted surveyor. The application w

Inspection for one month. the diagram shall lie for the inspection of the public for one month at the office of Mining Commissioner.

Day of hearing fixed. The Mining Commissioner shall thereupon issue a notice to the applicant, as possible in the form hereafter prescribed, wherein day and the date of hearing sh be fixed (between the date of publication of notice and the date of hearing there m be a period of at least one month.)

Publication of notice. This notice shall be published once in the *Staatscourant*, and twice in a lo newspaper, should there be one.

Where no objection, application granted. If before the said hearing no notice of objection has been given to the Min Commissioner and the applicant, and for the rest the law has been complied with, Mining Commissioner may grant the application, and the special registration sh

Stamp. then take place as is further set forth herein. A notice of objection shall bear stamp of five shillings, according to Article 71. When before the said hearing suc

When objection is made. notice of objection shall be received by the Mining Commissioner the special reg tration shall for the time being not be granted.

Legal proceedings within ten days of notice of objection. Within ten days after the notice of objection the person who objects must ta legal proceedings against the applicant to have his objection declared valid. T declaration of validity may be sought by application. The official charged with

Official charged with civil jurisdiction shall have jurisdiction. civil jurisdiction on the field shall have jurisdiction herein, and he shall give such order regarding the special registration as he shall deem necessary.

Special registration in separate register. If the application for special registration of a claim or claims is granted, su registration shall be effected in a separate register to be opened for the purpose, form of which shall be prescribed by the head of the Mining Department.

A certificate of such special registration shall be issued as far as possible rding to the form hereafter prescribed.

Certificate of special registration.

This certificate shall bear a stamp of a value calculated at the rate of ten ings per claim.

Stamp.

No certificate shall be issued unless all monies due on the claim or claims have paid.

101. The Mining Commissioner shall not be permitted to allow specially registered ns, on which a bond has been passed, to revert so as to be held under prospecting ces.

Specially registered claims cannot revert so as to be held under prospecting licences.

102. Article 86 is not applicable to specially registered claims.

Art. 86 not applicable to specially registered claims.

When the payment of digger's licences for such claims is six months or more in ar the Mining Commissioner shall demand payment thereof in the *Staatscourant*, , if considered desirable by the Government, also in a local newspaper.

When payment of digger's licences on specially registered claims six months in arrea.

The Mining Commissioner shall be obliged to make this demand immediately r the expiration of the said six months and at the same time to give written ce thereof to the bondholders per registered letter.

Demand.

If within three months after the date of publication of the demand the payment all monies due has not followed, the claim or claims may be publicly sold by the ernment in such a way as shall be decided upon by it.

If no payment within three months after demand, claims sold.

The date of sale shall be published in the *Staatscourant*, and, if deemed advisable the Government, also in a local newspaper, at least fourteen days beforehand.

Publication of date of sale.

Out of the proceeds all monies due to the Government shall first of all be paid. such monies shall be reckoned an amount of £2 10s. per claim as a fine and for s. If the claims realise more than the amount of the fine and expenses, half of remaining amount shall be paid out to the owner of the farm and the other half deposited in the State coffers.

Disposal of excess proceeds of sale.

103. Article 102 shall shall also be in force in regard to digger's claims or algamated blocks of digger's claims for the special registration of which application been made in terms of Article 100, but provisionally and only so long as progress made with the application, according to the provisions and within the terms laid n in Article 100, until such application shall be granted or refused.

Article 102 applicable to digger's claims for the special registration of which application has been made.

104. A mortgage can be created on specially registered claims just as on novable property. The same regulations shall hold good in this respect as in the e of mortgage of immovable property, such as, *inter alia*, with regard to the rights creditors and sales in execution, also as regards the drawing up of hypothecation and rtgage bonds and the persons entitled to do so. The stamp dues, as laid down by law in the case of fixed and immovable property, shall also be applicable here.

Mortgage on specially registered claims.

Stamp dues.

105. Stands on proclaimed township or townships approved by the Government y be specially registered in the same way as hereinbefore prescribed in respect of ger's claims; no publication of a notice shall, however, be necessary and the ing Commissioner may in this case immediately grant the special registration and e a certificate thereof if he has no objections against the same.

Special registration of stands on proclaimed ground. No notice.

106. With regard to the payment of the licences on specially registered stands rules prescribed in Article 102 with respect to specially registered claims shall ly.

Licences on specially registered stands.

107. A mortgage may be effected on specially registered stands under exactly the

Mortgage on specially registered stands.

same provisions as herein laid down with respect to mortgage on specially registe
claims.

Stands on a proclaimed gold-field, being leases *in longum tempus* for 99 years, partake of the natu
immovable rather than movable property. A mortgage of such stands, therefore, in order to be
against the debtor's creditors, must be effected, like any ordinary mortgage of immovable prope
coram lege loci. The mere deposit of the title deeds with the intended mortgagee is not suffici
Collins, N.O., vs. *Hugo and the Standard Bank* (C.L.J., Vol. X., p. 344), decided on the 16th of Aug
1893, *Coram* Kotzé, C.J., and De Korte and Ameshoff, J.J.

N.B.—Article 107 of this Law corresponds with Article 52*h* of the Gold Law as introduced
Article 20 of Law 9 of 1888.

Section 7. "*Bezitrecht*" (*Right of Possession*).

"Bezitrechten" indisputable. **108.** All "bezitrechten" granted according to law, shall be indisputable, and c
not be contested in law, unless they have been obtained through fraud on the part
the possessor thereof.

Diagram of developed diggings. **109.** The Government shall have the right, either after consultation with or
the recommendation of the head of the Mining Department, to instruct the Survey
General to cause worked or developed diggings or portions thereof, after notice of
least six weeks, in the manner defined in Article 110, second paragraph, to be survey
in such a way that every warer-right, "mijnpacht," watercourse, digger's claim,
block of diggers' claims, or any other right or privilege necessary for the developme
of the diggings, shall be properly delineated on a diagram, and further, be indicated
a general compilation diagram or plan.

Approval of by Surveyor-General. These diagrams shall be approved by the Surveyor-General in accordance wi
Article 74. When these diagrams are once approved and signed, no objection to t
boundaries established by this survey shall be taken into consideration by any Cou
Should it appear that such a diagram has been incorrectly framed the same shall
amended or cancelled by an order of the High Court, and a new diagram shall
approved in the usual way. Such cancellation shall be effected in accordance wi
Cancellation. Law No. 9, 1891, Articles 6 and 7 (General Survey Act), by the Surveyor-General,
the request of the owner.

Notice calling for objections. **110.** As soon as possible, after the survey, the Mining Commissioner concern
shall issue a notice containing the name of the owner or possessor of the rights, t
description of the rights, the number of the diagram relating to the same, and a
calling upon all persons who wish to make objections against the same.

Publication for three months. This notice shall be published for a period of three months in the *Staatscoura*
and such notice shall further be posted up at the office of the Mining Commission
within whose jurisdiction the ground is situated, or at the office of the nearest Lan
Inspection of diagram. drost, and the diagram or diagrams relating thereto shall, during such period, lie f
inspection at the office of the Mining Commissioner concerned.

When no objections. **111.** If within the appointed time no objections are filed the Mining Commission
shall issue to the person entitled thereto the diagram approved by the Surveyc
Certificate of "bezitrecht." General, in accordance with Article 74, registered and signed, besides a certificate
"bezitrecht," in the form to be prescribed by the head of the Mining Department.

Hearing of objections. **112.** When objections are filed with the Mining Commissioner he shall fix a d
on which the objection or case shall be heard by him. The Mining Commissioner sh
Action to be instituted within three months after decision of Mining Commissioner. decide, awarding the rights to the person who, in his opinion, is entitled to the same

If one of the parties is dissatisfied with this decision he shall be obliged, with
three months after the date of the decision of the Mining Commissioner, to institu
an action in the High Court or Circuit Court, in default of which the decision of t

ıg Commissioner shall be considered as final, and the diagrams and the certificate
ezitrecht " shall be issued in accordance with his decision.

113. The Mining Commissioner shall issue diagram and certificate of " bezitrecht," ꜱe of an action, in accordance with the judgment of the Court.

Certificate of " bezitrecht " in accordance with the judgment of the Court.

114. Parties interested are obliged, within two months after notice from the ıg Commissioner, to take out duplicates of the approved diagrams, on payment of ı to be fixed by the Government in proportion to the expenses incurred by the ꞇnment in connection therewith.

Duplicates of approved diagrams.

ꞇf the parties interested neglect to take out these diagrams within the two months ꞇbefore mentioned, they shall incur a penalty not exceeding £10. Notice shall be ꞇ to them by the Mining Commissioner that on failure to take out diagrams within ꞇonth after the date of the infliction of the fine, the renewal of their licences or ꞇrmation of their rights may be refused.

Penalty.

Renewal of licences may be refused.

115. A " bezitrecht " includes all rights obtained under the grant, contracts, or ꞇes, and may be duly transferred, wholly or in part, by those who have acquired right, and this " bezitrecht " shall be indisputable.

Transfer of "bezitrecht."

Indisputable.

116. Every person or company possessing a claim, block of claims, water-right, ꞇkways, machine stands, or watercourses, can make application to the Mining Com-ꞇioner in writing, properly signed, and accompanied with an approved surveyor's ꞇram, or, if possible, with a surveyor's diagram of the claims or water-right, etc., ꞇesting an investigation of his or their claims to a certificate of " bezitrecht."

Application in writing for certificate of "bezitrecht."

It shall thereupon be lawful and obligatory on the Mining Commissioner to ꞇtute an enquiry concerning such claims. Where it shall appear that the formal ꞇ proof of " bezitrecht " is defective owing to :—

Enquiry.

When formal legal proof of " bezitrecht " defective.

(a) Transfer not having been passed ; or

(b) Any defect in the competency or the authority of any person who may have given transfer, or may have pretended to give transfer ; or

(c) The death or absence of the person in whose name the rights in dispute may be registered ; or

(d) The inability, for any other reason, of the holder in possession of such property to obtain a certificate of " bezitrecht " in the manner hitherto prescribed by law ; or

(e) The original acquisition of claims through faulty or false powers of attorney or otherwise, provided the person who makes the application for the " bezitrecht," or who holds it, shall not have been a party to the making of such a false power of attorney, and is a *bona fide* possessor ;

ꞇ the Mining Commissioner shall have the right to issue a certificate of " bezitrecht " ꞇd by him to such applicant.

Before the issue of such certificate of " bezitrecht," however, it must first be shown ꞇ the applicant is in peaceful possession and enjoyment, and entitled to claim the ꞇts for which he has made application.

Applicant must be in peaceful possession.

And whether or no the right of the applicant is clear, the Mining Commissioner ꞇl not immediately issue a certificate of " bezitrecht " to him, but shall publish a ꞇce asking for objections to the issue of such certificate of " bezitrecht," to be made ꞇin one month from the date thereof.

When right not clear.

Notice calling for objections.

Publication.

Contents.

Such notice shall be published three times in the Dutch language in the *St.* *courant* and at least once in a local newspaper, should there be one, and shall ind as clearly as possible the situation of the property, the nature of the rights clai in respect thereof, the name of the person who makes the claim, and in case any o person is registered as the holder, the name of such person.

When no objections.

In case no objections are filed within such period of three months, the dec. of the Mining Commissioner shall be final.

When objections filed.

In case objections are filed, the Mining Commissioner as such shall decide cerning the same.

In case objections are filed the procedure shall be in accordance with the p: sions of Article 112.

Stamp duty.

On a certificate of "bezitrecht" for claims, or blocks of claims and mac stands a stamp of five shillings per claim and machine stand must be paid and other certificates of "bezitrecht" a stamp of ten shillings shall be placed on . certificate.

Section 8. Undermining Rights.

Where prospecting and digging is prohibited.

117. Prospecting and digging is prohibited on or in towns, villages, stand vill: public squares, streets, roads, railways, burial grounds, erven stands, locations, t commonages, gardens, storage sites, machine stands, water-rights, and places w] tailings are heaped up, and such grounds as in accordance with Articles 15 and may be pointed out by the Mining Commissioner.

> See the cases of *The Witwatersrand G.M. Coy.* vs. *Young*, referred to under Article 15, *Kempi: The Modderfontein G.M. Coy. and the Mining Commissioner of Boksburg*, and *Nicolls* vs. *Leyds*, *:* referred to under Article 15.
> See also the case of *Ginsberg* vs. *The Gauf Syndicate and the Mining Commissioner of Boksbu* Appendix C.

Grant of undermining rights.

118. The Government shall, however, be at liberty to award undermining rig in accordance with Article 117 of this law and in accordance with regulations dr: up by the head of the Mining Department, approved by the Government and o

Except on burial grounds.

firmed by the Second Volksraad, except under burial grounds.

Enquiry by Commission.

119. These rights shall be investigated by a Commission, consisting of the h of the Mining Department and two impartial persons to be nominated by the Gove ment, whose task it shall be to institute enquiries in such cases on the gold-fields : assist Government with their advice regarding underground mining.

Regulations to be confirmed by Second Volksraad.

The Government shall thereupon decide, but in no case shall action be ta herein before the regulations mentioned in Article 118 of this law shall have b confirmed by the Honourable Second Volksraad.

To whom granted.

120. Such rights shall be granted :—

Holder of stands.

(1). To the holder or possessor under this law of *bona fide* stands on wl buildings stand, machine stands and water-rights.

Holder of surface right.

(2). To the person or persons, holder or holders, possessor or possessors of surface right, where equity demands such.

Public sale of lease.

(3). In the remaining cases as follows :—On private proclaimed ground and Government ground these rights shall be disposed of by Government by w of public sale of leases, of which timely notice shall be given in the *Stac courant*. The working thereof shall be effected under digger's claim licer

Notice.

Of the proceeds of the lease and licence monies on private proclaimed ground half shall go to the registered owner of the farm or portion thereof or his assigns, and the remaining half to the State.

Digger's licence necessary.

Half of proceeds go to owner.

121. In the case of public squares, streets, roads, railways, and such like, a three-~~nthly~~ publication and proclamation as afore-mentioned in Article 41 of this law ~~ll~~ take place before a right to mine underground is granted.

In case of public squares, &c., three months' notice to be given.

122. Those who have obtained written permission to mine underground from the ~~·~~ernment, whether by way of lease or otherwise, shall, within a period to be fixed ~~~~the Government, have to deposit security to the satisfaction of the Government ~~~~the owner of the surface.

Security to be deposited.

123. This ground shall have to be paid for after the manner of claims, in accord- ~~~~e with Article 120 of this law, to be calculated according to the superficial area of ~~~~h ground obtained for underground mining. The licences for the same must be ~~~~en out immediately after the grant.

Payment same as for claims.

124. Regulations for the safe working of such underground mines shall be drawn ~~~~by the State Mining Engineer, after consultation with the head of the Mining ~~~~partment, and, after approval by the Government, the same may come into opera- ~~~~n until the next following session of the Volksraad, after which such amendments ~~~~improvements as shall be deemed desirable by the Hon. Volksraad may be made.

Licences after grant.

Regulations for safe working.

Section 9. Water-Rights.

125. Owners and occupiers of ground along rivers or other water courses shall ~~~~ve no right of action against the Government or any gold mining company or gold ~~·~~gers, or other companies or persons, exploiting mines or digging under protection ~~~~the laws of the land, for damages for disturbing or rendering muddy the water in ~~~~said rivers or watercourses by using it for mining purposes.

No action for making water muddy in course of mining operations.

The Government shall, however, have the right to take measures and to make ~~~~ulations in regard to the disturbing or rendering muddy of rivers or watercourses.

Regulations.

See the case of *Maré* vs. *The Mount Maré G.M. Coy.*, referred to under Article 55.

126. With regard to the distribution of water, it is left to the Mining Commis- ~~~~ner of each proclaimed field, subject to the further approval of the Government, ~~~~er consultation with the head of the Mining Department, to make such regulations ~~~~th reference to the distribution of water as according to the circumstances of such ~~~~ld may be considered fair and reasonable, regard being had to the rights of private ~~~~ners.

Distribution of water by Mining Commissioner.

With regard to public fields, it is expressly declared that no digger, under any ~~~~cumstances whatever, shall have any proprietory right in the water running in any ~~·~~er, watercourse or furrow. He shall only have the right to use the said water ~~~~cording to law or regulations. In cases where, under certain circumstances, dam- ~~~~es must be paid, the value of the water shall not be taken into consideration.

No ownership of running water.

Value of water not taken into consideration in estimating damages.

The Government may, by agreement, grant special water-rights on Government ~~~~ounds, and also, for public interests, on proclaimed private grounds.

Special water rights.

See the case of *Maré* vs. *The Mount Maré G.M. Company*, referred to under Article 55.

127. Holders of "mijnpachten" and properly developed digger's claims shall be ~~~~titled to obtain water-rights.

Who entitled to water rights.

Workers of tailings have the right to obtain and to make use of water-rights

Workers of tailings.

under such regulations as may be granted thereanent by the Mining Commission after consultation with the Head of the Mining Department.

Where K. had let certain ground with water thereon to S., K. and S. both being under the impression that the said ground had been reserved on the proclamation of the farm, and S. afterwards, on finding out that the ground had not been reserved, obtained a water-right from the Government to the same water during the currency of the lease :—Held that S. could not dispute K's title to the lease, and could not refuse to pay the monies due under the contract of lease. *The Salisbury G.M. Company* vs. *Klipriviersberg Estate and G.M. Company* (C.L.J., Vol. XI., p. 59, decided on the 21st of August, 189 *coram* Kotzé, C.J., and Jorissen and Morice, J.J.

The plaintiff Company allowed its tailings for two years to run down a creek and took no steps prevent them being entirely washed away. The defendant afterwards pegged off the ground on wh the tailings had been washed. The Company, in an action, claimed the tailings, but the Court held th had been total abandonment, and gave judgment for defendants. *Sheba G.M. Company* vs. *Vautin, M bourne and Steers*, decided on the 5th of March, 1889, *coram* Esselen, Jorissen and De Korte, J. (unreported).

Article 48*b* of Law 10 of 1891, enacted that :—"If before the taking effect of this amended la water-rights have been granted by Digger's Committees, whose regulations were not approved by t Government, this fact alone shall be no reason for cancellation or non-confirmation of these rights, b parties interested in such water-rights, as well as holders of water-rights which were not yet confirmed the Head of the Mining Department, shall be obliged, within six months after the taking effect of th amended law, to make application for a certificate of " bezitrecht " for such water-right, in accordan with Article 30*b*, or for confirmation by the Head of the Mining Department, in the manner hereinaft described."

Article 48*b*, of Law 18, of 1892, re-enacted the same thing. It was held that 48*b* of the Gold Law 1892, gives a further term of six months after the lapse of the term granted by Article 48*b* of Law 10, 1891. *Lindum G.M. Company* vs. *The Sexagon Syndicate*, decided on the 13th of April, 1895, *cora* Kotzé, C.J., and Jorissen, J. ; Ameshoff, J., dissentiente (unreported).

Where irregularities exist no certificate of " bezitrecht " issued.
128. Should it appear that irregularities have taken place, such as, for exampl when on the granting thereof they were not connected with claims, "mijnpacht," right to work tailings, or when such mining right for which they were granted ha already lapsed, then no certificate of " bezitrecht " shall be issued for such water-righ and they shall not be confirmed by the Head of the Mining Department.

Where two companies entered into an agreement to make a joint dam on a certain piece of grou for their joint use, and to amalgamate their respective water-rights for that purpose :—Held, that the was a trust and confidence established between the parties to the agreement, and their successors, to ho and use the amalgamated water-right jointly, and that neither party could set up the provisions of subsequent Statute in justification of its conduct in fraud of the agreement, unless the express langua of the Statute clearly sanctioned such a proceeding. *Van Ryn G.M. Company* vs. *New Chimes G.* *Company* (C.L.J. Vol. XII., p. 60), decided on the 12th of November, 1894, *coram* Kotzé, C.J., and I Korte and Ameshoff, J.J.

No water rights granted unless connected with claims, &c.
129. In future no water-rights shall be granted on proclaimed ground which ar not connected with claims, "mijnpacht," or a right to work tailings, except with th express consent of the Government.

Applications.
130. Applications for water-rights must be made to the Mining Commissione and every application must bear a stamp of the value of five shillings, and must b

Stamp.

Plans.
accompanied by plans in quadruple, framed by an admitted surveyor, which mus contain such connections and particulars as shall be desired by the Mining Commis sioner in accordance with Article 9 of the instructions for claim inspectors. Th

Signed by Claim Inspector.
plans must be signed by the Claim Inspector as correct with the beacons.

The applications must be made in such form as shall be prescribed from time t time by the Head of the Mining Department, and all particulars desired therein mus also appear on the plans.

Publication of notice by applicant.
131. Notice of these applications must be published by the applicant three time it the *Staatscourant*, and at least once in a local newspaper, should there be one. Thi notice shall be issued by the Mining Commissioner in the form prescribed by th Head of the Mining Department.

The application with plans shall, moreover, lie for one month at the office of the *Inspection for one month.* ng Commissioner for inspection of interested parties, who may send in their *Objections.* tions to the Mining Commissioner concerned within that period.

Should these objections be found groundless by the Mining Commissioner, after *Hearing of.* ng the parties, he may grant the application.

When more than one applicant makes application to obtain one and the same r-right, the Mining Commissioner, after hearing the parties, shall decide who is led thereto.

From the decision of the Mining Commissioner an appeal may be entered within *Appeal to Head of Mining Department.* teen days to the Head of the Mining Department, whose decision shall be final.

132. All grants of water-rights are sent up to the Head of the Mining Depart- *Grants of water rights confirmed by Head of Mining Department.* ; for confirmation, accompanied by a copy of the application, the plans, and the rt of the Mining Commissioner regarding the desirability, or otherwise, of the rmation, regarding the consideration of the objections, if there were any, etc.

In future no water-rights shall be considered valid unless confirmed by the Head *Not valid unless confirmed.* te Mining Department, or included in a certificate of "bezitrecht."

133. On all water-rights intended and used for motive-power the sum of 1s. per *Water rights for motive power.* th shall be paid for each horse-power for every water-right not exceeding ten e-power; and 2s. 6d. per month for each horse-power above ten horse-power. ms to which a water-right is attached and on which water-right payment, accord- *Claims cannot be renewed until monies due on water right have been paid* to this article, must take place, may not be renewed, unless the monies due on the r-right have been duly paid.

134. On the lapsing of claims or "mijnpacht," or of a right to work tailings, the *Lapsing of water right.* er-right granted for the working of such claims, "mijnpacht," or tailings lapses

The last holder of such water-right has, however, for the period of one month *Last holder preferent right for one month.* the date on which the abovementioned mining-right lapsed, a preferent right to ver the water-right for working other claims, "mijnpacht," or tailings belonging im, when he sends in a new application for the same in the ordinary way.

A water-right may also, on the representation of the Mining Commissioner, be *Lapses when not used for two years.* ared by the Head of the Mining Department to have lapsed, when within two s after the confirmation thereof the machinery for which the water-right was lied for is not in working order, or no proper use is as yet being made of the er-right.

135. No owner of a claim shall have the right to dam up natural or running *Running water may not be dammed up.* er for his own use to the detriment of other claim-holders unless a water-right is en out by him in accordance with this law. Water obtained artificially shall not under this provision.

Section 10. Right to Firewood and other Wood.

136. A permit may be obtained for the right to cut or carry firewood or other *Permit to cut wood on Government ground.* d on or from Government ground on payment of £1 (one pound) for a wagon load, 6d. (seven shillings and sixpence) for a Scotch-cart load, and 6d. (sixpence) for one son's load. The said permits may be obtained on Government grounds from the *Agreement with owner of private ground.* ing Commissioner or Responsible Clerk. With regard to the cutting of wood on vate ground an agreement must be entered into with the owner.

If a person pegs off a piece of ground as a claim on which would grows, he shall *Wood may not be cut for trading purposes.* be entitled to cut and to carry away such wood for sale or trading purposes. (a)

o 2

With regard to private grounds, these sums shall be paid to the private owner.

Penalty. person cutting or carrying away wood without a permit or without leave from owner shall be punished with a fine not exceeding £25, or in default imprisonment exceeding six months, besides and above liability for damages for the wood cu romoved.

Penalty for cutting more wood than allowed by permit. Should it be found that more wood is taken away on a permit than that pe gives the right to, the offender shall be punished with a fine not exceeding £50, o default with imprisonment, with or without hard labour, not exceeding twelve mo

Informer to be rewarded. The informer of the contraventions shall be entitled to the half of the fines pr

    (a) This provision does not apply to stone dug out of the mines in the course of mining operat Thus, where the defendants dug out stone in the ordinary course of gold mining operations and sold the Johannesburg Sanitary Board, and the plaintiff sued them for the value of such stone, it was that the *dominium* of the stone was in the defendants, the claim-holders, and not in the plaintiff owner of the soil. *Bezuidenhout* vs. *Worcester G. M. Co.* (C.L.J., Vol. XI., p. 305), decided on the 29 June, 1894, per Kotzé, C.J.

Firewood for domestic use. 137. Any white person or family shall, however, be allowed to obtain gratis his or their own domestic use firewood on Government ground under permit to obtained from the Mining Commissioner, Responsible Clerk, Justice of the Peace Permit. Field-Cornet, on payment of 1s. per permit per month, on which permit not more t one wagon-load of firewood may be carried away, such permits to be renewed mont

---

CHAPTER IV.

Miscellaneous Provisions.

Bridge must be constructed over water-furrow. 138. Anyone who digs a water furrow through a road or footpath which is u shall construct a sufficiently safe bridge ; if he does not do so, any official or priv person may fill up the furrow, and the offender shall further be liable to a fine of fr Penalty. £1 to £10, or in default of payment to imprisonment as laid down in Article 8.

He who closes or obstructs a road or footpath in any other way shall be liabl the same penalty.

Removal of quartz from claim of another. 139. Anyone who removes quartz from or out of the claim or " mijnpacht " another shall be responsible for all damages, and shall moreover have to pay as c pensation three times the value of what has been taken by him, apart from criminal prosecution to which he exposes himself.

Altering or removing beacons of claim. 140. He who makes himself guilty of altering, shifting, or removing the bead of a claim shall be punished with a fine not exceeding the sum of £100, or in defa of payment with imprisonment as laid down in Article 8.

Wilful injury to claims, machinery, &c. 141. Anyone who makes himself guilty of injuring or destroying a mine, cla machinery, watercourse, or other mining property or belongings, or who shall guilty only of an attempt to commit the said offences shall be punished with a fine from £100 to £1,000, or with imprisonment with hard labour for the period of fr one to ten years, according to the nature of the case.

Wilful pegging-off of another's claim. 142. Anyone who makes himself guilty of the wilful pegging off of claims wh belong to others, and which are in proper order according to law, shall be punish with a fine of not less than £25 and not more than £100 for every claim thus wilfu pegged off, or with imprisonment as laid down in Article 8.

    The word " *moedwillig* " is equivalent to " *malo animo.*" *Charlton* vs. *The State* (C.L.J., Vol. XI

, decided on the 3rd August, 1894, *coram* Kotzé, C.J., and Ameshoff and Morice, J.J.; *Sylvester* vs. *State* (Official Reports, L 2., p. 48), decided on the 4th June, 1894, *coram* Kotzé, C.J., and Jorissen Morice, J.J.

143. Every digger, inhabitant, or licence-holder shall, when called upon, render istance to maintain public order, under penalty of loss of licence and of a fine not eeding the sum of £25. *(Diggers must assist to maintain order.)*

144. Everyone within the boundaries of a proclaimed field being found guilty of crime of high treason or " gekwetste majesteit," or public violence, shall, above l besides the punishment provided by the law for such crime, forfeit all his goods, vable as well as immovable, in favour of the State. *(Treason and public violence on proclaimed fields.)*

Held, by the majority of the Court (Kotzé, C.J. and Ameshoff, J.; Morice, J.,diss.), that a bank unt falls within the terms of Article 148 of Law 19 of 1895. Held (per Morice, J., diss)., that Article refers to real rights to property, movable or immovable, situated within the Witwatersrand Gold ds, including shares in companies the property of which is situated within such gold fields, but does refer to bank accounts. *In re the State Attorney* vs. *Lionel Phillips and others* (C.L.J., Vol. XIII., p.

In January, 1896, an interdict was granted against all the property of the Reform Committee on the twatersrand Gold Fields. On the application of J. S. Curtis, one of the members of the Reform mmittee, it was held that his property did not fall under the interdict, because it was situated on an oclaimed portion of Doornfontein. *J. S. Curtis* vs. *The State*, decided 12th March, 1896, *coram* rice J. (unreported). See Article 144 of this law.

145. No person may carry on any trade whatever in unwrought precious tal, amalgam or precious stones, under which is included the buying or selling, the rtering or exchanging, of such unwrought precious metal, amalgam or uncut ecious stones, unless he has a special licence for the purpose, for which he must pay £10 year; provided, however, that the individual digger or company need not take out y licence for the sale of the unwrought precious metal, amalgam or uncut precious nes dug out or found by him or it personally or on his or its instructions. The vernment has the right to suspend, wholly or in part the working of the first rtion of this article with regard to one or more precious metals, amalgam or ecious stones. *(No trading in unwrought precious metal without special licence. Exception. Suspension of Article.)*

He who carries on trade in unwrought precious metal, amalgam or uncut precious nes as above described, without having a special licence to do so, is punished with a e not exceeding £100, or imprisonment with or without hard labour, or both gether, for the first offence; for the second offence a fine not exceeding £200 or prisonment for a period uot exceeding 12 months, with or without hard labour, or th together, and for any further offence a fine or imprisonment, or both together, in e discretion of the Court. *(Penalty.)*

146. Anyone who is found in possession of amalgam or unwrought gold or uncut ecious stones and can give no proof that he obtained possession of the same in a wful manner, shall be punished with a fine not exceeding £500, or imprisonment ith or without hard labour for a period not exceeding two years, or both together, cording to the nature of the case, for the first offence. For the second offence a fine t exceeding £1,000, or three years' imprisonment, with or without hard labour, or th together, and for any further offence, a fine or imprisonment, or both together in e discretion of the Court. besides forfeiture in favour of the State of the amalgam unwrought gold or uncut precious stones found in his possession. *(Being in possession of unwrought precious metal.)*

In *The State* vs. *James Bacon* (C.L.J., Vol. IX., p. 182), where B. was indicted for being in possession unwrought gold, it was held that it was the duty of the judge to define " unwrought gold," and that e question as to whether or not the gold was unwrought, was a question for the jury to decide. Decided the 23rd of February, 1892, *coram* Kotzé, C.J. and De Korte and Morice, J.J.

Licensed dealer in unwrought precious metal must keep proper books. 147. A licensed dealer in unwrought precious metal, amalgam or uncut precio stones, shall keep such books of his business as the Government from time to ti shall deem fit to prescribe, and the said dealer shall every month, on the first day each month, send up to the head of the Mining Department a true and sworn co of such books, and in such form as the Government from time to time shall prescri

Examination of books. The Government shall at any time have the right to cause such books to examined.

Penalty. Every contravention of this article shall be punished with a fine not exceedi £50, or in default of payment with imprisonment as laid down in Article 8.

Persons despatching, etc., unwrought gold must send in declaration in duplicate. 148. The managers of banks, store-keepers, agents and in general all persons w buy, sell, exchange, take or give for safe keeping, or despatch, unwrought gold, go amalgam, and other gold alloys are obliged to send in duplicate a declaratic thereanent, on or before the 15th of each month, for the preceding month, to the offi of the Mine Inspector concerned.

In case no Mine Inspector's office is established on or near the place where t transaction takes place, such declaration must be sent to the Mining Commission Responsible Clerk, or Landdrost of the district. These declarations must be ma according to the forms prescribed for that purpose by the State Mining Engineer.

Penalty. Contraventions of this provision shall be punished with a fine not exceeding £5 or in default of payment with imprisonment for a period not exceeding three month

Forms for returns. The persons who, according to this article, are obliged to make monthly returns, ca obtain the required forms for one or more months in advance at the offices of t officials to whom the declarations must be sent in, either by personal application or b written application posted, and are responsible for the consequences when they do n provide themselves with the forms early enough.

Sending in of returns. The sending in of the returns may be effected by personally handing them in the appointed office or by post, in which latter case the letter must be registered an the sending in shall be considered to have taken place on the day that the return w sent by post. Should the last day of the time for sending in fall on a Sunday holiday, the return must be made the day before.

Trading without licence. 149. Anyone trading without a licence to trade shall be liable to the penaltie laid down by the law of the land. Further, shall be punished with a fine of not les than £5, and not more than £25, or in default of payment, with imprisonment as lai down in Article 8 for every contravention :—

Penalty for digging or prospecting without licence. (a) He who digs or prospects for precious metal or precious stones without licence.

For pegging off claims without licence. (b) He who pegs off a claim or claims without prospecting or digger's licenc Moreover such pegging off shall be considered as unlawful, shall not b recognised, and shall entail no right whatever.

For digging or prospecting on unproclaimed Government ground. (c) He who with or without licence digs or prospects for precious metals o precious stones on Government grounds which have not been thrown ope for the purpose by the Government in accordance with Article 64 of thi law, unless special permission has been given by the Government. Thi **Special permission for twelve months.** special permission shall, however, not be given for longer than twelv months, and shall lapse if within six months after the date of the permissio no prospecting has been begun.

On the 13th of January, 1888, it was decided that a person could peg off claims and *then* get licence *Madeline Reef Syndicate* vs. *Coetzee and others* (C.L.J., Vol. V., p. 16 ; Official Reports, I. I., pp. 134, 135 'he law was altered by Law 9 of 1888, Article 30, which imposed a penalty for pegging off claims ut a licence.

)n the 20th of February, 1893, it was decided that if a person pegs claims without licences and then 1s licences, before anyone else with licences pegs the same ground, he will have a good title to the s notwithstanding Article 70 of Law 18 of 1892 (which corresponds with Article 149 of Law 21 of *Humphreys* vs. *The Claim Inspector of Heidelberg and Symons and Lys* (Official Reports, I. 1., 34, 135).

. person who pegs claims without licences always runs the risk of somebody else with licences 1ng the same ground before he can obtain his licences, as in the case of *Blomfield* vs. *Mining 1issioner of Johannesburg and F. J. Bezuidenhout, jun.* (Official Reports, I. 1., p. 132), decided on the of March, 1894, *coram* Kotzé, C.J. and Jorissen and Morice, J.J. There the plaintiff and defendant d off the same piece of ground as claims without licences, the plaintiff's pegging being prior to the dant's. The defendant then obtained licences and retrapped his pegs before the plaintiff could do [t was held that the defendant had a better title than the plaintiff. (Decided 17th of March, 1894.) le 70 of Law 14 of 1894, which corresponds with Article 149 of this law, enacted: "Moreover such ng off shall be considered as unlawful, shall not be recognised, and shall entail no right whatever." uld seem, therefore, that, as the law now stands, if a person pegged off claims without licences and obtained licences before any other person with licences pegged the same ground, he would not ire any title to the ground.

[t is not necessary that a person pegging off claims should have his licences with him. If his sentative takes out the licences and he pegs simultaneously, his pegging is good, though he be miles from his representative. But Article 39 (4th paragraph) of this law enacts: "No person shall have ight to peg off claims before he or his representative *is present with his licences on the ground* which he es to peg off." This new law came into force on the 1st of November, 1896.

150. No one shall be allowed to pay his servants in unwrought precious metal, lgam or uncut precious stones, under penalty of a fine not exceeding the sum of 0, or, in default of payment, of imprisonment as laid down in Article 8, besides a eiture of such unwrought precious metal, amalgam and uncut precious stones in ur of the State.

Servants may not be paid in unwrought precious metal.

151. Anyone who purchases, barters, or accepts unwrought precious metal, lgam or uncut precious stones, from coloured persons either on a proclaimed lic field or elsewhere within the borders of the South African Republic, shall be ished with a fine not exceeding £1,000 and imprisonment, with or without hard ur, for a period not exceeding five years, besides forfeiture of such unwrought cious metal, amalgam or uncut precious stones in favour of the State.

Purchasing unwrought precious metal from coloured persons.

152. A coloured person who sells, barters, delivers, or receives unwrought cious metal, amalgam or uncut precious stones, or is found in possession of vrought precious metal, amalgam or uncut precious stones, shall be punished with more than fifty lashes, and imprisonment for a period not exceeding five years, h or without hard labour, and forfeiture of such rough precious metal, amalgam or ut precious stones, in favour of the State.

Coloured person selling, etc., unwrought precious metal

153. Every coloured person within the boundaries of a public diggings must have 1onthly pass which is obtainable at the office of the Mining Commissioner or other sons appointed thereto, on payment of a sum calculated at one shilling per 1th, except in such cases where Law No. 23 of 1895 applies. For every contraven- 1 of this article the offender shall be punished with a fine of five shillings.

Coloured person must have pass.

This article is also applicable to coloured labourers exclusively employed in 1ing and digging on private unproclaimed grounds, and on private farms where in ordance with Article 26 written permission has been obtained, and on grounds ich are worked under concession or "mijnpacht," on Government as well as on specting grounds thrown open to the public, and on townships.

154. A coloured person who has entered into a contract, whether verbally or in ting, to serve his master as a domestic servant or as a servant in a shop or store, or assist him in working a claim, machinery or waterfurrow on any proclaimed field,

Coloured person leaving service without permission, or using insulting language to his master.

and who departs without leave from his master's service, or is negligent or refuse
do any work in discharge of his duty which can according to law be asked
required of him, or who uses threatening or insulting language to his master,
master's wife, or any other person lawfully placed over him, shall be punished wit
fine not exceeding the sum of £2, or with imprisonment, with or without l
labour, for a period not exceeding one month, or with lashes not exceeding twe
five in number.

Servant, not being a coloured person. A servant as above-mentioned, not being a coloured person, who is found gu
of any of the offences described in this article, shall be punished with a fine
exceeding the sum of £5 or with imprisonment, with or without hard labour, fo
period not exceeding three months. The Mining Commissioner shall further, wit
the limits of the field over which he is appointed, have the same duties and ri
which, according to Law No. 11 of 1892, Landdrosts have, except on such fields wl
Special Landdrosts are appointed.

Concluding provision.

Taking effect. 155. This law, as amended, comes into force from the 1st. November, 1896, v
the exception of Articles 118 to and including 124 (as now amended) which sl
remain in force until the further decision of the Hon. The First Volksraad.

S. J. P. KRUGER,
State President.

Dr. W. J. LEYDS,
State Secretary.

Government Office, Pretoria,
19th September, 1896.

APPENDIX A.

olution of the Hon. First Volksraad, Article 1,282, dated 20th September, 1895

The First Volksraad, with reference to the Executive Council's Resolution, Article
, contained in the Government missive, dated the 5th instant, with the proposal
·mitted therewith for amendment of Article 121, etc., of the Gold Law, as approved
the Hon. Second Volksraad, now under consideration; considering the fact that the
·d Law has been dealt with by the Second Volksraad, and that the First Volksraad
· not all the data before it which were laid before the Hon. Second Volksraad;
·ther, considering that there exist great differences, as well in the Second as in the
·st Volksraad, concerning the so-called undermining rights, and that it is therefore
· desirable to introduce amendments to the said law, where such great differences
·st; resolves that it can not agree with the resolution of the Hon. Government *Suspension of Articles 122 to*
·arding Articles 121, 122, and 124, but resolves to accept the resolutions of the *128 of Gold Law of 1895*
·ond Volksraad with regard to the Gold Law as notice, with the exception of Articles *(Law No. 19, 1895).*
·2 to 128 inclusive, and to hereby suspend the operation of the latter until the next
·inary session, and instructs the Hon. Government to collect the necessary informa-
·a, and to snbmit the same at the next session, in order to enable the Raad to become
·ter acquainted with the circumstances and with the feelings of the burghers of the
·public.

·B.—Articles 121, 122, 124, referred to in the above resolution, correspond to Articles
117, 118, and 120 in the Gold Law of 1896, and Articles 122 to 128 also referred
to above, correspond to Articles 118 to 124 in the Gold Law of 1896.

Appendix B.

No. 235.

GOVERNMENT NOTICE.

R/6963/95.

For general information are published herewith the following regulations with regard to the drawing of lots for claims on private and Government ground, approved by Article 1,129 of the resolutions of the Hon. Second Volksraad, dated 2nd August, 1895, which resolution was accepted as notice by the Hon. First Volksraad by Article 916 of its minutes, dated 14th August, 1895.

Dr. W. J. LEYDS,
State Secretary.

Government Office, Pretoria,.

15th August, 1895.

REGULATIONS.

For the drawing of lots for claims on private and Government ground.

Whereas it is necessary and desirable to make special provision for the pegging off of claims on the proclamation of some farms in cases where there are great gatherings of people, whereby serious irregularities might take place, now therefore it is laid down as follows:—

1. In future no private or Government ground, declared by proclamation to be a public diggings, shall be available for the pegging off of claims, before the proclamation has been read on the ground to be proclaimed, where also the licences shall be issued for the first time.

2. That, where in future it may appear to the head of the Mining Department that on the proclamation of private farms and Government ground, the circumstances require it, the Government, with the advice and consent of the Executive Council, shall have the power to instruct the Surveyor-General to cause such farms or Government ground to be surveyed in claims, and to have a diagram thereof made before the day of throwing open, which claims must be properly numbered on such diagram.

   On this diagram must further appear the situation of the claims mentioned in Articles 9, 10, and 14 of Law 14 of 1894, which must likewise be surveyed and numbered before the day of throwing open, as also the " mijnpachten," homestead, building and arable lands granted, and other grounds reserved under Article 20 of the said law, and the grounds reserved by the Mining Commissioner, in accordance with the second paragraph of Article 28 of Law 14 of 1894.

   Articles 9, 10, 14, 20, and 28 of Law 14 of 1894, correspond with Articles 47, 46, 48, 54, and 15 respectively of Law 21 of 1896.

3. The claims thus measured and reduced to diagram, with the exception of those mentioned in Articles, 9, 10, and 14 of the Gold Law, shall be given out by lot to the public on the day of throwing open, and if necessary on the following days.

The Mining Commissioner or his lawful representative shall at this drawing of lots and giving out of claims have to take into consideration:

(1) The number of claims available for the public.

(2) The number of persons present on the day of throwing open who wish to obtain claims.

In no case shall more than twelve claims be awarded to one person by lot, in connection with which Article 61A and 61c must be taken into consideration, or such other provision as may at present exist or in future be made thereanent in the Gold Law.

Article 61A of Law 14 of 1894 corresponds with Article 65 of Law 21 of 1896, while Article 61c is left out of Law 21 of 1896.

4. The expenses of surveying the claims thus surveyed shall have to be paid to the Government by the claimholder immediately on issue of the licence, in default of which the Mining Commissioner or responsible clerk is entitled to refuse the licence, in which case these claims shall be dealt with in terms of Article 61B of the Gold Law.

Article 61B of Law 14 of 1894 corresponds with Article 86 of Law 21 of 1896.

5. In case, on the day of throwing open, all the claims have not yet been surveyed, only the claims which have been surveyed or reduced to diagram shall be drawn for. The remaining claims shall however as speedily as possible be surveyed and drawn for on a day to be fixed by the head of the Mining Department, of which drawing at least three weeks' notice must be given in the "Staatscourant."

6. The manner of drawing lots shall be regulated by the head of the Mining Department in consultation with the Government, while after the termination of every drawing, a report must be sent in by the Mining Commissioner as soon as possible to the head of the Mining Department.

7. These regulations come into force immediately after publication in the "Staatscourant."

No. 247   R. 8030/95.

GOVERNMENT NOTICE.

For general information are herewith published the following Regulations for drawing lots for claims on private and Government ground in accordance with the resolution of the Executive Council, Article 603 of its Minutes, dated 20th August, 1895.

Dr. W. J. LEYDS,
State Secretary.

Government Office, Pretoria,
20th August, 1895.

REGULATIONS.

For the drawing of lots for claims on private and Government ground, approved by resolution of the Honourable Second Volksraad, Article 1,129, dated 2nd August, 1895, and accepted as notice by resolution of the Honourable First Volksraad, Article 916, dated 14th August, 1895.

In consequence of the above Regulations, and for the carrying out of the same, the Government has deemed fit to give out, by way of drawing lots, the claims on the portion of the farm " Witfontein," No. 572, formerly in the district of Potchefstroom, now in the district of Krugersdorp, and portion of " Luipaardsvlei," No. 682, formerly in the district of Potchefstroom, now in the district of Krugersdorp, and " Palmietfontein," No. 697, in the district of Potchefstroom, which will be proclaimed respectively on the 30th of August, 1895 ; 2nd of September, 1895, and the 27th August, 1895.

The manner in which the drawing for the claims must take place shall be as follows :—

(1) In accordance with the above-mentioned regulations, the claims, as surveyed and reduced to diagram, in blocks of six claims, on the above-mentioned farms, by the Surveyor-General, shall be drawn for.

(2) The person or persons who are present on the day of proclamation on the ground to be proclaimed, shall be entitled to obtain gratis one ticket for each person on each of the farms to be proclaimed, provided he produces his receipt or certificate to show that he has paid his personal taxes for the current year.

(3) The number of tickets shall be regulated according to the number of persons who, on the day of proclamation and after the reading of the same, shall be present on the ground to be proclaimed, and who shall be obliged to present themselves to the Mining Commissioner or responsible clerk, and to give him notice, after production of the receipt for personal taxes, that they wish to take part in the drawing.

(4) The drawing for claims takes place on the day of proclamation, and if necessary on the following days, and shall commence directly after the reading of the proclamation.

(5) When the number of persons present, who wish to take part in the drawing, exceeds the number of blocks of 6 (six) claims, blank tickets must be put into the drum after the tickets on which the blocks of 6 (six) claims in due sequence on each ticket have been noted have been placed in it.

(6) The names of the persons who wish to take part shall be placed in drum No. 1, and the tickets with the number and the numbers (six claims) and the blank tickets in drum No. 2. The official charged with the drawing shall have to draw a ticket out of drum No. 2, while an official to be named by the Head of the Mining Department shall have to draw a name out of drum No. 1.

(7) The Claim Inspector shall be obliged to point out to each person who has drawn a ticket representing claims the pegs and the situation of such claims.

(8) The Head of the Mining Department shall have to exercise due supervision and to instruct the officials from time to time in accordance with these regulations.

No. 255.   R. 8241/95.

GOVERNMENT NOTICE.

For general information is herewith published the following Article 1,408 of the resolutions of the Hon. Second Volksraad, dated 27th August, 1895, with regard to the taking part in the drawing for claims by youths of sixteen years, which resolution was accepted as notice by the Hon. First Volksraad by Article 1,023 of its minutes, dated 28th August, 1895, wherein it was laid down that this resolution should come into force immediately after publication in the *Staatscourant.*

DR. W. J. LEYDS,
State Secretary.

Government Office, Pretoria,
29th August, 1895.

Resolution of the Hon. Second Volksraad, Article 1,408, dated 27th August, 1895.

The Second Volksraad, having considered the Government missive, now on the order, including a letter from Field-Cornet Botha, and a telegram from Field-Cornet Cronjé, with regard to the drawing for claims, now to take place, by youths of sixteen years, the Second Volksraad, taking into consideration that this drawing is a special matter, resolves :

That in such special cases youths above the age of sixteen years, whose names appear on the Field Cornet's lists, and the taxes of whose parents have been paid for the current year, shall be entitled to take part in the drawing under the following conditions :—

(1) Each of them must be provided with a Field-Cornet's or Assistant Field-Cornet's certificate, showing the name and date of his registration in the Field-Cornet's books.

(2) A certificate from the official under whose jurisdiction his parents come showing that the taxes of his father or guardian for the current year have been paid.

(3) Each of them shall be present in person on the day of drawing.

This resolution shall only be of force on places for drawing of lots of claims, and shall not be applicable in any other case.

Appendix C.

On the 12th of June, 1891, J. S. Curtis bought 78 prospecting claims on Turffontein from a certain Rautenbach. On the 18th of June, the secretary of the Village Main Reef G.M. Company, on behalf of which Curtis had acquired the claims, applied to the Mining Commissioner of Johannesburg for digger's licences for the said caims. On the refusal of the Mining Commissioner to grant digger's licences, the secretary applied for renewal of the prospecting licences. This request was also refused. Thereupon Curtis, in his capacity of managing director of the said company, made an application to the Court to compel the Mining Commissioner to renew the licences, maintaining that the main reef ran through the ground in dispute, and that such ground was proclaimed ground. The Mining Commissioner alleged that he refused to renew the licences because in consequence of a contract between the Government and the Deep Level Developing and Mining Township Syndicate, dated the 29th of October, 1889, the ground had been reserved for a township.

A rule *nisi* having been granted, the Court (Kotzé, C.J., and Jorissen, J.) refused to confirm it, Kotzé, C.J., said:—"The Court is of opinion that the rule *nisi* must be set aside. Assuming that the Mining Commissioner can be ordered, under certain circumstances, to renew prospecting licences, or to change them into digger's licences, such circumstances are not present here. Under Section 67 of Law 8 of 1889, the Government has the right to grant stands, provided it be not on gold-bearing ground. It is here disputed, and it is not known whether the ground is gold-bearing or not. Moreover, the Government has the power to grant a piece of ground larger in extent than the size of a stand, and that under one licence. Of this right the Government has made use, and there is nothing to show that it has here made an unfair use of this power. More especially is this so because the respondent was, and is, in possession, and the applicant was warned of this fact, and, notwithstanding this, went and pegged off, well knowing that months before the ground had been granted to the respondent. The respondent is entitled to the costs."

Curtis N.O. vs. *The Mining Commissioner of Johannesburg, and the Johannesburg Township Compauy*, decided on the 12th of August, 1891 (unreported).

The farm Klein Paardekraal was proclaimed on the 11th of October, 1886 with the exception of such portion as had been beaconed off for a " mijnpacht." On the 8th of November, 1888, the plaintiff pegged off a claim immediately adjoining the southern line of the Alexandra " mijnpacht," on the said farm. Some days afterwards the defendants shifted the southern line of the Alexandra " mijnpacht," so as to take in a portion of the plaintiff's claim, and shortly afterwards again shifted the line so as to entirely include the said claim in the " mijnpacht." In an action instituted by the plaintiff, the defendants were ordered to move the southern line of their " mijnpacht " to the place where it was at the date of plaintiff's pegging, and interdicted from committing any trespass on the said claim in the future.

Cathcart vs. *The Main Reef G.M. Company*, decided on the 25th of November' 1889 (unreported), *coram* Kotzé, C.J., and Esselen and De Korte, J.J.

The beacons erected at the time of proclamation are the true boundaries, and they indicate the position of the "mijnpacht," and not the chart or diagram, when such does not agree with the beacons.

Substantial damages, assessed by the Court without evidence of special damage, ordered to be paid by trespassers who pegged, notwithstanding the fact that they saw the beacons which had been erected.

Nabob G.M. Company vs. *Phœnix G.M. Company.,* decided on the 1st of March, 1890 (unreported), *coram* Kotzé, C.J., and Esselen and De Korte, J.J.

Where certain lapsed claims had been bought from the Government, and the purchaser, from whom the defendants, Barnato Bros., derived their title, finding that some of these claims were not on the line of reef, on the advice of the Claim Inspector took certain other claims on the line of reef instead, without filing powers of attorney for the fresh claims thus taken. Held : That the plaintiff, who subsequently pegged off the said fresh claims according to law, had a better title to them.

When a lapsed claim is bought, a title is acquired to a certain definite piece of ground, and not to any indefinite piece the size of a claim.

Powers of attorney once used for the purpose of obtaining licences for claims cannot be used a second time, but are, as it were dead.

Underwood vs. *Barnato Bros. and the Mining Commissioners of Boksburg, coram* Kotzé, C.J., and Ameshoff and Gregorowski, J.J.; decided on the 13th of June, 1896, and reported in the *Cape Law Journal*, Vol. xiii., p. 226.

Where the Mining Commissioner of Boksburg had provisionally granted an application for a water-right made by the Gauf Syndicate, and the Head of the Mining Department had returned the said application to the Mining Commissioner to have a certain discrepancy between the application and the diagram eliminated, and the plaintiff pegged the ground, which was the subject of the application, before the publication of the amended application. Held, that, as the final confirmation of the water-right by the Head of the Mining Department was still pending, the ground was not open ground and could not be pegged.

Ginsberg vs. *The Gauf Syndicate and the Mining Commissioner of Boksburg,* decided on the 8th and 9th of July, 1896, *coram* Ameshoff, Morice and Gregorowski, J.J. (C.L.J. Vol. xiii., p. 225).

N.B. The application for a water-right in this case was made some time after the proclamation of the farm Leeuwpoort.

The plaintiff entered into a contract with the first defendant by which he acquired the right to *prospect* on a certain farm and the further right to purchase the said farm, within a certain period, for a certain price. The first defendant, notwithstanding this, sold the farm to the second defendant. The plaintiff sued the defendants for performance of the contract and rescission of the sale. The first defendant took the exception that the contract was *ab initio* null and void because it had not been *notarially* drawn. Kotzé, C.J., in delivering judgment, said : "The only question which the Court must decide is whether the contract is *ab initio* null and void under the Volksraad Besluit of August the 12th, 1886, Article 1,422. We are of opinion that the contract alleged in the summons does not fall under the terms of the V.R. Besluit or under the provisions of Article 14 of Law 7 of 1883. It is only said that the right to *prospect* or search for gold, etc., is granted to the plaintiff, with the further right to purchase the farm out and out. This is not a case of a grant of rights to minerals or regarding rights to dig (*afstand van regten of mineralen of omtrent regten om te delven*), of which Article 1,422 speaks, nor of a grant of a right to minerals which are supposed to be present or are actually present on any farm as laid down in Article 14 of Law 7 of 1883. All that is granted to the plaintiff is the *mere right to search* for gold and other minerals and, whether these are found or not, the further right to purchase the farm. There is no *grant or cession of mineral rights or rights to minerals*, and we are therefore of opinion that the exception must be set aside with the costs."

Pearce v. *Olivier and others*, decided on the 13th of November, 1889 (unreported), *coram* Kotzé, C.J., and De Korte and Ameshoff, J.J.

On the 28th of May, 1887, a certain contract was entered into between the plaintiff (and others) on one side and the defendant on the other, one of the clauses of which contract was as follows; " The owners of and parties interested in the half farm Welgegund adjoining Oudedorp and transferred to the name of J. P. K. N. Bezuidenhout have agreed as follows,—that all rights, profits, and privileges, arising out of the mineral rights on the said half farm Welgegund shall be divided as follows, etc."

The plaintiff sued the defendant to have the agreement drawn up *notarially* in accordance with one of the terms of the agreement. The defendant pleaded that the plaintiff was debarred from suing because the agreement on which he sued was not *notarial* in accordance with the Volksraad Besluit of the 12th of August, 1886. The majority of the Court (Kotzé, C.J., and De Korte, J.) held that judgment should be given for the plaintiff. Kotzé, C.J., gave as his reasons, (1) that the literal interpretation of the above-mentioned clause removed the contract from the operation of the Volksraad Besluit; (2) that the circumstances of the case showed that in the above-mentioned clause no grant of mineral rights, but only a division of the privileges and proceeds thereof was in the contemplation of the parties; (3) that even if the said clause fell within the terms of the Volksraad Besluit, still the defendant could not be heard when he attempted to make use of that Besluit to the prejudice of the plaintiff, for this would be equivalent to a fraud on him. The action was brought to compel the defendant to comply with the terms of the Volkraad Besluit, by executing a proper notarial agreement as contracted between the parties. De Korte, J., based his judgment on the last ground above-mentioned.

Esselen, J. (diss.) held that the said clause fell within the terms of the Volksraad Besluit.

Steyn vs. *Bezuidenhout*, decided on the 6th of March, 1890 (unreported).

The Paarl Pretoria Company, claiming to be the owner of certain claims on the farm Langlaagte, in November, 1888, sold all its right to the said claims to the Central Langlaagte Company. In January. 1889, Donovan, maintaining that the ground was open, pegged off the same claims and instituted an action against the Central Langlaagte Company for ejectment. The claims were awarded to Donovan. When the summons was served on the Central Langlaagte Company, this company's attorney wrote on the 21st March, 1889, to the attorneys of the Paarl Pretoria Company giving them notice of the action, and advising that the Paarl Pretoria Company should intervene, seeing that this company sold the claim to Central Langlaagte Company.

The Paarl Pretoria Company took no steps to intervene, and, after judgment was given in favor of Donovan, instituted an action against Donovan and Wolff, as representing the Royal Langlaagte Company, to whom Donovan had in the meanwhile sold the claims. The defendants (Donovan and Wolff N.O.) pleaded *Res judicata*, and this plea was upheld and the plaintiffs held to be estopped from instituting the action on the ground that they ought to have intervened in the action of *Donovan* vs. *The Central Langlaagte Company.*

The Paarl Pretoria G.M. Coy. vs. *Donovan and Wolff, N.O.*, decided on the 25th November, 1889 (unreported), *coram* Kotzé, C.J., and Esselen and De Korte, J.J.

On the 2nd February, 1889, certain Scott and Sparks pegged off 12 claims on ground afterwards known as Schweizer's Township, and on the 7th February, 1889, they pegged off 12 more claims. In April, 1889, those claims were amalgamated in blocks and registered in the name of the Non Pareil Syndicate consisting of Scott, Sparks and Thomas Whitty. On the 2nd and 7th of September, 1889, the Mining Commissioner of Johannesburg refused to renew the prospecting licences, because, as he stated, he wished to compel the Non Pareil Syndicate to take out digger's licences instead of prospecting licences. Scott and Sparks alleged that the renewal was refused because the Government wished to lay out a township on the ground. The Non Pareil Syndicate made no objection and lodged no protest against the refusal to renew.

On the 21st September, 1889, a contract was entered into between the Government and Schweizer, giving the latter the right to lay out a township on the ground held by him. Schweizer had pegged in July, 1889, and he caused a diagram to be made of all ground held by him, which included the 24 claims above-mentioned. In March, 1890, Schweizer caused a sale to be held of the stands laid out by him, but only a few were sold. He thereafter ceded all his rights to Hollard and Van Boeschoten, who again ceded to the Rand Exploring Syndicate. In 1893, on the advice of a Government Commission, the Government decided to change the stands into claims and to issue claim licences to the Rand Exploring Syndicate, and the syndicate had to indemnify the Government against any claims which might be set up by persons who had previously held portions of the ground included in Schweizer's Township. Thereupon the Non Pareil Syndicate sent in a claim for a block of 12 claims, but this was refused, and an action was consequently instituted against the Rand Exploring Syndicate in March 1895. After the closing of the pleadings the Non Pareil Syndicate ceded all its rights to the Schweizer's Claimholders Rights Syndicate, which obtained leave, with the consent of the defendant syndicate, to appear as plaintiff. The Court found that the renewal of the *prospecting* licences was refused because the Mining Commissioner wished to compel the Non Pareil Syndicate to take out *digger's* licences instead, under Article 17 of Law 10 of 1887, and held that this syndicate must be taken to have abandoned its rights on the ground that it did not protest either when the renewal of prospecting licences was refused, or when Schweizer put up the stands for sale. Judgment was, therefore, given for the defendant with costs. The Court considered that the taking over of the rights of the Non Pareil Syndicate by the Schweizer's Claimholders Rights Syndicate was impeachable on the ground of champerty, but did not think it necessary to decide the case on that ground.

Schweizer's Claimholders Rights Syndicate, Ld., vs. *The Rand Exploring Syndicate, Ld.,* decided on the 25th of August, 1896, *coram* Kotzé, C.J., and Gregorowski, J., (not yet reported).

Certain persons who alleged that they were entitled to certain claims (127 in all) on the farm Turffontein, in the possession of the Rand Exploring Syndicate, joined with certain other persons present who had no interest in these claims, and formed the

Schweizer's Claimholders Rights Syndicate, Limited, with the object of obtaining possession of the said claims and working them. The consideration received by those persons who alleged that they were entitled to claims consisted of shares in the Syndicate, while the working capital of the company, out of which the expenses of litigation were to be defrayed, was advanced by some of the other persons who had no interest in the claims. The syndicate instituted action against the Rand Exploring Syndicate, and the defendants raised the plea of champerty. The Court held that the articles of association of the syndicate were tainted with champerty and were, therefore, *contra bonos mores*, and granted absolution from the instance with costs.

Schweizer's Claimholders Rights Syndicate, Limited, vs. *Rand Exploring Syndicate, Limited,* decided on the 4th September 1896, *coram* Kotzé, C.J., and Ameshoff and Gregorowski, J.J. (not yet reported).

The plaintiff, Schuler, had certain prospecting rights over certain property. On the 27th February, 1895, he entered into a contract with the defendants Sacke and Saenger, the terms of which were contained in a letter written by Saenger on behalf of himself and Sacke. According to this agreement Schuler was to receive a certain sum of money and a certain number of shares on "flotation, sale, or otherwise" of the property. On the 24th of September, 1895, the defendants sold all their rights to George Albu as trustee for a certain company to be floated. The company was floated on the 1st of November, 1895, under the name of the Sacke Estates and Mining Company, Limited. The defendants, while admitting the agreement of the 27th of February, said that the property had never been sold or floated into a company, but that they had merely sold their rights under the agreement to George Albu Q.Q., and that, therefore, the Sacke Estates and Mining Company, Limited, stood in their shoes and would be liable to the plaintiff when the property was actually sold or floated.

Under these circumstances Jorissen, J., sitting at Johannesburg, held that there had been such a dealing with the property as was contemplated in the agreement and that, therefore, the plaintiff was entitled to the money and shares claimed. On appeal to the full Court in Pretoria this judgment was upheld.

Schuler vs. *Sacke and Saenger,* decided (on appeal) on the 4th of August, 1896, *coram* Ameshoff, Morice and Gregorowski, J.J. (not yet reported).

On the 19th of February, 1895, Jooste, who was the owner of certain 70 claims in the district of Potchefstroom, entered into an agreement with Carlis, under which the latter obtained the exclusive right to prospect for gold on these claims. It was further agreed that Carlis should "have the sole and exclusive right and power of purchasing, selling, floating into a limited liability company, or otherwise disposing of the said claims, provided that upon such purchase, sale, flotation, or disposal" he should pay to Jooste £100 or 100 fully paid-up shares for each claim so disposed of.

It was further agreed that the formation of a syndicate for the purpose of merely testing or exploiting such claims should not entitle Jooste to claim the above-mentioned consideration.

On the 26th of October, 1895, Carlis ceded his right or option under the agreement to Jacob Creewel, William Peter Taylor, and the firm of S. Neumann & Co On the 29th of October Creewel ceded his one-third share in the said right or option to the Klerksdorp Proprietary Mines, Limited. Thereupon Jooste sued Carlis for £7,000 or 7,000 shares in the Klerksdorp Proprietary Mines, Limited. It appeared in evidence that there was an understanding that W. P. Taylor and S. Neumann & Co.

would transfer their rights to the above-named company. Carlis contended that the claims had not been sold, floated, or otherwise disposed of, but that he had merely *ceded his right or option* under the agreement of the 19th of February.

The majority of the Court (Gregorowski and Kleyn, J.J., Morice, J., diss.) held that the plaintiff was entitled to succeed, on the following grounds:—That Carlis had made over all his rights and obligations to Creewel, Taylor, and S. Neumann and Co., for value received, but Jooste obtained no rights as against these persons. That it would be unfair to allow Carlis, by cleverly framing his agreement, to keep Jooste out of his money for an indefinite time and in the meanwhile enjoy all the benefits which he would have enjoyed in the case of an actual sale. That such was not the intention of the parties. That the fact that the formation of a syndicate to test or exploit the claims did not entitle the plaintiff to payment, showed that in this case he was so entitled, as the defendants did not allege that the Klerksdorp Proprietary Mines, Limited, was such a syndicate. That Carlis was more or less in the position of an agent for Jooste, and therefore in a position of trust. That under these circumstances such an alienation as was contemplated in the agreement must be considered to have taken place.

Morice, J. (dissentiente) held that this case could be distinguished from the case of *Schuler* vs. *Sacke and Saenger*, because in that case Schuler was not the owner of the ground. He merely had certain rights *in personam* against the owner of the ground. When Sacke and Saenger made over their rights under the agreement of the 27th February, 1895, to the company, they disposed of all the rights which Schuler had possessed in the ground, and there remained nothing further which he could have transferred, and therefore he was entitled to the stipulated consideration. But in this case Jooste was the owner of the claims, and when Carlis ceded his rights and liabilities to Creewell, Taylor, and Neumann & Co., he did not transfer Jooste's *jus in rem* in the claims. Jooste could not be prejudiced because the claims were registered in his name, and he was not bound to give transfer until he received the stipulated payment. Moreover, the use of the words "assignees" and "successors" in the agreement showed that it was contemplated that Carlis could cede his rights. As a matter of fact cessions of such options were of frequent occurrence as a speculation on the goldfields. As it did not appear that such an alienation as was contemplated in the agreement had taken place, his Lordship considered that the judgment should be absolution from the instance.

Jooste vs. *Carlis and Creewel*, decided on the 27th of August, 1896 (not yet reported).

The Plaintiff Syndicate alleged that Alfred Berriman, q.q. the Berriman Syndicate, on the 21st December, 1894, took out 100 licences and pegged off 100 claims on Block B, on the farm "Draaikraal," district Heidelberg, and renewed the licences till the 21st of September, 1895. Further, that on the 21st of February, 1895, he took out 115 licences, and on the 4th of March pegged off 115 claims on another portion of the same Block B, and renewed the licences till the 15th of September, 1895. That in March, 1895, Simpson, the defendant, lodged a protest against the numbering of the said claims. That thereupon the Mining Commissioner refused to allow the claims to be numbered, and in September refused the renewal of the licences.

The defendant alleged that on the 18th of February, 1895, he took out 100 licences and pegged the ground which the plaintiff alleged Berriman pegged in December, 1894, and that he still held the claims. That Berriman did not properly peg the ground in December, 1894, because he erected *corner* beacons *only*, and that the plaintiff

P 2

fraudulently held about 200 claims (viz. the whole of Block B) under only 100 licences. The 115 claims were not in dispute.

The Court found that Berriman pegged only the 100 claims in December, 1894; that he put in only *one centre* peg for each claim, and did not put in the corner pegs as required by law; and that in February, 1895, he placed an iron sign board at each corner of the block of 100 claims. It held that the provision of Article 63 of Law 14 of 1894, with regard to *two centre pegs* was unintelligible, and that the plaintiff had sufficiently complied with the law. Further, that as the plaintiff had· made a trench round the block of 100 claims there could be no doubt as to their exact situation, and that therefore the non-compliance with the provision of Article 63, with regard to corner pegs within seven days, was not fatal. Further, that the defendant was a "jumper," and that in a dispute between a "jumper" and a *bona fide* pegger the Court would not lightly deprive the latter of his claims on a mere informality, seeing that the law does not say that such informality shall entail forfeiture.

Judgment was therefore given in favour of the plaintiff for the 100 claims in dispute with costs.

Berriman Syndicate vs. *Simpson*, decided on the 4th of September, 1896, *coram* Kotzé, C.J., and Ameshoff and Gregorowski, J.J. (not yet reported).

On the 7th of December, 1894, the plaintiff, Dawe, pegged off 74 claims on the farm "Middelvlei." In February, 1895, he gave instructions to have the ground surveyed. On the 8th of March, 1895, the survey took place, and on the 28th of March he received the surveyor's diagram. He then for the first time found out that the ground pegged comprised 105 instead of 74 claims. On the 30th of March he applied to the Responsible Clerk at Doornkop, under Article 62*f* of Law 14 of 1894, for the surplus ground, *i.e.* 31 claims. This application was granted by the Responsible Clerk on the 6th of April, 1895, whereupon Dawe took out the necessary licences for the said 31 claims. On the 22nd of March, 1895, Cordeaux having found out that Dawe had pegged off more ground than his 74 licences entitled him to, provided with licences went and pegged off 25 claims on the said ground. He at the same time made application for these 25 claims, but the Responsible Clerk refused to give them to him. In July, 1895, however, these 25 claims were granted to him by the Head of the Mining Department. Dawe instituted an action for a declaration of rights. The Court assumed that Dawe had acted *bona fide* in pegging 105 claims instead of 74 under 74 licences, but held that, as he had only 74 licences, and intended to peg only 74 claims, whatever surplus there was above the 74 claims had to be looked upon as *open* ground, and as Cordeaux had properly pegged 25 claims on the 22nd of March, 1895, before Dawe applied for the surplus ground under Article 62*f*, he thereby acquired a good title to the said 25 claims. The Court further held that as Dawe had pegged first he was entitled to 74 claims, beginning from the place where he started pegging, and that Cordeaux was entitled to 25 claims on the remainder of the ground. Judgment was therefore given in favour of Cordeaux for 25 claims with costs.

Dawe vs. *Cordeaux and the Responsible Clerk of Doornkop*, decided on the 4th of September, 1896, *coram* Kotzé, C.J. (not yet reported).

On the 13th of June, 1888, all Government ground in the district of Heidelberg was thrown open. In March, 1893, the defendants pegged off a certain piece of ground on Vogelstruisbult under 800 licences. On the 10th of April, 1893. the Mining Commissioner refused to renew the licences because there was a dispute between the Government and one Botha, the owner of Daggafontein, as to whether the ground belonged to the Government or to Botha. The Mining Commissioner assured the defendants that if it should afterwards appear that the ground was Government ground they would retain their rights. In February, 1895, it was settled that the ground belonged to the Government, and the defendants thereupon on the 9th of March, 1895, renewed their licences. They, however, renewed only 600 licences. On the 29th of April, and 6th and 9th of May, 1895, the plaintiff pegged off the ground for which the defendants held the 600 licences under 1,173 licences. After the pegging by the plaintiff, the defendants had the ground surveyed, and found that it comprised 1,173 instead of 600 claims. They thereupon applied under Article 62*f* of Law 14 of 1894 for the 573 surplus claims, and their application was granted by the Head of the Mining Department in July. Thereupon, the plaintiff instituted action for a declaration of rights. He alleged that the defendants had no right to any of the 1,173 claims (1) because they in 1893 abondoned their rights, and did not peg again in 1895; (2) because they fraudulently held 1,175 claims under 600 licences.

The Court held that the defendants did not abandon their rights in 1893, and that when they renewed their licences on the 9th of March, 1895, their original pegging was still good. That when the plaintiff pegged in April, the defendants were in possession of the ground under 600 licences, and that it was not necessary to decide what would have happened if the plaintiff had pegged before the 9th of March, *i.e.*, before the defendants obtained renewal of their licences. Further, that although the defendants had pegged ground comprising 1,173 claims under 600 licences, there was no intention to defraud, and no one was prejudiced, and that therefore the defendants were entitled to 600 claims. With regard to the 573 remaining claims, the application for them was not granted (or made) until after the plaintiff's pegging, and consequently at a time when the ground was no longer open. Further, that, as the defendants had been the first to peg, they were entitled to choose their 600 claims first, and for this purpose they were allowed fourteen days, and that the plaintiff was entitled to the remaining 573 claims. Defendants were ordered to pay costs.

Neubauer vs. *Van Diggelen and Wilson* decided on the 4th of September, 1896 *coram* Kotzé, C.J., and Ameshoff and Gregorowski, J.J. (not yet reported).

On appeal from the decision of the Landdrost of Johannesburg, the Court held that digging a furrow to carry off water and cleaning it was sufficient working of the claims by the company holding them, and set aside the judgment of the Landdrost.

Henry Nourse G. M. Coy. vs. *Eland*, decided on the 5th of July, 1889, *coram* Kotzé, C.J., and Jorissen and De Korte, J.J. (unreported).

A person digging for gold on a proclaimed goldfield, under the Gold Law of 1875, without a licence, is a wrong-doer.

A gold-mining concession, granted by the Government and confirmed by the Volksraad, provided that all diggers at present digging on the farm embraced by the concession shall be compensated :—*Held*, that this did not entitle the diggers to peg out and work new claims on the farm, after the granting of the concession, and that they must be interdicted from so doing.

Gilbaud and Co. vs. *Walker and others*, decided on the 4th of December, 1883, *coram* Kotzé, C.J., and Burgers and Brand, J.J. (Kotzé's Reports, 1881-1884, page 82).

Digging for gold without a licence renders the digger a tresspasser under the Gold Law of 1875.

By virtue of the Volksraad Resolution of 11th June, 1883, Article 269, no one can dig for gold on private property without the consent of the owner or concessionaire.

Cohen, Goldschmidt, & Co. vs. *Stanley and Tate* (Kotzé's Reports, 1881-1884, page 133), decided on the 28th February, 1884, *coram* Kotzé, C.J. and Burgers and Brand, J.J.

A gold concession, granted to the respondents, contained a clause providing that all diggers on the farm, over which the concession was granted, shall be entitled to compensation, and in case the concessionaires and the diggers should not come to an agreement on the point, the Government shall fix the amount of compensation. The applicant, as digger, moved the Court for an order directing the respondents to proceed to arbitration as to the amount of compensation :—

Held, that the application must be refused, as there was no allegation that the applicant had applied to the Government to fix the amount of compensation.

Stanley vs. *Goldschmidt & Co.* (Kotzé's Reports, 1881-1884, page 155).

RESOLUTION OF THE HONOURABLE FIRST VOLKSRAAD, ARTICLE 1,261, DATED 25TH AUGUST, 1896.

The First Volksraad, having regard to the Government missive, dated 12th instant, and to all the memorials referring to the so-called undermining rights, at present under discussion ; considering that the First Volksraad, by Article 1282 of the 20th September, 1895. postponed this matter in order to hear the opinion of the public thereupon, and that the great majority have delared themselves in favour of reserving these undermining rights for the owner and also for the State : considering that digging under townships, storage stands (bewaarplatsen), etc., was always forbidden by the old Gold Law, Article 21, resolves to continue to maintain the prohibition clause (of Article 121 of the Gold Law of 1895) until such time as it shall appear necessary to the First Volksraad and to the Government to suspend the said prohibition clause, and thereupon to allow the working of such grounds under regulations framed by the First Volksraad, and subject to this proviso, that, when it is decided to do so, the preference with regard to such undermining rights shall be given to the highest bidder at a public sale, and half of the proceeds of such a sale shall, after deducting expenses, be awarded to the State and the other half to the lawful owner of such farm or ground, or his lawful heirs, and in the event of a special agreement having been made with regard to the licence monies, the person thus acquiring rights shall be entitled to the owner's half.

CORRESPONDING ARTICLES

OF THE GOLD LAWS OF 1894, 1895, AND 1896.

Law 21 of 1896. Article.	Law 19 of 1895. Article.	Law 14 of 1894. Article.
1	1	1
2	2	2
3	3	89 and 72a
4	4	35
5	5	88
6	6	90
7	7	58
8	8	—
9	9	3
10	10	4
11	11	25
12	12	26a
13	13	27
14	14	27a
15	15	28
16	16	28b
17	17	37
18	18	34
19	19	31
20	20	32
21	21	28a
22	22	33
23	23	26
24	24	29
25	25	7
26	26	8
27	27	12
28	28 and 52	18 and 21f
29	29	23
30	30	23a
31	31	24
32	32	24a
33	33	24b
34	34	50
35	35	59a
36	36	36
37	37	39
38	38	38
39	39	5
40	40	10
41	41	17
42	42	6
43	43	6a
44	44	6b

Law 21 of 1896. Article.				Law 19 of 1895. Article.				Law 14 of 1894. Article.
45	...	...	...	45	...	..	...	6c
46	...	...	...	46	...	...	..	10
47	...	...	...	47	...	...	...	9
48	...	...	...	48	...	..	...	17 and 14
49	...	...	...	49	...	...	...	11
50	...	...	...	50	...	...	...	13
51	....	...	...	51	...	...	...	15
(2nd part of Article).								
28	...	...	...	52	...	...	...	19
52	...	...	...	53	...	...	...	22
53	...	...	...	54	..	...	...	22a
54	...	...	...	55	...	...	...	20
55	..	...	...	56	...	...	...	20a
56	...	...	...	57	...	...	...	20b
57	...	...	...	58	...	...	...	20c
58	...	...	...	59	...	...	...	59b
59	...	..	...	60	...	...	...	60
60	...	...	...	61	...	...	...	28c
61	...	...	...	62	...	...	...	28d
62	...	...	...	63	...	...	...	59
63	...	...	...	64	...	...	...	61
64	...	...	...	65	...	...	...	53
65	...	...	...	66	...	...	...	61a
66	...	...	...	67	...	..	...	—
67	...	...	...	68	...	...	...	62
68	...	...	...	69	...	...	...	63
69	...	...	...	70	...	...	...	16
70	...	...	...	71	...	...	...	52
71	...	...	...	72	...	...	...	51
72	...	...	...	73	...	...	...	62a
73	...	...	...	74	...	...	...	62b
74	...	...	...	75	...	...	...	62c
75	...	...	...	76	...	...	...	62d
76	...	...	...	77	...	...	...	62e
77	...	...	...	78	...	...	...	62f
78	...	...	...	79	...	...	...	62g
79	...	...	...	80	...	...	...	62h
80	...	...	...	81	..	...	...	62i
81		...	...	82	...	...	...	63
82	...	...	...	83	...	...	...	64
—	...	...	...	84	...	...	...	75a
(Deleted from Law 21 of 1896).								
—	...	...	...	85	...	...	...	75
(Deleted from Law 21 of 1896).								
83	...	...	...	86	...	...	...	87
84	...	...	...	87	...	...	...	66
85	...	...	...	88	...	...	...	30
86	...	....	...	89	...	...	...	61b